November 11–14, 2012
Cambridge, Massachusetts, USA

Association for
Computing Machinery

Advancing Computing as a Science & Profession

ITS'12

Proceedings of the ACM Conference on
Interactive Tabletops and Surfaces

Sponsored by:
ACM SIGCHI

Supported by:
NSF, Wacom, 3M, Diamond Touch, Microsoft, Interaction Design Foundation, and Ideum

Association for
Computing Machinery

Advancing Computing as a Science & Profession

The Association for Computing Machinery
2 Penn Plaza, Suite 701
New York, New York 10121-0701

Notice to Past Authors of ACM-Published Articles
ACM intends to create a complete electronic archive of all articles and/or other material previously published by ACM. If you have written a work that has been previously published by ACM in any journal or conference proceedings prior to 1978, or any SIG Newsletter at any time, and you do NOT want this work to appear in the ACM Digital Library, please inform permissions@acm.org, stating the title of the work, the author(s), and where and when published.

ISBN: 978-1-4503-1209-7 (Digital)

ISBN: 978-1-4503-1932-4 (Print)

Additional copies may be ordered prepaid from:

ACM Order Department
PO Box 30777
New York, NY 10087-0777, USA

Phone: 1-800-342-6626 (USA and Canada)
+1-212-626-0500 (Global)
Fax: +1-212-944-1318
E-mail: acmhelp@acm.org
Hours of Operation: 8:30 am – 4:30 pm ET

Printed in the USA

Welcome to ITS 2012

We are pleased to welcome you to the *ACM International Conference on Interactive Tabletops and Surfaces (ITS) 2012*, held from November 11-14th, in Cambridge, Massachusetts. ITS 2012 marks the 7th anniversary of a series of annual research workshops and conferences that began in 2006 in Adelaide, Australia. In this short amount of time, the field of Interactive Tabletops and Surfaces has rapidly evolved. Hardware prices are falling, core sensing technology is improving, software toolkits are maturing, and interaction paradigms are beginning to solidify. As a result, interactive tabletops and surfaces are increasingly making their way beyond laboratories and appearing in a wide variety of private and public spaces including museums, offices, schools, airports, hotels, medical centers, and homes. Such surfaces employ a variety of technologies including capacitive sensing, computer vision, motion sensors, and appear in a variety of form-factors such as large walls and tabletops, tablets and slates, flexible materials, and on-demand projection.

Sponsored by ACM and generously supported by National Science Foundation and industry, the ACM conference on Interactive Tabletops and Surfaces brings together researchers and practitioners from a variety of backgrounds and interest areas. The intimate size of this single-track symposium provides an ideal venue for leading researchers, practitioners, and students to exchange research results and experiences.

This year we received 103 paper and note submissions (63 papers and 40 notes) of which we accepted 24 papers and 6 notes for an overall acceptance rate of 29%. We also introduced a new review process modeled after the 2012 ACM CSCW conference, in which papers and notes underwent two review cycles. After the first review by two external reviewers and one program committee member, submissions received either a "Revise" or "Reject" decision. Authors of papers in the "Revise" pool then participated in a second phase of the submission process, in which they had 3½ weeks to revise and resubmit their work based on the initial reviews (and also received an additional meta-review from a second program committee member). Revised submissions were then re-reviewed as the basis for final decisions. This is similar to a journal review process, except that it is limited to one revision with a strict deadline. We believe that this process has resulted in an extremely high quality papers and notes program, which we hope that you find enlightening and exciting!

In addition to the papers and notes program, the conference hosts several other programs. The Doctoral Symposium (DS) accepted seven doctoral students to discuss their research with peers and with a panel of experienced ITS researchers in an informal setting. The conference also includes an interactive hands-on reception that presents a juried selection of 21 posters and 18 demos. This year, ITS brings the theme of Beyond Flat Displays in our pre-conference venues with a tutorial and a workshop: four tutorials that offer novel practical experiences to conference attendees with diverse skills and backgrounds, and a pre-conference workshop that will challenge attendees to explore the realm Beyond Flat Displays. The National Science Foundation extends generous support for DS attendees and for student travel awards; this support will result in more opportunities for students to engage in this diverse and growing community.

The titles of the papers, notes, posters, and demos, reflect the diversity of ideas and perspectives that comprise the ITS community, ranging from large tabletop surfaces to non-flat displays, from pen and paper to free-space interaction, from education to surfaces "in the wild". What brings it all together is a commitment to innovation that expands our understanding of design considerations of ITS technologies and of their applications.

We are especially pleased to have two exciting keynote speakers this year. The conference kicks off with a keynote on "Thinking Outside of the (Computer) Box" by Pattie Maes of the MIT Media Lab, and we close the conference with our Capstone speaker Andy Wilson from Microsoft Research, discussing analog interactions.

A large number of volunteers offered dedicated effort to the organization, reviews, venue arrangement, web presence, and publicity for the ACM conference on Interactive Tabletops and Surfaces 2012. We would like to express our deep gratitude to everyone on the conference organizing committee and program committee, and to all the volunteers and reviewers whose efforts help enrich this community. We would like to thank ACM, NSF, and our corporate sponsors for their continued support for this conference.

Orit Shaer
ITS'12 Conference Chair
Wellesley College, USA

Chia Shen
ITS'12 Conference Chair
Harvard University, USA

Michael Horn
ITS'12 Program Chair
Northwestern University, USA

Meredith Ringel Morris
ITS'12 Program Chair
Microsoft Research, USA

Table of Contents

Session 5: Surfaces in Education

Session Chair: Sheelagh Carpendale *(University of Calgary)*

Session 6: Pens and Paper

Session Chair: Andrew Wilson *(Microsoft Research)*

Session 7: Touching with Precision

Session Chair: Alex Butler *(Microsoft Research Cambridge)*

Session 8: Interaction Techniques and Widgets

Session Chair: Raimund Dachselt *(Technische Universität Dresden)*

Session 9: Understanding Users

Session Chair: Niklas Elmqvist *(Purdue University)*

Session 10: Interacting with Information Using Surfaces

Session Chair: Jüergen Steimle *(Massachusetts Institute of Technology)*

Doctoral Symposium

Demo Session

Posters

ITS 2012 Conference Committees

Conference Chairs: Orit Shaer *(Wellesley College, USA)*
Chia Shen *(Harvard University, USA)*

Program Chairs: Meredith Ringel Morris *(Microsoft Research, USA)*
Michael Horn *(Northwestern University, USA)*

Treasurers: Clifton Forlines *(Draper Laboratory, USA)*
Anne Marie Piper *(Northwestern University, USA)*

Poster Chairs: Michael A. Evans *(Virginia Tech, USA)*
Eva Hornecker *(University of Strathclyde, United Kingdom)*

Demo Chairs: Daniel Leithinger *(Massachusetts Institute of Technology, USA)*
Jürgen Steimle *(Massachusetts Institute of Technology, USA)*
Anthony Tang *(University of Calgary, Canada)*

Tutorials and Workshops Chairs: Edward Tse *(SMART Technologies,Canada)*
Frederic Vernier *(South-Paris University, France)*

Doctoral Symposium Chairs: Raimund Dachselt *(Technische Universität Dresden, Germany)*
Mark Hancock *(University of Waterloo, Canada)*

Web Chairs: Consuelo Valdes *(Wellesley College, USA)*
Heidi Wang *(Stanford University, USA)*

Publicity Chairs: Petra Isenberg *(INRIA, France)*
YuanChun Shi *(Tsinghua University, China)*
Megan Strait *(Tufts University, USA)*

Mentoring Chairs: Changkyu Choi *(Samsung Advanced Institute of Technology, South Korea)*
Koji Yatani *(Microsoft Research Asia, Japan)*

Local Arrangements Chair: Consuelo Valdes *(Wellesley College, USA)*

Proceedings Chair: Consuelo Valdes *(Wellesley College, USA)*

Steering Committee: Sheelagh Carpendale *(University of Calgary, Canada)*
Shahram Izadi *(Microsoft Research, United Kingdom)*
Gerald Morrison *(SMART Technologies ULC, Canada)*
Chia Shen *(Harvard University, USA)*
Sriram Subramanian *(Bristol University, United Kingdom)*
Bruce Thomas *(University of South Australia, Australia)*
Andy Wilson *(Microsoft Research, USA)*

Program Committee: Alissa N. Antle *(Simon Fraser University, Canada)*
Alex Butler *(Microsoft Research, United Kingdom)*
Raimund Dachselt *(Technische Universität Dresden, Germany)*
Pierre Dillenbourg *(Ecole Polytechnique Federale de Lausanne, Switzerland)*
Kentaro Fukuchi *(Meiji University, Japan)*
Darren Gergle *(Northwestern University, USA)*
Michael Haller *(University of Applied Sciences Upper Austria, Austria)*
Mark Hancock *(University of Waterloo, Canada)*
Bjoern Hartmann *(University of California, Berkeley, USA)*
Pourang Irani *(University of Manitoba, Canada)*
Andruid Kerne *(Texas A&M University, USA)*
Paul Marshall *(University College London, United Kingdom)*
Christian Mueller-Tomfelde *(CSIRO, Australia)*
Miguel Nacenta *(University of St. Andrews, United Kingdom)*
Anne Marie Piper *(Northwestern University, USA)*
Jochen (Jeff) Rick *(Saarland University, Germany)*
Yvonne Rogers *(Open University, United Kingdom)*
Sriram Subramanian *(Bristol University, United Kingdom)*
Hong Tan *(Purdue University, USA / Microsoft Research Asia, Japan)*
Frederic Vernier *(South-Paris University, France)*
Daniel Vogel *(University of Waterloo, Canada)*

Additional Reviewers: Alexander, Jason *(Lancaster University, United Kingdom)*
Aliakseyeu, Dzmitry *(Philips Research Europe, The Netherlands)*
Anslow, Craig *(Victoria University of Wellington, New Zealand)*
Anthony, Lisa *(University of Maryland, Baltimore County, USA)*
Antti, Oulasvirta *(MPI-INF, Germany)*
Arif, Ahmed *(York University, Canada)*
Ashdown, Mark *(Thales, United Kingdom)*
Bailey, Brian *(University of Illinois-Urbana, USA)*
Bailly, Gilles *(Telekom Innovation Laboratories, Germany)*
Bao, Patti *(Northwestern University, USA)*
Benko, Hrvoje *(Microsoft Research, USA)*
Bérard, François *(University of Grenoble, France)*
Besacier, Guillaume *(University of Waterloo, Canada)*
Bezerianos, Anastasia *(LRI - U. Paris-Sud, France)*
Bi, Xiaojun *(Google Inc., USA)*
Block, Florian *(Harvard University, United Kingdom)*
Boring, Sebastian *(University of Calgary, Canada)*
Bowers, Chris *(University of Birmingham, United Kingdom)*
Buisine, Stephanie *(Laboratoire Conception de Produits et Innovation, France)*
Calvillo Gamez, Eduardo *(Universidad Politecnica de San Luis Potosi, Mexico)*

Additional Reviewers (continued):

Cao, Xiang *(Microsoft Research, P. R. China)*
Cauchard, Jessica *(Microsoft Research, United Kingdom)*
Chai, Jinxiang *(Texas A&M University, USA)*
Chang, Angela *(Massachusetts Institute of Technology, USA)*
Chen, Nicholas *(University of Maryland, USA)*
Cheng, Kelvin *(CSIRO, Australia)*
Collins, Anthony *(University of Sydney, Australia)*
Cowan, Lisa *(University of California, San Diego, USA)*
Coyle, David *(University of Bristol, United Kingdom)*
Dachselt, Raimund *(Technische Universität Dresden, Germany)*
Daiber, Florian *(German Research Center for Artificial Intelligence, Germany)*
Dowell, John *(University College London, United Kingdom)*
Echtler, Florian *(Siemens Corporate Technology, Germany)*
Edge, Darren *(Microsoft Research, P.R. China)*
Elmqvist, Niklas *(Purdue University, USA)*
Falcao, Taciana *(Institute of Education London, United Kingdom)*
Fisher, Danyel *(Microsoft Research, USA)*
Fitton, Daniel *(University of Central Lancashire, United Kingdom)*
Fjeld, Morten *(Chalmers University of Technology, Sweden)*
Fleck, Rowanne *(University College London, United Kingdom)*
Freeman, Dustin *(University of Toronto, Canada)*
Friedman, Whitney *(University of California, San Diego, USA)*
Genest, Aaron *(University of Saskatchewan, Canada)*
Gerken, Jens *(ICT Innovative Communication Technologies AG, Germany)*
Goel, Mayank *(University of Washington, USA)*
Graham, Nicholas *(Queen's University, Canada)*
Greenberg, Saul *(University of Calgary, Canada)*
Gustafson, Sean *(Hasso Plattner Institute, Germany)*
Gutwin, Carl *(University of Saskatchewan, Canada)*
Hachet, Martin *(LaBRI-INRIA University of Bordeaux, France)*
Hamilton, William A. *(Texas A&M University, USA)*
Hancock, Mark *(University of Waterloo, Canada)*
Hesselmann, Tobias *(OFFIS Institute for Information Technology, Germany)*
Hilliges, Otmar *(Microsoft Research, United Kingdom)*
Hinckley, Ken *(Microsoft Research, USA)*
Hinrichs, Uta *(University of Calgary, Canada)*
Hornecker, Eva *(University of Strathclyde, United Kingdom)*
Hourcade, Juan Pablo *(University of Iowa, USA)*
Huang, Elaine *(Georgia Institute of Technology, USA)*
Huber, Jochen *(TU Darmstadt, Germany)*

Additional Reviewers (continued):

Isenberg, Tobias *(University of Groningen, Netherlands)*
Isenberg, Petra *(INRIA, France)*
Itoh, Yuichi *(Osaka University, Japan)*
Izadi, Shahran *(Microsoft Research, United Kingdom)*
Jacucci, Giulio *(Helsinki Institute for Information Technology, Finland)*
Jetter, Hans-Christian *(University of Konstanz, Germany)*
Jota, Ricardo *(Inesc-ID, Portugal)*
Kalwar, Santosh *(Lappeenranta University of Technology, Finland)*
Kaplan, Frédéric *(EPFL, Switzerland)*
Karnik, Abhijit *(University of Bristol, United Kingdom)*
Kharrufa, Ahmed *(Newcastle University, United Kingdom)*
Khoo, Michael *(independent)*
Kildal, Johan *(University of Glasgow, United Kingdom)*
Kim, David *(Newcastle University, United Kingdom)*
Kim, Seokhwan *(University of Tsukuba, Japan)*
Kin, Kenrick *(University of California, Berkeley, USA)*
Klokmose, Clemens *(Aarhus University, Denmark)*
Koike, Hideki *(University of Electro-Communications, Japan)*
Kreitmayer, Stefan *(Open University, United Kingdom)*
Krüger, Antonio *(DFKI GmbH, Germany)*
Kuchenbecker, Katherine *(University of Pennsylvania, USA)*
Lank, Edward *(University of Waterloo, Canada)*
Leigh, Jason *(Electronic Visualization Laboratory, USA)*
Li, Nan *(EPFL, Switzerland)*
Li, Yang *(Google Research, USA)*
Lindeman, Robert *(Worcester Polytechnic Institute, USA)*
Löchtefeld, Markus *(German Research Center for Artificial Intelligence, Germany)*
Lopes, Pedro *(Hasso Plattner Institute, Germany)*
Lupfer, Nic *(Texas A&M University, USA)*
Luyten, Kris *(Hasselt University, Belgium)*
Lyons, Leilah *(University of Illinois at Chicago, USA)*
Malizia, Alessio *(University La Sapienza of Rome, Italy)*
Mandryk, Regan *(University of Saskatchewan, Canada)*
Marquardt, Nicolai *(University of Calgary, Canada)*
Marshall, Paul *(United Kingdom)*
Martinet, Anthony *(University of Lille, France)*
Martinez Maldonado, Roberto *(University of Sydney, Australia)*
Martinez Plasencia, Diego *(University of Bristol, United Kingdom)*
McGookin, David *(Scotland)*
Molyneaux, David *(Microsoft Research, United Kingdom)*
Oakley, Ian *(University of Madeira, Portugal)*
Olivier, Patrick *(Newcastle University, United Kingdom)*
Oppl, Stefan *(Johannes Kepler Universitaet Linz, Austria)*

Additional Reviewers (continued):

Pavlovych, Andriy *(University of Saskatchewan, Canada)*
Perin, Charles *(INRIA, France)*
Perrault, Simon *(TELECOM ParisTech - CNRS LTCI, France)*
Perry, Mark *(Brunel University, United Kingdom)*
Pfleging *(Bastian, Germany)*
Pielot, Martin *(Telefonica Research, Spain)*
Qin, Yongqiang *(Tsinghua University, P.R. China)*
Ramelin, Sonja *(University of Munich, Germany)*
Reilly, Derek *(Dalhousie University, Canada)*
Rekimoto, Jun *(University of Tokyo, Japan)*
Ren, Xiangshi *(Kochi University of Technology, Japan)*
Richter, Christoph *(Christian-Albrechts-Universität Kiel, Germany)*
Rick, Jochen *(Germany)*
Robinson, Peter *(University of Cambridge, England)*
Roudaut, Anne *(University of Bristol, Germany)*
Rukzio, Enrico *(Germany)*
Sakamoto, Daisuke *(University of Tokyo, Japan)*
Sandor, Christian *(Australia)*
Schmidt, Dominik *(Lancaster University, United Kingdom)*
Scupelli, Peter *(Carnegie Mellon University, USA)*
Shen, Chia *(Harvard University, USA)*
Shenfeng, Fei *(Texas A&M University, USA)*
Shizuki, Buntarou *(University of Tsukuba, Japan)*
Shotton, Jamie *(Microsoft Research, United Kingdom)*
Starner, Dr. Thad *(Georgia Tech University)*
Steimle, Jürgen *(Massachusetts Institute of Technology, USA)*
Steinicke, Frank *(University of Manchester, Germany)*
Stuerzlinger, Wolfgang *(York University, Canada)*
Sugimoto, Masanori *(University of Tokyo, Japan)*
Tabard, Aurélien *(University of Munich, Germany)*
Takatsuka, Masahiro *(University of Sydney, Australia)*
Tang, Anthony *(University of Calgary, Canada)*
Thomas, Bruce *(University of South Australia, Australia)*
Tse, Edward *(SMART Technologies ULC, Canada)*
Ullmer, Brygg *(Louisiana State University, USA)*
Villar, Nicolas *(Microsoft Research, United Kingdom)*
Wagner, Julie *(INRIA, France)*
Wallace, James *(University of Waterloo, Canada)*
Webb, Andrew *(Texas A&M University, USA)*
Weibel, Nadir *(University of California San Diego, USA)*
Weiss, Malte *(RWTH Aachen University, Germany)*
Wigdor, Daniel *(University of Toronto, Canada)*
Wilson, Andrew *(Microsoft Research, USA)*
Wolf, Katrin *(Deutsche Telekom Laboratories, Germany)*

Additional Reviewers (continued):

Yang, Xing-Dong *(University of Alberta, Canada)*
Yatani, Koji *(Microsoft Research, China)*
Young, Jim *(University of Manitoba, Canada)*
Yu, Chun *(Tsinghua University, China)*
Zancanaro, Massimo *(FBK-irst, Italy)*
Zhang, Yuru *(Beihang University, China)*
Zhao, Shengdong *(National University of Singapore, Singapore)*
Zufferey, Guillaume *(Simpliquity, Switzerland)*

ITS 2012 Sponsor & Supporters

Sponsor: SIGCHI

Platinum Supporter: NSF

Gold Supporter: wacom

Silver Supporters: 3M, Microsoft, DiamondTouch ... by Circle Twelve

Bronze Supporters: Interaction Design Foundation, ideum

Comparing Elicited Gestures to Designer-Created Gestures for Selection above a Multitouch Surface

Dmitry Pyryeskin, Mark Hancock, Jesse Hoey
University of Waterloo, Ontario, Canada
{dpyryesk, mark.hancock, jhoey}@uwaterloo.ca

ABSTRACT

Many new technologies are emerging that make it possible to extend interaction into the three-dimensional space directly above or in front of a multitouch surface. Such techniques allow people to control these devices by performing hand gestures in the air. In this paper, we present a method of extending interactions into the space above a multitouch surface using only a standard diffused surface illumination (DSI) device, without any additional sensors. Then we focus on interaction techniques for activating graphical widgets located in this above-surface space. We have conducted a study to elicit gestures for above-table widget activation. A follow-up study was conducted to evaluate and compare these gestures based on their performance. Our results showed that there was no clear agreement on what gestures should be used to select objects in mid-air, and that performance was better when using gestures that were chosen less frequently, but predicted to be better by the designers, as opposed to those most frequently suggested by participants.

Author Keywords

Multimodal interaction; natural human computer interaction; surface computing; multi-touch; gestures; hoverspace.

ACM Classification Keywords

H.5.2 [Information interfaces and presentation]: User Interfaces. - Graphical user interfaces.

General Terms

Human Factors; Design; Performance; Measurement; Experimentation.

INTRODUCTION

Multi-touch technology was conceived at least as early as 1965 [14], and since then has slowly become more reliable, accurate and commonplace. Nowadays, devices equipped with multi-touch screens are becoming ubiquitous on phones and tablets, and are being researched heavily on larger surfaces, such as tables and walls. This shift provides the potential for direct interaction with on-screen objects in a fashion familiar from the physical world [1,10,26].

Recent technology, such as the Microsoft Kinect, has made cheaper the possibility of extending this physical interaction into *hover space*—the space above or in front of a multitouch display. The addition of hover space input to touch input can provide another mode of interaction, while allowing smooth transitions from one mode to another [17]. This added dimension in the interaction space can be used for a variety of purposes, for instance to manipulate 3D artifacts [13], to provide shortcuts to applications via Hover Widgets [8], or to create occlusion-aware interfaces [24].

While this design space is promising, one of the most compelling aspects of direct touch interaction is the clear and understandable way in which on-screen targets can be selected—by touching them with your hands or fingers. This physicality, however, is lost in hover space, and it becomes no longer clear how digital artifacts can and should be selected. Will people expect to be able to grab objects in mid-air, point at objects from a distance, or will they understand the need to dwell over a 3D target to select it (for example)? Currently, little work has explored what gestures people expect to be able to use to select targets above a table. In this work we study target selection in this space, with respect to both people's expectations and performance.

In this paper, we explore interaction in hover space by focusing specifically on item selection in the space above a multi-touch surface. We first present the design of a system that can approximate the height of hands above a diffused surface illumination (DSI) device. We then present the results of a pair of studies: in the first, we elicit what gestures people expect to be able to use to select on-screen targets in hover space, and in the second we explore the performance of the gestures chosen from the first study compared to several of our own designs for selection. Some of the gestures identified in our first study were beyond the capability of our hardware system, though might be possible with additional hardware (e.g., a separate motion tracking system). Thus, the focus of our second study was on evaluating the performance of gestures that were practical to implement with minimal hardware. Our results show that not only do people disagree about how to select objects in this space, but also that the less-frequently chosen designs that we (the designers) predicted to perform better, in most cases did, when compared to the most frequently chosen gestures from the first study.

RELATED WORK

In this section we focus on four related areas: detecting movement above a surface, interaction in front of a surface, how others study gestures, and in-air target selection.

ITS'12, November 11–14, 2012, Cambridge, Massachusetts, USA.

Detection of Movement above a Surface

The subject of hover space interaction is already well researched and a number of hover detection techniques have been proposed. Some of these systems rely on multiple stereo cameras to calculate the 3D location of a person's hands and fingers [16,27]. These systems require much more computational power than other vision-based systems and also require very precise camera calibration. Other systems use depth cameras [3,25], such as that found in the Microsoft Kinect. Z-Touch uses multiple layers of lasers to estimate the position of a person's hands and fingers [22], and Shadow Tracking positions infrared emitters above the table to create and track shadows of people's hands together with touch regions [5].

Most of these methods require custom-built hardware or modifications of existing multi-touch tables. We add to this work by demonstrating how to use an existing DSI setup to track hands above a surface. Our approach uses computer vision algorithms to estimate hand distance and can be considered a special case of the more general shape from shading (SFS) problem. SFS techniques compute the shape of a surface using a single greyscale image as input [19]. The computed surface may be used to estimate the height of a hand above the surface and for gesture recognition.

Interaction in Front of a Surface

Many techniques already exist for interacting in front of a large display wall or interactive surface [3,13,25,27]. Some research investigates interactive widgets in the space above a table, such as Hover Widgets [8], which include the possibility of using the space above a surface to create a new command layer that is clearly distinct from the input layer on the surface. Hover space can also be used to create techniques for more natural manipulation of 3D artifacts on a multitouch surface [13], or for faster zooming interaction [9]. Our work expands this space and explores more specifically the target selection aspect of above-surface interaction techniques, once a widget has been acquired.

Studying Gestures

Gestures can be a rich, versatile, and natural way for people to interact with each other as well as with technology. With the wide variety of techniques that allow in-air hand tracking, gesture-based interaction has been studied in depth [7,17,21]. A common approach to evaluating these gestures is to first design them, based on experience or related work, and then evaluate their performance when compared to other alternatives. An alternative approach is to first elicit what gestures people expect to correspond to a given action [18,28], rather than have the system designer determine what gesture is best-suited to an action. Other researchers have used the same methodology to develop gesture sets for other domains [6,12]. Our work uses an approach similar to Wobbrock et al. [28] to elicit gestures from participants.

In-air Target Selection

Device-free interaction makes signalling selection non-trivial. One of the most basic solutions which has been adopted by many eye-tracking systems [11] is to use dwell time threshold to indicate a click event. Some of the other proposed gestures are: pinching in the air [13], *SideTrigger* [2], *AirTap* [23] and *ThumbTrigger* [23]. As Wobbrock et al. [28] put forward, while gestures defined by the system designers certainly produce good results, they may not reflect people's expectations, and their development may be influenced by concerns for reliable recognition [18].

Our work builds upon existing research in each of these areas by examining the specific domain of above-surface target selection. We present a technique to detect the height of a person's hand above the table, which we use to study above-surface selection. We draw from existing methodology by first eliciting preferred gestures, and then comparing their performance to designer-chosen gestures.

SELECTION ABOVE A MULTI-TOUCH SURFACE

The introduction of inexpensive hardware to detect the 3D shape of hands and fingers in mid-air has led to a surge in research that explores interaction in the space above a table. While this direction seems promising, the interaction space has some significant qualitative differences from on-surface interaction. One of the most salient of these differences is the inability to select on-screen targets by touching or clicking on them. A variety of gestures have been suggested in the research to perform such selections, but it remains an open question how people will expect selections to occur.

In this section, we first describe the design challenges associated with a person's expectations specifically about target selection in the space above a table, and then describe our system for detecting the height of a person's hand above the table, which can be used to make these selections.

Design Challenges for Above-Surface Selection

A number of factors make the design of above-surface selection particularly challenging. Many of these challenges have been raised in prior work on above-surface interaction, but we describe the most pertinent challenges specific to selection: non-physicality, the use of layers, the transition between above-surface and touch interaction, and fatigue.

Non-Physicality

One of the most important challenges when selecting objects in mid-air is the lack of a reference point. On a 2D surface, people can select artifacts such as buttons, menus, and images by touching the surface directly. In contrast, when a target is in hover space, it cannot be represented in the air (unless some sort of holographic or virtual reality technology is used); therefore the direct interaction paradigm breaks down. It is not clear how this lack of physical connection will manifest in a person's expectation about how to select on-screen targets.

Layers/Precision

Defining a number of layers in hover space can be useful for increasing the dimensionality of control space [22], and can provide an indication of the precision with which the system can detect hand height. Objects can be placed in separate layers above one another and selected by moving a hand up and down. However, it is not clear whether people will understand or expect these layers to exist, and whether such constraints will improve selection performance.

Transition between Hover and Touch

As discussed by Spindler et al [21], hover and touch data should be considered as a unified space. That is, there should be no separation between interactions in hover space and on the surface, and no need to switch the modality of interaction. Another challenge in designing a selection technique is to ensure that this seamless transition is supported. The most common selection technique on existing surfaces typically manifests at this point of transition (e.g., on touch down), and so the designer must still determine a suitable way of handling the response just before this event. It is again unclear what people's expectations are about how this transition should happen, and what gestures should cause on-screen changes.

Fatigue

Fatigue is a well-known issue with mid-air interactions. However, one common technique for mid-air selections is the use of a dwell time (e.g., Microsoft's Kinect interface on the Xbox). When multiple selections are required, this added wait time has the potential to exacerbate fatigue effects when a person is required to hold their hand steady. Ergonomics of the surface and the size of hoverspace are also important factors that affect users' fatigue. For example, Spindler et al. tried to reduce the effects of fatigue in their studies by limiting the height of hoverspace to shoulder height for standing users [21].

In our pair of studies, we attempted to determine what gestures people expect to be able to use to select targets above a table, and whether non-physicality, layers, transitions, and fatigue play a role in those expectations. To better elicit these expectations, we first developed a system to detect the height of a person's hand above a multitouch surface.

System Description

We implemented two techniques for estimating the height of hands and objects above a DSI multitouch table, both based on a vision-based tracker. While we found the second approach to be more simple and useful in our study of target selection, we include the description of the first as well, as it provides more information than just hand height, and could be useful in other applications.

Vision-Based Tracker

Our system is based on a common pipeline used in other vision-based multitouch trackers, for example, Community Core Vision (ccv.nuigroup.com) and reacTIVision (reactivision.sourceforge.net). We add one or more additional pipelines (in addition to the touch pipeline) to detect hands above the surface that each use a lower threshold (i.e., detects dimmer blobs) and a mean-shift filter [4] to reduce noise. Standard blob finding and tracking algorithms are applied to the result of all pipelines and the data is sent to client applications using the TUIO [15] protocol.

Hover Height Estimation

Currently, there are many methods that can be used to estimate the height of a palm above a surface: stereo cameras [16,27], depth cameras (like Kinect) [3,25], multiple layers of lasers [22], infrared emitters above a table [5] and so on. What distinguishes our tracker from other methods is the ability to estimate the height of a hovering hand above the surface of the table, without additional sensing technology. Some computer vision approaches, like shape-from-shading (SFS) techniques [19], may compute the shape of a palm using an image from a regular camera. In the process of software development, we explored two methods of palm height estimation based on the more general SFS problem.

Slices Method. This method uses nine additional hover pipelines instead of just one, gradually decreasing in cut-off value, and each representing a different slice of height above the table (the algorithm was adapted from [20]). This method presents interesting opportunities for gesture recognition, because it produces an approximate 3D surface of a hovering hand. A potential weakness of this method is the low resolution and high computational demand of the blob-finding algorithm run on each slice of the image.

Center-weighted Average Method. Another method that proved simpler and required much less processing power is a "center-weighted average" approach. This method computes an average value of the 16×16 pixel square located in the geometric center of each blob in the hover layer. The resulting value is then mapped to the height of a hovering hand using a formula derived from linear regression.

Our proposed height estimation methods inherit limitations and difficulties of other SFS techniques, such as the fact that the source image is heavily influenced by the properties of the surface (such as reflectivity) and lighting (direction and magnitude). To address these issues we have chosen to solve the problem empirically, not analytically. We have recorded 5-second videos of 16 participants holding their dominant hand at various heights above the surface (from 2cm to 20cm with a step of 2cm). An exponential function was then fitted to the relationship between the measured value and the actual height and was used in the tracker to estimate the height of a hand.

We used our system to perform two experiments to evaluate people's expectations of how to select targets in hover space, as well as the performance of techniques derived from these expectations and our own designs.

EXPERIMENT 1: EXPECTED SELECTION GESTURES

The purpose of the first study was to elicit expectations of how objects should be selected above a multitouch surface. We used the methodology of Wobbrock et al. [28] to elicit these gestures. Participants were asked to acquire targets in the space above a table, and then asked to perform the gesture that they expected would make a selection.

Apparatus

We used an unmodified DSI multi-touch table setup for the experiment. This setup uses EndLighten acrylic that scatters infrared (IR) light evenly throughout the table's surface. An 81cm × 61cm sheet of acrylic forms the surface of the table. It is edge-illuminated by a strip of 850nm IR diodes. The display is rear-projected with resolution of 1024×768 pixels. An Unibrain Fire-i™ camera equipped with an 850nm band-pass IR filter is mounted behind the screen. The table is powered by a Windows XP computer.

Participants

Sixteen paid participants (6 female) took part in the study. All were right-handed and the average age was 24.8 years ($SD = 5.08$). 13 participants had previously used smartphones equipped with a multitouch screen, and 7 had previously used tablet PCs and public multitouch devices such as bank machines or airport check-in kiosks.

Design

We used a within-participants factorial design with the following three factors:

- Widget (bar, circle, button, menu)
- Number of hands (one, two)
- Anchoring (screen, cursor)

Task

Participants were shown one of the four widgets (described below) and asked to interact by moving their hand in the 3D space above the multitouch surface. When the system detected a hand hovering above the surface, a cursor was displayed. The cursor is represented as a semi-transparent circle with its center directly below the geometric center of a hovering palm and its size proportionately related to the height of the palm above the surface. Participants were then asked to move this cursor to the target (which varied by widget) and then demonstrate what gesture they would use to select that target. The software did not attempt to recognize or act on the gestures performed by the participants; it only recorded activity above the surface. We also video recorded participants' hands using a camera positioned above the screen.

Participants were asked to perform gestures using four different visual widgets. These four widgets were designed to be both abstract representations of targets (bar and circle) as well as closer approximations of widgets that could be used in an application (button and menu). Each visual widget is controlled in the same way: by moving one's hand to a predetermined target in the 3D space above the table.

The *bar* widget (Figure 1a) is an abstract rectangular control with a small slider moving up and down along the midline. The distance of a person's hand above the table determines the position of this slider along the vertical axis. The target is represented as a differently-coloured portion of the rectangle, which turns red when the slider is placed inside.

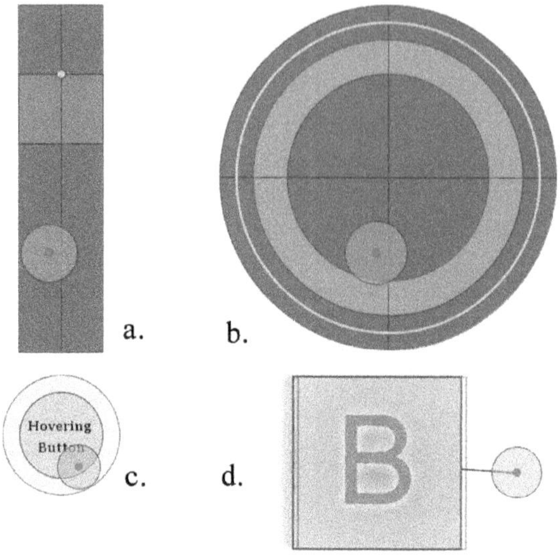

Figure 1: Above-surface widgets:
a. bar, b. circle, c. button and d. menu

The *circle* widget (Figure 1b) is similar to the bar widget, but shaped differently. The slider is represented as a ring and the target is represented as a differently coloured band, which turns red when the cursor is placed inside.

The *button* widget (Figure 1c) is a version of a standard circular GUI button, but adapted to be acquired by moving one's hand to a predetermined 3D position above the table. The circle changes colour when this correct location is acquired to indicate this hover state. Its height above the surface is represented by a grey band around the inner circle. The width of this band is the same as the radius of the cursor, when the cursor's height matches the button's height.

The *menu* widget (Figure 1d) is again adapted to hover space and is similar to the menu described by Benko et al. [25]. The current menu item is made visible by moving a hand up or down. Items that are located above or below the current item are blurred to simulate the way human eye focuses on objects. Items in our study are abstracted to the letters A through E.

Number of Hands and Anchoring

Participants were asked to demonstrate a gesture using both one hand and two hands separately. The widgets were also shown to be anchored either to the centre of the screen (i.e., remained stationary in x and y), or to the cursor (i.e., the x and y position of the widget moved with the hand).

Procedure

The order of events for each participant can be described algorithmically as follows:

1. The idea of hover space selection was introduced
2. For each widget (× 4):
   a. For each combination of hands and anchoring (× 4):
      i. Practice using the widget for as long as desired
      ii. When ready, demonstrate a gesture to select the corresponding target

Gesture	Description	Freq. 1 hand	Freq. 2 hands
Off-hand tap	Tapping the screen with a single or several fingers of the off hand	N/A	37.5%
Grab	Grabbing or pinching gesture with one or both hands	35.2%	23.4%
Push with a finger	Downwards motion of a single or several fingers	26.6%	10.2%
Snapping/Clapping	Clapping hands together or snapping fingers (sound-based interaction)	9.4%	7.0%
Spread/Expand	Both hands moving horizontally from the target to the edges of the surface	N/A	6.3%
Push	Downwards motion of a full hand, by bending wrist, elbow or shoulder joint. A version of the gesture was performed by bending all fingers downwards.	9.4%	3.9%
Tap	Tapping the screen with a single or several fingers	7.8%	0.0%
Dwell	A hand is held steady in the same place for a set period of time	6.3%	0.0%
Shake hand	A hand is held in the same place and shaken	3.9%	2.3%
Swipe	Horizontal motion above the surface	0.8%	6.3%
Other	Other gestures, such as rotating a palm or bumping palms together	0.8%	3.1%

Table 1. The frequencies with which each gesture was demonstrated in the first experiment.

The order in which the widgets appeared was counterbalanced using a random Latin square. The number of hands and target anchoring parameters were combined into a single 4-value parameter and counterbalanced using random Latin squares (one for every widget). Since the software had no means to recognize a gesture, participants were asked to indicate verbally when their gestures were complete. The experimenter then pressed a button to indicate to the software when to stop recording. With 16 participants, 4 visualizations, 1 or 2 hands and 2 anchoring methods, a total of $16 \times 4 \times 2 \times 2 = 256$ gestures were performed.

Gesture Classification

Once the gestures were collected we analyzed the videos recorded by the above-table camera. We manually classified the gestures performed along 3 dimensions: *palm shape*, *magnitude* and *motion*. Palm shape was specific to one hand; therefore the shape of the second palm was also analyzed in two-handed gestures. Examples of the *palm shape* category are: open palm, closed fist, closed fist with an extended index finger. The gesture *magnitude* describes how much of the palm was involved in the gesture; it ranged from full palm gestures to single finger gestures. The gesture *motion* category describes the path that the hand or a finger followed during the gesture. Depending on the magnitude of the gesture, the motion can describe the path of the full palm or a single finger.

Similar to the findings of [28], we noticed that participants did not attach significance to which fingers were used in a gesture and how many fingers were involved. Some participants performed gestures using their index finger interchangeably with their middle finger or thumb.

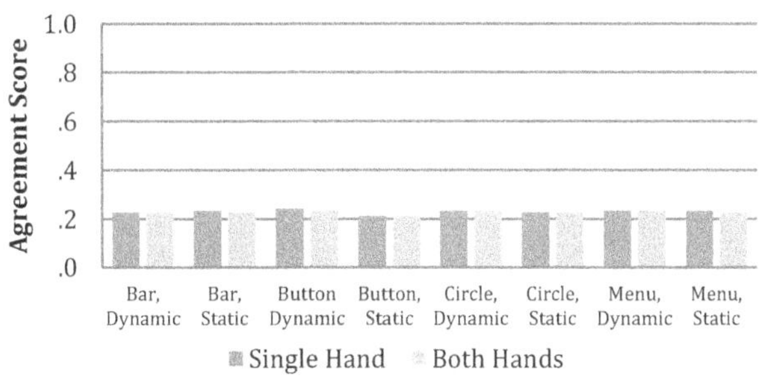

Figure 2. Agreement for each condition

Agreement Scores

We have grouped gestures with similar *palm shape, magnitude,* and *motion* into 11 groups (see Table 1). Group size was then used to compute an agreement score A that reflects, in a single number, the degree of consensus among participants (this process was adopted from [28]).

$$A = \sum_{P_i \subseteq P} \left(\frac{|P_i|}{|P|}\right)^2$$

P is the set of all proposed gestures for a certain condition (defined by widget, number of hands and anchoring) and P_i is a set of identical gestures from P.

Results

The average agreement score for each condition was .23 (SD = .008). This small variability indicates that the study factors had very little effect on agreement (see Figure 2). The overall agreement for one-handed and two-handed gestures was .22. In contrast, the agreement scores of most gestures selected for the user-defined set in [28], were between .30 and 1.0 for a single hand and between .30 and .60 for both hands. Our result indicates that there is no clear agreement between participants about how selection should be performed above a surface.

While the agreement scores were low, there were several gestures that were performed more often than others. With one hand, the *grab* gesture was performed 45 times (35.2%) and *push with a finger* was performed 34 times (26.6%). With two hands, *off-hand tap* (37.5%) and *grab* (23.4%) were performed more often than the others. Overall participants preferred one-handed gestures, as indicated either verbally or in the post-study survey. This finding agrees with the results of a gesture-elicitation study in [28].

We noticed that most participants (12 of 16) consistently used the same one-handed gesture and the same two-handed gesture for each experimental condition. Based on this observation, and in order to reduce the complexity of the factorial design, we opted to use only one visualisation in the second experiment, instead of testing all four.

EXPERIMENT 2: GESTURE PERFORMANCE

From the first experiment, we were able to identify *off-hand tap, grab* and *push with a finger* as possible candidates for a selection technique for targets above a multi-touch surface.

The second experiment was designed to measure the performance of these candidate methods of above-surface selection, as well as some techniques we suspected might be effective. We were interested in comparing three properties of each gesture: how fast it can be performed, how accurately it can be performed, and how difficult it would be for the computer to recognize and disambiguate the gesture. To do so, we designed an experiment where the human subject had to first *acquire* a target in hover space (above the screen), and then *perform* one of the gestures to select the target (like a button click). Unfortunately, the system we used was not accurate enough to recognize some of the gestures due to the low resolution and ambiguities inherent to shape-from-shading techniques. Too many factors can change the way a palm looks in greyscale apart from its height; for example the reflectivity of the skin on the top and bottom of the human palm is different, so the system would not be able to differentiate between a hand held palm-down higher above the table and a hand held palm-up closer to the surface. The *grab* gesture looks to our software exactly like lifting a palm higher above the surface. *Push with a finger* could not be recognized because the change in the image of the hand was too small to be differentiated from noise. We were similarly unable to include such designer-defined gestures as *SideTrigger* [2] or *ThumbTrigger* [23]. However, we hope these limitations will be addressed in future work using this research as a foundation.

As a result of these limitations, we decided to focus our second study on evaluating the performance of gestures that were practical to implement with minimal hardware. We chose *push* (as a close approximation to *push with a finger*) and selected the most common two-handed gesture suggested by the participants: *off-hand tap*. In contrast to elicited gestures, *dwell* and *tap* were also included in the experiment as those we expected to perform well based on our design experience (i.e., designer-defined), even though they were infrequently chosen by participants in our first study. We also used the same apparatus as in the first.

Participants

Sixteen paid participants (5 female) took part in the study. One participant was left-handed and the average age was 24.1 years ($SD = 3.17$). Some participants also took part in the first study. All participants were local university students and most majored in computer science or engineering.

Design

We used a within-participants factorial design with the following two factors:

- Gesture (dwell × 3, push, tap, off-hand tap)
- Location (dominant, middle, non-dominant)

Task

To begin each trial, the participant was asked to touch a specific area of the screen labelled "parking area" with their finger. When the participant touched this parking area, a target was displayed. The target is identical to the circle widget used in the first study, except for an adjustment in color scheme (see Figure 3). The participant was asked to acquire this target, using the same cursor as in the first experiment, by moving their hand so that the centre of their palm was directly above the centre of the ring (i.e., at the crosshair), and the height of their hand made the cursor radius match the target radius. Since the target was virtually located above the surface, the participants had to not only match its x, y position on the surface, but also its z position, or height above the surface. Once acquired, the participant then performed one of six selection gestures: *short dwell*, *medium dwell*, *long dwell*, *push*, *tap*, or *off-hand tap*.

The three dwell gestures required participants to hold their hand above the target for 500ms, 1000ms, and 2000ms, respectively. The push gesture required participants to move their hand rapidly in the downward direction, and was detected when the speed of the hand was above ~10m/s. To perform the tap gesture, a participant had to move their hand down rapidly (with the same speed as the push gesture) and then touch the screen. The last z position of the cursor prior to the start of this rapid motion was saved, and when a touch event was detected, it was used to determine if the target was activated successfully. Off-hand tap gestures were completed when the participant touched the table anywhere with a finger on the non-dominant hand.

Targets appeared in one of the three x, y locations: on the dominant side (right for right-handed participants, and left for left-handed), in the middle, or on the non-dominant side of the screen. The height and distance of the target from the "parking area" was kept constant, so that participants' hands had to be at 14cm above the table and 25.4cm from the start position along the table's surface. The participant was asked to acquire the target and perform a gesture as quickly as possible.

To indicate the state of the target, the following color scheme was used: initially the target was red, when the centre of the cursor was within 1cm of the crosshair, the target changed to yellow, and when a gesture was completed, the

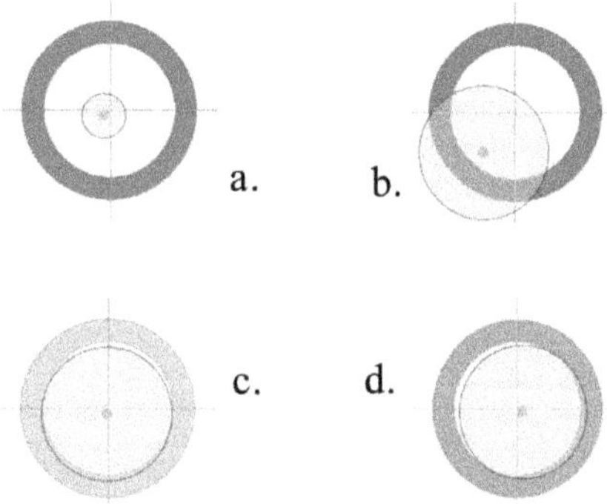

Figure 3. The targets (circular rings) and cursor used in experiment 2. Targets first appears red (a. & b.), turns yellow when acquired (c.) and green upon selection (d.). The radius of the cursor is determined by the height of the participant's hand above the table.

target changed to green (see Figure 3). For both the *push* and *tap* gestures, movement beyond the target boundaries was required to perform the gesture, and so once the target was first acquired (yellow), the target would not return to its non-acquired state (red).

Procedure

The order of events for each participant can be described algorithmically as follows:

1. The idea of hover space selection was introduced
2. For each gesture (× 6):
   a. The experimenter demonstrated the gesture
   b. The participant performed a practice trial
   c. For each trial (3 locations × 3 repetitions = 9), the participant was asked to:
      i. Move their hand to the "parking area"
      ii. Acquire and selected the target

As the dwell gestures all required only one explanation, the three dwell gestures were presented together (one after the other) in random order. The order of dwell, push, tap, and off-hand tap was then counterbalanced using a random Latin square. The order of the 3 locations was randomized.

The application recorded the path of the hand and the timing of events, as well as target loss and successful/failed gestures. The trial was considered successful when a gesture was recognized while the target was acquired. If a gesture was performed outside of the target or a gesture was never performed, the trial was marked as failed.

After each block of 9 trials, a participant answered three 7-point Likert scale questions about the ease of navigation to the target, performing the gesture and the overall experience. With 16 participants, 6 gestures and 9 repetitions, a total of $16 \times 6 \times 9 = 864$ gestures were performed.

Results & Discussion

Due to the shape and ergonomics of the experimental multi-touch table, most participants had difficulty acquiring targets on the side of the table opposite their dominant hand. The table was shaped as a coffee table and its small height (51 cm) forced participants to bend over the table or kneel next to it; which meant that to reach the left side of the screen, right-handed people had to rotate their torso and/or shoulders, making the target acquisition awkward and uncomfortable. We performed a one-way analysis of variance (ANOVA) on the location factor, which showed a significant effect ($F(2,30) = 32.19, p < .001$). Post-hoc pairwise comparison of the location factor showed a significant difference between the non-dominant location and both other locations ($p < .001$), while the middle and dominant locations were not significantly different ($p = .113$). We thus removed data from the non-dominant level of the location factor from the remainder of our analysis. Therefore, a total of $16 \times 6 \times 6 = 576$ gestures were considered in the analysis. We analyzed three main dependent measures: gesture speed, gesture accuracy, and participant preference.

Gesture Speed

The time to perform a gesture can be broken down into three parts: acquisition time, jitter time, and selection time.

Acquisition time was measured as the time it takes to move a hand from the starting area to the target. Using a 6 (gesture) × 2 (location) repeated-measures ANOVA, we found a significant main effect of gesture on acquisition time ($F(5,75) = 5.528, p < .001$). In particular, the *short dwell* gesture had significantly smaller acquisition times than all other gestures (*medium dwell*: $p < .01$, *long dwell:* $p = .024$, *push:* $p < 0.001$, *tap:* $p < 0.01$; *off-hand tap:* $p < 0.001$). Acquisition in the medium dwell was also significantly faster than *push* ($p = .035$), *tap* ($p = .028$), and *off-hand tap* ($p < .01$). The *long dwell* was also significantly faster than *off-hand tap* ($p = .039$). Acquisition times for *push, tap,* and *off-hand tap* were not significantly different ($p > .05$). There was also no main effect of location ($F(1,15) = 2.630, p > .05$), nor interaction between gesture and location ($F(5,75) = 1.544, p > .05$).

The differences in acquisition times were surprising, and cannot be easily explained, since the acquisition task did not differ for any of the gestures; all trials required acquiring a target at the same distance from the starting location. This indicates that people adjusted their behaviour depending on the gesture they were performing. Specifically, people moved more quickly toward targets that required only a dwell. We hypothesize that this was due to the inaccuracy of, in particular, the short dwell for selection (described below). This inaccuracy perhaps led to a speed-accuracy trade-off. That is, participants may have noticed an inability to accurately select targets, and so increased their speed. However, we note that this same trade-off did not occur for *off-hand tap*. Further studies are required to better isolate this effect.

Jitter time was measured as the time between the initial target acquisition and the final one. In other words, jitter represents a phase when the participant lost and reacquired the target (perhaps several times) before performing the gesture.

We performed a 6 (gesture) × 2 (location) repeated measures ANOVA on the jitter times. There was a significant main effect of gesture ($F(5,75) = 10.275, p < .001$). Post-hoc analysis revealed that jitter times for *long dwell* were not significantly different than *off-hand tap* ($p = .212$), and jitter times of both were significantly longer than jitter times of all other gestures ($p < .012$). *Short dwell* had significantly less jitter than both other dwells ($p < .002$), but similar to *push* and *tap* gestures ($p > .05$). Jitter times for *medium dwell, push* and *tap* were not significantly different. There was also no main effect of location ($F(1,15) = 0.065, p > .05$), nor interaction between gesture and location ($F(5,75) = 0.260, p > .05$).

The increase in jitter is expected as the length of dwell increases, since it is difficult for a person to hold their hand

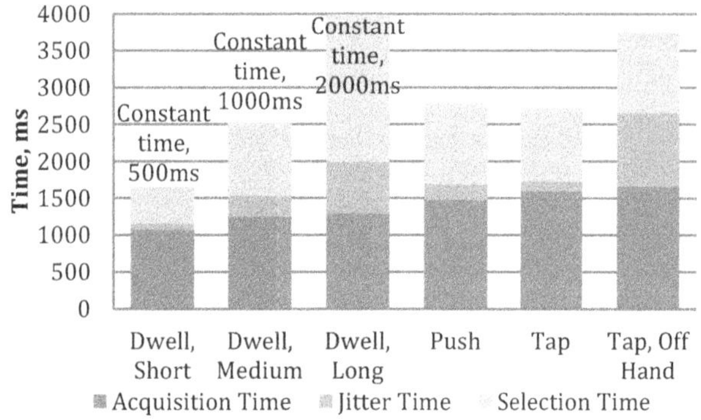

Figure 4. Acquisition, jitter, and selection times.

steadily in the same place. *Off-hand tap* had more jitter than all other gestures except for *long dwell*, perhaps due to the ergonomics of our table or to the fact that participants had trouble holding their main hand steady while touching the screen with the other hand. The same effect appeared in the number of times a target was lost (see below). The other four gestures had comparable amount of jitter.

Selection time was measured as the time it takes to perform the gesture after the last acquisition (i.e., after acquisition + jitter). For the *dwell* gestures, this selection time is constant, and so was not included in the analysis. We performed a 3 (gesture) × 2 (location) repeated measures ANOVA on the remaining three gestures, but found no significant main effects or interactions (gesture: $F(2{,}30) = 0.372, p > .05$; location: $F(1{,}15) = 0.252, p > .05$; gesture × location: $F(2{,}30) = 0.44, p > .05$).

Overall, although we broke down our analysis by acquisition, jitter, and selection time, Figure 4 shows how these times would accumulate in practice. *Short dwell* was the fastest to perform, while *long dwell* was the slowest. *Push*, *tap*, and *medium dwell* were comparable in speed, while *off-hand tap* performed almost as badly as *long dwell* (likely due to the high jitter times).

Gesture Accuracy

To evaluate the precision of each gesture we measured the number of times a target was lost when performing a gesture and the overall number of failed trials.

Target lost count was a measure of the difficulty in keeping one's hand on the target while selecting a gesture. This can be thought of as a count of the number of jitters per trial, rather than the time taken for jitter. The 6 (gesture) × 2 (location) ANOVA was performed on target lost count. There was a main effect of gesture ($F(5{,}75) = 12.947, p < 0.001$). Post-hoc analysis revealed that the target lost count of *long dwell* and *off-hand tap* gestures were significantly different from all others ($p < .034$). The target lost counts of *short* and *medium dwells* were also different from all others ($p < .030$) except for the *push* and *tap* gestures. There was also no main effect of location ($F(1{,}15) = 0.181, p > .05$), nor interaction between gesture and location ($F(5{,}75) = 0.368, p > .05$).

As expected, it becomes harder to stay on-target as the length of the *dwell* gesture increases. *Off-hand tap* again performed the worst for this measure. *Push* and *tap* performed as well as *short* and *medium dwells*.

Trial failure frequency was measured as the proportion of unsuccessful trials, which were recorded if (a) the target was never acquired, (b) no selection gesture was recorded, or (c) the target was not in its acquired state when the selection gesture was performed. We performed a Cochran's Q test to analyze this binary data (each trial was either successful or not) for the gesture factor, and included each location as a repetition. We found a significant difference between the failure frequencies of the gestures ($Q_{df=5,N=96} = 50.282, p < .001$). A Post-hoc McNemar's test revealed that the *short dwell* resulted in significantly more failures than the rest of the gestures ($\chi^2_{N=96} > 6.568, p < .01$); *long dwell* resulted in fewer failures than *push* ($\chi^2_{N=96} = 8.828, p < .01$); *tap* also had fewer unsuccessful trials than *push* ($\chi^2_{N=96} = 6.323, p = .012$).

The number of unsuccessful trials for the *short dwell* gesture was very high ($M = .47, SD = .502$). This high error rate was not unexpected as it has been noted before and dubbed the "Midas Touch" effect [11], which negates any speed benefit noted before by resulting in many unintentional selections. Moreover, the *tap* gesture resulted in fewer errors than the *push* gesture, and with a similar overall speed for these two gestures, this indicates that *tap*'s overall performance was better. While the *long dwell* had similarly few errors, the added time for dwell means that *tap* also outperforms *long dwell*.

Participant Preference

We also analyzed participants' preferences based on three

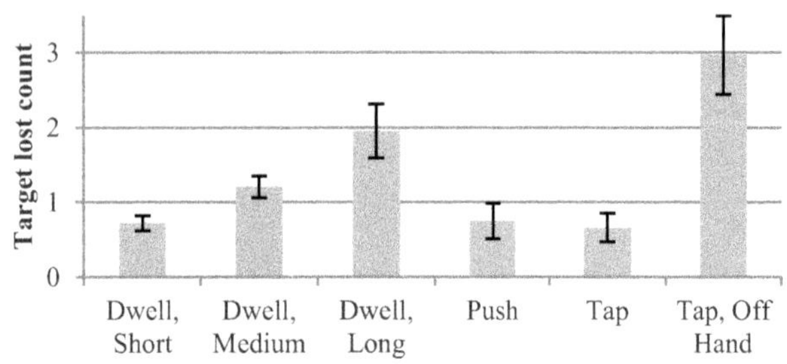

Figure 5. The target lost counts for each gesture.

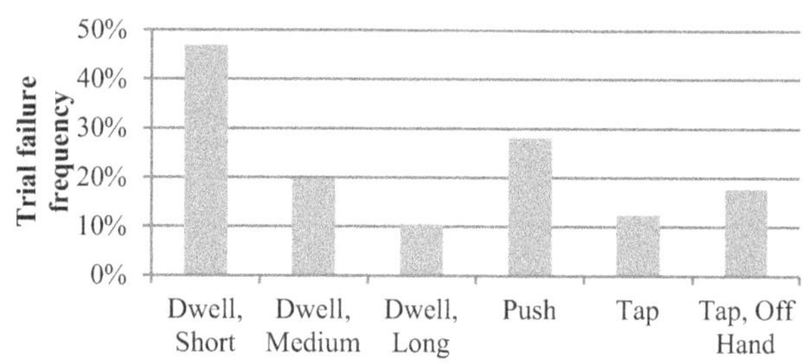

Figure 6. The frequency of unsuccessful trials.

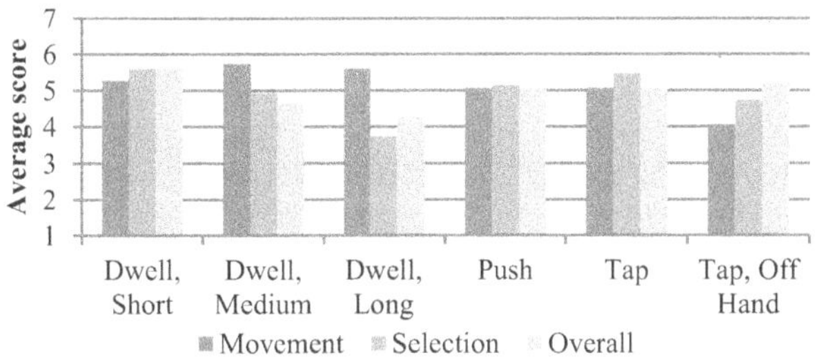

Figure 7. Participant preferences.

7-point Likert scale statements. The first was: "It was easy to ***move*** to the target", the second was: "It was difficult it to ***select*** the target" and the last was: "The selection technique is easy ***overall***". The words "easy" and "difficult" were used alternatingly to avoid influencing the responses; for clarity, we present the results of the responses to the scales with the word "difficult" backwards (i.e., answers 1 and 7, 2 and 6, 3 and 5 were interchanged). One of the participants did not rate one of the gestures.

A Friedman's test was performed on each of the three scales. Significant effects were found in the ***move*** and ***overall*** categories ($\chi^2_{N=15} = 17.509, p < .01$ and $\chi^2_{N=15} = 12.164, p = .033$ respectively). The ***select*** category's differences were only marginally significant ($\chi^2_{N=15} = 10.719, p = .057$). Post-hoc pairwise Wilcoxon tests were performed which revealed the following significant results:

- For ***move***, *off-hand tap* was rated significantly lower than all other gestures and *push* was rated lower than *medium dwell*.
- For ***select***, *long dwell* was rated lower than all other gestures except for the *off-hand tap*.
- For ***overall***, *short dwell* was rated higher than *medium* and *long dwells*.

The fact that most participants found moving a hand to a target in the *off-hand tap* gesture more difficult is consistent with our findings in performance. Selection using the *long dwell* gesture was rated low as expected, since two seconds is a long time to hold a hand steady in the same place. *Short dwell* was preferred to other dwells overall, but due to the unacceptably high false activation rate, we would not recommend that it be used in a real-world application. *Push* and *tap* were rated consistently high on all 3 scales.

Unlike the participants of the first experiment, the second experiment's volunteers had to perform a gesture multiple times while worrying about the speed and precision of their gestures. Therefore their preferences may be a better indication of which gestures are more suited for an application.

DISCUSSION

The results of this pair of studies provide some insight into the design of above-surface selection techniques. When selecting with one hand, people most frequently expect to be able to *grab* on-screen objects from a location in mid-air above that object, and with two hands expect to be able to *tap* with their other hand. However, this expectation was not agreed upon by all participants (35.2% and 37.5%, respectively; only between 1/3 and 2/5 of participants). Although, due to system limitations we could not easily investigate the preferred one-handed grab gesture, our investigation of a close approximation of their second choice in our *push* gesture and the *off-hand tap* two-handed gesture revealed that they underperformed when compared to the *tap* gesture, as expected by designers. More specifically, while we found no difference in selection time between *push* or *off-hand tap* and the one-handed *tap*, participants frequently drifted off of the target when using *off-hand tap*, and frequently missed the target with *push*.

In addition, the common *dwell* technique did not result in a suitable alternative. In particular, a trade-off between dwell time and accuracy was revealed; when the dwell time is low enough to improve speed beyond the best-performing *tap*, the number of errors increased dramatically.

Based on these results, we recommend the use of a single-handed tap gesture for selection of targets in hover space. However, we suggest some caution to designers in this interpretation, as our system was not capable of detecting *grab*, the most preferred selection gesture from the first experiment. Nonetheless, we note that accurate detection of a grab gesture is not simple in any of the existing hardware systems that we are aware of, whereas tap can easily be detected by tracking sudden acceleration and using the existing touch capabilities of an interactive surface. We demonstrate the use of tap to select colours from a colour palette in our example application.

EXAMPLE APPLICATION

We designed Hover Paint (Figure 8) using the results of our two experiments, which allows people to paint on a multi-touch surface using their fingers. Hover space interaction is used to control the colour and size of the brush. To activate the colour wheel, a person can lift their hand above the table. The x and y position of the hand can then be used to control the colour, and the height of the hand can control the brush size; the current selection is displayed as a circular cursor located under the palm. The selection can then be made by moving the hand down quickly and tapping the screen (i.e., the *tap* gesture).

CONCLUSION AND FUTURE WORK

We presented a system that can estimate the height of a person's hand above a DSI multitouch table. With this system, we performed two experiments, the results of which showed that people do not have a clear idea how to select

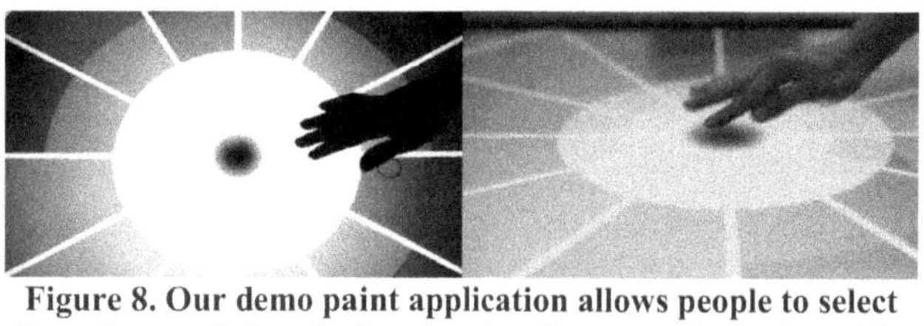

Figure 8. Our demo paint application allows people to select the colour and size of a brush using the space above the table.

objects in this hover space. In addition, gestures that were frequently chosen tended to underperform those both less-frequently chosen and predicted by designers to perform better. Specifically, based on our pair of studies, we suggest using a tap gesture. That is, people can perform selections by transitioning from the movement occurring above the table to tapping or touching the surface. In addition, our study shows that this technique will perform better than a tap with the other hand, a push gesture, and dwell. In the future we hope to address the limitations of our system that made us unable to analyze some of the gestures frequently selected in the first study or defined by other designers.

ACKNOWLEDGEMENTS

We would like to thank the Natural Sciences and Engineering Council of Canada (NSERC), NSERC Surfnet, and the Graphics Animation & New Media (GRAND) NCE for funding. We also thank the reviewers for their thoughtful and constructive suggestions.

REFERENCES

1. Agarawala, A. and Balakrishnan, R. Keepin' it real: pushing the desktop metaphor with physics, piles and the pen. *Proc. CHI*, ACM Press (2006), 1283–1292.
2. Banerjee, A., Burstyn, J., Girouard, A., and Vertegaal, R. Pointable: an in-air pointing technique to manipulate out-of-reach targets on tabletops. *Proc. ITS*, ACM Press (2011), 11–20.
3. Benko, H. and Wilson, A.D. DepthTouch : Using Depth-Sensing Camera to Enable Freehand Interactions On and Above the Interactive Surface. In *Technical Report MSR-TR-2009-23, Microsoft Research*. 2009.
4. Comaniciu, D. and Meer, P. Mean shift: a robust approach toward feature space analysis. *IEEE Transactions on Pattern Analysis and Machine Intelligence 24*, 5 (2002), 603–619.
5. Echtler, F., Huber, M., and Klinker, G. Shadow tracking on multi-touch tables. *Proc. AVI*, ACM Press (2008), 388–391.
6. Frisch, M., Heydekorn, J., and Dachselt, R. Investigating multi-touch and pen gestures for diagram editing on interactive surfaces. *Proc. ITS*, ACM Press (2009), 149–156.
7. Grossman, T. and Balakrishnan, R. The design and evaluation of selection techniques for 3D volumetric displays. *Proc. UIST*, ACM Press (2006), 3–12.
8. Grossman, T., Hinckley, K., Baudisch, P., Agrawala, M., and Balakrishnan, R. Hover Widgets: Using the Tracking State to Extend the Capabilities of Pen-Operated Devices. *Proc. CHI*, ACM Press (2006), 861–870.
9. Han, S. and Park, J. A study on touch & hover based interaction for zooming. *Proc. CHI*, ACM Press (2012), 2183–2188.
10. Hancock, M., ten Cate, T., and Carpendale, S. Sticky tools: full 6DOF force-based interaction for multi-touch tables. *Proc. ITS*, ACM Press (2009), 133–140.
11. Hansen, J.P., Tørning, K., Johansen, A.S., Itoh, K., and Aoki, H. Gaze typing compared with input by head and hand. *Proc. ETRA*, ACM Press (2004), 131–138.
12. Henze, N., Löcken, A., Boll, S., Hesselmann, T., and Pielot, M. Free-hand gestures for music playback. *Proc. MUM*, ACM Press (2010), 1–10.
13. Hilliges, O., Izadi, S., Wilson, A.D., Hodges, S., Garcia-Mendoza, A., and Butz, A. Interactions in the air: Adding Further Depth to Interactive Tabletops. *Proc. UIST*, ACM Press (2009), 139–148.
14. Johnson, E.A. Touch display—a novel input/output device for computers. *Electronics Letters 1*, 8 (1965), 219–220.
15. Kaltenbrunner, M., Bovermann, T., Bencina, R., and Costanza, E. TUIO: A protocol for table-top tangible user interfaces. *Proc. ISon*, (2005).
16. Leibe, B., Starner, T., Ribarsky, W., et al. The Perceptive Workbench: toward spontaneous and natural interaction in semi-immersive virtual environments. *Proc. VR*, IEEE Comput. Soc (2000), 13–20.
17. Marquardt, N., Jota, R., Greenberg, S., and Jorge, J. The Continuous Interaction Space: Interaction Techniques Unifying Touch and Gesture On and Above a Digital Surface. *Proc. INTERACT*, Springer-Verlag (2011), 461–476.
18. Nielsen, M., Störring, M., Moeslund, T.B., and Granum, E. A procedure for developing intuitive and ergonomic gesture interfaces for HCI. *Proc. GW*, Springer (2003), 409–420.
19. Prados, E. and Faugeras, O. Shape from shading. In Springer, ed., *Handbook of Mathematical Models in Computer Vision*. 2006, 375–388.
20. Pyryeskin, D., Hancock, M., and Hoey, J. Extending interactions into hoverspace using reflected light. *Proc. ITS*, ACM Press (2011), 262–263.
21. Spindler, M., Martsch, M., and Dachselt, R. Going beyond the surface: studying multi-layer interaction above the tabletop. *Proc. CHI*, ACM Press (2012), 1277–1286.
22. Takeoka, Y., Miyaki, T., and Rekimoto, J. Z-touch: An Infrastructure for 3D gesture interaction in the proximity of tabletop surfaces. *Proc. ITS*, ACM Press (2010), 91–94.
23. Vogel, D. and Balakrishnan, R. Distant freehand pointing and clicking on very large, high resolution displays. *Proc. UIST*, ACM Press (2005), 33–42.
24. Vogel, D. and Balakrishnan, R. Occlusion-aware interfaces. *Proc. CHI*, ACM Press (2010), 263–272.
25. Wilson, A.D. and Benko, H. Combining Multiple Depth Cameras and Projectors for Interactions On, Above, and Between Surfaces. *Proc. UIST*, ACM Press (2010), 273–282.
26. Wilson, A.D., Izadi, S., Hilliges, O., Garcia-Mendoza, A., and Kirk, D. Bringing physics to the surface. *Proc. UIST*, ACM Press (2008), 67–76.
27. Wilson, A.D. TouchLight: An Imaging Touch Screen and Display for Gesture-Based Interaction. *Proc. ICMI*, ACM Press (2004), 69–76.
28. Wobbrock, J.O., Morris, M.R., and Wilson, A.D. User-defined gestures for surface computing. *Proc. CHI*, ACM Press (2009), 1083–1092.

Direct Manipulation and the Third Dimension: Co-Planar Dragging on 3D Displays

Max Möllers, Patrick Zimmer, Jan Borchers
RWTH Aachen University, Germany
{moellers,borchers}@cs.rwth-aachen.de, patrick.zimmer@rwth-aachen.de

ABSTRACT

Recent advances in touch and display technologies are supporting a wide-spread use of touch-based direct manipulation techniques as well as 3D displays that give a perspectively correct view. Both techniques have consistency constraints including the following: With direct manipulation, a dragged object should stick to the finger tip. With viewer centered projection, head movement should update the scene's projection to preserve a sound 3D impression, e.g., leaning around a house should reveal its backyard. Unfortunately, these two contradict each other, making a combination, e.g., moving the head while touching or dragging an object, non-trivial. We introduce a design space of perspectively adjusted methods for direct manipulation to cope with this limitation, select nine different strategies from it, and evaluate six of them in depth. Participants dragged a box through a 3D maze with multiple, partially occluded levels. We identified one method to be among the fastest while yielding up to 32% less collisions than the other fast methods.

ACM Classification: H.5.2

Keywords: motion parallax; direct manipulation; co-planar dragging; 3D interactions; 3D tabletops

INTRODUCTION

More and more consumer displays are able to generate 3D output. One visual cue for this is stereoscopy: You render slightly different images for each eye and display them to each eye using shutter glasses or special lenses. Another important visual cue to perceive spatial relations is motion parallax: As soon as the user moves his head, a viewer centered projection is updated. This requires head-tracking but can be done using low-cost cameras found on devices such as smartphones, notebooks, or tablet PCs.

Orthogonal to this evolution, many current displays are touch enabled and employ the direct manipulation paradigm in which a dragged object always sticks to the finger. Our study looks into the combination of the two paradigms: Users touch and move the projections of 3D objects, thereby manipulating the objects themselves. To isolate our study from stereoscopic effects, such as the ones described in [18], we augmented our touch enabled tabletop exclusively with viewer centered projection.

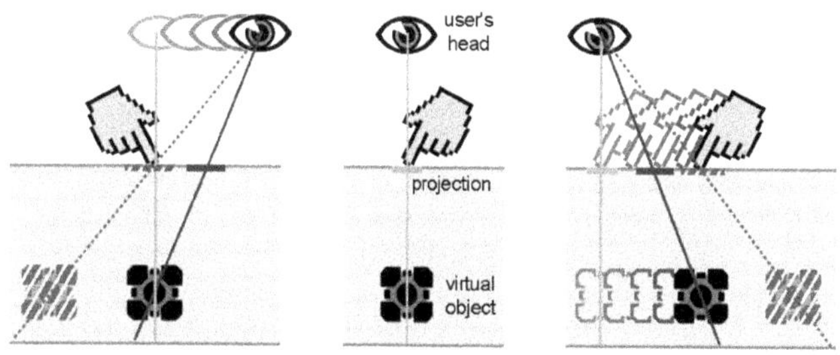

Figure 1: Direct manipulation in a naïve fish tank VR implementation. The colored lines show the gaze direction and the bars are the projections of the boxes. Bright blue is before and dark red after the movement; dotted green shows where the object would look to be "below" the finger from the user's point of view. Left) Moving the head does not change the 3D position of the object. Right) Moving the finger to the side moves the object equally. In both cases, the projections behave differently than the objects. Thus, the object is no longer below the finger, breaking the direct-manipulation metaphor.

One way to map the (x, y)-touch is to move the object in the same two dimensions and omit the third. We refer to this as *co-planar dragging*. Adding viewer centered projection causes head movement to change the projection of the 3D scene on the 2D display to provide a 3D impression. This means that the projections are moved on the display. In a naïve mapping (Fig. 1), touching one of these projections while moving your head will result in the projection of the touched object slipping off the finger—violating the sticks-to-finger property of direct manipulation. Another naïve option would be to move the touched object in 3D space based on the head movement—that way, the object would stick to the user's finger as expected, but now it would appear to move around in relation to its 3D environment as the user moves his head.

In this paper, we contribute new ways to perspectively adjust direct manipulation by presenting: (i) a design space for different input methods and (ii) a quantitative and qualitative analysis of six selected methods.

ITS'12, November 11–14, 2012, Cambridge, Massachusetts, USA.

RELATED WORK

Part of our research is related to the field of Virtual Reality (VR). While VR strives for perfect immersion covering multiple senses, we limit ourselves to a table size (150 cm x 80 cm) horizontal display, simulating 3D vision through motion parallax. These non-immersive systems are known as Fish Tank VR [19] and usually employ stereoscopy in addition to motion parallax. An early VR -motivated advance in the tabletop domain was the Responsive Workbench [1]. It featured a fully head-tracked stereo display for two users. However, its focus was on displaying content more than interacting with it as it only implemented indirect interaction through cyber gloves.

A comprehensive overview of other systems that use 3D technology on tabletops was done by Grossmann et al. in 2007 [6]. They defined a 3D tabletop taxonomy, differentiating systems by their physical properties as well as display and input properties. In this scheme, our setup joins the ImmersaDesk [5] in the group of table-sized systems with 2D input on a perceived 3D volume. While the ImmersaDesk was capaple of device-based input on its planar surface, its focus lay on interaction using six degrees of freedom flight sticks, also used in fully immersive VR systems like the CAVE [4]. Our setup differs as we strive for direct touch interaction [16], with no need for additional input devices.

Hachet et al. showed multitouch interaction with 3D objects hovering in the air [7]. They use an abstract 2D representation (based on handles) projected below the objects to allow for rotating, scaling, and translating them. We, however, focus on single touch direct manipulation and objects are shown beneath the physical interaction plane.

Steinicke et al. investigated the mix of stereoscopic and monoscopic content in a single GUI [17]. They also analyzed how people interact with stereoscopically rendered content [18], making it highly related to our work. However, we use view point correlation to monoscopically render our scene instead of showing fixed stereo images. While Steinicke et al. are trying to cope with the disparity of two different images displayed on the interaction surface, we are interested in the perceived alignment of touch point and virtual object.

Chan et al. [3] examined users' performance in 3D direct touch with an intangible reach-through display, realized with a fresnel lens. Similar to our motion parallax approach, the fresnel lens only displays a 2D projection, which is perceived as three dimensional. Chan et al. use two infrared cameras to calculate a 3D touch point above, on, or behind the image plane, which seems to be floating in mid air. Their results show that interaction in the z-axis (depth) is difficult, as there is no haptic feedback, neither active nor passive.

Interacting with 3D content does not necessarily require 3D displays; often 2D displays with a useful set of control options suffice. Recently, this field has branched towards tabletop displays with direct touch interaction. Interactions in the Air [12] controls content in three dimensions by additionally allowing contactless gestures above the table surface. Hancock et al. looked at direct touch gestures using one, two, or three contact points to manipulate objects with six degrees of freedom [9]. To keep interaction direct and feasible, they limited themselves to a shallow depth approach, where interactive content is reasonably close to the surface. Reisman et al. [15] present an in-depth analysis of the de-facto standard Rotate-Scale-Translate (RST) technique for manipulating 2D content and port it into the third dimension, using three or more contact points with novel interaction gestures.

Martinet et al. evaluated techniques for three dimensional object positioning on multitouch tabletops [13]. Their proposed Z-technique uses direct movement control on a plane with one finger, supported by a secondary indirect gesture to control depth. The use of single touch co-planar direct object movement gives a strong relation to our own work. Yet, we are facing the additional problem of a dynamic perspective and focus on techniques to cope with touch offset.

Hancock et al. showed how people (mis)interpret 3D orientation on tabletops when viewing off-axis [11] and offered insights in how to visualize content when perspectively accurate projection is not available or possible, e.g., when multiple users are involved [10].

An early version of the design space shown in this paper has been presented at a non-archival workshop at CHI 2012 [14].

INTERACTIONS IN A FISH TANK

It is an often used paradigm that dragging an object makes it follow the user's finger or cursor. However, in a head tracked fish tank VR system, the two-dimensional dragging input can not be mapped to the 3D object easily.

The problem is the offset between the touch point on the surface and an object's projection on the same surface (Fig. 2). The offset depends on the current system state, which consists of the current head or view position v, an object handle h, and a touch position t. During a dragging operation, the following happens: The hand moves from t_1 to $t_2 = t_1 + \vec{m}$. The object naïvely mimics the movement of the user's finger, thus, being far below the interaction surface, appearing to be moving slower. Consequently, the object does not stick to the finger. To describe this effect, we use the offset $\vec{a}$. Moving the object to h_i would eliminate the offset $\vec{a}$.

Furthermore, the illustration displays movement of the user's head from v_1 to v_2. The resulting additional offset is marked as $\vec{b}$. This offset is of special consideration when the user holds his hand still and tries to look around. By keeping track of head and touch movement, $\vec{a}$ and $\vec{b}$ can be easily distinguished. This gives us the option to deal with these effects either separately or in unison.

Design Space

Offset occurs when a set of v, t, h are not in a line. To compensate, we can either change the virtual object's position or we can change how the system takes the user's head into account by adjusting the virtual view point: Instead of moving the person's head, we move the digital representation of the head and ignore further updates (besides z movement, i.e., the person moving closer to the table). This means, we then have a new eye position and a changed viewport. This will shear the scene from the user's point of view. Table 3 shows

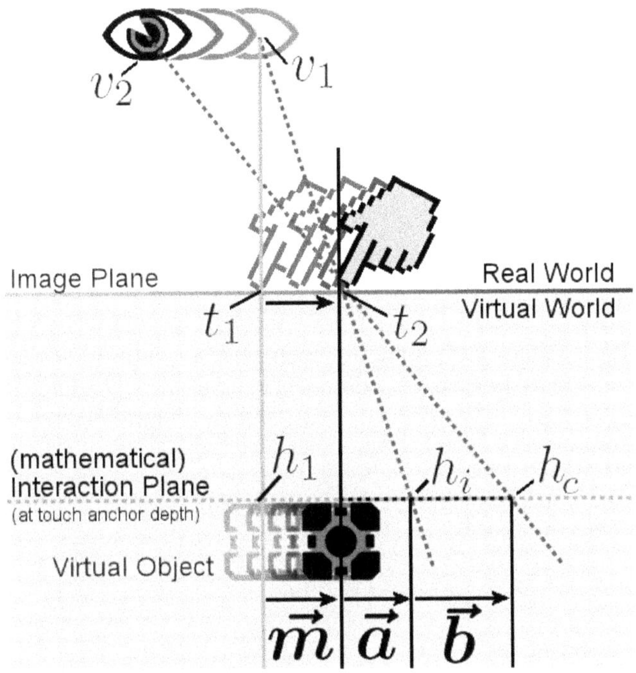

Figure 2: Offset created by dragging an object in a head tracked environment. Total offset can be split into a touch induced offset $\vec{a}$ and a head induced offset $\vec{b}$. From a graphics point of view, the near plane lies 60cm above the table, the projection plane matches the surface of the table, and the interaction plane is set to the top of the object.

a 2×2 matrix scheme where we oppose the offset triggers with the correction methods. For each type of offset we can choose one of two correction methods or none at all. This gives us three possible ways to deal with each offset: ignore the offset, move the object to compensate, or shear the scene to compensate. Linear combination of two corrections is an interesting field for future research.

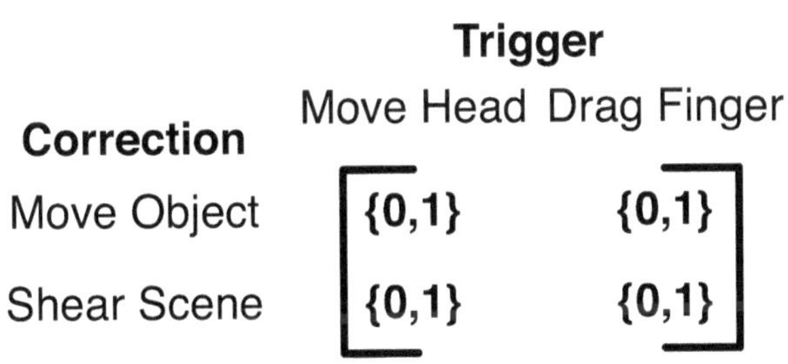

Figure 3: Design space for perspectively adjusted direct manipulation.

This leaves us with nine control methods in total, all of which were examined in a pilot study. Six promising methods were selected for further analysis regarding speed and accuracy. The following sections summarize all of the nine method's properties and implementation details as well as the reasons for the removal of the three.

Interaction Methods

The overall algorithm works as follows (cf. Figure 2):

0. Given positions last frame; head v_1, finger t_1, object h_1.
1. Drag finger to t_2 and move head to v_2. Note: $t_2 - t_1 = \vec{m}$.
2. Cast ray from v_1 over t_2. Intersection with object plane yields h_i. Note: $h_i - h_1 = \vec{m} + \vec{a}$.
3. Cast ray from v_2 over t_2. Intersection with object plane yields h_c. Note: $h_c - h_1 = \vec{m} + \vec{a} + \vec{b}$.
4. Move object to $h_1 + \vec{m}$.
5. Select method. Update offsets.
6. Move object by offset assigned for positional correction.
7. Shear scene by offset assigned to be shifted.
8. Draw. Update v_1, t_1, h_1. Repeat.

All nine methods perform the same direct object movement $\vec{m}$. They then differ in the way they treat the offsets $\vec{a}$ and $\vec{b}$. Their naming is loosely based on the following scheme:

- *Correction* if they move the object to compensate for offset,
- *Shift* if they shear the scene to compensate for offset,
- *Team* if they do both,
- *Adaptive* if offset is mitigated over time,
- *Cross* if the compensations are switched, e.g., head induced offset is corrected by object movement.

Additional impressions can be gathered from our supplemental video figure.

$\left[\begin{smallmatrix}0&0\\0&0\end{smallmatrix}\right]$ UNCORRECTED

No correction is applied and the resulting offset is tolerated. The object is naïvely moved only by vector $\vec{m}$.

$\left[\begin{smallmatrix}1&1\\0&0\end{smallmatrix}\right]$ OBJECTCORRECTION

This method can be found in literature under the term Sticky Finger [2]. The object position is constrained to a plane and determined based on head and touch position. In our model this correlates to an applied movement of

$$\vec{m} + \vec{a} + \vec{b}$$

This way, the object always appears to be precisely under the touch. The consideration of $\vec{b}$ leads to head movement alone causing the object to move. Offset can only be forced when this movement can not be applied due to other constraints, e.g., boundaries in the virtual world.

$\left[\begin{smallmatrix}0&1\\0&0\end{smallmatrix}\right]$ ADAPTIVECORRECTION

When the finger is moved, the object follows precisely. Head movement, however, does not cause the object to move and lets the touch slip off. This method is designed to appear to a user as $\vec{m} + \vec{a}$ object movement, yielding the described effects. However, mathematically the total applied object movement is:

$$\vec{m} + \vec{a} + |\vec{a}| \cdot f \cdot \frac{\vec{b}}{|\vec{b}|}$$

That means $\vec{b}$ is only corrected alongside $\vec{a}$ if the latter is dominant. This also causes an offset touch to ease back towards alignment while it is moved. This has been done to avoid an offset $\vec{b}$ to be retained indefinitely which would make the method feel indirect despite the $\vec{a}$ correction applied.

The factor $f \in [0, \infty]$ determines the dependance of $\vec{b}$ on $\vec{a}$, i.e., how quickly alignment is restored from an offset state. During our study, it was set to 0.8 as a trade-off between offset reduction and predictability.

$\left[\begin{smallmatrix}0&0\\1&1\end{smallmatrix}\right]$ SCENESHIFT

In this mode, we avoid the perceived offset between touch point and object without repositioning the object itself. While an object is grabbed, we take explicit control over the virtual view point to keep it in alignment with object and touch. This can make the scene look sheared from the user's point of view. However, from the manipulated view point the scene geometry is still soundly determined by the fish tank VR projection. This is the same effect a bystander would experience when another user's head position is tracked, not his own.

We achieve this viewpoint transformation by multiplying the projection matrix with the following shearing matrix:

$$\begin{bmatrix}1&0&0&0\\0&1&0&0\\x&y&1&0\\0&0&0&1\end{bmatrix};\ x = \frac{a_x + b_x}{z};\ y = \frac{a_y + b_y}{z}$$

When only the head is moved, this perspective correction exactly counteracts the perspective change created through head movement. This makes the scene appear frozen to the user, leaving him unable to look around obstacles. If the touch is moved, the object is naïvely moved along by $\vec{m}$, and the correction of the remaining offset $\vec{a} + \vec{b}$ causes a view point translation, making the scene shear in the direction of movement. In contrast to OBJECTCORRECTION, SCENESHIFT is even applied when the object is dragged into a boundary, never permitting the touch to be offset.

Releasing an object restores the correct perspective defined by the user's head position. Instead of snapping back instantly, we decided to ease back the scene using sine curve smoothing over a second.

$\left[\begin{smallmatrix}0&0\\1&0\end{smallmatrix}\right]$ ADAPTIVESHIFT

This method is derived from SCENESHIFT but differentiates between offsets. Without touch movement, the view point stays locked, maintaining alignment. Touch movement may cause offset, which is slowly mitigated by additional head movement. The same factor $f = 0.8$ applies, analog to ADAPTIVECORRECTION. The resulting values x and y fed into the shearing matrix are as follows:

$$x = \vec{b} + \frac{|\vec{b}| \cdot f \cdot a_x}{|\vec{a}| \cdot z};\ y = \vec{b} + \frac{|\vec{b}| \cdot f \cdot a_y}{|\vec{a}| \cdot z}$$

$\left[\begin{smallmatrix}0&1\\1&0\end{smallmatrix}\right]$ TAGTEAM

This method not only differentiates between offsets, it corrects them differently: additional object movement compensates touch induced offset; perspective shearing compensates head induced offset. That means, moving the touch causes the object to stick to the finger. Without touch movement the view point gets locked, as in SCENESHIFT. The total applied object movement, therefore, is:

$$\vec{m} + \vec{a}$$

The factors to be fed into the shearing matrix are

$$x = \frac{b_x}{z};\ y = \frac{b_y}{z}$$

During object movement, view point changes are limited, as the head-coupled projection only reacts to the user as long as it counteracts the touch induced offset. In this method, touch offset is only possible when objects get dragged against a boundary, although contrary to the OBJECTCORRECTION method, head movement can mitigate this offset to a degree.

$\left[\begin{smallmatrix}1&0\\0&1\end{smallmatrix}\right]$ CROSSTEAM

This method is an adaptation of TAGTEAM with switched roles. Here, touch induced offset is compensated by perspective adjustment and view offset by correcting object position. Note that the following formulas for total object movement and shearing show switched roles for $\vec{a}$ and $\vec{b}$, but otherwise are the same as for the TAGTEAM method. Total movement:

$$\vec{m} + \vec{b}$$

Shearing factors:

$$x = \frac{a_x}{z};\ y = \frac{a_y}{z}$$

Dragging the object in this environment automatically shears the scene, while moving the head has the potential of actively moving the object, depending on the direction of offset and existing projection adjustment.

$\left[\begin{smallmatrix}1&0\\0&0\end{smallmatrix}\right]$ CROSSCORRECTION

This methods applies adaptive positional correction, but unlike the ADAPTIVECORRECTION method, the correction here is linked to the other trigger, so here it is head movement that causes positional correction. Touch movement, on the other hand, causes no correction and can lead to offset. The offset is steadily corrected when the head is moved similar to other adaptive methods. The total applied object movement is:

$$\vec{m} + \vec{b} + |\vec{b}| \cdot f \cdot \frac{\vec{a}}{|\vec{a}|}$$

The known factor of $f = 0.8$ applies.

$\left[\begin{smallmatrix}0&0\\0&1\end{smallmatrix}\right]$ CROSSSHIFT

This methods applies adaptive projectional correction, but unlike the ADAPTIVESHIFT method, the correction here is linked to the other trigger. Touch movement drags the box along with $\vec{m}$ and shears the scene to preserve alignment. The factors used in the shearing matrix are the following:

$$x = \vec{a} + \frac{|\vec{a}| \cdot f \cdot b_x}{|\vec{b}| \cdot z}; \; y = \vec{a} + \frac{|\vec{a}| \cdot f \cdot b_y}{|\vec{b}| \cdot z}$$

Here, head movement causes no correction and can lead to offset, enabling the user to look around freely without loosing control of the box. When the touch is moved, existing offset is steadily corrected by shearing the scene, similar to adaptive methods.

STUDY

The aim of this study is to evaluate the aforementioned different control methods for object dragging. To analyze this (in)direct manipulation, we designed a task in which the user needs to move a box through a maze with several levels.

During initial testing that used a within-subject design, the three CROSS methods consistently received negative comments as touch induced offset could lead to viewport changes and head movement could move the object. All in all, users were very unhappy with (a) their head movement causing collisions, (b) the need to release the object to safely look around, and (c) the unexpected jumping of the box shortly after releasing it. Many users stated confusion and frustration. Some interpreted this kind of control as "moving the space around the object". CROSSSHIFT, e.g., was described as "weird", "unsettling", and "confusing".

Consequently, we focused on the remaining six methods: UNCORRECTED, OBJECTCORRECTION, ADAPTIVECORRECTION, SCENESHIFT, ADAPTIVESHIFT, and TAGTEAM.

System Setup

A sketch of the system used is displayed in Figure 4. The base of our system is a multi-touch table with outer measures of 155x136x92 cm. The visible size of the horizontal display is 140x80 cm. It is backlit by three Full-HD projectors, giving us a total resolution of 3240x1920 px on the tabletop. The table uses FTIR [8] for touch detection. Two 120 fps cameras with 640x480 px resolution scan the surface for reflected infrared light from the user's fingertips. This lead to an input resolution of 20dpi. The system is powered by a Mac Pro with a single ATI Radeon HD 5870 graphics card.

To augment the tabletop with head tracking, we used an industry grade tracking solution. Five cameras were mounted on a frame above and to the right of the table yielding sub

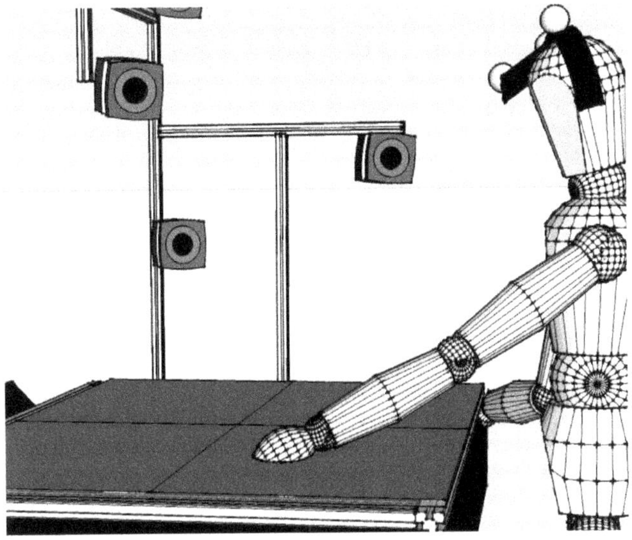

Figure 4: User standing in front of the tabletop. Infrared cameras in the background track the markers on the user's head. Head position is translated into a perspectively correct view of the virtual scene.

millimeter accuracy around and over the table. To be seen by the cameras, users had to wear a hair circlet on which four reflective markers were mounted.

Task

To accustom themselves with the hardware prior to the test, participants had two minutes to play around in a 2D dragging setting. Afterwards the previously assigned interaction method was activated and the participants could play around with it in a single level 3D playground for as long as they liked before they entered the maze itself. Participants had to drag a cuboid through this maze, avoiding collisions with its walls (Fig. 5). The maze was divided into three stages. Starting on the top level, participants progressed downwards by moving the box into a marked hatch on the end of each level. Levels did not disappear when finished, so participants had to deal with the added challenge of occlusion.

The box can be touched at one of two visible handles on its top (Fig. 5). Other objects would be controlled via similarly placed touch anchors or dynamically via ray casting to determine a touch anchor. We restricted grabbing the box to single touch interaction. The box follows the user's touch, according to the rules defined by the underlying design paradigm. While grabbed, the box is subject to a simple physics engine that allows it to pivot around its touch point depending on speed, direction, and friction. The physics layer is strictly two dimensional and works with the projections of the box and maze to calculate movement and collision behavior. When the box is released it immediately stops, so no flinging operations can be performed. However, to counteract touches getting lost while dragging, due to, e.g., bad tracking or blind spots, a small but noticeable delay is coded into the action of releasing an object. Yet, this allows for head induced box movement a few milliseconds after release.

The shape and physical movement model of the box gave the

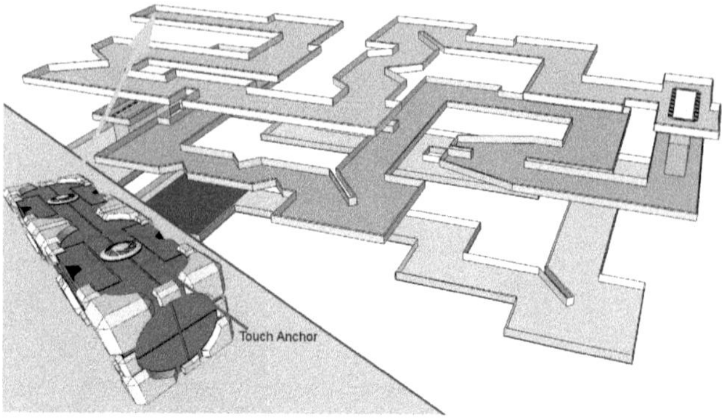

Figure 5: Task design: Participants had to drag the box through the maze, starting from the far left corner on top level to the green field on the bottom level. The boxes touch anchors are highlighted in blue.

users a task they found intriguing, challenging, and enjoyable. Many users described dragging the box as "driving a truck", referring to the tendency of the box's rear to cut corners when pulled behind. In case of collisions, a sound is played to encourage more careful behavior.

Procedure

We measured completion time in seconds, number of occlusions, and number of re-grabs. We used a between-subject design for the test with three repetitions. A within-subject design for six techniques was not feasible with the long task time and three repetitions. Before the test we collected demographic data: gender, age, height, prior experience with touch devices. During the playground settings, we encouraged participants to share their impressions. However, during the actual test we asked them to focus on moving the box without too many collisions or slowdown. Participants were offered breaks between each level of the maze and each of the three trials. Relax times were part of the schedule, as each level began at the first touch of the box.

Because users tended to cause multiple contacts or follow-up collisions due to the physical properties of the box, we decided to measure a maximum of one collision every two seconds. Besides time and collisions, we also recorded the number of re-grabs, counting one for every time the box is released and grabbed again, either to reposition it for corners, set back the perspective, unlock the camera to look around, reduce the touch offset, or personal preference. Participants were not told that re-grabs were tracked or in any way important for their performance.

The study host took notes based on the feedback during the playground and while observing. After the test, users filled out a questionnaire consisting of nine statements rated on a five point Likert scale: The input method (1) allows for precise control, (2) lets me control the box directly, (3) forces me to keep my head still, (4) allows for good orientation while dragging, (5) is taking away my control over the system, (6) is comprehensible, (7) causes unpredictable jumping of the box, (8) tempts me to re-grab often, (9) negatively influences my 3D impression.

While users were filling out the form, an open dialogue with the study host was offered to convey additional comments or answer open questions.

Participants

A total of 91 participants aged 18-30 ($M = 24.59$, $SD = 2.97$), 78 male, took part in our study. 91% were students, almost all of them computer science or related. 88% had previously experienced 3D vision, 87% had experienced mobile multi-touch, and 30% had already interacted with a touch-interactive tabletop. Half of the participants had some kind of vision impairment, but all of them had them corrected or only had minor impairments.

Results

Means and confidence intervals of time, collisions, and re-grabs are reported in Figures 6, 7, and 8. We opted to stack the bars for each level, but will point out significant effects between levels when they exist. To increase readability, we focus on significant and impactful results of our analysis, e.g., we do not elaborate on the fact that trial almost always had a (strongly) significant effect on every independent variable as this can be interpreted as a learning effect. The full factorial analyses as well as all pairwise comparisons for each method and independent variable can be found in the supplemental data.

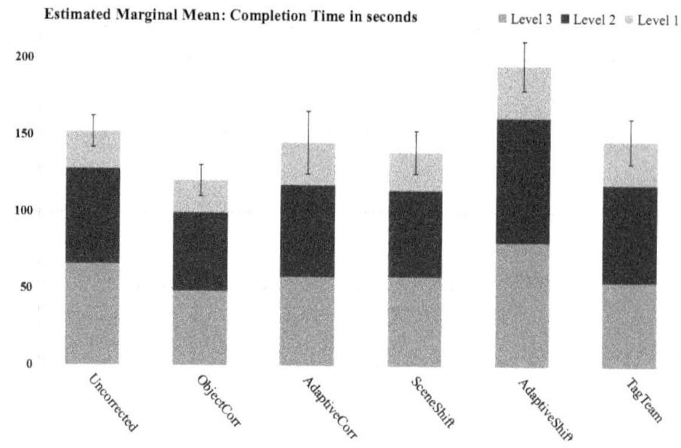

Figure 6: Mean completion time in seconds. Mean bars are sub-divided into single levels. 95% Confindence intervals are shown for the sum over all levels.

Time measurements were found not to be normally distributed (Shapiro-Wilk $W = .68, p < .0001$) but were sufficiently normal after a $log(y + 1)$ transform ($W = .99, p = .54$). Mixed effect analysis of variance (treating the user as a random effect) revealed significant main effects of method ($F_{(5,208.7)} = 3.49, p = .0048$) and level ($F_{(2,680)} = 471.56, p < .001$) on time. No interaction between method and level was found (Fig 6).

Collision was analyzed as Poisson distributed count data using Generalized Estimating Equations (reported as Wald's Chi-Square). We found a significant main effect of method ($\chi^2_{(5,N=91)} = 14.11, p = .015$) and level ($\chi^2_{(2,N=91)} = 390.32, p < .0001$) on the number of collisions. Interactions were found between method and level ($\chi^2_{(10,N=91)} =$

$\mathbf{57.75}, p < \mathbf{.0001})$. In level 1/2/3 the method had a significant main effect on the number of collisions $(\chi^2_{(5,N=91)} = \mathbf{24.98/12.46/15.39}, p < \mathbf{.0001}/ = \mathbf{.029}/ = \mathbf{.009})$.

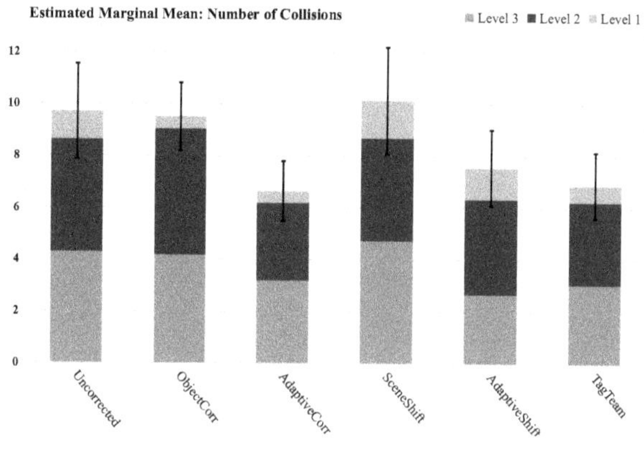

Figure 7: Number of collisions. Mean bars are subdivided into single levels. 95% Confindence intervals are shown for the sum over all levels.

Re-grabs were also analyzed as Poisson distributed count data using Generalized Estimating Equations (reported as Wald's Chi-Square). We found a significant main effect of method $(\chi^2_{(5,N=91)} = \mathbf{114.26}, p < \mathbf{.0001})$ and level $(\chi^2_{(2,N=91)} = \mathbf{557.56}, p < \mathbf{.0001})$ on the number of re-grabs. Interactions were found between method and level $(\chi^2_{(10,N=91)} = \mathbf{45.99}, p < \mathbf{.0001})$. In level 1/2/3 the method had a significant main effect on the number of collisions $(\chi^2_{(5,N=91)} = \mathbf{81.38/76.48/111.24}, p < \mathbf{.0001})$.

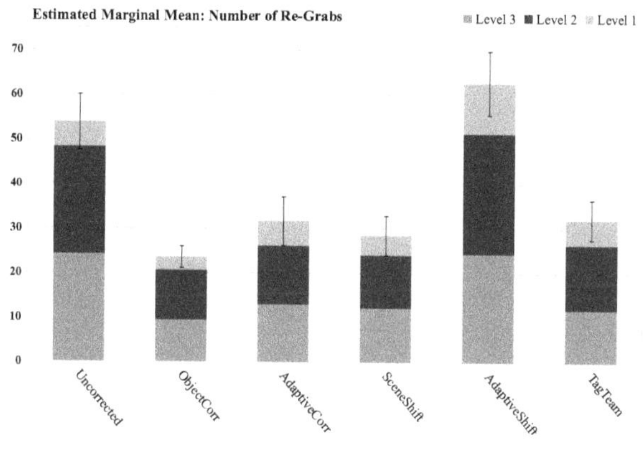

Figure 8: Number of re-grabs. Mean bars are subdivided into single levels. 95% Confindence intervals are shown for the sum over all levels.

The significant results of the pairwise comparisons for time, collisions, and re-grabs can be found in Fig. 9. All three independent variables are significantly correlated $(p < \mathbf{.0001})$: collisions and time, $r(\mathbf{89}) = \mathbf{.35}$, re-grabs and collisions, $r(\mathbf{89}) = \mathbf{.29}$, and re-grabs and time, $r(\mathbf{89}) = \mathbf{.79}$.

In our questionnaire, users rated statements on a five point Likert Scale from $\mathbf{1}$ (*strongly disagree*) to $\mathbf{5}$ (*strongly agree*) (see Table 1). Kruskal-Wallis revealed a significant effect

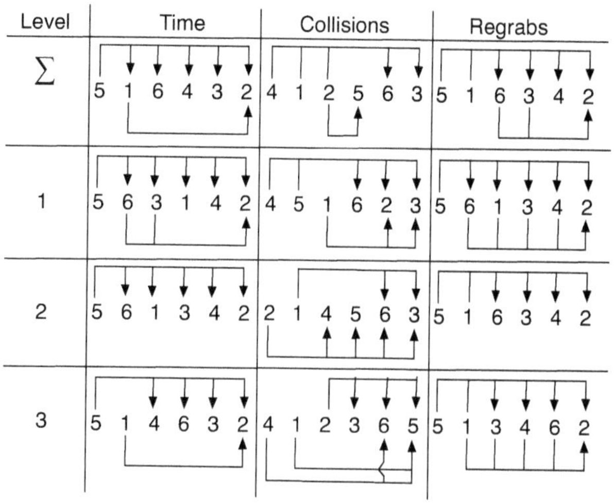

Figure 9: Results summed and by each level. Tukey's HSD for time and Wilcoxon signed rank sum test for collisions and re-grabs. Arrows denote a significant difference. Methods are sorted descending by their mean and are labeled as follows: (1) Uncorrected, (2) ObjectCorrection, (3) AdaptiveCorrection, (4) SceneShift, (5) AdaptiveShift, (6) TagTeam.

of the method on criterion (5) loss of control $(\chi^2_{(5,N=91)} = \mathbf{18.28}, p = \mathbf{.0026})$. For this criterion, a pairwise comparison using Wilcoxon rank sum test revealed that UNCORRECTED is lower than OBJECTCORRECTION, ADAPTIVECORRECTION, and ADAPTIVESHIFT. Also, OBJECTCORRECTION is higher than ADAPTIVECORRECTION.

	UNCORRECTED	OBJECTCORR	ADAPTIVECORR	SCENESHIFT	ADAPTIVESHIFT	TAGTEAM
precise control	3.0	3.7	**3.9**	3.5	3.3	3.5
direct control	3.3	4.0	4.0	**4.1**	3.7	4.1
keep head still	1.5	**2.6**	1.6	1.5	1.7	1.8
good orientation	3.9	3.3	**4.1**	3.1	3.4	3.4
loses control	1.3	**2.6**	1.9	2.4	2.4	1.7
comprehensible	4.3	4.5	4.2	3.9	3.6	**4.7**
unexpected jumping	2.0	**2.7**	1.8	2.1	1.9	2.6
requires re-grabs	**3.7**	3.4	2.5	2.6	3.3	2.9
lessens 3D impression	1.7	1.7	1.4	2.1	**2.3**	1.6

Table 1: Average ratings of the questionnaire statements. A five point Likert scale was used.

DISCUSSION AND DESIGN SUGGESTIONS

Before taking a closer look at each method, we can see that re-grabs and time have a tight connection. Obviously, performing a re-grab takes time. However, after a re-grab the offset is nullified, yielding more precise control, which in turn might speed up task time. The positive correlation ($\mathbf{.79}$) indicates that the former is the stronger effect, yet we recom-

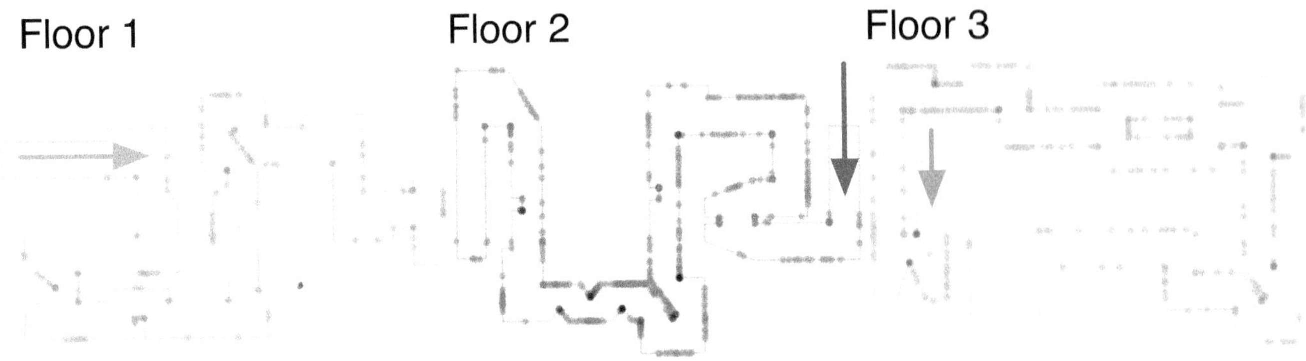

Figure 10: Collisions for each level across all methods. They primarily occurred at bottlenecks and in corners.

mend to allow methods to use re-grabs to let the user correct offset while minimizing the amount of re-grabs the user has to perform.

The number of collisions increased with the depth and primarily occurred at bottlenecks and in corners. This was similar for all methods. We observed that the box was mostly controlled using the front handle. However, to navigate around corners, some people used the back handle to rearrange the box.

OBJECTCORRECTION was in the group of fastest methods and its (insignificant) leader. They same is true for the number of re-grabs. However, many users stated confusion and frustration with OBJECTCORRECTION due to (a) their head movement causing collisions, (b) the need to release the object to safely look around, and (c) the unexpected jumping of the box shortly after releasing it. ADAPTIVESHIFT should be avoided regardless of the expected occlusion or interaction depth as it was slow and required a lot of re-grabs (Fig. 6,8,9). UNCORRECTED required many re-grabs but users did complete with average times. This could hint that re-grabs, though necessary, were easier and faster to execute for this method.

The number of collisions can vary greatly with the level due to the amount of occlusion and interaction-depth. However, SCENESHIFT and UNCORRECTED performed badly overall (Fig. 7,9). OBJECTCORRECTION worked well at least for the first level, but did have problems with lower levels due to the aforementioned implicit box movement. The ADAPTIVESHIFT method was one of the worst on the first level and the best on the last level regarding collisions. Participants also criticized the view snapping back, classifying the method as precise but weird. ADAPTIVECORRECTION performed great among all levels (32% fewer collisions), closely followed by TAGTEAM. Both methods offer direct control. While TAGTEAM is restrictive about object-finger alignment, ADAPTIVECORRECTION allows to break it in case the user just wants to look around a bit.

With ADAPTIVECORRECTION being received so well, we propose it to be the first choice. This method seems to be a confusion free, surprise free, accurate, low entry barrier approach to 2D direct manipulation of 3D media. Although OBJECTCORRECTION is (insignificantly) faster, the method received bad feedback on unexpected behavior. Also, ADAPTIVECORRECTION has a comparably low number of re-grabs, which might be important for some groups of users such as physically handicapped people.

All in all, we have identified head movement interfering with box control as one of the main problems. We also found that offset is a problem users struggle with and that performance seems to decline whenever offset is involved. However, not all methods that allow for offset perform poorly. Dealing with offset smartly seems to be a viable option, other than avoiding it completely.

Several extensions to our study setup may lead to further interesting results: using multiple fingers for single object control, controlling multiple objects at once, or adding stereoscopy to enhance the 3D impression. Further extensions to our methods are also possible by changing the adaptive correction factor f, or by trying to linearly combine correction methods for given offset triggers.

Another option would be to "zoom in" on the object to interact with. That means, we would set the projection plane to the object's top, thereby lifting it up and removing the problems introduced due to object depth. However, this would mean we would break the fish-tank metaphor thereby loosing context (e.g., the upper floors) and realism. Still, in other domains, this might be a feasible approach that would warrant further studies.

Non-flat objects could benefit from more sophisticated touch processing as people would expect or prefer objects to mimic physical behavior: start rotating (along the axis orthogonal to the plane defined by the drag begin point, drag end point and the object's center of gravity) until the object "tails" behind the finger. Separated manipulation modes could be another option, we would then try to adapt or compare some of the up to three finger combinations [9]. Another question is how to deal with varying heights of the scene, e.g., moving an object along a slope.

RepliCHI

As proposed in [20], we encourage replication of this study. To this end, all our datasets can be found at `http://tinyurl.com/buygrmq` for replication and further analysis.

CONCLUSION

In this paper, we presented a design space of interaction methods for touch-enhanced displays that use motion parallax for 3D. These methods address problems that arise with perspectively adjusted dragging in which users interact with an object's projection rather than the object itself. The two main problems identified are the perceived offset between touch and object projection, and head movement inferring object translation. We presented nine different control methods and evaluated six of them in depth. We identified the ADAPTIVECORRECTION method to be among the fastest, while yielding up to 32% less collisions than other fast methods.

ACKNOWLEDGMENTS

We thank our numerous study participants and Chatchavan Wacharamanotham for supporting us in analyzing the data. This work was funded in part by the German B-IT Foundation.

REFERENCES

1. Agrawala, M., Beers, A. C., McDowall, I., Fröhlich, B., Bolas, M., and Hanrahan, P. The Two-User Responsive Workbench: Support for Collaboration Through Individual Views of a Shared Space. *Proc. SIGGRAPH '97*, 332–388.
2. Bowman, D. A., Kruijff, E., and Laviola, J. J. *3D User Interfaces: Theory and Practice.* Addison-Wesley Longman, Amsterdam, 2005, 157.
3. Chan, L.-W., Kao, H.-S., Chen, M. Y., Lee, M.-S., Hsu, J., and Hung, Y.-P. Touching the Void: Direct-Touch Interaction for Intangible Displays. *Proc. CHI '10*, 2625–2634.
4. Cruz-Neira, C., Sandin, D. J., DeFanti, T. A., Kenyon, R. V., and Hart, J. C. The CAVE: Audio Visual Experience Automatic Virtual Environment. *Communications of the ACM 35*, 6, 64–72.
5. Czernuszenko, M., Pape, D., Sandin, D., DeFanti, T., Dawe, G. L., and Brown, M. D. The ImmersaDesk and Infinity Wall Projection-based Virtual Reality Displays. *Proc. SIGGRAPH '97*, 46–49.
6. Grossman, T., and Wigdor, D. Going Deeper: a Taxonomy of 3D on the Tabletop. *Proc. TABLETOP '07*, 137–144.
7. Hachet, M., Bossavit, B., Cohé, A., and de la Rivière, J.-B. Toucheo: Multitouch and Stereo Combined in a Seamless Workspace. *Proc. UIST '11*, 587–592.
8. Han, J. Y. Low-Cost Multi-Touch Sensing through Frustrated Total Internal Reflection. *Proc. UIST '05*, 115–118.
9. Hancock, M., and Carpendale, S. Shallow-depth 3D Interaction: Design and Evaluation of one-, two- and three-touch Techniques. *Proc. CHI '07*, 1147–1156.
10. Hancock, M., and Carpendale, S. Supporting Multiple Off-Axis Viewpoints at a Tabletop Display. *Proc. TABLETOP '07*, 171–178.
11. Hancock, M., Nacenta, M., Gutwin, C., and Carpendale, S. The Effects of Changing Projection Geometry on the Interpretation of 3D Orientation on Tabletops. *Proc. ITS '09*, 157–164.
12. Hilliges, O., Izadi, S., Wilson, A., and Hodges, S. Interactions in the Air: Adding Further Depth to Interactive Tabletops. *Proc. UIST '09*, 139–148.
13. Martinet, A., Casiez, G., and Grisoni, L. The Design and Evaluation of 3D Positioning Techniques for Multi-touch Displays. *Proc. 3DUI '10*, 115–118.
14. Möllers, M., Zimmer, P., and Borchers, J. Direct Manipulation and the Third Dimension: A Design Space for Co-Planar Dragging on 3D Displays . *CHI EA '12: Workshop on the 3rd dimension of CHI.*
15. Reisman, J. L., Davidson, P. L., and Han, J. Y. A Screen-Space Formulation for 2D and 3D Direct Manipulation. *Proc. UIST '09*, 69–78.
16. Shneiderman, B. Direct Manipulation: A Step Beyond Programming Languages. *Computer 16*, 8 (1983), 57–69.
17. Steinicke, F., Ropinski, T., Bruder, G., and Hinrichs, K. Interscopic User Interface Concepts for Fish Tank Virtual Reality Systems. *Proc. VR '07*, 27–34.
18. Valkov, D., Steinicke, F., and Bruder, G. 2D Touching of 3D Stereoscopic Objects. *Proc. CHI '11*, 1353–1362.
19. Ware, C., Arthur, K., and Booth, K. S. Fish Tank Virtual Reality. *Proc. INTERCHI '93*, 37–42.
20. Wilson, M. L., Mackay, W., Chi, E., Bernstein, M., Russell, D., and Thimbleby, H. RepliCHI - CHI should be replicating and validating results more: discuss. *CHI EA '11*, 463–466.

Evaluation of Depth Perception for Touch Interaction with Stereoscopic Rendered Objects

Dimitar Valkov, Alexander Giesler and Klaus Hinrichs
Visualization and Computer Graphics (VisCG) Research Group
University of Münster, Germany
[dimitar.valkov, alexander.giesler, khh]@uni-muenster.de

ABSTRACT

Recent developments in the domain of Human Computer Interaction have suggested to combine stereoscopic visualization with touch interaction. Although this combination has the potential to provide more intuitive and natural interaction setups for a wide range of applications, until now interaction with such systems is mainly constrained to simple navigation, whereas manipulation of the stereoscopically displayed objects is supported only rather rudimentarily.

In this paper we investigate the users' ability to discriminate depth or depth motion of stereoscopically rendered objects while she is performing touch gestures and discuss implications for object selection and manipulation. Our results show that there is a usable range of imperceptible manipulation, which - if properly applied - could support interaction with objects floating in the vicinity around the display surface without noticeable impact on a user's visual or touch performance.

ACM Classification: H.5.2 [Information interfaces and presentation]: User Interfaces – Input Devices and Strategies, Evaluation / Methodology.

General terms: Experimentation; Human Factors

Keywords: Touch, Depth perception, Stereoscopy.

INTRODUCTION

Recent developments in the domain of Human Computer Interaction (HCI) have suggested to combine touch input with stereoscopic visualization [18, 23]. Stereoscopically rendered content provides the user with additional depth cues, which usually decrease the overall cognitive load for understanding complex scenes [13]. This is of great importance in multiple application domains, e. g., geo-spatial applications, urban planning, architectural design [18], since often large amounts of data must be displayed on limited display size in such a way that it is instantly comprehensible even for untrained users. Recent investigations have revealed further benefits of the stereoscopic visualizations, such as the increased stereoscopic image quality, improved background separation, or enhanced emphasizing techniques [11, 16]. Moreover, adjusting the virtual point of view to the user's actual head or eye position, thus providing additional motion parallax cues, could further support the user's comprehension for complex content, since this enables her to explore the visual scene in a more natural way by just moving her head or eyes.

ITS'12, November 11–14, 2012, Cambridge, Massachusetts, USA.

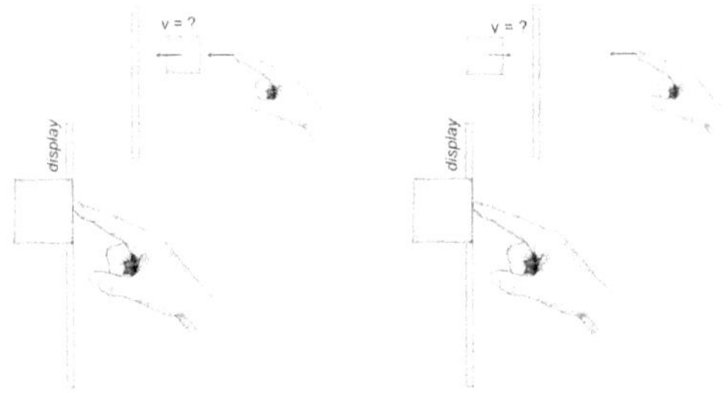

(a) (b)

Figure 1: Moving a stereoscopically rendered object starting with (a) negative and (b) positive parallax to the display surface, such that the object is aligned with the surface at the end of the touch gesture.

Although touch input has shown its potential for manipulation of both 2D and 3D content, interacting in *stereoscopically* rendered 3D environments is still a challenging task. Indeed, stereoscopic visualization introduces new kinds of problems, since the displayed objects are floating freely in the vicinity in front of or behind the display surface, while touches are only detected by direct contact with the display [18, 23]. While one could simply use a 3D tracking technique to capture the user's finger motions in front of the display surface, it has been shown that touching an intangible surface (i. e., *touching the void*) leads to confusion and a significant number of overshooting errors [6]. Furthermore, passive haptic has the potential to considerably enhance the user experience with touch or grasp based interfaces.

Existing approaches deal with these issues by either moving the interactive *surface* in the 3D space to become aligned with the floating object, e. g., using tangible views [20] or transparent props [17], or calculating a 3D position of a distant "cursor" as function of the positions of multiple touch points [2, 21]. The latter approach could be described figu-

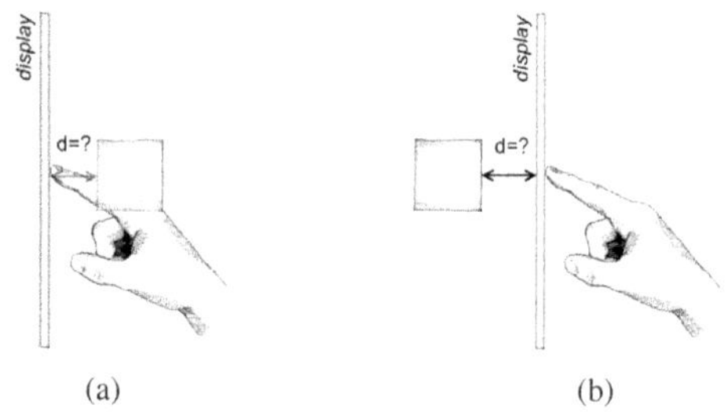

Figure 2: Discrimination of haptic and visual feedback for an object with (a) negative and (b) positive parallax.

ratively as moving the *touches* to the 3D space. In this paper we propose an alternative approach. In particular, as illustrated in Figure 1, we suggest to move a stereoscopic object toward the display surface while the user is reaching out to touch it in such a way, that:

(a) At the moment in which the user's finger reaches the display surface the object is aligned with this surface (s. Figure 1).

(b) The object's motion remains imperceivable for the user, i. e., the motion remains below the perceptional detection threshold of the user.

The feasibility of the second assumption is motivated by the findings of many perception research groups, revealing that there is a certain amount of induced object or scene manipulations, which (although perceivable) cannot be reliably detected by the human visual system (e. g. [4]).

Another interesting question is how sensitive humans are with respect to misalignment between visually perceived and tactually felt contact with a virtual object (s. Figure 2). For example, if an object is rendered at some small distance in front of the display surface, as shown in Figure 2 (a), is the user going to move her finger through the object until she receives tactile feedback due to the contact with the display, and how small may this distance be? In particular, this may allow touch (and possibly multi-touch) interaction within stereoscopic environments without loosing the advantages of common 2D techniques. Furthermore it relaxes the first requirement, since the objects need not to be *exactly* aligned with the display surface, but only within some range in front of or behind it.

In this paper we present the results of a series of studies in which we determine thresholds for the misalignment between visual and tactile contact (s. Figure 2), as well as the user sensitivity to small induced object motions applied while the user reaches for that object (s. Figure 1). Our findings show that there is a usable range stretching in front of and behind the display surface, in which *object shifts* can not be detected reliably, i. e., an object could be imperceptibly moved close to the display surface while the user is reaching out to touch it, and thus at the moment of touch passive haptic feedback is provided.

APPLICATION SPACE

Hancock et al. [9] mentioned several application domains in which *shallow-depth 3D*, i. e., 3D interaction with limited depth, would be sufficient. Assuming there is a usable range of imperceptible misalignments between visual and tactile touch (s. Figure 2), one could extend those applications with stereoscopic visualization without a need of complex 3D tracking of the user's finger. Through small induced object motions these ranges could be increased considerably. Although this comes at the cost of adding 3D finger tracking, in contrast to alternative techniques both direct object manipulation *and* haptic feedback are provided.

For instance, a map viewer could render markers or widgets stereoscopically above the display in order to improve visibility and (especially if head tracking is supported) reduce occlusion artifacts. Those widgets, if rendered within some range, would still be accessible for touch interaction. Going a step further, one could overlay the map itself on a (possibly flattened) height model in order to improve spatial understanding of the representation. Multiple applications, such as 3D desktops with stacked items on a tabletop setup, or graph visualizations, in which highlighted nodes are rendered with different depths, may benefit from the same approach. The combination of stereoscopic touch interaction with the tangible views paradigm [20] might also lead to a range of valuable interfaces. For instance, in a medical visualization a stereoscopic representation on the top of the tangible prop would support the tracking of long structures (e. g., veins, nerves) while touch interaction could be used to change the visualization properties at the same time (e. g., zooming, transparency). In general, there is a wide range of applications, especially in urban planning or data visualization, in which shallow-depth 3D is sufficient, but may still benefit from additional stereoscopic cues and more natural interaction interfaces.

At first glance, the approach suffers from its own inherit contradiction. On one hand, we claim that stereoscopic cues are precise enough to significantly increase the user's understanding of complex 3D scenes, i. e., the understanding "where the objects are" relative to each other, while, on the other hand, we suggest to change the depth of one particular object and assume that the user's depth perception is imprecise enough to not recognize this. The crucial point in our approach is the moment in which we apply the manipulation. Since touching is only a small part of the interaction process, we can assume that the user already has built a *cognitive map* [12] of the environment. In this case changing the position of an object would be perceived as object motion within a static scene rather than scene motion while the object is remaining static. Thus the spatial understanding for the scene would not be disturbed even if the object motion is detected. Furthermore, the total arm movement during reaching for an object consists of two distinct phases. During the *ballistic* phase the hand is moved close to the target, and during the subsequent *correction* phase the error between the hand or finger and the target is minimized under control of visual, haptic and proprioceptive feedback [15]. Thus the mechanical control in the correction phase, i. e., which muscle-control signal must be applied and what would be the result, is only approximative. Therefore, we expect that if we slightly move the target within the correction phase, the arm control would change to accommodate to the new target position. Since reaching is a very low-level task we expect that the user will not consciously detect the motion, provided it remains within certain thresholds.

RELATED WORK

In recent years the usability of stereoscopic displays has been reconsidered in multiple domains. For instance, Kooi and Toet [13] have shown that stereoscopic depth cues could improve the separation of details from their background, compensate for poor image quality or aid the decoding of complex visual data. Furthermore, it has been shown that stereoscopic objects better attract the user's attention [26], which has been further developed into an intuitive technique for adding emphasis to selected or searched content [11].

Nevertheless, existing approaches for extending multi-touch interaction techniques to the third dimension mainly focus on either monoscopic visualization or tabletop setups, (e. g. [9, 25]). For instance, extending the interaction space beyond the surface of a tabletop display has been investigated by Hilliges et al. [10]. The approach was further developed by Wilson and Benko, who used multiple depth cameras and projectors to augment interactive content on arbitrary physical surfaces [25]. To allow multi-touch interaction in the 3D space above the tabletop some indirect interaction techniques were also proposed, e. g., *triangle cursor* by Strothoff et al. [21]. Following that direction Grossman and Wigdor [8] proposed a taxonomy for 3D interaction in tabletop setups. As shown in their work, 3D volumetric visualizations are rarely being considered in combination with 2D direct surface input.

The hand and wrist trajectories during *reaching* and *pointing* tasks have been in the focus of many investigations (e. g., [15, 22]). The effect of scene manipulations during reaching for an object has been considered by Dvorkin et al. [7] and the effect of sudden object displacements is further investigated by Soechting et al. [19]. These contributions provide strong evidence for the widely accepted hypothesis that there is a (small) finite number of parametric functions for ballistic arm motions. In particular, after an object to be reached is determined, a particular ballistic function is selected, its parameters "calculated" and the motion is started without any further assistance or intervention from the visual system, provided no changes in the object or the scene are perceived [19]. The kinematics of the correction phase is more involved. It includes visual, tangible and proprioceptive feedback for error minimization between the finger and the object positions [7]. Multiple psychological studies have shown that humans tolerate a certain amount of inconsistency between visual and proprioceptive sensation [1, 4, 6] as well as between visual and tangible sensation [14]. Nevertheless, the large number of overshooting errors by touching an intangible surface [6] motivate the assumption that haptic may indeed dominate vision in the moment of touch, as discussed by Adams et al. [1]. The changes of the kinematics and control of the reaching tasks within virtual environments have been further investigated by Dvorkin et al. [7] and Viau et al. [24], and the relation between the 3D positions of a stereoscopically rendered object and the on-display touch point is considered by Valkov et al. [23].

a) b)

Figure 3: Parallax problem; while the occlusion cues (a) indicate that the user's finger is in front of an object, binocular disparity cues (b) are suggesting that the user's finger is behind the object.

While these results support the assumption that small induced object manipulations could not be reliably detected, there is few work on this in the context of pointing tasks.

PARALLAX PROBLEM

Virtual objects can be presented on stereoscopic displays with *positive*, *negative* or *zero* parallax, resulting in different visual impressions.

If an object is rendered with *zero* parallax it appears to be aligned with the plane of the display surface. Such objects are usually perfectly suited for touch-based interaction [18], especially if 2D interaction is intended (e. g., UI widgets).

Objects displayed with *positive parallax* are perceived to be behind the screen surface. Although several indirect manipulation techniques could be used (e. g. [3]), these objects cannot be accessed directly, since the user's reach is limited by the surface of the screen. Furthermore, since the display surface has usually no visual representation in a stereoscopically rendered scene, trying to reach an object with strong positive parallax may become unnatural and in some cases even harmful. Nevertheless, if an object is close to the surface, the only effect is that the user receives haptic feedback shortly before the visual representation of the object is reached (s. Figure 2 (b)), i. e., the haptic and visual feedbacks are misaligned. As mentioned above, we are interested in determining within which range this misalignment is still unnoticeable for the user.

Interaction with objects rendered with *negative parallax*, i. e., perceived as floating in front of the display surface, poses additional problems in this context. In order to receive haptic feedback a user has to touch the physical surface of the display, thus she has to reach through the object of interest to the display surface (s. Figure 2 (a)). In addition to the fact that users commonly consider this as unnatural, the stereoscopic perception may be disturbed, since the user's visual system is fed with contradicting information. Indeed, binocular disparity cues are suggesting that the user's finger is behind the

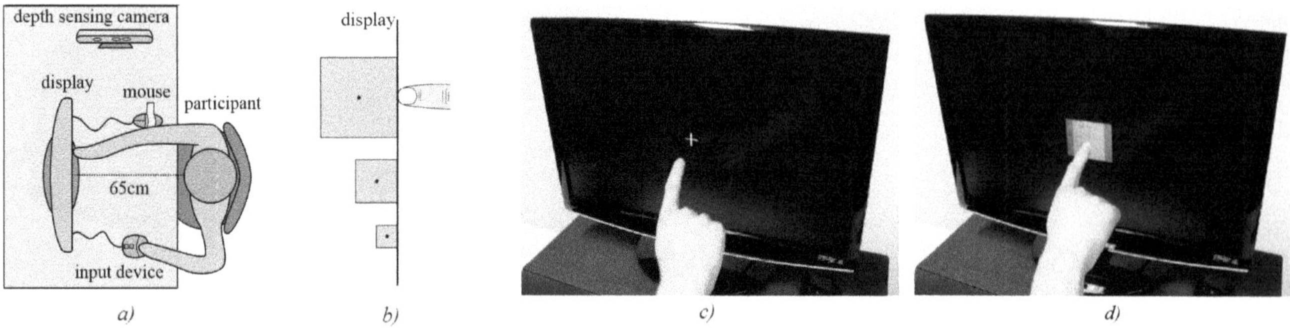

Figure 4: Illustration of E1; (a) the experiment setup; (b) object alignment to the parallax planes (here: zero parallax plane); (c) participant's hand motion during E1, a white cross in the middle of the screen indicates the point to be touched; (d) participant judged object parallax after a touch was detected.

object, while the finger is occluding parts of the object. Thus occlusion cues are confirming that the object is in front of the screen (s. Figure 3). Since occlusion cues usually dominate over disparity, disparity cues may be ignored and the images for the left and the right eye may not be merged any more, which results in loss of the stereoscopic impression. In addition, accommodation-convergence problems may further affect the perception and often lead to ambiguity [23].

EXPERIMENT 1 (E1): Discrimination of tactile and visual touch

The aim of this experiment was to provide information about the vicinity around the image plane in which displacement between object and the display surfaces cannot be detected reliably. In a *two-alternative forced-choice (2AFC)* task participants had to decide whether touched objects seam to appear behind or in front of the display, i.e., to discriminate if they went through the object before receiving tactile feedback or did not reach the object's surface due to the screen limiting their reach.

Experimental Setup

For the experiment (s. Figure 4) we used a 120Hz frame sequential stereoscopic visualization on a 22″ Samsung SyncMaster display with nVidia's 3D Vision shutter glasses. The screen size was $47.9cm \times 29.5cm$, and the resolution was 1680×1050 on the upright positioned display. The scene was rendered on a PC with Intel Core i7 processor, with 8GB of RAM and nVidia Quadro4000 graphic card. We occluded noticeable objects with a black board and performed the experiment in a dark room to avoid distraction. Input was performed with a Belkin n52te Speedpad and a fixed mouse at a convenient position for the dominant hand of the user. A subject's fingertip was tracked with our in-house tracker, based on the Microsoft Kinect. Our tests showed that the precision of the tracker is better than $5mm$, and its accuracy is better than $1mm$.

Participants

20 persons were invited to the experiment, but two of them failed the stereoscopy test and were excluded from participation. 17 male and 1 female subjects (age 20-36, ∅: 25.8, σ: 3.79) participated in the experiment. All were students or professionals from our department, and most of them reported to have experience with stereoscopic content, mostly due to 3D movies. All subjects were naïve to the experimental conditions. 14 have reported to be right-handed and 4 were left-handed. All subjects had normal or corrected to normal vision; 8 wore corrective glasses or contact lenses which they had to use during the experiment. The total time per subject including pre-questionnaire, instructions, training, experiment, breaks, and debriefing took about 30 minutes. Subjects could take breaks at any time. In addition, after each 50 trials subjects had to take a 2 minutes break in order to minimize errors due to exhaustion or poor concentration.

Materials and Methods

In a *within-subject designed* experiment, participants had to decide in a *2AFC* task whether objects appeared in front of the screen surface or behind it after performing a touch gesture.

At the beginning of the experiment each subject completed a simple stereoscopy test with our apparatus. Subjects were seated such that the center of the screen was at their eye level, at a distance of approximately $65cm$ (s. Figure 4 (a)). They were instructed to remain in this position during the entire experiment and to perform all trials with their dominant hand.

Subjects indicated the start of each trial by pressing the left mouse button, which guaranteed a consistent start position of the touch gesture throughout the experiment. After a trial was started, a white cross in the middle of the screen was displayed to indicate the position the user has to touch. Once touch on the cross was detected, an object was displayed for one second with a vertical offset of $1cm$ to avoid complete occlusion by the finger (s. Figure 4 (c) and (d)). Then a written description, displayed for at least $200ms$, forced the subject to decide with the Speedpad whether the object's surface appeared to be in front of the display surface or behind it; After all trials were accomplished, subjects were shortly interviewed to provide their subjective impressions or remarks.

As visual stimuli we used a textured box in order to provide sufficient amount of depth perception and stereoscopic disparity cues. The box was displayed with a light grey texture having a random, non-repetitive pattern on black background in order to reduce cross-talk artifacts. To test the effect of object size, boxes with edge lengths of $2cm$, $3.5cm$ and $5cm$

were displayed. We varied the distance between the display's and object's surfaces in the interval between $-10cm$ and $10cm$ with steps of $2cm$, resulting in a total of 11 parallax planes. Since we have used a *right-handed* coordinate system, *negative* depth values represent *positive parallax* and vice versa. Box positions were adjusted in depth such that the foremost surface was aligned to the specific parallax, i.e., positioning of the viewable surface instead of the center, as illustrated in Figure 4 (b). For this experiment the *method of constant stimuli* was used, i. e., the sizes and positions of the objects were not related from one trial to another, but presented randomly and uniformly distributed. Each position-size pair was presented exactly three times, resulting in a total of 99 trials per subject. Additional 5 training trials with strong parallaxes ($\pm 10cm$ and $\pm 15cm$) were added at the beginning of the experiment in order to ensure that participants understood the task and received some initial training.

Results

The data of one subject was excluded from evaluation since post interrogation with the subject revealed that he had misunderstood the task, evaluating the object's size rather then parallax.

The subject mean responses were evaluated with 3×11 repeated measurement ANOVA with Greenhouse-Geisser (G.-G.) correction, testing the within-subject effect of object size and parallax. We found a significant within-subject effect for object size (G.-G. $F^{1.32}_{22.48} = 17.09$, $p < 0.01$) as well as for parallax (G.-G. $F^{2.76}_{47.01} = 30.49$, $p < 0.01$) and therefore split the results for different object sizes and parallaxes.

The relation between mean subject estimations and parallax were evaluated for different object sizes with a parametric non-linear regression analysis, fitting psychological curves of the type $f(z) = a \cdot \arctan(b \cdot z + c) + d$ with real a, b, c and d with the non-linear Levenberg-Marquard least square iteration algorithm.

Figure 5 presents the fitted curves (top) and the residuals (bottom). The X-axis shows the start parallaxes, i.e., the distance between the object's front surface and the display surface, with positive values indicating objects in front of the screen, i. e., with negative parallax, and negative values indicating objects behind the screen, i. e., with positive parallax. The Y-axis shows the mean responses, where the judgment that an object appears behind the screen surface is valued as -1, and the judgment that an object appears in front of the screen surface is valued as 1. The solid curves show fitted sigmoid functions for object sizes $2cm$ (cyan), $3.5cm$ (orange) and 5cm (purple), and the dotted curves show the 95% confidence intervals. The crosses represent the means of subject responses, while the stars represent the fitting residuals. The standard error of the regression ($RMSE$) was 0.111 for objects with edge length of $2.0cm$ with summed square of residuals $SSE = 0.085$ and degrees of freedom adjusted R^2, i.e., $\hat{R}^2 = 0.929$. For object size $3.5cm$ the $RMSE$ was 0.108 with $SSE = 0.083$ and $\hat{R}^2 = 0.968$ and for object size $5.0cm$ the $RMSE$ was 0.079 with $SSE = 0.045$ and $\hat{R}^2 = 0.981$. These values and the random residuals show that the model functions are good fits of the data.

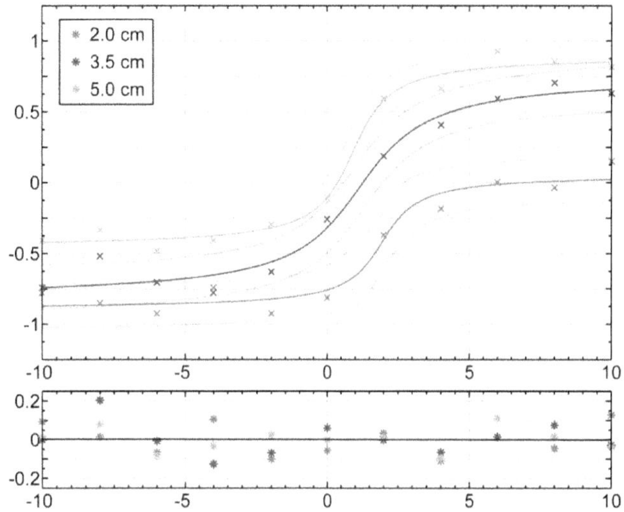

Figure 5: Mean responses for different object sizes; X-axis shows the depth of the object's surface in cm, Y-axis shows the mean of the responses; (top) solid curves show fitted psychological sigmoid functions, dotted curves show the 95% confidence intervals and crosses show the means of subject responses; (bottom) the fitting residuals

Usually a perceptual detection threshold is defined as the lowest intensity at which a stimulus can be detected at least 50% of the time, thus at least 75% of the answers were correct. Reflecting on the curves shown in Figure 5 one will see, that the line $Y = 0$ defines 50/50 guessing, if the object has positive or negative parallax, thus the detection threshold for positive parallax would be the cut point of the curve with the line $Y = -0.5$ and for negative parallax with $Y = +0.5$. We call these detection thresholds $DT_{0.5}$ for positive and negative parallax. Since some of the curves never reach these boundaries, we defined a second, more restrictive, interval in which the parallax is detected at least 25% of the time, i. e., at least 62.5% of the subject estimations were correct. Obviously these are the detection thresholds $DT_{0.25}$ for positive and negative parallax. The estimated points of subjective equality (PSE), and the $DT_{0.5}$ and $DT_{0.25}$ for positive and negative parallax are summarized in Table 1.

The detection thresholds in Table 1 show that subjects were accurate for parallaxes outside the interval $-1.27cm$ and $4.35cm$ for objects of size $3.5cm$. Participants detected positive parallaxes for $2cm$ objects below $2.54cm$ with a probability of at least 75%. In contrast they detected negative par-

Size $[cm]$	$DT_{0.5}$ behind, $[cm]$	$DT_{0.25}$	PSE $[cm]$	$DT_{0.25}$ in front of, $[cm]$	$DT_{0.5}$
2.0	1.69	2.54	7.02	–	–
3.5	-1.27	0.33	1.28	2.29	4.35
5.0	–	-0.94	0.38	0.99	1.67

Table 1: Detection Thresholds $DT_{0.25}$ and $DT_{0.5}$, and Points of Subjective Equality (PSE) for tactile and visual touch discrimination task.

allaxes for $5cm$ objects starting from $0.99cm$ with a probability of at least 75%. Participants were not able to accurately detect negative parallaxes for $2cm$ large objects and positive parallaxes for $5cm$ large objects. The PSE for $2cm$ large objects shows a strong offset of $7.02cm$, while the PSE for $3.5cm$ large objects shows a smaller offset of 1.28cm. Objects with $5cm$ size have a PSE of 0.38cm.

Discussion

Our results show that subjects tend to underestimate depth of an object relative to the object's size. In particular, subjects had problems in detecting positive parallaxes for large objects and negative parallaxes for small objects. The curves in Figure 5 show convergence below 75% detection in these cases. For instance, small objects ($2cm$) on the zero parallax plane were perceived behind the screen, but the same objects having negative parallax could not be discriminated clearly by subjects ($PSE = 5.9cm$). In contrast, subjects' detection for larger objects ($5cm$) was quite accurate for objects having negative or zero parallax, with PSE nearly zero ($PSE = 0.29cm$), while for objects behind the screen the subjects were somewhat uncertain.

The fitted curves show a stepwise shift towards negative parallaxes, i.e., $Z > 0$, and become flatter for smaller object size. One can explain the flatter curves with occlusion of objects by the finger. Objects with size of $2cm$ were in large part occluded by the finger such that depth impression was disturbed on negative parallaxes. This led to more uncertainty in discrimination for these objects, even though we applied small vertical offsets for objects displayed under the finger to reduce this effect. With increased object size stereoscopic perception had more surface to rely on, providing a more accurate detection even if a subject's finger occluded a part of the surface.

MANIPULATION OF STEREOSCOPIC OBJECTS

In order to move an object to the display surface one could shift either only the object of interest or the entire scene to the desired position. Shifting the entire scene has the advantage that the spatial relations between the objects remain unchanged. In particular, since the light sources are usually considered as part of the scene, lighting and shadows do not change either. Nevertheless, motion of an object close to the edge of the screen might be easier to detect, since the bezel of the display provides a non-manipulative reference for the object's depth. Although this technique might be suitable on a large display, which covers more than 60° of the user's horizontal field of view, it seems to be inappropriate in setups with limited display size, e. g., tabletops or desktops.

Moving a single object can reduce this problem, in particular if the object is far away from the display edge. Moreover, there is a wider range of manipulations that can be applied to a single object. For instance, an object could be moved along some curved path or along the line between its center and the position of the virtual camera, its size could be changed during the shift, etc. Nevertheless, since changes in the object's shading and its shadow's position and form may reveal the motion, the application should compensate for this. We consider investigation of object shifts as an important first step in this direction.

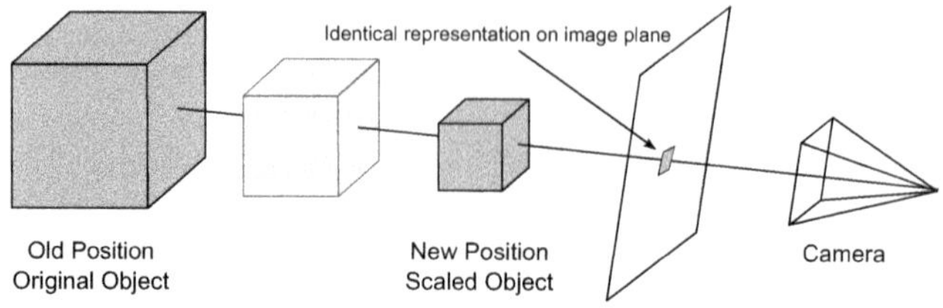

Figure 6: Illustration of the *scaled shift* manipulation technique. The object of interest is moved along the view line between its center and the camera position and scaled at the same time.

Scaled Shift Technique

In order to be able to imperceptibly shift an object to the display surface we choose to move it along the line between its origin and the position of the virtual camera (we consider the intermediate point between the cameras for the left and for the right eye as camera position). While [23] indicates that the intermediate eye point might be suboptimal and proposes a gradual shift (α shift) toward the user's dominant eye, the grade of this shift and the parameters on which it may rely are only vaguely defined. Thus we chose the intermediate eye point to confine variations due to inappropriate selection of the α shifts. While this ensures constant orientation of the object during translation, it still changes the size of its projection onto the image plane. Thus we have decided to simultaneously adjust the object's scale factor during translation relative to its motion. The manipulation technique is illustrated in Figure 6.

This technique, which we call *scaled shift*, reduces the number of motion cues on which the user may rely while still allowing us to use a number of visually different objects (e. g., different forms, textures, etc.). This is particularly important, because imperceptible scene or object manipulations should only be applied in the correction phase. Indeed, as mentioned previously, once initiated the ballistic phase is carried out without further assistance from the visual system, which is usually scanning for changes in the scene [5]. In the correction phase the vision is switched back and forth between the object and the user's finger, which allows manipulations [5]. Since the correction phase is entered shortly before reaching the object, stronger manipulations are desired to move objects with strong parallax to the display surface. To provide smooth, undetectable manipulation we move the object depending on the motion of the user's fingertip. Thus, if T_{finger} and T_{object} represent the translation magnitudes of the user's finger and the object of interest, we define an *object shift factor* σ as

$$T_{object} = \sigma \cdot T_{finger}$$

Thus for positive values of the shift factor ($\sigma > 0$) the object is moved in the same direction as the finger, while for negative values ($\sigma < 0$) it is moved in the opposite direction. For $\sigma = 0$ the object's position remains unchanged. For instance, with shift factor $\sigma = 0.5$ the object is moved with half of the speed of the pointing finger in the *same direction* as the finger, while with $\sigma = -0.5$ the object is moved again with half of the finger speed, but in the *opposite direction*.

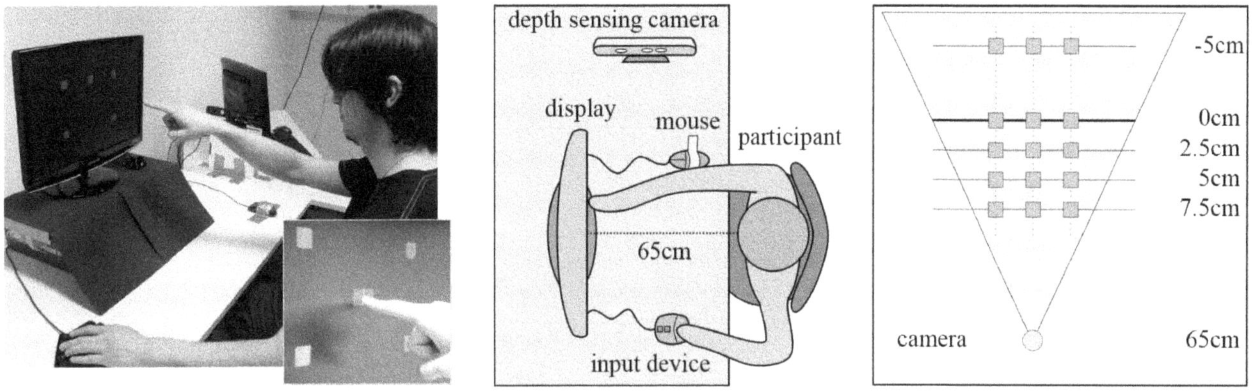

a) b) c)

Figure 7: Illustration of E2; (a) participant performing a touch gesture during E2; (b) experiment setup; (c) top-down view of object distribution in E2.

If P_{old} and P_{new} denote the object's position before and after the translation and P_{cam} the camera position, we obtain

$$P_{new} = P_{old} + \sigma \cdot T_{finger} \cdot v$$

with direction vector $v = (P_{cam} - P_{old}) / (\|P_{cam} - P_{old}\|)$. The new scale factor S_{new} of the object could then be calculated as

$$S_{new} = S_{old} \cdot \frac{D_{new}}{D_{old}}$$

with $D_{old} = \|P_{old} - P_{cam}\|$ denoting the old distance between object and camera and $D_{new} = \|P_{new} - P_{cam}\|$ the new distance between translated object and camera.

We assume the correction phase starts when the user's fingertip is $10cm$ away from the object. Dvorkin et al. [7] have shown that for virtual objects the correction phase is usually starting sooner than for real objects, which implies that our approximation may be too restrictive. However, precise determination of the start of the correction phase is beyond the scope of this work.

EXPERIMENT 2 (E2): Detection of object shifts

In this experiment we examined participants' ability to detect induced object shifts σ as described in the previous section. Our initial hypotheses are:

- $H_0^{(1)}$: The point of subjective equality (PSE) is at $\sigma = 0$ and does not change with the parallax.
- $H_0^{(2)}$: The position of the object has little or no effect on the detection thresholds for σ.
- $H_0^{(3)}$: The subject's handedness has little or no effect on the detection thresholds for σ.

Materials and Methods

Again a *within-subject design* was used, in which subjects had to decide in a *2AFC* task whether a highlighted object moved in the same direction as their fingertip or against it, while they were performing a touch gesture. As shown in Figure 7 (b), the same framework and experimental layout as in E1 was used. All 18 participants from E1 also participated in this experiment.

As visual stimuli (s. Figure 7 (a)) we used $2cm$ large boxes with a light grey texture with random non-repetitive pattern on black background. Four additional static boxes having the same size, but slightly darker texture, were displayed on the zero parallax plane as reference with screen-space (origin top-left) coordinates $(0.25, 0.25)$, $(0.25, 0.75)$, $(0.75, 0.25)$ and $(0.75, 0.75)$.

The applied *shift factors* varied from -1.0 to 1.0 in steps of 0.5, resulting in five different values. To test the effect of different object positions and depths we varied the object's *screen space coordinates* using unified positions $(0.25, 0.5)$, $(0.5, 0.5)$, $(0.75, 0.5)$, $(0.5, 0.25)$ and $(0.5, 0.75)$, as well as the object's *parallax* using the depth planes $-5cm$, $0cm$, $2.5cm$, $5cm$ and $7.5cm$ (s. Figure 7 (c)). We mainly considered negative parallaxes, since objects floating in front of the display surface introduces the main problem for touch interaction. As in E1 the method of constant stimuli was used, i. e., the applied shift factors as well as the object positions and parallaxes were not related from one trial to another, but presented randomly and uniformly distributed. Each combination of shift factor, position and parallax was presented exactly two times, resulting in a total of 250 trials per participant. Additional 10 training trials with strong shift factors (±1.0 and ±1.5) were added at the beginning of the experiment in order to ensure that participants understood the task and received some initial training.

Subjects started each trial by pressing the left button of a fixed mouse. Then an object was displayed, and the subject had to reach out and touch it with the pointing finger of her dominant hand. Once the subject's finger reached the display surface the object disappeared, and a written instruction forced the subject to decide whether the object moved in the same direction as her finger or in the opposite direction. Input was performed with the Speedpad using the 'up' button to indicate object motion in the same direction as the movement of the fingertip and the 'down' button for object motion in the opposite direction.

The total time per subject including pre-questionnaire, instructions, training, experiment, breaks, and debriefing took about 45 minutes. Subjects could take breaks at any time. In addition, after every 50 trials subjects had to take a 2 minutes break in order to minimize errors due to exhaustion or poor concentration.

Results

We excluded the data of two subjects, since we found strong deviations in their results (more than twice the standard error over all participants) in mean responses for shifts, parallaxes and screen positions.

Since we have not found a significant difference between left-handed and right-handed subjects (two-sided t-test, $T_{16} = -0.39; p = 0.702$), we pooled the results over all subjects. The subject mean responses were evaluated with $5 \times 5 \times 5$ repeated measurement ANOVA with G.-G. correction, testing the within-subject effect of shift factor, object size and parallax. We found a significant within-subject effect for shift factor (G.-G. $F^{1.82}_{30.87} = 37.19$, $p < 0.01$), but not for position (G.-G. $F^{2.98}_{50.69} = 2.50$, $p = 0.07$) and parallax (G.-G. $F^{1.47}_{25.00} = 1.30$, $p = 0.28$). Nevertheless, the combined effect of parallax and shift factor was significant (G.-G. $F^{5.63}_{95.72} = 3.07$, $p \leq 0.01$), while no significant effect of position and shift were found (G.-G. $F^{6.93}_{117.90} = 0.69$, $p = 0.68$). Therefore we split the results for different shift factors and parallaxes. The relation between mean subject estimations and shift factors were evaluated for different parallaxes with a parametric non-linear regression analysis, fitting psychological sigmoid curves as in E1.

Figure 8 presents the fitted curves and the residuals. The X-axis shows the applied shift factor σ, the Y-axis shows the mean responses, where $+1$ indicates a subject's judgment that an object moved in the same direction as the finger and -1 indicates judgment for the opposite direction. The solid curves show fitted sigmoid functions for positive (purple), negative (cyan) and zero (orange) parallax and the dotted curves show the 95% confidence intervals. The crosses represent the means of subject responses, while the stars represent the fitting residuals. The $RMSE$ for objects starting on positive parallax was 0.015 with summed $SSE = 2.27 \times 10^{-4}$ and $\hat{R}^2 = 0.999$. For objects starting on the zero parallax plane the $RMSE$ was 0.024 with $SSE = 5.98 \times 10^{-4}$ and $\hat{R}^2 = 0.998$, and for objects starting with negative parallax the $RMSE$ was 0.024 with $SSE = 5.57 \times 10^{-4}$ and $\hat{R}^2 = 0.996$. These values and the random nature of the residuals show that the model functions are good fits of the data and explain more than 99% of the variance. The estimated PSE, and the $DT_{0.5}$ and $DT_{0.25}$ for positive and negative shifts are summarized in Table 2.

The detection thresholds show that subjects were accurate in detection of object shifts outside the interval $[-0.75, 0.26]$ for objects starting with zero parallax and outside the interval $[-0.24, 0.32]$ for objects starting with negative parallax. Participants were not able to detect shifts for objects starting with positive parallax with a probability of at least 75%, but the $DT_{0.25}$ thresholds show that they had at least some good impression of the motion outside the interval $[-0.5, 0.14]$.

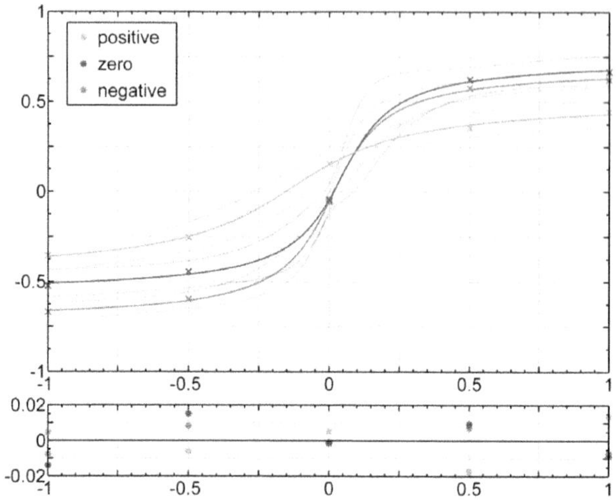

Figure 8: Fitted psychological functions for each parallax (top) and the fitting residuals (bottom). The X-axis shows the applied shift factor σ, the Y-axis shows the mean responses. The dotted lines show the 95% confidence interval and the crosses the means of subject responses.

Discussion

Our results support the initial hypothesis $H_0^{(3)}$ that the detection of induced object shifts does not depend on the user's handedness. While the hypothesis $H_0^{(2)}$ has also been supported, it is (at the current state) not clear, if it still holds for objects closer to the bezel of the display or in densely populated environments with multiple objects close to each other.

Contrary to our initial hypothesis $H_0^{(1)}$, participants judged objects starting on positive parallax and moving against their fingertip as static and thus underestimated the distances to those objects. The PSE for shift factors of objects starting on the zero or negative parallax planes is nearly zero, which indicates that subjects are more sensitive to the motion directions in these cases. In contrast to the steeply ascending curves for non-positive parallaxes, the flat curve for mean results of objects starting on positive parallax hints to detection thresholds outside the range of $[-1.0, 1.0]$. This may be explained with the smaller absolute object shift during reaching for objects on positive parallax. Indeed, since we start manipulating the object's position when the user's finger is approximately $10cm$ away from the object, the maximal hand motion until the finger reaches the display surface is only $5cm$. While the relative motion of the object is the same in all cases, the object is manipulated longer if starting on a negative or zero parallax. Thus the effective object motion

Parallax	$DT_{0.5}$	$DT_{0.25}$	PSE	$DT_{0.25}$	$DT_{0.5}$
	opposite			same	
positive	–	-0.50	-0.16	0.14	–
zero	-0.75	-0.11	0.02	0.10	0.26
negative	-0.24	-0.07	0.02	0.11	0.32

Table 2: $DT_{0.25}$, $DT_{0.5}$ and PSE for the shift discrimination task.

even with strong shift factors is smaller compared to the absolute object motion for the other parallaxes. For instance, a shift factor of 1.0 translates an object starting on the positive parallax plane a total of $5cm$, while the same shift factor translates an object starting on the zero parallax plane $10cm$.

GENERAL DISCUSSION AND DESIGN IMPLICATIONS

The results of E1 and E2 show that in both cases there is a usable range of detection thresholds, which could be used to enable touch interaction with stereoscopically rendered objects, with little or no impact on the depth perception or touch performance. Consistent with Chan at al. [6] the first experiment provides strong evidence for the fact that if tangible feedback is missing, humans are quite inaccurate in determining an object's depth at the end of the correction phase of a touch gesture. Nevertheless, the correction phase is only a small part of the interaction process itself. During task formulation, planning and the ballistic phase users usually focus attention on the visual scene and thus may benefit from the stereoscopy.

On the practical side, the subjects' inability to discriminate, if small objects are in front of the screen or not while performing a touch gesture, is quite interesting and motivates the possibility to design 3D interfaces without modifications of existing interaction techniques or the hardware. For instance, an interface designer could place some small widgets or anchors in front of the screen in order to improve their visibility and accessibility. Users could then directly interact with those widgets without noticeable impact on their performance, provided the accuracy is adjusted according to [23]. The detection thresholds derived in E1 define the narrow depth vicinity in which such objects could be scattered, i. e., if object size is under $3.5cm$, they may be placed at most at $4.35cm$ in front of the screen surface, but only at $1.3cm$ behind it. Although almost always perceived behind a touching finger, objects smaller than $2.0cm$ should be placed at most $10cm$ in front of the display, otherwise the start of the correction phase might be shifted, and thus the gesture might become unnatural and annoying. With objects greater than $5cm$ care must be taken, since users usually clearly detect if they are in front of the screen or not, being uncertain only in the range of about $1.0cm$.

The second experiment provides options to extend this depth vicinity. In particular, objects with negative or zero parallax, i. e., in front of or on the display surface, could be moved with the user's finger by about 25% of the total finger motion without the user noticing it. For instance, starting the manipulation when the pointing finger is at about $10cm$ in front of the screen for an object at depth $2.5cm$ will allow us to move the object exactly onto the display surface at the moment of touch contact, while this motion will remain imperceptible for most users. Although this extension comes at the cost of additional hardware equipment, it opens a range of new opportunities. For instance, combined with the approach proposed by Wilson and Benko [25], one could use stereoscopic rendering, thus augment non-planar content on the available surfaces or add objects floating in front of or beyond those surfaces. By shifting the virtual objects or application of some morphing technique on more complex surfaces, one could enable touch interaction while still providing passive haptic feedback in such a setup. Using solely the scaled shift technique with manipulations starting $10cm$ before the intended object or point is reached, the available interaction space could be seamlessly extended to a volume of $\pm 2.5cm$ around the display surface (see $DT_{0.5}$ in Table 2). Furthermore, the PSE shift of objects behind the display surface indicates that an interface developer might *need to* apply shifts such that the objects are perceived static.

Some of the test persons were first a bit confused when they were instructed to touch an object which is floating in front of the screen. Nevertheless, after a few test trials all of them adapted to the task and none found it unnatural or inconvenient. Usually more confusing for the users was the forced choice on objects' parallax or motion. Most of the users commented that in many cases they were not able to determine the right answer and pressed a button on gut instinct. Interestingly, those "instinctive" decisions were surprisingly consistent across the participants as the confidence intervals in Figures 5 and 8 confirm. This might be explained with the fact that disparity cues are used for planing a pointing gesture on a very basic cognitive level. Therefore it might be possible to detect such thresholds, that are independent from the cultural or educational background of the user.

CONCLUSION AND FUTURE WORK

In this paper we have addressed the challenge to enable touch interaction with floating objects on devices with stereoscopic displays. The results of E1 indicate that within some ranges touch interaction with stereoscopic objects is already possible without any additional hardware devices or changes of the 2D interaction techniques. The detection thresholds determined in E2 show that we can shift virtual objects closer to the display surface without users detecting this, thus enabling natural tangible feedback for these objects. From some initial application tests we conclude that touch interaction with objects floating in front of, or behind the display surface has the potential to provide significant enhancement of stereoscopically enabled devices. However, further research has to be done in this direction to provide generally applicable manipulation ranges and techniques. Nevertheless, we hypothesise that with more complex visualizations the results would differ only in quantity, e. g., point of subjective equality and detection thresholds, but the qualitative behavior would remain similar. For instance, the derived shift factors may be affected by the object's position in relation to the display's bezel, since the bezel provides a non-manipulative reference to the user. Additional problems could arise in dense 3D environments, where objects might be visualized at the same position with different depths, thus application of the *scaled shift* technique might lead to objects switching their depth position. The impact of those factors, as well as the possibility to apply rotational or curvature shift techniques, is currently not well assessable, and further research in this direction is needed to address it.

ACKNOWLEDGEMENTS

We would like to thank all participants of the experiments. This work was supported by a grant from the Deutsche Forschungsgemeinschaft in the scope of the iMUTS project.

REFERENCES

1. W. J. Adams, I. S. Kerrigan, and E. W. Graf. Efficient Visual Recalibration from Either Visual or Haptic Feedback: The Importance of Being Wrong. *Journal of Neuroscience*, 30(44):14745–14749, November 2010.
2. H. Benko and S. Feiner. Balloon selection: A multi-finger technique for accurate low-fatigue 3d selection. *IEEE 3DUI*, pages 79–86, 2007.
3. D. Bowman, E. Kruijff, J. LaViola, and I. Poupyrev. *3D User Interfaces: Theory and Practice*. Addison-Wesley, 2004.
4. E. Burns, S. Razzaque, A. T. Panter, M. Whitton, M. McCallus, and F. Brooks. The Hand is Slower than the Eye: A Quantitative Exploration of Visual Dominance over Proprioception. In *IEEE VR*, pages 3–10, 2005.
5. R. H. S. Carpenter. *Movements of the eyes*. Pion Limited, London, 1977.
6. L.-W. Chan, H.-S. Kao, M. Y. Chen, M.-S. Lee, J. Hsu, and Y.-P. Hung. Touching the void: direct-touch interaction for intangible displays. In *ACM CHI*, pages 2625–2634, 2010.
7. A. Y. Dvorkin, R. V. Kenyon, and E. A. Keshner. Reaching within a dynamic virtual environment. *Journal of NeuroEngineering and Rehabilitation*, 4(23), 2007.
8. T. Grossman and D. Wigdor. Going deeper: a taxonomy of 3d on the tabletop. In *IEEE TABLETOP '07.*, pages 137 – 144, 2007.
9. M. Hancock, S. Carpendale, and A. Cockburn. Shallow-depth 3d interaction: design and evaluation of one-, two- and three-touch techniques. In *ACM CHI*, pages 1147–1156, 2007.
10. O. Hilliges, S. Izadi, A. D. Wilson, S. Hodges, A. Garcia-Mendoza, and A. Butz. Interactions in the Air: Adding Further Depth to Interactive Tabletops. In *ACM UIST*, pages 139–148, 2009.
11. J. Huhtala, M. Karukka, M. Salmimaa, and J. Häkkilä. Evaluating depth illusion as method of adding emphasis in autostereoscopic mobile displays. In *ACM MobileCHI*, pages 357–360, 2011.
12. Robert M. K. Cognitive maps: What are they and why study them? *Journal of Environmental Psychology*, 14(1):1 – 19, 1994.
13. F. L. Kooi and A. Toet. Visual comfort of binocular and 3d displays. *Displays*, 25(23):99 – 108, 2004.
14. A. Lécuyer. Simulating haptic feedback using vision: A survey of research and applications of pseudo-haptic feedback. *Journal of Presence: Teleoperators and Virtual Environments*, 18:39–53, January 2009.
15. G. Liu, R Chua, and J. T. Enns. Attention for perception and action: task interference for action planning, but not for online control. *Experimental Brain Research*, 185:709–717, 2008.
16. S. Mizobuchi, S. Terasaki, J. Häkkinen, E. Heinonen, J. Bergquist, and M. Chignell. The effect of stereoscopic viewing in a word-search task with a layered background. *Journal of the Society for Information Display*, 16(11):1105–1113, 2008.
17. D. Schmalstieg, L. M. Encarnação, and Z. Szalavári. Using transparent props for interaction with the virtual table. In *ACM Interactive 3D graphics '99*, pages 147–153, 1999.
18. J. Schöning, F. Steinicke, D. Valkov, A. Krüger, and K. Hinrichs. Bimanual interaction with interscopic multi-touch surfaces. In *IFIP TC13 INTERACT '09*, pages 40–53, 2009.
19. J. Soechting and Laquaniti. Modification of trajectory of a pointing movement in response to a change in targer location. *Journal of Neurophysiology*, 49(2), 1983.
20. M. Spindler, C. Tominski, H. Schumann, and R. Dachselt. Tangible views for information visualization. In *ACM ITS*, pages 157–166, 2010.
21. S. Strothoff, D. Valkov, and K. Hinrichs. Triangle cursor: Interactions with objects above the tabletop. In *ACM ITS*, pages 111–119, 2011.
22. Y. Uno, M. Kawato, and R. Suzuki. Formation and control of optimal trajectory in human multijoint arm movement. *Biological Cybernetics*, 61:89–101, 1989.
23. D. Valkov, F. Steinicke, G. Bruder, and K. Hinrichs. 2d touching of 3d stereoscopic objects. In *ACM CHI*, pages 1353–1362, 2011.
24. A. Viau, A. G. Feldman, B. J McFadyen, and M. F. Levin. Reaching in reality and virtual reality: a comparison of movement kinematics in healthy subjects and in adults with hemiparesis. *Journal of NeuroEngineering and Rehabilitation*, 1(11), 2004.
25. A. D. Wilson and H. Benko. Combining multiple depth cameras and projectors for interactions on, above and between surfaces. In *ACM UIST*, pages 273–282, 2010.
26. Jeremy M Wolfe and Todd S Horowitz. What attributes guide the deployment of visual attention and how do they do it? *Nature Reviews Neuroscience*, 5(6):495–501, 2004.

Gradual Engagement: Facilitating Information Exchange between Digital Devices as a Function of Proximity

Nicolai Marquardt[1], Till Ballendat[1], Sebastian Boring[1], Saul Greenberg[1], Ken Hinckley[2]

[1]University of Calgary
Department of Computer Science, Calgary, AB, Canada
{nicolai.marquardt, sebastian.boring, saul}@ucalgary.ca, till@ballendat.info

[2]Microsoft Research
One Microsoft Way, Redmond WA 98052
kenh@microsoft.com

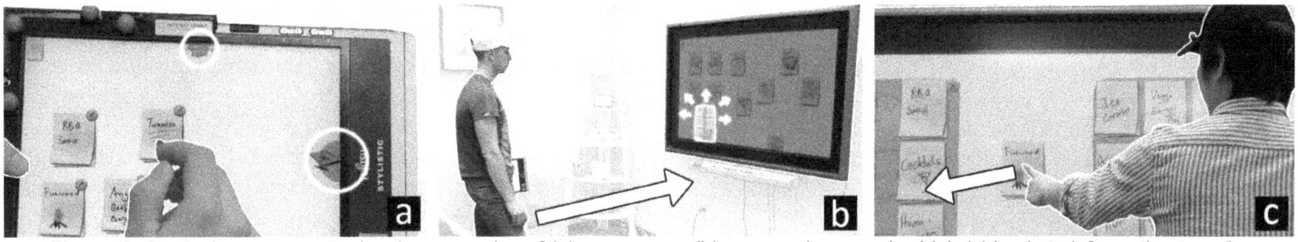

Figure 1. Gradual engagement, showing examples of (a) awareness, (b) progressive reveal, which (c) leads to information transfer

ABSTRACT

The increasing number of digital devices in our environment enriches how we interact with digital content. Yet, cross-device information transfer – which should be a common operation – is surprisingly difficult. One has to know which devices can communicate, what information they contain, and how information can be exchanged. To mitigate this problem, we formulate the *gradual engagement* design pattern that generalizes prior work in proxemic interactions and informs future system designs. The pattern describes how we can design device interfaces to gradually engage the user by disclosing connectivity and information exchange capabilities as a function of inter-device proximity. These capabilities flow across three stages: (1) *awareness* of device presence/connectivity, (2) *reveal* of exchangeable content, and (3) interaction methods for *transferring* content between devices tuned to particular distances and device capabilities. We illustrate how we can apply this pattern to design, and show how existing and novel interaction techniques for cross-device transfers can be integrated to flow across its various stages. We explore how techniques differ between personal and semi-public devices, and how the pattern supports interaction of multiple users.

ACM Classification: H5.2 [Information interfaces and presentation]: User Interfaces – Input devices and strategies

Keywords: gradual engagement; proximity; awareness; proxemic interactions; handhelds; interactive surfaces

INTRODUCTION

Personal mobile devices (e.g., phones, tablets) and semi-public stationary devices (e.g., information appliances, interactive surfaces) are an increasingly commonplace way for people to ubiquitously interact with digital information. Most of these devices are optimized for a seamless user experience when one uses them individually. Yet, using multiple devices in *concert* (such as for transferring information from a mobile phone to the device of a nearby person) is often tedious and requires executing complicated interaction sequences. This is why several projects in the area of ubiquitous computing (ubicomp) began introducing new techniques to facilitate transfer of content between nearby devices, e.g., [13,16,30]. However, significant challenges remain. People do not know *which* devices can communicate with one another, *what* information they contain that is exchangeable, and *how* information can be exchanged in a controlled manner.

To mitigate these problems, as our primary contribution we formulate a design pattern called *gradual engagement*, which we then refine to ease the information transfer task. As a design pattern [5,33], its strengths lie in (1) unifying prior work in proxemic interaction, (2) synthesizing essential, generalizable interaction strategies, and (3) providing a common vocabulary for discussing design solutions. Most importantly, the pattern informs and inspires future designs, but also allows for variations of the pattern applied to different domains.

As we will see, the gradual engagement pattern describes how devices can gradually engage the user by disclosing connectivity and information exchange capabilities as a function of proximity. That is, as people move and orient their personal device towards other surrounding devices [11,24], the interface progressively moves through three stages affording gradual engagement: (1) *awareness* of device presence and connectivity, (2) *reveal* of exchangeable digital content, and (3) interaction methods for *transferring* digital content between devices tuned to particular distances and device capabilities (cf. Figures 1 & 2).

As our secondary contribution, we illustrate how we can apply this pattern to design, and demonstrate how adapta-

ITS'12, November 11–14, 2012, Cambridge, Massachusetts, USA.

tions of existing interaction techniques flow across the three stages. In addition, we introduce novel interaction techniques that make use of this design pattern. In particular, we explore how gradual engagement techniques differ when the other device seen is personal (such as a handheld) vs. semi-public (such as a large display), and how gradual engagement applies to multi-user *collaborative* activities.

We begin with a brief review of proxemics and proxemic interactions, as these are the theoretical grounds behind our work. We then introduce the gradual engagement design pattern: how it emerges from prior work in proxemic interactions, and how we refine it to ease the information transfer task. We then describe particular interaction techniques, where our presentation is structured according to the three stages of the gradual engagement design pattern. The accompanying video illustrates these techniques in action.

PROXEMICS FOR UBICOMP INTERACTIONS

Proxemics – as introduced by anthropologist Edward Hall [12] – is one of the seminal theories for describing and studying people's use and understanding of spatial relationships in everyday encounters with others. People often use changes of spatial relationships – such as distance or orientation – as an implicit form of communication. Hall's studies, for example, revealed patterns in how certain physical distances correlate to social distance when people interact. Other observations further refined this understanding of people's use of spatiality. For example, spatial features of the environment (e.g., location of walls, doors, furniture) influence people's use of proxemics, and orientation relative to others when we communicate is another driving factor. Proxemics mediates many aspects of social interaction. For example, it influences casual and serendipitous encounters [20], is a nuance in how people greet one another [Ch. 6 in 19], and is a major factor in how people arrange themselves for optimal small group collaboration via spatial-orientational maneuvering [Ch. 4 & 7 in 19]. Proxemics as a social construct also helps people *gradually engage* with one another: people are spatially aware of others around them, how they approach each other to signal interest, and how they arrange themselves as they engage in conversation.

Within HCI, a variety of researchers used proxemics to motivate particular ubicomp system designs (e.g., [18,35]; see related work). This evolved *proxemic interactions* [2,24], a general construct that applies the insights of proxemic theory to the holistic design of ubicomp interaction. Proxemic interactions describe five important dimensions to consider when designing proxemic-aware ubicomp systems. These dimensions operationalize the relationships between people, devices, and objects as sensed or stored variables: the *distance* between entities, their relative *orientation* to one another, their relative *movement,* their *identity,* and *location* features that give further meaning to that setting [11].

PROXIMITY AND GRADUAL ENGAGEMENT

The vast majority of interfaces are premised on the notion that a person is fully attending it, i.e., the system is designed to support *foreground* activities and tasks. However, a variety of systems also recognize that the person may not be directly attending them (i.e., it is in the *background* of their attention), where they still try to be helpful by presenting an interface that selectively informs the user of information of interest.

One class of examples includes ambient displays [22] embedded in a physical environment. The display usually presents non-critical information unobtrusively, which a person can monitor at a distance and at the periphery of their attention (thus providing basic awareness). The display often contains a way for the person to easily transition to more in-depth information exploration if the person decides to engage with it; this normally occurs by the person approaching and directly interacting with that display. That is, such displays implicitly incorporate a *binary notion* of proximity: from afar, and within interaction reach.

Proxemic interactions provide another class of examples that use a much more refined notion of proxemics. Many proxemic interaction systems commonly interpret decreasing distance and increasing mutual orientation between a person and a device within a bounded space as an indication of gradually increasing interest of that person to interact with that device. Influential earlier work considered such gradual increasing engagement between a *person* and large interactive displays [2,18,35,36]. For example, Vogel et al. directly applied Hall's theory to a person's interaction with a public display [35]. They defined four discrete zones around the display that affect a person's interaction when moving closer: from far to close, interactions range from ambient display of information, to implicit, subtle, and finally personal interaction. Similarly, Ju's interaction techniques with a digital whiteboard remain public and implicit from a distance, and become increasingly more private and explicit when the person moves closer to that display. Ballendat et al. introduced proxemic interaction concepts illustrated with an interactive media player [2], where the device reacts to one or multiple people's proxemics relationships by varying displayed content and supporting diverse modes of interaction. Wang et al. described a proximity-based advertising display that changes its presentation of information not only to engage people for interaction, but to try to re-attract them if they appear distracted [36].

We generalize the sequence inherent in these (and other) systems as a design pattern we call *gradual engagement*[1]. The basic idea is that:

- background information supplied by the system provides awareness to the person about opportunities of potential interest when viewed at a distance;

[1] Jan Borchers describes an even more general pattern titled 'Attract-Engage-Deliver' [5]. The difference is that our pattern incorporates proxemics as a first-class element.

- the person can gradually act on particular opportunities by viewing and/or exploring its information in more detail simply by approaching it; and
- the person can ultimately engage in action if so desired.

This pattern is, of course, directly inspired by proxemic theory and by the systems that reflect that pattern. The pattern also characterizes what we thought was the 'best' of how proxemics was previously applied to ubicomp design.

APPLYING GRADUAL ENGAGEMENT TO CROSS-DEVICE INFORMATION TRANSFER

The previously mentioned systems are primarily focused on people's interaction with large displays, where the display's content changes as a function of a person's distance. However, the relatively recent explosion of smart phones and other hand-held devices, as well as the more general availability of computer displays embedded in the environment, mean that people are now living in a dynamic device ecology. This begs the question of how people can interact *across* such devices, where we focus on the particular problem of how people can transfer information between them.

We refine the *gradual engagement* design pattern by considering fine-grained proxemic relationships *between multiple devices* allowing seamless transitions from awareness to information transfer. Specifically, engagement increases continuously across *three stages* as people move and orient their personal device towards other surrounding devices (Fig. 2):

Stage 1. ***Awareness of device presence and connectivity*** is provided, so that a person can understand what other devices are present and whether they can connect with one's own personal device. We leverage knowledge about proxemic relationships between devices to determine when devices connect and how they notify a person about their presence and established connections.

Stage 2. ***Reveal of exchangeable content*** is provided, so that people know what of their content can be accessed on other devices for information transfer. At this stage, a fundamental technique is progressively revealing a device's available digital content as a function of proximity.

Stage 3. ***Transferring digital content between devices, tuned to particular proxemic relationships and device capabilities,*** is provided via various strategies. Each is tailored to fit naturally within particular situations and contexts: from a distance *vs.* from close proximity; and transfer to a personal device *vs.* a semi-public device.

We illustrate the application of this gradual engagement pattern between devices as a suite of interaction techniques, all based on providing a seamless transition leading from awareness, to reveal, to interaction. The remainder of the paper will revisit each of the three stages to introduce these techniques. First, however, we review prior work that relates to our derivation of the gradual engagement pattern.

PRIOR WORK APPLIED TO GRADUAL ENGAGEMENT

We briefly sample prior work that contributed to our derivation of particular stages of the gradual engagement pattern. Beyond the review, we also later explain how many of these prior techniques can be applied to people's interactions across all three stages of gradual engagement. Figure 2, bottom, summarizes how these works fit within and thus contribute to the pattern.

Awareness of Device Presence and Connectivity

Most systems define a discrete spatial region around devices, where a connection is established (and information transfer possible) once the distance becomes smaller than a certain threshold. Often, this distance depends on the actual sensing technology used (e.g., sensing range of RFID or Bluetooth).

Visualization of available devices becomes important in ubicomp environments, as an increasing number of diverse devices are present. Their presence, location, and ability to connect (or not) are rarely easily visible to a user. A few systems began exploring methods to inform a person about surrounding devices and possible connections. Most commonly, a map visualizes devices located in the environment (e.g., Sentient Computing [1]) or the same room (e.g., *ARIS* [4]). Gellersen et al.'s *RELATE* Gateways provide a similar visualization, but make use of sophisticated tracking systems to dynamically update the positions of all devices [10]. In an alternative view, icons at the border of a mobile device screen represent the type and location of surrounding devices [10,29]. Kray's *group coordination negotiation* introduced spatial regions for interaction around mobile phones [21]. Their scenario used these regions to negotiate exchange of information with others. Feedback about a phone's presence in any of the regions was visualized on a tabletop. Marquardt et al. observe F-Formations (i.e., patterns of how people stand in close proximity formations) to determine when to federate devices [25].

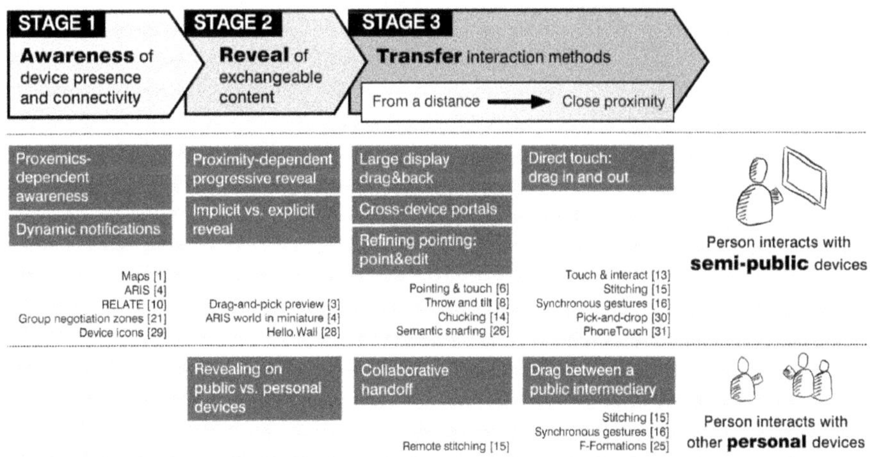

Figure 2. Three sequential stages of the gradual engagement pattern (top row) and interaction methods derived from the pattern supporting awareness and interaction in each stage: person interacting with *semi-public* devices (middle row) or *personal* devices of other people (bottom row).

Explicit Connections. Various systems allow people to manually associate two devices from a distance. This is usually done via pointing one device at the other. Swindells uses an infrared-emitting pen to point at a device to control it [32]. *Semantic snarfing* [26] also uses pointing to allow someone to take over temporary control of remote interfaces. Similarly, others have suggested ways to manually associate nearby devices that are all within reach. With Smart-its friends [17], a connection is established when two devices are shaken simultaneously and sense similar accelerometer values. In *Synchronous Gestures* people can bump devices [16] – including phones and interactive tabletops [31] – together to initiate a connection. In *Stitching*, users couple devices by drawing a stroke that begins on one display and ends on another [15]. Overall, Chong et al. confirmed that proximity is one of the 'big five' categories of how users associate devices [7].

Revealing Exchangeable Content.

Several systems visualized exchangeable content. *Hello.Wall* introduced the notion of 'distance-dependent semantics', where the distance (here: close, far, out of range) of a person's device from the wall screen defined the kind of information shown on the mobile display [28]. The aforementioned *ARIS* shows applications running on devices located in the same room in a world-of-miniature fashion [4]. In *Drag-and-Pick*, content that is located in the direction of an initial drag operation appears close to the point of interaction – even on other devices in that direction [3].

Transferring Digital Content

Once connected, diverse techniques allow information transfer. For example, Want's RFID-based technique allows detecting nearby objects and devices and associating/retrieving digital information [37]. In *Pick-and-Drop*, users pick up content on one display and place it on another with a digital pen [30]. *Touch & Interact* temporarily shift the interaction focus and content from a large display onto a mobile device [13]. Somewhat later, Marquardt et al. consider F-Formations and micro-mobility to drive device-to-device information transfer while people stand in close proximity formations [25]. Rekimoto combined near-field RFID and remote infrared communication for seamless information transfer [29]. Further examples for cross-device information transfer from a distance are: throwing gestures performed with a phone [8], touch and pointing gesture combinations [6], chucking motions towards the other device [14], or *corresponding Gestures* through cursor selections in multi-screen environments [27].

In summary, various techniques exist – most suited for particular discrete distances between devices – that fit into particular stages (but rarely all stages) of the gradual engagement pattern (see Figure 2). In the next sections, we use our design pattern to build on these earlier works. In particular, we illustrate interaction techniques that allow a person to move seamlessly from awareness at a larger distance, to gradually revealing more detail about devices and content when approaching, to direct interaction for transferring digital information between devices when standing in either close proximity or at a distance. By extending earlier work, we also consider how particular device types can influence this interaction, e.g., personal handhelds *vs.* semi-public stationary devices.

RUNNING EXAMPLE: PROXEMIC BRAINSTORMING

We use an example application throughout the paper as a running example to illustrate how our various techniques leverage proxemic interaction and follow gradual engagement to facilitate access to digital information. *Proxemic Brainstorming* is a multi-user, interactive digital brainstorming tool. Its users can create, change, and manage virtual sticky notes on their personal pen-enabled tablets. A large whiteboard provides a public sharing space for notes, and different techniques (explained shortly) allow temporary or permanent transfer of the digital notes between all devices. The video figure illustrates this application and the dynamics of the various methods described below. The video also demonstrates a second application, applying the pattern to facilitate transfer of digital photos from a network enabled digital camera to other devices, such as a large display or a digital photo frame.

STAGE 1: AWARENESS OF DEVICE PRESENCE & CONNECTIVITY

While ubicomp ecologies may contain many devices, only some of them – for a variety of reasons – are likely able to connect with a user's personal device to the point that the person can do useful work between them (such as transferring content). While these devices may sense this information (e.g., via service discovery protocols), the user is often left in the dark about these opportunities for inter-device interaction.

Consequently, we implemented methods that make a person aware of whether his personal device and other nearby devices can detect each other's presence and are able to connect. Building upon [1,4,10,29], the basic idea is that a person sees a visual indicator – a subtle notification – about which devices as well as their location in the surrounding environment can possibly interact with his handheld device (e.g., icons in Figure 3). People can then subsequently move toward a particular device to either establish that connection or to reveal further information and interaction possibilities (which would occur in stages 2 & 3, discussed shortly). This is particularly important in dynamically changing or unfamiliar environments: some devices may be hidden or disguised as a non-digital device (e.g., a digital picture frame appliance), or only some of the surrounding devices may allow connections to them (e.g., a device may not support a certain application). Information about these possible connections as well as simple ways to actually establish the connection is crucial if seamless interaction across devices is to occur.

Proxemics-dependent awareness. We use rules to determine when to trigger awareness of device presence and connectivity. By connection, we mean whether one device

Figure 3. Icons at the edge of the screen indicate the presence and location of other devices in close proximity (2 tablet computers).

should connect to another device based on human dynamics *vs.* whether a device is technically capable of connecting to another. We exploit the five aforementioned *proxemic dimensions* [11] as sensed factors: combinations of them allow us to create nuanced rules of connection behaviour.

Location informs devices if they (and the people using them) are in the same room. In almost all cases, devices present in the same room are far more relevant for interaction than the ones in another room. For example, when a person with a tablet enters a new room through the door, notifications can be triggered about other devices available in that particular room. Other devices in close proximity but in adjacent rooms (e.g., behind the walls) are not shown. In proxemics terms, doorways, walls and other boundaries are fixed features that further demark people's sense of social distance; we believe such fixed features are applicable to how devices determine possible candidates for cross-device connections. Location also informs context; some locations (e.g., public vs. home spaces) would afford quite different connectivity semantics.

Physical distance between devices is an essential factor we exploit for determining device connection and triggering notifications. Proxemic theory states that people naturally stand close to other people they are interested in and want to communicate with. Similarly, we believe that the distance between the user's personal device and other devices in the ecology is a natural indicator of whether a connection between the two should be signaled to the user and subsequently established. Distance measurements can also be applied as a filter that prevents too many notifications in environments with a large number of digital devices. In that case, awareness information is only shown of a limited number of devices that have the smallest distance (e.g., the five closest devices).

Movement – the change of distance over time – is an indicator of increasing or decreasing interest. When we are interested in something we move closer to it, while we move away when we are less interested. We can apply this to device-device connectivity. For example, if a person holding a tablet is approaching the large display, we can interpret this as increasing interest of that person to connect and ultimately interact with both devices in tandem.

Orientation of one device towards another is another indicator that the person wants to connect the two. This again mimics interpersonal interaction: when people interact, they orient themselves to either face the other person or stand side by side. Orientation between devices could simply be whether one device is facing towards or away from another device, or a finer measure that considers and acts upon the angle between the two (at the extreme, this becomes pointing [26,32]). For determining cross-device connections, we focus on all devices that are either located in front or at the sides of the device. We assume that if a person wants to interact with a device located behind them, they turn around to face this device, and if they are uninterested, they face away. For example, the visual feedback shown in Fig. 1a,b would appear or fade away as the person turns towards or faces away from the display.

Identity of devices functions as a filter for possible connections. Known devices can trigger the connection notification from a larger distance, while unknown devices need to be located next to each other to establish a successful (and more socially secure) connection. This technique follows the principle that "distance implies distrust" [9], and similarly that closer proximity between devices implies trust (although this depends on location context). Identity also distinguishes classes of devices, where (for example) connectivity to another person's personal device may be dealt with differently than to a semi-public device, as each suggests different social expectations.

The combination of these five proxemics factors informs the decision about device connectivity, and the corresponding visual/auditory/tactile feedback provided, that eventually allows a user to leverage this knowledge of device presence and connectivity for further interaction.

Dynamic notifications about device presence and location. Given the above, a broad variety of notification mechanisms can inform a person about the presence of other nearby devices and opportunities for interaction: audible signals, vibrotactile haptic feedback, visual notifications, etc. Yet, given the increasing number of devices in a ubicomp ecology, we opted for a visual approach, as such notifications can be displayed in a more ambient and distinguishable manner. Visuals can portray device identity and location, and – as we will shortly see – can also serve as containers showing content (stage 2) and act as portals for information exchange (stage 3).

In general, all device screens in close proximity display graphical icons representing the location of surrounding connectable devices (Figures 1a, 3, 4 & 5a). Each icon informs the user: where the device represented by the icon is physically located; that there is a potential connection between those devices; and that devices can interact with one other (e.g., allowing information transfer). Icon appearance can be informative, such as a graphic that represents the nearby tablet. Or they can be augmented with other information, such as the name of that device and/or its owner.

Figure 3 exemplifies this in Proxemic Brainstorming: as the two people move their tablets towards each other, icons at the edge of both screens show the other devices and the name of the device's owner. Extending earlier work (e.g., [2,10,29]), icon locations are continuously animated around the edge to represent the directional location of the corre-

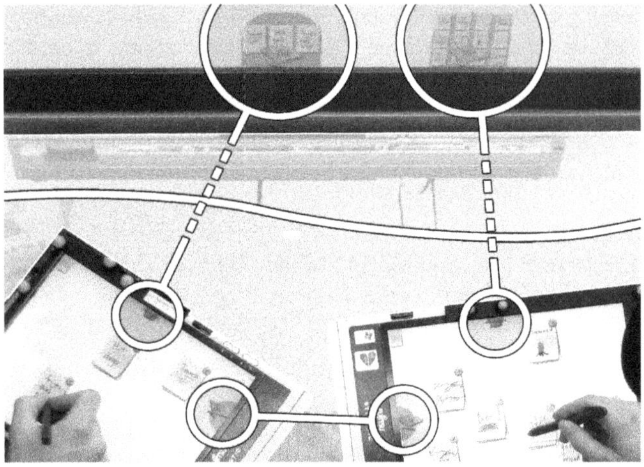

Figure 4. *Content awareness:* Proxy icons indicate the presence of nearby tablets and a large interactive display. Available content of the tablets is displayed as thumbnails atop these icons.

sponding device. In Figure 3, we see how both displays' icon locations illustrate their physical spatial relationship. Figure 4 is similar, except it shows how several locations are indicated in a multi-device environment, in this case of two handhelds and a large display. Again, this helps reducing ambiguity of which icon corresponds to which device in the environment.

Because icon location is dynamic, people can further identify the mapping of device icons to actual physical devices by changing their own device's distance and orientation and observing icon changes. If multiple devices are shown on a tablet's edge, for example, a person can move and/or rotate the screen and see the icons' positions updated in real-time. Naturally, the same continuous feedback applies when a person is moving closer to a cluster of devices. While approaching those devices, their corresponding icons on the tablet continuously change to reflect the new relationship between the tablet and each device. Thus, a person can move seamlessly towards and gradually engage the particular device desired for interaction.

STAGE 2: REVEAL OF EXCHANGEABLE CONTENT

As proximity increases, the gradual engagement pattern suggests that devices should reveal *content* available for exchange. Knowing what content a device offers for transfer is important information for a person to decide on further interactions. In fact, revealing content available for interaction or transfer to another device creates opportunities that invite a person to discover more about this content, eventually leading to more in-depth interactions.

Proximity-dependent progressive reveal. Importantly, revealing content is not all or none. Rather, the *distance* and *orientation* between two devices can directly affect the level of detail of content awareness information shown on other devices. Building upon work presented in [2], our *proximity-dependent progressive reveal* technique maps the distance between devices to the amount of information shared between them. The closer two devices are, the more information is shared between them. The level of detail shown (i.e., the amount of information shared) can change either at *discrete* distance levels, or *continuously* with changes in distance. As well, the level of detail can change depending on the orientation between devices. Again, this can happen at discrete angles (e.g., facing to or away from another), or through continuous changes of the orientation (e.g., from 0 to 180 degrees). Progressive reveal is important for three reasons. First, it presents people with opportunities as they approach another device; as with ambient displays, this could mediate the move from background peripheral awareness to foreground interaction [35]. Second, it gives them the chance to pull away, for example, if they see content about to be revealed that they would rather not make public. Third, it provides implicit security: in public contexts, fine details may appear in small size, and only when a person is (say) directly in front of other device, thus masking it from passersby.

For example, Figure 5 illustrates how Proxemic Brainstorming *continuously* reveals content during Stage 2 – in this case multiple sticky notes located on people's tablets – as they move closer to the large display. The wall display shows thumbnails of all sticky notes located on the tablets above the awareness icons (Fig. 5, right side). For the person sitting at a distance, the actual text on these notes is not yet readable, but the number of available notes is already visible. For the second person moving closer to the wall display, the thumbnails increase in size continuously (5b). For the third person standing directly in front of the display, the sticky notes are shown at full size (5c), allowing the person to read the text of all notes stored on the tablet and to pursue Stage 3 interactions, explained shortly.

Alternatively, instead of continuous growth of the awareness information, we can reveal content progressively at *discrete* distance thresholds. For example, the brainstorming application could first show only a device's awareness icon when at a larger distance (Stage 1), switch to showing

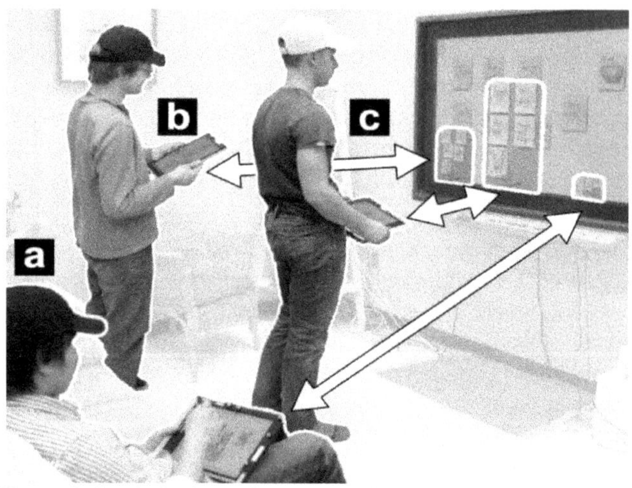

Figure 5. *Proximity-dependent progressive reveal* of personal device data of multiple users at different distances to the display: (a) minimal awareness of person sitting further away, (b) larger, visible content of a person moving closer, and (c) large awareness icons of person standing in front of the display.

a single thumbnail of the latest sticky note when the device is closer (Stage 2), and finally switch again to show all content once the person with the tablet stands in front of the screen. Furthermore, both continuous and discrete reveal can be combined, in a way that discrete stages trigger content changes and continuous distance changes affect the size of the currently displayed content.

Implicit vs. Explicit Reveal. The above method illustrates how content is revealed via a person's implicit actions. However, reveal can be complemented by explicit methods as well to fine-tune what is revealed. In this case, once content becomes revealed during Stage 2 the person can perform an explicit action to reveal more content. For example, tapping on the tablet screen allows cycling through multiple sets of sticky notes. Of course, alternative forms of explicit input (e.g., hand gestures, device movement) could be considered to cause similar explicit reveal behaviours (the video figure shows explicit reveal with a tilt-to-scroll technique for revealing additional photos of a camera).

Revealing content on personal vs. public devices. The information revealed about available content on the display of other devices should differ between *personal* and *semi-public* devices. For personal devices, we currently only provide an awareness icon of surrounding devices, but not their content. This is partially due to privacy reasons, but also size constraints: showing content on the small screens of *personal devices* may interfere with other content the user is viewing or interacting with. As we will see, we use other stage 3 methods to reveal content on personal devices during explicit information exchange.

Semi-Public devices (e.g., a wall-mounted display in a meeting room), however, reveal content located on one's *personal devices* as one approaches the display. For example, the wall display in Figure 4 shows both tablets' awareness icons at its lower edge, where each icon now contains small thumbnail images of all Proxemic Brainstorming notes on the corresponding tablet (i.e., 3 notes on the left tablet, 12 notes on the right one). Even though these thumbnails are too small to allow for full readability, they provide awareness information about the number of notes available for sharing on each of the tablets.

STAGE 3: TECHNIQUES FOR INFORMATION TRANSFER BETWEEN DEVICES

Stage 1 and 2 indicate device presence, connectivity and available content, eventually leading to Stage 3 of the gradual engagement pattern, where a person can interact with progressively revealed content. We now present a series of novel interaction techniques (and others from related work) that allow for sharing and transferring content between devices.

We stress that the power of these Stage 3 techniques is that they are used in conjunction with the Stage 1 and 2 methods *vs.* as stand-alone techniques similar to those found in the literature. Importantly, these techniques consider proxemic relationships between devices to drive the interaction, and come into play at particular points during Stages 1 and 2. We are particularly interested in two contexts:

- Whether information exchange is a single person activity (based on the proximity of a handheld to a semi-public display) or a cooperative multi-person activity (based on the proximity of at least two handheld devices).
- How they allow people to interact at different levels of proximity i.e., from a distance *vs.* within reach.

Single Person Transfer: from Personal to Public Device

First, we present a series of techniques that primarily allow a *single person* to share content from their personal device to a public display. We begin with distant-based interactions that could be performed in the early periods of progressive reveal, to within reach interactions at later periods.

Large display drag and back (from a distance) allows a person to temporarily show digital content from their personal device on a large *public* display. The idea is that the person owns the information, but is making it more convenient for others to view it. To share content temporarily on a large display, a person can drag content onto the awareness icon representing a nearby large screen. For example, Fig. 6 bottom shows a person dragging a note onto that icon. As he does so, a *viewing icon* appears atop the content (here: the 'eye' icon shown inside the circle of Fig. 6) indicating that one is about to share the note on that particular public display. As the person releases the note, the content appears in full screen view on the wall display (Fig. 6 top). To remove shared content, a person simply drags the content back from the device's awareness icon onto the tablet's canvas. Sharing also works for multiple people simultaneously: if others do similar actions, all shared content is shown side by side on the large display. This allows fast and easy sharing of digital content with all members of a group.

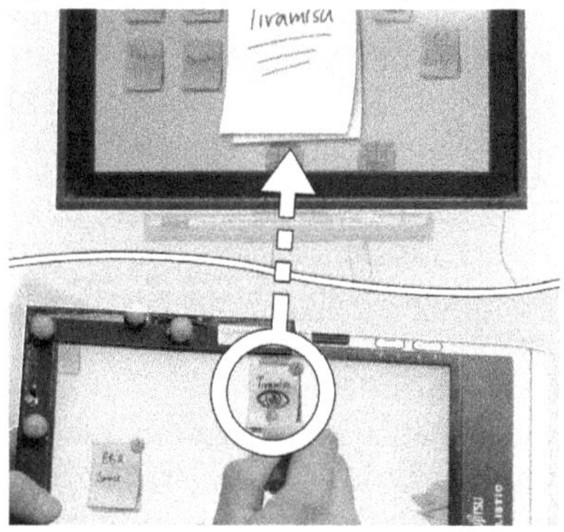

Figure 6. *Large display drag and back*: (bottom) dragging content on the wall display's awareness icon on the tablet, (top) content appears full screen on the large display. Notes from multiple users are shown side by side.

Cross-device portal drag to transfer (from a distance). We can also exploit the awareness icons of Stage 1 as portals to transfer information between them via drag and drop. This extension of the *portals* concept [34] supports transfer methods across *multiple* devices. Fig. 7 illustrates the transfer between a large display and a small screen; their awareness icons are visible at their borders. A person is

Figure 7. Cross-device *portal drag*

transferring content from the large display to the small screen simply by dragging a note onto the screen's portal, which then shows that note in full size on the small screen.

Integrating and refining pointing techniques: point & edit (from a distance). Considering all stages of the gradual engagement pattern also helps us integrate and refine existing gestural interaction techniques for information transfer.

For example, we integrated the *point & edit* technique as a refinement of *semantic snarfing* [26] and *touch+air* [6] pointing gestures from a distance. While content on a large display is convenient for viewing, editing may be more efficient on one's portable device. To select content for transferring back to the tablet, the tablet itself can function as a distant pointing device. A person holds the tablet away from his body and points it towards the display (the specific proxemic relationship of person and device is triggering the pointing mode). The system calculates the intersection of the pointing ray with the large display's surface. This action highlights the note (with a colored border) that is closest to that intersection point. To transfer the note to the tablet temporarily for editing purposes, the person taps on the tablet's screen. To place back the note on the large display, the person points at a location on the display and again taps the tablet's screen to confirm.

Direct touch: drag in and out (close proximity). In this technique, illustrated in Fig. 8, the tablet's content is progressively revealed in Stage 2 by growing it in size directly in front of the approaching person. (The area also follows the person's side-by-side movements). When within direct touch distance to the large display, this content becomes interactive, i.e., it allows that person to access his tablet's content by directly touching the large display. In particular, a person transfers content between the two devices (tablet & large display) by dragging items into or out of their personal area. Fig. 8 illustrate how Proxemic Brainstorming allows one to drag notes to an empty region on the screen, which transfers them across devices.

Figure 8. *Drag in and out in close proximity*

Again, we can integrate refinements of existing techniques at this stage. For example, inspired by *PhoneTouch* [31], the tablet itself can now be used as a physical pointing and selection device. Touching the device on the large screen will pick up or drop off information. Considering proxemics refines this technique: the pointing function of the tablet becomes active when a person stands within touch distance, and holds the tablet in a way that one of its corners points at content on the large display. As the device moves towards the display, a projected pointer highlights the currently selected note (thus providing continuous feedback before touching). When the person touches a note with a corner of the tablet, the note is picked up and temporarily transferred to the tablet device for editing. After editing, a person can quickly place that note back to a given location on the large display by touching that location with a corner of the tablet.

Collaborative Transfer

The next suite of techniques is tailored to multiple people collaboratively sharing content with each other through their *personal* devices, possibly including a large display. Unlike the single user techniques, these include coordination protocols that influence how handoffs are achieved.

Collaborative handoff (from a distance). In collaborative work scenarios, people may want to pass on digital information to another person. Often, this requires tedious sequences of tasks such as sending files by email or copying and retrieving content using portable media. Our notion of a *proxemic-aware collaborative handoff* (inspired by collaborative stitching [15]), represents a simpler method for transferring content between devices. The idea is that one person starts the gesture on his personal device, and a second person continues this gesture on his personal device to complete the handover process. That is, one person cannot transfer information without cooperation from the other person. Both must also be in close proximity before these techniques are activated. We expect people to monitor each other's actions in a way that mediates their social protocols.

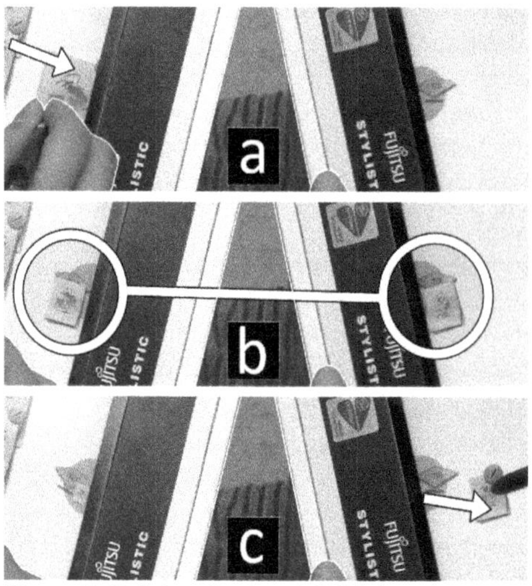

Figure 9. *Collaborative handoff*: (a) dragging content onto awareness icon representing the other tablet, (b) content appears on 2nd tablet, and (c) dragging content off the icon transfers it.

Figure 9 illustrates an example of content exchange in the Proxemic Brainstorming application between two people who have moved their tablets besides each other. As before, both are aware of connection availability via progressive reveal, where in this case the awareness icon size is larger as people move closer. Similar to our previously described 'portal drag to transfer', a person can initiate content sharing by dragging a sticky note onto the awareness icon of the second person's tablet (Fig. 9a). What is different is that a thumbnail of the content then appears on the second tablet, so that it is temporarily visible on both screens (Fig. 9b). If the second person drags the thumbnail image from the awareness icon onto his screen (thus *continuing* the first person's drag operation), the thumbnail on the first person's tablet disappears and the content is now permanently stored on the second person's device

Figure 10. *Drag between a public intermediary.* (a) person drags note out of his personal interaction area, (b) using the empty space between the interaction areas as a clipboard. (c) second person drags note into his interaction space of the tablet, and (d) the note is now moved to his tablet.

(Fig. 9c). Through this continuation of the gesture that was started by the first person, the second person '*accepts*' the content transfer action. If the person does not accept, the transfer is not performed. As well, if the transfer has not yet been accepted (i.e., phase 2; Figure 9b), the first person can cancel the transfer by dragging the content back onto his or her screen.

Drag between a public intermediary (close proximity). Two people can use the shared screen area of the large public display as a way to hand off content. The idea is that because information on that display is public, it implicitly gives permission to both actors to exchange information between their devices.

Figure 10 illustrates this. Two people are standing in direct touch distance in front of a large wall display with their tablet device in hand. Via progressive reveal, the personal content of both their devices are visible on the wall display as two interaction areas – one per person – in positions that reflect the side-by-side locations of both people (see the rectangular grey boxes containing sticky notes on the screen in Fig. 10). The large interaction areas on the screen make it easy to view and modify content.

Two different versions illustrate different ways of performing the transfer. In the handoff version, a person can drag a note to the shared public area (i.e., the regions not covered by individual interaction areas) on the large display (Fig. 10a,b), but not into the other person's area. The second person accepts that transfer by picking up this note and drag it to his own interaction area (Fig. 10c,d).

The second version does not require this handoff, relying instead on social protocol as augmented by the high visibility of all actions. Here, a person can move (or take) a note directly from one tablet to another by dragging it from one interaction area straight to the other.

DISCUSSION, FUTURE WORK, AND CONCLUSION

Gradual engagement, generalizability, limitations.

We believe that proxemic-aware interaction techniques following the gradual engagement pattern can help designing future ubicomp systems so that they drive the information transfer process in a way that more appropriately reacts to people's social understanding of personal space. Besides our presented application to cross-device transfers, the generalized gradual engagement pattern can be applied to other areas, e.g., interactive advertisements [36] or games [11]. In a similar way, these applications could benefit from (1) giving awareness notifications about presence, (2) reveal of content or possible interactions, and (3) providing a range of interaction techniques appropriate to the particular contexts as defined by distance, orientation, and group engagement. Overall, the gradual engagement pattern and our derived set of techniques is neither a complete or exhaustive set, nor do they handle all issues that will likely emerge. Rather, it is a starting point suggesting further exploration of patterns and interaction techniques for ubicomp system design.

Large ecologies of people and devices.

We believe the gradual engagement pattern will be more and more relevant as ubicomp ecologies emerge with an increasing number of personal and public devices featuring different form factors and capabilities. As shown, the pattern and the techniques we derived support a variety of 1-to-1 (e.g., *collaborative handoff, cross-portal drag*) and 1-to-many (e.g., *progressive reveal, large display drag and back*) collaborative settings. A major advantage of using the stages of gradual engagement is that it leads to an implicit *filtering* of choices presented to a user. For example, following the pattern prevents a system showing an overwhelming number of icons of all present devices in a large group, but instead fosters a design that only reveals the device presence between neighbours. Nevertheless, future work may extend our techniques to offer alternative 1-to-many sharing possibilities, e.g., by allowing dragging content on multiple device icons to share transfer content to all devices of a group (implemented as a cross-device group propagation technique in [25]).

Gradual engagement and privacy.

We recognize that the gradual engagement pattern for cross-device transfer can introduce privacy concerns in some situations. Thus, designs must incorporate safeguards to guarantee privacy of people's personal information. First, as mentioned in Stage 1, location information is essential to drive sharing behaviour. For example, while it is likely to have loose sharing between devices at home, only restricted sharing might be desired in the office, and no sharing (but maybe only device awareness) in public settings. Second, implicit protection rules can be applied to prevent sharing. For example, a device in a person's pocket stays invisible, but shares content when the person takes it out and points it towards other devices. Third, explicit actions and commands on the device can allow a person to manually stop sharing and close inter-device connections at any time (e.g., by pressing a button). This is a rich and fertile area for future work.

Pattern applied to different tracking hardware.

The principles of the gradual engagement design pattern can be applied to interactive systems using diverse *high-* and *low-fidelity* tracking systems. While the technology can limit or enhance how the design pattern is applied in a particular situation, the pattern itself goes beyond any specific technology.

At the high-fidelity end of the spectrum of possible hardware, our implementation uses an infrared-based motion capturing system [23]. The precise tracking information it provides of people and devices' distance or orientation allowed us to explore a large part of possible kinds of interactions. Such a system, however, is not suitable for wide deployments.

At the opposite side of the spectrum, a possible low-fidelity system using sensor fusion of depth-camera streams and wireless-radio signals for distance + orientation measurements (e.g., [25]) can similarly integrate gradual engagement methods. Despite its lower tracking fidelity, it would allow for applying diverse methods across all three stages of the pattern, such as progressive reveal, cross-device portals, and/or collaborative handoff.

Many other tracking systems would support gradual engagement as well. For example, eye-tracker based systems can provide interaction awareness, reveal information, and offer interaction methods depending on people's attention through eye contact. Likewise, a system using GPS based positioning and digital compass data could apply the pattern in a larger-scale outdoor deployment. Overall, the gradual engagement pattern has the potential of being applied to many other proxemic-aware systems with diverse tracking capabilities along this low-/high-fidelity spectrum.

REFERENCES

1. Addlesee, M., Curwen, R., Hodges, S., et al. Implementing a Sentient Computing System. *Computer 34*, 8 (2001), 50–56.
2. Ballendat, T., Marquardt, N., and Greenberg, S. Proxemic Interaction: Designing for a Proximity and Orientation-Aware Environment. *Proc. of ITS*, ACM (2010).
3. Baudisch, P., Cutrell, E., Robbins, D., et al. Drag-and-Pop and Drag-and-Pick: techniques for accessing remote screen content on touch- and pen-operated systems. *Proc. INTERACT*, IOS (2003).
4. Biehl, J.T. and Bailey, B.P. ARIS: an interface for application relocation in an interactive space. *Proc. of GI*, CHCCS (2004).
5. Borchers, J. *A Pattern Approach to Interaction Design*. Wiley, 2001.
6. Bragdon, A., DeLine, R., Hinckley, K., and Morris, M.R. Code space: touch + air gesture hybrid interactions for supporting developer meetings. *Proc. of ITS*, ACM (2011).
7. Chong, M.K. and Gellersen, H. How users associate wireless devices. *Proc. of CHI*, ACM (2011), 1909–1918.
8. Dachselt, R., Buchholz, R. Natural throw and tilt interaction between mobile phones and distant displays. *CHI EA*, ACM (2009).
9. Fishkin, K.P., Roy, S., and Jiang, B. Some Methods for Privacy in RFID Communication. *Proc. of SASN*, ACM (2005).
10. Gellersen, H., Fischer, C., Guinard, D., et al. Supporting device discovery and spontaneous interaction with spatial references. *PUC. 13*, 4 (2009).
11. Greenberg, S., Marquardt, N., Ballendat, T., Diaz-Marino, R., and Wang, M. Proxemic Interactions: The New Ubicomp? *ACM Interactions 18*, 1 (2011), 42–50.
12. Hall, E.T. *The Hidden Dimension*. Doubleday, 1966.
13. Hardy, R., Rukzio, E. Touch & interact: touch-based interaction of mobile phones with displays. *Proc. CHI*, ACM (2008).
14. Hassan, N., Rahman, M.M., Irani, P., and Graham, P. Chucking: A One-Handed Document Sharing Technique. *Proc. of INTERACT*, Springer (2009).
15. Hinckley, K., Ramos, G., Guimbretière, F., Baudisch, P., and Smith, M. Stitching: pen gestures that span multiple displays. *Proc. of AVI*, ACM (2004), 23–31.
16. Hinckley, K. Synchronous gestures for multiple persons and computers. *Proc. of UIST*, ACM (2003), 149–158.
17. Holmquist, L., et al. Smart-Its Friends: A Technique for Users to Easily Establish Connections between Smart Artefacts. *Proc. of Ubicomp*, Springer (2001), 116.
18. Ju, W., Lee, B.A., and Klemmer, S.R. Range: exploring implicit interaction through electronic whiteboard design. *Proc. CSCW*, ACM (2008).
19. Kendon, A. *Conducting Interaction: Patterns of Behavior in Focused Encounters*. Cambridge University Press, 1990.
20. Kraut, R., Egido, C., Galegher, J. Patterns of contact and communication in scientific research collaboration. *Proc. CSCW*, ACM (1988).
21. Kray, C., Rohs, M., Hook, J., and Kratz, S. Group Coordination and Negotiation through Spatial Proximity Regions around Mobile Devices on Augmented Tabletops. *Proc. Tabletop*, IEEE (2008).
22. Mankoff, J., Dey, A.K., Hsieh, G., Kientz, J., Lederer, S., and Ames, M. Heuristic evaluation of ambient displays. *Proc. of CHI*, ACM (2003), 169–176.
23. Marquardt, N., Diaz-Marino, R., Boring, S., and Greenberg, S. The Proximity Toolkit: Prototyping Proxemic Interactions in Ubiquitous Computing Ecologies. *Proc. UIST*, ACM (2011).
24. Marquardt, N. and Greenberg, S. Informing the Design of Proxemic Interactions. *In IEEE Pervasive Computing – Special Issue on Pervasive I/O.*, (2012), 14–23.
25. Marquardt, N., Hinckley, K., and Greenberg, S. Cross-Device Interaction via Micro-mobility and F-formations. *Proc. of UIST*, ACM (to appear, 2012).
26. Myers, B.A., et al. Interacting at a Distance Using Semantic Snarfing. *Proc. of Ubicomp*, Springer (2001), 305–314.
27. Nacenta, M.A., Aliakseyeu, D., Subramanian, S., and Gutwin, C. A comparison of techniques for multi-display reaching. *Proc. of CHI*, ACM (2005), 371–380.
28. Prante, T., Röcker, C., Streitz, N., et al. Hello. Wall–Beyond Ambient Displays. *Adjunct Proceedings of Ubicomp*, (2003).
29. Rekimoto, J., Ayatsuka, Y., Kohno, M., and Oba, H. Proximal Interactions: A Direct Manipulation Technique for Wireless Networking. *Proc. INTERACT*, (2003).
30. Rekimoto, J. Pick-and-drop: A Direct Manipulation Technique For Multiple Computer Environments. *Proc. UIST*, ACM (1997).
31. Schmidt, D., Chehimi, F., Rukzio, E., and Gellersen, H. PhoneTouch: a technique for direct phone interaction on surfaces. *Proc. of UIST*, ACM (2010), 13–16.
32. Swindells, C., Inkpen, K.M., Dill, J.C., and Tory, M. That one there! Pointing to establish device identity. *Proc. of UIST*, ACM (2002), 151–160.
33. Tidwell, J. Designing Interfaces: Patterns for Effective Interaction Design. O'Reilly Media, Inc., 2005.
34. Voelker, S., Weiss, M., Wacharamanotham, C., and Borchers, J. Dynamic portals: a lightweight metaphor for fast object transfer on interactive surfaces. *Proc. of ITS*, ACM (2011).
35. Vogel, D., Balakrishnan, R. Interactive public ambient displays: transitioning from implicit to explicit, public to personal, interaction with multiple users. *Proc. UIST*, ACM (2004).
36. Wang, M., Boring, S., and Greenberg, S. A Public Advertising Display that Captures and Preserves the Attention of a Passerby. *Proc. of Pervasive Displays*, ACM (2012).
37. Want, R., Fishkin, K.P., Gujar, A., and Harrison, B.L. Bridging Physical and Virtual Worlds with Electronic Tags. *Proc. of CHI*, ACM (1999), 370–377.

Eliciting Usable Gestures for Multi-Display Environments

Teddy Seyed, Chris Burns, Mario Costa Sousa, Frank Maurer, Anthony Tang
University of Calgary, Department of Computer Science
2500 University Drive NW, Calgary, Alberta, Canada, T2N 1N4
{teddy.seyed, chris.burns, smcosta, frank.maurer, tonyt}@ucalgary.ca

ABSTRACT
Multi-display environments (MDEs) have advanced rapidly in recent years, incorporating multi-touch tabletops, tablets, wall displays and even position tracking systems. Designers have proposed a variety of interesting gestures for use in an MDE, some of which involve a user moving their hands, arms, body or even a device itself. These gestures are often used as part of interactions to move data between the various components of an MDE, which is a longstanding research problem. But designers, not users, have created most of these gestures and concerns over implementation issues such as recognition may have influenced their design. We performed a user study to elicit these gestures directly from users, but found a low level of convergence among the gestures produced. This lack of agreement is important and we discuss its possible causes and the implication it has for designers. To assist designers, we present the most prevalent gestures and some of the underlying conceptual themes behind them. We also provide analysis of how certain factors such as distance and device type impact the choice of gestures and discuss how to apply them to real-world systems.

Author Keywords
Tabletop; gestures; multi-display environments; multi-surface environments; multi-display interaction; cross-device interaction; touch; mobile devices;

ACM Classification Keywords
H.5.2. Information interfaces and presentation: User Interfaces – Interaction styles, evaluation/methodology, user-centered design

General Terms
Design; Experimentation; Human Factors

INTRODUCTION
A multi-display environment (MDE) is a system where interaction is divided over several displays, such as digital tabletops, wall displays and personal devices like tablets or mobile phones. MDEs often include heterogeneous displays to take advantage of different capabilities such as their size, position, resolution or mobility to support the task at hand.

ITS'12, November 11–14, 2012, Cambridge, Massachusetts, USA.

Figure 1: A user performing a gesture to move an image from a tabletop to a tablet.

Yet, a number of socio-technical questions remain for designers of MDEs: what kinds of tasks are amenable to MDEs? How should tasks be distributed among and across displays? How do we enable effective collaborative work in MDEs?

A central MDE design problem is how to allow users to move applications and content across different displays. Addressing this problem allows users to distribute tasks across displays in an ad hoc fashion as their task needs change. Designers have proposed a wide range of solutions to this problem, including considering the space as continuous to allow dragging and flicking [19,21], "docking" and physical token approaches [5,14], menu-based approaches [25], world-in-miniature approaches [2], clip-board metaphors [22], approaches that involve "publishing" personal spaces to a shared space [17] as well as approaches that consider users as conduits for information [26]. These solutions arise from attempts to resolve users' conceptual model of MDEs with the technical constraints of such systems. A more recent approach has been to consider gestural interactions that leverage the spatial layout of displays in an MDE [1].

With the increasing popularity of gestures, several researchers have explored how these can be leveraged for cross-device communication. Some approaches involve on-device gestures such as pointing and flicking [4], while others involve flicking/moving the device itself [7,8]. This gestural approach shows promise, as it seems to provide a good mapping between users' spatial model of an MDE (i.e.

that there are multiple distinct displays) to a conceptual interaction model. While recent designs have often focused on moving content between specific devices (e.g. making a tossing gesture with a mobile device towards a large display [11]) it is often unclear how well they will generalize (e.g. how does one "toss" a tabletop display?). How do we design gestures for moving content that will be meaningful across various devices in an MDE that are discoverable, and map to users' conceptual model of the space?

To investigate these issues we conducted a user study to elicit gestures directly from potential users of MDEs. This follows previous work on tabletop gestures [9,10,27] and previous work regarding MDE gestures by [15,16]. We asked 17 participants to complete various commands or tasks in an MDE environment; they were also shown the outcome of the command across displays. We then asked them to create gestures they felt were appropriate to produce that outcome. These commands made use of three different displays (tablet, tabletop, wall display), and were illustrated using a Wizard of Oz approach. Participants were given a wide scope to create imaginative and creative gestures; in return, they generated 816 total gestures for the 16 commands. We then coded these gestures to identify common conceptual themes which underlie the gestures that users produced. We found that the gestures could be collected into four general themes: contact and closeness gestures, moving physical object gestures, identification gestures and borrowed metaphors gestures. These themes can be used by designers to derive new gestures or as a starting point for future research.

This paper makes several contributions. We confirm quantitatively that gestures elicited for MDEs show a low level of agreement. We consider the potential causes for this and the implications for applying gestures. The most prevalent gestures for each command and a convergence metric are presented. Second, we outline some conceptual themes behind the gestures and provide them as tools for designers to generate new gestures with. Third, we provide an analysis of how various factors such as the devices used and the distance involved in an interaction affected the gestures elicited from our participants. Finally, we provide a discussion of how a designer can use our findings in creating gestures for an MDE.

RELATED WORK

A main cocnern in MDEs is providing users with the ability to move content and applications across and between displays. Several researchers have proposed methods and system designs addressing this problem. An early approach was to consider all displays in an environment as being connected in a continuous space [14,19]. Other researchers considered a "bridging" interaction where a digital artifact would be bound to physical objects that could then be physically moved to other displays [23]. Other approaches took into account the ad hoc nature of the displays in the environment (in particular, mobile devices, such as tablets and PDAs). Rekimoto focused on extending the clipboard metaphor with a *pick-and-drop* interaction technique, whereby users could transfer digital items between displays by first picking it with a pen gesture, and then tapping on a target display to drop the content [22]. Hinckley explored a mechanism to recognize when multiple devices had been physically bumped together [13]. This bumping, combined with a simple gesture allowed devices to be temporarily linked for content transfer.

Proxemics for Cross-Device Information Transfer

Several recent approaches have considered how proxemics, or the spatial relationships between people and devices, can be leveraged for cross-device information transfer in MDEs. Generally, proxemics considers several factors such as position, orientation, movement and identity [13]. Voida et al., proposed a set of flicking, throwing and pointing gestures to move content between surfaces in an augmented MDE [24]. Wilson and Benko, explored how people could act as conduits for information: users could physically cup a digital photo and carry it with them to another display [26]. In another gestural interaction, users could touch an image displayed on the tabletop and create a 'bridge' between the two devices to transfer that content. In *Code Space,* a series of interactions are proposed for moving data to a wall display or other tablets, mainly through in-air pointing and on-device swiping gestures [4].

Some systems have also incorporated 'simulated proxemic' interactions, where the action a user performs in the system incorporates certain proxemic dimensions, even when the system itself is not able to track all these proxemic values. Several researchers have considered how rotating or moving the device itself can form a part of the gestural dialogue for transferring data [7,8,11]. For example, Dachselt et al. propose gestures for sending and retrieving content from a large display where users point their device towards it and mimic 'throwing' content towards the display [7].

Designing Gestures

Many of these interactions, particularly those that incorporate proxemics, are gestural. While these gestures may be effective and interesting, they were all developed by system designers, who may be unduly influenced by the underlying technical constraints of the system. At issue is that the conceptual models which designers form, may not match those of the users.

Nielsen et al. [20] propose a procedure for developing user defined gestures. Tasks for a system are first defined by the system designers. Gestures are elicited for these tasks from the users and are then extracted into a gesture vocabulary for the system. Benchmarking is then done to validate the gestures chosen for the system.

Wobbrock et al. employ the gesture elicitation procedure to construct a gesture set for general actions on interactive tabletops (e.g. move, copy, paste) [27]. Here, participants are exposed to the visual result of such an action, called a referent, and then asked to produce a gesture that would result in the outcome. A relatively high level of agreement was found among the gestures produced for a given task. This convergence allowed for a gesture set to be created. The gestures in this set were then evaluated in work by Morris et al. who showed that the elicited tabletop gestures were preferred by users, compared to those created by expert designers [18].

Frisch et al. [11] employ this gesture elicitation procedure to elicit a set of pen and touch gestures for diagram editing on tabletops. These gestures were then evaluated in a follow up work by Heydekorn et al [12], where the gestures were built into a real system and then evaluated with a usability study. It was found that implementing elicited gestures in a real world system requires careful consideration of how these gestures are applied.

Several researchers have applied a similar type of approach within the context of MDEs. For instance, Kray et al. explored how mobile phones could be used in a MDE environment comprised of a tabletop and a wall display, focusing on a wide range of tasks and content types (e.g. voting for content, synchronizing devices and rewinding interactions) [15]. In this work the elicited gestures were not categorized or labeled so no agreement statistics could be produced, however, the authors observed a wide variety of novel and diverse gestures.

Similarly, Kurdyukova et al. elicited a set of gestures from users specifically for transferring content between a tablet and fixed devices such as a wall display and tabletop [16]. The work presented here also focuses on the use of tablets rather than mobile devices, as these are likely to be used in a meeting/business scenario. The study found a number of interesting gestures and suggested that distance impacts the type of gestures, but this is presented as a qualitative observation and is not analyzed statistically.

Our approach extends this previous work by focusing on data transfer in an MDE, exploring how factors such as distance-to-target-display and impacts the nature of the gestures being performed. Finally, rather than producing a patchwork of unrelated gestures, we were interested in understanding the conceptual models that users were working with, thereby providing guidance to designers.

USER STUDY

Our primary interest in designing our user study was to understand users' conceptual model of interaction in an MDE. To what extent would this model be based on the spatial characteristics of the environment, or the characteristics/affordances of particular devices?

We focused primarily on tasks related to data transfer between the various components of an MDE. We based our tasks on those described in Voida et al., which all relate to moving content between components at varying distances [24]. We were interested in looking at gestures for transfer directions (sending and retrieving), different source and destination devices (tablet, tabletop and wall display) and at different distances (near and far). To ensure that the study could be completed in a reasonable amount of time, we selectively chose combinations that we thought would occur most commonly in a meeting/war-room scenario. Table 1 lists the final set of command combinations that we used in the study.

Apparatus

The study was conducted using an Apple iPad, Microsoft Surface 2, and a SMART Board Display. A specialized Node.js web application was written to visualize the outcomes of the commands. This application allowed us to simulate the transfer of images between devices. This was by showing the image disappearing from the originating device and, after a delay, appearing on the target device.

Video recording was used to capture each performed gesture along with notes taken by the authors. To consider distance consistently between studies, specific locations were marked on the floor and participants were asked to move to these locations for certain commands.

Participants

Seventeen paid volunteers participated in the study (10 male, 7 female). Participants were recruited using posters, email and word of mouth. The participants chosen had a variety of backgrounds, such as economics, education, business and engineering. However, participants were not excluded from the study based on experience with multi-touch systems, motion tracking systems or tabletops.

Procedure

At the beginning of the session, the participants were informed of the purpose of the study and given some background information on the type of gestures that were possible within an MDE. The participants were told they could produce gestures by rotating or manipulating their device, performing actions on the screen of the device or by performing gestures using their hands, arms or even their whole body.

At the start of each command, the intended outcome was displayed for each participant. Verbal instructions confirming the purpose of the task were also provided. Participants could also ask questions if they were unclear about what was required. They were then asked to create three distinct gestures for each command as a means of stimulating creativity. Participants were also encouraged to provide gestures they felt were appropriate without considering technological feasibility such as gesture recognition or positional tracking. This was done to ensure that users were not influenced into choosing gestures because they seemed easier to track or recognize. At this stage, participants were asked to explain their gestures while they were performing them and we also asked them to choose a preferred gesture.

Commands				
No	**Task**	**Source**	**Target**	**Distance**
Single Image Transfer				
1	Send	Tablet	Tablet	Near
2	Send	Tablet	Tablet	Far
3	Retrieve	Tablet	Tablet	Near
4	Retrieve	Tablet	Tablet	Far
5	Send	Tablet	Wall Display	Near
6	Send	Tablet	Wall Display	Far
7	Retrieve	Tablet	Wall Display	Near
8	Retrieve	Tablet	Wall Display	Far
9	Send	Tablet	Tabletop	Near
10	Send	Tablet	Tabletop	Far
11	Retrieve	Tablet	Tabletop	Near
12	Retrieve	Tablet	Tabletop	Far
13	Send	Tabletop	Wall Display	Fixed
14	Send	Wall Display	Tabletop	Fixed
Multiple Image Transfer				
15	Retrieve	Tablet	Wall Display	Near
16	Retrieve	Tablet	Wall Display	Far

Table 1: Commands for user study.

Classification of Gestures

The gestures collected were classified and guided by the *Descriptive Labeling* suggested by Nielsen [20]. In this sense, we described the gestures based on their motions and actions rather than their semantic meaning. Guided by work by Buxton [6] on chunking and phrasing, we looked for distinct phrases delineated by periods of tensions and relaxation. Such a phrase was considered an *atomic* gesture while several together were considered a *compound* gesture. Overall, this classification was motivated by the desire to find useful gestures for real world systems. This meant describing the gestures in a way that emphasized the physical action involved, thus allowing designers to build gestures easily recognizable by systems utilizing motion capture or vision sensing.

RESULTS

From our 17 participants, we collected a total of 816 gestures (17 participants' × 16 commands × 3 gestures). These were classified based on the previously described strategy.

What was striking about these gestures is that our participants, completely unprompted, frequently composed gestures that we considered to be *compound* gestures. That is, these gestures were clearly comprised of one or more *atomic* gestures performed sequentially. For example, in Figure 1 the participant is moving content from the table to his tablet. Here, he performed a *Position Down* gesture (moving the iPad close to the table) followed *by Swipe Away* gesture (swiping from the centre of the iPad to the edge, in a direction away from the iPad).

To address this complexity, we first consider the *atomic* gestures. We group these atomic gestures into a set of four conceptual themes that address users' mental models of the space. We then discuss how participants grouped these atomic gestures into *compound* gestures for the commands. Finally, we use participants' *preferred* gestures to explore the impact of distance and device type on the gesture set.

Agreement Scores and Prevalent Gestures

After classifying the gestures we determined the amount of convergence among different participants for each command. An elicited gesture set should have a large amount of agreement among the gestures as it shows that common gestures are independently created by different participants for the same command. We calculated agreement scores using the favorite gestures chosen by participants and applying the same metric used by Wobbrock et al. [27]. This equation is defined in Eq 1.

$$A = \frac{\sum_{c \in C} \sum_{Pi \subseteq Pr} \left(\frac{|P_i|}{|P_r|}\right)^2}{|R|} \quad (1)$$

The agreement scores calculated using our elicited gestures were substantially lower than those found by Wobbrock et al [27] in their study of gestures for tabletop computing. The overall agreement scores for the favorite gestures was calculated to be $A_{Favorite}$=0.16 compared to A_{1H}=0.32 and A_{2H}=0.28 for one-handed and two-handed gestures respectively. Our results demonstrate that participants showed very little convergence in the gestures they produced for the tasks. This

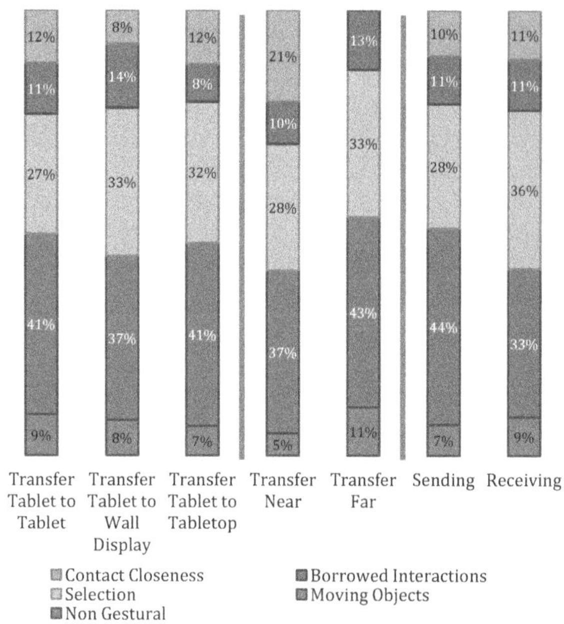

Figure 2: Percentage breakdown for metaphors for device conditions

result confirms qualitative suggestions made by earlier elicitation studies specifically for MDEs [16]. However, elicitation studies for tabletop gestures (e.g. [27]) saw a higher level of convergence and were able to build gesture sets based on that convergence.

While we do not have high enough convergence levels to propose a user-defined gesture set, we present the most prevalent gestures elicited for each command (see Figure 3). This set provides examples of gestures and the agreement scores calculated for each command gives a relative sense of the convergence for that command. To determine this set, we removed all gestures with n < 3 observations for each command. In some cases two gestures are presented for each command and we discuss the implications of gesture overloading and aliasing in the next section.

Conceptual Themes around Atomic Gestures

We first coded each atomic gesture for how the users positioned themselves relative to the devices, how devices were positioned/repositioned, the kinds of motions that were being made, how many fingers were used (if the device surface was contacted), etc. Through an iterative process of refinement, we arrived at four distinct conceptual themes that related the gestures with one another:

1. *Close contact:* Gestures based on close position or contact.
2. *Moving object*: Gestures based on the metaphor of moving of physical objects.
3. *Selection*: Gestures based on the act of uniquely identifying or selecting an object.
4. *Borrowed interactions*: Gestures based on existing interactions with other technologies.

These conceptual themes group the kinds of atomic gestures that we observed. Figure 2 illustrates how these different themes were used across commands. Table 2 describes the break down for the popular gestures by theme, and we illustrate some of these gestures in Figure 3.

Close Contact Theme

Users created many kinds of gestures that incorporated physical contact or physical closeness. Some users felt that positioning two devices close together or even touching together should cause data to be transferred. Atomic gestures specifically involving closeness had many variations. The *Position Above* gesture occurred when users placed one device directly over top of another device. A *Bump* gesture occurred whenever a user made temporary physical contact between two devices. These gestures were quite popular, being the underlying metaphor in 10% of users' preferred gestures. Because these gestures can only be performed when the user is physically close to their target device they are not generalizable across distance.

Moving Objects Theme

Data transfer lends itself naturally to the idea of moving object in physical space. People have a wide variety of experience with this because we live in a world filled with physical objects. Because there are many ways to move an object such as sliding, flicking or throwing, we saw considerable variety in this theme. These gestures were sometimes performed using hands, such as in the *Throw* gesture where a user would mimic the act of throwing an object. In other instances these gestures were performed using the device itself, such as in the *Chucking* gesture where the user would simulate the act of tossing the device.

Gestures in the *Moving Objects* theme has the largest number of variations with 24 distinct gestures, making up 40% of total gestures. While these gestures were popular, some users mentioned that repeatedly performing them would become fatiguing.

Borrowed Interactions Theme

Most of the previously described themes are based on activities and concepts from human interaction and everyday life. However, we also saw some gestures that were clearly borrowed from other experiences with existing technologies. In some cases, these interactions with technology can become a metaphor on which gestures are based. This was seen with two gestures, the *Camera* gesture and *Mirror* gesture.

In the *Camera* gesture, a user would hold their device up similar to using a camera. This gesture was overwhelmingly used for retrieving data (similar to [3]). Another gesture based on this idea was the *Mirror* gesture, where a user would reverse their tablet and expose the screen to their target device. Interestingly, this gesture was used for both sending and retrieving data.

Selection Theme

Gestures in this theme were often created by users for data transfer tasks. This was sometimes as simple as touching, either with a single finger or a whole hand. Another example of this identifying theme appeared in the *Point* gesture, which involved the user pointing with their finger or the *Devices Point* gesture, where users would use a device to point at a target. Often these interactions were used in conjunction with another gesture, an issue we discuss in the next section.

Compound Gestures

About 43% of the gestures we saw for commands were some kind of *compound* gesture. By this we mean that the gesture had several distinct phrases in the terminology of Buxton [6]. Each phrase can be considered as an *atomic* gesture, and taken all together as a *compound* gesture. In such a gesture the phrases are performed sequentially—one following another temporally. In some cases, users suggested that the command should be performed by two users, each performing a phrase simultaneously. We also considered these to be compound gestures and they clearly emphasize the social aspect of the task.

Gesture Name	Description	# times
Close Contact Theme		
Bump	Device is physically contacting another device for a brief period of time.	36
Position On	Device is placed down on top of a target.	26
Position Near	Device is placed very close to the target device, but not above or exactly beside or on top of.	12
Position Beside	Device is placed exactly beside target, such that the two devices line up.	11
Position Above	Device is placed over top or directly above its target.	10
Selection Theme		
Touch Five	Five fingers touch the device.	117
Point	User air-points with a single finger at target.	106
Single Tap	User taps device with one finger.	63
Point Device	Device is pointed toward target.	29
Touch Hand	Device is touched with a flat hand (palm or back of hand).	20
Double Tap	User taps device twice with a finger.	19
Borrowed Interactions Theme		
Camera	Device is held vertically, screen towards the user, mimicking the action of taking a picture with a camera.	52
Mirror	Device is held vertically, and inverted, exposing the screen to the target.	51
Lasso	The user traces and closes a distinct loop in the air with a finger.	11
Moving Objects Theme		
Throw	Performed in the air, a gesture mimicking the action of tossing or throwing an object.	99
Swipe Up	Performed on a device, with an arbitrary number of fingers, in the upwards direction.	96
Grab	Performed in the air, a gesture where the user mimics grabbing an object.	67
Swipe Down	Performed on a device, with an arbitrary number of fingers, in the downwards direction.	45
Shake Device	Performed with a device which is shaken in a rapid manner.	30
Swipe Device	Performed over two devices, a swipe which continues across a second device.	21
Rocking Device	Device is moved up and down in a rocking motion along its horizontal axis.	16
Chucking Device	User mimics a throwing action with the device.	12

For example a user might rotate their tablet and then use their tablet to point at a target device. We considered these as two individual atomic gestures (rotation, and the pointing). In one instance, a user suggested a *Touch Simultaneous* gesture, where two devices would be placed near one another, and then one (or two) users could tap the device screens simultaneously.

Pick & Drop Interaction Pattern

One particular pattern of compound gestures was very common, and following the pick-and-drop metaphor [21] very closely. These compound gestures involved two distinct atomic gestures, one for selecting content on the source device and the other for selecting the target device. This pattern was used for both the sending and retrieval of data, with users varying the individual gestures, depending on distance. For example, when a user was far away from the target they would perform *a Five Finger Touch* gesture to select an image on their tablet, followed by a *Throw* gesture in the direction of their target. But if the same user was close to a target device, they would again perform a *Five Finger Touch* gesture, but now would follow it with another *Five Finger Touch* gesture.

Two-Party Interactions

When a participant was asked to perform a gesture for tasks that involved another personal device (e.g. tablet to tablet), they would sometimes ask another user to perform a gesture on their device as well.

This was most prevalent in tasks where the user was asked to retrieve an image from the other user. Participants indicated that this was because actions that involved others' devices should be negotiated, rather than be unilateral actions.

Impact of Factors

In addition to the conceptual themes we wanted to investigate how the kinds of gestures users chose would change depending on certain factors. These factors were the device involved in the task, the distance at which the task was performed at and the action that the user was attempting to accomplish.

To focus our analysis, we considered only the gestures that participants identified as their favorite (recall that they

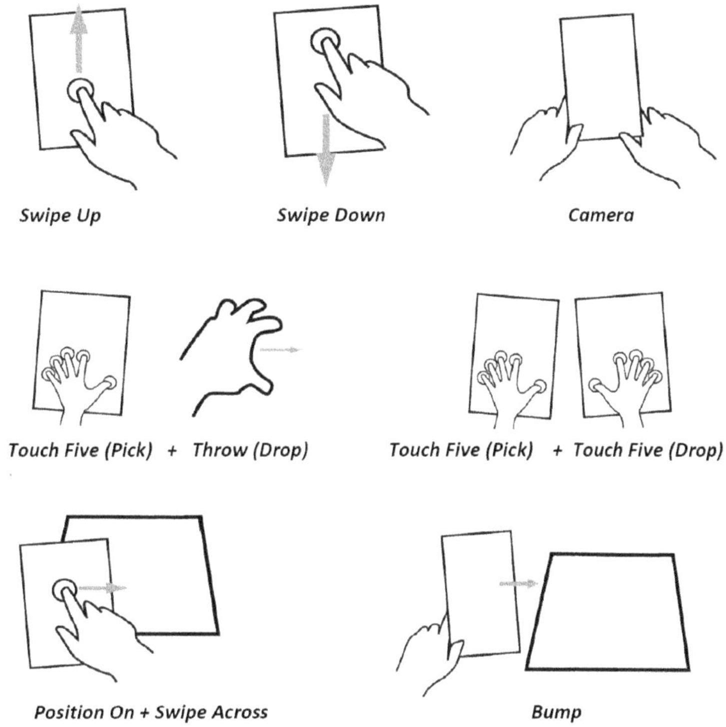

Task	Gesture 1	Gesture 2	Agreement Score
Send to Tablet (Near)	Swipe Up	-	0.26
Send to Tablet (Far)	Swipe Up	Touch Five (Pick) + Throw (Drop)	0.33
Retrieve from Tablet (Near)	-	-	0.11
Retrive from Tablet (Far)	Swipe Down	-	0.13
Send to Wall Display (Near)	Swipe Up	Bump	0.20
Send to Wall Display (Far)	Swipe Up		0.18
Retrive from Wall Display (Near)	-	-	0.07
Retrieve from Wall Display (Far)	Swipe Down	-	0.10
Send to Tabletop (Near)	Swipe Up	-	0.21
Send to Tabletop (Far)	Swipe Up	-	0.27
Retrieve from Tabletop (Near)	Position On + Swipe Across	-	0.09
Retrieve from Tabletop (Far)	Swipe Down	-	0.08
Send from Tabletop to Wall Display	Touch Five (Pick) + Touch Five (Drop)	-	0.08
Send from Wall Display to Tabletop	Camera	-	0.10
Retrieve from Wall Display with Multiple Images (Near)	Touch Five (Pick) + Throw (Drop)	-	0.10
Retrieve from Wall Display with Multiple Images (Far)	Touch Five (Pick) + Throw (Drop)	-	0.12

Figure 3: Prevalent gesture for each command. Generated by removing all gestures in a command with fewer than three observations.

performed three gestures for each command before selecting one as their favorite). Due to longitudinal nature of the study, we analyzed the data using the Generalized Estimating Equations (GEE) method using dummy variables for each of the categories in our proposed metaphor set. The data was aggregated and we used a Poisson distribution for the analysis.

Impact of Distance

A primary goal of our study was to investigate how the gestures users chose would change, depending on whether they were close to or far from a target device. This is important because an MDE can sometimes encompass an entire room and displays will not always be close to a user.

We found that far distances have a statistically significant impact on certain gesture types. Two gesture themes are significantly & positively predicted by far distances, *Borrowed Interactions* (B = .253, p = 0.045) and *Non-Gestural* (B = 0.799, p = 0.001). The *Close Contact* theme however was significantly & negatively predicted by far distances (B=-3.773, p<.001) as it was not possible to achieve contact at that distance. This suggests that using gestures which work on all displays might remove some gestures which users prefer.

Impact of Devices

Some of the gestures in our study were device specific and others could be used on any of the component devices. In addition to looking at how the preferred gestures were impacted by distance, we wanted to consider how they would be affected by the type of device.

Analyzing the data we found that only the *Close Contact* gesture theme was statistically significantly impacted by the overall device factor(χ^2(2)=15.144, p=0.001). Since there are three categories of the devices, therefore two dummy variables (i.e. one for the iPad & one for the wall display) are created & the tabletop is used as the reference category). This theme was negatively but not significantly predicted by the iPad condition (B=-3.26, p=0.117) and significantly & negatively predicted by the wall display condition (B=-0.622, p<0.001). This might suggests that contact gestures could be used for only the appropriate device types.

DISCUSSION

We designed our study around the procedure outlined in previous work [27,20] to develop a gesture set for moving content in multi-display environments. Our results show that unlike previous studies using this procedure, very little convergence was observed. This is an interesting result in itself and the implications of it are discussed in this section.

In spite of this lack of convergence our study produced several contributions which will be useful to system designers. The most prevalent favorite gestures were presented along with agreement scores to provide some concrete examples for designers. In addition the atomic gestures which participants created were classified into several thematic categories. These categories can serve as a basis for creating new gestures.

In this section, we discuss the direct implications of our results—that is, how designers can apply the thematic categories and example gestures to their systems. We then consider offering multiple gestures for each command or gesture aliasing. Finally we consider the notion of modifiers and feedback, issues that our participants brought up during the study.

Implications of Low Convergence

Wobbrock et al. present a metric of convergence called an agreement score which is a quantitative measure of the variability of gestures produced for a specific referent or command [27]. Low agreement scores imply a low level of convergence, which means that participants tended to produce different gestures for the same command. With sufficiently low agreement scores it is difficult to justify the creation of a definitive user-define gesture set for the commands being investigated.

Our results demonstrate that participants showed very little convergence in the gestures they produced for the tasks. This confirms some of the qualitative observations made by previous MDE gesture elicitation studies [15,16] but contradicts the results found in tabletop gesture elicitation studies [9,27]. While we cannot explain exactly why our participants' gestures did not converge, there are a number of possible explanations: the space of possibilities afforded by the MDE environment, the varying backgrounds of our participants, and possibly the lack of prior experience in an MDE space.

The previous elicitation studies for tabletop gestures have generally considered a single display surface - accordingly, most gestures occur on or near the display in a planar fashion. Our work explores a multi-display context meaning that the space of possibilities for gestures is much greater. Not only are some of the displays physically mobile, but there is also the space "between" displays that can be considered as part of the interaction space. That is, some of the implied "bounds" of what an appropriate gesture are taken away, freeing people to an even wider space of possible gestures.

Another explanation could be that participants, who did not have meaningful experiences with MDEs, accordingly did not have a strong and consistent mental model upon which to draw to create gestures. We strongly suspect that this is the case and our work in developing categories attempts to uncover the several different mental models which may be underlying the gestures. Rather than presenting a specific gesture set, we provide these categories. In so doing, we aim to give designers something to draw on to develop new gestures.

Applying the Gestures & Themes

Aliasing Gestures

Supporting multiple gestures for a specific command is one way of handling the divergence our study has found in the elicited gestures. Since we did not see any instances where gestures conflicted with one another in terms of their meaning, designers could provide aliases, where multiple gestures result in the same action. For instance, *Position {On, Near, Beside, Above}* were all expected to produce a similar result. Similarly several gestures, such as *Chucking*, *Swiping*, *Throwing*, etc. were expected to produce similar results, even though the specific nature of the gesture might be very different (with-device, on-device, in-the-air)—these can all be designed as aliases of one another.

Gestures and Themes

The themes that we identified for atomic gestures relate to the nature of these gestures. These themes can provide conceptual guidance for designers: gestures following these kinds of themes will likely be more easily discoverable as they map to users' conceptual model of how an MDE works. Of particular note, many of the conceptual models borrowed from an implicit understanding of the spatial relationships between devices in the room (i.e. proxemics [1] - that devices are considered as independent from one another, that they occupy certain parts of space, and so forth). One aspect that we did not consider deeply in this study was how these relationships might be changed if there are other people in such an environment. We saw indications that people would take social relationships into account (with the tablet-to-tablet transfers); however, this was not the central focus of our work.

Gestures for Distance & Device

Our analysis of the impact that the distance and device factors had on the type of gesture produced is useful when choosing gestures. Users often chose gestures of the *Borrow Interaction* type for far distances and a designer could pick a gesture such as *Camera* for those circumstances. Likewise *Close Contact* gestures were negatively associated (and not possible) with far distances and designers will need to provide an alternative for those situations. A gesture which can only work at a close distance such as *Bump* could be included along with a distance independent gesture such as *Swipe Up*. However *Close Contact* gestures are negatively predicted when a wall display is the target device, therefore designers might opt for different gestures if a wall display is a major component in their system.

Limitations and Future Work

While we encouraged participants to freely create gestures as they felt would be appropriate, it seems clear that their existing and current experiences with other technologies, limited (to some extent) the kinds of gestures that we saw. These experiences might include, but are not limited to, actual experiences with touch technologies, and also video games or movies. This may have resulted in a sub-optimal set of gestures; however, we are encouraged that the gestures they produced correspond to considerable prior work in this space, as well as to the spatial relationships between devices in the space. This suggests that proxemics may be a very fruitful way of thinking about MDEs.

In a future study, we would like to follow on work performed by Morris et al. by evaluating the metaphor set we have proposed in this paper [18]. This could be done by working with designers to create new gestures or by evaluating in a traditional way, a selection of the most common gestures found in our study. We also would like to work on evaluating complete MDE systems which can recognize and incorporate these kinds of gestures into their interactions.

CONCLUSION

In this paper, we designed a study to elicit gestures from potential users of MDEs. We looked specifically at gestures for data transfer tasks because of the importance of the problem in the MDE research space. We quantified the level of agreement between the gestures produced by participants for specific commands and found it to be low. We considered the potential causes for this low agreement and the implications for designers in creating systems. We classified the types of atomic gestures we saw into four conceptual themes that provide basis from which designers can design new gestures. Notably, these gestures often implicitly made use of the spatial relationships between devices in the environment. We also suggested that designers consider providing several different gestures for a single command (i.e. gesture aliasing). As multi-display environments become a reality, users will increasingly need to deal with the issue of moving content from one display to another. The results from this paper inform designers how to design gestural interactions that should be easily discoverable and usable by these users.

ACKNOWLEDGMENTS

We would like to thank our colleagues Abraam Mikhail, Daniel Sabourin, Abhishek Sharma, Rojin Vishkaie, Nadder Makhlouf, Patrick King and Nicole Sultanum for their useful discussions, edits and advice. We also thank the anonymous reviewers for their careful and valuable comments and suggestions. This research was partially funded by the NSERC/AITF/Foundation CMG Industrial Research Chair in Scalable Reservoir Visualization, and by the NSERC SurfNet Research Network.

We would also like to specially thank our colleague, Dr. Tak Fung, for his valuable help and steering us on the correct path with many discussions and support.

REFERENCES

1 Ballendat, T, Marquardt, N, and Greenberg, S. Proxemic interaction: designing for a proximity and orientation-aware environment. In Proc. of ITS '10,121-130.

2 Biehl, J T and Bailey, Brian P. ARIS: an interface for application relocation in an interactive space. In Proc. of GI '04, 107-116.

3 Boring, S., Baur, D., Butz, A., Gustafson, S., Baudisch, P.

Touch projector: mobile interaction through video. In Proc of CHI 2010,2287-2296.

4 Bragdon, A., DeLine, R., Hinckley, K., Morris, M. Code space: touch + air gesture hybrid interactions for supporting developer meetings. In Proc ITS 2011, 212-221.

5 Brignull, H, Izadi, S, Fitzpatrick, G, Rogers, Y, and Roddem, T. The introduction of a shared interactive surface into a communal space. In Proc. of CSCW 04, 49-58.

6 Buxton, W. Chunking and phrasing and the design of human-computer dialogues. In Human-computer interaction, Morgan Kaufmann Publishers In, pp. 494–499.

7 Dachselt, R., Bucholz, R. Natural throw and tilt interaction between mobile phones and distant displays. In Proc of CHI EA 2009, 3253-3258.

8 Döring, T, Shirazi, A, and Schmidt, A. Exploring gesture-based interaction techniques in multi-display environments with mobile phones and a multi-touch table. In Proc. of AVI '10, 419-419.

9 Epps, J.; Lichman, S. & Wu, M. A study of hand shape use in tabletop gesture interaction, Ext. Abstracts CHI 2006, 748-753.

10 Frisch, M., Heydekorn, J., Dachselt, R.: Investigating Multi-Touch and Pen Gestures for Diagram Editing on Interactive Surfaces. In Proc. of ITS 2009,149-156

11 Hassan, N., Rahman, M., Irani, P., Graham, P. Chucking: A One-Handed Document Sharing Technique. In Proc of Interact 2009, 264-278.

12 Heydekorn, J., Frisch, M., Dachselt, R.: Evaluating a User-Elicited Gesture Set for Interactive Displays, In Proc. of Mensch und Computer 2011, 191-200.

13 Hinckley, K. Synchronous gestures for multiple persons and computers. In Proc of UIST 2003 , 149-158.

14 Johanson, B, Fox, A, and Winograd, T. The Interactive Workspaces project: experiences with ubiquitous computing rooms. IEEE Pervasive Computing, 1, 2 (Apr-Jun 2002), 67-74.

15 Kray, C, Nesbitt, D, Dawson, J, and Rohs, M. User-defined gestures for connecting mobile phones, public displays, and tabletops. In Proc. of MobileHCI '10, 239-248.

16 Kurdyukova, E, Redlin, M, and André, E. Studying user-defined iPad gestures for interaction in multi-display environment. In Proc. of IUI '12, 93-96.

17 MacKenzie, R, Hawkey, K, Booth, K S, Zhangbo, L, Perswain, P, and Sukhveer, D S. LACOME: a multi-user collaboration system for shared large displays. In Proc. of CSCW '12 ,267-268.

18 Morris, M R, Wobbrock, J O, and Wilson, A D. Understanding users' preferences for surface gestures. In Proc. of GI '10, 261-268.

19 Nacenta, M A, Sakurai, S, Yamaguchi, T et al. E-conic: a perspective-aware interface for multi-display environments. In Proc. of UIST '07, 279-288.

20 Nielsen, M., Störring, M., Moeslund, T.B. and Granum, E. A procedure for developing intuitive and ergonomic gesture interfaces for HCI. In Proc. Int'l Gesture Workshop, 409-420.

21 Rekimoto, J., Saitoh, M. Augmented surfaces: a spatially continuous work space for hybrid computing environments. In Proc of CHI 1999 , 378-385.

22 Rekimoto, J. Pick-and-drop: a direct manipulation technique for multiple computer environments. In Proc. UIST'97, 31-49.

23 Streitz, N.A., Geibler, B. i-LAND: an interactive landscape for creativity and innovation. In Proc. CHI 2002, 120-127.

24 Voida, S, Podlaseck, M, Kjeldsen, R, and Pinhanez, C. A study on the manipulation of 2D objects in a projector/camera-based augmented reality environment. In Proc. of CHI '05, 611-620.

25 Wallace, J, Ha, V, Ziola, R, and Inkpen, K. Swordfish: user tailored workspaces in multi-display environments. In Proc. of CHI '06, 1487-1492.

26 Wilson, A D and Benko, H. Combining multiple depth cameras and projectors for interactions on, above and between surfaces. In Proc. of UIST '10, 273-282.

27 Wobbrock, J O, Morris, M R, and Wilson, A D. User-defined gestures for surface computing. In Proc. of CHI '10, 1083-1092.

MobiSurf: Improving Co-located Collaboration through Integrating Mobile Devices and Interactive Surfaces

Julian Seifert[1], Adalberto L. Simeone[2], Dominik Schmidt[3], Christian Reinartz[4], Paul Holleis[5], Matthias Wagner[5], Hans Gellersen[2], Enrico Rukzio[1,2]

[1]Ulm University, Ulm, Germany; [2]Lancaster University, Lancaster, UK; [3]Hasso-Plattner-Institut, Potsdam, Germany; [4]University of Duisburg-Essen, Germany; [5]DOCOMO Euro Labs, Munich, Germany

{julian.seifert, enrico.rukzio}@uni-ulm.de; a.simeone@lancaster.ac.uk; dominik.schmidt@hpi.uni-potsdam.de; christian.reinartz@uni-due.de; {holleis, wagner}@docomolab-euro.com; hwg@comp.lancs.ac.uk

Figure 1. MobiSurf supports co-located decision making through integrating personal devices and a shared surface. a) Users discuss their goals. b) They can decide to work on the surface or their personal device. c) Information can be shared easily for discussion on the surface.

ABSTRACT

One of the most popular scenarios for advertising interactive surfaces in the home is their support for solving co-located collaborative tasks. Examples include joint planning of events (e.g., holidays) or deciding on a shared purchase (e.g., a present for a common friend). However, this usually implies that all interactions with information happen on the common display. This is in contrast to the current practices to use personal devices and further, most people's behavior to constantly switch between individual and group phases because people have differing search strategies, preferences, etc. We therefore investigated how the combination of personal devices and a simple way of exchanging information between these devices and an interactive surface changes the way people solve collaborative tasks compared to an existing approach of using personal devices. Our study results clearly indicate that the combination of personal and a shared device allows users to fluently switch between individual and group work phases and users take advantage of both device classes.

Author Keywords

Interactive surfaces, co-located collaboration, smart phones.

ITS'12, November 11–14, 2012, Cambridge, Massachusetts, USA.

ACM Classification Keywords

H.5.m. Information Interfaces and Presentation (e.g. HCI).

General Terms

Experimentation, Human Factors.

INTRODUCTION

It is envisioned that the tables in our domestic environments will turn into interactive surfaces once the price per square meter is in the region of a few hundred Euro. One of the key reasons for buying and using them is the natural support for co-located collaboration, such as information visualization and retrieval or joint planning and decision making [2].

So far it has been widely assumed that users in such a setting will focus almost exclusively on the interaction with the interactive surface. However, this neglects the number of existing personal devices people currently have in use at home such as laptops, tablets, or smart phones and use them for co-located collaboration tasks. Our novel *MobiSurf* concept establishes a seamless integration of personal mobile devices and an additional shared interactive surfaces for co-located collaboration (Figure 1) extending existing interaction concepts and technologies.

The following scenario illustrates how MobiSurf supports collaboration: *Kim and John want to buy a new camera. After an initial discussion and joint web search on the interactive surface, they know what they want and what their needs are (Figure 1a). Then they start searching for offers individually using their personal devices (Figure 1b) as they would like to use different web sites, have differing ways of searching, want to check personal discounts, etc. As soon as they find interesting offers, they share them by dropping the web page on the common surface (Figure 1c). Now they can jointly view and discuss their options or go back to individual browsing.*

Using this approach, the mobile devices facilitate interaction in private while the interactive surface constitutes a shared space that is equally accessible to everyone (e.g., for placing information). This also turns mobile and personal devices at home into tools that support collaboration although they are primarily designed for a single user and usually relegate people nearby to mere observers.

The main contributions of the presented research are the results from a study which compared MobiSurf with the current practice of using laptops for co-located collaboration at home. When using MobiSurf, the participants interacted with the mobile devices twice as long as with the interactive surface itself. Furthermore, none of the groups in our study exclusively used the interactive surface or the mobile devices. This shows that the suggested combination of devices provides distinct advantages to the user which has not been exploited in existing systems. Furthermore, participants exchanged two to three times more web pages using MobiSurf than with the laptop-based approach further supporting the value of our approach.

RELATED WORK

MobiSurf mostly builds on work in co-located search in general as well as the combination of personal and shared displays and the way information is transferred between them.

Co-located Search

Collaboration in information seeking is very common. A recent web survey found that 97% of 204 respondents had already engaged in a collaborative web search activity [12]. Further, 88% of those who searched the web collaboratively reported doing so in a co-located setting. Similarly, in a diary study with 20 participants, Amershi and Morris observed 38 co-located collaborative web search sessions within one single week of which 45% occurred at home [2].

This motivates why there has been considerable research on supporting small-group co-located collaboration. Most of this has focused on the use of a single large interactive display. We basically follow this as it has been shown to support teamwork activities [25] and improve collaboration in general [3]. While Schneider et al. summarize advantages of using multi-touch tables for collaboration with respect to other systems [19], the successful integration of tabletop systems in the home has been frequently demonstrated (e.g., [24]).

Morris et al. have extensively studied tabletops for collaborative browsing and provide an overview of several projects using Microsoft Surface for collaborative search tasks, discussing the design space and challenges [13]. For instance, WeSearch has been designed for collaborative web search to leverage the benefits of tabletop displays for face-to-face collaboration [15]. A user study showed that tabletop displays facilitate collaborative web search. Furthermore, it revealed that they enhance the awareness of group members' actions and artifacts such as search criteria and allow fluent transitions between tightly- and loosely-coupled work styles.

A few studies have been conducted comparing collaboration when each user has a personal device to using a tabletop system only. Heilig et al. in [7], e.g., found that, with respect to a setting with synchronized laptops, their tabletop version fostered more simultaneous interactions, people were more likely to interrupt and engage in other users' actions, and they needed less short interruptions to notice and interpret "non-verbal expressions of the other group members". Yet, their study focused on a special tangible, physical token as an additional UI element on the tabletop and also did not incorporate cross-device sharing.

In the last years, some projects have begun to extend collaborative systems with several devices, especially multi display environments. These systems, however, usually involve high cost for acquisition, setup, and maintenance. They are thus mostly targeted at specific groups at a professional level and not suitable for home use (e.g., combining large vertical displays with a multi-touch tabletop to support scientific exploration of large data sets in teams [27]).

Personal and Shared Displays

A major theme in combining mobile and shared devices is that a personal screen can keep private documents or data such as passwords invisible and unreachable to other users. For example, Döring et al. used a tabletop as digital poker table while the cards of each users show up only "in their hands" on the mobile phone [5]. Other projects have shown additional promising uses of mobile displays in combination with large displays, e.g. the ability to present additional information [21, 27], enhance mobility of the overall system [9], improve control and security (e.g., for authentication [16]), leverage group discussions [22], and share information across different classes of displays [17].

Wallace et al. provide a comprehensive overview of projects that integrate heterogeneous devices [25]. Other research working with a combination of devices mostly focused on systems limited in some sense or concentrated on a specific issue. For example, the CoSearch system employs mobile devices mostly for cursor control and download of material [1]. Twidale also integrated phones into his system to upload images onto a shared display [24]. However, no further sharing or synchronization functionality has been envisioned.

Mobile Data Sharing Interaction

With respect to how data can be shared between a mobile device and an interactive surface, many approaches have been proposed: placing the phone on the table [28], using the phone's camera to detect its location with respect to a tabletop [4], or detecting dragging gestures across displays [8]. Also, gesture-based systems for moving data between screens have been implemented (e.g., [10]). In order to provide an easy to understand, quick interaction style for transferring data from a mobile device to the surface and back that requires little effort, we chose to employ *PhoneTouch* which is based on direct touch interaction between mobile and surface [18]. In order to transfer data using this technique, users simply touch the surface with their phone and selected data items are transferred and appear at the touch location on the surface. The technique allows users to transfer data from the surface to their phone (*picking them up*) through touching the corresponding item with their phone.

CONCEPT

The MobiSurf concept has been developed along the lines of various guidelines retrieved from related systems and projects: Amershi and Morris conducted a set of interviews leading to seven limitations of current co-located collaborative web search practices [1]; the last three (*Referential Difficulties*, *Single-Track Strategies*, and *Information Loss*) have also been stressed in the context of remote collaboration [14]. Besides these, Scott et al. identified three more guidelines for co-located collaborative tabletop systems [20] and Twidale et al. empirically derived guidelines for media surfaces in domestic environments [24]. Yuill and Rogers created a mechanism framework of factors for collaboration including *Awareness, Control,* and *Availability* [29]. Finally, studies with their WebSurface system lead Tuddenham et al. to a set of design goals for a tabletop-based co-located collaborative systems [23].

We summarized most of those issues and guidelines into five groups G1-G5. The following listing shows how the MobiSurf concept is built on top of them:

G1 The issues of *Difficulties Contributing* and *Pacing Problems* [1] as well as the feature *Independent Work* [23] are implemented by **giving each user a personal device**

G2 The issues of *Referential Difficulties* [1] and *Lack of Awareness* [1, 14, 23, 29] as well as features *Designing Activity Centers* and *Coordinate Displays* [24] are implemented by **using a shared device for all users**

G3 The issue of *Information Loss* [1, 14] is implemented by **using a tabletop as storage device for (intermediate) results**

G4 The features *Single-Track Strategies* [1, 14], *Flexible User Arrangements* [20], *Combining and Linking Heterogeneous Devices* [24], and *Transitions between Working Independently and Closely Together* [23] are implemented by allowing **easy switching between personal and shared device**

G5 The features *Natural Interpersonal Interaction* [20] and *Seamless Sharing of Results* [23] are implemented by an **easy to use cross device information sharing technique**

Thus, MobiSurf is based on the observation that collaborative searching and planning tasks often consist of individual and shared phases. People need to be able to follow their own strategies (**G1**) while at the same time be able to easily share their results with each other (**G2**). Accordingly, the concept includes one large, shared interactive surface (**G3**) and personal mobile devices for each user. For a seamless integration and supporting shifting between individual and joint work (**G4**), it is important, especially for ad-hoc meetings that often happen in the home, that information can be easily transferred from one device to another through a simple interaction technique (**G5**). This is provided by using a simple touch-based interface.

MobiSurf Application Design

From the user's perspective, the system consists of two main components: a web browser application running on the shared surface (Figure 2) and a web browser application running on the personal mobile device.

Figure 2. Two users jointly viewing and interacting with information on the shared surface.

The web browser application on the interactive surface allows users to open any number of browser windows on the surface which can be arranged freely using a corresponding handle at the top of the window (Figure 3). Browser windows support touch-based interaction with the web page content and controls (e.g., links, buttons, or scrolling) and a virtual keyboard is available for text input. Users can control the zoom level using corresponding buttons on the left of each browser window.

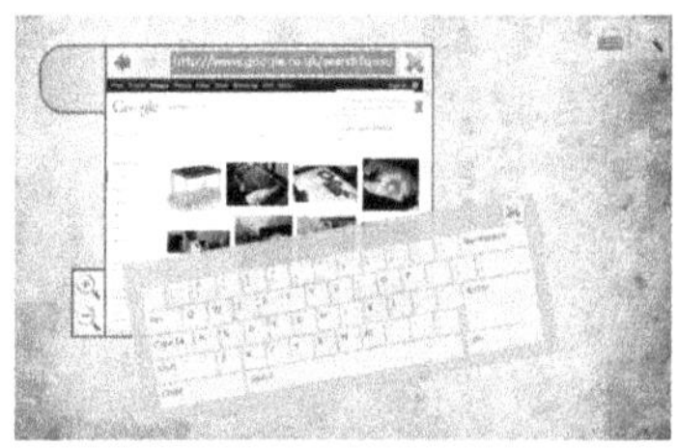

Figure 3. The shared browser application on the interactive surface.

The web browser application on the mobile devices (implemented for Android devices) allows the exchange of web pages with the interactive surface and other mobile devices through transferring URLs of the respective web pages (this implementation is limited to websites that encode session information in the URL). For instance, when a user wishes to transfer a web page from the mobile device browser (Figure 4) to the surface to share it with other users, the user simply touches the surface with the mobile device at the desired location (Figure 4(b)). The touch event gets detected, the URL of the page is transmitted in the background via WiFi, and the web page is loaded and displayed on the surface (Figure 4(c)). For picking up web pages from the surface in order to further review them on the personal device, the user just touches a displayed browser window on the surface with their phone.

After the touch event is detected, the page URL is transmitted, and the web page is loaded and displayed on the mobile device.

(a) (b) (c)

Figure 4. Transferring data from a mobile device to the surface. The web page shown in the mobile browser (a) is transferred to the surface using PhoneTouch [18], causing the system to create a new browser window (b). The received webpage is then immediately loaded (c).

In addition, users can exchange web pages directly between mobile devices. In order to do so, the *sending* device needs to display the web page which is to be shared (Figure 5(a)). The *receiving* device displays the home screen. As the users hold both device close to each other (Figure 5(b)), the web page is transferred and displayed on the receiving device (Figure 5(c)). For MobiSurf, we used Near Field Communication (NFC) to implement this functionality.

(a) (b) (c)

Figure 5. Transferring data between mobile devices. (a) The phone displays a web page (sender); the tablet shows the home screen (receiver). (b) Users hold their devices together for reading the NFC tag information. (c) The page is transferred from phone to tablet.

COMPARATIVE STUDY DESIGN

We designed and conducted a user study in order to gain in depth insights of how users interact with MobiSurf in comparison with current practice. The general aim of the study was to investigate to what extent MobiSurf facilitates collaboration. In doing so, we are particularly interested in its abilities to seamlessly integrate personal mobile devices and a shared large interactive surface to support varying collaboration styles. Also, how and to what extend are users taking advantage of different classes of devices offered simultaneously. We are further interested in how the provided shared space supports information sharing and discussion as basis for joint decision making

Current Practice

To guide the design of a the system which reflects current usage realistically we conducted a web-based survey about current practices and reasons for collaboration when performing planning or shopping tasks on the web. We advertised the questionnaire via a department email list (ca. 250 recipients) and posted it on a departmental discussion board. As incentive, participants could win one of five gift vouchers for 10 € each. In total, 54 persons (13 female), aged between 19 and 34 (M=24) completed the questionnaire. The majority of participants reported to *always* (18.5%) or *often* (40.7%) collaborate with others for online shopping. When planning holiday trips 35.2% reported to collaborate *always*, 24.1% *often*, and 31.5% *sometimes*. In general, 83.3% reported to be co-located with their collaborators. Laptop computers were most often used (90.7%) followed by desktop computers (57.4%), smart phones (46.3%), and tablet computers (11.1%). In response to the question whether they would share a single device with others during collaborative tasks, 13% stated *never*, 25.9% *rarely*, and the majority (42.6%) *sometimes*. Based on these results as well as on related settings reported in the literature (e.g., [1, 12]), we choose to compare MobiSurf with participants working side by side at a table using their individual laptop computers and allow for message exchange via instant messenger.

Practical Tasks

To familiarize participants with the systems, we arranged training tasks before working on the collaborative tasks. These tasks were system specific and covered all features that were available for performing the tasks. In case of MobiSurf, we asked participants to "Use the surface browser to look up your current location (use Google Maps)", "Use the mobile device and search your favorite movie DVD on Amazon. Then, share the results on the surface", and "Share a URL with the other participant using the 'beam' feature". Participants were told that they were allowed to move around the interactive surface. Further, the investigator pointed out that they were free to use the surface or the mobile devices. Participants were also told that they could switch their personal devices if they want to do so.

In case of the laptop-based approach, the training tasks included "Look up your favorite music album and share the link with the other participant by instant messaging". Participants were told that they are allowed to talk, to move and to share their laptop screens as they would like to do.

We designed two simple tasks, yet typical for domestic environments, that allow people to easily relate to in order to investigate co-located collaboration with both systems. Inspired by Morris who found travel planning and shopping to be the most common tasks for collaborative web browsing [12], we also chose these categories for our study.

The first task (T1) required participants to plan a weekend trip to London. Participants had to find options for flights, hotels, and museums they wanted to visit. In addition, participants were told that they had a budget of 700 €. The task was finished when they found a configuration they agreed on. The second task (T2) was to find a birthday present for a friend, which should cost not more than 40 €. Additional information about the friend was given (playing volleyball and badminton). In this task, participants were asked to make suggestions for presents, collect corresponding offers, and come to a final decision on how to spend the money.

In both cases, participants were free to decide by themselves when they were finished with the task. No goals were defined such as short completion time or money they spend. Accordingly, no quality criterion for the outcome of the group collaboration was defined.

Session Structure

We recruited eight pairs of volunteers (i.e. 16 participants in total; seven female) for our repeated measures design. Participants received 10 € as compensation for participation. In each study session two participants worked together. We omitted to include additional group sizes (e.g., triads or small groups) to avoid increasing the study complexity. The session was organized in three parts: 1) introduction, 2) tasks with the MobiSurf and laptop-based approach, and 3) post-hoc questionnaires.

Initially the participants were introduced to the study and gave their consent that recorded data may be analyzed and published. In the second phase, participants were asked to perform two tasks. One task using MobiSurf and another task using the laptop approach, preceded by training tasks with both systems. While working with the laptop approach, participants were sitting at a table and were free to change their position. During the MobiSurf condition, however, participants were standing at the interactive surface device as this makes it easier to reach for distance items on the surface. The order in which participants used the two systems was counterbalanced as well as the task assignment. All task instructions were read by the investigator. After giving the instructions, participants had the opportunity to clarify open questions with the investigator. Participants were allowed 10 min per task after which the investigator asked them to finish their discussion (which was not necessary in any case).

Apparatus

The hardware of the MobiSurf implementation consists of a custom-built interactive multi-touch surface able to support an arbitrary number of connected mobile devices. As mobile devices we used a Samsung Nexus S and a Motorola Xoom tablet. The former has a 4 inches screen with a resolution of 480×800 pixels. The latter has a 10.1 inches screen with a resolution of 1280×800 pixels. The interactive surface is based on frustrated total internal reflection (FTIR) technology using a rear-projected screen (1280×800 pixels on 65×105 cm). The whole system is controlled by a PC (Windows 7 (64), Xeon dual core 2.4 GHz, 4 GB RAM) that runs both the multitouch server and the browser application.

Communication between the interactive surface and the mobile devices was implemented based on the PhoneTouch technique [18]. Mobile devices and the interactive surface are connected via (wireless) network to a central server receiving events. Based on time correlation, the server matches accelerometer events from the mobile devices and corresponding visual events from the surface. Matching pairs of events are considered as *phone touch*. Depending on where the mobile device touches the surface a *picking up* (touch on open browser window on the surface) or *dropping* (touch free area on surface) action is performed. In this implementation of MobiSurf only URLs of webpages are transferred which are loaded on the receiving devices. Accordingly, only websites that encode session information in the URL are supported.

The touch-based transfer of web-pages between two mobile devices was implemented using NFC, whereas one device needs to be equipped with an NFC reader and the other device is equipped with an NFC tag on its back (see Figure 5(b)). For communication between the mobile devices the surface server is used to transfer webpage URLs.

The compared laptop-based approach consisted of two laptop computers (IBM ThinkPad, 15", 1400×1050 pixels) running Windows. As a web browser we installed Mozilla Firefox. To allow users to share information (e.g., a URL) not only verbally, Skype was installed and configured with a corresponding account to allow sharing via instant messaging.

Data Collection

We took notes during the study sessions and recorded videos for a post-hoc multi-pass analysis. We used *ChronoViz* for coding and annotation [26]. Repeated analysis passes allowed us to identify both high-level trends as well as subtleties of ongoing interactions between participants and with devices.

After performing the practical tasks with each system, participants answered questions concerning the systems' ability to support collaborative task performance and selected questions from the NASA TLX questionnaire [6]. As the last part of the user study, participants had to fill out a questionnaire about the two systems and their experiences with them. Participants were also asked to compare the two systems and to share any thoughts and observations they made.

STUDY RESULTS

The 16 participants were aged between 21 and 26 years (M=24). Three of the pairs were couples. Participants of two pairs were sharing an apartment while the remaining pairs were friends. Three were graduate students and the others were undergraduate students. The kind of relation between participants of each pair did not have any significant effects and no correlations to aspects such as verbal communication or sharing of information could be found.

All participants reported that they had prior experiences in collaborative tasks for which computers were used together with other users to achieve the common goals. Reasons for collaboration were ranging from gaming to working on course assignments together with other students. All participants had experiences with planning a trip or buying a product together with others. Each study session lasted for about one hour including the introduction, the tasks, and the completion of the questionnaires.

User Feedback

Initial Semi-Structured Interview

Concerning previously applied practices of the participants for collaborative shopping two themes were reoccurring: Eight participants reported that they used one personal computer together with others (sharing mouse, keyboard, and a single screen). Four participants pointed out that only one person is controlling the computer while the others are sitting nearby and participate in the discussion. In another approach that was described by six participants each user controls their individual device (e.g., the laptop) for searching offers online and discussing their search results with the others simultaneously.

One participant emphasized that using one computer that is shared with the others is quite comfortable because one can point at particular items in a web page. Another participant reported that he experienced the planning of a trip with friends where they set up a projector so that all could see comfortably the web browser while one person was controlling the computer.

Quantitative Feedback

After completing the two tasks with both systems, participants answered questions from a post-hoc questionnaire. The first part focused on aspects of collaboration support. Participants answered the questions on a five points Likert scale (1=very poor; 5= very good; Figure 6). Differences were tested for significance using the Wilcoxon signed ranked test.

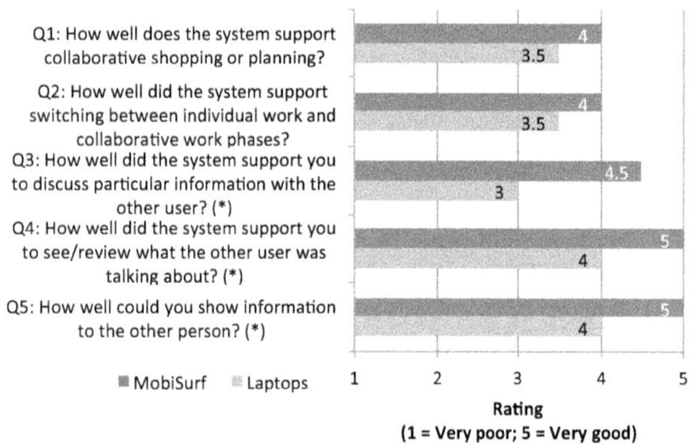

Figure 6. Results of the participants rating the tested systems regarding collaboration support ((*) indicate significant differences).

Answers to (Q1) "How well does the system support collaborative shopping or planning?" and Q2 "How well did the system support switching between individual and collaborative work phases?" indicate both a preference towards the MobiSurf (Mdn=4.0) over the laptop-based approach (Mdn=3.5). Yet, differences are not statistically significant. Question Q3 ("How well did the system support you to discuss particular information with the other user?") resulted in a significantly higher rating (z=-2.37; p=0.018; r=-0.53) in favor of MobiSurf (Mdn=4.5) compared to the laptop-based approach representing current practice (Mdn=3.0). Also Q4 ("How well did the system support you to see what the other user was talking about?") resulted in significant higher ratings for MobiSurf (Mdn_{MS}=5.0; Mdn_{Laptop}=4.0) (z=-2.83; p=0.005; r=-0.63). Accordingly, users rated MobiSurf significantly higher (Mdn_{MS}=5.0) in Q5 ("How well could you show information to the other person?") than the (Mdn_{Laptop}=4.0) (z=-2.7; p=0.007; r=-0.60). The large effect sizes (r) for Q3, Q4, and Q5 were expected considering that MobiSurf provides a shared display for shared reviewing of information.

Participants rated both systems using selected questions from the NASA task load index (TLX) questionnaire [6]. The results for one question show significant differences: ratings of "How physically demanding was the task using this system?" show that participants perceived MobiSurf as physically more demanding (Mdn=2.0) than the laptop-based approach (Mdn=1.0) (z=-2.109; p=0.035; r=-0.52). One probable reason for this different rating is while using MobiSurf, many participants held the mobile device in one hand and did the typing with other one. In particular, participants who used the tablet computer often placed their device on the rim of the surface partially due to the weight of the device. Also, direct touch interaction between mobile devices and interactive surface could be perceived as physically demanding as most users were very careful not to hit the surface too hard with the mobile device. Anther factor that influenced this rating is that users were standing while using MobiSurf and sitting during the laptop-based condition. However, we believe that this factor is rather small as none of the participants gave feedback indicating that standing while using MobiSurf was straining. In fact, standing while interacting with MobiSurf is of advantage as it is easier to reach for distant items on the surface.

Results of the remaining TLX questions do not show significant differences: on average the mental demand was rated to be equally moderate low (both systems with Mdn=2.0). Also the level of effort for accomplishing the level of performance was rated for both systems low (Mdn=2.0) and the success of accomplishing the tasks was rated equally for both systems (Mdn=4.0). The latter aspect indicates that MobiSurf allows participants to reach the collaboration task in to a satisfying level, event though participants were not familiar to use it,

Finally, we asked the participants to compare the two approaches they were using in the study with each other directly. 12 participants answered that in general they would prefer to use MobiSurf. 13 participants answered that MobiSurf allowed them to have a more active conversation and discussion with the other user. In addition, 15 decided that MobiSurf was more fun to use.

Qualitative feedback

To complement the quantitative data we collected qualitative feedback from the study participants, thereby drawing a more detailed picture of the user experience.

Seven participants emphasized that they liked the shared large display as one could show some information to the other user. For instance, P12 pointed out that "you could easily point at specific items on a website". Another aspect that was perceived as positive by three participants was how the system is supporting the discussion and conversation of the collaborators. For instance, P10 stated "the discussion is very direct", and "both had the same information available". Further, four participants identified as a positive aspect that users can start searching individually using the personal mobile device and collect valuable information on the shared screen. One participant highlighted that it was very easy to transfer information between different devices.

Concerning the laptop approach, seven participants indicated that they liked it because they were already familiar with it and have used it before. Four highlighted that exchanging links to webpages containing relevant information was something they liked. For instance, P1 emphasized that "one could share information by turning the screen towards the other person or simply send the link" via instant messaging. However, six participants expressed that the discussion support is not sufficient using individual laptops. For instance, P12 stated that "you cannot show what you are talking about, so one has to turn the screen and point to that piece of information". Also, three participants indicated that sharing of information using instant messaging did not suit their needs. For instance P9 expressed: "I did not know which link I should open and what the other one was talking about."

Video Analysis

Table 1 exhibits the results of our video analysis which are described in detail in the following.

Total duration	**MobiSurf**: 8:11		**Laptop Approach**: 8:49	
Conversation	27.6%	2:15 (1:26)	29.2%	2:34 (0:41)
Joint viewing	28.5%	2:20 (1:28)	5.45%	0:29 (0:30)
Mobile interaction	51.3%	4:12 (3:08)		
Surface interaction	26.1%	2:08 (0:41)		
Pointing		2.5 (2.0)		0.9 (1.4)
Dropping		5.4 (2.7)		
Picking up		0.8 (2.1)		
Instant messaging				1.0 (1.5)

Table 1. Video analysis results (times in minutes, SD in parenthesis): Device interaction, communication, and information exchange in both conditions.

Device Interaction

To complete the tasks, participants took on average 8:11 min with the MobiSurf, and 8:49 min with the system representing current practice. The number of average interaction phases we observed was similar with the mobile device (M=3.6 phases/session) and with the surface (M=3.7 phases/session). Interaction phases included all kinds of touch interactions (e.g., typing, scrolling) interrupted by reading information performed on one device. When a participant changed focus, the phase was considered to be ended. We observed, users interacted about twice as long with their mobile devices (4:12 min, or 51.3% of the average session length) compared to interactions with the surface (2:08 min, or 26.1%) in the MobiSurf condition. In the remaining time (1:51 min, or 22.6%) when participants did not actively interact with one of the two device classes, users mostly discussed with and observed the other participant's interaction. Moreover, participants frequently switched between mobile and surface interaction.

This difference in interaction time of the personal mobile and the shared device results from diverse reasons. First, in all study sessions, participants divided the task and decided to search for offers in parallel. Most participants started searching using the personal mobile device. Two participants decided right from the beginning to use the surface. The main reason appeared to be that the participants preferred to use the larger keyboard on the surface application. As they found satisfying offers they shared and collected them on the surface. When they had collected a set of selected web pages on the surface, the discussion about which option to chose was much shorter as all information were at hand and no time consuming typing was necessary. Second, during the discussion often only one participant interacted with the contents presented on the shared surface, while the other one followed the actions on the surface.

Figure 7. Using the mobile and surface system and using the laptop approach, users reviewed information together. (a) Participant actively sharing the laptop screen. (b) Participant leaning over to get a view on the screen of the other participant's laptop. (c) Participant looking at the screen of the mobile device used by the other participant. (d) Two participants reviewing a web page together on the surface.

Using MobiSurf, we observed that participants spent 2:20 min or 28.5% of a session to *jointly* view and interact with shared information on the surface. In contrast, joint information viewing accounted for 0:29 min or 5.45% in the laptop-based condition. This required either actively sharing the screen by turning the laptop towards the other participant (six instances, Figure 7(a)), or leaning over to get a view on the other screen (12 instances, Figure 7(b)).

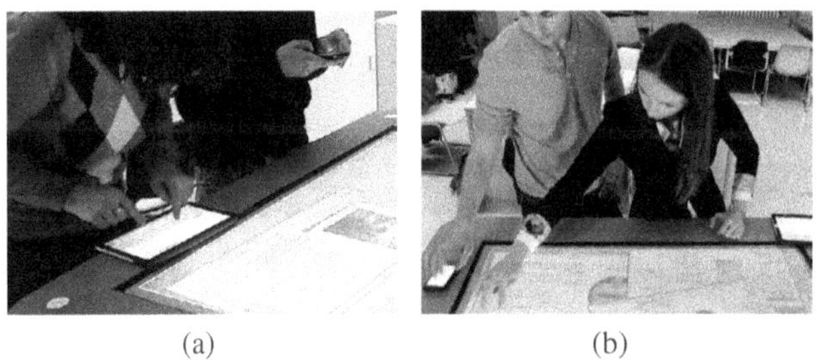

Figure 8. Users often put their mobile devices aside: (a) for typing with both hands and (b) for interacting with the surface.

Regarding mobile device usage, we observed in total 11 occurrences of participants depositing their devices on the surface rim (Figure 8) to free both hands for typing on the tablet

(Figure 8(a)) or interacting with the surface (Figure 8(b)), for example. Two times, both users deposited their mobile devices simultaneously while discussing their search results. In 9 cases, the time period of depositing the mobile device was less than a minute and succeeded by further interaction using the mobile device. In two cases, participants decided not to use the mobile device as they felt more comfortable using the surface application. Therefore, they placed their mobile devices on the surface rim after a short interaction period and continued to interact with the surface application.

Communication

Each participant spent on average 2:15 min for conversation using MobiSurf and 2:34 min in the laptop-based condition. This corresponds to roughly the same amount when compared to the mean session lengths, namely 27.6% (MobiSurf) and 29.2% (laptops). In both systems, the verbal communication was dominated by dialogs between users. Participants frequently articulated information they were looking at or commented on their current actions. For example, one participant stated "I found one [offer] for only 25.99" (MobiSurf). Another said "I just sent you a link", before actually doing so (laptop approach). We also observed an instance of reading out loud the entire text of an offer in the laptop-based condition for comparison with the other participant.

(a) (b)

Figure 9. For discussing information, users point to them on the surface (a), and while using laptop computers (b).

In addition, participants repeatedly used their hands to point out information in both conditions (Figure 9). This happened more frequently using MobiSurf than using the laptop computers, which required screen sharing or leaning over as discussed above.

Information Exchange

Both systems supported directly exchanging web links either by touching the surface with a mobile (MobiSurf) or by sending instant messages (laptop-based). In total, participants dropped 43 web pages (on average 2.7 per participant) but picked up only six with MobiSurf. Turning to the laptop-based approach, a total of 16 instant messages were exchanged (on average 1.0 per participant).

Analyzing the other participants' reaction to a drop interaction, we found that in 18 cases (41.9%) they were already focused on the surface. Another 10 drops (23.2%) interrupted the other participant's ongoing interaction with the mobile and drew their attention towards the surface. We could not observe any reaction for 14 cases (32.5%).

A percentage of 81.3% of sent instant messages resulted in immediately opening the included link on the other side. Two pairs of participants did not use instant messaging at all. Sharing links using instant messaging was accompanied by different actions. For instance, P6 sent a link to P7 to then lean over and discuss the content of the shared web page. In another case, sharing multiple links caused confusion since the receiver was uncertain as to what link the sender referred to in a subsequent conversation.

DISCUSSION

Our study results derived from user feedback and observations indicate that MobiSurf improves on a comparable laptop-based approach which represents current practice and which was identified in a preceding online survey.

MobiSurf successfully supported interleaving individual and group work as participants used both mobile devices (roughly 50% of the time) and interactive surface (roughly 25% of the time) to complete the tasks. Mobile devices were mainly used for individual searching while the surface was predominantly used for the shred discussion which was less time-consuming. They also made frequent use of the possibility to switch between those devices, strongly supporting our design decision **G5**. Especially notable here is that the usage of the mobile devices has been considerable thus confirming **G1** and marking the importance of the differences of MobiSurf to other systems. This is in line with the observation by Marshall et al. that collaborators often start with individual work phases and shift to shared work phases [11].

In particular, participants exchanged digital information more frequently in the MobiSurf condition (43 dropped and 6 picked up webpages) compared to using instant messages in the laptop-based approach (16 exchanged links) which confirms **G4**. Dropping information frequently caused the other participant to interrupt ongoing individual interaction on their mobile and switch the focus to the shared surface, leading to a better understanding of what the other user was engaged with. These findings suggest that users interacting with MobiSurf have a higher awareness of the current state of the workspace compared to the using individual laptops which is what **G2** asked for.

MobiSurf's interactive table proved indeed to be an effective area for shared storage and interaction (see **G3**). In particular, participants jointly looked at the surface for about one fourth of the overall task completion time. They were also substantially more likely to accompany their words with pointing gestures when using MobiSurf. Consequently, the *awareness* (c.f., [29]) of the other user's actions on the shared surface and presentation of information changes the quality of how users collaborate. Transitions between individual work phases and shared work phases are supported through the awareness of the shared surface as users can quickly decide whether they continue with their individual work or join the other user. While participants spent about the same time with verbal communication in both conditions, the majority felt that MobiSurf facilitated more active conversations and provided better support for discussions. This may be attributed to the availability of a common basis for discussion, as provided by the content shown on the shared surface. Further, the shared device creates a higher degree of *control* (c.f., [29]) compared to using individual laptops. As both users have access to displayed information and optionally picking them up with their mobile device allows them to interact with the corresponding web pages individually.

Participants rated MobiSurf to be more physically demanding compared to the laptop condition. The main factor appears to be holding the mobile device with one hand while typing with the other one. Also the direct touch interaction of dropping or picking up information from the surface seemed to be physically straining. Further, participants were standing while using the MobiSurf system as this allowed reaching for distant items more easily. We did not get feedback that indicated that users perceived the standing as unpleasant or tiring, yet, we cannot fully rule out that this as a factor, which we assume to be rather small.

Another interesting finding is that none of the participants used the device-to-device information sharing feature even though all participants were introduced to it during the training phase. It seems that the shared surface already provided an adequate place for sharing information without the direct and quite intrusive and especially interruptive means of pushing content to the other person's mobile device.

Although MobiSurf and particularly its integration of mobile devices with an interactive surface is novel and thus unfamiliar, participants were able to effectively use its features after a brief introduction. A few participants highlighted that they liked the laptop-based approach due to its familiarity, but MobiSurf was still rated as easy to learn and use with low mental demand required. This is also reflected in the similar average completion times and the throughout effortless interaction that we observed. As we allowed users to freely decide when they were finished with a task, we could not apply objective measures for the collaboration outcome. However, participants rated their successes of accomplishing their task when using MobiSurf equally high as in the laptop condition. When asked to state a preference, most participants favored MobiSurf and consistently rated it superior to the laptop-based approach with respect to information exchange and shared viewing.

CONCLUSION AND FUTURE WORK

As technology matures and prices fall, interactive surfaces are expected to become more pervasive in people's homes. In this paper we introduced MobiSurf which integrates an interactive surface into the interaction with people's own personal and mobile devices using existing interaction technologies and techniques.

In our study, we observed that even though participants used the mobile devices twice as long as the shared surface (e.g. for searching), the shared surface proved to be an integral part of the overall interaction. Using MobiSurf, participants shared more links and spend more time jointly viewing web pages compared to the laptop-based alternative. This shows that the mobile devices become central interaction devices and that the interactive surface is primarily used to share information for common discussions or later use.

This observation is very much in line with current situations at home when people discuss based on paper (e.g. holiday planning using various holiday catalogs or brochures) at a table in the kitchen or living room. People are used to take the material in their own hands to read it, show it to others by turning it towards them, place it on the table for discussion, and arrange it on the table to organize previously discussed aspects. People have different strategies and preferences when working in such a way. Some, for example, may prefer to read while holding a paper in their hands while others might prefer placing it on the table to read it. These types of familiar behavior have been taken into account during the design of MobiSurf and the results of our study confirm the need for adding and integrating shared interactive surfaces into interaction with personal mobile devices. Hence MobiSurf provides an environment allowing a user to seamlessly switch between individual and group work and easily share information between devices. As we have shown, these features made users more engaged in the task and helped them to have a better understanding of the current situation.

Our study design featured two specific tasks in a scenario of domestic environments. Although not investigated as yet, we envision MobiSurf to also facilitate co-located collaboration in office or educational situations (e.g., to support collaborative problem solving tasks in schools or planning meetings at work). In addition, surfaces in semi-public settings can serve as walk-up platforms for ad-hoc collaboration. For example, to schedule a meeting, the mobile devices can contribute personal appointments while the surface displays a joint calendar, hence facilitating finding a joint time slot. Besides using mobile devices for separate and private input, they also serve as source for personal data (e.g., documents or photos) that can readily be brought into the shared space.

In future work we will explore how to respond to some of the limitations that emerged during the post-hoc questionnaire in which users expressed the desire of having more discussion support at the feature-level of the system (e.g., organizing information or adding support for more than two concurrent users). Further, we are planning to investigate how MobiSurf can be used by triads and small groups for co-located collaboration.

ACKNOLEGEMEMNTS

This work was conducted within the MULTITAG project funded by DOCOMO Euro-Labs and the Emmy Noether research group Mobile Interaction with Pervasive User Interfaces funded by the German Research Foundation (DFG).

REFERENCES

1. Amershi, S., and Morris, M. R. CoSearch: a system for co-located collaborative web search. In *CHI '08*, ACM (New York, NY, USA, 2008), 1647–1656.

2. Amershi, S., and Morris, M. R. Co-located collaborative web search: understanding status quo practices. In *CHI EA '09*, ACM (New York, NY, USA, 2009), 3637–3642.

3. Buisine, S., Besacier, G., Aoussat, A., and Vernier, F. How do interactive tabletop systems influence collaboration? *Com. Hum. Behav. 28* (Jan. 2012), 49–59.
4. Cuypers, T., Francken, Y., Vanaken, C., Van Reeth, F., and Bekaert, P. *Smartphone localization on interactive surfaces using the built-in camera*, vol. 2. ACM, 2009, 3–4.
5. Döring, T., Shirazi, A. S., and Schmidt, A. Exploring gesture-based interaction techniques in multi-display environments with mobile phones and a multi-touch table. In *AVI '10*, ACM (New York, NY, USA, 2010), 419–419.
6. Hart, S. G., and Stavenland, L. E. Development of NASA-TLX (Task Load Index): Results of empirical and theoretical research. In *Human Mental Workload*, P. A. Hancock and N. Meshkati, Eds. Elsevier, 1988, ch. 7, 139–183.
7. Heilig, M., Huber, S., Gerken, J., Demarmels, M., Allmendinger, K., and Reiterer, H. Hidden details of negotiation: the mechanics of reality-based collaboration in information seeking. In *INTERACT'11*, Springer-Verlag (Berlin, Heidelberg, 2011), 622–639.
8. Hinckley, K., Ramos, G., Guimbretiere, F., Baudisch, P., and Smith, M. Stitching: pen gestures that span multiple displays. In *AVI '04*, ACM (New York, NY, USA, 2004), 23–31.
9. Kane, S. K., Avrahami, D., Wobbrock, J. O., Harrison, B., Rea, A. D., Philipose, M., and LaMarca, A. Bonfire: a nomadic system for hybrid laptop-tabletop interaction. In *UIST '09*, ACM (New York, NY, USA, 2009), 129–138.
10. Luyten, K., Verpoorten, K., and Coninx, K. Ad-hoc co-located collaborative work with mobile devices. In *MobileHCI '07*, ACM (New York, NY, USA, 2007), 507–514.
11. Marshall, P., Morris, R., Rogers, Y., Kreitmayer, S., and Davies, M. Rethinking 'multi-user': an in-the-wild study of how groups approach a walk-up-and-use tabletop interface. In *CHI '11*, ACM (New York, NY, USA, 2011), 3033–3042.
12. Morris, M. R. A survey of collaborative web search practices. In *CHI '08*, ACM (New York, NY, USA, 2008), 1657–1660.
13. Morris, M. R., Fisher, D., and Wigdor, D. Search on surfaces: Exploring the potential of interactive tabletops for collaborative search tasks. *Inf. Process. Manage. 46* (Nov. 2010), 703–717.
14. Morris, M. R., and Horvitz, E. SearchTogether: an interface for collaborative web search. In *UIST '07*, ACM (New York, NY, USA, 2007), 3–12.
15. Morris, M. R., Lombardo, J., and Wigdor, D. WeSearch: supporting collaborative search and sensemaking on a tabletop display. In *CSCW '10*, ACM (New York, NY, USA, 2010), 401–410.
16. Ratib, O., McCoy, J. M., McGill, D. R., Li, M., and Brown, A. Use of personal digital assistants for retrieval of medical images and data on high-resolution flat panel displays. *Radiographics 23*, 1 (2003), 267–272.
17. Rekimoto, J., and Saitoh, M. Augmented surfaces: a spatially continuous work space for hybrid computing environments. In *CHI '99*, ACM (New York, NY, USA, 1999), 378–385.
18. Schmidt, D., Chehimi, F., Rukzio, E., and Gellersen, H. PhoneTouch: a technique for direct phone interaction on surfaces. In *UIST '10*, ACM (New York, NY, USA, 2010), 13–16.
19. Schneider, B., and Shen, C. Enhancing tabletops: Multi-surface environments for collaborative learning. In *Proc. of ICLS Workshop* (2010).
20. Scott, S. D., Grant, K. D., and Mandryk, R. L. System guidelines for co-located, collaborative work on a tabletop display. In *ECSCW '03*, Kluwer Academic Publishers (Norwell, MA, USA, 2003), 159–178.
21. Shen, C., Everitt, K., Ryall, K., Dey, A., Schmidt, A., and McCarthy, J. UbiTable: impromptu face-to-face collaboration on horizontal interactive surfaces. In *UbiComp 2003: Ubiquitous Computing*, vol. 2864. Springer Berlin / Heidelberg, 2003, 281–288.
22. Sugimoto, M., Hosoi, K., and Hashizume, H. Caretta: a system for supporting face-to-face collaboration by integrating personal and shared spaces. In *CHI '04*, ACM (New York, NY, USA, 2004), 41–48.
23. Tuddenham, P., Davies, I., and Robinson, P. Websurface: an interface for co-located collaborative information gathering. In *ITS '09*, ACM (New York, NY, USA, 2009), 181–188.
24. Twidale, M. Over the shoulder learning: Supporting brief informal learning. *CSCW 14* (2005), 505–547.
25. Wallace, J. R., Scott, S. D., Stutz, T., Enns, T., and Inkpen, K. Investigating teamwork and taskwork in single- and multi-display groupware systems. *PUC 13* (Nov. 2009), 569–581.
26. Weibel, N., Fouse, A., Hutchins, E., and Hollan, J. D. Supporting an integrated paper-digital workflow for observational research. In *IUI '11*, ACM (New York, NY, USA, 2011), 257–266.
27. Wigdor, D., Jiang, H., Forlines, C., Borkin, M., and Shen, C. WeSpace: the design development and deployment of a walk-up and share multi-surface visual collaboration system. In *CHI '09*, ACM (New York, NY, USA, 2009), 1237–1246.
28. Wilson, A. D., and Sarin, R. BlueTable: connecting wireless mobile devices on interactive surfaces using vision-based handshaking. In *GI '07*, ACM (New York, NY, USA, 2007), 119–125.
29. Yuill, N., and Rogers, Y. Mechanisms for collaboration: A design and evaluation framework for multi-user interfaces. *ACM Trans. Comput.-Hum. Interact. 19*, 1 (May 2012), 1–25.

Tabletop Games for Photo Consumption at Theme Parks

Edward Anstead[1], Abigail Durrant[2], Steve Benford[1], David Kirk[2]

Mixed Reality Laboratory[1]
University of Nottingham, Nottingham, UK
{psxeja, pszsdb} @nottingham.ac.uk

Culture Lab[2]
University of Newcastle, Newcastle, UK
{abigail.durrant, david.kirk} @newcastle.ac.uk

ABSTRACT

This paper broadly explores novel tabletop interaction design opportunities for photo-souvenir consumption in a theme park context. We present the design and user evaluation of two tabletop applications for the playful triaging of photo collections within groups from a day trip to a UK theme park. Combining triaging with gameplay, the designs explore two distinct styles of user interaction, requiring either speed and dexterity or thoughtful strategy. Herein we discuss the rationale for the design process and the findings generated from our evaluation. Our study reveals the social impact of gameplay on user engagement with triaging tasks and implications for the deployment of interactive tabletop interfaces within theme parks to support photo consumption as part of the park experience.

Author Keywords

Theme parks; photography; tabletop; ludic interaction.

ACM Classification Keywords

H5.m. Information interfaces and presentation (e.g., HCI): Miscellaneous.

INTRODUCTION

The theme park is a site of increasing interest for the HCI community [17, 19, 20, 29]. These studies have looked at the analysis and manipulation of thrill and the use of theme park rides in the creation of story narratives, representing an interesting context for Human Computer Interaction (HCI) researchers to study ludic, social interaction. Attracting diverse populations and multiple generations of visitors, the theme park is a test-bed for state-of-the-art technologies, often manifest in roller coaster designs, and a commercial enterprise keen to deliver 'added value' services to visitors [13]. Our research presented herein explores the theme park as a relevant site for the deployment of tabletop interfaces.

Recent HCI studies have highlighted the significance of *photography* in the consumption of leisure experiences [25, 13, 24]. Therein, both the production and sharing of images was found to be very much part of the experience, of 'being at leisure' and of 'being social'. Theme parks already recognise the design opportunities around in-park photo-capture, with most providing their own on-ride photography systems and services to deliver personalised photo-souvenirs. Visitors to these attractions are starting to collaboratively use these in conjunction with their own personal mobile devices creating a rich 'photo ecology' [7] for the *real-time* consumption of photos that are both park and visitor created. Such ecologies are impacted by the forms of sociality engaged in by differing visiting groups.

ITS'12, November 11–14, 2012, Cambridge, Massachusetts, USA.

However, one issue that such prior work [ibid] has raised is that theme park visitors are only afforded limited 'windows of opportunity' to review and purchase photo souvenirs from the on-ride photo services. These photos are presented to visitors on a video display as they exit the ride, allowing them only a few seconds to make a buying decision. This process contrasts with visitors' real-time consumption of photos on personal devices. This leads to a clear design challenge: to consider new ways for visitors to review, display and consume photos taken of them or by them in theme parks, ways that leverage digital ubiquitous technologies to *widen* the windows of opportunity and enhance the provision of added value services; and supporting the sociality of the visitors through the process.

In this paper, we report on a prototype and evaluation exercise exploring the collective consumption of photo-souvenirs in the theme park. Building upon recent findings from field observations in this setting [6,7], we conducted a user evaluation of a tabletop photo browser that was envisaged as a 'sideshow game' attraction at the park. This attraction facilitated the collective reviewing and triaging of photos in the course of visiting, resulting in the production of a unique photo souvenir. This exercise was motivated by our overall aim to explore new approaches to supporting groups in selecting souvenir photos during theme park visits, responding to the previously identified design challenge. We explored this challenge by examining tabletop photo-triaging tasks for affording meaningful social interactions with photos in addition to the photos' consumption as part of a theme park visiting experience.

RELATED WORK: TABLETOP INTERFACES AND PHOTO SHARING

There have been a variety of tabletop studies that have focused on designing applications for photo triaging and sharing tasks. This work has covered a variety of topics from the role of tangible elements in triaging [31], new interaction metaphors for browsing [11], to considerations of collaborating around shared photo representations [9].

Work in this space has sought to consider how tabletop interfaces might support naturalistic interactions around photo sharing activities, considering both the sharing of photos and the sharing of narrative to accompany them [28]. In particular, such work has considered the means by which natural talk around photos can be supported [10] and the ways in which audio-narratives can be appended to digital photo files for around table reflection and story sharing [3]. Cao, et al. have extended notions of tabletop photo sharing in interfaces to support the collaborative development of photo-based multimedia animations [5].

Much of this work has broadly investigated the home setting. The family archive project [14,15] at MSR Cambridge is an example of research conducted in the home setting. A tabletop-based photo archiving and sharing application was developed and deployed in family homes for extended periods of time, demonstrating how a probe-like tabletop technology could be used in research. Results from its deployment showed how a tabletop photo-sharing interface was both disruptive, and revealing of, the social dynamics of domestic groups using the device. This work critically examined how technology should be shaped by the sociality of collaborative use, echoing work in other domains such as education [8,18] (that did not focus on photo sharing). Studies of gaming using tabletops have also considered collaboration at the interface, but they have tended to concern the simple mechanics of supporting collaboration and fostering engagement [30]. Such studies have begun to consider public tabletop gaming [2, 25, 32], which would be of relevance to theme park use. These studies have also started to address specific user groups such as the elderly [1], but this work lacks a focus on intergenerational collaboration, which would likely be of relevance to the diverse populations encountered in theme parks. Studies of tabletop gaming however rarely consider how aspects of gameplay and playfulness may fruitfully be used as interaction mechanisms within other tasks such as photo sorting and triage. In addition there has been extensive work that considers basic UI mechanisms for collaborative groupware on tabletops [22]. This has included issues as orientation of widgets [16], apportioning of surfaces to support territoriality [26], and the construction of mutli-user interaction gestures [21]. We have therefore considered such issues in our designs, but focus our reporting herein on higher-level issues.

Accordingly, there is more that needs to be understood about the specific sociality of photo-sharing activities in theme park contexts before designs in this space can be grounded. We investigate this through the paradigm of tabletop gaming, using playful interactions to support the diverse groups of theme park visitors.

APPROACH AND DESIGN RATIONALE

We sought to address the constraints of sorting and selecting photo media on mobile interfaces in the theme park context highlighted by Durrant, et al.'s field observations [7], incorporating a prototyping exercise and a lab based evaluation. Adopting a case study approach, our intention was to investigate divergent methods of tabletop interaction, to prompt critical user reflection on the prototypes core functionality, and to highlight areas for future interaction design research in the theme park domain and the leisure domain more broadly.

We iteratively developed a tabletop photo browser that allowed for the selection of individual photos to be included in a unique souvenir as a memento of a theme park visit. We fabricated an interactive tabletop device providing a 'walk-up' interface for groups of visitors to collectively triage their photos and select a representative photo-souvenir. The interface intended to facilitate ad-hoc review and consumption during 'a day in the park', akin to a 'sideshow' attraction. Prototype development focused on single elements of the interaction at a time to take place in the wider theme park photo ecology. Methodologically, our prototype was positioned as a probe for inviting users' critical reflections on their experiences of use [27].

Design Requirements

We elicited three key requirements from previous HCI studies in theme parks and related literature, which informed the design of the selection interface.

Playfulness and Fantastical Escapism Theme park experiences are playful and Machiavellian. These qualities are reflected through photos visitors take and are reminiscent of 'Candid Camera' photography, showing subjects scared or excited, inviting others to tease. This idea influences the next requirement. The term 'Fantastical Escapism' reflects the theme park's branding of attractions [6] and the sense of being in an 'extraordinary' place for 'escaping' from the mundane concerns of everyday life.

Group Collaboration and Negotiation– Given the playful, social nature of the theme park environs, we intended for each member of a visiting group to have equity in participation at the tabletop. We identify a process of group negotiation allowing for individuals to debate and enforce their preferences as the group moves towards making collaborative decisions on souvenirs.

Walk-up interaction: The selection process is spontaneous and lightweight enough to be distributed through the park infrastructure, allowing for *ad-hoc* visitor engagement with photo media and real-time souvenir consumption.

PROTOTYPE DEVELOPMENT

In supporting the design requirements above we developed a design metaphor that evoked the 'sideshow games' at theme parks and travelling fairs. We were inspired by how games such as 'Hook a duck' or 'Test your strength' offer playful experiences in keeping with notions of Fantastical Escapism. Visitors experience these sideshows as they walk around the theme park in between rides; the sideshows offer visitors the opportunity to 'try their luck' and 'test their skill'.

Design inspiration

We developed two interactive game designs evolved from traditional sideshow games found at many theme parks. In the traditional fairground game of *Arabian Derby*, a group of around 10 players compete against each other in a camel race. Players roll small balls toward a triangular grid of holes, the higher up the grid players manage to deposit the ball the further a small mechanical camel moves along a race track. The skill in the game is to avoid the holes lower down the grid which moves the camel along a smaller amount than the ones at the top. The winning player is the first whose camel crosses the finish line at the far end of the track. In *Remote Control Boats*, players take control of a remote control boat from the edge of a small pool of water often containing themed obstacles to navigate around. Although the game has no winning objective, negotiating rocks, lighthouses and other boats is difficult and skilful. Players who are more adept at steering can attempt to take the course at higher speeds and more daring routes.

Prototype sideshow games

Figure 1: Photo Derby interface.

'Photo Derby' (Figure 1) is inspired by the Arabian Derby sideshow attraction. This variation allows players to collectively decide the outcome of the race through voting for their individual favourites. Four camels compete in the race; however instead of a jockey each camel has a photo image upon its back. Players are asked to select their favourite photo from the four. The players make this selection by swiping their favoured photo towards a black hole at the edge of the screen, mimicking the rolling action required to play the Arabian Derby sideshow. Players are then asked to select their second, third and fourth favoured photo using the same interaction. Camels (photos) proceed down the race track based on how highly ranked they are by each player, the higher ranked photos moving the furthest distance. Those ranked second, third and fourth move shorter distances down the track relative to their ranking. The first camel to reach the end of the track is therefore the collective favourite and winner of the race. Players compete at the same time but there is no time limit to making selections. This allows for players to strategically wait for others to make their selection to allow their vote to have more sway, or to encourage a group of players to discuss the state of the race and make decisions together.

'Photo Boats' (Figure 2) develops the idea of the Remote Control Boats sideshow into a photo selection game. Four boats are rendered to the touch surface, each carrying a photo attached to its mast in place of a sail. The boats move toward the edges of the tabletop at increasing speed. Players attempt to keep their favoured photo on the screen by swiping it away from the edge. If a photo disappears out of view, the photo is removed from the game. The last photo to remain on-screen is rendered the group's favourite.

These two sideshow games were chosen for inspiration as they provide opposing styles of tabletop interaction. Photo Boats requires dexterity and skill from players in fast paced action, asking them to make split second decisions about photo *selection*. Photo Derby is more contemplative, and more about *triage*; skilful manipulation of the physical interaction is less likely to affect the outcome.

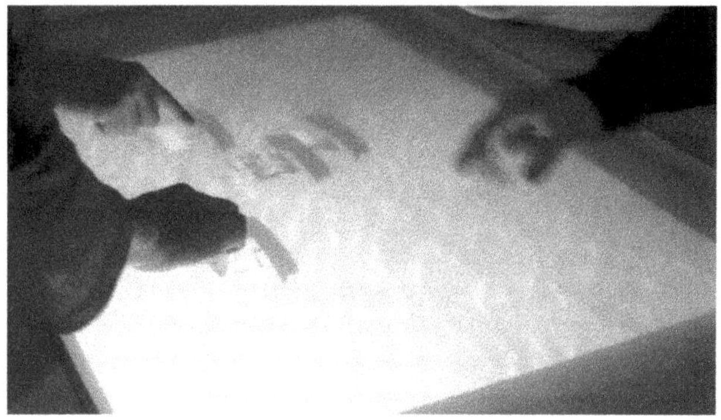

Figure 2: Photo Boats in use.

Prototype specifications

The prototype games were designed for use with a custom-built direct surface illumination touch-screen surface of approximately 50 inches, to accommodate four users. The game software was developed using the ActionScript3 (AS3) programming language. AS3 was chosen for its speed of development, mature graphics libraries and ability to communicate with Community Core Vision touch tracking software using the TUIO protocol.

STUDY METHODOLOGY

We studied our designs in use with a lab-based appraisal, evaluating their use against our stated design requirements. We adopted an ideographic, case study approach to carry out in-depth qualitative observation of a small sample of users, combined with semi-structured interviews. We recruited four groups of four participants who had recently visited Alton Towers Theme Park and Resort (UK) together and amassed a collection of photographs from their respective trips. Group A constituted an extended family, of two children (Jim (11) and Beth (9)), their mother (Maggie (38)) and grandmother (Helen 59)). Group B constituted a mix of family and friends; Linda (48) and her son Sam (11), and Anne (41) and her daughter Mel (7). Groups C and D comprised friends aged between 21 and 40. Each group had two male and two female participants. Group C comprised Marianne, Bella, Chris and Tim. Group D comprised Stuart,

Mike, Sarah and Lauren. In advance of using the prototype games, we invited users to conduct a 'pre-trial' exercise, to reduce their large collections of theme park photos down to the groups of *four* required for use in each game. We adopted a low-fidelity technique for this, providing users with a display of printed photos to collectively triage. The selection of four was then loaded into the prototype application. We chose to limit the number of photos used in the game to four to manage the potential complexity of the trial setting; future studies could utilise an increased number of photos and additional users. We asked our users to position themselves at the table with two participants on each long side. Initially we invited users to familiarise themselves with each prototype game, using stock photos before attempting to make selections with their own photos.

Subsequently players had the opportunity to use each game in turn to engage with four photos chosen from their original collections in the pre-trial triaging exercise.

We concluded each trial session with a semi-structured group interview, asking for users' reflections on the games, the appropriation of meaning of the selected souvenir photo, and how they saw this kind of sideshow activity fitting into the wider theme park environs and experience.

FINDINGS FROM THE EVALUATION

In this section we present key findings, organised around two foci: (i) tabletop photo triaging selection behaviours; and (ii) users' critical reflection on the deployment of tabletop interfaces in the theme park. As such, we analyse how an intergenerational sample of park visitors leveraged features of the tabletop interfaces and photo media in social, playful interaction, and how they critically explored the design space of our interests. More broadly, we consider how meaning making around photo triage and consumption could be supported by tabletop interaction and how the two methods of interaction compared in effecting this process.

Selection

First, we turn to findings relating to the observed methods of selecting photos that users made within the context of the research tasks. Overall, we found users' selections to be partly shaped by their preconceptions about tabletop interaction and the sideshow metaphors evoked by the prototype designs. We also found these methods led to the embodiment of meaning in the photos, which reflected the group social dynamics and the representation of individuals and the group. In some instances, selection was mediated by expressions of *social equity*, and in others by *joking*, teasing and *competitiveness* between users about portrayals of people and their theme park experiences.

Equity and fairness

A voiced feature of both games was that they fostered a sense of inclusiveness in the group activity. Maggie of Group A (GA) said of Photo Boats: "it was interactive as a family." She added that the game "made sense" as a means for group photo-selection: "Say you've got 10 photos and no one can decide what they want, you work together to pick the ones you like rather than the one no one likes."

The designs of both games afforded children the same opportunities to participate in the selection process as the adults. No one person could 'assume control' over the games and when a group selection was made it was seen as something that all would abide. Helen of GA highlighted how the games invited a relaxing of generational power relations: "And it gives a chance for all ages – it takes the discrimination out – it is purely who worked the hardest". The children also recognised this; Jim of GA said: "if you don't agree on what your family says you can just pick another - which is good cause you can just pick that one and not bother about what the others said."

Group B (GB) unanimously agreed that the Photo Derby made 'most sense' as a means for collectively selecting a photo; the game mechanism better enabled participant families to work closer together than that of Photo Boats. It also afforded more 'choice', participants referred to this as 'voting'. It was therefore considered 'fairer' because it was more usable by all, including those who had less or no experience using touch-screens.

The two friendship groups' (Groups C (GC) and D (GD)), evaluations of fairness echoed that of the family groups. However the promotion of equity in participation was observedly less relevant than in the families, because members were peers. Concerns for equity focused rather on balancing each member contributions to create 'fair' representations of individuals and the groups.

In both GC and GD, 'voting' was not seen as offering enough control to the individual participants to whittle out photos they didn't deem representative; concerns stemmed from worries about 'losing face' and the social impact of being negatively represented in a photo. As a result, some users in both groups wanted the right to "veto" certain photos that they thought made them look bad. This was exemplified by the photo selected by GC when playing Photo Derby. The image showed Chris being affectionate towards Marianne, untangling her hair after a log flume water ride. He was embarrassed as the photo was selected stating: "How is that winning? I picked that to go last." The other group members cheered as it was declared the winning photo, and used it to make fun of Chris during the rest of the trial. This is also an example of 'joshing' – or playful teasing, which we will discuss in detail shortly.

Overall, Photo Derby most efficaciously supported 'equity in participation' that didn't restrict less competent players, which is why many users preferred it for selecting a group souvenir. Photo Boats was less fair in this regard; the faster paced interaction in Boats enabled users to manipulate the game and demonstrate superior skill with it. Additionally, interaction was seen as being more fun; participants at time found interaction with Photo Derby to have pacing issues, with a *waiting time* between each photo selection as the camel moved down the track. The interaction with Boats allowed users to engage with the photos and each other in a more playful or competitive way, with implications for how meaning was inferred from the content. An extract from the interview with GB illustrates these findings well.

> Researcher 1: So if you had to pick one which made more sense as a way of selecting a photo, which one would you pick?
>
> All: Camels.
>
> Sam: But the Boats were more fun.
>
> Mel: Yeah, the Boats one was quite good. [...]
>
> Linda: The Camel one I think was fairer for the day out. Whereas the Boat one was more of a game. With Sam, he worked out which way it was going.
>
> Researcher 2: Why do you think the Camel game was fairer?
>
> Linda: Not sure if it's an ageist thing. Obviously I'm the oldest in the group and Mel perhaps is quite as [..] knowledgeable as Sam yet with touch screens.
>
> Researcher 2: So when you say fairer you mean interaction with the touchscreen?
>
> Linda: Yes with the screen. I do have a bit of knowledge. But if I went with grandparents they wouldn't. They're always going to lose aren't they? So technology-wise the Camel game was fairer for a broader party.

Indeed we observed an interesting tension in how the two designs afforded different forms of social interaction for balancing activities, of being at play whilst successfully completing a task – collectively selecting a group souvenir.

Family Participation and Help

In using the applications, the parents of the family groups expressed concern for demonstrating fairness to one other on how a group photo-selection was made. Jim's comment above on 'not bothering about what the others said' demonstrates how children differed from parents in their attitude to the nature of collaboration and participation. Parents also encouraged their children's collaboration with other group members. When Mel of Group B (GB) exclaimed: "that one's mine!" about a photo, her mother Anne replied: "You can share it, you can share it - Team work!" Parents facilitated their children's participation and fostered shared decision-making over content. Both Linda and Helen from GB and GA respectively were observed seeking consensus after people chose photos.

Parents also helped young children who didn't fully comprehend the nature of the task, to make sure they had a 'fair go'. Mel and Beth of GB struggled to comprehend associating a game interaction with the tasks. Upon completing a round of Boats, Beth asked "who won?" Maggie then reminded her that "the picture won, nobody one". The notion of fairness was a factor in the parents' perceived efficacy of the games for the task.

Notions of Gameplay

The applications were introduced to the participant users as sideshow games, so they were approached as games. The younger generations were excited at idea of playing games: "yay games!" (Mel). The older generations were familiar with the original game metaphors that were drawn upon for inspiration. For example, upon seeing the Derby interface, Linda exclaimed that the Arabian Derby game was a familiar feature of theme parks and fairgrounds.

Users brought preconceptions of 'gaming' to the table that led them to conceptualise themselves as individual players competing against each other. Children wanted to choose their own game element to play with. For example, Mel chose to manipulate the 'photo boat' closest to her on the table, rather than a favourite. At the end of the game she exclaimed: "I won, yay I won"! And, about the photo boat sprite said: "That one's mine".

Gameplay features of Boats arguably misled users about the selection task at hand; they saw the mechanism as more like a video game. Linda described the effect: "It's more like a competition who is going to beat who"; and later exclaimed: "It's funny we all went for different photos." It was not only children that oriented as individual 'players' to the games. After GC members completed the pre-trial of the Derby, Bella asked which camel she was and Marianne realised: "Oh, so it's the picture not the person!" In their interview afterwards, GC members stated that the game didn't make sense for them as a method of selection. They each took agency of the photo that came immediately towards them, at the start of the game as the photos spread out from the centre of the screen. This made them feel that they were competing with each other to be the last remaining player, instead of collaborating in the task.

> Marianne: I took it as a competitive game. So I couldn't pick the same as somebody else.
>
> Researcher 1: So you felt you had to take an individual role?
>
> Marianne: Yep, an individual role and whatever picture I had in front of me. I didn't really look at the picture I was just trying to keep the boat on the screen; it doesn't look at all like cooperation, more competition.

Subsequently, GC group members didn't feel that the photo that 'won the Boats game' represented their collective wishes for a group souvenir. This finding was a unique to this group, however; others were able to make sense of the game when using stock photos in the pre-trial.

Dexterity, skill and Strategy

For the boys Jim and Sam, Boats was in no small part about *exercising dexterity* as a feature of gameplay. Jim oriented to Boats as such: "Yeah if you can't decide you just try to keep the one on that you've got." In the case of Sam using Boats, he kept the photo he wanted to win, using his 'superior' knowledge of touch screen interaction to work out the method more quickly than his group members.

Indeed, the boys in the family groups demonstrated more skill in Boats than the others. Linda said she was: "letting go and seeing where it went before trying to move it". Sam told her how the touch interaction worked, that "you control which way it goes by sliding it" and that the game "was quite easy [...] if you just slide it with one finger then the other back and forth." Linda repeated her statements about Sam's superior knowledge of touch screens and that her difficulties "could be a generation thing as well."

By contrast, the triaging gameplay mechanism in Photo Derby facilitated gameplay-as-*strategy*. The comparatively slower interaction of Derby enabled users to wait for other members to make selections and then be strategic in selecting to influence the outcome of the game. This led to users showing greater interest in the resultant selected photo over the result of Photo Boats. Chris of GC explained why.

> The immediate thing with that one [Photo Boats] is to try to be competitive to try to save a boat regardless of the photo that's attached to it. Whereas with the second one [Photo Derby] you've have the static photos in front of you, you can work out which one you want to save.

However, for GC the Derby game mechanism invited other 'processual' issues that made it problematic (as a means for collaboration over content). Marianne said: "It's not really a collective activity; I mean you don't interact with other people you're just voting and then you can discuss the result with the group and then its fun." Tim added: "It's excluded in some way the collaborative element cause we decided on our own what we've taken, we could not find a solution for us four; there was no option for discussion." Bella recommended an additional stage in the design: "Maybe at the end, if we could see 'First', 'Second', 'Third', and then have a second decision process where you select: 'This is the one that won in the game, do you want to pick this one?' - then the people can agree or disagree with the list, cause otherwise it's just a mechanical its not a proper agreement."

We observed that, in the course of the evaluation both applications prompted participants to share their photos in ways that didn't necessarily engender collaboration, dexterity skill and strategy facilitated by gameplay changed the equity in selection. Issues were also found with attaching the sideshow metaphor to photo selection, as discussed in the previous section. However these behaviours allowed for sharing of content in other ways, in particular through *joshing*.

Joshing

Theme park photos are found to be evocative of 'Candid Camera' photography [6]. For example a ride photo may show a rider looking scared, overly excited or drenched in the case of water rides. In our prototype evaluation we observed that photos with these qualities propagated gentle, playful teasing – or joshing – between group members. This manifested itself as an inclusive experience for the participants in family groups, whereby the joke was shared, even by the target of the teasing.

Also, in family groups, joshing indicated the relaxing of generational power dynamics, as children made fun of their parents. Both Beth from GA and Sam from GB manipulated the gameplay to make fun of their mother and grandmother respectively. Sam used his superior dexterity with Photo Boats to ensure that the picture of his mum looking scared was selected. And Mel made fun of her guardian, Linda.

> Mel: Winner! The one with the crazy face wins!
>
> Linda: [In a comedy voice] Yeah, yeah, yeah, that crazy woman [pulls face at Mel]!"

Prior to this exchange, Sam had been subjected to joshing himself; during the paper selection stage of the trial, Linda selected a photo portraying him as being scared on a ride.

> Linda: what about Sam's funny face on that, do we like that?
>
> Sam: Nooo! [Sam grabs photo of Linda]
>
> Linda: [...] Oh no, not that one of me [*laughs*].

Sam acted in retaliation to Linda, and the Boats interface and his skill at the game allowed for this to happen. Joshing in friend groups was taken very differently. Users were concerned with self-representation through photographic portrayals. The process of teasing led to some group members feeling that they were 'losing face', and their dislike of certain photos was expressed vehemently. In more than one instance, participants swore at each other for drawing attention to particular photos. An example of this was when GD played Photo Boats. Stuart and Mike ensured that the selected photo was one of Sarah rubbing her nose and hence pulling a 'funny face'. The avoiding of social embarrassment was of particular importance to the friendship groups. Lauren of GD asked for what she considered to be a very unflattering photo of her to be removed from the social networking site that the photos had been uploaded to, even though the group had only made the photo collection privately available.

Tim of GC reflected at interview that joshing within his group, around Chris untangling Marianne's hair, was unfair and diminished the collaborative equity in the selection task at hand. Chris replied that he would have made different choices whilst playing, to ameliorate the possibility of the result. He said he would have appreciated the ability to deselect that photo from the game: "grab other people's photos away from them so they couldn't pick."

Participants found the games to be an engaging method of photo consumption and enjoyed playing them to triage photos from their trip. Although we uncovered issues with users understanding the nature of the tasks at hand, the game mechanisms allowed for playful interaction between group members and the attachment of meaning to content. This was particularly evident in Boats, where users with greater touch-screen skill were able to manipulate the result, to ensure other players were subjected to joshing.

Reflections on Theme Park Deployment

As a final exercise of the trial, we asked participants to use their experience of the prototypes to critically reflect on how they, more generally, envisaged tabletop sideshows like these fitting in with the infrastructure of theme parks like Alton Towers. We also invited reflection on the potential value of designing such games to fit in with the attractions and environs offered by theme parks.

The games within the theme park infrastructure
Alton Towers is divided into themed areas like many modern amusement parks. The tone, graphical styling and branding of rides, buildings and other attractions present a coherent product. Linda and Sam of GB voiced that this aesthetic design of the park environment was an important aspect of visiting and that the deployment of the games should be in keeping with the character of themed areas.

> Sam: So like with the Boats game, if a section of that was a water park, [...] you could have one like a little stall thing.
>
> Linda For each area you could have a different character, so like Dragons Fury have a dragon, instead of a camel.

At interview, Anne of GB talked about it being hard to keep children's attention whilst queuing for rides. Sam talked about how much he enjoyed the "little pots of Lego bricks" that were handed out in queues at the 'Legoland' theme park. He saw the possibility of deploying sideshow games within the queuing system to distract from waiting, but raised the issue of the tabletop interface's portability given the moving queue. He speculated that, in this instance, the touch-screen could be replaced with handheld devices.

The adults within GA suggested places in the park where they wait for other group members as possible locations for deploying sideshow games. Near toilet areas or refreshment areas; here, children could play with sideshow games whilst the adults take a break.

All groups took issue with the purchasing of park-provided ride photos. The photos were seen as expensive and visitors weren't given any opportunity to review or compare before making decisions. The ride photo booth is placed immediately after alighting at the ride station, and GD said they found that the service didn't allow them to consider their options and compare with other photos from the day. Lauren expressed her frustrations about this at interview.

> Lauren: Shouting at the thing, 'I want this picture' just as it goes off the screen. The decisions we were making were quite fast ones.

Anne of GB expressed a desire to be able to deliberate before buying up to the *end* of the visit, taking into consideration the set of photos amassed during the day. Linda added that making decisions about photo-souvenirs from the previous ride whilst in the queue for the next would give them time to decide upon purchasing.

The games within the theme park experience
Whilst theme parks are typically visited by groups, often the experiences aren't shared between all group members. Maggie and Beth of GA said that often they would be left waiting for others who went off to ride a flagship coaster. These times felt quite boring, they said, and they could be left "ambling around" the park. Maggie suggested that playing sideshow games akin to what we prototyped could actually become *part* of the spectator experience; whilst some of the family is still riding, the rest could be playing the games to *review* ride photos as they are captured, and select photo-souvenirs to present to riders upon alighting.

> Maggie: Like that will be ideal for me and her [Beth] where as Jim and her [Helen] go on the big rides me and Beth just basically walk round so to do anything there for an hour would be great fun.

Theme park experiences typically offer multi-sensory entertainment that, even in sideshow contexts aside from 'thrill rides', are relatively fast-paced and immersive. Critical reflection in the post-trial interviews sensitised the research team to the balance in pacing required in the design of the sideshow prototypes to afford the effective completion of the selection task whilst affording entertaining gameplay. For example, Photo Derby proved lacking in the 'thrill factor'. Linda suggested that the Derby ideally needed the kind of musical accompaniment that many traditional sideshow games have. Helen also commented on the pacing issues with the Derby, expressing that the user "needed more to do whilst waiting for the camel to move down the track." By contrast, numerous users in groups GC and GD echoed each other in saying that Photo Boats "was too fast" to be able to make selections effectively. Stuart responded to her comments saying that Boats "as a game though was more successful." For this reason, most participants felt that Photo Derby was more conducive to making group selections and working together, whilst Photo Boats was, in Anne's words, "a bit more working against each other – and a bit manic." Sam qualified Anne's statement: "Because the boats never stopped moving; the camels waited for someone to vote."

Overall, participants liked the tabletop as a game interface that "you can all gather around" (Helen). They preferred the orientation to a wall-mounted touch display, which Jim of GA thought, given the differing heights of family members, is "going to be really unfair, say if you have like a small person who is kind of like jumping up trying to get a photo." However participants were also conscious of the practicalities of using a tabletop surface in the physical locations they had suggested. Jim and Helen tried to imagine how the games could work on portable devices, speculating that a single player version of Photo Boats could be transferred to a mobile device.

DISCUSSION
We now discuss the design implications that follow from our findings and in particular the social dimensions of the tabletop gameplay we observed. In doing so we reflect back on our paper aims, frame our discussions around the three design requirements detailed previously, and offer novel insights to the related HCI literatures. This section concludes with a consideration of future design directions.

Group Collaboration and Negotiation
Our tabletop sideshow games allowed user groups to engage in social interaction around photo-souvenir content and facilitated differing methods of selection that reflected negotiation methods used by different generations of visitors. Interacting with the games and playing with the photos sparked reflection on social aspects of visiting.

Frequently, this took the form of *joshing*, and exploiting the Candid Camera nature of theme park photography.

Indeed, participants used the triaging component as a means to tease other members of the group. Recall, for example, Sam of GB selecting a 'candid' photo of his mother in the Photo Boats game. Competitive gameplay skills were enlisted for joshing, too; some participants – typically younger generations – used superior dexterity and prior knowledge of touchscreen displays to this end. We found that the frenetic interaction of Boats better enabled this behaviour in multigenerational groups. Joshing was enjoyed within families as a fun part of negotiation and selection.

Similar behaviours were observed in the friendship groups. In these cases, joshing was more explicitly linked to the preservation of self-image and 'saving face'; social embarrassment was more keenly felt in gameplay. Recall how Chris of was subjected to joshing in light of the result of the Derby game because he disliked the group selection.

This instance highlighted for the GC group what felt like a 'mechanical' photo-selection process, when playing Photo Derby, rather than a collaborative one. Whilst 'majority ruled' in this process, there was no option for veto, and also no option to 'discuss or act upon the selection process' as it unfolded. Chris wanted this affordance as part of gameplay; in the above instance he wanted the opportunity to "grab other people's photos away from them so they couldn't pick" the photo he didn't like. Two insights for collaborative tabletop design are revealed here: (i) support game design that makes the selection process visible for manipulation in gameplay; and (ii) afford users the opportunity to collaboratively and consensually make the final photo-selection *rather than* the system. These insights foreground the significance of interpersonal dialogue in collective photo-triaging activities.

Collaboration and consensus is discussed at length in the tabletop photo literature [10, 31]. We build upon this literature with our findings by observing a subtle distinction at play between collaboration and *participation*. Whilst our prototypes afforded our users equity in participation, they found different roles in the games that were not always *collaborative* ones and were most often *competitive*.

Playfulness and Fantastical Escapism

By focusing our designs with the sideshow game metaphor we developed an interactive experience that was characterised by playfulness and fun whilst engaging with a task of photo triaging. Whilst the combination of task and play activities may seem contrasting, our work intended to build on the tabletop and photo organisation literatures [3] to investigate the social aspects of task-selection. Specifically, by framing our designs within in the '*Fantastical Escapism*' requirement, we sought new perspectives on the social impact of introducing play into the task of tabletop triaging. However, our evaluation has uncovered interesting tensions in pursuing this endeavour. Some of the users struggled to ameliorate play and completing tasks and took time to establish their personal agency within the game, approaching the prototype as competitive players. This approach created a recurring issue during our trial, as players entered into competition without thinking about the *selection task* per se.

Our evaluation thus highlighted a tension in the design space, between providing a task and providing a playful interaction. Many participants found Photo Boats to be more fun and "more successful as a game" than Photo Derby. But, participants also struggled to use the Boats as a mechanism for photo selection. Many stated that the pace of the game was too fast and there wasn't time for discussion around the photos. Conversely the Derby was seen to offer a more efficacious means for selection and was preferred by three of the four groups for serving that purpose. However, in the given theme park context, participants wanted the Derby to offer a more exciting, immersive experience, requesting background music and higher-paced gameplay. We subsequently identified a key design challenge: the *pacing* of games must allow enough time for users to make selections, whilst being fast – frenetic – enough to foster excitement. On reflection, the race metaphor evoked by the Derby could've been exploited more in its design to build excitement towards a climax of decision-making.

Our results have led us to consider a more complex design space that embraces a wider photo ecology, in which the tabletop sideshow games are used to foster playfulness – including competitive play – within different forms of *participation* in an attraction for the shared consumption of photo-souvenirs. A key insight we've gained is that having a *goal-oriented* component to the sideshow prototypes was perhaps confounding in *playful* interaction; we suggest that the consumption of photos in this specific context should be oriented towards collective *review* rather than *triage*.

Walk-up interaction

The rationale behind our game design was inspired by previous findings on the mismatch between the flexibility of personal digital photography and the constraints of the park-provided systems for making photo-souvenirs of a park visit [7]. We sought to investigate this mismatch through the development and evaluation of a tabletop system that facilitated walk-up interaction within the theme park 'photo ecology'. Theme park goers wanted more time to be able to consider their purchase of ride photos and incorporate these into their personal photo collections. Within the theme park experience, users have considerable 'downtime' periods, which we've identified as opportune moments for consuming and reviewing photos. This was reiterated in the current study; participants spoke at length about the tedium of queuing for the rides and the difficulties of keeping children engaged during these times.

Reflection by our study participants after playing with our prototypes revealed a keen interest in the tabletop form factor for collectively consuming photo-media. One emerging challenge for designers is to consider how a tabletop sideshow game would fit into a broader ecology of interactive display surfaces and devices within the park infrastructure, and how it might connect with the designs and experiences of other in-park 'games' and entertainments. Building on the above discussion, a key consideration in future design work is how the potential 'steps' in a process of reviewing, triaging, and rendering photo-souvenirs would be afforded within the game design, taking into account issues of pacing and the balancing of ludic and task-based interaction. A related consideration is the extent to which this process is *group*-oriented.

Future design directions

Our initial designs combined concepts of *play* and a *collaborative* task into a 'sideshow' tabletop interface. Findings from our evaluation suggest that future designs should focus centrally on *play* as part of the *shared experience* of visiting. We found that the triaging task as a game mechanism created a tension that confused users who were intuitively associating gameplay with competition.

Taking inspiration from this, we may pursue future iterations of the prototypes that focus on creating an *exploratory* photo browser instead of a goal-orientated selection mechanism. Our aim through this would be to allow users to explore their photo collections and the meaning they attribute to them, through playful interactions that engender friendly competition. This design would allow for joshing as part of the theme park experience without the risk of a 'candid', embarrassing photo necessarily being rendered as a lasting souvenir. Any additional functionality in the design to facilitate group-selection, it seems, would best serve to afford interpersonal dialogue on triage rather than system control.

Finally, we consider the how a future prototype could be integrated within the theme park photo ecology. The tabletop form factor supports multiple simultaneous participants as a 'walk up attraction'. We envisage that follow-on prototyping and evaluative exercises in this design space would be conducted within that ecosystem, to establish the coupling between personal devices, park infrastructure and the tabletop. In addition we see that insights from this study maybe applicable to the wider domain of leisure and touristic visiting. Brown & Chalmers [4] discuss how technologies which the experience of leisure activities should also engage the social practices between the visiting groups of friends and family.

CONCLUSION

In this paper we have presented the prototyping and evaluation of a tabletop sideshow game for consuming photo-souvenirs within the theme park experience. The prototype designs were grounded in the fantastical nature of theme park entertainment and supported photo triaging tasks within groups of theme park goers that comprised a diverse, multi-generational sample. We summarise the findings of our trial in the following key points:

- Participation in gameplay did not ensure equity in collaboration. Joshing between participants meant that selections may not have reflected intentions to collaborate, rather to compete. Design of sideshow games should support these notions but limit impact on resulting souvenirs, playful interactions ought to allow for photo review rather than triage.
- We observed a tension between playfulness and completing collaborative tasks. Gameplay needs to be exciting and immersive to integrate with the theme park setting; however, allowing groups to make considered selection of photos requires careful pacing.
- The participants found the tabletop form factor to be in keeping and an enjoyable way of passing time between rides. Future studies could investigate suitable locations within the theme park environment for deployment.

From our results we offer new insights to the tabletop research literatures and HCI, on the social dimensions of tabletop gameplay, emphasising the significance of context in designing to support meaningful interaction.

ACKNOWLEDGMENTS

We thank our participants and the invaluable help of Anthony Brown. The first author is supported by the Horizon Doctoral Training Centre at the University of Nottingham (RCUK Grant No. EP/G037574/1). This work was funded by RCUK through the Horizon Digital Economy Research grant (EP/G065802/1)

REFERENCES

1. Al Mahmud, A., Mubin, O., Shahid, S. and Martens, J. Designing and evaluating the tabletop game experience for senior citizens. In *Proc. of NordiCHI 2008*, ACM Press (2008), 403-406.
2. Antle, A. N., Tanenbaum, J., Bevans, A., Seaborn, K. and Wang, S. Balancing act: enabling public engagement with sustainability issues through a multi-touch tabletop collaborative game. In *Proc. of INTERACT 2011*, Springer-Verlag, (2011),194-211.
3. Apted, T., Kay, J. and Quigley. A. Tabletop sharing of digital photographs for the elderly. In *Proc. of CHI 2006*, ACM Press (2006) 781-790.
4. Brown, B. and Chalmers, M. Tourism and mobile technology. In *Proc. of ECSCW 2003* Kluwer Academic Publishers (2003), 335-354.
5. Cao, X., Lindley, S., Helmes, J. and Sellen, A. Telling the whole story: anticipation, inspiration and reputation in a field deployment of TellTable. In *Proc. of CSCW 2010*, ACM Press (2010), 251-260
6. Durrant, A., Kirk, D.,S., Benford, S., Rodden, T., Pursuing Leisure: Reflections on Theme Park Visiting. *Computer Supported Cooperative Work (CSCW)*, (2011), 1-37.

7. Durrant, A., Rowland, D., Kirk, D.,S., Benford, S., Fischer J.,E. and McAuley, D. Automics: souvenir generating photoware for theme parks. In Proc. of *CHI 2011*, ACM Press (2011) 1767-1776.

8. Fleck, R., Rogers, Y., Yuill, N., Marshall, P., Carr, A., Rick, J. and Bonnett, B. Actions speak loudly with words: unpacking collaboration around the table. In *Proc. of ITS 2009*, ACM Press (2009), 189-196.

9. Hartmann, B., Ringel Morris, M., Benko, H. and Wilson, A.D. Pictionaire: supporting collaborative design work by integrating physical and digital artifacts. In *Proc. of* CSCW 2010, ACM Press (2010), 421-424.

10. Hilliges, O. and Kirk, D. S. Getting sidetracked: display design and occasioning photo-talk with the photohelix. In *Proc. of CHI 2009*, ACM Press (2009), 1733-1736.

11. Hilliges, O. Baur, D.& Butz, A, Photohelix: Browsing, Sorting and Sharing Digital Photo Collections. In *Proc. of Tabletop '07*, (2007)

12. Jacucci, G., Oulasvirt, A. and Salovaara, A. Active construction of experience through mobile media: a field study with implications for recording and sharing. Personal and Ubiquitous Computing. 11, 4 (2006), 215–234.

13. Jones, K. R. and Wills, J. *The Invention of the Park: From the Garden of Eden to Disney's Magic Kingdom.* Polity Press, 2005

14. Kirk, D. S., Izadi, S., Hilliges, O., Banks, R., Taylor, S. and Sellen, A. At Home With Surface Computing. in *Proc. of CHI 2012*, ACM Press (2012).

15. Kirk, D.S., Izadi, S., Sellen, A., Taylor, S., Banks, R. and Hilliges, O. Opening up the family archive. In *Proc. of CSCW 2010*, ACM Press (2010), 261-270.

16. Kruger, R., Carpendale, S., Scott, S. and Greenberg, S. How people use orientation on tables: comprehension, coordination and communication. In *Proc. GROUP '03*. ACM Press (2003), 369-378.

17. Marshall, J., Rowland, D., Rennick Egglestone, S., Benford, S., Walker, B., and McAuley, D., Breath control of amusement rides. In Proc of *CHI 2011*. ACM Press (2011), 73-82.

18. Marshall, P., Fleck, R., Harris, A., Rick, J., Hornecker, E., Rogers, Y., Yuill, N. and Dalton, N. S. Fighting for control: children's embodied interactions when using physical and digital representations. In *Proc. of CHI 2009*, ACM Press (2009), 2149-2152.

19. Pausch, R., Snoddy, J., Taylor, R., Watson, S. and Haseltine, E. Disney's Aladdin: first steps toward storytelling in virtual reality. In Proc. of *SIGGRAPH 1996*, ACM Press (1996), 193-203.

20. Rennick-Egglestone, S., Whitbrook, A., Leygue, C., Greensmith, J., Walker, B., Benford, S., Schnädelbach, H., Reeves, S., Marshall, J., Kirk, D., Tennent, P., Irune, A. and Rowland, D. Personalizing the theme park: psychometric profiling and physiological monitoring. *In* Proc. of *UMAP 2011*, Springer-Verlag (2011), 281-292.

21. Ringel Morris, M., Huang, A., Paepcke, A. and Winograd, T. Cooperative gestures: multi-user gestural interactions for co-located groupware. In *Proc. of CHI '06*, ACM Press (2006) 1201-1210

22. Ringel Morris, M., Paepcke, A., Winograd, T. and Stamberger, J. TeamTag: exploring centralized versus replicated controls for co-located tabletop groupware. In *Proc of CHI '06*, ACM Press (2006) 1273-1282.

23. Salovaara, A., Jacucci, G., Oulasvirta, A., Saari, T., Kanerva, P., Kurvinen, E. and Tiitta, S. Collective creation and sense-making of mobile media. In *Proc. of CHI 2006*, ACM Press (2006), 1211-1220.

24. Sarvas R., Oulasvirta A. and Jacucci, G. 2005. Building social discourse around mobile photos: a systemic perspective. *In* Proc of *MobileHCI* 2005. ACM Press (2005), 31-38.

25. Schild, J. and Masuch, M. Game design for ad-hoc multi-touch gameplay on large tabletop displays. In *Proc. of Futureplay 2010*, ACM Press (2010), 90-97.

26. Scott S., Sheelagh M., Carpendale T., and Inkpen M. 2004. Territoriality in collaborative tabletop workspaces. In *Proc of CSCW '04*. ACM Press (2004), 294-303.

27. Sengers, P., Boehner, K., David, S. and Kaye, J. Reflective design. In *Proc.* of *CC 2005*. ACM Press (2005), 49-58.

28. Shen, C., Lesh, N. and Vernier, F. Personal digital historian: story sharing around the table. *interactions* 10, 2 (2003), 15-22.

29. Schnädelbach, H., Rennick Egglestone, S., Reeves, S., Benford, S., Walker, B. and Wright, M. Performing thrill: designing telemetry systems and spectator interfaces for amusement rides. In *Proc. of CHI 2008*, ACM Press (2008), 1167-1176.

30. Speelpenning, T., Antle, A., Doering, T. and van den Hoven, E. Exploring how tangible tools enable collaboration in a multi-touch tabletop game. In *Proc. of INTERACT 2011*, Springer-Verlag (2011), 605-621.

31. Terrenghi, L., Kirk, D.S., Sellen, A. and Izadi, S. Affordances for manipulation of physical versus digital media on interactive surfaces. In *Proc. of CHI 2007*, ACM Press (2007), 1157-1166.

32. Van de Mortel, D. & Ju, H., Apartgame: a multi-user tabletop game platform for intensive public use. *Proc. of IUI conference*, (2007), 49–52.

Investigating Menu Discoverability on a Digital Tabletop in a Public Setting

A. Mindy Seto[1], Stacey D. Scott[1], Mark Hancock[1,2]
[1]Systems Design Engineering, [2]Management Sciences
University of Waterloo, 200 University Ave W, Waterloo, ON, Canada N2L 3G1
{mindy.seto, stacey.scott, mark.hancock} @uwaterloo.ca

ABSTRACT

A common challenge to the design of digital tabletops for public settings is how to effectively invite and guide passersby—who often have no prior experience with such technology—to interact using unfamiliar interaction methods and interfaces. We characterize such enticement from the system interface as the system's *discoverability*. A particular challenge to modern surface interfaces is the discoverability of system functionality: *does the system require gestures? are there system menus? if so, how are they invoked?* This research focuses on the discoverability of system menus on digital tabletops designed for public settings. An observational study of menu invocation methods in a museum setting is reported. Study findings suggest that discernible and recognizable interface elements, such as buttons, supported by the use of animation, can effectively attract and guide the discovery of menus. Design recommendations for improving menu discoverability are also presented.

Author Keywords

Digital tabletops; interactive surfaces; menu design; public setting; field study.

ACM Classification Keywords

H.5.2 [Information interfaces and presentation]: User Interfaces. - Graphical user interfaces. H.5.3 Group and Organization Interfaces: Computer Supported Collaborative Work.

INTRODUCTION

As large, interactive surfaces such as digital walls and tables become more feasible, they have begun to appear in public settings such as museums, airports, malls, and tourist centers. Studies examining the use of interactive surfaces in such public settings highlight the importance of a self-explanatory, 'walk-up-and-use' system that requires no prior training [7, 9, 10, 13-15, 18, 21, 24]. Such an experience requires "immediate apprehendability" [14, p. 124]. People need to experience success early, and quickly discover how to interact with the system [14, 18]. Thus, high *discoverability* of the system is important in public interactive displays. This discoverability includes attracting people to the system and informing them that the system is interactive. Attraction plays an important role in discoverability because, to interact with the system, one must first notice the system and then be enticed to interact with it.

To date, little interactive surface research has focused directly on designing for discoverability. Some commercial systems have integrated interaction design and visualization components to entice and encourage interaction, such as the water waves used on the Microsoft Surface. However, to our knowledge, the effectiveness of these techniques has not been empirically studied. A notable exception is Wigdor et al.'s [26] Ripples visualization, which provides feedback while touching a surface to help minimize ambiguity related to the success or errors of touch interactions. This approach helps to discover that a surface is interactive upon first touching, an important aspect of the overall discoverability problem. However, it does not address the initial enticement issue, nor does it help to discover the available system features (e.g., what gestures are possible or what system menus are available).

As a first step toward designing for discoverability of system features in interactive public surfaces, this research focuses on discovering system menus. As a key mechanism for accessing system functionality, menus have been the focus of considerable research for both traditional desktop computing and digital tabletops [e.g. 8, 17]. Although menus are a common graphical user interface (GUI) element, their use on digital tables is highly varied and non-standardized, creating challenges for discoverability.

This research examines how to improve the discoverability of menus designed for digital tables in public settings. More specifically, this paper presents a comparative study of several proposed menu invocation designs, conducted in a public setting. To set the context for this study, the relevant background on designing for discoverability on digital tabletops is first discussed. The proposed menu invocation designs are then presented. Next, the study method and analysis are described, and the results are presented. Finally, the implications of the study results are discussed.

BACKGROUND

Our research sits at the cross section of two streams of research in the literature: discoverability of novel technology in public settings and menu design on interactive surfaces.

ITS'12, November 11–14, 2012, Cambridge, Massachusetts, USA.

Discoverability in Public Settings

In a public setting, people tend to be unfamiliar with novel interactive devices. Unlike in a private setting, people are neither able to practice nor be explicitly instructed how to use the system. Discoverability is therefore of great importance when designing a digital tabletop for public use. In a study of a tabletop application in a public tourist centre, Marshall et al. [18] found that "visitors approached the tabletop quite tentatively...[and thus] designers need to grab their attention immediately to communicate its purpose and mechanisms of interaction" (p. 3041).

One approach to assist discoverability on public displays is to explicitly provide written instructions near the display to inform people of the purpose of the display and instruct them how to interact with the system [e.g. 9, 24]. Although this method provides an unambiguous approach to discoverability, Gaver et al. [11] argue that ambiguity in design can be used to initially draw people into interaction. This approach is echoed by Agamanolis [1] who found that ambiguity, or mystery, can entice users' natural curiosity and therefore more deeply engage them in interaction.

Gradual discovery with public displays is encouraged so as to not overwhelm users with instructions or a multitude of unfamiliar interactions [15]. Scaffolding is a gradual discovery method that breaks down larger activities into smaller steps on which to focus [27]. For example, the interface may only reveal a few elements at a time, therefore guiding the user through the exploration process.

Animation can also assist with discoverability. Previous public displays studies have used subtle movement of objects to inform users that they could manipulate these objects [e.g. 14]. The appearance and disappearance of objects has also been used to draw attention and invite interaction to these objects [e.g. 13, 14].

Discoverability of touch gestures is a particular challenge for interactive surface designers as no visible controls are typically presented for manipulation [22]. Self-revealing gestures [5, 27] use a combination of animation and visual affordances to scaffold user learning of gesture possibilities in a given interface context. This research applies similar animation and affordance techniques to improve the discoverability of individual interface elements such as menus.

Menu Design on Interactive Surfaces

Since the use of WIMP (Windows, Icons, Menus, Pointers) interfaces in the 1970's, graphical menus have been a common interface element. While many interactive surfaces utilize only gesture-based interaction, many surface applications include graphical menus to provide access to application functionality. For example, the X-Menu [3] and Occlusion-Aware Menu [6] are contextual, radial-style menus designed for digital tabletops that require people to tap the screen to invoke the menu. These designs, along with other touch-based contextual menu designs [e.g. 2, 16, 17], offer no visual indications that afford menu invocation.

While contextual menus can be invoked anywhere in the interface, other tabletop interfaces have employed edge-based menus, such as the adapted linear menu used in the Personal Digital Historian (PDH) application [25] and the semi-circular Stacked Half-Pie Menu [12]. The PDH menu was invocated from a visible control panel that could be moved anywhere along the perimeter of the table. This provided a highly visible design. The Stacked Half-Pie Menu could be invoked by tapping on a button at the edge of the table. The menu invocation button is always visible and clearly labeled with interaction instructions. This design uses a constant visual element, a button, on the display to indicate the presence and invocation method of the menu.

These evaluations have primarily focused on menu performance, particularly efficiency. Some studies also evaluated menu usability through standardized questionnaires. Although controlled studies are effective at assessing menu efficiency, particularly for user-trained scenarios, they do not assess *menu discoverability* and none of these evaluations were centred on the invocation stage. This research focuses on designing menus for digital tabletops with respect to a discoverable menu invocation experience.

DISCOVERING TABLETOP MENUS IN PUBLIC SPACES

To investigate menu discoverability, two menu invocation methods were designed: a button-based method, which leverages a conventional design concept, and an edge-based method, which uses a tabletop-specific design element. In addition to examining the effectiveness of the invocation method in fostering menu discoverability, we also explored the potential of animation to assist in menu discoverability, as suggested by the literature. Thus, we design both a proactive animation to entice and guide passersby, and a responsive animation to react to touch interaction on the table, as well as a glowing animation to highlight the invocation elements on the digital table. The menu invocation methods and animation designs are described below.

Buttons

Buttons are a common interface control element found on digital displays regardless of the medium. Modeled after physical push buttons, virtual buttons afford pushing (or touching). They are used with current menu designs such as drop-down menus. Similar to the invocation method used in the Stacked Half-Pie tabletop menu described above, the first invocation design is based on these tried and tested interface elements. This invocation design, shown in Figure 1 (left), allows people to invoke a menu by tapping or dwelling on triangular-shaped buttons situated along the interactive edge of the digital tabletop. A menu then opens in place of the button. The placement and quantity of the buttons can vary depending on the size of the digital table. This design helps to mitigate the chance of overlapping menus, and indicates the number of menus the digital tabletop provides. Menu invocation can be cancelled by dragging off the button before lifting one's finger.

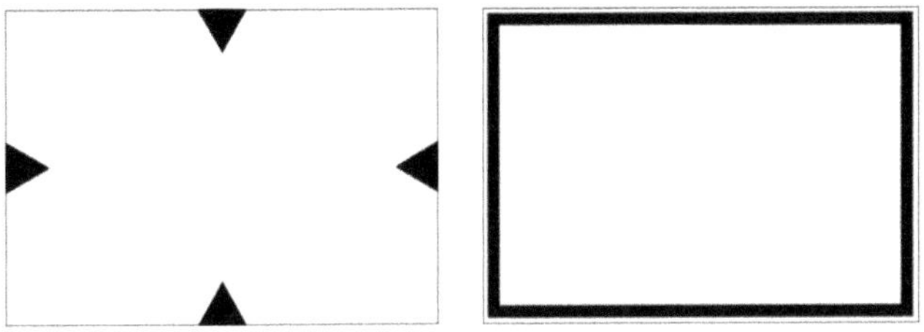

Figure 1. The two invocation type design concepts: buttons (left) and border (right).

In prior iterations of the button design, we attempted both circular and rectangular buttons, which we expected might leverage familiarity from desktop designs. However, informal user testing showed that triangular buttons were a more obvious visual element, as they bluntly protrude from the edge of table. The flat black coloring of the buttons was chosen so as not to introduce effects such as color and beveling to the observational study. Additionally, some styling effects, such as beveling a button to make it appear as though it is raised, can be misleading if viewed from an alternative orientation—a common phenomenon at a horizontal table that can be approached from any side.

Border

To provide more flexibility in positioning around the table, and in the number of menus that may be needed for a given session, an alternative invocation design was also investigated. The border design (Figure 1, right), allows the menu to be invoked anywhere along the interactive edge of the digital table by tapping or dwelling on the demarcated border. A menu then opens at the tapped location. Lifting the finger outside the edge will again cancel menu invocation.

Menu placement is particularly important to consider for shared tabletop and public settings, especially a walk-up and use setting, as investigated here. In this setting, people are free to approach the table from different directions, and position themselves as desired. It is also difficult to predict how many people may wish to use the table at once. Providing greater flexibility in where, and potentially how many, menus can be invoked may help to address these issues.

Animation

In public settings, many stimuli can compete for one's attention [20]. Sudden appearance of moving and/or luminous objects appeals to one's behavioral sense that the stimulus may be urgent information and thus attracts attention [4]. Therefore, animation was paired with the two invocation designs discussed above to attract passersby to the table and direct their attention to the appropriate invocation elements.

Floating Images

The first animation provided a proactive approach to attracting attention. It was designed to entice passersby to approach the table and to suggest the table contained interactive content. This animation consisted of non-interactive, translucent, floating images of the content available in the menus. The images spawned from the center of the table, enlarged as if rising, and then randomly drifted into the interactive edges of the digital tabletop (see Figure 2, left). This animation appeared whenever the table was in its "attract" state, that is, when no content was open. The images were designed to drift to the edges so as to direct people to the location of the menus. The images were also made non-interactive for the purposes of the study, as interactive floating images may have detracted from the discovery of the menus, and therefore may have affected our results. To help communicate to people that the floating images were non-interactive they were made translucent.

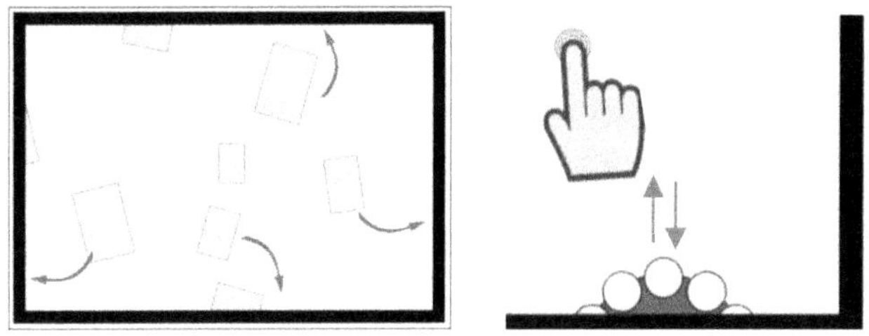

Figure 2. Design concepts for floating images animation (left) and pop-up menu animation (right).

Pop-up Menu Hints

The second animation provided a more reactive approach to indicating how to invoke a menu. When the digital tabletop was in the attract state and a person touched anywhere on the interface (other than the invocation elements), a pop-up animation would appear consisting of a partial menu coming rapidly out and then back into the edge of the table at the location of an invocation element (see Figure 2, right). This animation design was based on a self-revealing gesture to help teach people how to invoke a menu. The intention was to indicate the existence of a system menu, as well as to direct attention to the menu's location. The swift timing and movement of the animation was based on research showing that motion is effective at attracting attention, particularly if it occurs in a person's peripheral view [23].

Glow

To attract attention to the invocation elements and to indicate their interactivity, a glow effect was applied to each button and each edge. A pulsating blue gradient animation emanated from each element. The glow effect was designed so as to draw the attention of those who have not yet discovered the buttons, but not be too distracting to people already interacting with the digital tabletop. This effect only appeared on buttons and edges with no active menus, and thus also served the added purpose of indicating which sides of the table could still support additional menus.

STUDY

The goal of the study was to compare the discoverability of the different menu invocation designs for a public-use context. Thus, a realistic walk-up-and-use situation was incorporated into the study design: an observational study was conducted in a local children's museum.

Study Design

An observation-based field experiment was conducted, in which our proposed menu invocation designed were tested in a realistic setting. The study used a 2 (invocation type) × 2 (animation) between-participants factorial design.

The two invocation types were the *border* and *buttons* invocation designs. Both invocation designs invoked a system menu, described below. For the second factor, the floating images and pop-up menu hints animations were either both turned on (*animation*) or both turned off (*no animation*); however, the glow animation was kept on for all conditions.

The study was conducted across four consecutive days. Each day, observations were taken for a five hour period from approximately 10 AM to 3 PM. To ensure all four menu invocation designs obtained similar exposure to visitor traffic, the four conditions were counterbalanced using a Latin Square across the four days. To minimize disruption to participant interactions, breaks between conditions were chosen based on logical breaks in museum traffic flow, as determined by the experimenter. Conditions were presented for an average of 80 minutes per day.

Participants

Over the four-day observational period, 226 groups interacted with the digital table. Interaction times ranged from one second (e.g., a passing tap) to 20 minutes (e.g., opening and interacting with several menus and media items). Museum visitors included children aged 4 to 12[1], adolescents aged 13-18, and adults aged 25 to 75, including males and females of varying ethnic backgrounds. Visitors interacted with the table as individuals, and groups ranging from 2 to 8 people. Each visitor group typically consisted of one adult with multiple children, with the exception of kids' camp and daycare groups. In these cases, groups of only children were in the majority.

Equipment and Setting

The study took place at a local museum in August 2011. An observational area and the experimental equipment were set up on the second floor. Surrounding exhibits were primarily geared towards children. Directly across from the observational area was a motion-activated digital wall.

Within the observational area, a SMART Table[2] was set up to run our application. This table provides a child-friendly form factor (91.5×74×65.4 cm) and has a 71.5 cm (diagonal) interactive touch screen with 1024x768 pixel display resolution. The observation area also contained two small (non-digital) tables with two to three chairs situated nearby on either side of the SMART Table. The researcher sat at one of these tables to record field notes.

[1] All age classifications are the judgment of the researcher; no personal information was collected from the participants.

[2] http://smarttech.com

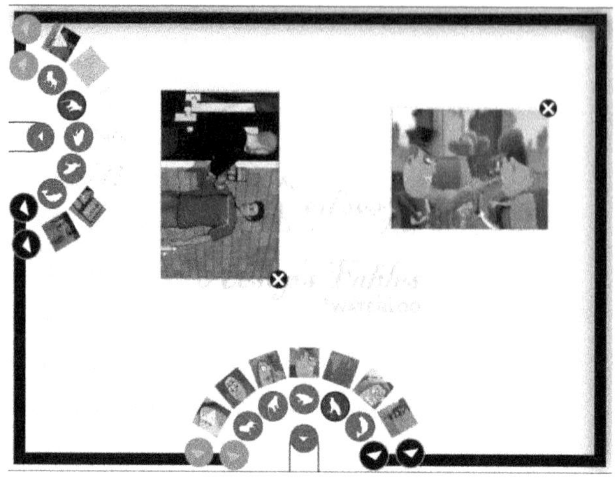

Figure 3: Media browsing application screenshot.

Experimental Application

To demonstrate the four study conditions, a media browsing digital tabletop application was developed. The application allowed up to four hierarchical, crescent-style menus (see Figure 3) to be opened (one on each edge of the table), from which a collection of videos and images could be opened. Multiple, replicated menus were provided based on Morris et al.'s [19] research that suggested they would better support multiple people, while reducing the discomfort and aversion of co-touching. Particularly in a museum setting, these were important factors to account for as museum visitors may not know one another.

The content in the media browsing application included images and videos representing interpretations of the fables by the author Aesop (e.g. The Tortoise and the Hare), created by local digital arts students. This content was selected for the study as it was appropriate for a broad audience (particularly children) and could be displayed as a stand-alone exhibit in a museum. The hierarchical organization of the crescent-style menu was leveraged to organize the content such that level 1 displayed the various fables, and level 2 displayed content pertaining to the selected fable. Text was avoided when possible for both the menu and the images to minimize orientation and display resolution issues. Figure 3 shows a snapshot of the application with two open system menus and two open content items. The application was developed in C#, .NET 4, and XAML.

Procedure

Although participants were not informed of any particular order of interaction with the SMART Table, a typical interaction consisted of the following events:

1. Noticing the SMART Table
2. Approaching the SMART Table
3. Interacting with the touch sensitive area of the table
4. Opening a system menu
5. Navigating through the menu
6. Selecting an item from the menu to open
7. Manipulating the open item

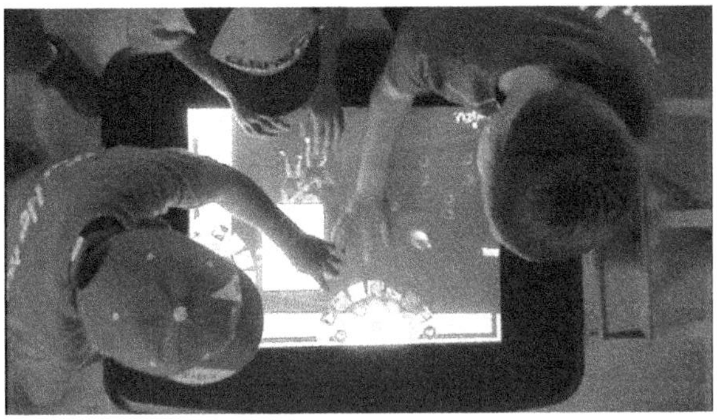

Figure 4: View from the above-the-table camera.

Participants were free to interact with the table for as short or long as desired. To help maintain the realism of a museum exhibit, a non-intrusive method of participant consent was used. A large sign posted directly behind the table informed museum visitors that by interacting with the table, they were implicitly consenting to study participation.

Data Collection

Three forms of data collection were used: field notes, computer logs, and video recording. Field notes were recorded from a nearby table. Observations focused on whether visitors noticed the table, attempted to interact with the table, successfully opened any menus, general details about their interaction with the table, and age of visitors. The experimental application automatically logged visitor's interaction with the tabletop interface. Finally, a digital camcorder was affixed directly above the table to capture a bird's eye view of the table and any interactions; audio data was captured along with the video. The video capture area extended approximately 0.5 m around the table (see Figure 4). This was useful in determining if visitors approached the digital table but did not interact with it.

Data Analysis

Visitors tended to interact with the digital tabletop in groups; therefore all analysis was conducted treating each group as one unit. Furthermore, as the focus of the study was discoverability, it was assumed that each individual in a group may be influenced by seeing other group members' interactions. Thus, the criterion used to differentiate groups was that there was no overlap in time between interacters from one group to the next.

Both quantitative and qualitative data analyses were performed. To validate the collected data, the video, log, and field data were amalgamated, verified against one another, and then sorted based on participant groups and study conditions. This data processing was conducted in conjunction with a multi-pass strategy for the video data and an open coding approach to identify behavior trends.

RESULTS

The data analysis revealed that discoverability of the system and of the system menu typically occurred in several phases. First, people noticed and approached the system, and then they began to explore the system and its interface. Finally, they began to discover the features of the system and of what the system was capable. The following sections describe how the tested invocation designs impacted discoverability through these different phases.

Initial Approach and System Use

When visitors first approached the digital tabletop, they either glanced around the system and surroundings prior to taking action or took action immediately. Actions included interacting with the system or leaving without interaction. Delay of action was often caused by people looking around the physical table (for example, looking for a physical 'start' button) or reading the consent signage. In some cases, visitors were deterred by the consent signage and left without interaction. System interaction was characterized as a person intentionally making contact with the table; this included looking around the physical tabletop and trying to find a button or tapping on the interactive surface of the digital tabletop. With a small number of groups, people interacted with the digital tabletop thinking it controlled the motion wall situated immediately across from the table. To compare the menu invocation conditions during this initial system interaction, the location of participant groups' first touches with the interactive screen was examined.

First Touches

Figure 5 shows the first tabletop interaction of each participant group across all menu invocation conditions. Each point represents the location of the first touch point of each group. Four categories of first touches were observed: invocation element, floating image, open space, and passing tap. 'Invocation element' points represent groups who first tapped on the invocation element (border or button). 'Floating image' points are only relevant for conditions with animation present as they represent groups who first tapped on a floating image (these elements were non-interactive). 'Open space' points represent groups who tapped in areas of the screen that contained no invocation elements or floating images. The last category, 'passing taps' is not shown, but represents groups who tapped on the table while walking or running by and did not stop or focus their attention to the table. Most first touches categorized as passing taps were children running by the table while dragging a hand across the surface. Often these interactions were too quick to be recognized by the system; all had no subsequent interaction. 42 groups were identified with 'passing taps' first touches. These interactions were omitted from the analysis; subsequent analysis was based on the remaining 145 groups.

As Figure 5 shows, most first touch points were located near where visitors first approached the table from the main corridor. Although this finding is likely influenced by the position of the table with respect to the visitor traffic, it suggests that people tended to first interact with the system interface within immediate reach.

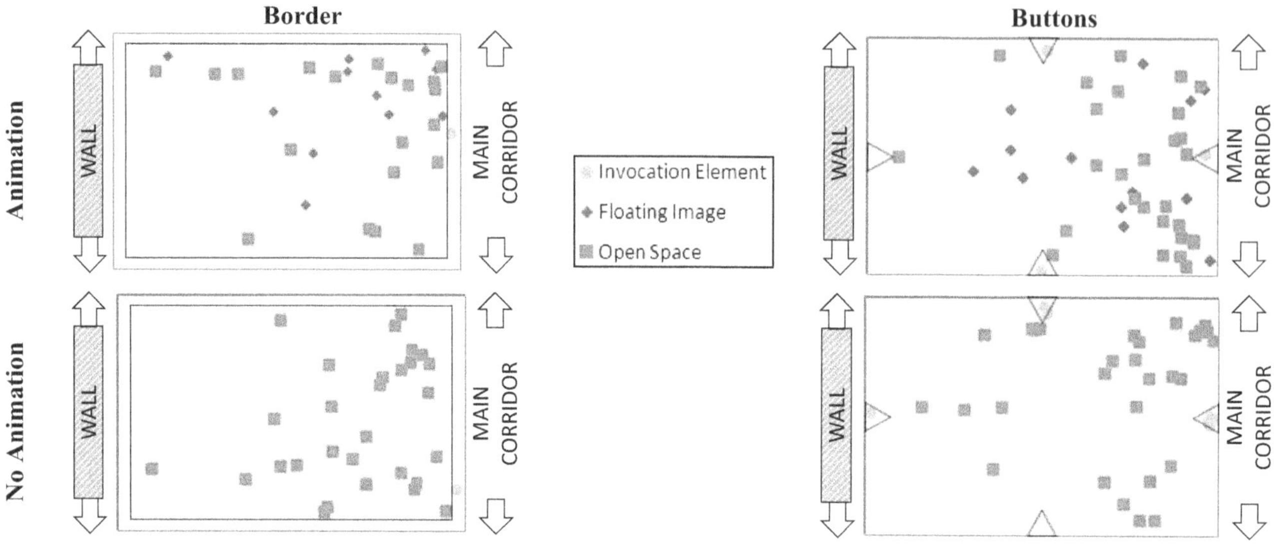

Figure 5: Location of participant groups' first touches.

In all conditions, the majority of the groups' first touches were located in the open space of the interface (107 out of 145 groups). During their initial explorations, the primary activity was to determine the purpose or use of the system. Observations suggest that people first tapped the screen to test if the digital tabletop was interactive. A difference was observed between how adults and children first interacted with the system. Adults tended to cautiously tap the table with one finger and paused for a response from the system. In contrast, most children were much less cautious and interacted with the table with their full palm (and sometimes two hands) while rubbing or hitting around randomly. Participants' explorations are presented in more detail next.

System Exploration

Timeline visualizations (Figure 6) were created for the three phases of discovery (*approach*, *explore*, and *discover*) for each group and condition to better understand these phases. Analysis of these timelines found that overall, groups with shorter *explore* times successfully transitioned to the *discover* phase. This suggests that groups with longer *explore* times often "gave up" and ceased interaction with the digital tabletop, possibly because they could not determine its purpose or find interactive content.

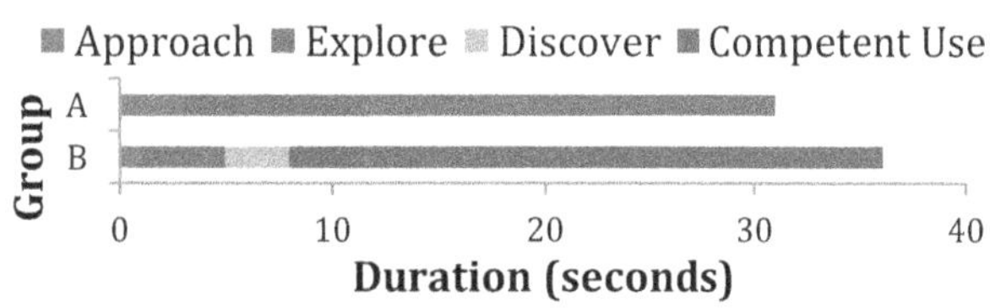

Figure 6. An example of the generated timeline visualizations.

While in the *explore* phase, many participants pondered out loud, "*what does this do?*"or "*does this thing do anything?*" If sufficiently intrigued, they continued to explore the table by continuing to tap on the screen until they either discovered something (i.e. invoked the system menu) or left. Some groups paused in this phase to read or re-read the consent and informational signage, perhaps seeking instructions on how to use the digital tabletop. Others called over other people to join in their interaction.

In exploring the digital tabletop, people either randomly tapped on the table without obvious direction or interacted with the displayed interface elements, such as tapping the floating images. Of those who interacted randomly without obvious direction, some notable interactions included a child who "hugged" the table and another one who rubbed his hands in the motion of windshield wipers.

In these random interactions, people appeared to be trying to determine the purpose of the system. If these people invoked a menu, they would often end their explorations with one person exclaiming "*oh I found something!*" to other group members. Some people's interactions appeared primarily guided by the interface elements; their interactions comprised tapping or trying to drag the floating images and, when displayed, trying to interact with the pop-up animation. These interactions are discussed in more detail below.

In the buttons condition, regardless of animation condition, many people tried to drag the buttons towards the center of the table. This behavior suggests that people may have interpreted the triangular button as an arrow pointing inward, suggesting dragging inward. Consistent with the groups' "first touch" interactions discussed above, exploratory interactions with the invocation element were not as common in the border condition.

Interactions with Animation

Groups' exploratory interactions included interaction with the floating images and the pop-up menu animations. The following statistical analysis of these interactions includes only the animation present conditions, including both the border and buttons invocation conditions.

Floating Images Animation. Overall, 51.3% of groups interacted with the floating images by tapping or trying to

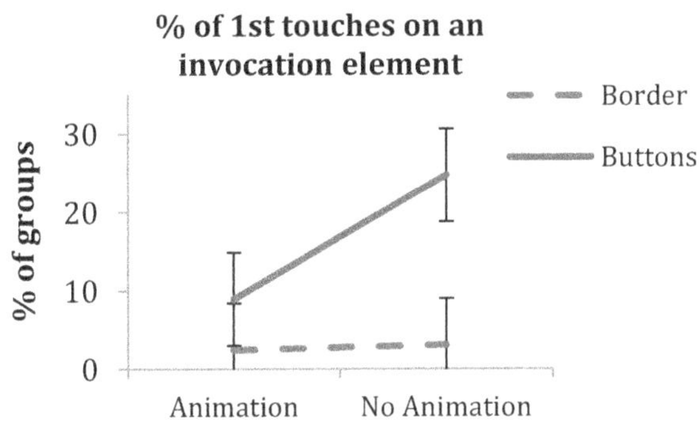

Figure 7: Percentage of groups whose 1st touch was on an invocation element (error bars based on standard error)

drag the images. This finding suggests that many people assumed that the floating images were interactive. The original intent of this animation was to provide a hint that the table contained interactive content, which could be accessed at the table's edge. However, observed interaction behavior suggests that this animation may have inadvertently distracted people by instead inviting interaction with the floating images. A t-test comparing interaction occurrences with floating images across menu invocation conditions found no significant difference ($t(6)=0.51$, $p=.63$, *n.s.*).

Pop-up Menu Animation. Of the 64 groups whose first touch triggered the pop-up animation[3], 42.2% interacted with the pop-up animation. These interactions included tapping or dragging on or near the pop-up. Of the groups that interacted with the pop-up, 51.9% of them successfully invoked a menu from their interactions. Thus, for those who noticed and were persuaded to interact with the pop-up animation, it appeared to help people successful discover and invoke the system menu. A t-test found that groups interacted with the pop-up animation significantly more often in the buttons condition (M=56.3%, SD=13.8%) than in the border condition (M=30.0%, SD=13.5%), ($t(6)=2.72$, $p=.04$). Thus, the pop-up animation appeared to be more attractive to system interaction in the buttons condition.

Feature Discovery

As groups explored the system, they began to discover the system features, including the system menu and the image and video content it invoked. To compare the effectiveness of the menu invocation conditions in this discovery process, the percentage of groups that invoked at least one menu per group and accompanying scenarios were examined.

Menu Invocations

Participants that first tapped the invocation element immediately transitioned into the *discover* phase. Figure 7 summarizes the percentage of groups whose first touch coincided with an invocation element by condition. A two-way ANOVA comparing invocation types found that the groups' first touches coincided with an invocation element significantly more often with the buttons (M=14.0%, SD=14.6%) than with the border (M=2.8%, SD=5.3%; $F(1,12)=4.89$, $p=.047$). This finding suggests that the buttons design initially attracted interaction more effectively than the border design for menu invocation. There was no significant difference found across animation conditions ($F(1,12)=2.42$, $p=.15$, *n.s.*) nor was there a significant interaction ($F(1,12)=2.05$, $p=.18$, *n.s.*).

Although no significant interaction was found, Figure 7 shows a trend for groups to first touch an invocation element in the buttons condition less often when animations were present. As the intention of including animation was to improve menu discoverability, this result suggests that animation may have actually impeded or distracted menu invocation in the buttons condition. This is further discussed below.

The video analysis revealed interesting observations of *how* participants interacted with the invocation elements. In the experimental application, a menu was invoked when a participant tapped on an invocation element. The video data revealed that some participants performed a variety of other gestures to try to invoke a menu. The most common alternative actions were to drag or dwell (i.e. touching and holding for a few seconds) on the invocation element.

Intentional Menu Invocation

Closer examination of *how* participants invoked menus revealed that there was a distinction between intentional and unintentional menu invocations. Intentional menu invocations were identified as invocations as a result of purposeful interaction while the participant's focus of attention was on the invocation element being interacted with. Unintentional menu invocations were identified as invocations as a result of an interaction when the participant's focus of attention was *not* on the invocation element being interacted with or as a result of an interaction intended for another item. Examples of interactions resulting in unintentional menu invocations are a participant resting or leaning his/her elbow/arm on the surface of the table, and a participant dragging an open image (menu content) around the screen.

Figure 8 shows the percentage of groups in which the first menu was intentionally invoked, of those that actually invoked a menu. The *first* menu is specified because it is the first menu per group that is invoked that demonstrates discoverability. Subsequent menu invocations are influenced by learning effects. A two-way ANOVA comparing these data across conditions found a significant difference across both invocation types ($F(1,12)=41.06$, $p<.01$) and animation ($F(1,12)=7.86$, $p=.02$). There was also a marginally significant interaction between invocation type and animation ($F(1,12)=4.58$, $p=.054$). Examination of the data reveals that across the invocation condition, significantly more

[3] Due to technical limitations, not all touch interactions were properly detected. Thus, not all first touches triggered a pop-up animation. Analysis of pop-up animation interactions was accordingly adjusted to include groups who successfully triggered a pop-up animation (64 of 78 groups).

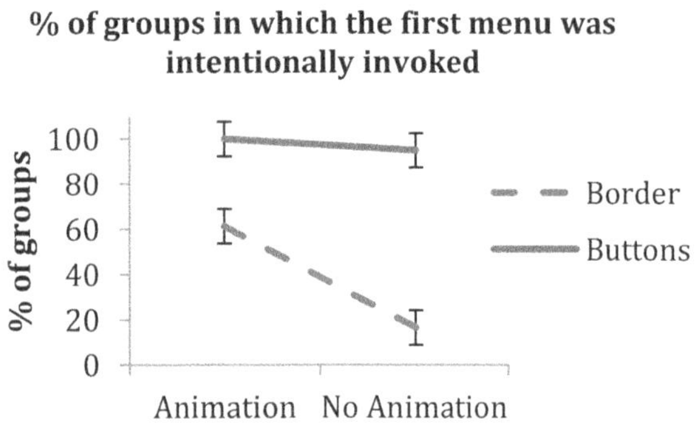

Figure 8: Percentage of groups in which the first menu was intentionally invoked (error bars based on standard error).

groups intentionally invoked a menu in the buttons condition (M=97.2%, SD=7.9%) in comparison to the border condition (M=43.6%, SD=30.3%). As Figure 8 shows, on average in the buttons condition, if a group invoked a menu, the first menu was intentionally invoked more than 90% of the time. Additionally across the animation condition, significantly more groups intentionally invoked a menu with the presence of animation (M=82.1%, SD=26.2%) than without (M=56.7%, SD=40.3%).

Further investigation of the marginally significant interaction was conducted for each invocation type across animation. An independent sample t-test comparing intentional menu invocation with the border condition found a significant difference across animation conditions ($t(6)=2.62$, $p=.04$). No difference was found for the buttons condition ($t(6)=1.00$, $p=.36$, *n.s.*). These results indicate animation had a greater impact with the border condition than with buttons; more groups in the border condition intentionally invoked a menu when animation was present (M=64.3%, SD=27.4%) than without (M=22.9%, SD=15.8%).

DISCUSSION

Invocation type and animation were introduced as two factors potentially influencing discoverability of system menus. The effectiveness of these factors are discussed below.

Invocation Type

The buttons invocation type design represented a familiar desktop-like interface element while the border design proposed an invocation method tailored to the horizontal orientation of digital tabletops.

Analysis of first touch interactions revealed that the majority of first touches coincided with open spaces or floating images, with a small percentage coinciding with the invocation elements. This finding suggests that most people were not initially drawn to the border or buttons. Of those who first interacted with invocation elements, significantly more were drawn to the buttons than the border. Since the same color and glow effect was applied to both the border and buttons, the results suggest that people recognized the buttons as an interactive interface element more easily than the border element. Each button distinctly protruded from the edge of the table, which appeared to be more effective at attracting and guiding interactions. The border design on the other hand was consistent all around the table and may have visually blended into the table edge, potentially making it difficult to distinguish as an interactive GUI element.

The examination of *intentional* versus *unintentional* menu invocation, revealed that significantly more groups intentionally invoked a menu with the buttons condition than with the border condition. These findings suggest that the buttons design was more discoverable for menu invocation. This result was likely due to the visual protrusion of the buttons, or the familiarity of most people with buttons as a GUI element. In contrast, a border is typically used to demarcate space on an interface and is not as commonly viewed as interactive. The higher frequency of border menu invocations in the raw data (though not statistically significant) was likely due to opportunistic accidents such as leaning on the table or random explorative gestures.

Although a simple aesthetic design for invocation conditions (black with blue glow) was used in the study for consistency across conditions and to control for possible confounding factors, it may have impacted recognition of the graphical elements. A flat aesthetic design (no shading or shadows) was applied to the buttons used in this study. This is unlike the classic design of buttons that mimics the physical button design, by using shading to make it appear 3D. The 3D effect is typically applied to a GUI button to imply the affordance of pushing. It is notable, that with the rise of touch interfaces, flat aesthetic designs are becoming more common, for example, as used in the Microsoft Windows Phone[4] interface. Due to the flat coloring of the buttons used in this study, it therefore cannot be definitively concluded whether the buttons design was the more discoverable design due to the use of a common interface element – a button – or, due to its more distinctive visual shape on the screen compared to the border design. Some people may not have initially recognized the triangular shape of the button as a GUI button, but instead just recognized it as a distinguishing and noticeable element on the screen. Further studies are warranted to separate these variables.

The border design appeared to be less recognizable as an interactive element, perhaps due to its classic use as a space divider. With the rise of mobile computing that uses border-based interactions (e.g. BlackBerry PlayBook[5]), people's experiences and perceptions of the GUI elements may change and thereby influence how they discover and interact with interactive systems. The design of affordances would need to account for these experiences. To better understand the impact of differing experiences on discoverability, further studies are warranted.

---

[4] http://www.windowsphone.com

[5] http://ca.blackberry.com/playbook-tablet

Animation

The data analysis showed that the groups' first tabletop interactions typically were attempts to determine whether the table was interactive; they often tapped or rubbed the table and then paused for a response. When animation was present, a small subset of groups first tried to interact with the floating images. More often, groups would attempt to interact with the floating images animation during further explorations on the table. However, this animation did not appear to be effective at guiding people to the system menus, as intended; no evidence was found that people noticed the trail of the floating images into menu invocation location (i.e. into the buttons or the border).

A trend was also found in the study indicating that groups' first touch event corresponded with the buttons invocation element less often when animation was present. As a proactive animation, only the floating images animation was visible prior to any system interaction. Thus, this trend indicates that the floating images animation may have distracted people from noticing the invocation element, despite its intention of assisting menu discoverability.

The study results showed that, of the groups that did trigger a pop-up animation, some tried to interact with it. This indicates that the pop-up animation did attract some attention. Moreover, it appeared to attract more attention, and was more persuasive at inviting interaction, in the buttons condition. This may have been the case due to the fact that the pop-up appeared at the button, which already attracted attention due to its distinctive shape. It is important to note that only the number of groups that *interacted* with the pop-up was measured. It is possible that others *noticed* the pop-up, but did not interact with it. A significant number of groups who interacted with the pop-up also successfully invoked a menu across invocation conditions. This suggests that when the pop-up animation was noticed and interacted with, it was effective in supporting menu discovery.

The analysis of intentional and unintentional menu invocation revealed that significantly more groups intentionally invoked a menu with the presence of animation. Moreover, the analysis revealed that the animation had a greater positive influence in the border condition. These findings suggest that animation is helpful for menu discoverability; however, they do not distinguish between the influence of the floating images and pop-up animation.

The study results suggest that the two animations, floating images and pop-up, served different purposes. The floating images animation was proactive – it appeared before any interaction was detected, and was unaffected by interaction (until a menu was invoked). This proactive nature appeared to help entice people to approach and engage with the system. In contrast, the pop-up animation only appeared in response to interaction. The feedback it provided appeared to make it more suitable for guiding interaction during the exploration and feature discovery phases. As the two animations were evaluated together in this research, further studies are needed to determine their individual influence on overall menu discoverability.

DESIGN RECOMMENDATIONS

The comparisons of the menu invocation designs evaluated in this research provided several implications for the design of future menu invocation techniques, as discussed below.

Immediate feedback to exploratory interactions. People's first interactions with the digital tabletop were often to test if it was interactive – tapping or rubbing the table and then pausing for a response. When available, people also tried to interact with the floating images animation. It is therefore recommended that in addition to using animation to draw attention, these animations should support interaction and respond to interaction to engage people into further action.

Use of discernible interface elements. The study results revealed the buttons design to be significantly more discoverable than the border design. It is posited to be due to its distinguishable shape in the interface and use of a common GUI element – a button. This finding suggests that the use of more universal GUI elements, such as the button which is already perceived to afford interaction, particularly one that has high visible contrast, facilitates discoverability. This finding is particularly important for public settings where people are typically novices. Special attention should be made, however, to ensure these elements are designed so as not to diverge so much from their original design that they become unrecognizable, while still taking heed to the digital tabletop interface considerations, such as orientation.

Animation as a guide. The study results also revealed that animation, especially the pop-up animation, was effective at guiding interaction. Animation is therefore recommended for assisting people to discover new interactions, or even to reinforce existing ones. This recommendation is consistent with the purpose and use of self-revealing gestures [5, 27].

CONCLUSION

This paper presented an exploratory study investigating the effectiveness of two menu invocation designs, border and buttons, and of the use of animation, to facilitate the discoverability of the system menus in a digital tabletop interface. As discussed, discoverability of the system features of a digital tabletop encompasses a number of phased interaction steps, beginning with the most basic step of first recognizing that the digital tabletop is interactive.

The study revealed that buttons with the use of animation was the most discoverable menu invocation design. Overall, buttons were found to be more discoverable than the border. The buttons design was based on a common GUI element and also used a more visually distinguishable design, which likely provided more affordance for interaction than the border design. As a result, more people intentionally invoked a menu with the buttons design.

The results regarding animation from this research are consistent with findings from previous research of the positive correlation between animation and attention [4, 23]. When discovered, the pop-up animation helped to guide a person's actions towards invoking a menu. The floating images animation was useful for attracting attention and interaction; however, results suggest that it may have also distracted from locating the invocation element. Further research is warranted on these different animation designs, specifically to better understanding how proactive and responsive animations can facilitate different phases of discoverability.

Overall, this was a first step toward understanding how to facilitate discoverability of tabletop menus in a public setting. Further studies are needed to clarify how to support the different phases of discovery, from attracting people to the table, enticing then to begin interacting with it, and to their eventual discovery of what the table has to offer.

ACKNOWLEDGEMENTS

This work was funded by NSERC (Natural Sciences and Engineering Council of Canada), Infusion Development, and NSERC SurfNet. We thank Robert Post, Justin Lin, and Trisha Villanueva for assistance with the experimental application and content, and Neil Randall and Lori-Ann Earl for assistance with the study setting.

REFERENCES

1. Agamanolis, S. (2002). Designing displays for Human Connectedness. *CSCW 2002: Workshop on Public, Community and Situated Displays*.
2. Bailly, G., Lecolinet, E., Nigay, L. (2008). Flower menus: a new type of marking menu with large menu breadth, within groups and efficient expert mode memorization. *Proc. of AVI 2008*, 15-22.
3. Benko, H., Wilson, A.D., Baudisch, P. (2006). Precise selection techniques for multi-touch screens. *Proc. of CHI 2006*, 1263-1272.
4. Bodenhausen, G.V. and Hugenberg, K. (2009). Attention, perception, and social cognition. In F. Strack and J. Förster (eds.), *Social cognition: The basis of human interaction*. Psychology Press: Philadelphia, 1-22.
5. Brandl, P., Forlines, C., Wigdor, D., Haller, M., Shen, C. (2008). Combining and measuring the benefits of bimanual pen and direct-touch interaction on horizontal interfaces. *Proc. of AVI 2008*, 154-161.
6. Brandl, P., Leitner, J., Seifried, T., Haller, M., Doray, B., To, P. (2009). Occlusion-aware menu design for digital tabletops. *Extended Abstracts of CHI 2009*, 3223-3228.
7. Brignull, H. and Rogers, Y. (2003). Enticing People to Interact with Large Public Displays in Public Spaces. *Proc. of INTERACT 2003*, 17-22.
8. Callahan, J., Hopkins, D., Weiser, M., Shneiderman, B. (1988). An empirical comparison of pie vs. linear menus. *Proc. of CHI 1988*, 95-100.
9. Cao, X., Massimi, M., Balakrishnan, R. (2008). Flashlight jigsaw: an exploratory study of an ad-hoc multiplayer game on public displays. *Proc. of CSCW 2008*, 77-86.
10. Correia, N., Mota, T., Rui Nobrega, Silva, L., Almeida, A. (2010). A multi-touch tabletop for robust multimedia interaction in museums. *Proc. of ITS 2010*, 117-120.
11. Gaver, W.W., Beaver, J., Benford, S. (2003). Ambiguity as a resource for design. *Proc. of CHI 2003*, 233-240.
12. Hesselmann, T., Stefan Floering, Schmitt, M. (2009). Stacked Half-Pie menus: navigating nested menus on interactive tabletops. *Proc. of ITS 2009*, 173-180.
13. Hinrichs, U. and Carpendale, S. (2011). Gestures in the wild: studying multi-touch gesture sequences on interactive tabletop exhibits. *Proc. of CHI 2011*, 3023-3032.
14. Hornecker, E. (2008). "I don't understand it either but it is cool": Visitor interactions with a multi-touch table in a museum. *Proc. of Tabletop/ITS 2008*, 121-128.
15. Jacucci, G., Morrison, A., Richard, G.T., Kleimola, J., Peltonen, P., Parisi, L., Laitinen, T. (2010). Worlds of information: designing for engagement at a public multi-touch display. *Proc. of CHI 2010*, 2267-2276.
16. Leithinger, D. and Haller, M. (2007). Improving Menu Interaction for Cluttered Tabletop Setups with User-Drawn Path Menus. *Proc. of Tabletop 2007*, 121-128.
17. Lepinski, G.J., Grossman, T., Fitzmaurice, G. (2010). The design and evaluation of multitouch marking menus. *Proc. of CHI 2010*, 2233-2242.
18. Marshall, P., Morris, R., Rogers, Y., Kreitmayer, S., Davies, M. (2011). Rethinking 'multi-user': an in-the-wild study of how groups approach a walk-up-and-use tabletop interface. *Proc of CHI 2011*, 3033-3042.
19. Morris, M.R., Paepcke, A., Winograd, T., Stamberger, J. (2006). TeamTag: Exploring Centralized versus Replicated Controls for Co-located Tabletop Groupware. *Proc. of CHI 2006*, 1273-128.
20. Mueller, J., Alt, F., Michelis, D., Schmidt, A. (2010). Requirements and design space for interactive public displays. *Proc. of Multimedia 2010*, 1285-1294.
21. Müller, J., Walter, R., Bailly, G., Nischt, M., Alt, F. (2012). Looking glass: a field study on noticing interactivity of a shop window. *Proc of CHI 2012*, 297-306.
22. Norman, D.A. (2010). Natural user interfaces are not natural. *interactions*, 17(3), 6-10.
23. Palmer, S. (1999). *Vision Science: Photons to Phenomenology*, Cambridge, MA: MIT Press.
24. Peltonen, P., Kurvinen, E., Salovaara, A., Jacucci, G., Ilmonen, T., Evans, J., Oulasvirta, A., Saarikko, P. (2008). It's Mine, Don't Touch!: interactions at a large multi-touch display in a city centre. *Proc. of CHI 2008*, 1285-1294.
25. Shen, C., Lesh, N., Frederic, V. (2003). Personal digital historian: story sharing around the table. *interactions*, 10(2), 15-22.
26. Wigdor, D., Williams, S., Cronin, M., Levy, R., White, K., Mazeev, M., Benko, H. (2009). Ripples: utilizing per-contact visualizations to improve user interaction with touch displays. *Proc. of UIST 2009*, 3-12.
27. Wigdor, D. and Wixon, D. (2011). *Brave NUI World: Designing Natural User Interfaces for Touch and Gesture*: Morgan Kaufman.

Re-Collision: A Collision Reconstruction Forensics Tabletop Interface

Marcel Tozser [1] Nicole Sultanum [1,2] Ehud Sharlin [1] Ken Rutherford [3] Colin Foster [3]
University of Calgary [1] IBM Research, Brazil [2] Calgary Police Service [3]
{mtozser, nbsultan, ehud}@ucalgary.ca {krutherford, pol4047}@calgarypolice.ca

ABSTRACT

In this paper we present the design, implementation and preliminary evaluation of *Re-Collision*, a prototype collision reconstruction tabletop interface. *Re-Collision* was developed through a participatory design process involving expert users from the Calgary Police Forensics Team and Collision Reconstruction Team. We briefly cover fundamental domain characteristics emerging from interview sessions and explain how these informed the design of *Re-Collision*. The paper details our current prototype implementation and discusses results of a design critique conducted with domain experts using our system, helping us assess the potential of tabletop interfaces as aids in the process of collision reconstruction, as well as delineate and discuss relevant design implications.

Author Keywords

Collision reconstruction; forensics; tabletops.

ACM Classification Keywords

H.5.2 [Information interfaces and presentation]: User Interfaces. - Graphical user interfaces.

INTRODUCTION

Among the many existing branches of police investigation, the field of collision reconstruction is focused on examining and solving traffic accidents, attempting to recreate vehicle crashes to find the sources and related circumstances of such events. Collision reconstruction shares many of the general characteristics of police work and forensics, such as involving critical decisions (both impact-wise, and time-wise), and requiring the processing of large amounts of evidence in a timely manner. However, unlike other sectors of police work, collision reconstruction received relatively little attention from the human-computer interaction community, leaving the idiosyncrasies of collision reconstruction practitioners generally unexplored from an HCI perspective, with little published insight on how to create and design better suited interfaces for this domain.

To fill this gap, as well as to guide design efforts for the creation of a domain-specific interface for collision reconstruction analysis, we sought feedback from experts at the Calgary Police Service (CPS), conducting interview sessions with the Collision Reconstruction team and the Forensics team. From these sessions we perceived, among other things, that the domain is potentially very collaborative, and relies heavily on spatiality with extensive usage of diagrams and schematics – characteristics for which tabletop interfaces can be particularly meaningful. We thus designed and developed a tabletop prototype system for collision reconstruction analysis, and conducted a preliminary design critique with the CPS domain experts to validate the design and the concept of tabletops to their work. We present our system and the study we conducted, and share the reflections and design implications which emerged from our evaluation.

ITS'12, November 11–14, 2012, Cambridge, Massachusetts, USA.

COLLISION RECONSTRUCTION

Collision reconstruction, a subfield of police work, relates to the investigation of traffic accidents and violent crashes through forensic science techniques, in order to understand how the event took place and what caused it. The workflow of collision reconstruction, as described by the CPS specialists, starts by *collecting evidence at the scene* (*e.g.* pictures, GPS location markups, witness reports, samples, and so on), which are *compiled and processed*. Then, evidence is *analyzed*, conclusions are drawn, and the case is prepared and *presented to court*. Among these, the *analysis* stage is arguably the most crucial one for collision reconstructionists. During this step, a top-down diagram of the scene is created, containing exact location of elements at the scene (e.g. vehicle, parts, victims, street posts, buildings), confirmed by precise GPS coordinates; car crash physics are taken into account, used to verify and simulate crash conditions. From our interviews, we found some of the fundamental characteristics of this process to include:

(I) Spatiality: Top-view diagrams describing the scene are an omnipresent element of the investigation, and denote the strong importance of spatial awareness.

(II) Emphasis on the facts: automatic simulations are sometimes used in-house to verify conjectures about a certain case. Nonetheless, a clear separation between the *consolidated facts* and the officers' *conjectures* (albeit strongly supported by data) is always clearly established, and only the factual layer (and what can be proven from it) is effectively brought to court for prosecution.

(III) Accuracy, with Efficiency: Police investigation often includes the processing of large volumes of evidence data. It also involves time-critical and impactful decision-making, while maintaining fair and prompt service to the citizens involved in the investigation. Therefore, it is essential to find

strategies to speed up analysis, while maintaining thoroughness.

(IV) Collaboration and group brainstorming: Although not necessarily present for all cases, investigation often becomes a collaborative process, with officers sharing insight and expertise to facilitate the task of analysis; one might see, in a typical session, white boards, diagrams and calculations being shared amongst experts for discussion and validation. Cooperation between investigators from different sectors might also occur.

From these four domain properties, we envisioned digital tabletops as notably suitable environments for collision reconstruction analysis, due to their inherent support of collaborative tasks and spatiality through direct, on-screen manipulation. Tabletops also naturally afford intuitive access to powerful automation, processing and storage, assets which are still often lacking in current police work practices. Our subsequent design efforts have focused on addressing these properties, and will be revisited in our system description.

RELATED WORK

A few off-the-shelf desktop tools are available to traffic accident reconstruction investigators for characterizing the crash scene. Mostly they feature top-view diagram creation tools containing scene description elements [11,12], while some also include 3D animation and crash simulation capabilities [1,10,14] . These tools are essentially WIMP-based desktop applications, targeted at the single-user scenario. Another spectrum of solutions focuses on supporting the overall experience and collaborative aspects of the police investigation analysis. For the traditional crime investigation and law enforcement, the work of Atzenbeck *et al.* [2] addresses team communication and collaborative analysis through the use of a spatial hypertext tool. Zhao *et al.* propose the integration of collaboration tools to a system they call COPLINK [4] – an IT system for crime investigation – focusing on both intra-agency [16] and interagency [15] cooperation. Studies have also been conducted for further understanding of the work and technology of police investigation from a user's perspective [3,6,9,16]. Nonetheless, to the best of our knowledge, our work is the first attempt to understand the forensics domain of collision reconstruction from a user perspective and focus on co-located collaborative analysis for the field.

Finally, there are a few instances of digital tabletops applied to peace and order civil service. Within command and control for emergency settings, tabletops were employed to time-critical decision making in orchestrating coordinated actions of several entities (including the police) [5], as well as a map-based emergency analysis system [13]. Recently, a more related instance within the police domain, Luderschmidt *et al.* [7] explore a graph-based interactive visualization on digital tabletops for traditional crime investigation; It covers, however, a very distinct class of police cases than the ones in this paper, not touch-basing on essential issues to collision reconstruction such as spatiality. Ultimately, we believe our work to be the first research effort attempting to apply interactive tabletops to the specificities of the collision reconstruction analysis.

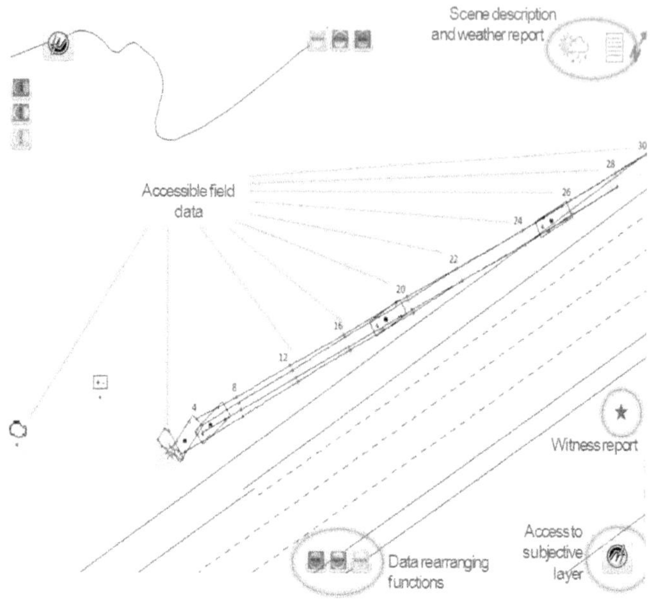

Figure 1. The main interface, featuring a schematic diagram depicting a car crash. Interface functions are indicated in blue.

RE-COLLISION

Re-Collision – developed for the Microsoft Surface – was designed to aid traffic collision investigators with an interactive and collaborative tool on tabletop, attempting to approach the many domain aspects observed for the task of analysis, namely: *(I) spatiality, (II) fact/hypotheses awareness, (III) efficiency and (IV) collaboration.* The system was populated with real data, provided by the CPS.

Taking in consideration the strong separation to be made between factual data and hypotheses, our interface design encompasses two distinct layers: the *factual* and the *sandbox* layer.

The *factual layer*: visualizing the evidence

The main view of *Re-Collision* consists of a traffic accident scene diagram along with visual representations of data/evidence pertaining to a specific accident (Figure 1). Field data collected at the scene – pictures, reports, videos, and so on – usually have an associated location on the map. Related evidences are grouped and made accessible through localized, semi-transparent green highlights; it can then be accessed via touch tap, and can also be toggled to appear or disappear on demand – thus facilitating evidence filtering. Other non-spatial data might be available (such as a weather report or a general description of the scene) and these were associated to special toggleable icons on the diagram as well, for the sake of consistency. Once certain data/evidence is visible, it can be moved, rotated, and scaled through touch (Figure 2(a)).

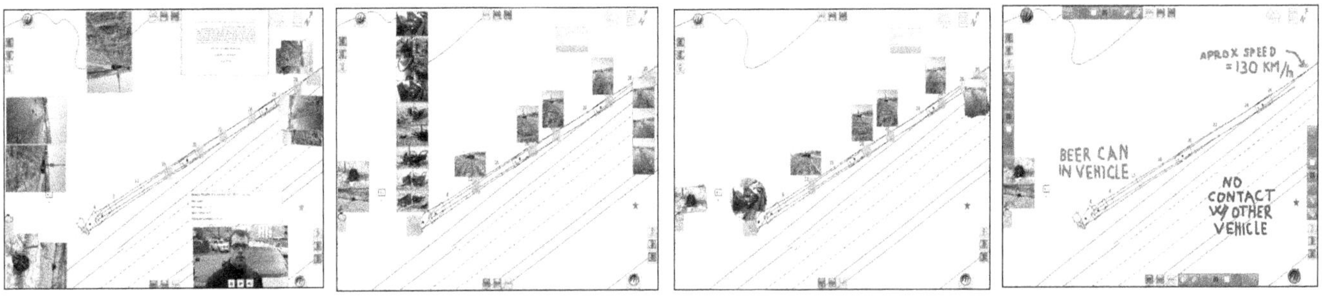

(a) (b) (c) (d)

Figure 2. (a) elements from the scene are selected for display; (b) *Order* function organizes photos side-by-side, oriented towards the lower side of the screen; (c) *Stack* function organizes the pictures in piles, associated to their respective location; (d) the sandbox layer is activated.

Due to the large amount of media to analyze at a time, quick rearranging functions were included to efficiently organize evidence – *Hide*, *Order*, and *Stack* – with respective buttons placed on each edge of the screen for facilitated access to all users. *Hide* closes all open media; *Order* organizes all displayed data side by side, near their respective location while reorienting them towards the edge button that triggered the action (Figure 2(b)); and finally, *Stack* places the opened data near their location, in a fanned stack also oriented towards the triggered edge (Figure 2(c)).

The *sandbox layer*: reasoning and sense-making

The evidence can be visualized, moved, stacked and resized. However, it cannot (and should not) be altered in any way. Nonetheless, during analysis, there are occasions in which one needs to augment or annotate the presented data, or even add new tentative elements to aid the analysis. To address this need, we created the *sandbox* layer allowing for the scene and the evidence to be more freely explored in collaborative brainstorming exercises. For our initial implementation we adopted a "drawing pad" approach, following inspirations from our initial meetings with the CPS teams who informed that white boards were extensively used in time-sensitive investigations.

To access the sandbox layer, two "sandbox" buttons were placed on opposite corners of the interface -- placed away from the rearranging buttons for clarity. Upon touching either of them, the interface activates the sandbox mode, with sketching tools appearing beside each of the three data rearranging buttons. Tools include the option of four different colors, an eraser, and a *Clear All* function. Drawings (Figure 2(d)) can be made via direct touch.

DESIGN CRITIQUE AND REFLECTIONS

To evaluate the concept of tabletop interfaces for collision reconstruction and discuss shortcomings and potential improvements of *Re-Collision*, we conducted a focus group session with the CPS, including the same officers who participated in our initial meetings. After a short introduction to the functionalities and features of the interface, the participants were invited to freely interact with the tabletop and critique, pointing out limitations and suggesting improvements. The session was videotaped for later analysis. We discuss some of the highlights of this session, from a perspective of validation of tabletops for the domain as well as relevant directions to guide subsequent design efforts.

Tabletops for Awareness, Communication and Collaboration

One of the discussed benefits of the interface included facilitated communication between non-experts, or experts from different domains, as stated by a collision reconstruction investigator: *"I can see the benefit of being able to show the forensic interview team exactly what the information is"*. It was also highlighted that the facilitated access and handling of data through tabletops could contribute to a better understanding of particularly complex and data-intensive cases. A member of the forensic unit acknowledged, *"I believe that this type of interface would benefit in the more complex protracted investigations"* and also *"(...) the volumes of information and to be able to continually collaborate for two years, to have information continually added, and to have a tabletop such as this where you can access information from day 'one' would be beneficial"*. Finally, with the use of tabletops, we hoped to provide an inviting medium to stimulate user's contributions, and thus spark positive collaboration amongst investigators. During the session, although users were not asked to simulate an investigation, they were actively interacting and reasoning with the data as a group. We considered this particularly meaningful, given that the forensics and the collision reconstruction teams work on completely different sectors within the CPS. We believe the tabletop environment might have contributed to empower and stimulate users to partake in the discussion and the interaction experience.

Potentializing Analysis – Implications for design

The focus group also generated many ideas for improvement, which at the same time embody fundamental concerns to domain users – also well aligned with topics such as clutter, awareness and sense-making brought forward by Morris *et al.* [8]. We reflect upon them in the form of a preliminary list of design implications to guide future efforts. We believe our guidelines may apply to not only to collision reconstruction but also to other forensics tabletop applications and possibly analogous domains.

1. Effectively de-clutter the visualization space: we observed that the members seemed comfortable manipulating the data and showed no problems correlating the collision scene diagram areas and associated evidence. However, the limited amount of surface area quickly became evident, as soon as all users started manipulating photographs simultaneously, and each decided to drastically enlarge their set of photographs. We suggest taking into account strategies to facilitate parallel evidence fetching, as well as effective evidence management for a coherent and organized workspace. Suggested ideas also revolved around the idea of external personal spaces (*e.g.* tablets), for individual manipulation.

2. Facilitate efficient sense-making through information correlation: the experts stated the importance of strengthening connections amongst stored data, for instance through user-defined data links between related pieces of evidence: *e.g.* associating the appearance of a witness on a surveillance video to the document containing her official written testimonial alleging icy road conditions, which in turn links to the corresponding weather report at the occasion. Alternatives for search mechanisms were discussed, as useful resources for facilitating navigation and retrieval to enable analysis of larger volumes of data.

3. Provide evolution awareness on the case: the officers emphasized the importance of awareness of the temporal progression of the case: for example, being able to load a scene and browse it over time, seeing its evolution from the initial investigation stages to later conclusion. This exercise of past recollection is often employed when briefing external people into a case, and direct support to this would be very beneficial.

4. Supporting hypothesis creation and testing: much of the reasoning process the officers described for an investigation relies on the evaluation of hypotheses – e.g. "*Mr. X claims not to be able to see Mrs. Y driving from the adjacent road; Is this possible? Where could he be located at that time?*". The *Sandbox* layer — which in this prototype was limited to sketching — in essence could encompass any reasoning over the evidence data, as well as resources to support and assess this reasoning, such as user-defined potential vehicle trajectories associated to physically-based simulations to visualize and compare the several outcomes.

CONCLUSION

In this work, we investigated the use of tabletops applied to the domain of collision reconstruction, with a focus on *spatiality*, *emphasis on the facts*, *efficiency*, and *collaboration*. Our design approach involved the participation of expert officers from the CPS, from initial brainstorming stages to the various prototyping stages of Re-Collision, and the focus group evaluation which helped provide insight into domain aspects, assess the potential of tabletops for the field and reflect on a set of implications for design. We hope these initial research efforts will trigger a greater interest on the domain from an HCI perspective, which we believe would be extremely beneficial for both fields and of great impact to society.

ACKNOWLEDGEMENTS

We would like to thank Staff Sergeant Jolayne Anderson and her colleagues from the CPS Forensic Crime Scenes Unit for their help and participation in our study, as well as the anonymous reviewers for their valuable feedback.

REFERENCES

1. Aras 360°. http://www.aras360.com/
2. Atzenbeck, C., Hicks, D. L. and Memon, N. Supporting emergent knowledge and team communication in police investigations. In *Proc. of the IEEE international conf. on Intelligence and security informatics*, (2009), 95-100.
3. Borglund, E.A.M. and Nuldén, U. Personas in uniform: police officers as users of information technology. In *Proceedings of ECIS* (2006), 1105-1116.
4. Chen, H., *et al.* COPLINK: managing law enforcement data and knowledge. *Communication of the ACM* 46, 1 (2003).
5. Cheung, V., Cheaib., N., and Scott, S. Interactive surface technology for a mobile command centre. In *CHI '11 extended abstracts on Human factors in computing systems*, ACM (2003), 1771-1776.
6. Colton, K.W. The impact and use of computer technology by the police. *Communications of the ACM* 22, 1 (1979).
7. Luderschmidt, J *et al.* Vispol: An Interactive Tabletop Graph Visualization for the Police. In *Mensch & Computer 2012: interaktiv informiert – allgegenwärtig und allumfassend!?*, Oldenbourg Verlag (2012), 63-72.
8. Morris, M.R, Lombardo, J., and Wigdor, D. WeSearch: supporting collaborative search and sensemaking on a tabletop display. In *Proc. of the ACM Conf. on Computer supported cooperative work*, ACM (2010), 401-410.
9. Nuldén, U. Investigating police patrol practice for design of IT. In *CHI '03 extended abstracts on Human factors in computing systems*, ACM (2003), 820-821.
10. PC-Crash. http://www.pc-crash.com
11. Quick Scene. http://www.cadzone.com
12. Smart Draw. http://www.smartdraw.com
13. Song, Y., Cummings, M. L., Ahmad, S. and Davis, R. Emergency Response System On a Pen- Based Tabletop Display. In *Conference on Interactive Tabletops and Surfaces (ITS'09)* (2009).
14. The Crash Zone. http://thecrashzone.com
15. Zhao, J.L., Bi, H.H. and Chen, H. Collaborative workflow management for interagency crime analysis. In *Proc. of the 1st NSF/NIJ conf. on Intelligence and security informatics (ISI'03)*, Springer-Verlag (2003), 266-280.
16. Zhao, *et al.* Process-driven collaboration support for intra-agency crime analysis. *Decision Support Systems* 41, 3 (2006), 616-633.

Investigating Mid-Air Pointing Interaction for Projector Phones

Christian Winkler
University of Duisburg-Essen, Germany
christian.winkler@paluno.uni-due.de

Ken Pfeuffer
University of Duisburg-Essen, Germany
ken.pfeuffer@stud.uni-due.de

Enrico Rukzio
Ulm University, Germany
Lancaster University, UK
enrico.rukzio@uni-ulm.de

ABSTRACT
Projector phones, mobile phones with built-in projectors, might significantly change the way we are going to use and interact with mobile phones. The potential of combining the mobile and the projected display and further the potential of the mid-air space between them have yet to be explored. In this paper we assess these potentials by reporting two user studies: First, an experimental comparison of four techniques for target selection on the projection, including interaction on the touchscreen of the projector phone as well as performing pointing gestures in mid-air around the phone. Our results indicate that interacting *behind* the phone yields the highest performance, albeit showing a twice as high error rate. Second, a follow-up experiment where we analyzed the performance of the two best techniques of the first study within realistic mobile application scenarios such as browsing and gaming. The results show that mobile applications benefit from the projection, e.g., by overcoming the fat-finger problem on touchscreens and increasing the visibility of small objects. Our findings speak for the integration of a tracking camera at the bottom of the projector phone to enable mid-air pointing interaction.

Author Keywords
Projector phone; selection; target; pointing; gesture.

ACM Classification Keywords
H.5.2 [Information interfaces and presentation]: User Interfaces - Input devices and strategies.

INTRODUCTION
An inherent issue of mobile phones with touch screens is their small size, which is on the one hand essential for their mobility but on the other hand significantly limits the available space for input and output of information. While some years ago miniaturization of mobile devices seemed to be the ultimate goal of mobile phone manufacturers, nowadays we see mobile phone sizes and resolutions expanding again. The emergence of pico projectors and in particular projector phones, i.e. phones with built-in projectors, provides a versatile solution for this issue: users can project and interact with a large display almost anywhere and at any time. Such projector phones also support various forms of collocated media viewing, browsing and interactions which are not possible with conventional mobile phones.

Currently available projector phones (e.g. Samsung Beam, Sharp SH-06C) or accessory projectors (e.g. the SHOWWX+ from Microvision) that can be connected via TV-out to a conventional phone only mirror what is usually shown on the touch screen [18]. Projecting the touch screen user interface while maintaining the same interaction style must lead to suboptimal interactions as it requires many context switches during operation and because those interfaces were designed for high resolution screens with small dimensions operated through direct touch input.

Using a pointer as an intermediate that marks the current position on the projection is a basic way to overcome some of these problems. In particular, using the touchscreen of the mobile phone for indirectly controlling a mouse pointer on the projection requires no additional hardware and has been the focus of various research projects and products, e.g. [15]. The conceptual disadvantages are the indirectness and the unavailability of the touchscreen for interaction or as information display since it is occupied as a touchpad.

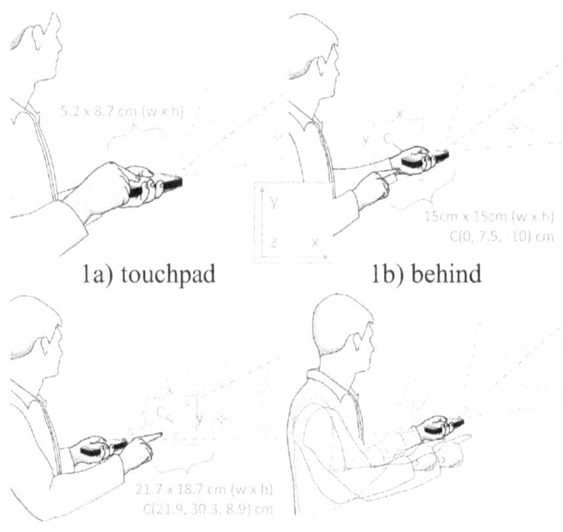

1a) touchpad 1b) behind 1c) group defined 1d) user defined

Figure 1. Compared pointing techniques. 'C' denotes the central point of the interaction area in relation to the projector phone position (0, 0, 0).

ITS'12, November 11–14, 2012, Cambridge, Massachusetts, USA.
Copyright 2012 ACM 978-1-4503-1209-7/12/11...$10.00.

Using mid-air finger-pointing techniques is an interesting alternative due to the more direct interaction and the possibility to use the mobile phone screen as secondary in-/output to the projection. Further, these techniques neither require the user to carry additional hardware nor do they require movement of the phone that interferes with the projection as accelerometer based interactions would do for instance. Thus they seem very suitable for typical ad-hoc mobile scenarios. However, the mid-air space around the user is quite large and unexplored considering the bimanual and interdependent control. So far it is unclear which interaction area will be optimal and how well users will be able to manage the dual-display, bimanual interaction.

To open this area of research we investigated the performance of three mid-air finger-pointing techniques leveraging different interaction areas (see Figure 1b-d) compared to the existing *touchpad* technique (Figure 1a). We compared the techniques through an experimental user study based on the ISO 9241-9 tapping task. Our results indicate that the interaction technique in which the user points *behind* the mobile phone to control a cursor on the projection performs significantly better than other mid-air techniques in all scenarios. Even more, it also performs ~15% faster than the *touchpad* option despite yielding ~2.5 times more errors. This makes it an interesting alternative interaction technique for a variety of application scenarios, even without considering its aforementioned advantage of keeping the touchscreen free.

In a follow-up experiment, we compared the interaction techniques *touchpad* and *behind* in common usage scenarios such as browsing, gaming, and drawing in order to analyze their performance in realistic contexts. Also, we included a standard smartphone without a projector in our comparison in order to analyze the performance of the projector phone interaction techniques in contrast to the current usage of a smartphone. Results of the second study confirm the familiarity of users with standard *touchscreen* phones but also highlight various advantages for the projector phone interaction techniques, e.g., in terms of not occluding targets on the screen, improved visibility, the usage in collaborative settings, and joy of use.

RELATED WORK

Interactions with a projector phone can be classified into four different categories: using controls on the phone, moving the phone, directly interacting with the projection and manipulation of the projection surface [18]. Most currently available solutions use the touchscreen of the mobile phone for input which requires no additional hardware but suffers from the separation of input (phone) and output (projection). This could lead to a large number of context switches as the user has to switch her focus constantly between the projection and the phone in case the phone screen is used for displaying information [6,8]. Moving the phone in order to perform interactions is another possibility but works mainly for simple commands and has the disadvantage that the projection moves as well [2,4]. Directly touching the projection of a projector phone or pico projector has recently been investigated but requires the user to be very close to the projection surface [9,22]. This limits the size of the projection through which collocated collaborations cannot be supported optimally.

The usage of the touchscreen as a *touchpad* is an effective approach for controlling a cursor on a remote screen (Figure 1a) [13]. The advantage of this concept is that it is already very familiar from touchpads found on laptops. Conversely, it has the disadvantage that while using the screen as a touchpad, there is no easy alternative to interact with the content on the mobile phone screen at the same time. One possible solution would be a hardware button on the side of the device to toggle between touchscreen and touchpad mode. While this seems feasible it still would not allow for interactions where both displays are simultaneously active, e.g. for seamless dragging of pictures from phone display to projection.

Recently researchers started to look at the usage of finger pointing and hand gestures for controlling interactions due to improved tracking technology. *SideSight* explored gestural interactions around a mobile phone to increase the input space on small devices [3]. Similarly, researchers looked at direct interactions with personal projections. Shadow interactions as described e.g. by Cowan and Li [7] are not applicable for single user scenarios as depicted in Figure 1, though, as the fingers are very close to the projector and this leads to very large shadows occluding a large area of the projection.

In the first study we aimed for investigating how well simple pointing tasks and target selections can be performed on the projection from a projector phone. Remote pointing has extensively been researched on large *fixed* projections. The *Pointable* facilitates remote interaction with distant targets on large tabletop displays through perspective pointing and ray-casting [1]. Pointing on vertical displays has been researched in regard to the influence of effects like parallax and control type, different ray pointing techniques [12] and different devices like laser pointers [17] or bare hands [20] including various mid-air selection techniques [1,20]. However, the findings from this research strand can only partially be applied within the context of personal projectors as the mobile scenario is substantially different: The projection is constantly moving with the device. The user has to hold the projector phone during the whole interaction, which introduces jitter to the projection and the interaction, limits the possible movement area per hand and makes the interaction bimanual by nature. Further, mobile users usually do not want to carry or use additional hardware like a laser pointer or air mouse, why mobile interaction techniques have to get by with the user's bare hands. Since interaction happens in unaltered environments, the gaze of the user cannot easily be made available why image-plane ray-pointing techniques are unpractical and pointing must usually be based on the relation to the projector alone.

Remote mid-air pointing nevertheless has shown good performance why we decided to compare the usage of the touchscreen as a *touchpad* against mid-air pointing techniques. Both have much potential to enrich interaction in various situations and do not interfere with the projection.

INTERACTION TECHNIQUES

The aim of our research is a first exploration of mid-air pointing for projector phones. Since the area around the user is quite large, we considered different spaces around the device including behind, before, above, below, and to both sides of the device. All spaces have substantial implications on the usability (cf. [11]) and technical feasibility of the approach.

Through two preliminary user studies we discovered that interacting in front of the projector phone is not a well-suited space. While this might work for projectors worn around the neck such as in [14], interacting with the right hand in front of the projector that is held with the left hand requires that the right hand must be held very far away from the body. Additionally, the shadow on the projection created by the finger close to the projection occludes large parts of the projection. In contrast, when pointing with the index finger *behind* the projector phone (Figure 1b) to control a cursor on the projection, the user does not interfere with the projection. Further, it might allow for a convenient posture as the user is able to rest the upper arm of the pointing hand on the upper part of the body. Also, this technique is more independent of the user's girth.

In contrast, interacting to the right side of the device (respectively left side for left handed users) as well as interacting above or below the device poses a more difficult challenge for a real implementation: the necessity for maintaining an input space that is planar to the projection surface ($x \times y$ in Figure 1) assumed, the device would require a depth camera facing to the side of the device, providing the finger's horizontal x-movement via depth sensing. Similarly, an upward facing depth camera would have to provide vertical y-movement via depth sensing for interaction above the device. Despite mobile depth sensing is gaining ground as recently presented by Omnitouch [9], commodity hardware with sufficiently precise depth sensing cannot be expected to become available on mobile devices soon. Therefore, we refrained from *specifically* designing input spaces above/below or beside the device.

Instead we wanted to learn and also lay more stress on participant's own likings for input (which could include any desired space around the device) following a user-elicited approach. Therefore, we derived the *group defined* technique from a separate previous assessment where we tracked pointing preferences of 27 people. Participants (7 female, 20 male) of this study were undergraduates with an average age of 23 and have not had any prior experience with our work. Each participant was asked to define their preferred input space by showing the pointing gestures they would perform when selecting the four corners of the projection by pointing at each corner three times while holding the projector phone (see Figure 2). Those pointing interactions were observed and measured by an optical tracking system. We calculated the average of those readings that led to an input space as specified in Figure 1c, which is on the top right side of the projector phone.

Figure 2. Pointing gestures performed for the definition of the input space for *group defined* and *user defined.*

The *user defined* technique (Figure 1d) is similar to *group defined* but here only the currently tested user defines her preferred input space by pointing three times at the four corners of the projection. *Group defined* and *user defined* follow the approach described by Nielsen et al. [16] in which users show how they would perform a certain interaction. As each user defined a different input area there was no common input space for *user defined* that we can provide. However, the average of users chose a 16.0 cm in width (SD=7.5) and 14.2 cm in height (SD=7.3) interaction space with its center lying at $\{6.8 \text{ cm x}, 20.3 \text{ cm y}, 9.7 \text{ cm z}\}$ (SD=9.8) away from the phone. In terms of size this would be similar to *behind* whereas the position would rather resemble *group defined.* Based on the different input sizes, the four techniques have slightly different control-display (C-D) gains. However, findings of Casiez et al. [5] indicate that C-D gain has a less important impact in studies modeled after Fitts' Law which our results will confirm as *behind* and *user defined* involved a very similar C-D gain but yielded significantly different results. Moreover, *touchpad*, in spite of having the highest C-D gain, was the slowest technique.

The actual selection of a target shown on the projection is in *all four* interaction techniques performed by a tap on any position of the touchscreen of the smartphone.

FIRST EXPERIMENT: TARGET SELECTION

The main goal of this experiment was to investigate whether finger pointing based techniques (controlled and user-elicited types) provide a similar performance in terms of target selection times and error rate when compared with *touchpad*. In addition, the experiment should clarify whether users perceive these techniques as beneficial. This experiment compares the previously described four techniques through a two-dimensional target selection task based on the ISO 9241-9 tapping test.

Participants

12 right-handed participants (6 female) took part in the experiment and were rewarded 10€ afterwards. All were undergraduate students and aged between 15 and 27 (mean = 23 yrs.). Their academic backgrounds were humanities, economics, and computer science.

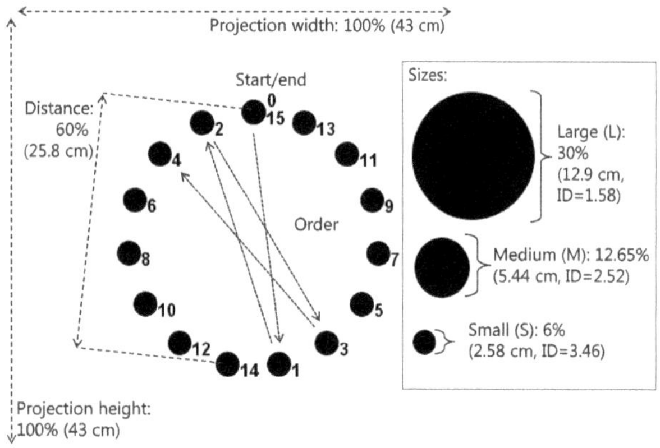

Figure 3. ISO 9241-9 task. Visualization of size and height of projection in relationship to the three target sizes.

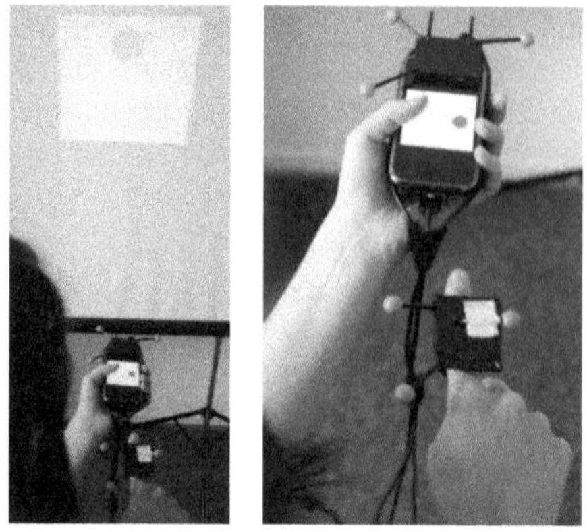

Figure 4. Study setting (for *behind*) and used hardware (participants did not look at phone display).

Experimental Design

The experiment used a within-subjects design, i.e. all participants participated in all conditions of the experiment (counterbalanced). The first independent variable *technique* contained four levels: *touchpad*, *behind*, *group defined* and *user defined*. The second independent variable *size* of targets contained three levels: small, medium, and large (see Figure 3). The smallest target size was defined through a preliminary test were we looked for the smallest size that could be comfortably selected with *touchpad*.

Prototype and Setup

We assume that the three finger pointing based interaction techniques can be realized through an additional camera on the bottom and / or side of the projector phone. Corresponding algorithms and approaches like coarse-grained depth tracking for background removal or IR-camera sensing have been reported previously, e.g. [9,14,21]. We used an external optical tracking system (OptiTrack V100:R2, 100Hz from NaturalPoint) and infrared markers attached to the user's finger and the projector phone in order to support accurate tracking of the index finger in relation to the phone (Figure 4). With this approach it is possible to compare the interaction techniques independently from a potentially inaccurate tracking solution. A SHOWWX pico laser projector from Microvision connected to a Samsung Galaxy S was used as no projector phone has been commercially available in the country where the study was conducted.

The software used for conducting the study was written in Java and executed on the Android phone. Apart from running the study tasks and logging phone properties such as acceleration sensor values, the software also performed the pointer calculations based on the input from the tracking system in real-time. Pointer movement worked instantly without any noticeable delay. For the *touchpad* technique we implemented pointer acceleration similar to the algorithm used in Microsoft Windows [24]. Thus, and because the screen size was notably bigger than the farthest distance between targets, clutching was not required with *touchpad* in the first study.

Procedure

The experiment was conducted in a light dimmed laboratory room. The position of the participant was marked with an X on the floor, facing a wall 100cm away, resulting in a projection screen size of 43x43cm (see Figure 3 and 4). A user standing in front of a nearby wall is considered as typical scenario for mobile usage of projector phones. Participants were asked to stay at this location throughout the study. Participants were holding the projector phone with their left (non-dominant) hand (see Figure 1 and 4), and pointing with the other hand. Participants were allowed to freely move the projector and their finger as only their spatial relation defined the position of the pointer.

Participants took part in the study individually. Initially, to define the *user defined* technique, the participant was instructed to point three times at each corner of the projection as they would want to point at them in the subsequent experiment. After that the experimenter explained and demonstrated the four interaction techniques and asked participants to rate each interaction technique on a 10-point Likert scale (1 – very bad to 10 – very good) based on their sole expectation. Then, each technique was tested with three different target sizes. For each of the 12 possible combinations of interaction technique × size the participant performed 1 test and 3 consecutive study rounds, each including 15 targets (see Figure 3). In each round, the user started with a click (tap any position of the phone screen) on the circle in the middle, then went to the first circle at the top from which on the time taken to every subsequent target was measured. After the user's click the target turned to green (hit) or red (miss) for 150ms and only one trial per target was allowed. After each round the user was shown their time taken and the percentage of hit and missed targets. In addition we logged hit locations and jittering of the phone using the built-in accelerometer. After each technique, participants rated the technique regarding perceived speed, precision, satisfaction, difficulty and fatigue. Finally, participants were asked to rate each interaction technique again on the 10-point Likert scale from before based on their actual experiences.

Results of first experiment

Movement times and error rates measured are depicted in Figure 5 and 6. Movement time (*MT*) is defined by the duration between the occurrence of the target on the projec-

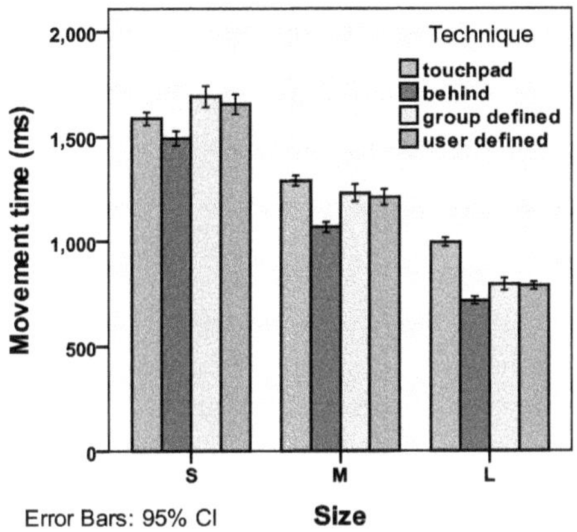

Figure 5. Movement times.

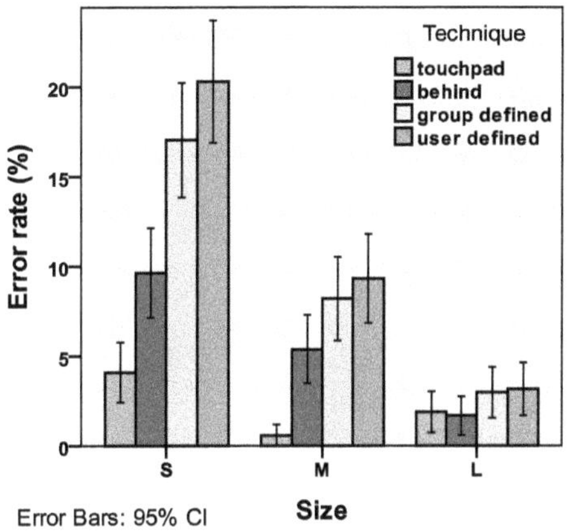

Figure 6. Error rates.

		Movement time	Error rate
Technique	η^2	161.850	162.925
	$\varepsilon_{G.-Geisser}$	.864	.857
	df	2.591	2.570
	df_{Error}	1386.343	1374.708
	F	73.587	38.147
Size	η^2	52.744	106.886
	$\varepsilon_{G.-Geisser}$	.914	.846
	df	1.828	1.693
	df_{Error}	978.017	905.705
	F	2251.249	95.670
Tech. x size	η^2	445.843	489.437
	$\varepsilon_{G.-Geisser}$	.767	.777
	df	4.603	4.663
	df_{Error}	2462.472	2494.854
	F	20.886	10.029

Table 1. ANOVA and post-hoc analysis of measured data.

tion and the selection of the target. An error is defined as click outside the target area. The results reveal *behind* to require a 15.4% shorter average movement time than *touchpad* when considering all sizes. The results also reveal a 2.55 times lower error rate of *touchpad* compared to the second best error rate of *behind* that we will discuss later.

Movement times (MT) and error rates (ER) were analyzed using a factorial repeated-measures ANOVA. Since sphericity had been violated for all effects, degrees of freedom were corrected using Greenhouse–Geisser estimates of sphericity (Table 1). According to this the main effects and the interaction effect were reported as significant ($p < .001$). The main effect *technique* and the interaction effect *technique × size* (split by *size*) were further post-hoc analyzed using pairwise comparisons of means with Bonferroni correction (for 6 and 18 comparisons respectively):

- $MT \times technique$: There were significant differences in movement time between all techniques ($p < .01$) except for *group defined* vs. *user defined*. Hence, users performed fastest with technique *behind* and slowest with *touchpad* ($MT_{touchpad} = 1291ms$, $MT_{behind} = 1092ms$, $MT_{group\ defined} = 1239ms$, $MT_{user\ defined} = 1217ms$).
- $ER \times technique$: The error rate significantly differed ($p < .001$) between all techniques except for *group* vs. *user defined*, revealing that users made the most errors with *group* and *user defined*, less with *behind*, and least with *touchpad* ($ER_{touchpad} = 2.2\%$, $ER_{behind} = 5.6\%$, $ER_{group\ defined} = 9.4\%$, $ER_{user\ defined} = 10.91\%$).
- $MT \times technique \times size$: No significant differences were found between *group* vs. *user defined* (S/M/L), *touchpad* vs. *group defined* (M) and *touchpad* vs. *user defined* (M). *Touchpad* vs. *user defined* on sizes S, M were reported significantly different ($p < .05$). Remaining differences were reported as significant ($p < .01$).
- $ER \times technique \times size$: On target size S, all pairs revealed significant differences ($p < .01$) except *group defined* vs. *user defined*. On size M, only *touchpad* vs. all other techniques showed significant differences ($p < .01$). Size L revealed no significant differences.

For further evaluation of the results we used the Fitts' Law model and calculated throughputs (TP) as described in [19,23]. First all measurements of the circular tapping task were rotated to horizontal 0° and 16 of 6480 targets (0.25%) were filtered out as spatial outliers. Then we calculated the effective index of difficulty (ID_e) individually for each subject and condition (technique and target size) based on the users trials (successful or not) over all test rounds of the condition (3 rounds × 15 targets) using equation

$$ID_e = \log_2(A_e/W_e + 1) \quad (1)$$

where A_e is the average actual movement distance over all rounds for a particular combination [19] and W_e reflects the standard deviation of endpoints as

$$W_e = 4.133 \times SD_{x,y} \quad (2)$$

where $SD_{x,y}$ is the bivariate endpoint deviation calculated as the spread of hits $\langle x_i|y_i\rangle$ around the center of mass $\langle \bar{x}|\bar{y}\rangle$

$$SD_{x,y} = \sqrt{\frac{\sum_{i=1}^{n}\left(\sqrt{(x_i-\bar{x})^2+(y_i-\bar{y})^2}\right)^2}{N-1}} \quad (3)$$

Having ID_es for each subject, technique and target size, we calculated the individual throughput for each subject and technique using the mean-of-means approach [19], and the grand throughput by averaging individual throughputs. The grand throughputs, depicted in Figure 7, show a similar picture as the movement times. *Behind* outperformed other techniques, especially showing a 28.5% higher TP than *touchpad*. Our measured throughput of 1.957 for touchpad is in line with measured throughputs of traditional touchpad usage in the literature, which agrees on values between 0.99 and 2.9 [19]. As pointing on movable displays has not been studied before we can relate the throughput of *behind* to fixed pointing only. The *fixed-origin* pointing described by Jota et al. [12] shares with *behind* the similarity that the pointing ray depends on the user's finger *and* another point in space, which albeit is fixed. They measured throughput of ~3.4b/s for *fixed-origin* pointing – for one-dimensional tasks only, though. In this light, the throughput of *behind* pointing might be slightly smaller than similar pointing on fixed projections, which can be explained by the increased complexity of the bimanual control.

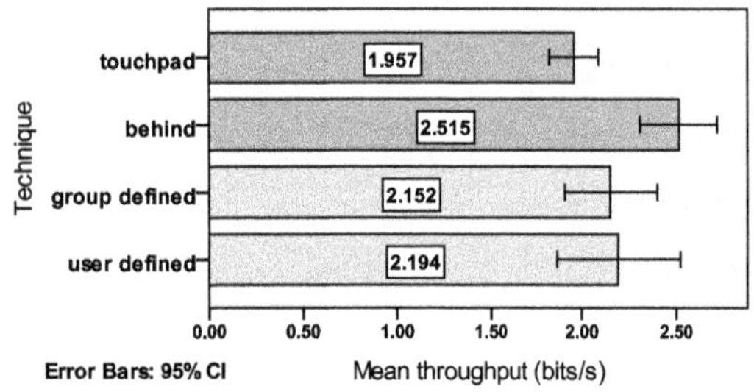

Figure 7. Grand throughput of interaction techniques (since *group* and *user defined* yielded a comparably high error rate close to or above 10% their calculated throughput values may be less meaningful).

A factorial repeated-measures ANOVA on throughput revealed a significant main effect of *technique* ($F_{3,33} = 6.219$, $p < .01$, $\eta^2 = 7.104$). Post-hoc pairwise comparisons with Bonferroni corrections showed no significant differences except for *touchpad* vs. *behind* ($p < .001$). Finally, we created Fitts' Law models of the form

$$MT_{Technique} = a + b \cdot ID_e$$

using linear regression. The average model fits (Pearson *r*) and parameters (*a*, *b*) are given in Table 2 and fit the measured results well: In particular, it shows the lower initial time required to start moving in mid-air (*a* of *behind*) as well as the smaller slope *b* of *touchpad* that indicates faster movement on the touchscreen for targets with a higher *ID*.

Technique	*a*	*b*	*r*
Touchpad	442.33	333.5	.953
Behind	-222.17	492.67	.937
Group defined	-735.42	795	.862
User defined	-563.25	741.58	.938

Table 2. Fitts' Law parameters and model fits.

After the study we asked participants to rate each interaction technique again on the 10-point Likert scale (1 – very bad to 10 – very good interaction) from before. Here *touchpad* performed best (average rating prior experiment 7.31, after the experiment 7.38) directly followed by *behind* (6.31, 7.31) that increased an entire point. Conversely, decreasing differences were found between *user defined* (7.46, 6.31) and *group defined* (6.46, 5.85).

We collected participants' ratings (Likert scale 1 – 7) after completing the tasks with each technique. Participants rated perceived speed, accuracy, fatigue of different body parts and selected questions from the Nasa TLX [10]. Participants' feedback delivered an overall similar picture to quantitative results in terms of speed, precision [*touchpad* (*MED* 6) slightly better than *behind* (*MED* 5)], difficulty and user satisfaction. As expected, overall fatigue was the lowest and almost non-existent with *touchpad. Behind* was rated the second best on fatigue scales overall (left/right finger, hand, wrist, and shoulder) but was rated one point worse than other pointing techniques for left hand, left arm, and left shoulder fatigue – the body parts involved in holding the projector. This can be explained by the fact that the projector had to be held slightly further away from the upper body

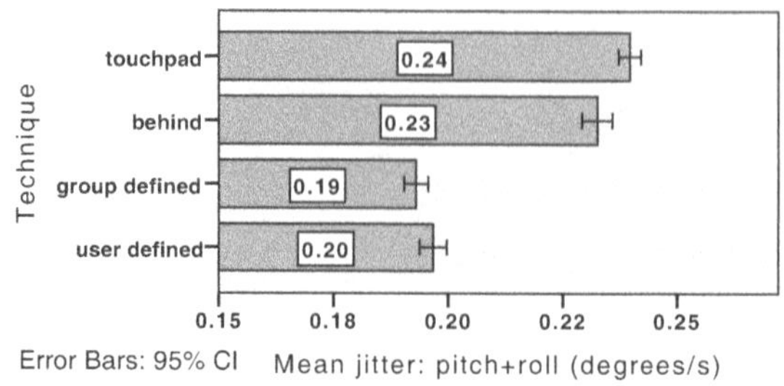

Figure 8. Mean phone jitter (pitch+roll) measured as the sum of differences over time.

to not interfere with the pointing right hand. The latter is supported by our analysis of phone jitter (Figure 8) which shows *behind* to cause the highest jitter among the mid-air pointing techniques. For right-sided body parts fatigue was rated as almost non-existent in contrast.

Discussion of first experiment

Contrary to our initial expectations, the experiment revealed a significant difference between *behind* and the other techniques. The difference between *behind* and *group defined / user defined* can mainly be explained by the fact that the independent group of 27 people who provided the information for the input space of *group defined* and the participants of our study preferred on average an area on the right top side of the projector phone. Users seem to choose this area because it allows them to move the right arm freely, unrestricted by the upper body or the projector phone. The negative implication of this area is that upper arm, lower arm, and finger have to be controlled simultaneously. Based on our results it seems that most participants were not able to control the attitude of their pointing arm exactly and steadily enough in those two interaction techniques. This caused pointing jitter, inaccurate pointing and arm fatigue.

When using the *behind* technique participants were able to rest their upper arm of the pointing hand on the upper part of their body. Therefore, they had to control only their lower arm and index finger, which allowed accurate and steady pointing and led to lower arm fatigue. The results show that those advantages outweigh the disadvantage of *behind* that is the slightly limited input space. For instance it is more difficult to select areas on the bottom-left of the input space (see Figure 9), especially for corpulent and female users.

Compared to *touchpad* the interaction technique *behind* has the significantly lower movement times because the user needs less time to start moving in the air whereas *touchpad* requires to place the finger on the screen and overcome the initial resistance on the surface. However, *behind* is more vulnerable to errors for small and medium sized targets because of hand jitter and arm fatigue. This is less an issue with *touchpad* because it is easier to brake or rest the finger on the touchscreen surface. In real usage scenarios it will likely depend on the type of application whether the faster movement time or the higher error rate will have the higher impact. For instance, *behind* will likely perform worse than *touchpad* for text entry on the projection as errors are very

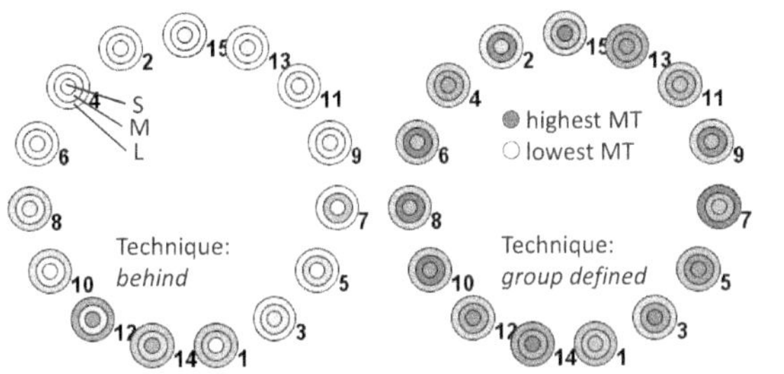

Figure 10. Target heat maps of *behind* and *group defined* averaged over all users showing movement times (MT) for the target sizes (S, M, L) and the overall benefit of *behind* despite the problematic area at the bottom left.

frustrating for the user in this scenario. During browsing a website on the other hand, being 15% quicker in general might easily compensate for missing every 18th link (5.6% error rate). Furthermore, if the application made good use of the dual-display setup enabled by mid-air techniques like *behind*, e.g. a browser showing an overview of open tabs on the touchscreen and the currently active tab on the projection, the user interface could benefit further in terms of speed, clarity and user satisfaction.

SECOND EXPERIMENT: APPLICABILITY

Before we can study dual-display mobile applications with projector phones, though, we need to test how the superior mid-air technique *behind* compares to the *touchpad* technique in real world application scenarios with *unaltered* mobile applications. We further added the standard mobile touchscreen usage as third technique that would allow participants and us to distinguish between the impact of the projection and the interaction technique.

Participants

For the second experiment we recruited the same 12 participants from the first experiment to ensure they had the same amount of practice with the projection techniques. All of them owned a laptop and were hence familiar with touchpads and all but P4 and P7 (10 of 12 participants) owned a touchscreen phone themselves (only a few featured multi-touch or VGA+ resolution screens, though).

Experimental Design

The second experiment comprised two independent variables *technique* and *application*. Techniques consisted of *touchscreen* (the application was used on the mobile touchscreen without projection), and *touchpad* and *behind* (application was used on the projection, controlled via a cursor). We decided to test three specific applications that are likely to benefit from the larger projection or the different input technique instead of fielding the projection in tasks that are optimized for and advantageous (like private text entry) on the touchscreen. The three applications (Figure 10) and reasons for choosing them were as follows:

1. Browsing

Browsing has become one of the most common tasks performed on smartphones. With mobile phones reaching display resolutions comparable to laptops, websites can be used in "full site" or "desktop view" mode instead of their usually very restricted mobile versions. However, due to the small physical display size, this requires several zooming and panning operations by the user. In contrast, on the projection even small text can easily be read without zooming.

We used the standard Android browser in full screen mode (Figure 10a) in all three techniques. The participant always started with a Wikipedia article about San Francisco. Starting on this web page the experimenter asked the participant to follow one of three predefined paths (counterbalanced). On every path the participant had to scroll down to the table of contents of the article, and then navigate to one of three predefined sections (e.g. museums). Then, the participant had to perform twice: following a link (e.g. to the Wikipedia article of the Museum of Modern Art) and finding a certain piece of information (e.g. when the museum was established). All tasks required roughly the same amount of scrolling, reading, clicking and time.

2. Gaming

As games are ultimately diverse we acknowledge that a single game cannot be representative. However, it can provide a preliminary sense for a particular group of mobile gaming applications. Since a shooting game resembles much of the Fitts' Law tapping task, yet in a completely different setting, the popular app "Drunken Hunting" seemed to be a reasonable candidate. The goal in this game (see Figure 10b) is simply to shoot flying ducks by touching or pointing and clicking on them respectively. In contrast to other similar simple shooting games, it features targets at different sizes with shooting smaller ones yielding more points than larger ones. We anticipated that smaller targets would be easier to see and hit while displayed on the (large) projection than on the (small) screen because of the bigger size and the eliminated fat-finger problem. Every participant played two levels with each level comprising 10 shots.

a) Fullscreen Android Browser **b) Drunken Hunting game** **c) Painting (post-painting outlines)**

Figure 9. Applications used in the 2nd experiment.

3. Painting

With mobile phones taking over increasingly more traditional PC tasks, accurate pointing *and* steering gains importance. Painting combines both requirements very well and the huge number of downloads of painting applications in the app stores shows their increasing distribution. One obvious problem with painting, though, is the lacking accuracy caused by the fat-finger problem. With this application we want to research if the usage on the projection with the presented techniques increases the accuracy during the task.

We used the – at the time of writing top ranking – application "Paint Joy" from the Android market store. The task of the participant was to post-paint the outlines of a snail with house (Figure 10c). This image was chosen because it combines horizontal, vertical, and circular lines – the basic subset of every more complex painting task.

Prototype and Setup

Hardware Setup

For the second experiment we employed a different prototype as we wanted to maximize the user experience of different display sizes between phone and projected display. We therefore used a Samsung Galaxy Nexus Android phone featuring 720p HD resolution. This phone has the highest physical display size and resolution currently available on mobile phones. Hence it seemed to be the strongest competitor against a projection. Similarly, we wanted to provide a large, bright, and high quality projection. Since none of the currently available pico projectors supported HD resolutions or a brightness beyond 50 Lumens, we opted for the palm-sized projector Qumi Q2 from Vivitek. This projector provides the same 720p HD resolution and a brightness of 300 Lumens while still only weighing 617g. Phone and projector thus weighed 742g together. While this was possible to hold in one hand and use for a short time, we decided to additionally uphold the projector from a rod affixed to a tripod moving freely in all directions. Thereby we equilibrated the weight of the projector to some extent, but it still had to be uphold and steered by the user as it would have without equilibration (Figure 11b). The phone was attached in landscape mode (Android's default when connected to a projector) on a flexible plastic attached to the bottom of the projector. This construction allowed the user to hold the "projector phone" with one hand in *behind* mode (Figure 11a) and two hands in *touchpad* mode (Figure 11c). Participants could stand and hold the device comfortably while looking on an almost leveled projection, yet were required the typical balancing to preserve the levelness and position of the projection and cope with hand jitter as with a real projector phone.

Software

The pointing software was realized as an Android background service, which showed a shiny green cursor on top of all other Android windows and applications and intercepted all user touch events. Our background service processed these events and based on the current mode of interaction (*touchpad* or *behind*) sent them as new touch events to Android's input system. The latter was accomplished using Android's built-in monkey service, which we hijacked on our rooted device to send arbitrary touch events to the system. Additionally we attached to the native Linux events from the touchscreen. Overall, this gave us full control over Android's touch input handling to send our own events to the Android system and its built-in applications.

In both projector interaction modes clicking anywhere on the device resulted in a click at the current position of the cursor. In *touchpad* mode the cursor position was changed relatively to movement of the finger on the device (same as in the first experiment). Scrolling in the browser application and painting in the paint application was initiated with a double click from where on movement of the finger was passed through to the application until the finger was lifted up again (in *browsing* the cursor position remained fixed during scrolling). In *behind* mode the cursor was moved by moving the finger in mid-air just as in the first experiment. In this case, scrolling and painting was executed while the finger was down on the touchscreen, i.e. the website was "grabbed" with the left hand's finger and moved up or down by moving the right hand's finger in the air. The game only required positioning and clicking to shoot.

Procedure

We employed a within-subjects design as in the first experiment. Each participant tried each of the three techniques with each of the three applications (counterbalanced). Each application was used with each technique between 2 and 3 minutes. We followed a qualitative analysis approach that would reveal differences that have not become apparent in the first study. We instructed participants to think aloud during all interactions, which we recorded for later analysis. After having tried all 9 combinations we asked participants for their feedback about speed, accuracy, liking, joy of use, advantages and disadvantages of each technique and the projection in general. We were also interested in when,

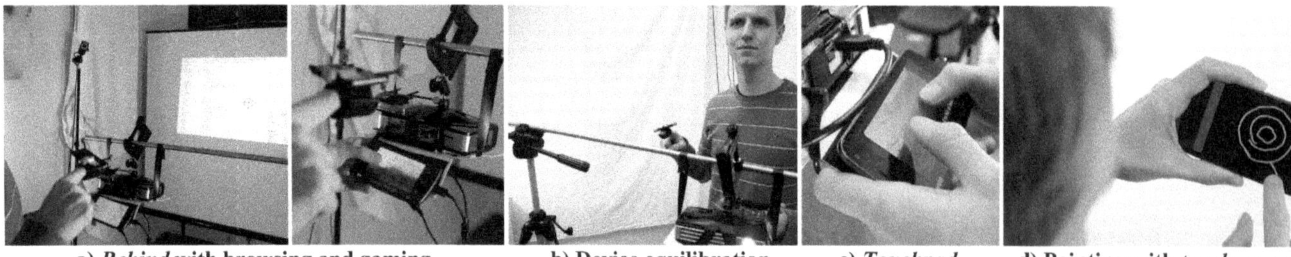

a) *Behind* with browsing and gaming b) Device equilibration c) *Touchpad* d) Painting with *touchscreen*

Figure 11. 2nd study prototype and techniques in use.

where, and for which applications participants would favor using the projection over using the touchscreen alone.

Results

Overall, the projection techniques were liked much by participants and more fun to use than *touchscreen* as reported by 9 participants. Partly, this has to be attributed to the novelty effect. Nevertheless, it indicates a positive user experience with both projection techniques, albeit being highly dependent on the application type.

In the browsing task *touchpad* was perceived as slower than other techniques by at least four participants since *touchpad* required a double-click to initiate scrolling which four participants perceived to slow down the interaction. In contrast, *behind* was reported to be very fast (P4, P5, P9) and precise (P3, P6, P10) as was *touchscreen* (7 and 8 participants respectively) despite the required zooming and panning steps. Especially in this task, those participants owning a high class smartphone and therefore being trained on getting by with the small screen for browsing performed much better with *touchscreen* while for novice smartphone users both systems seemed to perform equally well.

In the gaming task participants scored most successfully with the *behind* technique, which also felt intuitive (P1, P2, P8), but also became more aware of the freehand pointing jitter. P8 and P9 said "it was difficult to keep still". *Touchpad* was more affected by clutching than in other scenarios, as moving the pointer over long distances from a previous shooting target to the next required more than one movement. 4 participants said they felt constricted by the small touchscreen compared to the large projection (P6 said "I didn't know where I was on the screen with my finger"). But *touchpad* was on the other hand perceived as the most precise (6 participants) since targets that didn't move too fast could be hit more accurately than with any other technique. The *touchscreen* also performed fast but showed the problems that very small ducks could not be recognized on the small screen and that the finger occluded the targets at the expense of accuracy.

In the painting task 9 participants reported the fat-finger problem to hinder accurate painting on the *touchscreen*. Yet, *touchscreen* (Figure 11d) performed much better than *behind*, which was very unsatisfactory to use because of the comparably high jitter. Despite *behind*'s lower caused jitter compared to other mid-air techniques, the jitter is still too high for the technique to be qualified for steering tasks. Here, *touchpad* showed its huge advantage in that it, as P10 said, "combines the advantages of projection and touch-screen", namely the elimination of the fat-finger problem on one side and the haptic affordance of the touchscreen on the other that improves precision.

Further comments, independent of application, included that *behind* is an interactive performance like playing Wii (P5), which can be liked or disliked (as by P3 and P10 in our case). 3 participants also stated they would like to perform the click in the air, too, which we had thought about before but decided to stick to bimanual input as this will likely be the standard use case in future projector phone interaction. With *touchpad* participants liked that it feels familiar from laptops (P1, P3, P7) and requires little space (P2, P4) as well as little effort (P3, P5, P10) and therefore is more versatile in its application than *behind*. But it also requires a lot of movement on the touchscreen surface, which got uncomfortable over time for P7 and P9.

Discussion second experiment

The second experiment has shown that mobile applications indeed can benefit from a mobile projection. Despite private or public media broadcasting and collaboration, the projection can even enhance unaltered mobile applications that originally have been designed for touchscreens. Further, the advantages of the projection are very co-dependent on the usage scenario and can for instance be very useful to overcome the fat-finger problem on touchscreens or to increase the visibility and ease the selection of small objects on the display. Based on these findings we predict that new application-specific interaction techniques that sensibly integrate touch and mid-air interaction on both displays will largely enrich the projector phone experience.

LIMITATIONS

Even with comfortable arm postures such as with the *behind* technique, mid-air interaction might lead to higher fatigue than traditional solutions. Luckily, mobile situations rarely entail longsome series of interactions. Further investigation of fatigue, especially on larger mobile projections, also in respect to different C-D gains that might affect speed, accuracy, and fatigue, is required. In our studies we did not experiment with different C-D gains: the lower bound of C-D gain was set by the physical size of the touchscreen that we did not want to exceed to maintain comparability. Higher C-D gains in contrast might have decreased the accuracy of mid-air techniques further.

When testing the applicability of the techniques in common mobile scenarios we did not include all mobile factors such as interacting on the go or sudden breaks. In contrast to touch input, the mid-air techniques forbid pausing of the cursor as long as the user's hand is within the input area. Furthermore, we only evaluated existing mobile applications specifically designed for touch input. Studying applications designed for dual-display mid-air interaction will deliver further interesting results. Finally, people used to multi-touch performed the tasks of the second study quicker on the touchscreen, albeit acknowledging many advantages of the projection. However, the majority of participants were unacquainted with multi-touch for why we implemented *touchpad* interaction similar to laptop touchpads.

In terms of technical feasibility, the setup of both experiments used a precise external tracking system for position tracking during the mid-air techniques. A current implementation based on an embedded mobile camera with less hardware capabilities will likely not achieve the same accuracy/performance to the detriment of the mid-air techniques while touchpad performance could remain the same.

CONCLUSION

Projector phones raise various questions regarding their interaction design due to the large remote display, availability of various sensors, and movement of the projection. Most currently available commercial projector phones only mirror the information displayed on the phone display on the projection, involving frequent context switches and unsuited user interfaces. Using the *touchpad* interaction technique already provides a significant advantage as the user can focus primarily on the projection. But in real world scenarios the indirectness, the effect of clutching and the occupation of the screen diminish its applicability.

Our first study showed that more direct pointing using *behind* provides distinct advantages in terms of movement time and throughput when compared with *touchpad*, in particular when considering medium and large targets. The notably higher error rate of *behind* however makes it more suitable to application scenarios such as browsing and gaming and less to painting or text input. Interestingly, *behind* performed better than *group* and *user defined* although the latter two were gathered through a user-elicited approach.

The second study analyzed the user experience of *behind* and *touchpad* in relationship to conventional *touchscreen* usage. Here, we have seen that projection-based techniques (*behind, touchpad*) received overall equally good feedback as *touchscreen* despite not having been explicitly designed for the chosen applications. Furthermore, participants saw various disadvantages of touchscreens such as the fat-finger problem and numerous advantages of using a projection, e.g., for collaboration and application areas such as gaming.

Overall, our findings showed many advantages of the mid-air technique *behind*, which speaks for the integration of a camera at the bottom of the projector phone. Further, our research confirms that the interaction technique *touchpad* is an interesting option for future projector phones in particular as it comes for free. In our future research we will investigate *behind* further with dual-display mobile applications.

ACKNOWLEDGEMENTS

The presented research was conducted within the Emmy Noether research group "Mobile Interaction with Pervasive User Interfaces" funded by the DFG. We thank Markus Löchtefeld for helping proof-read the paper.

REFERENCES

1. Banerjee, A., Burstyn, J., Girouard, A., and Vertegaal, R. Pointable: an in-air pointing technique to manipulate out-of-reach targets on tabletops. *Proc. ITS 2011*, ACM (2011), 11–20.
2. Blasko, G., Feiner, S., and Coriand, F. Exploring Interaction with a Simulated Wrist-Worn Projection Display. *Ninth IEEE International Symposium on Wearable Computers (ISWC'05)*, 2–9.
3. Butler, A., Izadi, S., and Hodges, S. SideSight: multi-"touch" interaction around small devices. *Proc. UIST 2008*, ACM (2008), 201–204.
4. Cao, X., Forlines, C., and Balakrishnan, R. Multi-user interaction using handheld projectors. *Proc. UIST 2007*, (2007), 43.
5. Casiez, G., Vogel, D., Balakrishnan, R., and Cockburn, A. The Impact of Control-Display Gain on User Performance in Pointing Tasks. *HUMAN–COMPUTER INTERACTION 23*, 3 (2008), 215–250.
6. Cauchard, J.R., Löchtefeld, M., Irani, P., et al. Visual separation in mobile multi-display environments. *Proc. UIST 2011*, ACM (2011), 451–460.
7. Cowan, L.G. and Li, K.A. ShadowPuppets: supporting collocated interaction with mobile projector phones using hand shadows. *Proc. CHI 2011*, ACM Press (2011), 2707–2716.
8. Greaves, A. and Rukzio, E. Evaluation of picture browsing using a projector phone. *Proc. Mobile HCI 2008*, ACM (2008), 351–354.
9. Harrison, C., Benko, H., and Wilson, A.D. OmniTouch: wearable multitouch interaction everywhere. *Proc. UIST 2011*, ACM (2011), 441–450.
10. Hart, S.G. and Staveland, L.E. Development of NASA-TLX (Task Load Index): Results of Empirical and Theoretical Research. *Advances in Psychology 52*, (1988), 139–183.
11. Hinckley, K., Pausch, R., Goble, J.C., and Kassell, N.F. A survey of design issues in spatial input. *Proc. UIST 1994*, ACM (1994), 213–222.
12. Jota, R., Nacenta, M.A., Jorge, J.A., Carpendale, S., and Greenberg, S. A comparison of ray pointing techniques for very large displays. *Proceedings of Graphics Interface 2010*, Canadian Information Processing Society (2010), 269–276.
13. McCallum, D.C. and Irani, P. ARC-Pad: absolute+relative cursor positioning for large displays with a mobile touchscreen. *In Proc. UIST 2009*, ACM Press (2009), 153–156.
14. Mistry, P., Maes, P., and Chang, L. WUW-wear Ur world: a wearable gestural interface. *27th CHI extended abstracts*, ACM (2009), 4111–4116.
15. Myers, B.A., Stiel, H., and Gargiulo, R. Collaboration using multiple PDAs connected to a PC. *Proc. CSCW 1998*, ACM Press (1998), 285–294.
16. Nielsen, M., Störring, M., Moeslund, T., and Granum, E. A Procedure for Developing Intuitive and Ergonomic Gesture Interfaces for HCI. *Proc. GW 2003*, Springer (2004), 409–420.
17. Olsen,Jr., D.R. and Nielsen, T. Laser pointer interaction. *Proc. CHI 2001*, ACM (2001), 17–22.
18. Rukzio, E., Holleis, P., and Gellersen, H. Personal projectors for pervasive computing. *IEEE Pervasive Computing 11*, 2 (2012), 30 – 37.
19. Soukoreff, R.W. and MacKenzie, I.S. Towards a standard for pointing device evaluation, perspectives on 27 years of Fitts' law research in HCI. *International Journal of Human-Computer Studies 61*, 6 (2004), 751–789.
20. Vogel, D. and Balakrishnan, R. Distant freehand pointing and clicking on very large, high resolution displays. *Proc. UIST 2005*, ACM (2005), 33–42.
21. Wilson, A.D. PlayAnywhere: A Compact Interactive Tabletop Projection-Vision System. *In Proc. UIST 2005*, ACM Press (2005), 83–92.
22. Winkler, C., Reinartz, C., Nowacka, D., and Rukzio, E. Interactive phone call: synchronous remote collaboration and projected interactive surfaces. *Proc. ITS 2011*, ACM (2011), 61–70.
23. Wobbrock, J.O., Shinohara, K., and Jansen, A. The effects of task dimensionality, endpoint deviation, throughput calculation, and experiment design on pointing measures and models. *Proc. CHI 2011*, ACM (2011), 1639–1648.
24. Pointer Ballistics for Windows XP. http://msdn.microsoft.com/en-us/windows/hardware/gg463319.aspx.

Web on the Wall: Insights from a Multimodal Interaction Elicitation Study

Meredith Ringel Morris
Microsoft Research
Redmond, WA, USA
merrie@microsoft.com

ABSTRACT

New sensing technologies like Microsoft's Kinect provide a low-cost way to add interactivity to large display surfaces, such as TVs. In this paper, we interview 25 participants to learn about scenarios in which they would like to use a web browser on their living room TV. We then conduct an interaction-elicitation study in which users suggested speech and gesture interactions for fifteen common web browser functions. We present the most popular suggested interactions, and supplement these findings with observational analyses of common gesture and speech conventions adopted by our participants. We also reflect on the design of multimodal, multi-user interaction-elicitation studies, and introduce new metrics for interpreting user-elicitation study findings.

Author Keywords

Gestures, speech, multimodal input, user-defined gestures, participatory design, interactive walls, web browsers.

ACM Classification Keywords

H.5.m. Information interfaces and presentation (e.g., HCI): Miscellaneous.

INTRODUCTION

Marc Weiser's vision of ubiquitous computing [28] asserted that users would have access to an ecology of interactive devices at varying scales: "tabs" (small devices, a niche now filled by mobile phones), "pads" (mid-sized devices, a niche now filled by tablets and laptops), and "boards" (very large interactive surfaces). This last class of devices remains relatively rare, with large touch-screens such as those made by Perceptive Pixel [perceptivepixel.com], SMART [smarttech.com], and Microsoft [microsoft.com/en-us/pixelsense] costing several thousands of dollars, placing them out of reach of typical consumers. However, recent consumer technologies such as Microsoft's Kinect gaming device [kinect.com] can be used to cheaply add rich interactivity to user's televisions (the Kinect was introduced in 2010, costs about $150, and contains an array microphone and depth-camera). Unlike specialty multi-touch surfaces, TVs are quite common (96.7% of U.S. households had a TV as of 2011 [17]), and large-screen TVs (40'' diagonal and greater) are increasingly popular and cheap [25].

ITS'12, November 11–14, 2012, Cambridge, Massachusetts, USA.

Figure 1. Living room laboratory used in our study. Participants were seated on the couch facing the large-screen TV, which has a Kinect mounted on top.

In this paper, we employ a user-centered approach to investigate how the speech and gesture sensing afforded by devices like Kinect might support turning the TV from an entertainment device into one that enables casual interaction with more task-oriented applications. In particular, we focus on the use of a web browser, since the web is a rich and general platform whose uses span the gamut from leisure to productivity [9] and which is often used in a collaborative or social fashion [15], thereby making it suitable for multi-user settings like living rooms.

We conducted a study with 25 participants, many of whom described scenarios that have motivated them to desire the ability to interact with the internet on their TV from the comfort of their couch. We then describe an elicitation study in which these participants proposed speech and gesture interactions for fifteen common web browser functions (the *referents* [30]). We introduce two new metrics (max-consensus and consensus-distinct ratio) for analyzing user-elicitation studies, and present the most popular commands suggested by our participants. We also discuss common conventions and biases observed among our participants when designing and performing gesture and speech interactions.

RELATED WORK

We build upon prior work on web browser interaction techniques and on end-user interaction elicitation studies.

Browser Interactions

Researchers have considered various ways of updating the traditional web browser experience for large form-factor screens. For example, the WeSearch [14] and WebSurface [26] projects both reimagine the task of web search for a multi-user, multi-touch tabletop computer. The FourBySix system [12] illustrated how multiple mice and keyboards, combined with co-located projection when placed atop an interactive tabletop, could facilitate novel web search interactions. As in these projects, we are interested in the experience of web browsing and search in large-display, multi-user scenarios; however, we focus on interaction from a distance with a vertically-oriented television screen, rather than interaction with a tangible- or touch-sensitive horizontal surface.

WebGlance [19] was a prototype public electronic bulletin board (such as might be found in a train station), that enabled web browser interactions through the use of a cell phone – links were numbered so as to be selectable by a phone's keypad, enabling commuters to opportunistically engage with a browser on a public display. CoSearch [2] also allows a group of users to share control of a web browser on a single monitor (such as a public computer terminal in a library) through use of personal mobile phones. In contrast, we focus on using speech and gesture to control the browser, rather than mediation through a remote control or phone, and focus on a home-based rather than public use scenario.

Microsoft released a developer SDK for the Kinect in 2012 [kinectforwindows.org]. The DepthJS project [depthjs.media.mit.edu] is a JavaScript toolkit that augments the Apple Safari and Google Chrome browsers with the ability to recognize some Kinect inputs, such as gesture-based tab switching or button pressing. A 2011 competition by PrimeSense (developer of the Kinect depth camera technology) encouraged people to develop a "natural interaction based web browser app." The winning entry, SwimBrowser [swimbrowser.tumblr.com] allows users to use "swimming" gestures to perform functions such as forward/back navigation, zooming, and selecting bookmarks. In June 2012, shortly after we conducted our study, Microsoft announced the addition of web browsing functionality to its Xbox gaming system [27], controlled by a combination of voice commands and by the use of Windows phones and tablets as remote controls ("SmartGlass"). In this work, we consider how both the speech and gesture-recognition capabilities of a Kinect might be used to facilitate internet access on one's TV; however, we adopt a user-centered approach of interaction elicitation to gain insight into users' concerns and mental models surrounding this use case, as well as to identify interactions that are guessable [29, 30] by end users.

End-User Elicitation Studies

Participatory design [24] incorporates end-users into the design process. User-elicitation studies are a specific type of participatory design in which users are shown *referents* (an action's effects) and are asked to supply the corresponding *signs* (interactions that result in the given referent) [8, 30]. User-elicitation approaches are able to produce non-conflicting gesture sets [30], and to produce gestures that end-users find preferable to those designed by HCI professionals [16].

User-elicitation methodologies have been used to design a variety of gesture interface types, including multi-touch gestures [4, 5, 10, 18, 30], foot gestures [1], unistroke gestures [29], pen gestures [7], and mobile phone motion gestures [23]. In this work, we use this technique to design multimodal interactions enabled by a Kinect sensor, including speech and free-space gestures.

Some studies have used user-elicitation to generate vocabularies for speech-based interfaces, including [11, 21, and 22]. Mignot et al.'s study of a multimodal (speech + gesture) system for furniture layout [11] found that users preferred speech for more abstract commands and gesture for more straightforward ones. In this work, we examine when users choose to use speech, gesture, or both for the task of browsing the web on a TV in their living room, and identify common speech and gesture interactions for a set of fifteen browser functions, as well as discussing users' perceptions of the benefits and drawbacks of each modality.

STUDY DESIGN

To better understand users' current practices, desires, and concerns regarding the use of their television to browse the Web, we conducted a lab-based user study in April 2012. Because television-viewing is often a group activity, and because the appeal of using a large display for internet browsing (rather than a personal device such as a smart phone or tablet computer) is enhanced in multi-user settings [2, 15], we recruited groups of users to participate jointly.

The study took place in a lab set up to look like a living room, with a Kinect perched atop a wall-mounted 63'' TV. The TV was connected to a PC, and displayed output at a resolution of 1600 x 1200 pixels. Participants were seated on a sofa located 11 feet, 8 inches (3.56 meters) in front of the TV screen (Figure 1).

We recruited 12 groups of participants (11 pairs and 1 triad, for 25 total participants). Participants were external to our organization, and were paid for their time. Group members knew each other prior to the study, and played Kinect-based video games together at least once per month. Five groups consisted of spouses/romantic partners, four consisted of parents with their children, and three consisted of roommates/friends. Sample occupations included student, homemaker, network engineer, property manager, emergency medical technician, audio engineer, director of sales, and grocery cashier.

Ages ranged from 12 to 49 years old (mean of 25). 72% of participants were male. All participants had prior experience using Kinect (64% used it at least once per week; only 16% were self-described novices). All participants used a web browser at least once per day, and 92% used a search engine daily.

The study consisted of three parts. First, participants answered a series of interview questions about their current experiences and desires surrounding internet use while watching TV or playing Kinect. Next, participants participated in an elicitation exercise, in which they proposed speech and/or gesture commands for controlling a web browser on their television. Finally, participants individually completed post-study questionnaires.

For the elicitation portion of the study, participants were told that they would use their web browser on their television to plan a shared weekend activity. Participants were told that they could use any combination of speech and/or gestures that they felt a Kinect should be able to recognize in such a scenario, and that the experimenter would act as the "Wizard of Oz" and ensure that the system "reacted" properly to their envisioned commands.

The experimenter then walked the participants through a sequence of fifteen common browser functions, henceforth referred to as *referents* [30], in an order that would be plausible for the given scenario of weekend activity planning (Table 3). As in the methodology presented by Wobbrock et al. [30], for each command the experimenter stated the command name and demonstrated the *effect* of the command, then prompted the participants to suggest interactions that would *cause* this command to be executed. When participants demonstrated an interaction, the Wizard used the mouse and/or keyboard to produce the result of the command in the Web browser.

Participants were able to suggest more than one interaction, if desired, and were able to consult with each other during the elicitation process. Groups typically brainstormed several interactions together, and then identified which of the proposals they actually thought were "good" (these were the ones we recorded as proposed interactions). Note that group members did not always agree on what made a good interaction, and our methodology included noting which and how many members of each group "voted" for each proposal.

Participants, who had been seated on the couch for the interview portion of the study, were told that they were free to sit, stand, or otherwise move about, depending on what seemed most comfortable and realistic to them.

RESULTS

In this section, we present qualitative and quantitative results from our interviews with participants, the interaction-elicitation exercise, and the post-study questionnaire.

Use Scenarios

Participants were asked about scenarios in which they might find it beneficial to interact with a web browser on their TV both in an interview at the beginning of the study and on the post-study questionnaire.

Interview

During the pre-elicitation exercise interview, we asked participants whether they had ever had the experience of sitting together around their TV and wanting to use the web. Eight of the twelve groups (66.7%) indicated that this was a familiar scenario (and three indicated that they already attempted to use smartphones and/or laptops in their living room to fulfill such desires). These groups then described the information needs they had in this setting.

Gaming was a theme motivating living room search needs for four of the groups. This class of information need included looking up reviews of games the user was considering purchasing from their device's online game or app store, finding descriptions of new or upcoming games, and finding hints on how to beat current game challenges.

Television and movies was another common theme motivating a desire for living room search; this theme was also mentioned by four groups. Example tasks groups recalled wanting to complete included looking up a movie's show time in a local theatre, finding movies or TV shows the group might be interested in watching, looking up trivia about actors in programs currently being viewed, and accessing fantasy sports league websites and information while viewing live sports on TV.

A desire to use the internet to look up *general trivia* facts while in the living room was also relatively commonplace, being mentioned by three groups. Three groups also mentioned a desire to access *social media*, including social network sites and e-mail, as a supplement to their TV viewing or video-gaming experience.

Several groups also recalled more unique information needs that had prompted them to wish they could use their television as a platform for web browsing and search. One group mentioned that they often wished they could perform *online shopping* activities, such as further researching products seen in commercials during TV shows. Another described a desire to use their TV as a mechanism to *order food* for delivery while playing video games. One group mentioned a desire to use their TV to search for *music* (on services like Pandora or YouTube) in order to provide background atmosphere for activities like video-gaming.

Post-Study Questionnaire

On the concluding questionnaire, participants used a five-point Likert scale to indicate how likely they would be to use a gesture + speech enabled browser on their TV for each of several scenarios. Table 1 summarizes these ratings, which suggest that participants overall were enthusiastic about using the web on their TV. "Choosing a movie" was the most popular scenario, followed by "trivia," whereas

Scenario	Median	Mean
choosing a movie to see	5	4.5
looking up facts and trivia	4	4.2
using social networking applications	4	4.2
finding and viewing photos online	4	4.1
selecting a restaurant	4	4.0
shopping online	4	3.8
research for work or school projects	4	3.6

Table 1. Participants indicated enthusiasm for using a Kinect-enabled web browser for a variety of tasks on the post-study questionnaire (using a five-point Likert scale).

"research for work or school projects" garnered the least enthusiasm. A Friedman test to evaluate differences in medians was significant, $\chi2(6, N=25) = 28.68$, $p<.001$. Follow-up pairwise comparisons using Wilcoxon tests confirms that the research/school scenario was significantly less appealing than choosing a movie ($p = .003$) or looking up trivia ($p = .028$), perhaps because the form factor and setting do not lend themselves well to longer, more in-depth, or less playful activities.

User-Defined Multimodal Browser Control Techniques

Participants proposed a total of 357 interactions for the fifteen referents, 170 of which were distinct (considering distinctness on a per-referent basis). Table 2 shows the breakdown of proposed interactions by modality – speech interactions were the most common, and multimodal interactions were quite rare. Gesture interactions tended to be more agreed upon, as reflected in their lower representation among distinct gestures than total gestures.

Each referent had a mean of 23.8 proposed interactions (11.3 distinct interactions). On average, 3.7 distinct gestures, 6.9 distinct speech commands, and 0.7 distinct multimodal commands were suggested for each referent.

Wobbrock et al. [30] introduced a formula for an *agreement score* for a given referent, where P_r is the set of proposed interactions for referent r, and P_i is the subset of identical proposed interactions for that referent (Equation 1):

$$A_r = \sum_{P_i \subseteq P_r} \left(\frac{|P_i|}{|P_r|} \right)^2 \quad (1)$$

However, this notion of agreement was formulated for studies in which each participant was constrained to suggest exactly one interaction per referent. Since participants in our study suggested as many interaction synonyms for a referent as they felt were appropriate, comparing agreement scores across referents is not meaningful. Consider, for example, the case of the *open link in separate tab* referent. This referent received three distinct proposals for multimodal interactions, each of which were suggested by a single participant, resulting in a score $A_{multimodal} = 0.33$. This referent also received 8 distinct gesture interaction proposals, 7 of which were suggested by a single user and

	Total Proposed Interactions	Distinct Proposed Interactions
Gesture	40.9%	32.9%
Speech	56.0%	60.6%
Multimodal	3.1%	6.5%

Table 2. Proportion of the 357 total and 170 distinct proposed interactions employing each modality. Speech interactions were suggested most often, but gesture interactions exhibited greater consensus.

one of which was suggested by three separate users, resulting in a score $A_{gesture} = .16$. This lower score for agreement in the gesture modality as compared to the gesture + speech modality conflicts with our intuitive understanding of "agreement" – we would expect a higher score in the gesture modality in this case, since there was a proposed gesture that exhibited consensus from three users, whereas all of the multimodal suggestions were singletons. This example illustrates how the agreement score does not correctly account for situations in which the size of P_r varies for different referents (or modalities within a referent, if that is the desired comparison). We therefore introduce metrics that better capture the notion of "agreement" for elicitation studies in which participants can propose an arbitrary number of interaction synonyms for each referent: *max-consensus* and *consensus-distinct ratio*.

The *max-consensus* metric is equal to the percent of participants suggesting the most popular proposed interaction for a given referent (or referent/modality combination). The *consensus-distinct ratio* metric represents the percent of the distinct interactions proposed for a given referent (or referent/modality combination) that achieved a given *consensus threshold* among participants; the default assumption is a consensus threshold of two, meaning at least two participants proposed the same interaction. These two metrics together convey a sense of both the peak and spread of agreement, either (or both) of which may be of interest depending on the target goal of an elicitation exercise. For example, if the goal is to design a system with a single, highly guessable command per referent, then max-consensus may be more important, whereas if the goal is to understand diversity of opinion surrounding a referent, or conceptual complexity of a referent [30], consensus-distinct ratio may be more helpful. More generally, referents achieving high values for both *max-consensus* and *consensus-distinct ratio* can be considered highly suitable for representation using user-elicited interaction, as such scores would be indicative of strong agreement on a primary interaction with few other contender interactions. Raising the consensus threshold above two may be applicable in scenarios where very high agreement among users is desired in a final command set.

Table 3 provides max-consensus and consensus-distinct ratios for each referent in our study, as well as breaking these metrics down by modality on a per-referent basis.

Referent	Max-Consensus	Consensus-Distinct Ratio	Max-Consensus (Gesture)	Consensus-Distinct Ratio (Gesture)	Max-Consensus (Speech)	Consensus-Distinct Ratio (Speech)
Open Browser	32%	0.471	32%	1.000	20%	0.462
Search Engine Query	24%	0.500	**4%**	**0.000**	24%	0.750
Click Link	52%	0.375	52%	0.500	12%	0.333
Go Back	28%	0.444	28%	0.600	28%	0.250
Go Forward	24%	0.500	20%	0.600	24%	0.400
Open Link in Separate Tab	**12%**	**0.059**	12%	0.125	**4%**	**0.000**
Switch Tab	28%	0.385	28%	0.500	16%	0.333
Find In Page	16%	0.308	12%	1.000	16%	0.300
Select Region	24%	0.333	24%	0.667	4%	**0.000**
Open New Tab	24%	0.333	24%	0.250	20%	0.400
Enter URL	28%	0.300	20%	0.333	28%	0.286
Reload Page	36%	0.667	12%	0.500	36%	0.750
Bookmark Page	28%	0.500	28%	0.500	20%	0.500
Close Tab	20%	0.455	16%	0.250	20%	0.571
Close Browser	24%	0.353	24%	0.250	12%	0.385

Table 3. The fifteen referents used for the input elicitation exercise. The sequence was chosen to create a logical narrative for the task of planning a weekend activity. The overall max-consensus and consensus-distinct ratio are shown for each referent (using a consensus-threshold of 2), as well as being broken down within each referent according to modality. The highest-scoring referent(s) for each metric are indicated with grey shading, and the lowest-scoring are indicated with a bold font. Values for multimodal interactions are not shown, since these were rarely proposed and never achieved any consensus.

Across all referents and modalities, mean max-consensus was 26.7% and mean consensus-distinct ratio was .399 (using a consensus threshold of two).

Gestures tended to exhibit greater commonalities among participants than speech interactions. Gestures had a mean max-consensus of 22.4%, whereas speech interactions had a mean max-consensus of 18.9%. Gestures also had a higher mean consensus-distinct ratio (.472) than speech interactions (.381). However, these differences between metrics for gesture and speech were not statistically significant. For individual referents, however, the difference in our agreement metrics varied quite a bit across modalities, suggesting that some referents may be best mapped to certain modalities. For instance, the referent *select region* appears better suited to gesture rather than speech interactions, as it achieved no consensus among speech commands, yet had a max-consensus score of 24% for gesture interactions and a consensus-distinct ratio of .667 for proposed gestures.

Table 4 shows the proposed interactions from our study having a consensus threshold of three. Note that this is a list of popular interaction suggestions, but it is not a conflict-free interaction set – for example, conflicting directions for the flick motion for the "go back" and "go forward" commands would need to be resolved; the proper way to do this is not necessarily straightforward, due to strong individual preferences for each underlying metaphor, as discussed in the next section.

Themes in Elicited Interactions

Our observations during the elicitation exercise identified several common themes in participants' actions and comments. These observations relate to the perceived benefits and drawbacks of the available interaction modality, conventions commonly adopted by participants (and sources of bias that may have unconsciously influenced these), and areas in which participants' preferences diverged sharply.

Modality

Overall, very few participants proposed multimodal interactions, instead choosing one modality or the other for a given command (only 11 of the 357 proposed interactions were multimodal). However, though most did not create multimodal interactions, users often proposed *multi-modal synonyms*, i.e., creating both a speech interaction and a gesture interaction as alternatives for the same command. P18 noted, "it's nice to have both options." P22 echoed that, saying "it would be really nice if there were multiple commands to use," and P6 said, "I would actually want a few options [to issue this command]." This desire for multi-modal synonyms seemed to stem from users' perceptions that both speech and gesture had modality-specific

Referent	Interaction	#
Open Browser	hand-as-mouse to select browser icon	8
	"open browser"	5
	"internet"	3
	"<browser name>" (e.g., "Internet Explorer," "Firefox," "Chrome")	3
Search Engine Query	"<query>"	6
	"search <query>"	5
Click Link	hand-as-mouse to select link	13
	"<link #>" *(assumes all links have a number assigned to them)*	3
Go Back	"back"	7
	flick hand from right to left	7
	hand-as-mouse to select back button	5
	flick hand from left to right	4
Go Forward	"forward"	6
	flick hand from right to left	5
	flick hand from left to right	5
	hand-as-mouse to select forward button	3
Open Link in Separate Tab	hand-as-mouse hovers on link until context menu appears, then hand-as-mouse to select menu option	3
Switch Tab	hand-as-mouse selects tab	7
	"next tab"	4
	"tab <#>" *(assumes all tabs have a number assigned to them)*	3
	flick hand	3
Find in Page	"find <query>"	4
	hand-as-mouse to select a find button, then type on virtual keyboard	3
Select Region	hand-as-mouse sweeps out diagonal of bounding box	6
	hand-as-mouse acts as highlighter, sweeping over each item to be included in region	3
Open New Tab	hand-as-mouse to select new tab button	6
	"new tab"	5
	"open new tab"	5
Enter URL	"<url>" (e.g., "its2012conf.org")	7
	type on virtual keyboard	5
	"go to <url>"	3
Reload Page	"refresh"	9
	"refresh page"	9
	move finger in spiral motion	3
Bookmark Page	hand-as-mouse selects bookmark button	7
	"bookmark page"	5
Close Tab	"close tab"	5
	hand-as-mouse to select close button on tab	4
	"close tab <#>" *(assumes all tabs have a number assigned to them)*	3
Close Browser	hand-as-mouse to select close button on browser	6
	"close browser"	3
	"exit"	3
	"exit all"	3

Table 4. User-elicited gesture and speech commands for a web browser on a living room TV. Only interactions with a consensus-threshold of three or higher are included due to space constraints; the number of participants suggesting each is shown in the "#" column. Gesture interactions that use "hand-as-mouse" may be referring to either "palm-as-mouse" or "finger-as-mouse" postures, and may use either dwell, click, or push as the selection technique, as described in the "Common Conventions" section.

drawbacks that might make them unsuitable under particular circumstances.

The primary perceived drawbacks of gesture input were related to ergonomics and exertion. For instance, P20 noted "I feel like my arm would get tired," and "I'm a big fan of the voice commands, because it takes less arm movement." P1 noted that for switching tabs "the speech command would be easiest because you don't have to move your arm." P8 noted that for closing the browser, speech was preferable "because it's easier." The use of two hands seemed to be perceived as particularly burdensome, with P13 noting that for clicking a link "I wouldn't want to use two hands," and P14 commenting, "I wouldn't want to use two hands for browsing, either… I would want to be doing things as simply as possible with one hand." This echoes prior findings in the domain of surface computing, in which users preferred simpler, one-handed interactions [16]. The fact that all users chose to remain seated on the couch during the entire elicitation exercise despite a reminder from the experimenter that they could move about if they wished, also suggests that users view this scenario as one in which exertion is undesirable. Another drawback of gesture input for this use scenario was the possibility of large gestures to invade companions' personal space – several partners had to scoot apart from each other on the couch in order to avoid accidentally hitting each other while performing gestures.

Speech input had perceived drawbacks as well. In light of the living room scenario, in which multiple users are often present and conversing, many users were concerned about the ability of a speech system to detect whether an utterance was intended as an interaction or as part of a conversation. For example, P14 noted a preference for gestures since they "can't get misconstrued by the machine." Some users prepended signifiers like "command" or "xbox" to their speech interactions in order to make them distinct from casual conversation.

Users were also concerned that speech input might be disruptive to other members of their households, such as in the evening if other family members were sleeping. For example, P12 created a gesture synonym for the "bookmark" command, noting that they wanted a gesture alternative so that they "could just do it quietly." Other groups had the opposite concern, that other members of the household would be so noisy that a system would not be able to distinguish speech commands from the ambient noise. For example, P16 noted, "our house is always loud... it would never work."

Sources of Bias

As in past gesture-elicitation studies that found users' ability to suggest gestures for new form-factors was heavily influenced by their experience with WIMP interfaces [4, 30], we saw that several types of past experiences influenced the types of gesture and speech commands users proposed. Despite the Kinect being a relatively new device (launched in November 2010, about 18 months before our study was conducted), a series of conventions around its use have already emerged in the gaming community, and their influence on our users' creativity was apparent, such as preceding speech commands with the signifier "xbox," using the term "bing" to signify a desire to perform a web search, performing a dwell action to select items on-screen, and waving a hand around to get the device's "attention" before performing a gesture. Several participants also mentioned that their impression of speech interfaces was based on their experience using speech to operate their mobile phones (such as for hands-free driving scenarios), and that poor recognition in such settings biased them towards creating gestures rather than speech commands for this new scenario.

Biases from traditional desktop computing scenarios also influenced participants' behavior, despite the living room setting. The concept of a "cursor" was prevalent, with most participants assuming that a traditional mouse cursor would track their hands movements on-screen. P12 hesitated when inventing a bimanual gesture, expressing concern that the system "would probably have to have two cursors or something." Similarly, people often treated their hand as a virtual mouse by tapping and clicking; one participant in group 3 kept saying "the mouse" when referring to his hand. Several users also assumed virtual keyboards would appear on the TV, and their invented gestures consisted of typing on them by hunting and pecking with a single finger (rather than simulating keyboard-free touch-typing, e.g., [6]). Some gestures were metaphors based on imagined keyboards, such as when P8 pushed his hand forward after saying a search term out loud, explaining, "I'm trying to simulate hitting enter on the keyboard."

The influence of traditional desktop computing was so strong that several groups invented voice commands based on keyboard shortcuts. For example, P22 suggested the speech interaction "keyboard control F" for *find in page*, noting "if things could be as close to Windows as possible, it would make things a whole lot easier for everybody." P24 also suggested the voice command "control F" for the find in page function. For *reload page*, both P6 and P14 suggested the speech command "F5." P14 also used the spoken command "alt F4" for *close browser*.

Despite being influenced by prior systems, many participants seemed to recognize that legacy interactions could be modified to better suit this new scenario. For example, participants suggested that icons and buttons might be made larger to be more suitable as touch targets, that certain regions of the large-screen TV (such as corners or edges) might be set aside as dedicated menu areas, and that the need to exit applications might not be applicable, but rather that switching among a limited set of always-running applications might be more suitable in an entertainment scenario.

Common (and Divergent) Conventions

Several groups proposed the convention of assigning numbers to various components of the user interface, such as links within a web page, results returned from a search engine, browser tabs, and autocomplete or spell correction suggestions. This numbering system then formed the basis for simple speech commands to navigate the interface, e.g., "tab 4" or "link 2."

There were several cases in which participants displayed common but divergent patterns in their proposed interactions. Wobbrock et al. noticed this type of phenomenon in their study of user-elicited surface gestures, when different participants used either one, two, or three fingers to perform "single finger" pointing gestures [30]. In our study, diverging conventions were evident in the ways in which users mimicked the mouse, performed selections, specified regions, and performed flicking gestures.

Pretending that one's hand was a proxy for the mouse was a common metaphor in the gestures users invented. However, there were two distinct ways in which users mimicked the mouse with their hand, the *palm-as-mouse* gesture (in which the user held their hand with the palm parallel to the TV screen) or the *finger-as-mouse* gesture (in which users held their hand in a "gun" pose, with the index finger pointing at the screen).

When mimicking a mouse with their hand, users tended to adopt one of three conventions for selecting an item under the imagined projection of the mouse cursor: *dwell*, *click*, and *push*, with *dwell* and *click* being the most common (for example, for the *click link* referent, six users employed dwell and seven employed click). These three selection methods were compatible with either the *palm-as-mouse* or *finger-as-mouse* posture, and differed in the action performed once the imagined projection of the cursor was positioned over the desired on-screen target: the *dwell* gesture involved holding the "mouse" hand still for a few seconds, the *click* gesture involved rotating the wrist about the x-axis by 45- to 90-degrees, and the *push* gesture involved moving the hand along the z-axis toward the TV.

The *select region* referent (in which a user selected a two-dimensional on-screen region, such as a paragraph of text they wished to place on the clipboard) resulted in two different metaphors that users tended to adopt – *highlighter* and *bounding box*. The seven users employing the *highlighter* metaphor imagined that their "mouse" hand was selecting any item that they swept over individually, whereas the nine users employing the *bounding box* metaphor imagined that anything within a region whose outer limits they defined would be included in a selection.

Referents that tended to evoke "flick" gestures (particularly the *go back* and *go forward* referents) were the most problematic in terms of individual differences, in that the two most prominent metaphors users employed were in direct conflict with each other. The first flick metaphor users employed was the *book metaphor*, in which a flick from the right to the left would map to the forward direction (this is the motion one would use to turn a page when reading a book). The alternative metaphor was the *arrow metaphor*, in which a flick from right to left would map to the backward direction (since this motion would correspond to drawing an arrow pointing backward). Some users switched back and forth between which metaphor they employed, creating not only cross-user but also within-user conflicts for this gesture. For instance, P14, pondering both flick directions as possibilities for the *go back* command, wondered, "I don't know which way you'd want to go, which way makes sense." Similarly, P12 attempted to create *go back* and *go forward* commands that were inverses of each other, but switched metaphors in between, resulting in identical right-to-left flicks for both commands. The preference for these two metaphors was roughly equal, with five users employing a book metaphor for *go forward* and five employing an arrow metaphor.

Statement	Median	Mean
I would enjoy using a browser in this manner.	5	4.4
Gesture commands seem like an effective way to control the browser in this setting.	4	4.4
Speech commands seem like an effective way to control a browser in this setting.	5	4.3
I had fun operating the browser in this manner.	5	4.3
I cooperated with my partner(s) when operating the browser.	4	4.2
The interactions with the browser felt natural.	4	4.1
My partner(s) and I took on different roles in operating the browser.	4	3.6
The text in the web browser on the TV was difficult to read.	2	2.7
I felt tired after performing the activities.	2	2.6
My partner(s) and I got in each other's way when operating the browser.	2	2.3
I felt physically uncomfortable performing the activities.	1	1.6

Table 5. Participants' ratings of the usability of various aspects of the envisioned TV-web-browsing scenario (on a five-point Likert scale).

User-Suggested Referents
In addition to the fifteen referents that we presented to each group for the elicitation exercise (Table 3), several groups spontaneously proposed interactions for other functions that they felt would be important to their living room internet experience.

Three groups proposed a *scroll* referent. P10 and P15 accomplished this by extending an arm out to one's side or in front of one's body and moving it up and down; P22 used a spoken command, "scroll down."

Two groups proposed *zoom*, in order to make the text on the TV screen more readable. P16 accomplished this by moving two palms along the diagonals of an imagined rectangle, and P19 by spreading two palms out horizontally or using the voice command "zoom."

P13 observed that the large, widescreen TV form-factor would support tiling two tabs onto the two halves of the screen to support comparisons, and accomplished this by holding two palms together and then moving them horizontally in opposite directions.

P4 proposed *undo* by pulling a hand away from the screen along the z-axis. P16 used a similar backwards motion, combined with a finger-pinch of the moving hand, to represent *summon menu*.

Post-Study Questionnaire
The post-study questionnaire asked participants to reflect on the simulated TV-browser experience by using a five-point

Likert scale to rate their level of agreement with a series of statements, shown in Table 5.

Participants' responses indicated that, overall, they found the experience of using a web browser on a large-screen TV with Kinect control to be enjoyable. Participants disagreed with statements suggesting that gesture control of the browser was physically uncomfortable or tiring (a concern sometimes expressed in other studies of gesture interactions, e.g. [16]), nor did users' age correlate with their ratings of fatigue. Users also slightly disagreed that it was difficult to read the text displayed in the browser from their seated position on the couch; however, participants were generally not reading pages in depth. Additionally, two groups spontaneously invented a "zoom" gesture (which would increase font size), suggesting some desire for changes in web page readability for this form factor.

Participants rated both speech and gesture commands as effective ways to control a web browser in their living room; a Wilcoxon signed ranks test found that the difference in the overall ratings for speech and gesture was not statistically significant.

DISCUSSION

Our findings suggest that users would be highly receptive to the ability to use their TVs for web browsing. Two-thirds of participant groups readily identified scenarios when they had desired such interactions in the past, and all groups indicated enthusiasm for the scenarios proposed on the post-study questionnaire. However, the scenarios participants described and those they rated most highly suggest that living room internet use is likely appropriate for short-duration, casual tasks, more similar to the tasks labeled "lean-back internet use" by Lindley et al. [9] than to the multi-user productivity tasks often associated with collaborative web search (e.g., [2, 12, 14, 26]). Such casual, short-lived tasks seem particularly suited to computer-vision and speech-recognition based interactions, since these methods tend to be more lightweight than finding a dedicated interaction device, starting an appropriate application, etc. The recent addition of seated skeleton recognition by the Kinect technology [3] makes the gestures proposed by our participants (which they all chose to perform while seated) feasible to recognize. The difficulty of reading long articles from a distance, even on large-screen displays, and potential fatigue from performing gesture interactions for long periods [16] are usability challenges that would need to be overcome to make in-depth internet use tasks suitable for this form factor; offering multi-modal synonyms for interaction (i.e., speech alternatives to gesture commands) is one step toward expanding the suitability of this interaction platform to a broader array of scenarios.

Participants viewed neither gesture nor speech as ideal interaction methods, but rather saw pros and cons of each method depending on both situational factors (e.g., their current energy levels, or the locations and activities of other members of their household) and application-specific factors (e.g., the target referent). Wobbrock et al. [30] identified the benefit of including synonyms in a user-defined gesture set to increase guessability and coverage of proposed gestures; we found that a multi-modal elicitation study offers a related benefit of creating *multimodal synonyms*, which can support users' expressed desires to access the same functionality with different modalities in different circumstances. Our findings also provide some insight for designers as to which modalities may be more suitable for which referents – for example, the conflicting nature of the two popular metaphors for choosing flick gesture direction for the *go forward* and *go back* referents might suggest that a speech command would be less confusing to users.

Designing our study such that users could offer any number of interaction suggestions, using either (or both) modalities, offered challenges and benefits. Because this study design resulted in different numbers of proposed interactions for different referents, Wobbrock et al.'s agreement metric [30] was not applicable; however, we found that *max-consensus* and *consensus-distinct ratio* were useful alternative metrics for gaining insight into our data. Our less constrained study design allowed us to gain insight into which referents might be more suited to either speech or gesture control by examining differences in the total interactions proposed, max-consensus, and consensus-distinct ratio for each referent in each modality.

Our multi-user study design, in which groups of two or three previously-acquainted users simultaneously participated in the elicitation activity, had benefits and drawbacks. We chose this design to add ecological validity, since the target use scenario (interacting with a TV in the living room) is one in which multiple users are often present. We envisioned that pairs/triads participating together might propose cooperative interactions, such as cooperative gestures [13] or role-based collaborative web search actions [20], although users in our study did not do so (perhaps a fact which is noteworthy in its own right). Nonetheless, the multi-user design seemed to help shy users participate more actively by enabling them to build off of their partner's suggestions. Additionally, this configuration enabled relevant concerns to surface, such as the difficulty of performing large gestures without accidentally striking a companion seated nearby, or the likelihood of conversation being conflated with commands. However, it is possible that users were more likely to converge on suggestions in this arrangement; formally comparing single-user and multi-user elicitation methodologies to quantify tradeoffs between the two techniques is an area for future work.

CONCLUSION

In this paper, we explored appropriate gesture and speech interactions for enabling users to control a web browser on their television. Our contributions include interview and questionnaire results that illustrate the situations in which users wish to use the internet on their TV, user-elicitation results that identify popular suggestions for speech and gesture commands to support such interaction, and observational insights that identify common conventions and biases surrounding the use of speech and gesture interactions in this setting. We also offer a methodological contribution by introducing two new metrics for analyzing the results of user-elicitation studies, and reflecting on the benefits and challenges of multimodal and multi-user elicitation study designs.

REFERENCES

1. Alexander, J., Han, T., Judd, W., Irani, P., and Subramanian, S. Putting Your Best Foot Forward: Investigating Real-World Mappings for Foot-Based Gestures. *Proceedings of CHI 2012*.
2. Amershi, S. and Morris, M.R. CoSearch: A System for Co-located Collaborative Web Search. *Proceedings of CHI 2008*.
3. Cooper, D. Kinect for Windows SDK reaches v1.5, now works when you're sitting down. *Engadget*, 5/21/2012.
4. Epps, J., Lichman, S., and Wu, M. A study of hand shape use in tabletop gesture interaction. *Extended Abstracts of CHI 2006*.
5. Findlater, L., Lee, B., and Wobbrock, J.O. Beyond QWERTY: Augmenting Touch Screen Keyboards with Multi-Touch Gestures for Non-Alphanumeric Input. *Proceedings of CHI 2012*.
6. Findlater, L., Wobbrock, J., and Wigdor, D. Typing on Flat Glass: Examining Ten-Finger Expert Typing Patterns on Touch Surfaces. *Proceedings of CHI 2011*.
7. Frisch, M., Heydekorn, J., and Dachselt, R. Investigating Multi-Touch and Pen Gestures for Diagram Editing on Interactive Surfaces. *Proceedings of ITS 2009*.
8. Good, M.D., Whiteside, J.A., Wixon,D.R., and Jones, S.J. (1984) Building a User-Derived Interface. *Communications of the ACM*, 27(10), 1032-1043.
9. Lindley, S., Meek, S., Sellen, A., and Harper, R. "It's simply integral to what I do": Enquiries into how the web is weaved into everyday life. *Proceedings of WWW 2012*.
10. Micire, M., Desai, M., Courtemanche, A., and Yanco, H.A. Analysis of Natural Gestures for Controlling Robot Teams on Multi-Touch Tabletop Surfaces. *Proceedings of ITS 2009*.
11. Mignot, C., Valot, C., and Carbonell, N. An experimental study of future 'natural' multimodal human-computer action. *Conference Companion INTERCHI 1993*, 67-68.
12. Morris, M.R., Fisher, D., and Wigdor, D. Search on Surfaces: Exploring the Potential of Interactive Tabletops for Collaborative Search Tasks. *Information Processing and Management*, 2010.
13. Morris, M.R., Huang, A., Paepcke, A., and Winograd, T. Cooperative Gestures: Multi-User Gestural Interactions for Co-located Groupware. *CHI 2006*.
14. Morris, M.R., Lombardo, J., and Wigdor, D. WeSearch: Supporting Collaborative Search and Sensemaking on a Tabletop Display. *Proceedings of CSCW 2010*, 401-410.
15. Morris, M.R. and Teevan, J. Collaborative Web Search: Who, What, Where, When, and Why. *Morgan & Claypool*, 2010.
16. Morris, M.R., Wobbrock, J.O., and Wilson, A.D. Understanding Users' Preferences for Surface Gestures. *Proceedings of Graphics Interface 2010*.
17. NielsenWire. "Nielsen Estimates Number of U.S. Television Homes to be 114.7 Million." May 3, 2011.
18. Nielsen, M., Störring, M., Moeslund, T.B., and Granum, E. A procedure for developing intuitive and ergonomic gesture interfaces for HCI. *International Gesture Workshop 2003*.
19. Paek, T., Agrawala, A., Basu, S., Drucker, S., Kristjansson, T., Logan, R., Toyoma, K., and Wilson, A. Toward Universal Mobile Interaction for Shared Displays. *Proceedings of CSCW 2004*, 266-269.
20. Pickens, J., Golovchinksy, G., Shah, C., Qvarford, P., and Back, M. Algorithmic Mediation for Collaborative Exploratory Search. *Proceedings of SIGIR 2008*.
21. Robbe-Reiter, S., Carbonell, N. and Dauchy, P. Expression constraints in multimodal human-computer interaction. *Proceedings of IUI 2000*, 225-228.
22. Robbe, S. An empirical study of speech and gesture interaction: Toward the definition of ergonomic design guidelines. *Conference Summary CHI 1998*, 349-350.
23. Ruiz, J., Li, Y., and Lank, E. User-Defined Motion Gestures for Mobile Interaction. *Proc. of CHI 2011*.
24. Schuler, D. and Namioka, A. (1993) Participatory Design: Principles and Practices. Hillsdale, NJ: Lawrence Erlbaum.
25. Tarr, G. Large-Screen TV Sales Grow in Q4, FY 2010. *Twice*, Feb. 15, 2011.
26. Tuddenham, P., Davies, I., and Robinson, P. WebSurface: An Interface for Co-located Collaborative Information Gathering. *Proceedings of ITS 2009*.
27. Warren, C. Internet Explorer Coming to Xbox. *Mashable*. June 4, 2012.
28. Weiser, M. The Computer for the 21st Century. *Scientific American*, September 1991, 66-75.
29. Wobbrock, J.O., Aung, H.H., Rothrock, B., and Myers, B.A. Maximizing the guessability of symbolic input. *Extended Abstracts of CHI 2005*, 1869-1872.
30. Wobbrock, J.O., Morris, M.R., and Wilson, D. User-Defined Gestures for Surface Computing. *Proceedings of CHI 2009*.

Kinected Browser: Depth Camera Interaction for the Web

Daniel J. Liebling, Meredith Ringel Morris
Microsoft Research, Redmond, Washington, USA
{ danl, merrie }@microsoft.com

ABSTRACT
Interest in and development of gesture interfaces has recently exploded, fueled in part by the release of Microsoft Corporation's Kinect, a low-cost, consumer-packaged depth camera with integrated skeleton tracking. Depth-camera-based gestures can facilitate interaction with the Web on keyboard-and-mouse-free and/or multi-user technologies, such as large display walls or TV sets. We present a toolkit for bringing such gesture affordances into modern Web browsers using existing Web programming methods. Our framework is designed to enable Web programmers to incrementally add this capability with minimum effort by leveraging Web standard DOM structures and event models. We describe our framework's design and architecture, and illustrate its usability and versatility.

Author Keywords
Kinect, depth cameras, JavaScript, HTML, toolkits.

ACM Classification Keywords
H.5.m. Information interfaces and presentation: Misc.

INTRODUCTION AND RELATED WORK
Interest in input methods beyond the mouse and keyboard has recently accelerated as new, inexpensive sensing hardware has become widely available. Such input is particularly suitable to emerging form-factors, such as large display walls, which lack mice and keyboards.

In 2010, Microsoft launched the Kinect sensor for its Xbox 360 gaming platform [kinect.com], followed by Kinect for Windows in early 2012 [kinectforwindows.org]. The wide availability and affordability of these devices ($150 USD) make them a popular platform for experimentation among researchers, practitioners, students, and hobbyists. The Kinect device and accompanying SDK provide access to color and infrared (depth) cameras at 640 × 480 pixel resolution, 18-point skeleton tracking for multiple simultaneous skeletons, and a microphone array. The SDK provides programming APIs in both C++ and C#.

Researchers have quickly appropriated depth cameras such as Kinect for a variety of scenarios including 3D scene reconstruction [3], simulated touch sensing [7], facilitating interaction with multi-display environments [9], and enabling on-body sensing [2].

In this note, we describe a toolkit that enables developers to easily augment any Web page with gesture or speech input. Recent standards such as HTML5 and CSS3 enable richly interactive Web applications. Despite these recent updates, the browser interaction model is still based on keyboard, mouse, and simple multi-touch interactions (the latter due largely to the recent surge in adoption of touch-enabled smartphones and tablets).

We anticipate that in a few years, PCs, laptops, tablets, and perhaps even smartphones will include depth cameras as standard peripherals (much like webcams today). By supporting depth camera browser interactions in addition to standard mouse, keyboard, and touchscreen inputs, we envision that a user could choose the most natural and appropriate modality for a given task. Our toolkit also supports easily augmenting web pages with speech input via the Kinect's microphone array, but the main focus is on incorporating gesture input.

Using gestures to interact with the Web may be appropriate for a variety of reasons, such as for a collaborative web search where the users outnumber the traditional input devices [1]; for ergonomic reasons (to enable productivity during typing breaks) [5]; for situations where traditional input devices are not available such as for interactions with large display walls [6] or TVs; or for casual web-based experiences such as browser-based games or the use of the web for other casual or whimsical tasks (e.g., "lean-back internet" [4]).

There have been a few recent forays into using Kinects with Web browsers. In June 2012, Microsoft announced a version of Internet Explorer for Xbox, which is a customized browser that uses voice commands for navigation; in contrast, we present a framework applicable to standard web browsers, which includes gesture support. SwimBrowser [swimbrowser.tumblr.com] is a whimsical application that allows a user to navigate the Web via "swimming" gestures, recognized by a Kinect. It shows how a depth camera and browser might be used together, but does not expose control over the development of such interactions to page authors. DepthJS [depthjs.media.mit.edu] is an early Kinect–Web browser integration for the Safari and Chrome browsers. DepthJS provides some high level affordances such as gesture-based tab switching, list item selection, and button presses;

ITS'12, November 11–14, 2012, Cambridge, Massachusetts, USA.

```
<html>
<head>
    <script type="text/javascript" src="jquery-1.7.min.js"></script>
    <script type="text/javascript" src="KinectedBrowser.js"></script>                    ①
    <script type="text/javascript">
    $(document).ready(function () {
        Kinect.init();                                                                    ②
        $("#positions").on("rightHandOver.kinect", function (state) {                     ③
            $("#positions").text("Right hand @ " + state.clientX + ", " + state.clientY);
        });
    });
</script>
<body>
    <div id="positions" style="width:200px;height:200px;border:1px solid black">Wave here!</div>
</body>
</html>
```

Figure 1. Using HTML and JavaScript with jQuery to react to the right hand moving. Key portions are highlighted in gray. (1) including script library; (2) initializing object; (3) attaching event listener on the document.

developers use JavaScript to access this functionality. DepthJS focuses on providing reusable code for particular hand movement and gesture patterns; in contrast, our toolkit focuses on providing a more general integration of the depth camera and browser in order to provide more flexibility in interaction design. Additionally, our contribution in this paper goes beyond the features of the toolkit itself to encompass a reflection on the design rationale behind the architecture of Kinected Browser and an evaluation of its usability and versatility.

DESIGN CONSIDERATIONS

HTML and JavaScript are the common denominators of the Web; browsers exist on almost every modern platform and form factor. We believe that as depth cameras become cheaper, more common, and expand beyond PCs, researchers and developers will want to explore gestural interfaces that can scale across devices, from phones to wall displays. Our toolkit enables such scenarios.

Gesture integration with a browser can take two forms: high-level manipulation that translates specific gestures into existing events such as clicks and navigations (the approach taken by DepthJS), or mapping depth and skeleton positions into lower-level objects from which page authors can develop new experiences. The "high-level" approach limits the gesture vocabulary in ways that prevent page authors from developing novel or customized experiences and pushing the boundaries of interactive Web sites. In contrast, we aim to support *versatility* in terms of the range of experiences that can be created with Kinected Browser. Our "low-level" design approach avoids constraining Web page authors with assumptions. Kinected Browser does not assume that the entire page is interactive, that there is only one user, that the screen has a specific size or aspect ratio, that only a small set of element types support interaction, or that a specific gesture or speech vocabulary is standard. Also, to maximize flexibility, our toolkit allows access to raw data from the sensor. Although most page authors are unlikely to use raw depth data, one can imagine Web applications using depth data, e.g., to scan physical artifacts and input them into 3D printing services.

Existing Web experiences are built around single-user interaction paradigms. Multiple users sharing a PC are not uncommon, from classrooms in developing nations [7] to co-located search [5]. As large interface spaces lend themselves to social interaction and the Web becomes more pervasive, Web developers will increasingly need multi-user input support. Our design supports as many users as the underlying Kinect system, and every event fired by the system includes a user identifier. We explored adding uniqueness of user IDs in the toolkit, but leave this up to the developer, since "uniqueness" can be defined in different ways – a person, a team, a family, etc. Furthermore, with increased availability of face recognition systems, developers can easily leverage a third party service to perform their own identity assignment.

Despite the wealth of data that systems like Kinect provide, the toolkit should be easy to use by programmers. The system should leverage existing Web interaction programming facilities. Our toolkit maps the skeleton information provided by Kinect into scriptable browser events, as described in the next section.

ARCHITECTURE

Kinected Browser consists of two modules (Figure 2): a browser plugin linked to the C++ Kinect SDK, and a JavaScript library. The SDK provides low level data including the positions of users' skeletons and the color and depth images. SDK consumer applications choose to receive data when new frames are ready, or poll for new data on their own schedule. Our toolkit reads this data and interprets them as higher level events, freeing page authors from worrying about frame rates and hit testing.

The natural point of integration in a Web browser is its existing UI event system. Most visible Document Object Model (DOM) elements fire events in response to mouse and keyboard activity. Adding additional gesture events on

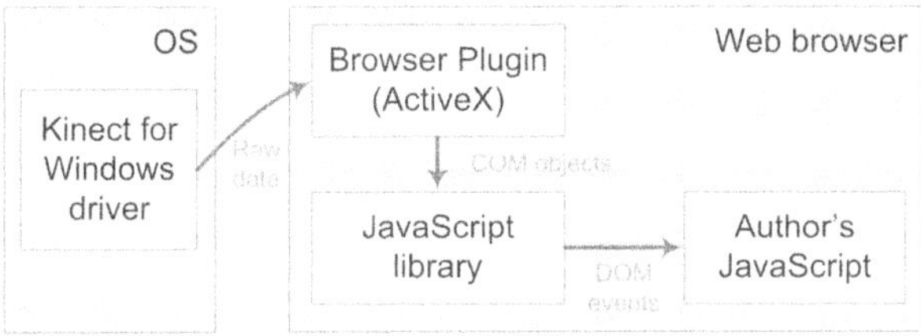

Figure 2. Kinected Browser toolkit architecture

each object is therefore consistent with the current programming model. Furthermore, it allows developers to reuse existing code if they simply want to use joints as virtual mouse cursors.

When Kinect data is ready, the browser plugin reads the raw data and assembles data structures that can also be read by scripting in the browser, since raw C-style interfaces are not usable there. We chose to implement most of the functionality in JavaScript to provide independence from the hardware and raw data; the browser-based portion of the code should work for new depth camera packages and new methods of providing data to the browser. For example, rather than a browser plugin, the low-level data could be read using the new WebSocket protocol, or the Kinect device might be on a remote machine. Furthermore, the JavaScript library is written to be browser platform neutral.

Pages enable use of the Kinected Browser system by placing a `<SCRIPT>` tag in the HTML that references the JavaScript library (Figure 1.1). After just as few as one lines of initialization code (Figure 1.2), authors can use data and events from the Kinect device using standard Web programming concepts.

Mapping Camera Space to Browser Space

In any vision-based application, the developer must choose how to map the camera coordinates into screen space. Kinected Browser provides two skeleton-to-screen-space mapping functions, but allows developers to specify custom mappers. By default, Kinected Browser maps screen space to the viewable area of the Web page rather than the entire scrollable page area. Since the camera space is in landscape aspect ratio, mapping to the entire page (the length of which may be several multiples of the width) would lead to severe vertical distortion. In practice, we find that users' browser viewports tend to have aspect ratios that are similar to the camera's; for such configurations, even when the horizontal and vertical multipliers are not precisely the same, the user experience is not adversely affected.

The system also supports the notion of egocentric mapping. That is, the centroid of the skeleton is roughly mapped to the center of the screen space. This allows multiple users to reach all controls on the page without having to occupy the same physical space. In egocentric mapping, we also scale the skeleton such that the user can physically reach any element in the viewport. To determine the outermost reachable points, we subtract arm length from the re-centered uppermost torso point in both the X and Y dimensions. These points, plus those of the feet, determine the physical skeleton bounding box. The system then scales between the physical bounding box and browser viewport. To aid debugging of skeleton interaction, the system supports drawing active skeleton mappings to an HTML canvas. We find this is useful for determining whether errors are due to camera noise or program bugs.

Controlling the DOM with Skeleton Input

Given the aforementioned camera-to-browser space mapping, the system uses skeleton points and motion to fire events on DOM elements. Page authors subscribe to skeleton movement events in a similar way to mouse events, adding event listener functions to any visual DOM element (Figure 1.3). Parallel to the DOM standard `mouseOver` and `mouseOut` events, the system publishes `jointOver` and `jointOut` events where *joint* is each of the 18 joints. The system hit tests skeleton points against a DOM element's bounding box, firing the appropriate event if necessary. Similarly, events in the `jointMove` family fire when a joint moves within an element's bounding box. The system can also map multiple joints into one "virtual joint" for scenarios where a set of joints is semantically equivalent. For example, we map *leftHand* and *rightHand* to a virtual *hand* joint. By using the virtual joint, authors can allow DOM elements to respond to either hand without duplicating event handlers; alternatively, developers can use the individual *left* and *right* versions of joints if they design interactions that make use of such distinctions.

In addition to having DOM elements respond to skeletal events, developers may also wish to associate input with geometrically specified regions of a page. For instance, a developer creating a game using only an HTML5 canvas might wish to make sprites react to joints moving over them. To support this scenario, Kinected Browser reuses the existing image map infrastructure. Web page authors use image maps to specify polygonal and circular regions of an image that respond to mouse interaction. Our system interprets the rectangular, circular, and polygonal areas to hit test for joint events.

Higher Level Inputs

In addition to over/out and movement events, Kinected Browser also supports joint hovers. Inspired by the Kinect for Xbox 360's hover selection mechanism, if a joint dwells above a DOM element and the joint's coordinates are fairly stable for 100 ms (allowing for noise and human joint wobble), the browser displays a large circle consisting of translucent arc segments that fill with a contrasting color as time progresses. If the hand remains over the target for 2.5 seconds, the system fires a target acquisition event and plays an audio cue. Target release occurs in the reverse manner; if a dwell occurs while the system is in an acquired state, then the target is released and a different audio cue plays. In one of our sample applications, we use acquisition and release to implement drag and drop.

Since our toolkit provides access to the underlying joint movement, developers can also easily incorporate an existing gesture recognizer such as the $1 Recognizer [10], which already has a JavaScript implementation.

Color and Depth Stream Data

Our toolkit also provides access to the color and depth camera image streams. Since the frame rate is up to 30 fps, the maximum bandwidth required across both streams is approximately 28.6 MB/sec. To reduce the load on JavaScript garbage collectors, we only copy data between the device and the browser on demand. This allows developers to request only as much data as they need without burdening the CPU unnecessarily. For convenience, the image data is available as a `CanvasImageData` object which can be drawn directly in the browser using the HTML5 Canvas API.

EVALUATION

To examine our toolkit's usability, we conducted a small informal user study. We recruited four participants from a Kinect interest mailing list at a large technology company. All participants were software professionals and had at least some experience using the Microsoft Kinect SDK as well as self-rated intermediate or expert experience with JavaScript and HTML. None were familiar with our toolkit.

We provided subjects with a short document describing the toolkit and detailing the available events. We then observed the developers completing two tasks each. In both tasks, participants were given an HTML file containing boilerplate code to initialize the framework (similar to Fig. 1, but without the event listener in Fig 1.3). In Task 1, we instructed them to update two regions of the page (`SPAN` tags) to display the X and Y coordinates of the right hand. All participants successfully completed the task in less than ten minutes. In Task 2, we created a simulated "scratch off" lottery ticket. In the HTML given to the participants, four rectangular `DIV`s with numbers were occluded by four opaque rectangular `DIV`s in front along the z-axis. Participants had to use the toolkit to make the opaque `DIV`s disappear so as to simulate scratching off the removable surface of a scratch-and-win lottery ticket. All participants successfully completed the task in 17 minutes or less.

After completing the tasks, subjects completed a post-study questionnaire. After less than an hour of exposure to the toolkit and minimal documentation, they expressed either Agree or Strongly Agree (on a 5-point Likert scale) that they understood how the toolkit mapped physical space into the browser and how to use the toolkit to respond to events. Furthermore, participants felt that expert proficiency was not required to use the system. We believe this is important given that Web development skill level varies and we want the system to be usable by a wide audience.

To illustrate the versatility of our toolkit, the authors and other members of our lab used Kinected Browser to create novel Web browser interactions. One team created an interactive information visualization that a user could manipulate using a combination of speech (to specify dimensions to manipulate) and gestures (to adjust the values of the target dimensions in the graph). Another developer used the system to build a multi-user search experience, in which voice queries directed to a search engine were color-coded based on user identity, and gesture recognition was used to implement voting to select a search result for viewing, by ensuring that all users simultaneously hovered over a common link in order to choose it. A third demonstration app let users select text on a page by pointing, then use the selected text to issue a search query initiated by speech control. These example applications showcase the flexibility that the Kinected Browser enables.

CONCLUSION

We introduced Kinected Browser, a toolkit that facilitates augmenting a Web browser with depth camera and gestural interactions using the familiar DOM-based event model of JavaScript programming, thus facilitating Web interaction for new form-factors such as large display walls, which may lack mice and keyboards or necessitate multi-user input. We discussed the design rationale and architecture involved in creating Kinected Browser and presented an initial evaluation of the toolkit's usability and versatility. Our toolkit is available for download at http://aka.ms/kib.

REFERENCES

1. Amershi, S. and Morris, M.R. CoSearch: A System for Co-located Collaborative Web Search. *CHI 2008*.
2. Harrison, C., et al. OmniTouch: Wearable Multitouch Interaction Everywhere. *UIST 2011*.
3. Izadi, S., et al. KinectFusion: real-time 3D reconstruction and interaction using a moving depth camera. *UIST 2011*.
4. Lindley, S.E., et al. "It's simply integral to what I do:" Enquiries into how the web is weaved into everyday life. *WWW 2012*.
5. Morris, D., et al. SuperBreak: Using Interactivity to Enhance Ergonomic Typing Breaks. *CHI 2008*.
6. Paek, T., et al. Toward Universal Mobile Interaction for Shared Displays. *CSCW 2004*.
7. Pawar, U.S., et al. Multiple Mice for Retention Tasks in Disadvantaged Schools. *CHI 2007*.
8. Wilson, A.D. Using a Depth Camera as a Touch Sensor. *ITS 2010*.
9. Wilson, A.D. and Benko, H. Combining multiple depth cameras and projectors for interactions on, above, and between surfaces. *UIST 2010*.
10. Wobbrock, J., et al. Gestures without libraries, toolkits or training: a $1 recognizer for user interface prototypes. *UIST 2007*.

A Collaborative Environment for Engaging Novices in Scientific Inquiry

Consuelo Valdes, Michelle Ferreirae, Taili Feng, Heidi Wang, Kelsey Tempel, Sirui Liu, Orit Shaer
Wellesley College
Wellesley, Massachusetts, United States
cvaldes@wellesley.edu

ABSTRACT
We describe the design, implementation, and evaluation of GreenTouch, a collaborative environment that enables novice users to engage in authentic scientific inquiry. GreenTouch consists of a mobile user interface for capturing data in the field, a web application for data curation in the "cloud," and a tabletop interface for exploratory analysis of heterogeneous data. This paper contributes: 1) the design, implementation, and validation of a collaborative environment which allows novices to engage in scientific data capture, curation, and analysis; 2) empirical evidence for the feasibility and value of integrating interactive surfaces in college-level education based on an *in situ* study with 54 undergraduate students; and 3) insights collected through iterative design, providing concrete lessons and guidelines for designing multi-touch interfaces for collaborative inquiry of complex domains.

AUTHOR KEYWORDS
Tabletop; multi-touch interaction; collaborative learning.

ACM CLASSIFICATION KEYWORDS
H.5.m. Information interfaces and presentation (e.g., HCI): Miscellaneous.

INTRODUCTION
The introduction and increasing availability of multi-touch, high-resolution displays in the form of handhelds, tabletops, and whiteboards open the opportunity to consider these technologies as a prominent alternative to current learning technologies. Several studies have examined the effects of interactive surface parameters on collaborative learning, investigating their benefits and deficits in the context of formal and informal learning; however, most of these studies have focused on children. To date, little research has been devoted to investigating the strengths and limitations of utilizing interactive surfaces in college-level learning. We are particularly interested in investigating the application of interactive surfaces for supporting collaborative inquiry of complex domains. Our main research question is: how can interactive surface technologies be used to help college students learn complex concepts through collaborative inquiry?

To address this question, we developed and evaluated GreenTouch: a pervasive environment that utilizes handheld and tabletop interfaces to mediate collaborative inquiry. GreenTouch enables undergraduate students to engage in authentic scientific inquiries in phenology – the study of how periodic plant and animal life cycle events are influenced by variations in climate.

Figure 1: Collaborative exploration of heterogeneous data using GreenTouch.

Engaging undergraduate students in authentic scientific inquiries has many documented benefits including improved ability to apply scientific thinking and complex problem solving, preparedness for graduate study, and increased retention rates [12,13,28]. Furthermore, it provides students an opportunity to engage in knowledge building [25], producing ideas that are of value to the broader scientific community. However, in data-intense fields [6] such as genomics, environmental studies, and phenology, scientific investigations rely on large data sets that can be understood only through the use of sophisticated computational methods and interfaces. Such interfaces do not support important aspects of college-level science learning such as inquiry-based high-level reasoning, the development of process knowledge, and collaborative learning [15, 29, 30]. As a result, in data-intensive areas, undergraduate students rarely engage in stages of the scientific inquiry beyond data collection [23]. We propose that emerging multi-touch and tabletop interaction techniques present an opportunity for

ITS'12, November 11–14, 2012, Cambridge, Massachusetts, USA.

enhancing learning in fields that require understanding complex data sets, which are difficult for non-experts to comprehend.

In this paper, we reflect on the design, development, and evaluation of GreenTouch. We describe our 18-month long effort from design strategy to iterations of design, development, and evaluation. The paper presents three main contributions: 1) the design, implementation, and validation of a collaborative environment which lowers the threshold for scientific data capture, curation, and inquiry; 2) empirical evidence for the feasibility and value of integrating interactive surfaces in college-level education; and 3) insights collected through iterative design, providing concrete lessons and principles for designing multi-touch interfaces for inquiry of complex domains.

This paper is organized as follows: we first discuss related work, followed by a description of the GreenTouch system. We then outline our multi-tiered *in situ* evaluation with 132 students and present results from a recent study with 54 students, focusing on users' engagement with data and learning through collaborative inquiry. We conclude with design implications for utilizing interactive surface technologies for collaborative inquiry of complex domains.

RELATED WORK

Ubiquitous and Mobile Systems for Field Study

A number of mobile applications have been developed to enhance field study [1, 4, 22, 23, 32, 34]. For example, LilyPad [23] is a mobile application for field study that promotes learning through integrating task-based and inquiry processes *in situ*. However, we found that extreme field conditions, as well as the complexity of the data set, often drive the separation of data collection in the field from inquiry processes in the lab. Out There In Here (OTIH) [1] is a distributed information resource system for learning geology in higher education settings. Similarly to GreenTouch, it utilizes a variety of devices to provide situated access to information. However, it was designed to support remote collaboration, while our focus is on design for co-located collaboration. ButterflyNet [38] is a mobile capture and access system for field biologists that integrates paper notes with digital photographs. It shares our challenge of collecting, transforming, and organizing heterogeneous field data. However, ButterflyNet was created to enhance the work of *expert* users (e.g. field biologists) and facilitate the collection of rich and expressive field data, while our goal is to enable *novice* users to collect concise, accurate, and consistent data. Thus, while ButterflyNet utilizes paper-based input to allow users to generate free-form data such as descriptive text and sketches during an extended stay in the field, we seek to guide and constrain user input to a well-defined data collection protocol determined by the primary investigator (PI). Our goal was to minimize the time required to collect field data, while accommodating extreme weather conditions. Thus, we chose to trade the rich affordance of the paper notebook in favor of a small device that can be easily protected from water and allows for quick touch input for selecting options in a strict data collection protocol, in addition to note, video, and photo capture. ButterflyNet also provides a desktop browser for accessing field data, allowing users to collaborate *asynchronously* through shared notebooks. Since our focus is on promoting the participation of novice users in scientific inquiry, we consider support for *co-located* collaboration essential.

Figure 2: Capturing data in the field using GreenTouch.

Tabletop Interfaces for Scientists and Learning

Several systems illustrate the potential of supporting science education through multi-touch and tabletop interaction: Augmented Chemistry [2] and CheMo [35] are tangible user interfaces for chemistry education. Schkolne et al. [26] developed a tangible immersive interface for the design of DNA molecules. However, these systems focus on the representation and manipulation of objects that have an inherent physical structure. Involv [7] is a multi-touch tabletop interface for exploring the Encyclopedia of Life that shares our challenge of creating effective interaction techniques for large data spaces. However, it targets museum and informal learning settings, which are different from formal learning environments. Piper and Hollan [19] conducted a study with undergraduate students, comparing the affordance of tabletop displays and paper handouts for studying neuroanatomy. However, their study utilized a tabletop prototype with minimal functionality. We present the design and evaluation of a feature-rich interface that supports complex analytical tasks and utilizes various devices. Schneider et al. [27] developed Phylo-Genie, a tabletop user interface for collaborative learning of college-level phylogeny. However, to date, this system has not been evaluated in authentic classroom settings. G-nome Surfer [29, 30, 31] is a tabletop interface that supports collaborative exploration of college-level genomics. While G-nome Surfer focuses on the hypothesis forming stage, we present the design and implementation of a pervasive system that supports data collection, curation, and exploratory analysis. Finally, to date, a few systems have been developed to facilitate collaboration among scientists across large displays and tabletops (e.g. [24, 37]). However, these systems target experts rather than novices.

Applications for Citizen Scientists

Numerous mobile and web applications have been created to engage non-scientists in scientific data collection. Several of these programs have demonstrated the value of mobile devices for data collection (e.g. OilReporter[1], and iNaturalist[2]). Here, we only discuss those most relevant to our work. Project BudBurst[3] engages citizen scientists in phenology data collection. It provides online reference, allowing users to collect data in different locations using standard paper-based journals or mobile phones. Creek Watch [11] is a mobile application for data capture that was designed to ensure the usefulness of the data collected. While empowering citizen scientists to collect data, both BudBurst and Creek Watch maintain a traditional model where citizen scientists collect data for scientists to study. Pathfinder [14] is an online collaboration environment for citizen scientists which challenges this traditional model. While Pathfinder shares our goal of empowering non-scientists to contribute to authentic research, it targets a distributed user population studying transportation patterns.

GREENTOUCH: DESIGN AND IMPLEMENTATION

Design Strategy

Our goal was to develop an interactive system for engaging novice users in both data collection and exploratory analysis of phenology research. Due to the complexity of this domain, our design strategy combined user-centered and participatory design methods. We established design partnerships with a botany research group led by the director of botanical gardens in our institution. The group consisted of four faculty members and six undergraduate student researchers. To formulate requirements and design goals, we collected data through a series of recurring individual hour-long meetings with members of this group. A review of related literature and teaching materials provided us with additional insight. Our design partners were an integral part of our team. They participated in brainstorming sessions and provided concrete feedback on a series of prototypes. This participatory and iterative process was instrumental for increasing the fidelity and ecological validity of our system. Based on the data we collected, we identified a set of requirements for supporting novice users in scientific inquiry of phenology:

R1: Simplifying and accelerating the capture of heterogeneous, consistent, and accurate data

Phenology researchers collect data about various biological events in specific locations repetitively over a long period of time. Researchers capture heterogeneous data that include GPS data, quantitative data (e.g. height), weather conditions, digital photos, and notes. We identified three core challenges for engaging students in data collection. 1) *Quality of data*: capturing scientific data requires observation, technical skills, and judgment that are often developed through experience and guidance. Thus, data collected by students are often less accurate and prone to errors. The quality of the data is also affected by varying levels of commitment and effort. 2) *Time*: repetitive data collection in the field is time consuming and often takes portions of class time that could have been dedicated to analysis activities. 3) *Field conditions*: data collection is often conducted under harsh conditions such as heavy rain or the presence of insects. Often, students are required to carry materials and instruments to access a remote site.

Considering these challenges, we defined R1: simplifying and accelerating the capture of heterogeneous data while increasing accuracy and consistency. A technological solution must also be flexible enough to accommodate various data collection protocols and instruments.

R2: Transforming disparate data into a cohesive collection

The current practice of data collection includes the use of paper journals along various instruments. Thus, a core challenge for data curation is transforming data into an analyzable form. Most often, this means manually typing or copying information into a spreadsheet, a process that is time consuming and error-prone. We found that data collected by students is often not used, since it is not transformed into digital form. Furthermore, there is only limited computational support for coordinating, associating, and organizing the heterogeneous data collected in the field [7, 40]. Thus, we identify R2: Providing a solution for transforming disparate data into a *cohesive* collection of analyzable and related data sets rapidly and reliably.

R3: Facilitating exploratory analysis of heterogeneous data by novices, and R4: Fostering collaborative learning, reflection and discussion.

To understand complex systems, biologists utilize various generic tools, including statistical and visualization software, image processing packages, and geographic information systems (GIS). While providing rich functionality, these tools pose high threshold and are often not suitable for novices. One of the instructors stated: "Our GIS system has the capability of multimedia, but it has a steep learning curve. It will take hours to get that far." In addition, generic tools do not support important aspects of college-level science learning such as high-level reasoning and collaborative learning. Another instructor describes: "For teaching research, having data analysis be more participatory is really important. It's something that is kind of a black box now for students." We thereby define R3: Facilitate exploratory analysis of heterogeneous data by novice users, and R4: Foster collaborative learning, reflection, and discussion.

Design Goals

In addition to the requirements above, we defined the following learning goals for GreenTouch:

---

[1] http://oilreporter.org
[2] http://inaturalist.org
[3] http://neoninc.org/budburst

L1 Developing observation and data collection skills
L2 Interpreting field data through critical examination
L3 Forming hypotheses based on exploratory analysis

We then translated our requirements and learning goals into specific goals aimed at informing our design:

G1 Allowing novices to collect, curate, and explore scientific phenology data.
G2 Reducing the mental workload associated with accessing and manipulating large amounts of heterogeneous data.
G3 Providing fluid transition between data collection, data exploration, and hypothesis forming.
G4 Fostering learning through discussion and reflection.

Following, we describe the development of GreenTouch; focusing on the rationale we followed to meet these goals.

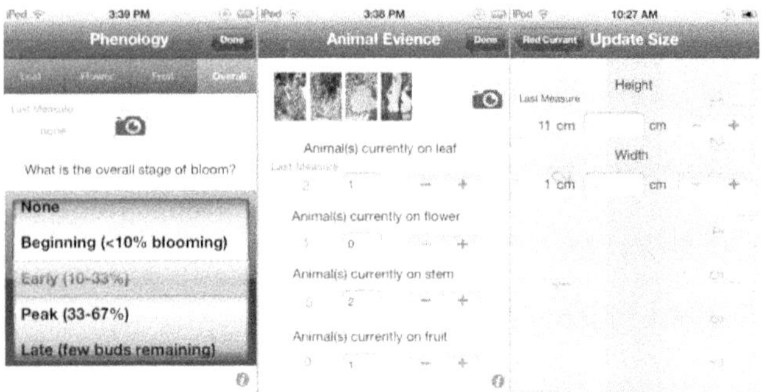

Figure 3: (a) A prompt to guide through categorical data collection. (b) A prompt for numerical data collection. (c) A ruler facilitates accurate measurements.

Design principles

In addition to our requirements and design goals, we propose the following generalizable design principles to foster collaborative inquiry of complex domains:

1) Reducing complexity - to lessen the mental workload associated with manipulating large amounts of information, we aimed to reduce the perceptive complexity of the interface while supporting rich inquiry cycles.

2) Supporting reflection - research indicates that reflection is essential for learning in the sciences [33]. Thus, we sought to support users in stepping back from "action mode" to achieve perspective, evaluate their experiences, and formally articulate insights.

3) Designing for large amounts of data - we aimed to create an environment that enables novice users to explore and make sense of large amounts of data. We applied various strategies including reducing clutter, highlighting connections, and supporting spatial manipulation.

4) Utilizing ecology of devices - to support fluid interaction across an inquiry cycle, we utilize ecology of devices, where each device used for a particular activity best supported by its affordance. For example, mobile devices facilitate portability and suit data capture in the field, while horizontal tabletops mediate collaborative discussion [4,6,10,24,35]. It is also important to consider metaphors for communicating relationships between different devices.

System Design

While there may be multiple ways to address each of these goals, our challenge was to find a way to address them all in a coherent design. Early in the design process, we realized that no single device is capable of meeting our design goals, so our system consists of three interconnected components: a mobile user interface for field data capture, a web application for automatic data curation, and a tabletop user interface for exploratory data analysis in the lab. Together, these components constitute a pervasive environment that enables novice science students to engage in scientific inquiry.

Mobile Interface for Heterogeneous Data Collection

The GreenTouch mobile interface augments traditional field data collection in several ways: 1) automatically tagging each entry with time, location, user names, and weather conditions (weather condition data is collected through Wi-Fi communication with a meteorological station on site); 2) presenting users with prompts that follow a particular field protocol while supporting the collection of heterogeneous data (e.g. measurements, photos, and notes); 3) applying mechanisms to ensure data quality.

To initiate interaction, users scan a QR code of a specific site or select a location from a list. Then, users are presented with a status update followed by a series of prompts that guide them through data collection. Figures 1 and 2 show data collection using GreenTouch. Upon completion, users submit their data via Wi-Fi.

Our design aims to reduce the threshold and provide guidance for capturing quality data (G1). To accelerate data collection under harsh weather conditions and to facilitate the collection of standardized data, we gave up the rich affordance of the traditional paper notebook in favor of a small computational device (i.e., iPod). Such devices can be easily protected from water and are capable of recording voice notes, capturing video, taking photos, and communicating through Wi-Fi. Through well-structured and standardized multiple-choice prompts, we reduced the need for text entry. However, users could choose to enter text in dedicated notes fields. We applied a multifaceted approach to ensure data quality, which considered completeness, consistency, and accuracy. To increase consistency and accuracy, we provided access to situated reference information, sample data, and an accurate ruler. We also checked for data completeness. To foster a sense of ownership, we associated a user name with each data entry (G4). Figure 3 shows screenshots of the mobile interface.

Figure 4: Map-based visualization with lenses for exploring heterogeneous data.

Web application for data curation

The web application makes data available in the "cloud" for both humans and machines. Data passes between mobile devices and the web application using a Wi-Fi network installed on campus (G3). The tabletop interface draws data from the web application and makes it available for users to manipulate. It then passes new information (e.g. users' annotations) back to the web application. Users can also access the data directly by downloading a spreadsheet. The application organizes the spreadsheet by data site. For each site, it curates quantitative and categorical data as well as links to relevant digital photos. The photos are stored on Flickr and can be accessed directly by users. Curating the data in the "cloud" lowers the threshold for maintaining, sharing, and accessing large amounts of data (G1).

Tabletop Interface for Collaborative Exploration

Based on existing research indicating that tabletop interfaces support collaboration through visibility of actions, egalitarian input and physical participation [5, 8, 20, 21, 30], facilitate active reading [16], and afford distributed cognition [18, 30], we decided to utilize tabletop interaction to facilitate collaborative data exploration (G4).

The GreenTouch tabletop interface supports the integration of heterogeneous data. To initiate interaction, users select a data set. The interface then displays a map-based visualization with highlighted sites. When a user touches a site, a semi-transparent circular "lens" appears around the site (see Figure 4). Each lens has several filters that can be applied to explore different facets of information. For example, Figure 4 shows two lenses: the first (right) displays an interactive time-series visualization, while the second lens (left) shows an interactive timeline of photos. Filters can be easily added or removed. The interactive time-series visualization in Figure 4 shows the overlay of two phenology data sets. The visualization also presents descriptive statistics for each time series that include mean, standard deviation, number of entries, and the minimum and maximum values. Users can pan left and right to explore large data sets and touch individual data points to display additional information (e.g. user name or weather).

The application provides the following filters: time series, interactive timeline, photo library, and hypotheses. Lenses can be moved and rotated upon the surface, as well as, easily removed. Users can annotate individual data points, particular time series, and different photos (see Figure 5). Users can also save photos or entire lenses for later reference by dragging the items into a "drawer" at the bottom of the surface. Users can "open the drawer" to revisit saved items at any point. Figure 5 shows a semi-open drawer. To combine data sets, users simply overlay two lenses, which are merged into a single lens.

Figure 5: A merged dataset and semi-open drawer with 3 annotated photos.

While the GreenTouch tabletop application eliminates some of the advanced functionality offered by existing statistics packages and GIS tools, the focus of our design was not on quantitative analysis but rather on enabling flexible but rich comparisons. Thus, we implemented: 1) seamless integration of quantitative and qualitative data, 2) fluid transition between data sets including merging data sets and side by side comparison, and 3) built-in visualizations that help users quickly see patterns.

Implementation

The GreenTouch mobile application is implemented using iOS and runs on iPod Touch devices. The QR code reading is implemented using the ZXing library. The application saves data locally until a Wi-Fi connection is available and then passes it to the web application. Photos are submitted to Flickr using the ObjectiveFlickr API. Photos are tagged by site, plant, and description. This allows users to view and share photos using any desktop computer. The tabletop interface is implemented using Microsoft Surface SDK 1.0 and updated to Surface 2.0 SDK for the SUR40. The web application is implemented in Python using Google ApPEngine. The application receives data in the JSON format and upon request prints out a comma-delimited document (.csv) that can be opened by various tools. The application can also print to a webpage as well as use JSON format to send data to the mobile and tabletop interfaces.

EVALUATING GREENTOUCH

Our goal was to gain an understanding of the strengths and limitations of GreenTouch in supporting college-level learning through collaborative inquiry. We thereby utilized a variety of quantitative measures and qualitative indicators, that combined together, highlight multiple facets of the collaborative learning process.

Throughout the development process of GreenTouch, we applied a multi-tiered evaluation framework [31], which consisted of three *in situ* studies with a total of 132 participants. All studies were conducted by deploying the interface in *intro to botany* courses in our institution; participants were undergraduate students enrolled in the course (all female, age range 18-22). GreenTouch was used to replace a paper-based *data collection* activity included in the syllabus. Due to the challenges discussed in the requirement analysis (R2, R3) the original syllabus did not include an *exploratory analysis* activity. However, during the three semesters in which GreenTouch was studied, the instructors added an exploratory analysis activity facilitated by GreenTouch. All studies took place in our institution's botanic gardens. Partial Wi-Fi coverage was available.

Study	Metrics & indicators	Methods	Iteration
Spring '11 (n=43) Usability	• Accuracy • Completion rates • Errors • Satisfaction • Time on task	• Logging • Observations • Questionnaires • Debrief	Mobile: • Navigation • Situated reference • Comments • Summary Surface: • Cloud metaphor • Lenses
Fall '11 (n=35) Usefulness	• Accuracy • Number and quality of hypotheses • Participation • Satisfaction • Time on task	(all of the above) • Video analysis • Interviews	Mobile: • Ruler • Sample data • Data checks Surface: • Drawer • Visualization
Spring '12 (n=54) Impact	(all of the above) • Talk categories • User actions • Information artifacts	(all of the above) • Discourse analysis	Surface: • Advanced statistics tools

Table 1: Metrics, methods, and design iterations.

The first study applied a micro-perspective - focusing on the *usability* and functionality of concrete interaction techniques; the second study applied a macro-perspective - studying the *usefulness* of the system in the context of a full-scale task; the third study applied holistic perspective – examining the *impact* of the system on the collaborative-inquiry process. Table 1 describes the metrics, collection and analysis methods used in each study, and the major features addressed in following design iterations. In this paper we report findings from the third, most recent, study.

User study: Spring '12

We deployed GreenTouch in an intro to botany course for a period of 4 weeks in which students collected spring phenology data. In each of 4 weekly lab sections (held on different days and lasting 3 hours each), students collected data in the field. Overall, 54 students (25 pairs and 4 singletons) participated in the data collection phase, collecting data on 5 species. In week 4, following data collection, each lab section was divided into smaller groups which used the tabletop interface to explore the entire data set. Participants were asked to form two hypotheses for future research based on exploratory data analysis. Overall 49 students, 24 groups participated in the data analysis activity (21 pairs, 2 triples, 1 single). Two Microsoft Surface 1.0 and one SUR40 devices were set up for this activity in the botany lab. While three groups used the tabletop interface, others completed an unrelated activity. Upon task completion, the groups switched activities.

Mobile

Satisfaction

We used post-task questionnaires and interviews to evaluate usefulness and satisfaction. Table 2 shows the questionnaire results. Overall, users found the interface useful and enjoyed using it. The results also show moderate confidence levels and an indication that the application helped users to reflect on the purpose of the study. Through post-task interviews and an investigation of the data collected we found evidence that users improved their observation and data collection skills (L1). For example, one user described: "The app made my observations more systematic and organized." Users also commented on the utility of the mobile device: "Much easier to collect data and it saved paper!" In face-to-face interviews, conducted in weeks 2 and 3, the instructors confirmed that the data collected is useful and that the curation method is effective for both teaching and research.

Question	Mean (SD)
Using the app made my observations better.	4.19 (0.96)
Using the app made me consider the relationship between climate and phenology.	3.66 (0.82)
Using the app let me collect data faster than without the app.	4.52 (0.95)
Using the app made it easier to collect heterogeneous data.	4.37 (1.06)
I enjoyed using this app to collect data.	3.49 (1.05)
I was confident in the accuracy of the data I gathered.	3.39 (1.03)

Table 2: Results of post-task questionnaire for mobile interface, scale of 1 (strongly disagree) to 5 (strongly agree).

Collaboration

To get insight into the collaborative process during data collection, we analyzed observations collected by investigators positioned in each data site and transcripts of user dialogs recorded for each pair in each session (total 79 legible recordings). We coded for verbal participation, data entry events, and physical interaction with plants of study.

We found that in the first session most pairs collaborated through *turn taking,* sharing control of the device while demonstrating similar levels of involvement. Decisions were made through critical discussion. In subsequent sessions however, in about *half* of the pairs the partnership became less equitable. One participant would take control of the device early on and "drive" for the session. The driver would think aloud while the navigator was participating verbally, interrupting the driver to express different ideas. In most *driver-navigator* pairs, the same participant assumed the role of the driver in all sessions. Overall, we found that most pairs (21/25) exhibited effective collaboration (turn-takers 13/25 or driver-navigator 8/25) that was motivated by the *opportunities for discussion* provided by the mobile interface, while in a small number of teams (4/25 driver-passenger) only the driver was involved in the task. The data collection prompts and the situated reference data encouraged students to reach decisions through discussion, which, in turn increased their confidence in the data collected. As one student described: "Today, my partner was absent. I find it easier to work with someone and get a second opinion. It would have made me more confident about the results."

Tabletop

Performance

The 24 groups spent on average 27:37 minutes using the system (SD 7:40 minutes). The relatively large standard deviation can be attributed to natural variation between participants and groups. At the end of each session, each group was required to formulate two hypotheses about the data for future research, while providing supportive evidence. The instructors rated 22 of the hypotheses on a scale of 1 to 5, where one was assigned to a shallow and simple observation, and five represented an exceptionally insightful hypothesis. The instructor ratings were distributed as follows: one (0%), two (27%), three (27%), four (36%), and five (5%). Overall 68% of the hypotheses formed by students were valuable and based on evidence. This indicates that users were able to utilize the interface to make sense of the heterogeneous data sets and derive useful insights (L3) within a short time frame.

Satisfaction

To gage user satisfaction, we utilized a post-task questionnaire, which asked users to rate enjoyment, confidence in their findings, difficulty of the task, and frustration using the interface. We used a Likert scale of 1 (low) to 7 (high). Users were also asked to comment on their experience. We found that users enjoyed (4.38 mean, 1.85 std) using the interface, had a moderately high confidence in their hypotheses (4.28 mean, 1.35 std) and low frustration (2.93 mean, 2.06 std). One participant shared: "I liked manipulating the data and exploring the ways in which it was possible to visually compare it. It made the analysis much less time consuming and probably more accurate." Users rated the difficulty of the task as moderate (3.43 mean, 1.56 std). Among SUR40 users, we found lower enjoyment (3.58, 2.27 std) and increased frustration (3.17, 2.44 std) caused by over sensitivity, which registered hovers as accidental touches.

Collaboration

To gain insight into *how* users collaborate and solve problems using GreenTouch, we conducted a manual video analysis of 24 recordings. Our coding scheme included verbal and physical participation (e.g. touch events, and "offline" gestures such as pointing, reaching, blocking, note taking). We calculated levels of physical participation per participant by summing the number of touch events and offline gestures. We calculated verbal participation levels per participant based on session transcripts. We also coded the interaction with information artifacts, recording their source, type, manipulation and configuration.

Based on this analysis, we found that during the session, each of the groups applied one of two distinct *problem solving strategies*: 1) Vertical (9/24) – where investigation focused on one heterogeneous data set (i.e., lens). The data was carefully examined using the various filters to explore multiple data facets of an individual site. Once several observations were made, another dataset was introduced and merged into a new data set. Conclusions were drawn through side-by-side comparison of the original data sets and careful analysis of the merged data set. The original data sets were stored on the surface or in the drawer. If needed other datasets were introduced one at a time for detailed examination. Data sets that were determined not interesting were discarded from the table. 2) Horizontal (15/24) - users brought up as many as four data sets at a time, and compared them to one another by aligning them next to each other. Users explored multiple facets of the data with the goal of identifying general trends from as much data as possible. Inter-coder reliability based on a random sample of 20% of the data was measured using Cohen's Kappa as 1.0 (95% CI: [0.12, 1.8]), indicating strong agreement. In both strategies we observed that participants moved information artifacts on the tabletop frequently and used the horizontal surface for spatially arranging the lens in meaningful ways, for example utilizing proximity to reflect potential connections. Also, side-by-side comparison was a key feature in both strategies. Some groups used the "drawer" as their workspace to arrange and compare lenses, while others used it for saving and revisiting information artifacts. Most teams didn't use the hypotheses filter for recording their observations through note taking until the end of the session when they were asked to record their hypotheses.

Studying physical and verbal participation data, we found that in the beginning of the session, often one user was unsure about trying out the new technology and thus waited until the partner took physical control of the system. When the timid user became comfortable with the technology, or was pushed into action due to their partner's inability to complete a task, they began interacting with the system physically. This would often result in turn-taking collaboration for the rest of the session. In other cases, users switched roles between driver (who participates both physically and verbally) and navigator (who guides the driver through verbal cues and "offline" gestures). We identified that in general, pair collaboration patterns could be described using 3 profiles (we excluded the singleton user): turn-takers (9 of 23), driver-navigator (10 of 23), and driver-passenger (2 of 23). The 2 groups of triples could be described as driver-navigator-passenger, and turn-takers and passenger. Inter-coder reliability based on a random sample of 20% of the data was measured using Cohen's Kappa as 0.62 (95% CI: [-0.19, 1.42]), indicating substantial agreement. These profiles draw on those presented by Shaer et al. [31] but were adjusted to describe interaction in triples. Interestingly, while most pairs collaborated effectively, in the triples one user was less engaged (i.e. passenger). This may result from our design, which uses a single orientation and thus affords side-by-side interaction leading to the exclusion of a third user.

To better understand the *nature of the dialogue* around the tabletop, we conducted a discourse analysis using transcripts of 23 groups (we excluded the singleton user). We iteratively developed a coding scheme that classifies talk into seven general categories. Table 3 defines each talk category and provides an example from the transcript for each. It also shows the proportional distribution of talk categories. Inter-coder reliability based on a random sample of 20% of the data was good with 81% agreement. These results suggest that users were mostly engaged in effective discussion, which focused on the task, as evident by the proportion of talk dedicated to problem solving and reflection (together 48%) and the low percentage of disengagement utterances (3%). We also found within the problem solving and reflection utterances evidence that users interpreted the data through critical examination (L2) (see examples in Table 3). Our discourse analysis further indicates that users established task division through continuous discussion as evident by the proportion of coordination talk (25%) and found the interface easy to use as evident by the low proportion of syntax talk (8%).

DISCUSSION

We applied holistic approach in examining the impact of GreenTouch on the collaborative-inquiry process, focusing on performance, satisfaction, and collaboration.

Our findings provide *empirical evidence for the feasibility and value* of utilizing ecology of devices for helping college students learn *complex* concepts through collaborative inquiry. In particular, we showed that GreenTouch: 1) allows novices to collect consistent and useful heterogeneous data that is curated automatically (G1); 2) enables novice students to participate in exploratory analysis that produces valuable insights through effective collaboration (G2, G4); and 3) facilitates nearly seamless transitions between stages across the workflow (pending connectivity) with no manual intervention (G3). While these results are specific, taken together they make up a compelling case study of using interactive surfaces for collaborative learning of complex concepts.

Category	Definition	Examples from transcripts
Problem Solving 43%	Planning, relevant questions or pointing out facts.	1: It didn't change degree. 3: Oh, okay. And then if we look at this, then we have quite a fluctuation, but both going towards a more positive trend upwards, so maybe over a longer period of time we can see an average upward
Coordination 25%	Turn taking, navigating, verbal shadowing, or task division.	2: Let's just focus on health because that is like growing 1: Wait, we should choose another plant. 2: OK. Let's compare it with 1: Which one?
Reflection 5%	Referring to the purpose of the exercise, the data collection, analysis, or hypothesis forming stages.	1: Okay, so it looks like someone didn't know what they were doing when they were doing the data. It's quite possible. Everybody was doing it for the first time and it's hard to know whether it is a leaf bud, a flower bud...
Peer Teaching 1%	One participant teaches the other how to analyze or interpret data.	1: Yeah, but she<the instructor> was saying that you already know the actual x-values...so you don't look at it as a line but rather as individual points so that gives you...there... <how to read a graph>
Syntax 8%	Referring to how to use certain features.	1: Oh. Wait. How'd you say you could combine them?
Brief Response 15%	Short responses to suggestions	1: Yeah 2: Yeah 3: mumbles
Disengagement 3%	Non-task related	2: And our report is due the 23rd. 3: No it said the 30th

Table 3: Dialogue coding scheme.

We also highlight *how users collaborate and solve problems* using handheld and tabletop interfaces in the context of college level inquiry-based learning. We showed that *mobile interfaces* could motivate effective co-located collaboration by providing *opportunities for discussion.* We also showed that mobile interfaces can guide users in complex inquiry through *situated reference*. We further demonstrated that the large size and shared workspace of a tabletop display provide benefits for collaborative problem solving. For example, side-by-side comparison and spatial interaction played an essential role in the problem-solving process mediated by GreenTouch: users accumulated, arranged, and moved information artifacts on the tabletop frequently. Also, we found that most pairs collaborated effectively through turn taking and role switching (driver-navigator). Such collaboration styles were mediated by the large horizontal multi-touch display and were established through continuous coordination (see Table 3). To date, few projects have explored the use of interactive surfaces with college-level learners (rather than children); thus, these insights shed light on how *older* users collaborate and solve problems using interactive surfaces. These findings are important for driving the discussion on educational benefits of interactive surfaces, for college-level learning, forward.

Finally, our study has several limitations that point towards future work: we neither provided participants with the opportunity to engage in iterative analysis nor measured learning outcomes in a way that enables to assess individual learning and participants' ability to apply their learning.

Designing for collaborative inquiry of complex concepts

Four generalizable guidelines shaped our design:

First, *reducing complexity*: we applied design strategies for eliminating complexity including traditional methods such as, reducing functionality and hiding complexity [10], as well as using reality-based metaphors [9] that draw upon interaction with the non-digital world, such as: lenses, filters, and drawers. Our evaluation shows that the use of lenses for displaying multi-faceted data combined with spatial interaction facilitated three aspects that were important for collaborative problem solving: incremental addition of complexity, seamless integration of quantitative and qualitative data, and fluid transition between data sets.

Second, *providing space for reflection*: to support reflection we provided physical space for the conceptual construction of ideas. On the tabletop interface, we implemented a "drawer," which allows users to deposit and revisit information. We found that while some users used the "drawer" for storing and revisiting data, others used it as their workspace, preferring to separate data retrieval from analysis. We also provided a space for formally articulating observations (i.e. hypotheses lens) through note taking. This space was not used often since users did not like typing using the multi touch keyboard. We suggest exploring alternative modalities for recording observations such as voice and pen input. On the mobile interface, we allowed users to reflect on their last data entry by presenting, upon request, a summary of the data collected. While some users used this feature to reflect on the data, most users were focused on collecting data. We plan to explore alternative designs to encourage users to step back from action mode.

Third, *designing for large amounts of data*: to mitigate the workload associated with manipulating large amounts of data, we designed for reducing clutter, highlighting the connections among information artifacts, and providing space for spatial manipulation. Our findings indicate that this approach allowed for both vertical and horizontal problem-solving strategies. We also considered the size of user interface elements, optimizing target size for touch while seeking to effectively utilize limited screen real estate. This required us to make tradeoffs such as overlaying information, and limiting the resizing of some tabletop information artifacts (e.g. lenses).

Finally, *utilizing ecology of devices*: our design facilitates nearly seamless transition across stages of the inquiry cycle by utilizing ecology of devices consisting of a mobile interface for capturing data, a web application for data curation in the "cloud," and a tabletop interface for group collaborative analysis. By making information available in the cloud, we also allow for new devices to be integrated into the GreenTouch device ecology. We experimented with various metaphors for communicating the relationship between the devices. For example, our early prototype (evaluated in the first study) was designed around the use of a "container" metaphor. When placing a mobile device on the tabletop, information appeared on the tabletop surface. However, users were confused by this metaphor and were not sure when it was safe to remove the device from the Surface. As a result, mobile devices were left on the Surface, covering important screen real estate. The current prototype uses the "site" metaphor, all data collected in a particular site is stored in the "cloud" and can be accessed by tapping the site on the map-based visualization. Users had no problems understanding the site and cloud metaphors and were readily able to find and retrieve data.

While we applied these guidelines to a particular domain they are generalizable and can be used to inform the design of other interfaces for college-level collaborative inquiry.

CONCLUSION

The increasing availability of commercial tabletop and handheld systems coupled with falling hardware prices remove major barriers for using interactive surfaces in educational settings. Within this context, this research makes three contributions that highlight possibilities for engaging novice users in activities that were previously available only for experts: 1) the design, implementation, and validation of a collaborative environment which allows novices to engage in scientific data capture, curation, and analysis; 2) empirical evidence for the feasibility and value of integrating interactive surfaces in college-level education; and 3) insights collected through iterative design, providing guidelines for designing multi-touch interfaces for collaborative inquiry in complex domains.

We intend to further evaluate GreenTouch in a longitudinal study by deploying it in a student research program.

ACKNOWLEDGMENTS

We thank our collaborators Kristina Jones, Marcy Thomas, Janet McDonough, and Alden Griffith. We also thank the Wellesley Botanic Gardens and all our study participants. This work is partially funded by HHMI through the Wellesley College Science Center.

REFERENCES

1. Adams, A., Coughlan, T., Lea, J., Rogers, Y., Davies, S., and Collins, T. (2011). Designing Interconnected Distributed Resources for Collaborative Inquiry Based Science Education. In Proc. of Digital Libraries.
2. Fjeld, M., Fredriksson, J., Ejdestig, M., Duca, F., Bötschi, K., Voegtli, B., and Juchli, P. (2007). Tangible User Interface for

Chemistry Education: Comparative Evaluation and Re-Design. In Proc. of CHI.
3. Fleck, R., Rogers, Y., Yuill, N., Marshall, P., Carr, A., Rick, J., and Bonnett, V. (2009). Actions Speak Loudly with Words: Unpacking Collaboration Around the Table. In Proc. of ITS.
4. Grant, W.C. (1993). Wireless Coyote: a Computer-Supported Field Trip. Commun. ACM 36, 5 (pp.57-59).
5. Harris, A., Rick, J., Bonnett, V., Yuill, N., Fleck, R., Marshall, P., and Rogers, Y. (2009). Around the Table: Are multiple-touch surfaces better than single-touch for children's collaborative interactions? In Proc. of CSCL.
6. Hey, T., Tansley, S., Tolle, K. (2009). The Fourth Paradigm: Data-Intensive Scientific Discovery, Microsoft Research, Redmond.
7. Horn, M.S., Tobiasz, M., and Shen, C. (2009). Visualizing Biodiversity with Voronoi Treemaps. In Proc. Sixth International Symposium on Voronoi Diagrams in Science and Engineering.
8. Hornecker, E., Marshall, P., Dalton, N.S., and Rogers, Y. (2008). Collaboration and Interference: Awareness with Mice or Touch Input. Proc. of CSCW.
9. Jacob, R. J., Girouard, A., Hirshfield, L. M., Horn, M. S., Shaer, O., Solovey, E. T., and Zigelbaum, J. (2008). Reality-based Interaction: a Framework for Post-WIMP Interfaces. In Proc. of CHI.
10. Janlert, L.E. and Stolterman, E. (2008). Complex interaction. ACM Trans. Comput.-Hum. Interact. 17, 2.
11. Kim, S., Robson, C., Zimmerman, T., Pierce, J., and Haber, E.B. (2011). Creek Watch: Pairing usefulness and Usability for Successful Citizen Science. In Proc. of CHI.
12. Lopatto, D. (2007). Undergraduate research experiences support science career decisions and active learning. CBE Life Science Edu. 6, (297--306).
13. Lopatto D. et al. (2008). Undergraduate research. Genomics Education Partnership. Science. 322:684-5.
14. Luther, K., Counts, S., Stecher, K.B., Hoff, A., and Johns, P. (2009). Pathfinder: an Online Collaboration Environment for Citizen Scientists. In Pro. of CHI.
15. Mirel, B. (2009). Supporting cognition in systems biology analysis: findings on users' processes and design implications. J Biomed Discov Collab. 27(2).
16. Morris, M.R., Brush, A.J.B., and Meyers, B. (2007). Reading revisited: evaluating the usability of digital display Surfaces for Active Reading Tasks. Proc. of IEEE Tabletop (pp.79-86).
17. Okada, T., and Simon, H.A. (1997). Collaborative discovery in a scientific domain. Cognitive Science (pp.109-146).
18. Patten, J., and Ishii, H. (2000). A comparison of spatial organization strategies in graphical and tangible user interfaces, Proc. of Designing Augmented Reality Environments.
19. Piper, A.M., and Hollan, J. (2009). Tabletop displays for small group study: affordances of paper and digital materials. In Proc. of CHI.
20. Rick, J., Rogers, Y., Haig, C., and Yuill, N. (2009). Learning by doing with shareable interfaces. Children, Youth and Environments, (pp.321–342).
21. Rick, J., Marshall, P., and Yuill, N. (2011). Beyond one-size-fits-all: How interactive tabletops support collaborative learning. In Proceedings of IDC.
22. Rogers, Y., Price, S., Randell, C., Fraser, D.S., Weal, M., and Fitzpatrick, G. (2005). Ubi-learning integrates indoor and outdoor experiences. Commun (pp.55-59).
23. Rogers, Y., Connelly, K., Hazlewood, W., and Tedesco, L. (2010). Enhancing learning: a study of how mobile devices can facilitate sensemaking. Personal Ubiquitous Computing (pp.111-124).
24. Ryall, K., Forlines, C., Shen, C., Morris, M.R., and Everitt, K. (2006). Experiences with and Observations of Direct-Touch Tabletops. In Proc. IEEE Tabletop.
25. Scardamalia, M., & Bereiter, C. (2006). Knowledge building: Theory, pedagogy, and technology. In K. Sawyer (Ed.), Cambridge Handbook of the Learning Sciences (pp. 97-118). New York: Cambridge University Press.
26. Schkolne, S., Ishii, H., and Schroder, P. (2004). Immersive design of DNA molecules with a tangible interface, Visualization, IEEE.
27. Schneider, B., Strait, M. Muller, L., Elfenbein, S., Shaer, O., Shen, C. (2012). Phylo-Genie: Engaging Students in Collaborative 'Tree-Thinking' through Tabletop Techniques. In Proc. of CHI.
28. Seymour, E., et al. (2004). Establishing the benefits of research experiences for undergraduates in the sciences: First findings from a three-year study. Science Education, 88(4).
29. Shaer, O., Kol, G., Strait, M., Fan, C., Grevet, C., and Elfenbein, S. (2010). G-nome surfer: a tabletop interface for collaborative exploration of genomic data. In Proc. of CHI.
30. Shaer, O., Strait, M., Valdes, C., Lintz, M., Feng, T., and Wang, H. (2011). Enhancing Genomic Learning through Tabletop Interaction. In Proc. of CHI.
31. Shaer, O., Strait, M., Valdes, C., Wang, H., Feng, T., Lintz, M., Ferreirae, M., Grote, C. Tempel, K., and Liu, S. (2012) "The Design, Development, and Deployment of a Tabletop Interface for Collaborative Exploration of Genomic Data", Int J of Human-Computer Studies.
32. Sharples, M., Corlett, D., and Westmancott, O. (2002). The Design and Implementation of a Mobile Learning Resource. Personal Ubiquitous Computing (220-234).
33. Singer, S. R., Hilton M. L., and Schweingruber, H. A. (2005). America's lab report: investigations in high School science, National Research Council.
34. Soloway, E. (2001). Log on education: Handheld devices are ready-at-hand. Commun (pp.15-20).
35. Song K, Kim G, Han I, Lee J, Park J, and Ha S. (2011). CheMO: mixed object instruments and interactions for tangible chemistry experiments. In Proc. of CHI.
36. Tanner, K., Chatman, L. S., and Allen, D. (2003). Cooperative learning in the science classroom - beyond students working in groups. Cell Biol. Educ.
37. Wigdor, D., Jiang, H., Forlines, C., Borkin, M., Shen, C. (2009). The WeSpace: The Design, Development and Deployment of a Walk-Up and Share Multi-Surface Visual Collaboration System. In Proc. of CHI.
38. Yeh, R., Liao, C., Klemmer, S., Guimbretiere, F., Lee, B., Kakaradov, B., Stamberger, J. and Paepcke, A., (2006). ButterflyNet: a mobile capture and access system for field biology research. In Proc. of CHI.

Orchestrating a Multi-tabletop Classroom: From Activity Design to Enactment and Reflection

Roberto Martinez-Maldonado, Judy Kay, Kalina Yacef
School of Information Technologies
The University of Sydney,
NSW 2006, Australia
{roberto, judy, kalina}@it.usyd.edu.au

Marie-Theresa Edbauer
Business School
The University of Sydney,
NSW 2006, Australia
medb1925@uni.sydney.edu.au

Yannis Dimitriadis
School of Telecommunications Engineering
University of Valladolid,
Paseo Belén 15, Spain
yannis@tel.uva.es

ABSTRACT
If multi-tabletop classrooms were available in each school, how would teachers plan and enact their activities to enhance learning and collaboration? How can they evaluate how the activities actually went compared with the plan? Teachers' effectiveness in orchestrating the classroom has a direct impact on students learning. Interactive tabletops offer the potential to support teachers by enhancing their awareness and classroom control. This paper describes our mechanisms to help a teacher orchestrate a classroom activity using multiple interactive tabletops. We analyse automatically captured interaction data to assess whether the *activity design*, as intended by the teacher, was actually followed during its *enactment*. We report on an authentic classroom study embedded in the curricula of an undergraduate Management unit. This involved 236 students across 14 sessions. The main contribution of the paper is an approach for designing a multi-tabletop classroom that can help teachers plan their learning activities; and provide data for assessment and *reflection* on the enactment of a series of classroom sessions.

Author keywords: User-centred design; Collaborative learning; Interactive Tabletops; Classroom Orchestration

ACM Classification: H5.2 Information interfaces and presentation: User interfaces, Input devices and strategies.

INTRODUCTION

Collaboration has proved successful in helping groups to achieve improved critical thinking and higher levels of thought that can lead to more effective learning outcomes [4]. This motivates teachers to use small group activities in their classrooms. However, group work also poses its own challenges, particularly in terms of the teacher's ability to support each group effectively. These include time constraints; class control skills; a different learning pace of each group; and limitations imposed by the activity [6].

ITS'12, November 11–14, 2012, Cambridge, Massachusetts, USA.

Interactive tabletops have significant potential to support a number of different aspects of education, spanning from providing a shared and enriched interactive space which can promote students collaboration [14, 20, 26, 27], to supporting teachers by improving their awareness [17, 18] or their control over a class [1, 10, 19]. Nonetheless, Muller-Tomfelde and Fjeld [21] warned about the initial overstated enthusiasm triggered by the novelty of interactive surface technologies that has not been followed by a broad adoption of such devices for real-world applications. Similarly, tabletops also offer diverse forms of educational promise [11]. However, there are still unanswered questions about the ways teachers can best take advantage of their affordances [5]. Research needs to be done to help teachers shape these technologies to match the learning objectives.

This paper describes an approach to exploit the affordances of interactive tabletops to provide a teacher the tools to monitor a classroom activity; *orchestrate* the whole class of students working in small groups; and reflect on the sessions for a possible re-design. The metaphoric term *classroom orchestration* is used to describe the role that teachers take as managers and coordinators of the cognitive, pedagogic and technological resources in the classroom, to help students achieve the intended goals of the learning activities [6, 24]. The effectiveness of orchestration and the extent to which teachers can respond to the ways students perform the class tasks is critical because it directly impacts these students' activities, and therefore, their learning [6]. The use of technology-based tools in the classroom can improve the teachers' management of the class and enhance their awareness of learners' activity. However, this requires the involvement of teachers' classroom practices in the design of the activities [2].

We report the key elements of an approach to help teachers to monitor and reflect on their classroom activity design making use of multi-touch tabletops. A series of 14 sessions of the same 1-hour tutorial were organised by a teacher to *enact* this design. These tutorials covered a topic in the formally defined set curriculum of an undergraduate-level subject. We explored the affordances of interactive tabletops to support the tutorial learning goals and to examine the consistency between the design intentions (specified by the teacher) and what actually occurred in each of the 14 classes. We evaluated our approach on three levels: assessment of how closely the class *script* was followed, measurement of *equality* of students' participation within each group, and evaluation of the achievement on the *learning outcomes*. The main contribution of the paper is an approach for designing multi-tabletop classroom systems that can help teachers to *plan* and *orchestrate* their classroom activities; and data to *assess* and *reflect* on the enactment of a series of classroom sessions. A secondary aim of this paper is to present our system, with its minimalist orchestration tools and interaction data capture functionalities, that enables a teacher to control and monitor a multi-tabletop classroom.

RELATED WORK

Several research projects have explored the use of interactive tabletops in learning contexts [13, 20, 25-27], but that previous work has been mostly limited to cases where students interact on a single table in a *controlled* learning environment, rather than on multiple tables in classroom scenarios [19]. Our work draws on some of these studies including the work done by Stock et al. [27] that explored the affordances of tabletops to help students discuss a challenging topic. We also build on the work by Kharrufa et al. [13], who described an approach for designing tabletop applications based on theories of scripted collaborative learning. Fleck et al. [8] also highlighted the importance of analysing both the verbal communication and students' physical actions with the shared device. Similarly, Rick et al's OurSpace [25] was used to investigate indicators of collaboration that could potentially be automatically measured from students interactions. Moreover, Schneider et al. [26] suggested that learning tabletop applications should provide support for reflection, engagement, and provision of feedback. Morris et al. [20] investigated the importance for groups to receive feedback at the tabletop with or without the presence of an instructor.

However, there are some important recent projects studying the role of multiple tabletops in classroom scenarios. One of the most relevant projects on multi-tabletop environments is SynergyNet [1]. This is a classroom with four multi-touch tabletops that has been used to run experiments with elementary school students engaged in an extracurricular problem solving activity (called Mysteries). This system permits the teacher to remotely control the classroom through a teacher's tabletop console. The teacher can visualise, interact with and control each group's tabletop screen from the console. The work involved qualitative observations of video-recordings to study how tabletops can support their collaborative learning interactions and the ways the teacher uses the system [19]. However, the task that students were asked to complete was outside their normal subjects and the teacher was not involved in the design of the class activity. Another reasonably similar learning environment was presented by Do-Lenh [7]. This consists of four non-multi-touch tangible tables that can keep track of fiducial markers attached to objects located on a flat surface. The learning activity was based on a simulation training application for logistics. The author presented a couple of tools to help a teacher orchestrate the classroom. These were a wall display that shows task progress and controls for the teacher to compare two groups' answers; and paper cards that a teacher could use to control individual tables. However, this work mostly focused on evaluating the *usability* of their tools on a specific case rather than integrating the teacher in the activity design or linking the task to the regular curricula. Martinez-Maldonado et al. [18] presented a dashboard that helps teachers monitoring up to three groups working at multi-touch tabletops. This dashboard showed live indicators about symmetry of verbal participation, amount of touches, progress on the task and interaction with others' objects. This project used real data from individual groups, but the evaluations were based on *simulated* concurrency.

In summary, these three previous approaches provided excellent background studies, but were not deployed in an authentic setting. This means that even when real students or teachers were involved in the studies, the tasks were not designed by the teacher and all sessions were experimental and not linked with authentic curricular activities. None of them addresses our key concerns of supporting a teacher in designing, orchestrating and reflecting on the design of an authentic activity as part of the curriculum. There was also limited automatic data capture. The information captured has mostly been targeted to researchers, designers or for in-class use only. Our work goes beyond these previous works by providing an approach to help teachers evaluate their classroom activities *design* in authentic tutorials using multiple interactive tabletops and orchestration tools. We also show that it is possible to pervasively capture rich classroom and students' data through the interactive tabletops. Then, these data can enhance the teacher's post-class *reflection* and *assessment* on the activity design and how it played out over delivered sessions.

SYSTEM OVERVIEW

We created a multi-tabletop classroom system using the following design guidelines, based on our critical analysis of previous work on classroom orchestration [6, 7], multi-tabletop classrooms [1, 18], and the specific requirements posed from the teacher in our study.

Teacher classroom control. All tabletops should be controlled by the teacher; this control should be simple and effective [6]. In particular it should be minimalist, so as not to add cognitive load to the teacher. It must be well integrated in the classroom, so the teacher does not get distracted from their teaching tasks.

User-friendly student user interface. The students' interface should be simple so that students can learn to use it within a few minutes, even on first use. This avoids wasting classroom time, considering a class session lasts only 50 minutes in our case.

Student action differentiation. It is important to distinguish which student performed each touch. This is needed to automatically identify each student's contributions or group dynamics such as dominance, leadership or disengagement.

Classroom activity capture and gathering. Distinguishing users and keeping track of all learners' actions is essential for creating monitoring tools that present overviews of students' actions or assess the match between the designed and actual enacted activities [15]. These monitoring tools should be able to access the captured information in real time and also make it available to the teacher for further activity re-design.

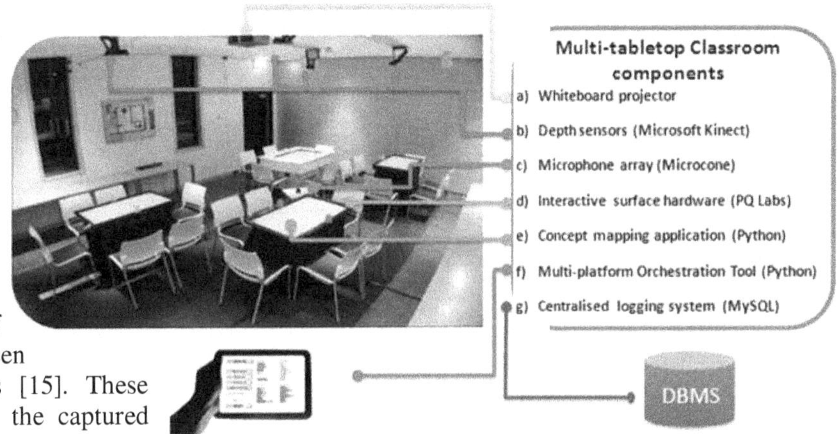

Figure 1. Multi-tabletop classroom components

Hardware

Based on these guidelines, we designed our multi-tabletop classroom. The classroom has a non interactive wall display connected to a teacher's laptop (Figure 1, a, shows the projector for this). Four multi-touch tabletops were placed in the room. These are composed of 46'' PQ Labs Multi-Touch overlays[1], placed over digital screens of the same size, which can detect up to 32 touches simultaneously (Figure 1, d). The hardware itself cannot distinguish the user who touches the screen. To obtain this information, we used a depth and vision-based system to distinguish each user's touches. This system tracks users' hands through overhead depth sensors[2] that are located on top of each tabletop (Figure 1, b). This touch identification system proved to be adequate in general terms with respect to the real world needs of this setting where students tended to stay seated at the same positions around the tabletops, as compared to the controlled environment studied in [15]. A directional microphone array was placed at the centre of the four tabletops to detect levels of sound that each group produced (Figure 1, c).

Software

We created a set of interconnected software that makes the classroom work as a single piece of technology, orchestrated by the teacher. Our two main applications, visible to the users, are: the teacher's orchestration tool and the learning application displayed in each tabletop.

Teacher's orchestration tool. The tabletops are controlled by the teacher through the *orchestration tool*. This is a multi-platform application that can be displayed on devices, such as a handheld, a desktop computer or at another tabletop. For the sessions described in this paper, it was displayed on the teachers' laptop computer. We used a participatory design process with iterative prototyping, with the teacher driving and responding to designs. This process identified five actions. The functions available are shown in Figure 2. The first is a synchronous *start* command that orders all the tabletops to start the activity. The second makes the tabletops *move from one phase to the next one* if the activity is divided in phases. Another functionality is the *freeze* feature, which blocks all tabletops in cases when teacher wants the attention of the class, and does not want students distracted by using the tabletop. The *broadcast a message* option can be used to, for example, send a time limit reminder that appears in front of each student. Finally, for the end of a class, the teacher can use the *reset* option to clear all tabletops and get them ready for the next class (with different students). Teachers can configure the dashboard to display a visualisation of each group's activity, as shown at the right of Figure 2. It shows a simple two-part bar that summarises the level of participation of each student in the activity, which was divided into two phases. It was designed to help the teacher identify individuals who may have low level of participation.

Learning application. Four interconnected instances of a minimal version of a *collaborative concept mapping application* [16] are loaded onto each tabletop (Figure 3). Concept mapping has proved effective in enhancing meaningful learning [22]. Through creating concept maps, students externalise their understanding by identifying relevant *concepts* and relationships between them, using *linking words* to create *propositions or links.* These can be read as statements. In the domain of Management, some examples of propositions are: "HR Director – reports to - CEO" or "HR Director –fires 25 of the- Low level staff".

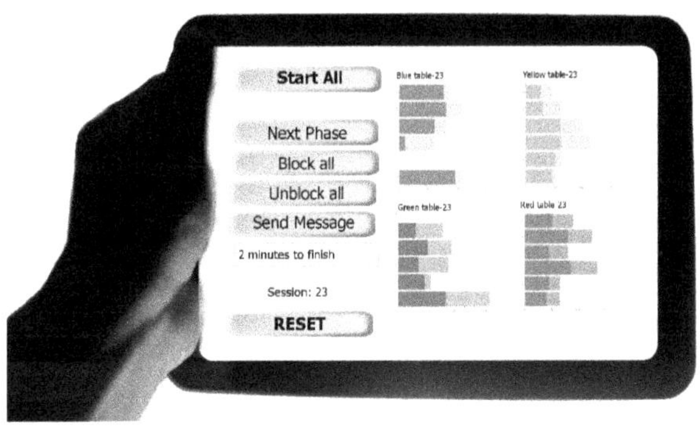

Figure 2. Teacher's orchestration tool.

[1] PQ-labs, Multi-touch http://multi-touch-screen.com/

[2] Microsoft Kinect. http://www.kinectforwindows.org/

Users can create a complete concept map about a topic in minutes by performing three possible actions: 1) *adding a concept,* by selecting it from an initial list of key concepts provided by the teacher (Figure 3, A); 2) *creating a linking word* that joins two different concepts, by dragging and dropping one concept onto the other, and then selecting a word from a list of suggested links provided by the teacher (Figure 3, B); or 3) *editing a concept/linking word,* that is fired when a student dwells on any concept or link. This brings up a virtual keyboard in front of the user who performed the selection (as resolved by the depth camera). Students can also perform other intuitive actions such as moving, deleting and resizing elements to create a concept map similar to the one shown in Figure 3, D. All captured applications logs are recorded on a central common repository (Figure 1, g).

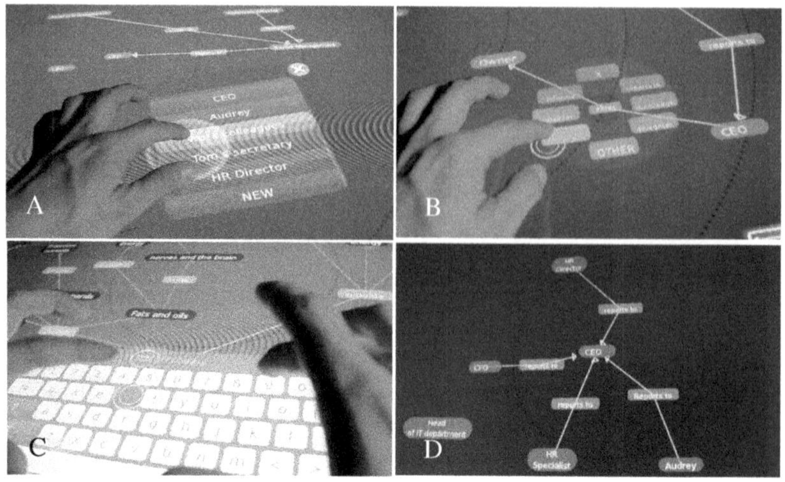

Figure 3. Minimal application for concept mapping

SMALL-GROUP CLASSROOM ACTIVITY

A learning activity was designed to fit into tutorial sessions with undergraduates in the unit: *Foundations of Management* taught in the School of Business at the *University of Sydney.* This has weekly fifty minutes tutorials that involve discussion of a previously defined case-study. Tutorials are often run as a teacher-led class discussion or by organising students in small groups. The teacher decided to use interactive tabletops to support these small group discussion activities for all the tutorials in Week 9. Importantly, the class design involved collaboration between the teacher and tabletop team to ensure that the design of the classroom activities was carefully crafted to make effective use of the multi-tabletops. Next, we describe the phases of the learning activity in terms of the timing, tools, tasks and learning objectives as intended for each repeated tutorial. Figure 4 shows the formalisation of the design using a representation developed by Prieto et al. [23]. This very concise form is gaining increased use by researchers to document orchestration plans. In this diagram we observe teacher and students actions that occur at different social levels *(classroom and small groups).* We explain each part of it in the next sub-section with special emphasis on the various *tools* available and the *atomic actions* performed by the teacher during the enactment.

Activity Design

1-Objectives explanation (10 minutes). First, the teacher explains the structure and goals of the tutorial (1a in Figure 4). Here, the objective of the tutorial is to solve a problematic scenario within an organisation. This is described in two pages provided to students one week earlier, and which they have to read as preparation. Then, the teacher explains the main concepts of the topic, and how to use the tabletop application to build a concept map (1b). The teacher makes sure that everybody understands this by walking around and stopping to check each table.

2- Activity 1 at the tabletop (15 minutes). For this activity, students are asked to *create a concept map that represents the case study organisational hierarchy and the stakeholders' power level.* This first concept mapping task enables students to establish shared understanding of their approaches to the problem, based on their preparatory reading and thinking. The tabletop application provides students with a list of the main concepts extracted from the

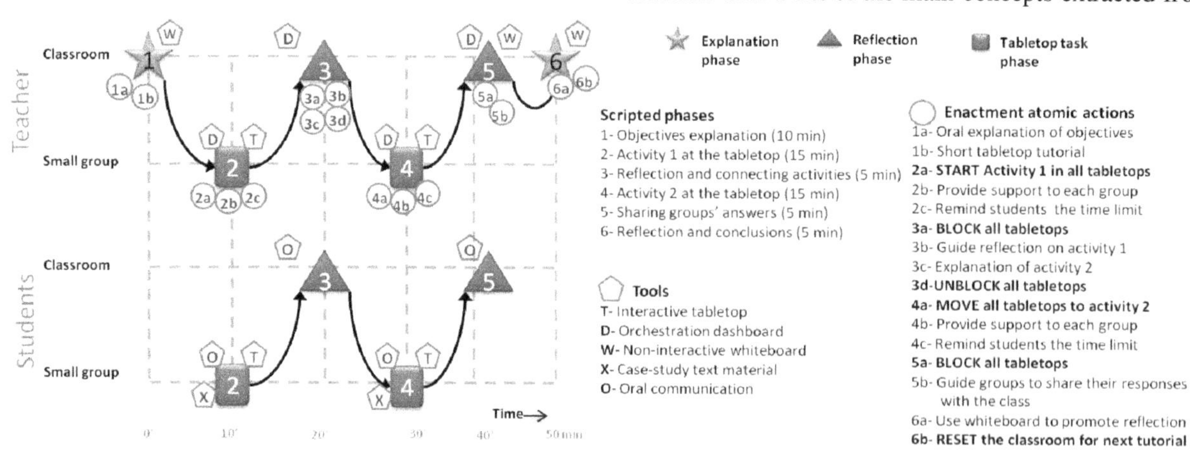

Figure 4. Design plan for the activity using the multi-tabletop classroom. This is scripted in 6 phases. Two are performed at the interactive tabletops (blue squares). The actors are students in small groups (lower), and their teacher (upper). The right half shows the phases, tools and atomic actions.

text material by the teacher. These correspond to different role players within the organisation (e.g. CEO, HR Director, Low level staff). Students can also create their own new concepts. The provision of starting concepts is important for ensuring the class to focus on the creation of the relevant propositions in the limited time available.The final product should contain the key concepts of the problem, their relationships and reflect the distribution of power within the organisation. The teacher starts the activity (2a), walks around reviewing progress and joins the discussion of some groups (2b). The teacher makes sure students are always updated on how much time they have left, by verbally reminding the class or by sending a message to all tabletops through the orchestration tool (2c).

3-Reflection and connecting activities (5 minutes). After about 15 minutes from the start of *Activity 1* the teacher stops students' activities by blocking all tabletops (3a), leads the reflection on *Activity 1* (3b), and then describes *Activity 2* (3c) explaining how it builds on *Activity 1.* When finished, the teacher unblocks all tabletops (3d).

4- Activity 2 at the tabletop (15 minutes). To start Activity 2, the teacher uses the orchestration tool to send a command to all tabletops (4a). *Activity 2* called on students to *provide a new piece of information about the problem by modifying the concept map built in the Activity 1.* Students are provided with additional concepts and different linking words to use in new types of propositions. The teacher moves around the class, meeting each group (4b). The teacher can send a time limit reminder through the orchestration tool (4c).

5- Sharing groups' answers (5 minutes). After about 15 minutes of the *Activity 2,* the teacher stops students by *freezing* all tabletops (5a). The teacher asks each group to share their solutions with the rest of the class (5b).

6- Reflection and conclusions (5 minutes). The teacher uses the notes on the whiteboard to summarise the key ideas students should take away from the tutorial and also to link it to the theories on this topic (6a). Then, the teacher resets all tabletops using the orchestration tool, ready for the next class (6b) that sometimes starts in the next 5 minutes.

Next, we describe an evaluation that highlights the affordances of our system for monitoring the match between, teacher's intentions as captured in the design shown in Figure 4 as well as those in the second column of Table 1, and the enactment of the 14 tutorials.

PRACTICAL EVALUATION: *from design to enactment*

We aimed to enable the teacher to evaluate how well the actual class matched the design intentions, particularly those that were specifically designed to exploit the tabletops affordances. Our approach did not simply adapt the pre-existing learning activities to an interactive surface: this may not translate into an improved experience and can lead to force activities that may not be ideal for these devices

Figure 5. Multi-tabletop classroom enactment

[3]. Interactive tabletops offer new opportunities for helping students and people to collaborate [13] but they also introduce new challenges. If well exploited, the affordances can create opportunities to foster collaborative learning. One key part of the appeal for a teacher to undertake this project was the opportunity to evaluate and reflect on the way the design played out in the real classroom.

The tutorials unit had 236 students scheduled in 14 tutorial slots. In each tutorial session small groups were formed to give diversity in terms of gender and international versus domestic students at each table. Students knew their peers well as they had met over several weeks before. In each tutorial session, there were at least three students per table and a maximum of six. Data from sessions was captured, including: application logs with user information, snapshots of the evolution of each group's concept map solution, and the actions performed by the teacher on the orchestration tool. Figure 5 shows one of the sessions. During classes, the teacher freely moved among the tabletops, reviewing each groups' concept map and identifying groups that needed help. The teacher had access to the orchestration tool through a personal computer. Three semi-structured interviews were held with the teacher after the tutorials to investigate the teacher's observations of the enactment. One of these included the presentation of the results described in the next section to collect the teacher's reflections and considerations for future re-design. Additionally, we used participant's data, as well as observations, in order to capture teachers' intentions, actions and reflections.

Table 1 shows the teacher's design intentions (Column 2) and the data that our system captured during the enacted tutorials to assess how well these intentions were met (Columns 3, 4). These were grouped into three categories: *collaboration* and *equality* of student participation (A), the adherence to the class *script* over all the sessions (B), and the achievement of the *learning outcomes* (C). The first two aspects apply to other contexts. The *learning outcomes* are connected to the particular activity of this study.

Collaboration and equality. Multi-touch tabletops offer equal opportunity for each user to provide input. One of the priorities for the teacher was to encourage and foster groups' collaboration. The intention of the teacher was that all groups could engage in productive discussions with all the students involved in the co-construction of the solution. The capture of this dimension of collaboration is beyond the scope of our system (Table 1, Rows A3, A4). Another more modest attribute of collaboration, that has proven to be important for teachers to be aware of, is the amount of participation of each student in their group activity [12]. For this, our system can automatically capture and analyse the balance of the physical participation (touches) and the contributions of each group member to the shared product (i.e. to the group map) (Table 1, Rows A1, A2). We used application logs and the analysis of group products to determine the equality within each group.

Adherence to the class script. The second set of teacher's intentions was associated with the effectiveness of the teacher to stay on track, following the planned sequence of activities (Figure 4) and the time limit for each task. One possibility is that the time planned for a certain activity is actually an over or under estimate, so requiring a change in the design. It could also be the case that the teacher inadvertently modifies the way the script is followed for some sessions, therefore, impacting on students' learning goals. Interactive tabletops and the orchestration tools can improve awareness of the process the teacher actually followed in the classroom. We investigated three design intentions set by the teacher. The first two relate to the time the teacher spends orchestrating each activity (Rows B1, B2). The third design intention is about the student response to the time allowed for each activity (Row B3). The logs of the orchestration tool indicate the teacher's behaviour and the tabletop application logs show students' task progress.

Learning outcomes of activities 1 and 2. Two learning goals were set for the tutorials. The aim for the first activity was two-folded: students should identify the key concepts of the case problem and visually represent the relationships between them (C1) and the distribution of power within the example organisation (C2). The tabletop application can validate the concepts and the propositions contained in each group map by comparing them with a *master map*. This contains the key concepts, linkages and hierarchical layout that the teacher expected from students' maps. For *Activity 2,* the learning goal was to discuss about possible solutions to the case and justify why they chose a final solution for the situation within the example organisation by augmenting the concept map produced in *Activity 1* (C3).

RESULTS: *...and reflection*

We now report results of the evaluation of the teacher's design intentions based on data from the 196 students, who agreed to make their interaction data available. They were organised in 40 groups: 10 had six students, 17 had five, 12 had four and 1 had three. Data from interviews with the teacher, as well as from non-participant observations were used to triangulate evidence.

Collaboration and equality

Each member should participate equally (A1). We assessed whether groups' physical participation and contribution were balanced within each group. In practice, it is hard for groups to achieve exact balance. Groups may be influenced by a number of factors and the individual style of group members. One indicator of group symmetry in tabletops is the *Gini index* [9]. This is a measure of dispersion that represents the inequality among values in a frequency distribution with a single number between 0 and 1, where 0 is perfect symmetry and 1 total inequality. Figure 6 shows the extent to which physical participation (meaningful touches on the surface) and contribution (parts of the final product added by each student) were equally distributed among group members. On *equality of participation* in *Activity 1* (A1), more than half of the groups (26 groups out of 40) had high levels of equality (Gini index <=0.4). But in *Activity 2* this equality dropped to only 15 out of 40 groups. This difference was statistically significant ($t(47) = 2.71$, $p < .0094$) indicating physical activity on the table was more egalitarian in *Activity 1* than in *Activity 2*. After looking at these results, the teacher commented that in Activity 1

	Teacher's design intention	Data collected during the enactment	A
	Collaboration and equality (general)		
A1	Each member should participate equally to some extent	Equality in participation from application logs	YES
A2	Each member should contribute equally to the group solution	Equality in contribution from the final maps in activities 1 and 2	YES
A3	All groups should participate in in-depth group discussions	-	NO
A4	All groups should demonstrate collaboration between team members	-	NO
	Adherence to the class script (general)		
B1	Each class activity at the tabletop should take the planned amount of time	Orchestration logs show the duration of the activities and the impact on groups' performance	YES
B2	The explanation and reflection phases should keep to the time	Orchestration logs show the duration of the phases and the impact on the duration of the activities	YES
B3	All groups should start discussing and visually representing their ideas as soon as the tabletop activities start	Application logs show the time and evolution of the physical construction of groups' products	YES
	Learning outcomes activity 1 (concept mapping)		
C1	All groups should identify the key concepts of the topic and their relationships, and avoid irrelevant concepts.	Application logs show the key concepts and relationships created by each group	YES
C2	All groups should understand the power distribution of the key concepts/players of the case	Final products logs indicates the physical arrangement of objects in the tabletop surface indicating power distribution	YES
C3	All groups should have discussions of different possible solutions and be able to justify their solution	-	NO

Table1. Teachers' intentions and data that captured from our system (A=Is it possible to assess it from the captured data?).

"everyone starts with the same basis so at the beginning they don't know who's the leader, who understood the case … I am not surprised that groups tended to be equal in activity one". This difference can also be explained by the nature of *Activity 1.* This consisted of building the organisational structure, working in a group, and drawing on each individual's preparation for the class. For *Activity 2,* it was observed that there was typically more oral discussion, since team members had already reached a consensus on the concept map and were aware of its structure. The few new actions were typically performed by the *spokesperson* or *delegated* in the team.

For the goal of *equality of contribution* (A2), we observed a different situation. The contributions to the product of *Activity 2* only included the portion of actions that changed the previous map from its state at the end of Activity 1. The number of groups with high *equality of contribution* for both *Activities 1 and 2* (Gini index < 0.4) was 18 and 17 out of 40 respectively. A deeper analysis of both *participation and contribution* showed that groups where students participated more equally also tended to produce final products with parts added by all group members (Corr. 0.509). These results can be useful for the teacher to have an overall view of groups' equality. The teacher commented that, for further tutorials, *"this is an interesting result,… [next time] I should emphasise and make sure that everyone is fine to use the tabletop and include their ideas to minimise the non equality aspect"*. However, other groups' strategies can be also valid. We observed during the tutorials that some groups agreed that they all were going to discuss the topic and only one student would perform the physical actions. This brings up the limitation of what can currently be captured by the tabletop and what cannot. The teacher cannot be present with each group but can infer the levels of learning from students' discussions. Previous work on tabletops used basic automatic speech detection in enclosed settings [18]. In the near future, new technology may capture this aspect of group work to study and support collaboration in the classroom.

Adherence to the class script

The design intended that both activities associated with the use of the tabletops would take similar time, permitting the teacher to explain and encourage reflection between and after these (Table 1, rows B1, B2). Multiple factors can affect the time actually taken by the teacher to move from one phase to the other, even when tabletops can help to coordinate the enactment of the script. For example, different groups may work at different rates, some students arrive late, ask the teacher more questions, or the teacher can just take more time explaining key points [6]. Timing differences can have serious effects on students' learning experiences, especially if key phases need to be skipped when the class ends and students must leave. Interactive tabletops, orchestrated through our system, can help teachers monitor the actual enactment and assess whether the script was followed in the classroom. Figure 7 shows the planned script for the learning activities (upper line): 10 minutes (') for initial explanations, 15' for each tabletop activity (blue lines), and 5' for each reflection phase, between and after the tabletop activities. Results over the 14 class sessions are shown underneath. For the initial explanation, the teacher took slightly longer than planned (mean of 11', against planned 10'). *Activity 1* and the reflection before *Activity 2* matched closely with the design (mean of 15' and 5' for most of the sessions respectively). However, the time for *Activity 2* was shortened in most of the sessions to 11'. This partly caught up time from the initial explanation and also gave a little time for students to share and reflect about what they did in the classroom (7') forcing the teacher to use more time than the 50 minutes allowed. This had an impact on the learning experience as it was explained by the teacher: *"Even when Activity 2 was the most interesting from a learning perspective, I couldn't make Activity 1 shorter because Activity 2 depended on what they did in Activity 1."* This may be acceptable for the teacher if time initially allocated for *Activity 2* (11' instead of 15') still allowed enough time for students to complete the task. If this information is available after the first classes of the week, the teacher could revise the design for future tutorials or for other tutors. The teacher suggested a possible re-design of the tutorials script: *"This is a very good reminder... maybe the structure for the next tutorials should be changed to give more time for Activity 2"*

Another potential group issue that can be detected from the students' application logs is whether the time allocated for the activities was enough for the students to complete the goal (Table 1, Row B3). Figure 8 (left) shows the relationship between time (average time for *Activity 1* = 15 minutes, std=1.3) and the number of links (or propositions) created by the 40 groups for *Activity 1.* Most groups started creating links by minute 5, and finished with an average of 20 links in their maps. The teacher had expected that all

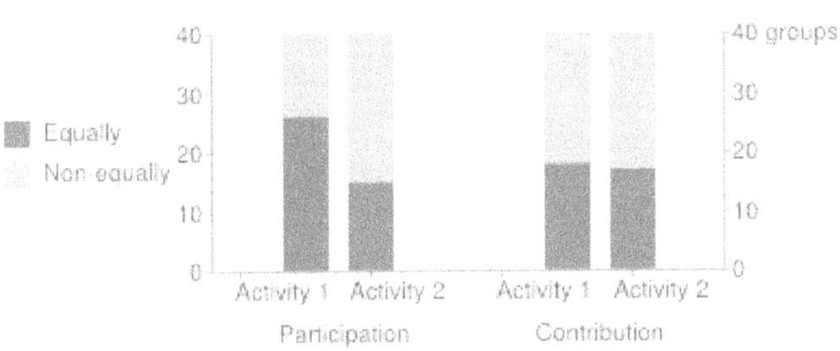

Figure 6. Proportions of groups in terms of equality of physical participation and contribution for activities 1 and 2

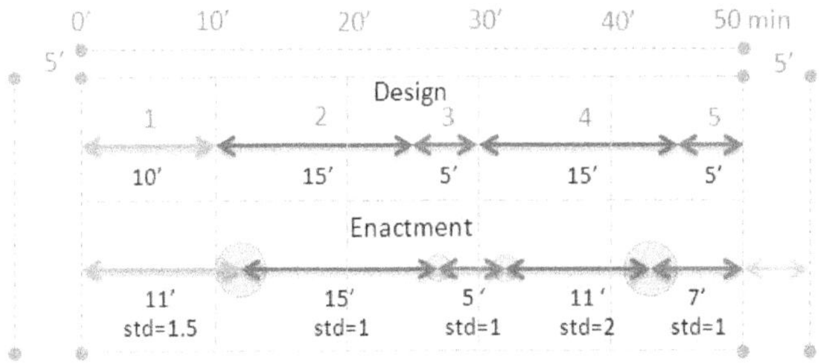

Figure 7. Comparison between the planned time limits and the enactment of the design for the 14 tutorials.

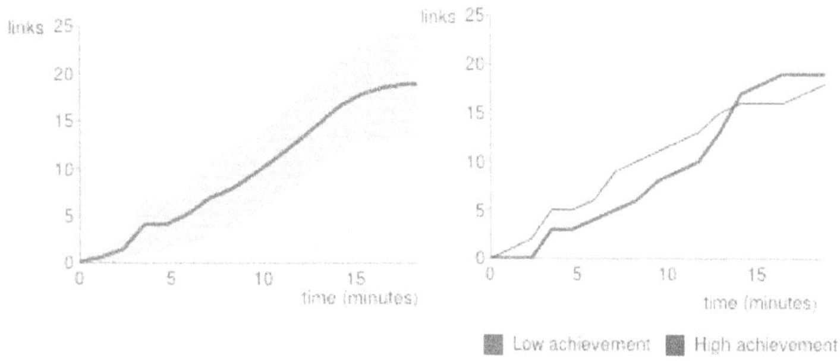

Figure 8. Left) Relationship between time and number of links created by the 40 groups for Activity 1. The shaded area represents the standard deviation. Right) Relationship between time and number of links created comparing high and low achieving groups.

groups would get started much faster than they did since there was no previous experience with this concept mapping activity in the classroom. Figure 8 (right) shows the *time- versus number of links*, comparing high achieving groups with low achieving groups. For measuring the level of achievement, each student map was assessed by counting the number of propositions matching the teacher's master list of crucial propositions for *Activity 1*. Groups were rated high achieving if they had more than 50% of these crucial propositions. This analysis suggests the low achieving groups took longer to get started. The high achieving groups started to create links in minute 1 and kept adding them at a constant pace (blue line in Figure 8, right). By contrast, low achievers only started creating links in minute 3 on average. This gives a weak statistical difference ($t(16) = 1.8$, $p < .087$). The teacher responded that, even when it can be possible to find some trend between groups that start building the solution late and their low final outcome, it is not possible to generalise the cases. "*It would be more valuable to get this information per each group during the tutorials*". A striking feature of these graphs is that the rate of creation of propositions appears to be rather steady over the first 15 minutes, the time allowed in the design. This is valuable information for the teacher's reflection on their design, even if the time constraints of the class make it challenging to perform big changes on the original plan.

Learning outcomes for activities 1 and 2

The goal of *Activity 1* was that groups should *identify the key concepts* of the topic and *their relationships or links* (Table 1, row C1). At the same time groups should not have *irrelevant concepts*. To measure this, each group map was compared with the teacher's map. This listed the concepts and links that were crucial to solve the case. Results showed that the 40 groups added an average of 50% of teacher's concepts (std=.15), meaning they missed half. In terms of essential links, 60% (std=.30) of group maps' links matched with the master map's. The number of *non relevant concepts* added was also high. The 60% (std=11) of the concepts students added were not essential concepts. Without expert analysis, we cannot conclude that these were not relevant. But in words of the teacher, "*this indicates a lack of knowledge from some students. More training is needed for students to understand how to differentiate what is important from what is not in a case*". This suggests the potential value of a new functionality that would provide the teacher, in real time, overview comparisons of *desired* and *actual* maps. This information may enable the teacher to react and adapt the strategies of the activity. For example, in this case, the teacher mentioned that "*one possible strategy to make them look at the case more carefully would be to have a sort of punishment for including non relevant information*".

Also in *Activity 1*, groups should have represented the power distribution of the key concepts by choosing a hierarchical reference between two options suggested by the teacher: concentric or linear/top-down (Table 1, row C2). This means that the player within the company with the highest level of power (the CEO in the case study) should be placed either in the centre or by one of the sides of the tabletop. The analysis showed that 18 groups chose the concentric hierarchy, 16 a linear one, and 4 did not show any hierarchical arrangement. Figure 9 depicts examples of a concentric hierarchy *(left)*, and a top-down hierarchy *(right)*. From a learning perspective, both types of hierarchy can correctly represent the levels of power. Results showed that groups that chose the concentric arrangement were partly correlated (Corr 0.4) with higher levels of equity of participation (low Gini factor). This was informative for the teacher to re-design future tutorials, and it was expressed as: "*now that I know there is some relation between layout and participation, next time I would ask students to use a circular layout*".

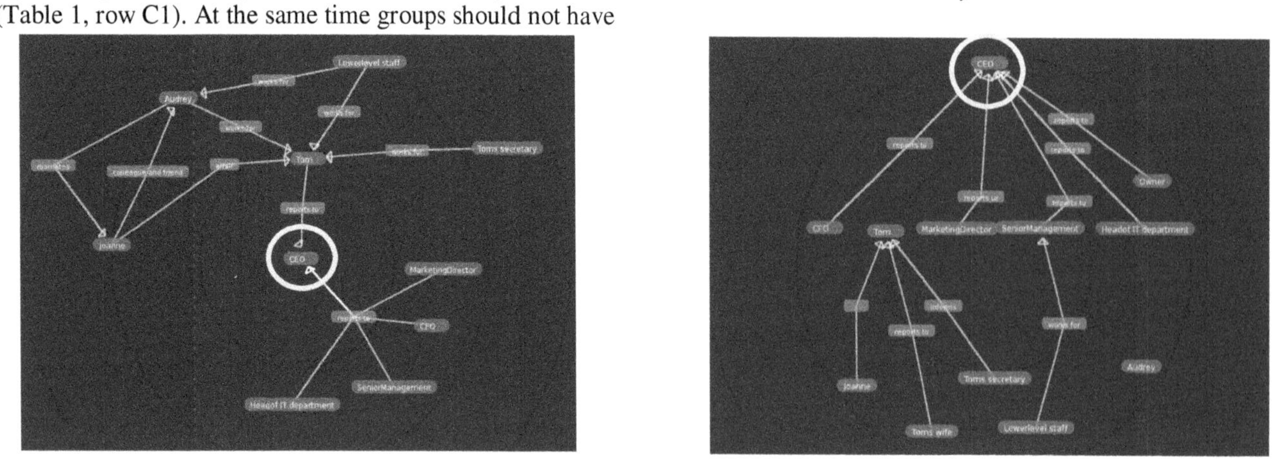

Figure 9. A) Concentric map arrangement. B) Linear map arrangement. The yellow circle indicates the most general concept.

DISCUSSION

The system presented in this paper aims to help a teacher design collaborative learning activities for students in authentic classroom tutorials. It also enables the teacher to orchestrate the activities during tutorial sessions, in real time. At a different level, the system offers functions to capture and centralise rich information about students' actions. This can be used in two ways. First, the real time and carefully curated information is displayed to help the teacher run the class. Secondly, the full data are made available for post-hoc analysis; this enables the teacher to assess the design and perhaps re-define it. We now summarise the outcomes of the enactment and our analysis.

Interactive tabletops can give teachers new ways to address challenges in orchestrating an 'authentic' classroom. Our study is in line with previous work (such as [1, 7]). We demonstrate that interactive tabletops, combined with other technologies, can give the teacher both enhanced control over, and improved awareness of, the multiple groups of students in a real classroom. Our work goes beyond previous research by providing mechanisms for the teacher to evaluate their classroom activity design, based on what actually happened in the enactments, as found in the data that can be captured by the interactive tabletops. Our design of the orchestration functions (e.g. freezing the tabletops, broadcasting messages to all tabletops, and flow control) primarily addressed needs that the teacher identified; we also took account of previous work [1, 19]. This gave opportunity to develop an environment for classroom orchestration and focus on the tools and data to help design, monitor and assess the authentic classroom activities.

Interactive tabletops, and relatively simple technologies, can be used to capture sufficiently rich data to allow teachers monitor the effectiveness of such classroom orchestration. This is aligned with our work showing that even simple interaction data could be useful for teachers to evaluate group work and performance [12,17]. Interactive tabletops can help teachers monitor the effectiveness of their design by reflecting on data about groups and class performance, such as the rate at which propositions were created. In the classroom, there are many factors that can affect the enactment of the teacher's plans from one tutorial to the next. Our approach proved helpful in enhancing the teacher's awareness of the execution of each tutorial. For example, for the timing problems found, the teacher commented: *"These results are very good as a reminder that the structure for the next tutorials should be changed to give more time for activity 2 and final take away message. Ideally by making activity 1 shorter or making some variation in the activity itself"*.

Interactive tabletops can address real classroom orchestration problems that could not be addressed without this technology. To justify use of interactive tabletops, they need to provide useful services that are not otherwise possible [5]. The classroom activity, the system's functionalities and information provided should be adapted or designed according to teachers' learning intentions. The classroom activity, and more specifically, the orchestration commands, should be provided to the teacher under their request. In our study, the options to freeze the tabletops and control the flow of the whole class were specifically requested by the teacher. Similarly, the teacher valued the understanding she gained about the class enactment, information that the teacher would not normally have. This is exemplified by one of teacher's comments on reviewing the results: *"I could probably know if the groups are working too slow[ly] but I wouldn't know straight away if they are introducing the 'important' concepts"* (from the teacher's master map) or if *"the contribution is lower for some students"*.

Our approach includes generic features (e.g. some orchestration and data capture functions can be used in other contexts), customisable features (e.g. the orchestration tool and some classroom indicators), and features specific to the domain of the activity (e.g. concept mapping). Choosing the right tabletop learning application depends heavily on the subject and particular learning goals. In our case, the teacher considered that concept mapping was suitable for a management case-study solving activity. Concept mapping has long been used in many learning contexts. This indicates that our system is likely to be useful for many other domains and contexts. The indicators of *collaboration and equality; and adherence to the class script,* can be generalised to other contexts. For other types of activities requiring different learning software, the indicators of *learning outcomes* would have to be identified accordingly. Further research should be done to define the levels of generalisation of available tools for classroom orchestration among various contexts.

CONCLUSIONS AND FUTURE WORK

Interactive tabletops offer new affordances for collaborative learning activities. They are progressively making their way in a wide variety of learning settings, such as group work rooms, training centres and schools. This paper describes an authentic case, a multi-tabletop system and the data analysis that show some challenges of orchestrating classrooms. Our goal was two-folded. 1) To propose an approach to provide support for teachers to design and orchestrate classroom activities with multi-touch tabletops. 2) To exploit the affordances of these devices to assess this design and promote reflection by analysing activity data captured during the enactment. Our approach was tested in a series of 14 authentic tutorials where students engaged in a collaborative activity that was part of their normal curriculum. This work can serve as a foundation for future richer analyses of data that draw upon different sources, more devices and tools involved in the classroom, with multiple sessions, and combinations of physical and virtual interactions. The next step in this research includes the evaluation of different ways to visually represent information about groups' performance, for example in private for the teacher, or at a wall display to lead class reflection. We also aim to explore the rich data that can be collected to analyse the collaborative interactions and look for patterns associated with high or low achieving groups so that these can drive alerts to the teacher in real time about potential problems in the classroom.

REFERENCES

1. AlAgha, I., Hatch, A., Ma, L. and Burd, L. Towards a teacher-centric approach for multi-touch surfaces in classrooms. In *Proc. ITS 2010*, ACM (2010), 187-196.
2. Bielaczyc, K. Designing Social Infrastructure: Critical Issues in Creating Learning Environments With Technology. *Journal of the Learning Sciences*, 15, 3 (2006), 301-329.
3. Coppin, G., Corré-Nicolas, C., Diverrez, J. M. and Legras, F. Evaluation methods for collaborative multi-touch support. Tutorial in *ITS 2011* (2011).
4. Dillenbourg, P. What do you mean by 'collaborative learning'? Collaborative Learning: Cognitive and Computational Approaches. *Advances in Learning and Instruction Series.* Elsevier Science (1998), 1-19.
5. Dillenbourg, P. and Evans, M. Interactive tabletops in education. In *IJCSCL*, 6, 4 (2011), 491-514.
6. Dillenbourg, P., Zufferey, G., Alavi, H., Jermann, P., Do-Lenh, S., Bonnard, Q. Classroom orchestration: The third circle of usability. In *CSCL 2011*, (2011), 510-517.
7. Do-Lenh, S. Supporting Reflection and Classroom Orchestration with Tangible Tabletops. École Polytechnique Federale De Laussane, 2012.
8. Fleck, R., Rogers, Y., Yuill, N., Marshall, P., Carr, A., Rick, J. and Bonnett, V. Actions Speak Loudly with Words: Unpacking Collaboration Around the Table. In Proc. *ITS 2009* ACM (2009), 189-196.
9. Harris, A., Rick, J., Bonnett, V., Yuill, N., Fleck, R., Marshall, P. and Rogers, Y. Around the table: are multiple-touch surfaces better than single-touch for children's collaborative interactions? In Proc. *CSCL 2009* (2009), 335-344.
10. Hatch, A., Higgins, S., Joyce-Gibbons, A. and Mercier, E. NumberNet: Using Multi-Touch Technology to Support Within and Between Group Mathematics Learning In Proc. *CSCL 2011* (2011).
11. Higgins, S., Mercier, E., Burd, E. and Hatch, A. Multi-touch tables and the relationship with collaborative classroom pedagogies: A synthetic review. In *IJCSCL, 6, 4* (2011), 515-538.
12. Kay, J., Maisonneuve, N., Yacef, K. and Reimann, P. The Big Five and Visualisations of a Team Work Activity. *Intelligent Tutoring Systems* (2006), 197-206.
13. Kharrufa, A., Leat, D. and Olivier, P. Digital mysteries: designing for learning at the tabletop. In Proc. *ITS 2010* ACM (2010), 197-206.
14. Kharrufa, A. S. Digital tabletops and collaborative learning. Newcastle University, 2010.
15. Martinez, R., Collins, A., Kay, J. and Yacef, K. Who did what? who said that? Collaid: an environment for capturing traces of collaborative learning at the tabletop. In Proc. *ITS 2011*, ACM (2011), 172-181.
16. Martinez, R., Kay, J. and Yacef, K. Collaborative concept mapping at the tabletop. In Proc. *ITS 2010*, ACM (2010), 207-210.
17. Martinez, R., Kay, J. and Yacef, K. Visualisations for longitudinal participation, contribution and progress of a collaborative task at the tabletop. In Proc. *CSCL 2011* 2011), 25-32.
18. Martinez, R., Yacef, K., Kay, J. and Schwendimann, B. An interactive teacher's dashboard for monitoring multiple groups in a multi-tabletop learning environment. *Intelligent Tutoring Systems* (2012), 482-492
19. Mercier, E., Higgins, S., Burd, E. and Joyce-Gibbons, A. Multi-Touch Technology to Support Multiple Levels of Collaborative Learning in the Classroom. In Proc. *ICLS 2012* (2012).
20. Morris, M. R., Piper, A. M., Cassanego, A. and Winograd, T. Supporting Cooperative Language Learning: Issues in Interface Design for an Interactive Table. 2005.
21. Müller-Tomfelde, C. and Fjeld, M. Tabletops: Interactive Horizontal Displays for Ubiquitous Computing. *Computer, february* (2012), 78-81.
22. Novak, J. Concept maps and Vee diagrams: two metacognitive tools to facilitate meaningful learning. *Instructional Science, 19, 1* (1990), 29-52.
23. Prieto, L. P., Dimitriadis, Y. and Villagra, S. Representing learning design and classroom orchestration using atomic patterns. In Proc. *ASLD 2011* (2011).
24. Prieto, L. P., Dlab, M. H., Gutiérrez, I., Abdulwahed, M. and Balid, W. Orchestrating technology enhanced learning: a literature review and a conceptual framework. *International Journal of Technology Enhanced Learning*, 3, 6 (2011), 583-598.
25. Rick, J., Harris, A., Marshall, P., Fleck, R., Yuill, N. and Rogers, Y. Children designing together on a multi-touch tabletop: an analysis of spatial orientation and user interactions. In Proc. *ICDM 2009*, ACM (2009), 106-114.
26. Schneider, B., Strait, M., Muller, L., Elfenbein, S., Shaer, O. and Shen, C. Phylo-Genie: engaging students in collaborative 'tree-thinking' through tabletop techniques. In Proc. *CHI 2012*, ACM(2012), 3071-3080.
27. Stock, O., Zancanaro, M., Koren, C., Rocchi, C., Eisikovits, Z., Goren-bar, D., Tomasini, D. and Weiss, P. A co-located interface for narration to support reconciliation in a conflict: initial results from Jewish and Palestinian youth. In Proc. *CHI 2008* ACM (2008), 1583-1592.

Combinatorix: A Tangible User Interface that Supports Collaborative Learning of Probabilities

Bertrand Schneider
Stanford University
Stanford, CA, USA
schneibe@stanford.edu

Paulo Blikstein
Stanford University
Stanford, CA, USA
paulob@stanford.edu

Wendy Mackay
INRIA
Orsay, France
Wendy.Mackay@lri.fr

ABSTRACT

Teaching abstract concepts is notoriously difficult, especially when we lack concrete metaphors that map to those abstractions. *Combinatorix* offers a novel approach that combines tangible objects with an interactive tabletop to help students explore, solve and understand probability problems. Students rearrange physical tokens to see the effects of various constraints on the problem space; a second screen displays the associated changes in an abstract representation, e.g., a probability tree. Using participatory design, college students in a combinatorics class helped iteratively refine the Combinatorix prototype, which was then tested successfully with five students. Combinatorix serves as an initial proof-of-concept that demonstrates how tangible tabletop interfaces that map tangible objects to abstract concepts can improve problem-solving skills.

Author Keywords

Education; Probability; Tabletop; Tangible User Interfaces; Collaborative Learning.

ACM Classification Keywords

H.5.m. Information interfaces and presentation: User Interfaces.

General Terms

Human Factors; Design; Measurement.

INTRODUCTION

Many decisions benefit from understanding probability, e.g., when a patient must interpret the meaning of a medical test result or when a politician must weigh the costs and benefits of a particular policy. Unfortunately, Tversky and Kahneman [11] demonstrated that everyone, even professional statisticians, suffer from systematic biases in their intuitive judgements of probability. Students make a variety of identifiable mistakes when solving probability problems [1] and even graduate students who plan to teach mathematics retain strong misconceptions [6].

The challenge is how to help students develop an intuitive grasp of these abstract concepts. We are particularly interested in combinatorics, a branch of probability that deals with the enumeration, combination, and permutation of sets of elements and their mathematical relationships, because it results in a combinatorial explosion: even simple problems result in hundreds of possibilities that cannot be represented simply with physical objects, virtual or otherwise. Although some interactive tabletops offer a one-to-one mapping between physical objects and virtual concepts to support learning [2], there is a paucity of TUIs supporting learning of complex, *abstract* concepts.

Figure 1. Combinatorix: Tangible objects control a tabletop display (left) and corresponding probability tree (right screen)

This paper describes the design and development of Combinatorix (Fig.1), a tangible tabletop interface in which users manipulate physical objects to obtain deeper insights into complex mathematical relationships. Our goal is not to transform virtual into physical objects but rather to use physical objects to explore fundamentally abstract concepts in combinatorics. We discuss the benefits and the challenges of our approach and conclude with an analysis of how tabletops and tangible user interfaces can affect education.

DESIGN PROBLEM

The original motivation for this project stemmed from observations of students in a university-level course in combinatorics. Faced with only paper and pencil, many had difficulty developing intuitions about probabilities [4] and suffered from the 'stereotype threat' [10] that they are poor in math. We hoped that letting students manipulate concrete objects while simultaneously observing the corresponding changes in deep structure, e.g. a probability tree, would reinforce their intuitions about the underlying mathematical

ITS'12, November 11–14, 2012, Cambridge, Massachusetts, USA.

principles. Our goal was to create an engaging and playful environment that avoids excessive mathematical notations and encourages discussion.

We support Fast's [3] constructivist approach, which emphasizes "overcoming misconceptions through supportive frameworks such as a series of anchoring situations". Our approach builds upon the "Preparing for Future Learning" (PFL) framework [9] in which students begin by analyzing contrasting examples of a concept to isolate important "deep features" of a combinatorics problem, in contrast to the "surface features" or superficial characteristics of a model [5]. Rather than limiting the number of cases, students should be able to express a variety of cases, each with their own visual representations.

Combinatorix is not designed to teach probability per se, but rather to provide a learning environment that encourages small groups of students to explore and discuss combinatorics problems. They should be able to express ideas and hypotheses, struggling with concepts in a productive way. Ideally, they will build their own theories, appreciate the challenges of defining an elegant formula and understand what their personal strengths and weaknesses are.

The learning environment should provide students with tools for reasoning about probabilities, including visualizations that support their reflections. Students should be able to associate common features of a problem with accepted mathematical representations, e.g., a probability tree. This implies that students need two interactive spaces: one for manipulating concrete, physical objects to explore the problem space and one for displaying the corresponding abstract representation of the problem space. The specific learning goals are to:

- learn the concepts of sample and event spaces, with probability defined as a ratio of the two;
- compute sample and event spaces using factorials, permutation and combinations with various constraints; and
- identify the deep structure of a problem as a probability tree and transfer this understanding to new situations.

Participatory Design Study

We began by conducting ten one-hour semi-structured interviews with students currently enrolled in a probability class. We found that less proficient students:

- crave concrete examples and visualizations,
- attempt but often fail to create their own representations, due not only to their lack of domain expertise but also to the limitations of pen and paper: one cannot draw a probability tree with 100 leaves,
- jump too quickly to abstract representations, e.g., formulas and mathematical notations, a major barrier to conceptual understanding,
- experience anxiety and cognitive load when faced with mathematical notations, and
- do not know where to start, often asking the teaching assistant to effectively solve the problem for them.

We next created a mockup with cardboard letters representing the building blocks of combinatorial problems. Participants could address questions such as: How many possible combinations of A, B and C are there? We also provided cardboard constraints to address questions such as: How many combinations obtain if A and B must be next to each other? Participants formed questions by combining physical letters and we created a corresponding visual representation (Fig. 2) with paper or on a whiteboard. One student suggested an innovative visualization, a kind of fractal representation that we tried with other students (Fig. 2, bottom). Based on these explorations, we designed Combinatorix, a custom-made tabletop with tangible objects that students manipulate to express and explore combinatorial problems.

Figure 2. Participatory design: Cardboard mockup with paper-based tree (left) and graph representations (right)

COMBINATORIX

Hardware

Combinatorix (Fig. 4) supports several input techniques: a camera detects the location of fiducial markers and a wiimote provides the position of multiple infra-red pens. A projector displays additional information around the tangible objects. The interactive surface is 60 x 45 cm. and can accommodate up to four students at the same time.

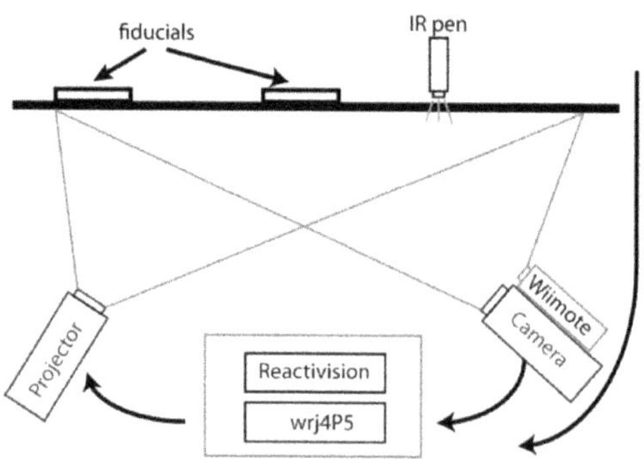

Figure 3. Combinatorix setup: The webcam detects location of fiducial markers; the wiimote detects position of infra-red pens

Software

The underlying application is written in Java and uses the Reactivision engine to detect fiducial makers [7]. Additional libraries, e.g., wrj4P50, communicate with the wiimote. The system is modular and can easily accommodate the creation of additional operators for constraining the sample space.

The current version displays two kinds of information: first, the tabletop interface shows a specific number of placeholders for objects. Letters can be placed on those spots to form a new combination. At the same time, the remaining number of letters for each step is displayed on top of each placeholder. A second screen displays a probability tree reflecting the current state of the problem. Letters can easily be replaced by other elements, including virtual, laser-cut and 3D-printed physical objects. Combinatorix supports up to 10 tangible objects and 20 virtual ones.

Interaction Techniques

Students can interact in two ways: 1) Use tangible letters to form combinations or to add constraints, e.g., fixing the position of a particular element. For example, Fig. 4 (top) shows the number of combinations when A and B are attached to each other. 2) Use a pen to annotate the probability tree. For example, Fig 4 (bottom) shows how to "prune" certain sections, which is equivalent to dividing a factorial number with the combinations that don't satisfy the constraint.

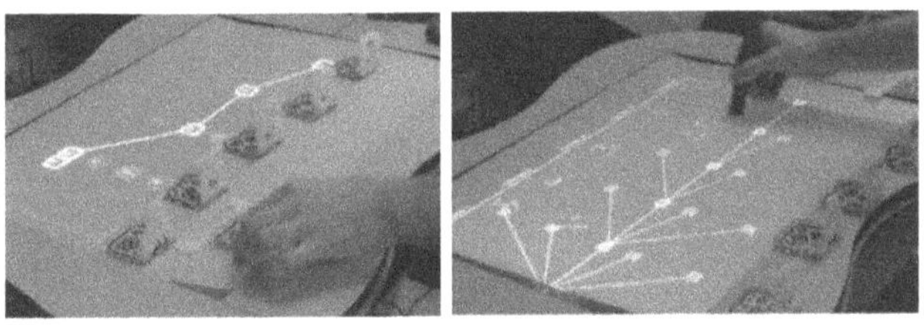

Figure 4. Users can switch between building combinations using physical objects (left) and annotating a probability tree (right).

Rational for Using Tangibles

We built on the results of Schneider, Jermann, Zufferey and Dillenbourg [8] to design the tangible part of our system. They found that compared to a multi-touch surface, a TUI better supported collaborative learning, users' exploration of a problem space, playful learning and problem-solving strategies when working on a logistic problem. Our contribution is to go beyond those results and explore how the mapping of a specific concept to a tangible affects 1) problem-solving skills, and 2) transfer of those concepts to a new situation (that does not share the superficial features of a "school-type" problem). Ultimately, our goal is to provide students with a physical "toolbox" that encompasses all conceptual tools they can use to solve a probability problem. Table 1 summarizes the concepts that our system currently supports.

Concepts	Example	Tangible / action
1.Factorials *(multiplying the branches of the tree)*	"How many different linear arrangements are there of the letters A, B, C, D, E?"	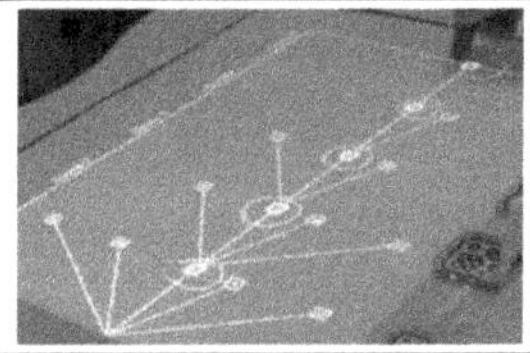
2.Grouping *(connecting two objects to group them)*	" ...for which A must be next to B?"	
3.Symmetry *(using a treemap to divide the sample space)*	" ...for which A is before B?"	
4.Position *(removing an object from the linear arrangement)*	" ...for which A is last in line?"	
5.Subtraction *(removing a subpart of the sample space)*	" ...for which A is not last in line?"	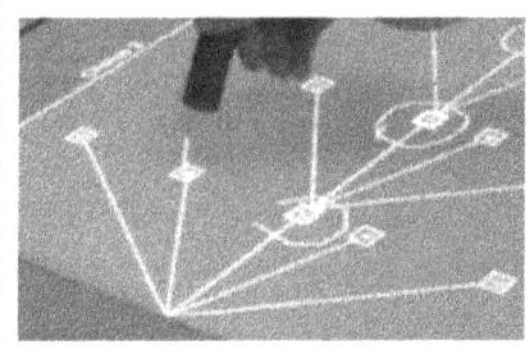
6.Permutation *(pruning the tree)*	"... with 4 placeholders?"	

Table 1. Conceptual mapping to physical objects and actions.

INFORMAL EVALUATION

Five participants tested Combinatorix, including two high-school students and three university students. We asked them to use the table to solve five problems of increasing difficulty: "The letters A, B, C, D, E form how many different linear arrangements?" 1) in total, 2) for which A and B are next to each other, 3) where E is not last in line, 4) for which A is before B, and 5) where A and B are next to each other and C is not first in line?".

General reception

Users were enthusiastic about using the system to solve the problems and were generally able to come up with the right solution after a few minutes. Problem four was the most difficult since the system does not provide any relevant hints. Instead, students tried a brute force solution, exhaustively counting the number of possible cases. The university students eventually realized that the problem was about symmetry: there is an equal number of combinations in which A is before B and B is before A. The solution is thus to divide the total number of combinations by two, e.g.

5! / 2. High school students required more support, in the form of prompts from the experimenter, to find this solution. Such prompts could easily be integrated into the system as automatic feedback; for instance, if a student spends too much time on a particular problem, Combinatorix could display a small hint to unblock the situation.

Participants found the current prototype very useful for certain types of problems: Ann[1] noted that "All the functionalities you could add should not do the thinking for the student; if I use this piece, it's telling what the solution is... well not really. It's more like a hint". Interviewer: "So do you think it's too much help?"; Ann: "I think it's a good level of help, because it conveys the notion that in this situation there are only four combinations that can be here".

However, Combinatorix clearly does not support all types of combinatorics problems. Henry said that "this is a really elegant way to show the concept of factorials; but for some problems I feel like I need to already know that concept to figure it out to get the solution". He also noted "it would be excessive to build a new model for each problem". This is the main challenge for our approach: some classes of problems can be supported easily, but others might require a totally different interface.

Although Combinatorix currently supports high-school level problems, future versions will address college-level problems including conditional probabilities (Bayes' theorem), independence of events, statistical indices (expected value, variance, standard deviation), discrete distributions (binomial, multinomial, geometric, hypergeometric, negative binomial), continuous distributions (uniform, normal, exponential, beta), law of large numbers and central limit theorem. We plan to support specific problems, such as the ones described, rather than creating a fully open-ended system, providing additional scaffolding to extend basic functions.

CONCLUSION

Due to the complexity of the domain i.e. combinatorics, and more generally probability, we do not envision Combinatorix as a stand-alone teaching tool. Rather, we consider it as a platform for students to reflect on problems, offload the cognitive burden of picturing all possible options and as a tool to provide small hints when students are stuck on a problem. Initial user testing revealed that students thought of it as a useful tool, but also mentioned important challenges that need to be addressed.

Our contribution is to develop a direct mapping between tangibles and concepts in combinatorics. To our knowledge, no previous work has studied the direct association of a concept to an arbitrary object in a learning environment. In the long run, our goal is to let students build their own objects and bring them home with them. They could then use those objects (that have been imprinted with a specific concept) to help them think about probability problems or transfer their knowledge in a different domain. These tangibles could be used as "reminders" of students' conceptual toolbox and thus be an ideal scaffold for transfer problems. For future studies and versions of Combinatorix, we intend to further develop its potential as a collaborative tool in a formal learning setting.

ACKNOWLEDGMENTS

Blank for blind review.

REFERENCES

1. Batanero, C. and Sanchez, E. What is the Nature of High School Students' Conceptions and Misconceptions About Probability? In G.A. Jones, ed., *Exploring Probability in School*. Springer US, 2005, 241–266.
2. Dillenbourg, P. and Evans, M. Interactive tabletops in education. *International Journal of Computer-Supported Collaborative Learning 6*, 4 (2011), 491–514.
3. Fast, G.R. Using analogies to overcome student teachers' probability misconceptions. *The Journal of Mathematical Behavior 16*, 4 (1997), 325–344.
4. Garfield, J. and Ahlgren, A. Difficulties in Learning Basic Concepts in Probability and Statistics: Implications for Research. *Journal for Research in Mathematics Education 19*, 1 (1988), 44–63.
5. Goldstone, R.L. and Son, J.Y. The Transfer of Scientific Principles Using Concrete and Idealized Simulations. *Journal of the Learning Sciences 14*, 1 (2005), 69–110.
6. Jendraszek, P.A. Misconceptions of probability among future teachers of mathematics. *Dissertation Abstracts International-A, 69*(01), 2008.
7. Kaltenbrunner, M. and Bencina, R. reacTIVision: a computer-vision framework for table-based tangible interaction. *Proceedings of the 1st international conference on Tangible and embedded interaction*, ACM (2007), 69–74.
8. Schneider, B., Jermann, P., Zufferey, G., et Dillenbourg, P. Benefits of a tangible interface for collaborative learning and interaction. *IEEE Transactions on Learning Technologies, 99*, 1–1
9. Schwartz, D.L. and Martin, T. Inventing to Prepare for Future Learning: The Hidden Efficiency of Encouraging Original Student Production in Statistics Instruction. *Cognition and Instruction 22*, 2 (2004), 129–184.
10. Steele, C.M. A threat in the air: How stereotypes shape intellectual identity and performance. *American Psychologist 52*, 6 (1997), 613–629.
11. Tversky, A. and Kahneman, D. Judgment Under Uncertainty: Heuristics and Biases. *Science* 185 (4157): 1124–11.

[1] All participant names have been anonymized.

Tangible Paper Interfaces: Interpreting Pupils' Manipulations

Quentin Bonnard, Patrick Jermann, Amanda Legge, Frédéric Kaplan, Pierre Dillenbourg
CRAFT, École Polytechnique Fédérale de Lausanne
{first.last}@epfl.ch

ABSTRACT
Paper interfaces merge the advantages of the digital and physical world. They can be created using normal paper augmented by a camera+projector system. They are particularly promising for applications in education, because paper is already fully integrated in the classroom, and computers can augment them with a dynamic display. However, people mostly use paper as a document, and rarely for its characteristics as a physical body. In this article, we show how the tangible nature of paper can be used to extract information about the learning activity. We present an augmented reality activity for pupils in primary schools to explore the classification of quadrilaterals based on sheets, cards, and cardboard shapes. We present a preliminary study and an in-situ, controlled study, making use of this activity. From the detected positions of the various interface elements, we show how to extract indicators about problem solving, hesitation, difficulty levels of the exercises, and the division of labor among the groups of pupils. Finally, we discuss how such indicators can be used, and how other interfaces can be designed to extract different indicators.

Author Keywords
Paper interface; Manipulation; Computer Supported Collaborative Learning;

ACM Classification Keywords
H.5.m. Information Interfaces and Presentation: Misc.

INTRODUCTION
Paper interfaces have the potential to integrate computing in schools more seamlessly than mice, keyboards, and screens. Paper is already omnipresent in schools. In general, paper has a lot of affordances that cannot be replaced by digital technologies [18]. For example, paper is freely annotated, easy to navigate, can be transported and duplicated easily, etc. In the case of geometry, paper is an essential ingredient to learning the use of fundamental tools like compass or protractors.

ITS'12, November 11–14, 2012, Cambridge, Massachusetts, USA.

Following the seminal work of Wellner [23], many authors have used paper interfaces to bridge the digital divide between a paper document and its electronic form. Paper is used to bridge the digital divide because it often embodies documents. What matters in this context is the content it carries. Yet paper is also a physical body which can be moved, rotated, and flipped. Paper can thus be used to implement Tangible User Interfaces (TUI) that integrate seamlessly into classroom environments, where paper is ubiquitous. This is especially true for practical reasons: as demonstrated by Costanza et al. [2], a paper-based TUI can be produced with basic tools, such as printers, scissors, and glue. Furthermore, paper-based interfaces have the same properties as flat objects, making them perfectly compatible with 2D geometry, the main part of the curriculum in primary schools.

This article focuses on the tangible nature of paper. We present Quads, an activity based on the manipulation of pieces of paper to learn the classification of quadrilaterals. A pilot study and an in-situ study in primary schools revealed that the very manipulation of the elements of the interface can be analysed to generate indicators about the learning process. We explain how the traces of the interaction can be used to measure the progress of the activity, hesitation when doing the activity, difficulty level of the activity, and how the work is divided among a group of pupils during the activity. Finally, we discuss how these indicators can be applied in different Technology Enhanced Learning approaches.

RELATED WORK
Traditional geometry education, based on regular paper, has a major shortcoming: only static figures can illustrate the concepts. However, Garcia et al. [9] claimed that students appreciate the ability to repeat and play a geometrical construction as allowed by a computer. Furthermore, Dynamic Geometry Software (DGS) such as Cabri Géomètre [13] and GeoGebra[1] enable learners to explore the dynamic behaviour of a geometrical construction, i.e. what is free to move and what remains fixed under given constraints. Straesser [22] explains how DGS opens new possibilities in geometry education by enabling geometric constructions not easily possible with pen and paper. However, the use of interfaces based on windows, icons, menus and pointers involves the risk of spending more time learning software than learning geometry [12], as these interfaces are completely different from the typical geometry tools frequently used in classrooms such as a pen, ruler,

[1] `www.geogebra.org`

or compass. Paper is a less distracting interface: Oviatt et al. [15] showed that the more interfaces mimic pen and paper (digital pen, graphic tablet), the less they induce an extraneous cognitive load.

There are several examples of digital pen and paper systems used for education. They are often based on Anoto technology, which consists of printing a microscopic pattern on paper which is detected by a camera embedded in a pen, such that the strokes can be acquired. For example, Pietrzak et al. [17] presented a system augmenting note taking in the classroom. They concluded from interviews with teachers that augmented paper could address the separation of digital content shown in the classroom, oral explanations, and notes. CoScribe [21] integrates pen-and-paper-based interaction techniques that enable users to collaboratively annotate, link, and tag both printed and digital documents. Other systems are commercially available.

Paper interfaces are not limited to interactions based on a digital pen. Books are a popular way to control Augmented Reality applications. For example, Martín-Gutiérrez [14] and his colleagues designed a book combined with a screen to develop spatial abilities among engineering students. They measured a positive impact on the spatial abilities, and the users found the system easy-to-use, attractive, and useful.

Paper interfaces can further rely on their tangible nature by using artefacts that are more important for their presence and position than for their content, such as gaming cards. Perlman [16] made programming in Logo accessible to children by ordering cards in rows, which represent commands in sequences. Do-Lenh et al. [7] used paper tokens to build a concept map on an augmented tabletop system.

The tangible and document nature of paper interfaces are not mutually exclusive. For example, Song et al. [20] used a paper cube and a digital pen to combine the advantages of physical and digital modelling tools in the early stages of architectural training. Zufferey [24] proposed an interface that combines tangible and paper elements to teach logistics. The mix of tangibles and paper is particularly powerful in education, where manipulation is often key to experimentation, and documents help make reflection become persistent.

To create paper interfaces, it is thus possible to use one of the several frameworks analysing TUI's (e.g. [8]). Particularly, Hornecker and Buur [10] broadened the scope of TUI to *tangible interaction*, by describing more than the *data-centred* view of TUI. They add the *expressive-movement-centred* and the *space-centred* views of tangible interaction. The former focuses more on the interaction itself than the physical-digital mapping. The latter focuses on the position of the user in space. This is interesting if we draw parallels in the pedagogical context. The *expressive-movement-centred* view of tangible interaction can be seen as a way for pupils to enact a concept to learn. For example, discovering angles can be done by rotating a piece of paper, or by making it follow a circular course. The *space-centred* deals with aspects like the division of labour, which can result naturally from the spatial disposition of tangible resources, which orient the roles of learners in a group, as shown by Jermann et al. [11].

This leads us to believe that studying the tangible interaction of a group brings useful insights about the learning activity. This is the field of research called Interaction Analysis [6]: it consists of automatically analysing a computer-mediated activity to produce indicators to be reused, to qualify, or to adapt the activity. These indicators are typically computed from the traces of an interaction between learners and computers via a mouse and keyboard. However, this is also possible with tangible interactions, and these indicators are even richer, because interaction happens in the real world.

This paper shows four indicators that can be drawn from the tangible interaction with a paper interface, which we present in the next section. Based on the positions of the pieces of paper (which are tracked by a camera), we can deduce which problem solving step the pupils are on, how much they hesitate in the activity, how much difficulty they have on an exercise, and how they distribute the roles within the group.

DESCRIPTION OF THE SYSTEM

Technology

Our system for geometry education is built on the TinkerLamp, a tabletop system developed at our laboratory [24]. The TinkerLamp, shown in Figure 1, incorporates a camera and a projector directed to the tabletop surface via a mirror. The augmented surface is of dimension 70 $\times$ 40 centimetres. The camera and projector are connected to an embedded computer, so that the interaction with the hardware is minimum for the end user: switch on or off. It only needs to be plugged into an electric outlet.

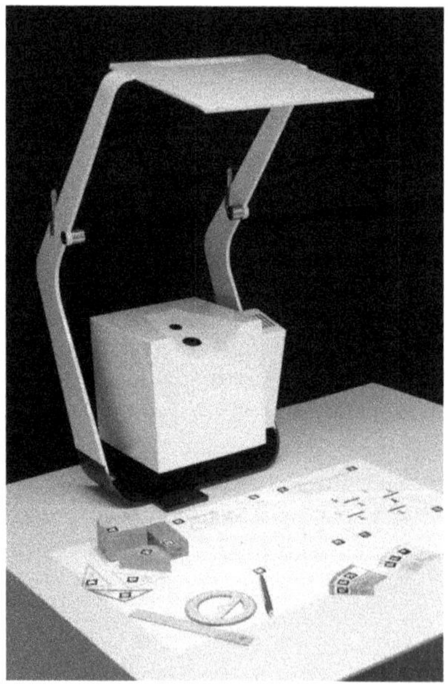

Figure 1: Our camera-projector system on a table, along with various types of objects which can be augmented: sheets, cards, tools and wooden blocks. In Quads, only sheets, cards and cardboard shapes are used.

The interface mainly consists of *sheets* and *cards* and cardboard *shapes*. The properties and behaviours of these interface elements are identified by the system using the fiducial markers printed on them. We use fiducial markers, which are similar to ARTags[2], to identify and precisely track the various elements of the interface. Since the interface is projected from the top, it is possible to use interface elements (paper sheets and cards) as a projection surface in addition to the tabletop surface. We refer to this kind of interface as a *scattered interface* [3], because it allows for interaction and distribution in space and among people. This characteristic is central to gather the indicators.

Description of the Activity

We designed the first activity as a pedagogical script to introduce the classification of quadrilaterals (squares, rhombuses, trapezoids, etc.) as shown in Figure 2. The script consists of *sheets*, four *cards*, and a set of quadrilateral cardboard *shapes*. We discuss the properties of each type of element in detail in another article [1]. Each of these elements has a fiducial marker to identify it and was produced with a regular printer. The cardboard shapes were numbered, so that they could be referenced with the sheets.

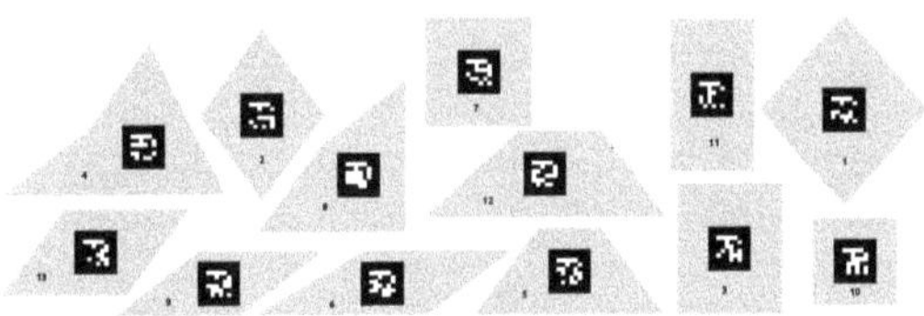

Figure 2: The numbered cardboard quadrilaterals used in the study.

The sheets, which include activity instructions, are shown in the left part of Figure 3. They consist of a short instructional text and two areas (marked with different colors - gray and white) denoting two different classes of quadrilaterals. For the last page, related to the classification of a square, a rhombus, and a rectangle, the two areas overlap because the square shares the properties of the two others. The text instructs the learner to use the three cards shown in Figure 4 to find a common characteristic in a subset of shapes, and separate them into two classes. The cards have a small text describing their function. When a specific card is brought close to a shape, the system will display the given characteristic of the shape (such as side length, angle measures, or parallel sides).

The learner is instructed to place a fourth card next to the current page once the shapes are placed in the classification areas (see the top right part of Figure 3). If all shapes have not been placed in the areas, the learner will be reminded to do so. If the grouping is not the expected one, the learner will be invited to try again. If the grouping into areas is correct, the formulation of the answer will appear, e.g. *"Good job! Quadrilaterals with a pair of parallel sides are called trapezoids"*. Feedback is intentionally trivial; the cards are not meant to replace teachers.

[2] `http://www.artag.net`

Figure 3: The components of Quads. (Left) Five cardboard quadrilaterals are classified into two groups on the instruction sheet; a card displays the measure of the angles of a rectangle. (Right) The feedback card displays the validation text.

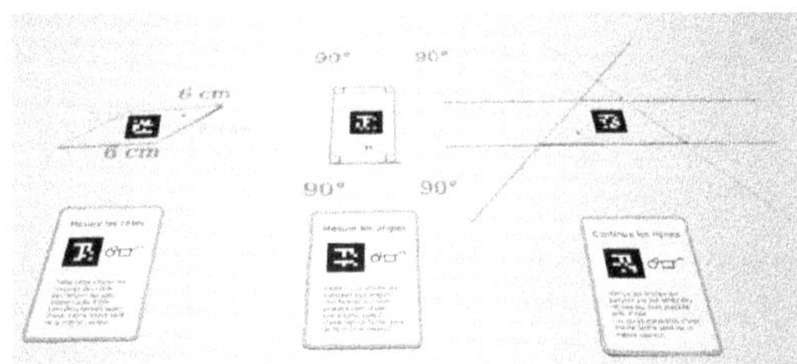

Figure 4: An example of the information displayed by each of the cards.

The seventh (last) page of the sheets is a recapitulation exercise that does not use the TinkerLamp. In the first part, the pupils have to write the names of the shapes under a figure representing them. In the second part, pupils have to link a list of quadrilateral names to a list of properties (four right angles, two pairs of parallel sides, one pair of parallel sides, four sides, and four equal sides).

Scenario

We illustrate the intended use of Quads with the following scenario. This scenario allows us to introduce three steps in the problem solving process, which will be revealed from the manipulation of the paper interface: *inferring*, *applying*, and *validating*. First, pupils have to *infer* a classification rule, i.e. make a hypothesis about the criteria that discriminates one set of shapes from another. Second, pupils can check their hypothesis quickly by *applying* the tool card related to the rule on the shapes. Third, if it fits, they can *validate* their classification rule by placing the shapes in one of the two areas of the exercise sheet and placing the validation card.

The scenario is as follows: Jim and Sarah are two sixth graders who are trying to learn the classification of quadrilaterals. They already know about most names and the appearance of quadrilaterals (square, rectangle, rhombus, parallelogram, trapezoid). They also know how to measure a side, and the meaning of perpendicular and parallel, but they do not know how to check these properties or measure angles.

They are given the leaflet of six exercise sheets, the 13 cardboard shapes, and the four cards. Jim reads the instructions of page 1 aloud and selects the corresponding cardboard shapes. Jim guesses (*infers*) that the shapes with equal sides belong together. Sarah reminds him to use the tool cards. She takes the tool card measuring sides and tries it on the shapes (*applies*). After Sarah places the shapes on the sheet, Jim takes the validation card for feedback (*validates*). He reads it aloud, and Sarah repeats the name of the category (rhombuses). The pair goes on through each exercise sheet, until they reach the final recapitulation one, and return to their respective desks to complete it.

PILOT STUDY

In this section, we report on the first deployment of this activity outside of the laboratory. A school agreed to host a demonstration of the system to its pupils. The demonstration occurred on a Friday afternoon, during the period of time normally allocated to homework. Three classes participated: two fifth grade classes and one sixth grade class; i.e. the pupils were 10 to 12 years old. The goal was to validate the design of the activity.

Ten groups of variable sizes (one individual, six groups of two, two groups of three, and one group of four) were given five minutes to go through the first page of Quads. They were given the sheet, the five cardboard shapes shown in Figure 5, and the three tool cards, but not the feedback card. They were simply asked to use the tool cards on the shapes and place the shapes into two groups. After five minutes, we asked them why they grouped the shapes in the way that they did. We then asked them to explain the purpose of each card.

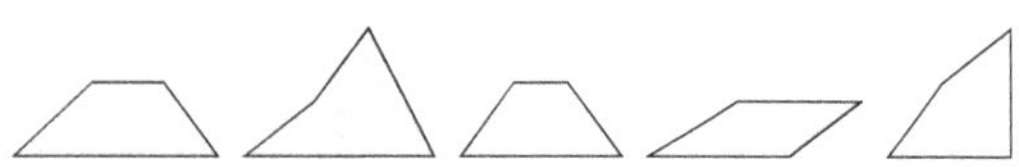

Figure 5: The five quadrilaterals used in the pilot study.

Supporting exploration

The classification expected by the design was the distinction between trapezoids (Shapes 1, 3, and 4 in Figure 5) and non-trapezoids (Shapes 2 and 5 in Figure 5), using the card that shows the lines passing along the sides of the quadrilaterals where parallel lines are coloured the same. Of course, any classification can be made as long as it comes with a justification.

The classifications produced are shown in Figure 6. We see that this activity supports exploration surprisingly well: five different classifications were produced and eight different justifications were given (the pupils could find the expected classification with a different justification). For example, a group used the fact that Shapes 2 and 5 can be assembled like a tangram, and that they both had five centimetre sides as classification criteria. Other groupings were geometrically sound. For example, shape 5 has a right angle, as opposed to 1, 2, 3, and 4, which do not.

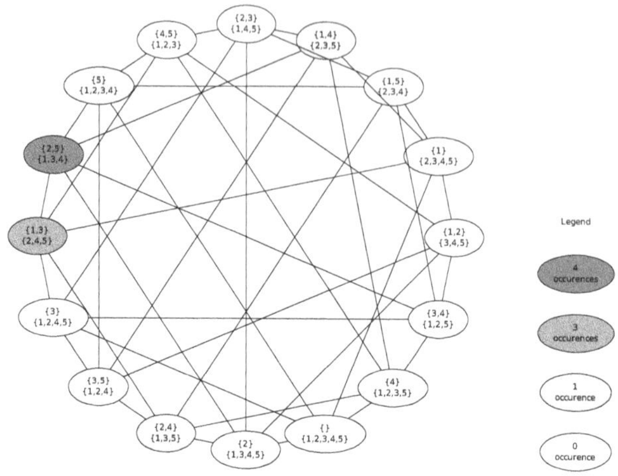

Figure 6: The classifications proposed by the pupils out of the 16 possible classifications. Each node represents one possible classification. Their colour indicates how often they were proposed by a group. Each classification is linked to the classifications that are possible after changing one element.

This five minute activity could have been followed by a rich discussion among the pupils, directed by a teacher. The augmentation contributed to the diversity of the answers: it is likely that pupils would have based their classifications on the appearance of the shapes rather than the characteristics revealed by the tool cards (e.g. the length of the sides). The artefacts produced by the augmentations, such as the line continuing the sides which formed a triangle, were also interesting from a pedagogical point of view: the teachers could explain the difference between the pertinent properties of a *figure* (e.g. the sides of a cube remain parallel in an isometric representation) and the artefact linked to the *drawing* (e.g. not all the sides of a cube have the same length in an isometric representation). This distinction is central in geometry education.

Observations

The interactions were based on the position of the paper elements: when a card was brought close to a shape, it would display additional information. There were two ways to do that: either move the shape towards the card, or move the card towards the shape. The latter seems more intuitive, as cards are usually kept in the hands. However, four groups out of ten moved the shapes towards the cards.

Within the groups moving the shapes rather than the cards, an interesting interaction emerged. Three groups created a test bench by placing all of the tool cards together, and bringing the cardboard shapes in the common neighbourhood of the cards to show all of the related information at once, as shown in Figure 7.

We also observed another emerging interaction pattern that addressed technical limitations of the system. Indeed, there was a perceptible lag (of a few hundred milliseconds) between a card being close to a shape, and the display of the

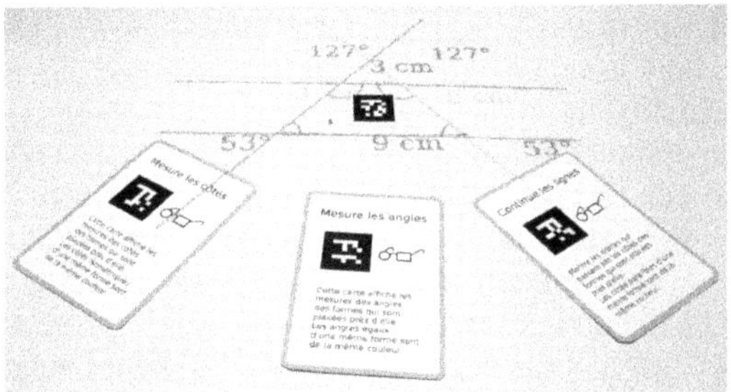

Figure 7: The single display of the cards shown in Figure 4 can be combined into a "test bench", where cardboard shapes are placed to display all of their characteristics at the same time.

related information. Moreover, the single marker on the cards and shapes was often occluded (e.g. by the hands of the pupils), preventing the detection of the elements of the interface, and thus the resulting display. To address this, some groups interacted in two steps: they would first manipulate the cards and shapes, and then leave the interface alone for the system to display the information. We suppose that this technical limitation can have a pedagogical value, and, for this reason, we decided not to 'fix' this limitation for the in-situ study. Indeed, the fact that the pupils stop their manipulation to wait for feedback might actually foster an observation time that could be beneficial for their reflection [4].

Finally, we observed that the size of the group had a strong impact on the course of the activity. On one extreme, the pupil manipulating the interface alone seemed very intimidated by our presence and did not dare interact too much. On the other extreme, the four pupil group was easily distracted and focused less on the task. Three pupils per group seemed like the best compromise.

IN-SITU STUDY

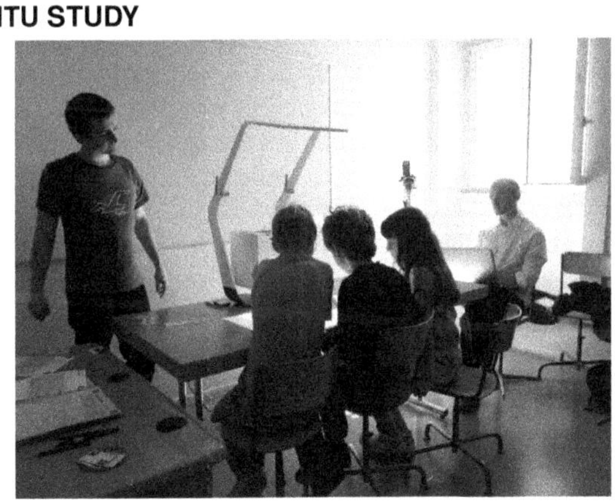

Figure 8: The physical set-up of the experiment: three pupils sitting under the TinkerLamp, in a spare room of their school.

We deployed the activity in another study, which took place in a spare room of another primary school (see Figure 8). The pupils came from two sixth grade classes (i.e. 11-12 year-old pupils). We could only extract pupils from workshop-like activities related to mathematics. As a consequence, our study was limited to two periods (of 45 minutes) per class. We decided to have the groups go through the whole activity, which meant that only one group per period could take part in the study. Two groups from each class tried the system during one period each, after a brief presentation to the whole class.

Based on the lessons drawn from the pilot study, we asked the teachers to form groups of three pupils. For each teacher, the first group was composed by higher performing students than the second group. Each group was asked to complete pages one to six with the TinkerLampand then complete page seven (the recapitulation exercise) individually on separate desks. The expected classifications for each of the pages are shown in Figure 9. We did not reserve time at the beginning of this study for the pupils to get familiar with the system, because in the pilot study, they immediately understood how to use the interface.

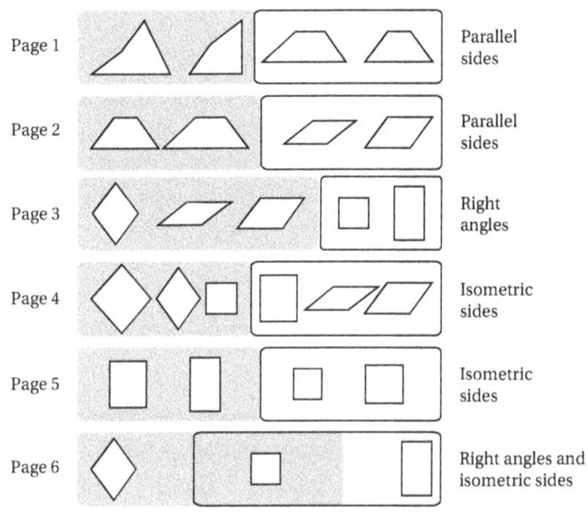

Figure 9: Expected classifications for the first six pages of the study. The criteria for each classification is shown on the right. The classification of page 6 is not a partition: a square is in both the rectangle and rhombus classes.

We provided the feedback card to the pupils, with a mechanism to make intensive trial and error strategies difficult: the feedback card had to be placed on the sheet, i.e. on top of the shapes, which prevents from moving them. The experimenter gave one exercise sheet and its related cardboard shapes to the group at a time, after the feedback card validated the classification for that particular exercise.

During the experiment, we recorded the position of the fiducial markers detected by each image captured by the TinkerLamp. This allowed us to replay the augmentations projected during the study. More importantly, it allowed us to trace the trajectory of each element of the paper interface. We also recorded a video of each group, but do not report on the analysis of the dialogues, since we focus on indicators that can be collected automatically.

We first analyze two simple measures of performance: a pre/post-test, and completion time. These measures will then be used as a reference to compare indicators computed from properties of the manipulation of the various elements of the paper interface: the presence of the various pieces of paper indicate which step of the problem solving process the pupils are in; the speed of the pieces of paper indicate how much the pupils hesitate; the vertical transitions indicate how much difficulty the pupils have on an exercise; and the horizontal transitions indicate how the pupils dispatch the roles among the group.

Performance

We used page 7 of the activity as a pre-test and post-test. The score was computed as the number of quadrilaterals that could be named correctly. For nine out of twelve pupils, the score did not change, mostly because of a ceiling effect: the answers were already correct in the pre-test. Three pupils improved their score from four to six, from two to four, and from three to four, respectively. These three pupils were in groups 3 and 4; groups 1 and 2 scored perfectly on both tests. The explanation lies more in the group formation than in the activity: groups 1 and 2 came from one class, while groups 3 and 4 came from another.

More importantly, the teacher purposely formed the groups of homogeneously performing pupils: pupils from groups 1 and 3 were higher performers than those from groups 2 and 4. This is reflected in the completion times: the time to solve the exercises (excluding exercise 4) was 515, 631, 819, and 911 seconds for groups 3, 1, 4, and 2, respectively. Exercise 4 was excluded from the calculation, because group 3 did not receive this exercise: the experimenter erroneously skipped the page.

All the groups managed to go through the activity in less than 40 minutes, which is important, because it fits the 45 minute periods between the two breaks. Figure 10 shows the time spent on each exercise, from the presentation of the page by the experimenter to the positive feedback given by the validation card.

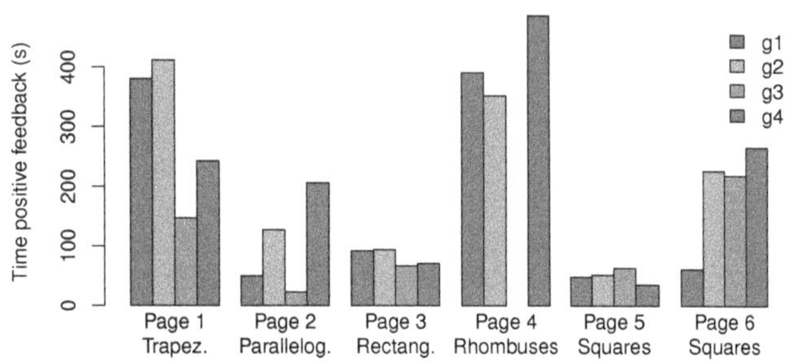

Figure 10: Time spent by each group on each activity.

Figure 10 highlights the differences between the exercises: pages 2, 3, and 5 were more obvious, since they could be completed on a perceptual basis (compare with Figure 9). This helped the pupils formulate a hypothesis very quickly, but they double-checked their hypothesis with the tool cards in most cases before viewing the feedback. Only one pupil tried to validate a classification immediately without using the tool cards.

Page 4 stands out in completion time. This is due to the fact that the appearance was misleading: the first intuition of the pupils was to group the square and the rectangle together because they have equal angles, but the expected classification was actually based on the length of the side. Pupils tried several hypotheses before correctly classifying the shapes. Page 1 also stands out, mostly because it was the first exercise: pupils were still discovering the activity and the interface of the system to solve it. Finally, page 6 was grouped with the more challenging exercises, because it was slightly different: the two areas of the page in which to classify the shapes were actually overlapping, and one shape (the square) was in the overlap of these two regions. We now present indicators that corroborate these explanations.

Use of the Augmentations as Problem Solving Step Indicator

The most basic information regarding the manipulation of an interface element is its use, i.e. whether it is activated or not. In the case of a tool card, it means that its functionality was being used by being close to a shape. Not all of the cards were useful for completing each exercise. For example, the card showing the lengths of the sides was useful to distinguish rectangles from squares, but not to distinguish squares from rhombuses. A mixed effect anova with the group as a random factor showed that the useful cards were used significantly more than the others ($F[1, 64] = 7.24, p < 0.01$). In general, it informs us that the pupils were not toying with the system, and understood which cards could help them. More particularly, it is a first indicator on the learning activity: by detecting which tool card is activated, it is possible to determine whether the pupils are trying to *infer* the expected classification, or whether they are still guessing.

The associations between the tool cards and the cardboard shapes can bring more information. Theoretically, this association is many-to-many: a card can display the attributes of several shapes at once, and a shape can have several of its attributes displayed. In practice, it is a one(-card)-to-many(-shapes) relationship: a card often displayed the attributes of several shapes at the same time, but a shape very rarely had several of its attributes displayed at the same time. Throughout the whole experiment, cards were associated to one shape 1.6 times more often than to multiple shapes, while shapes were associated to one card 10.5 times more often than to multiple cards. We assume that when a tool card is activated on one shape, the pupils are still trying to *infer* the rule. If the card is applied to multiple shapes, the pupils are more probably in the *applying* step, because they have grouped shapes together, and can compare the characteristics displayed by a card. Of course, it is easy to know when the pupils are in the *validating* step: the shapes are on top of the exercise sheet.

Average Speed as Hesitation Indicator

We kept a trace of the position of each piece of paper throughout the study. This allows us to recreate the trajectory of the various pieces of paper (see Figure 11). This is very rich information. To exploit it, we concatenated the trajectories of paper elements of the same type: shape, validation card, tool card, and sheet, for each exercise of each group. Dividing this cumulated length by the time each group spent on each exercise gives an average speed of a type of interface component.

This average speed is a quantity of movement performed by the pupils on the interface, normalized over the length of the exercise; it does not correspond to any actual speed.

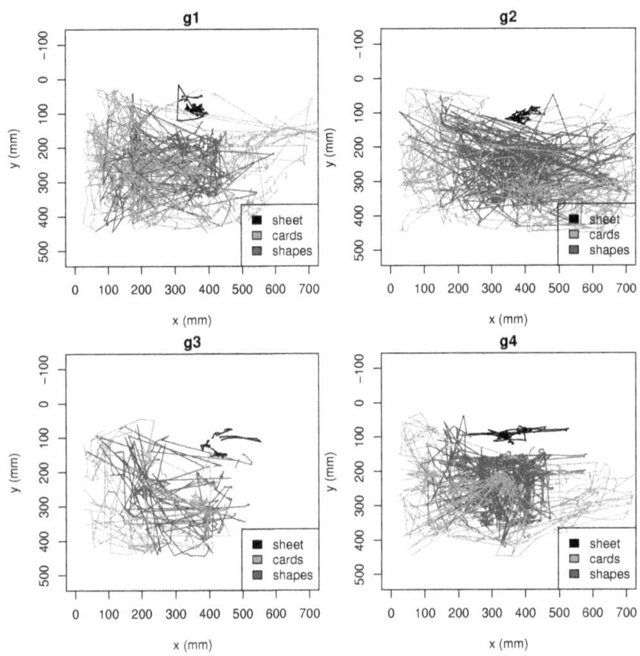

Figure 11: The traces of the various pieces of paper.

Figure 12 shows the average speeds of each kind of component. A mixed effect anova with the group as a random factor showed that each kind of component had a significantly different average speed from the others ($F[3, 84] = 32.40$, $p < 0.0001$). On average a sheet moved by 7 mm/s. It is the most stable element. The augmented area under the TinkerLamp, delimited by the projected white background, defines a virtual border for the exercise sheet, out of which it is hard to move. Anyway, moving the sheet away from the centre would mean excluding one of pupils who are sitting on the side. Second comes the validation card, at 18 mm/s, which is simply brought above the sheet when needed. Third come the tool cards, at 32 mm/s, which are manipulated more often. The most mobile element are the shapes, at 52 mm/s; they have to move between the areas of the exercise sheets and the neighbourhood of the tool cards.

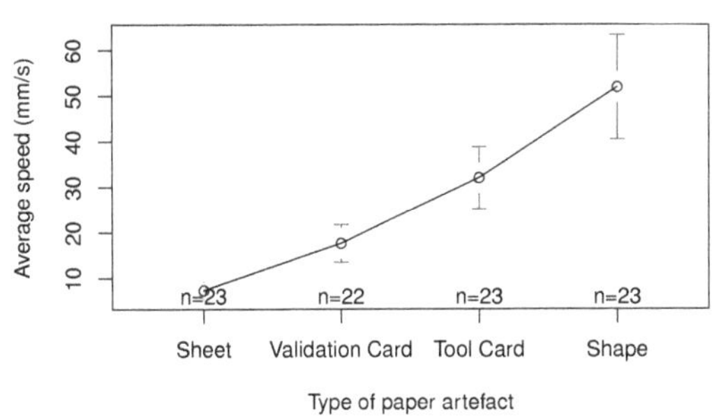

Figure 12: Average speeds of the different kinds of paper artefacts.

We now consider the average speed of the shapes, the most mobile interface element. More time-consuming pages (1, 4 and 6) see a decrease of this average speed. A mixed effect anova with the group as a random factor showed that this decrease is significant ($F[5, 14] = 8.34$, $p < 0.001$). The speed can thus be used as an indicator of the hesitation of the pupils: on trivial pages, they will obviously move the cardboard shapes more than on pages where they hesitate. This may be because the exercise is new, as with page 1, or because the exercise is harder, as with pages 4 and 6.

Verticality as Difficulty Indicator

We can refine the grain of our analysis by only observing the y-coordinate of the positions of the cardboard shapes relative to the y-coordinate of the position of the sheet. Indeed, the goal of the activity is to place shapes in one of two boxes which are on top of each other. Figure 13 shows an example of this data. It actually corresponds to the path taken by a group towards a solution. One way to formulate the exercise is the following: shapes are associated to a binary type for each sheet, and the goal is to place the ones of a same type within the boundary of areas that stretch over the whole width of a page. The problem is thus solved when all shapes of a given type are within the vertical range of an area.

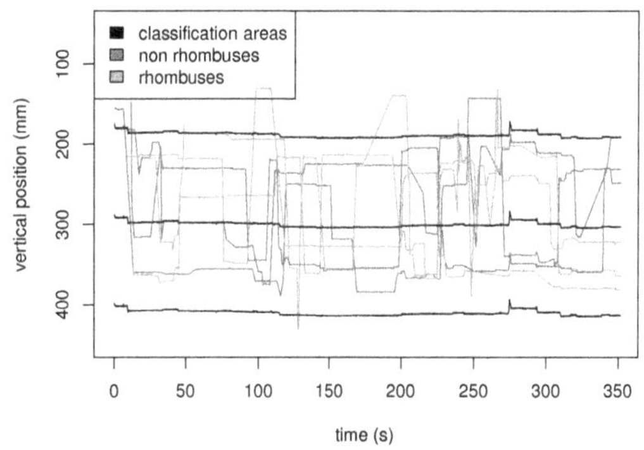

Figure 13: The y-coordinate of the position of the various elements of the paper interface as a function of time, for one group and one exercise. This allows us to visualize the position of the cardboard shapes (blue and orange, depending on the expected classification) relative to the areas on the exercise sheet (delimited in black).

We can then make the y-coordinate of a cardboard shape discrete by defining one value per classification area on the sheet (i.e. two values for the first five sheets, and three values for the sixth sheet, which has two areas and their overlap). What is interesting then is the number of transitions from one area to another, because it means that a shape was moved to another category. In other words, the more transitions that happen on the discrete vertical coordinate of a cardboard shape, the more changes have been made to a solution. The number of vertical transitions is thus an indicator of the amount of difficulty that the pupils are having. As seen in Figure 14, pages 4 and 6 stand out from the other pages. The finding here is that page 1 does not stand out. This means that the increased time needed for solving page 1, and the increased average speed of the paper elements previously found, are not related to the difficulty of the task. On the first page, pupils are beginning to discover the activity and the interface and do not yet know how to manipulate the interface elements. The fact that we did not reserve time for the children to familiarize themselves with the interface allowed us to make this distinction: pupils can spend more time on an exercise because they are having difficulties with the exercise (as indicated by the number of vertical transitions) or because they are hesitant about how to use the interface (as indicated by the lower speed of manipulation).

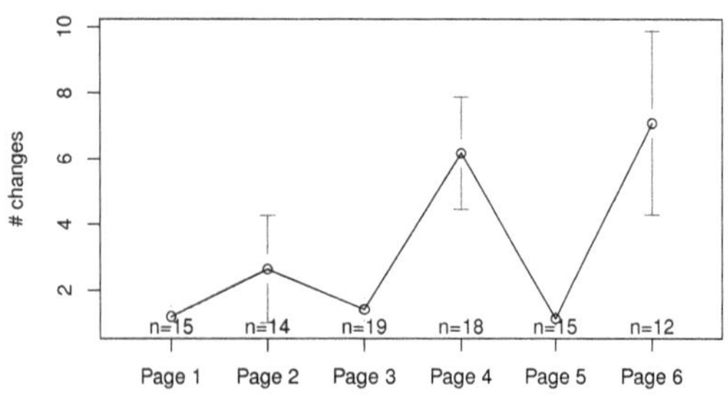

Figure 14: Number of vertical transitions per exercise sheet.

We fitted several models to explain the number of vertical transitions, and the best fit is a mixed effect model (the group being a random variable) with the difficulty of the exercise sheet being a factor ($F[1, 87] = 126.51$, $p < 0.0001$), the group performance level being a factor ($F[1, 2] = 43.92$, $p < 0.05$), and the interaction of the two of these factors ($F[1, 87] = 25.78$, $p < 0.0001$). This model is visualized in Figure 15. It categorizes the exercise sheets into two difficulty levels (reflected in Figure 14), and the groups into two performance levels (based on the group's composition by the teachers, corroborated by previous observations). We see that the number of vertical transitions significantly increases on difficult pages, and with lower performing groups. Furthermore, when these two conditions are met, the increase is even higher. The number of vertical transitions is thus a measure of the difficulties that a group of pupils faces on an exercise.

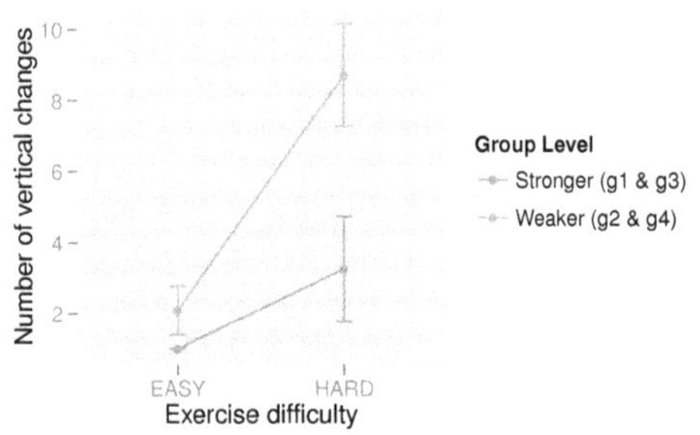

Figure 15: Number of vertical transitions per exercise sheet.

Horizontality as Division of Labour Indicator

Similar to the verticality of pieces of paper that we just investigated, we define the horizontality as the x-coordinate of the position of a piece of paper (card of shape) relative to the sheet. We show that it allows us to visualize the participation of each pupil. As shown in Figure 16, the three pupils sat next to each other. The exercise sheet was always in front of the MIDDLE pupil. The experimenter stood to the LEFT of the group, distributing the cardboard shapes from the LEFT of the group. The position of the pieces of paper was hence a hint at the balance of participation: the pupil on the RIGHT had to request or otherwise fetch the interface elements.

(a) Three pupils sitting in front of the augmented area, with the sheet in the middle.

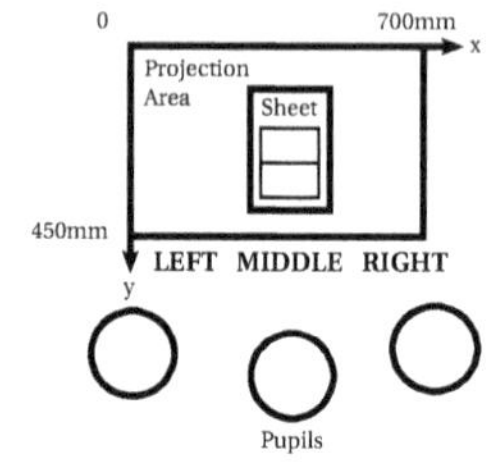

(b) A schema of the positions of the pupils revealing the three areas defined by the position relative to the exercise sheet.

Figure 16: The positions of the pupils.

For example, Figure 17 shows the positions of the cardboard shapes and cards relative to the first exercise sheet. This allows us to observe the difference in collaboration between groups 2 and 4: the use of the cards was more balanced between the members of group 2. In both cases, the pupil on the RIGHT started far away from the pieces of paper. However, in group 2, the pupil on the RIGHT grabbed a cardboard shape after three minutes, and a card after 4 minutes, in order to do measurements. The pupil on the LEFT took them back, but the pupil on the RIGHT took the validation card, and used it twice, before the pupil on the LEFT took it back. In group 4, the pupil on the RIGHT was more shy and did not participate in the exercise.

First, observing the time spent by the pieces of paper in the three sections relatively to the position of the sheet (LEFT, MIDDLE, and RIGHT), we can see three kinds of collaboration types (see Figure 18). The collaboration of groups 1 and 2 happened naturally; it is unbalanced in favour of the LEFT pupil because the shapes and sheets were initially placed by the experimenter on the left side. Group 3 shows another kind of collaboration: the RIGHT pupil did not manipulate anything in her section. Instead, she was monitoring and leading the manipulations of the other members of the group. Finally, Group 4 was artificially balanced: the experimenter imposed a turn-taking rule for the pupils to manipulate, after realizing that the RIGHT pupil was not participating at all.

Similar to the vertical changes, we can define the horizontal transitions as the number of time a piece of paper changes sections (LEFT, MIDDLE, or RIGHT). This corresponds to a pupil exchanging (either by taking or giving) pieces of paper. This provides an important complement to the previous data, by indicating how much the pupils cooperate. This is different from the division of labour: if the pupils evenly dispatch the elements of the interface among them and work independently, there is an even distribution of labour, but no cooperation. Group 2 showed the other extreme: they exchanged the

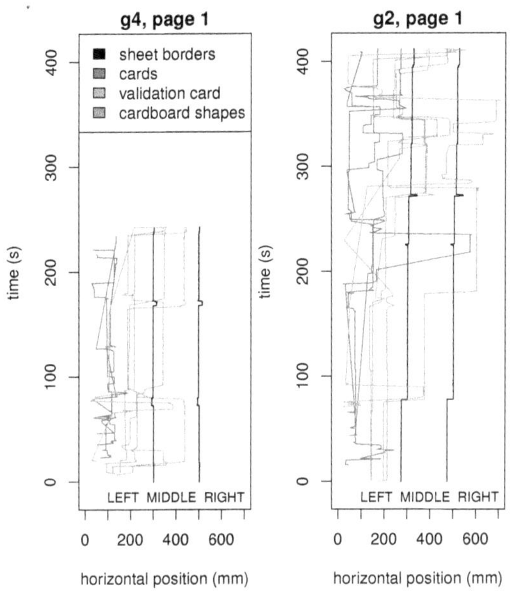

Figure 17: The x-coordinate of the position of the various elements of the paper interface as a function of time, rotated horizontally. This shows the position of the pieces of paper relative to the first exercise sheet (see Figure 16b)

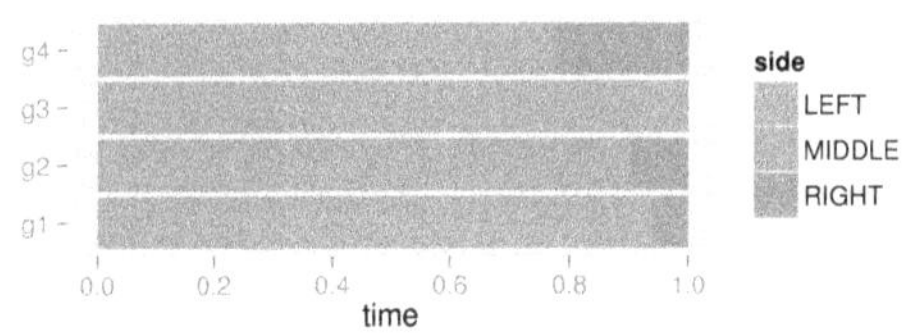

Figure 18: Time spent on each section of the collaboration surface by the pieces of paper.

pieces of interface about twice as much as the other groups. This is to contrast with Group 4, who had a more even repartition of the interface elements due to the intervention of the experimenter, but this did not significantly increase the cooperation. Note that a higher cooperation is not by itself a sign of a good collaboration. In the two higher performing groups, two pupils were manipulating, and one was overseeing, while the two other groups were less coordinated and worked more separately. Indicators can only be used after being interpreted, as we will discuss in the next section.

DISCUSSION

In summary, we found four indicators that could be extracted from the manipulation of the paper interface for Quads. These indicators are derived from the position of the various pieces of paper. First, the position of the tool cards relative to the cardboard shapes gives an indication about the problem solving step. Using the right tool card is a hint that the pupil is close to the solution, and applying it to multiple shapes indicates that the pupil has a hypothesis on how the quadrilaterals should be grouped. Second, the speed of the various elements of the interface shows how much the pupils hesitate. Increased hesitation was seen when doing the first page, when the activity was unknown, and when doing the more challenging pages. Third, a projection of the position of the cardboard shapes on the vertical axis of the exercise sheet indicated how much difficulty the pupils had in the construction of the solution, even if they did not request feedback. We showed that this was different from the time spent on or the hesitation when doing an exercise: the first exercise was trivial, i.e. the pupils did not have much difficulty, but they hesitated to use the interface because it was new to them. Fourth, the horizontal projection of the position of the pieces of paper was an indicator of the distribution of the roles among the groups of pupils.

These indicators are not automatically applicable, because they do not directly qualify the learning activity. For example, hesitation is a good thing if it corresponds to a reflection, but too much hesitation is not productive; too little hesitation is acceptable if it is the result of an exercise being too easy for a group, but not if it is the result of a lucky guess. Indicators are thus the basis of a retroactive loop on the learning group. The indicators need to be interpreted within their context, and this interpretation can be used to generate feedback on the group.

Many TEL approaches are based on this principle, explained in more detail by Soller et al. [19]. They show three families of systems that support the management of collaborative learning interaction, which differ in the exploitation of the indicators. In a mirroring tool, pupils are shown the indicators and left free to decide what to do with them. Meta-cognitive tools are similar, but also show a desired value for the indicators, so that the pupils aim at a desired state of interaction. Finally, guiding tools actually process the indicators and propose a remedial action for the pupils to reach a desired interaction state.

Orchestration [5], a more recent trend in Computer Supported Collaborative Learning, can also profit from the extractions of indicators from the manipulation. Orchestration refers to the tasks of teachers to identify and exploit learning opportunities and constraints in real time. This task is very challenging in a classroom: teachers have to integrate tight time constraints, expectations of the curriculum, practical matters (e.g. a forgotten book), the energy of the pupils, etc. A big part of this task consists of monitoring the class to acquire information. In this context, computing indicators from the manipulation of pupils on a tabletop can support the teacher in the orchestration task. It would even give a sense of activities based on paper without augmentation: the added value could be the tracking of the various pieces of paper, in order to provide indicators to the teacher in real time about the learning activity comparable to the one achieved if a teacher was monitoring only one group continuously.

CONCLUSION

We presented Quads, a pedagogical activity based on a paper interface utilizing augmented reality for pupils to explore the classification of quadrilaterals. In a preliminary study, we illustrated how Quads supported this exploration, and observed how pupils used the paper interface. In a following in-situ study, we investigated how the manipulation of a paper interface can be used to compute indicators on the learning activity. We compared these indicators to various performance data (tests, completion time, and evaluation of the groups from the teachers) to explain how they can be interpreted. We then discussed how these indicators can be applied as the input of a variety of TEL systems to manage the collaboration of pupils.

By observing how pupils manipulate a paper interface, we extracted some features that can be used as basic design guidelines. For example, cards are easily used as a function that can be applied to several objects. More importantly, the way Quads was designed allowed for easy extraction of the indicators we described. For example, the exercise sheets are laid out in a way that the y-coordinate of cardboard shapes maps directly to the solution state, and the changes of this value map to the difficulty. The workspace is set up in a way that the x-coordinate maps directly to the 'owner' of a piece of the interface, and the changes of this value show the coordination among the group. Finally, the tools are dispatched into independent pieces of paper, which allows us to know which function is being used and how, indicating where the group is on the path to a solution.

We do not claim that our interpretation of the indicators is perfect. Instead, our contribution is to inspire designers of TEL to use paper interfaces as a way to easily design activities that highlight targeted characteristics of a TEL activity. For example, the simple design of the exercise sheets supported the extraction of features related to the difficulty of and the collaboration in an activity. We hope that this approach will inspire other TEL researchers to tailor interfaces to help them investigate their own questions.

In future work, we believe that it would be possible to use further indicators from the manipulation of a paper interface. We could exploit the scattered aspect of paper interfaces to model the cognition of the pupils with a higher granularity, revealed by which element of the interface is being used, or how. Furthermore, there are many other features that can be exploited from the manipulation of a paper interface, such as the trajectory of the pieces, how they are stacked, how they can be combined, etc. This opens a wide range of possibilities as to the design of paper interfaces that makes indicators easily collectable.

ACKNOWLEDGMENTS

The authors wish to sincerely thank the teachers for their precious collaboration, as well as Olivier Guédat for building the TinkerLamp, and Chia-Jung Chan Fardel for her help with the second study.

REFERENCES

1. Bonnard, Q., Verma, H., Kaplan, F., and Dillenbourg, P. Paper interfaces for learning geometry. In *7th European Conference on Technology Enhanced Learning* (2012).
2. Costanza, E., Giaccone, M., Kueng, O., Shelley, S., and Huang, J. Tangible interfaces for download: initial observations from users' everyday environments. In *CHI '10* (2010).
3. Cuendet, S., Bonnard, Q., Kaplan, F., and Dillenbourg, P. Paper interface design for classroom orchestration. In *CHI '11* (2011).
4. Cuendet, S., Jermann, P., and Dillenbourg, P. Tangible interfaces: when physical-virtual coupling may be detrimental to learning. In *BCS '12 Proc. of the 25th BCS Interaction Specialist Group Conference* (2012).
5. Dillenbourg, P., and Jermann, P. Technology for classroom orchestration. *New Science of Learning: Cognition, Computers and Collaboration in Education* (2010).
6. Dimitrakopoulou, A., Bollen, L., Dimitriadis, Y., Harrer, A., Jermann, P., Kollias, V., Marcos, J. A., Martínez, A., and Petrou, A. State of the art of interaction analysis for metacognitive support & diagnosis, 2006.
7. Do-Lenh, S., Kaplan, F., and Dillenbourg, P. Paper-based concept map: the effects of tabletop on an expressive collaborative learning task. BCS-HCI '09 (2009).
8. Fishkin, K. P. A taxonomy for and analysis of tangible interfaces. *Personal and Ubiquitous Computing 8*, 5 (2004).
9. García, R. R., Quirós, J. S., Santos, R. G., González, S. M., and Fernanz, S. M. Interactive multimedia animation with macromedia flash in descriptive geometry teaching. *Computers & Education 49*, 3 (2007).
10. Hornecker, E., and Buur, J. Getting a grip on tangible interaction: a framework on physical space and social interaction. In *CHI '06* (2006).
11. Jermann, P., Zufferey, G., Schneider, B., Lucci, A., Lépine, S., and Dillenbourg, P. Physical space and division of labor around a tabletop tangible simulation. In *CSCL '09* (2009).
12. Kortenkamp, U., and Dohrmann, C. User interface design for dynamic geometry software. *Acta Didactica Napocensia 3* (2010).
13. Laborde, C., Keitel, and Ruthven, K. The computer as part of the learning environment: the case of geometry. In *Learning from computers:Mathematics education and technology*. Springer-Verlag, 1993.
14. Martin-Gutiérrez, J., Luis Saorin, J., Contero, M., A., M., Pérez-López, D. C., and Ortega, M. Design and validation of an augmented book for spatial abilities development in engineering students. *Computers & Graphics 34*, 1 (2010).
15. Oviatt, S., Arthur, A., and Cohen, J. Quiet interfaces that help students think. In *UIST '06* (2006).
16. Perlman, R. Using computer technology to provide a creative learning environment for preschool children. Tech. rep., M.I.T., 1976.
17. Pietrzak, T., Malacria, S., Tabard, A., and Lecolinet, E. What do u-note? an augmented note taking system for the classroom. In *PaperComp 2010: 1st International Workshop on Paper Computing. Workshop at Ubicomp 2010* (2010).
18. Sellen, A. J., and Harper, R. *The Myth of the Paperless Office*. MIT Press, Cambridge, MA, USA, 2003.
19. Soller, A., Martínez, A., Jermann, P., and Muehlenbrock, M. From mirroring to guiding: A review of state of the art technology for supporting collaborative learning. *International Journal of Artificial Intelligence in Education 15*, 4 (2005).
20. Song, H., Guimbretière, F., Ambrose, M., and Lostritto, C. CubeExplorer: an evaluation of interaction techniques in architectural education. In *INTERACT '07* (2007).
21. Steimle, J., Brdiczka, O., and Muhlhauser, M. CoScribe: integrating paper and digital documents for collaborative knowledge work. *IEEE Transactions on Learning Technologies 2* (2009).
22. Straesser, R. Cabri-géomètre: Does dynamic geometry software (DGS) change geometry and its teaching and learning? *International Journal of Computers for Mathematical Learning 6*, 3 (2002).
23. Wellner, P. Interacting with paper on the DigitalDesk. *Communications of the ACM 36*, 7 (1993).
24. Zufferey, G. *The Complementarity of Tangible and Paper Interfaces in Tabletop Environments for Collaborative Learning*. PhD thesis, 2010.

Empirical Evaluation of Uni- and Bimodal Pen and Touch Interaction Properties on Digital Tabletops

Fabrice Matulic, Moira C. Norrie
ETH Zurich, Institute of Information Systems
8092 Zurich, Switzerland
{matulic|norrie}@inf.ethz.ch

ABSTRACT
Combined bimanual pen and touch input on digital tabletops is an appealing interaction paradigm enjoying growing popularity among many HCI researchers. Due to its relative novelty, its properties are still relatively unexplored and many hypotheses emerging from intuition and extrapolations from studies about touch and other pointing devices remain to be verified. We present an empirical evaluation consisting of three experiments aimed at investigating a few important issues of pen and touch interaction on horizontal surfaces. Specifically, we examine the compromise between speed and accuracy for the two input modalities in positioning and tracing contexts, the influence of palm-resting on pen precision and bimanual coordination for pen mode-switching via postures. We report on quantitative and qualitative results obtained from these trials and discuss their potential impact on the design of pen and touch systems.

Author Keywords
Pen and Touch interaction; Digital tabletops

ACM Classification Keywords
H.5.2

General Terms
Design; Human Factors; Experimentation

INTRODUCTION
Bimanual pen and (multi)touch input on digital tabletops has received increased attention from the HCI community recently, as researchers discover the benefits of combining the two modalities enabling richer interaction possibilities. It has been generally observed that touch input through the non-dominant hand (NDH) lends itself to coarser manipulations such as panning, zooming, and moving objects on the surface, while pen interaction via the dominant hand (DH) is more suitable for precise actions such as sketching and writing [11]. There are mainly two advantages of pen and touch input being available together: in sequential interaction patterns, it enables seamless and almost instant context switches between the two modes (users are able to effortlessly transition from touch to pen actions) and in coupled bimanual operations, one modality can serve to modify the functional context of the second through parallel activation or gestural actions (e.g. placing a flat hand on the surface to constrain the pen to draw straight lines [2]).

The benefits of pen and touch interaction have materialised in a few interesting applications that demonstrate the potential of a synergistic use of the two input methods [2, 7, 10, 17, 29]. This interaction paradigm is still relatively novel and it is only very recently that commercial (and relatively costly) hardware supporting simultaneous and differentiated pen and touch have come onto the market (e.g. Perceptive Pixel [18] and Wacom [23]). The field is therefore fairly open and, notably, we observe that empirical research investigating the properties of bimanual pen and touch interaction is still relatively scarce compared to the quantity of studies dedicated to mice and other pointing devices [6, 13, 30]. We also note that most of the studies about different and potentially competing pointing methods and devices are mode-comparative by design and so do not examine the interplay of those input techniques when coexisting in a single cohesive environment [3, 15, 21, 22, 28].

In this paper, we report on an empirical investigation of certain aspects of pen and touch interaction in different contexts through a set of three user experiments, from which we derive a number of observations and lessons that we hope will inform the design of future systems and applications based on this interactive ecosystem. Our first set of experiments tackle issues that have been studied for touch and other pointing devices, and we revisit the tests and adapt them for the context of pen and touch tabletop interfaces. Concretely, we consider tasks such as widget targeting and positioning as well as shape-tracing, through which we compare direct (multi)touch input to pen and touch configurations. The difference to previous comparative studies is that, in all our pen conditions, we assume the copresence of touch, either for assisting manipulations as in our first experiment (panning and zooming the workspace), or as a possible hindrance as in our second test (palm resting causing interference). Our third and last experiment addresses problems more specific to asymmetric pen and touch interaction: bimanual coordination and synchronisation. Here we examine how effectively the NDH can change the pen's function on-the-fly via postures compared to classic button tapping on a toolbar.

ITS'12, November 11–14, 2012, Cambridge, Massachusetts, USA.

While we certainly make no claims to exhaustiveness, we believe those aspects cover important ground of the still under-explored problematics of two-handed pen and touch input and hence add to the body of work on the topic.

RELATED WORK

The problem of bimanual interaction and coordination has been widely studied in the field of cognitive sciences [20], but is also of great interest to HCI researchers wishing to exploit knowledge of cognitive and kinaesthetic processes governing human motor skills to design more intuitive NUIs (Natural User Interfaces). Following Guiard's early work on the role of the DH and NDH and the development of his kinematic chain model for two-handed action [9], many researchers have attempted to apply those findings to multitouch and more recently to pen and touch interaction.

Yee describes how a tablet PC can be augmented by a touch screen to support asymmetric pen and touch input as a way to place "both hands and the display in the same reference frame using inexpensive, portable hardware" [27]. Wu et al. propose a set of design principles for multi-hand gestures and include observations of how gesture registration by the NDH can be applied to modify the function of a stylus (e.g. to transition from writing to selecting and vice versa) [26]. Brandl et al. present the pros and cons of pen vs. touch input and lay out the groundwork for a reflection on the assignment of those two interaction modes to the DH and NDH [2]. This reflection is pursued more extensively by Hinckley et al. who, through a design study, explore the roles best adopted by each input type [11]. Their observations of people working with paper notebooks and various stationery items led them to advocate a framework of divided labour in which the unimodal pen mainly writes or inks, unimodal (multi)touch manipulates and multimodal pen and touch provide new tools.

As for applications utilising those principles, proof-of-concept prototypes have been developed to support tasks and scenarios such as sketching [10], painting [2], diagram editing [7], laying out widgets [8], equation writing [29] and active reading [17].

As mentioned above, there is still a relative paucity of solid empirical evidence to buttress many of the design principles formulated by the aforementioned authors. Brandl et al.'s maze task shows that pen+touch is superior to bimanual/ unimodal input combinations (i.e. touch+touch and pen+pen), but does not examine the individual properties of each mode further [2]. Frisch et al. conduct a user study to elicit gestures suitable for node-link diagram editing from which they obtain high-level qualitative results for the purpose of their system [7]. More recently, an evaluation by Zabramski compares mouse, pen and touch input in the context of a freehand shape-tracing task somewhat similar to our second experiment [28]. The author reports that participants using touch input performed fastest but were less accurate compared to other input methods. Another recent study by Tu et al. measures temporal and geometrical characteristics of stroke gestures when executed by the pen vs. the finger [22]. While potentially relevant for pen and touch systems, the findings concern complex single-stroke gestures, an aspect not addressed here. Finally, while not directly related to pen and touch input, Forlines et al.'s evaluation of touch vs. mouse [6] with targeting and docking tasks informed the design of our first experiment.

STUDY DESIGN AND ENVIRONMENT

When designing our evaluation and its constituent tasks, we decided to approach the problem from a low to mid-level perspective. We wanted to integrate both fine-grained per-action and per-pointer indicators, such as target pointing and tracing errors as well as higher-level aspects pertaining to user interface elements such as mode-switching and two-handed shortcuts for the design of our tasks. This choice was motivated by our belief that it is hard to generalise and provide ecological validity for measurements obtained from strictly low-level trials that focus on isolated input techniques in a heavily controlled and constrained interactive context. Similarly, it is difficult in higher-level experimental settings to validate individual design choices for more complex applications comprising several features and interaction capabilities. We therefore tried to strike a compromise between these two considerations in order to obtain meaningful results that can be of use to the community.

Following the above rationale, we devised a set of three relatively simple tasks that we thought could be performed more or less easily by users familiar with touch interfaces as well as those with less or even no experience with touch devices. For all three tasks, we created three different interaction contexts that we hereafter refer to as configurations. These configurations represent the three levels of the independent variable that is considered in each experiment (in each case, a particular interaction method).

Apparatus

As enabling hardware, we used a DiamondTouch [4] augmented with Anoto technology [1], i.e. a layer placed on the touch surface with a printed dot pattern to recognise the position of a digital pen. For the latter, we used one of Anoto's DP-301 "streaming" pens, which have the required level of reactivity for such real-time situations. This experimental platform combining a responsive multitouch tabletop with high-resolution pen-sensing technology [12] is a popular choice among researchers [2, 14, 17].

The resolution of the display was 1600x1200 which yielded a dpi value of roughly 48.

The system was carefully calibrated before each session in order to guarantee the accuracy of the measurements.

Study Design

We opted for a between-subjects design for our experiments, as we felt that people could become confused if they had to successively perform the same tasks using different interaction techniques. While imposing a logistic burden regarding the number of participants to be recruited, this choice allowed us to have volunteers carry out all three experiments in one session, where each person executed one task set to one particular configuration. This design also enabled us to use identical protocols for each configuration, hence direct comparisons were possible without randomising the particulars or orders of the subtasks, which would otherwise have been required to mitigate learning effects.

Participants

30 participants - 19 males and 11 females aged between 20 and 65 years old (median: 28 years old) - were recruited among students and staff of our department to take part in the study. Three people were left-handed, which justified our adopting a symmetrical design for our interfaces (UI widgets and shapes were mirrored about the middle vertical axis for those users).

The overwhelming majority of participants owned one or more touch device(s) such as a modern smartphone and/or a tablet computer, with only four people declaring that they did not possess such machines. No one owned a stylus-operated appliance, except for one user who said he occasionally used a special pen to write notes on his touch tablet.

Since the first three tasks had three configurations, an even assignment of those configurations to participants yielded three groups of 10 users. Before executing the actual task of each experiment, for which measurements and observations were recorded, participants were given as much practice time as they desired to become acquainted with the work to be done and the different gestures to accomplish it.

For all tasks, we recorded the time to complete it as well as the time taken to execute each individual subtask (a task constituted of 20 subtasks in each case). For each experiment, we further logged a number of task-dependent metrics that we describe in the relevant sections. These values were then summed up for all subtasks to yield a total that was included in the data set used to compare the different configurations in the analysis phase.

After each trial, users were presented with a questionnaire, in which they had to rate on a linear scale (using a slider) how easy it was for them to execute the task and report any problems they had encountered.

EXPERIMENT 1

Description

As mentioned above, this experiment was inspired by Forlines et al.'s study of direct-touch vs. mouse input [6], which somewhat departs from a traditional Fitts' law-based target acquisition test. Our goal was similarly to mimic situations encountered in graphics or publishing software where widgets need to be manipulated and placed in specific positions. Our task involved docking a draggable rectangular shape inside a given target. We merged Forlines et al.'s two experiments so that the rectangles had to be moved and resized in all cases. In our setting, however, we included a virtual sheet in the shape of a blank document (hereafter referred to as "the worksheet") in the middle of the workspace area. This worksheet could be panned and zoomed using classic multitouch gestures, a facility that is commonly available in such kind of interfaces and whose influence on the docking task we were curious to see. All shapes appeared and were to be manipulated on this designated space. Users could also drag and release the rectangles as many times as they wished.

As soon as an edge was positioned within 2 pixels (with a worksheet scaling factor of 1) of the corresponding target edge, its colour changed to green (Figure 1). Contrary to Forlines et al's experiments, shapes could only be "validated" after fully releasing them. This allowed us to measure a possible displacement-on-release effect, i.e. the slight translation of the contact point registered by the sensing hardware upon lifting the finger or pointing device. Without any smoothing or thresholding filters, this displacement can cause an object held down by dragging to move away from its target position when the finger or pointing device is released [24].

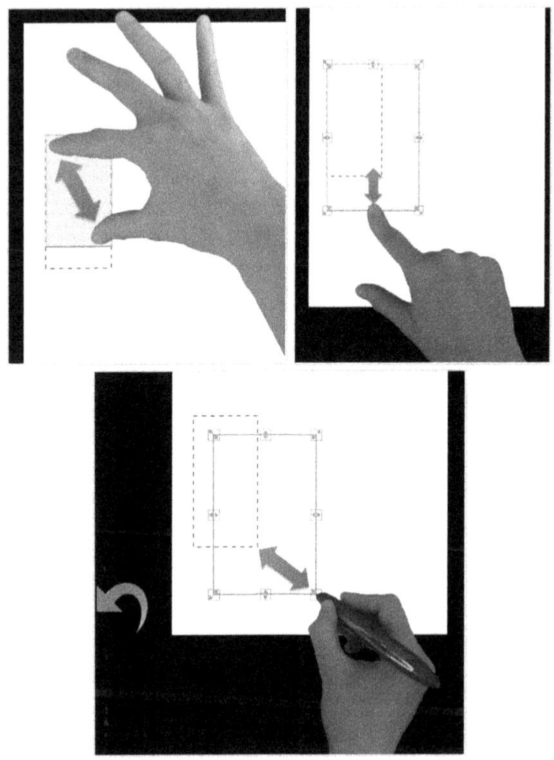

Figure 1. Positioning task with pinch-spread moving and scaling (top-left), unimodal handle manipulation with finger (top-right) and pen (bottom).

In our implementation, we defined this displacement factor as the distance covered by the contact points registered by the system *t* milliseconds before the finger or the pen was lifted from the surface. We chose a value of 200ms for *t* and recorded this displacement only for release events that led to a correctly positioned shape in order to ensure that the user was finalising a docking action. We also ensured an equal number of contact events were considered to account for the sampling rate differences between pen and touch.

In the first configuration, the rectangles had to be moved and resized using two-finger pinch and spread gestures, where the changes of the bounding box formed by the two contact points of the fingers were mapped to the affine transform affecting the position and size of the rectangle to be dragged in place (Figure 1 top left). Hence, the gesture commanded translation as well as the two independent scale factors of each axis of the dragged shape. It was left to the user whether to use fingers from the same hand or from both hands to perform the manipulations.

In the second and third configurations, rectangles were supplemented with handles along their edges and corners. These handles could be tapped and dragged with the pen (second configuration, Figure 1 bottom) or finger (third configuration, Figure 1 top right) to move the associated edges thereby scaling the rectangle. This type of widget manipulation is commonly found in graphics and design software. The handle dimensions were varied from shape to shape using three different set sizes: small (15px), middle (25px) and large (35px). The size of the handles scaled along with all objects contained in the worksheet in accordance to the latter's zooming factor. This meant that users could use the scaling feature of the worksheet to increase their targeting accuracy if they wished (but possibly at the cost of more time required to complete the task). Each set handle size was used an equal number of times for the task, specifically 6 times each for a total of 18 rectangles to be positioned.

For the configurations with handles, we recorded the number of times users missed the latter. Recalling that our target scenario is a graphic design program on a pen and touch system, we considered the situation in which the pen is mainly used for inking and direct stroke input. Therefore, in the second configuration where the pen is also used for handle manipulations, a miss caused a stroke to appear on the worksheet. To be able to resume the positioning operation, users had to tap an undo button located at the bottom left (or bottom right for left-handed people) of the workspace (Figure 1, bottom). For the third configuration, where handles were manipulated by the finger, a missed handle only caused the user to move the worksheet instead of the object, which we considered to be of lesser impact than accidental inking. Therefore, in this condition, we only registered an error without imposing additional time-consuming penalties. Because it was difficult to algorithmically differentiate an intentional worksheet pan from a handle miss, we simply observed users and manually recorded an error when it was obvious they were off target when intending to select a handle.

Results

Figure 2 shows task completion times and difficulty ratings chosen by users after performing the test. The charts show a similar pattern, with the two-finger positioning configuration (Pinch/Spread) appearing to be the most inefficient and difficult.

ANOVAs performed on these results confirmed there were significant effects in both cases ($F_{2,27} = 6.41$, $p = 0.005$ for completion time and $F_{2,27} = 14.34$, $p < 0.001$) so post-hoc Tukey tests were conducted. These tests revealed significant mean differences for completion time between Pinch/Spread and the two others ($p < 0.001$ in both cases), however no main effects were observed between the two handle configurations ($p = 0.49$). Similar conclusions can be drawn with respect to the difficulty ratings. Hence, we were not able to confirm that pen was significantly faster than touch [3].

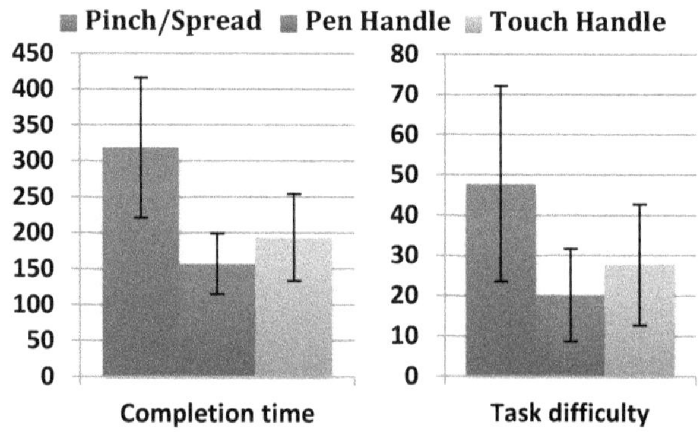

Figure 2: Task completion times (in sec.) and user ratings of task difficulty (from 0=extremely easy to 100=extremely difficult). Error bars show standard deviation values.

Digging deeper into the results and relating them to our observations of participants executing the task, we recall that especially the last docking operation was difficult for users as it required precise positioning of the rectangle edges. The displacement-on-release effect caused the rectangle position controlled by the held down finger(s) or pen to slightly move when lifting it/them up, leading to correctly positioned rectangles being misaligned after release. The average value for this displacement was evaluated at 1.18 pixels for the pen (SD=0.44) and 2.26 pixels for single-finger touch (SD=0.54), which are significantly different values, as confirmed by a t-test ($p<0.001$).

This reduced accuracy of touch and multitouch translated in increased uses of the worksheet's zooming feature. All participants of Pinch/Spread made use of it, with an average of 7.4 operations per user (SD=4.48), while 7 did for Touch Handle with 5.1 zoom actions on average (SD=4.1) and only 2 people for Pen Handle.

Our observations also showed that users tended to favour sequencing simple actions and separating degrees of freedom rather than attempting to perform one complex operation controlling several factors at a time. Many participants of the "Pinch/Spread" group said in their feedback that they would have liked to have been able to "fix" correctly placed edges so that they could then concentrate on working with the others. The configurations with single-point interaction with handles controlling only one or two edges fulfilled that requirement and users were more efficient in these conditions and felt the task was easier. Those observations are consistent with previous findings on control allocation of degrees of freedom [16].

Turning to the comparison of the handle configurations, specifically the handle targeting errors, we recorded an average of 1.6 errors for the pen (SD=1.84) and 6.2 errors for touch (SD=3.61), again with significance easily confirmed by a t-test ($p < 0.001$), which confirms previous studies reporting that pen or stylus is more accurate than touch [3]. As expected, most errors occurred for the smallest handles (68% and 80% respectively) and edges (25% and 13%). As for positioning strategies adopted by participants, we did not observe any differences, as the numbers of move and resize operations were roughly equal for both configurations (38.2 vs. 39.8 and 13.5 vs. 16 respectively).

In our qualitative feedback session, we asked participants of the pen handle group if they would have preferred to use touch and vice-versa, but generally, users of each group did not express any dissatisfaction with their assigned interaction method. Only two people in the Touch Handle condition said that a pen would perhaps have been better to hit the smaller handles, but this was less a problem of touch than a problem of the interface (and a deliberate design choice for the experiment).

We derive essentially four lessons from this experiment:

1. The pinch-spread gesture is not particularly suitable for precise positioning and hence is best reserved for coarse zooming functions of browsing windows and viewports with a single common scale for both axes.
2. The pen can also be an appropriate tool for widget manipulations, both in terms of precision/efficiency and the perspective of (some) users' preference.
3. A succession of simple operations that each controls a limited amount of degrees of freedom is preferred to one complex action that attempts to fulfil multiple operational requirements simultaneously.
4. To achieve precise positioning with touch, the displacement-on-release effect needs to be suppressed with adequate filtering and smoothing techniques. Other assisting functionality such as snap features (a suggestion made by a few participants, but contrary to the intent of this experiment), rulers and other constraint-based mechanisms [8, 25] can also be utilised.

EXPERIMENT 2

Description

In the second experiment, we considered tracing precision with the finger and the pen, a problem also crucial for drawing and design applications as well as interfaces requiring a certain level of stroking accuracy such as text input pads with handwriting recognition. We observed that among applications available for devices operated by touch only, there exist a number of sketching and freehand note-taking programs. This further motivated us to examine how the two modalities compared in such contexts. For pen tracing in particular, we wanted to determine whether not allowing resting of the palm or the arm on the tabletop surface had a noticeable influence on precision. Our three configurations were therefore: finger tracing, pen tracing with and without palm resting (Figure 3). We used simple geometrical shapes for the tests to allow users to easily execute single-stroke tracing movements with minimal cognitive effort.

Figure 3: Shape-tracing task with a finger (left) and with the pen (right). The grey filler shows the passing time (shade emphasised in the figure for illustration purposes).

As in the first experiment, the shapes to be drawn appeared on a document-like virtual worksheet, which this time was static and hence could not be panned or zoomed. The task for the participants consisted of trying to trace over the given shapes in one stroke as precisely as possible. In the third configuration (pen tracing without palm resting), if the user touched the surface with his/her hand or arm, the background colour would change to red and tracing with the pen would be blocked until the hand or arm was lifted.

A further constraint was added to the task in that, for some of the shapes, tracing had to be performed within a specific time limit. We included these time constraints in an attempt to artificially model rapid stroking situations. To provide users with appropriate awareness of this time pressure without disrupting the tracing task, we materialised the passing time as a light grey area that gradually fills the worksheet from top to bottom (Figure 3 right). A time constraint was constructed as a function of the perimeter of the shape to be drawn, a fixed offset and a modifier. We created three time settings for the task: unlimited (i.e. no time constraint, users could take as much time as they wanted to draw over the shape), moderate and fast. Typical times for the fast setting would be less than 1.8 seconds, so users were forced to draw the shapes very rapidly, presumably with a significantly reduced ability to concentrate on precise tracing. The moderate parameter corresponded to times between 4 and 7 seconds, depending on the size of the shape to be drawn.

A series of 18 different shapes was thus generated for all configurations and, as in the first experiment, the three time settings were evenly assigned to the individual subtasks. Shapes that a user could not finish drawing within their associated time constraints (i.e. a timeout occurred while the pen was down) were repeated at the end of the set.

We calculated two precision errors for this task, a pointer-down error, which was the distance from the first contact point to the closest point on the target shape, and a shape error, which we computed as the area of the space obtained by applying an exclusive OR operation to the two areas of the target and user-drawn shapes (so that if the shape was perfectly traced, the two areas overlapped completely and therefore the error was 0). The contact point error modelled the accuracy of initial targeting of the shape by the user, whereas the shape error represented overall tracing precision for the entire stroke. Our hypothesis was that the pointer-down error would be higher for finger tracing, but that the shape errors might not turn out to be significantly different, since users could automatically adapt their tracing movement as they visualised where the stroke appeared.

Results

We consider first the global results over all subtasks, i.e. all shapes to be traced, disregarding the time constraints. Figure 4 shows users' difficulty ratings and the two errors described above.

We see that this task received a range of assessments regarding its difficulty, with average ratings for all three configurations between 40 and 50 and evidently no significant differences. In the discussion session after the task, participants who judged the experiment relatively difficult gave the time pressure imposed on them for some of the shapes as the reason for their ratings. This consideration overshadowed the differences between the three input methods and so we asked users directly how comfortable they had been with pen or finger tracing and if they would have preferred an alternative technique. While 5 participants of touch tracing said they would rather have used a pen, there were also people in the pen conditions (2 in each group), who expressed a preference for direct touch input, which somewhat surprised us. Regarding palm resting, 4 participants of the third group explicitly stated they would have liked to have had that possibility.

As for precision, the error charts of figure 4 seem to confirm our hypothesis that only the pointer-down errors would exhibit considerable disparities between touch and the two pen configurations. At first glance, it does not seem as if palm resting had any significant influence. We verify this observation and expand our analysis using the results of the tracing subtasks broken down according to their associated time settings. Figure 5 shows the separated error values.

We conducted ANOVAs on the 6 dependent measures to identify significant differences. The numeric results of those analyses and of the post-hoc pairwise comparisons (when relevant) are reported in Table 1, with significant values highlighted in bold and values close to the common α-level of 0.05 (specifically before and after Bonferroni correction) in italics.

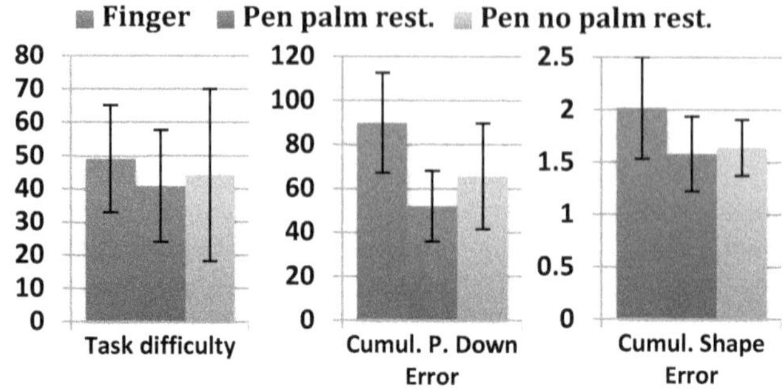

Figure 4: User ratings of task difficulty (from 0=extremely easy to 100=extremely difficult), cumulative pointer-down error (in px) and cumulative relative shape error.

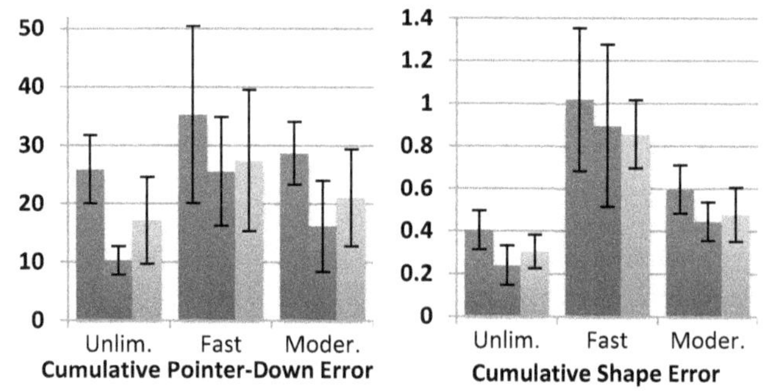

Figure 5: Cumulative pointer-down error (in px) and cumulative relative shape error for the three time constraint settings unlimited, fast and moderate.

	P.-Down Error	Shape Error
Unlim.	**F=19.08, p<0.001**	**F=9.17, p=0.001**
Fast	F=1.72, p=0.199	F=0.75, p=0.482
Moder.	**F=7.48, p=0.003**	**F=5.13, p=0.013**

ANOVA

	P.-Down Error		Shape Error	
	Unl.	**Moder**	**Unlim.**	**Moder**
Fing vs. Pr	**<0.001**	**=0.002**	**=0.001**	**0.014**
Pr vs. no Pr	*=0.030*	=0.307	=0.233	=0.790
Fing vs no Pr	**=0.005**	=0.068	*=0.040*	=0.061

Post-hoc Tukey tests

Table 1: F and p-values for ANOVAs and p-values of post-hoc Tukey tests (when applicable) for the pointer-down and shape errors in the three time-constraint settings.

The data reveals interesting results, most strikingly that there is no significant effect of palm resting on overall tracing precision. Even the pointer-down error in the unlimited time setting is not significant enough (after Bonferroni adjustment) to draw clear-cut conclusions. Furthermore, it appears that, in fast drawing contexts, finger or pen perform equally well (or rather equally badly), although the large standard deviations indicate that this varies considerably among users. We notice, however, that pen with palm-resting is always more accurate than touch input in conditions with no or moderate time pressure, which is consistent with our expectations.

If we attempt an interpretation of these results and what they could imply for pen vs. touch interfaces involving rapid tracing, opting for one or other input method has no or little consequence on accuracy (a consideration that arguably is not all that important in those types of scenario anyway). In more relaxed situations, such as artistic drawing and painting, the pen is clearly superior, even more so if those activities involve executing several short strokes rather than long freeform paths as in our task (i.e. the pointer-down error becomes a much more important factor). As for palm-resting, the influence on precision is less pronounced than we had initially thought, at least on a digital platform with all its imperfections (see Discussion section).

After establishing those results, we performed an informal experiment with a similar task using real pen and paper. We asked 6 people to trace over a set of shapes and short lines printed on two sheets (without time constraints), where they had to lift their arm while drawing for one of the sets. The results more or less mirrored what we experienced on the tabletop. The shapes were drawn relatively accurately overall in both conditions but the short lines less so (Figure 6). It seems therefore that the most significant precision discrepancy between the two conditions is the initial targeting and placing of the pen. An initial firm stand on the surface allows more precise pointing than a shaky hand making an unsteady approach. But once contact has occurred, the necessary support is established and the tracing movement can continue with relative stability, albeit with slight fluctuations and irregularities.

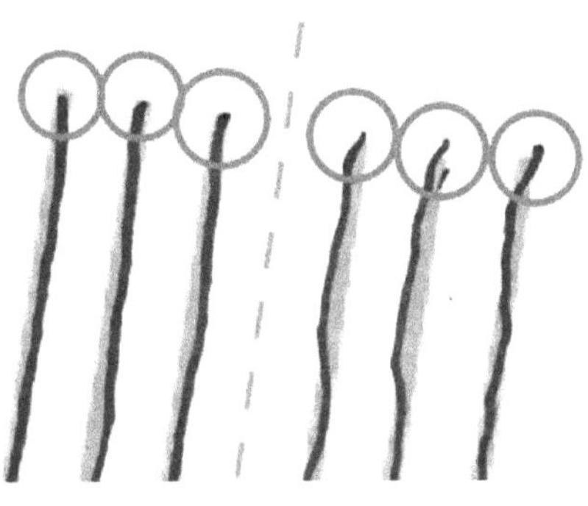

Figure 6: Lines traced on paper with arm rested on the drawing surface (left) and lifted (right). Starting portions of the line are circled in red.

We hasten to add that the ability to rest the hand or the arm on the surface while executing drawing tasks is very important for comfort and fatigue. Protracted pen use with a lifted limb causes exhaustion and pain and so we think this problem needs to be addressed if only for that reason.

To summarise our findings in this experiments:

1. Pen and touch have comparable, low precision in rapid tracing tasks.
2. Palm resting mainly affects initial targeting and pointing accuracy of the pen. Overall tracing precision is also diminished, but to a lesser extent.
3. A majority of users agree that the pen is more adequate for a tracing task. There are, however, a few people who prefer direct touch input.

EXPERIMENT 3

Our third experiment was devoted to bimanual coordination, specifically how the pen-holding DH could be affected by changing frames of reference triggered by the touching NDH, to borrow Guiard's terminology. We observed that, in most existing applications for pen and touch tabletops, pen mode-switching occurs through simple function selections or postures performed by the NDH. Most notably, the activation of pen functions through the touching hand is largely static, i.e. the switch to a different pen mode is almost never triggered by a gesture requiring a complex motion of the NDH. For their "new tools" obtained by combining pen and touch primitive operations, Hinckley et al. employ mostly tapping and holding actions for touch, while the pen can also draw strokes and drag objects [11]. This is in accordance with Guiard's kinematic model and we also followed this principle for the design of our task.

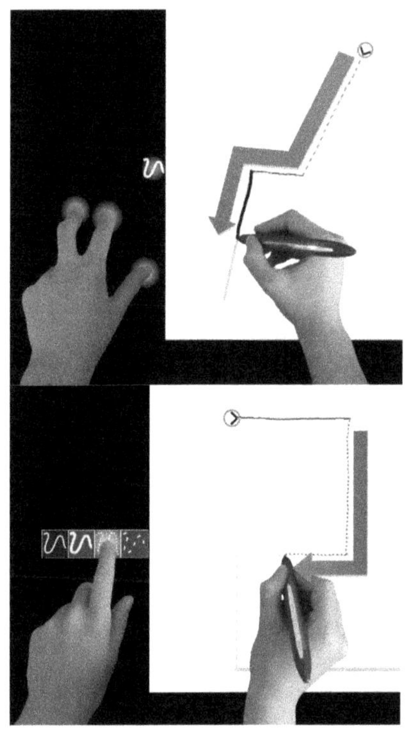

Figure 7: Bimanual coordination task with style changes controlled by postures (top) and toolbar selection (bottom).

To test people's ability to switch modes effectively, while mainly focusing on the pen-tracing task, we devised the following experiment: we asked participants to trace over a polyline, whose segments had different line styles, in a single stroke. Users had to change the style on-the-fly using the NDH to correspond to that of the segment they were currently drawing with the pen-holding DH, without lifting the latter. The goal here was less to trace over the polyline as precisely as possible, as in the previous experiment, than to execute the stroke quickly enough while correctly matching the styles of the target segments.

We adopted a similar interface to the previous task, with a static worksheet in the centre of the display on which the polyline appeared and tracing was to be performed. To keep the experiment tractable and easy to learn in a few minutes, we used four different stroke styles only: normal, dotted, dashed and bold. The three configurations that we set up controlled the way the NDH could activate the style changes. In the first two configurations, styles had to be activated using specific touch postures performed on the surface surrounding the worksheet (Figure 7 top). The difference between the two settings was that, in the first case, postures had to be maintained, i.e. fingers had to be held down to keep a non-normal stroke style selected (the normal stroke was activated by default when there was no touch contact), whereas, for the second configuration, a simple tap on the surface was sufficient to change styles (including normal style). This distinction between style selection methods was motivated by our desire to test whether quasimodes [19] were perhaps more appropriate for pen mode-switching and activation than normal tap-once selection actions.

We used the following mappings for the four different styles: one finger down for dotted, two fingers for dashed, three fingers for bold and a gentle palm press for normal style in the second tap-to-select configuration. The currently selected stroke style was shown in an icon placed close to the worksheet. For the third configuration, a classic toolbar was displayed with tappable buttons corresponding to each style (Figure 7 bottom). In all configurations, palm resting on the worksheet was allowed.

Other than the measurements common to all tasks, we recorded three important pieces of data: the total line-tracing error, the number of stroke style errors and the pen dwell time. The first quantity represented the total tracing error when attempting to draw the polyline regardless of style. It was computed by simplifying the user-traced curve into a fixed number of points and calculating the distance between those points to the closest segment on the target polyline. The second value, the stroke style error, measured how many mismatches occurred between the style of the current portion of the user curve and that of the corresponding segment of the target polyline. Specifically, we registered an error each time the distance between the current styled point on the user curve and the nearest point with the same style on the polyline exceeded a particular threshold value (this distance was infinite if the currently selected style was not present in any of the segments of the polyline). This was only done for distinct pairs of mismatched styles, i.e. no new error was logged if the next point on the user curve had the same mismatched style as the previous one.

The third quantity that we kept account of was the pen dwell time, which we defined as the amount of time the pen did not move (or moved very little) during the tracing movement and mostly occurred during pauses when the user was changing styles between segments. This time could then be compared to the total stroking time of the polyline, given the number of required style changes to trace it. A high dwell time for a stroke indicated longer periods of style change activations and more coordination effort. We suspected that we would witness higher dwell times for the toolbar configuration, where users had to momentarily shift their gaze and concentration from the tracing hand to the operating hand that had to select the correct style button on the toolbar. In the posture configurations, however, we conjectured people would remain focused on the tracing activity and trigger the different styles without looking by using the appropriate finger/palm combinations (almost as if playing the piano). If users were able to master that technique, we believed it would lead to shorter pauses between segments, yet we wondered if such rapid and unchecked switching activity might also negatively impact accuracy and hence cause the error rates to increase.

Results

Here also completion time and task difficulty results exhibit a similar pattern, with the first "Posture maintain" configuration seeming to be both the easiest and the fastest (Figure 8). ANOVAs reveal, however, that only the former has statistically significant differences, using 0.05 as the cut-off α-value ($F_{2,27} = 4.06$, $p = 0.029$ vs. $F_{2,27} = 2.76$, $p = 0.082$). Tukey tests show that the lowest p-value between "Posture Maintain" and the toolbar configuration is 0.025, which is higher than the threshold value after Bonferroni adjustment (0.017) but only marginally. We can therefore only discern a trend, but no clear general distinctions between the three configurations.

Feedback from the participants was also very diverse. For the posture configurations, people appreciated the ability to concentrate on the pen-holding hand actually performing the tracing motion, although a few users felt the need to constantly check whether the correct tool had been selected. 3 people critiqued some of the mapping choices between postures and styles (e.g. the palm posture in "Posture tap" to revert to the normal style) and 2 suggested that the visual clues to maintain awareness of the currently selected style should be improved. For the toolbar configuration, we received fewer comments relating to the input method, which is understandable considering its commonness.

The detailed tracing times and errors, reveal more telling disparities (Figure 9). The charts show that while users were mainly quicker with the posture configurations they were also more careless. Interestingly, forcing the selecting posture to be maintained in the first configuration seems to have encouraged that behaviour even more, compared to the second configuration that required only simple tapping to change the style. This is consistent with our observations of users performing the task, as we noticed that, in the first case, participants checked less often that their finger postures triggered the right style selections, compared to the other two tapping configurations. Those shorter coordination times for "Posture Maintain" are reflected in the pen dwell times, which average only 20% of the total time the pen was in contact with the surface, compared to roughly 33% for the other configurations. We think the difference between those proportions is also partly due to the fact that a retained posture sometimes only required lowering or lifting fingers (e.g. to switch from dotted to dashed style), whereas a full tapping gesture necessitated a movement of the whole hand with correct placement of the fingers.

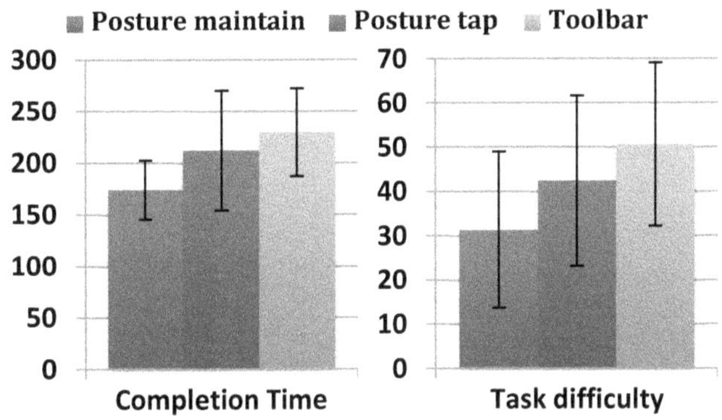

Figure 8: Task completion times (in sec.) and user ratings of task difficulty (from 0=extremely easy to 100=extremely difficult)

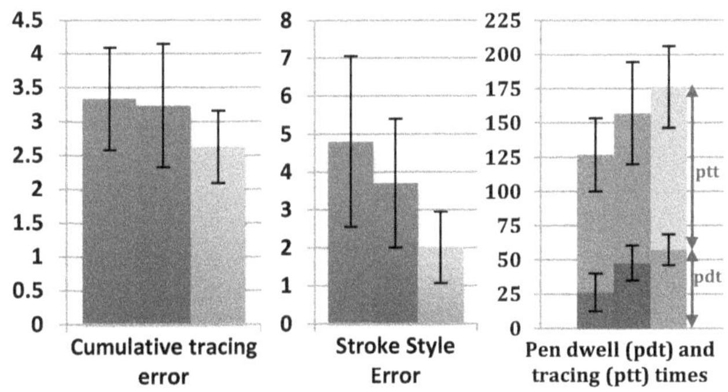

Figure 9: Cumulative relative tracing error, number of stroke style errors and pen dwell and tracing times.

Statistical tests for the three metrics confirmed main effects only for the stroke style error ($F_{2,27} = 6.74$, $p = 0.045$) and pen dwell times ($F_{2,27} = 15.75$, $p < 0.001$) (for the tracing error $F_{2,27} = 2.64$, $p = 0.09$), with post-hoc comparisons yielding significant mean differences between "Posture Maintain" and "Toolbar" for the style error ($p = 0.003$) and between "Posture Maintain" and both other configurations for dwell time ($p = 0.002$ and $p < 0001$ respectively).

We therefore learn the following from those results:

1. Pen mode-switching or function activation through postures can speed up bimanual coordination and synchronisation but at the cost of increased errors. We believe, however, that this is mainly a question of practice and postures can prove effective as functional shortcuts in bimanual pen and touch applications once the necessary finger and hand positions have been acquired. To some extent, this process can be likened to learning how to coordinate the hands when playing the piano.
2. Maintained postures encourage further speed increases and less coordination effort.
3. Adequate awareness mechanisms are needed when employing non-focused NDH interaction techniques so that users can make sure their actions produced the desired response from the UI.

DISCUSSION AND CONCLUSION

In light of our empirical results, we now take a broader view of the topic and discuss their direct and indirect implications for pen and touch systems. Essentially, we see two relevant and interrelated issues that need to be addressed to further the cause of these platforms. The first is determining the scope of the competitive advantage of pen and touch vs. unimodal paradigms, especially the currently prevailing input model of multitouch. With the proliferation of tablets, smartphones and other touch-only devices, the interactive ecosystem is heavily biased towards the latter. In this changing ergonomic context influenced by touch-operated appliances, people are gradually developing a habit of using their fingers for all kinds of interactions, including quite a few that one would think would be more adequately performed with a pen (see for example the success of the social drawing game "Draw Something" [5]). This preference was explicitly voiced by some of our participants, who declared they felt more comfortable tracing lines using direct touch than with a stylus. The majority, however, agreed that the pen is more suitable for those types of tasks. It is hard not to embrace the compelling advantages of the pen for activities such as note-taking, artistic drawing, professional design etc. But then, the question becomes: what does pen and touch bring to the table, as it were, compared to interfaces entirely commanded by a stylus?

Before attempting to answer this question we would like to bring up another reason why pen input is not earning wider mainstream appreciation and that is current hardware. Digital pens for interactive screens have the disadvantage compared to touch that people have experience with traditional writing implements and therefore expect digital counterparts to meet similar levels of precision, handiness and responsiveness. Current digital pen technology, however, is not yet up to par. Anoto pens are still very bulky and cannot be tilted beyond a certain angle for input to be detected. Response lags and insufficiently high resolutions are further problems that hamper users' natural experience on interactive displays, even, but to a lesser extent, in professional (and expensive) solutions such as those provided by Wacom [23]. Thus, it is no wonder that many commercial solutions for digital pens involve regular paper, which arguably still provides the best affordance.

At present, we think the most compelling argument in favour of pen and touch interaction is the "new tools" proposition [9]. The combination of the two modalities creates a new experience that is hard to match in a unimodal system.

In addition to what other authors have demonstrated [2, 7, 8, 10, 29], our third experiment provides a further example of increased efficiency in coordinated bimanual contexts (with a certain level of practice). The ability to rapidly trigger mode-switches and functional changes of the DH responsible for fine-grain operations via coarse-grained activations of the NDH without disrupting the user's focus on the former is an asset hard to replicate in unimodal environments.

The second issue that we wish to touch upon concerns the practical challenges posed by the copresence of pen and touch input on a single, shared interactive surface. In our second experiment, we evaluated the influence of palm-resting on tracing precision and observed that the impact was most significant on the pen's first contact point. But we would also like to raise a design question that follows from our first discussion point about the functional roles assigned to each input mode. Our first experiment showed that the pen is also very effective at performing manipulation tasks and most people do not find it incongruous. While touch is the preferred modality to perform such actions according to the accepted interpretation of Guiard's kinematic model for pen and touch interaction, what if some users would like to also be able to use the pen to activate buttons, select menus and move objects? In fact, in another test that we conducted involving a mock paint program with a toolbar whose functions could be triggered either by touch or pen, 4 participants used touch only, 5 pen only and one both to select tools. This indicates that the division of labour is not always clear-cut as far as users' preferences are concerned [7]. There are cases where touch is the only obvious possible input method, for example operations involving multipoint gestures (zooming, rotating etc.) and interactive spaces where touch and pen cause different actions to take place (e.g. on a worksheet: touch pans while pen inks). However, for clearly monofunctional areas such as toolbars, buttons, and menus, limiting activation to touch seems like an arbitrary and overly restrictive design choice. We leave it to future work to prove whether this is indeed a good decision or not.

REFERENCES

1. http://www.anoto.com
2. Brandl, P., Forlines, C., Wigdor, D., Haller, M. and Shen, C. Combining and measuring the benefits of bimanual pen and direct-touch interaction on horizontal interfaces. In *Proc. AVI 2008*, 154–161.
3. Cockburn, A., Ahlström, D. and Gutwin, C.: Understanding performance in touch selections: Tap, drag and radial pointing drag with finger, stylus and mouse. In *International Journal of Human-Computer Studies*, vol. 70, issue 3, Elsevier (2012), 218–233.
4. Dietz, P. and Leigh, D. DiamondTouch: a multi-user touch technology. In *Proc UIST 2001*, 219–226.
5. http://www.omgpop.com/drawsomething
6. Forlines, C., Wigdor, D., Shen, C. and Balakrishnan, R: Direct-touch vs. mouse input for tabletop displays: In *Proc. CHI 2007*, 647–656.
7. Frisch, M., Heydekorn, J. and Dachselt, R. Diagram Editing on Interactive Displays Using Multi-Touch and Pen Gestures. In *Proc. Diagrams 2010*, 182–196.
8. Frisch, M., Langner, R. and Dachselt, R. Neat: a set of flexible tools and gestures for layout tasks on interactive displays. In *Proc. ITS 2011*, 1–10.
9. Guiard, Y. Asymmetric division of labor in human skilled bimanual action: The kinematic chain as a model. In *Journal of Motor Behavior* (1987). 19(4), 486–517.
10. Hinckley, K., Yatani, K., Pahud, M., Coddington, N., Rodenhouse, J., Wilson, A., Benko, H., Buxton, B. Manual deskterity: an exploration of simultaneous pen+ touch direct input. In *Proc. CHI 2010*, 2793–2802.
11. Hinckley, K., Yatani, K., Pahud, M., Coddington, N., Rodenhouse, J., Wilson, A., Benko, H. and Buxton, B. Pen + Touch = New Tools. In *Proc. UIST 2010*, 27–36.
12. Kauranen, B. The ANOTO pen - Why light scattering matters. http://www.acreo.se/Global/Meet-us-at/OE2000/00-KAURANEN.pdf.
13. Kin, K., Agrawala, M., and DeRose, T.: Determining the benefits of direct-touch, bimanual, and multifinger input on a multitouch workstation. In *Proc. GI 2009*, 119–124.
14. Leitner, J., Powell, J., Brandl, P., Seifried, T., Haller, M., Dorray, B., To, P. Flux - a tilting multi-touch and pen based surface. In *Proc. CHI 2009*, 3211–3216.
15. MacKenzie, S., Sellen, A., and Buxton, W.: A comparison of input devices in elemental pointing and dragging tasks. In *Proc. CHI 1991*, 161–166.
16. Masliah, M. R. and Milgram, P. Measuring the allocation of control in a 6 degree-of-freedom docking experiment. In *Proc. CHI'00*, 25-32.
17. Matulic, F. and Norrie, M.C. Supporting active reading on pen and touch-operated tabletops. In *Proc. AVI 2012*, 612–619.
18. http://www.perceptivepixel.com/products/active-stylus
19. Raskin, J. *The Humane Interface: New Directions for Designing Interactive Systems*, Addison-Wesley (2000).
20. Swinnen, S. and Wenderoth, S. Two hands, one brain: cognitive neuroscience of bimanual skill. In *Trends in Cognitive Sciences Vol. 8 issue 1*, Cell Press (2004), 18–25.
21. Tränkle, U. and Deutschmann, D. Factors Influencing Speed and Precision of Cursor Positioning Using a Mouse. *Ergonomics, 34(2)*, Taylor & Francis Ltd. (1991), 161–174.
22. Tu, H., Ren, X. and Zhai, S. A comparative evaluation of finger and pen stroke gestures. In *Proc. CHI 2012*, 1287–1296
23. http://www.wacom.com
24. Wang, F. and Ren, R. Empirical evaluation for finger input properties in multi-touch interaction. In *Proc. CHI 2009*, 1063–1072.
25. Wigdor, D., Benko, H., Pella, J., Lombardo, J., and Williams, S. Rock & rails: extending multi-touch interactions with shape gestures to enable precise spatial manipulations. In *Proc. CHI 2011*, 1581–1590.
26. Wu, M., Shen, C., Ryall, K., Forlines, C., and Balakrishnan, R. Gesture Registration, Relaxation, and Reuse for Multi-Point Direct-Touch Surfaces. In *IEEE Tabletop 2006*, 183–190.
27. Yee, K. Two-handed interaction on a tablet display. In *Proc. CHI 2004*, 1493–1496.
28. Zabramski, S.: Careless touch: a comparative evaluation of mouse, pen, and touch input in shape tracing task. In *Proc. OZCHI. 2011*, 329–332.
29. Zeleznik, R., A. Bragdon, F. Adeputra, and H.-S. Ko. Hands-on math: a page-based multi-touch and pen desktop for technical work and problem solving. In *Proc. UIST 2010*, 17–26.
30. Zucco, J. E., Thomas, B. H. and Grimmer, K. Evaluation of three wearable computer pointing devices for selection tasks. In *Proc. ISWC 2005*, 178–185.

Hand-rewriting: Automatic Rewriting similar to Natural Handwriting

Tomoko Hashida
The University of Tokyo
7-3-1 Hongo, Bunkyo-ku
hashida@nae-lab.org
+81-3-5841-6781

Kohei Nishimura
The University of Tokyo
7-3-1 Hongo, Bunkyo-ku
nishimura@nae-lab.org
+81-3-5841-6781

Takeshi Naemura
The University of Tokyo
7-3-1 Hongo, Bunkyo-ku
naemura@nae-lab.org
+81-3-5841-6668

ABSTRACT

We have developed a hybrid writing and erasure system called Hand-rewriting in which both human users and computer systems can write and erase freely on the same piece of paper. When the user writes on a piece of paper with a pen, for example, the computer system can erase what is written on the paper, and additional content can be written on the paper in natural print-like colors. We achieved this hybrid writing and erasure on paper by localized heating combined with handwriting with thermochromic ink and localized ultraviolet-light exposure on paper coated with photochromic material. This paper describes our research motivation, design, and implementation of this interface and examples of applications.

Author Keywords

Paper Computing; Handwriting; Automatic rewriting; Thermochromic Material; Photochromic Material

ACM Classification Keywords

H.5.m. Information Interfaces and Presentation (e.g., HCI): Miscellaneous

INTRODUCTION

More and more researchers are looking into paper computing, in which papers and printed materials are connected to the digital world, enriched with additional content, and even transformed into interactive interfaces [1]. In this field, we are particularly interested in approaches for combining computing with handwriting using pen and regular paper, something with which all generations are familiar.

As an example, digital pens can capture handwriting on plain paper and make the data available to computer systems. Captured handwritten content can be edited and processed automatically by using Optical Character Recognition (OCR) and image processing to produce and display things such as graphical effects on drawings and add extra information related to the original handwriting. However, output in this case is usually done through a separate medium such as an LCD.

ITS'12, November 11–14, 2012, Cambridge, Massachusetts, USA.

(a) Automatic erasing

(b) Automatic painting and duplication

Figure 1. Automatic rewriting on paper

There are also systems that project the computer-generated content directly onto paper. Even though the latter approach may enable real time dynamic display and interaction on paper as the user writes, it may also result in the following inconveniences.

- Content written by pen cannot be modified (e.g. physically erased).
- Visualization via selective absorption of uniformly applied lighting (e.g. uniform ambient light shines on paper and is selectively absorbed by ink) and that via selective projection of non-uniform light (e.g. lights of different wavelengths and strengths are projected selectively pixel by pixel) do not combine naturally.

We believe that an erasing-based interaction supported by a computer system on the paper would expand possibilities of handwriting on paper. Moreover, non-emissive information displaying (displaying dynamic information in print-like color) is more suitable than emissive information displaying for natural augmentation of handwriting on paper. To solve problems described above reflecting our motivations, this paper proposes a novel system called Hand-rewriting that enables both human users and computer systems to write and erase freely on the same piece of paper. The system has the following features.

- Handwritten content can be selectively erased by the computer system without an eraser, as shown in Figure 1(a).
- Additional content related to hand drawn sketches can be dynamically displayed on paper in print-like color as shown in Figure 1(b).

To achieve the above features, we focused our attention on chromic material, in which the appearance and disappearance of color can be controlled by external stimuli. Specifically, we used thermochromic material and photochromic material, both of which can be controlled without contact by heating or by exposing light. We achieved this hybrid writing and erasure on paper by means of localized heating in combination with handwriting with thermochromic ink and localized ultraviolet-light exposure on paper coated with photochromic material. The current system has several limitations. Drawings by a computer only last from 10 to 30 minutes, and only one color appears on paper. However, we chose this system design for first prototype. In the following sections, the authors explain the concept, design (including experiments), and implementation of the Hand-rewriting system. In addition, we present examples of interactive applications.

RELATED WORKS

Computer supported handwriting

Approaches for combining handwriting acts and control by computer are classified into three general types: the pen tablet, the digital pen, and the support system for handwriting using projection onto paper. A pen tablet approach, like Bamboo tablet [2], and a digital pen with an electronic paper display approach, like Broadsheet AM300 [3], can display drawing effects and additional information related to that information in addition to being able to capture and display handwritten information. Both data input and data output by this approach, however, can only be handled by digital displays including electronic paper. The "digital pen" approach, like the Anoto pen [4] and Airpen [5], enables handwritten information on paper to be captured, digitized via Optical Character Recognition (OCR), and automatically stored in a database. Data output by this approach, however, can also be handled by digital displays like LCD or a projection screen, which is different from paper on which users handwrite. The support system for handwriting using a projector on paper is represented by Datadesk [6] and Yamada's system [7], in which handwriting on paper can be tracked and information related to the acquired handwriting is displayed on paper in appropriate positions. Information displayed by a tabletop projection system that emits light, however, is not natural when it is put down with handwriting and a print graphic on paper that displays reflected light. Moreover, with this approach, one of the most important characters of paper mobility is lost.

The proposed Hand-rewriting automatically performs rewrite processing on paper. Hand-rewiring is different from the above approaches in that it displays dynamic information on paper in print-like color. This displaying method has the advantage of being natural since its display form is a refraction mode based on the color-forming control of paper. Moreover, it does not interfere with paper mobility since displayed information can be retained over several minutes. Moreover, our system performs rewrite processing, including erasing written information on paper physically, although none of the above-described approaches take into account paper-based erasing interaction.

Information presentation system using chromic material

To display information dynamically on paper in natural print-like color, we focus on chromic material. The phenomenon of color change is known as chromism, and the materials that show color change are known as chromic materials. Such color change in materials can be brought about by some external stimuli, such as an electric field, temperature, pressure, solvent, light, etc. As for using electrochromic material in information systems, E Ink [8], which is a commercial electronic paper manufactured by E Ink Corporation, is a pioneer work. We utilize thermochromic material and photochromic material in terms of contact-less control and high-resolution control. A display system using these two materials is described in detail below.

Displaying Systems using thermochromic ink

The use of thermochromic material for information systems has been reported. AmbiKraf [9] is a non-emissive fabric display using thermochromic ink controlled by semiconductor Peltier arrays. Mosaic Textile [10] and Fabcells [11] are also non-emissive fabric displays where authors use liquid crystal inks actuated by a conductive yarn that works on the same principle as thermochromic ink. Anabiosis [12], an interactive pictorial art, enables dynamic color change on paper when people touch its surface by using thermochromic ink controlled by carbon heating pastes. Thermo-Pict neo [13], which is an information display that uses a thermograph sheet, enables control of 80 pixels in a 8x10 configuration occupying a 15-mm x 15-mm area using Peltier elements. Yamada et al. [14] also achieved a thermochromic display that has 64 pixels with infrared LED installed within a section of 3.54 mm. The above-described systems mainly utilize temperature control of thermochromic for displaying information (e.g. controlling color-forming of thermochromic ink). In contrast, we utilize temperature control of thermochromic material for erasing information. Our proposed system is intended to erase handwritten sketches freely by a combination of a thermochromic ink pen and a laser for heating control. Moreover, in contrast to previously proposed control methods, ours enables control in high spatial resolution, which is suitable for handwriting. As Olberding and Steimle [15] pointed out, adding erasing capabilities to pen-and-paper based interactions is an important future challenge in paper computing.

Displaying Systems using photochromic material

Some systems have used photochromic material and UV light to display information. KAMI CHAT [16], which enables users to chat on paper with handwriting, uses an ultraviolet

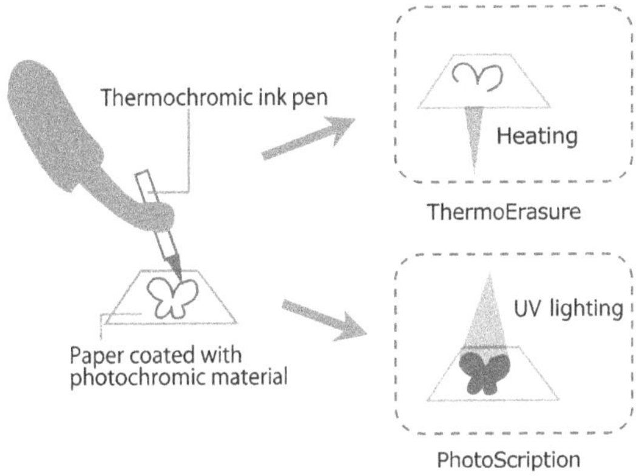

Figure 2. Overview of the process of Hand-rewriting

LED array. Hino et al. [17] also uses an ultraviolet LED array to control the reflectivity of photochromic surface in a high contrast display system. Slow Display [18], which displays dynamic information in high spatial resolution in print-like color and at a low refresh rate, uses a UV laser. Fade-out [19], an installation art that generates gradational pictures, also uses a UV laser. SolaColor [20] and The Solar Annual Report [21], which displays dynamic information in a non-emissive way outdoors, utilize solar light as an ultraviolet light source. Previously proposed optical control devices and light sources such as the UV LED array, UV laser, and solar light have the following problems: spatial resolution of UV LED array is low, information can be only displayed sequentially if a UV laser is used, and stable supply of ultraviolet light is not easy when solar light is used. In contrast to previous works, our system can display a 2D pattern at once in high resolution by developing an UV projector. Note that most previous systems were not concerned with the paper's material or the wavelength of the light source, which provokes light emissions. Our system achieves natural print-like color without emitting light by examining and choosing the suitable paper and light source for this purpose.

CONCEPT OF HAND-REWRITING

Overview of the system

Hand-rewriting is a hybrid writing and erasure system in which both human users and computer systems can write and erase freely on the same piece of paper. The following functions frame the essence of Hand-rewriting. When the user writes on a piece of paper with a pen, for example, the computer system can erase what is written, and additional content can be written on the paper in natural print-like colors, as shown in Figure 2.

To achieve this concept, we focused our attention on chromic material, in which the appearance and disappearance of color can be controlled by external stimuli. Specifically, we used thermochromic material and photochromic material, both of which can be controlled without contact by heating or exposing light. We achieved this hybrid writing and erasure on paper by combining two technical innovations: ThermoErasure and PhotoScription. The first technology can automatically erase specific areas on paper without using an eraser by selectively heating thermochromic ink using a laser. The second can repeatedly display additional content on the paper in color by projecting UV light on paper coated with photochromic material. We kept external stimuli for erasing and displaying separate so that they do not interfere with each other.

System design issues

Before implementing the handwriting system, we have to solve some issues.

ThermoErasure system

ThermoErasure system is comprised of temperature control of a thermochromic ink pen ("FriXion", Pilot Pen Co., Ltd.). Our basic plan does not clearly specify detailed temperature property of FriXion, though specifications indicate FriXion's ink is colorless at 65 $^\circ$ C and colored at -20 $^\circ$ C. Thus, we should examine the appropriate temperature at which the colors of thermochromic ink can be reliably erased. We convert laser light controlled by a galvanometer scanner into heat to control temperature. When light hits a black surface, it is easily absorbed and converted into heat. However, the color of the paper for handwriting is white, so we needed to place a black surface in contact with the white paper in the light path. Depending on the design of the black surface placement, temperature rises differently. We must examine the design of the black surface that can convert laser light into heat efficiently.

PhotoScription system

PhotoScription system is comprised of controlled ultraviolet-light exposure on a paper coated with photochromic material. Of the photochromic materials, we choose spiropyran, which produces color under UV light and returns gradually to colorless and transparent when the UV light is blocked. For the PhotoScription system of Hand-rewriting, first, we have to examine what kind of paper is good for coating with the spiropyran. Preliminary research indicated that most normal white paper and high-quality paper is not suitable for achieving natural print-like color in our system since they emit light under UV light. In addition, characteristics of spiropyran's color-forming under UV light are not well known since these materials have mainly been dealt with in the chemical field, where a material's characteristics are analyzed on the molecular level. Thus, we should examine how color strength changes depending on the irradiance of UV light and speed of appearance and disappearance of color under a common indoor environment.

EXPERIMENTS FOR THERMOERASURE PART

Temperature for stable erasing

In this experiment, we examined the temperature needed to erase FriXion's ink stably. According to the preliminary research, FriXion's ink starts to lose color when the temperature reaches about 50 $^\circ$ C (140 $^\circ$ F). At this temperature, however, the colorless state of FriXion's is unstable, and color is produced again at normal temperature after heating. This phenomenon implies that FriXion's ink should be heated at higher temperature in order to erase it stably.

The experimental conditions were as follows. FriXion's ink coated on the $1cm^2$ paper was heated from 59° C to 66° C. After the paper surface reached the target temperature, the paper coated with FriXion's ink was left at normal temperature for one minute and the surface of the paper was photographed. For heating, we used a Peltier device, which is an electrically operated device that becomes hot on one side when voltage is applied. Surface temperature of the paper was measured by a thermo-camera (Thermo Shot F30S, NEC/Avio Co., Ltd.). Figure 3 shows the results. When FriXion's ink is heated from 59° C to 63° C, it produces color again at normal temperature. On the other hand, when FriXion's ink is heated above 64° C, it does not produce color at normal temperature. Therefore, in the Hand-rewriting system, thermal source should provide heat over 64 ° C in order to erase FriXion's ink stably.

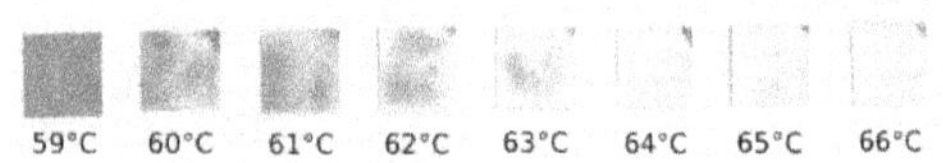

Figure 3. Color re-appearance after heating to various temperatures

Comparison of black surface configuration

In this experiment, we compared different designs of black surface configuration for effectively converting laser into heat. In ThermoErasure, a UV laser is applied from underneath a transparent plate on which a piece of paper for writing is placed. We think there are at least three configurations for placing a black surface in the light path in contact with the paper while satisfying the above condition.

configuration1 a white paper coated with FriXion's ink is put on the transparent board whose surface is coated with black paint as shown in Figure 4(a).

configuration2 a white paper coated with FriXion's ink is put on the black paper over the transparent board as shown in Figure 4(b).

configuration3 a white paper whose surface is coated with FriXion's ink and underside is coated with black paint is put on the transparent board as shown in Figure 4(c).

In this experiment, we examined which configuration enables the fastest rise in temperature. For the thermal source, laser light (405-nm wavelength and 0.07-mm laser diameter) was used. Surface temperature of the paper was measured and recorded for a minute by a thermo-camera (Thermo Shot F30S, NEC/Avio Co., Ltd.). This trial was repeated five times. Average transition of temperature for a minute is shown in Figure 5. The results of the experiment show that the third configuration enables a fast increase in temperature. Thus, the Hand-rewriting system should use a white paper whose surface is coated with FriXion's ink and underside is coated with black paint for effective thermal conversion of laser light.

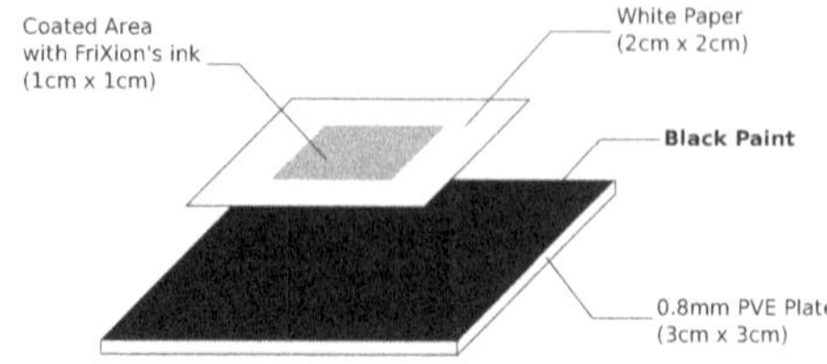

(a) Configuration1: transparent board coated with black pain

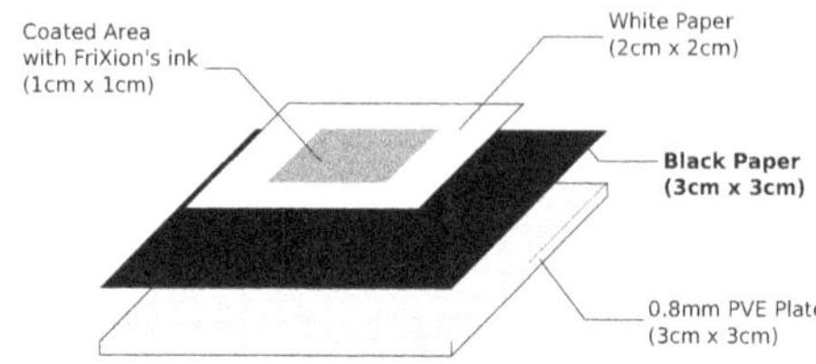

(b) Configuration2: black paper over the transparent board

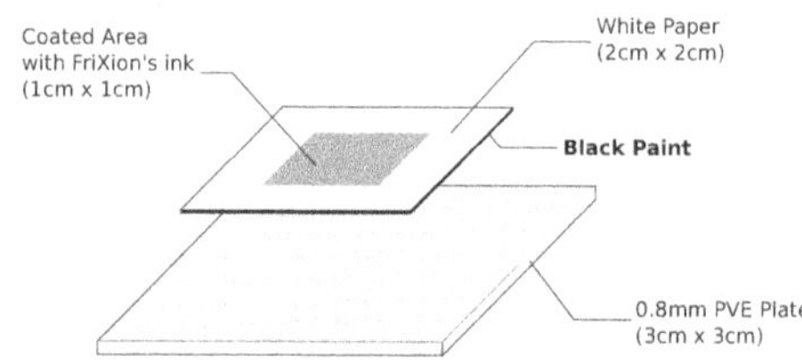

(c) Configuration3: a white paper's underside is coated with black paint

Figure 4. Comparison of black surface configurations

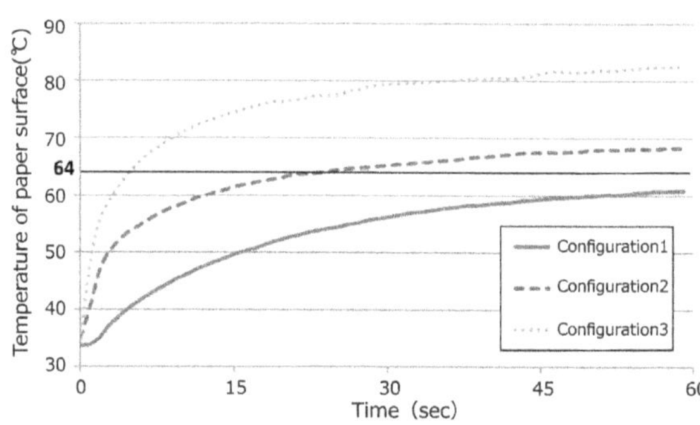

Figure 5. Transition of temperature in each black surface configuration

EXPERIMENTS FOR PHOTOSCRIPTION PART

Selection of paper that does not emit light

We examined what kind of paper is suitable as a substrate for coating with spiropyran. On the basis of the results of our preliminary research, where we consulted a printing company for

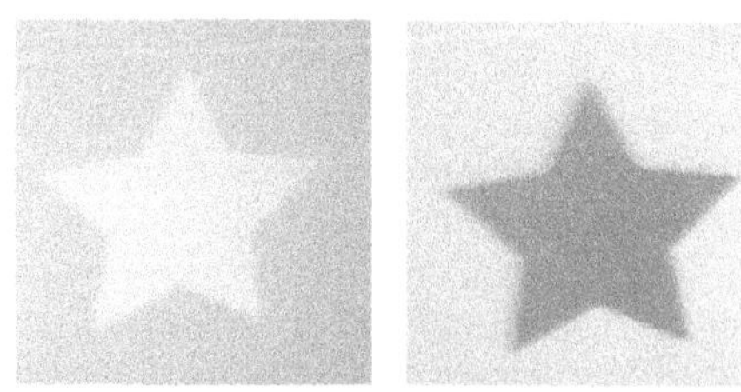

(a) Ordinary paper with bleach show fluorescence

(b) Bleach-less paper coated with spiropyran indicate forms color

Figure 6. Behavior of paper under UV light

paper that did not contain a bleaching agent, we discovered that some synthetic paper from the Yupo Corporation called Yupo paper, made mostly from polypropylene film, satisfied the above condition.

Figure 6 shows simple experimental results for the reaction of paper under UV light. Figure 6 (a) shows high-quality paper under UV light. Figure 6 (b) shows Yupo paper coated with spiropyran (Yupo SGS80-SN, Nichiei Kakoh Co., Ltd.) under UV light. High-quality paper generates a fluorescence reaction and emits light. On the other hand, the Yupo paper neither emits light nor generates color naturally. Therefore, in the Hand-rewriting system, we use this Yupo paper coated with spiropyran in order to achieve natural print-like color.

Color strength depending on the irradiance of UV light

In this section, color strength depending on the irradiance of UV light is examined in order to determine the appropriate irradiance of UV light for controlling color-forming. Here, we measured chromaticity of four different spiropyran when UV light was irradiated from $0\mu W/cm^2$ to $1500\mu W/cm^2$. Irradiance was changed by changing the distance between the UV light source and paper. Four different colored types of spiropyran were used: blue, purple, pink, and yellow. These were purchased from (Kirokusozai Co., Ltd.). Spiropyran, whose concentration in coating material is at 0.5%, is coated on the above described Yupo paper, which was white.

Chromaticity of spiropyran paper was measured by Luminance Color Meters (CS-100A, Konica Minolta Co., Ltd.). The timing of measurements was decided by visual judgment when spiropyran paper did not seem to change its color even though the UV light is shining at each irradiance. Figure 7 shows the results. In this figure, xy Chromaticity Scale is converted into u ' v ' Uniform Chromaticity Scale. This is a chromaticity diagram in which the coordinate scales are chosen with the intention of making equal intervals represent steps of discrimination as equal was possible for colors of the same luminance at all parts of the diagram.

As a guide, irradiance value of UV light is shown near blue spiropyran's u' v' Uniform Chromaticity Scale. Moreover, u' v ' Uniform Chromaticity value of white Yupo paper without spiropyran is denoted by an asterisk in Figure 7. As shown in this figure, when UV light is not irradiated ($0\mu W/cm^2$), most types of spiropyran are transparent. Then, chromaticity of different spiropyran paper overlaps since Yupo paper's white surface is measured and plotted. Because irradiation power is strong, color strength changes. Pink and purple produce enough color under relatively low irradiance around $1000\mu W/cm^2$, but since even stronger UV light is irradiated, the plotted dots overlap. On the other hand, blue and yellow produce stronger colors as irradiance becomes strong like $1500\mu W/cm^2$. This indicates that blue and yellow spiropyran paper need stronger irradiance than pink and purple spiropyran paper.

Time for appearance and disappearance of color

We examined time for producing and losing color to find out the time characteristics of spiropyran. To reveal them, we

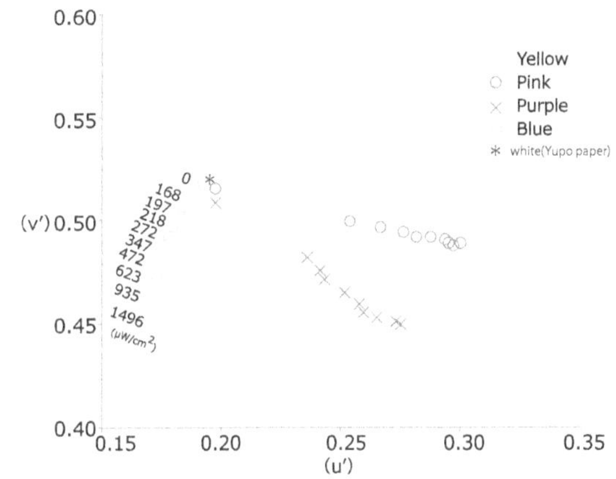

Figure 7. u ' v ' Uniform Chromaticity Scale of spiropyran under various irradiance strengths of UV light.

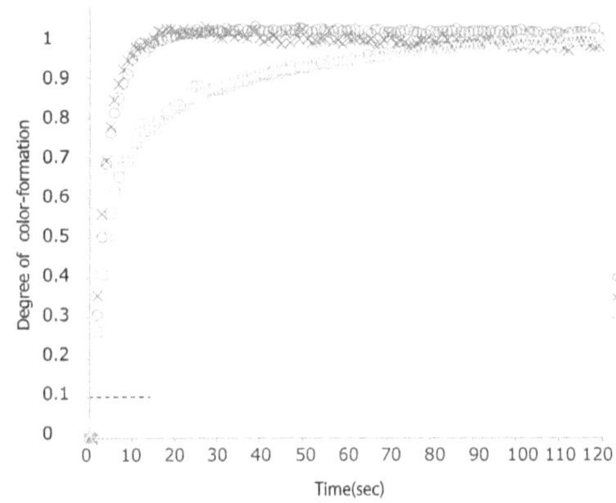

(a) Rate of color formation indicated as degree of color formation plotted against time.

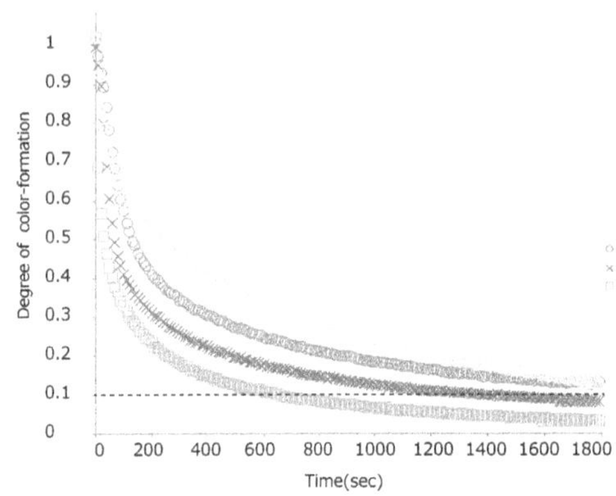

(b) Rate of color disappearance indicated as degree of color formation plotted against time after UV light has been cut off.

Figure 8. Time characters

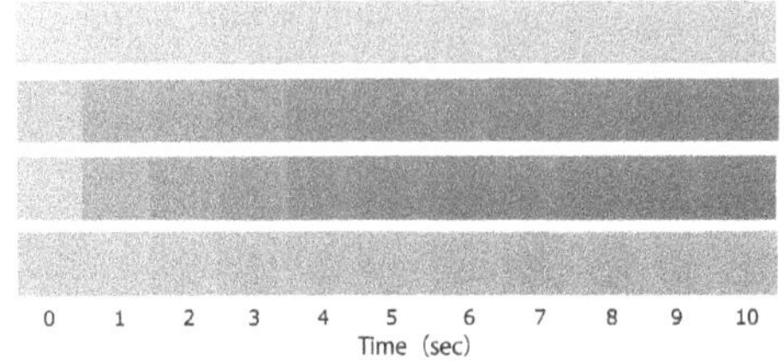

Figure 9. Transition of color formation from 0 to 10 seconds when shining UV light at $1500\mu W/cm^2$

analyzed transition of xy Uniform Chromaticity of spiropyran paper depending on the irradiating time. Here, we used $1500 \mu W/cm^2$ UV light irradiance. We measured xy Uniform Chromaticity Scale every second up to 120 seconds, when it produced colors (when UV light was irradiated), since preliminary research indicated that color-forming is quick. On the other hand, we measured xy Uniform Chromaticity Scale every 10 seconds up to 1800 seconds, when it lost color (when UV light was blocked), since preliminary research indicated that color-loss is slow.

Here, we define chromaticity as (u'_0,v'_0) when spiropyran paper losing color with UV light is blocked. We define chromaticity as (u'_∞,v'_∞) when spiropyran paper produces enough color. We define chromaticity as ($u'_{(t)}$,$v'_{(t)}$) when the spiropyran paper changes color. Depending on the above definitions, the fraction of distance $DR(t)$ can be calculated by the following expression.

$$DR(t) = \frac{\sqrt{(u'_{(t)} - u'_0)^2 + (v'_{(t)} - v'_0)^2}}{\sqrt{(u'_\infty - u'_0)^2 + (v'_\infty - v'_0)^2}} \quad (1)$$

$DR(t) = 1$ means that spiropyran produces enough color, and $DR(t) = 0$ means that spiropyran loses its color. Based on the visual judgment, however, spiropyran seems to be color-less when $DR(t) = 0.1$. Therefore, we judge that when $DR(t) = 0.1$, spiropyran loses color. We define color-forming time as from $DR(t)$=0 to $DR(t)$=0.1. We define color-loss time as from $DR(t)$=1 to $DR(t)$=0.1.

Judging from these definitions, color-forming time when $DR(t)$ becomes 0.1 from 0 is about one to two seconds (see Figure8(a)). For reference, Figure 9 shows the surface of spiropyran paper under UV light from 0 to 10 seconds. Shot images also indicate that spiropyran paper produces color at one or two seconds. These color-forming times seem to be quick enough for natural interaction. Meanwhile, color-loss time differs among four spiropyran papers, as shown in Figure 8(b). For pink and yellow, color-loss time is more than 30 minutes ($DR(1800)$=0.13). Color-loss time is 22 minutes and 30 seconds for purple and 10 minutes and 30 seconds for blue.

SYSTEM DESIGN

Figure 10 shows the system configuration of Hand-rewriting. A camera, a UV projector, and a UV mirror are installed over the drawing space. A galvanometer scanner, a UV laser, a mirror, and a transparent glass heater plate are installed under the drawing space. A thermochromic ink pen and a white paper coated with spiropyran on the front surface and black paint on the back surface are used as shown in Figure 11. In the following section, we divide the explanation of Hand-rewriting's hardware design into three parts: handwriting recognition using camera, erasing handwritten sketches, and displaying information on paper in print-like color.

Recognition of Handwriting

A camera installed over the drawing space can capture the position and direction of a white paper coated with spiropyran (spiropyran paper) and pattern of handwriting. There are

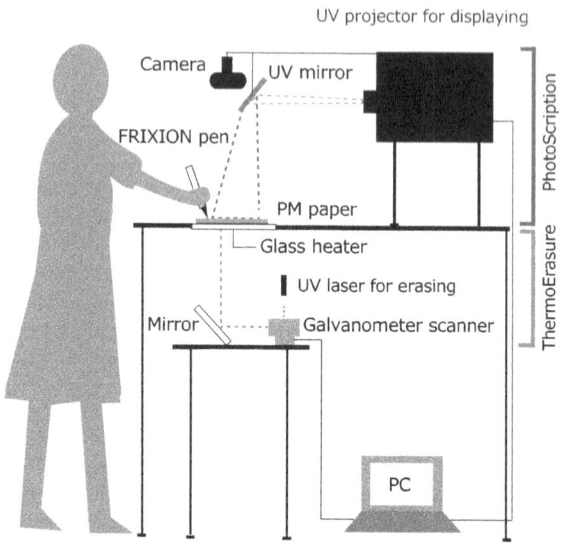

Figure 10. System configuration of Hand-rewriting

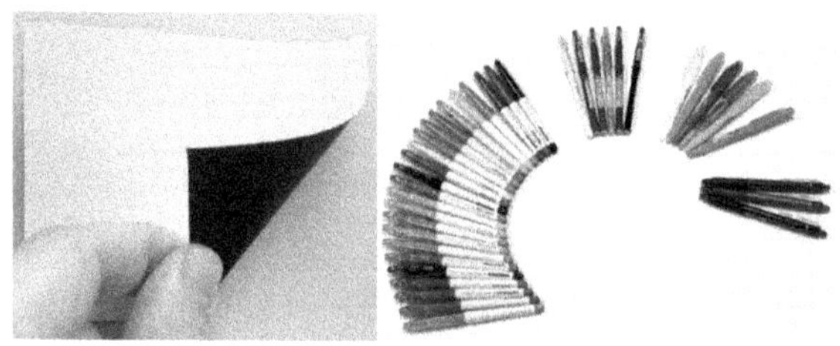

Figure 11. (Left) White paper coated with spiropyran on the top surface and black paint on the back surface (Right) Thermochromic ink pens

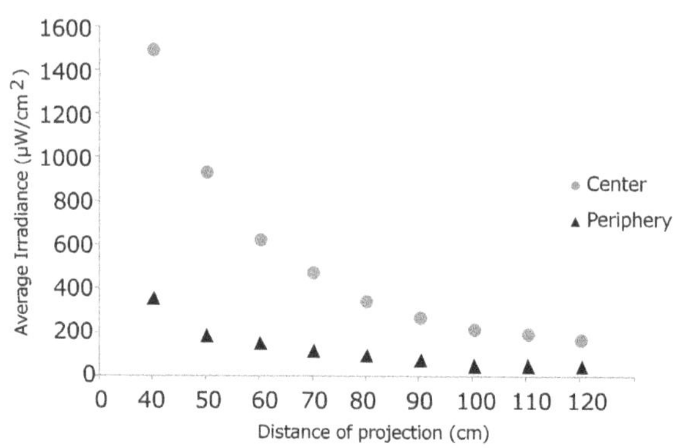

Figure 12. UV irradiance strengths at various projection distances

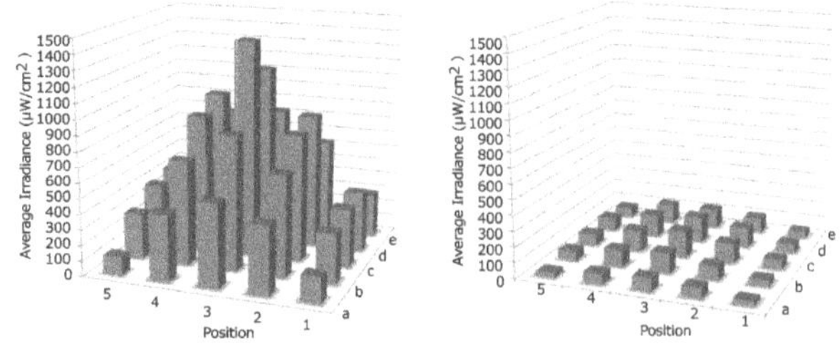

(a) Surface at 40cm from projector (b) Surface at 120cm from projector

Figure 13. UV irradiance strengths at different areas of paper.

some preconditions for camera recognition. The distance between the UV projector and spiropyran screen must be fixed. Moreover, the colors of the background of spiropyran paper (surface of desk), spiropyran paper, and pen must be known in advance.

On the basis of the preconditions, a rectangle region of spiropyran paper is detected via the lightness filtering and a pattern of handwriting is detected via the hue filtering. The start timing of recognition of spiropyran paper and handwriting is automatically decided by the system. Specifically, the start timing of recognition is decided by existence or non-existence of a hand, which is also detected via the hue filtering. When fingers disappear from over the spiropyran paper, spiropyran paper recognition starts. When fingers disappear from over the spiropyran paper with handwriting, handwriting pattern recognition starts. Moreover, to project information obtained by a camera onto the paper surface appropriately, a camera coordinate system is transformed into a projector coordinate system by perspective projection transformation.

ThermoErasure system

The ThermoErasure system is comprised of a FriXion pen with 24 colors (including black, blue, purple, and pink), a spiropyran paper whose underside is coated with black paint, a 405-nm laser controlled by a galvanometer scanner, and a glass heater. For temperature control, we use thermal conversion of laser light. A galvanometer scanner is then used to control the irradiating position of the laser light in high resolution. When the light hits the black paint coated on the underside of the paper, it is converted into heat, and when the temperature reaches about 64 ° C, the colors of local areas are erased. The galvanometer scanner can control a laser beam to an accuracy of 0.068 mm (in the case of letter-size paper). To accelerate the speed of the color erasure, a glass heater warms up the paper from below. A picture of the paper is captured with an overhead camera, and the erasure area is automatically determined by computer processing. This automatic determination of the erasure area based on a camera image has a variety of potential applications.

PhotoScription system

The PhotoScription system is comprised of spiropyran-coated paper, a UV mirror, and a UV projector. A single color appears locally on the paper when UV light pattern is projected. Color is determined by the kind of spiropyran applied on the paper, and not by the wavelength of the UV light. In this implementation, we prepared four types of spiropyran-coated paper (blue, purple, pink, and yellow). To project any type of invisible UV pattern locally, we have developed a UV projector with the following features.

- It has an invisible 365-nm wavelength light source (ZUV-C20H, omron Co., Ltd.)
- It can illuminate in units of pixels by means of digital micromirror (DLPD4X00KIT(UV), Texas Instruments Co., Ltd.)
- It has high resolution (1024 × 728)

Projection UV pattern can be controlled by a computer with a black-and-white image signal in which the white area indicates projected UV light.

To examine how the developed UV projector works, we measured irradiance at several distances and at each position. As shown in Figure 12, irradiance at the surface of spiropyran paper becomes weak as a function of distance from an UV projector. As shown in Figure 13, center irradiance and peripheral irradiance are different even at the same projection distance. As indicated in the above described experiments, pink and purple spiropyran need UV irradiance around $1000\mu W/cm^2$ and blue and yellow spiropyran need irradiance around $1500\mu W/cm^2$. To achieve $1500\mu W/cm^2$ irradiance on a paper surface, projection distance should be $40cm$. In this distance, the size of projection is about $10cm \times 12cm$.

How Hand-rewriting works

We confirmed the operation of Hand-rewriting. When a user writes something by hand in the roman alphabet as shown in Figure 14(a), one of the characters that system specifies can be automatically erased as shown in Figure 14(b), and written characters are replicated in the manner of a stamp as shown in Figure 14(c).

As described in Concept, we combined temperature control of a thermochromic ink pen as the erasing process and ultraviolet-light control of photochromic material as the displaying process since we think external stimulus should differ between the erasing and displaying processes so that they do not interfere with each other. We confirmed that a handwritten sketch by a thermochromic ink pen is not affected by UV light and color-forming of spiropyran paper is not affected by heating at about 64° C. Therefore, we confirmed the possibility of natural local erasing and displaying in print-like color without any interference.

(a) Handwriting (b) Erasing (c) Duplication

Figure 14. Automatic rewriting on paper

APPLICATIONS

By applying the above-described control technologies, several types of interactive applications of the Hand-rewriting system have been developed. In the following section, we have divided the explanation of the Hand-rewriting application into three parts.

ERASING APPLICATIONS

We implemented the followings three applications that focus on erasure of colors. The first adds effects to a handwritten drawing. As shown in Figure 15(a), when a user writes something by hand in the Roman alphabet, parts of the characters are automatically erased and transformed into ornamental writing. The erasure area is determined by shifting the written area obtained by thresholding the camera image. As shown in Figure 15(b), when the user draws a rough sketch, the second application automatically erases unnecessary parts of the sketch and transforms it into a finished drawing. This application would be of great help in creative projects. To determine which of the lines are necessary, we implemented a new algorithm in which multiple lines in the binary image are gathered by morphological closing and thinning and dilation is executed to equalize and optimize the width of the finished drawing. The third application is a pencil-and-paper questionnaire that has conditional branching. The questionnaire is prepared with FriXion ink, and the application erases unnecessary questions depending on the user ' s answers. In the example shown in Figure 15(c), when user checks " Japan " for the upper question, the application recognizes this and erases the " State " option of the lower question. In contrast, when the user checks " U.S. " , the system erases " Prefecture " . This content of the questionnaire can be changed dynamically, even on paper

(a) Decorating characters by partial erasure

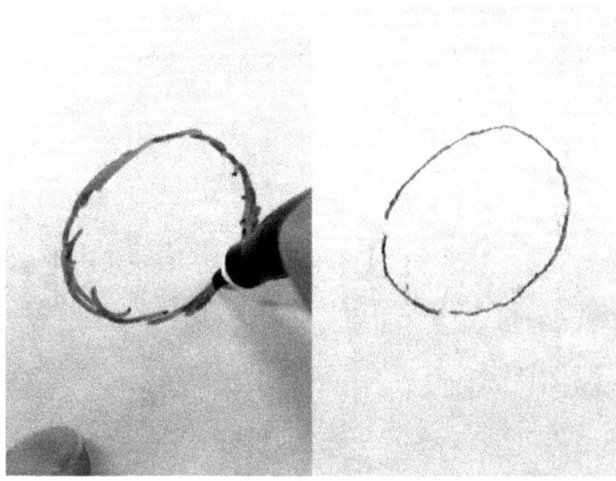

(b) Finishing a rough sketch

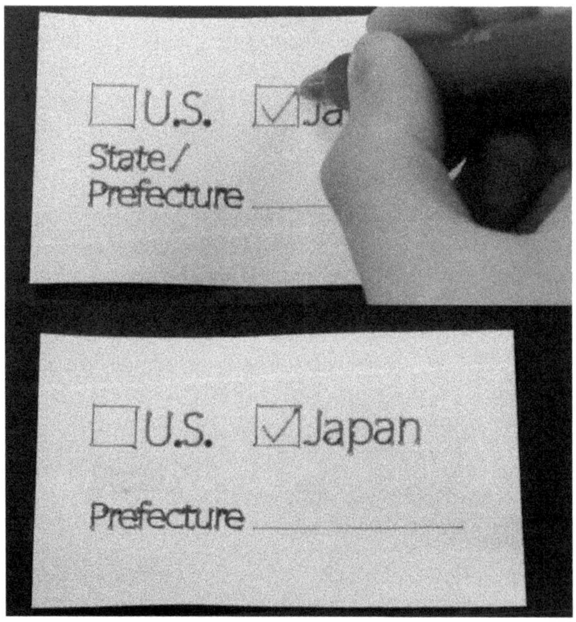

(c) Interactive paper questionnaire

Figure 15. ThermoErasure erasing applications

COLOR-FORMING APPLICATIONS

We implemented the following applications that generate colors. The first automatically colors the interior of the outline sketch when the user sketches something by hand, and the effect is to replicate the sketch itself in the manner of a stamp as shown in Figure 16(a). This application would also be useful in creative projects. The second enables remote users to interact over and co-edit the paper in real-time using a shared real paper. In other words, this application is like an online-whiteboard. In the example shown in Figure 16(b), when User A writes " 4/15 System Meeting " on User A's paper, the application automatically replicates the sketch onto User B's paper as shown in pink. In turn, when User B writes some figure on User B's paper, the application automatically copies the sketch onto User A's paper as shown in pink in Figure 16(c). This application is intended to be used in collaborative editing.

ERASING AND COLOR-FORMING APPLICATIONS

The third application generates and erases colors at the same time as shown in Figure 17. When a user writes something by hand in the Roman alphabet, parts of the characters are automatically erased, transformed into ornamental writing, and replicated in the manner of a stamp. Using these applications, the user can enjoy performing various creative activities on the paper by freely using both kinds of control (i.e., generation and erasure of colors).

DISCUSSION OF APPLICATIONS

We will now discuss and reflect on some issues raised in the implementation of the applications. First, in this implementation, the choice of effects and timing of running the effects are automatically decided by the system. A user can enjoyably perform various creative activities on paper freely if he/she lets the system take these decisions. Second, for the PhotoScription system, we do not take into account erasing or

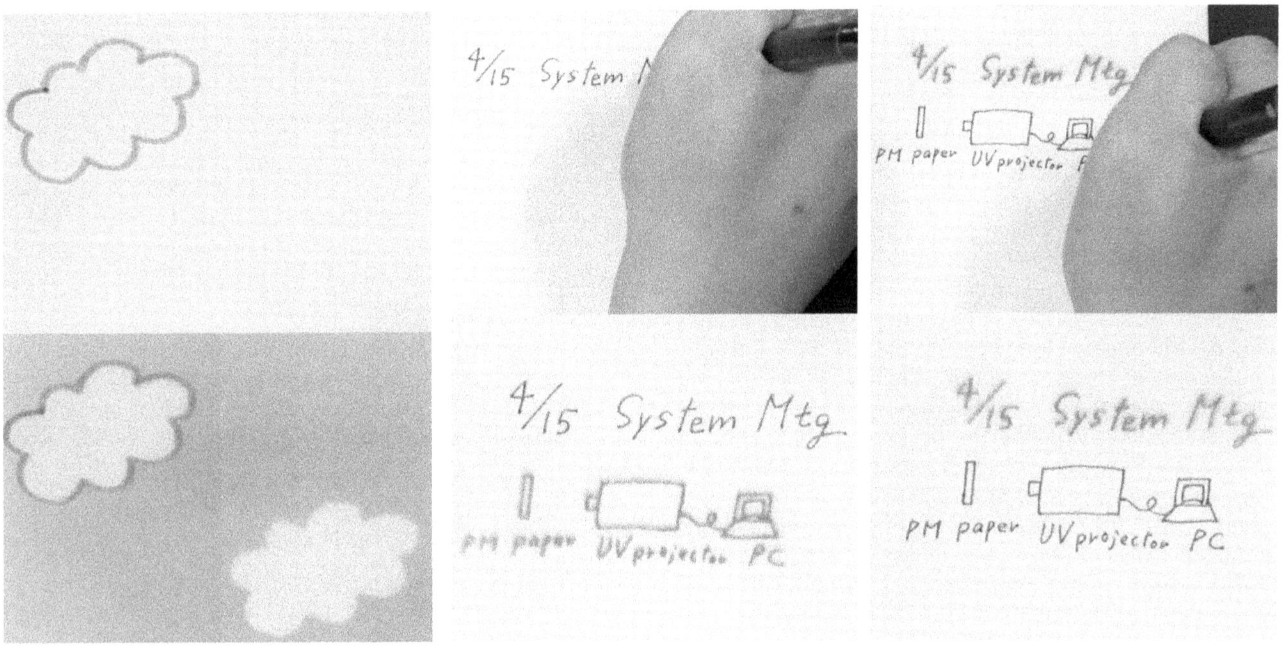

(a) Automatic painting (b) Co-editing on User A's paper (c) Co-editing on User B's paper

Figure 16. PhotoScription color-forming applications

recording of color-forming effects by photochromic material or UV light. In truth, the color-forming of spiropyran can actively be erased by heating. Thus, in the future, we should utilize thermal control not only for erasing thermochromic ink but also for erasing spiropyran freely. Third, if we introduce OCR technologies, we can develop erasing and color-forming applications. For example, when the user makes a mistake while writing something, this application automatically erases the incorrect part and displays a guide giving the correct entry in color. This function may be useful.

Figure 17. Combined application for ThermoErasure and PhotoScription

CONCLUSION

We developed a hybrid writing and erasure system called Hand-rewriting in which both human users and computer systems can write and erase freely on the same piece of paper. To achieve this concept, we combined two technical innovations: ThermoErasure and PhotoScription.

Through experiments, we have identified the following requirements for efficiently comparing systems: 1) Temperature at which colors of thermochromic ink FriXion can be reliably erased is 64 ° C. 2) Directly coating the bottom side of the paper with black paint enables fast increase in temperature in thermal conversion of laser light. 3) Irradiance of UV light from $1000 \mu W/cm^2$ to $1500 \mu W/cm^2$ enables spiropyran paper to produce sufficient color. 4) Color-forming time of spiropyran paper is approximately one or two seconds under $1500 \mu W/cm^2$ UV light, and color-loss time after UV light is blocked is approximately 10 to 30 minutes. On the basis of the experimental results, we have implemented the Hand-rewriting system that includes our original UV projector. Moreover, three types of interactive applications of the Hand-rewriting system have been developed. The first concentrates on erasure of colors, the second focuses on generation of colors, and the third utilizes generation and erasure of colors in combination. Using these applications, users can enjoyably perform various creative activities on paper.

Some issues must be addressed for Hand-rewriting to be more practical. First, we have to improve the quality of color-forming in images. Our original UV projector generates color variability within a designated pixel since center irradiance and peripheral irradiance are different even at the same projection distance because of hardware (DMD) structure as previously mentioned. We may improve this, however, by controlling the illumination time pixel by pixel by means of software. Second, as mentioned in the Application section, we should implement functions that enable users to choose effects, to command when to apply the effects, and to erase or fix the effects. These functions will improve user experience. Third, we have to make the entire system much smaller so that we can benefit from the flexibility of usage as with ordinary pen and paper such as portability. In this implementation, all three systems i.e. Paper Recognition, ThermoErasure, and PhotoScription, are non-portable. For Paper Recognition, we may achieve a more portable recognition by utilizing a digital pen such as AnotoPen, which contains a small camera. However, its ink would have to be replaced with FriXion ink. For ThermoErasure, we have been discussing localized heating utilizing conductive ink on the paper, which would require only a simple power unit instead of a large laser system. However, we may have to sacrifice the resolution of localized heating. For PhotoScription, ultraviolet light patterns may be portably projected if a DLP Pico Handheld Projector is developed for Ultraviolet light. However, DLP Pico Projector Development Kit currently available is for visible light only.

In future work, we plan to solve the above-described issues and re-evaluate our system. We are also considering the possibility of linking this system with other electronic pen devices. Additionally, we will continue to propose and implement new types of interaction and specific applications and test and verify their effectiveness.

ACKNOWLEDGMENTS

This project is supported by JST-CREST project "Harmonized Inter-Personal Display Based on Position and Direction Control".

REFERENCES

1. Signer, B. and Norrie, M. C. Interactive Paper: Past, Present and Future In *Proceedings of Paper Computing*, 2010
2. Bamboo Tablet http://www.wacom.com/GlobalSites.aspx
3. Broadsheet AM300 http://www.wacom-components.com/english/news/20080520.html
4. Anoto Pen http://www.anoto.com.
5. Air Pen http://www.airpen.jp/
6. Datadesk http://news.mynavi.jp/news/2003/06/16/10.html
7. Yamada, K. and Takahashi, M. Support system for handwriting using projector, In *Proceedings of SICE Annual Conference 2011* pp.2869-2872, 2011
8. e-Ink http://www.eink.com/
9. Peiris, R. L., Cheok, A. D., Teh, J. K., Fernando, O. N., Yingqian, W., Lim, A., Yi, P., Polydorou, D., Ong, K. P., Tharakan, M., and Hoogendoorn, K. AmbiKraf: an embedded non-emissive and fast changing wearable display, In *Proceedings of SIGGRAPH2009*, Emerging Technologies, Article No, 2009
10. Wakita,A. and Shibutani,M. Mosaic textile: wearable ambient display with non-emissive color-changing modules, In *Proceedings of Advances in Computer Entertainment Technology 2006*, Article No.48,2006
11. Shibutani,M. and Wakita,A. Fabcell: fabric element, *Proceedings of SIGGRAPH2006*, Emerging Technologies, Article No.6, 2006
12. Tsuji, K. and Wakita, A. Anabiosis: An Interactive Pictorial Art Based on Polychrome Paper Computing. In *Proceedings of ACE' 2011*, Creative Showcase and Interactive Art, Article No. 80, 2011
13. Kushiyama, K., Baba., T., Doi, K., and Sasada, S. Thermo-Pict neo, In *Proceedings of SIGGRAPH2010*, posters, Article No.42, 2010.
14. Yamada, H., Nishimura, K., and Hirose, M. Development of Interactive Inky Image Display-Paper-made Display with Thermochromic Ink and Temperature Control System, In *Proceedings of 3rd International Conference on Computer and Electrical Engineering (ICCEE 2010)*, Vol. 10, x332, 2010.
15. Olberding, S. and Steimle, J. Towards Understanding Erasing-based Interactions: Adding Erasing Capabilities to Anoto Pens. In *Proceedings of Paper Computing*, 2010.
16. Okada, A., Takeshita, A., Miyahara, M., and Inakage, M. KAMI CHAT, In *Proceedings of Advances in Computer Entertainment Technology 2008*, p403, 2008.
17. Hino, N., Iwai, D. and Sato, K. High Contrast Projection Display by Surface Reflectivity Modulation using Photochromic Material, In *IEICE Tech. Report*, vol. 111, no. 380, MVE2011-70, pp. 145-150, 2012
18. Saakes, D., Chiu, K., Hutchison, T., Buczyk, B., Koizumi, N., Inami, M., and Raskar, R., Slow Display, In *Proceedings of SIGGRAPH '10*, Emerging Technologies, Article No.22, 2010.
19. Manabe, D. and Ishicashi, M., Fade Out, http://www.ycam.jp/art/2011/03/ycam-scopic-measure11-12-parti.html
20. Hashida,T., Kakehi, Y. and Naemura, T. SolaColor: space coloration with solar light, In *Proceedings of the fifth international conference on Tangible, embedded, and embodied interaction*, pp.417-418, 2011
21. The Solar Annual Report http://goo.gl/LFdUX

Towards the Keyboard of Oz: Learning Individual Soft-Keyboard Models from Raw Optical Sensor Data

Jörg Edelmann* **Philipp Mock†** **Andreas Schilling†**

Peter Gerjets* **Wolfgang Rosenstiel†** **Wolfgang Strasser†**

* Knowledge Media Research Center, Schleichstr. 6, 72076 Tübingen, Germany
† University of Tübingen, Sand 13, 72076 Tübingen, Germany

ABSTRACT

Typing on a touchscreen display usually lacks haptic feedback which is crucial for maintaining finger to key assignment, especially for touch typists who are not looking at their keyboard. This leads to typing being substantially more error prone on these devices. We present a soft keyboard model which we developed from typing data collected from users with diverging typing behavior. For data acquisition, we used a simulated perfect classifier we refer to as *The Keyboard of Oz*. In order to draw near to this classifier we used the complete sensor data of each keystroke and applied supervised machine learning techniques to learn and evaluate an individual keyboard model. The model not only accounts for individual keystroke distributions but also incorporates a classifier based on the images obtained from an optical touch sensor. The resulting highly individual classifier has remarkable classification accuracy. Additionally, we present an approach to compensate for hand drift during typing utilizing a Kalman filter. We show that this filter performs significantly better with the keyboard model which takes raw sensor data into account.

Author Keywords

Typing, optical touch sensor; soft-keyboard; machine learning; hand drift estimation

ACM Classification Keywords

H5.2 [Information interfaces and presentation]: User Interfaces - Input devices and strategies.

INTRODUCTION

Entering text into computer applications is an essential task in human-computer-interaction (HCI). Though many different devices and key layouts were presented in the history of HCI-research, the QWERTY keyboard – initially introduced in the 19th century – today still is the most common way for text input. Touchscreen devices ranging from smartphones to tabletop devices usually implement a soft-keyboard with this key layout. Compared to hardware keyboards, typing on virtual keyboards lacks tactile feedback from the key profile and is therefore less precise and more error-prone [23]. However, soft keyboards offer the chance to adapt to a user's individual typing behavior and additional classifiers such as language models [1, 8, 9] can be incorporated. Moreover, sensor data from today's touchscreens provide a rich data set from occurring touch events. In contrast, hardware keyboards consist of discrete switches at a low spatial resolution whereas devices with optical touch sensors like Samsung SUR40 capture a complete 2D grayscale image of touching fingers. To the best of our knowledge, this raw sensor information has not been used to improve typing on a touchscreen device.

Goals and Contribution

In this paper we focus on the improvement of key classification accuracy on regular sized soft-keyboards for tabletop devices with optical touch sensors. We present a data-driven approach with minimal prior assumptions on the typing process, to create individually trained keyboard models which adapt to users' typing behaviors. In particular, we focus on the incorporation of raw touch sensor data from optical sensors to improve typing accuracy and the design of a robust classifier utilizing machine learning techniques. This classifier yields high accuracy and can be combined with a classifier based on individual touch locations [6, 8] in order to improve overall accuracy significantly. To create and evaluate such a model, we captured a rich data set of typing patterns from 12 users with different typing styles. Since we are interested in individual users' typing preferences, we simulated a nearly perfect soft-keyboard classifier we call the *"Keyboard of Oz"* which increases the active area of the forthcoming key substantially. This data set was used to build and validate individual keyboard models with the goal of achieving the accuracy which was simulated with the *Keyboard of Oz*.

This paper is structured as follows: First, we discuss related research to present the general idea, concept and approach of this work. Second, we describe the data acquisition process and depict the model generation procedure and correspond-

ITS'12, November 11-14, 2012, Cambridge, Massachusetts, USA.

ing results from the novel classifier. Then, we present an application of the obtained classifier to enable hand-drift estimation in order to further improve typing accuracy. Finally, we conclude the paper with a discussion of the results and limitations of our approach.

RELATED WORK

A large body of research exists in the field of text input with keyboards. Numerous layouts have been proposed for all kinds of electronic devices [19, 31]. For this paper we discuss related work regarding typing on tabletop devices. An overview over other techniques like speech recognition is given by Himberg *et al.* [13]. The lack of good text input methods for these devices was highlighted in various studies [6, 25]. According to Benko *et al.*, hardware keyboards are actually the most-missed desktop feature when using such a device [3]. However, in a long term study, Wigdor *et al.* found no negative impact on the quality of composed email messages produced with soft-keyboards, highlighting the potential of tabletop devices for everyday tasks [30].

A practical approach to improve typing on tabletop devices is the use of hardware keyboards. Hartmann *et al.* augmented a large interactive table with mice and keyboards and present linking techniques for multi-user scenarios [11, 12]. A similar method is presented by Weiss *et al.*, introducing a translucent silicone keyboard [28]. However, screen space is occluded with this approach and is therefore only feasible for devices with a larger screen estate. Morris *et al.* highlighted the problems of spatial arrangement on interactive horizontal displays with additional input devices in an office scenario [21]. In contrast, on-screen keyboards require no additional hardware and allow for better integration into the screen design of tabletop applications.

However, one major drawback of on-screen keyboards is the lack of tactile feedback [23]. To compensate for this, different methods were proposed to improve haptic sensation on tabletop devices [2, 27]. Using these techniques the user can "feel" the virtual keys and adapt typing behavior accordingly. McAdam and Brewster could show that adding distal tactile feedback from vibration induced at the wrist or upper arm can increase text entry accuracy on a tabletop device. Again, additional hardware or actuators are required, not available in regular tabletop devices.

In order to deal with imprecise keystroke positions, language models are used to improve key classification accuracy. Letter based language models allow for immediate corrections when the keystroke occurs [8], whereas word based models are usually applied when the word has been typed completely. The change of letter probabilities can also be visualized on the virtual keyboard [1, 14] though improvements in accuracy or typing speed could not be shown. The performance of language models heavily depends on the type of text input and can even degrade accuracy [9]. Gunawardana *et al.* therefore presented and evaluated a method to limit the effect of a language model on the keyboard layout [9].

Soft-keyboards also allow the adaption to users' individual typing positions and hand anatomy. Virtual keyboards, which change the key positions according to the initial finger posture (e.g., [7, 15, 26]) showed no performance improvements compared to regular QWERTY soft-keyboards. Individual key positions can also be adopted from previous keystrokes by computing a mean position [6] or by modeling full bivariate normal distributions from the samples per key [24] which has been shown to improve typing accuracy significantly, especially for touch typing. This adaption can be visualized though it has not shown to improve performance over invisible adaption [5].

Our work is motivated by research from by Findlater *et al.* who analyzed the potential of individual keyboard models for touch typing on tabletop devices [6]. A second user study, utilizing individually trained keyboard models, showed improvements in typing speed over regular soft-keyboards [5]. For the individual keyboard model additional features obtained from the touch event were examined, but only few were used in the final model. In contrast to Findlater *et al.* we focus on the benefit from the complete feature set, which can be obtained from optical touch sensors. We present methods on how to combine this additional information effectively in order to improve overall typing accuracy. Additionally, we account for hand drift that potentially occurs during touch typing. This was intentionally avoided in the above data acquisition procedures.

APPROACH

On the lowest level, a keyboard's purpose can be described as transforming user input into a string of characters. A physical keyboard consists of discrete switches, which are directly mapped to characters. In contrast, touch devices use different sensor techniques to detect fingers. As a result, a virtual keyboard has to transform the touch sensor information into the currently pressed key. Consequently, the starting point for this work was to regard the usage of a virtual keyboard as a machine learning problem: Each finger touch corresponds to a press of one of the keys of the on-screen keyboard. Finding out which one a user intended to hit is the critical problem. Regular soft-keyboards only operate on the 2D-touch positions to classify the intended key. However, an optical touch sensor provides a huge amount of data, which is collected upon each finger interaction, due to it's high spatial resolution. Given the assumption that sensor data differs for each key, e.g., keys are pressed with different fingers, this can potentially improve key classification. Thus, sensor information can be considered as features to describe touch events. In order to obtain a model trained from this feature set we use a supervised machine learning approach which requires keywise labeled data. The purpose of such a model is to adapt to the user's individual typing preferences.

To gather information on how users would like to type on a soft-keyboard, we present them a text-entry system we call the *Keyboard of Oz*: in analogy to the "Wizard of Oz"-technique [18] this keyboard simulates a perfect classifier which reports the user's input as correct, as long as no obvious errors are made. Actual typing errors the user is aware of are still indicated as false input. The *Keyboard of Oz* should therefore classify input perfectly, but avoids to act against a user's expectations. Following this procedure, data sets are generated that a perfect classifier would ideally be able to

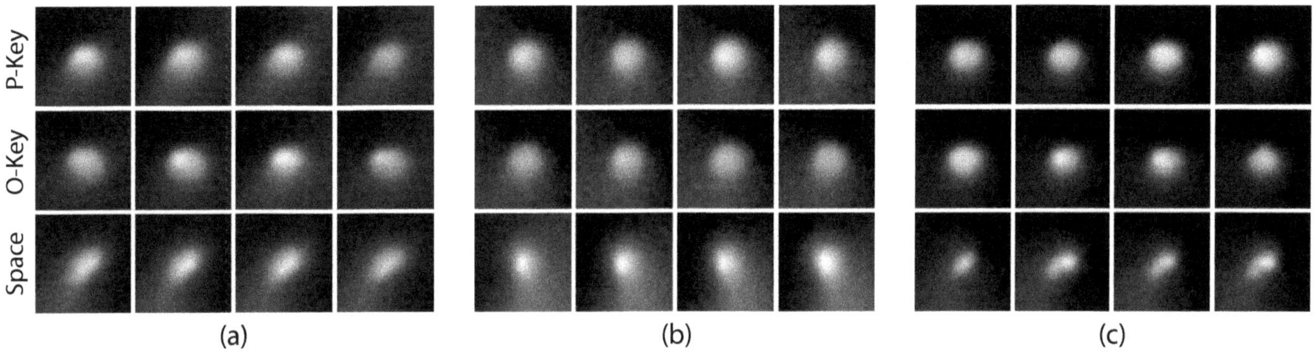

Figure 1: Raw data from optical sensor for keystrokes on two adjacent keys (O, P) and the space key of users with different typing styles: (a) touch typist, (b) 4-8 finger typist, (c) hunt-and-peck typist

transform into correct input. Of course, this behavior can only be simulated, if the text which the user has to type is predetermined.

With the human in the loop, the development of an adaptive keyboard model is usually an iterative process: each developed model or changed parameter requires additional user studies which makes the process of developing such a model cumbersome and time-consuming. The presented *Keyboard of Oz* approach allows to collect realistic typing data without having to design the keyboard model in advance. Moreover, with this approach the model generation and evaluation is decoupled from the text input procedure. Thus, the problem can be treated as a supervised machine learning problem and allows to optimize a models parameters offline.

A drawback of this procedure is that users adapt to an input system and thereby alter their typing behavior. This might lead to users interacting differently with the developed system and the simulated classifier. This becomes more likely, if the classification accuracy and thus the behavior of the resulting model differs substantially from the simulated classifier. In this case, a subsequent user study with an online operating system is required in order to determine how the system performs with the user in the loop. However, the *Keyboard of Oz* procedure allows to determine the potential of differing approaches for model generation more precisely.

We chose this approach to determine the potential of utilizing raw touch sensor data for key classification. From the recorded data an individual keyboard model is generated. This keyboard should not only be able to classify the user's input as accurately as possible, but also keep the user in control over the interface. Therefore, in this work we did not include dictionary based language models which change the input subsequently.

DATA ACQUISITION

The goal of the data acquisition procedure was to collect a large data set of individually preferred typing schemes using the aforementioned *Keyboard of Oz* technique: We implemented a soft-keyboard where the key for the forthcoming letter has an active area of four times the regular size. The developed model should be able to correctly classify imprecise keystrokes and we therefore need them to be reported as correct input. In addition, some hand drift was anticipated and we wanted the simulated classifier to be able to handle this. Since no values are available on the amount of potential hand drift, this size was chosen, so that all adjacent keys are within the acceptance area. Thus, this keyboard allows for very imprecise keystrokes and substantial hand drift during text input. A comparable approach for data acquisition was used by Gunawardana *et al.* [9].

Participants

We recruited 12 participants (average age: 30.3 years, 2 female) from the local university community. In order to gather a rich data set from different individual typing patterns, we selected 4 participants with hunt-and-peck typing behavior, 4 participants with an individual typing style using 4-8 fingers and 4 users capable of touch typing on a regular hardware QWERTY keyboard to ensure generalization of the obtained model. Group assignment was based on users' subjective assessments which matched our observations during the data acquisition process. The participants had only little or no prior experience with a tabletop device, though five regularly used a tablet computer with a standard QWERTY soft-keyboard.

Apparatus

For data acquisition we used a custom built standing-height camera based tabletop system based on the FTIR touch sensing technique [10]. The screen surface is captured in the infrared-spectrum from behind by a camera with a resolution of 640x480 pixel at 60 frames per second. The vision software to process the camera image is based on reacTIVision [17] and has been modified to save 42x42 pixel images of the detected fingers (see Fig. 1).

The application presented to the users displayed a text box and a standard on-screen keyboard (see Fig. 2) with standard key width and height of 0.750". The keyboard was rendered with all keys of the regular QWERTY layout to present to the user a familiar layout known from hardware keyboards.

Procedure

Each participant received a short 5 minute introduction to the tabletop system and the typing task and afterwards completed 4 typing sessions of 10 minutes each with 5-10 minute breaks in between. The first session was a test run for the participant to get familiar with both the system and the task and was discarded for data analysis and model generation. The text consisted of the standard phrases from MacKenzie and Soukoreff [20] interspersed with pangrams at a 4:1 ratio. Including the pangram sentences ensured that sufficient information was collected for every key. For correct keystrokes, i.e., touch input within four times the key size, the keyboard highlighted the correct key green and played an unobtrusive beep-sound and the cursor was forwarded.

For touch events that occurred outside of the acceptance area, the actual touched key was highlighted red, an error-sound was played and the cursor remained at the current letter until the user correctly typed the required character. For actual typing errors on adjacent keys, the system still reported a correct keystroke (see Fig. 3). This behavior was noticed and mentioned afterwards by some of the participants. Nevertheless, users did not perceive the classifier to be simulated. To complete a phrase the user had to push the Enter-Key which allowed to continue typing without looking at the keyboard. No numeric, uppercase or punctuation characters were included in the phrases and the corresponding keys on the soft-keyboard were not active although rendered for consistent keyboard representation. Users typed at an average rate of 40 words per minute (WPM, $SD = 9.8$), ranging from 22 WPM to 52 WPM, depending on the typing style. Keystrokes outside of the tolerance area resulted in an average error rate of $3.6\% (SD = 2.62)$ across all participants. The complete information for each session gathered from occurring touch-events was stored in a xml-file together with the corresponding finger-images obtained from the vision software.

LEARNING INDIVIDUAL KEYBOARD MODELS

In order to draw near to the classification accuracy simulated by the optimal classifier that was used in our typing sessions, we recorded a large amount of data for every single keystroke. The following set of features was collected for every touch event:

- 42x42 pixel grayscale images of the touch area around the center of each keypress
- weighted center of the touch location (x- and y-location)
- timestamp for each starting touch event
- area of the detected finger on the screen
- intensity of the detected finger, correlating to pressure of touch

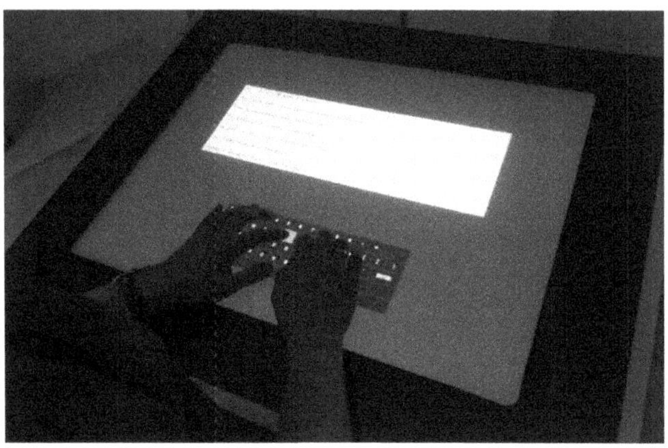

Figure 2: Typing application for data aquisition.

Figure 3: For data acquisition, correct feedback was given for imprecise keystrokes.

- principal direction of the detected finger on the screen

This includes common features for training an individual keyboard model [5] but is expanded by the complete set of features that an optical sensor provides. Area, intensity and principal direction of the touch events are calculated from the touch-region images. Thus, the 42x42 features, that correlate to each of the pixels in the grayscale images, comprise this information but provide additional details on the appearance of a finger. Accordingly, the combination of touch position and sensor images contains all of the available information and is therefore used for key classification. The image size of 42x42 pixels was determined from the largest possible touch area of a single fingertip on the screen which was used for data acquisition. This value is device dependent and has to be adjusted to the resolution of the specific sensor. Using this raw sensor data leads to highly accurate classification results, as will be described in detail later in this section. Due to the diverging characteristics of position and touch images concerning linear separability, they are modeled and classified individually.

For data analysis, we implemented a Matlab toolkit for model generation and evaluation. The data obtained from the three ten-minute runs per user has been split into two equal parts of which the first half was used as a training set and the second half as a test set for evaluating the classifiers. This follows the idea of having a mere fifteen-minute training session for each new user who can subsequently use an individually trained keyboard.

A combination of two classifiers is used for each occurring keystroke: The first one is a multiclass support vector machine (SVM) that has been trained with the grayscale images. The second one uses touch position information using multivariate normal distribution functions.

Image Classification Using Support Vector Machines

SVMs are binary large margin classifiers. This means, that an SVM constructs a hyperplane or a set of hyperplanes that separate two classes of data (potentially in high-dimensional space) with the largest possible margin to all of the data points. The points closest to the hyperplane which define the parameters of the hyperplane are called support vectors.

A linear SVM uses a linear combination with parameter vector α of the feature vector X to define this hyperplane. If linear separation does not perform well on a given dataset, it is also possible to map the feature space to a higher dimensional space using kernel functions. Multiclass classification using SVMs is achieved by using multiple two-class SVMs and joining the individual results by majority voting.

We chose support vector machines as a classifier for grayscale touch area images because of their capabilities to handle large amounts of features. This allows us to use the whole images with each pixel as one feature without the need of dimensionality reduction which comes along with possible loss of information. In our implementation we used the libSVM [4] toolbox for Matlab. The classes of our multi-class SVM each correspond to one key on the keyboard. Since our feature space of 42x42 values is considerably large in comparison to the amount of samples that were collected during data acquisition, a linear SVM was chosen. Additionally, a linear kernel has lower computational cost compared to a more complicated kernel function (e.g. Gaussian kernel) and is less prone to overfitting the model to the training set. These characteristics make it the best choice for our given feature set. To optimize the SVM kernel cost parameter C, cross validation was performed on the complete data set. This value turned out to be stable across data sets from different participants. Thus, the same value ($C = 2$) was used for all individual classifiers. From the initial training sets of each test proband, only those touch events were used for training the SVM that occurred within a distance of 2.5 times key size around the key center. This was done to rule out some of the false positive input. Thereby, 0.56% ($SD = 0.3$) samples were removed on average across all users. For model evaluation the complete test data set was used as labeled by the simulated classifier. The resulting training sets contained, on average, 3491 keystrokes ($SD = 947$). Here, a fixed text length would have been more appropriate. However, for reasons of scheduling during data acquisition, we opted for fixed typing duration instead.

Position Based Classification

Of course, touch position is a powerful feature for key classification, but it has to be mapped properly to a keyboard model in order to make the best possible use of it. The most naïve approach to position based classification is to simply check the key-boundaries of the visual representation of the on-screen keyboard and choose the respective key. Our data, however, indicates that keys are usually not hit that precisely and that the average touch positions per key most often deviate from the actual key centers. Simulation results [6] confirm these observations and demonstrate the benefits of a closest centroid approach that adapts to the users. Furthermore, we found that key centroids also vary heavily in between users – especially when comparing ten-finger to non-ten-finger typists. Figure 4 illustrates the differences in performance between the own individual model and the classification accuracy when applying the models of other participants.

Accordingly, utilizing user specific distributions further increased performance of the position based classifier. In the end, we used bivariate Gaussian functions to also take correlations between x- and y-direction into account. Figure 5 shows the normal distribution functions of keypresses for one user. The covariances are clearly visible as skewed distributions. Furthermore, bivariate Gaussian distributions have the advantage of naturally providing probability values for a decision which is needed for combining the results from the single classifiers.

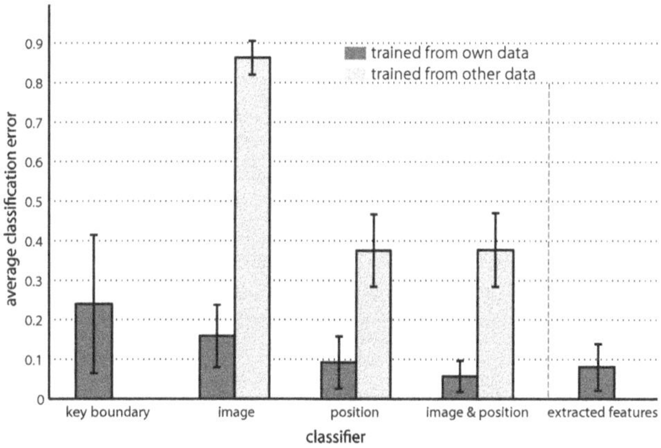

Figure 4: Average classification error for different classifiers. Blue bars illustrate error for individually trained models compared to error using individual models of other users (green). (Error bars represent standard deviation.)

Classification Results

In order to combine the classifiers, decision probabilities for each class are calculated. For position data, the likelihood of a decision can directly be taken from the normal distribution functions as

$$p_{pos}(k) = \frac{f(\boldsymbol{x}; \mu_k, \Sigma_k^2)}{\sum_{i=1}^{K} f(\boldsymbol{x}; \mu_i, \Sigma_i^2)}$$

where f denotes the normal density function with parameters μ and Σ of key k evaluated at $\boldsymbol{x}$ and K is the total number of keys. For the image based SVM, probabilities are calculated according to [22], which has already been implemented in libSVM. The class c with highest multiplied probability is taken as the overall decision:

$$c = \arg\max_{k=1..K}(p_{pos}(k) \cdot p_{image}(k))$$

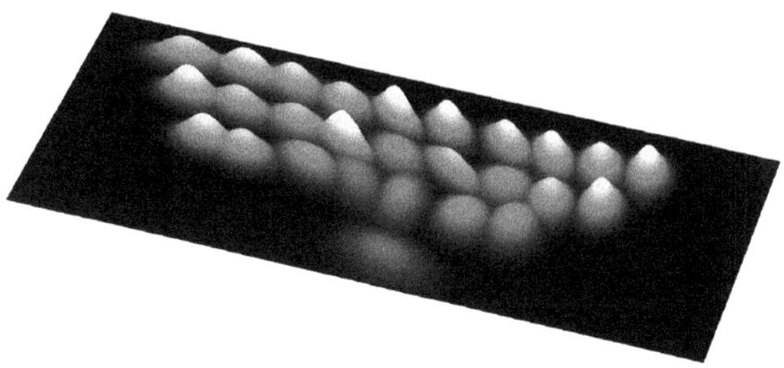

Figure 5: Bivariate normal distribution functions for every key obtained from a touch typist's individual keypress locations

By multiplying the probability values and thus treating them as independent, we make the assumption, that the touch images for one key are independent from the touch position on the key. This simplification is true for complete hand displacement but might not hold for positional deviation due to different finger postures. In order to model this dependence without introducing spurious correlations, much more training data would be required with presumably minor impact.

Figure 6 visualizes the effect on the keyboard layout of the combined classifier for users with different typing styles. Since sensor data of hunt-and-peck typists is less discriminable for different keys, the image classifier's impact on the overall classification process is reduced. Nevertheless, no errors are induced, therefore the presented approach degrades gracefully.

To review the results of our approach, the two classifiers described above have been validated both singularly and in unison. The results have been compared to the naïve classifier based on key boundaries.

Previous work [5] included extracted geometrical features from the touch event to improve key classification. Our model in contrast uses the complete available sensor data. In order to validate whether the raw sensor data contains more information and thus improves classification accuracy, we also evaluated an additional classifier with the following feature set:

- touch position
- orientation
- major axis length
- touch contact area

We extracted these features from our dataset and trained and evaluated a separate SVM with a Gaussian kernel and optimized parameters.

A repeated-measures ANOVA with *Key Boundaries*, and classifiers based on *Position*, *Images*, *Images + Position* and *Extracted Features* as the five different measures showed significant differences between the measures ($F_{4,44} = 10.02, p < .001$). Bonferroni adjusted post hoc tests revealed that *Position* and *Images + Position* performed significantly better than *Key Boundaries* ($p = .04$ and $p = .02$, respectively). More importantly, *Images + Position* also performed significantly better than *Position* and *Images* ($p = .05$ and $p = .02$, respectively). *Images* did neither differ significantly from *Position* nor from *Key Boundaries* ($p = .35$ and $p > .99$, respectively). Furthermore, *Extracted Features* also performed significantly better than *Key Boundaries* ($p = .03$), but significantly worse than *Images + Position* ($p = .04$). It did not differ significantly from *Position* ($p = .14$).

Despite the image based SVM performing better for ten-finger typists as a fixed key-to-finger assignment helps to distinguish between keys, it also slightly improved overall accuracy for non-ten-finger typists. This is because vertical angle of a finger and hand orientation vary depending on which key is hit, which is reflected in the touch images. Overall, the image classifier showed strong results and significantly improved overall classification performance, especially for participants using many fingers for typing. See Figure 8 for a comparison of the results across user groups.

APPLICATION: ESTIMATING HAND DRIFT

In the previous section, we showed, that the results of a combined classifier using finger images can account for imprecise keystrokes (see Fig. 4). However, for keystrokes with a larger displacement from the intended key centroids, the classifiers might not agree upon a classification result. With increasing distance, the probability obtained from the Gaussian distributions decreases rather rapidly to nearly zero. Therefore, combined probability for the intended key will degrade as well, leading to a possible classification error. Such a larger displacement of keystroke positions can occur from hand drift – especially in the case of typists which do not look at the virtual keyboard for a longer period of time. Hand drift leads to similar displacements from the intended key centroids for subsequent keystrokes. This induces a systematic error. Since the test persons were not given any restrictions but were instructed to type freely across the whole session, hand drift has to be expected. As the participants still received positive feedback for displacements within the tolerated distance, they also did not correct themselves immediately.

However, it is impossible to measure precise ground truth data for hand drift directly, since small hand movement is an integral part of the typing process. Even if the hand position is measured precisely with an additional sensor (e.g., camera, depth sensor), there is no possibility to distinguish between regular motion that is part of typing and inadvertent hand drift. Therefore, the observed hand drift measurements are superimposed by a noisy process that results from the regular typing motion.

Depending on the touch sensor, coarse hand contours can be obtained directly from the sensor image, which could be used for hand drift estimation (e.g., with diffused illumination approaches). However, since fingers move rapidly during typing and thereby change the hand contour substantially, position estimations are expected to be rather imprecise. More important, other touch sensor techniques like FTIR [10]) do not provide sensor information from objects above the surface. In order to maintain generalizability of the presented approach, we work with touch contact information only.

However, keystroke positions are not that precise and thus hit locations are scattered around the key centers (or more precisely, around the individual key centroids). Therefore, we have to estimate the hand drift from noisy input. In a previous section, we showed that these touch distributions can be modeled as bivariate Gaussian functions. From a signal processing point of view, this problem can be formulated as the estimation of a hidden system state from measurements containing normal distributed noise. Here, the Kalman filter [16] computes the optimal solution. We therefore propose this filter to compensate for structural errors induced by hand drift.

A Kalman filter model without control-input model estimates the true state – in our case hand drift h_t – at time t to be:

$$h_t = A_{t-1}h_{t-1} + w_{t-1}$$

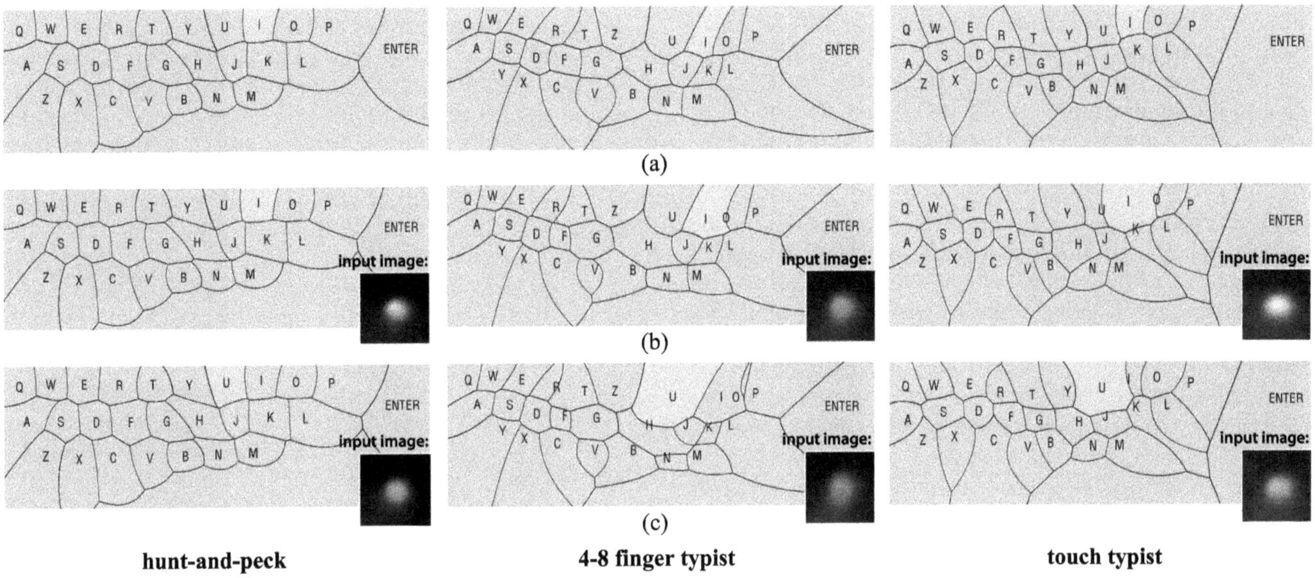

Figure 6: Individual keyboard models from three users with different typing styles (a) key regions trained with individual position data, (b) modified key regions for keypress 'i' with additional information from the image based classifier, (c) modified key regions for keypress 'u'

A denotes the state transition matrix, w the process noise from a bivariate normal distribution with zero mean and covariances Q. In our case, the state vector h_t is four-dimensional and contains position and velocity. The transition is assumed to be linear motion with low process noise. Observations are described as:

$$d_t = H_t h_t + v_k$$

with d_t describing our measurements of finger displacements and H_t denoting the observation model which maps true space into observed space. v_k is the observation noise from a zero mean normal distribution with covariances R. As explained earlier, this can be approximated by using the normal distribution function of the current key k. For temporarily irregular measurements, the resulting state estimate $\hat{h}_t^-$ after each time update step scaled with time step Δt is:

$$\hat{h}_t^- = A\hat{h}_{t-\Delta t}\Delta t$$

and estimated error covariance P_t^- accordingly:

$$P_t^- = AP_{t-\Delta t}A^t + Q\Delta t^2$$

For more detailed explanations of the mathematics behind Kalman filtering we refer to Welch and Bishop [29]. The estimated hand drift is reset whenever the time between two keystrokes is above a predetermined threshold of $100ms$. This follows the assumption that hands are repositioned after a longer break (e.g. after an error occurred). The value was chosen according to presumptions and is subject to further optimization.

Hand drift compensation has to be treated separately for both hands. Therefore for each new keystroke the corresponding hand needs to be determined. In practice, the Kalman model is integrated into the main classification loop as depicted in Figure 7.

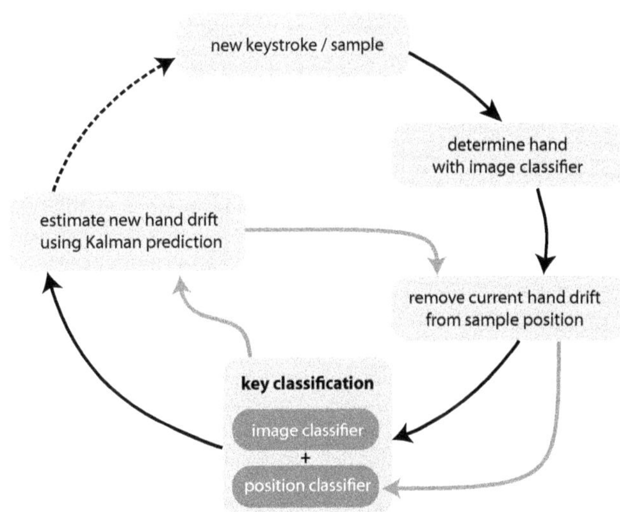

Figure 7: The main classification loop containing Kalman based hand drift estimation. Red arrows indicate dependencies between the individual components.

Estimating the hand drift utilizing a Kalman filter, however, suffers from immanent problems: Evidently, key labeling has to be correct for a given keystroke, because else the observed displacement is calculated using a wrong centroid (resulting in wrong displacement values) and additionally observation noise is modeled with a wrong distribution function. This means, each misclassification of keys leads to a faulty measurement and thus may induce errors into hand drift estimation. If a faulty estimation is used to correct touch locations of future keystrokes, this will have a negative impact on future position based key classifications. Consequently, the overall accuracy of the *Position* classifier was degraded using Kalman filter to estimate hand drift. Since our evaluation was conducted offline, the user received no feedback for these consequential errors. If the user had noticed the misclassification, he or she would presumably have corrected the error leading to a reset of the Kalman filter.

However, adding the image classifier compensates for the faulty hand drift estimates and leads to a superior performance of the overall system. This is due to two reasons: on the one hand, key labeling performs significantly better with the combined classifier. Therefore, the input for the Kalman filter is more accurate and less erroneous measurements are induced in the filter. On the other hand, wrong estimates from the Kalman filter can immediately be corrected and thus error accumulation over time is avoided. This is because the image classifier does not depend on position information. A paired-sample t-test showed that *Kalman + Images + Positions* performed significantly better than *Images + Position* without Kalman ($t(11) = 2.54$, $p = .03$). The maximum hand drift that the Kalman filter corrected was a hand displacement of 1.42 times the key size of the displayed keyboard. The mean maximum drift across all participants was 0.95 times the key size ($SD = 0.4$). The estimated drift in x-direction was generally larger than in y-direction with a ratio of 1.92 ($SD = 0.83$).

DISCUSSION AND LIMITATIONS

Our results show that the rich set of features that can be obtained from an optical touch system significantly improve key classification for virtual keyboards. The results of our image based classifier alone showed no significant difference compared to the position based classifier using individual bivariate Gaussian functions. Even more important, overall accuracy could be improved by combining image and position based classifiers. In order to determine whether the complete blob images contain substantially more information than extracted geometrical features, we evaluated a classifier with such a feature set. We could show, that the image based classifier performs significantly better, which means that the features contained in the pixel intensities of the image data are not redundant with geometrical features for keystroke classification. Additionally, a method for hand drift estimation using a Kalman filter was presented. In combination with our image based classifier, Kalman filtering can be used to further improve overall performance.

We acquired data from touch typists, but also from 4-8 finger typists and participants that only use their forefingers to press keys (so called *hunt-and-peck*-method). The classifiers performed differently across the user groups. Figure 8 shows the varying performances of the applied techniques for all user groups: For each pair of classifier and user group a bar for average classification error is shown (lower is better). Variance analysis was not performed here, as the number of test persons per group was only four. Still, average results can give a good impression of the differences between classification performance depending on a user's typing habits. As anticipated, the image based approach has inferior performance for hunt-and-peck typists (22.56% average error compared to 8.16% and 16.94% for the other groups). As this group of users looked at the keyboard while typing, results were already satisfying using naive boundary checking (4.85%). Yet, our combined classifier still improved performance slightly (3.46%). The other groups' results improved more drastically from the naïve approach to using individual positions and finally the combined classifier (30.66% → 8.77% → 4.26% and 36.47% → 14.92% → 9.40% respectively).

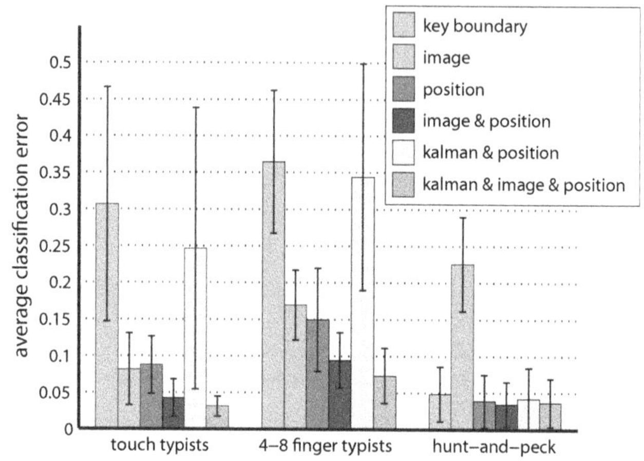

Figure 8: Average classification error of different classifiers ordered by typing style. (Error bars represent standard deviation.)

Concerning hand drift estimation using a Kalman filter, average classification error was reduced for touch and 4-8 finger typists when combined with the image based classifier (4.26% → 3.13% and 9.40% → 7.33% respectively). For hunt-and-peck typists it remained virtually the same. Therefore, our hand drift estimation approach degrades gracefully and does not induce further errors. Overall, we could show, that a Kalman model can be used to estimate hand translation from finger displacements. However, hand rotation, which results in concentrical movement of the respective fingers, is not supported. In order to account for such motion, the model would have to be expanded with additional parameters. Most likely, measurements of only finger displacements will not be enough to support a more complicated model.

Since ground truth data for hand drift is not available we cannot specify how well the true underlying process is approximated. However, the presented Kalman filter approach for hand drift compensation improves overall classification results significantly, which means that a systematic error of typing positions is corrected for subsequent keystrokes. According to how the Kalman filter was adjusted to the problem, this error is certainly induced by hand drift. Thus, the presented approach compensates for the adverse effects of unintentional hand drift.

The *Keyboard of Oz* data acquisition approach allowed us to generate and evaluate different adaptive keyboard models. However, during data acquisition, some mistypings the users were aware of were recorded as false positives due to the large acceptance area of 4 times the key size. This can not only irritate the user but also decrease the quality of the obtained model. Due to our findings from hand drift estimation we would reduce this area to approximately 3.5 times the key size in x-direction and 2 times the key size in y-direction. This would reduce the potential of false positives but still allow for substantial hand drift.

With the applied techniques we can only account for errors that are a result of imprecise input or the lack of haptic feedback. The latter containing such errors as hand drift or continuous hits outside the visual boundaries of some of the keys. With the way the used data was collected, some faulty insertions by the users could not be ruled out. For example, two succeeding letters corresponding to two adjacent keys could be interchanged, if a user actually hit them in the wrong order. In order to remove such errors, the incorporation of a language model would be a promising inclusion. To maintain the immediateness of typing, a word based language model would not be preferable. Instead, a letter based n-gram model [8] could be used as a fallback whenever the other classifiers do not agree upon a decision. That way, even letter sequences that are not represented in the language model can be typed as long as the user's input matches the trained model.

As stated before, our approach is data-driven. This means it could also be applied to other keyboard layouts just by presenting another keyboard visualization during training. Though developed with an optical touch device, the machine-learning framework is potentially suitable for other touch systems since no specific assumptions on the sensor data are made. However, the impact of the classifier depends on the discriminability of the raw sensor data. Instead of a dedicated training session, the data could be collected during regular typing first and a model would not be created until enough samples have been obtained. The corrected text input would be used as labels for the training of the model. A final implementation should capture typing data continuously and update the model periodically in order to adapt to a users changing typing behavior.

Other optical tabletop devices like the Samsung SUR40 are equipped with a sensor with equal or higher resolution than our camera-based system with 640x480 pixels. Our approach can be used directly with the larger blob images from these sensors. Classification accuracy will presumably increase or remain constant at least. If the computational cost becomes too high due to the larger feature space, the blob images can either be scaled down, or can be compressed with less loss of information utilizing Principle Component Analysis. A refresh rate lower than 60fps should still be acceptable, as long as a sensor image can be obtained for every keystroke. Multiple images per keystroke can be averaged in order to reduce noise.

Another important aspect is the realtime capability of the presented approach. The presented keyboard model has been developed and evaluated offline from recorded user data. The computation of the model from training data takes several minutes. Of course, this has to be done only once for each new user model. Our complete classification loop implemented in Matlab consisting of Kalman filtering and evaluation of both position and image based classifiers takes about 80 ms per keystroke on a regular PC. To determine the potential speedup for an online system we implemented the image classification procedure in C, resulting in a computational time of about 12 ms per keystroke. This allows up to 5000 keystrokes per minute. Accordingly, the performance of the used algorithms is sufficient for an online implementation.

Still, extensive user-studies will be necessary to determine how users interact with the developed model which has to be extended to a complete keyboard. Eventually, there might be mutual impacts that should be investigated. Also subjective feedback from users might give indications, whether they generally feel comfortable with a keyboard that behaves like the one presented here. Nevertheless, the main contribution of this work is the formal evaluation of the value of using complete sensor information for typing on optical touchscreen devices. Since typing data from real users was used for model generation and evaluation and due to high classification accuracy, we proceed to the assumption that an online implementation of the presented method would perform comparably well.

CONCLUSION AND FUTURE WORK

In this paper we presented a data-driven approach to create individual keyboard models. In particular we presented a classifier based on raw data from an optical touch sensor which improves classification accuracy obtained from an image based classifier significantly. Additionally we proposed a Kalman filter to account for hand drift.

As mentioned above, for future work we plan to investigate the incorporation of a language model to further improve typing accuracy. For real-world application, the model has to be extended to all available keys. Additionally, the keyboard classifier should also learn from a user's typing habits: For example, adapt to a user's most common mistakes. This might involve to learn, which characters get mixed up most often, how varying periods of time in between touches affect accuracy, or how errors influence the likelihood of the occurrence of other errors. For all this, a much larger amount of data would have to be collected to reduce the risk of spurious correlations. Since the touch images are highly individual features we consider using the image classifier for user authentication on a tabletop device. We are also curious whether the presented machine learning approach can be used with raw data from other touch sensors (e.g., capacitive sensing) to use the proposed methods to improve typing on tablet computers.

ACKNOWLEDGMENTS

This project is funded in part by the "Wettbewerbsfonds 2011" of the Leibniz Association.

REFERENCES

1. Aulagner, G., François, R., Martin, B., Michel, D., and Raynal, M. Floodkey: increasing software keyboard keys by reducing needless ones without occultation. In *Proc. ACS'10* (2010), WSEAS, 412–417.

2. Bau, O., Poupyrev, I., Israr, A., and Harrison, C. Teslatouch: electrovibration for touch surfaces. In *Proc. UIST '10* (2010), ACM Press, 283–292.

3. Benko, H., Ringel, M. M., Brush, A. B., and Wilson,

A. D. Insights on interactive tabletops: A survey of researchers and developers. Tech. Rep. MSR-TR-2009-22, Microsoft Research, March 2009.

4. Chang, C.-C., and Lin, C.-J. LIBSVM: A library for support vector machines. *ACM Transactions on Intelligent Systems and Technology 2* (2011).

5. Findlater, L., and Wobbrock, J. O. Personalized input: improving ten-finger touchscreen typing through automatic adaptation. In *Proc. CHI '12* (2012), ACM Press, 815–824.

6. Findlater, L., Wobbrock, J. O., and Wigdor, D. Typing on flat glass: examining ten-finger expert typing patterns on touch surfaces. In *Proc. CHI '11* (2011), ACM Press, 2453–2462.

7. Go, K., and Endo, Y. Catkey: customizable and adaptable touchscreen keyboard with bubble cursor-like visual feedback. In *Proc. INTERACT'07* (2007), Springer-Verlag, 493–496.

8. Goodman, J., and Venolia, G. Language modeling for soft keyboards. In *Proc. AAAI 2002* (2002), AAAI Press, 419–424.

9. Gunawardana, A., Paek, T., and Meek, C. Usability guided key-target resizing for soft keyboards. In *Proc. IUI '10* (2010), ACM Press, 111–118.

10. Han, J. Y. Low-cost multi-touch sensing through frustrated total internal reflection. In *Proc. UIST '05* (2005), ACM Press.

11. Hartmann, B., Morris, M. R., Benko, H., and Wilson, A. D. Augmenting interactive tables with mice & keyboards. In *Proc. UIST '09* (2009), ACM Press, 149–152.

12. Hartmann, B., Morris, M. R., Benko, H., and Wilson, A. D. Pictionaire: supporting collaborative design work by integrating physical and digital artifacts. In *Proc. CSCW '10* (2010), ACM Press, 421–424.

13. Hinrichs, U., Hancock, M. S., Collins, C., and Carpendale, S. Examination of text-entry methods for tabletop displays. In *Proc. Tabletop'07* (2007), IEEE, 105–112.

14. Hinrichs, U., Schmidt, H., Isenberga, T., Hancock, M. S., and Carpendale, S. Bubbletype: Enabling text entry within a walk-up tabletop installation. Tech. rep., Department of Computer Science, University of Calgary, Canada, February 2008.

15. Hirche, J., Bomark, P., Bauer, M., and Solyga, P. Adaptive interface for text input on large-scale interactive surfaces. In *Proc. TABLETOP 2008* (2008), IEEE, 153–156.

16. Kalman, R. E. A new approach to linear filtering and prediction problems. *Transactions of the ASME – Journal of Basic Engineering 82* (1960), 35–45.

17. Kaltenbrunner, M., and Bencina, R. reactivision: a computer-vision framework for table-based tangible interaction. In *Proc. TEI '07)* (2007), ACM Press.

18. Kelley, J. F. An empirical methodology for writing user-friendly natural language computer applications. In *Proc. CHI '83* (1983), ACM Press, 193–196.

19. Kölsch, M., and Turk, M. Keyboards without keyboards: A survey of virtual keyboards. Tech. rep., Proc. of Sensing and Input for Media-centric Systems, 2002.

20. MacKenzie, I. S., and Soukoreff, R. W. Phrase sets for evaluating text entry techniques. In *Ext. abstracts CHI '03* (2003), ACM Press, 754–755.

21. Morris, M., Brush, A., and Meyers, B. A field study of knowledge workers' use of interactive horizontal displays. In *Proc. TABLETOP 2008* (2008), IEEE Computer Society, 105–112.

22. Platt, J. C. Probabilistic outputs for support vector machines and comparisons to regularized likelihood methods. In *Advances in Large Margin Classifiers* (1999), MIT Press, 61–74.

23. Rabin, E., and Gordon, A. M. Tactile feedback contributes to consistency of finger movements during typing. *Experimental Brain Research 155*, 3 (2004), 362–369.

24. Rashid, D. R., and Smith, N. A. Relative keyboard input system. In *Proc. IUI '08* (2008), ACM Press, 397–400.

25. Ryall, K., Forlines, C., Shen, C., Morris, M. R., and Everitt, K. Experiences with and observations of direct-touch tabletops. In *Proc. TABLETOP '06* (2006), IEEE Computer Society, 89–96.

26. Sax, C., Lau, H., and Lawrence, E. Liquidkeyboard: An ergonomic, adaptive qwerty keyboard for touchscreens and surfaces. *Electrical Engineering* (2011), 117–122.

27. Weiss, M., Wacharamanotham, C., Voelker, S., and Borchers, J. Fingerflux: Near-surface haptic feedback on tabletops. In *Proc. UIST '11* (2011), ACM Press, 615–620.

28. Weiss, M., Wagner, J., Jansen, Y., Jennings, R., Khoshabeh, R., Hollan, J. D., and Borchers, J. Slap widgets: bridging the gap between virtual and physical controls on tabletops. In *Proc. CHI '09* (2009), ACM Press, 481–490.

29. Welch, G., and Bishop, G. An introduction to the Kalman filter. Tech. rep., Chapel Hill, NC, USA, 1995.

30. Wigdor, D., Perm, G., Ryall, K., Esenther, A., and Shen, C. Living with a tabletop: Analysis and observations of long term office use of a multi-touch table. In *Proc. TABLETOP '07* (2007), 60–67.

31. Zhai, S., Hunter, M., and Smith, B. A. The metropolis keyboard - an exploration of quantitative techniques for virtual keyboard design. In *Proc. UIST '00* (2000), ACM Press, 119–128.

Finger and Hand Detection for Multi-Touch Interfaces Based on Maximally Stable Extremal Regions

Philipp Ewerling **Alexander Kulik** **Bernd Froehlich**
Bauhaus-Universität Weimar
Bauhausstrasse 11, 99423 Weimar, Germany
philipp.ewerling@gmail.com, kulik@uni-weimar.de, bernd.froehlich@uni-weimar.de

ABSTRACT
We propose a new approach for touch detection on optical multi-touch devices that exploits the fact that the camera images reveal not only the actual touch points, but also objects above the screen such as the hand or arm of a user. Our touch processing relies on the Maximally Stable Extremal Regions algorithm for finding the users' fingertips in the camera image. The hierarchical structure of the generated extremal regions serves as a starting point for agglomerative clustering of the fingertips into hands. Furthermore, we suggest a heuristic supporting the identification of individual fingers as well as the distinction between left hands and right hands if all five fingers of a hand are in contact with the touch surface.

Our evaluation confirmed that the system is robust against detection errors resulting from non-uniform illumination and reliably assigns touch points to individual hands based on the implicitly tracked context information. The efficient multi-threaded implementation handles two-handed input from multiple users in real-time.

Author Keywords
Multi-touch input; hand detection; finger detection.

ACM Classification Keywords
H5.2 [Information interfaces and presentation]: User Interfaces; I.4.9 [Image Processing and Computer Vision]: Applications

INTRODUCTION
Research and development on multi-touch interfaces has come up with an ever growing number of multi-touch input gestures. However, the expressiveness of touch input remains limited without additional context information. Most existing hardware platforms assume that all simultaneous touches belong to the same gesture, hence they support only a single user. This may be sufficient for small form factor devices like smartphones. Large touch screens, on the other hand, can accommodate more than one user and thus require hand detection at the very least in order to minimize interferences. It is therefore prudent that input processing should take into account the fact that input may be induced by different hands

ITS12, November 1114, 2012, Cambridge, Massachusetts, USA.

Figure 1. Detection of multiple hands and fingers. Note that the system is robust against false positives from contact with the palm of the hand.

or even by different users. If we could additionally distinguish individual fingers, the design space of new multi-touch interaction techniques would be greatly enhanced.

We developed a processing pipeline for multi-touch detection on large touch screens that detects finger touches, groups finger touches into hands and distinguishes left from right hands for full-hand input (Figure 1). Our pipeline is based on the *Maximally Stable Extremal Regions* (MSER) algorithm which has previously been used primarily in stereo image matching and visual tracking. We use this algorithm to compute a hierarchy of extremal regions, which in conjunction with a set of local descriptors forms the basis for fingertip detection. Fingers are assigned to hands using agglomerative hierarchical clustering of a small subset of touch points provided by the MSER component tree. Our processing pipeline even performs hand and finger registration for situations in which all five fingers of a hand are detected.

Our approach is motivated by the observation that the captured image data of optical multi-touch systems clearly conveys the outlines of a hand even if the hand is only hovering above the surface while one or more fingers are touching the screen. Surprisingly little research exists on how to exploit this additional context information. Most existing systems perform simple contact point detection based on image filtering and thresholding that ignores any further image information.

Our main contribution is a new approach for multi-touch processing based on an adapted version of the well-established MSER algorithm in combination with on-the-fly clustering of fingertips into hands. We evaluated our prototypical implementation with four simultaneously interacting users. The evaluation confirmed the excellent detection of touch points with over 97% true positives and the reliable assignment of touch points to individual hands with over 92% true positives while false positives fall in the range of 1% for both cases. Initial observations also indicate that our heuristic for finger and hand registration performs well. However, it is limited to situations in which all five fingers of one hand are in contact with the touch surface in a natural hand pose.

Our efficient multi-threaded implementation focuses on image regions containing potential touch points and processes up to 40 fingertips in less than 10 ms with a total latency of less than 50 ms on our hardware. While we have implemented our prototype on a system based on diffuse illumination, the processing pipeline can also be used with other touch sensing systems that provide some sort of depth map of the region above the touch screen. Examples include Thinsight[9], the current Microsoft Surface tabletop device and systems based on depth-sensing cameras.

RELATED WORK

Diffuse back-illumination is arguably the most widely used approach to multi-touch finger tracking. Nevertheless, surprisingly little literature can be found on the actual image processing. The processing pipeline, described in the following, is considered the default approach which has been extracted from prototypes described in the literature and techniques used in the open-source multi-touch community, namely the Community Core Vision framework[1].

In most setups based on infrared illumination, the detection accuracy can be negatively affected by ambient infrared light such as stray sun light. The use of high-frequency modulated light can eliminate this problem almost completely [17]. However, this is not always possible and thus the first step generally is to remove interfering noise using a *background subtraction* and *image normalization*. In certain cases the camera image is then filtered such that only objects of a certain size, typically that of a fingertip, remain. To this end, band-pass filters are applied (usually *Mid-Gauss* or *Mid-Box*). Given the assumption that in diffuse illumination setups objects appear brighter the closer they are to the surface, contact points can now be detected by a simple image thresholding.

The benefits of exploiting additional information regarding the association of touch points to individual hands and users for more expressive multi-touch interaction have been shown earlier [4, 25, 18, 19, 22, 15, 13]. Most of this research has been performed using the DiamondTouch system [4]. This commercially available multi-touch device achieves the association of touch input to respective users by coupling electric signals from the tabletop through the user's body to a distinct receiver for each user. Unfortunately, the system limits the choice of display components only to front projection and requires the users to remain in physical contact with their receiver unit. For the purpose of grasp- and posture-recognition with capacitive touch-sensing devices, Sato et al. recently proposed a novel technology called Swept Frequency Capacitive Sensing [24].

Optical systems for extracting additional context information have also been proposed. For instance, [3] and [28] use the orientation of the contact area's bounding ellipse to infer the relationship between hands and fingers, which requires users to touch the surface with the finger pad instead of the tip. Hilliges et al. [7] proposed interleaving common touchscreen interaction based on diffuse illumination with image acquisition beyond the surface. Their setup requires the projection surface to be a high frequency switchable diffuser. Other approaches utilize an overhead camera for context tracking [5, 14, 12, 8, 15]. Echter at al. proposed an additional ceiling mounted light source to enable shadow tracking of hands hovering above the input surface [6]. Both approaches require additional hardware which thwarts the compactness of the setup while also causing significant additional processing overhead to the pipeline [5].

It has been suggested to use a depth sensing camera as an all-in-one sensor both for touch detection with defined interaction surfaces and context awareness [29, 11]. Since the same sensor that is exploited for touch sensing covers the entire surrounding area in depth, touch data could directly be associated with tracked users. A drawback of this concept is that the relatively low resolution of current depth cameras impede accurate multi-touch input.

Roth et al. propose attaching small IR-emitting devices to the users' hands for cryptographically sound user identification [23]. This is obviously the most secure implementation of user tracking for tabletop interaction, but requires the users to wear an electronic device, which interferes with the walk-up-and-use paradigm of most tabletop applications.

Proximity sensors embedded to the frame of the tabletop device may also be used for integrated context tracking at tabletop interaction devices [26, 1]. This approach provides rough user tracking and even hand distinction for many purposes. Based on an heuristic, touch points can be assigned to the individual hands of several users.

With the objective of registering hands and fingertips in optical multi-touch interfaces, Walther et al. recently proposed a decision tree to classify fingertip configurations [27]. To the best of our research and knowledge, their system is currently unique in providing fingertip registration with less than five fingers present. However, their approach can only be considered a starting point for further research as the accuracy of approximately 80% is still too low for productive use.

PROCESSING PIPELINE

At the core of our processing pipeline lies an algorithm introduced by Matas et al. called Maximally Stable Extremal Regions that reveals the hierarchical structure of extremal regions in an image. An extremal region is a particular type of distinguished region and can be defined as a set of connected pixels that are all either of higher or lower intensity than pixels on the region's outer boundary. Given the fact that objects in diffuse front illumination setups appear brighter the closer they get to the surface, the representation of image content in terms of extremal regions provides two compelling advantages:

- An extremal region only defines a relative relationship between the contained pixels and those surrounding the region. Since it is independent from absolute intensity values,

[1]see `http://ccv.nuigroup.com/`

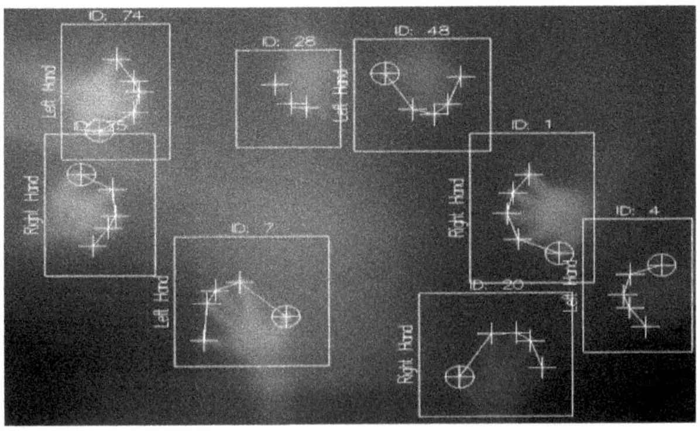

Figure 2. Finger and hand detection with our novel processing pipeline.

it is more robust in the presence of non-uniform illumination than approaches relying on a global threshold.

- Each extremal region can include further extremal regions, thereby organizing distinguished image regions in a tree structure. That structure is later used to reveal relationships between objects such as grouping contact points belonging to the same hand.

A processing pipeline usually starts with *distortion correction* and *illumination correction* in order to normalize the camera image. However these steps are considered basic image processing operations and have therefore been omitted for the sake of clarity. Our novel processing pipeline (Figure 2) comprises the following steps:

1. **Region of Interest Detection** to reduce the computational cost of subsequent processing steps
2. **Maximally Stable Extremal Regions** analysis to create a hierarchical structure
3. **Fingertip Detection**
4. **Hand Distinction** to group all revealed fingertips from the same hand into clusters
5. **Hand and Fingertip Registration** if all fingers of a hand are simultaneously touching the surface and
6. **Tracking** to follow fingers and hands across multiple frames

Step 1: Region of Interest Detection

Usually only a limited area of the tabletop surface is utilized at a time, making it appear as unnecessary overhead to process the complete camera image at every frame. Performing a simple region of interest detection first provides the following advantages:

- Applying the fingertip detection algorithm only to the relevant image areas that might represent an object or a hand on or above the surface significantly reduces computational costs.
- Several resulting regions of interest are independent and can be processed in parallel, in order to take full advantage of the threading capabilities of modern CPUs.

As the tabletop surface is illuminated from below, objects above the surface appear brighter the closer they get to the surface. Hence a simple *thresholding* operation on the intensity values seems appropriate in order to reveal regions of interest in the image. We apply a very small brightness threshold, rejecting all pixels less than 2% brighter than the background. In our setup, hands hovering less than 20 cm above the interaction surface are on average 5% brighter than the background and can thus still be detected. A drawback of this conservative approach is that illumination changes may erroneously be interpreted as user interaction. However, this only reduces the performance advantage of our processing pipeline without affecting the actual detection accuracy.

Step 2: Maximally Stable Extremal Regions

Maximally Stable Extremal Regions (MSER) is a widely used blob detection algorithm first described by Matas et al. in [16]. It robustly detects distinguished regions (i.e. regions that can be detected in image sequences or multiple views of the same scene with high repeatability). In their algorithm, Matas et al. introduced a new type of distinguished region called a maximally stable extremal region. This concept is an extension of extremal regions which are defined as follows:

Extremal Region

Given a region R in an image I, this region is called extremal if and only if all pixels within this region are either of higher or lower intensity than the pixels on the region's outer boundary Ω_R:

$$(\forall p \in R, \forall q \in \Omega_R \mid I(x_p, y_p) < I(x_q, y_q)) \quad \vee$$
$$(\forall p \in R, \forall q \in \Omega_R \mid I(x_p, y_p) > I(x_q, y_q))$$

The concept of maximally stable extremal regions additionally includes a stability criterion based on a region's relative growth.

Maximally Stable Extremal Region

Be R_{i-1}, R_i, R_{i+1} regions in an image I such that $R_{i-1} \subset R_i \subset R_{i+1}$. Region R_i is a maximally stable region if and only if R_{i-1}, R_i, R_{i+1} are extremal regions and the following stability property attains a local minimum in i:

$$s_\Delta(i) = \frac{\mid R_{i+\Delta} \mid - \mid R_{i-\Delta} \mid}{\mid R_i \mid}$$

with Δ defined as a user-defined constant.

Matas et al. describe the detection process of these regions informally as follows (Figure 3). Assume I a gray-level image thresholded on all possible intensity values $i \in \{0, \ldots, 255\}$ resulting in 256 binary images B_i. B_0 contains only black pixels while in B_{255} all pixels are white. Hence, when iterating through B_i with ascending i, the initial black image gradually turns into a complete white image with new white blobs appearing and existing blobs increasing in size. Considering the connected components from all thresholded images, each of them corresponds to an extremal region. Furthermore, each extremal region R_i at intensity threshold i is contained by exactly one extremal region from each B_j with $j > i$, since connected components do not decrease in size with increasing intensity threshold. As a result, extremal regions can be organized in a tree-like structure where the root node consists of an extremal region that covers the entire image area.

This structure is called a *component tree*. Their proposed algorithm runs in quasi-linear time with respect to the number of pixels.

In 2008 Nistér et al. proposed a different algorithm that reveals maximally stable extremal regions in true linear time [21]. Unlike the original algorithm, it does not resemble a rising waterfront continuously filling holes in the intensity height image, but rather a flood-fill spreading across the image.

In layman's terms, the algorithm can be described as pouring water into a height field that is derived from the brightness values in the camera image. Water is poured on an arbitrarily chosen point from which water starts flowing downhill. Once the lowest point of a sink is reached, water starts filling up. The filling of a sink would correspond to the growing of a connected component. Whenever the water surface of the sink did not notably change in size after filling to a certain amount, this connected component can be considered stable according to the above definition. Once a sink is fully filled, water starts pouring into adjacent sinks. The algorithm is finished after the whole image has been flooded.

Linear-time algorithm

The algorithm relies on the following data structures that describe the current state of execution:

- A binary mask marking the already visited pixels
- A priority queue of pixels on the outer boundary of the currently flooded image region. The queue is prioritized based on the pixels' intensities (lower intensities first).
- A stack of components. A component corresponds to a sink that is currently being filled with water. Therefore a component is not always necessarily an extremal region. The topmost component on the stack corresponds to the currently considered component. Whenever a sink is filled and adjacent sinks exist, a new component is pushed onto the stack and the neighboring sink is explored. Therefore the maximum stack size is equal to the number of gray levels in the image, which at most would total 256.

The algorithm proceeds as follows [21].

1. Choose an arbitrary starting point, make it the current pixel and mark it as visited.
2. Initialize a new component with the current pixel's intensity and push it onto the stack.
3. Examine all neighboring pixels of the current pixel and mark them as visited.
   - If the intensity is higher than the current pixel's intensity, then the neighboring pixel is added to the priority queue of boundary pixels.
   - If the intensity is lower, then the current pixel is added to the priority queue and the neighboring pixel is made the current pixel. Continue with 2.
4. All neighboring pixels of the current pixel have either been visited or have higher intensity. Therefore accumulate the component with the current pixel.
5. Retrieve the next pixel from the priority queue.
   - If its intensity is equal to the current pixel's intensity, continue with 3.
   - If its intensity is higher than the current pixel's intensity, all components on the stack are merged until the intensity of the topmost component is greater or equal to the next pixel's intensity. Continue with 3.
   - If the queue is empty, the algorithm terminates.

Modifications of the algorithm

In order to accelerate the subsequent processing steps, the algorithm has been modified to gather additional information on extremal regions and their spatial structure during its execution.

Extension to reveal all extremal regions

The standard algorithm only reveals extremal regions that are maximal according to the stability criterion. Hence a number of intermediate extremal regions are being discarded and do not appear in the component tree. However, these additional regions might convey important information as to the spatial relationship among regions that will be exploited extensively in the hand distinction processing step. Thus, the algorithm design has been changed in order to identify all available extremal regions.

Characterization of extremal regions

In order to be able to use the identified regions for fingertip recognition, a set of local descriptors will be used. Due to the incremental growth of components, the following features can be efficiently computed during execution of the algorithm.

Intensity statistics

The mean and variance of the intensity distribution characterize the pixel's intensity values within a component. During the sequential growth of components through accumulation of new pixels and merging of existing components, these statistics can be efficiently computed.

Image moments

In [10], Hu described a widely used set of shape descriptors based on image moments that are invariant to translation, rotation and scale. In our algorithm the first of his 7 shape descriptors will be used:

$$\phi_1 = \nu_{20} + \nu_{02}$$

where ν_{pq} denotes the *normalized moment* of order $(p + q)$ with $p, q \in \mathbb{N}$ (see [20] for a detailed description).

Bounding volumes

Image moment based shape descriptors provide a performant yet unintuitive way of describing a region's shape; however, it is sometimes useful to find a simpler representation based on geometric primitives. Therefore a region's shape will be additionally described using the oriented bounding ellipse. A non-optimal approximation can easily be derived using *image moments* of zeroth, first and second degrees [20].

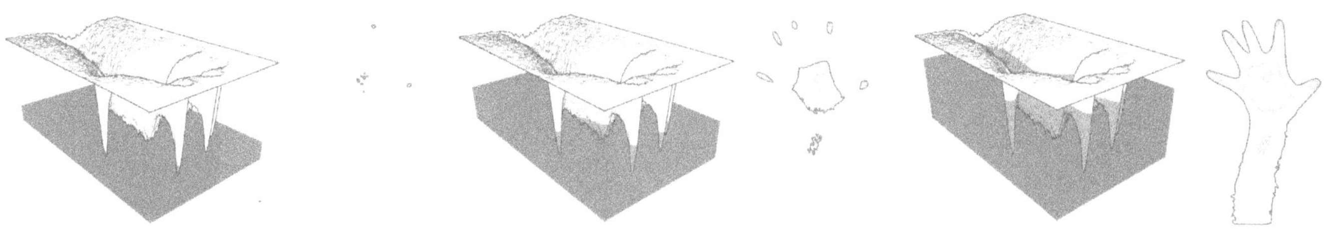

(a) (b) (c)

Figure 3. Visualization of the *Maximally Stable Extremal Region* algorithm as a rising waterfront(from a to c). On the left hand side of each illustration, the raw camera image is represented as a height map with the waterfront indicating the level of the current intensity threshold. The isolines on the right hand side show the outlines of the image at the current and previous threshold levels.

Step 3: Fingertip Detection

The component tree resulting from the MSER processing serves as the foundation of the fingertip detection and the following processing steps. This tree structure has two important properties with respect to its contained *extremal regions*:

- The darkest and simultaneously largest extremal region forms the root of the component tree.
- For all child-parent relationships maintains the property that the child is smaller in size and has brighter intensity than its parent.

As fingertips in contact with the surface create the brightest spots in an image, it follows that only leaf nodes of the component tree can be considered fingertip candidates.

These fingertip candidates are evaluated as follows:

1. Identify the extremal regions that represent the finger of a fingertip candidate. This applies to all parent regions of the candidate up to a maximum size and as long as these do not have siblings (i.e. the candidate region is the only leaf contained in the parent's subtree). The largest of these regions will subsequently be referred to as *finger*.
2. For each candidate region a feature vector is compiled containing the following properties:
   (a) Bounding ellipse of the candidate region.
   (b) Bounding ellipse of the finger region.
   (c) The maximum value of the first of the seven shape descriptors introduced by Hu for all regions below the finger region.
   (d) The depth of the subtree having the finger region as its root node.
   (e) The maximum relative growth in pixel size of any child-parent relationship between the candidate and the finger regions.
   (f) The relative growth in pixel size of the finger region with respect to the candidate region.
   (g) The ratio of the intensity ranges of the candidate and finger regions respectively.
   (h) The number of pixels within a defined distance that have an intensity of less than 10% of the candidate region's mean intensity. This feature is based on the observation that pixels within a fingertip's contact area are close to a certain number of background pixels, hence resulting in a significant intensity fall-off within the vicinity.

   Properties 2a, 2b and 2c are used to discard candidate regions that do not exhibit the typical, rounded shape and average size of fingertips. Using property 2h, the algorithm is able to discern fingertip contacts from bright regions at the wrist and palm in case the hand is resting on the surface during interaction. The remaining properties describe the characteristic intensity fall-off around the contact area due to the oblique or vertical finger orientation. They are hence able to distinguish fingertip contacts from contact areas of similar size and shape.
3. Calculate a confidence score C using the weighted sum of the feature vector:
   $$C = \sum_{f_i} w_i \cdot f_i \quad (1)$$
   The weights have been chosen such that range differences between features are compensated for without awarding any of the features too high of an influence on the final score. We adjusted these values manually and achieved convincing results. A machine learning approach would certainly ease setting up the system under varying conditions.
4. Two thresholds have been defined on the confidence score to classify candidate regions either as *no confidence*, *low confidence* or *high confidence*. However, having a *high confidence* score in a single frame is not sufficient for a region to be considered as a fingertip. A temporal hysteresis has been implemented that requires a candidate region to achieve at least once a *high confidence* and never a *no confidence* score in three consecutive frames in order to be classified as a fingertip. Note that this does not require the finger to be stationary during these three frames as candidates are continuously tracked while moving.

Step 4: Hand Distinction

In this approach, the grouping of fingertips is robustly established solely using the information from the previous processing steps, that is the component tree and the identified contact points that to a given degree of confidence correspond to fingertips. These fingertips may or may not belong to the same hand or even the same user. As the respective extremal regions are leaves in the component tree, they are contained in a number of regions of higher level until all of them are contained in the root region. Hence there already exists a spatial clustering of these regions based on intensity values. Therefore, fingertips could simply be grouped gradually while ascending in the component tree until a homogeneity criterion such as the maximum distance between fingertips or the maximum size of the parent region is violated. While that approach generally works reasonably well, problems arise under certain conditions. In the case of excessive ambient light such as from stray sun light, the amount of contrast in the camera image is heavily reduced. However, with reduced contrast less extremal regions are revealed resulting in a sparse component tree. That loss of spatial information might lead to an erroneous clustering or a dead-lock situation in which too many fingertips are children of the same region.

Therefore a more robust approach will be presented here that combines the advantages of the idea described above combined with agglomerative hierarchical clustering. Hierarchical clustering itself would be unsuited in our scenario because of its high computational complexity. Tabletop surfaces continually grow in size, hence enabling the simultaneous interaction of multiple users. Due to the large number of resulting touch points, unaided nearest neighbor clustering would be highly inefficient for real-time application.

The idea is to only cluster a small subset of touch points at a time using agglomerative hierarchical clustering thereby reducing the impact of the polynomial complexity. The spatial clustering provided by the component tree, although erroneous at times, can serve as a reasonable input. The outline of the algorithm is as follows:

1. Traverse the component tree in postfix order. This ordering ensures that all children have been processed before the node itself is processed. For each node do:
   - If the node is a leaf node and has been classified with at least low confidence as a fingertip, create a new cluster containing this node.
   - Otherwise create the current set of clusters from all child nodes and process these as follows:
     (a) Compute the distance matrix among all pairs of clusters of this node using a distance function $d(C_1, C_2)$.
     (b) Find the pair of clusters C_1, C_2 with the lowest distance $d_C(C_1, C_2)$ that still satisfies the distance criterion $\mathcal{D}(C_1, C_2, d_C)$.
       - If such a pair of clusters exists, merge the two and continue with 1a
       - Otherwise the clustering is finished.

The *complete-link* (furthest neighbor) distance function is used in this instance as it takes into account the distance to the fingertip that is furthest away. It is defined as follows:

$$d_C(C_1, C_2) = \max_{u \in C_1, v \in C_2} d(u, v) \quad (2)$$

with d being a distance measure. Here Euclidean distance is used as distance measure. Combining *complete link* with an appropriate *distance criterion* $\mathcal{D}$ that places a constraint on cluster growth has been found to work best to cluster fingertips into hands.

$\mathcal{D}$ is set to the maximum expected distance between any two fingertips of the same hand. The maximum distance is usually the one between the thumb and the little finger. However, as user interaction using only these two fingers is rather rare, the criterion has been restricted further based on the combined number of fingertips in the clusters. The lower the number of fingertips contained in both clusters, the smaller the maximum allowed distance is. Hence fingertips that are at an unusually large distance from each other will only be merged once fingertips in intermediate positions have been found. Therefore this extension makes the criterion more robust as it alleviates negative effects of the chosen maximum finger distance as being considered too large or too small.

As a result of this image analysis, every detected touchpoint is assigned to a certain parent region that corresponds most probably to a single hand. The hand distinction is robust until individual hands physically touch each other. In case this accidentally happens, the problem can be eliminated based on frame-to-frame coherence. If instead this state of touching or crossing hands remains present over several frames, all involved touch events will be assigned to the same cluster. Given that the situation of touching hands is also very salient to users and generally not desired during interaction, we consider this to be a minor issue.

As a result of this step, every node in the hierarchical structure has a unique ID assigned that remains valid until the system looses track of it. Our system is able to keep track of hovering hands up to almost 20 cm above the screen due to their relatively large size. Applications allowing the users to choose between different tools should thus assign the selected interaction tool to the parent node that constitutes the hand rather than the selecting finger in order to keep the association when the user removes the finger from the screen.

Step 5: Hand and Fingertip Registration

The hand and fingertip registration comprises the following steps (Figure 4):

1. Order the five fingertips along the hand such that either the thumb or the little finger comes first.
2. Identify the thumb from the set of fingertips. The fingertip registration of the remaining fingertips follows from the previous ordering.
3. Infer from the fingertip registration whether the considered fingertips are from a left or right hand.

The first step is crucial as an erroneous ordering cannot be corrected at later stages of the registration process. Au et al. for instance propose an angular ordering around the centroid of the five fingertips [2]. However, the centroid usually deviates too much from the perceived center position as the index, middle, ring and little fingers are generally located very closely to each other. While this approach is robust if fingertips are aligned as an arc on the surface, considering if one of the fingers is moving (e.g. the index finger performs a sliding gesture downwards), the ordering might swap the thumb and index fingers. Hence another ordering will be proposed

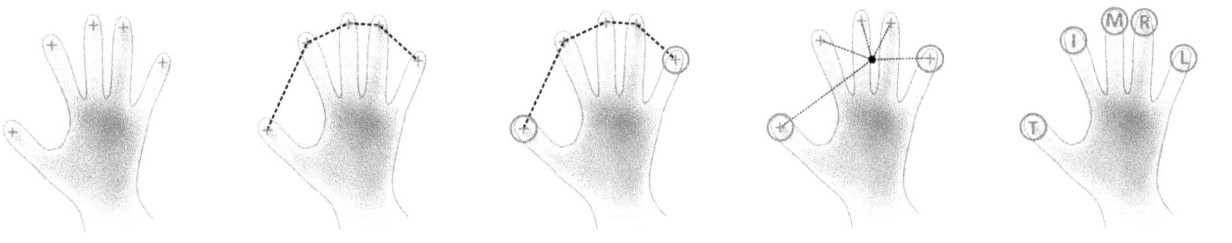

(a) Initial fingertip positions of a hand in resting position. (b) Fingertip ordering along shortest path. (c) Endpoints are identified as either thumb or little finger. (d) Identify thumb as the finger furthest away from the centroid of all five fingertips (e) Fingertips can now all be identified given the thumb (T) and the ordering.

Figure 4. Steps of the fingertip registration process. The hand shape and fingertip positions used in the drawing were copied from an actual camera screen shot of the prototype.

here based on the shortest path along the fingertips which is computed as follows:

1. Be $\mathcal{F}$ the set of all fingertips f_i. The set $\mathcal{D}$ is defined as the distances among all possible pairs of fingertips:
$$\{\{d(f_i, f_j), f_i, f_j\} \mid (f_i, f_j) \in F \times F\}$$
with $d(f_i, f_j)$ denoting the Euclidean distance between f_i and f_j.
2. For each fingertip f_i assign a unique label $L(f_i)$.
3. Iterate $\mathcal{D}$ in increasing order of $d(f_i, f_j)$. Be $\mathcal{C}$ the set of all edges forming the fingertip contour. For each pair (f_i, f_j) do
   - If $L(f_i) \neq L(f_j)$:
     (a) Add (f_i, f_j) to $\mathcal{C}$.
     (b) Assign a common unique label to all fingertips f_k that either fulfill $L(f_k) = L(f_i)$ or $L(f_k) = L(f_j)$.
   - If $\mid \mathcal{C} \mid= 4$:
     (a) All fingertips have been included in the contour. (f_i, f_j) denotes the pair of fingertips on the contour that are furthest apart from each other. f_i and f_j define the endpoints of the contour which by definition of the ordering correspond either to the thumb or the little finger.

The above ordering relies on the assumption that along the shortest path the thumb and little finger are the two fingertips that are furthest apart from each other. Since a rather unnatural hand pose would be required to violate that property, it was deemed a valid assumption for regular use.

The next step in the registration process is to uniquely identify the thumb. As the previous ordering already reduced the number of candidate fingertips, the task is equivalent to distinguishing thumb from little finger. Since the index, middle, ring and little finger influence the position of the centroid as mentioned above, thumb and little finger can be distinguished with respect to their distance to the centroid. The little finger is the one located closer to the centroid while the thumb is the one positioned further away.

Finally the registration of the set of fingertips as belonging to the left or right hand remains to be done (Figure 5). Be

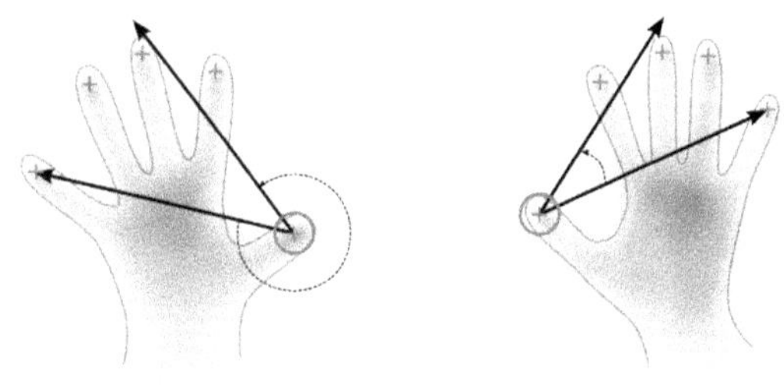

(a) (b)

Figure 5. Hand registration using the angle between the little finger and the remaining fingertips with respect to the thumb.

f_T, f_I, f_M, f_R and f_L the thumb, index, middle, ring and little finger respectively. Based on the angle between the the vectors $\overrightarrow{f_T f_L}$ and $\overrightarrow{f_T f_I}$, left and right hand can be easily distinguished. If that angle is smaller than 180°, the set of fingertips is classified as right hand, otherwise as left hand. In order to make the registration more robust in presence of finger movement such as the aforementioned sliding down gesture of the index finger, the vector $\overrightarrow{f_T f_{IMR}} = \overrightarrow{f_T f_I} + \overrightarrow{f_T f_M} + \overrightarrow{f_T f_R}$ will be used instead of $\overrightarrow{f_T f_I}$ only.

Hence the registration is defined as follows:

$$\begin{aligned} \mid \overrightarrow{f_T f_L} \times \overrightarrow{f_T f_{IMR}} \mid &< 0 \Rightarrow \text{Left Hand} \\ \mid \overrightarrow{f_T f_L} \times \overrightarrow{f_T f_{IMR}} \mid &> 0 \Rightarrow \text{Right Hand} \end{aligned} \quad (3)$$

where $\times$ denotes the cross product of two vectors.

Note that finger and hand identification is only possible if the hand touches the screen in a relaxed posture with all fingers in direct contact. However, we consider this feature a mere add on to our processing pipeline providing robust multi-touch tracking with finger and hand detection. We believe that the additional information on involved fingers and hands, although limited to certain postures, can be beneficial in many applications like system control (cf. [2]).

Step 6: Tracking

The clustering of fingertips greatly reduces the complexity of matching fingertips in consecutive frames. Instead of computing all possible combinations, this step is being accelerated by only considering fingertips for nearest-neighbor matching whose containing clusters intersect. The tracking of clusters is inferred from their contained fingertips. In case fingertips have been clustered erroneously, clusters from previous frames will be merged or split if that condition persists over a small number of frames. A window of 5 frames has worked well in our implementation.

EVALUATION AND RESULTS

In a pilot study we tested the limits of the proposed processing pipeline in terms of execution time and finger detection rate. Four students (all male, aged 24 - 27) from our research group were asked to perform multi-touch gestures on the surface. However they were reminded to not only use common gestures involving a small number of simultaneous touch points but to also use both hands with randomly changing configurations of fingers touching the surface, hence resulting in a maximum number of 40 simultaneous finger touches (and possibly even more evaluated touch points considering that users were allowed to rest their palm on the surface). We did not include intensive variability of background illumination as an independent variable as our laboratory is generally artificially illuminated. More than 4000 camera frames were captured during the interaction process that now could be replayed to the processing pipeline in order to properly measure execution times and finger detection rate.

Execution Time

As performance is dependent on the number of simultaneous user actions performed on the surface and surfaces continuously increase in size, processing pipelines have to deal with an ever increasing number of simultaneous touches. Therefore, evaluating the detection performance for up to 40 simultaneous fingers touching the surface is being considered a well-suited performance indicator of the processing pipeline.

We evaluated the performance of our algorithm on a machine with an Intel Core i7-940 CPU (2.93GHz, 4 cores) and 5.8GB of available memory running Ubuntu Linux 10.04. The camera delivered frames at a resolution of 640 x 480 at 60Hz. The reported execution times include all steps of the pipeline as well as required image preprocessing. Measuring was started just after the image had been loaded into memory and stopped when all processing and memory clean-up steps had been executed. The recorded user interaction was processed five times and we averaged the corresponding performance measures in order to minimize the influence of external factors such as the operating system.

Given the measurements shown in Figure 6, the most important result is that even for single-threaded execution, a processing performance of at least 60 frames per second was achieved. Most notably that performance was achieved even during the simultaneous interaction of 4 users, 8 hands and up to 40 fingers. Furthermore using four processing threads, processing time is capped at around 10ms regardless of how many fingers of the 8 hands simultaneously touch the surface.

Although the performance measurements prove very satisfying, it is important to keep in mind that this is only a part of the processing that is performed between a user action and the corresponding visual feedback. What determines the user's

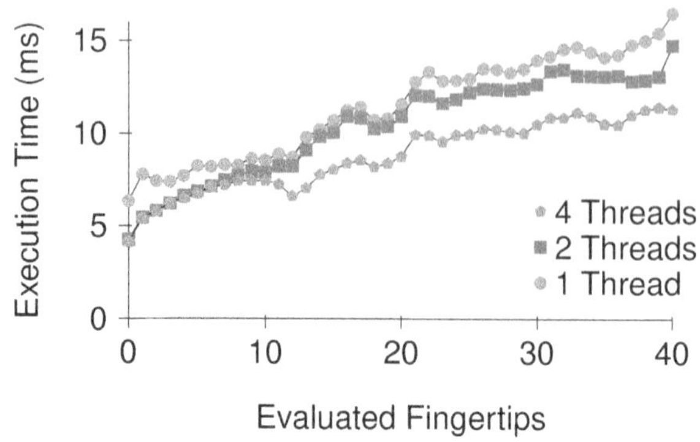

Figure 6. Execution times with respect to the simultaneous number of finger touches for different numbers of threads involved in the processing.

impression of responsiveness of our prototype is the end-to-end latency that stems from the following contributing factors (values from our prototype in brackets):

- The image acquisition, in particular the exposure time (~16 ms)
- The transmission of image data from the camera to the computer (~16 ms w. a Firewire camera)
- The processing of camera images (~10 ms w. 10 threads)
- The protocol used to communicate detection results over a network interface (TUIO[2])
- The response of the application software that updates the display

Latency introduced by the individual components can also temporarily vary due to unfavorable process scheduling as a result of the operating system. We achieved an overall latency of under 60 ms with our prototype. Further improvements can be achieved with a faster camera interface such as USB3.0 and the impact of the exposure time could be reduced by pulsing the infrared light. Since the light's intensity can be much higher during the pulse, the exposure time could be significantly shortened. This would additionally reduce the influence of ambient illumination.

Finger Detection Rate

Measuring the finger detection rate is particularly difficult as it requires a ground truth as a basis for comparison. In this case the first 1500 frames from the interaction process were considered. Given the extensive manual work required to label all visible fingertips in these camera images, this number has been further reduced to only consider every fifth frame. Hence, a total of 300 camera images were analyzed that contained on average more than 21 visible fingertips.

In order to quantify the finger detection rate, two basic measures are used. Firstly, the number of visible fingertips which have been correctly detected by the pipeline will be considered. This measure is usually called the *true positive* or *hit rate*. Secondly, given the total number of detected fingertips,

[2]Open protocol for tangible multi-touch surfaces, see `http://www.tuio.org`

how many of these have been falsely considered to be in contact with the surface will be evaluated. This second measure is usually referred to as *false positive* rate. We achieved the following results:

True Positive Rate

$$\frac{\text{Correctly detected fingertips}}{\text{Total number of visible fingertips}} = \frac{6449}{6628} \approx 0.973$$

False Positive Rate

$$\frac{\text{Wrongly detected fingertips}}{\text{Total number of detected fingertips}} = \frac{88}{6537} \approx 0.0135$$

The high *true positive rate* shows the potential of the proposed pipeline. The *false positive* rate also seems reasonably low given the constraints of the prototype, in particular the significantly uneven illumination (Figure 2). We assume that the *false positive* rate as well as the *false negative* rate could be further reduced by applying machine learning techniques to the fingertip detection.

The accuracy of the hand distinction was analyzed as well. For this purpose, more than 450 camera images were manually classified which were extracted from the interaction process at five frame intervals. The evaluation measured the success rate of the hand distinction process, defined as the percentage of hands that were correctly clustered. Hand distinction was regarded as successful if all detected fingertips from the same hand were attributed to the same cluster. However, if these fingertips were contained in more than one cluster, the clustering for this hand was considered invalid. Furthermore, if two hands were erroneously contained in the same cluster, both were regarded as unsuccessful. The results are as follows:

Success Rate

$$\frac{\text{Correctly clustered hands}}{\text{Total number of visible hands}} = \frac{2681}{2909} \approx 0.922$$

The hand distinction usually failed in the presence of *false positives* from the fingertip detection. Since cluster size was capped at five fingers, *false positives* resulted in surpassing that limit and hence interrupted the merging of clusters. This in turn reduced the *false positive* rate of the fingertip detection step, which would have positive effects on hand distinction in terms of *success rate*.

The accuracy of the hand and fingertip registration has only informally been tested. In total eight students, all male aged in their mid-twenties, from our research group were asked to place both of their hands on the surface. While no restrictions were imposed on the exact hand posture, the students were asked to adopt a position that felt natural to them. In these short tests the hand and fingertips were correctly registered for all participants. Hence the assumptions used to infer these properties appear to be reasonable. Although only a static hand position was tested, it currently seems to be the most convincing use case in which a gesture is started in this position allowing proper registration.

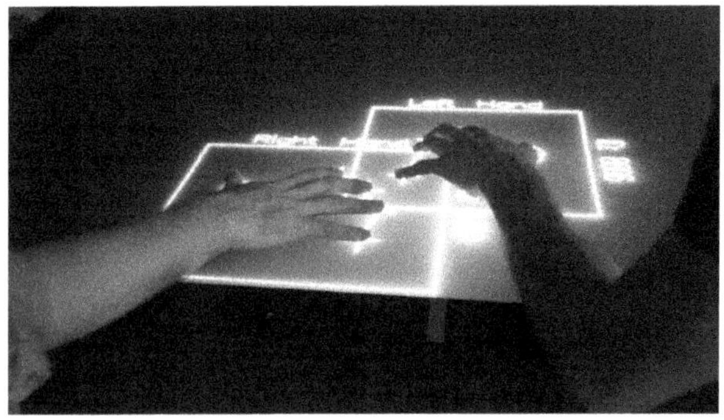

Figure 7. Close hands can still be differentiated.

CONCLUSION

We presented a novel processing pipeline for optical multi-touch surfaces that relies on Maximally Stable Extremal Regions for fingertip detection rather than on simple thresholding. Extremal regions are defined as a relative relationship between an image region and its border, which renders the detection robust in the presence of non-uniform illumination. Furthermore, extremal regions can be organized into component trees which represent the spatial relationship among surface contacts and also consider further information of the captured camera images such as the hand and the arm. The leaf nodes of these trees are candidates for fingertips, which are evaluated by a set of image features and an appropriate confidence score. Using the component tree and agglomerative clustering, fingertips are merged into hands. Hand and fingertip registration for these clusters of fingertips can be performed if all five fingers of a hand are on the touchscreen in a natural pose.

We found the system to be very stable even in situations where palms and elbows were resting on the table (Figure 7) since the detection relies on the identification of the fingertips and the hand regions. Our evaluation confirms this reliability of the finger and hand detection with high true positive rates. While our approach is more computationally intensive than basic blob detection, our efficient implementation indicates that it can perform in real-time on current multi-core CPUs. We believe that advanced touch processing is at the core of further development in the realm of multi-touch interfaces. Our results clearly demonstrate novel interaction opportunities that can be achieved with smarter processing of input data from multi-touch systems which acquire some sort of depth information above the surface.

ACKNOWLEDGMENTS

This work was supported by the German Federal Ministry of Education and Research (BMBF) under grant 03IP704 (project Intelligentes Lernen). We thank the participants of our study. We also thank the reviewers of this paper for their constructive comments.

REFERENCES

1. Annett, M., Grossman, T., Wigdor, D., and Fitzmaurice, G. Medusa: a proximity-aware multi-touch tabletop. In *Proc. UIST 2011*, ACM Press (2011), 337–346.

2. Au, O., and Tai, C. Multitouch finger registration and its applications. In *Proc. OZCHI 2010*, ACM (2010), 41–48.

3. Dang, C., Straub, M., and André, E. Hand distinction for multi-touch tabletop interaction. In *Proc. ITS 2009*, ACM Press (2009), 101–108.

4. Dietz, P., and Leigh, D. Diamondtouch: a multi-user touch technology. In *Proc. UIST 2001*, ACM Press (2001), 219–226.

5. Dohse, K., Dohse, T., Still, J., and Parkhurst, D. Enhancing multi-user interaction with multi-touch tabletop displays using hand tracking. In *Proc. ACHI 2008*, IEEE (2008), 297–302.

6. Echtler, F., Huber, M., and Klinker, G. Shadow tracking on multi-touch tables. In *Proc. AVI2008*, ACM Press (2008), 388–391.

7. Hilliges, O., Izadi, S., Wilson, A. D., Hodges, S., Garcia-Mendoza, A., and Butz, A. Interactions in the air: adding further depth to interactive tabletops. In *Proc. UIST 2009*, ACM Press (2009), 139–148.

8. Hirsch, M., Lanman, D., Holtzman, H., and Raskar, R. Bidi screen: a thin, depth-sensing lcd for 3d interaction using light fields. In *Proc. SIGGRAPH Asia 2009*, ACM Press (2009), 159:1–159:9.

9. Hodges, S., Izadi, S., Butler, A., Rrustemi, A., and Buxton, B. Thinsight: versatile multi-touch sensing for thin form-factor displays. In *Proc. UIST 2007*, ACM (2007), 259–268.

10. Hu, M. Visual pattern recognition by moment invariants. *Information Theory, IRE Transactions on 8*, 2 (1962), 179–187.

11. Izadi, S., Kim, D., Hilliges, O., Molyneaux, D., Newcombe, R., Kohli, P., Shotton, J., Hodges, S., Freeman, D., Davison, A., and Fitzgibbon, A. Kinectfusion: real-time 3d reconstruction and interaction using a moving depth camera. In *Proc. UIST 2011*, ACM Press (2011), 559–568.

12. Jota, R., Marquardt, N., Greenberg, S., and Jorge, J. A. The continuous interaction space: Interaction techniques unifying touch and gesture on and above a digital surface. In *Proc. INTERACT 2011* (2011), 5–9.

13. Klinkhammer, D., Nitsche, M., Specht, M., and Reiterer, H. Adaptive personal territories for co-located tabletop interaction in a museum setting. In *Proc. ITS 2011*, ACM Press (2011), 107–110.

14. Leibe, B., Starner, T., Ribarsky, W., Wartell, Z., Krum, D. M., Singletary, B., and Hodges, L. F. The perceptive workbench: Toward spontaneous and natural interaction in semi-immersive virtual environments. In *Virtual Reality* (2000), 13–20.

15. Martínez, R., Collins, A., Kay, J., and Yacef, K. Who did what? who said that?: Collaid: an environment for capturing traces of collaborative learning at the tabletop. In *Proc. ITS 2011*, ACM Press (2011), 172–181.

16. Matas, J., Chum, O., Urban, M., and Pajdla, T. Robust wide-baseline stereo from maximally stable extremal regions. *Image and Vision Computing 22*, 10 (2004), 761–767.

17. Moeller, J., and Kerne, A. Zerotouch: an optical multi-touch and free-air interaction architecture. In *Proc. CHI 2012*, ACM Press (2012), 2165–2174.

18. Morris, M. R., Huang, A., Paepcke, A., and Winograd, T. Cooperative gestures: multi-user gestural interactions for co-located groupware. In *Proc. CHI 2006*, ACM Press (2006), 1201–1210.

19. Morris, M. R., Ryall, K., Shen, C., Forlines, C., and Vernier, F. Beyond "social protocols": multi-user coordination policies for co-located groupware. In *Proc. CSCW 2004*, ACM Press (2004), 262–265.

20. Mukundan, R., and Ramakrishnan, K. *Moment functions in image analysis: theory and applications*. World Scientific Publishing, 1998.

21. Nistér, D., and Stewénius, H. Linear time maximally stable extremal regions. *Computer Vision–ECCV 2008* (2008), 183–196.

22. Ringel, M., Ryall, K., Shen, C., Forlines, C., and Vernier, F. Release, relocate, reorient, resize: fluid techniques for document sharing on multi-user interactive tables. In *Ext. Abstracts CHI 2004*, ACM Press (2004), 1441–1444.

23. Roth, V., Schmidt, P., and Güldenring, B. The ir ring: authenticating users' touches on a multi-touch display. In *Proc. UIST 2010*, ACM Press (2010), 259–262.

24. Sato, M., Poupyrev, I., and Harrison, C. Touche: enhancing touch interaction on humans, screens, liquids, and everyday objects. In *Proc. CHI 2012*, ACM Press (2012), 483–492.

25. Shen, C., Vernier, F. D., Forlines, C., and Ringel, M. Diamondspin: an extensible toolkit for around-the-table interaction. In *Proc. CHI 2004*, ACM Press (2004), 167–174.

26. Teichert, J., Herrlich, M., Walther-Franks, B., Schwarten, L., and Krause, M. User detection for a multi-touch table via proximity sensors. *Proc. ITS 2008* (2008).

27. Walther-Franks, B., Herrlich, M., Aust, M., and Malaka, R. Left and right hand distinction for multi-touch displays. In *Proc. Smart Graphics 2011*, Springer (2011), 155–158.

28. Wang, F., Cao, X., Ren, X., and Irani, P. Detecting and leveraging finger orientation for interaction with direct-touch surfaces. In *Proc. UIST 2009*, ACM Press (2009), 23–32.

29. Wilson, A. D. Using a depth camera as a touch sensor. In *Proc. ITS 2010*, ACM Press (2010), 69–72.

Measuring the Linear and Rotational User Precision in Touch Pointing

Francois Berard
University of Grenoble
LIG, Grenoble-INP
BP 53, 38041 Grenoble Cedex 9, FRANCE
francois.berard@imag.fr
+33-476-514-365

Amelie Rochet-Capellan
GIPSA-lab, UMR 5216 CNRS
Grenoble INP/UJF/U. Stendhal
BP 46, 38402 Grenoble Cedex, FRANCE
ameliecapellan@free.fr
+33-476-574-850

ABSTRACT
This paper addresses the limit of user precision in pointing to a target when the finger is already in contact with a touch surface. User precision was measured for linear and rotational pointing. We developed a novel experimental protocol that improves the estimation of user's precision as compare to previous protocols. Our protocol depends on high-resolution measurements of finger motions. This was achieved by the means of two optical finger trackers specially developed for this study. The trackers provide stable and precise measurements of finger translations and rotations. We used them in two user experiments that revealed that (a) user's precision for linear pointing is about $150dpi$ or $0.17mm$, and (b) user can reliably point at sectors as narrow as 2.76° in $2s$ in rotational pointing. Our results provide new information for the optimization of interactions and sensing devices that involve finger pointing on a surface.

Author Keywords
Touch, Precision, Human Precision, Finger Rotation, Computer Vision, Tracking

ACM Classification Keywords
H.1.2 [User/Machine Systems]: Human factors; H.5.2 [User Interfaces]: Input devices and strategies

General Terms
Measurement, Performance, Experimentation, Human Factors

INTRODUCTION
With the emergence of large interactive surfaces, and the widespread adoption of mobile interactive devices (e.g., smartphones, tablets), touch interaction is becoming a major way to interact with computers. As touch devices evolve into fully capable computers, with display's pixel count matching that of desktop monitors[1], they can support complex tasks, which require increased input precision from users. In this context, a challenging question to address is users' precision in finger pointing gestures. In this paper, we report new methods and empirical results to evaluate the precision achievable by users with touch interaction, both in linear and rotational pointing.

Direct touch pointing is the prime interaction for touch surface. In direct touch, the finger is initially *above* the touch surface. The target is acquired upon landing the finger directly on top of it (or shortly after, on takeoff). This mode of pointing is characterized by a *discrepancy in the location of the active point* of the finger, as imagined by the user and as measured by the touch surface. Holz et al. studied this phenomenon carefully and showed that, with an ideal sensing mechanism and user calibration, targets have to be more than $4mm$ in diameter for reliable selection [11, 12]. This is 40 times the size of pixels of recent touch computer displays[1]. In other words, direct touch is not immediately usable for precise tasks such as positioning a cursor between letters, or acquiring small targets in a dense display. One way to allow accurate pointing with touch devices is to use a virtual pointer controlled by finger motions when the *finger is already in contact* with the device [1, 3, 21, 24]. With the user focusing on the position of the virtual pointer, instead of some particular point of the finger, the active point discrepancy issue disappears. The achievable precision is then restricted by other factors such as the sensing device precision, the visual acuity, the interaction technique involved, and the limit of human's precision when moving a finger in contact with a physical surface. Our work focuses on the latter.

The first contribution of this work is to provide a new method to estimate the smallest targets *in the motor space* that can be acquired by a finger already in contact with a surface. We focus on user's motor capabilities. We neutralize the effect of the visual acuity and interaction technique factors by providing a magnified graphical feedback (Figure 6), and by using the identity as the transfer function between motor and visual spaces (constant gain = 1). In order to neutralize the device sensing precision factor, we developped the second contribution of this work: two high precision trackers, one for linear finger motions and one for finger rotations. The precisions of these trackers are substantially better than users' precision.

[1]Recent tablet computers carry displays with 2048x1536 pixels, see for example http://www.apple.com/iPad/

ITS'12, November 11–14, 2012, Cambridge, Massachusetts, USA.

The third contribution of this work is to provide first estimations of user's precision in linear and a rotational pointing.

Users' maximum achievable precision is key information for *interaction designers* of touch systems. It is informative to design pointing interactions on very small devices [2], or indirect input technique for games on mobile devices (e.g. virtual joystick, slingshot, etc.). It provides an estimate of the "limb precision" required to optimize the C/D gain[6] or to design subpixel interactions [22]. It also defines the requirement for the precision of any touch sensing device and, as such, it is an important information for *input device designers* as well: if we can state that a device already saturates users' precision, research effort should be allocated on other parameters than the precision of the device. Conversely, a device that measures finger pointing with less precision than users' abilities is introducing a bottleneck in the input bandwidth. This is especially important in the case of the finger orientation, which has many potential applications in novel interaction designs [17, 20, 25], but for which the empirical knowledge on user's precision is limited.

After a review of the previous work, we present a new experimental protocol meant to estimate user's precision. We then introduce the two optical finger tracking techniques aimed at very high precision and low latency measurement of finger linear and rotational motions, as required by the experimental protocol. These trackers and protocol were used in two user studies that provide first empirical estimations of the limits of user's precision in linear and rotational touch pointing. Finally, we discuss the results of the experiments and conclude.

PREVIOUS WORK

The limit of user's precision in manipulating input devices has been investigated through various approaches. Chapuis et al. systematically questioned the effect of visual scale, motor scale and quantization of the acquisition of small targets [7]. They found that users' performance degraded at small scale, in particular in the motor space and for target size in the range $0.1-0.2mm$. Casiez et al. studied the impact of the control-display gain on user's performance. They identified a "limb precision problem" when using a high CD gain for reciprocal target acquisition [6] and evaluated, the resolution of the hand and fingers at $0.2mm$. In Chapuis et al. and Casiez et al., the limit of precision in the motor space was not the main focus, and the input device was a high-resolution computer mouse. Rahman et al. developed a more systematic approach to estimate the limit of users' precision in wrist rotations for wrist-based input [19]. In their protocol, targets were defined on various discretization of a semi-circle. Berard et al. compared users' precision when pointing with a mouse, to user's precision when pointing with two 3D devices [4]. They found wide variations in user's precision according to the device. Berard et al.'s experimental protocol also involved a discretization of target sizes. In the next section, we point to the issue of the discretization approach and describe a new experimental protocol that solves this issue.

To our knowledge, the limit of user's precision in finger pointing while in contact with a touch device has never been specifically studied. Studying the limit of user's finger pointing precision requires a precise device to track finger motion. In a recent work, Rogers et al. showed that both the yaw and the pitch angle of a finger landing on a touch surface could be inferred from the signal sent by a capacitive sensing device [20]. Yet, their system was designed in order to improve the precision of pointing from above the surface. Wang et al. also inferred finger orientations from the higher resolution signal provided by an FTIR touch surface [25]. They estimated the precision of their system to $\pm 1^{\circ}$, which is still too broad for our purpose. Inferring parameters from a rough signal is interesting when one is constraint by the input device. However, an accurate estimation of user's precision requires a precise input device. Many finger tracking approaches have used direct visual sensing (see Erol et al., for a review of several approaches reported in the literature [8]). Most of these visual finger tracking systems, though, are directed towards the creation of novel forms of interactions, not towards measuring precise positions. For example, Oka et al., used a thermal camera to facilitate the segmentation of the hand from the background [18]. They analyzed the extracted information for finger pointing and multi-finger gestures recognition. Yet, thermal imaging is restricted in term of resolution and sampling rate: their camera provided only 512×512 pixels at $30Hz$. Letessier et al. detected the position of many fingers in a multi-users scene recorded with a regular visual camera. They used background subtraction and shape filtering [14], but they did not estimate the orientations of the fingers. Malik et al. measured fingertip position and finger orientation from two webcams positioned close to the interactive surface [17]. Their system also relied on background subtraction to extract the contour of the hands. The contour was then filtered to infer the position and the orientation of the fingers. In the present work, we build on this last approach to develop a high precision tracking system. The precision of the tracker was increased by using a more precise camera and by improving the models of the finger contour.

MEASURING THE LIMIT OF USER PRECISION

The central idea to measure user's precision limit for a given task is to find a threshold in the task precision above which user's performance drops, showing that user's precision limit has been reached. Fitts' law [9] is a powerful tool to evaluate user's performance in pointing tasks. Fitts' law predicts that the mean time to acquire a target (MT) is a function of a single parameter: the ratio between the initial distance to target, also called *amplitude* (A), to the target *width* (W). Fitts' law also predicts a linear relationship between MT and the Index of Difficulty (ID) as expressed in the following equations [15]:

$$ID = log_2(A/W + 1) \quad (1)$$

$$MT = a + b.ID \quad (2)$$

Assuming that there is a width below which targets become significantly more difficult to acquire than "normal" targets, mean acquisition time should become significantly higher than the Fitts' prediction for these targets and Equation 2 should be broken. This break in linearity could be taken as an indicator of the saturation of users' precision.

Limits of previous approaches

Following this rational, Berard et al. designed an experimental protocol to evaluate user's precision for 3 different devices [4]. In their protocol, participants acquired targets of various sizes, some assumed to be above and some below the limit of user's precision. The authors expected to observe the linear relation of Equation 2 for target sizes above the threshold, but to witness acquisition times significantly above the prediction for sizes below the threshold. This was the case for the mouse, while the results for the two other devices were not as clear, and required to consider both MT and the error rate to evaluate the threshold.

We identified two shortcomings in this protocol. The first one is related to the discretization of target size: the user's precision limit is bracketed by two of the experiment's target widths. Because participant time is constrained, only a limited number of target widths can be included in the experiment, resulting in a broad estimation of the user's precision limit. In other words, the protocol does not provide a direct estimation of the user's precision limit. For example, if participants' performance drops between targets of width 2 and 3 ticks (the smallest reported motion of the device) for a $1200dpi$ device, then the estimation of the user's precision limit is in the rather broad range $400 - 600dpi$.

The second shortcoming of Berard et al.'s protocol is related to its sensitivity to the speed-accuracy tradeoff. Careful participants will fight to acquire the targets that are above their precision ability, at the cost of an increase of the acquisition duration. In contrast, faster and less careful participants will simply race through difficult targets, yielding no significant time increase, but substantially increasing their error rate. As participants in an experiment tend to be distributed along this speed-accuracy scale, the identification of the performance drop is blurred between an increase in the acquisition time and the error rate. The speed-accuracy tradeoff is handled in classical Fitts' experiments using the *effective width* [15] (*ew*) achieved by the participants, instead of the requested target width (W), in the computation of ID (Equation 1). When the distribution of error (final distance to target) is known, the effective width is computed according to Equation 3.

$$ew = 4.133 \times stddev(error) \quad (3)$$

With the effective width, slow and careful participants will have ew smaller than W, while fast participants will have larger ew. This approach does not impose a speed-accuracy tradeoff to participants, but it takes into account the tradeoff adopted by each participant into the computation of ID. This is fine for regular Fitts' experiments, where the goal is to improves the fit of Equation 2 to experimental data. When searching for user's precision limit, what is needed is a homogenization of the participants' strategies.

A new protocol: unpredictable controlled durations

In order to solve the problems of speed-accuracy tradeoff we *impose* the duration of the pointing. Imposing a pointing duration puts every participants on the same level for a given task: they all have to make the best of the time they are given to point to the target. In particular, participants cannot slow down the task for accuracy, nor speed it up for efficiency. Hence the control of the speed-accuracy tradeoff is transferred from the participant to the experimenter. Indirectly, controlling time also solves the discretization problem by switching the roles between pointing time and target width in the experimental design. Pointing time becomes a factor controlled by the experimenter, and target width becomes a dependent variable measured from the participant' performances.

In our protocol, participants point at the smallest possible target (1 tick width) with as much accuracy as possible within the allocated duration, i.e. we ask them to minimize the distance between the pointer and the target. This distance is recorded at the end of the duration controlled by the system, when the target disappears. As a consequence, there is no validation from the participants at the end of a trial and so, no *error rate*. Thus, we name the experimental task "target pointing" instead of "target acquisition". We estimate the precision of the pointing as the distribution of end distance to the target. This distribution is translated to an equivalent target width using the computation of ew according to Equation 3. ew yields a continuous estimate of the precision achieved by the participants for a given duration, which allows an accurate measure of the limit of user's precision.

Previous works have controlled the pointing time, using ew as a measure of users' performance [23], or keeping a set of discrete target sizes as in more classical Fitts' paradigm [26]. In both cases, the limit of pointing precision was not the scope, and subjects were aware of the duration available for pointing. Similarly to these approaches, in pilot studies, we trained participants to the duration of the trials with a visual and auditory metronome [26]. We observed that participants reduced their speed of motion in order to reach the target exactly at the end of the trial and minimize corrective motions. We removed this bias in our protocol by insuring that the allocated duration to reach the target is unknown to participants, in contrast with previous approaches. This was done by randomizing the presentation order of trial durations. The final protocol includes the following steps:

- Participants move the screen pointer within a *start area* shown on screen as a grey region (Figure 6, left). The start area has a large width to make it an easy target.
- As the pointer is moved, the location of the *next target* is shown as a thin grey line, offset from the pointer by the *amplitude* of the next trial. Thus, the next target moves with the pointer until the pointing task actually starts, which helps participants to plan their pointing gesture.
- The pointing gesture starts when the pointer has remained within the start area for some time set by the system. The time is randomly chosen within the range $500 - 1500ms$. This prevents anticipation from the participants.
- When the pointing task starts, the start area is hidden and the moving thin grey line of the next target is replaced by a fixed thick red line (Figure 6, right).
- Participants move the pointer as close as possible to the target. The duration of target presentation is set by the system

and unknown to the participants who are induced to rush to the target and then try to stabilize the pointer.

- The target is hidden at the end of the trial duration, the distance to the target (error) and the distance from the starting point (trial amplitude) are recorded. The next trial is initiated by showing the start area again.

We predicted that the longer the pointing duration, the better the pointing precision achieved by the participants. However, this linear relationship should only apply until a duration that is long enough for the participants to reach their limit of precision. From this duration and above, we should not see any improvement in precision. As a result, when plotting *ew* against pointing durations, we should see a curve that decreases until it reaches a plateau. The *ew* associated with the plateau will represent the limit of users' precision.

As the precision *limit* is only related to the target width, not to the distance to target, Berard et al. [4] used a single amplitude in their protocol. Here, we used two amplitudes in order to introduce an additional evidence that participants have reached their precision limit. For short durations, the small amplitude should yield better precision than the large one because of the extra time provided by the smaller distance to cover. This extra time should serve to stabilize the pointer on the target. However, once the pointing duration is long enough for participants to reach their precision limit, the extra time should be of no use. As a result, when plotting *ew* against pointing durations for both amplitudes, we should see the curve of the larger amplitude *above* the one of the smaller amplitude, until they converge at the precision limit.

The experimental protocol focuses on the limit of pointing precision, not on pointing in the general case. Consequently, the amplitudes should be chosen small enough such as they only require the *final* pointing gesture from the participants. If pointing with a mouse for example, they should not require clutching. In the case of linear touch pointing, amplitudes must be chosen so that the pointing can be performed in the common precision pointing way: by a small deformation of the finger on the surface, without actual sliding of the finger. For rotational pointing, amplitudes must be small enough so that the rotation of the finger and the wrist can be performed in a single gesture, without clutching.

In order to implement this experimental protocol, we needed to measure finger motions with great precision. We developed two optical finger trackers for this.

HIGH PRECISION OPTICAL FINGER TRACKING

Measuring the limit of user precision is a task that has very high requirements in term of the precision of the input device. Devices are usually designed to support Human-computer interaction. As such, they only need to provide a precision that is similar to what users can achieve. Consequently, we were not aware of any commercial or experimental touch-sensing device that could satisfy the requirements of a *measuring* device. We built two devices for the measurement of finger motion especially designed to optimize precision. Our experiments also required that the devices had low latency, as lag is well known to degrade Human performance [16], and that they would be robust enough to run without failure during the experimental sessions. These demanding requirements were counterbalanced by the low requirements on the range of motion and by the possibility of operator supervision. Optical sensing was a natural choice because of the flexibility it offers in term of tracking approaches and parameters.

Image sensing

For image sensing, we used an AVT Marlin F-131B camera with a 12*mm* C-Mount lens. The camera has a CMOS sensor of resolution 1280x1024 that has high sensitivity in the near infrared (IR) spectrum. In order to have a strong control on illumination, we chose to work in the IR spectrum: a filter was mounted on the camera to block the visible light spectrum, and a RayLed RayMax 25 infrared illuminator was used to light the finger.

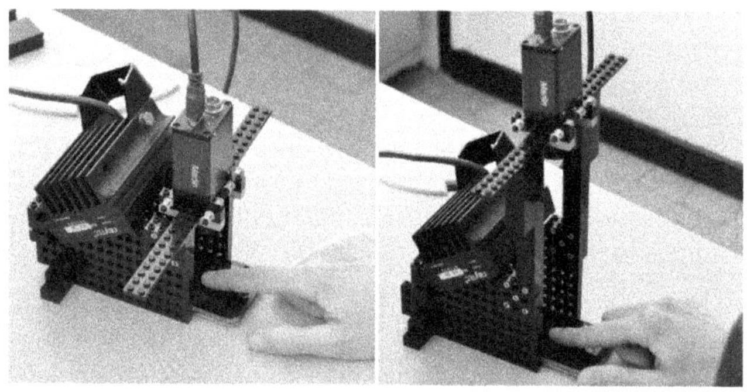

Figure 1. Camera setups for linear tracking (left) and rotational tracking (right).

The camera was mounted vertically above a touch device using a custom made frame built from Lego^{TM} blocks, as shown in Figure 1. The frame also supported the IR illuminator oriented towards the finger. The close proximity of the light source allowed the use of a short exposure time on the camera, a requirement for high frame rates. The touch device was only used as a compliant touch surface and was not switched on. The frame had two different configurations allowing different fields of view for the camera. When measuring the finger linear position, the tip of the finger was tracked on a very limited range. The camera was set very close to the finger to increase measurement precision. There was a minimal distance, though, where the image became too blurry for correct tracking. We found this distance at 60*mm* between the lens and the touch surface. For the measurement of the finger rotations, a larger field of view was needed to see the sides of the finger. We set the lens at 175*mm* from the touch surface.

CMOS sensors have the ability to provide the reading of only a subpart of the sensor. This "Region Of Interest" (ROI) is set by sending commands to the camera. This gives great flexibility in choosing a tradeoff between the size of the captured image and the frame rate. We used two different settings for linear and rotational tracking. For linear tracking, we only needed mono-dimensional tracking in the left-right direction. The ROI was thus set to 600×300 pixels, which allowed a frame rate of $83Hz$. The rotational tracking required a more square ROI, we set it to 500×400 pixels which translated to a frame rate of $78Hz$.

The video signal was processed by an Apple Mac Pro computer equipped with 2 quad-core 3 GHz Xeon processors. We made sure that no buffering occurred in the video acquisition pipeline in order to minimize latency. Tracking was monothread for the linear tracking, but was parallelized for the rotational tracking as detailed below.

Tracking linear finger motion

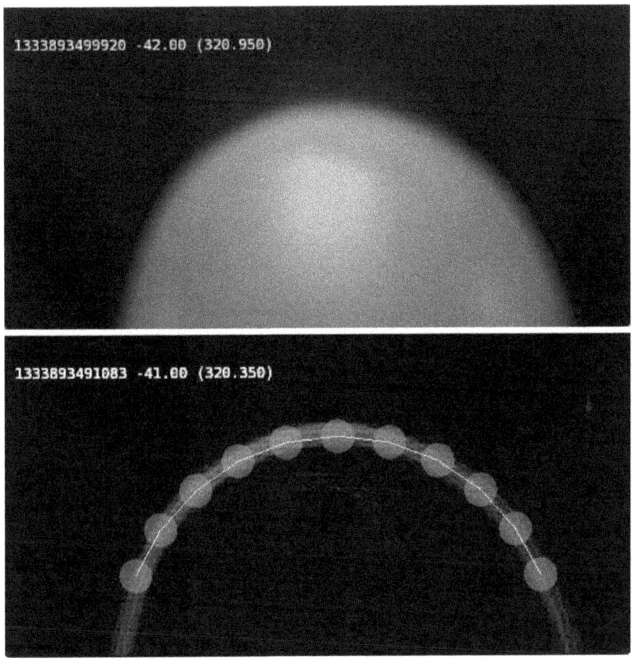

Figure 2. Linear tracking. The out of focus input image of the tip of a finger (top). The arc of a circle model with 11 control points, fit to the Sobel edge image (bottom).

The Arc model

The main objective of our tracker was to achieve high *precision*. With our setup, the 600 pixels wide image covered 25mm of the surface, hence the measurement at the pixel level was roughly 600dpi (dot per inch). But video signals are known to be noisy at the pixel level, reducing the measurement precision if noise is not handled properly. Moreover, pilot studies revealed that 600dpi would not be enough for an accurate measurement of user's precision. We dealt with the noise problem, and the need for higher precision, by fitting a simple model to the image. The model was an arc of a circle with an angle of 135°. It was fitted to the image through 11 control points, as illustrated in Figure 2 (bottom). Each control point had a mask of size 33x33 pixels with values defined by a 2 dimensional Gaussian with a standard deviation of 16 and centered in the mask.

To fit the model to the image, we first processed the greyscale input image by a Sobel filter [10] to generate an edge image (the background in Figure 2, bottom). We defined the "score" of the model, at any (x, y) location, as the sum of the scores of each of its control points. The score of a control point is the sum of the edge image values at locations covered by the control point's mask, weighted by the mask's Gaussian coefficients. The model was fitted to a new frame by an exhaustive search of the maximum score for all possible locations in the 2D neighborhood of the model's previous position.

In order to cope with various finger sizes, the radius of the model was adapted by the operator for every new participant of the experiment. Still, an arc of a circle is only a rough approximation of the shape of a finger, especially when the finger is rotated along its own axis, for example to reach the edges of the work surface. We observed, however, that the arc model allowed our tracking to be very stable, even when the fingertips were not circular anymore. Here, we should emphasize that the tracker did not need to be *accurate* in estimating the shape of the finger. It was only required to be stable and precise such that participants could make precise corrections when aligning their cursor to a small target.

Sub pixel tracking

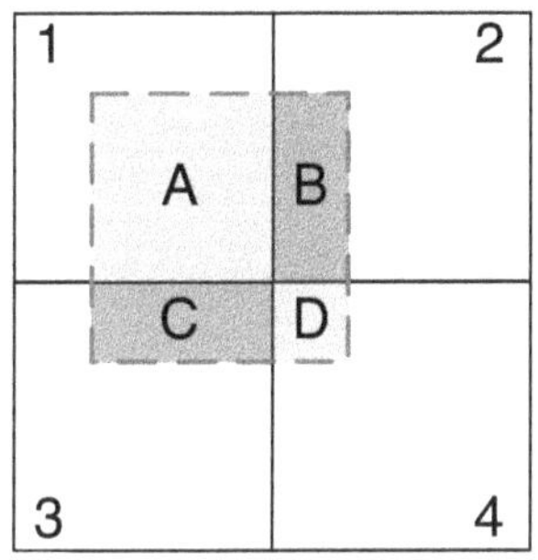

Figure 3. Sub pixel score computation for one particular mask pixel. In the general case, a mask pixel (thick dashed red square) intersects 4 image pixels (numbered thin black square). The contribution of this mask pixel to its control point's score is the sum of the products of the mask pixel Gaussian value by the image pixel values, weighted by the surface of the area of intersection (labeled A to D here).

The first benefit of the model is to handle noise at the pixel level: the score of the model depends on 11 control points, each of those points depending on 33x33 pixels. Hence the global position estimation averages the uncorrelated noise of 11969 pixels. The second benefit of the model is to allow the measurement of sub-pixel accuracy: control point score computation was implemented for any floating point position in the image, as illustrated in Figure 3. The model's maximum search was thus performed on a grid of $1/2$ pixel. In order to maintain computation time compatible with the input frame rate, we optimized the search by making it hierarchical: the search was first performed on a grid of 9x9 (horizontal and vertical) locations separated by 4 pixels and centered on the model location on the previous frame. We divided the grid spacing by 2 at each level, resulting in only 3x3 locations having to be searched around the maximum location found at the previous level. The search was thus performed on 3 levels in order to reach a grid spacing of $1/2$ pixel. To get confidence that this approach did not miss any local maximum, we plotted a set of score maps at the $1/2$ pixel grid spacing on a 2×2 pixel wide area around the found maximum. We observed that the maps had a smooth dome-shaped surface with a single maximum. Finally, the raw output of the tracker was multiplied by 2, so that the tracker outputted integer number of "ticks".

We verified that the first level of search, in a 36×36 pixel wide area, combined with the $83Hz$ frame rate, was large enough to track very fast finger motions. During the experiments, we never observed any tracking failure. Tracking only had to be bootstrapped when the finger first appeared in the image: at the beginning of a session, or after participants had removed their finger during pauses. Bootstrapping was performed by an automatic algorithm that found the topmost line in the edge image having a sum of pixel greater than a threshold, and then initializing the model at the barycenter of this line.

Evaluation of stability and precision

As a tool for measuring precision, instead of a tool for an interactive system, our tracker has a specific set of requirements. Namely, its output must be perfectly stable, and its precision has to be accurately measured.

For static stability, we cut a piece of cardboard in the shape of a finger. We then simply put the cardboard finger in several different locations under the camera, and checked that a perfectly stable object yielded a perfectly stable output from the tracker. For dynamic stability, we recorded the output of a finger moving at roughly constant slow speed and verified that the trajectory was regular and spanning all tick positions.

To evaluate the precision, we used the cardboard finger again, this time to point at two different graduations, as far as possible of each other, on a ruler put on the touch surface. We used the tracker control window to align the center of the model to the two graduations and to read the tracker's reported position. A physical distance of $22mm$ yielded a distance of 1040 ticks of the tracker. The tracker precision was thus evaluated at $1040 \times 25.4/22 = 1200dpi$. We estimated that our measurement error was within $0.5mm$ on both positions, hence we estimated the physical distance in the range $21-23mm$ and the tracker's precision in the range $1150-1260dpi$.

Tracking rotational finger motion

The Snake Model

The arc of circle model was good enough to extract the position of the fingertip, but not to extract the orientation of the finger because it did not track the sides of the finger. We thus used a snake [13] model in order to track more of the participants' fingers, while adapting to their various shapes. The snake model shared its structure with the circular arc: it consisted in a set of control points connected with each other at fixed distance. As the *scale* of the scene was smaller (in order to see more of the finger), the control points were smaller too: their mask had a size of 9x9 pixels with coefficients from a 2D Gaussian of standard deviation 4. The model fitted to a finger is shown on Figure 4 (right).

The model was initialized by the operator clicking on the center of the tip of the finger while in vertical orientation. From this point on, the system found the control points on the edge of the finger as detailed in Figure 5. For increased precision, we used the same sub-pixel score maximization approach as with the arc model.

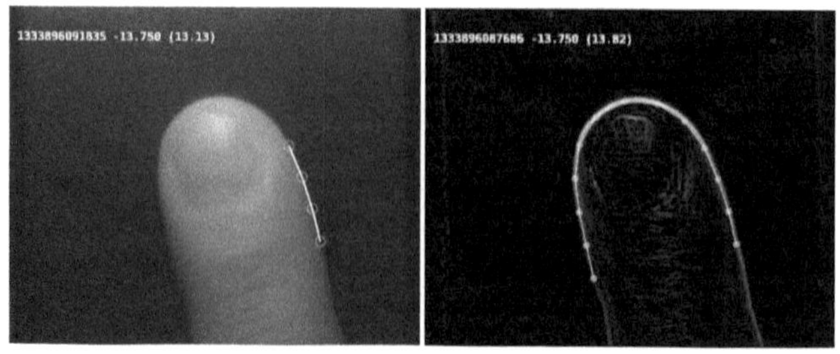

Figure 4. Rotational tracking. (right) The snake model with 13 control points, fit to the Sobel edge image. (left) The finger's orientation is computed as the mean of the 3 orientations defined by the 4 last controlled point. Only the well-lit side is used.

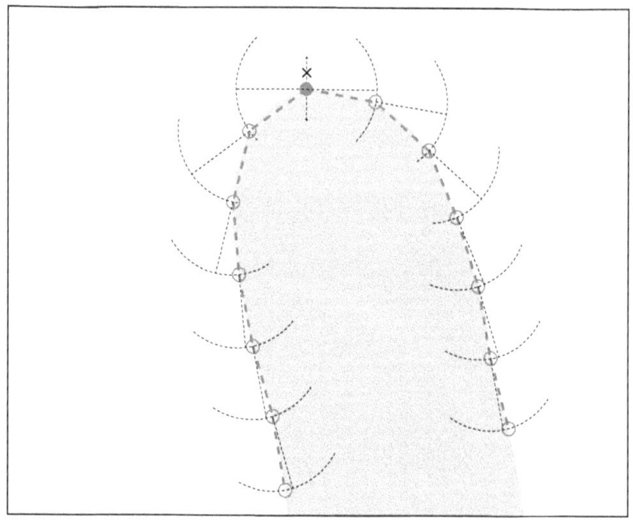

Figure 5. Defining the snake shape (thick dashed red line) on the edge of the finger (grey shape). The operator clicked on the "x". The first "anchor" control point (red disk) is searched on a vertical neighborhood. The other control points, on each side of the anchor (red circles), are searched at 40 pixels, on 90° arcs oriented from the two previous control points, except for the 2 first which are search at orientations 0 and 180°.

Once the model had been initialized, its shape was *frozen* and it was only allowed three degrees of freedom: (x, y, θ), θ being the rotation in the surface plane. The snake's U shape had to be frozen to prevent it to drift along the finger edges, which would prevent the reliable tracking of (x, y), and ultimately of θ.

Tracking

Tracking was performed, as with the arc model, by an exhaustive search in the neighborhood of the previously found position. The neighborhood was now 3-dimensional, which significantly increased computation cost. However, the search parameter space was easily split and distributed on the 8 cores of the computer. We used the same hierarchical approach, this time with 3 levels, to optimize the search as with the arc model. Initial search was performed on a grid of 16×16 locations spaced by 2 pixels, and $22°$ of angle by steps of $1.15°$. At the third level, the resolution of the search was 0.1 pixels in position and $0.06°$ in rotation. Here again, the wide search area of the initial level, combined with the $78Hz$ frame rate, allowed the tracker to never fail during the experiment.

We first planned to use the θ angle found in the tracking as the orientation of the finger. But we observed that this fixed snake model would not be stable enough for our experiments: using the cardboard finger, we computed the standard deviation of the output for a perfectly stable finger, and found that it would not allow a stable output below 1°. We attributed this problem to the inability of the fixed snake to adapt to slight shape variations along the finger edges during large rotations. Orientation estimation was thus implemented in two stages. In the first stage, the fixed snake was searched as described above. In a second stage, the shape constraint was released and the side control points were searched using the same approach as shown in Picture 5, only this time the anchor point was defined by the first stage instead of the click of the operator. The role of the fixed snake was thus to reliably track the anchor control point at the tip of the finger, so that an accurate snake could be fit in the second stage.

Once the accurate shape of the finger had been extracted, we computed the finger's orientation from the last control points at the end of each side of the snake. On each side, we averaged the 3 orientations of the segments defined by the 4 last control points, as shown in Figure 4 (left). We initially averaged the two resulting orientations from both sides. We observed however that on large rotations, due to the light source coming from the top of the image, the side of the finger closer to the bottom of the image was in the shadow and could become unstable. We thus simply estimated the finger orientation from the well lit side of the finger.

Precision

Using the cardboard finger and plotting the output of rotating fingers, we found that setting a threshold at 0.25° before reporting a new rotation produced a stable and continuous output. We thus estimated the rotational tracker's resolution at 0.25°.

EXPERIMENTAL EVALUATION OF FINGER POINTING PRECISION

We used the trackers to run two experiments aimed at measuring the linear and rotational limit of user's precision in finger pointing. We implemented two *duration controlled target pointing* experiments as defined and motivated in the third section of this paper.

Visual feedback

The visual feedback was displayed on a $120Hz$ Samsung SyncMaster 2233RZ 1680×1050 pixels monitor. The visibility of the pointer and target was improved using a zoom factor of 4 (a 1 tick target was represented by 4 pixels). As Bohan et al. have shown, increasing visual magnification essentially amounts to zoom-in to the precision limits of the effector, after which performance asymptotes[5]. The visual feedback of the experiments is shown on Figure 6.

Experiment design

Twelve volunteers participated in each experiment, aged 32.5 (mean) ± 10.8 (stddev) for the linear experiment and, 29.1 ± 5.53 for the rotational experiment. Six users participated in both experiments. All of the participants had extensive

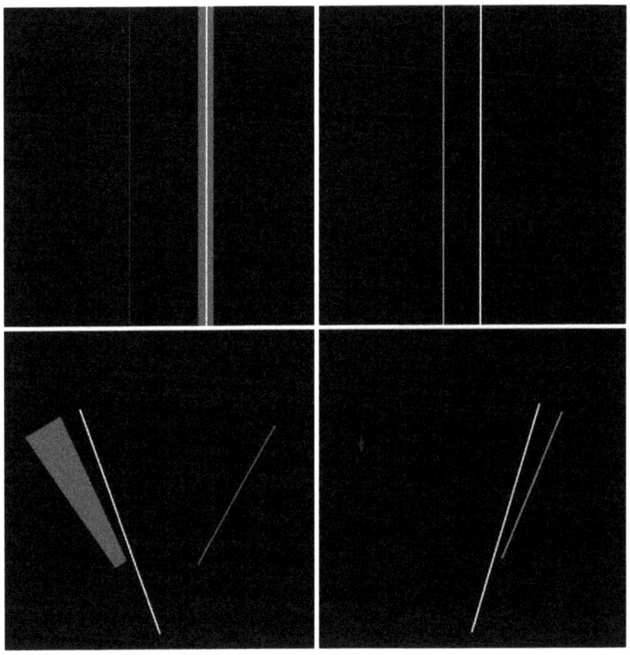

Figure 6. Visual feedback of the linear (top) and rotational (bottom) experiments.

previous experience with laptops' touchpads. Nine of them in each experiment had extensive previous experience with direct touch devices (such as smartphones).

Participants were asked to position their index finger on the touch device, below the camera, in a comfortable posture. Most participants adopted a posture with the finger close to the horizontal, but a few preferred a more vertical posture with the finger at around 45°. Participants were given a few trials to understand the task and to find their most comfortable posture.

Participants were asked to be as precise as possible in pointing to 1 *tick* wide targets at two different amplitudes: $(80, 120)$ ticks and $(30, 50)$ degrees for the linear and the rotational experiment respectively. For the linear experiment, both amplitudes allowed pointing by a *slight roll of the finger* leading to a slight deformation, i.e. without any sliding. For the rotational experiment, both amplitudes required a significant motion of the palm of the pointing hand.

Targets were displayed with 8 different durations: (800, 900, 1000, 1100, 1200, 1400, 1600, 2000) ms. All combinations of amplitude and durations were presented 5 times within a block, in random order, with different orders in each block. Directions (left/right, clockwise/counterclockwise) were reversed after each trial. Participants performed 6 blocks with a 1 min break between blocks. The total number of trials was 5760 for each experiment and each experimental sessions lasted $1/2$h.

Data processing

For each group (subject X amplitude X duration combination, 30 trials) we rejected trials for which the error was greater than 3 times the error mean of the group (in total, 2.3% of

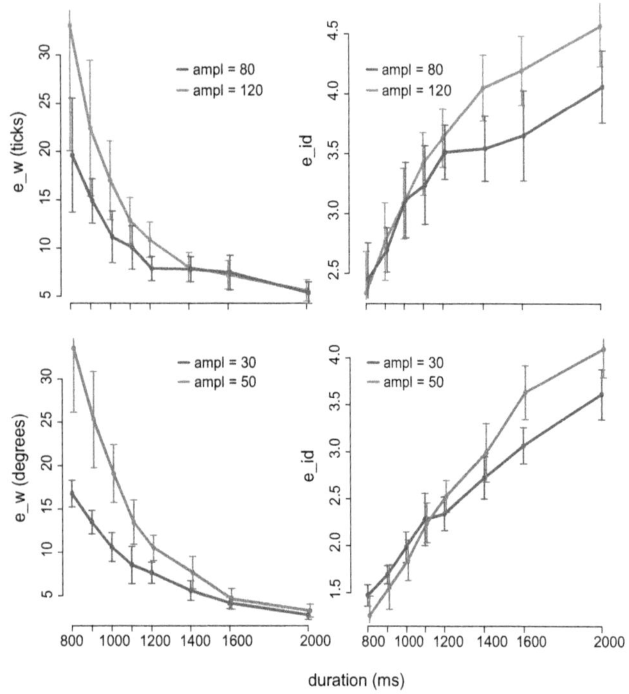

Figure 7. Result of the linear experiment (top) and rotational experiment (bottom). Average effective width (left) and effective ID (right) achieved by all participants as a function of the trial duration, with 95% confidence intervals, for amplitude 80 and 120 ticks (top) and 30 and 50 degrees (bottom).

the trials for the linear experiment, 1.3% for the rotational experiment). We then computed two parameters: the effective target width (*ew*), according to Equation 3; and the effective index of difficulty $eid = log_2(ea/ew+1)$, with *ea* being the effective amplitude, computed as the average of the pointing amplitude.

Results

Results of the two experiments are summarized in Table 1 and illustrated in Figure 7. Distances are expressed in ticks of our $1200dpi$ linear tracker ($1tick = 2.12 \times 10^{-2}mm$).

The effects of Amplitude and Duration on the effective width (*ew*) were tested for each experiment using 2-ways within subjects Analyses of Variance (ANOVA). Post-hoc comparisons of *ew* and *eid* between amplitude were run for the 8 levels of duration using paired t-tests with Bonferroni correction (testing using $8 \times p$).

Linear experiment

In the linear experiment, between 800*ms* and 1200*ms*, *ew* decreases from 20 *tick* to 8 *tick* for Amplitude 80 *tick* and from 33 *tick* to 11 *tick* for Amplitude 120 *tick*. For both amplitudes, *ew* stabilizes at about 8 *tick* between 1400*ms* and 1600*ms*, but then improves again to reach about 5 *tick* at 2000*ms* (Figure 7). ANOVA shows that *ew* changes with Duration [F(7, 77)]=23.7, p<.0001] and with Amplitude [F(1, 11)=14.4, p<.01]. The effect of Amplitude also interacts with the effect of Duration [F(7,77)=7.59, p<.0001]. Post-hoc comparisons show significant differences in *ew* between

Table 1. Results of the experiment. Average on all participants of the effective width (ew) and effective ID (eid) across durations, for the two amplitudes and the two experiments (top and bottom). Amplitude (A) and *ew* are expressed in ticks for the linear experiment and in degrees for the rotational experiment.

	Linear experiment					
duration (ms)	**ew A=80**	**ew A=120**		**eid A=80**	**eid A=120**	
800	19.62	33.03	*	2.45	2.34	
900	14.89	22.43		2.70	2.77	
1000	11.17	17.03	*	3.11	3.08	
1100	10.08	12.85		3.24	3.42	
1200	7.88	10.88	**	3.51	3.63	
1400	7.82	8.04		3.54	4.05	*
1600	7.46	7.24		3.65	4.20	*
2000	5.36	5.60		4.06	4.57	**
	Rotational experiment					
duration (ms)	**ew A=30**	**ew A=50**		**eid A=30**	**eid A=50**	
800	16.77	33.55	**	1.47	1.26	
900	13.48	25.30	**	1.69	1.56	
1000	10.59	19.07	**	1.98	1.85	
1100	8.54	13.50	**	2.28	2.24	
1200	7.64	10.53	**	2.34	2.53	
1400	5.58	7.66		2.72	2.99	
1600	4.15	4.63		3.07	3.63	**
2000	2.76	3.26		3.61	4.10	*

* $8p < .05$, ** $8p < .01$, post-hoc comparisons between amplitude

the two Amplitudes for durations smaller than 1200*ms* but not for longer durations.

Similar *eid* are observed for both amplitudes for durations from 800*ms* to 1200*ms*. For durations longer than 1200*ms*, the improvement of *eid* with duration then changes according to the Amplitude, from 3.54 at 1400*ms* to 4.06 at 2000*ms* for Amplitude 80 *tick* and from 4.05 to 4.57 for Amplitude 120 *tick*. ANOVA shows a significant effect of Amplitude [F(1,11)=20.97, p<.001] and Duration [F(7,77)=95.7, p<.0001] on *eid* and a significant interaction of the two factors [F(7,77)=5.42, p<.0001]. Post-hoc comparisons show that differences in *eid* between the two amplitudes are significant only for durations greater than 1200*ms*.

Rotational experiment

The rotational experiment does not show the same stabilization of *eid* as with the linear experiment for durations in the range $[1200-1600ms]$: *eid* appears to improve regularly up to the longest duration of 2000*ms*. However, the convergence of the curves of the 2 amplitudes is still observable (at duration 1600*ms*). ANOVA shows a significant effect of Amplitude [F(1,11)=57.6, p<.0001] and Duration [F(7, 77)=107, p<.0001] and Amplitude X Duration [F(7, 77)=19.2, p<.0001] on *ew*. Post-Hoc comparisons show that *ew* is significantly different for Amplitude 50° as compare with Amplitude 30° only for durations shorter than 1400*ms*.

ANOVA shows a significant effect of Amplitude [F(1,11)=8.04, p<.05], Duration [F(7,77)=247, p<.0001] and Amplitude X Duration [F(7,77)=8.84, p<.0001] on *eid*. *eid* linearly increases with the duration and similar values are observed between 800*ms* and 1400*ms*, the difference being only significant at 1600*ms* and 2000*ms*.

Discussion

Our users' studies were a first effort to evaluate the user resolution of finger pointing on a touch surface. Our results are partially consistent with our expectations, as threshold in precision is not as clear as predicted, especially for the rotational pointing. However, our results provide a first objective measurement of users' precision.

Linear experiment

In the linear experiment, we observe a stabilization of users' performance at about 8 *tick* for durations between 1200*ms* and 1600*ms*: for Amplitude 80 *tick*, this 400*ms* increase in duration only yields a precision improvement of 0.42 *tick*, while the previous 400*ms* duration increase (from 800*ms* to 1200*ms*) yields an improvement of 11.74 *tick*. Also, at duration 1400*ms* and above, the effect of Amplitude seems to disappear as the achieved *ew* is similar for both amplitudes. Hence, around 1400*ms*, users' performances move away from Fitts' Law prediction. Consistently with this observation made from *ew*, *eid* curves for the two Amplitudes overlap for duration smaller or equal to 1200*ms*, as predicted by Fitt's law. The two curves then diverge starting at 1400*ms*, as the increase in duration doesn't improve user's precision anymore for the smaller Amplitude. In addition, the slope of *eid* curves for the two amplitudes are less steep after 1400*ms*, indicating that participants become substantially less efficient than with lower durations. Using the tracker's precision evaluated at around 1200*dpi* (see the above section "Evaluation of stability and precision"), the 8 *tick* translate to a precision of $1200/8 = 150dpi$. In other words, users can point at targets as small as 0.17*mm* within 1.4 *sec*, for amplitudes of movement up to 120 *tick* (2.54*mm*).

The surprising outcome of the linear experiment is that precision can still be improved *after ew* has stabilized: when the duration increased past 1600*ms* to 2000*ms*, *ew* improved by about 2 *tick* for Amplitude 80 *tick* and by about 1.6 *tick* for Amplitude 120 *tick*. With the highest amount of time and lowest amplitude that they were given, our participants where able to point at targets as small as 0.11*mm* (equivalent to 224*dpi*). Our experiment indicates that even though there is a threshold in precision achievable in a "regular" amount of time (i.e. predictable by Fitts' Law), when the duration available to reach the target increases, users probably enter another mode of control. This mode only materialize for long pointing durations, where the time for initial approach to target is minor compared to the time for final adjustments, hence the effect of Amplitude disappears in the achieved pointing precision. However, due to the large amount of time required, this mode of operation might not be suitable for frequent interactions such as positioning a cursor or acquiring small buttons in a dense display.

Rotational experiment

The rotational experiment does not show the same profile as the linear experiment. Rather than stabilizing at some precision level, the curves *ew* for the two amplitudes show a regular improvement up to the last duration (Figure 7, bottom). However, a divergence of the *eid* curve is here again visible, as indicated by the significant differences of *eid* for the two amplitudes at Duration 1600*ms* and above. The lack of precision stabilization in our rotational experiment could be attributed to the fact that the two angular amplitudes used in this experiment may have been too high, inducing the major part of the pointing time to be allocated to the approach of the target, and so, not enough time for final adjustements. This point to the necessity to investigate the effect for smaller amplitudes.

However, as a first attempt to evaluate user's precision in rotational pointing, our study provides a guideline for the development of interaction on touch surface using rotational movement of the finger. Hence on Table 1, designer can find the user's precision that can be expected depending on the duration and on the amplitude of the pointing. To our knowledge, this constitutes the first empirical evidence that users can be quite precise in rotational pointing, down to 3.26° for duration of 2 sec and Amplitude 50°. This indicates, for example, that reliable selection of 1 sector among 15 in a 50° pie menu could be performed by direct pointing.

CONCLUSION

In this paper, we contributed with the design and evaluation of two high precision optical finger trackers, one for linear motions and one for rotations. The trackers run at frame rates above 70*Hz*, they provide robust and stable outputs, and their precisions were evaluated at 1200*dpi* for the linear tracker and 0.25° for the rotational tracker. These characteristics make them valuable experimental tools that could be useful to address other properties of finger gestures and to evaluate interactions that rely on precise finger motions. In addition, our trackers open the way to improvements in their tracking range and autonomy, which would have direct applications in the design of interactive systems.

The main objective of this work was to estimate the limit of users' precision in linear and rotational touch pointing. We found this limit at 150*dpi*, or 0.17*mm* for linear pointing. It appears that we did not reach the limit for rotational pointing, and additional research will be required here to decide if there is a threshold. Still, we discovered that for rotational pointing, users can be quite precise, achieving for example 2.76° of precision for a 2*s* pointing duration and 30° of amplitude. This result should motivate the design of new interactions based on precise pointing, and the design of new devices that are able to sense this level of precision in rotational pointing.

ACKNOWLEDGMENTS

The authors wish to thank Renaud Blanch for his contributions to this work.

REFERENCES

1. Pär-Anders Albinsson and Shumin Zhai. High precision touch screen interaction. In *ACM Conference on Human Factors in Computing Systems (CHI)*, pages 105–112. ACM, 2003.

2. Patrick Baudisch and Gerry Chu. Back-of-device interaction allows creating very small touch devices. In

ACM Conference on Human Factors in Computing Systems (CHI), pages 1923–1932. ACM, 2009.

3. Hrvoje Benko, Andrew D. Wilson, and Patrick Baudisch. Precise selection techniques for multi-touch screens. In *ACM Conference on Human Factors in Computing Systems (CHI)*, pages 1263–1272. ACM, 2006.
4. François Bérard, Guangyu Wang, and Jeremy R. Cooperstock. On the limits of the human motor control precision: the search for a device's human resolution. In *IFIP Conference on Human-Computer Interaction, INTERACT*, pages 107–122. Springer-Verlag, 2011.
5. Michael Bohan, Daniel S. McConnell, Alex Chaparro, and Shelby G. Thompson. The effects of visual magnification and physical movement scale on the manipulation of a tool with indirect vision. *Journal of Experimental Psychology: Applied*, 16(1):33–44, March 2010.
6. Géry Casiez, Daniel Vogel, Ravin Balakrishnan, and Andy Cockburn. The impact of control-display gain on user performance in pointing tasks. *Human-Computer Interaction*, 23(3):215–250, 2008.
7. Olivier Chapuis and Pierre Dragicevic. Effects of motor scale, visual scale and quantization on small target acquisition difficulty. *ACM Trans. Comput.-Hum. Interact.*, 18(3), 2011.
8. Ali Erol, George Bebis, Mircea Nicolescu, Richard D. Boyle, and Xander Twombly. Vision-based hand pose estimation: A review. *Computer Vision and Image Understanding*, 108(1–2):52 – 73, 2007. Special Issue on Vision for Human-Computer Interaction.
9. Paul M. Fitts. The information capacity of the human motor system in controlling the amplitude of movement. *Journal of Experimental Psychology*, 47(6):381–391, 1954.
10. Rafael C. Gonzalez and Richard E. Woods. *Digital Image Processing*. Addison-Wesley Longman Publishing Co., Inc., Boston, MA, USA, 2nd edition, 2001.
11. Christian Holz and Patrick Baudisch. The generalized perceived input point model and how to double touch accuracy by extracting fingerprints. In *ACM Conference on Human Factors in Computing Systems (CHI)*, CHI '10, pages 581–590, New York, NY, USA, 2010. ACM.
12. Christian Holz and Patrick Baudisch. Understanding touch. In *ACM Conference on Human Factors in Computing Systems (CHI)*, CHI '11, pages 2501–2510, New York, NY, USA, 2011. ACM.
13. Michael Kass, Andrew Witkin, and Demetri Terzopoulos. Snakes: Active contour models. *International Journal of Computer Vision*, 1:321–331, 1988.
14. Julien Letessier and Francois Berard. Visual tracking of bare fingers for interactive surfaces. In *ACM Symposium on User Interface Software and Technology (UIST)*, pages 119–122, 2004.
15. I Scott MacKenzie. Fitts' law as a research and design tool in human-computer interaction. *Human-Computer Interaction*, 7:91–139, 1992.
16. I Scott MacKenzie and Colin Ware. Lag as a determinant of human performance in interactive systems. In *ACM Conference on Human Factors in Computing Systems (CHI)*, pages 488–493, 1993.
17. Shahzad Malik and Joe Laszlo. Visual touchpad: a two-handed gestural input device. In *ACM International Conference on Multimodal Interfaces (ICMI)*, pages 289–296. ACM, 2004.
18. K. Oka, Y. Sato, and H. Koike. Real-time fingertip tracking and gesture recognition. *Computer Graphics and Applications, IEEE*, 22(6):64–71, Nov/Dec 2002.
19. Mahfuz Rahman, Sean Gustafson, Pourang Irani, and Sriram Subramanian. Tilt techniques: investigating the dexterity of wrist-based input. In *ACM Conference on Human Factors in Computing Systems (CHI)*, pages 1943–1952. ACM, 2009.
20. Simon Rogers, John Williamson, Craig Stewart, and Roderick Murray-Smith. Anglepose: robust, precise capacitive touch tracking via 3d orientation estimation. In *ACM Conference on Human Factors in Computing Systems (CHI)*, pages 2575–2584. ACM, 2011.
21. Anne Roudaut, Stéphane Huot, and Eric Lecolinet. Taptap and magstick: improving one-handed target acquisition on small touch-screens. In *Proceedings of the working conference on Advanced visual interfaces*, AVI '08, pages 146–153, New York, NY, USA, 2008. ACM.
22. Nicolas Roussel, Géry Casiez, Jonathan Aceituno, and Daniel Vogel. Giving a hand to the eyes: Leveraging input accuracy for subpixel interaction. In *ACM Symposium on User Interface Software and Technology (UIST)*. ACM, 2012.
23. Richard A. Schmidt, Howard Zelaznik, Brian Hawkins, James S. Frank, and John T. Quinn Jr. Motor-output variability: A theory for the accuracy of rapid motor acts. *Psychological Review*, 86(5):415–451, 1979.
24. Daniel Vogel and Patrick Baudisch. Shift: a technique for operating pen-based interfaces using touch. In *ACM Conference on Human Factors in Computing Systems (CHI)*, pages 657–666. ACM, 2007.
25. Feng Wang and Xiangshi Ren. Empirical evaluation for finger input properties in multi-touch interaction. In *ACM Conference on Human Factors in Computing Systems (CHI)*, pages 1063–1072. ACM, 2009.
26. Jacob O. Wobbrock, Edward Cutrell, Susumu Harada, and I. Scott MacKenzie. An error model for pointing based on fitts' law. In *ACM Conference on Human Factors in Computing Systems (CHI)*, pages 1613–1622. ACM, 2008.

SnapRail: A Tabletop User Interface Widget for Addressing Occlusion by Physical Objects

Genki Furumi[1], Daisuke Sakamoto[1&2] and Takeo Igarashi[1&2]
[1]The University of Tokyo
7-3-1 Hongo, Bunkyo, Tokyo
113-0033 Japan
[2]JST ERATO Igarashi Design Interface Project
1-28-1-7F Koishikawa, Bunkyo, Tokyo
112-0002 Japan
{furumi, d.sakamoto, takeo}@acm.org

ABSTRACT
The screen of a tabletop computer is often occluded by physical objects such as coffee cups. This makes it difficult to see the virtual elements under the physical objects (visibility) and manipulate them (manipulability). Here we present a user interface widget, called "*SnapRail*," to address these problems, especially occlusion of a manipulable collection of virtual discrete elements such as icons. SnapRail detects a physical object on the surface and the virtual elements under the object. It then snaps the virtual elements to a rail widget that appears around the object. The user can then manipulate the virtual elements along the rail widget. We conducted a preliminary user study to evaluate the potential of this interface and collect initial feedback. The SnapRail interface received positive feedback from participants of the user study.

Author Keywords
Tabletop; avoiding; occlusion; interaction.

ACM Classification Keywords
H.5.2 [Information Interfaces and Presentation]: User Interfaces – User-centered design.

INTRODUCTION
A table is a place where people perform daily activities such as having coffee, reading a book, and enjoying a hobby. During those activities, people place various objects, such as paper, books, and coffee mugs, on the table. Tabletop computers and displays are expected to enhance these activities, and many applications have been presented [9,11].

There is, however, a fundamental problem with tabletop computers: physical objects often hide virtual elements on the tabletop display, making it difficult for the user to see (visibility) and handle them (manipulability).

As a solution, we present a user interface widget called "SnapRail". For visibility, the system automatically rearranges the occluded virtual elements along a ring-shaped rail widget that appears around the object. For manipulabilbity, the rail widget allows the user to manipulate the virtual elements. We created a proof-of-concept prototype system to demonstrate the feasibility of the idea and conducted a preliminary user study to evaluate the potential of this interface and collect initial feedback from participants. The SnapRail interface received positive feedback from the participants in the user study.

ITS'12, November 11–14, 2012, Cambridge, Massachusetts, USA.

Figure 1. The SnapRail interface identifies the virtual elements under a physical object on a tabletop surface and places them along the ring-shaped rail widget. The user can also manipulate the virtual element by using with the widget.

RELATED WORK
Interactive environment-aware display bubbles [3] move projected display images by means of simple physical simulation until no more collisions exist. This technique enables the user to avoid obstacles on a tabletop. In this system, the screen changes its form as a whole according to the position of the physical objects, whereas our approach rearranges the virtual elements individually.

Vogel and Baudisch proposed a novel pointing technique, Shift [12], which creates a callout showing a copy of the occluded screen area in order to avoid occlusion. This technique and ours are similar in that they use a non-occluded space in a display. An occlusion-aware interface [13] lets the user see the information occluded by the user's own hands, for example, when the user inputs information directly with a pen input interface. This technique regards the user's hands as obstacles and uses a using a bubble-like callout approach to solve the problem. Leithinger and Haller introduced novel context menus for a cluttered tabletop setup. The user draws these context menus while avoiding obstacles on the tabletop [8]. Our system further automates the processes and also uses physical objects as handles to manipulate the virtual elements.

Steimle et al. investigated usage patterns for grouping and sorting physical and digital items on a tabletop surface [10]. In their case, sheets of paper were the physical objects and digital documents were the virtual elements. Javed et al. introduced occlusion management techniques, which included the rearrangement of virtual objects under a physical object [6]. However, they did not address virtual element manipulation with physical objects.

Some tangible user interface systems allow the user to manipulate virtual elements by rotating physical objects [5, 7]. For example, items in a pie menu that appears around a tangible object can be selected by rotating the object. However, forcing the user to arrange a physical object in a contrived way, such as having the grip of a coffee mug facing away from them, might be inconvenient. The SnapRail interface enables the user to manipulate virtual elements without rotating the actual coffee mug.

USER INTERFACE DESIGN

The SnapRail interface detects physical objects and user interactions (e,g., touch, drag) on an interactive tabletop surface. If it finds virtual elements occluded by the physical objects, the SnapRail interface places the virtual elements along the rail widget appearing around the physical object. With only this feature, the physical object is just an obstacle for the SnapRail interface. The system, however, tracks the physical object on the table, and the virtual elements snapped into the rail widget move together with the object. The object also serves as a handle for manipulating the virtual elements.

We focus on occlusion of a manipulable collection (selectable, movable, groupable, etc.) of virtual discrete elements such as icons. We do not address large virtual elements, such as maps. We often manipulate discrete elements on not only computer screens but also on tabletop displays. This paper addresses the occlusion avoidance problem with discrete elements on a tabletop display. In the SnapRail interface, physical objects are everyday objects, such as a wallet, a smart phone device or coffee mug.

Recovering the Visibility of Virtual Elements

Our system uses an infrared (IR) camera to track the location of a physical object placed on the tabletop. Then, a ring-shaped rail widget appears around the object. The diameter of a physical object plus the maximum size of the virtual objects determines the diameter of the rail. The virtual elements under the object snap into the rail widget after the rail widget appears (Figure 2). Each virtual element moves and snaps into the nearest part of the rail widget.

When two physical objects exist in close proximity and the rails touch each other, the two rail widgets are unified into one (Figure 2). The trigger for unification is the contact of the two rails. The unified rail widget consists of arcs and tangential lines enclosing the two objects. A tangential line is

Figure 2. Avoiding a physical object (top). Two rail widgets united (bottom).

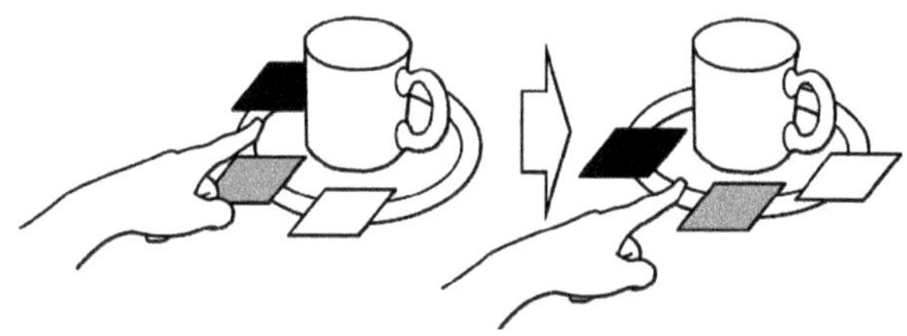

Figure 3. Scrolling virtual elements on the rail widget.

the outer common tangent for some two arcs and connects an arc with another one. This feature prevents a physical object from hiding the virtual elements on the rail widget around another physical object. Once the user separates the two objects, the unified rail widget is split automatically. The threshold distance for splitting of the rail widgets is the same as for their unification. Each element on the unified rail is uniformly distributed.

Manipulation of Virtual Elements

The user can manipulate the virtual elements snapped into the rail widget. The user touches the rail widget and drags it to slide all virtual elements on it (Figure 3).

The user can add and remove an additional virtual element to and from the rail widget by performing a drag-and-drop operation. This interaction enables the user to assign a physical object as a handle for grouping virtual elements (Figure 4). When the user slides a physical object on the surface, the rail widget and the virtual elements on it automatically follow the object (Figure 4). The virtual elements on the path where the physical object has been slid are snapped into the rail widget.

The group manipulation on the rail widget represents a unique approach for interaction on a tabletop. A variety of interaction designs is possible for object avoidance: virtual elements simply avoid as soon as the physical object is moved. We choose the group manipulation technique as a prototype because it gives the physical object an additional function, which might be useful for the user.

When the user lifts a physical object from the table, the rail widget disappears and the virtual elements are remapped.

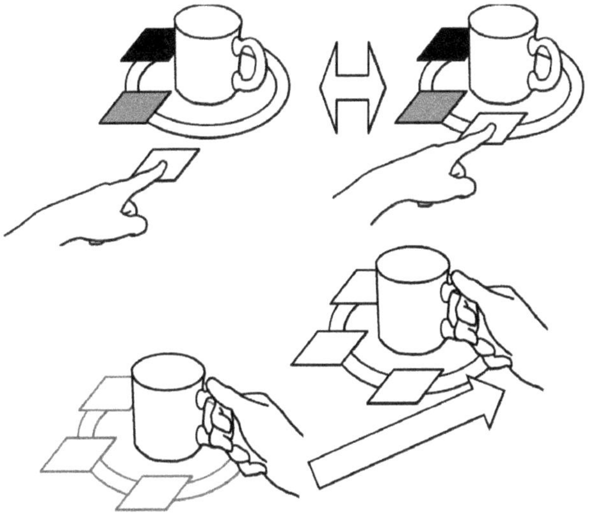

Figure 4. Snap and release (top). The rail widget automatically follows the object (bottom).

When elements are snapped into a rail, the system saves only the distance and angle from their original position. When they are remapped, each element moves the relative distance and angle back from its position on the rail regardless of ring modifications.

IMPLEMENTATION

We constructed a tabletop display device that detects a user's finger and physical objects. We used the low-cost method developed by Han [4] as the foundation of our tabletop device. The shape of the touch surfaces can be detected by an IR camera set under the panel. We needed to obtain two blobs separately: a finger blob and a physical object blob. We measured the blob sizes and determined that a blob with a diameter of less than 2 cm would be detected as a finger. This means that a finger-sized object is not detected as a physical object; however, a finger-sized object might not be considered as an obstacle on the table. We used the Qcam Pro 4000 (Logicool) as an IR camera for blob detection. It had a frame rate of 30 frames per second and pristine video quality. We replaced its infrared cut-off filter with an IR pass filter. The tabletop device was 80-cm wide, 50-cm long, and 105-cm high. The display was 62-cm wide and 46-cm long, with resolution of 1024 × 768 pixels. We built the system on the Windows 7 and .NET Framework.

USER STUDY

We conducted a preliminary laboratory-based user study. The aim of this test was to assess the potential of this interface and gather feedback from participants who practically used this interface.

Study Design

Participants

Five volunteer students (all males) with a mean age of 21.4 (range [21, 22], *SD* = 0.55) participated in this study. It took each participant 20-30 minutes to complete the task (described below). All of them had experience with a touch device, such as Android-enabled phones or iPhones. None of them, however, had used a tabletop computer before.

Figure 5. Two physical objects and 150 virtual cards on the SnapRail interface. Virtual cards are rearranged with the physical object.

Procedure

While participants stood around the tabletop computer, the experimenter gave an overview of the SnapRail interface and explained the details of each feature. The participants were then given a few minutes to try it out on their own before moving on to the main task. While the participants were performing the task, the experimenter carefully observed their behavior. We asked the participants to fill evaluate the usability using a 10-item questionnaire based on the System Usability Scale (SUS) [2] after the test. Finally, we conducted open interviews with the participants.

Task

The task was to find a specific set of cards among 150 virtual cards displayed on the tabletop computer screen. There were two physical objects on the surface, and participants were able to move these physical objects arbitrarily. The cards were numbered between 0 and 49 and there were three cards of each number in the set. All cards were 100 × 100 pixels. The physical objects were shaped in the form of a cylinder and were 10 cm in diameter and 15 cm in height. Participants were given two numbers and asked to start looking for the six cards among the 150 cards. The six cards were intentionally placed under or behind the physical object in order to force participants to use the SnapRail interface. The other cards were placed dispersed randomly. Each participant performed the task two times.

Result

Questionnaire results

The combined score from the SUS-based questionnaire was 76.7 on average (*SD* = 5.9). According to Bangor et al. [1], this score can be considered "good." Even though the SnapRail interface is still in the prototyping stage, the SUS score was high enough to show the potential for its practical use. Table 1 shows the scores for selected questionnaire items. Our questionnaire consisted of ten items and was based on the SUS (7-pt Likert scale; 7 is "Strongly agree," 1 is "Strongly disagree.").

#	Questionnaire items	Mean	SD
3	I thought the system was easy to use	6.4	0.55
9	I felt very confident using the system	6.2	1.10
10	I needed to learn many things before I could use this system	1.4	0.55

Table 1. The scores of selected questionnaire items

The participants reported that the SnapRail interface was easy-to-use (item 3) and that they felt confident using the interface (item 9). Most participants reported that they would be able to use it without training beforehand (item 10). The other questionnaire items also received positive scores. From these results, we consider the SnapRail interface to be evaluated as a usable device for the participants.

Qualitative result

We conducted open interviews with each participant after their trials. One participant said, *"The rail widget was good because the user does not have to move his or her eyes while searching for the virtual cards."* While searching for the virtual cards around the physical objects, it seemed to be natural for the participants to fix their eyes on the place through which the virtual cards passed when rotating the rail widget.

Another participant expressed a desire to be able to change the size of the rail widget flexibly and easily. In addition to this improvement, he requested a method for scrolling the virtual elements continuously because he had found having to scroll the virtual elements repeatedly to be tiring.

CONCLUSIONS

We presented a user interface widget for addressing occlusion by physical objects. This interface is aimed to allow the user to see the virtual elements occluded by the physical objects (visibility) and handle them (manipulability). We conducted a preliminary laboratory-based user study, and the SnapRail interface received a System Usability Scale rating of 76.7 from participants, who reported that they were satisfied with the SnapRail interface.

Our prototype implementation has some technical limitations. The touch surface is not sensitive enough, the size of each rail widget is fixed at the time it first appears, and the system cannot distinguish a small physical object from a finger. We are planning to improve the interface according to the feedback from the participants.

ACKNOWLEDGMENTS

This work was supported by JSPS KAKENHI Grant Number 24700112.

REFERENCES

1. Bangor, A., Kortum, P. T., and Miller, J. A. An Empirical Evaluation of the System Usability Scale. *Intl. Journal of Human-Computer Interaction*, 24(6):574–594, 2008.
2. Brooke, J. *SUS-A quick and dirty usability scale*. Taylor and Francis, London, 1996.
3. Cotting, D., and Gross, M. Interactive environment-aware display bubbles. In *Proc. UIST 2006,* ACM Press (2006), 245-254.
4. Han, J. Y. Low-cost multi-touch sensing through frustrated total internal reflection. In *Proc. UIST 2005*, ACM Press (2005), 115-118.
5. Ishii, H., and Ullmer, B. Tangible bits: towards seamless interfaces between people, bits and atoms. In *Proc. CHI 1997*, ACM Press (1997), 234-241.
6. Javed, W., Kim, K., Ghani, S., Elmqvist, and N. Evaluating Physical/Virtual Occlusion Management Techniques for Horizontal Displays. In *Proc. INTERACT2011*, (2011), 391-408.
7. Jordà, S., Geiger, G., Alonso, M., and Kaltenbrunner, M. The reacTable: exploring the synergy between live music performance and tabletop tangible interfaces. In *Proc. TEI 2007*, ACM Press (2007), 139-146.
8. Leithinger, D., and Haller, M. Improving Menu Interaction for Cluttered Tabletop Setups with User-Drawn Path Menus. In *Proc. TABLETOP 2007*, IEEE Press (2007), 121-128.
9. Seifried, T., Haller, M., Scott, S. D., Perteneder, F., Rendl, C., Sakamoto, D., and Inami, M. CRISTAL: a collaborative home media and device controller based on a multi-touch display. In *Proc. ITS 2009*, ACM Press (2009), 33-40.
10. Steimle, J., Khalilbeigi, M., Mu□lha□user, M., and Hollan, J. D. Physical and digital media usage patterns on interactive tabletop surfaces. In *Proc. ITS 2010*, ACM Press (2010), 167-176.
11. Tabard, A., Hincapié-Ramos, J. D., Esbensen, M., and Bardram, J. E. The eLabBench: an interactive tabletop system for the biology laboratory. In *Proc. ITS 2011*, ACM Press (2011), 202-211.
12. Vogel D., and Baudisch P. Shift: a technique for operating pen-based interfaces using touch. In *Proc. of CHI 2007*, ACM Press (2007), 657-666.
13. Vogel, D., and Balakrishnan, R. Occlusion-aware interfaces. In *Proc. CHI 2010*, ACM Press (2010), 263-272.

HandyWidgets: Local Widgets Pulled-out from Hands

Takuto Yoshikawa, Buntarou Shizuki, and Jiro Tanaka
University of Tsukuba, Japan
{yoshikawa,shizuki,jiro}@iplab.cs.tsukuba.ac.jp

ABSTRACT

Large multi-touch tabletops are useful for collocated collaborative work involving multiple users. However, applying traditional WIMP interfaces to tabletops causes problems where users cannot reach GUI elements, such as icons or buttons, on the opposite side with their hands, and they sometimes have difficulty in reading the content of GUI elements because their view does not match the orientation of the content. To solve these problems, we present HandyWidgets that are widgets localized around users' hands. The widgets are quickly invoked by a bimanual multi-touch gesture which we call "pull-out". This gesture also allows users to adjust the position, orientation, and size of the widgets, in a continuous manner after invocation.

ACM Classification Keywords

H.5.2 [Information interfaces and presentation]: User Interfaces. - Interaction styles, Graphical user interfaces.

Author Keywords

multi-touch; tabletops; gestures; bimanual interaction; crossing.

INTRODUCTION

Large multi-touch tabletops are useful for collocated collaborative work involving multiple users. Users surround tabletops extend their hands and touch the screen at their location. However, applying traditional WIMP interfaces to tabletops causes problems where users cannot reach GUI elements, such as icons or buttons, on the opposite side with their hands, and they sometimes have difficulty in reading the content of GUI elements because their view does not match the orientation of the content. These problems impose extra actions on users, such as having to extend their hands to reach the desired elements, walking toward them, or tilting their heads to read the content. Furthermore, the first two actions might obstruct other users' line of sight or their territory.

Our approach to these problems is to localize the GUI elements around each user's hand as illustrated in Figure 1. This paper presents HandyWidgets, which are widgets (combinations of GUI elements) that are localized around users' hands. The widget are quickly invoked by a bimanual multi-touch gesture which we call *pull-out*. This gesture also allows users to adjust the position, orientation, and size of the widgets, in a continuous manner after invocation.

ITS'12, November 11–14, 2012, Cambridge, Massachusetts, USA.

Figure 1. Overview of HandyWidgets. Each user can simultaneously display HandyWidgets.

RELATED WORK

Localization of widgets has previously been studied. In such research, where and how widgets appear and how users invoke widgets are important design factors and they have been intensively investigated.

Popup menus and localized widgets [1,4,5,7–10,12,16] can be displayed at any position, but their orientation is fixed. This is because their designs assume users interact with a constant view, and they have not been designed for tabletops where multiple-users touch the screen at each location. Research such as [2,3,6,13,15,17–20] allows users to not only determine the position of widgets, but also their orientation. Using orientation enables each user to match his/her view and the orientation of widgets.

In contrast, HandyWidgets' users can not only adjust the position and orientation of widgets, but also additional parameters, such as their size and type, through invocation gestures. Further, they can also adjust their parameters in a continuous manner by using the gestures, after they have invoked them.

On-screen buttons or physical buttons [7,16] are wide-spread techniques of invocation. Stroke gestures have also been used as invocation techniques [1,12,19] . Further, multi-stroke gestures have been used. Benko et al. utilized a secondary finger to invoke a widget [4]. The number of touches has also been used for invocation [15,20]. In addition, the rotation of pinch gestures has invoked widgets [9]. Additional states, which are provided by special devices, are also used for invocation. In [5, 8, 10] the hover states of styluses or hands have been used. Further, the contact shape of hands have invoked widgets [3,6,13,18]. Guimbretière and Nguyen used the gesture of a hovering hand for invocation [11].

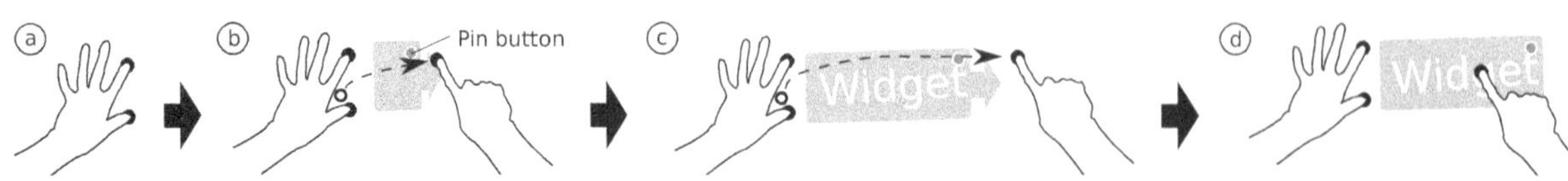

Figure 2. Basics of HandyWidgets. User a) touches tabletop with two fingers of non-dominant hand (base-fingers), b) places one finger of dominant hand (pull-finger) inside non-dominant hand, and drags pull-finger outside non-dominant hand to cross segment between base-fingers (base-segment), c) moves base-fingers and pull-finger to obtain desired position, orientation, and size of shown widget and d) releases pull-finger and executes command with widget using pull-finger.

HandyWidgets are invoked by a bimanual multi-stroke gesture combined with other gestures to avoid conflict with traditional gestures. HandyWidgets are robust to casual touching because users do not generally unintentionally perform this gesture. Moreover, this design requires no special devices and can be applied to conventional multi-touch screens that detect three or more coordinates of touches.

HANDYWIDGETS

HandyWidgets are invoked by a bimanual multi-touch gesture that we call pull-out. Widgets are displayed by using the following procedure (Figure 2), where the behavior of fingers in steps a) and b) is pull-out:

a) Touch the tabletop with two fingers of the non-dominant hand (base-fingers).

b) Place one finger of the dominant hand (pull-finger) inside the non-dominant hand, and drag the pull-finger outside the non-dominant hand to cross the segment between the base-fingers (base-segment).

c) Move the base-fingers and the pull-finger to obtain the desired position, orientation, and size of the shown widget.

d) Release the pull-finger, and execute a command with the widget using the pull-finger.

Once the pull-finger is lifted from the tabletop, the position, orientation, and size of the widget are fixed. Users can then interact with the widget. The widget is removed by releasing the base-fingers from the tabletop. This design provides ad-hoc use of HandyWidgets. However, if users need to keep the widget visible even after their fingers have been released, a pin button on the widget allows it to be pinned to the tabletop. This design allows users to interact with the widget with both hands in a relaxed way. In addition, it is possible to simultaneously display two or more widgets.

Features

Fluidity. Pull-out does not conflict with traditional multi-touch gestures, such as pinch or swipe, and can coexist with them. This means that pull-out represents a new interaction vocabulary. Thus, as seen in Figure 3, users can invoke a widget and fluidly execute commands with their dominant hand while using pinch gestures with their non-dominant hand to adjust the scale, rotation, or translation of objects.

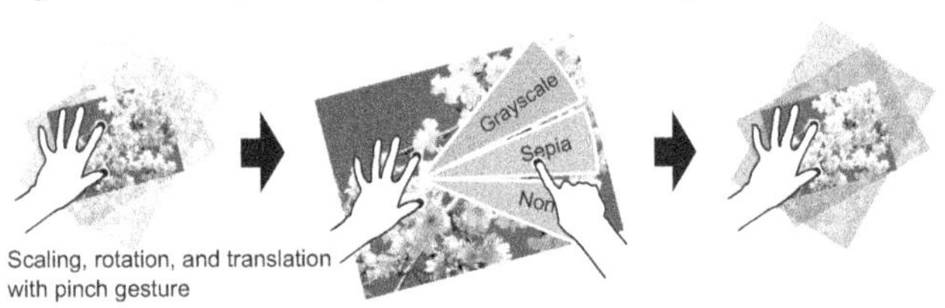

Figure 3. Fluid manipulation of objects. Note that non-dominant hand keeps pinching.

Robustness against casual touching. Pull-out is distinctive, that is, users do not generally perform this gesture unintentionally. Therefore, HandyWidgets are hard to be accidentally invoked by casual touching.

Occlusion aware design. The design of HandyWidgets and pull-out gestures avoids occlusion in a similar manner to those found in previous works [6, 13, 18, 19], where the interaction technique itself has been designed to avoid the widget from being occluded. The hands that invoke widgets in HandyWidgets do not occlude the widgets because they appear between the hands. Because dragging the base-fingers can also adjust the position, orientation, and size of the widgets, it helps users to invoke widgets even if they are near the edge of the screen (Figure 4).

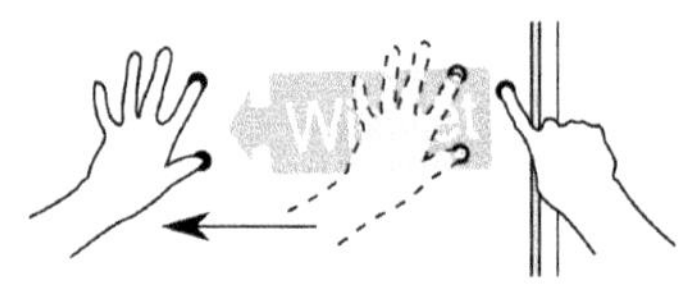

Figure 4. Showing widget near the edge of the screen.

ADVANCED INTERACTION DESIGN

This section presents advanced interaction design that enhances the basics of HandyWidgets we previously described.

Pull-in. Dragging an object with the pull-finger to cross base-segments can be used as a gesture (Figure 5). We called this gesture *pull-in*. Users can copy objects to their clipboards with pull-in, and they can then choose a copied object from the widget invoked by pull-out and paste it.

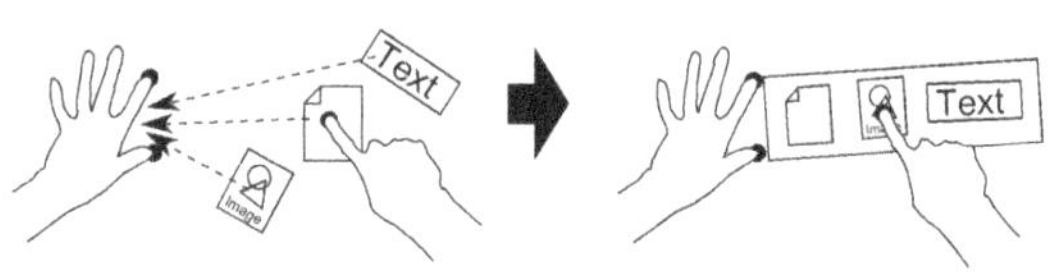

Figure 5. Pull-in.

Object specific widget. While pull-out on the background can be assigned to invoke a general widget, pull-out on a foreground object can be assigned to invoke its specific widget. It is possible in this way to display an effect menu on an image while a tool set is being displayed on the background, for example.

Various pull-outs. Various pull-outs are available. This enables users to select types of widgets corresponding to each pull-out. For example, the additional use of single crossing with two pull-fingers (Figure 6) or double crossing with one pull-finger (Figure 7) enables users to display a system menu with the former and a keyboard with the latter, while basic pull-out invokes a tool set. Thus, users can invoke various widgets using various pull-outs depending on their purposes.

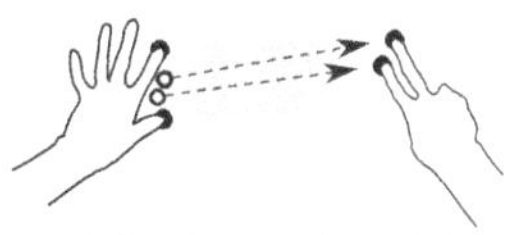

Figure 6. Single crossing with two pull-fingers.

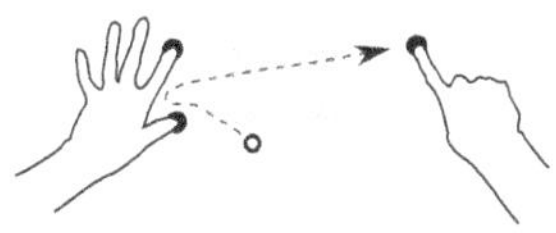

Figure 7. Double crossing with one pull-finger.

Figure 8. Widget that transforms from Numeric keypad into QWERTY keyboard.

Dynamic widgets. Users can dynamically transform the structure of a widget according to the positional relation of a base-segment and a pull-finger, which determines the position, orientation, and size of the widget. This enables adaptive use of the widget depending on the required functions. Figure 8 shows such usage, where the widget transforms from a Numeric keypad into a QWERTY keyboard. While users can input numbers quickly with the former, the latter is available for long texts.

EXPLORING DESIGN SPACE

Pull-out gestures not only allow users to determine the position, orientation, and size of widgets, but they also add a degree of freedom to the design space of widgets. We implemented four *widget models* to explore the design space of HandyWidgets. Each model is outlined in Figure 9.

The Drawer Model (Figure 9a) is the model in which items of the widget are displayed from one side according to the length between the base-segment's center and the pull-finger, which we called the distance-pulled. In this model, placing frequently used items on one side of the widget allows fast access to the items, while providing on-demand access to the items rarely used by opening it further. This model is suitable for a tool palette in which frequency of use differs greatly between items, such as those in painting or CAD applications.

The Popup Model (Figure 9b) is the model in which the widget is immediately displayed when pull-out is performed, regardless of the distance-pulled. Although this model causes occlusion by the user's hand, it minimizes the time to access the widget. The model is thus suitable for widgets that only include some frequently-used items. We used the model for pie-menus, which can be used quickly without depending on visual cues once users have become familiar with them.

The Scale Model (Figure 9c) is the model in which the widget is scaled according to the distance-pulled. In this model, users can adjust the size of widgets, which is needed to determine their area on the screen, by using pull-out. The model is suitable for widgets that require definitions of areas, such as zoom lenses or shape tools.

The Transform Model (Figure 9d) is the model in which the structure of the widget dynamically transforms according to the distance-pulled. This model is suitable for widgets in which users want to modify usage depending on their purpose such as that illustrated in Figure 8.

While these four models only utilize the distance-pulled, more parameters are available, e.g., the rotation and length of a base-segment. This indicates that HandyWidgets have a broad design space.

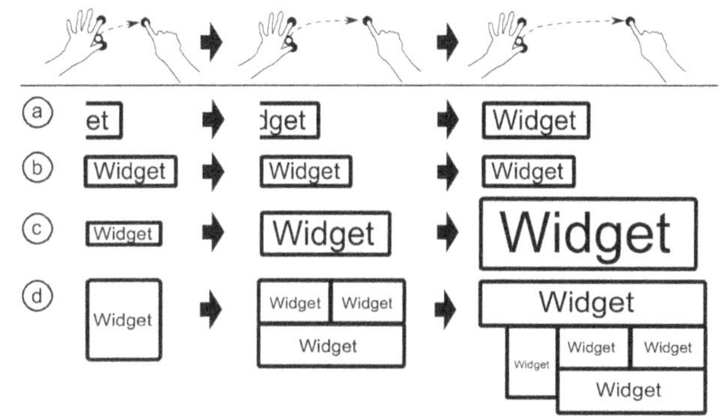

Figure 9. Four models of widgets we implemented.

IMPLEMENTATION

Invoking HandyWidgets needs to recognize the crossings of pull-fingers through base-segments. Base-segments are defined to fit the users' hand shapes shown in Figure 10. This technique can be applied to conventional multi-touch screens that detect three or more coordinates of touches. We describe the recognition technique below.

First, the system tries to find the nearest touch point within a threshold distance (15 cm in our current implementation) for each touch point. If such points are found, then the system defines the segment between them as a base-segment. These segments are updated dynamically. Second, the crossing of pull-finger is detected. The system regards touch points that are within a half length of the base-segment from its center as pull-fingers. Touches farther than the threshold from the other touches are also regarded as pull-fingers. Next, crossing through the base-segments of pull-fingers is detected. After that, the system estimates users' locations. Lines through base-segments roughly point to users when they place their index finger and thumb on the tabletop as base-fingers. Based on this observation, our system defines the nearest intersections of the lines with four sides of the screen as users' locations. Finally, the system determines which hand has pulled out the widgets by using the users' locations. If a pull-finger has crossed a base-segment from left to right from the viewpoint of each user's location, then our system determines the right hand has pulled out the widget, and vice versa. This allows users to pull-out widgets from both right and left hands.

HandyWidgets are rendered within the rectangular area between the base-segment and the pull-finger. Our system defines the side of the area nearest to the users' location to be the widgets' floor to display the widgets. This makes their orientation suit the users' view.

There have been some multi-touch systems that have used the segment defined by users (e.g., [20]), but we utilized the segments as targets of crossing.

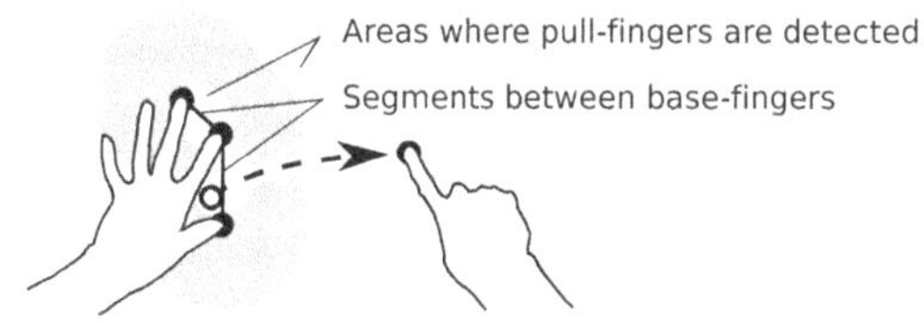

Figure 10. Definitions of base-segments, and detection of pull-finger.

APPLICATION

We developed an application (Figure 1), similar to [14], that supports collocated collaborative work such as discussions or meetings. In this application, each user can annotate images or text documents. Users can invoke HandyWidgets at any position and orientation, and they display images or text documents in a shared folder with file browsers embedded in the widgets. Annotations by painting or texts, and zoom lenses are also available with the widgets. Users can scale, rotate, or translate objects. Objects including images, texts, and paintings can be stored in a shared clipboard by using pull-in.

Object specific widgets are available. Pull-out with one finger single crossing on images or annotations invokes a pie-menu of the Popup Model, which determines image effects, or background colors. Moreover, pull-out with one finger single crossing on the background invokes a tool set of the Drawer Model; pull-out with two fingers single crossing on the background invokes a system menu of the Drawer Model; pull-out with one finger double crossing on the background invokes a keyboard (Figure 8) of the Scale and Transform Model.

EXHIBITION

We demonstrated a prototype system at an open house at our university. We used a 60-inch tabletop, and prepared a simple diagram-drawing application with HandyWidgets. Twenty three participants used the system and their behaviors were recorded during the exhibition. Participants used the system simultaneously with one of the authors. Many participants failed to invoke the widget at first because they did not know how far they should place the pull-finger between base-fingers. However, they immediately learned how to do it after being instructed to place their finger further. This observation may indicate the ease of learning HandyWidgets. Still, accidental invocations were observed when users quickly swiped more than three fingers, and invocation failures were also observed. However, these problems seemed to be due to failures in finger detection by the optical multi-touch display we used, because when we carried out tests with a smaller, more accurate multi-touch display, no problems were observed.

DISCUSSION

Fatigue is an issue that needs to be further studied because pull-out gestures involve three fingers, although we did not observe any fatigue in users at the exhibition. Our system allows users to touch the tabletop with more than two fingers of their non-dominant hand, thus they can stably pull-out and use widgets with less fatigue by allowing their non-dominant hand touch with all fingers for invocation. Further, allowing users to place their palms in contact with the tabletop will also reduce fatigue.

CONCLUSIONS AND FUTURE WORK

We presented HandyWidgets, which represented widgets localized around hands. The widgets are invoked by a distinctive bimanual multi-touch gesture, called pull-out, which can coexist with traditional gestures and is hard to be accidentally invoked by casual touches. Moreover, various pull-outs can be defined, each of which can be used to invoke their corresponding widgets.

One direction for future work is to explore the properties of pull-out. We will use more parameters, such as the rotation and length of base-segments, to add more degrees of freedom to widgets. Another direction we plan is to utilize the geometry of hands. This will realize four widgets corresponding to four base-segments defined by five fingers. It can thus allow users to relate spatial memory to widgets. Moreover, arranging the elements of a widget along the strokes, similiar to [17], of pull-out achieves ergonomical design, because the strokes follow the range of motion of one's arm and hand. We could, for example, develop a curved tool set or keyboard.

REFERENCES

1. G. Apitz and F. Guimbretière. CrossY: A crossing-based drawing application. In *UIST '04*, pp. 3–12.
2. N. Banovic, F. C. Y. Li, D. Dearman, K. Yatani, and K. N. Truong. Design of unimanual multi-finger pie menu interaction. In *ITS '11*, pp. 120–129.
3. T. Bartindale, C. Harrison, P. Olivier, and S. E. Hudson. SurfaceMouse: supplementing multi-touch interaction with a virtual mouse. In *TEI '11*, pp. 293–296.
4. H. Benko, A. D. Wilson, and P. Baudisch. Precise selection techniques for multi-touch screens. In *CHI '06*, pp. 1263–1272.
5. A. Bragdon, R. DeLine, K. Hinckley, and M. R. Morris. Code Space: touch + air gesture hybrid interactions for supporting developer meetings. In *ITS '11*, pp. 212–221.
6. P. Brandl, J. Leitner, T. Seifried, M. Haller, B. Doray, and P. To. Occlusion-aware menu design for digital tabletops. In *CHI EA '09*, pp. 3223–3228.
7. J. Callahan, D. Hopkins, M. Weiser, and B. Shneiderman. An empirical comparison of pie vs. linear menus. In *CHI '88*, pp. 95–100.
8. G. Fitzmaurice, A. Khan, R. Pieké, B. Buxton, and G. Kurtenbach. Tracking Menus. In *UIST '03*, pp. 71–79.
9. D. Freeman and R. Balakrishnan. Tangible Actions. In *ITS '11*, pp. 87–96.
10. T. Grossman, K. Hinckley, P. Baudisch, M. Agrawala, and R. Balakrishnan. Hover Widgets: using the tracking state to extend the capabilities of pen-operated devices. In *CHI '06*, pp. 861–870.
11. F. Guimbretière and C. Nguyen. Bimanual marking menu for near surface interactions. In *CHI '12*, pp. 825–828.
12. K. Hinckley, P. Baudisch, G. Ramos, and F. Guimbretiere. Design and analysis of delimiters for selection-action pen gesture phrases in Scriboli. In *CHI '05*, pp. 451–460.
13. K. Hinckley, K. Yatani, M. Pahud, N. Coddington, J. Rodenhouse, A. Wilson, H. Benko, and B. Buxton. Pen + Touch = New Tools. In *UIST '10*, pp. 27–36.
14. U. Hinrichs, S. Carpendale, and S. D. Scott. Evaluating the effects of fluid interface components on tabletop collaboration. In *AVI '06*, pp. 27–34.
15. K. Kurihara, N. Nagano, Y. Watanabe, Y. Fujimura, A. Minaduki, H. Hayashi, and Y. Tutiya. Toward localizing audiences' gaze using a multi-touch electronic whiteboard with spiemenu. In *IUI '11*, pp. 379–382.
16. G. Kurtenbach and W. Buxton. User learning and performance with marking menus. In *CHI '94*, pp. 258–264.
17. D. Leithinger and M. Haller. Improving menu interaction for cluttered tabletop setups with user-drawn path menus. In *TABLETOP '07*, 121–128.
18. J. Rekimoto. SmartSkin: An infrastructure for freehand manipulation on interactive surfaces. In *CHI '02*, pp. 113–120.
19. V. Roth and T. Turner. Bezel Swipe: conflict-free scrolling and multiple selection on mobile touch screen devices. In *CHI '09*, pp. 1523–1526.
20. S. Strothoff, D. Valkov, and K. Hinrichs. Triangle Cursor: interactions with objects above the tabletop. In *ITS '11*, pp. 111–119.

Pseudo-Weight: Making Tabletop Interaction with Virtual Objects More Tangible

Chantal Keller
INRIA Saclay–Île-de-France at École polytechnique
Laboratoire d'informatique (LIX), UMR 7161
F-91128, Palaiseau, France
Chantal.Keller@inria.fr

Renaud Blanch
Université Joseph Fourier–Grenoble 1
Laboratoire d'Informatique de Grenoble, UMR 5217
F-38041, Grenoble, France
blanch@imag.fr

ABSTRACT
In this paper we show that virtual objects manipulated on a tabletop interaction device can be augmented to provide the illusion they have a weight. This weight offers a supplemental channel to provide information about graphical objects without cluttering the visual display. To create such a *pseudo-weight* illusion on a passive device, the pressure applied with the fingers during the interaction has to be captured. We show that this pressure can be estimated without hardware modification on some touch sensitive tabletop setups (e.g., MERL's DiamondTouch). Two controlled experiments show that *pseudo-weight* is perceived effectively. The first one demonstrates that users, without training and without previous knowledge of the system, can accurately rank virtual objects according to their pseudo-weights, provided they are sufficiently distinct. The second controlled experiment investigates more formally the relation between the pseudo-weight and the actual perception of the users.

Keywords: Tabletop interaction, pseudo-weight.

ACM Classification: H.5.2 [**Information Interfaces and Presentation (e.g., HCI)**]: User Interfaces – *Graphical user interfaces, Input devices and strategies.*

INTRODUCTION
Over the past few years, tabletop interaction turned from prototypes into commercial products (e.g., the MERL DiamondTouch [4], or the Philips Entertaible [6]), and the software editor Microsoft Corp. has coined the term "surface computing" to refer its first touch-enabled products: the Surface table from 2007. These systems are significant steps towards the merge of the digital and physical worlds envisioned twenty seven years ago by Krueger et al. [8].

However the illusion of manipulating real objects on a table is not yet complete. Some physical properties such as tactile and haptic feedback are still missing when users are interacting with virtual objects. To provide feedback through these mechanical perception channels, the output device would have to be actuated. The hardware involved would be more complex, consume more power, and be more prone to failure.

In this article, we investigate the psychophysics of a software technique that creates the illusion of a weight for virtual objects. This weight is a pseudo-perception: the channel by which the feedback is provided is not the regular one (tactile or haptic) but a substituted perception channel (namely vision) coupled to a passive (force) sensor.

We first review previous works related to our research. Then we present how we have implemented the pseudo-weight on a tabletop interaction device. Two experiments are then reported: the first one demonstrates that users perceive the pseudo-weight and can use it to accurately order virtual objects. The second experiment characterizes more formally the relation between the pseudo-weight assigned to objects and its perception by the user.

RELATED WORK
Previous works have introduced the notion of pseudo-haptic feedback: haptic properties such as stiffness, friction, or feeling forces, bumps or holes, can be simulated without haptic devices. Pseudo-haptic friction/stiffness feedback was initially obtained by coupling a force sensor with a perturbed visual feedback [10]. Sugimoto et al. and Lecuyer et al. proposed to simulate forces and bumps or holes by simply varying the control to display ratio of the cursor [14, 9]. With tabletop interaction, such techniques can not be used because of the colocation of the cursor and the finger.

Early work on using the pressure on a touch sensitive device dates back to the eighties (e.g., [2]). But even recent works (e.g., [1, 12]) use the pressure as a supplemental input channel only. The coupling of the pressure with a tactile feedback is investigated by Rekimoto & Schwesig [13], but they used an actuated device to provide the feedback. Physical constraints on tabletop interaction is investigated by Patten & Ishii [11], but with mechanically enforced constraints. More recently, physical models have been used to add plausible collision and friction [5] but without using the pressure as input. ShapeTouch [3] already explored the design space for interactions using pseudo-weight (which Cao et al. call *virtual force*), but we are rather focused on understanding the psychophysics of this kind of interactions.

PSEUDO-WEIGHT
In order to substitute a sensory channel with a pseudo-perception, we have to understand the actual perception. For doing so, we have observed users moving real objects with different weights (e.g., sheet of paper, books, etc.) on the surface of a table using one finger. The actual physics in-

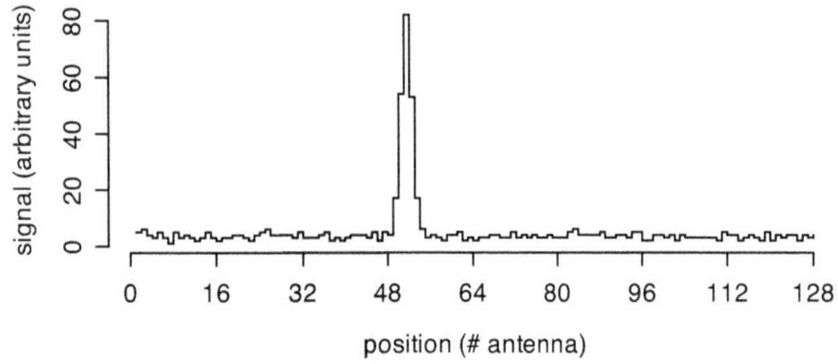

Figure 1: Typical signal reported by the MERL DiamondTouch antennas when a finger touches the table.

volved is surprisingly complex, drawing upon tribology, the science of friction. In our particular case, we observed two distinct modes: either the pressure on the object is sufficient, the object sticks to the finger and follows its movements, or the pressure is not sufficient, and the object sticks to the table and does not move regardless of the finger movements.

To simulate this behaviour, we have solved three problems, two of them were identified a priori while we did not anticipate the third one:

- capture the pressure applied with the finger to the table during the interaction (technological challenge);
- create the pseudo-weight illusion by simulating the behaviour of the virtual objects according to this pressure and to the weight assigned to them (design challenge); and
- provide insights that the system is reliable to avoid misinterpretation of an immobile object (design challenge).

Capturing Pressure

To conduct this study, we have used a MERL DiamondTouch coupled with a video projector. The DiamondTouch does not include any pressure sensor but we found that pressure can be estimated from the raw data captured for finger tracking. Fingers position is achieved by detecting variations of the capacitance caused by the fingers in an array of antennas embedded in the table [4]. We observed that the capacitance varies according to the surface of the finger in contact with the table. In turn, this surface varies according to the squeeze applied to the table. Since the DiamondTouch API gives access to the row values read from the antennas (Figure 1), we have access to a quantity that varies according to the pressure. This quantity is not a real measure of the pressure, but it allows us to create the pseudo-weight illusion as the experiments described below show (measuring the real relation is not an option because placing a force sensor between the finger and the table disturbs the capacitance measure).

The DiamondTouch uses two orthogonal arrays of antennas that produce two monodimensional images of the table projected on the x-axis and y-axis. These images consist of 128 (resp. 96) values measured periodically by the vertical (resp. horizontal) antennas. Figure 1 shows the vertical antennas that give a projection of the table on the horizontal axis. The reported values are integers ranging from 0 to 255. We consider the x-axis array only since it provides sufficient data to compute the pressure. We define the pressure, in arbitrary units, as the sum of the values that pass a threshold of 10. This threshold is necessary because the signal reported by the antennas is noisy, and is never a true 0 even in the absence of contact on the table. The sum performs a spatial integration of the signal so as to cover the whole contact surface (the spatial resolution of the antennas grid is 5 mm, and a finger typically activates 4 successive antennas).

Creating the Pseudo-Weight

Based on our preliminary observations, we have implemented the pseudo-weight by adding a *weight* attribute to each draggable object. At the beginning of an attempt to drag an object (when a finger touching the table enters an object) the current pressure is compared to the weight of the object. The object starts to move only when the pressure exerted exceeds its own weight. This makes heavy objects hard to move whereas light objects are easily dragged as in real life.

Pressure is monitored continuously during dragging. Dragging ends when the pressure falls below the weight of the object reduced by a constant. This constant is introduced so that the noise in the signal does not affect the interaction. It also models the hysteresis observed in the physical world known as static friction: friction forces are stronger when the object is immobile than when it has started to slide.

The objects are thus made sensitive to the pressure: according to their weight, the user has to drag them more firmly if they are heavier. Since more effort is needed to move the heavy object, the user should perceive it and associate this perception to a physical attribute of the virtual objects.

Providing Visual Feedback of the System Reliability

When we first confronted naive users to the system previously described, some of them did not perceive anything. They interpreted the fact that some objects did not move when they tried to drag them as a malfunction of the finger tracking. We did not anticipate that our users are used to tactile systems, like automatic dispensers, that often miss user inputs. We solved this issue by providing an additional feedback: a circle is projected at the position of the tracked fingers. Since the finger tracking is very robust, these circles follow the fingers in real time without noticeable lag. This makes the user unconsciously aware of the reliability of the tracking system and re-enables the illusion.

EXPERIMENTAL VALIDATION

To test our hypothesis, we have conducted two experiments. 12 master students volunteered to take part in this study, they all did both of them. The first experiment is designed to check that the pseudo-weight is perceived and that it can be used as an output channel for a digital table. The second experiment is designed to explore more deeply the relationship between the pseudo-weight and its perception.

Proof of Concept

Our initial informal experiments convinced us that the pseudo-weight was actually working, but we wanted to evaluate if (and how) a user would perceive the effects of the system if she is not aware of the system internals. The participants were only told that they "would take part in an experiment designed to evaluate a new interaction technique on a digital table". Each one was familiarized individually with finger interaction on the tabletop display by using a non pseudo-weight enhanced photo-shuffler application until she was able to manipulate the photos easily.

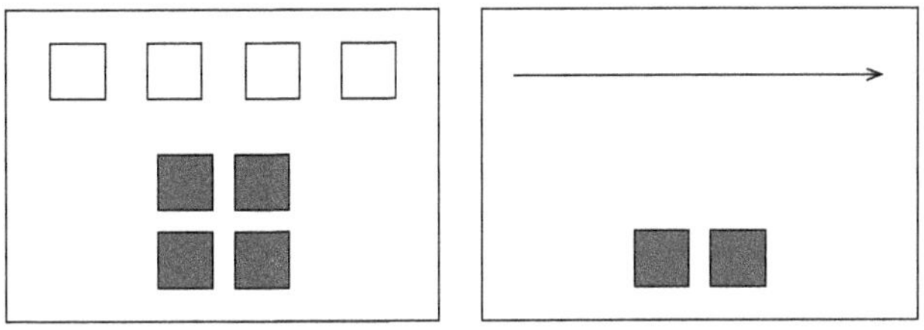

Figure 2: Experimental setups. (left) first: 4 places at the top, 4 blue squares to order at the bottom; (right) second: 2 squares to place on an axis.

Setup When the participant is ready, the experiment begins. A text displayed on the table invites him to sit conformably and provides the following instructions:

> "In the next screens, 4 squares looking identical will be presented together with 4 places to put them. The squares behave differently while interacting with them. You can try to manipulate the square below."

Four draggable squares with different weights are placed at this place. The instructions then continue:

> "Please move the squares into the places, and arrange them from left to right in growing order. When you are done, press the *next* button to start a new task."

As our goal was to test if the pseudo-weight is perceived by untaught people, the text was intentionally left vague and did not explicitly state what is the difference between the squares nor which criterion should be used to sort the squares.

When the participant depresses the *go* button, a series of 10 trials starts. Each one presents the same visual aspect: 4 blue squares grouped in front of the user and 4 places horizontally aligned on the top of the screen (see Figure 2 left). For each trial, the weights of the square are evenly distributed between 2 random extremal values. These values are constrained in a range compatible with the interaction determined a priori.

Results After the tests, the participants were asked to name the criterion they used to order the squares. Two of them did not notice any effect and could not find a name, but the 10 others cited: "force", "friction", "power" or "surface". Those terms are all related to the action of the user rather than to a property of the objects. When we suggested "weight" as a characteristic of the objects, the participants agreed upon it. We choose this term because it also has an abstract meaning.

Despite involving only 120 trials, the qualitative results are interesting. All of the 10 participants who felt something ordered spontaneously the objects in ascending weights from the left to the right: the object on the left is lighter than the one on the right in more than 70% of their trials. When considering all the participants, the heaviest object is correctly placed 66.67% of the time, the lightest one 60%. There is more confusion for the average objects: the second heaviest (resp. lightest) object is correctly placed 54.17% (resp. 51.67%) of the time. The whole 4 objects are positioned in the correct order 39.17% of the time.

These results depend highly on the difference between the weights of the objects presented simultaneously. If we redo the same analysis considering only the half of the data produced by the trials where the weights were the most separated, the order is correct 48.33% of the time. The heaviest (resp. lightest) object is correct 81.67% (resp. 68%) of the time (61.67% and 58.33% for the two other objects).

These results show that users perceive the pseudo-weight without being taught and that some information can be transmitted through this channel. It also shows that the more the weights are separated, the more they are discernible.

Controlled Experiment

The goal of the second experiment is to better understand the perception of the pseudo-weight.

Setup The experiment is roughly similar to the previous one, but only two squares are presented to the participant at each trial, and a directed axis is displayed at the top of the screen (Figure 2 right). The axis is depicted to the user as an axis "where the lightest object should be on the left side, and the heaviest on the right side". The participant is then instructed to place the two squares on the horizontal axis according to their respective weights.

Two factors are used to determine the weights of the squares: the median weight (w) and the difference between the two weights (Δw). The two variables have three possible values: $w_0 = 80$, $w_1 = 95$, $w_2 = 110$ (arbitrary units); and $\Delta w_0 = 4$, $\Delta w_1 = 8$, $\Delta w_2 = 12$. Nine possible couples of weights are then possible ($w_i \pm \Delta_j/2$, $(i, j) \in [0,2]^2$). To balance order effects, a pseudo-random series of 81 trials consisting of 9 time each couple was constructed using a 9×9 latin square.

Results The final abscissas of the light and heavy squares (x_l and x_h) are recorded and two dependent variables are computed: the median abscissa around which the two objects have been positioned $x = (x_l + x_h)/2$; and the signed deviation that separates them $\Delta x = x_h - x_l$.

We first test the hypothesis that the squares are placed in the right order (i.e. $\Delta x > 0$). As in the first experiment, there is a lot of inter-subject variability: the least effective participant is only slightly better than random (55,56% of correct ordering), whereas the highest success rate was 90,12%. On average, the success rate is $68.52 \pm 9.56\%$[1]. A repeated measure analysis of variance (ANOVA) shows that the only significant effect on the success is the difference between the weight of the two objects Δw ($F = 10.69$[2]).

The mean position x also depends highly on the user. A repeated measure ANOVA shows that the main factor affecting the position x is the weight w ($F = 175.12$). Figure 3 shows x as a function of w with the means connected. They form a quasi-straight line ($r^2 > 0.998$ for the linear fit). Similarly, Δx is essentially a function of Δw ($F = 11.62$). The linear fit is also very good ($r^2 > 0.98$).

These results show that the discriminability of two pseudo-weights is directly linked to the amplitude of the difference separating the weights, which was expected. A more notable result is that the mapping between the weight assigned to the

[1] $m \pm \sigma$: the mean (m) and standard deviation (σ) across users.
[2] Reported F statistics all have a p value smaller than 0.0001.

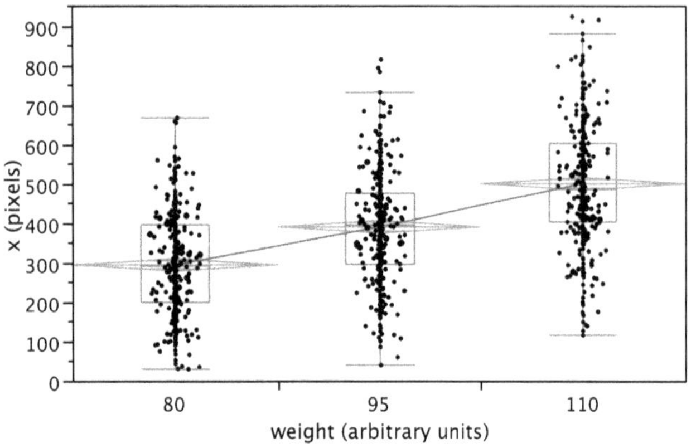

Figure 3: Position vs. weight (diamonds show 95% confidence intervals, box plots .25 and .75 quantiles).

objects and the position where the participants put them is linear. It means that the arbitrary weight scale created by our software implementation of the pseudo-weight is the same as the psychophysical scale the user has modeled after her experience of the real world. This result validates a posteriori our definition of the pressure as a function of the capacitance signal, and the physical model on which we have based the pseudo-weight implementation.

CONCLUSION & FUTURE DIRECTIONS

We have shown that virtual objects can be augmented with a pseudo-weight on a passive touch sensitive surface provided that pressure can be monitored. We have shown that on a regular DiamondTouch table, this information can be deduced from the raw capacitance. We have shown that this input channel, coupled with an adequate visual feedback, can provide a pseudo-perception. In addition, pseudo-weight conveys information: our experiments show that it allows users to rank objects which are visually identical.

The technique has some weaknesses. The first one is that the real tactile signal is contradictory with the simulated behaviour: the real object below the finger (the table) is immobile, even when the virtual objects is dragged. This limits the palpability of the illusion, but this limitation seems impossible to overcome without introducing tangible objects [11] or active feedback [7]. The second weakness is that the perception scale depends on the user. Several factors affect the range of pressure computed from the capacitance: a different finger size or a dryer skin changes the capacitance while the same real pressure is exerted. A sensor really responsive to the pressure would solve this problem.

This technique is nonetheless promising since it offers a supplemental channel to provide information about graphical objects without cluttering the visual display. It can be used to transmit weights in a broad sense i.e. any attribute that can be mapped on a continuous scale (e.g., for an icon, the size of the file it represents). We have observed that, contrarily to other interaction techniques involving a smart coupling in the perception-action loop, the pseudo-weight is noticeable for spectators of the interaction. They easily interpret the visual feedback provided by the degree of flexion of the finger as it is totally natural. This property is valuable since tabletop devices are often used for collaborative work.

In the future, we would like to study how the pseudo-weight could be exploited in collaborative environments (e.g., making objects harder to move if they are in someone else focus could improve awareness of such situations). On a more theoretical side, studying how the visual clues (e.g., size, shape or texture of the objects) interfere with the pseudo-weight could provide interesting results.

ACKNOWLEDGEMENTS

The authors would like to thank F. Bérard for the GIL toolkit[3] used to conduct the experiments and S. Coquillart.

REFERENCES

1. H. Benko, A. D. Wilson, and P. Baudisch. Precise selection techniques for multi-touch screens. In *Proc. CHI'06*, pages 1263–1272, 2006.
2. W. Buxton, R. Hill, and P. Rowley. Issues and techniques in touch-sensitive tablet input. In *Proc. SIGGRAPH'85*, pages 215–224, 1985.
3. X. Cao, A. D. Wilson, R. Balakrishnan, K. Hinckley, and S. E. Hudson. ShapeTouch: Leveraging contact shape on interactive surfaces. In *Proc. Tabletop'08*, pages 129–136, 2008.
4. P. Dietz and D. Leigh. DiamondTouch: a multi-user touch technology. In *Proc. UIST'01*, pages 219–226, 2001.
5. O. Hilliges, A. Butz, S. Izadi, and A. D. Wilson. Interaction on the tabletop: Bringing the physical to the digital. In *Proc. Tabletops'10*, pages 189–221, 2010.
6. G. Hollemans, T. Bergman, V. Buil, K. van Gelder, M. Groten, J. Hoonhout, T. Lashina, E. van Loenen, and S. van de Wijdeven. Entertaible: Multi-user multi-object concurrent input. In *Adj. proc. UIST'06*, pages 55–56, 2006.
7. J. Kildal. 3D-Press: haptic illusion of compliance when pressing on a rigid surface. In *Proc. ICMI'10*, 2010.
8. M. W. Krueger, T. Gionfriddo, and K. Hinrichsen. VIDEOPLACE–an artificial reality. In *Proc. CHI'85*, pages 35–40, 1985.
9. A. Lécuyer, J.-M. Burkhardt, and L. Etienne. Feeling bumps and holes without a haptic interface: the perception of pseudo-haptic textures. In *Proc. CHI'04*, pages 239–246, 2004.
10. A. Lécuyer, S. Coquillart, A. Kheddar, P. Richard, and P. Coiffet. Pseudo-haptic feedback: Can isometric input devices simulate force feedback? In *Proc. VR'00*, pages 83–90, 2000.
11. J. Patten and H. Ishii. Mechanical constraints as computational constraints in tabletop tangible interfaces. In *Proc. CHI'07*, pages 809–818, 2007.
12. G. A. Ramos and R. Balakrishnan. Pressure marks. In *Proc. CHI'07*, pages 1375–1384, 2007.
13. J. Rekimoto and C. Schwesig. PreSenseII: bi-directional touch and pressure sensing interactions with tactile feedback. In *Ext. abstr. CHI'06*, pages 1253–1258, 2006.
14. M. Sugimoto and I. Fujishiro. Enhancement of virtual interaction devices using pseudo force sensation. In *Sketches and Applications, SIGGRAPH'00*, 2000.

[3] http://gil.imag.fr, GIL: a Toolkit for Novel Human-Computer Interactions.

Touch, Click, Navigate: Comparing Tabletop and Desktop Interaction for Map Navigation Tasks

Elham Beheshti, Anne Van Devender, Michael S. Horn
Computer Science and Learning Sciences
Northwestern University, Evanston, IL
beheshti@u.northwestern.edu

ABSTRACT
Multi-touch tabletops and desktop computers offer different affordances for interaction with digital maps. Previous research suggests that these differences may affect how a person navigates in the world. To test this idea we randomly assigned 22 participants to one of two conditions. Participants used the interfaces to complete a series of tasks in which they interacted with a digital map of a fictitious city and then attempted to navigate through a corresponding virtual world. However, based on participant performance, we find no evidence that interface type affects navigation ability. We discuss map navigation strategies across the two conditions and analyze multi-touch gestures used by participants in the tabletop condition. Finally, based on these analyses, we consider implications for the design of interactive map interfaces.

Author Keywords
Map interfaces; spatial ability; navigation; multi-touch tabletops; interactive surfaces; gestures.

ACM Classification Keywords
H.5.2 Information interfaces and presentation (e.g., HCI): User Interfaces - *Input devices and strategies (e.g., mouse, touchscreen), Interaction styles.*

INTRODUCTION
As multi-touch tabletops make their way into public spaces such as museums, hotels, and travel agencies [1, 13, 14, 19], we expect that digital map applications specifically designed for interactive tabletops will become increasingly common. These tabletop interfaces will likely differ from more general-purpose map applications (e.g. maps on mobile devices) in several key ways. First, they will be situated in a specific location and context. As such, the maps provided to users might be confined to a specific geographical area such as a theme park or a historical district. Second, the interfaces will be tailored for collaborative, walk-up-and-use scenarios. Finally, they will be customized for that given location, showing maps of both indoor and outdoor spaces, and providing information on specific points of interest. For example, maps might show wait times for rides at an amusement park, menus for restaurants near a hotel, or flight status information at an airport. For these reasons tabletop map interfaces might be thought of as specialized information kiosks.

Previous studies of geographical map interfaces have considered design challenges such as economizing limited screen real estate on mobile phones [23], supporting social navigation through connected devices [3], combining mobile devices and public displays [5, 24], and providing location context through augmented reality [23]. Some studies have also considered the use of maps on large interactive surfaces such as multi-touch tabletops and display walls [9, 10]. The current study considers user interaction with tabletop map interfaces as compared to more traditional kiosk-style interaction (e.g. mouse or trackball).

We are interested in two questions related to tabletop map interfaces. First, what advantages, if any, does tabletop interaction offer for way-finding activities? And, second, in what ways do people interact with kiosk-style maps—what way-finding strategies do they use and what kinds of multi-touch gestures do they employ? To begin to explore these questions, we conducted a controlled study in which individual participants completed map navigation tasks in one of two conditions: using a desktop computer with mouse input (Figure 1a) and using an interactive tabletop with touch input (Figure 1b).

BACKGROUND
Map Interaction and Interfaces
The ways in which people interact with maps have been well studied in the fields of Applied Geography, Geographic Information Systems, and, more recently, Human-Computer Interaction. However, most work on map interaction and navigation has focused on how interaction varies when the visual appearance of the map is altered. Such alterations include changing the colors [22], the amount of information displayed [8], and the types of information displayed [18]. Relatively little work has focused on how changing the type of interaction affects people's use of digital maps. Work in the area of mobile navigation systems [12, 23, 26] has focused mainly on maximizing the limited real estate available on a mobile

ITS'12, November 11–14, 2012, Cambridge, Massachusetts, USA.

Figure 1a. In the desktop condition participants interacted with a map on a desktop computer with a standard keyboard and mouse.

Figure 1b. In the tabletop condition, participants interacted with a map using multi-touch input on an interactive tabletop computer.

display. Other research has considered the use of maps on large interactive surfaces [9, 10]. Forlines et al. [10] presented a multi-display system built on Google Earth with each display augmented with a different layer of information. Their design aimed to support multi-user interaction in a co-located environment. Research comparing input-type (e.g. direct touch vs. mouse input) for map interaction is limited. The current study addresses open questions involving the effect of input type on map navigation performance of single-user interactions.

Mouse vs. Touch Input Comparisons

In recent years, the use of direct-touch interactive surfaces has grown to include many different applications. Accordingly, several studies have explored the benefits of touch compared to mouse input [11, 15, 16, 21, 27]. Forlines et al. [11] compared mouse vs. touch input on tabletop displays for both unimanual and bimanual tasks. Their results indicate that users in the touch condition perform better for bimanual tasks. However, for single-user, unimanual input, users may benefit more from a single-mouse. Kin et al. [16] found that participants using direct-touch input performed better on a multi-target selection task than those using mouse input. In a study of a collaborative learning task, Shaer et al. [27] found that tabletop interaction had several advantages compared to a multi-mouse desktop condition.

Tan et al. [28] compared users' ability to recall the positions of objects on a screen using a touch or mouse input. They found a 19% increase in spatial recall for users with touch input based on error rate of placed objects. However, they found no significant difference between conditions in the percent of objects correctly identified and time spent on learning and recall. They also found that, while men performed significantly better than women in the mouse condition, there was no significant difference in the touch condition. This suggests that the kinesthetic cues offered by touch input might narrow the gender gap for spatial tasks. Likewise, Czerwinski et al.'s work on virtual world navigation provides evidence that a slight alteration in the interface (field of view in their case) could have a significant effect on users' ability to navigate [8]. In that same vein, altering the input type (tabletop vs. desktop) might have an effect on how well users are able to navigate. In this study we aim to investigate whether these results also apply to users of touch-based map interfaces.

Multi-Touch Gestures

There is a growing body of research that provides design insights for a variety of direct touch interfaces. Wu and Balakrishnan [33] presented a set of multi-touch gestures for interactive tabletops. They implemented interaction techniques employing single-finger, two-finger, and multi-finger gestures. Their evaluations of these techniques suggest that learning and applying these gestures effectively required only limited practice.

Wobbrock et al. [32] presented a set of user-defined gestures based on users' agreement over a thousand of gestures. Their findings show that users rarely care about the number of fingers touching the display, and that they prefer unimanual rather than bimanual interactions. They also suggest including desktop widgets along with touch input to support ease of use. Based on this work, Morris et al. [20] compared the previously created user-defined and researcher-defined surface gestures [32] to better understand users' preferences. Their findings indicate that physically and conceptually simpler gestures were highly preferred to more complex gestures. For example, users preferred single-finger gestures over multi-finger or whole-hand gestures and unimanual gestures over bimanual ones. Most recently, Urakami [29] studied the differences between novice and expert users' choice of gestures for a tabletop map application. Their observational data suggest that the choice of gestures was affected by the users' experience and, to some degree, by the size of the manipulated object and nature of the command. Furthermore, their findings show that surface gestures should focus on the motion pattern of the hand or fingers and not depend on the use of specific hand shapes or fingers.

Due to the appearance of tabletop displays in public spaces, several studies have explored both multi-user gestures and gestures in the wild. Ryall et al. [25] conducted longitudinal observations of tabletop users in four contexts and discovered a number of common behavior patterns. More recently, Hinrichs and Carpendale [13] conducted a field study at the Vancouver Aquarium investigating visitor gestures on two tabletop exhibits. They compared gesture types for children and adults, and reported on a variety of gestures for different actions. Their findings indicate that the choice of gesture depends not only on the specific action, but also on interaction context and social context. To our best knowledge, there is very little research on exploring the gestures used in the context of map interaction on tabletops.

RESEARCH QUESTIONS

We imagine that tabletop map interfaces in real-world settings will often be used simultaneously by multiple people (as in [19]). However, in this study, we are interested in comparing the effects of tabletop and desktop interfaces on map navigation performance. As such, we chose to focus on individual users in a controlled laboratory setting guided by the following research questions:

RQ1. What strategies do people use to support navigation when interacting with kiosk-style digital maps?

RQ2. What type of the multi-touch gestures do users employ while interacting with tabletop map applications?

RQ3. Do individuals who interact with the map in a tabletop condition perform better on the subsequent navigation tasks than users in a desktop condition?

STUDY DESIGN

We conducted a between-subject study with two conditions: mouse input with a desktop display (Figure 1a) and touch input on a tabletop display (Figure 1b). We selected a between-subject design to keep participant time commitments manageable. We measured participant map interaction time and navigation time. We also video recorded participants during the study to understand their map interaction and way-finding strategies at a more detailed level. After interacting with the map, participants navigated in a corresponding virtual world with a three-dimensional, first-person view. All participants used a desktop computer to navigate in the virtual world (Figure 2).

Participants

For this study, we recruited 22 participants aged 18 to 70 years (M=25, SD=12.8). We randomly assigned participants to one of the study conditions (11 desktop and 11 tabletop). In the tabletop condition there were 5 women and 6 men (average age 29, SD=17.46), and in the desktop condition there were 7 women and 4 men (average age 20.9, SD=2.39). The participants were recruited from the local university community, and 19 of them were students. Participants were paid $10 to take part in the study, which took around one hour to complete. We also conducted a pilot study with 10 people using a set of simpler tasks (for both map interaction and navigation tasks).

Figure 2. First-person perspective of navigating through the virtual world, built with Microsoft XNA Game Studio.

Apparatus

The study was conducted with two devices. The desktop computer had an 18.5×11.5 inch monitor (1680×1050 pixels). This device was used for navigation in the virtual world (for both conditions) and also the desktop map condition. For the tabletop map condition, we used a first-generation Microsoft Surface with a 24.5×18.5 inch display (1024×768 pixels).

Procedure

At the beginning of the experiment, we asked participants to complete a simple practice task to become familiar with the map interface and with navigating in the corresponding virtual world. Once completed, we asked the participants to accomplish three increasingly difficult tasks, each consisting of two sub-tasks: (a) map interaction and (b) virtual world navigation. For both map interaction and virtual world navigation, we asked participants to think out loud while they were working. All sessions were video recorded.

All tasks were completed in a fictitious city called Laketown. For each task, we first gave the users a note card with a specified start and end point and then instructed them to locate each point on the map and find a route between those points in the order specified. For example, the note card for the first task read:

"*Here is a map of a fictitious city. You will have up to ten minutes to study this map to learn the way to get from the southwest corner of the dome to the dinosaur.*"

After verbal confirmation of completion of this phase (or up to 10 minutes interaction with the map), participants then navigated in a virtual world from the start point to the end point (Figure 2), relying on their memory alone to find the route. Participants entered the virtual world at the start point but did not know which direction they were facing, requiring them to use streets and landmarks to orient themselves.

Navigation Tasks

The first task (A) involved traveling from a start point to an end point with a minimal number of intermediate turns. The end point for this task was a highly recognizable landmark (a dinosaur statue). The second task (B) was similar to the first task, but it involved more turns. To make it slightly more difficult, the landmark at the end point (a lighthouse) was harder to identify than in the first task—there were three lighthouses in the virtual world, all similar in appearance. Finally, the third task (C) asked participants to find two intermediate points in addition to an end point. The intermediate points were specific houses located in a group of similar looking buildings. Our results show that mean participant navigation times increased from one task to the next, suggesting that the tasks were increasingly difficult.

Map Interaction

The digital map was presented on a tabletop (for touch condition) and a desktop (for mouse condition). On the tabletop, participants could use one or more fingers to pan the map and two or more fingers to zoom and rotate the map (using standard pinch gestures). Zooming revealed more detailed information on the map. The names of buildings and landmarks did not appear at the lowest level of zoom, meaning that users must zoom in to complete each task. Tapping and double tapping were not mapped to any action in the tabletop interface.

On the desktop, participants could click and drag to pan the map and use the scroll wheel to zoom in and out. To rotate the map, participants had to hold down the control key while manipulating the scroll wheel. As was the case in the tabletop interface, single and double clicks in the desktop condition were not mapped to any interface action.

Each condition also included a panel with standard button widgets to pan, zoom, and rotate the display (inset, Figure 1a). We instructed participants on how to use the interface, and we provided a practice task prior to the start of task A.

Virtual World Interaction

The navigation subtask was conducted within a virtual world corresponding to the map (Figure 2). Participants were given a first-person perspective as if the user were walking through the world:

"This computer shows the same fictitious city that you saw on the map in 3D. You are "standing" on the southwest side of the dome now. Use the arrow keys to "walk" to the dinosaur. Let us know when you get to the end point. You will have up to ten minutes."

All participants used a desktop computer to navigate in the virtual world using arrow keys on a standard keyboard. The up and down arrow keys were mapped to forward and backward motion respectively (with constant velocity and instant acceleration). The left and right arrow keys allowed for turning in place at a constant angular velocity. We built the world using Microsoft XNA Game Studio. In pilot testing, we developed our world in Alice as in Czerwinski et al. [7], but the final world was too large for fluid use in Alice.

After completing all three tasks, the participants took a standard mental rotation test to assess spatial reasoning abilities [30]. The participants then completed a brief experience questionnaire in which they reported their previous experience with different input techniques, virtual worlds, maps and navigation.

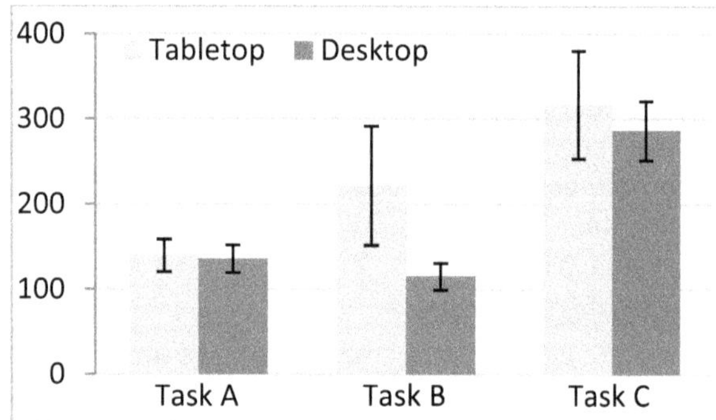

Figure 3. Mean map interaction time in seconds for the three tasks with standard error shown.

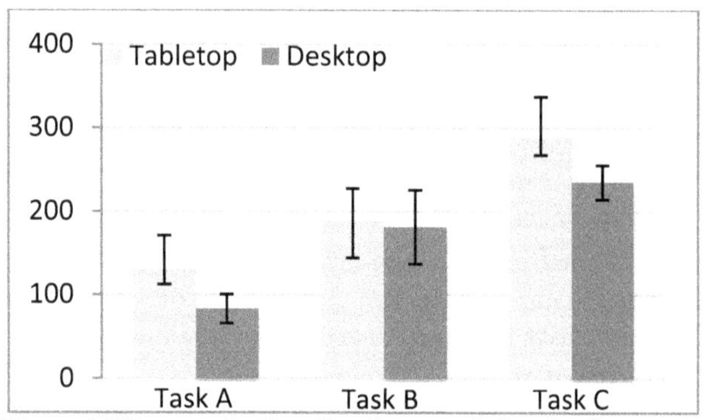

Figure 4. Mean navigation time in seconds for the three tasks with standard error shown.

RESULTS

To answer our research questions, we analyzed both quantitative and qualitative data. In this section, we first report our quantitative results, which address our third research question (RQ3). Afterwards, we consider RQ1 and RQ2 using qualitative data from video recordings.

Quantitative Results

To determine whether individuals in the tabletop map condition performed better on the navigation tasks, we considered participants' map interaction time, navigation completion time, age, and spatial ability scores. Interaction times were determined by measuring the time between the user's first interaction with the interface (click, touch, etc.) and his or her verbal confirmation of completion. One participant in each condition did not complete the third task. Additionally, we lost video data for one participant in the desktop condition for the second task (task B). These three data points were omitted from our analysis.

Spatial Ability

The average spatial ability score for the tabletop condition was 10.1 (SD=4.99) while the average score for the desktop condition was 8.73 (SD=4.29). There was no significant difference between spatial scores between the two conditions, $t(20) = 0.69$, $p = 0.34$. We also found little to no correlation between spatial ability and navigation performance (ρ = -0.3 for task A; -0.18 for task B; and 0.02 for task C). Unlike previous studies [2, 6, 8, 17, 28], we also found no significant difference between sex and spatial ability, $t(20) = 1.64$, $p = 0.117$. The average score for women was 8.0 (SD=4.1) while the average score for men was 11.1 (SD=4.8).

Map Interaction Time

Figure 3 shows mean map interaction time for the three tasks for the two conditions. There was no significant difference between the conditions for any of the tasks. For task A: $t(20) = 0.153$, $p = 0.88$; task B: $t(20) = 1.49$, $p = 0.15$; and task C: $t(19) = 0.434$, $p = 0.67$.

Navigation Performance

Figure 4 shows mean navigation times for the three tasks. Again, there was no significant difference between the conditions for any of the tasks. For task A: $t(20) = 1.03$, $p = 0.34$; task B: $t(19) = 0.12$, $p = 0.9$; and task C: $t(18) = 0.99$, $p = 0.33$. We also constructed a composite performance score for each participant consisting of individual average completion time across the three tasks. Using this composite score as a dependent variable, we performed an ANCOVA with spatial ability and age as covariates. This test revealed no main effect of interface type ($F(1,18) = 1.23$, $p = 0.28$), spatial ability ($F(1,18) = 0.96$, $p = 0.34$), or age ($F(1,18) = 1.59$, $p = 0.23$). There was also no interaction between condition and spatial ability ($F(1,18) = 0.43$, $p = 0.52$), and condition and age ($F(1,18) = 3.29$, $p = 0.09$). We also found no significant effect of sex on navigation performance. Using sex as the independent variable, women had an overall average completion time of 203 (SD=92.97), while men had an average completion time of 154.9 (SD=84.9), $t(20) = 1.26$, $p = 0.22$.

Qualitative Results on Way Finding Strategies

Qualitative data were obtained from video recordings of both the users' map interaction and virtual world navigation. We coded the video recordings for users' map interaction styles and navigation strategies. Map interaction style refers to the way in which participants used the map interface, while navigation strategy refers to the way in which participants navigated in the virtual world on the desktop computer. Tables 1 and 2 summarize the codes for map interaction styles and navigation strategies, respectively.

Map Interaction Styles

Independent of input type, most users (86.6%) either traced street paths with their finger (or mouse) or dragged the map along their route from point A to point B. We define *tracing* as following a route without touching the screen or directly interacting with the interface in anyway. Meanwhile, dragging a route involved directly touching/clicking the screen and dragging the map. Tracing was more frequent in the mouse condition, while dragging was more frequent with the touch condition. This is likely because there is no equivalent of "mouse-over" input for the Microsoft Surface.

Counting the streets occurred when users either directly touched/clicked the screen or held their finger close to the screen while counting streets or intersections. There were 7 desktop users (63.6%) who counted streets in one or more tasks, while only one tabletop user counted streets. Almost half of the participants (45%) traced a route using the panel, which mostly happened at the end of a task.

Map Interaction Styles	
Drag Route	Dragging the interface along a route
Trace Route	Tracing finger/mouse along a route
Panel Route	Using the panel to trace a route
Visual Trace	Tracing a route by looking at the map (no finger/mouse tracing)
Counting	Counting streets, intersections, or buildings

Table 1. Codes for map interaction styles

Navigation Strategies

Participants used a variety of strategies to navigate in the virtual world for different tasks (see Table 2). Strategies for navigating in the virtual world did not appear to be related to the condition in which users interacted with the map. We observed that 21 of 22 participants used at least one of these two strategies: landmark and cardinal directions. Most users (86%) used one or more landmarks on the map to find their ways, which were mostly natural landmarks (e.g., a city park, the lake, or a green path). There were also some specific buildings on the map used as a landmark (e.g., a cathedral and a pyramid). 19 of 22 users (86%) used cardinal directions in which they were heading as one of their main strategies (e.g., North, or West). Some instances of using these two strategies are:

- "*I just go west until the end of the city park*" [Cardinal, Landmark]
- "*I need to turn left, when I get to the north of the little bay area*" [Cardinal, Relative, Landmark]
- "*So I need to go north first for six blocks*" [Cardinal, Counting]

Participants who combined both landmark and cardinal direction strategies seemed especially successful. Almost half of the users (45%) counted the number of streets, intersections, or buildings between landmarks. For example:

- "*I need to cross eight streets this way before I turn right*" [Counting, Relative]

There were also a few users (27%) who used experiences from prior tasks to guide their navigation:

- *"Oh, I see the dome, so I know I'm heading to the north"* [Landmark, Cardinal, Previous Experience]

Navigation Strategies	
Cardinal	Using cardinal direction words (e.g. *North)*
Landmark	Using landmarks on the map
Counting	Counting streets, intersections, or buildings
Relative	Using the words such as *left, right, next to,* and *between.*
Prev. Experience	Words about experiences with prior tasks

Table 2. Codes for navigation strategies

Qualitative Results on User Gestural Interactions

Analyzing our video data, we observed a variety of gestures for the three actions supported by our tabletop map: drag, zoom in/out, and rotate.

Drag

Due to the nature of tasks (locating points of interest and finding a route), dragging the map was the most common action used by the participants. Most users relied on single-finger, one-handed gestures to drag the map. The choice of finger was not limited to index or middle fingers—one participant dragged the map with his pinky finger (Figure 5e). The simultaneous use of both hands for drag occurred occasionally in two cases: (a) as a trouble-shooting use after one or several unsuccessful dragging with one hand, and (b) when users had less previous experience with direct touch interfaces. We found a number of other gestures that participants used for drag, which we have not seen reported in the literature. This set of gestures is reported below.

Zoom In/Out

Participants occasionally zoomed in to see more details on the map and find a specific point, and zoomed out to have an overview of the whole map to find or review a route between those points. To zoom in and out 82% of participants made use of a two-finger pinch using either thumb/index fingers or thumb/middle fingers. Some participants (64%) also made use of a bimanual pull apart gesture and, in a few instances, a single-handed splay gesture (18% of users). Wobbrock et al. [32] found the same set of user-defined gestures for enlarge/shrink actions. However, we also observed users employing the less common fingers for the pinch gesture, such as index/middle fingers (Figure 5c) or thumb/pinky fingers.

Zooming was the most difficult action for participants on the tabletop, and participants who reported having little experience with touch input devices most commonly used the button panel to zoom instead of touch. In other cases, participants had to try a variety of gestures to succeed. Some users also tried to tap on the map in order to zoom in, which was not supported by the system. One participant even gave up using the touch-mode after tapping on the surface a few times to zoom in, and used the button panel instead for all the three tasks. This observation suggests that users will try to tap on the display when they are struggling to understand the interface, possibly due to prior experience with touch or mouse input devices.

Rotate

We only observed unwanted rotations as a result of dragging the map or zooming in/out. Consequently, users rotated the map to its default state (i.e. the facing-North state). The most common rotation gestures included touching the map with two fingers and rotating the wrist (64% of users), and touching the map with one finger from each hand and rotating the fingers relative to one another (55% of users). Participants used a variety of fingers for these two gestures. Some interesting gestures include rotating the wrist with index/middle fingers touching, and rotating thumb finger of left hand relative to index finger of right hand. Hinrichs et al. [13] found that the most common rotation gesture for a media item is rotating the wrist using all five fingertips, but we did not see any instance of this gesture in our study.

Other Interesting Gestures

Much of gesture variety that we observed has been reported in previous studies [13, 32, 33]. However, we also observed a number of new gestures that we have not seen reported elsewhere. We believe some of these gestures resulted, in part, from the nature of the map interaction task, and the differences between whole screen and media object interaction.

Let Your Fingers Do the Walking

This gesture was used by one participant while tracing a route on the map, which involves dragging the map by walking on it, using two (index/middle) or three (index/middle/ring) fingers of one hand and moving the fingers back and forth after each other (Figure 5a).

Itsy-Bitsy Spider and Bimanual Drag

Hinrichs et al. [13] reported that people mostly applied single-handed gestures for drag, and that only a few bimanual instances occurred in which four or five fingers were used. However, we observed some tabletop participants who frequently used one finger from each hand to drag the display (18% of users). Specifically, they dragged their fingers one by one to "walk" across the map, both to locate points of interest and to find routes, which we refer to as the "itsy-bitsy spider" gesture (see Figure 5b). Similarly, we observed two other participants using one finger from each hand (most commonly the index finger) to simultaneously drag the map (Figure 5f). We speculate that because users are interacting with a map that covers the entire display (rather than smaller media objects), the resulting gesture sets are correspondingly different.

Doggie Paddle

One participant used a bimanual whole hand gesture to drag the map (see Figure 5d). He used both his hands simultaneously to drag the surface, but many times, it was an unsuccessful gesture. The user was 70 years old and he reported having very little previous experience with direct touch input. We noted that he switched to a single-finger gesture a few times, but interestingly only for trouble-shooting.

Pinky Drag

Existing studies suggest that users rarely care about the number of fingers they use for tabletop interaction [32]. We also observed that the users tended to use different fingers for different instances of an action, such as dragging with pinky finger (see Figure 5e). In this instance, one user had found the start and end points and was retracing the route. During this process he frequently switched from finger to finger including his pinky in an improvisational manner.

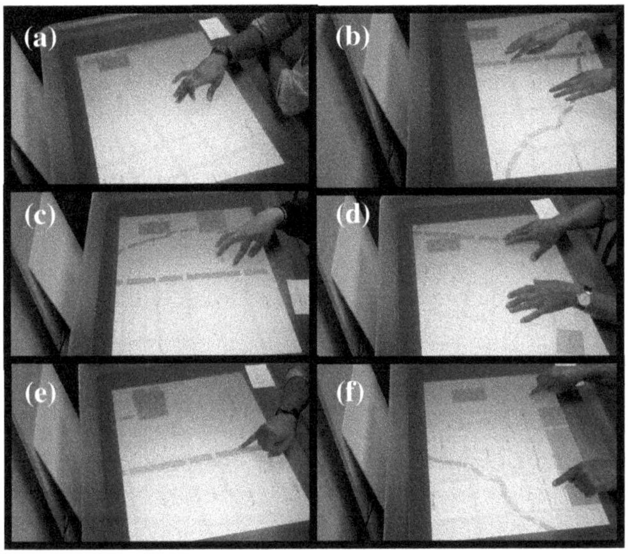

Figure 5. Some gestures used in the tabletop map condition: (a) walk with three fingers; (b) itsy-bitsy spider drag; (c) index/middle pinch; (d) doggie paddle drag; (e) pinky drag; and (f) bimanual drag.

Influence of Prior Experience on Gesture Choices

Previous studies suggest that users' choice of gestures is affected by experience with touch-input devices [20, 29]. We examined this effect by comparing gestures that novices and experienced users applied on the tabletop while interacting with the map. We determined user experience level based on self-report data from a pre-test questionnaire. In the touch condition, four participants reported that they frequently or very frequently used touch input devices; six reported that they rarely or never used a touch device; and one participant reported occasional use.

Comparing user interaction based on experience level, we observed that more experienced users applied a variety of multi-finger gestures, while novices tended to use simpler gestures with a single finger. This is in agreement with Urakami's [29] observation that experts used two-finger gestures more often than did novices. Urakami's findings also suggest that novices prefer using bimanual gestures for interacting with the entire map, while experts prefer unimanual gestures. While our study involved a small number of participants, we did observe that more experienced users were able to skillfully interact with the system using only one hand.

We also observed that less experienced users tended to keep their hands off the table while rehearsing and memorizing the route, while more experienced users tended to keep their hands on the table while rehearsing the route, often making continuous small adjustments in the process.

Button Panel Use

The button panel added an additional input option for users. Panel use occurred in two cases: (a) voluntary use and (b) trouble-shooting use in response to difficulty using touch input. Not surprisingly, less experienced participants used the button panel for trouble-shooting more often than those with more experience. However, voluntary panel use was also more common for less experienced users, suggesting that the panel use is, in some cases, a more comfortable choice for novices and may lead to a better user performance. For example, one participant struggled with the touch-input. She gradually increased the number of times she used the panel, from an exclusive trouble-shooting use (task A) to an exclusive voluntary use (task C). Her navigation performance enhanced accordingly from getting completely lost (task A) to accomplishing the task with just a few wrong turns (task C).

We observed that the most common use of button panel overall was for the action of zooming in and out. Many users even started each task by zooming in with the button panel, and then later switched to direct gesture interaction to zoom. These observations were similar across experience level. The use of button panel for dragging occurred mostly for trouble-shooting.

DISCUSSION

Although our results provide some insight into the relationship between map interaction, input type, and navigation, many factors remain unclear. Among our open questions are: Why there was no correlation between spatial ability and navigation performance? Why did some users outperform others? And what factors contributed to success? These factors could be differences in familiarity and comfort with the interface type, differences in navigation ability not accounted for with the spatial ability test, choice of navigation and orientation strategies, and differences in route choice.

Quantitatively, the fact that there were no significant differences in navigation performance between the two conditions suggests that designers might concentrate on other aspects of map design, rather than input type. In addition, the fact that spatial ability did not correlate with navigation performance suggests that other skills and strategies might be more important for navigation.

On the qualitative side, there were some prominent patterns in users' map interactions. Notably, people frequently trace and drag routes along the map, count street intersections, and keep the map at a fixed orientation. Current map interfaces provide users with a pre-traced route (typically a colored line between points A and B), but there seems to be something gained by users tracing the route themselves. For non-mobile maps, adding the ability for users to trace their own route in either touch or mouse conditions might enhance the user experience.

In this study, we explored gestures in the context of map interaction on tabletops. Comparing our findings with the gestures reported in the literature [13, 32, 33], we found several new gestures. We think participants used these new gestures for several reasons. First, the map took up the entire screen, while other media objects have usually smaller sizes. Second, the nature of task (i.e. using a map to navigate) might result in certain types of gestures, such as using fingers to walk along a route (see Figure 5a and 5b), that simply don't make sense when manipulating a picture, movie, or drawing object on the table.

We observed a variety of multi-touch gestures that participants used for drag, zoom, and rotate operations. Participants with more direct touch interface experience tended to use their dominant hand while interacting with the surface and used a greater variety of fingers and touch-points. Less-experienced users gravitated toward using single-finger gestures, which is in agreement with Ryall et al.'s [25] observation that users, at first, tend to use single-finger gestures, simulating the mouse or stylus inputs. In addition, novice users employed less effective gestures such the *doggie paddle* gesture (see Figure 5d).

Novices and users with less touch-input experience may not be comfortable using the touch-mode and may not be familiar with all gestures supported by the system (e.g., the tapping instances that we saw for zooming in). Marshall et al. [19] examined the in-the-wild use of multi-touch tabletops; their study showed that when users approach a tabletop their first touch tended to be a single tap or a double tap. They also suggested that users would give up quickly if they weren't able to receive an immediate feedback from the first touch interactions. In all, our observations in this study support difficulty of designing *crowd interaction* [4] tabletop interfaces for public spaces. Subtle touch feedback such as those suggested by Wigdor et al. [31] might also improve the understandability of the interface for novices. In addition to touch input, we provided the participants with a button panel that they used voluntarily or for trouble-shooting. We think having an additional input option in the digital map interfaces has benefits for users' performances (similar to the conclusion of Wobbrock et al. [32]).

An additional option for the digital map users is the ability to pin points and locations on the map. In some cases users, who found start and end points, had to search for those points a second time. Being able to pin the points could decrease the users' map interaction time and could possibly enhance their overall performance. This feature is provided by standard digital map interfaces that offer direction services (e.g. Google maps). However, placing pins on points of interest might also be useful in kiosk-style map applications, suggesting intriguing opportunities for augmenting tabletop interfaces with tangible interaction.

CONCLUSION AND FUTURE WORK

The current study offers some insight into the relationship between spatial ability, map interaction, and input type. Map interaction styles on tabletops and desktops were similar. And, despite our hypothesis, there was no significant difference in performance between users in the two conditions. Additionally, spatial ability did not predict navigation performance. Instead users seemed to rely on a variety of other skills to complete the navigation tasks.

Tabletop users employed a variety of gestures to interact with the map, some of which have not been previously reported. This suggests that there may be task-dependent differences in users' gesture choices. In other words, interacting with a map is different than manipulating media objects on the display, which makes gestures such as walking on the table with two fingers more convenient and intuitive. More research is needed to explore the underlying principles of gestures that can be applied to a map application on a tabletop, which enables developing a more user-friendly system.

In the future we hope to extend our study to real-world settings with multi-user collaborative interactions on tabletop and desktop map interfaces. We are mostly interested in exploring the effects of collaboration on users' navigation performance and the way-finding strategies in both conditions.

ACKNOWLEDGMENTS

We thank David Utall and David Rapp for providing valuable input for this study. We also thank Robert Houyi for his help in analyzing qualitative data.

REFERENCES

1. Antle, A.N., Bevans, A., Tanenbaum, J., Seaborn K., and Wang, S. Futura: Design for collaborative learning and game play on a multi-touch digital tabletop. In *Proc. TEI'11*, ACM Press (2011), 93-100.

2. Astur, R.S., Ortiz, M.L., and Sutherland, R.J. A characterization of performance by men and women in a virtual Morris water task: A large and reliable sex difference. *Behav. Brain Research, 93* (1998), 185-190.

3. Bilandzic, M., Foth, M., and De Luca, A. CityFlocks: Designing social navigation for urban mobile information systems. In *Proc. DIS'08*, ACM Press (2008), 174-183.

4. Block, F., Wigdor, D., Phillips, B. C., Horn, M. S., Shen, C. FlowBlocks: A multi-touch UI for crowd interaction. To appear in *Proc. UIST'12*, ACM Press (2012).

5. Boring, S., Jurmu, M., and Butz, A. Scroll, tilt or move it: Using mobile phones to continuously control pointers on large public displays. In *Proc. OZCHI'09*, ACM Press (2009), 161-168.

6. Chai, X. J., Jacobs, L. F. Effects of cue types on sex differences in human spatial memory. *Behav. Brain Research 208*, 2 (2010), 336-342.
7. Chase, W.G. Spatial representation of taxi drivers. In R. Rogers & J.A. Sloboda (eds.), *The acquisition of symbolic skills,* Plenum Press (1983), 391-405.
8. Czerwinski, M., Tan, D.S., and Robertson, G.G. Women take a wider view. In *Proc. CHI'02*. ACM Press (2002), 195-202.
9. Forlines, C., Shen, C. DTLens: Multi-user tabletop spatial data exploration. In *Proc. UIST'05*, ACM Press (2005), 119-122.
10. Forlines, C., Esenther, A., Shen, C., Wigdor, D., Ryall, K. Multi-user, multi-display interaction with a single-user, single-display geospatial application. In *Proc. UIST'06*. ACM Press (2006), 273-276.
11. Forlines, C., Wigdor, D., Shen, C., and Balakrishnan, R. Direct-touch vs. mouse input for tabletop displays. In *Proc. CHI'07*. ACM Press (2007), 647-656.
12. Hang, A., Rukzio, E., and Greaves, A. Projector phone: A study of using mobile phones with integrated projector for interaction with maps. In *Proc. MobileHCI'08*. ACM Press (2008), 207-216.
13. Hinrichs, U. and Carpendale S. Gestures in the wild: Studying multi-touch gesture sequences on interactive tabletop exhibits. In *Proc. CHI'11*, ACM Press (2011), 3023-3032.
14. Hornecker, E. "I don't understand it either, but it is cool": Visitor interactions with a multi-touch table in a museum. In *Proc. Tabletop'08* ,IEEE (2008), 121-128.
15. Hornecker, E., Marshall, P., Dalton, N.S., and Rogers, Y. Collaboration and interference: Awareness with mice or touch input. In *Proc. CSCW'08*, ACM Press (2008), 167-176.
16. Kin, K., Agrawala, M., and DeRose, T. Determining the benefits of direct-touch, bimanual, and multifinger input on a multitouch workstation. In *Proc. Graphics Interface'09*, ACM Press (2009), 119-124.
17. Lawton, C.A. Gender differences in way-finding strategies: Relationship to spatial ability and spatial anxiety. *Sex Roles 30* (1994), 765-779.
18. MacEachren, A.M. *How Maps Work,* Guilford Press, New York NY, 1995.
19. Marshall, P., Morris, R., Rogers, Y., Kreitmayer, S., and Davies, M. Rethinking 'multi-user': An in-the-wild study of how groups approach a walk-up-and-use tabletop interface. In *Proc. CHI'11*, ACM Press (2011), 3033-3042.
20. Morris, M. R., Wobbrock, J. O., and Wilson, A. D. Understanding users' preferences for surface gestures. In *Proc. Graphics Interface'10*, ACM Press (2010), 261-268.
21. Müller-Tomfelde, C. and Schremmer, C. Touchers and mousers: Commonalities and differences in co-located collaboration with multiple input devices. In *Proc. CHI'08*, ACM Press (2008), 1149-1152.
22. Robinson, A. H. *The look of maps: An examination of cartographic design.* Wisconsin Press (1952).
23. Rohs, M., Schöning, J., Raubal, M., Essl, G., and Krüger, A. Map navigation with mobile devices: Virtual versus physical movement with and without visual context. In *Proc. ICMI'07*, ACM Press (2007), 146-153.
24. Rukzio, E., Müller, M., and Hardy, R. Design, implementation and evaluation of a novel public display for pedestrian navigation: the rotating compass. In *Proc. CHI'09*, ACM Press (2009), 113-122.
25. Ryall, K., Morris, M., Everitt, K., Forlines, C., Shen, C. Experiences with and observations of direct-touch tabletops. In *Proc. Tabletop'06*, IEEE (2006), 89-96.
26. Schöning, J., Rohs, M., Kratz, S., Löchtefeld, M., and Krüger, A. Map torchlight: A mobile augmented reality camera projector unit. In *Proc. CHI'09*, ACM Press (2009), 3841-3845.
27. Shaer, O., Strait, M., Valdes, C., Feng, T., Lintz, M., and Wang, H. Enhancing genomic learning through tabletop interaction. In *Proc. CHI'11*, ACM Press (2011), 2817-2826.
28. Tan, D. S., Stefanucci, J. K., Proffitt, D. R., and Pausch, R. Kinesthetic cues aid spatial memory. In *Ext. Abstracts CHI'02*, ACM Press (2002), 806-807.
29. Urakami, J. Developing and testing a human-based gesture vocabulary for tabletop systems. *Human Factors* (2012) doi:10.1177/0018720811433052.
30. Vandenberg, S.G. and Kuse, A.R. Mental rotations, a group test of three-dimensional spatial visualization. *Perceptual and Motor Skills 47, 2* (1978), 599-604.
31. Wigdor, D., Williams, S., Cronin, M., Levy, R., White, K., Mazeev, M., and Benko, H. Ripples: Utilizing per-contact visualizations to improve user interaction with touch displays. In *Proc. UIST'09*. ACM Press (2009), 3-12.
32. Wobbrock, J.O., Morris, M.R., and Wilson, A.D. User-defined gestures for surface computing. In *Proc. CHI'09*, ACM Press (2009), 1083-1092.
33. Wu, M. and Balakrishnan, R. Multi-finger and whole hand gestural interaction techniques for multi-user tabletop displays. In *Proc UIST'03*, ACM Press (2003).

Microanalysis of Active Reading Behavior to Inform Design of Interactive Desktop Workspaces

Matthew K. Hong[1], Anne Marie Piper[1], Nadir Weibel[1], Simon Olberding[2], James D. Hollan[1]

[1]University of California, San Diego
9500 Gilman Dr., La Jolla, CA, USA
{m1hong, apiper, weibel, hollan}@ucsd.edu

[2]MIT Media Laboratory
20 Ames St., E14-548K. Cambridge, MA 02139, USA
simon_o@media.mit.edu

ABSTRACT
Hybrid paper-digital desktop workspaces have long been of interest in HCI [5, 39], yet their design remains challenging. One continuing challenge is to support fluid interaction with both paper and digital media, while taking advantage of established practices with each. Today researchers are exploiting depth cameras and computer vision to capture activity on and above the desktop and enable direct interaction with digitally projected and physical media. One important prerequisite to augmenting desktop activity is understanding human behavior in particular contexts and tasks. Here we study active reading on the desktop. To better understand active reading practices and identify patterns that might serve as signatures for different types of related activity, we conducted a microanalysis of single users reading on and above the desktop workspace. We describe the relationship between multimodal body-based contextual cues and the interactions they signify in a physical desktop workspace. Detailed analysis of coordinated interactions with paper documents provides an empirical basis for designing digitally augmented desktop workspaces. We conclude with prototype design interactions for hybrid paper-digital desktop workspaces.

Author Keywords
Active Reading; Microanalysis; Paper-Digital Workspaces

ACM Classification Keywords
H.5.2 [Information interfaces and presentation]: User Interfaces. - Graphical user interfaces.

General Terms
Human Factors; Design

INTRODUCTION
Designing hybrid workspaces that support fluid interaction with both paper and digital media is a central area of HCI research. Early seminal visions of an interactive desk to enable simultaneous work with paper and digital information were proposed by Wellner [39] and MacKay and colleagues [20]. More recently researchers have developed many techniques to support interaction across paper and digital media [12, 19, 35, 33, 38, 41]. One particularly promising focus for digitally enhanced paper documents is to better support active reading [1]. How might observing the coordination of one's body and materials while engaged in active reading provide insights into the design of hybrid workspaces that better support this cognitively demanding task?

Active reading is a critical task of knowledge workers. Knowledge workers spend substantial time in office environments, where information is spread between digital devices (computers, smart phones, tablets, etc.) and physical media (paper documents, whiteboards, books, printed photos, etc.) [24]. Furthermore, collaborative interaction and information sharing with others is often central to the accomplishment of tasks. The introduction of mobile devices, interactive tabletops, multitouch surfaces, and digital paper presents many challenges for designing workspaces that support fluid natural interaction with information spanning the physical and digital worlds.

In this paper we present a detailed microanalysis of reading paper documents positioned on and above a physical desktop. Our analysis looks closely at coordination of the body and materials. We identify opportunities for leveraging naturally occurring behaviors such as body position, pen grip posture, and paper document manipulation to serve as signatures of the micro-task structure of active reading. We use these observations to derive design insights and prototype digitally enhanced interactions with paper documents. Our aim is to learn from people's existing reading behaviors how a digitally augmented system might integrate with and support focus of attention and the immediate task at hand.

This research is part of a larger project to explore novel paper and digital desktop surface interactions. We are iteratively developing a system that tracks body movement, hands on and above the desktop surface, and the presence and orientation of other materials, particularly paper documents, in the workspace. The present paper presents a detailed analysis of behavior during active reading tasks to inform the development of current and future systems aimed at softening the boundaries of paper and digital media.

RELATED WORK
Considerable prior work guides our analysis of body movements and reading behaviors with paper documents. Behavioral models from experimental psychology provide the foundation for analysis. We briefly review related work and then discuss research on *active reading*.

Descriptive Models of Manual Behavior

The left hand knows what the right hand is planning, and the right hand knows what the left hand just did.

—Frank R. Wilson [40, p. 160]

One of the earliest detailed analyses of manual behavior is Napier and Tuttle's [26] description of prehensile movements, in which an object is held by a gripping or pinching action between the digits and the palm. Along with the classification of power and precision prehensile grips, they also observed that, "during a purposive prehensile action, the posture of the hand bears a constant relationship to the nature of that activity." In our analysis of active reading, we observe unique prehensile actions that are consistent with this description, especially regarding pen usage.

Guiard [11] investigated the differential roles of dominant and non-dominant hand in a shared task. Of particular interest is his identification of writing (previously conceived of as a unimanual one) as a bimanual task, showing how the non-dominant hand performs a complementary role of continuously repositioning the paper with respect to the motion of the writing hand. Based on his observation of a range of bimanual activities (such as writing, drawing, and sewing), Guiard concluded that "there is a logical division of labor between both hands that appears to govern the entire range of human bimanual activities," of which movement of the non-dominant hand both precedes and sets the spatial context for the activity of the dominant hand [11]. Many of the behaviors observed in our analysis consist of asymmetric bimanual movements and can be described within this framework.

Both models of manual behavior (see [40] for a thorough review) share a characteristic property: *the movement of the hands often anticipate and signal the nature of activity.* This parallels gesture in face-to-face conversations, in which hand movements or conversational gestures tend to precede semantically-linked speech utterances [6, 17, 23]. Such identifications promise to aid activity recognition, and an important aspect of this involves examining bimanual interaction.

Bimanual Interaction

Bimanual interaction with a computer was first introduced by Engelbart and English in 1968. Their NLS system supported simultaneous use of a chorded keyboard in the non-dominant hand and a mouse in the dominant hand [9]. However, it was not until the mid-80s' that Buxton and Myers [7] first detailed the efficacy of two-handed input. They compared unimanual with bimanual input, demonstrating that two-handed input readily outperforms the former. Although independent of Guiard's work (published a year later), and providing little discussion of the differential roles of each hand, their research increased awareness of the importance of bimanual input mechanisms. Somewhat later Bier el al. [3], took guidance from Guiard's work to develop the *Toolglass* metaphor – a semi-transparent palette-like interface controlled by simultaneous but functionally asymmetric two-handed input (see also Kabbash et al. [16] for an informative discussion of two-handed input in a compound task). Inspired by the Toolglass metaphor and the affordances of physical paper [30], Song looked at bimanual interaction techniques that render the non-dominant hand as a frame of reference by controlling the visual feedback projected onto paper [32].

Two-handed mode switching techniques have been explored extensively, especially involving combined use of pen and touch interactions. Li et al. [18] conducted an experimental analysis of five different mode switching techniques for pen-based user interfaces and concluded that pressing a button with the non-dominant hand yields the best performance in terms of speed, accuracy, and user preference. This study stimulated a body of research [4, 15, 32] that further confirmed the importance of understanding bimanual interaction and the asymmetric division of labor between hands. Brandl [4] describes several examples of bimanual pen plus multitouch gestures, assigning pen to the dominant hand and multitouch to the non-dominant hand. Hinckley [15] explored a wider vocabulary of pen+touch techniques that considers the interleaving assignment of pen and touch manipulation to either hand, depending on usage context. Based on certain grip postures used by artists, Song et al. [31] explored mode switching techniques that incorporate various postures and multitouch gestures. Inspired by the way artists manipulate a conté crayon, Vogel [37] recently investigated mode switching techniques that leverage various contact points of an interactive prism-shaped crayon with a multitouch table.

The reciprocity between visual attention and the cognitive cost of switching between subtasks has also been discussed in terms of Guiard's theory of bimanual interaction. For example, exploring bimanual vs. unimanual interactions with a "doll's head" neurosurgical interface, Hinckley [14] demonstrated the naturalness and cognitive benefits of two-handed manipulation. The use of both hands, afforded by the tangibility of the interface, resulted in a low transaction cost for switching between subtasks. Finally, Bederson [2] asserts that the flow [8] experience in human-computer interaction may be subject to interruptions when visual feedback and the associated need for attention becomes a requirement for task execution. This is something that can be minimized by bimanual interaction.

Active Reading and Tablet Displays

Research efforts from both experimental psychology and human computer interaction have great significance for informing the design of hybrid paper-digital desktop workspaces. One such domain is Active Reading [1], a form of knowledge work that requires high level of interconnectivity among reading-related tasks to retain a "flow experience" for the reader. Such activity is characterized by fluid transitions between immersive reading (the primary task) and a set of subtasks that support the active reading experience. These secondary tasks involve information creation and organization, including annotation [22], content browsing [27], file organization [21], and cross-referencing [28] between multiple documents. Due to the interlacing of interactions involved, active reading serves as an important testbed for exploring interaction techniques that are cognitively less demanding.

Many prior systems have attempted to support active reading by mimicking paper forms of interaction with digital

Categories	Description	Duration	Contact point	Symmetricity
Reading	reading with intense concentration	long	hand (both)	symmetric
Visual Tracking	quick skimming for overview of contents	moderate	finger, pen, other	N/A
Pointing	place-marking gesture for quick references	short	finger	N/A
Piling	chopping motion to stack group(s) of papers	short	hand (both)	symmetric
Flipping	turning to previous or next page	short to moderate	hand (single/both)	asymmetric
Writing	producing an explicit marking	moderate to long	pen	asymmetric
Annotating	producing telegraphic markings	short	pen, highlighter	asymmetric

Table 1. Coding scheme evolved from iterative analysis of video corpus. Short interactions usually last 1-5 seconds, moderate interactions are longer continuous activities in the range of 5-15 seconds, and long interactions last 15 seconds to several minutes.

technology. For example, XLibris [29] was one of the first efforts that explored pen-based gestural interactions to simulate a paper-like experience on a tablet display. LiquidText [36] explored bimanual multitouch interactions on a tablet PC along with flexible visual representations to recreate experiences that were previously unique to physical paper, such as viewing two disparate areas of text in a single pane. GatherReader [13] describes a bimanual pen+touch system that supports fluid interleaving interactions between reading and writing without requiring explicit specification or organization of content. Finally, Morris et al. [25] investigated active reading in the context of both horizontal and vertical displays. Still, the tangibility and materiality of paper often outweigh the benefits afforded by computers. Simply mimicking key affordances of paper digitally is unlikely to be sufficient. Detailed understanding of how people interact with paper documents is fundamental to the design of more effective digitally-augmented desktop workspaces.

METHODS

To better understand the context of active reading, we collected 333 minutes of overhead video data of three PhD students (age 25-35, 1 left handed) at their desk during standard paper reading and reviewing activities. Our research goal is to characterize movements of the body and artifacts during the task of active reading to inform the design of a digital environment. After inspecting the whole video corpus for active reading activities, we selected from each participant's data one representative 30 minute segment where active reading was most salient. Our research team conducted an analysis of the larger corpus as well as a detailed microanalysis of the focused video segments. Through the microanalysis we characterize the nuances of human activity during active reading, often by examining moment-to-moment interaction on a millisecond timescale. Our goal is to understand the richness of body and material coordination and identify interactions that may be augmented in a hybrid paper-digital workspace, including indicators of specific active reading behaviors.

Coding Scheme

Active reading is a broad category description for behaviors that aid in understanding and retaining written content, and encompasses both writing and reading activities. In order to investigate these dimensions two researchers analyzed the entire video corpus and iteratively developed a common coding scheme, informed by Marshall's previous analysis of annotations [22] by selecting the most redundant actions, activities, and behaviors (Table 1). Inter-coder reliability for this coding scheme and our data set was calculated with Cohen's Kappa coefficient of 92%[1].

Video Annotation

Video data was analyzed using ChronoViz [10], a software tool that aids annotation, visualization, and navigation of multimodal time-coded data (see Fig. 1). Each video clip was annotated using the above coding scheme (Table 1), and all annotations were visualized in a single timeline. We also included the acoustic patterns generated in the activities. Thus, adjacent to the annotations, a timeline of an audio waveform was added and incorporated into the analysis. All hand-coded annotations were sorted according to the categories.

[1]Cohen's Kappa coefficient was calculated over a 36 min. session where the two researchers coded a total of 177 events.

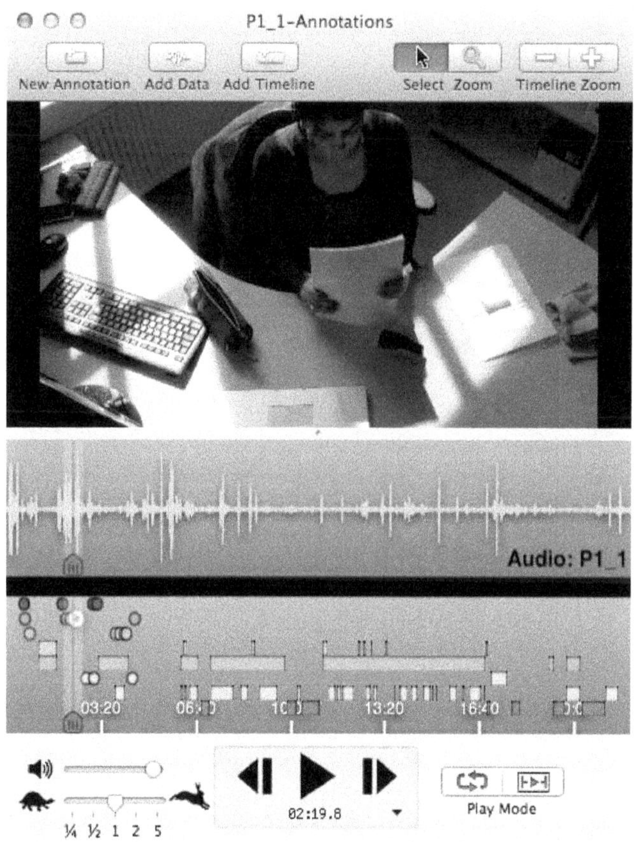

Figure 1. Analysis of a specific activity in ChronoViz. Multiple categories can be assigned to single events and events of varying duration. Filtering and reordering annotations enables visualization and identification of new patterns of behavior.

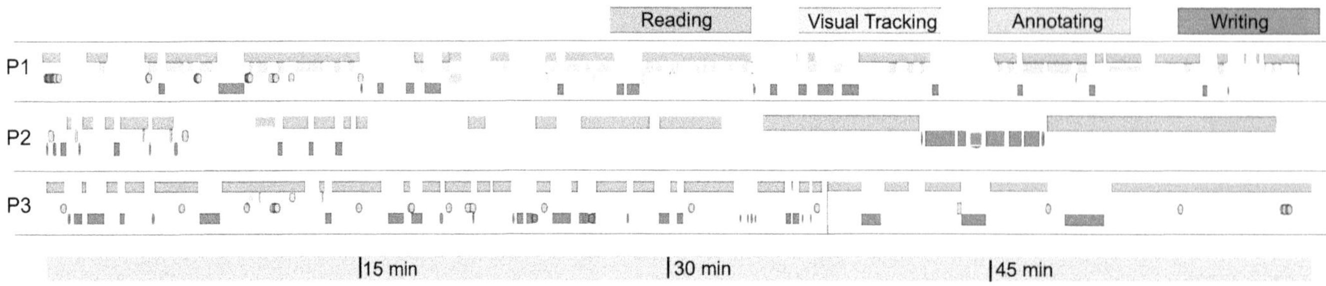

Figure 2. Distribution of the reading and writing activities for the three participants over one hour of observation. For each participant, four rows of annotations show (top to bottom) reading, visual tracking, annotating and writing. Notice that activities are evenly distributed across the session and that reading and writing are intertwined in a repetitive pattern.

Once sorted, navigation among annotated video segments was feasible within and between categories. Our analysis focused on identifying contextual cues that are consistently present during various active reading activities.

Microanalysis

Following high-level analysis of the larger video corpus, one 30 minute segment for each of the three participants was analyzed in further detail. As part of this microanalysis, we identified additional dimensions based on body interaction (i.e. single hand vs. bimanual), artifacts handled (i.e. pen, paper, computer), document gestures (i.e. underlining, highlighting, circling), physical gestures (i.e. holding, flipping, tucking), or high-level activity (i.e. searching, browsing).

RESULTS

The first level of analysis of the video corpus (333 minutes total; P1=160.6 min., P2=71.9 min., P3=100.5 min.) focused on the overall dynamics of reading activity and associated behaviors. In this section we describe the patterns that emerged from this analysis, the temporal distribution of the main reading and writing activities, and the summary statistics of the observed interactions. We then describe the results from the microanalysis.

Quantitative Analysis

High-level analysis of the video corpus indicates that reading and writing behaviors were fairly evenly distributed across the recorded sessions and among participants. Figure 2 illustrates the distribution of reading and writing for one hour of observation for all three participants. Table 2 illustrates the amount of time each participant spent on writing and reading activities as well as the frequency of actions such as annotating, pointing, piling, flipping and moving. The repetitive pattern of reading/writing was observed across participants. Annotating was a frequent activity and the durations of each contributes to the total time engaged in writing, revealing the importance of general writing interactions interspersed among reading. Flipping was also present across participants, although P3 showed much more flipping activity in conjunction with more writing and annotations. Long reading activities were interrupted by typically shorter periods of writing (between a few seconds and 1.5 minutes). Brief annotations (1-5 seconds) were generally integrated as part of the reading activity, as well as longer visual tracking sessions (2-100 seconds), that were often performed with a finger, a pen, or a highlighter. Participants varied considerably in use of visual tracking.

Qualitative Analysis

Building on the high-level analysis of user behavior, we examined the qualitative details of active reading activities. Findings of the analysis are organized into four sections: reading, annotating, navigating, and organizing. These are derived from the coding categories described in the methods section.

Reading

Reading is a rich cognitive activity that requires intense concentration. Although the extent of concentration may vary depending on the goal (e.g., reading for learning, to obtain an overview, find a specific piece of information, etc.), it remains cognitively expensive. Overall, the nature of interaction during reading involved a fixed position and was of longer duration than the rest of the observed activities (see also Table 2).

Immersive Reading: We observed two major postural configurations that indicated immersive reading. In general, the readers inclined to maintain a close proximity to the reading materials, which was accomplished in two ways. The first and most prevalent posture was made after bending and moving their heads closer to the desk. For almost all of these instances, the readers' elbows were on the desk either making a cross-arm posture or providing support with hands to rest their heads (Fig. 3). This particular variation of arm posture

Activity	Measure	P1	P2	P3
Reading	% of total time	55.94%	50.04%	68.97%
	Max (sec)	408.3	223.6	505
	Min (sec)	5.9	15.5	4
Writing	% of total time	7.77%	6.03%	12.95%
	Max (sec)	77.3	22.7	97.4
	Min (sec)	3	6.2	1.6
V. Tracking	% of total time	30.83%	-	2.35%
	Max (sec)	99.8	-	22.1
	Min (sec)	2.1	-	7.7
Annotating	occurrences / hour	24.28	8.34	38.99
Pointing	occurrences / hour	4.11	8.34	3.00
Piling	occurrences / hour	5.23	1.67	2.40
Flipping	occurrences / hour	11.21	5.00	29.99

Table 2. Duration and frequency of coded active reading behaviors. Over 50% of time is dedicated to reading activities while writing occurs between 6% and 13% of the time. We normalize frequency counts to the average number of occurrences per hour.

Figure 3. Examples of immersive reading. Leaning over with elbows bent on the physical desktop (*top*) and papers brought closer to reader's head (*bottom*)

Figure 4. Visual tracking with a pen or pencil. The instrument is held loosely towards the top, providing precise index with minimal occlusion. People shift easily from this grip to a closer grip for marking the paper.

may counter muscle strain coming from prolonged periods of neck and head flexion [34]. In these configurations, we also observed subtle continuous movements of the hands, such as the persistent fidgeting of fingers or twirling of a pen. The second posture was made while holding the reading materials with both hands in mid-air, and drawing them closer to the reader's head. This posture was also maintained when one participant switched to a leaned-back position by placing both legs on the desk. Detecting this sustained orientation of body and materials through an overhead camera or sensing device (e.g., depth camera) promises to be an effective index of immersive reading. Also, we noticed the overwhelming presence of symmetry in the readers' use of arms and hands, yet another strong contextual cue and identifying feature.

Visual Tracking: In the midst of each reading session, readers (especially P1) exhibited visual tracking activities, involving the dominant hand and an object of thin profile (i.e., a pen) or a finger to serve as a transient focal point of visual attention. A typical tracking activity took the form of a hovering gesture, in which the tip of an object was seen as hovering (less than half a centimeter) above parts of the text in a linear fashion. While using a marking tool as the main mode to aid linear reading of the text, such as a pen or pencil (Fig. 4), all participants exhibited a high tendency to switch between visual tracking and annotating or writing activities, leveraging the same tool for different activities.

It was sometimes difficult to determine whether the reader was hovering above or making slight marks on the paper, until we noticed a fundamental visual cue that served to signify visual tracking. For most tracking activities, the grip posture was relaxed and the tip of the object protruded such that it was visible at any orientation and the angle was less acute than when marking. We also observed that the orientation of the pen tip changed relative to the area of text that was being read. Detecting this loose grip posture coupled with the angle and movement over the page will help identify visual tracking.

Visual tracking was also often accompanied by an indexical gesture, performed with the non-dominant hand (Fig. 5, left). While reading, participants placed their index finger on the margins to the left of a particular line or paragraph of interest, and moved up or down in relation to the area of text being read. This is an example of using the non-dominant hand as a frame of reference for guiding visual attention and dominant hand activity, functioning as a place marker. Attending to the placement of the non-dominant hand provides important cues for recognizing activities and focus of attention.

Annotating

Marshall's extensive study [22] of annotated materials reveals that annotations provide a permanent frame of reference for guiding the reader's visual attention. It is also known to aid encoding activities and memory. According to Marshall, the major functional roles of annotations include procedural signaling for future attention, place marking and aiding memory, in situ locations for problem solving, and visible traces of reader's attention. We observed annotating practices in our video corpus that fit these descriptions. In the remainder of this section we outline explicit (short notes) and telegraphic annotations (underlining, highlighting, circling).

Figure 5. Reader uses the non-dominant hand in coordination with the dominant hand to focus attention on segments of the document (*left images*), while they use the non-dominant hand to control the position and orientation of paper while writing (*right images*).

Short Notes: In our data short notes were written on a notebook, margin of a paper, or a Post-It. Marginal and Post-It notes were written in relation to the spatial location of a specific paragraph, line, or word of interest, rendering manual search and navigation less difficult. This was apparent, for example, when one participant (P1) quickly identified and selected a document with a Post-It note from a large pile of similar looking documents.

Underlining, highlighting, and circling: Other forms of annotations, including underlining, highlighting and circling (telegraphic marking), also increase the saliency of particular areas of text. Underlining activities were often preceded, or followed by visual tracking. Unlike tracking, annotating activities involved the use of a tripod grip, which is a characteristically rigid and tense grip posture. Calculating pen-to-surface angle in addition to pen grip posture may help a system discriminate between tracking and annotating activities. A common pen-to-surface angle was a consistent signature of annotation instances.

Dominant vs. Non-dominant hand: We also observed a fundamental difference in the relationship between the dominant and non-dominant hands during annotating activities. According to Guiard's description of asymmetric bimanual interaction [11], the dominant hand moves relative to the motion of the non-dominant hand, which is an instance of setting a frame of reference. Consistent with Guiard's observation, we found all annotating activities to be carried out by an asymmetric division of labor between the hands, in which the non-dominant hand served as an anchor point by holding down the paper while the dominant hand performed the functional role of the annotating activity (Fig. 5, right). This interaction was also preserved when one participant wrote a brief note on a small Post-it. Yet again we note that detecting the location and posture of the non-dominant hand provides important cues about readers' attention and frame of reference.

Navigation

We observed multiple instances of paper navigation behaviors that were typical of content browsing, searching, and cross-referencing activities within and between source documents (Fig. 6). These behaviors were typically observed in the beginning of reading activities as well as in transitional phases in which the reader switched between different reading materials. They include holding, flipping, and tucking (Fig. 7), which all involved a coordinated asymmetric division of labor between the dominant and non-dominant hands. Many of these activities are afforded by the tangibility of paper and its physical properties of being thin, lightweight, and flexible [30]. We see many opportunities in tracking the position of paper documents with respect to one's hands as a way of indexing attention and activity.

Holding: A holding gesture was defined as any instance of holding or lifting an object (i.e. paper) from the surface of the desk. This gesture marked the beginning of most paper navigation activities. Almost all navigational activities were

Figure 6. Readers hold documents or objects while cross-referencing between multiple source documents. Preserving the non-dominant hand's position on a mouse (*top*) or holding a group of papers (*bottom*) may indicate intention to return to a previous state or frame of reference.

(a) Holding (b) Flipping (c) Tucking

Figure 7. Examples of paper navigation.

preceded by the holding gesture, since any paper, or stacks of papers, had to be picked and held in mid-air before it could be acted upon. For example, page turning was most likely preceded by a holding gesture, in which an edge of a page was picked up and held in advance before the reader turned the page. Importantly, its duration was short-lived, except a few occasions in which a paper was held in "stand-by" mode during an ongoing activity.

However, in a few cases, a paper was moved or manipulated without being lifted from the surface of the desk. One example was a dragging gesture, in which a paper, once read, was dragged by the participant (P3) across the desk and away from the center space. Minor positional adjustments were made via panning and rotating gestures.

Long term usage of the hold gesture was observed during cross-referencing or content browsing activities. We observed one such behavior (P2) that seemed to be characteristically slow and fine-grained, indicating a decision making process. This behavior was observed when readers have narrowed down their search to a smaller number of items. During this process, one or more papers were held in mid-air for close inspection, and readers looked back and forth between the papers on the desk and the ones they were holding.

Flipping: A flipping gesture was used when a reader turned over a page in order to navigate between the previous or next page. As mentioned earlier, a typical page flip started with a holding gesture, or a pinch grip of the edge of a paper, followed by two different variations of the flipping gesture depending on the state of the document. When the papers were stapled together, readers typically exhibited a bimanual asymmetric interaction. In general, the dominant hand picked up the tip of the paper (hold gesture), passing it over to the non-dominant hand to turn the page.

In contrast, a single paper sheet was flipped single-handedly, typically using the non-dominant hand. In both cases, the non-dominant hand was used to perform the flipping gesture, which was typically due to the fact that the dominant hand was occupied with a marking tool for performing annotating activities. However, there was another difference in the execution of the flipping gestures. With stapled papers, readers turned the page by rotating the entire forearm. With unstapled pages, the same gesture was performed by only rotating the wrist. This difference seemed to emerge as a result of the use of staples, which limit the paper's range of motion.

Tucking: Another consistent use of the holding gesture involved tucking. This gesture seemed to cue within-document cross referencing or search activities, in which readers were often seen as making quick comparisons between multiple pages. Instead of making a full page turn, readers searching for a particular page used one hand to lift the edges of a paper while using the other to hold onto multiple pages in "standby". During this phase, one reader (P1) used her "holding hand" as a place marker by inserting one or two fingers between several prematurely turned pages. This action seemed to facilitate within-document search or referencing processes by allowing the reader to easily return to one of the target search pages while accessing those pages in full view.

Organization

After an extensive study of desktop organization behaviors, Malone [21] concluded that documents are organized into piles and files. We observed various multimodal cues that appear to signify piling activities, including the stacking motion, spatial layout of document piles, acoustic pulse patterns, and searching behaviors.

Stacking: A stacking gesture was always followed by a formation of a paper pile. It may be followed by a stapling activity that binds multiple single pages into one group. The stacking gesture was consistently identified as a symmetric bimanual interaction, and all readers performed the gesture in three simple steps: first, multiple papers were gathered together and held in mid-air with both hands in a vertical fashion; second, while maintaining the vertical hold gesture, papers were let loose from the fingers to slide down until they touched a flat surface; and finally, further adjustments were made with both hands to ensure alignment in the vertical and horizontal directions. This gesture leverages gravity and the flatness of the desk surface to yield a near-perfect alignment of a group of papers.

Spatial layout: While the most actively read documents are placed in the immediate vicinity of the reader, other documents and piles were arranged to the periphery. In addition, a dense region of piles and documents often formed towards the non-dominant side of the reader (see Fig. 6). This particular arrangement seemed to be influenced by the placement of the reader's personal computer (both laptop and desktop), positioned so as to be able to use the mouse with their dominant hand. Since piles are by no means arranged in systematic order, recognizing the spatial location and activity history of each pile will provide additional cues to the organization of physical documents in space.

Search: Because of the nature of piling activities, with papers stacked on top of each other, finding a particular document or page can be a serial and time consuming process. When looking for a particular document from a pile of papers, participants typically performed the search by removing one paper at a time, beginning from the top of the pile, until they found the paper of interest. Interestingly for the purpose of recognizing this activity, we noticed that a secondary pile was created by virtue of the activity, later to be combined with the previous pile once the reader completed the search. Participants also demonstrated well-coordinated asymmetric bimanual interaction. Although we have not observed any particular role bias between the dominant and non-dominant hands, there was clearly an asymmetric division of labor between hands in which one hand was in charge of lifting while the other did the moving.

Audio waveform: We observed an interesting phenomenon while analyzing acoustic pulse patterns generated from the above activities. To our surprise, most peaks in the audio waveform were associated with paper manipulation activities (see Fig. 1 for an example of stacking behavior aligned with a peak in the audio signal). We now suspect that there may be unique ranges of frequency amplitudes associated with various paper activities. Detecting and processing such audio signals may provide additional cues and signatures of the structure and organization of activity on the desktop.

IMPLICATIONS FOR DESIGN

When, where, and how digital technology should be used to augment active reading are central questions of our research. We argue that detailed understandings of the structure and patterns of active reading activities are needed in order to be able to augment them in effective and natural ways. The contribution of the current work is a microanalysis of active reading, focusing primarily on identifying patterns and practices that might serve as activity and context signatures. By applying the outcomes of our analysis as part of a system able to recognize and track body movement and activity on and above the desk, we aim to develop feedback mechanisms that support novel augmented active reading experiences. While the integration of those findings in the system we are developing is part of our future work, in this section we detail the implications of active reading activity recognition, and we sketch four possible interactions that can be implemented by leveraging the recognized activity.

Recognizing Activities

We identified various types of activities involved in active reading. One central task involves immersive reading. It requires intense concentration and may be susceptible to the slightest of interruptions. Annotation is another central task commonly associated with immersive reading, serving to assist subsequent activity. We identified several peripheral tasks that provide support: visual tracking, underlining and highlighting, cross-referencing between multiple documents, content browsing, and document organization. Of particular importance for design, we identified how the position and movement of the body and hands with respect to the material workspace might serve as signatures for these activities.

Sustained Body Positioning: A salient cue for automatically identifying immersive reading is the presence of a sustained body position (leaning over desk, elbows on desk, or feet propped up). Another feature of this activity is the proximal distance of a document to the reader's head. From a design perspective being aware of this state is particularly important since it is particularly vulnerable to interruptions.

Hand Positioning and Contact Points: The position and document contact points of the hands provide considerable information about the focus of attention. Most activities center around gestures that involve hands in contact with paper documents. Knowing which hand is in contact with which document is critical, but additional resolution at the paragraph or word level is also necessary. Sustained contact between hands and documents may indicate place-marking and holding, both of which provide a spatial frame of reference that guides attention to facilitate peripheral activities (e.g. visual tracking, cross-referencing, searching). Furthermore, visual tracking and cross-referencing are accompanied by a place-marking gesture (Fig. 5, left) while cross-referencing and searching are accompanied by a place-holding gesture (Fig. 6).

Positioning of Non-Dominant Hand: Detecting the location and document contact points for the non-dominant hand working in coordination with the dominant hand provides a different view into the person's frame of reference for their current activity. The non-dominant hand serves as a pointer, index, and guide to direct attention, possibly at a higher level or with different temporal qualities than the dominant hand. Using the non-dominant hand to temporarily hold a group of documents or other object may preserve a past frame of reference to which the person intends to return.

Pen Grip Posture: While both visual tracking and annotating activities frequently involve the use of pens, the associated postures differ (i.e. relaxed vs. tripod grip). The angle of the pen-to-surface may also differ during visual tracking and annotating. These different configurations may be used to identify when participants switch between writing and tracking, subsequently providing different user interface facilities depending on the activity.

Acoustic Properties: The stacking gesture used in piling activities has a unique acoustic property. Other paper navigation techniques such as flipping pages and searching through a pile of documents also seems to generate unique frequency amplitudes. In combination with tracking document movement and placement via an overhead camera, processing these acoustic signals may provide a robust method of helping to detect grouping or navigation actions without additional user input. More work is needed to explore the specific acoustic properties of each interaction.

Envisioned Interactions

The microanalysis of active reading behavior and identification of signatures of component activities provides a basis for

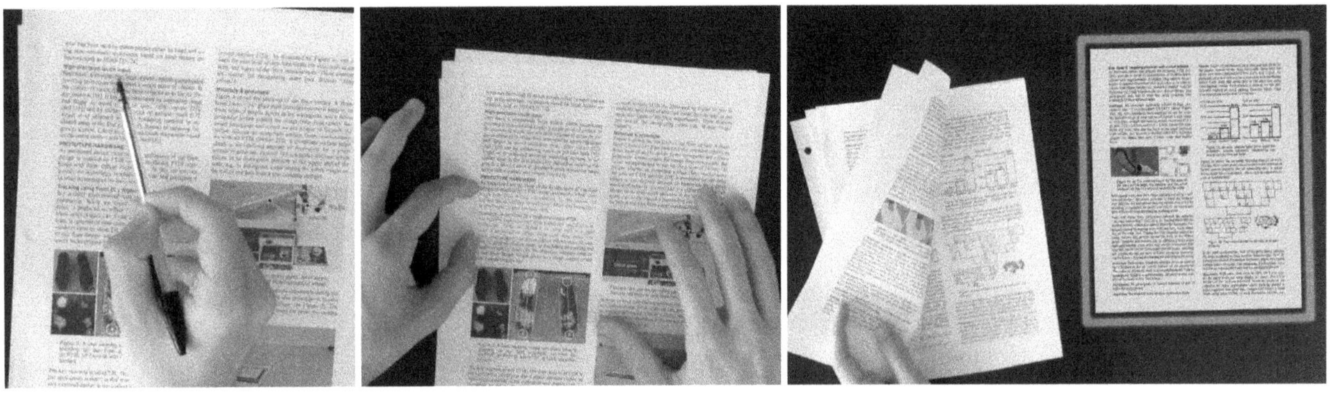

Figure 8. Envisioned interactions. ***Left:*** **Visual tracking with a pen or finger temporarily highlights text on the paper document.** ***Center:*** **Pinch-to-select gesture persistently highlights blocks of text.** ***Right:*** **Tucking a page provides an auxiliary view on the digital surface.**

the design of a range of novel interaction techniques to augment interactive desktop workspaces. We have prototyped several interactions based on our microanalysis of active reading (see Fig. 8). Note that while we plan to implement these interactions as part of the desktop workspace we are currently developing, the figures are mockups that give concrete design ideas to demonstrate how our results may inform augmented paper-based interactions.

Visual Tracking: To provide a supplementary visual cue to guide attention while engaged in active reading, the tip of the pen or the finger used to track the information on the paper document can be augmented with a focused high-intensity light cast on the entire line of text. This can function as a transient focal point of attention, with the highlight fading away as the reader moves his pen or finger away from the line to another line, and the focused light following (see Fig. 8, left).

Pinch-to-Select: To create an artificial highlight of the reader's visual attention while they work elsewhere, readers can use the index and thumb finger, similar to the "pinch-to-zoom" gesture on mobile phones, with their non-dominant hand next to a portion of text they want to highlight or select. The selection results in a persistent highlighting that can remain on the page while reading the document (see Fig. 8, center). Selected text can be used also in other interactions with the system, such as copying and transferring.

Drag to Copy: The reader can drag selected text or an image from the paper document onto the interactive workspace. Flicking an image with one finger can send the image to the nearest display monitor in the direction of the flicking motion.

Parallel View: To support within-document cross-referencing, a duplicate page is projected onto the desktop when readers flip a page that is tucked in between their fingers more than once. This enables reading two pages in full view regardless of the source location of each page (see Fig. 8, right).

CONCLUSION

This paper describes the process of active reading in detail as a foundation for designers of augmented desktop workspaces. Our research team is iteratively developing a novel augmented desktop workspace that uses a depth camera to track movement of the body and hands on and above the desktop surface, captures video of activity, and can project onto the desk surface. The main contributions of the work reported here are a detailed microanalysis of active reading, identification of potential signatures of component activities, and concrete examples of how these insights should drive interaction design. We stress the importance and significance of asymmetric bimanual interaction and the need for digital augmentations that fit naturally with everyday active reading practices and support fluid interaction with both paper and digital media. The broader impact of our analysis is to inform the development of novel interaction techniques based on the recognition of specific features of active reading components, opening up new avenues for exploring augmentation of active reading on and above the desktop.

REFERENCES

1. A. Adler, A. Gujar, B. L. Harrison, K. O'Hara, and A. Sellen. A diary study of work-related reading: design implications for digital reading devices. In *Proc. CHI '98*, pages 241–248, 1998.
2. B. B. Bederson. Interfaces for staying in the flow. *Ubiquity*, pages 1–1, Sept. 2004.
3. E. A. Bier, M. C. Stone, K. Pier, W. Buxton, and T. D. DeRose. Toolglass and magic lenses: the see-through interface. In *Proc. SIGGRAPH '93*, pages 73–80, 1993.
4. P. Brandl, C. Forlines, D. Wigdor, M. Haller, and C. Shen. Combining and measuring the benefits of bimanual pen and direct-touch interaction on horizontal interfaces. In *Proc. AVI '08*, pages 154–161, 2008.
5. V. Bush. As we may think. *The Atlantic Monthly*, 176(1):101–108, 1945.
6. B. Butterworth and G. Beattie. Gesture and silence as indicators of planning in speech. *Recent advances in the psychology of language: Formal and experimental approaches*, 4:247–360, 1978.
7. W. Buxton and B. Myers. A study in two-handed input. *SIGCHI Bull.*, 17(4):321–326, Apr. 1986.
8. M. Csikszentmihalyi. *Flow: The Psychology of Optimal Experience*, volume 8:1. Harper Perennial, 1991.

9. D. Engelbart and W. English. A research center for augmenting human intellect. In *Proc. AFIPS '68*, pages 395–410, 1968.

10. A. Fouse, N. Weibel, E. Hutchins, and J. D. Hollan. Chronoviz: a system for supporting navigation of time-coded data. In *Extended Abstracts of CHI 2011*, pages 299–304, 2011.

11. Y. Guiard. Asymmetric division of labor in human skilled bimanual action: The kinematic chain as a model, 1987.

12. F. Guimbretière. Paper Augmented Digital Documents. In *Proc. UIST '03*, 2003.

13. K. Hinckley, X. Bi, M. Pahud, and B. Buxton. Informal information gathering techniques for active reading. In *Proc. CHI '12*, pages 1893–1896, 2012.

14. K. Hinckley, R. Pausch, and D. Proffitt. Attention and visual feedback: the bimanual frame of reference. In *Proc. I3D '97*, pages 121–ff., 1997.

15. K. Hinckley, K. Yatani, M. Pahud, N. Coddington, J. Rodenhouse, A. Wilson, H. Benko, and B. Buxton. Pen + touch = new tools. In *Proc. UIST '10*, pages 27–36, 2010.

16. P. Kabbash, W. Buxton, and A. Sellen. Two-handed input in a compound task. In *Proc. CHI '94*, pages 417–423, 1994.

17. A. Kendon. Gesture. *Annual Review of Anthropology*, 26:pp. 109–128, 1997.

18. Y. Li, K. Hinckley, Z. Guan, and J. A. Landay. Experimental analysis of mode switching techniques in pen-based user interfaces. In *Proc. CHI '05*, pages 461–470, 2005.

19. C. Liao, F. Guimbretière, K. Hinckley, and J. Hollan. PapierCraft: A Gesture-Based Command System for Interactive Paper. *ACM TOCHI*, pages 1–27, 2008.

20. W. MacKay, G. Velay, K. Carter, C. Ma, and D. Pagani. Augmenting reality: Adding computational dimensions to paper. *Communications of the ACM*, 36(7):96–97, 1993.

21. T. W. Malone. How do people organize their desks?: Implications for the design of office information systems. *ACM Trans. Inf. Syst.*, 1(1):99–112, Jan. 1983.

22. C. C. Marshall. Annotation: from paper books to the digital library. In *Proc. DL '97*, pages 131–140, 1997.

23. D. McNeill. So you think gestures are nonverbal? *Psychological Review*, 92(3):350–371, 1985.

24. T. Moran and S. Zhai. Beyond the desktop metaphor in seven dimensions. *Designing integrated digital work environments*, pages 335–354, 2007.

25. M. Morris, A. Brush, and B. Meyers. Reading revisited: Evaluating the usability of digital display surfaces for active reading tasks. In *Proc. TABLETOP '07*, pages 79 –86, 2007.

26. J. Napier and R. Tuttle. *Hands*. Princeton Science Library. Princeton University Press, 1993.

27. K. O'Hara and A. Sellen. A comparison of reading paper and on-line documents. In *Proc. CHI '97*, pages 335–342, 1997.

28. K. O'Hara, A. S. Taylor, W. M. Newman, and A. Sellen. Understanding the materiality of writing from multiple sources. *Int. J. Hum.-Comput. Stud.*, 56(3):269–305, 2002.

29. B. N. Schilit, G. Golovchinsky, and M. N. Price. Beyond paper: supporting active reading with free form digital ink annotations. In *Proc. CHI '98*, 1998.

30. A. J. Sellen and R. H. Harper. *The Myth of the Paperless Office*. MIT Press, Cambridge, MA, USA, 2003.

31. H. Song, H. Benko, F. Guimbretière, S. Izadi, X. Cao, and K. Hinckley. Grips and gestures on a multi-touch pen. In *Proc. CHI '11*, pages 1323–1332, 2011.

32. H. Song, F. Guimbretière, T. Grossman, and G. Fitzmaurice. Mouselight: bimanual interactions on digital paper using a pen and a spatially-aware mobile projector. In *Proc. CHI '10*, pages 2451–2460, 2010.

33. J. Steimle, O. Brdiczka, and M. Mühlhäuser. CoScribe: Integrating Paper and Digital Documents for Collaborative Knowledge Work. *IEEE Trans. on Learning Technologies*, 2009.

34. L. Straker, C. Pollock, R. Burgess-Limerick, R. Skoss, and J. Coleman. The impact of computer display height and desk design on muscle activity during information technology work by young adults. *Journal of Electromyography and Kinesiology*, 18(4):606 – 617, 2008.

35. A. Tabard, W. Mackay, and E. Eastmond. From individual to collaborative: the evolution of prism, a hybrid laboratory notebook. In *Proc. CSCW '08*, 2008.

36. C. S. Tashman and W. K. Edwards. Liquidtext: a flexible, multitouch environment to support active reading. In *Proc. CHI '11*, pages 3285–3294, 2011.

37. D. Vogel and G. Casiez. Conté: multimodal input inspired by an artist's crayon. In *Proc. UIST '11*, pages 357–366, 2011.

38. N. Weibel, A. Ispas, B. Signer, and M. C. Norrie. PaperProof: A Paper-Digital Proof-Editing System. In *Proc. CHI '08*, 2008.

39. P. Wellner. Interacting with paper on the digitaldesk. *Communications of the ACM*, 36(7):87 – 96, 1993.

40. F. Wilson. *The Hand: How Its Use Shapes the Brain, Language, and Human Culture*. Vintage Series. Vintage Books, 1999.

41. R. Yeh, J. Brandt, J. Boli, and S. Klemmer. Interactive Gigapixel Prints: Large, Paper-based Interfaces for Visual Context and Collaboration. In *Proc. Ubicomp 06*, 2006.

Interaction and Recognition Challenges in Interpreting Children's Touch and Gesture Input on Mobile Devices

Lisa Anthony[1], Quincy Brown[2], Jaye Nias[2], Berthel Tate[2], Shreya Mohan[1]

[1]UMBC
Information Systems
1000 Hilltop Circle
Baltimore MD 21250 USA
lanthony@umbc.edu

[2]Bowie State University
Computer Science Department
14000 Jericho Park Road
Bowie MD 20715 USA
qbrown@bowiestate.edu

ABSTRACT

As mobile devices like the iPad and iPhone become increasingly commonplace, touchscreen interactions are quickly overtaking other interaction methods in terms of frequency and experience for many users. However, most of these devices have been designed for the general, typical user. Trends indicate that children are using these devices (either their parents' or their own) for entertainment or learning activities. Previous work has found key differences in how children use touch and surface gesture interaction modalities *vs.* adults. In this paper, we specifically examine the impact of these differences in terms of automatically and reliably understanding *what kids meant to do.* We present a study of children and adults performing touch and surface gesture interaction tasks on mobile devices. We identify challenges related to (*a*) intentional and unintentional touches outside of onscreen targets and (*b*) recognition of drawn gestures, that both indicate a need to design tailored interaction for children to accommodate and overcome these challenges.

Author Keywords

Touch interaction; surface gesture interaction; child computer interaction; mobile devices; touchscreens; Android; $N; gesture recognition.

ACM Classification Keywords

H.5.m. Information interfaces and presentation (e.g., HCI): Miscellaneous.

INTRODUCTION

As mobile devices like the iPad and iPhone become increasingly more commonplace, touchscreen interactions are overtaking other interaction methods such as keyboard and mouse in terms of frequency and experience for many users. Furthermore, educators and researchers are identifying mobile devices as a powerful platform to provide personalized learning environments, games and entertainment for kids [6,20,26,27]. However, most of these devices are mass-market, consumer-oriented products that have been designed for the general, typical user. Trends indicate that children are using these devices (either their parents' or their own) for entertainment or learning activities (Figure 1) [27]. Children have smaller fingers, weaker arms, less fine motor control, less manual dexterity, and (typically) less experience with technology than adults. These factors, among potentially others, contribute to key differences in how children can, expect to, and do use touch and gesture interaction and impact their success with mobile devices. So far, this impact has not been examined thoroughly for design implications.

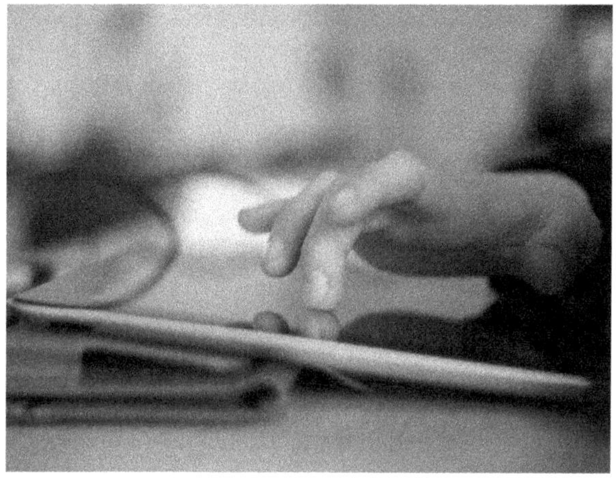

Figure 1. A child using an iPad. Image courtesy of Lexie Flickinger. http://www.flickr.com/photos/56155476@N08/6660076003/

Previously we have found key differences in how children use touch and surface gesture interaction modalities when compared to adults [4]. That work was a small study focusing on characterizing differences and theorizing about their impact, *e.g.*, in terms of missed touch events and bad recognition. In this paper, we expand on that work with a larger study of children and adults performing similar touch and surface gesture interaction tasks on mobile devices, in which the goal is to identify interaction and recognition challenges in *interpreting users' intended input*, especially for children. Given a touch event, can we be reasonably certain of which target the child intended to hit? Given a drawn gesture, can we confidently recognize and interpret the desired command? Similar issues may occur for adults, but in our study, we find much higher proportions of challenging input from kids.

We specifically find issues related to (*a*) intentional and unintentional touches outside of onscreen targets and (*b*) recognition of drawn gestures, both of which indicate a need to design tailored interaction for children to accommodate and overcome these challenges. We analyze patterns of touches for onscreen targets, and we present recognition accuracy results of a modern user interface gesture recognizer called $N [1,2] on the gestures generated by children and adults. Understanding these challenges, and designing interactions and implementing algorithms to overcome them, is critical to providing children the most successful user experience possible on mobile devices.

RELATED WORK

Touch and Surface Gesture Interactions

Prior work has examined the usability of touch and surface gesture interaction for *adults* on a variety of platforms, *e.g.*, PDAs and mobile devices [31], Tablet PCs and tablet computers [28,29], tabletop and surface displays [10,23,25], but *children* have been largely overlooked. In studies that did include children, analysis grouped children and adults together [25], focusing on general factors rather than on *differences* between children and adults that could be used to design better interactions. Some research has investigated only children, impeding the comparison of adults' and kids' interaction patterns [10,23]. More recently, researchers are specifically acknowledging and investigating differences between children and adults as users of such devices [4,11], but more work is needed in this area.

Children's Pointing Interactions

Prior studies have been conducted comparing differences in how children and adults acquire targets using mice or other pointing devices by studying how well Fitts' law (developed for adults) applies to children [7,12,16]. Typically, performance on pointing tasks increases for older children. Prior work has also found consistent evidence that children have difficulty with drag-and-drop interactions [14,15], implying that simple pointing is preferable. Pointing-based studies must be updated and extended to include modern touchscreen interactions with finger-based touch and surface gesture input.

Children's Gestures and Mobile Interactions

Stylus-based handwriting interaction has been extensively studied with children with the goal of comparing to analogous investigations with adults (*e.g.*, [22]). So far, work that looks at direct touch and gesture interaction for children has examined this question primarily on tabletop surfaces [10,11,23], and we do not yet know whether those findings will also apply to smaller-screen mobile devices.

Recent past work has examined children's direct touch and gesture interactions on mobile applications [4,5], and found that children experience different challenges in each interaction mode (*e.g.*, touch *vs.* gesture). For example, swipe gestures, which must be executed in one smooth stroke, are difficult for children, who tend to lift their fingers during the stroke [5]. Also, children have trouble accurately touching small onscreen targets, requiring larger interactors onscreen (*e.g.*, widgets and icons) and reducing the amount of onscreen information that could be displayed [4,5]. These findings form a good foundation but must be deepened to allow us to design interactions and technology that will be successful for the range of children's abilities.

Gesture Recognition Approaches and Performance

Once we can characterize the gesture input we can expect to see from children for various tasks, we can develop recognizers that are tailored to kids' input patterns. Current common gesture recognition approaches for user interfaces such as $N perform at reasonably high accuracy levels (*e.g.*, 95 to 99%) [1,2], but testing of such recognizers has used gestures from adults only, not children. Prior published benchmark datasets for gestures and handwriting recognition have only included samples from adults, not children [1,8,13,30]. No systematic testing of gesture recognition for children yet exists. These recognition benchmarks must be extended to represent the broader population of potential users of such technology.

APPROACH

To prepare for this work, a survey of mobile applications in the Android Marketplace was conducted. The surveyed applications were evaluated to identify the interaction modes employed in mobile games. Of the 23 surveyed game apps, 21 utilized touch as the primary mode of user interaction. Six applications employed surface gestures as a second mode of interaction, and only three employed tilting as an interaction mode. When examining children's education apps specifically, we find that tracing or handwriting practice activities using letters and numbers are commonly used, for example, Jaloby's AlphaCount[1], gdiplus' I Write Words[2], or Critical Matter, Inc.'s ABC Letter Tracing[3]. Additionally, prior work has found that users prefer gesture short cuts for commands that are character-based [18]. Given these results, we have chosen to focus our current investigations on touch and surface gesture interactions. We have developed two controlled tasks that resemble real-world touch and gesture interaction activities such as tapping, sketching and writing [4]. These abstracted tasks simplify the interaction to basic elements and eliminate any possible effects of application context.

PRELIMINARY STUDY

This work extends a preliminary study we conducted [4]. In that study, 8 children (aged 7 to 11 years) and 6 adults

---

[1] http://itunes.apple.com/us/app/alphacount/id359046783?mt=8

[2] http://itunes.apple.com/us/app/iwritewords-handwriting-game/id307025309?mt=8

[3] http://itunes.apple.com/us/app/abc-letter-tracing-free-writing/id416326981?mt=8

(aged 18+ years) participated. This work seeks to expand on that investigation by considering a wider range of users. We briefly review that study and its findings, pointing toward where this study replicates *vs.* improves on the previous work. In the preliminary study, two tasks were used: (1) a touch target acquisition task; and (2) a surface gesture interaction task. This study uses similar tasks with a few significant changes, which we now describe.

Preliminary Study: Touch Target Acquisition Task

This task involved users touching targets drawn onscreen [4]. The preliminary study used 43 square targets of 4 different sizes: extra-small (20 pixels), small (40 pixels), medium (60 pixels), and large (100 pixels), in 13 different interface positions [4]. In this study, we use the same four target sizes but define them based on absolute physical size rather than pixels, to account for varying screen resolutions and pixel densities (see Study Design section). In the preliminary study, participants tapped the target on the screen; the software automatically advanced to the next target upon registering a tap event, even if the tap was not within the target [4]. In this study, we require the user to touch the target correctly before moving on, recording every touch event generated per target.

Preliminary Study: Gesture-Based Interaction Task

This task involved users drawing samples of eight different gestures, *e.g.*, letters or shapes [4]. In this study, we expand the set to 20 gestures, allowing us to examine more types of gestures such as numbers and symbols. In the preliminary study, no visual feedback was given to the users as they drew gestures [4]; in this study, we show a trace of the user's finger path on the screen to more closely mimic real-world touch and gesture sketching and drawing activities. Lastly, in the preliminary study, users only drew one example per gesture type, limiting the types of gesture recognition testing that could be performed [4]. In this study, we collect six samples per gesture type to enable exploration of within-user recognition and consistency.

Preliminary Study: Results

In general, the preliminary study found several significant differences between children and adults in how they completed the two tasks. For example, children missed targets 50% more often than adults, by a greater distance, and had more trouble with smaller targets than did adults [4]. The children in the preliminary study also made significantly smaller touch points but exerted significantly less pressure than did adults [4]. Also, recognition of children's gestures in the preliminary study was more challenging for modern recognizers than recognition of adults' gestures, likely due to the inconsistencies in how children made gestures (*e.g.*, generating more individual strokes, writing with a slower input speed) [4]. In addition to these findings, touches that were located in the vicinity of the previous target, *holdovers*, were also observed. These results point to several promising avenues for exploration of tailored interactions for children, but the small sample size and limited task set restrict the scope of the findings. Therefore, we have extended this preliminary study and addressed these limitations in order to yield broader results.

STUDY DESIGN

The study consisted of two phases: (1) a touch task designed to gather data on touch target acquisition; and (2) a gesture task designed to gather data on gesture-based interaction. The target acquisition task was intended to investigate interactions similar to those required when performing tasks such as tapping in a game or pressing an interface widget (*e.g.*, checkbox, menu item). The gesture task was designed to examine users' surface gestures entered with visual gesture feedback. All participants did both tasks in the same session, with breaks between tasks.

Participants

A total of 30 participants (16 children, 14 adults) participated in the study. The ages of the children varied from 7 to 16 years (mean: 11.5 yrs, stdev: 2.8 yrs), and all of the adults were over the age of 18 (mean: 22.5 yrs, min: 18 yrs, max: 29 yrs, stdev: 3.6 yrs). Of the 14 adults, 6 were female, and of the 16 children, 8 were female. The large majority of our participants were right-handed (24 of 30); three considered themselves ambidextrous, and three were left-handed.

In terms of self-reported familiarity with touchscreen devices, the adults rated themselves "average" (5 of 14, or 36%) or "expert" (9 of 14, or 64%), whereas 2 of the 16 (13%) children rated themselves as "beginners," 5 of 16 (31%) rated themselves "average," and 9 of 16 (56%) rated themselves "expert." For the children, these self-ratings were not correlated with age (r=-.08, *n.s.*, N=16). Table 1 shows the percentage of participants (adults and children) that owned and used various touchscreen devices. These demographics reflect the increased pervasiveness of touchscreen devices such as smartphones and iPads. We did not ask about tabletops and surfaces in our study because they are still very uncommon in the home environment.

		Mobile Phone	Tablet	MP3 Player	Tablet PC
Adults	Own it	79%	21%	7%	7%
	Use it daily	79%	29%	7%	0%
Children	Own it	50%	19%	44%	6%
	Family owns it	75%	56%	31%	6%
	Use it daily	63%	19%	38%	0%

Table 1. Distribution of ownership and usage of touchscreen devices among our participants. Note that, in our sample, no children under age 10 owned their own touchscreen devices.

Equipment

Both phases of the experiment were performed on Samsung Google Nexus S smartphones running the Android 4.0.4 operating system; the phones measured 4.88 x 2.48 x 0.43

inches (123.9 x 63 x 10.9 mm) with a 4-inch (101.6-mm) screen, measured diagonally. The display resolution was 480 x 800 pixels, with a pixel density of approximately 233 pixels per inch (ppi). The study interfaces and software were designed in Eclipse using the Android SDK. Note that this particular Android device does support multitouch interaction, but our apps were not designed to respond to it.

Phase 1: Touch Interactions

The goal of the touch task was to extend the previous study's findings regarding differences between the touch patterns of adults and children for specific targets of varied sizes and locations. The goal was to learn whether it was possible to reliably correlate users' touches to the desired targets, *e.g.* figure out what target they meant to touch, and to compare these patterns for kids and adults.

Design

This phase of the study used 104 targets of 4 different sizes: very small, small, medium, and large, in 13 different interface positions. Because a user's finger remains a constant size no matter what device he or she is using, we aimed for cross-platform uniformity in the absolute physical sizes of the targets: (a) large: half-inch squares (12.7 mm); (b) medium: three-eighths-inch squares (9.5 mm); (c) small: quarter-inch squares (6.35 mm); and (d) very small: one-eighth-inch squares (3.175 mm). The device-specific pixel size of each target was computed based on the device-reported ppi. We hypothesized that size of the target would be inversely related to difficulty: smaller targets were expected to be harder than larger targets. We used data from the pre-study mobile game app survey to determine the appropriate target sizes for the study. Additionally, Android recommends 7 to 10 mm. Thus, we also selected targets slightly smaller and larger than what we found in practice and in the guidelines in order to probe the boundaries of acceptable target sizes.

The 13 possible target locations were defined by dividing the display into a 3 x 5 grid. Of the 15 areas, 13 were selected using locations frequently identified in the surveyed apps, *e.g.*, along edges, in corners, in the center of screen. Half the targets were drawn with edge padding, causing them to appear slightly inset from the edge of the screen, whereas the other half were drawn exactly aligned with the edge of the screen. Edge padding was a constant value of 10 pixels. Thus, we had 4 sizes x 13 locations x 2 edge padding conditions = 104 possible targets. Every combination was represented once in the study stimuli. The order of targets was designed to evenly represent all possible transitions between target positions and sizes, and no two consecutive targets had the same size or position.

The participant's task for each discrete target trial was to tap the target drawn on the screen. All tasks were performed sitting and using the hand that the participant preferred. The participants were told to perform the tasks as naturally as they could and were allowed to hold the phone or rest it on the table as they preferred. Each touch on the screen was recorded. If a registered touch was not located within the bounds of the onscreen target, nothing happened and the participant had to try again. The software would not advance to the next target unless the user was able to register a touch within the current target. Figure 2(a) shows an example target (small). All participants were shown the targets in the same order. In our study, only one person (an adult) gave up on a target and needed help to move on.

Measures

Application logs recorded the *x*-coordinate, *y*-coordinate, time, touch pressure, and touch size of each down event, *i.e.*, touch, by the participants. Additionally, other measures were calculated from these data, including (1) whether the touch occurred within the boundaries of the target, (2) the distance a touch occurred from the center point of the target (in both pixels and inches), (3) the time delay from the time of the appearance of the target to the time the user successfully touched it, and (4) the attempt number of this touch for the current target.

Phase 2: Gesture Interactions

The goal of the gesture interaction phase was to explore whether there were differences between adults and children creating free-form gestures that may create challenges in recognizing and interpreting these gestures.

Design

In this phase of the study, participants were shown an interface screen with text indicating which gesture to make and a "Done" button. A screenshot of this interface for one gesture is shown in Figure 2(b). Users were asked to use their finger to draw gestures on the device screen and press the "Done" button when finished. The complete gesture set (20 in all) included letters (A, E, K, Q, and X), numbers (2, 4, 5, 7, and 8), symbols (line, plus, arch, arrowhead, and checkmark), and geometric shapes (circle, square/rectangle, triangle, diamond, and heart). These gestures were chosen

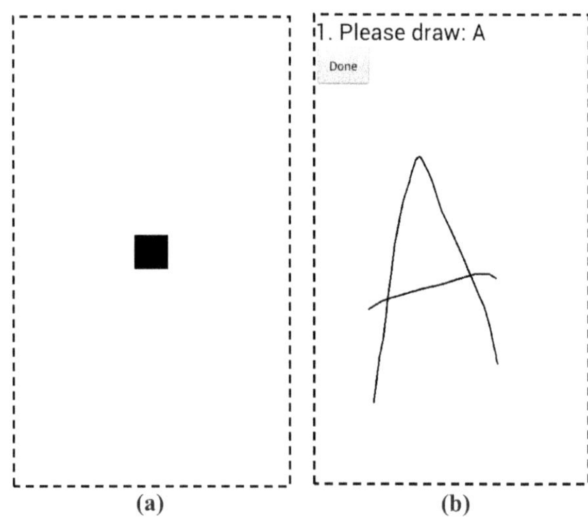

Figure 2. Example of the two task interfaces. (a) Touch target task: the user was required to touch the target with his or her finger. (b) Gesture data capture interface: the prompt at the top of the screen tells the participant what symbol to draw.

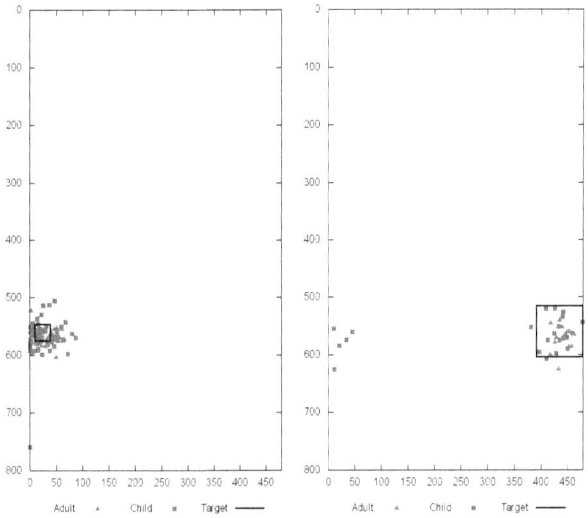

(a) (b)

Figure 3. Holdovers from target (a) to target (b).

based on a survey of existing gesture datasets for adults [2,9,13,32], and gesture / shape generation literature from educational psychology [3]. Participants were given a paper sheet showing what each gesture should look like, in case they were not familiar with every symbol by name, but were asked to make the gesture however they normally would and not to focus on copying the gesture sample. Participants entered one example of each gesture type one after another, and repeated this five times, yielding a total of six examples of each gesture type. As participants drew each gesture, a trace appeared under their finger of the gesture, but they were not able to edit their gestures. This decision was made to prevent users from becoming overly concerned with making perfect gestures.

Measures

To aid in the understanding of users' stroke patterns, the application logs recorded the *x*-coordinate, *y*-coordinate, time, touch pressure, and touch size for each down, move, and up event as the user made the gesture. All strokes made before hitting "Done" were counted as part of one gesture and stored together. After the session, other measures were calculated from these data, such as (1) the size of the bounding box containing each gesture (height, width, area), (2) the length of the gesture, (3) the duration in milliseconds that it took the user to enter the gesture, (4) the speed at which the gesture was entered (length over time), (5) the number of points sampled during the gesture, and (6) the number of strokes made. We also ran the gestures collected in this task through a gesture recognizer, discussed in more detail later, and computed recognition accuracy for kids *vs.* adults, as well as identifying commonly confused gestures.

DATA ANALYSIS AND RESULTS

We have analyzed both tasks to understand challenges that may occur in understanding what kids meant to do in touch and gesture interaction tasks, and compare them to adults.

Phase 1: Touch Interactions

Log data from two participants were lost for the target task (1 child, 1 adult), so the analysis in this section includes only the other 28 participants (15 children, 13 adults).

Because we initially intended to examine time to acquire targets, we removed specific targets from analysis if participants took a break in the task before completing that target, or if the task software had to be re-started, inflating the time taken to touch the target. The first target for every person was counted as practice and excluded from analysis. Thus, after removing 43 attempts for these reasons, we had 4650 attempts across 28 participants and 103 targets.

Users of touchscreen devices commonly register unintentional touches due to a slip of the finger, contacting the surface with other parts of the hand, or other reasons. We coded the touch locations based on the target location, and occurrences on the very edges of the device occurred only 8 times in our dataset (all done by children). We retained them in our analysis because we expect similar behaviors to occur during use of mobile devices.

Touch Target Acquisition: Holdovers

In this task, we observed a category of touches that were located within the vicinity of the *previous* target, which we call *holdovers*. These touches occurred because the targets automatically advanced when a successful touch was registered; users often hit the screen a few more times before noting the target had changed. This behavior occurred most often on the very small targets (81% of the time), as users had the most difficulty with these targets on a variety of measures. Interestingly, children exhibited this behavior far more often than adults (96% of all holdover occurrences were children), indicating a greater challenge in discerning a touch event's intended target for kids than for adults. Figure 3 shows an example of several holdovers occurring after a "very small" target (a) advances to a "medium" target (b). As users of mobile devices ourselves, we have noted similar behavior occurs in real tasks: touchscreen devices may be slow to register a touch and so we touch again intentionally in the same location, but the interface has already moved on, causing unintentional effects. Note that our prior study [4] also found that holdovers occurred at a similar rate and contributed to a large proportion of the missed targets, since in that task the target advanced on any touch. We discuss qualitative implications of this behavior in the Discussion section.

Touch Target Acquisition: Misses

Not counting the holdovers, children's touches were not within the target on the first attempt 23.1% of the time (*misses*), whereas adults only missed 16.9% of the time. The per-user average proportion of targets missed on the first try separated by target size is shown in Figure 4. A repeated measures ANOVA was performed on the per-user proportion of first-attempt misses with a within-subjects factor of *target size* (large, medium, small, very small) and a between-subjects factor of *participant type* (adult or

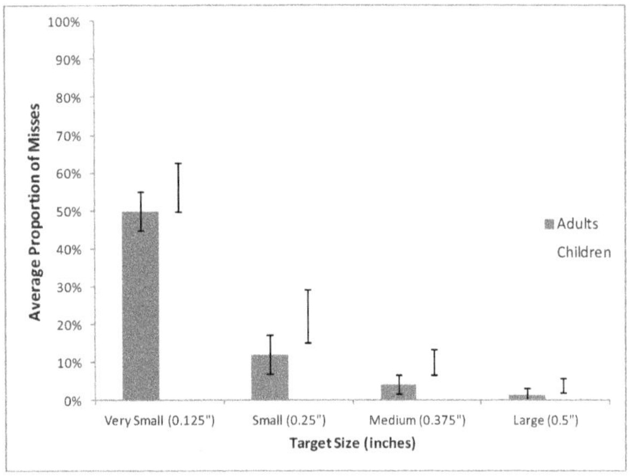

Figure 4. Average proportion of misses by target size for adults and children over all targets. Error bars show 95% confidence interval.

child). Multivariate tests indicate no significant interaction between *participant type* and *target size* ($F_{3,24}$=1.73, *n.s.*), but there are significant main effects of *target size* ($F_{3,24}$=209.6, p<0.0001) and *participant type* ($F_{1,26}$=6.57, p<0.05). Both children and adults experienced the most difficulty with the "very small" targets, and the difference in proportion of mistaken touches between adults and children was smallest with the "large" targets (though the interaction is not significant). Figure 5 shows a representative target for each size and all the touches that occurred within or outside the target for both children and adults. In these typical examples, kids make many more misses than do adults, indicating another challenge for discerning desired targets in kids' interactions.

The presence or lack of edge-padding on targets also contributed to the proportion of misses per target. In the presence of edge padding, the proportion of first-attempt misses nearly doubled (children: 30.2% and adults: 22.0%) compared to no edge padding (children: 17.8% and adults: 11.9%). A repeated measures ANOVA was performed on the per-user proportion of first-attempt misses with a within-subjects factor of presence of *edge padding* (yes or no) and a between-subjects factor of *participant type* (adult or child). Again, no significant interaction was found between *participant type* and *edge padding* by multivariate tests ($F_{1,26}$=0.542, *n.s.*), but significant main effects of both *edge padding* ($F_{1,26}$=52.54, p<0.0001) and (consistent with prior tests) *participant type* ($F_{1,26}$=7.05, p<0.05) were found. Note that nearly all (99%) of the misses on edge-padded targets occurred within the edge padding "gutter" itself (the space between the target and the edge of the screen). Kids and adults both had difficulty with edge-padded targets, and the prevalence of this problem indicates we must account for this challenge during touch interaction.

Touch Features

The Android operating system can sense the size and pressure exerted during a touch event. In unpaired samples two-tailed t-tests on the per-person average touch point size and pressure, we found that children make significantly smaller touch points (t(27)=2.67, p<0.05) and exert significantly less touch pressure (t(27)=2.37, p<0.05) than adults do, replicating our earlier study's findings [4]. An implication of this finding is that apps that use touch size or pressure to change pen color or thickness (such as using Adobe Photoshop with a Wacom pressure-sensitive pen) may need to be calibrated separately for kids. As long as the touch events are registered by the hardware, these results do not point to a technical challenge for interpreting input.

Phase 2: Gesture Interactions

In total we collected 3600 gesture samples from 30 people over 6 samples of 20 gestures each. The first round of gestures was considered practice, leaving 3000 gesture

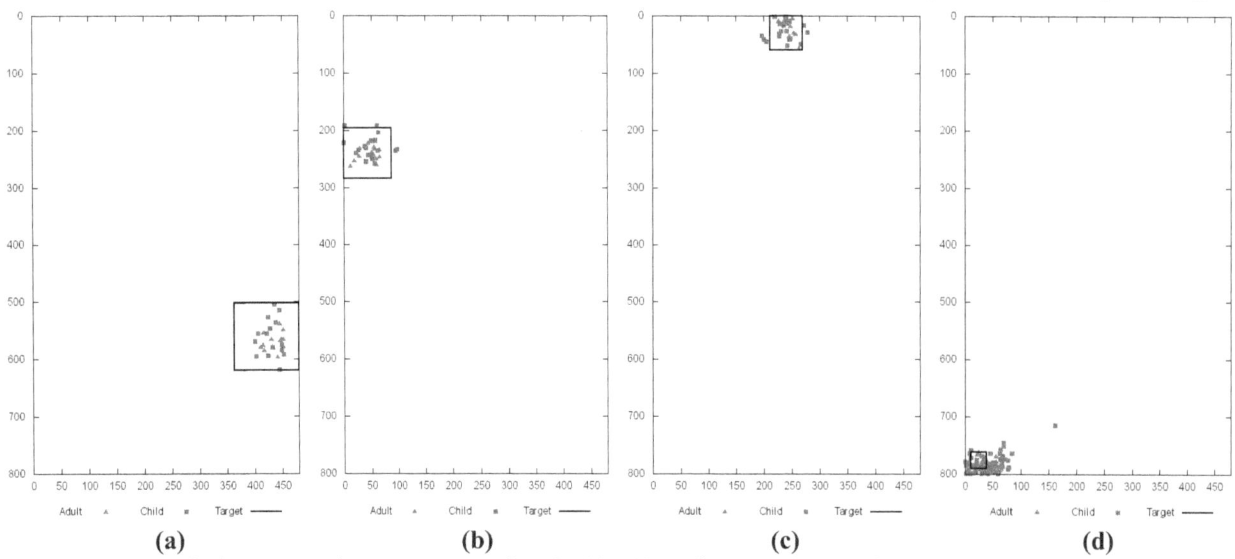

Figure 5. Examples of miss patterns in our target touch task: (a) a "large" target with no misses; (b) a "medium" target with a few misses from children; (c) a "small" target with several misses, mostly from children; and (b) a "very small" target with many misses from both children and adults, many of which appear in the gutter between the target and the screen's edge.

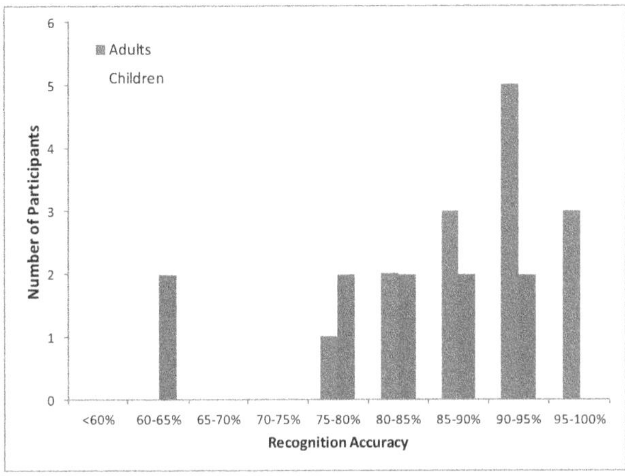

Figure 6. Histogram showing recognition accuracy distribution for gestures drawn by children and by adults.

samples for our analysis. We noted several gesture anomalies that were artifacts of the task, such as extra touches on the canvas near the "Done" button, that we could reasonably infer were not part of the user's intended gesture sample (something a real app could take into consideration through simple heuristics). In total we removed 5.8% of the samples due to such issues, leaving 2825 gestures for our analysis.

Gesture Recognition: Accuracy

Before we can act on gesture input, we must first interpret it. To determine how recognition of gestures performed by children might be different than of gestures performed by adults, we conducted recognition tests of the gestures collected in this study using the popular $N-Protractor recognizer [2]. We performed *user-dependent* testing, meaning the recognizer was trained and tested on data from the same user one at a time; final recognition accuracy rates are averaged across all children or all adults.

On average, children's gestures were recognized more poorly (mean: 81%, min: 61%, max: 92%, stdev: 9%) than adults' (mean: 90%, min: 76%, max: 98%, stdev: 6%), and this difference is significant by an unpaired samples two-tailed t-test on per-user recognition accuracy ($t(26.6)=3.18$, $p<0.01$). This result supplements the finding in our previous study [4] that *user-independent* recognition testing (*i.e.*, training the recognizer on different users than it is tested on) also shows significantly worse performance on children's gestures than on adults' gestures [4]. In this case, the effect size is smaller because user-dependent testing is in general more accurate. However, in both cases, interpretation of kids' intended gestures is more difficult.

Figure 6 shows a histogram of the number of children and adults whose gestures were recognized in bins of 5% intervals: children tend to be less accurately recognized. We theorized that recognition accuracy might be correlated with a participant's actual age. Indeed, there was a strong positive correlation between age (in years) and average recognition accuracy ($r=.59$, $p<0.01$, $N=30$).

Gesture Recognition: Confusions

When recognition of a drawn gesture is not correct, the recognizer typically returns some other gesture (rather than "[no result]"). How can we be sure the recognized gesture is what the user meant to draw? Confidence scores are used in recognition approaches to enable some sense of "degree of certainty" that the recognition result matches the intention [21]. $N [1,2] does not return a confidence score, but we can look at the confusable gestures to understand any patterns that may occur. Gestures that are commonly confused for each other should reduce our confidence that recognition results returning these gestures are correct.

Table 2 shows the top five most highly confused pairs of gestures for children and adults. Because recognition for children is lower, there are more instances of the confused pairs than for adults. It is interesting to note that in the top five, only A-to-K is common between children and adults.

	Tested Gesture	Confused Gesture	No. of Confusions	% Tests Confused
Adults	A	K	268	6.5%
	E	[no result]	246	6.0%
	rectangle	E	195	4.8%
	arrowhead	7	184	4.5%
	diamond	triangle	167	4.1%
Children	plus	X	503	14.4%
	A	K	353	10.1%
	K	4	206	5.9%
	X	plus	203	5.8%
	triangle	diamond	191	5.5%

Table 2. Top five most highly confused gestures for children and adults. Total number of tests for adults per gesture type is 4100 and for children is 3500.

Figure 7 shows an example (for an adult) of how A and K as written (a) can be confused after $N-Protractor performs its pre-processing steps (b) used to match multistroke gestures [1,2]. Because they are confused for both adults and children, this finding indicates that gesture sets must be defined based on knowledge of what gestures are confusable by particular recognizers.

Also, for children, plus and X are confused for each other in both directions, *i.e.*, plus is often recognized as X and X is often recognized as plus, but the same is not true for adults. Based on knowledge of how the $N-Protractor recognizer works [1,2], we would expect these two symbols to be highly confusable because they are rotations of each other. In our tests, $N-Protractor was configured with a bounded rotation invariance of ±45° (meaning that it would only consider two gestures to be the same if they were within 45° of rotation from each other). For children, plus and X were often within this rotation bound, but for adults, this was not common. Figure 8 shows one child's plus and X (a)

(a) A and K as written by an adult participant.

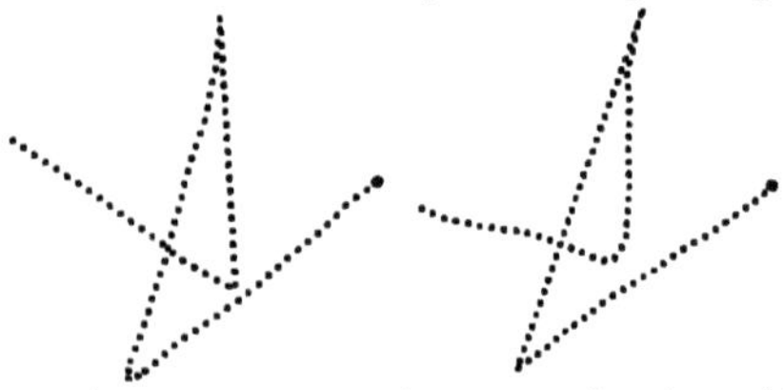

(b) Recognizer pre-processing steps for A and K yield two gestures that it cannot distinguish.

Figure 7. Illustration of how the recognizer's pre-processing steps can create highly confusable pairs of gestures.

that were confused for each other by the recognizer, and one adult's (b) that were not. This finding may indicate that children do not tend to write their gestures oriented to an expected upright rotation. This factor can be used to tweak parameters for gesture recognizers and to select the best gesture set so as to avoid such rotation-induced conflicts, increasing confidence that we will know what was meant.

DISCUSSION AND DESIGN IMPLICATIONS

The results of this work have important implications both for designing touchscreen interfaces for children and adults and for implementing recognizers for children's gestures. The technical challenges we identify focus on understanding and interpreting what the user meant to do:

- Prevalence of *holdover* touches and *misses* create challenges for identifying the user's intended target; and,
- Low recognition accuracy on some gestures creates challenges for interpreting the user's intended gesture.

These challenges are more pronounced across the board for input from kids *vs.* adults. We now discuss implications for design and implementation that follow from our findings.

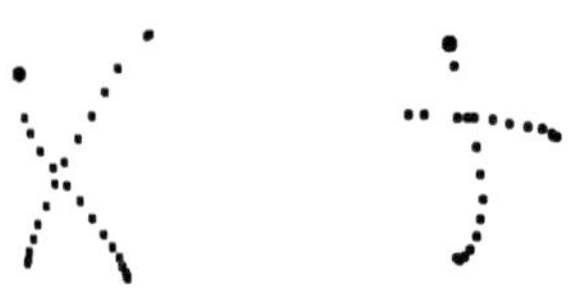

(a) X and plus as written by a child participant.

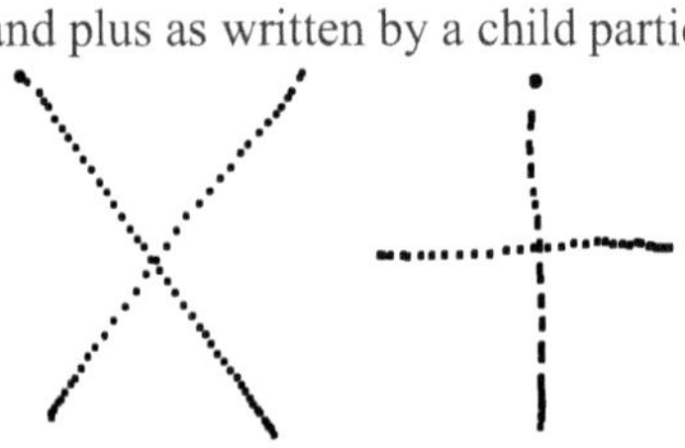

(b) X and plus as written by an adult participant.

Figure 8. Example of a pair of gestures (X and plus) that were highly confused for children but not for adults.

Touch Interactions

The target task results lead to several recommendations for designing touch interfaces for kids.

Use timing and location of touches and interface widgets to identify and ignore holdover touches (corollary: improve interface responsiveness to prevent holdovers). Consider the *holdover* touches observed for many of the targets, especially the "very small" ones. Although the holdover phenomenon of intentional touches in the location of the previous target was exhibited by both children and adults, the vast majority of occurrences (96%) were caused by children. This difference suggests that there may be cognitive processing delays preventing children from noticing as quickly that their target has activated. This phenomenon also occurs in real world use of mobile devices, from the authors' own experiences, and makes it challenging for the system to understand the user's intended action: was it an intentional or unintentional touch? If the touch was very close to the last activated target in space or in time, it is probably a holdover and can be ignored.

Use consistent, platform-recommended target sizes. Our data revealed that the "very small" targets, 0.125" square, are too small for both children and adults. However, we found that the other target sizes (0.25", 0.375", and 0.5") were large enough that on average only one attempt was needed, pointing to a possible floor effect. Because of the limited screen space on a mobile device such as a smartphone, smaller interactors allow more information to be onscreen at once. It is possible that there may be a minimum acceptable target size between 0.125" and 0.25" that has yet to be discovered. The Android design guidelines specify targets should be between 7 to 10 mm in size (0.275" to 0.39"), which is supported by our findings.

Increase active area for interface widgets to allow slightly out-of-bounds touches to count. The target size impacts the number of recorded misses for both children and adults. For the smallest targets, touches appear in a scattered distribution centered on the target itself; making this space also an active area will improve touch accuracy.

Align targets to edge of screen, or count edge touches. Our data also shows that many of the missed touches for edge-padded targets appear in the "gutter" between the target and the edge of the screen. Thus, we find Fitts' law's recommendation (for desktop pointing applications) to have interactors at screen edges also applies to mobile devices.

Gesture Interactions

The gesture task results also lead to recommendations for implementing recognition for kids.

Train age-specific recognizers to improve accuracy on kids' gestures. Recognition and interpretation of children's gestures was more difficult than of adults' gestures, and recognition accuracy was positively correlated with participant age: the recognizer had the most trouble interpreting the youngest kids' gestures. Previously we have found significant differences in the characteristics of children's and adults' gestures such as height, width, and stroke count [4]. We analyzed similar features of the gestures collected in this study and did not find any significant discriminators between children's and adults' gestures. However, we did observe higher recognition error and gesture confusion among children's input than among adults'. This data suggests that there are other characteristics, yet to be discovered, of gestures that differ between adult and child users that do affect recognition accuracy. We intend to investigate other potential feature spaces to identify these characteristics in order to implement recognition algorithms that can accommodate them. For example, measures of the total curvature, sharpness, or global orientation of the gesture [24], or movement variability within the gesture (*e.g.*, "wiggliness") [19] may be effective discriminators for children's gestures.

Design gesture sets to avoid confusions caused by recognizer limitations (corollary: train recognizers specifically to problematic pairs). Our data shows that children's writing and drawing styles can affect recognition and interpretation of what they meant to draw. We found that the recognizer's most frequently confused gestures differed for kids and for adults, both in terms of frequency and in terms of whether they were reciprocal (*i.e.*, in both directions). Since we found that recognition accuracy is related to age, we expect that, as children age and improve their fine motor skills and penmanship, not only will the recognition accuracy gap narrow, but recognizer confusions will be more similar to those for adults.

LIMITATIONS

This study represents an important next step in our research agenda of understanding how children use touch and gesture interaction differently than adults, in order to better design and implement such interfaces for kids. Building on prior work, this study expands the ages of the children and the task we have studied. This study does have some limitations, which we acknowledge here and plan to address in future work. First, this study expands on our prior study [4] by looking at older children. It may be that younger children will pose more challenges for touchscreen interfaces and recognizers, and wider recruitment is needed to find kids with varying touchscreen expertise levels. Therefore, we plan to expand to younger children. Working with younger children will require further modification of the tasks to engage young kids during the study session.

Second, we focused on a relatively narrow age range for adults (18 to 29) in this study. This choice was partly because we expect this age range of adults to have the smoothest performance compared to older demographics, and we wanted to compare children to adults for whom the biggest performance differential would result. However, based on prior work on mouse pointing performance [17], we anticipate that touchscreen interaction performance will reach a peak in early to middle adulthood and then begin declining with age. We plan to explore this relationship in future studies by including older adults, people with disabilities, and users with less touchscreen expertise.

FUTURE WORK

We previously found significant differences in other touch and gesture characteristics, as well as target accuracy and gesture recognition [4]. In this paper, we focused on understanding and interpreting what the user meant by his or her input. The visual feedback provided in this study in the gesture task may have impacted our findings, since we did not see the same gesture feature differences. Plans for future studies include comparing the task both with and without visual feedback to understand the potential effects of providing such feedback. Also, 93% of participants in this study considered themselves either average or expert users of touchscreen devices. In future studies, we plan to include users who consider themselves beginners to explore the effects of users' familiarity with touchscreen devices on gesture characteristics and touch target acquisition. To investigate possible impact of the recognition approach, we also plan to explore other recognizers, such as the Microsoft Tablet PC recognizer. Ultimately, tailored recognition may be required to confidently interpret kids' gestures.

CONCLUSION

We have presented results of a study that identifies specific challenges in understanding what kids meant to do in touch and gesture tasks on mobile touchscreen devices. We have found frequent intentional and unintentional touches outside of onscreen targets for children, and age-related challenges in recognizing children's gestures, both of which will impact the success of children's interactions. For example, children miss a greater proportion of targets than do adults, and generate a larger amount of *holdover* touches after an onscreen target has been selected. Also, gesture recognition of children's gestures is more challenging than for adults, especially for younger children. These challenges indicate a need for tailored interaction for children. The results of this work inform the types of interaction or recognition adaptations that would be necessary for children's successful interaction with mobile touchscreen devices.

ACKNOWLEDGMENTS

This work was partially supported by Department of Education HBGI Grant Award #P031B090207-11 and National Science Foundation Grant Awards #IIS-1218395/IIS-1218664. Any opinions, findings, and conclusions or recommendations expressed in this paper are those of the authors and do not necessarily reflect these agencies' views.

REFERENCES

1. Anthony, L. and Wobbrock, J.O. A lightweight multistroke recognizer for user interface prototypes. *Proc. GI 2010*, Canadian Information Processing Society (2010), 245–252.
2. Anthony, L. and Wobbrock, J.O. $N-protractor: a fast and accurate multistroke recognizer. *Proc. GI 2012*, (2012), 117–120.

3. Beery, K., Buktenica, N., and Beery, N.A. *The Beery-Buktenica Developmental Test of Visual-Motor Integration, 5th Edition.* Modern Curriculum Press, New Jersey, 2004.
4. Brown, Q. and Anthony, L. Toward comparing the touchscreen interaction patterns of kids and adults. *ACM SIGCHI EIST Workshop*, 4pp.
5. Brown, Q., Bonsignore, E., Hatley, L., Druin, A., Walsh, G., Foss, E., Brewer, R., Hammer, J., and Golub, E. Clear Panels: a technique to design mobile application interactivity. *Proc. DIS 2010*, ACM (2010), 360–363.
6. Chiong, C. and Shuler, C. *Learning: Is there an app for that? Investigations of young children's usage and learning with mobile devices and apps*. The Joan Ganz Cooney Center at Sesame Workshop, New York, NY, 2010.
7. Donker, A. and Reitsma, P. Aiming and clicking in young children's use of the computer mouse. *Computers in Human Behavior 23*, 6 (2007), 2863–2874.
8. Guyon, I., Schomaker, L., Plamondon, R., Liberman, M., and Janet, S. UNIPEN project of on-line data exchange and recognizer benchmarks. *Proc. ICPR 1994*, IEEE (1994), 29–33.
9. Hammond, T.A., Logsdon, D., Paulson, B., Johnston, J., Peschel, J., Wolin, A., and Taele, P. A sketch recognition system for recognizing free-hand course of action diagrams. *Proc. IAAI 2010*, AAAI Press (2010), 1781–1786.
10. Harris, A., Rick, J., Bonnett, V., Yuill, N., Fleck, R., Marshall, P., and Rogers, Y. Around the table: Are multiple-touch surfaces better than single-touch for children's collaborative interactions? *Proc. CSCL 2009*, International Society of the Learning Sciences (2009), 335–344.
11. Hinrichs, U. and Carpendale, S. Gestures in the wild. *Proc. CHI 2011*, ACM (2011), 3023–3032.
12. Hourcade, J.P., Bederson, B.B., Druin, A., and Guimbretière, F. Differences in pointing task performance between preschool children and adults using mice. *ACM Transactions on Computer-Human Interaction 11*, 4 (2004), 357–386.
13. Hse, H.H. and Newton, A.R. Recognition and beautification of multi-stroke symbols in digital ink. *Computers & Graphics 29*, 4 (2005), 533–546.
14. Inkpen, K.M. Drag-and-drop versus point-and-click mouse interaction styles for children. *ACM Transactions on Computer-Human Interaction 8*, 1 (2001), 1–33.
15. Joiner, R., Messer, D., Light, P., and Littleton, K. It is best to point for young children: a comparison of children's pointing and dragging. *Computers in Human Behavior 14*, 3 (1998), 513–529.
16. Jones, T. An empirical study of children's use of computer pointing devices. *Journal of Educational Computing Research 7*, 1 (1991), 61–76.
17. Keates, S. and Trewin, S. Effect of age and Parkinson's disease on cursor positioning using a mouse. *Proc. ASSETS 2005*, ACM (2005), 68–75.
18. Li, Y. Gesture search: a tool for fast mobile data access. *Proc. UIST 2010*, ACM (2010), 87–96.
19. MacKenzie, I.S., Kauppinen, T., and Silfverberg, M. Accuracy measures for evaluating computer pointing devices. *Proc. CHI 2001*, ACM Press (2001), 9–16.
20. Norris, C. and Soloway, E. Envisioning the handheld-centric classroom. *Journal of Educational Computing Research 30*, 4 (2004), 281–294.
21. Pitrelli, J.F. and Perrone, M.P. Confidence-scoring post-processing for off-line handwritten-character recognition verification. *Proc. ICDAR 2003*, IEEE (2003), 278–282.
22. Read, J.C., MacFarlane, S., and Casey, C. Pens behaving badly-usability of pens and graphics tablets for text entry with children. *Adj. Proc. UIST 2002*, ACM Press (2002), 21–22.
23. Rick, J., Harris, A., Marshall, P., Fleck, R., Yuill, N., and Rogers, Y. Children designing together on a multi-touch tabletop: An analysis of spatial orientation and user interactions. *Proc. IDC 2009*, ACM (2009), 106–114.
24. Rubine, D. Specifying gestures by example. *SIGGRAPH Computer Graphics 25*, 4 (1991), 329–337.
25. Ryall, K., Morris, M.R., Everitt, K., Forlines, C., and Shen, C. Experiences with and observations of direct-touch tabletops. *Proc. Tabletop 2006*, IEEE (2006), 8pp.
26. Shin, N., Norris, C., and Soloway, E. Effects of handheld games on students learning in mathematics. *Proc. ICLS 2006*, International Society of the Learning Sciences (2006), 702–708.
27. Shuler, C. *Pockets of Potential: Using Mobile Technologies to Promote Children's Learning*. Joan Ganz Cooney Center at Sesame Workshop, New York, NY, 2009.
28. Vatavu, R.-D., Vogel, D., Casiez, G., and Grisoni, L. Estimating the perceived difficulty of pen gestures. *Proc. INTERACT 2011*, Springer (2011), 89–106.
29. Vogel, D. and Balakrishnan, R. Direct pen interaction with a conventional graphical user interface. *Human–Computer Interaction 25*, 4 (2010), 324–388.
30. Willems, D., Niels, R., Van Gerven, M., and Vuurpijl, L. Iconic and multi-stroke gesture recognition. *Pattern Recognition 42*, 12 (2009), 3303–3312.
31. Wobbrock, J.O., Aung, H.H., Rothrock, B., and Myers, B.A. Maximizing the guessability of symbolic input. *Ext. Abstracts CHI 2005*, ACM (2005), 1869–1872.
32. Wobbrock, J.O., Wilson, A.D., and Li, Y. Gestures without libraries, toolkits or training: a $1 recognizer for user interface prototypes. *Proc. UIST 2007*, ACM (2007), 159–168.

Branch-Explore-Merge: Facilitating Real-Time Revision Control in Co-Located Collaborative Visual Exploration

Will McGrath,[1] Brian Bowman,[1] David McCallum,[2] Juan David Hincapié Ramos,[2] Niklas Elmqvist[1], Pourang Irani[2]

[1]Purdue University
West Lafayette, IN, USA
{wbmcgrat, bowmanb, elm}@purdue.edu

[2]University of Manitoba
Winnipeg, MB, Canada
@umanitoba.ca

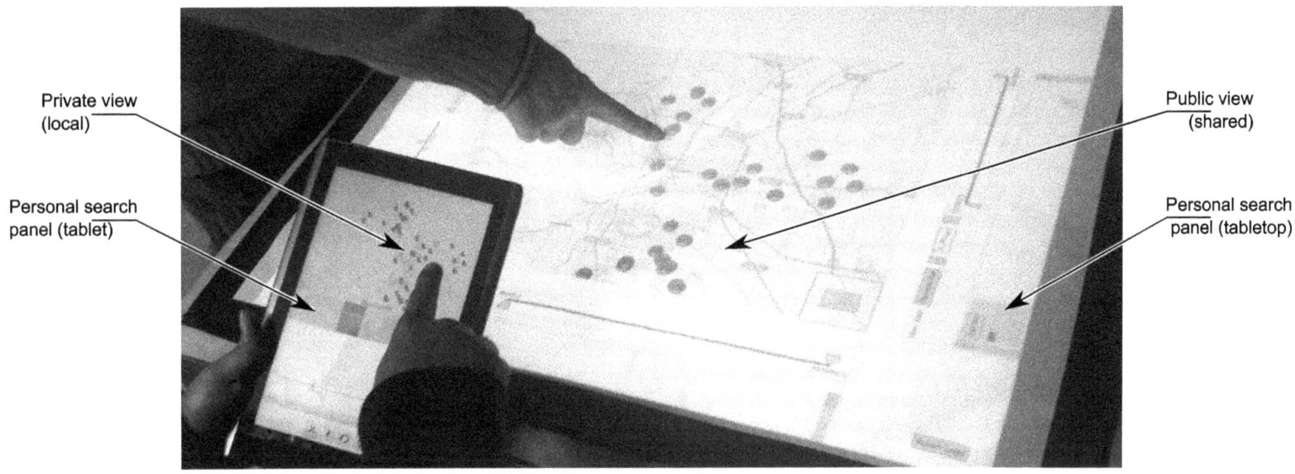

Figure 1: Our BEMVIEWER implementation of the branch-explore-merge protocol showing tabletop (public view) and tablet (private view). Two users are exploring a real estate dataset using a visual query formula as the shared state.

ABSTRACT

Collaborative work is characterized by participants seamlessly transitioning from working together (coupled) to working alone (decoupled). Groupware should therefore facilitate smoothly varying coupling throughout the entire collaborative session. Towards achieving such transitions for collaborative exploration and search, we propose a protocol based on managing revisions for each collaborator exploring a dataset. The protocol allows participants to diverge from the shared analysis path (branch), study the data independently (explore), and then contribute back their findings onto the shared display (merge). We apply this concept to collaborative search in multidimensional data, and propose an implementation where the public view is a tabletop display and the private views are embedded in handheld tablets. We then use this implementation to perform a qualitative user study involving a real estate dataset. Results show that participants leverage the BEM protocol, spend significant time using their private views (40% to 80% of total task time), and apply public view changes for consultation with collaborators.

ACM Classification: H.5.2 [Information Interfaces and Presentation]: User Interfaces—*Interaction styles*

Keywords: Public views, private views, collaborative visualization, coupling, computer-supported collaborative work.

INTRODUCTION

In collaborative settings, multiple users working together routinely engage in both *coupled* (working together) and *decoupled* (working alone) activities to solve a problem at hand [2, 21]. The degree of coupling varies along a continuum where on one end, the participants are working together in lockstep on a task, and on the other end, they are solving it independently. These coupling transitions happen constantly and seamlessly in any collaboration [11, 12, 26, 28].

These findings are particularly interesting for the field of *visualization* (the use of interactive graphics to convey large, complex, and/or abstract data [5]), where collaboration has recently been named a grand challenge for research [27]. Of course, collaborative visualization must overcome the same challenges in supporting varying degrees of coupling as discussed above [8]. As a result, designers of collaborative visualization tools have considered various methods of integrating smooth transitions in coupling styles into the workflow. For example, coordinated multiple views [28] can be used to create a link between a private workspace for decoupled activity, and the public shared view for coupled collaboration. Another approach is to simply make the other participant aware of common work and similarities [9]. Other visualization systems have provided restricted access control to parts of the data to enforce a specific degree of coupling [13].

While such solutions can greatly enhance collaborative efforts, they are limited in a number of ways. Adding private views to a tabletop display consumes valuable screen real-estate and thereby counters the collaborative nature of this medium which is already taxed by displaying crucial information. More importantly, private views on shared displays have to be managed as the user moves around, and is even more challenging in the context of multiple users, each in need of a private view consuming space on the shared display. The overhead in managing coordinated views can be significant [28], suggesting that new styles of linking private and public views are necessary. Additionally, private views on a shared workspace are still visible by all users, thus limiting the degree of decoupling (i.e. users around the display can still interfere with actions on the private views of others).

To allow for seamless transitions between coupled and decoupled work styles, we propose an approach where these two forms of interaction are interlinked but distinct. Our approach, referred to as Branch-Explore-Merge (BEM) is inspired by solutions used for asynchronous software subversion systems, such as CVS, Subversion, or RCS. With BEM, participants can view and work together on the shared workspace, but can also branch away from the current state of the visualization, allowing them to explore the data separately and independently from other participants. Results obtained from working on their private decoupled workspace can then be merged back into the shared display. Branching allows participants to deviate from the shared state, while merging is an operation that changes the shared state of the visualization. To make a clear distinction between coupled and decoupled activity, to address real-estate constraints of private views on a shared display, and to alleviate concerns of combining multiple private views on the shared view [28], BEM offloads decoupled work and places it on private views on mobile devices such as smartphones or tablets, leaving the collaborative surface to be used exclusively for shared work.

We have implemented a multivariate visualization system for tabletop displays and multitouch tablets that support the BEM model. We demonstrate the capability of the system through a qualitative evaluation involving a collaborative analytic activity. In the study, participants are asked to explore a multidimensional dataset of real-estate properties using a scatterplot. They are assigned a distributed task for finding a home with specific pre-defined constraints split between participants. A map view supports progressive filtering through faceted browsing, where the collaborators can iteratively filter out items in the dataset using range selections for each attribute in the dataset. The resulting visual query consists of a conjunction of such set selections and forms the shared state that the BEM model operates on. Users can branch off from any state of the public display to explore the dataset without affecting the work of the entire group. Updates can then be merged back onto the shared space.

The study yielded several qualitative observations: (a) users tend to branch very early on in the collaborative process; (b) participants spend considerable time working in decoupled style on the tablets; (c) in scenarios where the results are ambiguous, i.e. no homes found for the collective constraints, users return to the table for more inquiry; and (d) participants almost always end the search process by discussing results in the shared space over the tabletop.

BACKGROUND

Our work lies at the intersection of computer-supported cooperative work (CSCW), information visualization, and novel computing platforms. Below we review each of these areas and highlight the important messages for each of them.

Computer-Supported Cooperative Work

CSCW research centers on theory, design, and implementation of *groupware*: software used concurrently by multiple users. The CSCW field has formally existed since the 1980s, and numerous groupware systems have been developed over the years. An exhaustive survey of this body of work is outside the scope of this paper, and we will instead describe only directly relevant research in the discussion below:

- **Coupling:** A group's *collaborative coupling style* has been defined as the mutual involvement of its participants in each other's work [26]. Research has shown that coupling ranges from fully coupled to fully uncoupled modes, and that groups transition between different degrees of coupling throughout a collaborative session [11, 26, 28].
- **Coordination:** Coordination mechanisms are used to effectively manage shared resources, and are critical for efficient collaboration and for minimizing the impact of interference [22, 26]. The multi-user coordination policies proposed by Morris et al. [18] are particularly useful here.
- **Territoriality:** People collaborating in the same physical space tend to automatically form *territories* that are used for personal work, shared work, or for storage [22]. However, short of systems that explicitly support *personalized views*, these territories are generally ad hoc in nature.

Collaborative Visualization

Visualization is the graphical representation of data to aid human cognition [5], and collaborative visualization is accordingly the shared use of visualizations by multiple users (often called *analysts*). Studies have shown that involving multiple analysts in the analysis process generally improves the results (in quality or in time, or both). For example, Mark et al. [16] found significant benefits for collaborative visualization in both distributed and co-located settings. Balakrishnan et al. [3] show that a shared visualization significantly improves performance compared to alternative settings. Isenberg et al. [8] give a comprehensive overview of collaborative visualization and its connections to CSCW and HCI.

Several frameworks and toolkits for collaborative visualization exist. Scientific visualization has devoted much effort towards collaboration, mainly for distributed settings (see the survey by Brodlie et al. [4]). For information visualization, the Command Post of the Future [27] was one of the earliest examples. In summary, we take away several findings:

- **Flexible organization:** Isenberg et al. [11] study individuals, pairs, and triples in paper-based analysis tasks. Their results highlight the dynamic nature of collaborative visualization that demand highly flexible tools which support many different strategies for reaching a particular goal.

- **Common ground:** A key coordination task in collaborative visualization is to establish *common ground* [6], i.e., a shared understanding of the state of the analysis. Robinson [20] observed analysts working in pairs to complete an information synthesis task using paper artifacts and note that a significant time during the beginning of each session was spent establishing such a common understanding.

Interactive Surfaces for Visualization

Novel input and output surface technologies are poised to make a significant impact on visualization research. We can derive the following messages from this topic:

- **Tabletop displays:** Digital tabletop displays have been shown to be particularly well-suited to collaborative information visualization; examples include Isenberg and Carpendale's tabletop visualization system for tree comparison [7], the Cambiera system [9] for face-to-face collaborative analysis of documents, and the Hugin toolkit [13] for mixed-presence visualization. However, none of these systems distinguish private and public views.
- **Public and private views:** The Lark system [28] extends the concept of coordinated multiple views (CMV) to multi-user collaboration. This practice is supported by general knowledge about territoriality on collaborative surfaces. However, Lark's private and public views are still virtual spaces that compete for space on the tabletop surface.
- **Multi-device environments:** Combining several co-located devices facilitates both solitary and collaborative work, such as in the i-LAND [24] system. ConnecTables [25] explicitly supports dynamic coupling through pen-based displays for both individual or group work. The UbiTable [23] is a "scrap display" where documents and laptops can be bridged using visual means. However, they all rely on social protocols [18] for coordinating the work.

Collaborative Browsing, Filtering and Search

People working together on a common problem often have shared information needs, and so collaborative browsing and search is a common task in many collaborative sessions [17, 29]. With the exception of the Cambiera [9] system reviewed above, very few collaborative visualization systems are designed for collaborative search. The system perhaps most relevant to our work is Facet-Streams [12], where multiple participants use physical widgets on a tabletop display to construct visual queries. However, while the Facet-Streams system does support independent work, the private workspace of each participant is limited by the overall size of the tabletop. Regardless, we can learn the following:

- **Personal and shared devices:** Most systems for co-located collaborative search provide participants with their own device, often supplemented with a shared display [17]. This provides a natural physical partitioning for uncoupled and coupled work. For example, Maekawa et al. [15] present a collaborative web browsing system that partitions a webpage across several mobile devices. Paek et al. [19] propose a system for control of shared displays using PDAs, such as for web browsing, polls, and games. CoSearch [1] provides each user with a mobile phone as well as a shared PC display. Again, while supporting both private and public views, none of these existing projects explicitly tackle merging and revising collaborative state.

Summary: Contributions

As can be seen from the above literature review, much work has been done on the intersection of these fields. We can summarize the unique contributions of our work as follows: (a) a novel model for clearly separating as well as merging coupled and decoupled activity around a shared dataset; (b) an implementation of this model for collaborative visual search using tablets as private views and a tabletop display as a public view; (c) improved understanding of how coupling patterns affect performance in a collaborative search task; and (e) initial qualitative results supporting the new model.

BRANCH-EXPLORE-MERGE

The motivation for the Branch-Explore-Merge (BEM) protocol is to embrace the continually changing coupling in collaborative work to allow for participants to seamlessly move from closely to loosely coupled work. This is achieved by adopting a revision control mechanism for interactive visual exploration where the metaphor is that of the user's exploration taking a path that iteratively veers off, travels alone, and joins traffic. Below we discuss the BEM data model and the three protocol components (Figure 2).

Model

Branch-Explore-Merge (BEM) assumes a collaborative application with a shared state S, a visual representation $V(S)$, and a set of interaction techniques I that operate on the state to produce a modified state ($I(S) \rightarrow S'$). In a concrete implementation of the BEM protocol, the visual representation $V(S)$ would be rendered on a shared display that all participants can see (and typically interact with). Meanwhile, all participants also have a private display that shows the visual representation and supports interacting with the state.

Upon starting a BEM session, all private displays are *synchronized*, meaning that they are using the same shared state S, and the private displays will update as that state is changed.

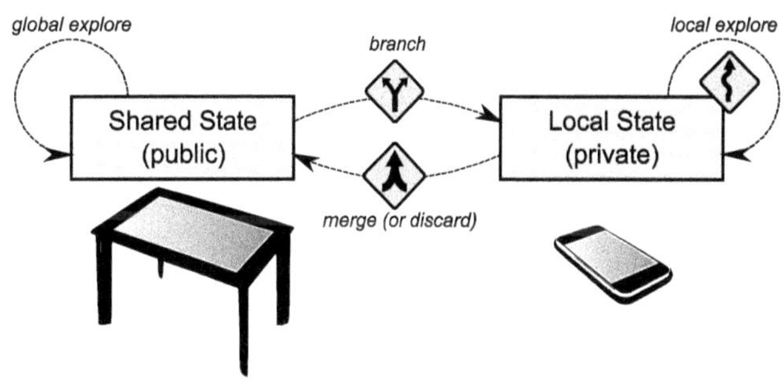

Figure 2: State diagram for branch-explore-merge.

Branch Operation

Branching in the BEM protocol is a local (i.e., non-conflicting) operation that only affects the particular participant who initiated the branch. The result of a branch operation is simply to *desynchronize* the participant's private display from the shared display; in other words, the global shared state S is copied to a local state S_i for that participant.

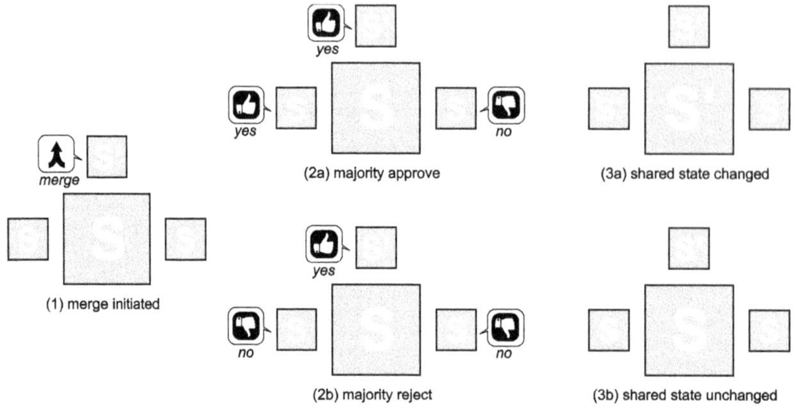

Figure 3: Example of two possible outcomes of a merge operation for three collaborators using a shared surface.

Branching is explicitly invoked by, e.g., clicking on a button, but an implementation may also allow implicit branching; for example, automatically branching (and desynchronizing) a participant who starts to modify the visual representation on their private view instead of on the shared view.

Explore Operation

After having desynchronized from the shared state using a branch operation, the participant's private view will henceforth render the visual representation $V(S_i)$ instead of $V(S)$. Furthermore, any interaction performed on S_i is specific to that view only. In other words, the participant is now free to independently explore data in uncoupled mode.

Merge Operation

Merging is invoked by a participant with a desynchronized private view when the participant wants to add his or her results back to the shared state (alternatively, the participant can always revert back to the shared state if they decide that a branched exploration is not worth pursuing further). During the merge operation, the shared display is transformed into a *visual merge* which shows the proposed changes to the shared state. Designing the visual merge is an important aspect, but is specific to the particular visual representation. One useful approach may be to take inspiration from visual diffs for source revision control systems such as SVN or CVS; here, items who are to be removed are colored red, whereas items to be added are colored green. Invariant items that do not change have no color highlighting.

Unlike branching, merging is a global operation that may potentially cause conflicts with other participants as well as the shared state. For this reason, we need to introduce a conflict resolution mechanism to handle this situation.

There are several ways to resolve conflicts, ranging from pure social protocols [18] to system-supported mechanisms; examples of the latter include splitting the screen to show alternatives, allowing people to vote on a particular alternative, or simply overwriting shared state but maintaining an easily accessible history to revert back. Although the BEM protocol is not tied to any one mechanism, we will discuss voting here (Figure 3). The voting policy can vary on the application; simple majority is the most straightforward and useful one. Of course, even if a proposed visual merge is voted down, the participant who initiated the merge will retain that proposed state on his or her own private view. The participant can then choose to refine the state or persuade other participants to accept the change, or simply discard that state. Furthermore, for situations where a visual merge is accepted by simple majority, any naysayers may choose to automatically desynchronize from the new shared state and receive the old state on their private views to continue their work.

IMPLEMENTATION

We have implemented the BEM protocol in a prototype collaborative visualization system called BEMVIEWER (Figure 1 and 4) for collaborative visual search in multidimensional datasets using geospatial displays. The system consists of a tabletop display, representing the public view, and individual tablets for collaborators, representing private views. Below we describe the details of the system.

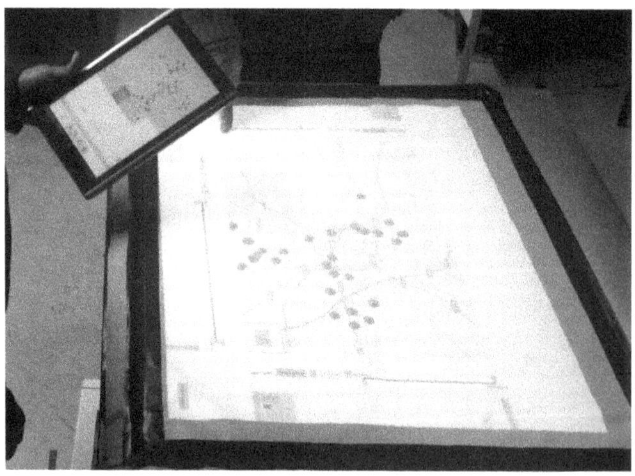

Figure 4: Our BEMViewer prototype setup.

Visual and Interaction Design

The shared visual representation in the BEMViewer is a geographical map that can be panned and zoomed on both the tabletop display and the tablets using multitouch gestures such as pinch and drag. The data visualized on the map is represented by a multidimensional dataset where two of the dimensions specify a geospatial position using longitude and latitude. These dimensions are used to plot each item in the dataset on the map. Any geospatial dataset can be visualized using the tool, such as real estate, restaurants, hotels, etc.

Query Formula

Because the BEMViewer is a tool for collaborative visual search, its shared state is actually **not** the dataset, but instead the *query formula* used to filter the dataset. Our query formula is a simple conjunction of terms, where a term can be any logical expression; similar to the classic Dynamic HomeFinder [30], our implementation supports simple intervals of the format [min, max], i.e., which constrain item values for a given dimension to be within a particular interval.

Of course, changing the query formula for the BEMViewer geospatial visualization will cause houses to potentially appear and disappear on the map. For this reason, it is the query formula that is branched, explored, and merged using our BEM protocol. We implement the operations as follows:

- **Branch:** Copy the user's query formula to the user's tablet and detach them from the shared state.
- **Explore:** Allow the user to independently add, modify, or remove terms from the query formula on their private device without affecting the shared display.
- **Merge:** Upload the proposed changes to the query formula to the shared tabletop display.

In our implementation, we sidestep the need for an explicit vote upon merge by using *consensus icons* that convey the filters of all participants simultaneously (see below). For branching, there are several ways to implement the copying of shared state from tabletop to tablet; in the interest of simplifying the interface, we chose to copy only the user's own query formula to the tablet, but users were still able to copy the formula of any of their collaborators as well.

Interactions

Upon joining a collaborative session, each participant gets assigned a *personal search panel* on the tabletop (Figure 1 shows three such panels, one per connected user). This search panel is also replicated on their tablet, i.e. their private view (Figure 1). The panel consists of a visual representation of the current query formula, buttons to branch, discard, and merge your personal state, and a simple filter interface. The filter interface is a drop-down menu where the user can choose which dimension in the dataset to operate on, and a dynamic query range slider [30] for defining an interval. The panel also allows for selecting, modifying, and deleting query terms in the query formula.

Interacting with the personal search panel on the shared tabletop will cause the global query formula to change for all users. This is implied in the fact that the panel is located on the shared surface. Interacting with the panel on the tablet, on the other hand, carries a more personal connotation and will thus only affect the local device.

Consensus Icons

Our BEMViewer has two modes of managing the shared state: (1) a master query formula, as described in the BEM protocol, which is reached by consensus for all participants, or (2) individual queries, conveyed using consensus icons. A consensus icon is simply a visual glyph representing an item's filter status in the dataset where different parts of the glyph convey whether a given collaborator has filtered out the icon or not. Ideally, the different parts are oriented towards each user as well. Figure 5 shows this for four collaborators; here, the presence of a circle sector indicates that the item is within the query formula of a that user (i.e. not filtered).

(a) All agree. (b) Even split.

Figure 5: Consensus icons for four collaborators.

Implementation Notes

We have implemented the tabletop display version of the BEMVIEWER as a Java application that uses the Piccolo2D structured vector graphics library. The map on the tabletop is implemented using the OpenStreetMap API. The application also provides a TCP/IP server port that accepts connections from BEMViewer clients on the network, lets them choose a seat (the system currently provides four sets, one on each side of the table), transmits the dataset to the client over the network, and then adds them to the current session.

The BEMVIEWER client is designed to be used on an Android tablet and uses the Android Canvas and Drawable APIs for graphical rendering. The client can connect to any BEMViewer server, support choosing a seat, and then provides the full set of interactions for collaboratively branching, exploring, and merging the exploration. The map view here is implemented using the Google Maps API.

QUALITATIVE EVALUATION

A standard approach used in prior systems to evaluate collaborative search systems is to ask groups of two or more participants to solve a set of collaborative search tasks [1, 12, 17]. Assessment is generally conducted through a combination of observational and objective metrics (often using datasets with ground truth [10]). To stimulate discussion and consensus, participants may each receive slightly conflicting search criteria that requires negotiation [12].

We applied a similar methodology to gain insight about the usability and utility of BEM and to collect data about usage patterns of this model. In general, our study was inspired by the methods used to evaluate the Facet-Streams [12] system. We observed the use of BEM during a realistic collaborative search task using a geospatial real estate visualization. Group members were required to collaborate to negotiate on compromises we introduced in the study (compromises were controlled for the experiment). In particular, we wanted to gauge how participants would engage in collaborative search strategies on both an individual and group level.

Participants

We recruited 4 groups of 3 participants each from an advanced HCI course at our university. All participants were experienced computer and touch interaction users.

Task and Dataset

We chose a multidimensional dataset consisting of 150 real-estate properties organized into 8 dimensions: price, square footage, acreage, number of bedrooms, number of bathrooms, distance to university, distance to shopping center, and distance to factory (i.e., a workplace). We presented participants with the scenario wherein they were asked to purchase a house in which they would live in together. Each participant was given a different set of constraints. For example, one would be concerned about the price, the other about the size and distance to the factory. While each person's constraints were personal, we did not prevent them from sharing their constraints with other participants. However, participants were told to treat their own personal constraints as more important than that of other members in the triad.

The objective of the study was to solve the collaborative search tasks using our BEMViewer software on a tabletop and three tablets, one per participant. Participants were asked to complete 5 tasks of increasing difficulty. For the first task, participants would be able to locate a home that met all criteria. In the second task, several homes would match their constraints and participants were asked to choose one from the list. In the last three tasks, no one house matched all criteria. Participants were required to relax their constraints to satisfy the conditions. Table 1 shows all five tasks.

#	User 1	User 2	User 3
1	BR $>$ 3 Univ $<$ 4.5 mi	SqFeet $<$ 1900	Price $<$ \$175k
2	Price $>$ \$100k Price $<$ \$200k	BR $\geq$ 3 Acreage $>$ 2	Shops $<$ 3 mi Factory $<$ 4 mi
3	Price $<$ \$240k Acreage $>$ 3	Shops $<$ 3 mi Univ $<$ 3 mi	SqFeet $>$ 1900
4	$2 \leq$ Bedrooms ≤ 6 Acreage ≤ 1 Price $<$ \$105k	SqFeet $>$ 450 Shops $<$ 3.5 mi	Univ $<$ 4.5mi Factory $<$ 2 mi
5	Less than \$150k, maximize bedrooms for cost (≥ 2).		

Table 1: The real estate search tasks given to users in our qualitative evaluation on collaborative search.

Solving a task implied arriving at a consensus on which house to purchase. For the tasks where no perfect house existed, the participants were asked to negotiate amongst themselves and find the house that most closely matched their collective constraints. We informed participants that we would weigh each of the dataset dimensions equally.

Performance Metrics

Our study was qualitative and observational. As indicated earlier, some of the more salient questions we were investigating concerned such things as "do users comprehend and use the BEM model for solving such tasks?", "If the model is used, how early/late do users branch off to do decoupled work?", "when users merge their results, do they continue to branch off again to filter further, or is further filtering performed on the tabletop?", etc. We used concession distance to measure how closely their results matched ground truth.

Concession distance is the normalized distance between the house selected by the group and the subset S of the search space defined by their collective constraints. For simplicity, we use the rectilinear distance between the search subset $S = [s(i)_{min}; s(i)_{max}]$ and the house h in all dimensions i of the dataset, normalizing using the range $D(i)$ of each dimension. We designed most trials so that a concession distance of 0 (all constraints fulfilled) is not possible. In other words, this would model situations where the search subset S contains no house, but where the house that is closest to S is optimal (we assume all dimensions have equal weight).

Note that our concession distance method is different from the discrete concession/fail metric used by Jetter et al. [12], but we think it better captures typical search behavior.

Equipment

We evaluated the systems using a 40-inch FTIR tabletop display equipped with a projector, having a resolution of 1280×800 pixels. For the mobile devices, we used three Acer Iconia tablets running the Android 3.0 operating system. The tablets communicated wirelessly with the server. The experimental software used for both tabletop and tablets was the BEMViewer prototype described previously.

Experimental Design

Given that our approach was qualitative and designed to understand patterns of coupling better, we asked groups of participants to do all the tasks using the full BEMViewer system. Group dynamics can change over time as people get to know each other and this could influence the outcomes and performance. Therefore, we paid attention to how these patterns change over the length of the study. The outcomes were observed as discussed above.

Procedure

Each session consisted of a group of three participants (a *triad*). Upon arriving in our lab space for an experimental session, participants were asked to read and sign a consent form which broadly outlined the study. The experimenter gave a brief background, answered questions, and allowed participants to make introductions with each other.

The group first performed a test task to get them familiar with the interface and the tasks. The experimenter explained and demonstrated how to use the interface to filter in a sample real estate dataset. Tools for filtering, adding filters, and removing filters were demonstrated to the participants. Participants were also taught how to branch off from the shared display, how to perform queries on their mobile device, and how to discard or merge their findings with the shared display. Participants were allowed to practice until they felt comfortable. Questions about the functionality of the tool were allowed throughout the trials.

All search trials began with the BEM tool initialized with no filters active and all points representing houses visible on the shared geographic map. Participants were given a sheet of paper listing their individual constraints for each task and were allowed to commence the collaborative search task. We did not set a time limit as we were not concerned with efficiency with the task. Instead participants were allowed as much time as possible to complete the tasks. A trial ended when the group reached consensus on a target home.

After completing all tasks, each participant filled out a personal questionnaire about their subjective assessment of the system. Each session lasted about 60 minutes in total, including filling out the post-test questionnaires.

RESULTS

Here we describe the results in terms of observations, branch-explore-merge patterns, and the concession distances.

General Observations

All group sessions were characterized by lively interaction, both verbal and gestural (pointing to the tabletop or to tablets), as well as common and consistent switching between the shared tabletop and the private tablets. The transitions were quick and often seamless. Some participants would also use their tablet to show certain aspects of the dataset to other participants. This seems to confirm that collaborative coupling was indeed smoothly transitioning from decoupled to coupled states during the collaboration [26].

We did note that different participants attributed different weights to various dimensions; for example, most participants took price criteria as being serious, whereas dimensions such as distance to work or square footage seemed to have varying importance to participants. A common method of searching was for participants to use the tablets to configure filters, merge their changes, and then look together on the tabletop for houses matching the global criteria.

BEM Patterns

To further understand how users engage in collaborative practices in a search task, we developed a visualization technique, BEMViz, inspired by visuals such as TimeNets [14] and Minard's map of Napoleon's March. BEMViz displays the branching and merging patterns using a timeline with a specific line for each participant involved in a collaborative session. Color is used to identify each user and line thickness indicates the percentage of currently visible items. The diagram has a baseline, which is set to a central filter state. The distance of a user's line from the baseline is an indication of how many items are in common; if all the user's items exist on the central entity, the lines are overlaid.

We utilize BEMViz with the tabletop as the ground truth, shown in dark grey (Figure 8). As users filter on their tablets, their lines diverge from the tabletop. The lines merge with the tabletop when users interact with their personal tabletop controls, or when they upload filters from the tablet. The line thickness shows the percentage of visible houses for each device. These are the houses that match the criteria in the relevant filters. A change in line thickness indicates that a filter was modified, created or deleted. The line thickness of the ground truth also changes when users merge their filters.

Our results show that the branch-explore-merge protocol seemed straightforward for users to adopt in the context of both public and private views; the ratio of device use for tablet vs. tabletop ranged between 40:60% to 80:20% of the total task time. Analysis of the BEM patterns (see below) clearly indicate that participants often transitioned between coupled and decoupled work when solving a task, which would seem to indicate that the protocol facilitated collaborative search. Whether this translates to a higher-quality solution is difficult to say (see below for concession distance results), but we think that this at least is an indication that the collaborative process is facilitated by the BEM protocol.

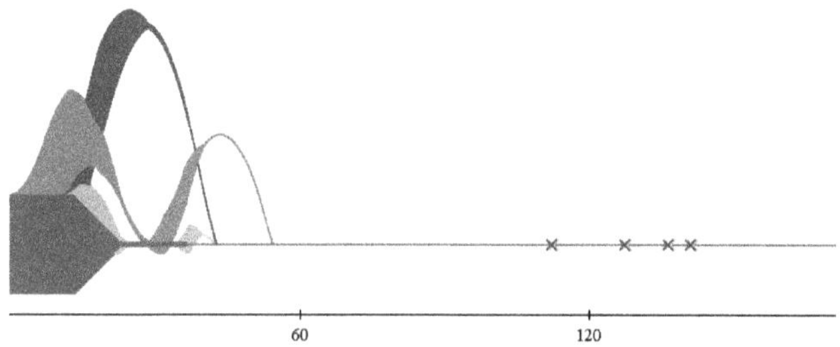

Figure 6: Example of early branching.

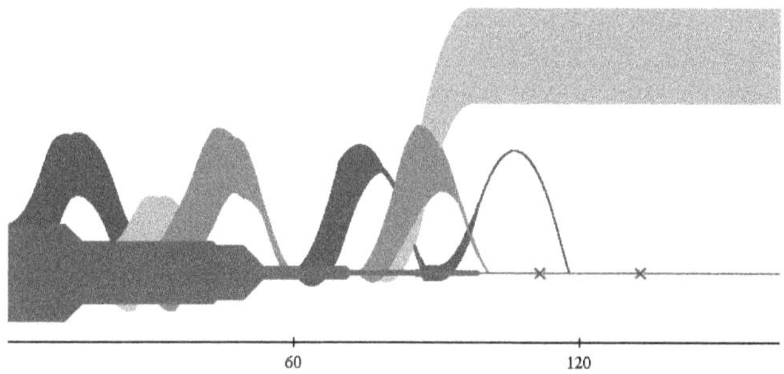

Figure 7: Green user branched off but did not merge.

Early branching. In about 80% of the tasks, participants would branch off to work on their tablet interface within the first 10% of the total task time. Figure 6) shows two cases where such early branching takes place. Early branching can be interpreted to suggest that: (a) users are more comfortable querying on the tablet interface; (b) decoupled work for collaborative search takes place very early on; and (c) users may wish to not overwrite the global state of the search, and instead perform local searches until they feel comfortable with their personal results. This outcome suggests that the BEM model's ability to decouple is useful for collaborative search.

Abandoning the merge. Our observations suggest that in some cases users merge, but then abandon their merged state without refreshing the global state. This also happens much later in the collaborative process, often nearly toward the end (Figure 7). This seems to also happen when the other active users are mostly operating on the shared display and not on their tablets. One reason for this might be that users may have reached a consensus without needing the local search results of the user that has abandoned the merge operation. Another explanation might be that the user gets involved with refinement on the tabletop and does not need to branch to resolve the query, essentially letting their private view languish. This usage model is well supported in BEM as it provides sufficient flexibility to move seamlessly between devices.

Resolving conflicts. To resolve conflicts, all participants invariably discussed potential solutions on the shared display. In over 90% of all tasks, the final decision took place after adjusting filters on the tabletop (Figure 8). Interestingly, for complex tasks we noticed a number of repeated branches and

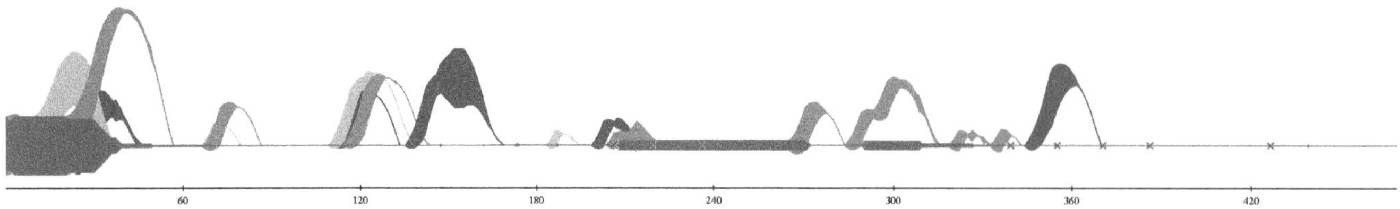

Figure 8: Patterns showing conflict resolution in several branches and merges for two participants (blue and red).

merges among participants. Usually one participant would take an active role in such activity. This was particularly the case with tasks 3 and 4 where the resulting set could lead to a large number of potential solutions and users would need to filter repeatedly to arrive at a satisfactory solution.

In the same pattern above, we notice a number of branches that take place simultaneously, i.e. that all three users have branched off. However, later in the same task, branching happens sequentially, where one user branches off, filters the dataset, and the other user picks up from the filtered dataset. Such patterns emerged in complex tasks where all users were relaxing their constraints, either together or in sequence.

Minimal concession. We also observed cases wherein a participant would not relax their constraints in response to other participants. Instead they would rely on the other users to relax their filter options before making changes. They would also view the outcome of the collective results after seeing a user modify their query set but would not necessarily branch off (the blue user in the figure below).

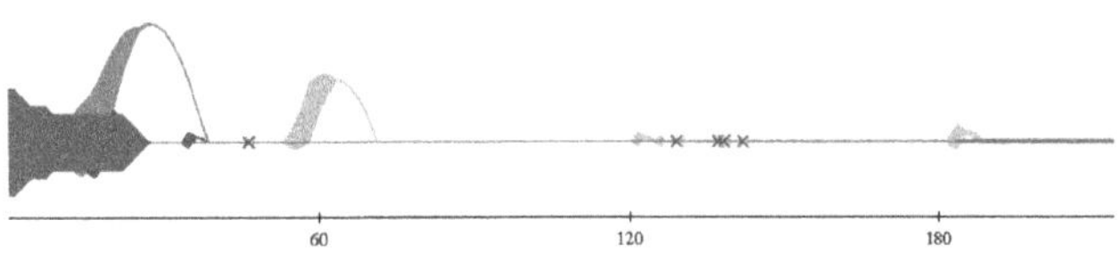

Figure 9: The blue user is not relaxing their constraints despite the task requiring mutual concessions.

Concession Distance

The purpose of our experiment was not to compare the results to some ground truth of what would be the best trade-off, particularly since people tend to weigh different dimensions differently. Instead, we use the average concession distance metric as an informal indication of performance. For example, an average concession distance of .059 means that the group ended up relaxing their given constraints by 5.9% when determining an answer. Our data shows that the collaborative search tasks were fairly accurate; on average across all tasks, the participants only had to relax their constraints by approximately 2% in finding an answer to the tasks.

DISCUSSION

The results from our qualitative evaluation clearly show the utility of the branch-explore-merge protocol. Participants in our study split their time between tabletop and tablet, and they frequently branch, explore, and merge results back to the shared state. We found that the quality overall was very high; solutions were within less than 2% of the search parameters.

Generalizations

Ample research has shown that collaborative coupling is a continuous scale ranging from uncoupled to tightly coupled work, yet it can be argued that our BEM system only explicitly supports two discrete points along this scale—the two extremes. However, while it is true that our public and private views are implemented using two very different types of devices, we observed that users would freely share the content with their tablets to other participants while solving the common task. In other words, even a private device such as a tablet can be used in a collaboratively coupled fashion.

Furthermore, the intention of our collaborative protocol is not to **limit** the users, but to **empower** them. Thus, even if our protocol has certain stipulations on the nature of uncoupled and coupled work, and even if our BEMViewer implementation strictly used physical devices for private views, this is not to say that we think a real-world collaborative application need be this literal. Our intention in this paper was to control the collaborative setting to study certain phenomena related to collaborative coupling, but these controls need not stay in place for a real system. For example, we can easily see such a system supporting "hybrid" private views that still are rendered on the shared display, but which the user can easily bring onto a physical device with a simple operation.

Our work has so far considered only co-located and synchronous collaborative sessions, and the BEMViewer supports only up to four participants. However, there is no reason to believe that—given appropriate visual design—the protocol will not support more than four participants, or that it will not be just as suitable for distributed, mixed-presence, and/or asynchronous collaborative modes. Furthermore, our focus in this paper has been on collaborative search, whereas visual exploration can include many other tasks such as sensemaking, decision-making, and planning. Exploring these parameters is left for future work, however.

We used concession distance to evaluate our results from the user study, summing up the normalized distances for each dimension between a chosen house and the boundaries of the search space given in the constraints. However, this model assumes that all dimensions have equal weight, but our observations from the experimental sessions clearly showed that this is not the case; for example, people tend to be particularly sensitive about money (spending less is often perceived as better). Therefore, it is likely that such biases played a role in choosing what was perceived to be the closest house given a search space where no "perfect" house existed. However, we speculate that the BEM protocol may even have helped participants in identifying and discussing these biases.

Another interesting observation is that device preference given the choice of two devices—tablet vs. tabletop—is a very fickle phenomenon. In early pilot testing, our tablet interface was not fully developed and as aesthetically pleasing as in the current version, and the result was that participants preferred the tabletop interface and basically did not interact with the tablets at all. However, in the evaluation, as can be seen from the data, participants preferred the tablet, most likely because of the higher relative screen resolution (DPI) as well as the more responsive touch detection. This leads us to speculate that small differences (or imbalances) in interaction design between devices in a multi-device environment may have a large impact on the device affinity of the users. This is an interesting claim for future studies of such systems.

Finally, this evaluation was primarily qualitative in nature, and in particular, we did not perform a controlled comparison with a baseline condition. Conceivable baseline comparisons would be a tabletop only, or even a desktop computer interface with a single mouse and keyboard. However, the BEM protocol provides new affordances that simply did not exist previously, making such comparisons potentially lopsided. Instead, our qualitative evaluation provides more useful findings on the protocol's utility for collaborative search.

Beyond Maps

The visualization components in our BEMViewer prototype are relatively simple: a geospatial map with some graphical embellishments. This was done to let us study the effectiveness of the BEM protocol without visual complexity getting in the way of users understanding the visualizations.

However, there is nothing in the branch-explore-emerge protocol that limits the nature of the visual mapping. The only requirement is the capability to, given two visualization states, render their difference as a visual difference, and then supporting the merge operation. This leaves the space open for using virtually any visualization design in the protocol. For example, a social network visualization tool may support expanding and collapsing the node-link diagram as filtering operations, and a visual difference would highlight the topological changes to the network that a merge would cause. Or, an intelligence analysis tool could be adapted for collaborative work by placing a common report on the shared display and allowing participants to contribute to this report.

As a case in point, we have also implemented a slight variation of the BEMViewer that uses 2D scatterplots with dynamically controllable axis mappings as the main visual representation (Figure 10). This tool can be used for general visual exploration in multidimensional datasets for situations when the data does not have an intrinsic geospatial position. Unlike the map-based version, the scatterplot BEMViewer has an explicit vote protocol and uses a simple visual merge operation where nodes to be added by a merge are highlighted in green, and nodes to be removed are highlighted in red.

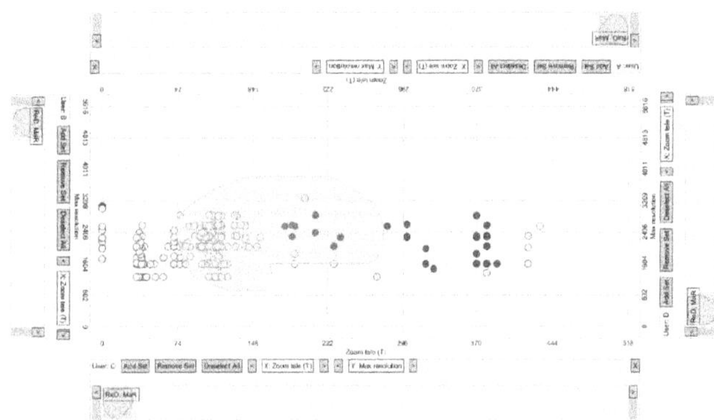

Figure 10: BEMViewer for multidimensional data.

CONCLUSIONS AND FUTURE WORK

We have proposed Branch-Merge-Explore, a new collaborative protocol for explicitly supporting varying degrees of coupling styles in co-located collaborative visualization settings. Our approach incorporates both public and private views and allows participants to temporarily desynchronize their private views from the main visualization state to perform independent work. Synchronizing the new state to the shared and public display consists of a visual merge and a common vote among all participants. An informal evaluation compared search behavior for the branch-explore-merge protocol using a prototype implementation using a tabletop display as a public view and individual tablets as private views. Results indicate that the protocol appeared to facilitate collaboration, particularly where no perfect result existed.

Our future work will consist of implementing BEM in the context of other visual representations, interactions, and datasets. In general, we think that there is tremendous potential in pairing mobile devices with large displays, be it tabletops or wall-mounted ones, and we are working on software toolkits for supporting such ubiquitous visualization spaces.

ACKNOWLEDGMENTS

This work is partly supported by the U.S. National Science Foundation grants IIS-1249229 and TUES-1123108. We thank the user study participants for their time and effort.

REFERENCES

1. S. Amershi and M. R. Morris. CoSearch: a system for co-located collaborative web search. In *Proceedings of the ACM Conference on Human Factors in Computing Systems*, 1647–1656, 2008.
2. K. Baker, S. Greenberg, and C. Gutwin. Empirical development of a heuristic evaluation methodology for shared workspace groupware. In *Proceedings of the ACM Conference on Computer-Supported Cooperative Work*, 96–105, 2002.
3. A. Balakrishnan, S. Fussell, and S. Kiesler. Do visualizations improve synchronous remote collaboration? In *Proceedings ACM Conference on Human Factors in Computing Systems*, 1227–1236, 2008.
4. K. W. Brodlie, D. A. Duce, J. R. Gallop, J. P. R. B. Walton, and J. D. Wood. Distributed and collaborative visualization. *Computer Graphics Forum*, 23(2):223–251, 2004.
5. S. K. Card, J. D. Mackinlay, and B. Shneiderman, editors. *Readings in Information Visualization: Using Vision to Think*. Morgan Kaufmann Publishers, San Francisco, 1999.

6. H. H. Clark and S. E. Brennan. Grounding in communication. In L. B. Resnick, J. M. Levine, and S. D. Teasley, editors, *Perspectives on Socially Shared Cognition*, 127–149. Amer. Psych. Assoc., 1991.
7. P. Isenberg and S. Carpendale. Interactive tree comparison for co-located collaborative information visualization. *IEEE Transactions on Visualization and Computer Graphics*, 13(6):1232–1239, 2007.
8. P. Isenberg, N. Elmqvist, J. Scholtz, D. Cernea, K.-L. Ma, and H. Hagen. Collaborative visualization: definition, challenges, and research agenda. *Information Visualization*, 10(4):310–326, 2011.
9. P. Isenberg and D. Fisher. Collaborative brushing and linking for co-located visual analytics of document collections. *Computer Graphics Forum*, 28(3):1031–1038, 2009.
10. P. Isenberg, D. Fisher, M. R. Morris, K. Inkpen, and M. Czerwinski. An exploratory study of co-located collaborative visual analytics around a tabletop display. In *Proceedings of the IEEE Conference on Visual Analytics Science and Technology*, 179–186, 2010.
11. P. Isenberg, A. Tang, and M. S. T. Carpendale. An exploratory study of visual information analysis. In *Proceedings of the ACM Conference on Human Factors in Computing Systems*, 1217–1226, 2008.
12. H.-C. Jetter, J. Gerken, M. Zöllner, H. Reiterer, and N. Milic-Frayling. Materializing the query with facet-streams – a hybrid surface for collaborative search on tabletops. In *Proceedings of ACM Conference on Human Factors in Computing Systems*, 3013–3022, 2011.
13. K. Kim, W. Javed, C. Williams, N. Elmqvist, and P. Irani. Hugin: A framework for awareness and coordination in mixed-presence collaborative information visualization. In *Proceedings of the ACM Conference on Interactive Tabletops and Surfaces*, 231–240, 2010.
14. N. W. Kim, S. K. Card, and J. Heer. Tracing genealogical data with TimeNets. In *Proceedings of ACM Conference on Advanced Visual Interfaces*, 241–248, 2010.
15. T. Maekawa, T. Hara, and S. Nishio. A collaborative web browsing system for multiple mobile users. In *Proceedings of the IEEE Conference on Pervasive Computing and Communications*, 22–35, 2006.
16. G. Mark, A. Kobsa, and V. M. González. Do four eyes see better than two? Collaborative versus individual discovery in data visualization systems. In *Proceedings of the International Conference on Information Visualization*, 249–255, 2002.
17. M. R. Morris, J. Lombardo, and D. Wigdor. WeSearch: supporting collaborative search and sensemaking on a tabletop display. In *Proceedings of the ACM Conference on Computer Supported Cooperative Work*, 401–410, 2010.
18. M. R. Morris, K. Ryall, C. Shen, C. Forlines, and F. Vernier. Beyond 'social protocols': multi-user coordination policies for co-located groupware. In *Proceedings of the ACM Conference on Computer Supported Cooperative Work*, 262–265, 2004.
19. T. Paek, M. Agrawala, S. Basu, S. Drucker, T. Kristjansson, R. Logan, K. Toyama, and A. Wilson. Toward universal mobile interaction for shared displays. In *Proceedings of the ACM Conference on Computer-Supported Cooperative Work*, 266–269, 2004.
20. A. C. Robinson. Collaborative synthesis of visual analytic results. In *Proceedings of the IEEE Symposium on Visual Analytics Science and Technology*, 67–74, 2008.
21. K. Schmidt and C. Simone. Coordination mechanisms: Towards a conceptual foundation of CSCW systems design. *Computer Supported Cooperative Work*, 5(2/3):155–200, 1996.
22. S. D. Scott, M. S. T. Carpendale, and K. M. Inkpen. Territoriality in collaborative tabletop workspaces. In *Proceedings of the ACM Conference on Computer Supported Cooperative Work*, 294–303, 2004.
23. C. Shen, K. Everitt, and K. Ryall. UbiTable: impromptu face-to-face collaboration on horizontal interactive surfaces. In *Proceedings of the International Conference on Ubiquitous Computing*, volume 2864 of *LNCS*, 281–288. Springer, 2003.
24. N. A. Streitz, J. Geissler, T. Holmer, S. Konomi, C. Müller-Tomfelde, W. Reischl, P. Rexroth, P. Seitz, and R. Steinmetz. i-LAND: An interactive landscape for creativity and innovation. In *Proceedings of the ACM Conference on Human Factors in Computing Systems*, 120–127, 1999.
25. P. Tandler, T. Prante, C. Müller-Tomfelde, N. Streitz, and R. Steinmetz. ConnecTables: Dynamic coupling of displays for the flexible creation of shared workspaces. In *Proceedings of the ACM Symposium on User Interface Software and Technology*, 11–20, 2001.
26. A. Tang, M. Tory, B. Po, P. Neumann, and S. Carpendale. Collaborative coupling over tabletop displays. In *Proceedings of the ACM Conference on Human Factors in Computing Systems*, 1181–1190, 2006.
27. J. J. Thomas and K. A. Cook, editors. *Illuminating the Path: The Research and Development Agenda for Visual Analytics*. IEEE Computer Society Press, 2005.
28. M. Tobiasz, P. Isenberg, and S. Carpendale. Lark: Coordinating co-located collaboration with information visualization. *IEEE Transactions on Visualization and Computer Graphics*, 15(6):1065–1072, 2009.
29. M. Twidale, D. M. Nichols, and C. D. Paice. Browsing is a collaborative process. *Information Processing and Management*, 33(6):761–783, 1997.
30. C. Williamson and B. Shneiderman. The dynamic HomeFinder: Evaluating dynamic queries in a real-estate information exploration system. In *Proceedings of the ACM SIGIR Conference on Research and Development in Information Retrieval*, 338–346, 1992.

Use Your Head: Tangible Windows for 3D Information Spaces in a Tabletop Environment

Martin Spindler[1], Wolfgang Büschel[2], Raimund Dachselt[2]
[1] User Interface & Software Engineering Group, University of Magdeburg, Germany
[2] Interactive Media Lab Dresden, Technische Universität Dresden, Germany
{martin.spindler, bueschel, dachselt}@acm.org

ABSTRACT
Tangible Windows are a novel concept for interacting with virtual 3D information spaces in a workbench-like multi-display environment. They allow for performing common 3D interaction tasks in a more accessible manner by combining principles of tangible interaction, head-coupled perspective, and multi-touch techniques. Tangible Windows unify the interaction and representation space in a single device. They either act as physical peepholes into a virtual 3D world or as physical containers for parts of that world and are well-suited for the collaborative exploration and manipulation of such information spaces. One important feature of Tangible Windows is that the use of obtrusive hardware, such as HMDs, is strictly avoided. Instead, lightweight paper-based displays are used. We present different techniques for canonical 3D interaction tasks such as viewport control or object selection and manipulation, based on the combination of independent input modalities. We tested these techniques on a self-developed prototype system and received promising early user feedback.

Author Keywords
Tangible windows; head interaction; head tracking; multiple views; magic lenses; tabletop displays; multi-surface user interfaces; fish tank virtual reality; head-coupled perspective; 3D interaction.

ACM Classification Keywords
H.5.m. Information Interfaces and Presentation (e.g. HCI): Miscellaneous

INTRODUCTION
Interacting with 3D content on tabletops has received considerable attention in the past, e.g., [3, 16, 18, 29]. One reason for this is the desire to transfer advantages of touch-based interfaces – which are associated with being natural and intuitive – to a variety of application domains that deal with complex 3D data. Examples include the architectural design of 3D buildings and their surroundings, surgical planning based on 3D imagery, and interactive 3D scientific visualizations. Inevitably, these types of applications implicate challenges that

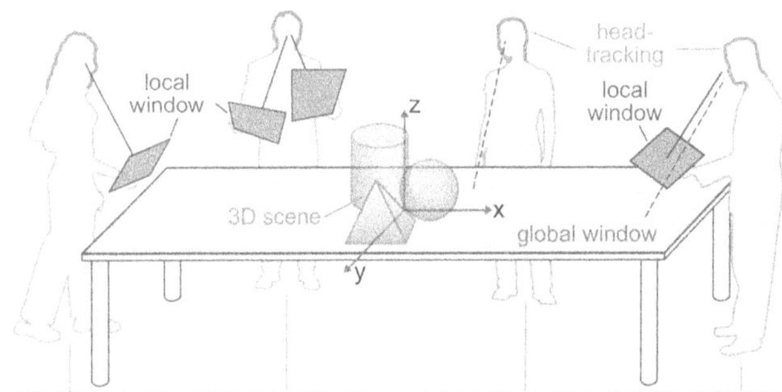

Figure 1. A tabletop (*global display*) serves as the shared view of a virtual 3D scene that is spatially aligned with room and table. This setup is enriched by multiple tracked mobile *local displays* that act as personal views into this scene. The system is also capable of tracking head positions & orientations, which is the basis for head-coupled perspectives on local and global displays.

are caused by mapping 3D spaces onto a 2D surface. Therefore, extending the tabletop to a third dimension was and still is a major goal of many research projects. Grossman and Wigdor [15] compiled a taxonomy of prevalent approaches that come from areas as diverse as interactive 3D graphics, e.g., [38], virtual reality, e.g., [25], and augmented reality, e.g., [7]. In their taxonomy, they distinguished between the "actual" and the "perceived" display space and identified unexplored gaps for several combinations of both parameters.

With Tangible Windows, we fill one of these gaps. In particular, we address stereo spatial augmentation [15] in multi-display tabletop environments. This is the combination of projecting imagery onto physical proxies and the tabletop and using head-coupled perspectives to provide a 3D volumetric perception anywhere in the working volume. Tangible Windows are lightweight paper-based displays like in [30] that are coupled with a user's head for the purpose of auto-perspective. They act as peepholes into a virtual 3D information space or serve as tangible containers for parts of it and are controlled by physically moving them through the volume on or above a tabletop surface (see Figure 1).

The primary contributions of this paper are: (1) The integration of three independent input modalities, i.e., display locations/orientations, head locations/orientations, and touch/pen input, into a unifying interaction model. (2) A set of novel 3D interaction techniques. (3) A technical solution for lightweight spatially aware displays, associated with a virtual 3D information space (or parts of it), supporting multiple displays for both single users and collaborative work. Although various solutions for head-coupled perspectives already exist, e.g., [1, 4, 14, 26, 38], an integration into a single, flexible multi-display system, suitable for co-located collaboration, has not been done before.

The remainder of this paper is organized as follows. After presenting an overview of related work, we discuss the design space from which we derive the Tangible Windows concept. Based on that, we introduce basic 3D interaction techniques, present example application scenarios and summarize our technical setup. We conclude with a discussion of initial user experiences and an outline of future work.

RELATED WORK

Volumetric Displays

Perception of 3D in the real world is accomplished by a number of visual depth cues, such as occlusion, perspective, shading, shadows, parallax, etc., which can be conveyed by 3D displays. 3D display technologies can be categorized as volumetric or geometric (see [12] for an overview). Volumetric displays directly present 3D information by illuminating points in real-world spatial locations, e.g., cubic static-volume implementations with visible gas suspended in glass [11]. Although such technology provides very realistic results, it is still too limited in many ways, e.g., in terms of resolution, mobility, weight and brightness, as well as by high costs.

Geometric Displays & Head-coupled Perspective

Geometric displays render images on one or more 2D displays with a perspective corrected to the user's view (head-coupled perspective). In this context, Ware et al. [38] coined the term Fish Tank Virtual Reality (FTVR) that either provides monocular or stereoscopic views for one perspective (or user) on a vertical display (desktop monitor). Here, shutter glasses are used to multiplex multiple perspectives, either to provide monocular views for two users or a single stereoscopic view. The concept of FTVR has been applied to a variety of form factors. The Responsive Workbench is one variation that uses FTVR on a horizontal tabletop with support for one [25] or two users [1] simultaneously. Unlike our approach, however, their setup does not include the projection on mobile displays. Hancock et al. [17] show that a neutral center of projection combined with parallel projection geometry provides a reasonable compromise for multi-user tabletop setups, which we make use of in our system. In the last years, FTVR has become more popular on consumer electronics, such as the Wii [26] and the iPad [14]. Another example for recent commercial products making use of FTVR is the NettleBox[1] tabletop display. Recently, de Almeida et al. [10] used head-coupled perspective to allow looking "behind" the bezels of multi-display walls.

See-Through Interfaces & Tangible Magic Lenses

The see-through interface, as introduced by Bier et al. [5], is a virtual interface (the Magic Lens) that appears between users and 2D applications for the purpose of local presentation/manipulation of data. It was later extended to 3D [37] and has also been widely adopted in 3D virtual reality (VR) systems. Head-mounted displays (HMD) provide immersive see-through-like stereo views by using small displays located directly in front of the eyes. Although there are lightweight projector-based variants of HMD [7] that help attenuate physical exhaustion that occurs with active HMD [33], HMD systems often suffer from significant mismatches between the virtual and real world.

With spatially-aligned displays these problems are less distracting (but still present) because they are used farther away from the eyes. With their metaDesk [36] system, Ullmer and Ishii introduced a tangible version of the Magic Lens concept that allows users to physically interact with a see-through interface. Here, tracked mobile displays that users can hold in their hands serve as physical peepholes into a VR workspace. As demonstrated by Fitzmaurice [13], moving these displays, e.g., around the user in a donut-like shape, allows users to explore these workspaces. Yee [41] later extended this idea by combining spatial input with pen input. Another prominent example is Boom Chameleon [35], where a single pen-enabled touch screen is mounted on a mechanical arm for the purpose of exploring/annotating a virtual car model.

Recent trends show an increased use of passive (projective) handheld displays, where digital image content is projected onto tracked paper-like screens, e.g., as shown by PaperWindows [22]. This type of passive handheld display technology has been integrated into tabletop environments where it was used, e.g., for the exploration of various information spaces by moving the tangible lenses through the physical 3D space on or above a tabletop surface [30, 31]. With their SecondLight, Izadi et al. [23] presented a more self-contained approach by using switchable diffusers to allow rear-projection on both a tabletop and passive mobile displays above it. This approach also allows for Frustrated Total Internal Reflection (FTIR) touch input on both tabletop and mobile displays, something that our system is not capable of. Chan et al. [9] combine a normal RGB- and an IR-projector to display invisible markers on a tabletop. Using an IR-camera on a mobile device, they can provide 6DOF tracking of the device's position above the tabletop. In comparison, our setup, employing a second projector, provides a bigger interaction volume and allows using handheld displays not only above but also next to the tabletop. Furthermore, these systems have not integrated the use of the head as an additional input channel or address the special requirements of 3D manipulation within a VR environment.

3D Interaction on the Tabletop and beyond

There has been extensive research in the field of multi-touch for 3D interaction, which has proven to be an excellent basis for many powerful 3D interaction techniques, e.g., [3, 16, 29]. Hilliges et al. [21] use an IR-transparent diffuser to facilitate such interaction above the table screen by tracking finger gestures as input. Wilson et al. [40] presented a system for interaction on and above non-instrumented surfaces using consumer depth cameras and a projector setup. A comparable setup, albeit for mobile indoor projections, has recently been shown by Molyneaux et al. [27]. Benko et al. [4] presented the MirageTable, which consists of a curved screen, a depth sensor, and a stereo projector and provides head-coupled perspective through the tracking of shutter glasses worn by the

[1] http://www.nttl.ru

user. Although differing in terms of interaction, these systems share some characteristics with our approach. Tracking with depth cameras, however, still has limited precision and reliability. Thus, we decided for a more traditional optical tracking of IR-reflective markers.

DESIGN SPACE

We envision a system that enables users to directly interact with a virtual 3D world or parts of it in a more accessible manner, compared to traditional setups. Our intent is that users are not required to wear any obtrusive hardware, such as HMD or heavy display/tracking equipment. Instead, all necessary hardware shall be hidden so that users are not aware of its presence. This is to ensure a high degree of immersion combined with an experience as natural as possible.

This goal shall be accomplished by using mobile spatially-aware lightweight displays and additional – much larger – stationary displays that are spatially aligned with the environment. Although vertical wall-sized screens, the CAVE™and other large 360° displays are possible alternatives, we primarily focus on a horizontal tabletop setup that we will briefly introduce in the following.

General System Design and Components

We propose a multi-display system that consists of two basic types of displays (see Figure 1): a single stationary tabletop screen (*global display*) and one or multiple mobile screens (*local displays*) that provide independent views into a *3D information space*. The system keeps track of the *heads* of *one or multiple users*. The main components of the system are:

3D Information Space According to Bowman et al. [6], typical interaction tasks that users intend to accomplish within virtual 3D environments (3D information spaces) are *navigation*, *selection* and *manipulation*. They commonly involve changing the viewpoint and applying transformations onto individual objects or the whole 3D scene. The purpose of the system shall be the exploration and manipulation of a global *virtual 3D scene* that is (dynamically) aligned with the physical room and is seen from an exocentric (outside-in) view (see Figure 2). This 3D information space can be associated with global and local displays in various ways. For this purpose, a *global coordinate system* is defined with the center of the table surface being the origin and the Z-axis pointing to the ceiling (see Figure 1).

Global Display The horizontal tabletop display features a large interactive screen that usually shows global context information shared by all users. For example, this can be a view into parts of the global 3D scene that virtually resides below, on, or even (partly) above the table surface (see Figure 2).

Local Displays Local displays are spatially-aware lightweight interactive displays that share some similarities with the tangible magic lenses introduced in the PaperLens project [30]. Our system supports different sizes and shapes, such as rectangles and circles. The main objective of local displays is to provide several users with personal views into the virtual 3D world. These can be views that are either in complete synchronicity with the global scene, show some local modifications (e.g., annotations), or provide alternative representations (e.g., wireframe rendering, see Figure 5, right) and perspectives/mappings (e.g., fisheye distortions). They can even show a completely different virtual 3D scene or an object that is exclusively attached to it. We support the simultaneous use of multiple local displays to facilitate co-located collaboration.

Heads Chan et al. [8] found that their head-controlled document zooming was fairly ineffective and that document manipulation and interaction should rather be handled as an active process than a passive process, e.g., by supporting iconic gestures [24]. In contrast, using the head for secondary tasks, e.g., by providing users with the right perspective [28] or by presenting different levels of detail depending on the distance of head and display [20], can help making interaction more natural. One important characteristic of the head is that it becomes more meaningful when it is coupled with a single local display (see Figure 1a) or the tabletop (see Figure 1c), e.g., for the purpose of head-coupled perspectives. These basic combinations in turn can arbitrarily be combined again, such as by coupling one user's head with either multiple local windows (see Figure 1b) or with a local and the global window simultaneously (see Figure 1d).

One vs. Multiple Users The number of users is another defining factor of the system and does not necessarily match the number of local displays in use. In fact, the combination of (typically one) global display and multiple local displays for one or many users opens up additional exciting possibilities. For example, two users could temporarily share a single local display for collaboration purposes. Alternatively, a single user could use two local displays, e.g., for bimanual interaction that could be used for comparison tasks (see Figure 1b). Beyond that, if only one user is present, the tabletop display is not shared anymore and thus becomes a personal view. This allows to provide the only user with special views directly on the tabletop screen that could, e.g., depend on where the user is standing or looking at.

General Types of Input

There are three fundamental types of input that constitute the interaction space of our proposed system: *on-surface input*, *spatial input*, i.e., *with-device input*, and *head input*.

On-Surface Input Interaction can be performed directly *on* the surface of displays. This applies to both local (mobile) displays and the global (tabletop) display. In particular, we consider different variants of touch and digital pen input.

Spatial Input One important feature of local displays is that they are being tracked in physical space with six degrees of freedom (6DOF). This allows users to directly interact *with* a local display by grabbing it with their hands and then moving or rotating it through the physical space. This way, a rich set of interaction techniques becomes available. As a first but non-exhaustive attempt, see the interaction vocabulary described in [31].

Head Input Heads can be considered as input devices with 6DOF. In this respect, they provide an additional interaction modality that is useful, e.g., for the purpose of head-coupled

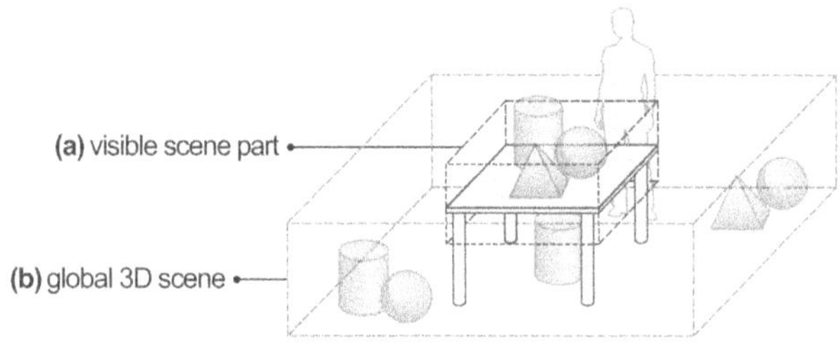

Figure 2. The 3D scene is situated around the table. Only a part of this larger scene is shown on the tabletop at any time.

perspectives [38]. Beyond that, observing head movements also helps to distinguish between users in terms of user ID and user position, which can be a valuable information for systems supporting user collaboration.

THE TANGIBLE WINDOWS CONCEPT

After having introduced the general design space and system components, we will now provide a definition of Tangible Windows and discuss some of their properties.

A Definition of Tangible Windows

We define a Tangible Window as a spatially-aware display that is typically coupled with a user's *head*. This coupling between display and head is particularly intended for the purpose of interacting with a virtual 3D information space in such a way that Tangible Windows are peepholes into it or that they act as physical proxies for parts of it. For this purpose, Tangible Windows serve as physical handles that users can grab and move around with their hands. In this regard, they are not only a tool of direct *representation*, but also a tool of direct *interaction*, seamlessly integrating input and output.

Windows into Virtuality

We distinguish between two basic types of Tangible Windows that differ in how they are associated with virtual 3D scenes (see Figure 3): *fish tank windows* and *peephole windows*.

Fish Tank Windows One way of linking a virtual 3D scene with a Tangible Window is to attach the 3D content so that both always remain aligned with each other ("scene in hand" metaphor [39]). For this purpose, a *fish tank window* provides its own local coordinate system, as illustrated in Figure 3. Moving or rotating a fish tank window through the physical space also moves and rotates the attached 3D content with it. Hence, a fish tank window can be thought of as a visual and physical container for arbitrary virtual 3D scenes.

Peephole Windows Another way of associating a Tangible Window with a virtual 3D world is the *peephole window* that employs the "eyeball in hand" metaphor [39]. Such *peephole windows* serve as windows into the virtual 3D environment that show what virtually exists behind them [13]. Moving or rotating a *peephole window* directly influences its view frustum and view orientation into the virtual 3D space. The see-through effect is usually achieved by maintaining a direct one-to-one spatial mapping between the real and virtual space so that both spaces share the same global coordinate system. However, other mappings are also possible. This may include position and orientation offsets, clipping planes (e.g., useful for slicing), and simulating a mirror.

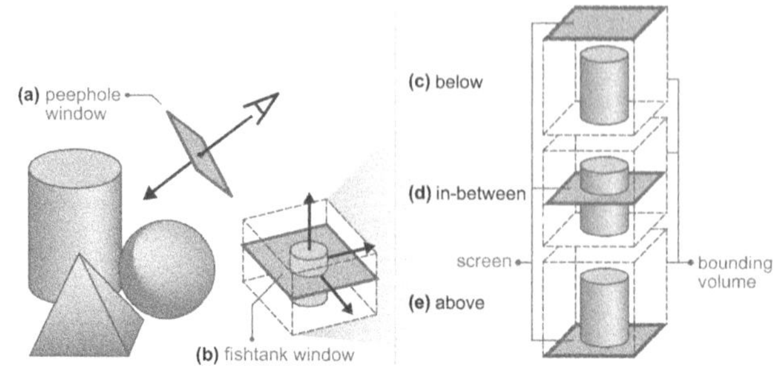

Figure 3. Tangible Windows can be associated with virtual 3D content in two principle ways: as *peephole windows* (a) that serve as physical peepholes into a virtual world, or as *fish tank windows* (b) acting as physical containers for virtual 3D objects that can reside below the display surface (c), above it (e), or somewhere between the two extremes (d).

Mapping 3D Volumes Onto 2D Surfaces

Each Tangible Window employs a canonical 3D bounding volume in the shape of an extruded surface geometry. Typically, with rectangular-shaped displays this will be a box, although we explicitly support different shapes, e.g., circles. The XY-plane of the bounding box always remains aligned with the 2D display and the Z-axis is defined to be orthogonal to the display plane, see Figure 3.

This describes an extent into the third dimension that we can use for mapping arbitrary 3D content onto the 2D surface. Motivated by the *zero-parallax-plane* (see Section Head-coupled Perspectives), three canonical cases are possible: Considering the window surface as a dividing plane held horizontally, we distinguish between objects residing completely *above* it, objects being attached entirely *under* the window, and objects that *intersect* the window plane, i.e., some parts of the 3D content lie below and others above it (see Figure 3).

Head-coupled Perspectives

While VR displays often allow for stereoscopic rendering of 3D scenes, we will not focus on this aspect. Instead, we will use monoscopic views that only address cues that are processed by one eye. Such *monocular cues* involve relative size, texture gradients, linear perspective, occlusion, and motion parallax. Head-dependent control of camera parameters (*head-coupled perspective*) is a technique that allows for reproducing such cues. With it, a more realistic simulation of perspective effects can be created that comes close to what users would expect from their real-world experiences and thus helps making the overall interaction experience more natural.

Technically, this is achieved by setting the *zero-parallax-plane* – a determinant factor for off-axis perspective projections – in such a way that it remains aligned with the window surface. This ensures that no visual shifts occur within this particular plane and thus parts of the 3D object that precisely fall onto the window plane appear to be fixed to it. Opposed to that, the farther away an object part resides from the display plane (in terms of positive or negative Z-distance), the more it is being shifted. For example, when users move their head to the right,

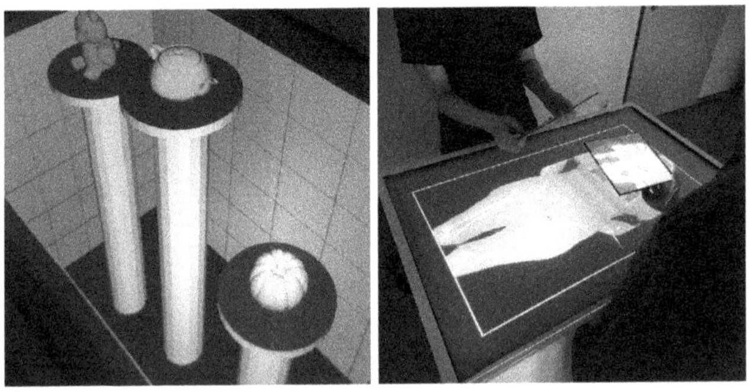

Figure 4. Head-coupled perspective allows users to look at the global 3D scene from arbitrary sides by simply walking around the table (left). One use case is the exploration of medical volume data (right, mockup).

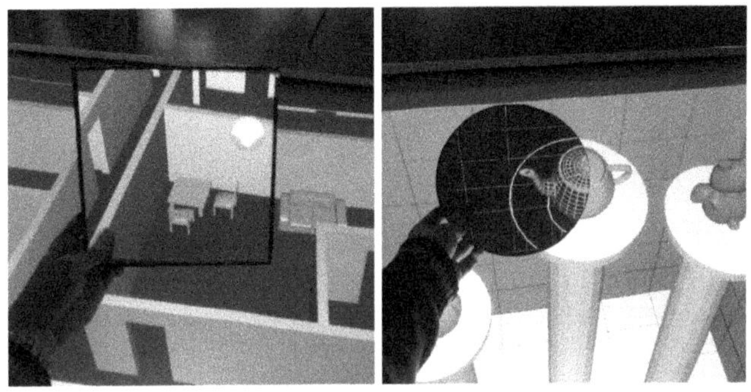

Figure 5. Users can independently explore a virtual 3D world with mobile *peephole windows* that either show photo-realistic views (left) or alternative representations, such as wireframe renderings (right).

objects above the table will appear to move left while those behind it will seem to move right (motion parallax).

We distinguish between two major effects that are based on the head-coupled perspective: the *fish tank VR* effect and the *head-coupled peephole* effect. Both effects are controlled by moving the head and/or a display with respect to each other.

Fish Tank VR Effect The illusion of holding a virtual object physically in the hands by using a fish tank window as a visual container can further be improved by applying the concept of fish tank VR [38]. With it, 3D objects are always shown from the correct viewpoint – the one of the user (observer). While the original fish tank VR technique only addressed conventional desktop monitors, it was later used for horizontal workbench-like VR stereo displays [25], which is similar to what we do with our tabletop. More recently, fish tank VR was shown for the iPad [14] that enabled users to hold 3D objects virtually in their hands. We extended this approach by providing a seamless integration into a multi-display tabletop environment, where every display can provide an individual fish tank view for each user. Beyond that, we support passive displays allowing us to project image content not only onto the front side of a Tangible Window but also onto the back side. This is necessary, e.g., for interaction techniques that employ display flipping.

Head-coupled Peephole Effect Using head-coupled perspectives for *peephole windows* reverts the "eyeball in hand" metaphor into something that could be called "eyeball in place" metaphor. Here, the *peephole window*'s own orientation does not effect the view direction anymore. Instead, the viewer's position defines which part of the scene is visible through the peephole window. This also allows users to hold a *peephole window* less accurately, e.g., when they look at a particular object of the global scene.

INTERACTION TECHNIQUES

We will now illustrate how users can accomplish the most common 3D interaction tasks with Tangible Windows: object selection and manipulation, including moving, copying and deleting objects, as well as viewport control and global navigation. To support this set of basic interaction techniques, we employ the three major input modalities provided by Tangible Windows, *on surface input* (pen/multi-touch input), *spatial input* (moving/rotating a window through the physical space), and *head input* (moving/rotating the head). We will focus on interaction techniques that are mostly based on head-assisted *spatial* input. We believe that such kinesthetic techniques will help users by utilizing their spatial memory, as supported by evidence presented in, e.g., [34]. This implies that while the physical interaction is taking place, users unconsciously acquire spatial knowledge about the overall virtual 3D scene. This supports them in recalling (wayfinding) and coming back (traveling) to a certain region of interest in a natural way.

Global Viewpoint Control on the Tabletop

The tabletop display plays an integral role for the interaction with Tangible Windows and serves as a physical reference that can be used for constraining the interaction to a particular 2D plane. Therefore, defining the tabletop's view is among the most important interaction tasks. With head-coupled perspective enabled, global camera parameters such as viewpoint and angle of aperture are solely controlled by using head positions with respect to the table. This enables the user to explore the global scene from different sides by walking around the table (see Figure 4). Head-coupled perspectives do not work well when two or more users look at the same display (tabletop). In such scenarios, averaged head positions could be used for people standing very close together or the shared tabletop display could be divided into partitions that provide a unique view for each user [19]. For our system, we decided to provide a single movement-independent default view that is a good compromise for most users. As suggested by [17], we opted for orthographic projections with the center of projection being directly above the table.

Scene Exploration (with Mobile Peephole Windows)

Scene exploration as one very basic task of 3D interaction is not only supported by changing the tabletop's view. We also use mobile *peephole windows* that serve as personal peepholes into the global scene to enable multiple users to examine the virtual 3D world independent from each other (see Figure 5). They provide easy viewport control by allowing users to physically move/rotate them through the space above the tabletop, while their physical orientation usually coincides with their view orientation. By this means, for instance, it is possible to orbit around a single virtual object within the overall virtual 3D world by just walking around its fixed virtual

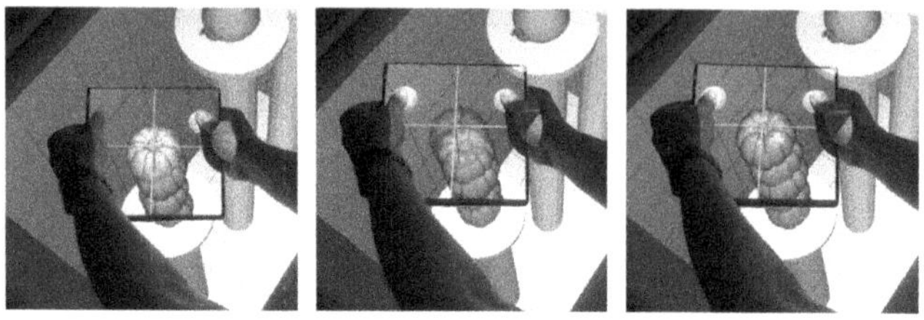

Figure 6. Object selection with a *peephole window*. The object targeted by the selection stick of the 3D cursor-stick gets highlighted (left). Once selected, the object can be moved (center) or copied (right).

Figure 7. Mobile *fish tank windows* serve as physical proxies for virtual objects that users can inspect by moving/rotating the display. The back-side of an object can be inspected by flipping the window.

center in physical space. Various systems have demonstrated similar capabilities, with the Boom Chameleon [35] being a prominent example. In contrast to others, our solution does not require mechanical arms for tracking, supports multiple displays simultaneously, and provides a seamless integration into a tabletop environment. Besides conventionally rendered views (see Figure 5, left), *peephole windows* can also show filtered representations, such as non-photorealistic or wireframe renderings (see Figure 5, right).

Object Selection (with Mobile Peephole Windows)

A common interaction task is selecting (picking) a particular object that is currently visible in a *peephole window*, e.g., for further inspection or manipulation. For this purpose, a 3D cursor-stick is displayed in the center of the window (see Figure 6). It can be thought of as a virtual stick that extends into the scene and keeps traveling along with the window. The 3D cursor-stick is activated by slightly pushing a pressure-sensitive button on the window and it is deactivated as soon as the user releases the button again. It serves both as a visual cursor and a ray that a user can point to any near or distant object. Objects appearing under the 3D cursor-stick automatically get visually highlighted. For this purpose, a ray is cast into the global scene. This makes it possible to select remote objects, e.g., objects below the table surface, which otherwise would be difficult to reach. We currently only consider the object that is closest to the window. However, more sophisticated approaches are possible, such as considering all available targets or letting users choose from a sorted list, see also [6]. Once an object is visually highlighted, it is a candidate for *snap-to-hand selection* and *snap-to-stick selection*.

Snap-to-Hand Selection Snap-to-hand selection is triggered by double-tapping a button on the window (see Figure 7). Then, a copy of the candidate object is created. The view changes and the copy is displayed in a hand-held *fish tank window*. For users, this has the effect that the object is brought from the distance directly into their hands in an animated way, allowing them to further examine and manipulate it.

Snap-to-Stick Selection Snap-to-stick selection (see Figure 6) is activated by pushing the pressure-sensitive button a little harder than before (remember that the 3D cursor-stick is only visible as long as the user slightly presses this button). Once the candidate object becomes selected, a half-transparent ghost object will be created that gets fixed to the ray at the current hit point and will remain there until the user releases the button again. In a way, this is similar to the real-world example of spiking a strawberry with a chopstick. As we will see next, this "fruit on a stick" metaphor is useful for various manipulation tasks.

Object Manipulation (with Mobile Peephole Windows)

Snap-to-stick selection implies that while a user is maneuvering a *peephole window* through the physical space, the object's ghost will be moved along with it, while always keeping the same distance to the window surface. At the same time, the original object is still visible at its original position in the global scene serving as a visual reference (see Figure 6, center). We use this configuration as the basis for the following manipulation tasks that are also inspired by the "drag and drop" metaphor employed on conventional desktop computers. For simplicity, we only address standard manipulation tasks, such as *moving*, *duplicating*, and *deleting* an object.

Object Moving Once the user is satisfied with the new position and orientation of the ghost, s/he only needs to release the button in order to permanently replace it with the original object. Along with this, the object at its original position is being removed and the 3D cursor-stick fades out. At any time, users can cancel the entire move operation by shaking the *peephole window* for more than one second.

Object Copying The above technique can also be used to create a duplicate of an object and to place it somewhere into the global scene. For this purpose, a special modifier button on the display needs to be pressed with the non-dominant hand. This is similar to holding a modifier key when performing a drag and drop operation in a file browser. As long as the button is pushed, a special copy icon appears on the *peephole window* indicating the changed interaction mode. As soon as the modifier button is released, the old interaction mode is restored. This allows users to seamlessly switch between MOVE and COPY operations.

Object Deletion A selected object can be removed from the global scene by dragging and then dropping it into the physical area besides the table. This is accomplished with the move operation as explained above. Once the proxy is released into the void, an icon on the window indicates that the object is to be deleted. In order to prevent unintentional object removals, the user can confirm or cancel the operation by pushing a button.

Beyond these standard operations, other more complex types of manipulation could be realized, too, for example, by using a second Tangible Window as a knife that cuts away parts of the objects or deforms it (two-hand interaction).

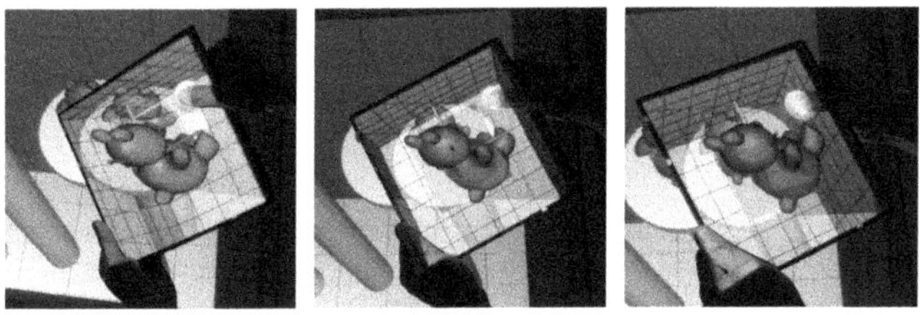

Figure 8. For precise control of how an object is oriented on a display we use *object clutching* that temporarily decouples the object from the window. It is activated by pressing (and holding) a button on the display.

Figure 9. With the help of tangible World in Miniature views, *scene-on-stick-dragging* (left) and *scene-in-hand-dragging* (middle, right) allow users to control what parts of the scene are displayed on the table.

Object Inspection (with Mobile Fish Tank Windows)

After having selected a particular object with the *snap-to-hand selection* technique, a user can examine the selected object from various sides by simply holding, moving and rotating the *fish tank window* with the hands (see Figure 7). Along with head-coupled perspectives this usually results in a convincing experience.

Object Flipping Due to the window's flat nature, usually only one hemisphere of an associated object can be shown on a window's screen, e.g., the front side of a virtual teddy bear. To lessen this problem, we support window flipping, i.e., the object's back side will be displayed on the window after it is flipped (see Figure 7).

Object Clutching For more precise object rotations on the window we use clutching [13], which enables users to control how an object is aligned to the display in terms of orientation. This is achieved by pushing a button on the window. As long as this button is pressed, any rotation of the window will not affect the object's orientation with respect to the physical world, see Figure 8.

Global Navigation on the Tabletop

The global scene can reach far beyond the physical boundaries of the table and thus often only parts of it are displayed on the tabletop (see Figure 2). In order to allow users to explore all parts of the scene, they need to be able to change its overall position with respect to the physical location of the table. This usually involves panning and lifting/lowering the global scene until a particular region of interest shows up. To provide users with such functionality, we utilize the concept of World in Miniature (WIM) [2, 32] – an overview & detail technique that we propose to make *tangible* with Tangible Windows. This is achieved by showing an overview map of the entire scene on the mobile *fish tank window*, where the parts of the scene that are currently displayed on the tabletop are visually highlighted by a semi-transparent box (see Figure 9). We support the following two techniques.

Scene-on-Stick-Dragging During scene exploration with a *peephole window*, a user can select (virtually harpoon) the entire scene by using the *snap-to-stick selection* technique. This is achieved by pointing the 3D cursor-stick to the background of the scene. When the pressure-sensitive button is pushed hard enough, a small overview map appears in the left upper corner of the *peephole window* indicating that the user has control over the position of the global scene (see Figure 9, left). Since the scene is now locked to the handheld window, moving it also moves the scene with respect to the table until the user releases the button again.

Scene-in-Hand-Dragging While *scene-on-stick-dragging* allows for a more precise control of the global scene, it is not suitable for adjustments on a more coarse level, e.g., consider a global scene that consumes 20 m of physical space. For this reason, we developed *scene-in-hand-dragging* that allows users to hold a miniature version of the entire scene physically in their hands by using the *object inspection* technique. Besides providing an overview, the WIM also visually highlights the part of the scene that is currently visible on the table by enclosing it with a semi-transparent box. Similar to *object clutching*, users can temporarily fixate the semi-transparent box in the physical space by pushing and holding a button. While the box is fixated in real-world space, moving the window will move the miniature map with respect to the box (see Figure 9, middle and right). This directly affects what parts of the scene are displayed on the tabletop.

EXAMPLE APPLICATION SCENARIOS

Tangible Windows provide a functionality that is suitable for a variety of application domains. Examples are manifold: a team of architects and urban designers could reshape an historic factory site on the basis of a virtual 3D model; a new car could be designed and then inspected virtually; doctors could plan a surgery with a virtual 3D representation of a patient's body. The key strengths of Tangible Windows are their generality, their support for parallel activities and collaboration, and their natural way of interaction. In order to demonstrate these benefits, we built two simple example applications – the *Virtual Sandbox* and the *Interior Designer* – that we used as a testbed for studying and improving the interaction with Tangible Windows. We also propose Medical Visualization (MedVis) as one particular domain for the application of Tangible Windows.

Virtual Sandbox The Virtual Sandbox is a static virtual 3D space that can exist above, on, and also below a tabletop surface (see Figure 4). It is filled with several simple 3D objects (triangle-based surface geometry) of different sizes and complexity. These objects can be viewed, selected, moved, rotated, and copied individually with Tangible Windows by using the interaction techniques previously described. It does not impose constraints on the location and orientation of the objects. In this way, the Virtual Sandbox acts as a simple virtual playground that allows for arrangement and manipulation of virtual 3D objects.

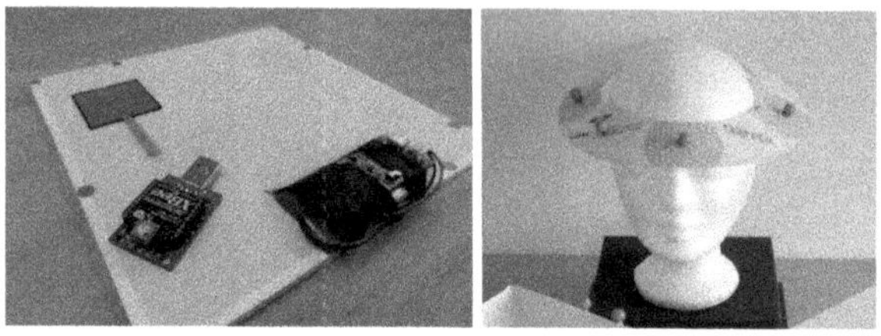

Figure 10. Pressure-sensitive buttons and crown.

Interior Designer Interior design is one of the use cases for our approach. Designers can use Tangible Windows to present different arrangements of furniture to their customers. This may help them to understand the design proposals and facilitate their decision. The Interior Designer scene consists of a large three-dimensional floor plan filled with several pieces of furniture (see Figure 5, left). Compared to the Virtual Sandbox scene, which emphasizes the possibilities of unconstrained three-dimensional interaction, it focuses on a 2D map that extends into the 3rd dimension. Due to its size, not the whole layout can be shown at once. This example thus benefits from the global navigation interaction techniques presented earlier. For example, the bedroom of a virtual apartment in the Interior Designer may be shown on the table display. Should the user decide to examine the kitchen, he or she might opt for using the *scene-in-hand-dragging* to change the viewpoint, because it allows a coarse and quick navigation. The pieces of furniture placed in the scene's rooms can be moved, rotated and copied. Two principle modes are possible on the tabletop: a 2D map of the floor plan, well suited for multiple users, and a 3D view of the rooms on or below the table. Seamless switching between the two modes is supported by lifting and lowering the global scene.

Medical Visualization While the former two examples demonstrate the interaction with Tangible Windows, they do not fully show the potential benefits for collaborative work. One of the domains that we envision to benefit from our approach is Medical Visualization (MedVis). Here, volume data sets often need to be examined by several medical professionals, e.g, for therapy planning (see Figure 4, right). By using multiple displays, we can combine different projections of the same scene. This can be used to provide individual, personalized head-coupled perspectives for each user, displayed on their own peephole window. This may help to present 3D-spatial relations more realistically than normal displays. At the same time, the tabletop can show a general view, e.g., a planar projection or an outline of the patient's body which serves as a frame of reference. Additionally, different visualization techniques can easily be combined. For example, by showing both a direct 3D-volume rendering and a 2D-slice projection (freely defined by the orientation of the Tangible Window), we can support a fast comparison of different views of the same data set using multiple handheld displays. MedVis is also a good use case for the annotation of data, supported by pen input, directly on the Tangible Window.

TECHNICAL SETUP

In the future, Tangible Windows could be implemented as self-contained (active) displays, e.g., by using organic light emitting diode (OLED) technology that provides high-resolution views and high-accuracy multi-touch/pen input. Due to current technical limitations and availability, we chose a passive display approach that uses cardboard as projection material. Besides immediate availability, these passive displays have the advantage of being a straightforward and cost-effective way of integrating and customizing new displays in arbitrary shapes for several users once the system is built.

Principle Setup Inspired by [31], the principle components of our technical setup are: a back-projected tabletop, an infrared (IR) optical tracking system, a ceiling-mounted projector, and several pieces of cardboard serving as mobile displays (Tangible Windows). We extended this setup with the ability to track users' head positions by using tracked crowns.

Tracking of Mobile Displays and Heads Twelve IR cameras (Optitrack FLEX:V100R2) allow for precise determination of position and orientation (6DOF) of mobile displays and crowns at 100 Hz with a tracking error of less than 3 mm. We glued small and unobtrusive IR reflective markers onto all tracked devices. Besides calibration of the overall tracking system, every tracked devices has to be initially registered once. In order to ensure a robust tracking, only four out of six markers needed to be visible for a successful recognition. Unique marker designs ensured a reliable distinction between individual devices.

Mobile Displays Mobile displays were made of circular- and rectangular-shaped pieces of cardboard with edge lengths between 15 and 25 cm. The ceiling-mounted short-throw projector (HD) is used to project arbitrary image content onto them. For this purpose, we wrote an OpenGL-based graphics engine that simulates the physical space above the table surface with each mobile display being represented by a textured polygon. In practice, we achieved an overall projection error of less than 5 mm (measured as the offset of handheld cardboards and the projections onto them).

Touch and Pen Input In order to provide basic touch input on mobile displays, we applied two physical pressure-sensitive buttons (Arduino XBee) to some of them (see Figure 10, left). All touch input currently done in our setup (mainly confirming actions and switching between interaction modes) is realized this way. For digital pen input, we attached Anoto pattern[2] to the tabletop and all mobile displays. Though implemented, we did not use digital pen input in the prototypes.

INITIAL USER EXPERIENCE & DISCUSSION

Although still being in an early stage of implementation, experiences with our system were encouraging. Three computer science students and two members of our institute (22 to 35 years old, 1 female) were invited to test our *Virtual Sandbox* and *Interior Designer* prototypes. After a brief demonstration, they were immediately able to successfully interact with the system. They liked the concept of viewing and manipulating parts of a virtual 3D world by simply grabbing and moving small lightweight paper screens. Users particularly found it easy to explore the global 3D world by looking through a *peephole window*. All five users stated that they were impressed by

[2] Anoto Group AB, http://www.anoto.com

the 3D appearance of virtual objects displayed on the handheld *fish tank windows*. The valuable feedback which we received helped us to identify several new ideas and approaches for further improvements and also revealed limitations of our current implementation.

Limitations

Although users generally appreciated the overall impression of Tangible Windows and in particular the intuitive way of interacting with them, four of the five users complained about unpredictable behavior or a non-responsive system. We identified the following causes for this. First, touch input was preliminary with only two pressure-sensitive buttons on each display that do not provide any haptic feedback. Our experiences suggest that real physical buttons with tactile feedback would have been a much better choice, in particular for techniques that heavily rely on holding a button for a longer time, such as *object clutching*, *object moving*, etc. Second, we implemented all techniques as described in Section Interaction Techniques in a prototypic way, not paying much attention on the interplay between them. This required us to frequently reset the prototype during the tests, which impaired the overall interaction experience. One example for this is the hard-coded mapping of head-coupled perspectives and Tangible Windows. Also, head-coupled perspectives on the tabletop were automatically replaced by a default orthographic perspective as soon as two users (recognized by their crowns) were using the system. However, this did not affect the mobile displays. Fourth, the physical interaction zone was restricted due to our technical setup (single projector, limited tracking volume). This could be mitigated by including additional projectors, an extended tracking setup or using active displays, e.g., the iPad. The latter would also help with the problem of limited buttons and provides a higher display quality. In contrast, passive (projected) displays have several advantages regarding their cost and flexibility. For example, interaction techniques like *object flipping* cannot be easily implemented for active displays without using special hardware. For these cases, alternatives need to be found, e.g., providing a button that triggers *object flipping* or replacing it with *object clutching*.

Precision and Constraints

Users sometimes complained about having problems with adjusting an object's orientation and position. Constraints can be employed to facilitate such object manipulation. Especially the Interior Designer prototype shows how certain application domains may provide inherent constraints. For example, most pieces of furniture are placed on the ground, none are floating in mid-air. Other solutions, e.g., grids, object snapping or alignment guides may also improve the user experience but are beyond the scope of this paper. Another problem arises from a lack of depth perceptibility. As the system does not feature stereoscopic displays, depth clues like projected shadows could be used to support the user, especially when working with parts of the scene floating above the table's surface.

More Permanent Representations

Frequently, users asked for a more permanent representation of virtual content. This is because Tangible Windows are mostly temporary in nature and instantly change their view as soon as they are moved. However, due to their flat shape, Tangible Windows do not lend themselves to be fixed in upright positions. A possible solution would be to provide little support stands that could be used for fasting the displays in arbitrary orientations. Similarly, but for virtual scene parts floating higher above the table surface, tripods could allow for fixation of *fish tank windows* in mid-air. One user proposed fixating and using a *peephole window* similar to a watchmaker's magnifying glass that would provide additional contextual views into the global 3D scene in a more permanent manner, which resembles the Boom Chameleon [35].

Head-coupled Perspectives and Head Input

Head-coupled perspectives were not always perceived as superior to manual perspectives. The best effects were achieved with one eye closed, which is due to the monoscopic display approach. Although users generally liked the fish tank VR-like views, there are situations in which it is preferable to switch off auto-perspectives, e.g., when sharing a view on a mobile display with somebody else. We conclude that the ability for a seamless de- and reactivation of head-coupling is a fundamental requirement of a Tangible Window system. One user suggested to use the head for other interaction purposes, e.g., to fade in text labels or to show more detailed geometry when a user comes closer to a display.

CONCLUSION & FUTURE WORK

With Tangible Windows, we have contributed a novel concept for interacting with virtual 3D information spaces in a tabletop environment that goes beyond conventional multi-touch input. This was achieved by adding a spatial component to the interaction and combining tangible interaction, head tracking, and multi-touch as well as pen input techniques. For this purpose, we built a multi-display environment that features a true unification of physical interaction and output space by using multiple handheld displays providing haptic affordances. They serve as visual proxies or peepholes into a virtual 3D world. Multi-user collaboration and the seamless transition between local and distant control of 3D scenes are especially supported by Tangible Windows. Head input is mainly utilized for auto-perspective effects that help making the interaction more natural and intuitive by approximating what users would expect from real-world experiences. We received promising initial user feedback that makes us confident that Tangible Windows are a valuable tool for many 3D tasks operating above, on, or even below a table surface.

With our contribution of several basic 3D interaction techniques, we have only set first steps into a rich interaction space. We foresee a variety of follow-up work that will extend our techniques to additional collaborative work scenarios and specific application domains, e.g., by addressing the issues discussed in the last section, among them the usage of constraints. While in this work we mainly used Tangible Windows for parallel activities, specific concerns regarding collaboration, such as exchange of data between displays or dynamic mapping of head-coupled perspectives to tangible windows to allow changing their ownership have to be examined. Besides simulating real-world effects with head-coupled perspectives, "unnatural" effects, such as exaggerated zooming or distortion effects (fisheye, etc.), are another promising field of research. Other issues to investigate are accuracy and hand fatigue when working with Tangible Windows over a longer period of time. Finally, technical progress provides new possibilities, e.g., marker-less tracking of users and displays, or affordable volumetric displays.

ACKNOWLEDGEMENTS

This work was funded by the German Ministry of Education and Science (BMBF) project ViERforES-II (01IM1000 2B).

REFERENCES

1. Agrawala, M., Beers, A. C., McDowall, I., Fröhlich, B., Bolas, M., and Hanrahan, P. The Two-user Responsive Workbench: Support for Collaboration through Individual Views of a Shared Space. In *Proc. of SIGGRAPH*, ACM Press (1997), 327–332.
2. Bell, B., Höllerer, T., and Feiner, S. An annotated situation-awareness aid for augmented reality. In *Proc. of UIST*, ACM Press (2002), 213–216.
3. Benko, H., and Feiner, S. Balloon Selection: A Multi-Finger Technique for Accurate Low-Fatigue 3D Selection. In *Proc. of 3DUI* (2007), 79–86.
4. Benko, H., Jota, R., and Wilson, A. MirageTable: Freehand Interaction on a Projected Augmented Reality Tabletop. In *Proc. of CHI*, ACM Press (2012), 199–208.
5. Bier, E. A., Stone, M. C., Pier, K., Buxton, W., and DeRose, T. D. Toolglass and Magic Lenses: The See-through Interface. In *Proc. of SIGGRAPH*, ACM Press (1993), 73–80.
6. Bowman, D. A., Kruijff, E., LaViola, J. J., and Poupyrev, I. *3D User Interfaces: Theory and Practice*. Addison Wesley Longman Publishing Co., Inc., 2004.
7. Brown, L. D., Hua, H., and Gao, C. A Widget Framework for Augmented Interaction in SCAPE. In *Proc. of UIST*, ACM Press (2003), 1–10.
8. Chan, C., Lai, S., and Zhan, Y. Evaluation Of A Head Tracked 3-D Document Visualization. In *Proc. of Human Interface Technologies Conference* (2006).
9. Chan, L.-W., Wu, H.-T., Kao, H.-S., Ko, J.-C., Lin, H.-R., Chen, M. Y., Hsu, J., and Hung, Y.-P. Enabling beyond-surface interactions for interactive surface with an invisible projection. In *Proc. of UIST*, ACM Press (2010), 263–272.
10. de Almeida, R. A., Pillias, C., Pietriga, E., and Cubaud, P. Looking behind bezels: French windows for wall displays. In *Proc. of AVI*, ACM Press (2012), 124–131.
11. Downing, E., Hesselink, L., Ralston, J., and Macfarlane, R. A Three-Color, Solid-State, Three-Dimensional Display. *Science 273*, 5279 (1996), 1185–1189.
12. Favalora, G. Volumetric 3D Displays and Application Infrastructure. *Computer 38*, 8 (2005), 37–44.
13. Fitzmaurice, G., Zhai, S., and Chignell, M. Virtual Reality for Palmtop Computers. *Trans. Inf. Syst. 11*, 3 (1993), 197–218.
14. Francone, J., and Nigay, L. Using the User's Point of View for Interaction on Mobile Devices. In *Actes de la Conference francophone sur l'Interaction Homme-Machine (IHM)*, ACM Press (2011), 25–31.
15. Grossman, T., and Wigdor, D. Going Deeper: A Taxonomy of 3D on the Tabletop. In *Proc. of Tabletop*, IEEE (2007), 137–144.
16. Hancock, M., Carpendale, S., and Cockburn, A. Shallow-Depth 3D Interaction: Design and Evaluation of One-, Two- and Three-Touch Techniques. In *Proc. of CHI*, ACM Press (2007), 1147–1156.
17. Hancock, M., Nacenta, M., Gutwin, C., and Carpendale, S. The Effects of Changing Projection Geometry on the Interpretation of 3D Orientation on Tabletops. In *Proc. of ITS*, ACM Press (2009), 175–182.
18. Hancock, M., ten Cate, T., and Carpendale, S. Sticky Tools: Full 6DOF Force-based Interaction for Multi-touch Tables. In *Proc. of ITS*, ACM Press (2009), 133–140.
19. Hancock, M. S., and Carpendale, S. Supporting Multiple Off-Axis Viewpoints at a Tabletop Display. In *Proc. of Tabletop*, IEEE (2007), 171–178.
20. Harrison, C., and Dey, A. K. Lean and Zoom: Proximity-aware User Interface and Content Magnification. In *Proc. of CHI*, ACM Press (2008), 507–510.
21. Hilliges, O., Izadi, S., Wilson, A. D., Hodges, S., Garcia-Mendoza, A., and Butz, A. Interactions in the air: Adding further depth to interactive tabletops. In *Proc. of UIST*, ACM Press (2009), 139–148.
22. Holman, D., Vertegaal, R., Altosaar, M., Troje, N., and Johns, D. Paper Windows: Interaction Techniques for Digital Paper. In *Proc. of CHI*, ACM Press (2005), 591–599.
23. Izadi, S., Hodges, S., Taylor, S., Rosenfeld, D., Villar, N., Butler, A., and Westhues, J. Going Beyond the Display: A Surface Technology with an Electronically Switchable Diffuser. In *Proc. of UIST*, ACM Press (2008), 269–278.
24. Kjeldsen, R. Head Gestures for Computer Control. In *Proc. of ICCV Workshop on Recognition, Analysis, and Tracking of Faces and Gestures in Real-Time Systems*, IEEE (2001), 61–68.
25. Krüger, W., Bohn, C., Fröhlich, B., Schüth, H., Strauss, W., and Wesche, G. The Responsive Workbench: A Virtual Work Environment. *Computer 28*, 7 (1995), 42–48.
26. Lee, J. Hacking the Nintendo Wii Remote. *Pervasive Computing 7*, 3 (2008), 39–45.
27. Molyneaux, D., Izadi, S., Kim, D., Hilliges, O., Hodges, S., Cao, X., Butler, A., and Gellersen, H. Interactive environment-aware handheld projectors for pervasive computing spaces. In *Pervasive*, vol. 7319 of *Lecture Notes in Computer Science*, Springer (2012), 197–215.
28. Nacenta, M. A., Sakurai, S., Yamaguchi, T., Miki, Y., Itoh, Y., Kitamura, Y., Subramanian, S., and Gutwin, C. E-conic: A Perspective-aware Interface for Multi-Display Environments. In *Proc. of UIST*, ACM Press (2007), 279–288.
29. Reisman, J. L., Davidson, P. L., and Han, J. Y. A Screen-Space Formulation for 2D and 3D Direct Manipulation. In *Proc. of UIST*, ACM Press (2009), 69–78.
30. Spindler, M., Stellmach, S., and Dachselt, R. PaperLens: Advanced Magic Lens Interaction Above the Tabletop. In *Proc. of ITS*, ACM Press (2009), 77–84.
31. Spindler, M., Tominski, C., Schumann, H., and Dachselt, R. Tangible Views for Information Visualization. In *Proc. of ITS*, ACM Press (2010), 157–166.
32. Stoakley, R., Conway, M. J., and Pausch, R. Virtual Reality on a WIM: Interactive Worlds in Miniature. In *Proc. of CHI*, ACM Press (1995), 265–272.
33. Szalavri, Z., and Gervautz, M. The Personal Interaction Panel - A Two-Handed Interface for Augmented Reality. In *Proc. of EUROGRAPHICS*, ACM Press (1997), 335–346.
34. Tan, D. S., Pausch, R., Stefanucci, J. K., and Proffitt, D. R. Kinesthetic cues aid spatial memory. In *Proc. of CHI Extended Abstracts*, ACM Press (2002), 806–807.
35. Tsang, M., Fitzmaurice, G., Kurtenbach, G., Khan, A., and Buxton, B. Boom Chameleon: Simultaneous Capture of 3D Viewpoint, Voice and Gesture Annotations on a Spatially-aware Display. In *Proc. of UIST*, ACM Press (2002), 111–120.
36. Ullmer, B., and Ishii, H. The metaDESK: models and prototypes for tangible user interfaces. In *Proc. of UIST*, ACM Press (1997), 223–232.
37. Viega, J., Conway, M. J., Williams, G., and Pausch, R. 3D Magic Lenses. In *Proc. of UIST*, ACM Press (1996), 51–58.
38. Ware, C., Arthur, K., and Booth, K. Fish Tank Virtual Reality. In *Proc. of INTERACT and CHI*, ACM Press (1993), 37–42.
39. Ware, C., and Osborne, S. Exploration and Virtual Camera Control in Virtual Three Dimensional Environments. *SIGGRAPH Comput. Graph. 24* (February 1990), 175–183.
40. Wilson, A. D., and Benko, H. Combining multiple depth cameras and projectors for interactions on, above and between surfaces. In *Proc. of UIST*, UIST '10, ACM (New York, NY, USA, 2010), 273–282.
41. Yee, K. Peephole Displays: Pen Interaction on Spatially Aware Handheld Computers. In *Proc. of CHI*, ACM Press (2003), 1–8.

TouchWave: Kinetic Multi-touch Manipulation for Hierarchical Stacked Graphs

Dominikus Baur[1], Bongshin Lee[2], Sheelagh Carpendale[1]

[1]Innovis Group, University of Calgary
2500 University Dr NW, Calgary, AB, Canada
dominikus.baur@gmail.com, sheelagh@ucalgary.ca

[2]Microsoft Research
One Microsoft Way, Redmond, WA, USA
bongshin@microsoft.com

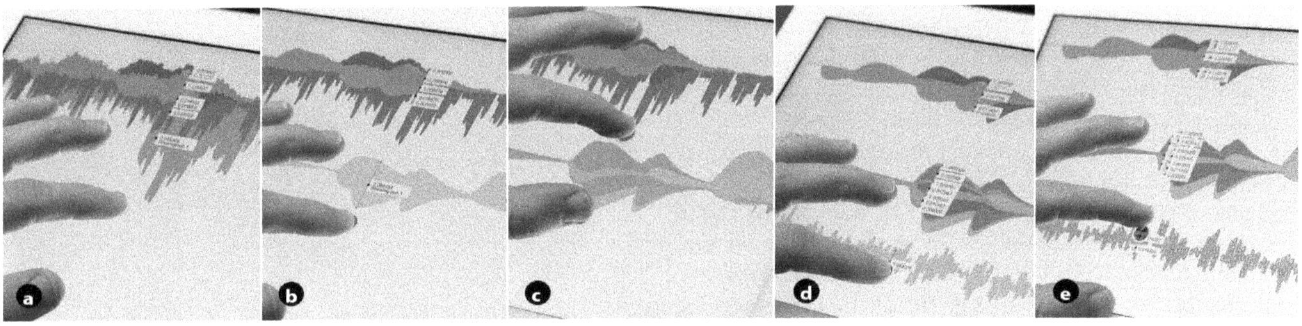

Figure 1: TouchWave: (a) reading specific values with the vertical ruler, (b) extracting a layer from its parent by dragging, (c) showing sublayers by pinching, (d) extracting a layer containing atomic items, and (e) pinching to show the underlying items.

ABSTRACT

The increasing popularity of touch-based devices is driving us to rethink existing interfaces. Within this opportunity, the complexity of information visualizations offers particular challenges. We explore these challenges to bring multi-touch interactions to a specific visualization technique, stacked graphs. Stacked graphs are a visually appealing and popular method for presenting time series data, however, they come with associated problems—issues with legibility, difficulties with comparisons, and restrictions in scalability. We present TouchWave, a rethinking and extension of stacked graphs for multi-touch capable devices that provides a variety of flexible layout adjustments, interactive options for querying data values, and seamlessly switching between different visualizations. In addition to ameliorating the main issues of stacked graphs, TouchWave also integrates hierarchical data within stacked graphs. We demonstrate TouchWave capabilities with two datasets—a music listening history and movie box office revenues—and discuss the implications for weaning other visualizations off mouse and keyboard.

Author Keywords

Stacked graphs; Visualization; Multi-touch; tablets.

ACM Classification: H.5.2 [Information interfaces and presentation]: User Interfaces. - Graphical user interfaces.

ITS'12, November 11–14, 2012, Cambridge, Massachusetts, USA.

INTRODUCTION

In the last few years, multi-touch has become the default mode of interaction not only for portable devices such as smartphones and tablets, but also for interactive tabletops and wall displays. Changes are also expected to happen with desktops as touch-enabled monitors become more affordable and readily available. Controlling everything with fingers instead of a single, indirect mouse cursor drastically changes the requirements and capabilities of interfaces. These changes present both opportunities and challenges for information visualization, where interactions are still predominately mouse and keyboard; we need to rethink those interfaces. Given the wide variety and complexity of existing visualization techniques, it is probably not feasible to create a single set of multi-touch interactions that can cover all visualizations. To consider generalizing touch interactions across visualizations, we therefore need more concrete practical examples. In this paper, we add to the small set of multi-touch enabled visualizations [6,8,13,18,22,23] by extending one specific visualization technique, stacked graphs, which is commonly used and yet could significantly benefit from multi-touch interactions.

Despite their popularity, stacked graphs suffer from issues with legibility, enabling comparisons, and scalability. With the design and development of TouchWave (Figure 1), we show how bringing stacked graphs to multi-touch capable tablet computers to address their inherent issues requires a complete rethinking of the visualization, in both representation and interaction. In addition, we demonstrate how we address stacked graph issues with a simple yet comprehensive set of touch-based interactions.

The main contributions of this paper are: TouchWave, which extends capabilities of stacked graphs by introducing a set of consistent multi-touch interactions that mitigate several basic stacked graph problems; a collection of touch interaction design goals, which consider particularly the issues of creating a hands-on-data visualization experience; and the concept of *kinetic manipulation*, which encourages combining the active physical finger, hand, and body motions with the animated responses of the visualization to enhance an experience of virtual tangibility.

STACKED GRAPHS AND THEIR PROBLEMS

Stacked graphs are a popular method for visualizing socially relevant time-changing data mostly due to their organic and flowing visual qualities. Examples include news stories [11], music listening histories and movie box office rates [1], email messages [10], twitter postings [5], and names people give their babies [24]. Stacked graphs are composed of several *layers* of time series data on one common timeline (Figure 2). Each layer stands for one specific attribute of the data (e.g., the number of tweets for a given keyword or the stock price of one specific share), providing its value at a given point in time. Values are encoded as the height of a layer at a given horizontal point. Compared to other types of time series visualization such as line charts or small multiples [20], stacked graphs form one cohesive chart: all layers are stacked on top of each other without intermediary whitespace. The outer hull of a stacked graph therefore depicts the sum of the values of all contained layers. The layout of a stacked graph depends on the form of its *baseline*: a straight baseline leads to a regular stacked graph, but its shape can also be adjusted to the data at each position. This leads to layouts such as symmetrical Themerivers or Streamgraphs that optimize the variation in slope based on a layer's thickness [1]. Stacked graphs are popular, but their approach to representing the data faces three types of problems: (1) *legibility,* (2) *comparisons*, and (3) *scalability* (Figure 3).

The *legibility* of a graph describes the ease with which the human visual system is able to extract values from it and whether the graphical representation exceeds a human perceptual threshold [16]. Visualizations are based on turning numerical data into visual shapes and legibility issues can arise in the process when choosing a problematic or unsuitable chart type [20]. Stacked graphs in their non-interactive form suffer from the fact that human perception makes reading and comparing curved slopes difficult [2] (Figure 3a). Also, stacked graphs are usually based on discrete data samples, but their representation suggests that the data was continuous. Finally, stacked graphs often lack explicit scales; they might show a horizontal time axis but the vertical axis is usually missing. The reason is that explicit scales would have to be visible at every point of the graph, which would lead to overlap and visual clutter.

Comparing values is common in information visualization scenarios but problematic with stacked graphs. While they provide a good overall "feeling" for the growing and shrinking of layers over time, explicitly comparing layers is difficult (Figure 3b) and practically impossible if all layers have roughly the same size. Common comparison tasks that are difficult with stacked graphs include comparisons between layers overall, between different parts of one layer, between different parts of different layers and even between all layers at one point in time.

In common with many visualizations, stacked graphs also have *scalability* issues. Simply stacking all layers means that only a certain number of them can be visible and stay interactive at one time for a given screen resolution. Tens

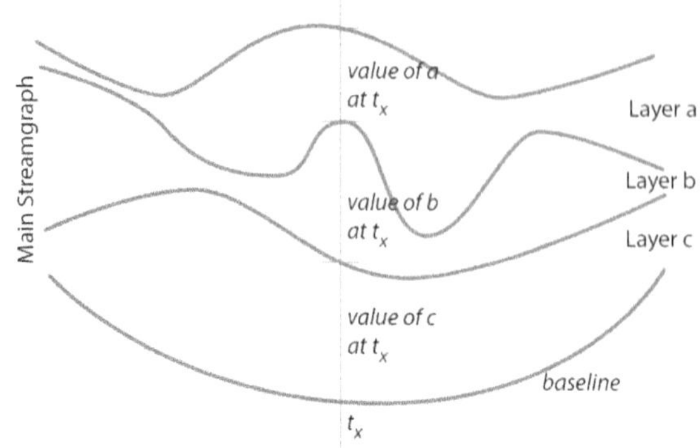

Figure 2: The structure of a stacked graph (here: a streamgraph). Each graph is made up of the sum of the values of its sublayers.

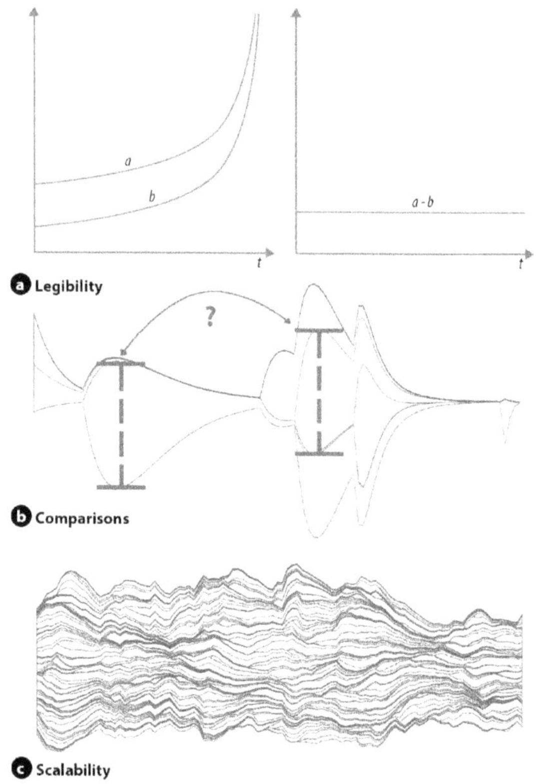

Figure 3: Three main issues of stacked graphs.

or hundreds of layers quickly lead to visual clutter and makes interacting with layers nearly impossible (Figure 3c). Current solutions rely on simple panning and zooming, or hiding some layers; filtering by text query (hiding layers based on their attributes in NameVoyager [24]) or filtering by additional control widgets (BookVoyager's separate tree-control can show and hide specific layers [25]).

Only a few projects (e.g., BookVoyager [25], ManyEyes [21]) incorporate hierarchical data into a stacked graph to address scalability. Those that do support hierarchical data rely on separate (e.g., tree) views to show the hierarchy. This use of two views not only uses additional screen space but also requires the viewer to make the cognitive links between the two representations of the same data.

RELATED WORK

Interaction in Stacked Graphs and Streamgraphs

The challenges of stacked graphs caused even early projects to incorporate interaction with the visualization. ThemeRiver [11] shows the flow of document themes on a timeline and enables displaying and hiding labels, scales, and underlying numbers, and navigating the stream by zooming and panning. NameVoyager [24], an interactive stacked graph showing the popularity of baby names, enables rapid exploration of more than 6,000 time series based on prefix text search. Its filtering capability combined with smooth animations and aesthetically pleasing visual representations led to a popular response from the general public. BookVoyager extends NameVoyager to handle hierarchical time series by integrating it with an additional standard tree control used to navigate the hierarchy of the data [25]. Muse [10] provides similar filtering capabilities through additional on-screen elements for navigating email archives. Color-coding was used to make the hierarchical structure more visible in the stacked graph of ManyEyes [21]. Cui et al. merge time-series visualization with topic analysis in TextFlow [4] and create interactive and animated ways to explore this information. However, they emphasize topic development over time and relax some of the constraints of stacked graphs (e.g., having no whitespace between layers). ColourVis [15] provides considerable functionality but does not consider interaction. Finally, while sense.us [12] does not suggest new ways to directly improve on stacked graphs, it supports the social aspects of asynchronous collaborative visualizations.

Looking at the types of tasks supported by interaction with stacked graphs, they clearly focus on details-on-demand and filtering: based on Yi et al.'s taxonomy of seven high-level interaction goals in information visualization [26], all visualizations support such *abstraction/elaboration* (mostly by hovering over an item [4,11,12,21,24,25] or clicking [10]) and *filtering* (through text input [12,24,25] or clicking [4,12,21]). Yet, other tasks such as *exploration* (i.e., showing different subsets of the data, e.g., through pan & zoom [11]) or *reconfiguration* (i.e., showing the same data in a different layout [25]) are only rarely supported. Enabling similarly complex manipulations in one consistent widget-less set of simple touch-based interactions requires a different approach with a stronger focus on *reconfiguration* to keep the visualization object consistent.

Multi-touch Interactions for Information Visualization

With the rapid advances in technologies, some research projects are specifically exploring multi-touch interactions for information visualization. For example, Voida et al. present two interaction techniques, *i-Loupe* and *iPodLoupe*, and a set of design considerations to address the challenges of designing interaction techniques for information visualizations on tabletops [23]. Valming et al. explore tabletop touch interaction for 3D information visualization [22]. Spindler et al. explore the implications of a secondary, passive display device above a tabletop surface for information visualization [19] without extending touch-based manipulations.

There also have been several efforts to provide more fluid interactions for node-link graph visualizations. For example, Schmidt et al. focus on multi-touch interactions for link manipulation [18]. They broaden interaction possibilities by presenting a set of multi-touch interaction techniques (e.g., plucking, pinning, strumming, and bundling) that can be effectively combined. Frisch et al. discuss a rich set of individually-elicited pen and touch gestures for editing node-link diagrams, and provide insights into the suitability of gestures and bimanual interactions on tabletops [8]. Dwyer et al. investigate interaction techniques people use while they are optimizing node-link graph layouts [6]. Multi-touch interactions are also used to provide high freedom of expression when entering queries. For example, Facet-Streams harness the expressive power of facets and Boolean logic with tangible and multi-touch interactions without requiring people to use complex formal notations [14]. More generally, Isenberg et al. discuss how multi-touch interactions could be applied to visualizations [13].

We extend this research direction by demonstrating with TouchWave how bringing multi-touch to a visualization can go beyond mapping touches to cursor input, and start to reveal how touch interactions can improve the visualization.

TOUCHWAVE

TouchWave provides touchable stacked graphs that offer a set of integrated interaction techniques and the ability to display hierarchical data within streams. In this section, we first describe the underlying design considerations, followed by TouchWave's interaction techniques and then explain its hierarchical capabilities.

Design Goals

This section contains our main design goals for TouchWave: creating a full interaction set with kinetic manipulations and integrated interaction but without complex gestures and on-screen widgets.

Support Kinetic Manipulation

Touch-based interaction invites people to interact directly with the on-screen visuals. The idea behind *kinetic manipulation* is that a person's fingers, hands, and perhaps arms and body together with the visualization form a coherent kinetic whole. Kinetic manipulation suggests that a visualization reacts in a consistent, learnable manner to touch interaction. This consistency is usually arrived at via physically-based metaphors, but could also use a type of virtual consistency as in the concept of alternate interface physics [17]. In any case, kinetic manipulation enables exploration and learning the "rules" to which a visualization obeys by touching and dragging parts of it. The visualization becomes a tangible, virtual object that enables data exploration through its manipulation.

Kinetic manipulation also works with the concept of momentum, harmoniously linking physical touch movement to visualization movement. In this regard, kinetic manipulation follows similar ideas as the increasingly popular concept of fluid interaction [7] by avoiding abrupt switches between states and developing animated transitions. Kinetic manipulation goes further, however, in that it more strongly emphasizes the stability and existence of virtual objects. The intention here is to have consistent and active behavior and predictable malleability in touch-based adjustments.

Create Integrated Interactions

Integrated interactions mean that interactions are triggered directly on the visualization itself instead of a control panel, etc. Visualizations have had a long history of being manipulated in software where the visual representations and the interaction controls are spatially separate. Mapping these touch interactions directly to parts of the visualizations and creating a visual response that is expected is non-trivial. The intention with integrated interactions is to keep the interactions located within the visualization's screen space.

Another way interactions have been developed for visualizations is through the use of additional on-screen widgets. While this can be a powerful idea, the use of additional widgets can pull cognitive attention away from the visualization. In supporting the idea of integrated interactions, we work towards both limiting the use of additional widgets and making those that are used adhere with the kinetic manipulation concept. That is, they should be spatially situated appropriately within the visualization and their actions and reactions should be kinetically in harmony with those of the visualization.

Avoid Complex Gestures

One possible approach to creating touch-based interactions is to develop touch-traced patterns, which can then be recognized and used to trigger specific system responses. These touch-gestures can quickly become complex and can be hard to learn and remember. Instead, our goal is to keep the touch interactions simple, to when possible use established touch interactions (touch-and-drag, tap, double tap, long press, swipe, and pinch).

Consider the Viability of the Interaction Set

Creating a set of touch interactions that work together is harder than creating individual interactions. Performing the same touch interactions on the same on-screen element should lead to the same result. As a touch usually produces a reaction of the visuals even before the gesture itself is finished, interactions have to be able to handle ambiguity (touching an object can lead to touch-and-drag, swipe, or two-finger pinch gesture, etc.).

Interacting with TouchWave

In this section, we present interaction techniques available in TouchWave. For each technique we discuss the extent to which it mitigates particular aspects of the stacked graph problems. We address the legibility issues by introducing vertical rulers, supporting comparisons through adjustable layouts and temporarily extracting layers from their original positions, and provide navigation techniques for overcoming the scalability problems.

Vertical Rulers On Demand

The legibility problems of stacked graphs come on the one hand from the visual, curve-based data mapping but also from the lack of suitable scales. This is mostly due to the visual clutter that can be introduced by permanent scales. Offering scales on-demand for horizontal points allows reading explicit values while not overburdening the visualization. Our *vertical rulers* (Figure 4a) are an aid for these legibility issues. Touching the background behind a stacked graph in TouchWave creates a ruler that is bound to the position of the finger. Each ruler shows the size of all layers that it crosses at its current position by providing the numerical values. Moving the finger horizontally updates the labels correspondingly. Vertical rulers can be generated for more than one finger supporting both reading and comparing. This detail-on-demand technique can also be used to show additional information for each layer (e.g., movie names, see the box office case study).

Automatic Sorting and Adjustable Layouts

Vertical rulers allow reading absolute values, but sometimes only the relative order of layers is important (e.g., Which layer has the highest or lowest value for a given horizontal position? At which point is the layer no longer the largest?, see the box office case study). With *automatic sorting* (Figure 4b) TouchWave solves this comparison problem interactively. Press-and-hold a stacked graph in TouchWave sorts its layers based on their values at that horizontal position. This quickly shows the most influential layer for the position. Once the sorting is invoked, the finger can also be moved along the horizontal axis to continue sorting the layers based on the values at other horizontal positions.

In their discussion on stacked graphs [1], Byron and Wattenberg present several approaches that rely on changing a stacked graph's baseline to create a new layout.

Different layout approaches enable different comparisons; ThemeRivers help in comparing layers above and below the central timeline, while a basic stacked graph avoids the problems of curvature at least for the lowest layer. In order to quickly change between different layouts for a stacked graph, TouchWave enables *adjustable layouts* (Figure 4c) triggered by double tapping (the default layout is a streamgraph). As a transition between different layouts only changes the baseline, TouchWave uses an animated transition to help people keep track of points and layers.

Extracting Layers

Comparing two layers for different horizontal positions (e.g., if layer A's value at a certain point in time is larger/smaller than layer B's at a different point) can still be difficult even after adjusting the layout and using vertical rulers. TouchWave therefore makes it possible to *extract layers* from a stacked graph by dragging (Figure 4d). Touching a single layer and moving it far enough removes it from its parent. The parent stacked graph in TouchWave then adjusts the layout so that the remaining layers fill the gap. Since this works for multiple layers simultaneously and both fingers automatically create vertical rulers, rearranging and holding the layers against each other supports comparison of different sections. This interaction would be cumbersome to perform using a mouse in conjunction with keyboard modifiers which might be the reason why such deconstructions have not been done before. When a layer is dropped on the background canvas by lifting the finger, it creates a new single-layer. If a layer is dropped on an existing stacked graph it lands right above the layer it is currently over. This allows manual sorting and grouping of stacked graph, if automatic approaches such as sorting do not bring the expected results.

Navigation through Focus+Context

The main interaction technique that current stacked graphs provide to overcome the scalability problem is zooming & panning. Using this navigation for something as uniform as a stacked graph can, however, become disorienting. Also, losing the context makes it hard to perform comparisons. The concept of focus+context displays [9] addresses some of the problems of zooming & panning and works well in TouchWave through the availability of multiple input points. TouchWave bases its navigation on two-finger pinching gestures that are by now commonly used for scaling objects on multi-touch devices.

Horizontally pinching a stacked graph in TouchWave activates *horizontal scaling* (Figure 4e). The two vertical slices that the two fingers touch at the beginning of the gesture can be freely dragged towards the left or the right while the ends of the stacked graph stay fixed at the screen borders. The rest is distorted accordingly. So if, for example, the left vertical slice is dragged towards the left side of the screen, all horizontal values left of it are compressed, while all positions to its right are expanded. Similarly, moving the left vertical slice towards the right

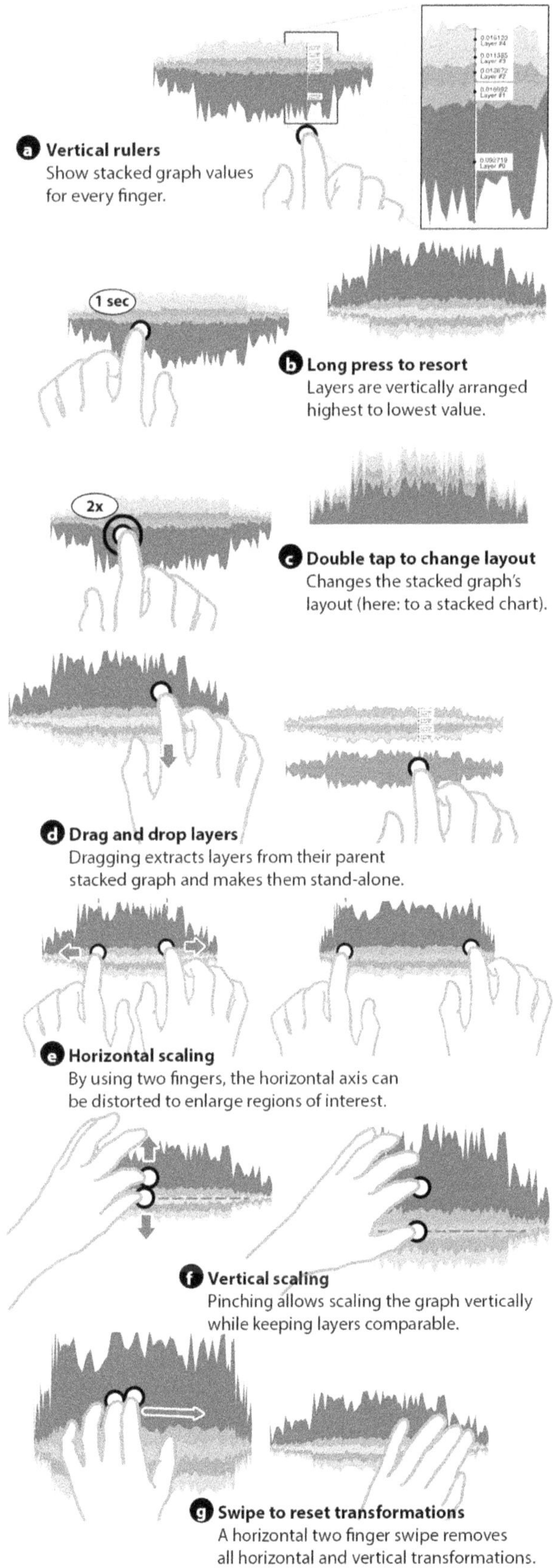

Figure 4: Interaction techniques for stacked graphs in TouchWave.

screen border compresses all values to the right of it, while expanding the ones to its left. The ends of a stacked graph in TouchWave are pinned to the left and right borders of the screen, preserving visibility of all parts at all times even though certain regions may be distorted. Thus two fingers can quickly adjust the size of a horizontal section while keeping the context intact. The view remains distorted until it is reset. All other interactions (e.g., changing the stacked graph's layout) preserve the distortion. The horizontal pinching gesture can be repeatedly applied to focus on even smaller horizontal regions.

Vertically pinching a stacked graph in TouchWave enables *vertical scaling* (Figure 4f). While using the same pinching gesture, there is one major difference between vertical and horizontal scaling. In horizontal scaling, the context is compressed but kept intact while the focus region is expanded. Using the same notion for vertical scaling would make the height of some layers bigger, while other layers would be shrunk. This would introduce a distortion of the layers' values and aggravate legibility by distorting the data representation. TouchWave therefore scales the vertical axis uniformly for vertical pinching to keep the relative sizes of the layers intact. As with horizontal scaling, other operations still work (changing the layout and reading values with the vertical rulers) and the vertical pinching gesture can be repeated multiple times to increase the scaling. This vertical scaling partially overcomes problems with too many layers and interacting with layers that would otherwise be too small because of the fat finger problem.

Both horizontal and vertical scaling introduce distortions to the graph that are non-trivial to revert using these techniques themselves. TouchWave therefore introduces a two-finger horizontal swiping gesture to *reset the scales* (Figure 4g). This removes all horizontal and vertical transformations and resets a stacked graph.

Introducing Hierarchy to TouchWave

Our set of interaction techniques addresses legibility and comparison issues of stacked graphs. However, our approach to scalability with focus+context only ameliorates some of the scalability issues. Once the number of layers crosses a certain threshold it is still difficult to see them all.

Extracting and re-organizing the layers in TouchWave helps with scalability. To take this further, introducing a hierarchy allows hiding unnecessary details; layers of interest can be expanded into sub-layers while other, less interesting layers can hide their sub-layers. Introducing a hierarchy also makes the underlying elements in TouchWave accessible, such as individual songs or tweets.

In this section, we present interaction techniques that enable conveniently working with hierarchical stacked graphs and reorganizing their layers. While BookVoyager [25] used an additional on-screen tree control for the hierarchical data structure, we build on integrated interactions with the stacked graph itself for our techniques.

Hierarchical and Item-based Stacked Graphs in TouchWave

Hierarchical stacked graphs contain multiple nested layers instead of a list of coequal layers. The underlying data structure is therefore a tree, with a single main stacked graph acting as root node and containing all other layers, each of which may in turn contain sub-layers and so on. At the lowest level, simple layers do not contain other layers but only values (leaf nodes). A layer's value at a given horizontal position is therefore either a specific numerical value (for a leaf node) or the sum of all its sub-layers' values at that position.

Previously, stacked graphs contained abstract numerical values, even if the underlying data is based on discrete items. For example, popular stacked graphs such as music listening histories or twitter data are based on atomic units (e.g., songs, tweets) but converted to numerical representations that allow displaying them in such a graph. Hierarchical stacked graphs in TouchWave, however, can display the numerical overview data and the atomic units: a leaf node can either contain discrete numerical values (e.g., stock prices) or atomic items (Figure 5). These items are bound to their horizontal position (e.g., their timestamp) but can move vertically and also have a range of influence depending on how much a single song is "worth." This influence is expressed through a radius for the item. Items have to be rearranged vertically to prevent overlap, which establishes a height value for the layout at that horizontal position. Listening to two songs in quick succession, for example, would lead to an overlap between the items. Moving one of them one item radius up prevents the overlap and creates a correct height reading (the layer is twice as high at that position as at positions with single songs, Figure 6). Displaying atomic units therefore does not introduce distortion to the graph and with the right range of influence, atomic unit and numerical value layers can be combined in the same stacked graph.

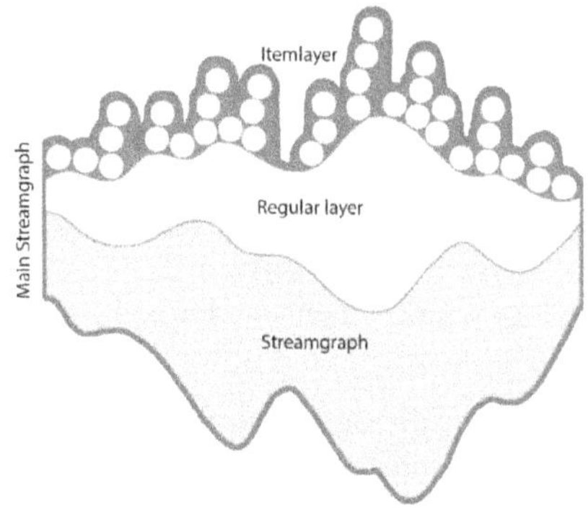

Figure 5: Hierarchical stacked graphs in TouchWave can contain regular layers, other stacked graphs or item layers consisting of atomic items (songs, tweets).

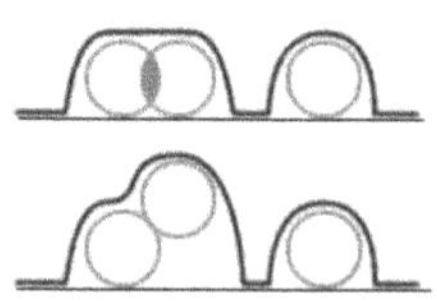

Figure 6: Resolving collisions between items in item layers.

Data Organization

Working with hierarchical stacked graphs in TouchWave requires adjustments to our existing techniques and the introduction of new ones for managing the information. These new techniques allow showing/hiding sublayers, panning the background for more space and creating/removing copies of layers and sublayers.

Vertical scaling of a stacked graph now does not only adjust its size but also *shows its sublayers*, once a certain amount of scaling is reached (Figure 7a). Similarly, shrinking a layer's vertical size through pinching hides visible layers and reduces visual clutter. The lowest layers not only show single values but can also contain items which are represented as small, semi-transparent circles.

Panning the background (Figure 7b) by dragging it moves all stacked graphs in TouchWave up or down. Panning only works vertically, as all stacked graphs are fixed to the left and right borders of the screen. The background also starts to pan while dragging a layer if the dragged layer gets too close to the lower or upper screen borders. This allows finding an empty spot for dropping the layer without having to pan the background first. This gesture is identical to triggering a vertical ruler, which means that while panning a ruler is displayed as well. We decided to put up with the ambiguity instead of introducing a more complex gesture, as rulers are not too distracting.

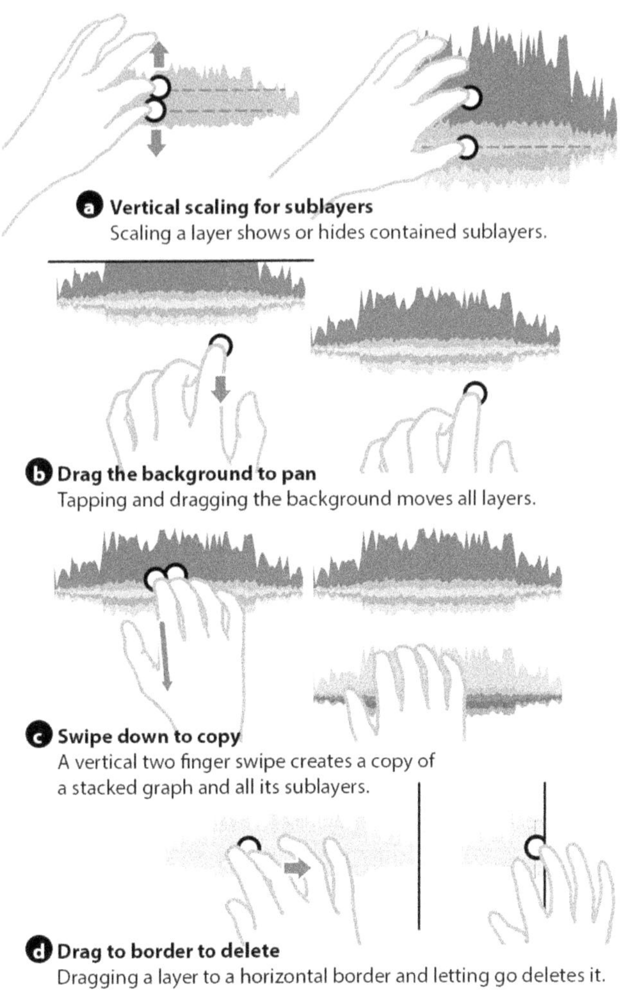

Figure 7: Extended interaction techniques for hierarchical stacked graphs in TouchWave.

Extracting a layer from a stacked graph in TouchWave by dragging and dropping is still possible and now also affects all contained sublayers; removing a layer from its parent and dropping it in another stacked graph moves it and all of its sublayers to that new position. This allows building new stacked graphs on-the-fly, simply by dropping and combining layers of interest on the background.

All layer re-organization changes the original order of a stacked graph. Therefore, a two-finger vertical swipe allows *copying a stacked graph* and all its sublayers (Figure 7c). In a fluid transition, the newly created copy is hurled in the direction of the swipe and stops at the lower or upper screen border. The way to *delete a copy* is to drag it to the vertical screen border and let it go (Figure 7d).

Implementation

TouchWave was written in Objective-C for iOS 5. We deployed TouchWave on a 3rd generation iPad with a resolution of 2048 x 1536 pixels on a 9.7 inch display. For this configuration, TouchWave supports up to 1,000 horizontal sampling points and 100 parallel layers at interactive frame rates. Reducing the number of sample points allows showing more layers and vice versa. The actual number of layers can be far greater, as non-visible layers do not have any impact on the performance.

The basic layout algorithms for our Objective-C code were derived from Byron and Wattenberg's 2008 paper [1] and their Processing drawing code (available as open-source on Github[1]). Fluid transitions between different states and layouts were enabled through the use of Apple's CoreAnimation framework, and graphical output was built using CoreGraphics. One TouchWave-specific implementation issue was creating a suitable layout for items within an item layer. A single item is defined by its horizontal position pos_x, its radius r, and a vertical position pos_y. Both pos_x and r are fixed and only pos_y can be adjusted to prevent overlaps (Figure 6). As we wanted to have this layout working on a portable device, we went for a non-optimal, but simple solution to solving collisions. Our algorithm works as follows. Each round the item with the largest radius is picked and dropped on the horizontal axis (y=0). Afterwards the item "bubbles up" (y is increased in steps whose length determines the accuracy of the layout) until it no longer collides with any other existing item. The algorithm finishes after placing all items.

CASE STUDIES

Stacked graphs are popular for various datasets, so we decided to demonstrate the possibilities of TouchWave with existing use cases from literature [1]. Two exemplary datasets we used are music listening histories and movie box office results.

[1] https://github.com/leebyron/streamgraph_generator

Music Listening Histories

One of the first widespread examples of a stacked graph is Byron's music listening history visualization. Discussions about layout approaches and implications for stacked graphs were published by Byron and Wattenberg [1]. The listening history stacked graph is based on creating a layer for each artist in the history. The values for each horizontal sampling point for one layer corresponds with the number of times a song by that specific artist has been listened to in one week. The result represents the changes in musical taste over time, but makes it difficult to read clear values and is completely static.

A music listening history in TouchWave provides multiple ways to interact with the data. Figure 8 shows a screenshot of two months of listening history data as interactive stacked graphs. Compared to the original, the data is hierarchical, with genres as the top level (visible at the top). Each genre layer consists of layers for artists that are in turn based on single songs. When enlarging an artist layer far enough, the single underlying songs become visible. In this example they appear as oval shapes, due to the non-uniform scaling (middle layer). The two most popular genres have been extracted from the overarching stacked graph and placed below it for further analysis (indie and electronic as blue and green layer, respectively in Figure 8). We work with 1,000 horizontal sample points in this example which means that each sample corresponds to roughly 80 minutes of the two months. The average song length of four minutes leads to much overlap between the song items and explains the stacked look of the middle layer. Pinching horizontally allows focusing on certain periods in time and pinching vertically controls the visible level of the hierarchy (genre, artists, songs). More detailed exploration is enabled through the possibility to deconstruct the stacked graph and drag interesting layers out. Additionally, the TouchWave version clearly shows the "burstiness" of music listening behavior: people listen to several songs before stopping again. This is apparent in the visualization as empty spots between stacked sets of songs. The free-flowing layout of the original Listening History visualization hinted at these gaps but brushed over them. The more realistic representation in TouchWave leads to worse results for the streamgraph layout however (there is no clear horizontal axis). Double tapping on the stacked graph allows switching to a different layout - ThemeRiver, for example, makes sure that all layers above and below the time axis form a symmetrical shape. Another aspect that is enabled through the hierarchical view is the comparison between different genres. It is interesting to see that the listening history is dominated by several main genres (indie, electronic, alternative (red color)) while other genres are more niche with only few songs.

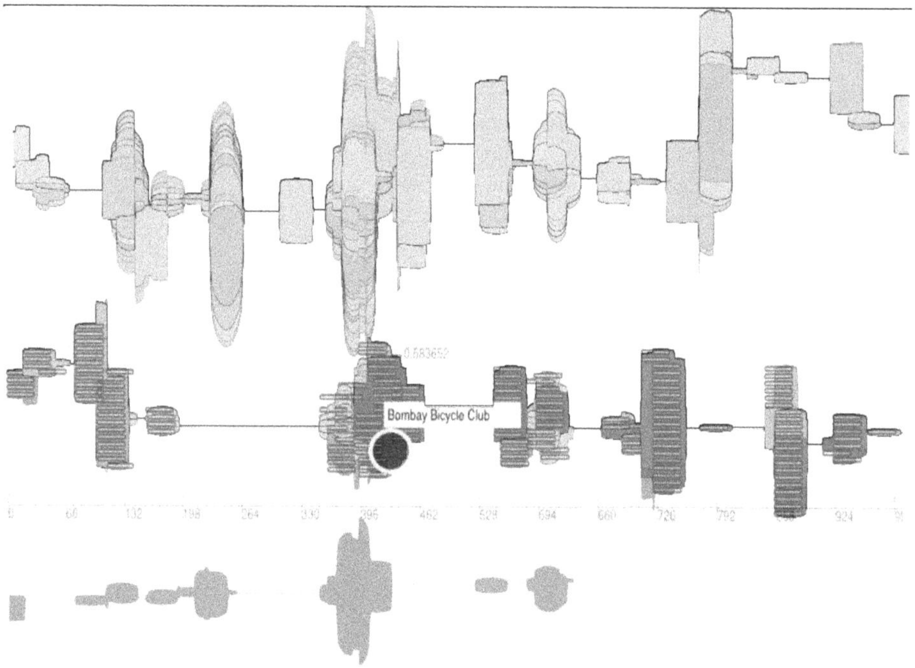

Figure 8: Two months of a listening history with genres and single artist layers.

Movie Box Office Revenues

Another popular example of a stacked graph is the New York Times' 'The Ebb & Flow of Movies' [3], a visualization of box office results from 1986 to 2008 (also in Byron and Wattenberg [1]). Each film is depicted as one layer and the stacked graph shows the development over time. Movies typically make the most money in the first few weeks and then start to slowly lose drive until they disappear from the theatres. The elongated shapes of single films fold into an overarching stream whose shape depicts the overall box office. The outer stacked graph shows seasonal shifts (summer blockbusters).

We used a similar dataset in TouchWave, showing the box office results for 52 films over 80 weeks (Figure 9). We applied a similar color coding to Byron and Wattenberg where more saturated red colors depict higher grossing films [1]. This allows a rough estimate of which films were the most successful. Interaction in the web version of the New York Times' graph[2] allows clicking on a layer to see a story synopsis and horizontal panning for navigation. While we did not integrate detail information about a movie into

[2] http://www.nytimes.com/interactive/2008/02/23/movies/20080223_REVENUE_GRAPHIC.html

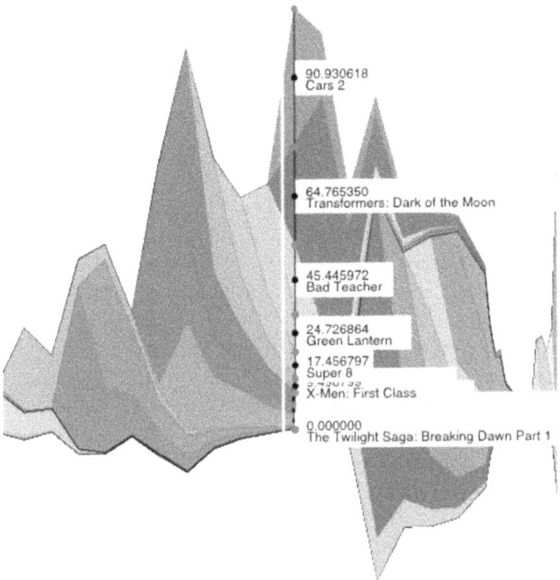

Figure 9: Section of box office results for movies. A vertical ruler allows reading the numerical values.

the TouchWave version, our two finger horizontal scaling enables focusing on specific regions of the graph while keeping the context. This allows comparing the current section to the top-grossing films of the whole dataset. Visually comparing a film's performance to others is difficult if they were not released at the same time. Relying on the color coding allows comparing the overall gross revenue, but even finding the number of weeks that both films were in the theaters is difficult. In TouchWave, two films can be compared by extracting their layers from the stacked graph with two fingers. Even if they were released at different times, both layers can be aligned to compare the films' shapes and their time at the box office. Focusing on a certain couple of weeks is possible through horizontal pinching. Additionally, while the color coding only depicts a rough estimate for the overall revenue, the vertical rulers show the specific box office results for a given week. Moving a ruler along the time axis or creating a second one with a second finger enables explicit comparisons. Finally, resorting the stacked graph at one specific horizontal position sorts all film layers by their revenue in that week.

DISCUSSION AND CONCLUSIONS

TouchWave is an example of rethinking an existing visualization technique to make a suitable, multi-touch based interaction. Our design goals can be valuable for extending other visualization techniques from the desktop:

- *Support kinetic manipulation*: endeavour to respond to a person's physical motions during interaction with harmonious interactive animation and responses.
- *Create integrated interactions*: look to spatially locate one's fingers and hands in contact with the visual representation whenever possible. The notion is to develop a hands-on data experience. Also, to leverage the full potential of touch interactions, avoid simply copying an interface with existing on-screen widgets. Instead, minimize widgets and integrate the widgets within the visual representation whenever possible.
- *Avoid complex gestures*: while the temptation might be to replace complex widget and menu systems with complex gestures, the challenge is to enable the same rich interaction with simple touch interaction.
- *Consider the viability of the interaction set*: when working towards simple, kinetic, integrated interactions it is important to pay attention to the creation of unambiguous interactions that where possible can be provided in a modeless interface.

TouchWave's kinetic interaction with the visualization uses fluid, animated transitions [7], to convey a natural, pseudo-physical feeling for the data. All interactions are integrated where touches are placed directly on the visualization. Our only additional widget, touch-based vertical rulers are also placed in situ. We adhere to simple touch actions, such as those that are becoming commonly accepted. Within the immediacy of integrated interaction TouchWave supports a mode-less approach to working with the data. Every type of manipulation and measurement can be triggered at any point without locking people into modes. This general approach has the advantage of maximizing the usage of available screen space for representing the data instead of filling some of it with buttons and other widgets. The downside is discoverability; figuring out what the system supports for the first time may not be easy as functions cannot be discovered by trying all the buttons. Suitable help mechanisms such as tutorials and in-place help would alleviate this problem and once learned, re-discovering interactions options might not be too difficult because everything is based only on simple touch gestures.

A main challenge while designing TouchWave was coming up with a consistent interaction set: a mapping between elementary touches, on-screen visuals and changes to the visualization that would lead to consistent and expected results. Ad-hoc mappings between touches and visuals usually lead to conflicts and ambiguities in the results. We found that creating a suitable combination of all these factors is a challenging problem in itself. Our approach was to first decide on a list of manipulations that we would make available. We then made two lists of all available visual categories (single layers, stacked graphs, background) and all available elementary interactions (tap, pinch, etc.). Finally, we determined what manipulation would happen for each combination of a visual category and an elementary interaction (e.g., background + touch ➔ vertical ruler and panning). This allowed us to pick suitable interactions for each manipulation without (unwanted) collisions. This process may prove useful to apply to other visualization techniques for multi-touch interactions.

We addressed the fat finger problem by initially scaling stacked graphs in TouchWave to the maximum available screen size. Also, sublayers in each stacked graph in TouchWave are only shown for a certain size of stream. Vertical scaling allows increasing the size of a stacked graph and its layers to make reaching them easier. Still, for some cases, a single layer can just be too small and for these cases, having an on-screen widget such as a type of virtual magnifying glass [21,22] could help.

As multi-touch capable devices such as interactive tabletops, walls and tablet computers become more and more popular the demand for more complex applications such as visualization tools for those devices will also rise. With TouchWave we have demonstrated that multi-touch can provide a more fluid and modeless interaction with data that extends the existing technique. For example, TouchWave offers an integrated representation for hierarchical data in stacked graphs. Enabling interactive exploration through multi-touch gestures can ameliorate some of the issues arising from legibility, comparisons, and scalability. Even though TouchWave was developed for tablets, the proposed interaction techniques are applicable to all larger multi-touch devices (tabletops, wall displays).

With touch-capable devices available everywhere the formerly fringe case of touch-based visualization will continue to become more generally relevant. Other visualization techniques can equally benefit from the advantages of having a more immediate interaction with the data representations. Kinetic manipulation, integrated interaction and a consistent set of interactions based on simple gestures can improve the overall experience of a multi-touch visualization.

ACKNOWLEDGEMENTS
This research was supported in part by NSERC, AITF, CFI and SurfNet.

REFERENCES
1. Byron, L. and Wattenberg, M. Stacked Graphs - Geometry & Aesthetics, *IEEE TVCG (InfoVis 2008)*, vol. 14, no. 6, 2008, pp. 1245–1252.
2. Cleveland, W.S. and McGill, R. Graphical Perception: Theory, Experimentation, and Application to the Development of Graphical Methods, *Journal of the American Statistical Association*, vol. 79, 1984, pp. 531–554.
3. Cox, A. and Byron, L. The Ebb and Flow of Box Office Sales, *The New York Times*, February 23, 2008.
4. Cui, W., Liu, S., Tan, L., Shi, C., Song, Y., Gao, Z., Tong, X., and Qu, H. TextFlow: Towards Better Understanding of Evolving Topics in Text, *IEEE TVCG*, vol. 17, no. 12, 2011, pp. 2412–2421.
5. Dörk, M., Gruen, D., Williamson, C., and Carpendale, S. A Visual Backchannel for Large-Scale Events. *IEEE TVCG (InfoVis 2010)*, vol. 16, no. 6, 2010, pp. 1129–1138.
6. Dwyer, T., Lee, B., Fisher, D., Inkpen, K., Isenberg, P., Robertson, G., and North, C. Understanding Multi-touch Manipulation for Surface Computing, *IEEE TVCG (InfoVis 2009)*, vol. 25, no. 19, 2009, pp. 961–968.
7. Elmqvist, N., Vande Moere, A., Jetter, H.-C., Cernea, D., Reiterer, H., and Jankun-Kelly, T.J. Fluid interaction for information visualization, *Information Visualization*, vol. 10, 2011, pp. 327–340.
8. Frisch, M., Heydekorn, J., and Dachselt, R. Investigating multi-touch and pen gestures for diagram editing on interactive surfaces, *Proc. ITS 2009*, 2009, pp. 149–156.
9. Furnas, G.W. Generalized fisheye views, *Proc. CHI 1986*, 1986, pp. 16–23.
10. Hangal, S., Lam, H., and Heer, J. Muse: Reviving memories using email archives, *Proc. UIST 2011*, 2011, pp. 75–84.
11. Havre, S., Hetzler, B., Whitney, P., and Nowell, L. Themeriver: visualizing thematic changes in large document collections, *IEEE TVCG*, vol. 8, no. 1, 1999, pp. 9–20.
12. Heer, J., Viégas, F., and Wattenberg, M. Voyagers and voyeurs: supporting asynchronous collaborative information visualization, *Proc. CHI 2007*, 2007, pp. 1029–1038.
13. Isenberg, P., Hinrichs, U., Hancock, M., and Carpendale, S. Digital Tables for Collaborative Information Exploration, Tabletops - Horizontal Interactive Displays, C. Müller-Tomfelde, ed., Springer-Verlag, 2010, pp. 387–405.
14. Jetter, H.-C., Gerken, J., Zöllner, M., Reiterer, H., and Milic-Frayling, N. Materializing the Query with Facet-Streams – A Hybrid Surface for Collaborative Search on Tabletops, *Proc. CHI 2011*, 2011, pp. 3013–3022.
15. Lynch, S., Haber, J., Carpendale, S. ColourVis: Exploring Colour in Digital Images. *Computers & Graphics*, vol 36, no. 6, 2012, pp. 696-707.
16. Pentland, A. Maximum likelihood estimation: The best PEST, *Attention, Perception & Psychophysics,* vol. 28, no. 4, 1980, pp. 377–379.
17. Perlin, K. and Fox, D. Pad: An Alternative Approach to the Computer Interface, *Proc. SIGGRAPH 1993*, 1993, pp. 57–64.
18. Schmidt, S., Nacenta, M., Dachselt, R., and Carpendale, S. A Set of Multitouch Graph Interaction Techniques, *Proc. ITS 2011*, 2011, pp. 113–116.
19. Spindler, M., Tominski, C., Schumann, H., and Dachselt, R. Tangible Views for Information Visualization, *Proc. ITS 2010*, 2010, pp. 157–166.
20. Tufte, E. The Visual Display of Quantitative Information. Graphics Press, Cheshire, CT, USA 1983.
21. Viégas, F., Wattenberg, M., van Ham, F., Kriss, J., and McKeon, M. ManyEyes: a Site for Visualization at Internet Scale, *Proc. InfoVis 2007*, 2007, pp. 1121–1128.
22. Vlaming, L., Collins, C., Hancock, M., Nacenta, M., Isenberg, T., Carpendale, S. Integrating 2D mouse emulation with 3D manipulation for visualizations on a multi-touch table. *Proc. ITS 2010*. 2012 221-230.
23. Voida, S., Tobiasz, M., Stromer, J., Isenberg, P., and Carpendale, S. Getting Practical with Interactive Tabletop Displays: Designing for Dense Data, "Fat Fingers," Diverse Interactions, and Face-to-Face Collaboration, *Proc. ITS 2009*, 2009, pp. 109–116.
24. Wattenberg, M. Baby Names, Visualization, and Social Data Analysis, *Proc. InfoVis 2005*, 2005, pp. 1–7.
25. Wattenberg, M. and Kriss, J. Designing for Social Data Analysis, *IEEE TVCG*, vol. 12, no. 4, 2006, pp. 549–557.
26. Yi, J., Kang, Y.A., Stasko, J.T., Jacko, J.A. Toward a Deeper Understanding of the Role of Interaction in Information Visualization, *IEEE TVCG (InfoVis 2007)*, vol. 13, no. 6, 2007, pp. 1224–1231.

Perception and Reality: Exploring Urban Planners' Vision on GIS Tasks for Multi-Touch Displays

Rojin S. Vishkaie, Cand. Phil., Computational Media Design
University of Calgary
2500 University Drive NW,
Calgary, AB, T2N 1N4, Canada
rsalehiv@ucalgary.ca

Richard M. Levy, PhD. MCIP, EVDS
University of Calgary
2500 University Drive NW,
Calgary, AB, T2N 1N4, Canada
rmlevy@ucalgary.ca

Abstract
For urban and transportation planners, GIS has become an essential tool in land use planning and in the design of urban infrastructure. The use of PC-based GIS software has made it possible to analyze massive data sets on an urban scale. Although there is a wide availability of new multi-touch displays such as smart-phones, tablets, tabletops and large wall displays, they are rarely used by planning professionals. This research explores the role that such displays may have with GIS experts, specifically urban planners. In conducting this research, interviews with GIS professionals focused on how they analyzed GIS data, as well as their perceptions of the types of tasks that maybe suitable for multi-touch displays.

ITS'12, November 11–14, 2012, Cambridge, Massachusetts, USA.
ACM 978-1-4503-1209-7/12/11.

The primary tasks identified from the participants in the study were collaboration, visualization and data analysis. This research will further analyze the tasks, with respect to urban planners and consider the properties of various multi-touch displays to explore the role of multi-touch displays in the GIS context.

Author Keywords
Multi-Touch Displays; GIS; Urban Planning; Multi-Modal Interaction; Visualization.

ACM Classification Keywords
H.5.2. Information interfaces and presentation: User Interfaces; User-Centered Design.

Introduction and Motivation
Geographic information systems (GIS) are useful socio-technical tools that provide support for solving geographic problems in everyday tasks such as locating the nearest train station, as well as complex tasks in a wide variety of disciplines such as urban planning [6]. More recently, there have been significant improvements in professional GIS tools such as ESRI's ArcMap [4], which is used by experts to enter, access and evaluate geographic information. Alternatively, these improvements have also benefitted non-expert

GIS users, with tools such as Google Earth [5], allowing them to perform simple geospatial tasks [12], such as trip planning or direction-finding. In both cases, these tools facilitate spatial problem-solving, decision-making processes, save critical time in planning and for GIS experts, evaluation of new GIS related projects.

Interactive multi-touch displays are increasingly being used for work and in public settings [11]. These collaborative multi-touch displays are becoming important tools for solving problems in various fields including geography, urban planning, oil and gas, agriculture, transportation and healthcare. However, despite the improvements in the modern GIS tools, there is a disconnect between these two technologies, as neither truly benefits from the other. Although many researchers have explored interactions on multi-touch displays, more research is needed to determine how GIS applications can fully capitalize on the benefits of new types of multi-touch displays. Specifically, there is an absence of research on how GIS experts can benefit from using multi-touch displays to solve their everyday tasks. The result is a lack of design specifications for interaction with GIS on multi-touch displays.

Planned Research Contributions

The goal of this dissertation research is to explore how urban planners could potentially interact with GIS if provided multi-touch displays in a collaborative environment.

In particular, this research focuses on the following questions:

- Understand what urban planners currently do with PC-based GIS system and explore what they see as potential usages for multi-touch displays.
- Explore high-level goals that can be supported by GIS on multi-touch displays.

Methodology. This study relies on a methodology that employs a range of approaches within the Contextual Design framework [2].

Domain Analysis. Consulting with urban planners in local city government and academia to gain an understanding on how multi-touch displays are used currently. This will include a literature review as an initial exploration, followed by a set of empirical studies to identify tasks (e.g., zoning, subdivision approval, granting of variances) that would benefit from multi-touch displays used in a collaborative setting. The goal is to understand expert GIS users, their primary tasks and methodologies and accordingly, describe how it relates to GIS interaction design.

Comprehensive Toolset Analysis. Identify the current GIS tools that are available to GIS users, from novice to expert. This will include looking at platforms of the tools such as iOS, android and Windows, their capabilities and limitations. Additionally, this research will examine tools that are available for multi-touch displays and how GIS users interact with them. A major objective is to understand the toolsets GIS users use and how they may potentially use these tools. Other issues that will be explored include the impact of skill level on use and the availability of multi-touch displays in the workplace.

Design Guidelines. Develop a set of specifications and guidelines for GIS users that use multi-touch displays. This will be achieved by analyzing and evaluating the collected data from previous empirical studies. A follow up study will also be conducted where users will be asked to rank the complied list of specifications taking into account the skill levels of users. These specifications and guidelines will also address technological factors as well, such as the capabilities of the multi-touch displays (e.g. size, features and mobility). The goal is to develop a set of guidelines and specifications for GIS interaction with a variety of multi-touch displays. These guidelines and specifications could then be used as a basis for designing interactions and applications in a wide variety of domains that utilize GIS.

Related Work

Planners, scientists and business executives working collaboratively would benefit from a GIS designed to work effectively on multi-touch displays. Currently, GIS tasks are not designed for collaboration [7]. In order to improve geographic information system's interface, an approach using the Dialogue-Assisted Environment for Geoinformation (DAVE_G) addressed the issue of human-centered approach for designing a collaborative, multi-modal, multi-user and dialogue-enabled system integrated with large multi-touch displays and speech-gesture interaction [8]. Other researchers considered tangible user interfaces (TUIs) as a novel means for interfaces in GIS. Such systems take advantage of a tactile user interface combined with the numerical simulations to allow the user to interact with the tangible objects. These interfaces suggest a more effective use of GIS by non-experts in distributed decision-making processes [10].

Other research has shown that the visualization of geospatial information (geovisualization) could support GIS decision-making [6]. Understanding the fundamentals such as how GIS can be perceived by human cognition; how users think about time and space; and how computer and digital data can be utilized to better represent the spatial environment are key concerns to geovisualization [6]. Functions such as pointing, clicking and dragging windows and icons and more recently, data and map manipulation and zooming are some of the most important gestures for interacting with geographic data on multi-touch devices [6]. Further research also shows that multiple displays for projecting maps are being used increasingly in advanced GIS applications [6].

It has been shown that utilizing virtual reality (VR) can be used to help visualize spatial phenomena and can also be an effective means to improve the understanding of real-world patterns and processes [6]. The use of multi-user VR worlds can also provide access to GIS data [6]. These environments typically don't have expert GIS users and highlights the effectiveness of VR when combined with GIS. For example, Second Life provides an environment with the potential for connecting information, action and controlling objects, which could be utilized to improve collaboration in the various aspects of urban planning in an online virtually collaborative environment [6].

Research to Date

Examining peer-reviewed literature that focused on interaction design, GIS and multi-touch displays, served as the starting point to address the research objectives. In addition, a literature review of relevant sources, provided a better understanding of the role of multi-touch displays for use by GIS professionals. A series of empirical studies that involved semi-structured interviews with thirty participants including GIS experts from geography, urban planning, oil and gas, GIS, IT and computer science were used to evaluate the needs and abilities of GIS professionals. From this data, a list of criteria were constructed that could be used to evaluate GIS applications designed for multi-touch displays. Identified were two key areas:

Hardware and Software. The analysis of the interview and survey data showed that the vast majority of participants agreed that the advance of (small) mobile multi-touch displays such as smart-phones and tablets have had a significant impact on the way users interact with traditional GIS environments (e.g., paper maps vs. Google maps application for smart-phones). Alternatively, (large) fixed multi-touch displays such as tabletops and large wall displays are not accessible to many of these users currently and hence they have not had a significant impact on the way users interact with GIS.

Also discovered during the course of this research was that hardware and software are two primary contributing factors that influence the users' interaction with GIS on multi-touch displays. In most cases, participants had difficulty grasping details of anticipated uses of tabletops and large wall displays because they had little experience with these new technologies. For most of the participants, multi-touch interactions on digital displays were considered more natural as opposed to the traditional mouse-keyboard paradigm. Consequently, participants mentioned that they would like more multi-touch technology to help them in their professions. However, from a software perspective, multi-touch displays neither supports current GIS applications designed for PC's with keyboards and mice, nor does it take any advantage of multi-touch interactions.

Several participants suggested that multi-touch displays and most importantly tabletops and large wall displays should be more accessible to GIS users. Specifically, tabletops and large wall displays must support the wide range of users' perceived task types such as data analysis, data management, visualization, collaboration, decision-making, presentation, navigation and natural user interface operation in the GIS context. Additionally, training of planners on the appropriate use and operation of such devices to the GIS experts should be high priority for the manufacturers of this equipment.

Urban Planning Tasks and Multi-Touch Displays. While the initial focus of this research was on the GIS experts, other participants from professions were added to this study. One discovery was that urban planners have concerns, which overlap those of GIS professionals.

Typically, urban planners deal with a variety of tasks such as zoning reviews, land use studies, area structure planning, transportation studies, environmental reviews and visual impact assessments, where collaboration with the public and landowners is critical [1, 9, 13]. Currently, these tasks are performed on a conventional PC-based GIS software environment.

From the early stage of data analysis two central issues emerged: *Perception: "What do urban planners want to do with GIS on multi-touch displays?"*. *Reality: "Is what urban planners want to do with GIS already possible with the current technology?"* and *"How do urban planners currently interact with multi-touch displays?"* Furthermore, the analysis of the interview and survey data showed that urban planners' expectations and requirements go beyond the existing set of GIS tools. Hence, the most direct approach to future studies is to interview urban planners about their software and hardware needs.

From the study and analysis of the data collected in this research, *collaboration such as interaction, data input, interaction with data, map-making on the fly*; *visualization such as 3D visualization and map*; and *data analysis such as modeling and spatial analysis* were urban planning tasks that would be best served by GIS on multi-touch displays. Furthermore, many of these tasks typically involve conflict resolution with a number of different stakeholders such as city planners, developers and the community. For example, rezoning a parcel of land from residential to commercial can have an impact on adjacent properties, such as a need for parking and increased traffic. Visualizing plans in 3D, by translating them from 2D (typically in the form of maps) allow stakeholders to collaborate and analyze information and potentially resolve future conflicts.

Development of a Prototype: Interactive Design Review Application for Google Earth Pro. Using the specifications derived from the empirical study of urban planners, a test environment will be created for a specific set of urban planning tasks such as collaboration, visualization and data analysis, using high-fidelity prototyping. A specific problem, that this test environment will address, is allowing urban planners to evaluate the design of a tall building in a collaborative environment. Benefits of such a tool would be less time spent on approval processes. This would allow both developers and members of a community to have input into planning their cities. As many urban planners have little knowledge of CAD or GIS [3], the test environment will work on a familiar platform such as Google Earth Pro on multi-touch displays such as smart-phones and tablets, providing all urban planners with an inexpensive platform accessible to all.

The next phase of this research will focus on the evaluation of tasks and the development of a set of specifications for the design of the proposed prototype.

Future Research

One aspect of this dissertation research included asking participants to envision higher-level GIS interactions and user scenarios on multi-touch displays. After analyzing the interview and survey data, several issues have emerged:

Collaboration. Co-located and distributed collaborations that utilize GIS data could be further enhanced by utilizing mobile multi-touch displays, supported by synchronous interaction. Additionally, investigating synchronicity with regards to GIS data and collaboration is also important to this study, as it may provide techniques for seamless interactions for GIS users of all skill levels and not just urban planners.

Visualization. Providing a means for urban planners, as well as GIS users, to present the outcomes of their GIS exploration could potentially improve the customizable user interfaces over mouse-keyboard interaction. Furthermore, this research will explore approaches to the integration of intelligent features such as audio and video recording capabilities and voice recognition with current multi-touch displays' systems.

Date Analysis. Examining possible techniques of embedding geoprocessing functionality, such as buffering and measurements to work effectively with multi-touch displays. As was suggested several times by participants in the study, looking at the feasibility of new approaches to solving urban planning problems could have an impact on the design of cities.

Summary

This dissertation research will provide a set of design specifications and guidelines for the development of tools used by GIS experts, specifically urban planners in collaborative environments. These guidelines are focused on the use of multi-touch displays that are becoming more readily available. This work expands on prior research by examining the tasks that GIS users, specifically urban planners must conduct on a daily basis. A test environment for urban planners will be developed, which will provide a test-bed for evaluating the proposed guidelines and specifications. This will provide the foundation for creating GIS tools that promote collaboration, visualization and data analysis in future urban planning projects.

References

[1] Babcock, R.F. *The Zoning Game: Municipal Practices and Policies.* Lincoln Inst of Land Policy, Cambridge, IN, USA, 1966.

[2] Beyer, H. and Holtzblatt, K. *Contextual Design – Defining Customer-Centered Systems*. Morgan Kaufmann Publishers, San Francisco, IN, USA, 1998.

[3] Edwards, M.M. and Bates, L.K. Planning's Core Curriculum: Knowledge, Practice and Implementation. *Journal of planning Education and Research 31*, 2. 172-183.

[4] ESRI. http://www.esri.com/software/arcgis.

[5] Google Earth. http://www.earth.google.com.

[6] Longley, P.A., Goodchild, M.F., Maguire, D.J. and Rhind, D.W. *Geographic Information Systems and Science 3e.* John Wiley and Sons, New Jersey, IN, USA, 2011.

[7] MacEachren, A.M. and Brewer, I. Developing a conceptual framework for visually-enabled geocollaboration. *International Journal of Geographic Information Science,* (2003).

[8] MacEachren, A.M., Cai, G., Sharma, R., Rauschert, I., Brewer, I., Bolelli, L., Shaparenko, B., Fuhrmann, S. and Wang, H. Enabling Collaborative Geoinformation Access and Decision-Making Through a Natural, Multimodal Interface. *International Journal of Geographical Information Science 19*, (2005), 293-317.

[9] Nassar, J.L. *The Evaluative Image of the City*. Sage Publications, IN, London, UK, 1988.

[10] Ratti, C., Wang, Y., Ishii, H., Piper, B. and Frenchman, D. Tangible User Interface (TUIs): A Novel Paradigm for GIS. *MIT Transactions in GIS, 8*, 4. 1361-1682.

[11] Rogers, Y. and Lindley, S. Collaboration around vertical and horizontal large interactive displays: which way is best?. *Elsevier Interacting with Computers 16,* 6. 1133-1152.

[12] Schöning, J., Hecht, B., Raubal, M., Krüger, A., Meredith, M. and Rohs, M. Improving Interaction with virtual Globes through Spatial Thinking: Helping Users Ask "Why?". *in 13th annual ACM Conference on Intelligent User Interfaces (IUI),* ACM Press (2008), 129-138.

[13] Shirvani, H. *The Urban Design Process.* Van Nostrand Reinhold Company, New York, IN, USA, 1985.

Scalable Interaction Design for Collaborative Visual Exploration of Big Data

Ioannis Leftheriotis[1,2]
iolef@acm.org

[1]Ionian University
Tsirigoti Sq. 7
Corfu, Greece

[2]Norwegian University
of Science and Technology
Sem Sælands vei 7-9
Trondheim, Norway

ITS'12, November 11–14, 2012, Cambridge, Massachusetts, USA.
ACM 978-1-4503-1209-7/12/11.

Abstract
Novel input devices such as tangibles, smartphones, multi-touch surfaces etc. have given impetus to new interaction techniques. In this PhD research, the main motivation is to study novel interaction techniques and designs that augment collaboration in a collocated environment. Furthermore, the main research aim is to take advantage of scalable interaction design techniques and tools that can be applied in a variety of devices so as to help users to work together on a problem with an abstract big data set, using visualizations on a collocated context.

Author Keywords
Interaction design; collaboration; big data; visual exploration; user interfaces; scalability

ACM Classification Keywords
H.5.2. Information Interfaces and Presentation: User Interfaces: Interaction Styles

Introduction
Input devices that allow multiple points of interaction have become popular during the last years. The advent of devices such as smartphones, tablets, larger multi-touch surfaces (tabletops or vertical surfaces) or other

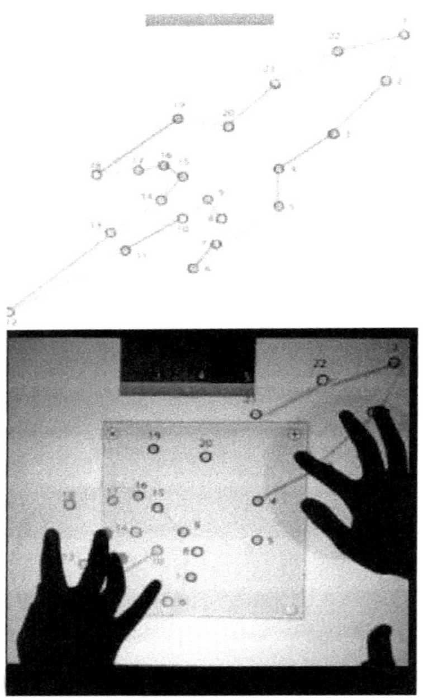

Figure 1. The collaborative drawing dot-to-dot task. Multiple users are asked to connect the dots. They make use of chords in order to select the appropriate color and action windows so as to draw the respective lines. In the upper photo, the task is completed while in the lower photo, an experiment with two users working with chords and windows in order to complete the task is demonstrated.

types of input devices such as tangibles or multimodal interfaces raised new issues in the interaction design area. In contrast to the traditional indirect input device, the mouse, these devices present some unique characteristics. They are input devices allowing multiple contact points (instead of the single point interaction found in mouse) and moreover, they alter the way user interacts with a system along with the user experience. Besides, these interaction surfaces and input devices are able to present multi-user interaction. For instance, there have been studies that propose that multi-touch surfaces enhance multi-user collaboration and awareness or studies that show that tangibles improve user experience. However, it seems that the traditional WIMP (Window, Icon, Menu Pointer) paradigm that is widely used by developers, is not adequate for this type of devices.

Moreover, as most applications for these novel devices and surfaces denote, a unique opportunity of presenting images or data and information in a way that allow user to navigate using fingers (e.g. [4]) and gestures or tangible objects (e.g. [2]), making user interaction more natural or even magical [10]. In this research, our main aim is to study new interaction techniques and kinds of software user interfaces more appropriate for these devices allowing multi-user interaction in order to more easily explore or navigate a large data set. Considering the diversity of devices as far as the technology or the size is concerned, these user interfaces should be flexible and scalable.

Collaborative Collocated User Interfaces

Collocated simultaneous use of a computer by multiple users is not a new idea. Multiple input devices can be connected to a desktop so as to have multiple users working on a single screen (Single Display Groupware). However, with the advent of novel input devices, multiple contact points can be identified by the system, making them a promising technology for multi-user interaction. In an exploratory study [5] we have been focused on multi-touch input technology and we have investigated its promises in comparison to traditional mouse input and showed that multi-touch surfaces have positive impact to the user experience and user performance. More importantly, two users working concurrently on the same problem seem to perform better. There have been also laboratory studies or studies in the wild investigating how groups of people work on this type of surface. In addition, researchers have described a number of factors that influence group work (e.g. group size or positioning of a multi-touch surface). It seems that these surfaces enhance multiuser interaction even if in most multiuser applications multiple users work in parallel and not collaboratively because both developers and users are used to traditional desktop interaction [6].

From our perspective, we have developed a novel interaction technique that allows for collocated and simultaneous multiuser interaction on large surfaces. Particularly, we have been focused on vertical multi-touch surfaces. In an exploratory design study [4], we examined alternative selection techniques on a large multi-touch screen based on chord interaction. Chording is a novel interaction technique consisting of chords, simultaneous touch of more than one finger on the screen. In addition, a toolkit that allows multiuser interaction was presented [6]. It was designed and documented with the perspective of being easily embedded in collocated multiuser applications.

Moreover, window-based interaction is being investigated as a tool that helps identifying which user interacts on a larger surface, or just enables different actions depending on the user. In Figure 3, a drawing application that employs the developed techniques in a large multi-touch wall is presented.

Since the aim of this research is primarily the use of tools that enhance collaboration among the users in a collocated context, we conducted a number of laboratory experiments investigating whether new interaction techniques support multiuser interaction. In our preliminary qualitative results, a number of factors apparent in tabletop interaction such as partitioning of the screen, space negotiation among the users and alternative conflict resolution techniques were found and analyzed. In addition, a novel collaborative task was designed in order to evaluate the developed user interfaces on a vertical multi-touch screen (Figure 1).

Scalability

Due to the high diversity of input devices concerning the technology (e.g. systems based on cameras and infrared light, resistive multi-touch screens, etc.), concerning the style of interaction (e.g. tangible objects, wearable, mobile or static devices), concerning the size of input devices (smartphones, tablet pc, tabletop computers, large MT wall installations), we investigate the development of user interfaces that can be applied in a variety of devices. We have found that developers are not focused on a general framework of scalability including hardware, software and human factors [1]. In addition, we propose that configuration along with efficient simulation is indispensible part of the development process. We also investigate whether different applications or user interfaces could be simulated with different devices, at least during the development process. In Figure 2, the preliminary results based on our experience are demonstrated.

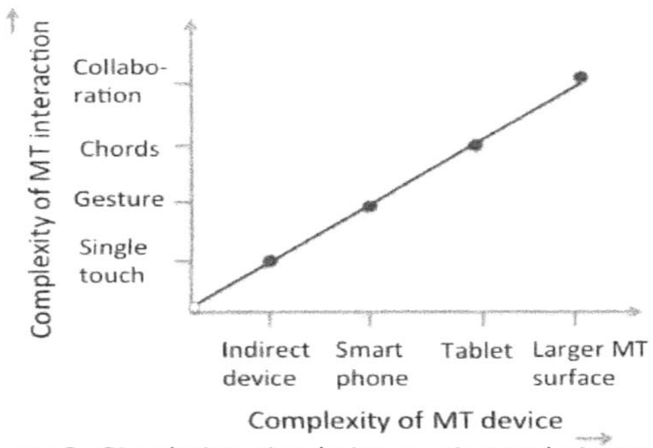

Figure 2. Simulating simple interaction techniques such as a single touch can be done with an indirect device such as mouse. For more complex interaction, more complex devices are needed.

Exploration of Big Data

The development of collaborative user interfaces is not an end in itself. My main research motivation is to develop user interfaces that support collocated collaboration so as to be easier for multiple users to work efficiently on a surface and interact effectively or even intuitively with objects and amounts of data. Wigdor and Wixon [10] claim, "One part of the promise of the NUI (Natural User Interface) is to make interaction with technology seem like magic". In our experiments [5] users argue about feeling a kind of flow when interacting on a multi-touch surface. We seek to employ novel user interfaces so as to use these feelings for efficiently data exploration.

According to Keim [3], visual data exploration deals more easily with highly inhomogeneous and noisy data, is intuitive and requires no understanding of complex mathematical or statistical algorithms or parameters. There are some studies such as the tabletop interface for collaborative exploration of genomic data [8] or the WeSearch [7], a collaborative web search system, that indicate that collocated collaboration is facilitated provided that novel user interfaces and interaction techniques are used.

Selecting different actions, widgets or contextual menus using chords.

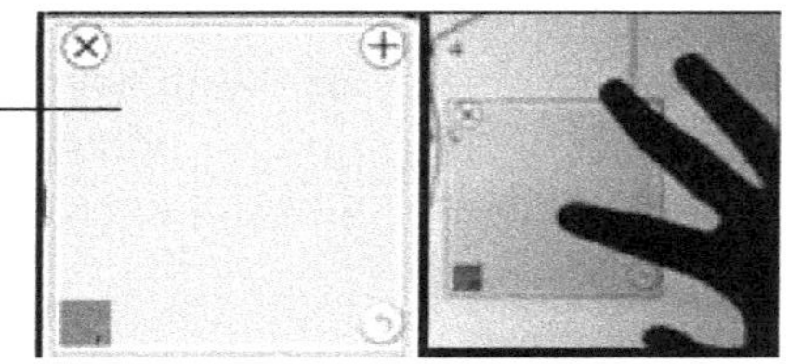

A window interface allowing different users doing different actions simultaneously on the multi-touch surface. In addition, these windows can be used for giving a specific characteristics to the covered objects (e.g. magic lenses), or simply help us identify users.

Figure 3. An exploratory drawing application that employs chords and windows in a large MT surface: It is shown how multiple users can work simultaneously doing different actions. With chords, users select a color and within the limits of the appropriate window that pops-up, they are able to draw in the respective color.

Future Work

We believe that multimodal collocated interaction have more to offer in collaborative exploration of big data. We will conduct further laboratory experiments with users in order to investigate our developed techniques quantitatively and qualitatively with the designed collaborative task or other experimental collaborative tasks such as task scheduling [9]. In addition, we plan to do comparative studies between different interaction techniques such as physical, graphical and tangible user interfaces (e.g. [11]) investigating the effect of different input devices or software interfaces on collaboration.

Finally, apart from testing the developed user interfaces on our implemented applications (multiuser drawing, multiuser word construction or image editing app) we will focus on a case study where multiple users are going to interact with visualizations of a large data set. We are searching for the appropriate data set, being open source:

- biology (e.g. Encyclopedia Of Life)
- social networks (e.g. SMR foundation)
- web multimedia
- smart grid data (e.g. electricity consumption data)
- spatial data (e.g. GPS tracks)

Expected Contribution

In this research, we are dealing with the issue of developing novel interaction techniques and interfaces for enhancing collocated multiuser collaboration so as to allow multiple users to explore large amounts of data. Hence, multiuser decision support and collaborative problem solving are the vision of this work.

We consider that the results of this PhD research will be valuable to both the academic community and practitioners. The main outcome of this research will be a set of collaborative interaction techniques, applications and tools that will be effective and suitable for multi-user use. These tools will be available to other researchers to conduct other experiments, or to simply embed them in their own experimental applications. In addition to the software interface, collaborative tasks such as the drawing dot-to-dot task (Figure 1), that were designed in order to evaluate our tools, will be available for evaluation of other multiuser interaction techniques or tools by researchers. Apart from the tools, the whole philosophy of building scalable interaction techniques and application bearing in mind simultaneously the software, hardware and human factors will be proven to be an effective and stable procedure of developing interactive applications from a collaborative perspective. On the other hand, practitioners will have tools that can be easily embedded in their own collaborative applications for scalable interactive surfaces. In addition to the tools, there will be guidelines and measurable effects that these tools had on the users.

Finally, the use of these software tools on a specific case study with large amount of data will demonstrate their effectiveness and give impetus to the development of novel multiuser techniques and applications that exploit the fact that multiple people work simultaneously on the same surface for a common goal and thus, producing valuable results or decisions.

References

[1] Chorianopoulos, K., Leftheriotis, I., and Pandis, P. 2011. Design of Scalable Collaborative Multi-touch Screens. EICS'11. Second Workshop of Engineering Patterns for Multi-Touch Interfaces, Pisa, Italy.

[2] Hancock, M., Hiliges O., Collins C., Baur D., Carpendale S., 2009. Exploring Tangible and Direct Touch Interfaces for Manipulating 2D and 3D Information on a Digital Table. ACM Conference on Interactive Tabletops and Surfaces. ACM Press. New York, NY, USA.

[3] Keim A. Daniel. Visual Exploration of Large Data Sets. Communications of the ACM 44 (2001), 8, pp. 28-44.

[4] Leftheriotis, I. and Chorianopoulos, K., 2011. Multi-user Chorded Toolkit for Multi-touch Screens,

Proceedings of EICS ' 11. ACM SIGCHI Symposium on Engineering Interactive Computing Systems, ACM Press. New York, NY, USA.

[5] Leftheriotis, I. and Chorianopoulos, K., 2011. User Experience Quality in Multi-touch tasks, Proceedings of EICS ' 11. ACM SIGCHI Symposium on Engineering Interactive Computing Systems. ACM Press. New York, NY, USA.

[6] Leftheriotis, I., Chorianopoulos, K., and Jaccheri L. 2012. Tool Support for Developing Scalable Multiuser Applications on Multi-touch Screens. ACM Conference on Interactive Tabletops and Surfaces. ACM Press. New York, NY, USA.

[7] Morris M. R., Lombardo J., and Wigdor D. 2010. WeSearch: Supporting Collaborative Search and Sensemaking on a Tabletop Display. ACM Conference on Computer Supported Cooperative Work. ACM Press. New York, NY, USA.

[8] Shaer, O., Strait, M., Valdes, C., Wang, H., Feng, T., Lintz, M., Ferreirae, M., Grote C., Tempel, K., and Liu, S. 2012. The Design, Development, and Deployment of a Tabletop Interface for Collaborative Exploration of Genomic Data, *Int. J. Human-Computer Studies*. http://dx.doi.org/10.1016/j.ijhcs.2012.05.003

[9] Tan D. S., Gergle D., Mandryk R., Inkpen K., Kellar M., Hawkey K. 2008. Using job-shop scheduling tasks for evaluating collaboration. *Personal Ubiquitous Computing* (2008) 12:255-267.

[10] Wigdor, D., and Wixon, D. 2011. Brave Nui World: Designing Natural User Interfaces for Touch and Gesture. Morgan Kaufmann publications. ISBN: 978-0-12-382231-4.

[11] Xie, L., Antle, A. N., Motamedi N., 2008. Are tangibles more fun? Comparing children's enjoyment and engagement using physical, graphical and tangible user interfaces. ACM Conference on Tangible and Embedded Interaction. ACM Press. New York, NY, USA.

Spatially Aware Tangible Display Interaction in a Tabletop Environment

Martin Spindler
User Interface & Software Engineering Group
Faculty of Computer Science, University of Magdeburg
Universitätsplatz 2, 39106 Magdeburg, Germany
martin.spindler@acm.org

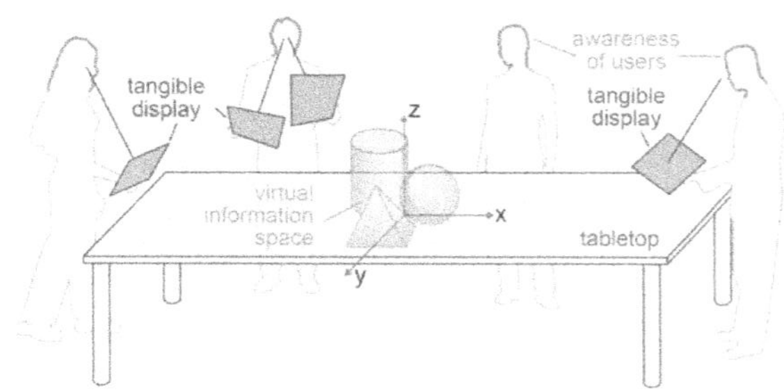

Figure 1. A multi-display tabletop environment consisting of following entities: a large tabletop, multiple spatially aware handheld displays, spatial awareness of users, virtual information spaces, and non-digital spatially aware objects.

Abstract

One limiting factor of digital tabletops is that interaction is usually restricted to a single 2D surface. I propose to extend this interaction space to the 3D space above the table by using spatially aware handheld displays. Utilizing the spatial position and orientation of such tangible displays provides an additional dimension of interaction that allows users to interact with complex information spaces in a more direct and natural way. The simultaneous use of multiple tangible displays explicitly supports collaborative work. My research includes the identification of basic interaction principles, the design and implementation of a technical framework, and the development and evaluation of interactive systems demonstrating the benefits of tangible displays for different application domains.

ITS'12, November 11–14, 2012, Cambridge, Massachusetts, USA.
ACM 978-1-4503-1209-7/12/11.

Author Keywords

Tangible magic lenses; PaperLens; digital tabletops; mobile displays; tangible interaction; user interfaces

ACM Classification Keywords

H.5.2. [Information interfaces and presentation]: User Interfaces: Input devices and strategies

General Terms

Human Factors, Design

Introduction and Motivation

Current technical developments in the smartphone and tablet market show that a fusion of input and output within the same device results in a more direct and natural interaction. While the majority of current approaches focuses on interacting *on* the surface of such mobile displays, e.g., by using multi-touch or pen input, interacting *with* handheld displays, i.e., by using their spatial relationships, still plays a rather minor role. When applied to a digital tabletop environment, the usage of handheld displays offers exciting new possibilities not only in terms of an enlarged presentation space but also as an increased interaction space. First, the tabletop display can act as a global view that can be shared by all users, whereas individual handheld displays can serve as personal views for single users. Thus the simultaneous use of multiple

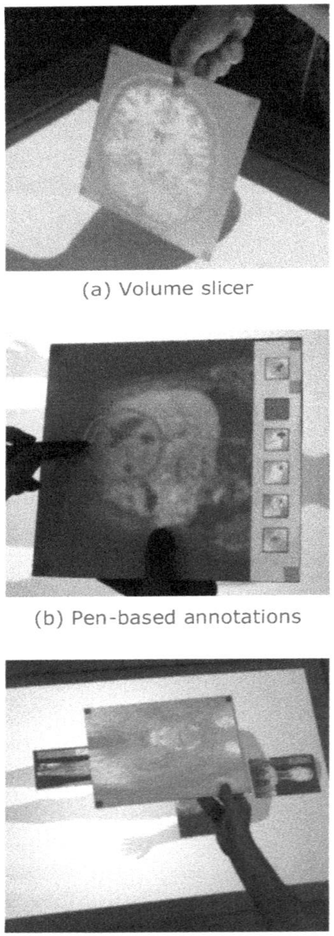

(a) Volume slicer

(b) Pen-based annotations

(c) Thumbnails on the table

Figure 2. Exploration of medical volumetric datasets with our tangible display system

handheld displays can explicitly support collaborative work. Second, the spatial position and orientation of tangible displays, e.g., with reference to the table surface, can be used as a valuable form of input to the system. In this way, the previous 2D interaction space of the table display can effectively be extended to the physical 3D space above the table surface, thus better matching the volumetric character of complex 3D information spaces, such as medical MRI scans or 3D virtual environments. Third, tangible displays serve as a tool of representation (output) and interaction (input) at the same time. Fourth, the users' natural understanding of spatial relationships between everyday objects can be leveraged towards a more seamless and natural interaction with complex information worlds by using tangible displays. Building and studying such multi-display tabletop environments is the subject of my dissertation research.

Related Work

Merging the digital world with the physical (analog) world is the vision of ubiquitous computing, as defined by Weiser [16]. This concept was adapted by Ishii's and Ullmer's tangible user interfaces (TUIs) [4], where interaction with digital information is provided through physical manipulation of real-world objects. Inspired by the notion of see-through interfaces [1], these objects can also be spatially aware handheld displays (e.g., mobile phones) that serve as tangible magic lenses into the virtual world. One of the first mobile displays for ubiquitous usage has been proposed by Fitzmaurice, who presented a spatially aware palmtop computer for exploring 3D-situated information spaces for revealing virtual information associated with arbitrary objects in an office environment [2]. With the metaDESK project, Ullmer and Ishii [15] applied this idea to a tabletop environment, where users can freely navigate through polygonal 3D models by moving an arm-mounted LCD display through the space above the tabletop that is also responsible for providing contextual graphical information.

In many situations, active display solutions, such as LCD panels, do not provide suitable form factors for a seamless integration into a tangible display system. This is because active displays are often too heavy, too thick, too big, too rigid, and sometimes even too expensive if many devices are needed. This lack of technology motivated researchers to come up with a variety of lightweight display solutions that can easily be customized in terms of shape and size. Most of these solutions use a passive approach, i.e., image content is projected onto spatially aware projection screens in one or another form. Lee *et al.* [6], Holman *et al.* [3], and we [12] presented such systems that all use ceiling-mounted projectors for projecting dynamic video content onto optically tracked paper-like displays. SecondLight by Izadi *et al.* [5] is technically more complex in that it is based on electronically switchable diffusers. It supports dual back-projections on both a tabletop surface and tangible lenses above it. Another promising technological development are organic LEDs (OLED) that one day might unify the advantages of active and passive displays.

Research Question & Planned Contributions

In my research I address the question of how to extend the interaction and representation space of digital tabletops into the third dimension by using the concept of spatially aware handheld displays. For this purpose, I propose a multi-display tabletop environment that supports following entities (see Figure 1): a large

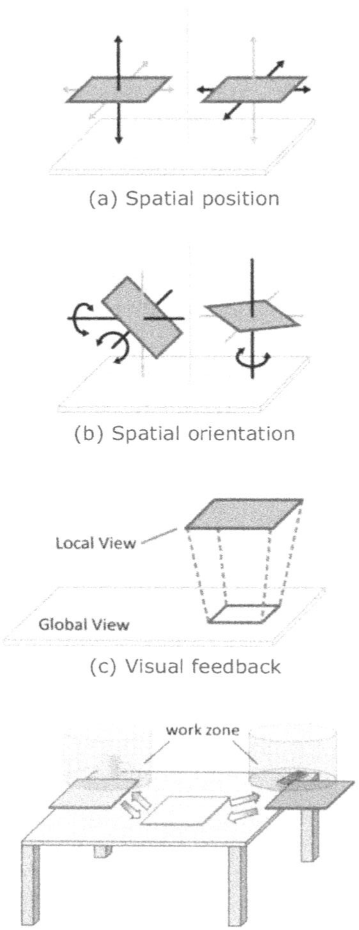

(a) Spatial position

(b) Spatial orientation

(c) Visual feedback

(d) Spatial work zones

Figure 3. Some of the interaction principles that we derived for tangible displays

digital tabletop, multiple spatially aware handheld displays, the spatial awareness of users (e.g., head positions and orientations), virtual information spaces, and non-digital physical objects. I want to understand how such environments can leverage the user's natural understanding of spatial relationships of everyday objects aiming at making the overall interaction experience more seamless and natural. To address this research question, I plan to make the following three interdependent contributions:

(1) Conceptual Framework: My work will provide insights into the fundamental interaction principles a tangible display system should employ to meet the users' needs. These insights will be presented in the form of a conceptual framework and general design guidelines that unify different input modalities such as spatial relationships between displays, objects, and users as well as pen and multi-touch input. This includes the description of the main design variables, physical boundaries, and how they relate to tangible display interaction design.

(2) Technical Toolkit: The findings of Objective 1 will define technology requirements for designing and building a technical framework that make tangible display functionality accessible to developers. This includes tools for the spatial tracking of devices, the seamless communication between devices, and a programming framework for developing applications.

(3) Prototypes and Demonstrators: To evaluate and illustrate tangible display interaction principles (Objective 1), interactive prototypes and demonstrators need to be developed for different application domains. They will be built using the technical toolkit (Objective 2). Experiences with these systems will be used to refine the conceptual framework.

Research Status: Conceptual Framework

With PaperLens [12], we developed the basic concept of tangible displays that employs the height and the horizontal position of handheld displays above the table as a means of interaction. This can be used, e.g., for zooming (by lifting/lowering a display) and panning (by horizontally moving a display) of large 2D pictures. We extended this concept and derived an interaction vocabulary [10] that describes essential dimensions for interacting with tangible displays. This includes spatial position and orientation (see Figure 3a/b), freezing, gestures (e.g., flipping and shaking), toolbox metaphor (e.g., the shape and size of displays), direct pointing (e.g., touch and pen based), visual feedback on the table (see Figure 3c), and the support of multiple displays. We also introduce the concept of spatial work zones (see Figure 3d) for pooling functionality, documents, and other digital content that is accessible by moving tangible displays into and through a work zone. In addition, we propose to leverage the spatial relationships between users and handheld displays, e.g., for the purpose of head-coupled perspective.

We distinguish between two basic groups of modes of how spatial movements can be interpreted. First, the system either can *implicitly* respond to positional changes of a tangible display or it can react only when the user *explicitly* says so, e.g., by pressing a button. Second, the interaction space associated with a particular tangible display either can move along with the display like a floating *bubble* that surrounds it or it can be *fixed* in space allowing the display to enter and leave the interaction space.

One way of using the 3D space above a horizontal surface is to divide it into discrete parallel layers stacked upon each other. Horizontal and vertical display movements are essential tasks for the style of multi-layer interaction associated with it. We conducted a comprehensive user study [8] with 18 participants investigating fundamental issues such as optimal number of layers and their thickness, movement and holding accuracies, and physical boundaries of the interaction volume.

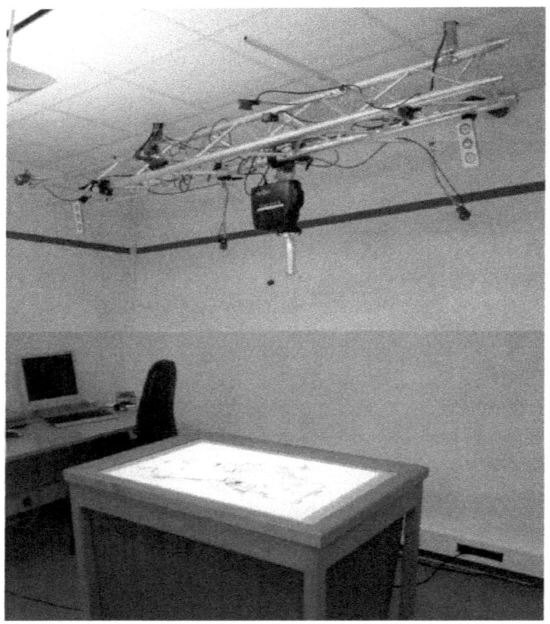

Figure 4. Technical setup of the tangible display system in our lab

Research Status: Technical Toolkit

We decided on using a projective display approach as the technical basis for tangible displays. This gave us high flexibility in terms of form factors for the design of handheld displays – an important advantage for a research prototype. Examples for this are displaying content on the displays' backsides (required for flipping), arbitrarily shaped displays in different sizes (e.g., discs), the avoidance of display frames, and digital pen input [www.anoto.com].

Figure 4 shows the technical setup in our lab, see [12] and [10]. It consists of a back-projected tabletop, several infrared cameras, and a ceiling-mounted projector. The setup is enriched with various tangible displays made of cardboard in different sizes and shapes that can be freely moved through the space on or above the tabletop. To bring such a system alive, several problems need to be solved: tracking of tangible displays, projecting image content onto them, recognizing gestures, support for direct pointing, and providing application functionality. Many of these tasks can be tackled independently and thus have been split up between different computers. For the purpose of inter-computer communication, we use public protocols for streaming device states and remote procedure calls.

Research Status: Demonstrators

A multitude of application domains in fields like science, education, and entertainment can benefit from tangible display interaction principles. We developed several demonstrators illustrating and showcasing their use.

Exploration of Scientific 3D Datasets

One particular field of application for tangible displays is the exploration of large three-dimensional data. Besides geological or biological data, prime examples are medical volume datasets acquired from MRI or CT. With tangible displays in a tabletop environment, such data sets can be understood as residing in the space above the tabletop. The tabletop acts as a global view, providing reference for the users. For example, it can show an outline of the patient or a specific slice of the data set. The handheld displays provide local, personal views (see Figure 2a). When a user moves a display through the interaction volume, arbitrary, user-defined cutting planes can be computed in real-time and displayed, as showed by us in [12]. This form of direct interaction allows for fast and flexible exploration of the whole dataset or specific structures within. In addition, conspicuous structures can be annotated by using digital pen or finger based interaction techniques (see Figure 2b/c), as demonstrated by us in [13].

Information Visualization

In many fields of scientific research, large amounts of data have to be visualized and examined. Such

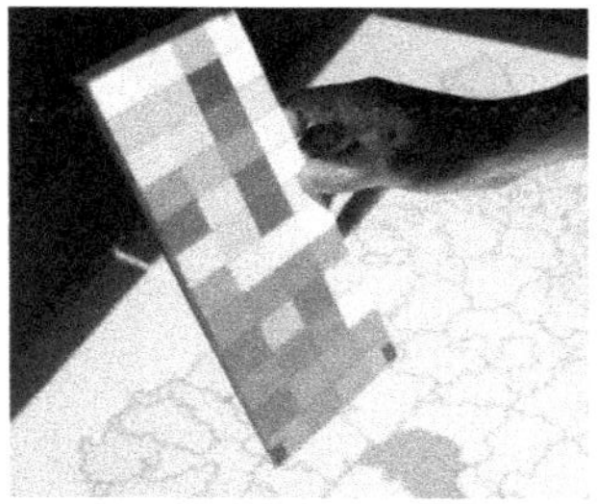

(a) Slicing the space-time-cube vertically to get an overview of time

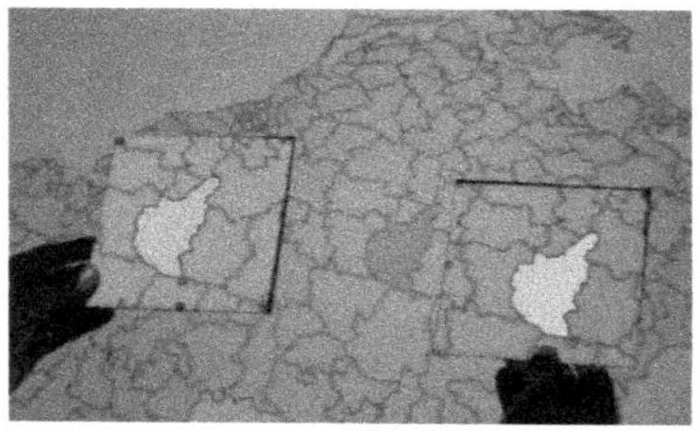

(b) Two-handed comparison

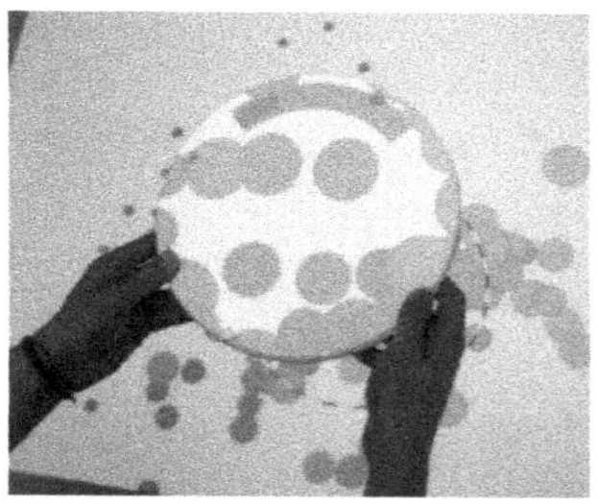

(c) Tangible fisheye lens

Figure 5. Tangible displays used for the purpose of information visualization

complex datasets usually cannot be presented in a single image without the risk of cluttering. Filtering or presenting multiple views on the data can mitigate this problem. Tangible displays naturally support this by providing both additional display space and a new means for interaction, combined in single tangible objects, as described by us in [10].

One good example for this is space-time-cube visualization, which is an approach to integrate spatial and temporal aspects in a single visual representation. The analogy between a space-time-cube and the 3D presentation space of tangible displays motivated this idea: the tabletop shows the spatial context as a geographic map, and the dimension of time (e.g., 12 months) is mapped to the height above it. Tangible displays are used as physical viewports into the space-time-cube. Interactive exploration is driven by horizontal and vertical translation to navigate the map and the time axis, respectively. When held in a horizontal orientation, a tangible view shows the data for a selected month, i.e., a horizontal slice through the space-time-cube. To get an overview for all months (i.e., a vertical slice), users can rotate a tangible view into upright orientation (see Figure 5a). The support for multiple independent handheld displays allows for collaboration between users or the visual comparison of portions of the data (see Figure 5b).

Beyond that, tangible displays support the focus and context concept. The tabletop serves as a reference, showing the contextual background in a main view. The handheld displays on the other hand provide additional physical display space that can be used to show local views into the information space. Here, the relative height of a tangible display may encode the zoom factor or, for a semantic zoom, a specific level of abstraction. Other examples include changing the parameters of a fisheye lens by rotating the display (see Figure 5c).

Collected User Experiences

We have given a number of demos of our tangible display system at international HCI conferences, e.g., at ACM ITS in Banff [14] and Saarbrücken [11], and we also frequently presented our system at public events at our local university. In total, several hundred visitors have tried out our prototypes, including average users, domain experts, and children. Overall, the feedback was very positive. Visitors appreciated how easy it was to learn the interaction techniques and to use the system. Since working with the system only requires users to grab one or more pieces of cardboard and move them through the space above the tabletop, which dynamically changes the image content displayed on them, a common comment was that the interaction was very natural and even felt somehow magical. Our experiences from qualitative users studies, e.g., [12], confirm this.

Summary And Further Research

A majority of research in the field of tangible user interfaces (TUI) focuses on input aspects by means of physical objects. In contrast, the goal of my dissertation is on making the output directly manipulable by using spatially aware displays. By allowing users to hold and move one or more lightweight handheld displays through the space above a tabletop, novel forms of interaction become possible providing a more natural and seamless way of interacting with complex information spaces, e.g., virtual 3D worlds [7] (see Figure 6).

(a) A tangible peephole window

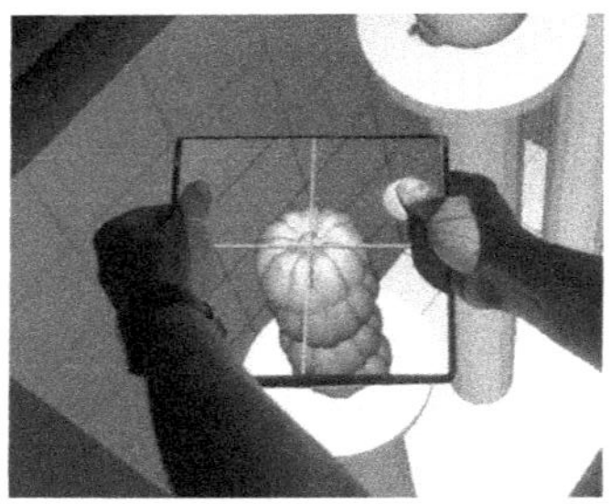

(b) Remote object selection

(c) Object inspection

Figure 6. Tangible displays combined with head-coupled perspectives (see [7])

My dissertation research is already in an advanced stage and I intend to submit and defend my thesis in 2013. In the future, lightweight organic displays (OLED) and simple spatial tracking solutions (e.g., optical depth sensors) are likely to replace the complex technical setup used for my work. This can help making the interaction techniques available for a broader audience one day. To take a first few steps towards this future, I am currently working on a less complex and easy to build technical setup [9] that is based on affordable consumer hardware, in my case the iPad and MS Kinect. Besides the future usage of lightweight smartphones and tablets as tangible displays, the interaction with digitally augmented everyday objects, such as coffee mugs, is another promising research objective for tangible displays.

Acknowledgements

My research is funded by the German Ministry of Education and Science (BMBF) project ViERforES-II (01IM10002B).

References

[1] E. A. Bier, M. C. Stone, K. Pier, W. Buxton, and T. D. DeRose. Toolglass and Magic Lenses: The See-Through Interface. *Proc. SIGGRAPH 1993*, ACM Press (1993), 445-446.

[2] G. W. Fitzmaurice. Situated Information Spaces and Spatially Aware Palmtop Computers, *Communications of ACM*, 36, 7 (1993), 39-49.

[3] D. Holman, R. Vertegaal, M. Altosaar, N. Troje, and D. Johns. Paper Windows: Interaction Techniques for Digital Paper. *Proc. CHI '05*, ACM Press (2005), 591-599.

[4] H. Ishii and B. Ullmer. Tangible Bits. Towards Seamless Interfaces between People, Bits and Atoms. *Proc. CHI 1997*, ACM Press (1997), 234-241.

[5] S. Izadi, S. Hodges, S. Taylor, D. Rosenfeld, N. Villar, A. Butler, and J. Westhues. Going Beyond the Display: A Surface Technology with an Electronically Switchable Diffuser. *Proc. UIST '08*, ACM Press (2008), 269-278.

[6] J. C. Lee, S. E. Hudson, J. W. Summet, and P. H. Dietz. Moveable Interactive Projected Displays Using Projector Based Tracking. *Proc. UIST '05*, ACM Press (2005), 63-72.

[7] M. Spindler, W. Büschel, and R. Dachselt. Use Your Head: Tangible Windows for 3D Information Spaces in a Tabletop Environment. *Proc. ITS '12*, ACM Press (2012).

[8] M. Spindler, M. Martsch, and R. Dachselt. Going Beyond the Surface: Studying Multi-Layer Interaction Above the Tabletop. *Proc. CHI '12*, ACM Press (2012).

[9] M. Spindler, W. Büschel, and R. Dachselt. Towards Spatially Aware Tangible Displays for the Masses. Workshop on Designing Collaborative Interactive Spaces for e-Creativity, e-Science and e-Learning at AVI '12. ACM Press, 2012.

[10] M. Spindler, C. Tominski, H. Schumann, and R. Dachselt. Tangible Views for Information Visualization. *Proc. ITS '10*, ACM Press (2010), 157-166.

[11] M. Spindler, C. Tominski, M. Hauschild, H. Schumann, and R. Dachselt. Novel Uses for Tangible Displays above the Tabletop. TechDemo at ITS '10.

[12] M. Spindler, S. Stellmach, and R. Dachselt. Advanced Magic Lens Interaction above the Tabletop. *Proc. ITS '09*, ACM Press (2009), 77-84.

[13] M. Spindler and R. Dachselt: Towards Pen-based Annotation Techniques for Tangible Magic Lenses Above a Tabletop. In *Accompanying DVD of ACM ITS '09*.

[14] M. Spindler and R. Dachselt. Advanced Magic Lens Interaction Above the Tabletop. TechDemo at ITS '09.

[15] B. Ullmer and H. Ishii. The metaDESK: Models and Prototypes for Tangible User Interfaces. *Proc. UIST '97*, ACM Press (1997), 223-232.

[16] M. Weiser. The Computer for the 21st Century. *Scientific American*. 265, 3 (1991), 66-75.

Improving Awareness of Automated Actions within Digital Tabletops

Y.-L. Betty Chang
Systems Design Engineering
University of Waterloo
200 University Ave. W
Waterloo, ON, N2L 3G4, Canada
betty.chang@uwaterloo.ca

ITS'12, November 11–14, 2012, Cambridge, Massachusetts, USA.
ACM 978-1-4503-1209-7/12/11.

Abstract
My research investigates information visualization techniques that improve the awareness of complex automated activities within digital tabletop interfaces. As a case study, I am exploring digital tabletop board gaming as the context to enable rapid design cycles and easy manipulation of variables, such as level of complexity. Preliminary work has revealed that automation reduces workload; however, it also increases the potential for confusion, restricts flexibility, and may negatively impact the gaming experience. Through a series of laboratory studies, my dissertation research will investigate the impact on awareness and decision making processes of following three factors: 1) persistent display of automation results, 2) animation of automated actions, and 3) user control of automated actions. Finally, a field study is planned to deploy and validate the design concepts explored in the laboratory studies.

Author Keywords
Awareness; Automation; Digital Tabletops; Collaboration

ACM Classification Keywords
H.5.2 [User Interfaces]: Graphical user interfaces (GUI).

General Terms
Design, Experimentations, Human Factors

Figure 1: The physical Pandemic game.

Introduction

Working together around a table provides people cues that can be used to maintain awareness of collaborators and the progress of joint work. This collaboration can be enhanced via a digital tabletop. These devices combine the advantages of traditional tables and of digital media, and provide the opportunity to automate some of the complex tasks during face-to-face collaborative activities. My research investigates the use of automation on digital tables in complex collocated collaboration by examining a specific application scenario: collaborative board games. This scenario enables the rapid prototyping of new design ideas, evaluation of these ideas in a controlled setting, and easily adjustment of parameters such as the level of complexity.

To support the collaborative gaming scenario, digital utilities and automation features can be provided. For example, a game can provide save and load functions, and handle game mechanics, such as setup, cleanup, scorekeeping activities, and shuffling of card decks. The collaboration quality of a game can thus be improved since players can focus on the tactics rather than game mechanics. However, complex automation of activities can leave players out of the loop, as they may not be constantly watching for changes on the digital tabletop while they engage in face-to-face interaction with other people at the table. In addition, complex automation triggered by a collaborator's actions can also create confusion for others.

In previous work focused on mitigating the loss of awareness of automated actions, Endsley [3] found that awareness can be improved by adjusting the level of user control through increased interactivity and balanced manual control and automation. Providing appropriate feedback through animation can help by drawing people's attention [1] and guiding them through changes [5].

My research aims to investigate the use of such strategies, e.g., animation and user control, to improve awareness of automation during collaborative tabletop gaming. Animation, of course, requires people to be looking at the display when the animation occurs. As mentioned above, during a collaborative tabletop activity, people may instead be interacting with others around the table. Thus, I will investigate alternative design strategies for improving awareness, such as the use of persistent information displays, which can provide a reference point if people were looking away when automatic changes occur [6,7].

To investigate these design strategies, I propose a series of studies to investigate the effectiveness of the three factors: 1) persistent display, 2) animation, and 3) user control. The first two studies, which will be laboratory based, will determine the best candidate information visualization technique. A third, field-based, study will validate the selected technique—in the wild.

My dissertation is expected to result in information visualization techniques that improve the awareness of complex automated activities through an investigation of the aforementioned three factors. The contribution includes the design of the visualization techniques and empirical data from both laboratory and field studies on the effectiveness of these techniques. The results can benefit other complex collaborative tabletop activities beyond gaming, including collaborative planning and decision-making applications.

The Pandemic Game

Overview: The three or four players are on the same team trying to defeat the game board together. The losing conditions include running out of time (the set number of cards they draw from a pile) or failing to keep the outbreaks in control (exceed allowable number of outbreaks).

Player's turn: The current player has four actions including treating diseases, exchanging cards, traveling to different cities, and building research stations. Then, he/she draws two cards, which can be exchanged for cures or for travelling.

Game's turn: More disease cubes are placed onto the game board during the game's turn. With certain probability, an *epidemic card* will be drawn, and it is resolved by following several specific steps including stacking and shuffling decks of cards as well as drawing cards. The epidemic event makes the game state more chaotic.

Preliminary Research

An exploratory study using a collaborative board game, Pandemic (see Figure 1), provides the foundation for this research. As a collaborative game, Pandemic requires three to four players to strategize and work together as a team to save the world from epidemic outbreaks. To win the game, players have to find cures to four diseases while managing limited resources within the time constraint

Three conditions that vary the amount of automation were tested, including the physical version of the game and two digital tabletop versions with low- and high-automation. The physical version uses the traditional paper-based version of the Pandemic. The low-automation version is a direct translation of the physical game to the digital tabletop, and it provides very little automation help. All the game pieces can be moved freely, and players are allowed to carry out any actions they wish even if it violates the rules, just like the physical game. Only actions cumbersome to perform on a 2D surface were automated, such as shuffling the deck of cards. The high-automation version (see Figure 2) handles most of the game mechanics, such as distributing disease cubes and resolving special events. Then, the automation results are displayed through animations. Moreover, unlike the low-automation version, this game also enforces rules.. Players have more time for strategizing and they only need to perform their moves.

The exploratory study revealed that the low-automation version requires too much effort to play, and thus, does not take full advantage of the digital computation. On the other hand, the high-automation version requires less work, but the enjoyment of the game was negatively affected. There were more instances of confusion, and the rule enforcement reduces the flexibility in the game. Players' confusion increased because the brief animation was not enough to communicate the changes in game state resulted from automation. Players often need to engage in intense discussion to catch up to the game state. Players may also miss the animation completely because they were strategizing or conversing. Persistent displays can provide game state change information over a longer period of time and help players to refer to and find game state changes. However, the animation can still be helpful to direct players' attention to changes on the board and guide their understanding of the changes.

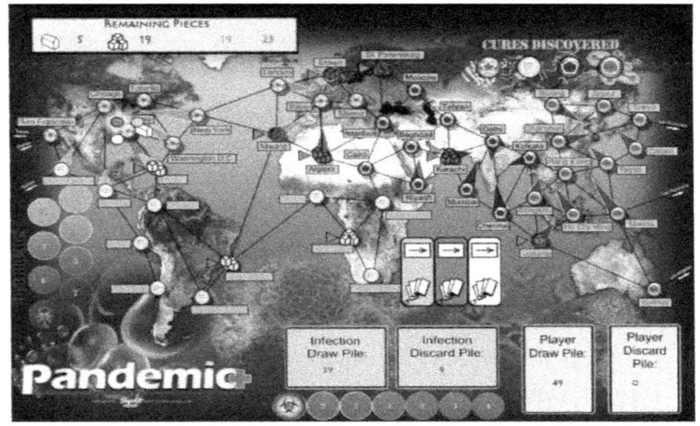

Figure 2: The high-automation Pandemic game.

Furthermore, the system needs to support players' decision-making process through increasing flexibility and players' control in the game. Players often move game pieces to mock up their strategies. However, in the high-automation version, players would accidentally perform the action while mocking up their strategies.

As the game does not allow undoing actions to prevent the breaching of rules, this inflexibility frustrates players and decreases their ability to strategize. One solution is to provide an undo function. Moreover, the animation displays all the changes simultaneously right after players finish their actions, and more user control over automation could allow players to manage the game pace and increase the enjoyment in the game. This can be done through segmenting the automation to smaller steps and allowing players to step through the changes. To summarize, the exploratory study illustrated three areas for future investigation: 1) persistent display, 2) animation, and 3) user control. The following sections will outline my research plan to investigate these three factors.

Research Plan

My research aims to improve players' understanding of automation results and the decision-making process through the development of information visualization techniques that will be evaluated in a series of studies. The first study will investigate the use of persistent displays as a way to provide information on automation result over time and as a means to enable flexible undos to support the decision-making process. The second study will investigate the effectiveness of different animation and user control to improve players' awareness of the game state and provide better control of the game pace. Finally, a third study will be conducted to validate the developed techniques in the wild and to elucidate why the designs is or is not effective.

Research approach

Collaborative work is so rich that it cannot be fully described by numbers alone. Therefore, a mixed-methods approach [2] will be taken so that both qualitative and

		Local	
		Absence	**Presence**
Peripheral	**Absence**	1 (none)	2 (local only)
	Presence	3 (peripheral only)	4 (both)

Table 1: Conditions for Study 1.

quantitative data are used to understand and evaluate the complex user experience. The studies will collect video and audio recordings of the game sessions and analyze them using an open-coding process [8]. The background and post-condition questionnaires in Likert scale will be analyzed using statistical tests.

Study 1 – persistent displays

Study 1 will investigate the use of persistent information displays during gameplay. Persistent displays provide players a reference point for information on game state changes. In addition, persistent displays can keep track of the history of the gameplay, and be used to provide the undo function to increase the flexibility and facilitate the decision-making process. Thus, Study 1 will investigate persistent displays as a way to enhance players' understanding of game state changes and the trade-off between rule enforcement and flexibility during gameplay.

Persistent information can be displayed locally, directly on the digital tabletop and right next to the changes. The information can also be presented on the peripheral, such as tablets. The information on the tablet will be interactive to support history navigation and automation result exploration. Study 1 will investigate the impact persistent displays on gameplay as well as their ability to support undo actions. The measurements to the effectiveness of the persistent displays include self-rated awareness, enjoyment, and collaboration quality as well as game event resolving time, confusion, and instances of long pauses. The study will also reveal how players make use of persistent displays based on their locations and options available. As described in Table 1, four conditions will be tested: none, both, only peripheral, and only local. The results of Study 1 will help inform which condition is the most effective and how the design can be improved. The revised design will feed into Study 2.

Study 2 – animation and user control
Based on the revised design of Study 1, the second study will further improve players' understanding of automation results and increase the flexibility in the gameplay. Animation can be used to guide players' attention on a large display, and thus help them understand the game state changes. However, animation presents all the game state changes at once, and the players have less control of the game pace. By segmenting the animation and providing ways for players to step through the animation can increase the flexibility and the excitement during gameplay. However, there is a trade-off between providing powerful control for a single person and the group's awareness of the system state [4]. When one player is controlling the game pace, other players may be lost or confused of the current game state. Thus, Study 2 will also look at group control vs. single user control of the game pace in addition to studying the use of animation.

As described in Table 2, four conditions will be tested. Animation can be played all at once (i.e. simultaneously) or sequentially. When the animation is played sequentially, it can also be stepped through by a single user or collaboratively by a group of users. The results of Study 2 will reveal the impact of different animation types and user control types on players' understanding of the automation results and their gaming experience. It will also help improve how the automation results are being divided.

		Animation	
		Simultaneous	**Sequential**
User Control	**None**	1 (control)	2 (sequential animation)
	Single User		3 (sequential animation single user)
	Group		4 (sequential animation group

Table 2: Conditions for Study 2.

Study 3 – field study
The final study will be a field study that places the refined digital game from Study 2 in a home or public gaming environment. The environment may be full of distractions that are not present in the laboratory environment, but players may feel more comfortable to act normally. The result will reveal the distracting factor and a more realistic gameplay. More importantly, Study 3 will validate the information visualization techniques developed in the laboratory setting, and provide insights on why the techniques work or fail.

Expected Benefits of Attending
My main goal for attending the doctoral symposium is 1) to receive feedback on the current proposed disserta-

tion direction and 2) to gain insight on the application of my research to the general tabletop community. This valuable opportunity of hearing the opinions from experts in the tabletop community will help me refine my dissertation direction and provide a new perspective on my research. Moreover, I would like to hear the work from other attendees and learn of new research methodologies that may help improve my own work.

Expected Contributions

Through my investigations to improve the awareness of automated actions and decision-making process, my research is expected to contribute in a deeper understanding of how to present automated actions on digital tabletop interfaces. Moreover, it will provide insights on reaching a balance between providing flexibility and automating mundane activities. In addition to information visualization techniques that will be developed, my research will help understand the use of digital tabletops in the field with an emphasis on the automation so that the digital capability of digital tabletops can be utilized. The result of my dissertation will also be applicable to other fields that require collaborative decision-making.

Acknowledgements

I would like to thank the Natural Science and Engineering Research Council of Canada (NSERC) and the NSERC Digital Surface Software Application Network (SURFNET). I thank Dr. Stacey Scott, Dr. Mark Hancock, James R. Wallace, Joseph Pape, Phillip J. McClelland, Dr. T.C. Nicholas Graham, Chris Cooper, Dr. Neil Randall, Matt Leacock, Z-Man Games, and Todor Doychev.

References

[1] Bodenhausen, G.V. and Hugenberg, K. Attention, perception, and social cognition. In F. Strack and J. Förster, eds., *Social cognition: The basis of human interaction*. Psychology Press, Philadelphia, 2009, 1-22.

[2] Creswell, J.W. and Clark, V.L.P. *Designing and conducting mixed methods research*. Sage Publications, Inc, California, USA, 2010.

[3] Endsley, M.R. Automation and situation awareness. *Human Factors*, (1996), 1-11.

[4] Gutwin, C. and Greenberg, S. Design for individuals, design for groups : Tradeoffs between power and workspace awareness. *CSCW'98*, (1998), 207-216.

[5] Heer, J. and Robertson, G. Animated transitions in statistical data graphics. *IEEE transactions on visualization and computer graphics 13*, 6 (2007), 1240-7.

[6] John, M., Smallman, H.S., and Manes, D.I. Recovery from interruptions to a dynamic monitoring task: The beguiling utility of instant replay. *Proceedings of the Human Factors and Ergonomics Society 49th Annual Meeting*, (2005), 473-477.

[7] Scott, S.D., Mercier, S., Cummings, M.L., and Wang, E. Assisting interruption recovery in supervisory control of multiple UAVS. *Proceedings of the Human Factors and Ergonomics Society 50th Annual Meeting*, (2006), 699-703.

[8] Strauss, A.L. and Corbin, J.M. Basics of qualitative research: Techniques and procedures for developing grounded theory. Sage Publications, Inc, Thousand Oaks, CA, 1998.

Designing Tabletop Activities for Inquiry-Based Learning: Lessons from Phylogenetics, Neuroscience and Logistics

Bertrand Schneider
Stanford University
Stanford, CA, USA
schneibe@stanford.edu

Abstract
In this paper I discuss the lessons learnt from designing learning environments for science education. More specifically, I describe four projects I designed and (or) evaluated: Walden, a multi-touch multi-displays for informal science education; the Tinker Table, a Tangible User Interface for students in logistics; Phylo-Genie, a learning scenario for collaborative learning of phylogenetics; and finally BrainExplorer, a pen-based tabletop environment that enables direct interaction with a small-scale brain. I summarize my findings by defining 3 ways in which technology can enhance knowledge building for inquiry-based learning: via a "Representational Effect", by providing rich interaction techniques and by preparing for future learning.

ITS'12, November 11–14, 2012, Cambridge, Massachusetts, USA.
ACM 978-1-4503-1209-7/12/11.

Author Keywords
Tabletops; Collaborative Learning.

ACM Classification Keywords
H.5.m. User Interfaces. - Graphical user interfaces.

Interactive Tabletops in Education
Over the last decades researchers in the Learning Sciences and Computer Science have begun to explore how interactive surfaces can improve learning [5]. More specifically, multi-disciplinary teams have tried to translate findings in Data Visualization and HCI (Human-Computer Interaction) to education. In my own work, I have explored how interactive surfaces improve learning for science education: Four projects from my own research (Figure 1, 2, 3 and 5) describe the promises of technology for inquiry-based learning. I discuss how novel representations can affect users' perception and group collaboration. I then provide a few examples of rich interaction techniques for exploring a problem space. Following, I discuss how

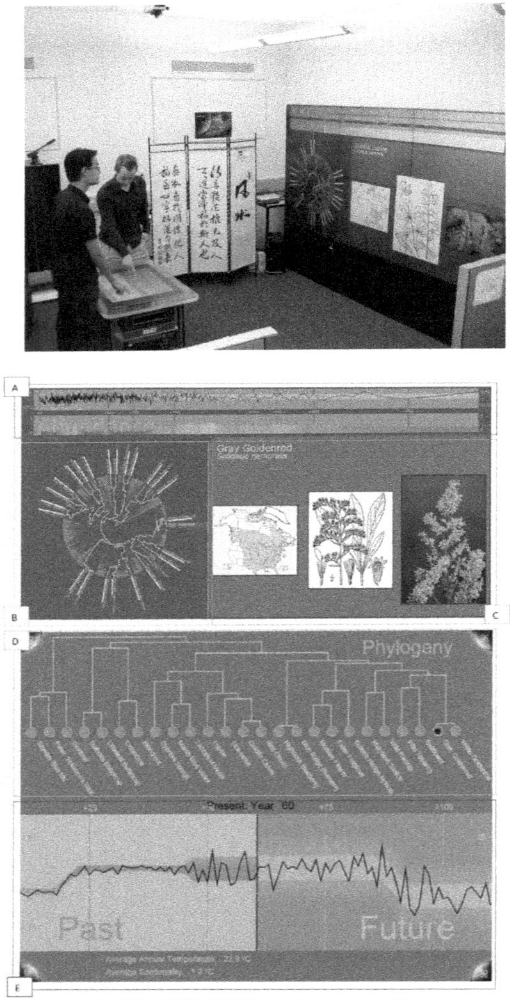

Figure 1: The WALDEN environment (top: two users interacting with the system; bottom, the interface on the large display and on the tabletop)

fostering inquiry-based learning in interactive learning environments can build strong foundations for future learning. I finally describe the limits of those approaches and highlight a few areas of concern.

Learning via Data Visualization Techniques

For decades, cognitive psychologists have investigated how external representations influence cognition. The general findings are summarized by Zhang [12], and referred to as the representational effect. It is defined as "the phenomenon that different representations of a common abstract structure can generate dramatically different representational efficiencies, task complexities, and behavioral outcomes". A classic example mentioned by Zhang is the shift from roman numerals to Arabic numbers: in the 13th century, the adoption of the later representation led to a tremendous development in economics and mathematics because it allowed people to perform complex computations in a faster and more efficient way. In other words, the shift to a new representation (Arabic numbers) changed people's perception of numbers; this, in turn, opened doors to practical and intellectual developments. This is a powerful idea, and education can benefit from this insight: by providing adequate representations, we can enable students to do things they would not otherwise be able to do. This is important in discovery learning settings, where asking the right question or perceiving a problem from different perspectives allow students to conduct successful inquiries [6].

In my own research, I have evaluated a visualization of scientific findings on a multi-surface multi-display environment [2]. This simulation, WALDEN (Fig.1), provides ways of exploring the impact of climate change on phylogenetically related species of Thoreau's Wood in Concord, Massachusetts. Taking advantage of Data Visualization techniques and multi-touch interactions, the system allows group of users to investigate how evolutionary relationships shaped patterns of species loss. The goal of this project was to make scientific findings accessible to the general public, in an attempt to increase awareness of environmental changes. Results from a pilot study (N = 10) suggest that large visualizations are prone to cognitive overload. Indeed, individuals reported being "overwhelmed" by the amount of information and produced few comments illustrating a conceptual understanding of the domain. We also compared how dyads interacted with WALDEN, and interestingly we found that pairs of users were more active, produced more hypotheses, predictions and comments reflecting a deep conceptual understanding. Those results suggest that complex visualizations may offer an interesting space for collaborative knowledge building as opposed to individual exploration. The key lesson from this project was that different users perceive different details, and providing more information than necessary has the potential of creating productive debates among users. Future studies are needed to investigate how simpler visualizations impact student's inquiry of a domain.

Another way to create rich representations is to blend physical and virtual information. In another project (the "Tinker Table"[4] – Fig. 2), students in logistics had to create small-scale warehouses where they interacted with the simulation in groups. We showed that compared to a multi-touch table (N = 82), the physical

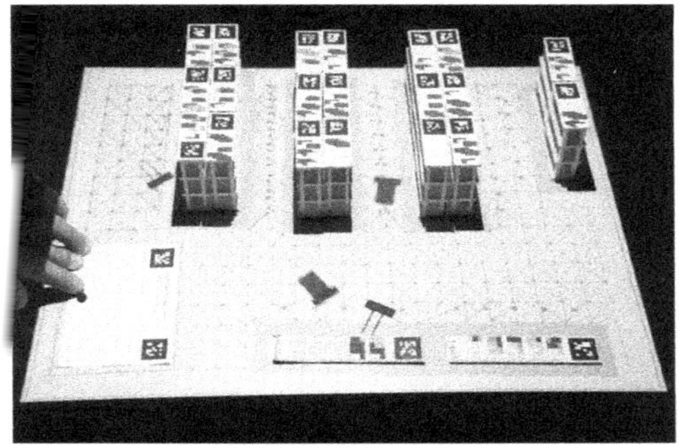

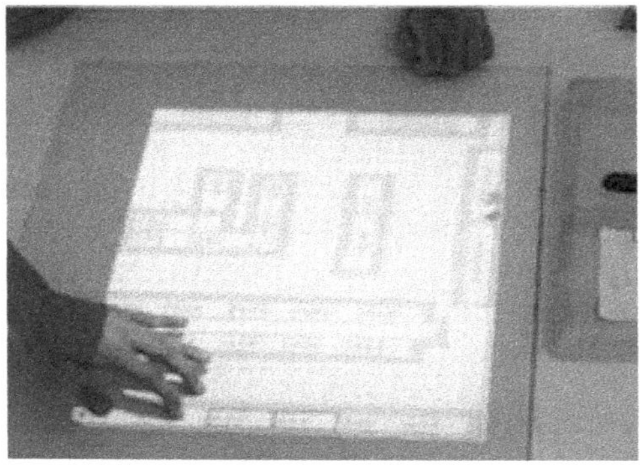

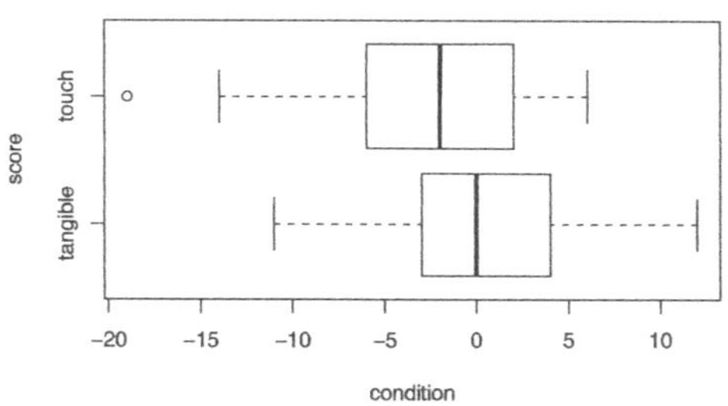

Figure 2: The Tinker Table (top) compared to the same system using a multi-touch interface (middle). On the bottom, the results of the learning gain.

dimension of the simulation fostered collaboration, playfulness, exploration of the problem space in addition to increasing learning gains. I argue that educational designers can take advantage of augmented reality (AR) techniques to create rich external representations. Those representations have the potential to foster collaborative learning and exploration of a problem space. In our evaluation, exploration (how many configurations the students explored) played a crucial role for problem-solving processes: a mediation analysis showed that exploration was the most important factor in assuring high learning gains.

Embodied Interactions – Increasing Engagement and Exploration in a Problem Space

In addition to designing novel kinds of external representations, recent advances in HCI allow users to interact with interactive simulation in original ways. Computer vision algorithms can easily track bodies, objects and various signals (e.g. infra-red light). Those technological developments opened doors to new kinds of learning.

For instance, I developed several projects where users interact with a Tangible User Interface (TUI; [7]). In BrainExplorer [3], for instance, students interact with a small-scale model of the brain on a tabletop surface. Users can move individual parts of the brain and cut neural pathways with an infra-red pen. Those lesions are reflected on the bottom right part of the table, where subjects observe how their action impacted the visual field of the brain. We conducted an ecological evaluation of this system, where one group of participants read a text on this topic while another group freely investigated this question using BrainExplorer. We found that subjects in the "tabletop" condition outperformed their peers on three different kinds of learning: terminology questions, conceptual learning and transfer of their knowledge to a different situation (N = 28). Future studies are needed to investigate which factors caused this positive effect; however this study shows that directly interacting with a simulation of a dynamic system has the potential to support learning on different dimensions.

Another example of using tabletop interaction techniques for education is a project called Phylo-Genie [1]. Phylo-Genie is a learning scenario that fosters collaborative learning of phylogenetics. During the activity, students learn about evolutionary-related snakes and built phylogenetic trees based on morphological and genomic data. Participants interact with the interactive surface with their fingers and by manipulating tokens representing different species of snakes. The tabletop implementation of this scenario provides support by providing a structured activity in which students build their own trees from scratch, and make them evolve based on morphological or genomic data. We compared this scenario with a pen and paper activity, where participants are provided with the same instructions and follow the same steps as in the tabletop implementation. We found that dyads using Phylo-Genie learnt more, collaborated more, were more engaged and reported a lower cognitive load while completing the activity (N = 56). An additional analysis of our data (mediation analyses) showed that engagement fostered collaboration, which in turn was associated with higher learning gains. Sub-dimensions of the engagement questionnaire also suggest that a novelty effect was not correlated with higher learning

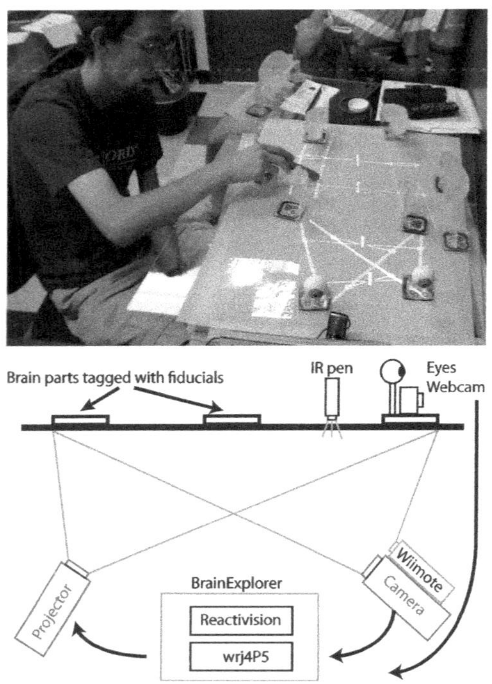

Figure 3: The BrainExplorer project, a tabletop environment where users learnt about the visual pathways of the brain by severing connections.

gains. The main lesson from those results can be summarized as follows: structured inquiry-based activities on interactive surfaces have the potential to increase engagement and collaboration, which in turns positively impact knowledge building.

Finally the Tinker Table also illustrates a case where TUIs provide interesting ways to interact with a simulation. By moving shelves, users can actively create a warehouse and then test its efficiency. The resulting simulation provides a rich way to investigate students' understanding of logistics' concepts. Additionally, my results from those projects helped us formulate the following hypotheses: learning environments that blend physical and virtual information have the potential to foster collaboration, for instance by facilitating joint attention on key objects.

Preparing for Future Learning by Creating Prior Knowledge

So far I have described how technology potentially enhance knowledge building by providing rich visualizations and effective interactions. We argue, however, that the most interesting educational benefit of technology is to prepare students for future learning. More specifically, I believe that the potential of inquiry-based learning approaches coupled with technology is not promote learning per se, but to provide a space for students to build solid foundations for future learning. In the next paragraph, I describe how our data supports this hypothesis.

In the BrainExplorer project (Fig. 3), I evaluated how sequencing different learning activities impacted conceptual understanding of neuroscience. Following an AB/BA cross-over design, I assessed how sequencing different learning activities influenced the way participants learnt. In one conditions subjects used the tabletop for 15 minutes, took a test, then read a textbook chapter on the same topic for 15 minutes, and finally completed a post-test. In the other condition, participants followed the same procedure, except that they read the text first and then used the tabletop for 15 minutes.

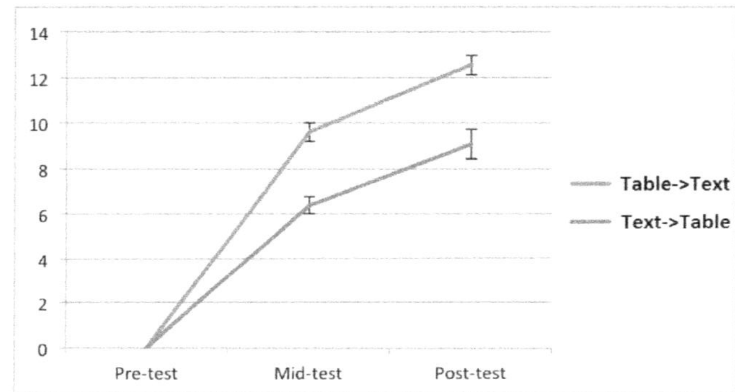

Figure 4: The results from the BrainExplorer project: students learnt more when using the table first and then reading a text on the same topic.

My results (Fig. 4) suggest that correctly sequencing learning activities had a tremendous impact on subjects' learning. We believe that two effects are taking place: the first one (blue line) shows a positive effect where using BrainExplorer prepared participants to learn. By freely exploring the problem space, users developed a set of questions and pre-concepts that helped them make sense of the textbook chapter. This can be explained by the "dual coding theory" [9]: since executing physical actions with BrainExplorer does not impede the verbal channel, subjects can develop their own, personalized story on how the brain processes visual information. This self-generated knowledge is, in

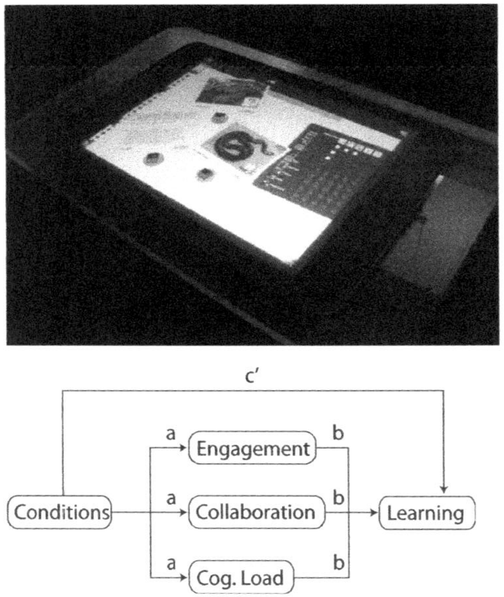

Figure 5: The Phylo-Genie project, an inquiry-based learning scenario implemented on the Microsoft Surface. Below, I found that dyads of students learnt and collaborated more on the tabletop compared to the same paper activity; only collaboration was a significant mediator.

turn, more likely to be remembered by our subjects (cognitive psychologists call this the "Elaboration Effect" [11]). On the other hand, participants in the other condition used their verbal channel to read the text, and thus did not have the opportunity to build prior knowledge on the domain. We propose that in some cases, reading a textbook chapter with a clear description of a concept has a negative impact on knowledge building; this idea is supported by lower-level experiments in cognitive psychology (e.g. the "verbal shadowing effet" [8]), where retrieval of verbal information negatively impacts recognition.

In summary, learning environments have the potential to provide a first hands-on experience in a domain. By letting students engage with the learning material in an alternative way, they get the opportunity to build "pre-concepts" that will support future learning [10].

Limits and Concerns

One main concern in using new technologies to promote discovery-based learning can be summarized by the "novelty effect" – namely, the fact that students are temporarily more engaged in learning activities because the technology is new and interesting. This reflects a major issue in using new interaction techniques for education: students may not necessarily continue to react in a positive, because they lose interest in the technology. This issue should be addressed by longitudinal studies or self-reports from users.

A different concern is the cost of building complex learning environments. For instance in the BrainExplorer, Tinker Table or Phylo-Genie project, the cost of building those environments was high in terms of time or monetary cost. Educational researchers need to be strategic when it comes time to implement those environments in real classroom: key concepts need to be targeted first, especially when misconceptions are likely to arise. Additionally, those environments may be more relevant for offering a space where students discover a concept for the first time; as previously described, active exploration of a problem space may provide unique contributions for future learning.

Conclusion

In this paper we have articulated three views in which technology can positively affect discovery-based learning. More specifically, we discussed 1) how providing rich visualizations may increase the way people collaborate, 2) how rich interactions techniques have the potential to foster engagement and exploration of a problem space, and 3) the fact that the main benefit of technology-enhanced learning environments may not be learning per se, but to prepare for future learning.

References

[1] Schneider, B., Strait, M., Muller, L., Elfenbein, S., Shaer, O., Shen, C. (2012). Phylo-Genie: Engaging Students in Collaborative 'Tree- Thinking' through Tabletop Techniques. In Proc. *ACM Conference on Human Factors in Computing Systems (CHI'12)*,ACM Press.

[2] Schneider, B., Tobiasz, M., Willis, C. & Shen, C. (accepted). WALDEN: Multi-Surface Multi-Touch Simulation of Climate Change and Species Loss in Thoreau's Woods. *ACM International Conference on Interactive Tabletops and Surfaces*, ITS '12. Boston, MA, USA: ACM.

[3] Schneider B., Wallace J., Pea, R. & Blickstein P. (under review). Preparing for Future Learning with a

Tangible User Interface: the Case of Neuroscience. *IEEE Transactions on Learning Technologies.*

[4] Schneider, B., Jermann, P., Zufferey, G., & Dillenbourg, P. (2011). Benefits of a Tangible Interface for Collaborative Learning and Interaction. *IEEE Transactions on Learning Technologies, 4*(3), 222–232.

[5] Dillenbourg, P., & Evans, M. (2011). Interactive tabletops in education. International Journal of Computer-Supported Collaborative Learning.

[6] de Jong, T. (2006). COMPUTER SIMULATIONS: Technological Advances in Inquiry Learning. *Science*, *312*, 532-533.

[7] Ishii, H., & Ullmer, B. (1997). Tangible bits: towards seamless interfaces between people, bits and atoms. Proceedings of the SIGCHI conference on Human factors in computing systems, CHI '97 (pp. 234–241). New York, NY, USA: ACM.

[8] Meissner, C. A., Brigham, J. C., & Kelley, C. M. (2001). The influence of retrieval processes in verbal overshadowing. Memory & Cognition, 29, 176-186.

[9] Paivio, A. (1990). Mental Representations: A Dual Coding Approach. Oxford University Press.

[10] Schwartz, D. L., & Bransford, J. D. (1998). A Time For Telling. Cognition and Instruction, 16, 475-5223.

[11] Stein, B. S., & Bransford, J. D. (1979). Constraints on effective elaboration: Effects of precision and subject generation. Journal of Verbal Learning and Verbal Behavior, 18(6), 769-777.

[12] Zhang, J., & Norman, D. A. (January). Representations in distributed cognitive tasks. Cognitive Science, 18(1), 87-122.

3D Touch Panel Interface Using an Autostereoscopic Display

Takehiro Niikura
The University of Tokyo
Hongo 7-3-1
Bunkyo-ku, Tokyo, Japan
takehiro_niikura@ipc.i.u-tokyo.ac.jp

Takashi Komuro
Saitama University
255 Shimo-Okubo
Sakura-ku, Saitama City, Japan
komuro@mail.saitama-u.ac.jp

ITS'12, Nov. 11–14, 2012, Cambridge, Massachusetts, USA.
ACM 978-1-4503-1209-7/12/11.

Abstract
We propose a 3D touch panel interface using an autostereoscopic display and a high-speed stereo camera. With this system, the virtual objects are stereoscopically-presented, and the objects respond to the hand movement captured by a stereo camera, which makes users feel like they are touching the objects directly. Since we used high-speed camera for detecting the fingertip, it can realize more accurate synchronization between the real object and virtual object without a feeling of strangeness.

Author Keywords
3D user interface; vision-based UI; high-speed camera

ACM Classification Keywords
H.5.2 [**Information interfaces and presentation**]: User Interfaces. - Input devices and strategies.

Introduction
Recently, touch panels are widely used everywhere in our living environment. As well as touch panels are easy to use, they can be used for general purposes since screen layout and UI components can be changed depending on the situation. However, since presentation and operation of the objects are restricted on a 2D surface, we can not feel much like we are operating the objects directly.

Therefore, we propose a 3D touch panel interface using an autostereoscopic display. With this system, the objects are stereoscopically-presented, and the objects respond to the hand movement captured by a stereo camera, which makes users feel like they are touching the objects directly.

Though many approaches to realize the interaction with 3D virtual objects using cameras have been proposed[1, 3, 4], these system may cause position gaps between the real object (e.g. the operating hand) and the virtual object because standard cameras have long latency. Therefore, we aim more accurate synchronization between the real object and virtual object using high-speed cameras, which reduce the latency due to image output and transfer.

SYSTEM OVERVIEW

Hardware Configuration

We developed a system shown in Fig. 1. We put a black board on the right side of the display so that the cameras, which are placed on the left side of the display, can extract the finger region easily and stably.

The stereo camera consists of two monochrome IEEE1394 high-speed cameras Grasshopper (Point Grey Research Inc.) with a lens having a focal length of 5mm. We used the cameras at the frame rate of 120 fps (frame per second) and the image size is 640 x 480 [pixels].

Since a high-speed camera has shorter latency than standard cameras, a high-speed camera can reduce the position gap between real object and virtual object. In other words, it can realize more accurate synchronization between the real object and virtual object without a feeling of strangeness.

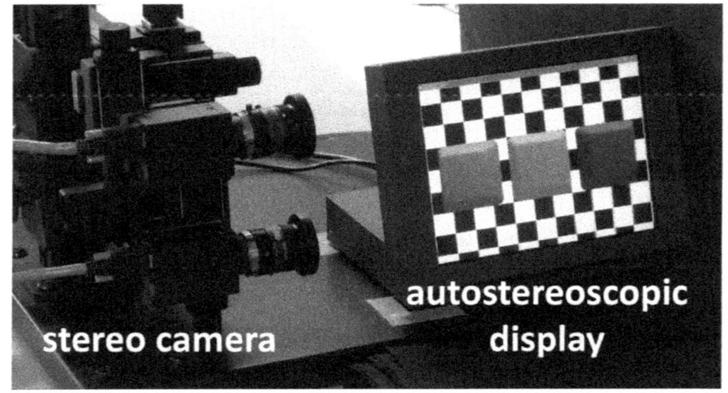

Figure 1: The prototype system

There are some types of autostereoscopic displays. We chose an 8.4" parallax barrier autostereoscopic display (VMJ Inc.), which has good stability of autostereoscopy and proper 3D viewing distance. The specifications of the display is shown in Table1. The minimum 3D viewing distance of the display is 0.65m, which is short enough for users to operate the 3D virtual object by the hand. We used OpenGL for drawing, and the SDK, which is provided by the manufacturer of the display, generates CG images of all views.

Display	Spec
Size (inch)	8.4
Barrier type	Parallax barrier
Resolution	1024×768
Display type	XGA
Response time (ms)	25
The number of views	5
Min & max 3D viewing distance (m)	0.65-1.5

Table 1: The specifications of the display

Processing Flow

In this system, we assumed that users keep their finger stretched during operation. Therefore, each camera detects the position of the fingertip in the following algorithm. At first, the system binalizes the captured stereo images with an appropriate threshold and obtains the finger images. Then, from left to right, the system counts the successive white pixels in each column of the images. When the number of successive white pixels exceeds than a certain threshold, the pixel at that moment is set to the position of the fingertip. The 3D position of the fingertip is calculated from estimated positions of the fingertip in stereo images. The stereo camera is calibrated using Camera Calibration Toolbox for Matlab[2].

Collision detection between the fingertip and the virtual object is performed using the estimated 3D position of the fingertip. When the position of the fingertip gets to the appropriate distance from the display, where the surface of the virtual object is displayed, the system detects the collision between the fingertip and the virtual object. After the collision, the virtual object moves according to the position of the fingertip, which gives users a sense of touching the real object.

3D TOUCH PANEL INTERFACE

Using the developed system, we created a 3D graphical user interface of a touch panel, in which user can push three buttons which are displayed stereoscopically. Figure 2 shows the operation experiment using the system. When the subject brought his finger close to a button, the collision between the finger and the button was detected at a certain distance, and then the buttons moved according to the distance of the finger from the display until he touched the surface of the display.

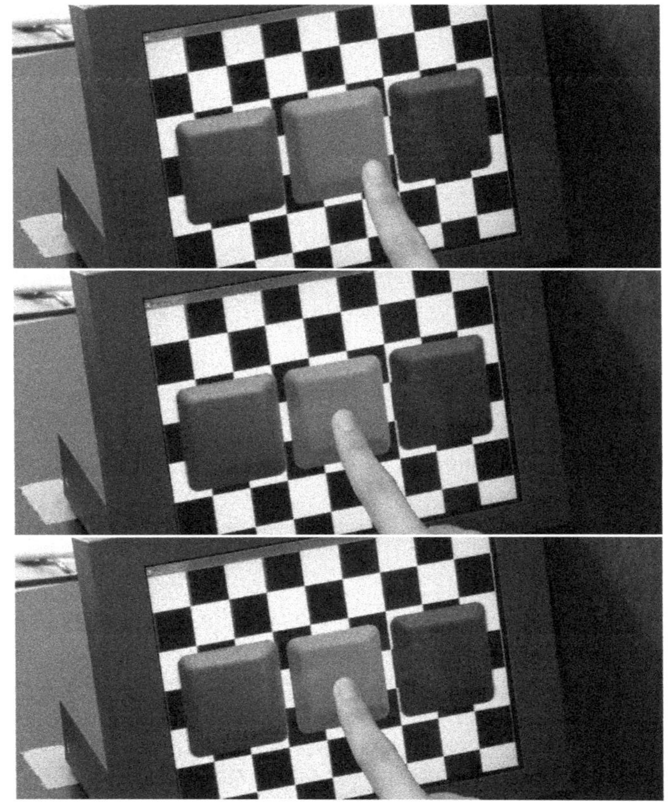

Figure 2: The operation experiment.

When the subjects experienced our system, at first they were surprised that they felt no tactile feedback at the finger even though they "touched" the surface of the button. After that, when they really touched the surface of the display, the feeling of touching the real button was sensed. Additionally, when we changed the camera's frame rate, they felt that the movement of the buttons was more synchronized to the movement of the fingertip in the case of at the higher frame rate.

CONCLUSION

In this paper, we proposed the 3D touch panel interface using an autostereoscopic display and a high-speed stereo camera, and developed the prototype in which users can push the buttons with their finger as if they touch real buttons. In the future work, we will create more advanced interface by adding other UI components, and also we are planning to evaluate the feeling of reality by performing a subjective evaluation experiment.

References

[1] Benko, H., Jota, R., and Wilson, A. D. Miragetable: Freehand interaction on a projected augmented reality tabletop. In *Proc. CHI'12* (May 2012).

[2] Bouguet, J.-Y. Camera calibration toolbox for matlab.

[3] Hoshi, T., Takahashi, M., Iwamoto, T., and Shinoda, H. Noncontact tactile display based on radiation pressure of airborne ultrasound. *IEEE Transactions on Haptics* (2010), 155–165.

[4] Yoshida, T., Kamuro, S., Minamizawa, K., Nii, H., and Tachi, S. Repro3d: full-parallax 3d display using retro-reflective projection technology. In *ACM SIGGRAPH 2010 Emerging Technologies* (2010).

FloTree: A Multi-touch Interactive Simulation of Evolutionary Processes

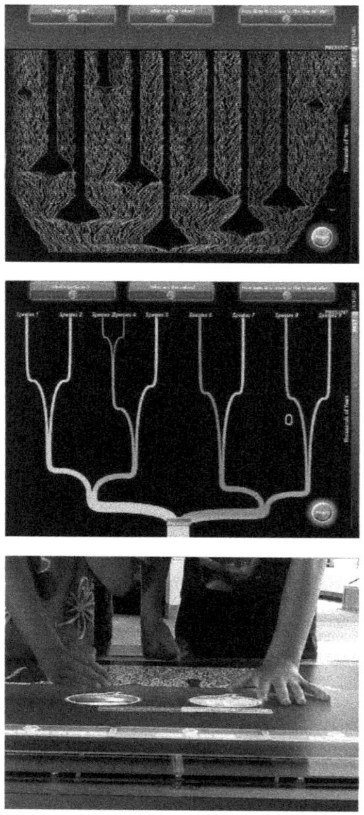

Figure 1. *FloTree* interactively simulates evolutionary processes at the population-level (top), and then links to the species-level (middle). The bottom figure shows visitors interacting with *FloTree*.

Kien Chuan Chua[1, 2]
cchua@alumni.nus.edu.sg

Yongqiang Qin[1, 3]
qyq08@mails.tsinghua.edu.cn

Florian Block[1]
fblock@seas.harvard.edu

Brenda Phillips[1]
phillips@seas.harvard.edu

Judy Diamond[4]
jdiamond1@unl.edu

E. Margaret Evans[5]
evansem@umich.edu

Michael S. Horn[6]
michael-horn@northwestern.edu

Chia Shen[1]
cshen@seas.harvard.edu

[1] School of Engineering and Applied Sciences, Harvard University Cambridge, 02138 USA.
[2] Department of Computer Science, National University of Singapore 117417 Singapore.
[3] Department of Computer Science, Tsinghua University Beijing, 100084 China.
[4] University of Nebraska State Museum Lincoln, 68588 USA.
[5] Center for Human Growth & Development, University of Michigan Ann Arbor, 48109 USA.
[6] Computer Science and Learning Sciences, Northwestern University Evanston, 60208 USA

ITS'12, November 11–14, 2012, Cambridge, Massachusetts, USA.
ACM 978-1-4503-1209-7/12/11.

Abstract
We present FloTree, a multi-user simulation that illustrates key dynamic processes underlying evolutionary change. Our intention is to create a informal learning environment that links micro-level evolutionary processes to macro-level outcomes of speciation and biodiversity. On a multi-touch table, the simulation represents change from generation to generation in a population of organisms. By placing hands or arms on the surface, visitors can add environmental barriers, thus interrupting the genetic flow between the separated populations. This results in sub-populations that accumulate genetic differences independently over time, sometimes leading to the formation of new species. Learners can morph the result of the simulation into a corresponding phylogenetic tree. The free-form hand and body touch gestures invite creative input from users, encourages social interaction, and provides an opportunity for deep engagement.

Author Keywords
Interactive, simulation, population genetics, evolution

ACM Classification Keywords
H5.2: User Interfaces. - Graphical user interfaces.

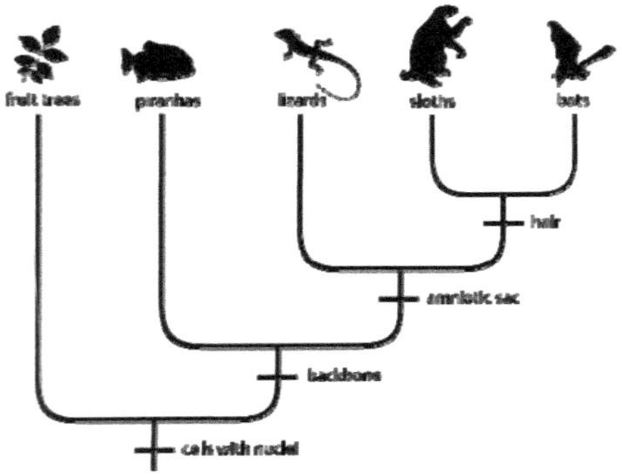

Figure 2. A phylogenetic tree illustrating the macro-evolutionary descent of species.

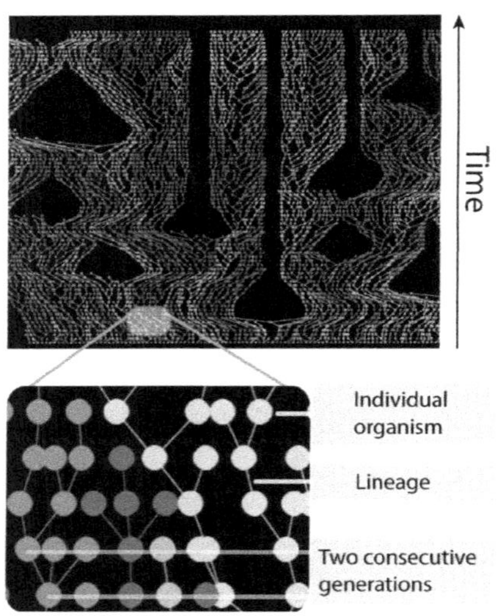

Figure 3. Population view: Organisms give birth to new generations that spread upwards on the display. The lines between organisms indicate lineages.

General Terms

Design, Human Factors

Introduction

Conveying concepts of evolutionary biology to the general public is a key feature of many natural history exhibits. One challenge to understanding evolution is grasping how micro-evolution—processes at the population level—and macro-evolution—speciation and biodiversity—are connected [2]. One way in which speciation might occur is through geographic isolation. Over time populations are split, preventing them from interbreeding, which interrupts the exchange of genetic material. Gradually, the separated sub-populations accumulate genetic differences that may eventually result in separate species. These processes lead to the biodiversity seen on earth today, which is often represented by evolutionary trees (Fig. 2).

Although other interactive applications have focused on helping the general public understand population-level processes [1] and speciation [4], conveying the link between micro- and macro-evolution remains a challenge [2].

In this demo, we present FloTree–a collaborative museum exhibit deployed on a multi-touch tabletop. The FloTree allows visitors to experiment with simulated populations to see how such interactions can lead to the emergence of new species. Visitors experience the relationship between micro- and macro-evolutionary processes firsthand. The following sections describe the FloTree exhibit, interaction design and implementation.

The FloTree Exhibit

As museum visitors approach the exhibit, they see colorful animated dots spreading across the display (Fig. 1, top). The dots emerge from the bottom of the screen and repeatedly "produce" new lines of dots that steadily "grow" upward. Each dot appears to emerge from a dot in the previous group, to which it stays connected (Fig. 3, bottom).

As visitors observe the emerging pattern, virtual "instructional" hands appear on the screen (Fig. 4) encouraging visitors to put their hands or arms somewhere on the surface (Fig. 1, bottom). As visitors' hands touch the table they split a single column into two—creating two independent groups of growing dots (Fig. 5). As long as groups of dots remain separated, color patterns on each side of the hand start to change. If hands are removed prematurely, both columns of dots merge back into a single population, eventually converging to a uniform color pattern. If the hands remain in place for a time, the color patterns diverge, and the two independent columns will no longer merge, even after the hand are released. This process can be repeated until all columns have reached the top of the screen.

After each simulation run, visitors are presented with a "Tree" button. When the button is pressed, the pattern of dots merge into a solid area (Fig. 6), which then morphs into a phylogenetic tree (Fig. 1, middle). Visitors can then switch back and forth between the "population" view and the "tree" view. Visitors are also presented with expandable information bubbles (Fig. 7) that explain the exhibit visualization (e.g. "*What's going on?*", "*What are the colors?*").

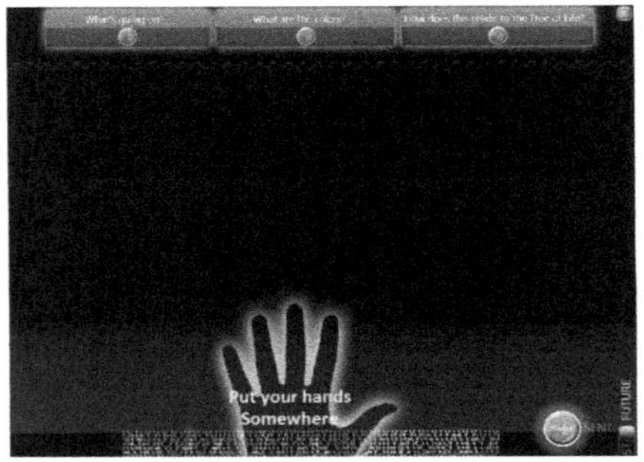

Figure 4. An "instructional" hand (bottom) encourages visitors to place their hands or arms on the surface to split the population.

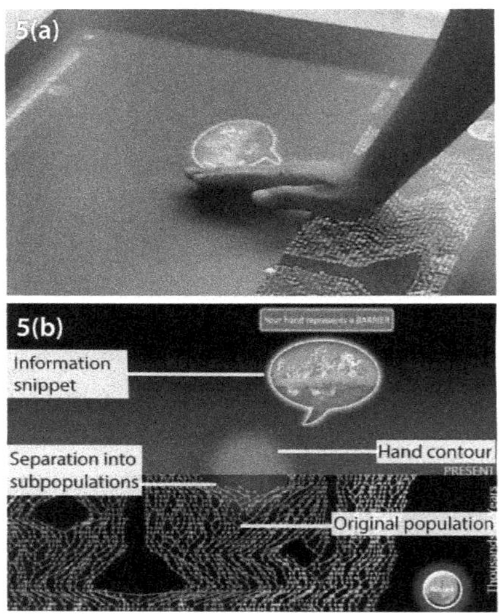

Figure 5. Interaction design: People put hands or arms on the surface (a) and the recognized contour separates population into subpopulations (b).

Visualization
The FloTree uses visual representations to illustrate key evolutionary concepts. As indicated in Figure 3 and Table 1, in the population view, the small dots represent individual organisms and their colors indicate traits passed down from generation to generation. Dots in a single horizontal line represent a generation. Dots in different generations are connected by vertical lines, which help visitors track filial relationships. This also makes it possible for visitors to track a color to its origin. When populations of organisms are separated by geographic and/or reproductive barriers, the colors slowly change. This change results from different environmental pressures. In response to these pressures, organisms with certain traits have a higher probability of producing more offspring, effectively changing the color distribution—and thus the distribution of traits—in a sub-population. When sufficient differences between sub-populations have accumulated, so that interbreeding is no longer possible, they can be considered different species.

Interaction Design
The FloTree is a simulation with different outcomes for each run [5]. Because each run is different, users are encouraged to restart the simulation and explore alternative outcomes. The goal is to spark visitors' curiosity and to encourage exploration and active prolonged engagement [3].

Interaction with the FloTree is based on free-form input. Any object that is put down on the surface is detected, and its contours are extracted. The contours then act as "obstacles" for the dots. This free-form input has three advantages. First, it allows multiple people to collaborate (Fig. 1, bottom). Secondly, free-form input encourages creativity. For example, we observed visitors placing their whole arms on the table and using their hands to make shapes. Thirdly, the free-form input creates opportunities for "deep" engagement:

Visual	Biological
Dots	Individual organisms
Colors	Traits
One row of dots	One generation
Dots close to each other	Groups of related individual organisms
All dots	Populations

Table 1. Mapping from visual elements to corresponding biological models.

Visitors can experiment by making barriers with different shapes and sizes. This provides them with the opportunity to see how their interactions affect the outcome (e.g. a larger obstacle is more likely to lead to speciation than a smaller one). In our interactive visualization, the horizontal size of an obstacle represents the physical size of the barrier (e.g. a mountain range vs. a small river), while its vertical size constitutes the duration of an obstacle (short vs. long separation). This maps input to meaningful parameters in the population simulation, allowing visitors to playfully experiment with the way in which different factors affect evolutionary outcome.

Hardware and Implementation
The FloTree runs on a Samsung SUR40 multi-touch tabletop [7]. FloTree was developed using the Windows Presentation Foundation (WPF), Microsoft Surface SDK, and the .NET Framework 3.5. We are currently

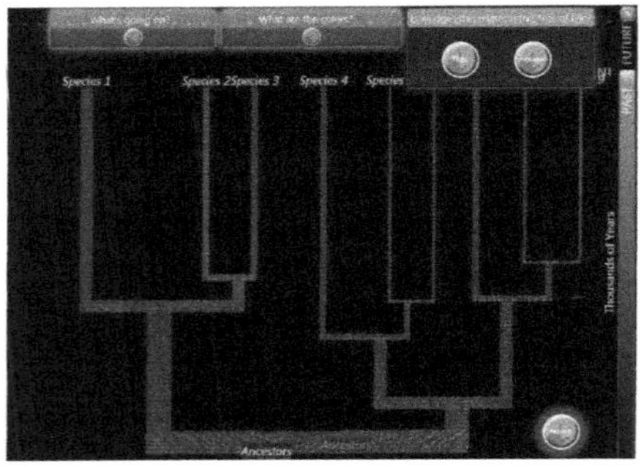

Figure 6. Morph: Intermediate step in the morph from population-level to speciation-level view.

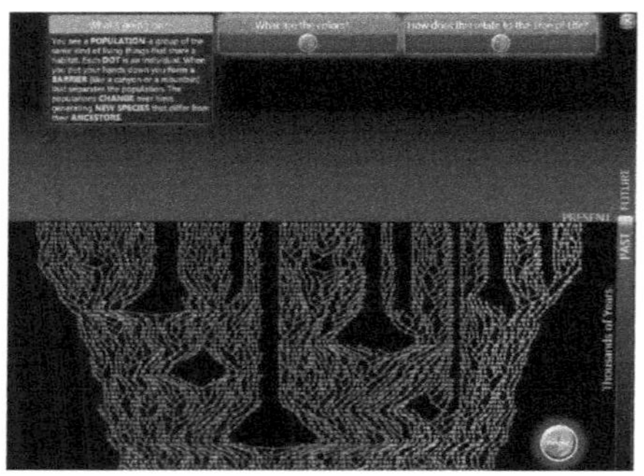

Figure 7. Expandable information bubbles (top) explain the exhibit visualization in easy-to-understand language.

conducting studies that examine how well visitors learn evolutionary concepts via the FloTree exhibit in both the Harvard Museum of Natural History (HMNH) and the Field Museum of Natural History in Chicago (FMNH).

Conclusion

Designed as a platform for collaborative learning, the FloTree combines the high-bandwidth input of today's multi-touch tabletops with a population genetics simulation to let visitors playfully experience the relationship between micro- and macro-evolution. The simulation-based nature of the game, coupled with open-ended free-form input, creates an interaction that invites deeper engagement. The FloTree is part of an exhibit that will soon be disseminated to five museums, with an estimated 4.5 million visitors in the next year.

Acknowledgements

We thank our science advisers Gonzalo Giribet, James Hanken, Hopi E. Hoekstra, and Jonathan Losos. Sebastian Velez provided valuable feedback and discussions throughout the design of the FloTree. Larry Kyrala, Tanja Gesell, Hanspeter Pfister contributed to the design of an earlier version of the population genetics visualization.

This work is part of the "Life on Earth" project (https://lifeonearth.seas.harvard.edu/), which is partially funded by the National Science Foundation (DRL-1010889). Any opinions, findings and conclusions or recommendations expressed in this material are those of the authors and do not necessarily reflect the views of the National Science Foundation.

References

[1] Evans, E. M., Frazier, B., Hazel, A., Kiss, A., Lane, J. D., Spiegel, A., & Diamond, J. (2010, August). Treethinking: do pictorial representations of phylogenetic relationships help or hinder museum visitors' understanding of evolution? In Understanding the tree of life conference. Carnegie Museum of Natural History.

[2] Evans, E.M., Spiegel, A.N., Gram, W., Frazier, B.N., Tare, M., Thompson, S., and Diamond, J. A conceptual guide to natural history museum visitors' understanding of evolution. Journal of *Research in Science Teaching* 47, 3 (2010), 326–353.

[3] Horn, M.S., Leong, Z.A., Block, F., Diamond, J., Evans, E.M., Phillips, B.C., Shen, C.. Of BATs and APEs: Designing an interactive tabletop game for natural history museums. In Proc.CHI'12, ACM Press.

[4] Schneider, B., Strait, M., Muller, L., Elfenbein, S., Shaer, O., Shen, C. (2012). Phylo-Genie: Engaging Students in Collaborative 'Tree- Thinking' through Tabletop Techniques. In Proc. CHI'12, ACM. 3071-3080.

[5] Wilensky, U. & Stroup, W. (1999). Learning through Participatory Simulations: Network-Based Design for Systems Learning in Classrooms Computer Supported Collaborative Learning (CSCL '99). Stanford University: December 12-15, 1999.

[6] Hartl, D., & Clark, A. (2006). Principles of population genetics. Sinauer Associates. Retrieved from http://books.google.com/books?id=SB1vQgAACAAJ

[7] Samsung SUR40 with Microsoft PixelSense http://www.pixelsense.com/

[8] The history of life: looking at the patterns. http://evolution.berkeley.edu/evolibrary/article/evo_03.

SynFlo: An Interactive Installation Introducing Synthetic Biology Concepts

Kimberly Chang
Wellesley College
Wellesley, MA 02481
kchang2@wellesley.edu

Wendy Xu
Wellesley College
Wellesley, MA 02481
wxu2@wellesley.edu

Nicole Francisco
Wellesley College
Wellesley, MA 02481
nfrancis@wellesley.edu

Consuelo Valdes
Wellesley College
Wellesley, MA 02481
cvaldes@wellesley.edu

Robert Kincaid
Agilent Technologies
5301 Stevens Creek Blvd.
Santa Clara, CA 95051
robert_kincaid@agilent.com

Orit Shaer
Wellesley College
Wellesley, MA 02481
oshaer@wellesley.edu

ITS'12, November 11–14, 2012, Cambridge, Massachusetts, USA.
ACM 978-1-4503-1209-7/12/11.

Abstract
SynFlo is an interactive installation that utilizes tangible interaction to help illustrate core concepts of synthetic biology through outreach programs. This playful installation allows users to create useful virtual life forms from standardized genetic components, exploring common synthetic biology concepts and techniques. The installation consists of Sifteo cubes, which are used to modify virtual *E. coli* to serve as environmental biosensors. The modified bacteria can then be deployed into an environment represented by a tabletop computer, where they detect environmental toxins. The goal of this research is to explore ways to develop effective interactive activities for outreach in STEM and to communicate the excitement and constraints of cutting-edge research.

Author Keywords
Tangible user interfaces; Sifteo cubes; Microsoft Surface; E. chromi; synthetic biology

ACM Classification Keywords
H.5.2 [Information Interfaces and Presentation]: User Interfaces.

General Terms
Design, Human Factors.

Introduction
Synthetic biology is an emerging research area at the intersection of science and engineering that enables the

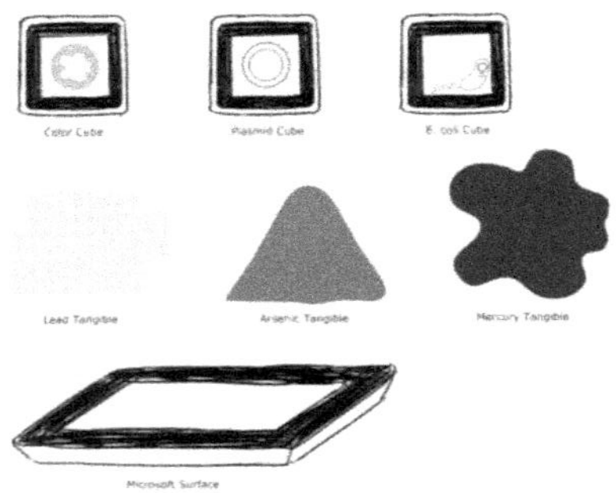

Figure 1: The components of SynFlo

Figure 2: "Contamination" between two *E. coli* cubes

design and construction of new biological systems. The field applies engineering principles such as abstraction and modularity into biological research, treating genetic material as standardized parts, "BioBricks," which can be combined and swapped in a plug-and-play manner before they are inserted into host organisms. The ability to create tailored biological systems can shed light on particular phenomena or solve specific problems. For example, synthetic biology is used in the development of low-cost anti-malarial drugs, in the production of alternative energy or biofuel from bacterial, and in the study of infectious diseases such as tuberculosis [2]. However, considering the ethical and social questions that the field raises, the public and media has eyed the field with concern and slight skepticism. Making synthetic biology more accessible and transparent to the public will allow better understanding of the fields' promises and challenges.

SynFlo is an interactive installation, designed to illustrate core concepts of synthetic biology through a playful tangible interface as well as making the ideas behind synthetic biology more accessible to the general public. SynFlo mirrors actual protocols used in wet labs to manipulate the genome of *E. coli*, the most common model organism in synthetic biology and microbiology. SynFlo consists of triplets of Sifteo cubes, which can be used to modify the genome of virtual *E. coli* to serve as biosensors for environmental toxins. The virtual bacteria can then be deployed into an environment represented by a tabletop computer. In this environment, the *E. coli* can interact with other bacteria and with environmental toxins. The remainder of this paper discusses the design, implementation, and preliminary evaluation of SynFlo in informal science learning settings.

Related Work

Numerous artists have embraced synthetic biology as a theme, tool, and an inspiration. Oron Catts and Ionat Zurr created their sculptures *Semi-living Worry Dolls,* consisting of cells grown on a scaffolding of degradable polymers, as an exploration of the relationship between the living and the non-living [3]. Tuur van Balen designed bacteria that turn pigeon feces into window soap as a commentary on the ethical issues surrounding synthetic biology [1]. However, while these projects have attempted to emphasize the societal and ethical questions raised by the field, we seek to communicate both the opportunities and the challenges of synthetic biology while making its methods more transparent to non-scientists. The visual and interactive components of SynFlo were inspired by several interactive games. Thatgamecompany's *flOw* and Japan Studio's *LocoRoco* informed the simple aesthetics and engaging quality that aimed for [10] [6]. Maxis's *Spore* was also a game that we looked at for the creature creation aspect of SynFlo [8]. The bright colors of the installation were inspired by Brainbow, Harvard's research project on fluorescent neurons [7], and the block interaction was inspired by Zigelbaum and Coelho's *Six-Forty by Four-Eighty* [4].

Design and Concept

SynFlo's design is a result of close collaboration with synthetic biologists. Our design goal for SynFlo is to help illustrate core concepts of synthetic biology in outreach programs. We focus on three core concepts including 1) *abstraction*, the representation of genetic materials with known functionality as standard biological parts with common interfaces, called BioBricks; 2) *modularity*, the construction of biological systems composed of reusable mix-and-match BioBricks; and 3) *protocols*, the use of predefined standardize laboratory procedures to ensure

Figure 3: Clicking through the BioBrick library

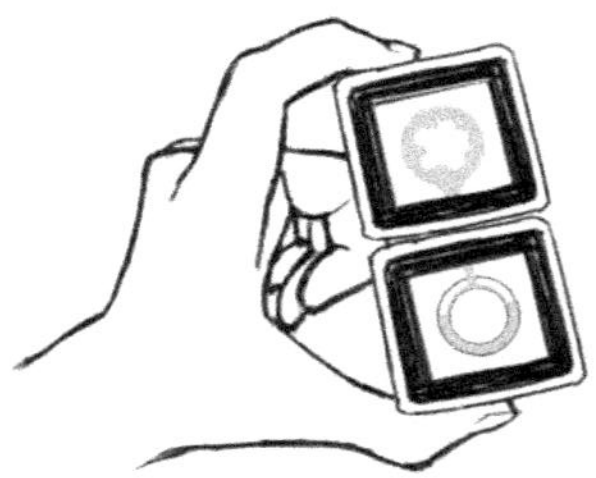

Figure 4: Shaking the DNA material into the plasmid cube

safety and successful replication of results by others. We also aim to provoke further inquiry about the everyday implications of synthetic biology while experiencing some of its excitement and constraints.

To accomplish these goals, SynFlo draws upon a well-known synthetic biology experiment called E. chromi [5], in which genetically engineered *E. coli* bacteria act as biosensors, indicating the presence of certain environmental toxins. This experiment has three basic procedural tasks: 1) Combining biological parts to create a genetic element capable of producing a particular color in response to the presence of a particular toxin; 2) Inserting the selected BioBrick into a plasmid, a circular DNA strand that replicates independently from chromosomal DNA; 3) infusing *E. coli* bacteria with the engineered plasmids; and 4) deploying the modified bacteria into a testing environment.

SynFlo utilizes tangible and embodied interactions to allow users to experience an interactive and playful simulation of the E. chromi experimental process. The installation consists of triplets of Sifteo cubes, a tabletop computer (Microsoft Surface SUR40), and tangible objects that represent environmental toxins (see Figure 1). Each triplet of Sifteo cubes consists of a BioBrick cube, a plasmid cube, and an *E. coli* bacterial cell. We chose to use Sifteo cubes [9] to implement the interaction with BioBricks because Sifteo Cubes support a variety of gestures and actions including moving, shaking, flipping, rotating, and neighboring. These allow us to mimic physical aspects of laboratory work. Also, the form factor of the cubes communicates the idea that BioBricks are modular. We represent the testing environment using a tabletop computer. Multiple users can deploy modified *E. coli* into the surface and interact with the deployed bacteria through touch. In addition, users can add tangibles that represent different environmental toxins and observe their effects on the existing bacteria. Following, we describe interaction with SynFlo.

When two *E. coli* cubes are placed next to each other, the *E. coli* interact by "contaminating" the neighboring cube (see Figure 2). Then, following SynFlo experimental protocol users choose a BioBrick from a library of biological parts that encode for a particular color the *E. coli* turns when detecting a certain toxin. The user presses the Sifteo cube screen to scroll through a library of three colors and toxin shapes (see Figure 3). Similar to the biologists preforming the E. chromi experiment, users add the BioBrick to a plasmid and mix by vortexing: the BioBrick cube is placed on top of the plasmid, then the two are shaken together while the color drips into the plasmid (see Figure 4). Then, just as a biologist would pipette, mix, and eject the newly-infused plasmid onto the waiting biological vessel, SynFlo allows the user to place the now colored plasmid cube next to the awaiting *E. coli* cube and then flip the plasmid cube as if pouring or pipetting into the *E. coli*.

Finally, users can deploy their *E. coli* to the testing environment by placing the *E. coli* cube on the Microsoft Surface and flipping the cube (see Figure 5). Users can then interact with the *E. coli* by adding tangibles to the surface that represent different environmental toxins (see Figure 6); the modified *E. coli* sensitive to particular toxins will respond by changing their color. Touching the *E. coli* results in a color change (see Figure 7).

Figure 5: Flipping the *E. coli* cube on the Surface

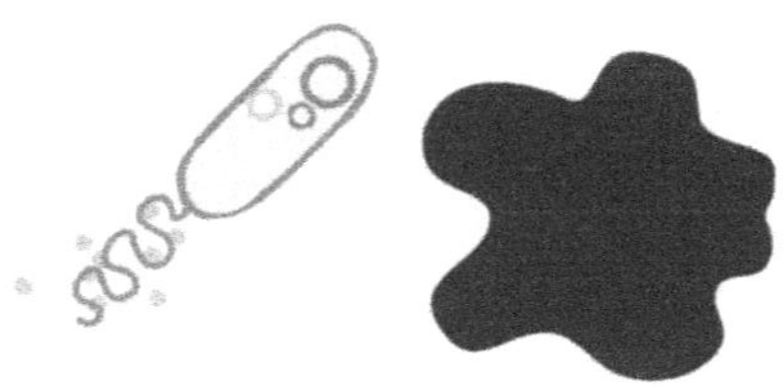

Figure 6: Placing a tangible on the Surface

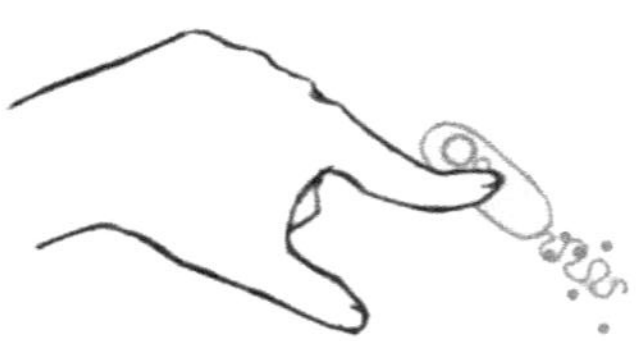

Figure 7: Touching the *E. coli* on the Surface

Implementation

SynFlo uses Sifteo cubes [9], a commercially available, clickable 1.5 inch block micro-computers that can interact with each other. Sifteo cubes communicate with a computer via proprietary 2.4GHz radio protocol. The current prototype of SynFlo supports up to 6 Sifteo cubes. The interaction and animation is programmed using the Sifteo SDK written in C#. The tabletop application is implemented on the Microsoft Surface SUR40 device using the Microsoft Surface 2.0 SDK. The communication between the Sifteo cubes and the SUR40 is implemented using Client-Server communication between the Surface and Sifteo applications.

Evaluation

We conducted preliminary user studies with 18 high-school students (10 female) participating in a science outreach program. The students were given a 10-minute presentation explaining basic synthetic biology concepts, then interacted with SynFlo for about 20 minutes. The users picked up the interaction quickly and found the Sifteo and tabletop interaction especially engaging. While in the first few minutes the users were focused on experimenting with the technology, later in the session they also reflected on the connection between SynFlo and the synthetic biology concepts discussed.

Conclusion and Future Work

We present SynFlo, an interactive installation that utilizes tangible interaction to help illustrate core concepts of synthetic biology in outreach programs. We plan to further refine SynFlo to more accurately portray the scientific protocol used in E. chromi. We also plan to evaluate the effectiveness of SynFlo in informal science learning settings.

Acknowledgments

We would like to thank David Olsen from Wellesley College, Traci Haddock and the Boston University iGEM team. This work is partially funded by the NSF grant no. IIS-1149530.

References

[1] Balen, T.V. (2010). *Pigeon D'Or*. Retrieved from http://www.biofaction.com/synth-ethic/#tuur-van-balen

[2] Carlson, R.H. (2010) Biology is Technology, Harvard University Press.

[3] Catts, O. and Zurr, I. (2000). *Semi-living Worry Dolls* [Sculpture]. Retrieved from http://www.biofaction.com/synth-ethic/#tissue-culture-and-art-oron-catts-ionat-zurr

[4] Coelho, M., Zigelbaum, J., and Kopin, J. (2011). *Six-Forty by Four-Eighty: The Post-Industrial Design of Computational Materials.* In Proc.of TEI '11.

[5] Davies, M., et al. (2009). *E. chromi Cambridge*. Retrieved from http://2009.igem.org/Team:Cambridge

[6] Japan Studio. (2006). *LocoRoco* [PlayStation Portable game]. Tokyo, Japan: Sony Computer Entertainment.

[7] Livet, J., et al. (2007). *Transgenic strategies for combinatorial expression of fluorescent proteins in the nervous system.* Nature, 450, 56-62.

[8] Maxis. (2008). *Spore* [PC game]. Redwood City, CA: Electronic Arts.

[9] Sifteo, Inc. https://www.sifteo.com/

[10] Thatgamecompany. (2007). *flOw* [PlayStation 3 game]. Foster City, CA: Sony Computer Entertainment.

MoClo Planner: Supporting Innovation in Bio-Design through Multi-touch Interaction

Sirui Liu
Wellesley College
sliu@wellesley.edu

Kara Lu
Wellesley College
klu2@wellesley.edu

Nahum Seifeselassie
Massachusetts Institute of Technology
nahumseife@gmail.com

Casey Grote
Wellesley College
cgrote@wellesley.edu

Nicole Francisco
Wellesley College
nfrancis@wellesley.edu

Veronica Lin
Wellesley College
vlin@wellesley.edu

Linda Ding
Wellesley College
lding@wellesley.edu

Consuelo Valdes
Wellesley College
cvaldes@wellesley.edu

Robert Kincaid
Agilent Technologies
robert_kincaid@agilent.com

Orit Shaer
Wellesley College
oshaer@wellesley.edu

ITS'12, November 11–14, 2012, Cambridge, Massachusetts, USA.
ACM 978-1-4503-1209-7/12/11.

Abstract
Synthetic biology is an emerging field that promises to revolutionize biotechnology through the design and construction of new biological constructs useful for medicine, agriculture, and industry. Software tools for this field are currently immature. Our research investigates how interactive tabletops and surfaces could be utilized to enhance innovation in biological design. Here, we present the MoClo Planner, a multi-touch interface, which supports the design and construction of complex biological constructs. MoClo planner was developed in close collaboration with domain scientists to simplify the design stage of a cutting-edge laboratory method.

Author Keywords
Interactive surfaces, multi-touch interaction, molecular cloning, synthetic biology.

ACM Classification Keywords
H.5.2 [Information Interfaces and Presentation]: User Interfaces.

Introduction
The emerging research field of synthetic biology offers the promise to transform biotechnology through the

Figure 1: The Primer Designer used to actualize genetic constructs, can be accessed from Levels 0-2.

design and construction of novel biological systems useful for medicine, agriculture and industry [5].

The field applies engineering principles such as abstraction and modularity into biological research, treating genetic elements as standardized biological parts, which can be combined and swapped in a plug-and-play manner before they are inserted into host organisms. However, a limiting factor in synthetic biology research is the ability of current methods to assemble complex DNA molecules encoding multiple genetic elements [9].

Golden Gate Modular Cloning (MoClo) [9] is a novel laboratory method that allows the efficient creation of multi-gene constructs from a library of biological parts. Using this method, biological parts are permuted and joined together in a tiered fashion to create new synthetic biology constructs, which are called BioBricks. While the MoClo method reduces the number of laboratory steps required for the assembly of multi-gene constructs, it requires careful design and planning. Planning for the MoClo method includes: browsing a library over 2200 biological parts; selecting biological parts based on their function, genetic sequence, and other biological characteristics; computing possible permutations of parts in predefined arrangements; and designing primers and fusion recognition sites (a task that involves the identification and testing of short sequences of DNA marking the start and end of a particular region of DNA, which are necessary for amplifying and assembling DNA). Currently, there is no computational support for the MoClo design process. Thus, biologists use a combination of existing web-based databases and tools as well as spreadsheets in order to retrieve, store, synthesize, and organize the information required for MoClo design. This process is time consuming, error-prone, and is rarely understandable for novices in the field (e.g. student researchers).

The MoClo Planner application that we present in this paper, utilizes multi-touch interaction to simplify the design process of complex biological constructs. The application provides an interactive visualization of the MoClo process; facilitates an integrated yet flexible workflow; and utilizes direct and spatial interaction to give users more control over the design process. The application also supports co-located collaboration through multiple touch points. The goal of this research is to investigate how interactive tabletops and surfaces could be utilized to enhance innovation in biological research. Following, we describe the design, implementation, and preliminary evaluation of MoClo Planner. We begin with related work.

Related Work

Existing computational tools do not provide comprehensive support for biological design. Biologists often use a variety of existing web-based and commercial bioinformatics tools in order to retrieve, compare, and study genetic elements. Several studies indicate that current web-based bioinformatics tools show severe limitations in supporting users to gain deep insights [6]. A number of projects have been undertaken by the synthetic biology community to support data management and storage (e.g. MIT Registry of Standard Biological Parts), and facilitate the development of applications for the synthetic biology domain [Xia et al. 2011]. The Synthetic Biology Open Language [2011] and Eugene [2] are domain specific languages for synthetic biology. In addition, several research prototypes were developed to support the design of biological systems including GenoCAD [3] and Tinkercell [4]. However,

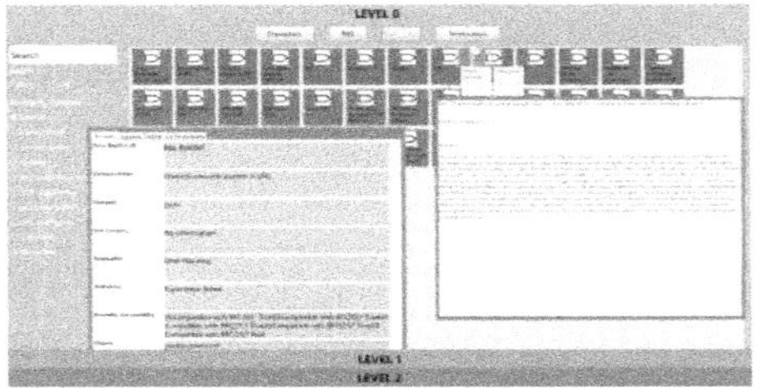

Figure 2: Level 0 design of the MoClo Planner

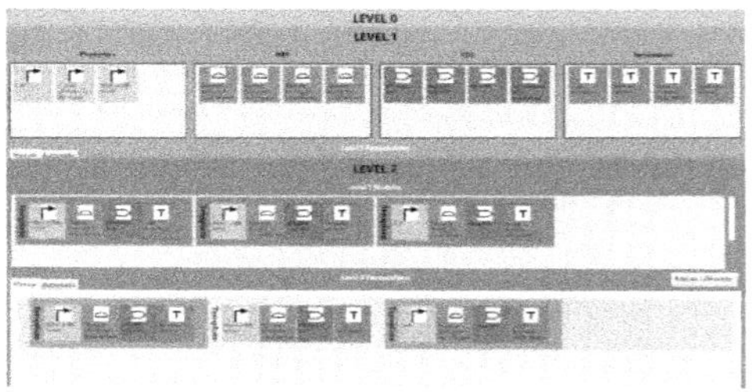

Figure 3: Level 1 and Level 2 of the MoClo Planner

these prototypes are limited in their functionality and compatibility with other community efforts such as the MIT Registry of Standard Biological Parts and SBOL.

Design Process and Goals

MoClo Planner is the result of a participatory design process in which we partnered with two groups of investigators and students from Boston University and MIT, who conduct research in synthetic biology. In collaboration with our design partners we defined the following design goals for MoClo Planner: 1) Lower the barriers for MoClo design, making it available for the growing community of novice synthetic biology researchers [8]; 2) Facilitate an integrated and flexible workflow; 3) Provide users with control over the design process while eliminating errors; and 4) Fostering collaborative problem solving.

MoClo Planner

The current prototype of MoClo Planner is implemented using a multi-touch vertical surface (SUR40). Our decision to use a vertical interactive surface was informed by current work practices of our users (side-by-side work on the white board or a shared screen), and by recent theories in the cognitive sciences, such as embodied cognition, that illustrates the importance of the body, external artifacts, and the environment in reasoning and learning [1].

MoClo planner organizes the design process using three "shutters"; each shutter provides a workspace corresponding to a particular level of the MoClo design process: In Level 0, the application allows users to browse a collection of biological parts (curated by the MIT Registry of Biological Parts). Upon demand (indicated by touch) the application generates a data sheet characterizing the part's behavior, retrieving its genomic sequences, and displaying PubMed and iGEM abstracts related to that part drawing information in real time from the Registry of Biological Parts. Users can select parts of interest and save them by dragging them into the Level 1 shutter. Figure 2 shows the Level 0 shutter.

Parts that were saved by the users into Level 1, are automatically organized according to their biological function. In Level 1, users design transcription units (i.e. biological constructs that contain a single gene) from the basic parts selected in Level 0. The design of transcription units must satisfy several constraints that are expressed to users in the form of a template. The application enables users to automatically or manually create constraint-based permutations of the selected parts so that all possible transcription units can be considered. Users can then select those transcription units of interest and drag them to level 2. Figure 3 shows the transcription units created in Level 1 and saved to Level 2.

Finally, in Level 2 users can create multi-gene constructs that consist of series of transcription units. Again, the application enables users to automatically or manually create constraint-based permutations of selected transcription units so that all possible constructs can be considered. Figure 3 illustrates the permutations created in Level 2.

On each of the levels, users can launch the built-in primer designer, which allows users to convert abstract parts or constructs into concrete genetic elements by generating primers and protocols to facilitate construct assembly in the lab. Unlike many existing primer design applications, our primer designer provides users with full control, allowing them to customize primer sequences and to select computational tests. Figure 1 shows a user interacting with the primer designer.

In order to facilitate an integrated and flexible workflow, the application allows users to move back and forward between levels, keeping one or multiple shutters open at any given time, and dragging elements between shutters. Leveraging this fluid interaction, users can iterate on their design, go back to select additional parts, explore information, or trace previous design decisions.

Implementation

The MoClo planner is implemented on the Microsoft Surface SUR40 device using MS SDK 2.0 and C#. Information is drawn from the MIT Registry of Biological Parts, PubMed, and the iGEM archive [8]. Eugene is used for testing and validating permutations.

Evaluation

24 undergraduate Biology and Biological Engineering student researchers from Wellesley College, Boston University, and MIT participated in our evaluation process, using MoClo Planner to conduct an inquiry-based modular cloning task in pairs. Preliminary analysis of the quantitative and qualitative data collected indicates that users found the multi-touch interaction intuitive and the process visualization clear. Further user suggestions provide inspiration for the next iterations for our designs.

Conclusion

We presented MoClo Planner, a multi-touch interface for supporting the design of complex and useful biological constructs. We plan to iterate on the design of MoClo Planner and evaluate its use and impact by deploying it in a synthetic biology research lab. Our goal is to understand how interactive tabletop and surfaces can support innovation in biological design.

Acknowledgements

We would like to thank Traci Haddock, Swapnil Bhatia, the Boston University and MIT iGEM teams. This work is partially funded by the NSF grant no. IIS-1149530.

References

[1] Anderson, M. L. (2003). Embodied cognition: A field guide. Artificial Intelligence, 149: 91-130

[2] Bilitchenko, L., et al. (2011). Eugene- A Domain Specific Language for Specifiying and Constraining Synthetic Biological Parts, Devices, and Systems. PLoS One, 6(4).

[3] Cai Y, Wilson ML, Peccoud JL. (2010) GenoCAD for IGEM: a grammatical approach to the design of standard-compliant constructs. Nucl. Acids Res., 38 (8).

[4] Chandran D, Bergmann FT, Sauro HM. (2009). TinkerCell: modular CAD tool for synthetic biology. Journal of Biological Engineering, 3:19.

[5] Carlson, R.H. (2010). Biology is Technology, Harvard University Press.

[6] Bolchini,D.,et al. (2009). Better bioinformatics through usability analysis, Bioinformatics, 25(3), 406-12.

[7] Mirel, B. (2005). Supporting cognition in systems biology implications, J Biomed Discov Collab, 27(2).

[8] International Genetically Engineered Machine Foundation: http://igem.org/About

[9] Weber E, Engler C, Gruetzner R, Werner S, Marillonnet S (2011). A Modular Cloning System for Standardized Assembly of Multigene Constructs. PLoS ONE 6(2): e16765. doi:10.1371/journal.pone.0016765

Fluid Surface: Interactive Water Surface Display for Viewing Information in a Bathroom

Figure1. Fluid surface

Yoichi Takahashi
Graduate School of Information Systems,
University of Electro-Communications
1-5-1, Chofugaoka, Chofu, Tokyo 182-8585, JAPAN
Yo---1---yo@vogue.is.uec.ac.jp

Yasushi Matoba
Graduate School of Information Systems,
University of Electro-Communications
1-5-1, Chofugaoka, Chofu, Tokyo 182-8585, JAPAN
matoba@vogue.is.uec.ac.jp

Hideki Koike
Graduate School of Information Systems,
University of Electro-Communications
1-5-1, Chofugaoka, Chofu, Tokyo 182-8585, JAPAN
koike@is.uec.ac.jp

ITS'12, November 11–14, 2012, Cambridge, Massachusetts, USA.
ACM 978-1-4503-1209-7/12/11.

Abstract
Information is becoming accessible everywhere in everyday life due of the spread of smart phones and portable personal computers; however are very few methods in accessing contents in a bathing environment. Sometimes smart phones can be carried into a bathroom but it is unnatural to be holding a device at during bathing, so a suitable technique for information browsing in a bathing environment is required. We propose an interactive water surface display system, which uses image-recognition techniques. By using water, the system can perform an intuitive interaction peculiar to water such as poking a finger up from under the water surface, stroking the water surface and scooping up water. In this paper, we discuss interaction design in a bathroom, describing an implementation of our system and its applications.

Author Keywords
Bathtub; fluid interaction; gesture recognition; interactive surface; water surface display

ACM Classification Keywords
H.5.2. Information interfaces and presentation (e.g., HCI): Graphical user interfaces.

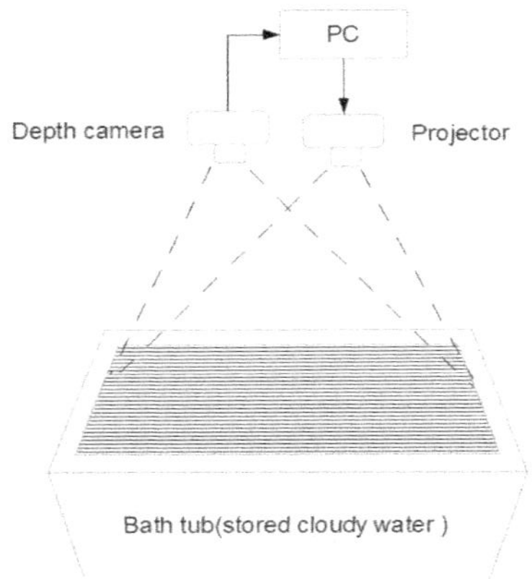

Figure2. System configuration

Figure3. Usage scenario

Introduction

The accessibility of data and contents has changed a great deal with the development of portable computers and hand held devices; however, in a bathing environment it is still scarce. In Japan, idling in a hot water bath has become a part of everyday life, and bathing has long been a very common method for health maintenance and relaxation. Therefore, the needs for the entertainment or information at the time of bathing is growing; sometimes a TV set is installed in a bathroom or a smart phone is carried into a bathroom to view information. Holding a remote control or a device at the time of bathing is very unnatural, so information browsing technique of having been suitable for bathing environment is required. Thus we proposed interactive water surface display system. This system can interact with information without any markers and devices. We specifically focus on input and output techniques which use the characteristics of water. In related research, there are some systems that use water as a display, but the projection of images onto the water surface is not common neither is interaction with the water's surface [1]. Hirai proposed Bathtub touch user-interface [2]. But, this system is using a frame of bathtub, and is not projecting on to the water surface. In addition, some systems suggests flexible surfaces like sand, which is a radical alternative to conventional rigid screens and the interaction with this suggestion uses the physical features of the surface material [3]. Following this approach, the physical feature of water was also considered for the interaction of our system.

System

System configuration of our system is shown in figure 2. Hardware construction of our system is consists of a Microsoft Kinect depth camera for finger recognition, a projector for image projection and PC for processing. We use cloudy water made from bath salts for the water screen. It is reasonable to consider the cloudiness of water in a bathing situation from soaps, etc. Given the expectations of a standard bathing environment, the surface of the bath is wide and allowed for a large screen for information presentation. The bathroom lighting should also have sufficient lighting for visibility. Usage scenario is shown in figure 3.

Interaction

In this section, we propose the intuitive interaction technique and information display techniques that can be used during bathing. A feature of this system is the input using the unique characteristics of fluids. We suggest three gestures which use features of water, such as poking finger out from water surface, stroking water surface and scooping up water. A comparison of these gestures and their mappings with traditional input interfaces can be shown in Table 1. In our system, pointing gestures can be poking a finger from under the water surface, scrolling gestures from making a stroke water surface and dragging by scooping up water. Details of each input technique are given below.

· Poking a finger from under the surface

Although the input in a legit touch display system is a touch input from the upper part of a display surface, during bathing, it is possible to use gestures from semi-submerged hands under the surface. Using this method, single touch gestures as well as multi-touch gestures with two or more fingers can be detected much like conventional touch screens through interactions unique to water, such as submerging fingers underwater, etc. Since it is common to move hands in and out of water

Figure6. Example of top menu

Figure7. Example of movie playback mode

Application

We created a multimedia viewer as interactive application using our system. The appearance of application is shown in a figure 6 and figure 7. This application consists of a top menu and a viewer/playback mode. In the top menu, both videos and image stills appear floating on the water via the fluid simulation effect. User can interact with media files being previewed in this mode using the gestures mentioned in the previous section: poking will move the position of the displayed information, pinching (multi-touch) can be used to zoom and a three-finger submerge will switch modes. In addition to these interactions, stroking gestures will create ripples in the information via the fluid simulation and scooping can be used to select the target information. Moreover, scooping the information into various locations such as shared folders (Dropbox) is also possible. In the viewer mode, the user can watch movies and images selected in the top menu full-screen and in playback mode the user can control the movie sequence by stroking the water surface. Since the slider moves with time across the water, stroking this slider to move it along can be considered natural. Playback, pause, volume control and back can be performed using icons using finger interactions. When viewing image stills, stroking gestures are used to scroll the image; icons are available for finger interactions to return back to the top menu.

Conclusions

In this research, we proposed interactive water surface display system for intuitive information browsing during bathing - the result was a multimedia viewer a top of a cloudy water surface. In this application example, the information displayed was prepared beforehand. We would like to expand this by connecting the application with media available online such as YouTube and Twitter to be presented on the water's surface - this allows the user to be connected, even while bathing. Another area of development is the accuracy of the system, specifically in finger recognition, when the user has erratic movements within water, which is typical during bathing.

References

[1] M. R. Mine, Dustin Barnard, B. Yang, D. Baker. Thermal Interactive Media. ACM SIGGRAPH 2011 Emerging Technologies, Article No. 18, Vancouver, Canada, 2011.

[2]Y. Sakakibara, S. Hirai. TubTouch: Bathtub touch user-interface toward curved surfaces and unaffected by water. In Japanese.

[3]B. Piper, C. Ratti, and H. Ishii. Illuminating clay: a 3-d tangible interface for landscape analysis. Proc. of CHI'02, pages 355–362, New York, NY, USA, 2002. ACM.

[4] The Mega Super Awesome Visuals Company, Available at: http://www.msavisuals.com. Accessed August 5, 2012.

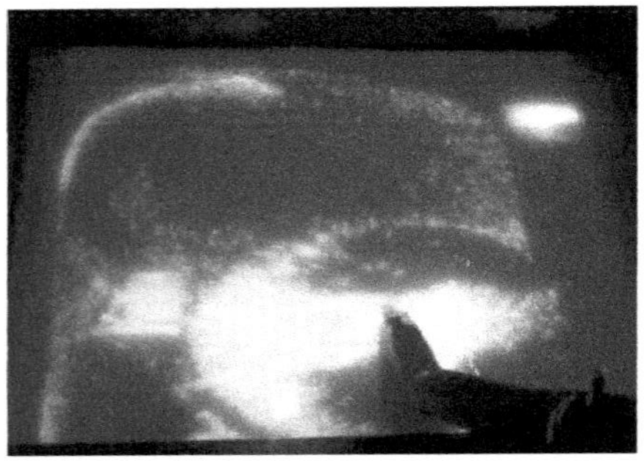

Figure4. Fluid simulation

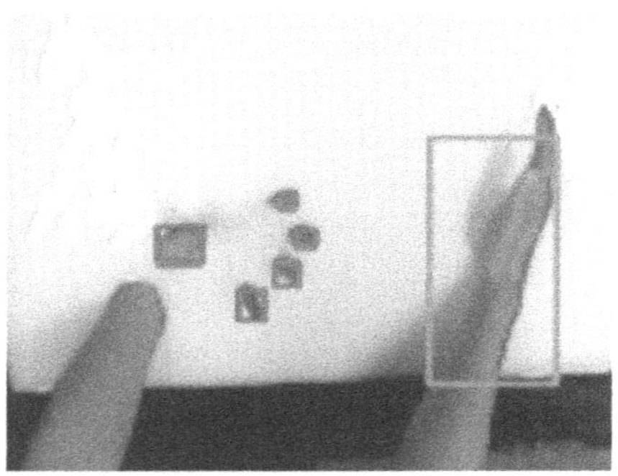

Figure5. Recognition of fingertips and hand

during bathing, it can be assumed that poking one's fingers out from the water's surface, which uses very few movements, will give a very simple input method to the users. Furthermore, since the inputs (and outputs) will follow the user's finger positions it is easy on the human cognition.

· Stroking the water's surface

Using one's hand to stroke water in this context is a natural movement, which can also be used for both expression and input - we suggest using this interaction for scrolling information. By adopting this method, an intuitive input interaction can be obtained.

· Scooping up water

Since water is a physical object, the tactile feeling that comes with holding a real object and the visual effect make the user feel like they are holding information in their hand. It can be thought that the operations like scooping up water can be used for choosing and moving information projected on the water surface that also makes good use of the characteristics of water. The 'drag' metaphor is a perfect interaction equivalent for the moving of information.

Table1. Comparison of proposal gesture and traditional input interface

	PC	Touch pad	Our system
Pointing	Click	Touch	Finger poking
Scroll	Move a mouse wheel	Swipe	Stroking water
Drag	Click and move	Touch and move	Scooping up water

Display using Fluid Simulation

Modification of the projection image is also applied before the projection. In this system, we apply a fluid simulation to the information to 'warp' the image such that it appears to be floating on water. An example of a fluid simulation is shown in figure 4. We use ofxMSAFluid library for a fluid simulation [4]. The reason for this is that when interaction is applied to the water's surface, the surface shape changes dynamically, thus making the information move in a similar fashion will bring about a more 'natural' impact.

Implementation

An example of sample detection of fingertip and hand recognition (of two of the three interaction metaphors) is shown in Figure 5. Using color recognition with a common RGB camera tends to be very sensitive to illumination change, and recognition with markers (IR) require some type of attachment, which, in this context is very difficult. To solve this, we use a depth camera which is resilient to illumination change as well does not require wearable markers. The use of cloudy water allows the depth sensor to be able to measure the water surface, applying background subtraction to this will allow us to recognizing fingertips and hands on the water surface. Because area of detection region in a fingertip is smaller than a hand, we apply simple threshold processing to area of detection region for distinction between fingertips and hands. In addition, there were some cases that noise is recognized as fingertips because user's body moving made water surface change. By using a time-based filter for this noise, it is possible to keep reduce this noise and detect only fingers and hands above the surface.

Flexible Surfaces for Interactive Audio

Jess Rowland
Center for New Music and Audio Technology, Dept. of Music,
1750 Arch St. &
Department of Art Practice, 345 Kroeber Hall, UC Berkeley,
Berkeley, CA 94720 USA
jessrowland@berkeley.edu

Adrian Freed
Director of Research
Center for New Music and Audio Technology, Dept. of Music,
1750 Arch St.
Berkeley, CA 94720 USA
Adrian@cnmat.berkeley.edu

Abstract
We present here flat flexible audio speaker surface arrays, which are transparent, formed to various environments, and allow for user interaction. These speaker arrays provide an alternative to traditional models of sound reproduction, which often involve discreet point source systems and bulky hardware passively received by the user. The surface array system opens up new possibilities for acoustic spaces, creativity, and sound interactivity

ITS'12, November 11–14, 2012, Cambridge, Massachusetts, USA.
ACM 978-1-4503-1209-7/12/11.

Author Keywords
Paper Speakers; Flexible Audio Array; Interactive Electronics

ACM Classification Keywords
J.5 arts and performing

Introduction
Planar speaker technology has been well-known and studied for many years, though such systems are generally built on the same design concerns as traditional loudspeaker, and use bulky magnets (1, 2). However, it is possible to build a sound system from an alternative aesthetic that is applied only on the surface, distributed, stochastic, continuous, multimodal, with potentially unlimited channels and allows for new practical and artistic possibilities. We have developed a flat flexible speaker array system that was motivated by these interests. The surface depth of our flexible array is reduced from centimeters (in traditional planar speakers) to up to less than a millimeter, and the surface for these speaker arrays are potentially unlimited by curvature or folding. Furthermore, our speaker array is both more lightweight and cost-effective than standard loudspeaker designs. These speakers afford creative and practical uses, interactions, and sound spaces that are not available to standard speaker design.

System Design

Our system of flexible audio driver arrays is based on conductive materials suitable for flexion and flat surfaces, such as conductive inks and thin foils. Surface substrates consist of flexible magnetic strips, paper, foams, plastics such as clear acetate, and other lightweight flat surfaces which allow small rare earth magnets of 1 mm depth, or magnetic particles, to be attached or embedded in the material. Our 2-D voice coils are made from machine-cut copper sheets (.001" thick), or by inkjet printing and electroless copper plating onto flat surfaces. Figure 1 shows a typical array system using copper foil adhered to paper.

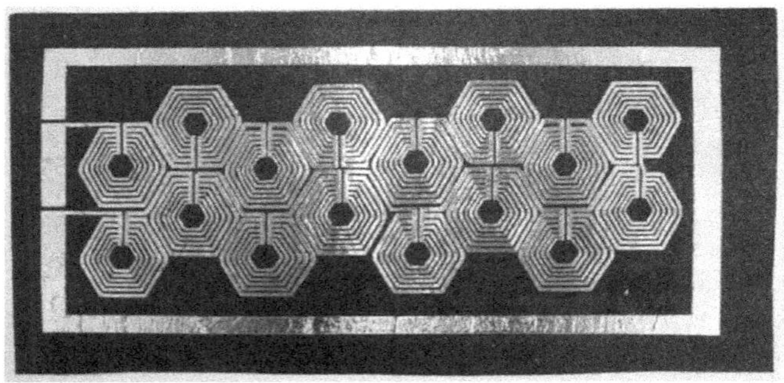

Figure 1. A flat speaker array of copper foil on paper

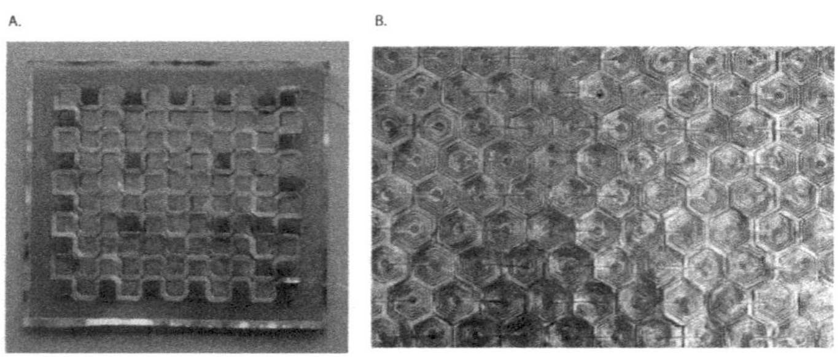

Figure 2. Two flat speakers designs using maximal tiling A. Square speaker. B. Hexagram speaker

The effectiveness of these surface speaker designs relies on maximizing the potential magnetic field and magnetic flux at the level of the surface itself. For maximum efficiency on the surface, the interaction of the electromagnetic field and the permanent magnetic field is strongest at the boundary of the magnet and drops off rapidly thereafter. Therefore, maximizing this boundary across the sheet or surface is optimal for the strongest audio response. We used regular tilings, such as these ones using squares, or hexagrams, to create a dense sheet of copper foil arrays on a clear acetate backing (Figure 2).

Geometric patterns which maximize packing, such as regular tilings and Archmidean tilings, and –at a theoretical ultrafine resolution - space-filling curves (e.g. the Sierpinski Curve), can be utilized to best drive this response.

Applications

In addition to performing the function of a diffuse and distributed audio loudspeaker system, these arrays allow for interactivity through the use of magnetic gloves, and provide for multiple configurations of multichannel input and output.

Figure 3. A Sound Glove with Magnet Attached

By mounting the magnets in gloves worn by the listener, an active experience is created in which gestures control sounds from the speaker array. These "sound gloves" consist of every-day gloves with a permanent neodymium rare-earth magnet attached (Figure 3). Since there is no wiring or electrical system involved in the gloves themselves, users have the full use of movement freedom to explore the arrays. Sound is generated in proportion to the proximity of the user's hand to the array. Since there is no computation, data measurement, or information control involved in this process, the glove provides a natural and unmediated alternative to the same functionality available in wireless proximity sensors generating audio feedback. Arrays can also guide users to interaction points where the electromagnetic field is maximized, opening up possibilities for haptic, tactile, and audio feedback from the glove.

Figure 4. 4-Channel Speaker Utilizing Artistic Possibilities of the Surface

Figure 5. "Uncle Bill". A one-channel flat speaker on flexible magnetic sheeting.

Multiple channels can be incorporated into the system with user interaction. Figure 4 presents a four-channel system that blends elements of sound installation and visual art to produce an interactive sound environment.

Note that the geometry of the electromagnetic field production been intentionally obscured by artistic concerns. With these 2-d speaker arrays, artistic and design possibilities open up for sound art, sound installation, patterning and graphic design, which are not part of standard sound reproduction aesthetics.

It is also possible to explore photographic material as a basis for flat audio circuitry design. Using commonly available rubberized ferrite magnetic sheets with a circuitry design maximized to respond to the vagaries of the anisotropic ferrite deposition on the flexible magnetic sheet, photographic half-tone strategies can be employed on the surface, such as in this speaker/image of William Burroughs (Figure 5).

Discussion

Flexible audio speaker arrays are a useful alternative to standard models of loudspeaker design. Because of their flexibility, ability to form, and wrap, new multimodal and interactive possibilities emerge. Sound surfaces allow for haptic and tactile feedback, as well as auditory feedback, without requiring direct contact.

Audio speaker design has been used as part of auditory aesthetics at least as early as the Ondes Martinot, which utilized multiple speaker outputs to adjust timbre and sound quality (3). More recently, sound artists have explored manipulated traditional speakers as part of their practice (4, 5).

Our current work shows that visual aesthetics and sound art can also be explored on surfaces in a way that 3D speaker design does not allow. DIY paper speaker design has been pioneered by Hannah Perner-Wilson (6) and Marcelo Coehlo (7). In the same spirit as their work, the technology explored here can be designed and implemented by anyone with some basic supplies available at their local art store, rather than requiring industrial machinery.

This rethinking of the fundamental properties of audio circuitry design shows alternative ways to imagine our relation to sound. Explorations of circuitry geometries can open up new possibilities for sound applications to be embedded in real environments and embodied in our interactivity.

Acknowledgements

This work was supported by Pixar and Meyer Sound Labs.

References

[1] Planar electrodynamic electroacoustic transducer, Nakaya; Takao (Hamamatsu, JP), United States Patent: 4337379, June 29 1982

[2] Planar speaker driver, Igor Levitsky Bohlender Graebener Corporation. Patent United States Patent: 8116512, Sep 13, 2007

[3] Orton R & Davies H. "Ondes Martenot". *The New Grove Dictionary of Music and Musicians*, 2nd Ed. Eds. Sadie S and Tyrrell J. London: Macmillan Publishers. 2001.

[4] http://christinesunkim.com/

[5] Pigott J. Vibrations, Volts and Sonic Art: A practice and theory of electromechanical sound.

Proceedings of the International Conference on New Interfaces for Musical Expression, 2011.

[6] http://web.media.mit.edu/~plusea/?p=265

[7] http://web.media.mit.edu/~marcelo/paper/index.html

8D Display: A Relightable Glasses-Free 3D Display

Matthew Hirsch
MIT Media Lab
75 Amherst St.
E14-348
Cambridge, MA 02139 USA
mhirsch@media.mit.edu

Henry Holtzman
MIT Media Lab
75 Amherst St.
E14-348A
Cambridge, MA 02139 USA
author5@anotherco.com

Shahram Izadi
Microsoft Research UK
7 JJ Thompson Avenue
Cambridge, UK CB3 0FB
shahram@microsoft.com

Ramesh Raskar
MIT Media Lab
75 Amherst St.
E14-474G Cambridge, MA
02139
raskar@media.mit.edu

ITS'12, November 11–14, 2012, Cambridge, Massachusetts, USA.
ACM 978-1-4503-1209-7/12/11.

Abstract
Imagine a display that behaves like a window. Glancing through it, viewers perceive a virtual 3D scene with correct parallax, without the need to wear glasses or track the user. Light that passes through the display correctly illuminates the virtual scene. While researchers have considered such displays, or prototyped subsets of these capabilities, we contribute a new, interactive, relightable, glasses-free 3D display. By simultaneously capturing a 4D light field, and displaying a 4D light field, we are able to realistically modulate the incident light on rendered content. We present our optical design, and GPU pipeline. Beyond mimicking the physical appearance of objects under natural lighting, an 8D display can create arbitrary directional illumination patterns and record their interaction with physical objects. Our hardware points the way towards novel 3D interfaces, in which users interact with digital content using light widgets, physical objects, and gesture.

Author Keywords
3D Display, interactive lighting

ACM Classification Keywords
H.5.2 [**INFORMATION INTERFACES AND PRESENTATION (e.g., HCI) - User Interfaces**]: Input Devices and Strategies.; I.3.1 [**COMPUTER**

GRAPHICS - Hardware Architecture]: Input Devices; I.3.3 [**COMPUTER GRAPHICS - Picture/Image Generation**]: Display Algorithms

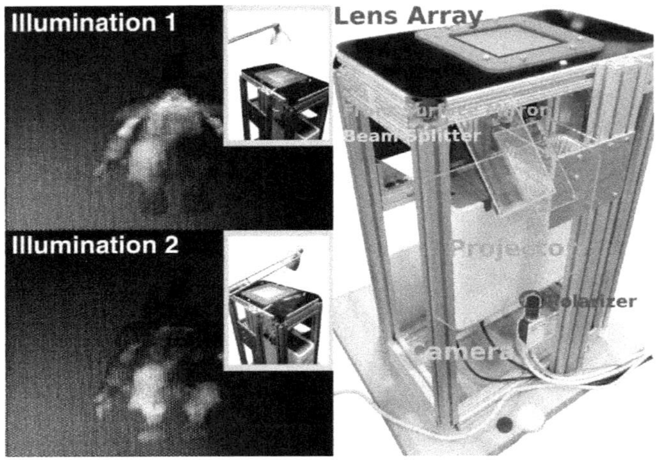

Figure 1: (Left) One view of the output of the 8D Display under two different lighting conditions (Left, Inset). (Right) The hardware composition of the 8D Display prototype.

Introduction

Our 8D display prototype is a general purpose light transducer. With limitations, it is capable of mapping 4D lighting between the physical environment in front of the display and the digital environment behind it. Nayar et al. [6] create a lighting sensitive display, though it cannot accurately map shadows and specularities. BRDF displays can simulate flat surfaces with a particular Bi-Directional Reflectance Distribution Function [4]. 6D displays that demonstrate 4D relighting of 2D images have been shown in both active [3] and passive [2] modes. A 7D display that allows real-time relighting from a single tracked 3D point was recently demonstrated[7]. Our work contributes a real-time 8D display, composed of off-the-shelf optical elements and a new GPU rendering and capture pipeline, to make simultaneous real-time 4D lighting and 4D capture feasible for the first time.

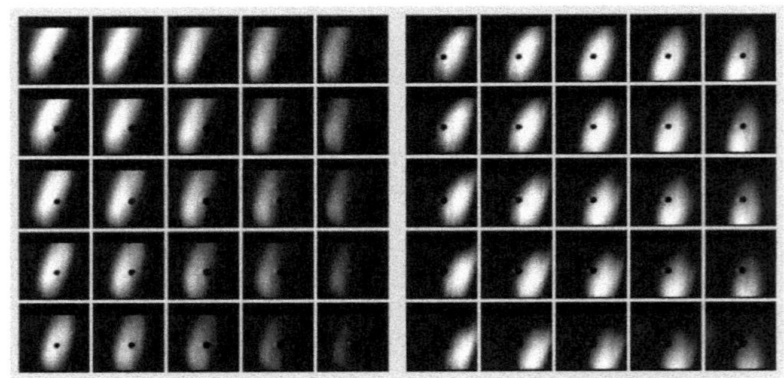

Figure 2: The 4D input light field captured by the 8D Display under two different lighting conditions, shown in Figure 1.

8-Dimensional Rendering

To achieve real-time rendering and decoding of light fields we have developed a new 8D GPU pipeline. We implement diffuse lighting in our prototype, which can be efficiently mapped to projective texture lookups. We implement a simplified version of the rendering equation, neglecting BRDFs.

$$L_o(\mathbf{x}, \omega) = \int_{\Omega} L_i(\mathbf{x}, \omega')(-\omega' \cdot \mathbf{n}) d\omega' \qquad (1)$$

where L_i is the measured incident light field, L_o the displayed light field, and ω' the incoming lighting direction. Though in our model local regions are invariant in outgoing light direction, ω, each light field view is generated with a view matrix corresponding to a virtual skewed orthographic camera viewing the scene from ω. To capture a 4D light field we deinterlace images recorded from the back of the lens array in our GPU pipeline.

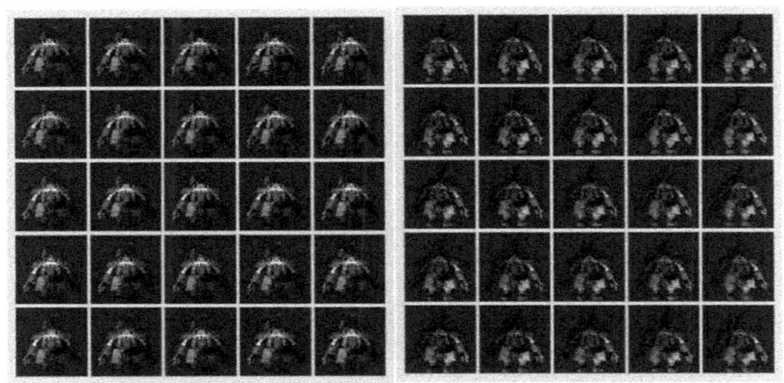

Figure 3: The 4D output light field displayed by the 8D Display under two different lighting conditions, shown in Figure 1.

Optics and Implementation

A hexagonal lens sheet (Fresnel Tech. #360), is placed atop a high-resolution sensor and display panel, composed of a 2048×2048 Point Gray Gazelle camera and 1080P Optoma projector, respectively. We achieve a $150mm$, $325dpi$ display by modifying our projector lens. The camera and projector are focused on a diffuser placed behind the lens sheet. A beam splitter system is used to overlap the projector and camera views (Figure 1). We prevent cross-talk between the camera and projector by multiplexing through crossed linear polarizers. The projector-camera system introduces unwanted calibration complexities, which are addressed in supplementary material. In all cases, an angle limiting material, such as privacy film, can be included in the optical system to prevent angular aliasing.

The light field rendering and decoding necessary for the 8D display is implemented in DirectX 11 HLSL. According to the above 8D rendering equation, for each output light field view, the camera matrix is updated to an appropriate shifted off-axis projection [5], and the scene geometry is rendered and interlaced for the lens sheet. At each rendering stage, each view of the captured and resampled incident light field is used for illumination. This step is accomplished through a projective texture map.

Results and Discussion

The included video demonstrates our display simultaneously showing realistic horizontal and vertical parallax, without tracking or glasses, as well as relighting effects. A 3D model can be illuminated and shadowed by various light sources.

Interaction
Abundant interactive possibilities include: using an off-the-shelf light source as 6DoF input controller, direct manipulation of physical lights to cause relighting of 3D scenes, accurately mimicking surfaces with exotic BRDFs, and applying non-realistic physics to real lighting sources. Though work in the area of HCI using an 8D display is nascent, one near-term area for exploration is in the application of light-emitting widgets with non-physical results. In one example, a low intensity light illuminates an object as described above, while a higher intensity reveals subsurface details of the model such as venous or skeletal structure.

Sensor-In-Pixel LCD Displays
Much of the potential impact of this project is predicated on the existence of Sensor-In-Pixel (SIP) Liquid Crystal Displays (LCDs). In recent years LCD manufacturers have begun to introduce a variety of semiconductor

technologies that combine light sensitive elements into the driver matrix for typical liquid crystal displays [1]. While our real-time prototype was certainly enabled by high-end computer graphics hardware, the optical configuration of the presented camera and projector implementation is somewhat unremarkable. However, in combination with collocated, thin, optical capture and display elements, such as those provided by a SIP LCD, this work suggests a straightforward route to achieving a thin, low-cost, commercially realizable, real-time, 8D display.

Acknowledgments

The authors thank the members of the Computer Mediated Living Group at Microsoft Research, and the Information Ecology and Camera Culture groups at the MIT Media Lab for their helpful discussions.

References

[1] Brown, C., Kato, H., Maeda, K., and Hadwen, B. A continuous-grain silicon-system lcd with optical input function. *Solid-State Circuits, IEEE Journal of 42*, 12 (dec. 2007), 2904 –2912.

[2] Fuchs, M., Raskar, R., Seidel, H.-P., and Lensch, H. P. A. Towards passive 6d reflectance field displays. *ACM Trans. Graph. 27*, 3 (Aug. 2008), 58:1–58:8.

[3] Hirsch, M., Lanman, D., Holtzman, H., and Raskar, R. Bidi screen: a thin, depth-sensing lcd for 3d interaction using light fields. *ACM Trans. Graph. 28*, 5 (Dec. 2009), 159:1–159:9.

[4] Hullin, M. B., Lensch, H. P. A., Raskar, R., Seidel, H.-P., and Ihrke, I. Dynamic display of brdfs. *Computer Graphics Forum 30*, 2 (2011), 475–483.

[5] Lanman, D., and Hirsch, M. Build your own glasses-free 3d display. In *ACM SIGGRAPH 2011 Courses*, ACM (2011), 4.

[6] Nayar, S. K., Belhumeur, P. N., and Boult, T. E. Lighting sensitive display. *ACM Trans. Graph. 23*, 4 (Oct. 2004), 963–979.

[7] Tompkin, J., Muff, S., Jakuschevskij, S., McCann, J., Kautz, J., Alexa, M., and Matusik, W. Interactive light-field painting. *ACM SIGGRAPH Emerging Technologies Demonstration* (Aug. 2012).

Skin Games

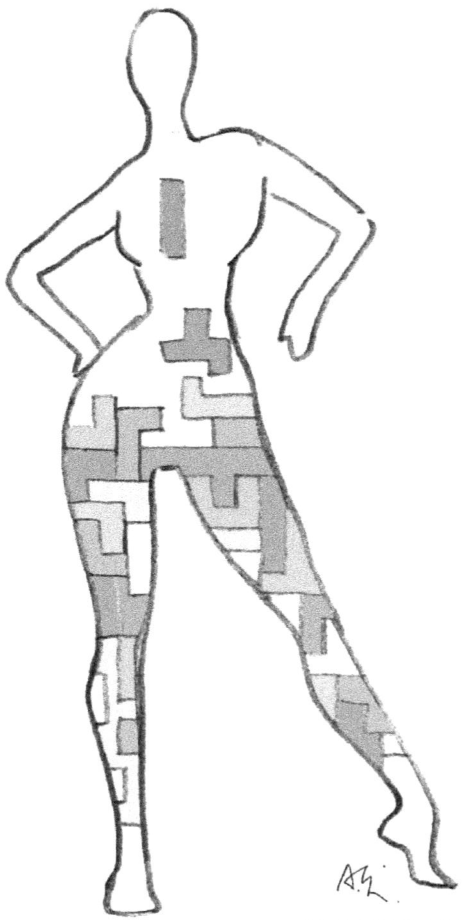

Alvaro Cassinelli
Ishikawa-Oku Laboratory
University of Tokyo
cassinelli.alvaro@gmail.com

Jussi Angesleva
The Berlin University of the Arts
jussi.angesleva@iki.fi

Yoshihiro Watanabe
Ishikawa-Oku Laboratory
University of Tokyo
Yoshihiro_Watanabe@ipc.i.u-tokyo.ac.jp

Gonzalo Frasca
Powerful Robot Games
frasca@powerfulrobot.com

Masatoshi Ishikawa
Ishikawa-Oku Laboratory
University of Tokyo
Masatoshi_Ishikawa@ipc.i.u-tokyo.ac.jp

ITS'12, Nov. 11–14, 2012, Cambridge, Massachusetts, USA.
ACM 978-1-4503-1209-7/12/11.

Abstract

Recent developments in computer vision hardware have popularized the use of (free hand) gestures as well as full body posture as a form of input control in commercial gaming applications. However, the computer screen remains the place where the eyes must be placed at all times. Freeing graphic output from that rectangular cage is a hot topic in Spatial Augmented Reality (SAR). Using static or dynamic projection mapping and 'smart projectors' [11], it is possible to recruit any surface in the surrounding for displaying the game's graphics [17, 18]. The present work introduces an original interaction paradigm building on kinetic interfaces and SAR: in 'Skin Games' the body acts simultaneously as the controller and as the (wildly deformable) very projection surface on which to display the game's output.

Author Keywords

proprioception; spatial augmented reality; dynamic projection mapping; laser sensing display; gestural control; entertainment; computer games

ACM Classification Keywords

H.5.2 [Information interfaces and presentation]: User Interfaces - Input devices and strategies; B.4.2 [Input/output and Data Communications]: Input/Output Devices - Image display;

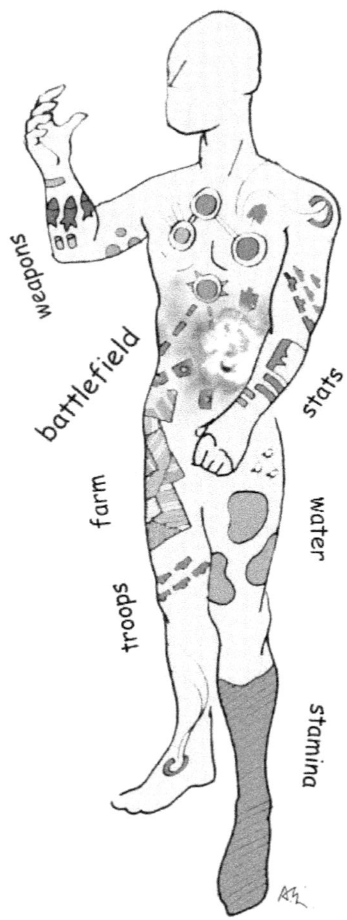

Figure 1: Wearing the game map and fighting a simulated 'infection' on the body.

The skin is the battlefield

We are interested here in the ludic possibilities opened up by harnessing the body not only as a kinetic user interface controller (using Kinect for instance), but also as the *displaying surface*. This creates a tighter connection between gesture, body posture and game control. Posture not only triggers particular game actions, but also distorts and modifies the game map *as a whole*. Construction and management simulations games (CMS) such as SimCity may be an attractive scenario for this interaction paradigm. Indeed, proprioception and 'body mnemonics' [1] can be exploited to better manage and organize game resources (see Figure 1). Simple arcade games may also be revisited in this light: instead of controlling a spaceship or hitting a ball, the player actually *moves the whole scene around* (Figure 2).

Technical challenges

There are different possible ways to materialize Skin Games. One approach is to actually wear the screen. This is technically feasible as demonstrated in numerous art/entertainment projects (see for instance Waldemeyer 'video jacket' [15]). A wearable, full body display can easily integrate kinetic sensors (accelerometers, gyros), biosensors or simple switches thus providing appropriate input, as demonstrated in [16]. A different approach is to use external tracking and projection. In the case of a traditional projector/camera setup, this requires relatively sophisticated hardware and significantly computer power because the system must realize real-time dynamic projection mapping while maintaining minimum delay and spatial mismatch. Although several techniques have been proposed in the framework of HCI [8], telepresence [14] or to augment stage performances by projecting on the actor's costumes [12], it is safe to say that to date no system providing perfect registration on deformable surfaces with unnoticeable time delay exists beyond very experimental setups such as [10].

Figure 2: Changing the topology of the soccer field

Since 2005 we have been developing a technology that is capable of displaying simple graphics with perfect registration and insignificant time delay: the Laser Sensing Display (LSD) is basically a laser projector, in which the displaying beam is simultaneously used as a *rangefinder* [3]. The information gathered by this beam can be used to adjust the geometry and color of the projected image (pre-warp when projecting on slanted or curved surfaces and color compensation when the background is uneven). The sensing beam can also be used as an input interface capable of recognizing gestures [4] or following lines [6]. The LSD fits in many ways the definition of a 'smart projector' or 'sensor-enhanced display' [2, 11] but presents a number of advantages with respect to a classical projector/camera implementation. Indeed, the sensing and the projection beam share the

Figure 3: Vector graphics games on clothing.

same optical path, and both sensing and displaying operations are realized simultaneously. The most important advantage is therefore that *camera-projector calibration is not needed at all, and misalignment is impossible by construction*. Moreover, since there is no image processing or video buffering, very fast feedback is possible (our latest prototype takes no less than 10k measurements per second).

Figure 4: Towards 'playable' clothing?

Skin Games on LSD

In this (proof-of-principle) demo we will demonstrate some simple arcade games based on the LSD technology. Each game uses here a *fixed* background printed on a T-shirt - in a way reminiscent of the translucent plastic overlays used in the Magnavox Odyssey, the first home video game console [9]. One or more 'laser sprites' interact with this printed support by following contours or bouncing. The gamer interacts by the system by jumping, contorting and/or spinning, but also can use her hands to pick the sprites and replace them over her own body - or transfer them to another player. The applications demonstrated here are a 'circular' Pong game, a simplified Pac-man and a Pinball game (see Figure 3). A video demo can be seen here [13]. Although very simple, these applications already demonstrate the fundamental shift in how to engage in a game with a full body interface. Body movement can not only shift the playground in response to the interactive graphics, but also transform the topology of the "game level", by connecting patterns on the sleeve to the one in the torso for example.

Conclusion and future work

Skin Games takes the concept of 'immersion' to a whole new *physical* level: you are litterally *covered* by the game. The fact that the user needs to contort to see the graphics on her own body is perceived here as an interesting inherent feature of the Skin Games paradigm (Figure 4). It encourages a form of gymnastics more extreme that the one promoted by kinetic based interfaces such as Xbox Kinect, where the real body movement is often a subdued gesture to elicit super human behavior within the game world. The paradigm also forces to reconsider the representation and the role of the player: as in CMS, the gamer is omnipresent and does not have an 'avatar'; but more interestingly, here the gamer *impersonates the whole game* instead. In the present implementation, the dynamic graphical elements are externally projected, while the game background is printed on clothing (for extreme game lovers it could even be permanently tattooed on the skin; or existing tattoos could gain new meaning in a game context). An obvious improvement would be to project complex and dynamic backgrounds: this would require higher resolution, raster scan projectors (presumably many of them to cover the whole body surface). As explained in the technical discussion, this is not possible nowadays - at least not for games requiring relatively unconstrained and fast interaction. However, it is conceivable that in the near future fast cameras and tracking/projection hardware, coupled with GPU processing will push delay and spatial misalignment under the threshold of human perception. Another fascinating direction would be to produce multi-modal stimuli such as vibration or sound, and restrict these to different areas of the body - the player could perform with her eyes closed. This would be easier to do in the case of a 'wearable display' implementation [7], but it is also possible using directive sound projectors [19].

Acknowledgements
The authors would like to thank Alexis Zerroug, Stephane Perrin and Daito Manabe who participated at various stages in the development of the LSD technology in the past.

References

[1] Angesleva J. et al: Body Mnemonics - Portable device interaction design concept, Proceedings of UIST'03, 2003.

[2] Bimber O. et al: Embedded Entertainment with Smart Projectors, Computer, vol. 38, no. 1, pp. 48-55, Jan. 2005.

[3] Cassinelli A. et al.: Camera-less Smart Laser Projector, ACM SIGGRAPH 2010 Etech, Article No.9.

[4] Cassinelli A. et al: Smart Laser-Scanner for 3D Human-Machine Interface, SIGCHI 2005, pp: 1138-1139.

[5] Cassinelli A. et al: Sticky Light, Ars Electronica 2008 / Campus Exhibition (HYBRID EGO), Exhibition catalog.

[6] Cassinelli A. et al: scoreLight: playing with a human sized laser pickup, Int. Conf. on New Instruments for Musical Expression (NIME2010), pp:144-149.

[7] Cassinelli A. et al.: Augmenting spatial awareness with Haptic Radar, Tenth International Symposium on Wearable Computers (ISWC 2006), pp.61-64.

[8] Harrison C. et al.: OmniTouch: Wearable Multitouch Interaction Everywhere. UIST 2011.

[9] Magnavox Odyssey, 1972 (http://en.wikipedia.org/wiki/Magnavox_Odyssey)

[10] Okumura K. et al: Lumipen: Projection-based Mixed Reality for Dynamic Objects, ICME 2012, pp: 699-704.

[11] Raskar R. et al: iLamps: Geometrically Aware and Self-configuring Projectors, SIGGRAPH 2006. TR2006-103.

[12] Sauter J.: The Jew of Malta virtual opera (1999-2002) (http://www.joachimsauter.com/en/work/thejewofmalta.html)

[13] skinGames exerpt video demo: http://www.k2.t.u-tokyo.ac.jp/members/alvaro/skinGames/skinGames1.wmv

[14] Tachi S.: Telexistence and Retro-reflective Projection Technology (RPT), Proc. Virtual Reality International Conference (VRIC 2003) pp.69/1-69/9.

[15] Waldemeyer M.: LED Dress (http://www.waldemeyer.com/)

[16] Wilde D. et al.: LightArrays, CHI EA 2012, pp. 987-990.

[17] Willis K. et al.: Motionbeam: a metaphor for character interaction with handheld projectors. ACM CHI 2011, pp: 1031-1040.

[18] Willis K. et al.: SideBySide: Ad-hoc Multi-user Interaction with Handheld Projectors. ACM UIST 2011, pp: 431-440.

[19] Zerroug, A. et al: Invoked computing: Spatial audio and video AR invoked through miming, Proc. Virtual Reality International Conf. (VRIC 2011), pp. 31-32.

Quantitative Evaluation of an Illusion of Fingertip Motion

Hiroyuki Okabe
The University of Electro-Communications.
1-5-1 Chofugaoka,
Chofu, Tokyo Japan
h.okabe@kaji-lab.jp

Taku Hachisu
The University of Electro-Communications.
1-5-1 Chofugaoka,
Chofu, Tokyo Japan
hachisu@kaji-lab.jp

Michi Sato
The University of Electro-Communications.
1-5-1 Chofugaoka,
Chofu, Tokyo Japan
michi@kaji-lab.jp

Shogo Fukushima
The University of Electro-Communications.
1-5-1 Chofugaoka,
Chofu, Tokyo Japan
shogo@kaji-lab.jp

Hiroyuki Kajimoto
The University of Electro-Communications.
1-5-1 Chofugaoka,
Chofu, Tokyo Japan
kajimoto@kaji-lab.jp

ITS'12, November 11–14, 2012, Cambridge, Massachusetts, USA.
ACM 978-1-4503-1209-7/12/11.

Abstract
In recent years, touch panels have become widespread as an intuitive means to activate device operations. Because the touch panel has a space over which a finger and a corresponding cursor moves, certain actions become intuitive compared to force input-type devices such as a pointing stick. If we could add an illusory feeling of finger motion with the force input interface, it would become more intuitive. We have found a new haptic illusion of "motion", which occurs when an electrical tactile flow is presented on the fingertip while experiencing a shearing force. We have also investigated occurrence conditions, focusing on the relation between shear force and movement speed of the electrical tactile stimulation. In our study, we investigated directional characteristic focusing on the illusory position of the finger perceived using a new electrocutaneous display mounted on a six-axis force sensor.

Author Keywords
Electrocutaneous display; haptic illusion; slip sensation; input interface

ACM Classification Keywords
H.5.2. [Information interfaces and presentation]: User Interfaces - Haptic I/O;

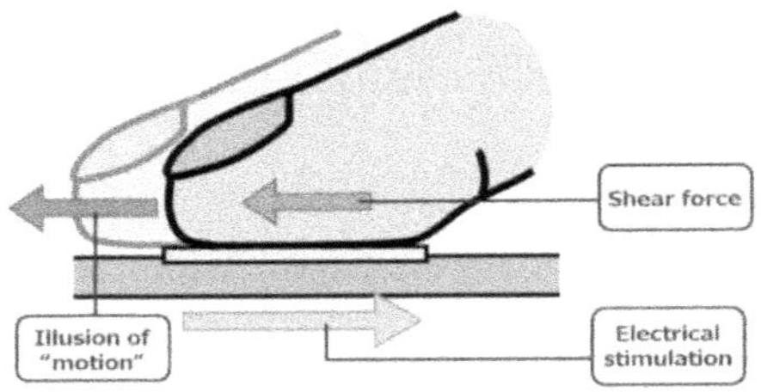

Figure 1. Conceptual image of the illusion

Figure 2. Electrocutaneous display [8]

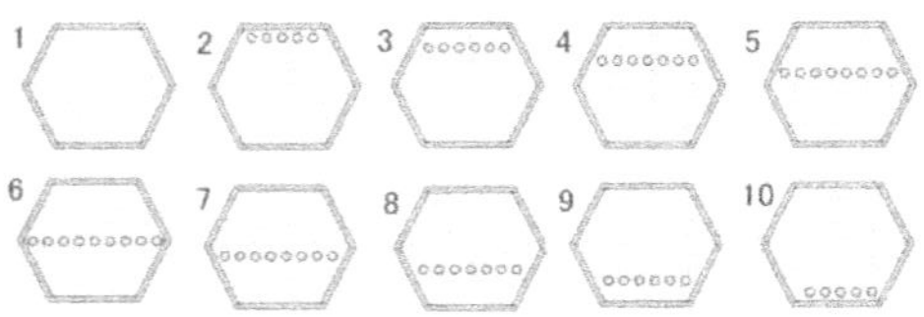

Figure 3. Electrical tactile flow

Figure 4. A six-axis sensor

Introduction

Currently, the touch input interfaces such as a touch panel or a touchpad are widely used in PCs or mobile phones. These are position-sensing-input devices, which require a large area for finger activation, with finger and cursor motion being intuitively related. Nevertheless, there are other types of input interface, such as joysticks and pointing sticks that are regarded as force-sensing-input devices. These require relatively small installation areas. Here, with finger force related to cursor motion, our idea is that if we could add a feeling of finger motion without the large input area, the trade-off between intuitiveness and area will be resolved. We focused on our newly found haptic illusion of finger motion [1], which is perceived when a moving cutaneous sensation is applied to a fingertip surface. However, a quantitative evaluation of the illusion has not been conducted. In this paper, we investigate directional characteristics, using a new electrocutaneous display mounted on a six-axis force sensor.

Previous work

Conversion of input methodology

There has been work on converting characteristics of input method. Kurita et al. presented a small touchpad with a fingerprint sensor [2] to produce a motion input device with relatively small installation area. Although micro-movements can be measured, it is subjectively a force input device because the finger barely moves. Harrison et al. equipped a pointing stick under the touch panel to add force inputs [3]. Our concept is to do the opposite by adding a feeling of motion to a force input type device.

Self-motion illusion by cutaneous input

Pasquero and Hayward showed that a cutaneous motion of a pattern presented on a finger augments the feeling of motion, and reduces time in scrolling and selection tasks [4]. In further developments, other research showed that the feeling of self-motion becomes stronger by presenting simultaneously cutaneous motion and proprioceptive sensation, with the latter predominating in perceiving self-motion [5][6][7]. Our finding is one such cross-modal presentation of a proprioceptive and cutaneous sensation that uses tactile flow with an electrocutaneous display and user-explicit force inputs (Figure 1) [1]. In our study, we investigated the illusion quantitatively, focusing on the illusory position of the finger.

Experiment

Experimental system

An electrocutaneous display that we developed was used to present cutaneous sensation on a finger (Figure 2) [8]. The display has 61 electrodes arranged hexagonally. The distance between each electrode is 2.0 mm, and the electrode diameter is 1.0 mm. A moving line pattern is presented (Figure 3). To measure the fingertip force, we used a six-axis force sensor (NITTA Corp., TFS12-10) (Figure 4). This sensor is situated 20 mm under an electrode substrate, and measures shear and vertical force applied to the display. A linear potentiometer was placed next to the electrocutaneous display for participants to gauge illusory finger position.

Experimental conditions

Four participants (2 males including experimenter and 2 females, aged between 21–25 years) took part in the experiment. The moving line pattern was applied to each participant's right index finger using electric pulses with amplitude of 0.0–5.0 mA (adjusted by each

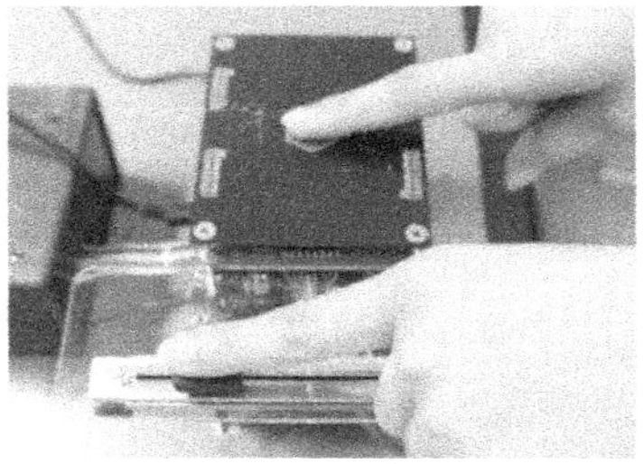

Figure 5. Answer the position of finger

Table 1. Combination of experimental conditions

Total moving distance [mm]		Velocity of the electrical stimulation [mm/sec]			
		-20	-10	+10	+20
Direction and amplitude of shear force	+ High				
	+ Low				
	- Low				
	- High				

Table 2. Experimental results

Total moving distance [mm]		Velocity of the electrical stimulation [mm/sec]			
		-20	-10	+10	+20
Direction and amplitude of shear force	+ High	6.48	6.54	5.09	10.13
	+ Low	6.51	5.01	3.61	8.09
	- Low	-6.51	-6.42	-6.94	-7.38
	- High	-7.84	-5.59	-8.68	-8.64

Table 3. Standard deviations

		Velocity of the electrical stimulation [mm/sec]			
		-20	-10	+10	+20
Direction and amplitude of shear force	+ High	7.51	7.39	5.81	9.19
	+ Low	5.21	6.50	5.80	7.72
	- Low	5.29	5.92	5.24	5.33
	- High	5.87	4.85	6.69	6.89

participant), a pulse width of 0.05 ms, and a pulse frequency of 50 Hz. Participants were also asked to exert designated vertical and horizontal forces. When participants perceived a finger motion, they were asked to slide a potentiometer with their left index finger so that subjectively left and right fingers were at the same location (Figure 5).

We prepared four stimulus conditions that combined two line pattern velocities (10.0 mm/sec, 20.0 mm/sec) and two directions (positive (+), negative (-), positive means fingertip direction). Moreover, we prepared four shear force conditions that combined two amplitudes (Low (0.0-1.0 N), High (1.0-2.0 N)) and two directions (positive (+)/negative (-)). There were four trials for each combination, resulting in 64 (=4×4×4) trials conducted in random order (Table 1).

Experimental procedure

To unify the vertical force during the experiment, the participants were trained to keep the vertical force within the range from 1.0 to 3.0 N by an electronic force balance, assuming a touch-type operation as input interface. During trials, a partition panel covered both fingers and visual cues were eliminated. The participants were asked to keep shear force within a designated range by watching a color bar. Setting a certain constant shear force, the experimenter began presenting electrical stimulations. The position of the slider was recorded for 10.0 seconds from 1.0 to 11.0 seconds after the start of each stimulation.

Results

The results and the standard deviations are listed in Tables 2 and 3. The value of each cell shows the total moving distance of the slider. Positive values (red cells) mean that the finger subjectively moved towards the positive direction. Figures 6 and 7 are graphs of Table 2. The vertical axis gives the total moving distance; and the horizontal axis shows the velocity of the electrical stimulation pattern.

Discussion

The result showed that the direction of the illusory movement always coincides with the direction of the applied shear force; in Fig. 6, all results indicate positive directions, whereas in Fig. 7 all results indicate negative directions. The correlation agrees with previous observations that proprioceptive sensation predominates over cutaneous sensation in the feeling of self-motion. Moreover, the perceived moving distance was affected by the velocity of the electrical stimulation although its relationship seems nonlinear.

In our previous study, we supposed that the direction of the finger shear force and the cutaneous pattern movement must be in the opposite direction to generate a consistent illusion; i.e. when the finger moves, the cutaneous pattern movement must be in the opposite direction to the exerted force. However, even if these cues were not consistent, the illusion persisted and its perceived movement was also by no means small. After the experiment, some participants commented: "In the inconsistency conditions, I had a strange feeling in that my finger was being pushed in the direction of exerted force". That is, there is a possibility of interpreting various cutaneous sensations in accordance with the proprioceptive cue. Random cutaneous sensations might even be effective, although the

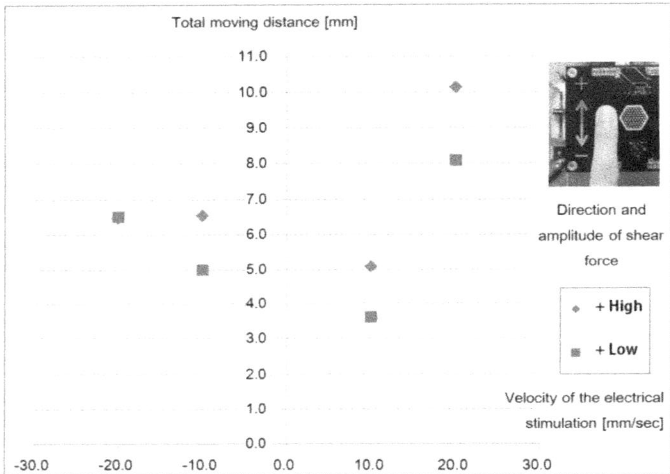

Figure 6. Result of positive shear force

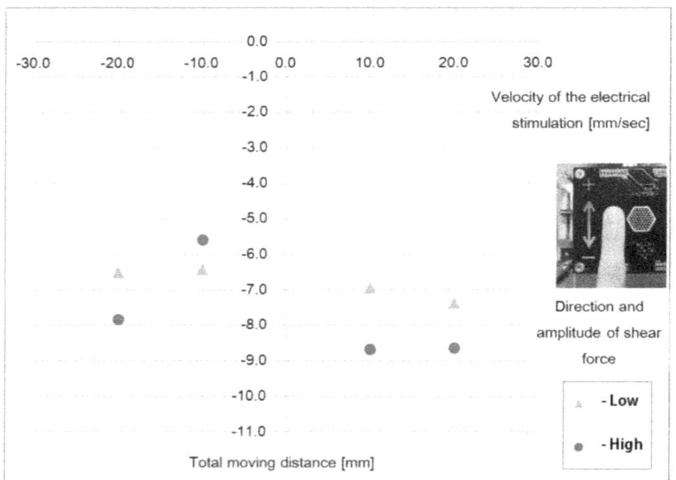

Figure 7. Result of negative shear force

current result seems to support that cutaneous pattern velocity affects the illusion. To verify these possibilities, we will need to make comparison with conditions under random or absence of cutaneous stimulations.

Conclusions and future work

In devising a position sensing input device with small installation area, we employed the haptic illusory finger movement. We conducted an experiment to quantify the effect of force and cutaneous pattern speed on the illusion by measuring the subjective position of finger. The result suggested that the sense of finger motion always occurs in the direction of the applied shear force, whereas movement speed of the cutaneous pattern affects the magnitude of the illusion. Our future work will include an in-depth study of the relationship between proprioceptive and cutaneous cues on the illusion, in particular adding conditions of random and absence of cutaneous stimulations. We will also prototype an input interface and compare with conventional interfaces.

References

[1] Okabe, H., Fukushima, S., Sato, M., and Kajimoto, H. Fingertip Slip Illusion with an Electrocutaneous Display. In *Proc. The 21th International Conference on Artifical Reality and Telexistence*, ICAT (2011).

[2] Kurita, Y., Ikeda, A., Ueda, J., and Ogasawara, T. A Fingerprint Pointing Device Utilizing the Deformation of the Fingertip during the Incipient Slip. IEEE Transaction on Robotics, IEEE Robotics and Automation Society Press (2005), vol. 21, no. 5, 801–811.

[3] Harrison, C., and Hudson, S. E. Using Shear as a Supplemental Two-Dimensional Input Channel for Rich Touchscreen Interaction. In *Proc. The 30th Annual SIGCHI Conference on Human Factors in Computing Systems*, ACM Press (2012), 3149–3152.

[4] Pasquero, J., and Hayward, V. Tactile Feedback Can Assist Vision During Mobile Interactions. In *Proc. 2011 Annual Conference on Human Factors in Computing Systems*, ACM Press (2011).

[5] Tiest, W.M.B., van der Hoff, L.M.A., and Kappers, A. M. L.. Cutaneous and Kinaesthetic Perception of Traversed Distance. In *Proc. The IEEE World Haptics Conference*, IEEE Press (2011), 593–597.

[6] Collins, D.F., Refshauge, K.M., Todd, G., and Gandevia S. C. Cutaneous Receptors Contribute to Kinesthesia at the Index Finger, Elbow, and Knee. *Journal of Neurophysiology*, APS Press (2005), 1699–1706.

[7] Blanchard, C., Roll, R., Roll J-P., and Kavounoudias, A. Combined contribution of tactile and proprioceptive feedback to hand movement perception. *Brain Res. 1382*, ELSEVIER Press (2011), 219–229.

[8] Kajimoto, H. Electro-tactile Display with Real-time Impedance Feedback. In *Proc. EuroHaptics 2010*, Springer Press (2010), 285–291.

Seamless Integration of Mobile Devices into Interactive Surface Environments

Andreas Dippon
Technische Universität München
Boltzmannstr. 3
85748 Garching
dippona@in.tum.de

Norbert Wiedermann
Technische Universität München
Boltzmannstr. 3
85748 Garching
wiederma@in.tum.de

Gudrun Klinker
Technische Universität München
Boltzmannstr. 3
85748 Garching
klinker@in.tum.de

ITS'12, November 11–14, 2012, Cambridge, Massachusetts, USA.
ACM 978-1-4503-1209-7/12/11.

Abstract
This poster abstract describes the seamless integration of uninstrumented mobile devices into an interactive surface environment. By combining a depth camera with a RGB camera for tracking, we are able to identify uninstrumented mobile devices using visual marker tracking. We describe the technical details of combining the two cameras and an example application for the integration of mobile devices.

Author Keywords
Multitouch; Depth-sensing cameras; Object tracking; Interactive Surface.

ACM Classification Keywords
H.5.2 [Information interfaces and presentation: User Interfaces. - Graphical user interfaces.]

INTRODUCTION
With the introduction of the Kinect, depth cameras got a lot of attention recently. It was shown, that such cameras can be used to detect touches on arbitrary displays [12, 2]. In addition, tangible objects on surfaces can be detected. Yet the depth data has the drawback that similar looking devices (e.g. mobile phones) can't be distinguished. This drawback can be reduced by combining the depth camera with the

built-in RGB camera and computer vision algorithms. Using this combination we can detect and distinguish different mobile devices (e.g. mobile phones, tablet computers) without any additional instrumentation. This can be used to seamlessly integrate mobile devices into an interactive surface environment.

RELATED WORK

One interesting approaches from Wilson [12] was to use a depth camera for sensing touches on an arbitrary surface. He already mentioned the possibility of tracking objects in addition to finger touches. Klompmaker et al [8] developed object tracking by using a history of depth images and additional background images. With this method, they can already detect touches, arbitrary objects and touches on objects very consistently. Yet it is not possible to distinguish similar objects from each other.

Combining mobile devices and interactive surfaces has already seen a lot of attention in recent years [6, 10, 11, 4]. Wilson used a visual handshaking process on the BlueTable [11] where mobile phones have to be placed on the surface and be visible for an above mounted camera. Echtler [4] improved the system by identifying the phone using the signal strength of the bluetooth connection instead of a visual handshake. Yet both systems have the drawback that the phones have to be placed and stay on the surface, which causes privacy issues and an inferior usability of the mobile phone. Chehimi et al [1] improved the approach by creating a proxy circular area on the surface when a phone connects to it. This area is created in the middle of the surface and users have to be aware that the created proxy is representing their mobile phone. While this method is already well integrated, the mental load on the user is increased as users are part of the registration process. Additionally the identification of the correct proxy becomes difficult when several users want to join at the same time.

Schmidt et al [9] used a different solution, where the mobile phones have to touch the surface to trigger an interaction. By using timestamps, different mobile phones can be distinguished if they don't touch the surface at the same time. The system works quite well, yet users were uncomfortable touching surfaces with their mobile devices. The same drawback can be found in the system used by Izadi et al. [7], where the built-in camera of the mobile phone is used to identify itself with the bluetooth connection to the surface.

DEPTH AND RGB TRACKING

We use the depth data for tracking objects and fingers on and above any surface by calculating the difference between the depth values in the image and a previously captured background image [12, 2]. To be able to combine the tracking data of the RGB camera and the depth camera, the two images have to be aligned in order to match marker and blob positions. As the Kinect has the RGB camera built-in, this alignment is approximately the same for all devices. As the accuracy of the tracked marker positions in the RGB image is not critical, a predefined calibration for shifting the RGB image to the depth image is sufficient. This approximation has the advantage that the system doesn't have to be calibrated for different Kinects. For the tracking of visual markers we integrated a very robust visual marker tracker from the Ubitrack library by Huber et al. [5] into the libtisch framework [3]. This combination enables us to reliably track the positions, rotations and identification numbers of visual markers in the image.

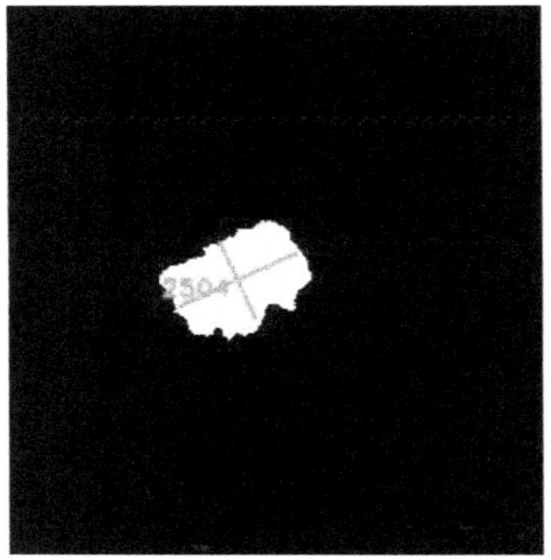

Figure 1: Detected Blob in Depth Image.

Figure 2: Detected Marker on Mobile Phone in RGB Image.

The next step is to combine the information of a marker with an object blob of the depth camera. This is done for each detected marker position by searching for the nearest blob within a modifiable search radius. If a blob is found, the marker information is added to the other characteristics of the blob. If no blob is found in the vicinity of a marker, the system can be adjusted to simply discard the marker or to automatically generate a blob on the projected position on the surface. The position of the generated marker blob won't be as accurate as an object tracked by the depth camera because of the predefined camera calibration. Yet it can still be useful especially if you want to track reflective displays (e.g. mobile phones) which often can't be detected reliably by the depth camera.

EXAMPLE: DATATRANSFER WITH PHONES

User Experience

Friends want to share and exchange pictures from their mobile phones with each other on a large interaction surface. They simply start the application on their mobile phone to connect to the surface display. By holding their mobile phone above the surface, it gets automatically registered by the depth camera which is mounted above the interactive surface. During the registration of the mobile phones, a visual representation of each phone is generated on the surface at the position of the corresponding phone. The users can now select pictures on their mobile phones that they want to share with their friends without the requirement to be tracked anymore. The selected pictures will be shown on the surface next to the users' mobile phone representation. The friends can now look at and interact (zoom, rotate, move) with the pictures on the interactive surface. If they want to copy the picture to their phone, they simply can drag it on their mobile phone representation on the surface. Alternatively they can hold their mobile phone above a picture and press a copy button on the mobile application.

Implementation

We developed an Android application (AA) and an application for the interactive surface (ISA). The user simply needs to install and run the Android application to be able to instantly work with the interactive surface. When started, the AA sends a greeting message to the already running ISA. The ISA responds by sending an available random marker identification number (ID) from a predefined ID list to the device and locks this marker ID. The AA generates a visual marker from this ID, shows it on its display and waits for a confirmation message of the ISA. As soon as the ISA detects the marker and combines it with a blob (or creates a new blob for this marker), it sends a confirmation message to the mobile phone that the connection is established and the application is ready to use. Additionally the ISA creates a visual representation for the mobile phone on the position of the blob with the corresponding marker ID. After receiving the confirmation message of the ISA, the AA shows a menu with different pictures instead of the generated marker. Then the user can select pictures which should be shown on the interactive surface. The selected pictures are shown on the interactive surface and can be scaled, moved and rotated by touch interaction. In order to copy pictures to another phone, the pictures can simply be dragged onto the visual representation of another phone which was created during the registration process for each mobile phone. Pictures can also be copied by holding

Figure 3: User interacts with his mobile phone and the interactive surface.

a mobile phone above a picture and pressing the copy button in the AA. This will show the previously generated marker on the display of the mobile phone until it is detected by the ISA. The ISA then sends the picture and as soon as the mobile phone receives the data, it will show the pictures menu again. If a user wants to leave, the user can simply quit the AA which will send a farewell message to the ISA. The visual representation and all data coming from the corresponding phone will be removed from the interactive surface and the locked marker ID will be available again for another phone.

DISCUSSION

For the identification process of a mobile device it is sufficient, that the marker is detected in only one frame. Therefore this process is often not even recognized by the users and enables a seamless integration of mobile devices. Due to the simple registration process of the mobile devices, this method could also be very well integrated into games (e.g. card games) that use the interactive surface as the playground and the mobile devices as private displays to show the cards of a player [10].

CONCLUSION

We presented a technique to seamlessly integrate uninstrumented mobile devices into an interactive surface environment. We believe that the combination of the two cameras has a lot of potential in upcoming applications and think that the described fundamentals help other researchers to develop further ideas.

ACKNOWLEDGMENTS

Part of the CRUMBS project, funded by BMWi.

References

[1] Chehimi, F., and Rukzio, E. Throwing Gesture as a Way for Photo Sharing between Mobile Phones and Interactive Tables. In *4th Intermedia Open Forum* ('10).

[2] Dippon, A., and Klinker, G. KinectTouch: Accuracy Test for a Very Low-Cost 2.5D Multitouch Tracking System. In *ITS '11* (Nov. 2011).

[3] Echtler, F., and Klinker, G. A multitouch software architecture. In *NordiCHI '08* (Oct. 2008).

[4] Echtler, F., and Klinker, G. Tracking mobile phones on interactive tabletops. In *MEIS '08* (Sept. 2008).

[5] Huber, M., Pustka, D., Keitler, P., Echtler, F., and Klinker, G. A system architecture for ubiquitous tracking environments. In *ISMAR '07* (Nov. 2007).

[6] Izadi, S., Brignull, H., Rodden, T., Rogers, Y., and Underwood, M. Dynamo: A public interactive surface supporting the cooperative sharing and exchange of media. In *UIST '03* (Nov. 2003).

[7] Izadi, S., Butler, A., Hodges, S., West, D., Hall, M., Buxton, B., and Molloy, M. Experiences with building a thin form-factor touch and tangible tabletop. In *Tabletop 2008* (Oct. 2008).

[8] Klompmaker, F., Nebe, K., and Fast, A. dSensingNI: A Framework for Advanced Tangible Interaction using a Depth Camera. In *TEI '12* (Feb. 2012).

[9] Schmidt, D., Seifert, J., Rukzio, E., and Gellersen, H. A Cross-Device Interaction Style for Mobiles and Surfaces. In *DIS '12* (June 2012).

[10] Shirazi, A. S., Döring, T., Parvahan, P., Ahrens, B., and Schmidt, A. Poker surface: Combining a multi-touch table and mobile phones in interactive card games. In *MobileHCI '09* (Sept. 2009).

[11] Wilson, A., and Sarin, R. Bluetable: connecting wireless mobile devices on interactive surfaces using vision-based handshaking. In *GI '07* (May 2007).

[12] Wilson, A. D. Using a depth camera as a touch sensor. In *ITS '10* (Nov. 2010).

Control of Ridge by Using Visuotactile Cross-Modal Phenomenon

Maki Yokoyama
The University of Electro-Communications.
1-5-1 Choufugaoka.
Choufu Tokyo Japan
m.yokoyama@kaji-lab.jp

Taku Hachisu
The University of Electro-Communications.
1-5-1 Choufugaoka.
Choufu Tokyo Japan
hachisu@kaji-lab.jp

Michi Sato
The University of Electro-Communications.
1-5-1 Choufugaoka.
Choufu Tokyo Japan
michi@kaji-lab.jp

Shogo Fukushima
The University of Electro-Communications.
1-5-1 Choufugaoka.
Choufu Tokyo Japan
shogo@kaji-lab.jp

Hiroyuki Kajimoto
The University of Electro-Communications.
1-5-1 Choufugaoka.
Choufu Tokyo Japan
kajimoto@kaji-lab.jp

ITS12, November 11–14, 2012, Cambridge, Massachusetts, USA.
ACM 978-1-4503-1209-7/12/11.

Abstract
Currently, touch panels are used in many devices, and there have been many proposals to add tactile sensation to touch panels, which require additional electro-mechanical components. In this paper, we propose a simple method of adding a tactile sensation of a ridge, using just a thin sheet. The sheet has ridges that are haptically imperceptible, but once a visual cue such as a line is presented, visuotactile cross-modal response induces a haptic ridge. We tested the effects of the visual cue and height of the ridge. The result showed that the visual cue definitely enhances feeling of a ridge.

Author Keywords
Cross-modal; Interface; Ridge sensation; Tactile illusion; Visuotactile

ACM Classification Keywords
H.5.2. [Information interfaces and presentation]: User Interfaces - Haptic I/O;

Introduction
In recent years, touch panels have become pervasive on for many devices. They display visual information

and respond to touch input, but lack sufficient tactile capability, that constrains device operations. One example of this tactile deficiency is "bumps" for buttons and keys.

To solve this problem, there have been many proposals to add tactile sensation to touch panels. Bau et al. proposed TeslaTouch, which can change surface friction by controlling the electrostatic force on touch panels [1]. Jansen et al. proposed MudPad which can present tactile sensation by controlling the viscosity of a magnetic fluid in electromagnets [2]. Saga et al. presented virtual bumps by pulling a user's finger laterally using SPIDAR system [3]. Tactus Technology, Inc. proposed a method to form real ridges on the touch panel by controlling a micro fluid [4]. However, it is still not easy to mount these devices on mobile terminals because they require additional electro-mechanical components such as motors or electromagnets.

In this study, we propose to simply put a thin sheet with ridges for keys on the touch panel. Of course, normal ridges will interfere with operations when they are not necessary. However, we discovered that visual cues added to the ridge will dramatically increase the perception of the ridge, and consequently, we can switch between a "ridge" and "no ridge" status by just changing visual information.

For this paper, we measured a basic property of this cross-modal phenomenon and verified the validity of our proposal.

Method

We preliminary observed the following phenomenon; the ridge of a few μm is just below the perception threshold, and normally cannot be perceived when we trace the ridge with a finger (Figure 1, left panel). However, when a visual cue such as a line is added over the ridge, the ridge suddenly becomes perceivable (Figure 1, right panel). This phenomenon is considered to be one of the visual-tactile cross-modal phenomena.

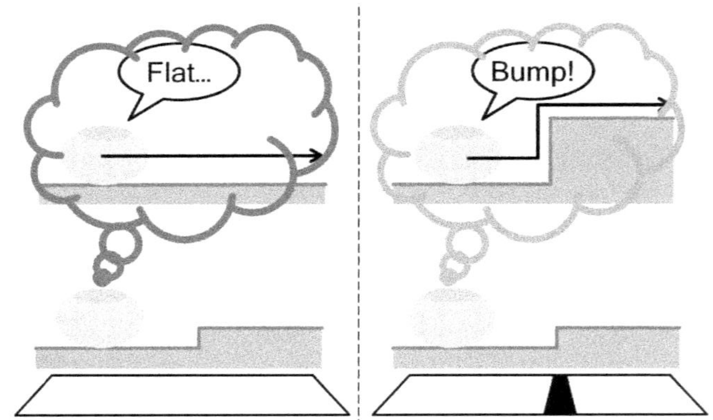

Figure 1 Proposed method. (Left) without visual cue, a user feels a flat surface; (Right) with visual cue, a user feels a tactile ridge.

Our idea is to apply this phenomenon to add ridges to the touch panel. Our scenario is as follows; we put a thin transparent sheet with ridges below the perception threshold, forming keyboard or buttons. When the user needs keyboard, an image of the keyboard is displayed, and the ridges is perceived. In other words, the subjective ridge height is controlled by visual modality.

There have been many studies on the cross-modal relationship between visual and tactile stimuli and its

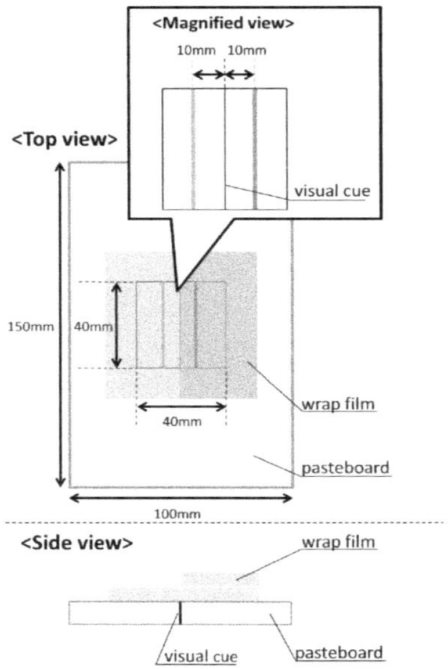

Figure 2 Experimental setup

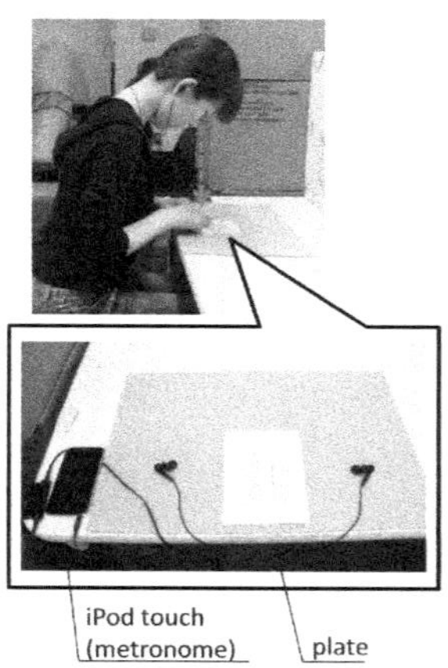

Figure 3 Environment of the experiment (This picture was taken under lighting)

effect on perception threshold. Taylor et al. reported that if the tactile stimulation site is visually observed by the participant, the discrimination threshold is decreased [5]. Kennett et al. reported that even if a visual cue that was unrelated to the tactile stimuli was added to the body surface at the tactile stimulation site, the two-point discrimination threshold was improved [6].

However, these studies cannot substantiate our proposal, because in our situation, users gaze at the tactile stimulation site and the visual cue is hidden by the user's finger (a visual cue is presented under the user's finger). Therefore, we conducted an experiment to establish the validity of our proposal.

EXPERIMENT

We examined the relationship of the subjective ridge height and visual cue.

Experiment setup

We made a transparent plate with a ridge using a wrap film (Asahi Kasei Home Products Corporation, Saranwrap20m) and a pasteboard (Figure 2). A plate is made with a ridge, created from the texture of the wrap film, running down the center. We prepared ridges of various thickness (of 0, 1, 2 wrap film thicknesses). A 40 mm square was drawn on the square plate, and a blue and a red line (line width 1.0 mm) were printed at a spacing of 20 mm on each side of the step. Participants move a finger between these two lines at a designated velocity.

There were two visual conditions; with and without visual cue. The visual cue is a 0.1 mm-wide black line, which was printed midway between the two lines just under the step (Figure 2 Side view). In total, we prepared six types of plates (3 different ridge heights, 2 different visual cues). Actual ridge heights were measured using a micrometer (Mitutoyo Corporation, M320-25AA, Range: 0.000-25.000 mm, Accuracy: 0.001 mm), and the three thickness conditions were 0.000, 0.014±0.001, and 0.021±0.002 mm.

Procedure

Figure 3 shows the environment of the experiment. Because ridges were visible under normal lighting conditions, the illumination of the room was set down to 2.3 Lux. Before the experiment, participants confirmed whether they could see the visual cues. They were asked to trace the plate from the blue line to the red line with their right index fingers. To control speed, we asked participants to move their fingers according to the beats of a metronome (iPod touch software) so that sounds were only heard when the fingers were on blue or red lines. By this means, the duration in moving the finger from the blue line to the red line was 0.75 sec, giving a speed of 26.7 mm/s.

Participants traced two plates (plate1 and plate2) and were asked which ridge was higher with three alternative responses ("plate1", "plate2", or "same"). We paired the six types of plates, giving 36 randomized trials in total for each participant. Participants were 5 laboratory members composed of 3 males and 2 females, aged between 22and 24 yeas, right handed, with 4/20-20/20 eyesight.

Result and Discussion

Figure 4 shows a partial result. It compares the same ridge height with or without visual cue. The horizontal axis is the physical ridge height from 0.000 to 0.021

mm, and the vertical axis is the answer rate. For example, when the ridge was 0.000 mm, 90 % of the participants answered that two specimens (with or without visual cue) has the same height, while 10 % answered that a specimen with visual cue was higher.

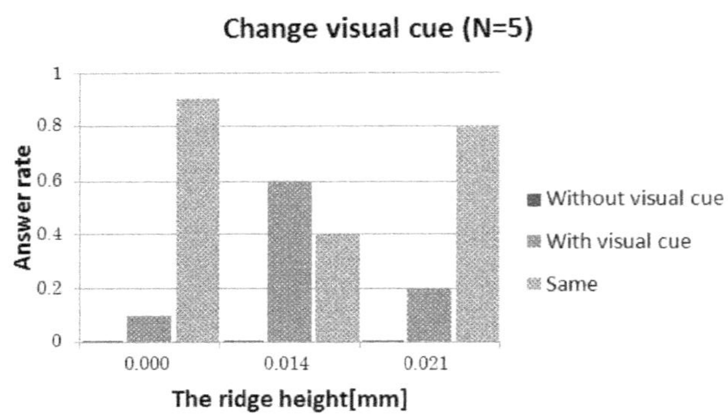

Figure 4 Average answer rate when changing visual cues.

When the ridge height was 0.000 and 0.021 mm, the subjective ridge height was not affected by the visual cue (i.e. most participants answered that two specimens had the same height). However, when the ridge height was 0.014 mm, the subjective ridge height was affected by visual cue.

This result clearly indicates that the subjective ridge height became higher by adding a visual cue. However, because the participants could perceive the lowest in ridges (0.014 mm) we had prepared, the result did not fully validate our proposal; when a visual cue is added, the ridge which normally cannot be perceived can become perceivable. Therefore, as a next step, we will use lower ridges that are normally unperceivable.

CONCLUSION

In this paper, to add a tactile sensation of ridges to touch panels with a simple set up, we proposed to control the subjective ridge height using a visualtactile cross-modal phenomenon, and partially confirmed the validity of our proposal.

Our next step is the sophistication of the experiment using ridges below a certain threshold height. In the future, we will prepare design guidelines that state optimum parameters such as ridge height, visual line width and luminance.

References

[1] Bau O., Poupyrev I., Israr A. Harrison C. Tesla-touch: Electro vibration for touch surfaces, UIST 2010.

[2] Jansen Y., Karrer T., Borchers J. MudPad Tactile Feedback for touch screen, CHI 2011.

[3] Saga S., Deguchi K. Lateral-force-based 2.5-dimensional tactile display for touch screen. In Proceedings of Haptics Symposium 2012.

[4] Tactus Technology, Inc. Taking touch screen interfaces into a new dimension, A tactus technology white paper, 2012.

[5] Taylor M. C, Kennett S., Haggard P. Persistence of visual-tactile enhancement in humans, Neuroscience Letters, 354, pp. 22-25, 2004.

[6] Kennett S., Clarke M. T., Haggard P. Noninformative vision improves the spatial resolution of touch in humans, Current Biology, Vol.11, No.15, pp.1188-1191, 2001.

Touch-Consistent Perspective for Direct Interaction under Motion Parallax

Yusuke Sugano
Institute of Industrial Science
The University of Tokyo
4-6-1 Komaba, Meguro-ku
Tokyo, 153-8505 JAPAN
sugano@iis.u-tokyo.ac.jp

Kazuma Harada
Institute of Industrial Science
The University of Tokyo
4-6-1 Komaba, Meguro-ku
Tokyo, 153-8505 JAPAN
dani@iis.u-tokyo.ac.jp

Yoichi Sato
Institute of Industrial Science
The University of Tokyo
4-6-1 Komaba, Meguro-ku
Tokyo, 153-8505 JAPAN
ysato@iis.u-tokyo.ac.jp

ITS'12, November 11–14, 2012, Cambridge, Massachusetts, USA.
ACM 978-1-4503-1209-7/12/11.

Abstract
A 3D display is a key component to present virtual space in an intuitive way to users. A motion parallax-based 3D display can be easily combined with multi-touch surfaces, and it is expected to bring a natural experience of viewing and controlling 3D space. However, since virtual objects are rendered in accordance with the head position of the user, their projected positions are not fixed on the display surface. We propose a novel formulation of head-coupled perspective that adaptively changes the position of the projection image plane to maintain touch consistency of direct interaction.

Author Keywords
Head-coupled Perspective, Direct Manipulation

ACM Classification Keywords
H.5.2 [**Information interfaces and presentation**]: User Interfaces. - Graphical user interfaces..

General Terms
Theory, Human Factors

Introduction
Techniques for intuitive interaction with 3D virtual environments have long been investigated. Direct 3D interaction is expected to provide the most natural user

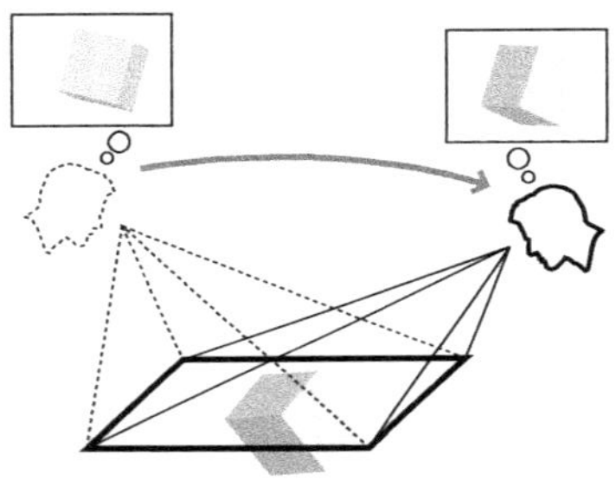

Figure 1: Illustration of head-coupled perspective

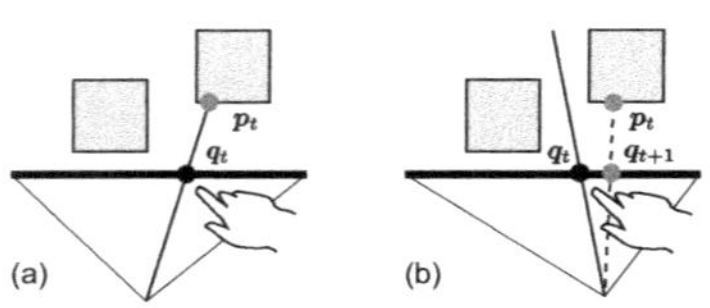

Figure 2: Touch inconsistency during viewpoint change with head movement

experience in many scenarios, such as 3D desktop environments, and to appeal to not only novices but also experts.

Technical elements for 3D interaction are mainly divided into two components: display and input [1]. For the display technique, a 3D display is obviously the most intuitive way to present the 3D space to users. Many existing techniques utilize the mechanism of binocular stereopsis for depth perception; however, monocular cues like motion parallax are another important factor for humans to perceive the 3D space.

To present motion parallax cues, the eye or head position of the viewer is used to render 3D objects under a perspective consistent with the viewpoint, which we refer to as *head-coupled perspective* (Figure 1). Conventionally, head-coupled perspective has been studied in the context of VR under the name of Fish Tank VR [8]. Owing to the recent advance in head tracking technologies, it is becoming much easier to achieve head-coupled perspective without forcing users to wear additional devices.

For the input technique, a multi-touch surface provides a great advantage by providing an experience of direct manipulation on virtual objects. Several research efforts have attempted to utilize 2D touch to directly manipulate 6-DoF position and orientation of 3D objects [5, 3, 4]. As discussed in [5], one of the key factors in designing touch-based 3D interactions is directness. It is easy to define pointing and manipulation gestures separately, but such indirect interaction significantly spoils the benefit of touch-based interaction.

However, as illustrated in Figure 2, the projected position of virtual objects are not fixed on the display surface under head-coupled perspective and direct touch interaction technique cannot be applied in a straightforward manner. In other words, if the user moves her head while touching a 3D object, projected position of the object moves away from the touched position. Since most existing touch-based 3D manipulation techniques implicitly assume a static projection mapping, they cannot handle the touch inconsistency problem and the interaction cannot be direct under head-coupled perspective. Some researches have studied 3D manipulation on stereoscopic displays [2, 7, 6]. However, the case of head-coupled perspective has not been discussed well in previous researches. The view of a virtual camera is closely related to users' depth perception, and it is not a trivial task to resolve the touch inconsistency problem without affecting rendered scene.

Our basic idea is adaptively changing the depth of the image plane so that the projected position of the target virtual object is always fixed on the display surface. Similar techniques are sometimes used in the context of VR and 3D user interfaces. However, since the position of the virtual camera always have to be consistent with the user's view position, it is not clear how to incorporate the depth adjustment into head-coupled perspective. In our formulation, the rendered image does not change depending on the touch action, and can be naturally combined with touch-based interaction techniques.

Touch-consistent Perspective

Touch Inconsistency

As briefly discussed earlier, the problem arises when the head-coupled perspective is combined with touch-based interaction. At the time of the initial touch (Figure 2 (a)), touched 2D position $\boldsymbol{q}_t$ can be mapped to a 3D position $\boldsymbol{p}_t$ through back projection. When the viewpoint moves to a new position (Figure 2 (b)), $\boldsymbol{p}_t$ is also projected to a new position $\boldsymbol{q}_{t+1}$, and the initial position $\boldsymbol{q}_t$ does not

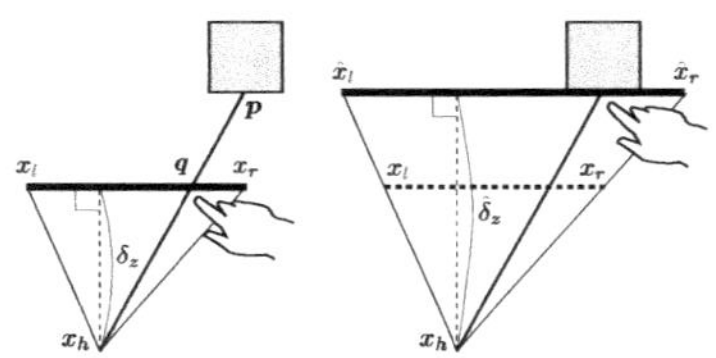

Figure 3: Touch-consistent perspective with adaptive relocation of the target plane

correspond to $\boldsymbol{p}_t$. If the one-to-one mapping is forced, i.e., the target object is moved in accordance with the viewpoint change so that $\boldsymbol{p}_t$ is projected to $\boldsymbol{q}_t$, the user's head movement can produce unintended object movement. In both cases, interaction techniques that rely on the one-to-one mapping between $\boldsymbol{p}$ and $\boldsymbol{q}$ cannot be direct.

Touch-consistent Relocation of the Image Plane
Let us denote the 3D head position of the viewer in the virtual world coordinates as $\boldsymbol{h} = {}^t(x_h, y_h, z_h)$. The virtual camera is assumed to be directly placed at $\boldsymbol{h}$ and facing the negative Z direction in a right-hand coordinate system. The target plane, which is perceived as fixed on the screen, is defined as a rectangle parallel to the X-Y plane whose four corners in the world coordinates are $\boldsymbol{a} = {}^t(x_l, y_t, z_d)$, $\boldsymbol{b} = {}^t(x_r, y_t, z_d)$, $\boldsymbol{c} = {}^t(x_l, y_b, z_d)$, and $\boldsymbol{d} = {}^t(x_r, y_b, z_d)$. The distance from $\boldsymbol{h}$ to the target plane becomes $\delta_z = z_h - z_d$.

Our key observation is that the inconsistency does not occur when and only when the target position $\boldsymbol{p}$ is on the image plane. To resolve the touch inconsistency problem, we propose changing the position of the target plane adaptively during touch-based interaction. As illustrated in Figure 3, the depth z_d of the target plane is set to be the same as the depth $\hat{z}_d$ of the back-projected 3D position $\boldsymbol{p}$ of the touched position $\boldsymbol{q}$.

To maintain the current visual field of the camera and to avoid the jump of the rendered image depending on the touch action, the size of the target plane is also changed as $\hat{x}_l = x_h + \frac{\hat{\delta}_z}{\delta_z}(x_l - x_h)$ and $\hat{x}_r = x_h + \frac{\hat{\delta}_z}{\delta_z}(x_r - x_h)$, where $\hat{x}_l$ and $\hat{x}_r$ are the new values of x_l and x_r, and $\hat{\delta}_z = \hat{z}_d - z_h$. y_t and y_b are also changed in the same way in accordance with y_h.

Experiments
To compare user experience, users were asked to execute a 3D positioning task with and without the proposed head-coupled perspective. The task was to align the pose of the target dice whose initial position and orientation were randomly defined to the goal. A translucent dice indicates the goal object, and users were asked to align both position and orientation of the dice. If both position and orientation errors became lower than a predefined threshold, the color of the goal dice changed to red. Then users could finish the task in their own time at the best position. There were also randomly placed obstacles, and users were instructed to avoid them as much as possible, so that depth perception of the 3D space had more importance during the experiments.

Reisman et al.'s screen space formulation [5] was used as the baseline method for touch-based 3D manipulation. In their method, 6-DoF position $\boldsymbol{t}$ and orientation $\boldsymbol{r}$ of the target object can be directly controlled by 2D touch through projection error minimization. By changing the projection function at each time step in accordance with the current head position and the target plane, this method can be combined with our proposed touch-consistent perspective without any restriction.

The system consisted of a 3M Multi-Touch Display M2256PW, and a Logitech QuickCam Pro 9000. faceAPI library from Seeing Machines [1] was used to obtain users' 3D head positions $\boldsymbol{h}$. The system runs at more than 60 [fps] with a desktop PC with Intel Core i7 3.33GHz processor, 8GB RAM, and nVidia GeForce GT230 graphics.

Ten people took part in the experiments, and each person

[1] http://www.seeingmachines.com/product/faceapi/

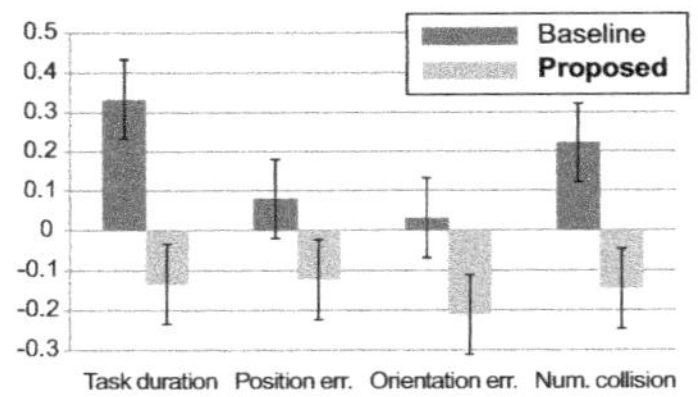

Figure 4: Mean scores of five criteria (duration, position and orientation error, and number of collisions to the obstacles). Since the criteria of the task completion was left to each user's decision and relative difference between modes is important. Absolute values of each criterion were first normalized per user so that they have zero mean and one variance. Lower scores indicate better performance. Error bars indicate standard errors.

executed ten trials for two modes alternately. In the first mode, Reisman et al.'s original method was used as it is and users' head poses were not used to change viewpoint. Instead of using head poses, users could change the camera position using arrow keys. For fair comparison, however, the camera was not allowed to be rotated more than 45 degrees from the initial orientation. The second mode corresponded to the proposed method.

As shown in Figure 4, proposed method achieved better scores in task duration (t-test: $t(99) = 3.21$, $p < 0.01$) and number of collisions (t-test: $t(99) = 2.36$, $p = 0.02$) while pose errors remained the same. After experiments, five-grade subjective scores from 5 (best) to 1 (worst) were collected from each user. The score of the proposed method ($M = 3.7$) was higher than the score of the baseline method ($M = 2.5$) (Wilcoxon signed-rank test: $p = 0.02$).

Conclusion

This paper presented a novel projection method suited to touch-based interaction under head-coupled perspective. In the proposed formulation, The position of the image plane is adaptively changed without causing change of the rendered virtual scene. The consistency between touched positions and target 3D positions is maintained during interaction, and any kind of touch-based interaction techniques can be naturally combined with the motion parallax-based 3D display. Through a user study, interaction using the proposed formulation was shown to enable more smooth and natural user experience for 3D manipulation.

References

[1] Grossman, T., and Wigdor, D. Going deeper: a taxonomy of 3D on the tabletop. In *Proc. Second Annual IEEE International Workshop on Horizontal Interactive Human-Computer Systems* (2007), 137–144.

[2] Hachet, M., Bossavit, B., Cohé, A., and de la Rivière, J. B. Toucheo: multitouch and stereo combined in a seamless workspace. In *Proc. 24th annual ACM symposium on User interface software and technology*, UIST '11 (2011), 587–592.

[3] Hancock, M., ten Cate, T., and Carpendale, S. Sticky tools: full 6DOF force-based interaction for multi-touch tables. In *Proc. ACM Intl. Conf. on Interactive Tabletops and Surfaces*, ITS '09 (2009), 133–140.

[4] Martinet, A., Casiez, G., and Grisoni, L. The effect of DOF separation in 3D manipulation tasks with multi-touch displays. In *Proc. 17th ACM Symposium on Virtual Reality Software and Technology*, VRST '10 (2010), 111–118.

[5] Reisman, J. L., Davidson, P. L., and Han, J. Y. A screen-space formulation for 2D and 3D direct manipulation. In *Proc. 22nd annual ACM symposium on User interface software and technology*, UIST '09 (2009), 69–78.

[6] Valkov, D., Steinicke, F., Bruder, G., and Hinrichs, K. 2D touching of 3D stereoscopic objects. In *Proc. 2011 annual conf. on Human factors in computing systems*, CHI '11 (2011), 1353–1362.

[7] Valkov, D., Steinicke, F., Bruder, G., Hinrichs, K., Schöning, J., Daiber, F., and Krüger, A. Touching floating objects in projection-based virtual reality environments. In *Proc. Joint Virtual Reality Conference (JVRC 2010)* (2010), 17–24.

[8] Ware, C., Arthur, K., and Booth, K. S. Fish tank virtual reality. In *Proc. INTERACT '93 and CHI '93 conf. on Human factors in computing systems*, CHI '93 (1993), 37–42.

Perceived Intensity of Click Sensation for Small Touchscreen Devices

Jeong Mook Lim
Smart Interface Research Team
Electronics and
Telecommunications Research
Institute
161, Gageong-no, Yuseong-gu,
Daejeon, Korea
Jmlim21@etri.re.kr

Heesook Shin
Smart Interface Research Team
Electronics and
Telecommunications Research
Institute
Hsshin8@etri.re.kr

Jong-uk Lee
Smart Interface Research Team
Electronics and
Telecommunications
scinfuture@etri.re.kr

Ki-Uk Kyung
Smart Interface Research Team
Electronics and
Telecommunications Research
Institute
kyungku@etri.re.kr

Abstract
'Click' and 'Tap' are one of the most commonly used gestures UI on touchscreen. There were many studies that aimed to provide realistic tactile feedback when user touched a graphic object on touchscreen. In this study, we analyzed perceived intensity levels of tactile sensation that can be utilized in clicking or tapping gesture on touchscreen. Two experiments were conducted to investigate the number of perceived intensity levels. The first was to find the range of accelerations for our new haptic device. The second experiment was to measure the number of intensity levels that can be reliably identified in the acceleration ranges. Four stimuli were used in this experiment. The result showed average information transfer of 1.34 bits for intensity identification, or equivalently, 2.53 correctly identifiable intensity levels.

ITS'12, November 11–14, 2012, Cambridge, Massachusetts, USA.
ACM 978-1-4503-1209-7/12/11.

Author Keywords
Touchscreen; Touch Gesture; Tactile Feedback

ACM Classification Keywords
H.5.2. [Information interfaces and presentation]: user interface, Haptic I/O

Introduction
The growth rate of the smartphone market is rapidly increasing compared to that of the feature phone market. One of the main features of the smartphone is to use touchscreen as their main input interface. The use of touchscreen enables the direct interaction of users with what is displayed, rather than using any other input devices such as mouse or keyboard. As the touchscreens are used in the mobile devices, touch gesture has become a common UI. Because touch gesture operates by touching the panel with a finger, users can feel tactile feedback naturally when they touch the panel. Even though it provides tactile feedback naturally, there were many efforts to create

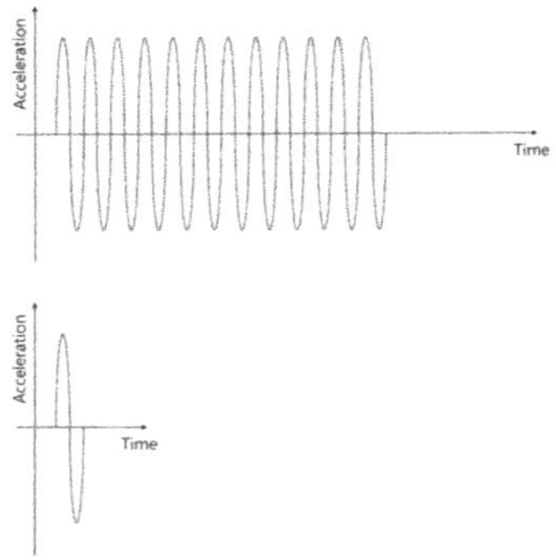

Figure 1. Vibration stimuli (Upper), Single Pulse stimuli (Lower)

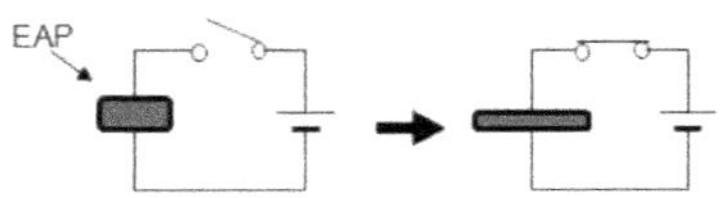

Figure 2. Working principle of EAP

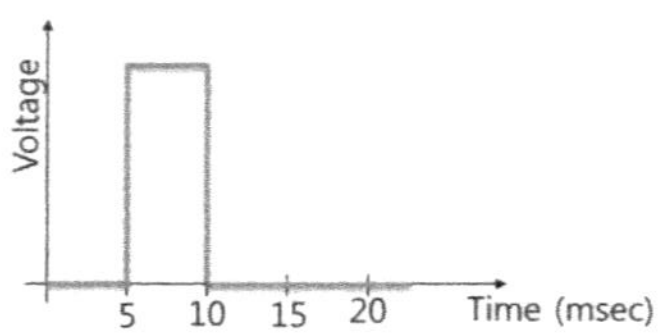

Figure 3. Input Voltage

artificial tactile feedback that goes well with GUI objects on the screen. Because the user can interact with the computing device more naturally, when the system feedback is presented in the form of combining visual, auditory and even tactile modalities. Fukumoto et al. introduced 'Active Click' that was a short vibration whenever user tapped the touch panel with their finger [1]. A short vibration was felt as clicking sensation so that it was helpful to improve the usability of touch panel, especially in noisy situation. Since 'Active Click' was introduced, several technologies have been implemented to generate tactile feedback for providing confidence of key typing on touchscreen. Nashel and Razzaque made virtual button's spring force as in increase the vibration frequency, depending on position of finger or force of pressing [2]

Despite the rich literature in this area, a lot of studies focused on vibration stimuli, not single pulse stimuli (Figure 1). According to a recent study, single pulse stimuli are more suitable to resemble the clicking sensation than vibration stimuli in aspect of reality [3]. The present study addresses how a user perceives the single pulse stimuli. More specifically, we investigated how many intensity levels of clicking sensation can be identified. Since we found the relationship between acceleration changes and perceived intensity levels, we can design diverse clicking sensations with different intensity on the touchscreen devices

Experiments

Apparatus

We developed a new type of actuator and haptic device as the test apparatus, named SHIFT. SHIFT is a typical smartphone case with an electro-active polymer (EAP) actuator. EAP actuator is advantageous to generate single pulse stimulation, because it has a fast response time and a short settling time. EAPs are polymers that exhibit a change in size or shape when stimulated by an electric field [4] (Figure 2). We attached a mass on the EAP, and the tactile stimuli are made by the motion of the mass on the EAP. The inner structure of SHIFT is shown in Figure 4. The experiment was conducted while a participant clicked button images on a smartphone equipped with SHIFT.

Stimuli

We used a square wave for input signal, a time duration from rising edge to falling edge is 5ms (Figure 3.). Fig. 4 shows averaged peak accelerations responding to input signal and a cubic regression curve with R2 value of 0.9944. According to equation (Figure 5), the acceleration range is from 0 to 1.347G for input voltage range 0 to 3.021V.

Procedure

Two preliminary experiments were conducted before the main experiment. The first experiment was designed to find the minimum stimulus. The second experiment was to determine the number of stimuli and their intensities to be used in the main experiment. The minimum stimulus was determined as the absolute threshold in acceleration. Six participants (PT1-PT6, 2 females, 4 males, age 26 ~ 42) took part in the first experiment. All of the participants were new to the tactile experiment, except for PT1 who was research staff. They wore a noise-canceling headphone to eliminate the influence of sound during the experiment. We used adaptive staircase method (1-Up 3-Down) to find the absolute threshold (reference stimulus = 0 m/s^2, Test Stimulus = Maximum acceleration). As a

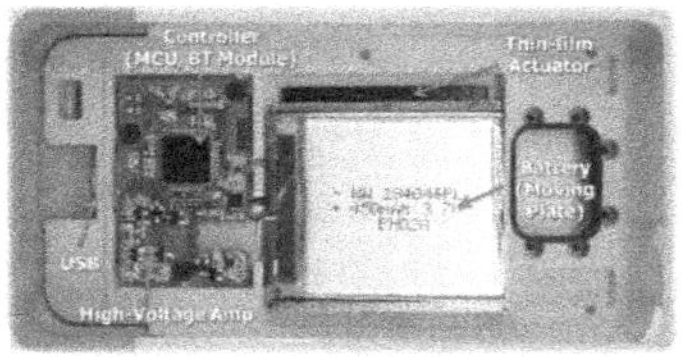

Figure 4. Inside structure of SHIFT

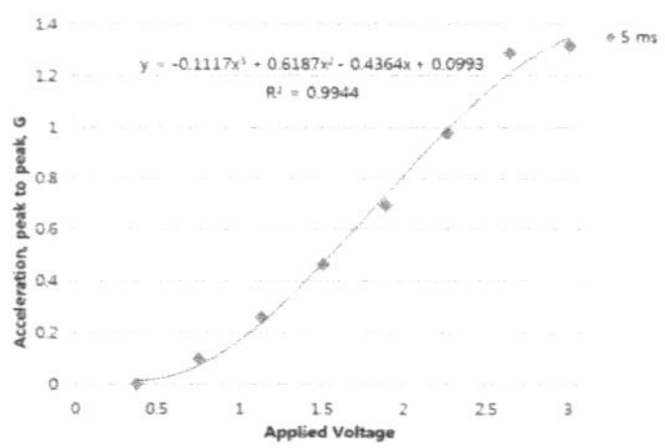

Figure 5. Acceleration response for input voltage

Equation 1

$$\mathrm{IT} = \sum_{j=1}^{k}\sum_{i=1}^{k}\frac{n_{ij}}{n}\log_2\frac{(n_{ij}\cdot n)}{(n_i\cdot n_j)}$$

, where k is the number of stimulus alternatives, n is the total number of trials, n_{ij} is the cell entry in the i_{th} row and j_{th} column of the confusion matrix.

result of the first experiment, the absolute threshold was measured 0.244G in average. However, 0.244G was too small stimulus to perceive for the participant who has poor sense. Thus, we determined 0.423G[1] and 1.347G so that all participants can feel the stimulus.

The second experiment was conducted to determine the number of stimuli alternatives and their intensities. To determine the number of stimuli alternatives, we investigated how many intensity levels were distinguished by the participants in the acceleration ranges (0.423G ~ 1.347G). The test was conducted in 2 directions, from the minimum intensity to maximum intensity, and vice versa. The intensity of test stimulus was set to smaller or bigger 1dB than the reference stimulus, depending on the test direction. If the participant found any difference between two stimuli, then the reference stimulus was reset to the test stimulus, and the intensity of the test stimulus was increased or decreased by 1dB. Twelve subjects (PT1-PT12, 3 females, 9 males, age 26 ~ 42) participated in the preliminary experiment.

The main experiment was designed to measure the number of intensity levels that can be reliably identified in the acceleration ranges. As a result of the preliminary experiment, the participant could distinguish 3.44 levels in average. Therefore, we used four stimuli alternatives in main experiment. And the intensity of stimuli alternatives was set to acceleration evenly divided with four of the acceleration ranges. The participants received one stimulus that was randomly chosen with equal probabilities, when they clicked a button on screen. The participant's task was to identify the intensity level of the presenting stimulus. Each participant completed a total of 80 trials per the experiment. In order to get an unbiased estimate of information transfer, a total of trials should be at least $5 \mathrm{x} k^2$, where k represents the number of stimulus alternatives (k=4 in the present study).

Data Analysis

The result of the main experiment was recorded in a 4-by-4 stimulus-response confusion matrix. Each cell in the confusion matrix represented the accumulated number of times the specific pair (S_i, R_j) occurs. The information transfer (IT) was calculated by applying Equation 1 to the confusion matrix. The quantity of the IT measures the amount of information transmitted from the stimuli to the responses. The number of intensity levels that can be identified without error could be 2^{IT} [5].

Results

The correct response rate was 81% for all stimuli in average. In cases of S3 and S4, the correct response rate tended to be lower. Estimated *IT*s for all participants along with averages and standard deviations are listed in Table 2. The average IT was 1.34 bits and STD was 0.11, it means that the participants could correctly identify 2.53 intensity levels ($2^{1.34bits}$ = 2.53). PT9 and PT2 scored the higher IT value than other participants, PT9 is one of the youngest participants, and PT2 was research staff and very experienced with tactile stimuli.

Discussion

Result from the preliminary experiment shows that the participants could distinguish 3.44 stimuli in average.

[1] 0.423G is the minimum acceleration for the participant who is not sensitive.

Table 1. Stimulus-Response Confusion Matrix

		Response			
		R1	R2	R3	R4
Stimulus	S1	225	15	0	0
	S2	33	201	6	0
	S3	0	19	194	27
	S4	0	1	73	166
Correctness Rate (%)		94	84	81	69

Table 2. IT value for Intensity Identification

Participants	*IT(bits)*
PT9	1.56
PT2	1.55
PT6	1.39
PT5	1.37
PT4	1.36
PT1	1.32
PT7	1.29
PT8	1.28
PT3	1.25
PT12	1.24
PT11	1.24
PT10	1.22
Average	1.34

Therefore we expected that the participants could identify at most 3 intensity levels of stimuli. However, the number of intensity levels that the participant could correctly identify was 2.53. The reason why the score is down is that the participant's task was changed from distinguishing a different stimulus to identifying a specific stimulus. The participants were also tended to more confuse stimuli between S3 and S4 than S1, S2 and S3. This is because the difference of the intensity of each stimulus was uniform. In order to identify better the each stimulus, the difference between each stimulus should be larger in proportional to the intensity of the reference stimulus. And the fatigue also affected the confusion.

Conclusion

In this paper, we analyzed perceived intensity of tactile stimuli that can be used in clicking sensation on small touchscreen devices. Tactile stimuli were generated by the EAP actuator, and a smartphone having a 4.3 inch touchscreen was used in the user experiment. We used the single pulse stimuli for a realistic clicking sensation rather than vibration stimuli. Acceleration range of the stimuli was 0.423G ~ 1.347G, the experimental results shows that the user can distinguish the stimuli into 3.44 levels and they can also identify 2.53 stimuli in the same range.

It means that the users are able to distinguish the meaning of the buttons on small touchscreen device, by adjusting the intensity of haptic feedback even though they click the same sized button image. The user can sense their typing error instantly while they are typing, by applying the different intensity of clicking sensations to character keys, numeric keys or function keys. Therefore we can enhance the key typing speed on the small sized touch screen device.

Acknowledgements

This work has been supported by the S/W Computing R&D program of MKE/KEIT (10035360, TAXEL: Visio-haptic Display and Rendering Engine).

References

[1] Fukumoto, M. and Sugimura, T. 2001. Active Click: Tactile feedback for Touch Panels. In Proc. of the CHI EA'01 on Human Factors in Computing Systems, CHI'01.

[2] Nashel, A. and Razzaque, S. Tactile virtual buttons for mobile devices. 2003. In Proc. of the CHI EA'03 on Human Factors in Computing Systems, CHI'03.

[3] Shin, H., Lim, J., Lee, J., Kyung. K, and Lee, G. 2012. Tactile Feedback for Button GUI on Touch Devices. In Proceeding of the CHI'12 on Human Factors in Computing Systems, CHI'12.

[4] Carpi, F., Rossi, D., Kornbluh, R., Pelrine, P. and Sommer-Larsen, P. Dielectric elastomers as electro-mechanical transducers: Fundamentals, Materials, Devices, Models and Applications of an Emerging Electroactive Polymer Technology. Elsevier, 2008.

[5] H.Y.Chen, Information transfer of tactile signals on mobile devices. Masters' thesis, Purdue University, USA, May 2009.

Novel Interaction Techniques Using Touch-sensitive Tangibles in Tabletop Environments

Saphyra Amaro
Interaction Technology Laboratory
The University of Tokyo
7-3-1 Hongo, Bunkyo-ku,
Tokyo, JAPAN
saphyra@itl.t.u-tokyo.ac.jp

Masanori Sugimoto
Interaction Technology Laboratory
The University of Tokyo
7-3-1 Hongo, Bunkyo-ku,
Tokyo, JAPAN
sugi@itl.t.u-tokyo.ac.jp

ITS'12, November 11–14, 2012, Cambridge, Massachusetts, USA.
ACM 978-1-4503-1209-7/12/11.

Abstract
In this work, we propose techniques for interaction that use a touch-sensitive tangible to assist 3D manipulation in tabletop applications. The objective of this research is to investigate the effectiveness and user satisfaction with this combination for performing virtual object manipulation in tabletop environments. A prototype of a touch-sensitive tangible was constructed and some of the proposed techniques were implemented, namely 3D translation and rotation. We conducted a pilot study to compare 3D manipulation on the tabletop with and without the tangible, from which we found that the touch-sensitive tangible was useful for 3D manipulation tasks.

Author Keywords
Touch-sensitive tangible; input device; Tangible User Interface; TUI; HCI; Tabletop; 3D interaction

ACM Classification Keywords
H.5.2 [Information interfaces and presentation]: User Interfaces. Input devices and strategies..

Introduction
Tabletop interfaces impose physical constraints to interaction because they are flat and allow only 2D touch inputs on their surface. As a consequence, tasks with high DOF such as 3D manipulation require specific

Figure 1: The touch-sensitive tangible.

implementation methods. Researchers have been spending significant effort to design intuitive ways for perfoming 3D manipulation – some works are introduced in the next section.

Touching is one of the simplest and most intuitive ways of interacting with objects. In tabletop systems, though, as concluded by Hancock et al. [4], tangibles are usually preferred over direct touch interaction for tasks that require fine control. As also stated in the same work, "an alternate method for manipulating 3D objects would be to combine the best aspects of both techniques".

In our work, we propose combining direct touch and tangibles for manipulating 3D objects in tabletop environments in a different fashion – by combining direct touch on tabletops and touch-sensitive tangibles. For achieving this, we built a touch-sensitive tangible, and designed and implemented a set of interaction techniques. Finally, we conducted a pilot study to evaluate our proposal. The results show that users found the touch-sensitive tangible interface easier to use, more effective and more satisfactory for 3D manipulation than utilizing a interface which only used touch on the tabletop surface for the same purpose.

Related works

Several researches propose techniques for 3D manipulation. Reisman et al. [5] and Au et al. [2] propose touch-only techniques on tabletops.

Some works propose the utilization of tangibles, as we do – Wu et al. [8] employ a tangible in combination with a tabletop to navigate a 3D world. The tangible's position is determined by fiducial tracking when on the tabletop's surface and by a camera mounted over the tabletop when lifted. We utilize, instead of position, acceleration data, and our tangible also recognizes finger gestures on its surface. Aguerreche et al. [1] created extensible tangibles, whose manipulation is reflected in an associated virtual object. Our proposal also associates a tangible to a virtual object. Though, we propose a small and light tangible, which can be held by only one hand, leaving the other free for touching the tabletop.

However, even though 3D manipulation has been largely discussed, there are few researches regarding touch-sensitive tangibles. One is Pulse [3], which is a concept interface. TZee [7] and SlapWidgets [6] are transparent tangibles that can detect user touches by using the tabletop's and the tangible's lighting properties. So, if taken away from the table's surface, both cannot recognize touch. This restricts their usage, differently from our tangible, which is made for mid-air manipulations and not limited to the tabletop's surface.

Interface design

Our interface proposal for 3D manipulation is that the user transfers control of a virtual object from the tabletop to the touch-sensitive tangible and manipulates it in mid-air. Therefore, the tangible works as an avatar of the virtual object. For designing the interface, we adopted the following guidelines:

- *Size:* the tangible should be held with only one hand without causing any discomfort.
- *Weight:* the tangible should be of low weight so it does not tire the user's arms.
- *Accuracy:* users should accurately manipulate 3D objects on tabletops.
- *Cost:* the implementation cost should be low.

We decided to use a tangible because of affordance. We believe that it improves the 3D manipulation experience

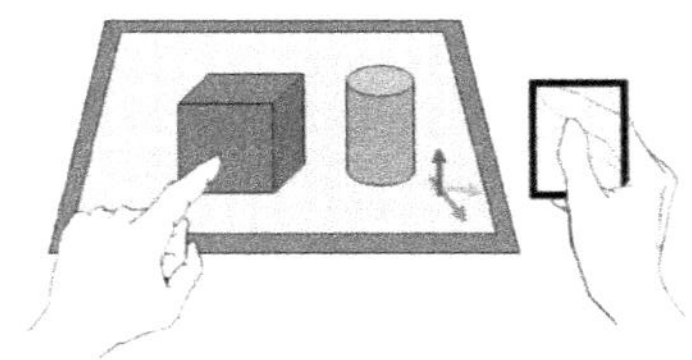

Figure 2: Transferring control of a 3D model from the tabletop to the tangible by touching them simultaneously.

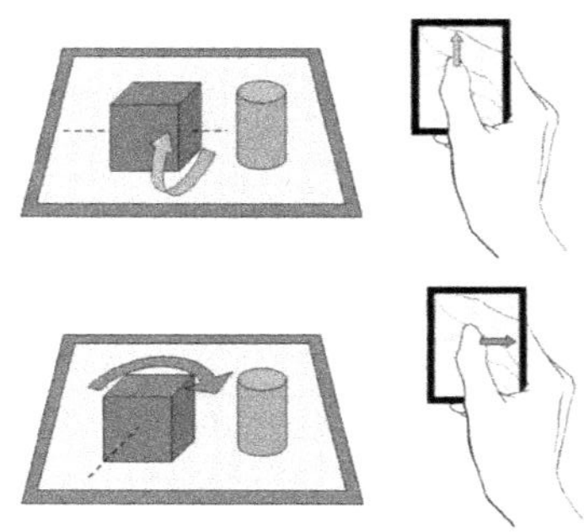

Figure 3: Rotations are performed by a scrolling gesture on the tangiblefs surface. Top: rotation about the X-axis. Bottom: rotation about the Y-axis.

because the user feels that s/he is actually holding and manipulating something, even though it is a virtual object. It is known, though, that adding a device limits the flexibility of the interface. In the future, we want to quantify how negative this addition is.

Touch-sensitive tangible prototype

The prototype comprises a 3-axis accelerometer breakout from SparkFun Electronics attached to a Nintendo DS touch screen (2.2″ x 2.75″). Both are connected to an Arduino Mega board, which is connected to the tabletop. The prototype is shown in Figure 1. Movement is detected by determining the peaks of acceleration using derivatives. The relative amplitude of each peak is used as a multiplicative factor for changing the velocity of the translation/rotation.

The touch gestures supported for now are scrolling gestures. When touch is detected, the algorithm determines if the touch is being held or if it is the start of a gesture. The touch points are approximated by a straight line and its slope determines whether it was a horizontal or a vertical scroll.

Even though this prototype resembles a smartphone, we prefer this implementation because we want to develop interaction techniques that utilize the transparency of the tangible, such as transferring a pattern from a printed image to the application by drawing on the touch-screen. Also, we want to propose a simple tangible with low implementation cost.

Interaction techniques

The user interacts with the tabletop application by concurrently using touch on the tabletop screen and manipulation/touch on the touch-sensitive tangible. The user should hold the tangible as shown in Figure 1. The thumb should be used for gestures and touches.

To start manipulating 3D models using our interface, first the user has to to transfer control of a virtual object to the tangible. This is done by touching a specific object on the tabletop's surface and touching on the tangible at the same time. This procedure is illustrated in Figure 2. After control is transferred, the user is able to perform the following actions:

- *Translation of a selected component.* To translate the object along the X-, Y- or Z-axis, the user has to touch the tangible, hold the touch and move the tangible in the desired direction. To end the translation, the user just has to stop touching the tangible.
- *Rotation of a selected component.* To perform a rotation about the X-axis, the user makes a horizontal scroll gesture on the tangible's surface. For the Y-axis, a vertical scroll gesture is used. This action is illustrated in Figure 3.

Our proposal involves also other interaction techniques, such as rotation of the world-coordinate axes, extrusion, rotation by tilting and cancelling the control of a component by shaking the tangible.

Preliminary evaluation

We conducted a preliminary evaluation of our proposal with 5 users, all men, aged 23-40. One tabletop application that offered only on-screen elements for performing manipulation (touchable GUI) and one that used the touch-sensitive tangible were introduced to the subjects. They were given as much time as desired for verifying the interfaces' limitations. Afterwards, they rated each interface in a 0 to 10 scale regarding how easy it was to use, how well it worked for 3D manipulation and how

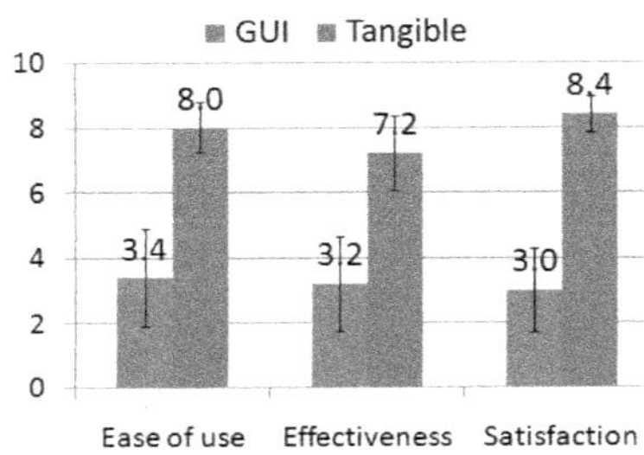

Figure 4: Results obtained from the user study. Y-axis shows the score obtained, while the X-axis shows the aspects of the interface evaluated. The touchable GUI application got an average of 3.4 points for ease of use, 3.2 for achieving is purpose and 3.0 for satisfaction with the interface. The touch-sensitive tangible got 8.0, 7.2 and 8.4 points, respectively.

satisfied they felt with it. The results can be seen in the Figure 4. The touch-sensitive tangible got higher scores in all items. Also, all users answered positively when asked whether introducing a touch-sensitive tangible in a tabletop interface for 3D manipulation was valid, and if they felt the tangible was useful for that purpose.

Discussion

During the evaluation, we obtained positive comments from the users, most regarding the intuitiveness of the manipulation using the tangible, the fact that the manipulation does not require exhausting arm movements, and that manipulation can be done without memorizing a complex gesture set. One user suggested implementing tilt detection in the tangible, which allows rotation guided by the applications current view, similar to the "trackball" rotation mode in Blender.

The biggest problem pointed out was accuracy. The movements are detected only by processing the accelerometer's readings. Since they fluctuate, sometimes the virtual object would move a little in a wrong direction. Another problem pointed out was the fluctuation of the control-display ratio, also caused by the accelerometer's imprecision.

Conclusion & Future work

In this work, we propose and implement an interface for 3D manipulation in tabletop interfaces utilizing touch-sensitive tangibles. For that, we created a tangible that recognizes touch, developed and implemented interaction techniques using it. In a preliminary evaluation of the interface, we found that our touch-sensitive tangible is, in fact, a valid idea for 3D manipulation and that users felt it was useful for such purpose.

As future work, we want to improve our system's accuracy by adding another sensor to the tangible. Afterwards, we will add the interaction techniques not implemented yet, design new ones if necessary and perform a user study.

References

[1] Aguerreche, L., Duval, T., and Lécuyer, A. Reconfigurable tangible devices for 3d virtual object manipulation by single or multiple users. In *Proc. VRST '10* (2010), 227–230.

[2] Au, O., Tai, C., and Fu, H. Multitouch gestures for constrained transformation of 3d objects. *Computer Graphics Forum: special issue of Eurographics 2012.* (2012).

[3] Gupta, G. Pulse: tangible touch. In *Proc. MobileHCI'10* (2010), 471–472.

[4] Hancock, M., Hilliges, O., Collins, C., Baur, D., and Carpendale, S. Exploring tangible and direct touch interfaces for manipulating 2d and 3d information on a digital table. In *Proc. ITS '09* (2009), 77–84.

[5] Reisman, J. L., Davidson, P. L., and Han, J. Y. A screen-space formulation for 2d and 3d direct manipulation. In *Proc. UIST '09* (2009), 69–78.

[6] Weiss, M., Wagner, J., Jansen, Y., Jennings, R., Khoshabeh, R., Hollan, J. D., and Borchers, J. Slap widgets: bridging the gap between virtual and physical controls on tabletops. In *Proc. CHI '09* (2009), 481–490.

[7] Williams, C., Yang, X. D., Partridge, G., Millar-Usiskin, J., Major, A., and Irani, P. Tzee: exploiting the lighting properties of multi-touch tabletops for tangible 3d interactions. In *Proc. CHI '11* (2011), 1363–1372.

[8] Wu, A., Reilly, D., Tang, A., and Mazalek, A. Tangible navigation and object manipulation in virtual environments. In *Proc. TEI '11* (2011), 37–44.

Tangible Interactions on a Flat Panel Display Using Actuated Paper Sheets

Kota Amano
The University of Tokyo
7-3-1 Hongo, Bukyo-ku
Tokyo, 113-8656, JAPAN
amano@aml.t.u-tokyo.ac.jp

Akio Yamamoto
The University of Tokyo
7-3-1 Hongo, Bukyo-ku
Tokyo, 113-8656, JAPAN
akio@aml.t.u-tokyo.ac.jp

ITS'12, November 11–14, 2012, Cambridge, Massachusetts, USA.
ACM 978-1-4503-1209-7/12/11.

Abstract
This paper describes active tangible interactions on a flat panel display using plain paper sheets as tangible media. A prototype system employs transparent planar electrostatic actuators that cover the surface of a flat-panel display to realize co-located tangible and visual interactions. In a demonstration program, users can interact with animated computer graphics through plain paper sheets actuated by the electrostatic actuators.

Author Keywords
Interactive surface; tangible tabletop interface; transparent electrostatic actuator; paper sheet

ACM Classification Keywords
H.5.2 [Information interfaces and presentation (e.g., HCI)]: User Interfaces

General Terms
Design

Introduction
Tangible tabletop interfaces realize intuitive human-computer interaction using real tangible objects placed on computer screens as communication media [1,2]. In typical tangible interface systems, a user communicates with a computer by handling passive tangible objects, through which uni-directional interaction is realized.

The user experience would be enhanced considerably if the tangible objects can actively respond to the users' operations. Such active tangibles can be realized by using screen-embedded actuators [3,4]. As embedded actuators, most of the reported systems employed electro-magnetic motors. Although the use of electro-magnetic motors can provide high actuation power and high motion controllability, the resultant systems tend to have heavy and bulky structures due to the heavy use of ferromagnetic materials in those actuators. Another solution is to use self-moving tangibles that have built-in motors [5]. This allows easier integration of actuators but requires large and complicated tangible objects. For better integration of actuators to computer screens, another actuator solution would be preferred.

One promising alternative is electrostatic surface actuators [6,7]. Electrostatic surface actuators are characterized by its thin and light-weight structure, possible optical transparency, and actuation capability for everyday materials, such as plain paper sheets. In [8], a simple tangible interaction was demonstrated using an electrostatic actuator. The work emphasized its compact structure; the actuator is simply put on a flat panel display, which is not possible with typical electromagnetic motors. Although the work successfully showed the potential of the electrostatic actuators for active tangible interfaces, its demonstration was limited due to the opaqueness of the actuator used. The opaque actuator impeded visual rendering in the actuation area. To avoid this problem, the actuator covered only a limited area of the screen, and a special interaction scenario, *interactive shadow play*, was tailored, in which tangible and visual interactions took place at different locations.

This work tackles on this problem and realizes co-located tangible and visual interactions. Transparent electrostatic actuators are manufactured using indium-tin-oxide (ITO), a transparent conductive material. The use of transparent actuators allows to use a whole display as the interaction area, as well as to render computer graphics directly below the actuator to realize tangible action and visual rendering at the same place. This paper reports on the system structure of the prototyped tangible interface system and a demonstration program that realizes bi-directional user-computer interaction. It demonstrates an intuitive interaction with an animated character through a plain paper sheet as a tangible. The paper also mentions the potential simple force feedback in the prototype.

Transparent planar electrostatic actuator

Several actuation principles have been proposed for electrostatic surface actuators and this work utilizes induction actuation principle, which is realized by multi-phase electrode structure [7]. This work fabricated a three-phase electrode pattern using ITO on a transparent sheet of polyethylene terephthalate (PET) as shown in Figure 1. The three-phase electrodes and two bus lines for voltage feeding were made by ITO in the same layer, but the third bus line needs to be made in a different layer and was made by conducting silver paste, which is not transparent. The whole surface of the electrodes was covered with another PET sheet for insulation.

Actuation in one degree-of-freedom (DOF) is realized on the three-phase electrode area, whose size is 200 mm long and 100 mm wide. For induction actuation of a paper sheet, three-phase sinusoidal signals are applied to the three-phase electrodes [7]. The voltage

Appearance of the transparent actuator.

Note:
As reported in [7], performance of this actuation principle is sensitive to humidity. The experiments of this work were performed at relative humidity of 45-60%. Driving signal frequency was adjusted depending on the condition.

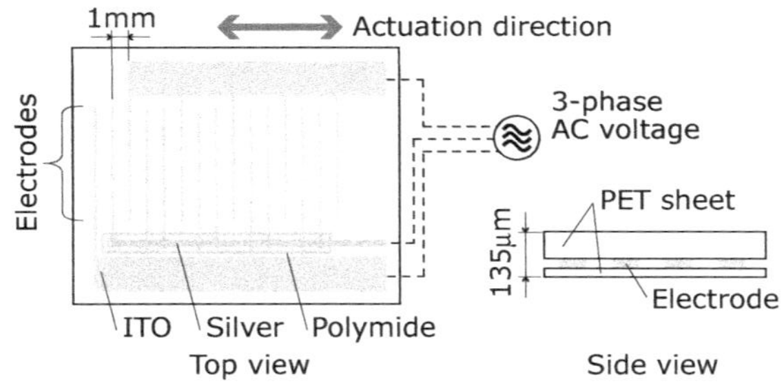

Figure 1: Structure of transparent electrostatic actuator.

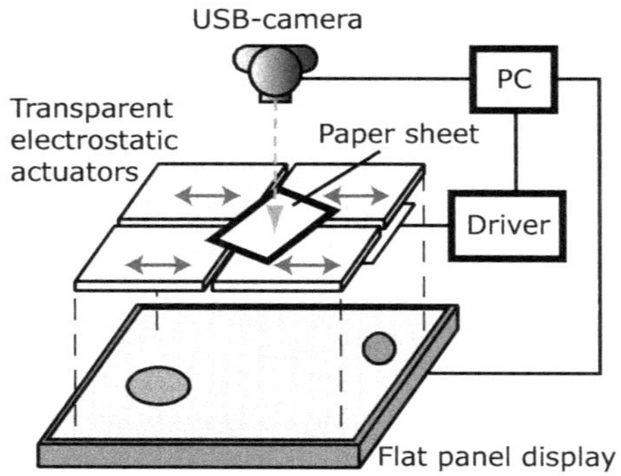

Figure 2: Setup overview of the interaction system.

amplitude and frequency in this work range between 600 V to 800 V and 100 Hz to 1 kHz, respectively. The motion of the actuated sheet is asynchronous and requires feedback control. This work utilizes a camera as a position sensor. To cope with the limited operation speed of the camera (30 frames per second), the actuator was intermittently activated.

Active tangible interface system

System overview

Figure 2 shows the schematic of the prototype system. Four electrostatic actuators are placed on a flat panel display to cover a most part of the surface of 24.1 inch wide liquid crystal display. All the actuators have 1-DOF motion capability in lateral direction and thus the motion of tangible objects is restricted in the lateral 1-DOF, in this particular work. On the surface of the actuators, glass beads with 100 µm diameter are scattered to keep spacing with the actuated objects and to reduce the surface friction. The resultant friction coefficient was about 0.07. Tangible objects are sheets of plain paper, on which illustrations are printed by a laser printer and are cut into corresponding shapes. For actuation of a tangible paper sheet, a computer program sends actuation commands to the driver electronics. In this particular system, the driver electronics activates all the four actuators at the same time in the same actuation condition.

Co-located tangible interaction using plain paper

A pilot application program was implemented to demonstrate active tangible interactions. The program draws an animated cat, which wanders around in the whole screen. At the same time, the program detects the position of a paper sheet by using the overhead camera. The animated cat is programmed to rush to the detected paper sheet. As any collisions occur between the paper sheet and the animated cat, the program issues an actuation command so that the paper sheet will be moved in an appropriate lateral direction.

With the implemented program, a user can play with the animated cat through the paper sheet. User experience may differ depending on the design of the paper sheet. For example, if the paper sheet is a ball, a user can play catch with the cat; as the user throws the ball to the cat, the cat hits it back to the user (see

Figure 3). Or, if the sheet is designed as a foxtail, a user can pat the cat as shown in Figure 4.

Force perception

The electrostatic force generated on the paper sheet is just enough to move the paper sheet and cannot be clearly perceived by a user in direct touch as in Figure 3. However, with a long sheet such as foxtail as in Figure 4, the force can be amplified by a lever mechanism, and the user could feel as if the animated cat was pushing back through the sheet.

Conclusion

This paper demonstrated that transparent electrostatic actuators and plain paper sheets as tangible media can realize co-located tangible and visual interactions with a simple system structure. Although this particular work dealt with a simple interaction in 1-DOF motion, future studies will address more sophisticated interactions by multi-DOF motion and multi-objects actuation.

Closeup of application view. Silver bus lines are visible, but not so eye-catching.

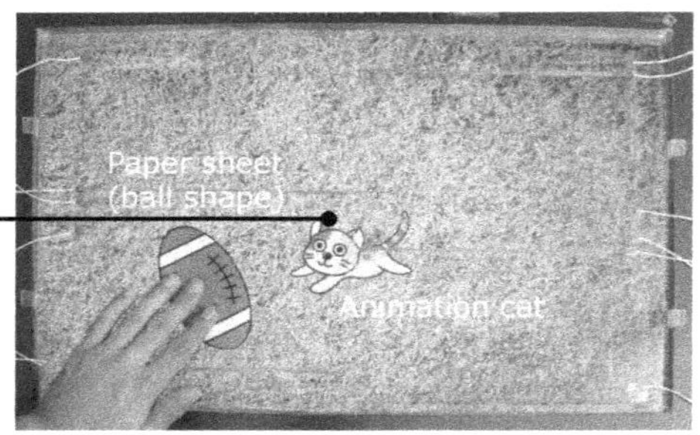

Figure 3: Example of the active tangible interaction. The user is playing catch with animation cat.

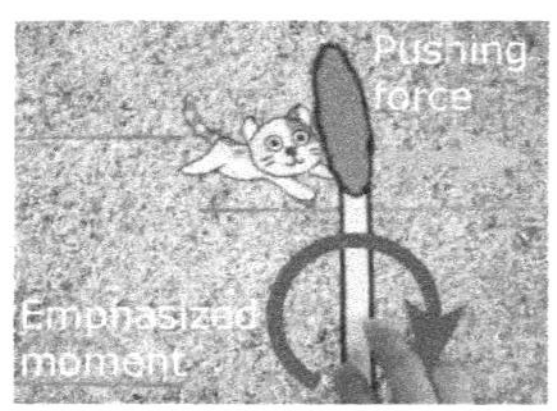

Figure 4: Force amplification for force perception.

Acknowledgement

This work was supported by Funding Program for Next Generation World-Leading Researchers (LR013) from JSPS, Japan.

References

[1] Brave, S., Ishii, H., and Dahley, A. Tangible Interfaces for Remote Collaboration and Communication. Proc. CSCW'98, 169-178, 1998.

[2] Avrahami, D., Wobbrock, J.O., and Izadi, S. Portico: Tangible Interaction on and around a Tablet. Proc. UIST'11, 347-356, 2011.

[3] Pangaro, G., Maynes-Aminzade, D. and Ishii, H. The Actuated Workbench: Computer-Controlled Actuation in Tabletop Tangible Interfaces. Proc. UIST'02, 181-190, 2002.

[4] Yoshida, S., Noma, H., and Hosaka, K. Proactive Desk II: Development of a New Multi-object Haptic Display Using a Linear Induction Motor. Proc. IEEE Virtual Reality Conference 2006, 2006.

[5] Richter, J., Thomas, B. H., Sugimoto, M., and Inam, M. Remote Active Tangible Interactions. Proc. TEI'07, 39-42, 2007.

[6] Egawa, S., Niino, T., and Higuchi, T. Film Actuators: Planar Electrostatic Surface-Drive Actuators. Proc. 1991 IEEE MEMS, 9-14, 1991.

[7] Yamamoto, A., Tsuruta, S., and Higuchi, T. Planar 3-DOF Paper Sheet Manipulation Using Electrostatic Induction. Proc. 2010 IEEE ISIE, 493-498, 2010.

[8] Amano, K., and Yamamoto, A. An Interaction on a Flat Panel Display Using a Planar 1-DOF Electrostatic Actuator. Proc. ITS 2011, 2011.

Revisiting Hovering: Interaction Guides for Interactive Surfaces

Victor Cheung
victor.cheung@uwaterloo.ca
Collaborative Systems Laboratory
Systems Design Engineering
University of Waterloo
Waterloo, Ontario, Canada

Stacey D. Scott
stacey.scott@uwaterloo.ca
Collaborative Systems Laboratory
Systems Design Engineering
University of Waterloo
Waterloo, Ontario, Canada

Jens Heydekorn
jheyde@isg.cs.uni-magdeburg.de
User Interface & Software
Engineering Group
Otto-von-Guericke-Universität
Magdeburg, Germany

Raimund Dachselt
raimund.dachselt@tu-dresden.de
Interactive Media Lab
Technische Universität Dresden
Dresden, Germany

ITS'12, November 11–14, 2012, Cambridge, Massachusetts, USA.
ACM 978-1-4503-1209-7/12/11.

Abstract
Current touch-based interactive surfaces rely heavily on a trial-and-error approach for guiding users through the interaction process. In contrast, the legacy WIMP (Windows, Icons, Menus, Pointer) paradigm employs various methods to provide user assistance. A commonly used strategy is the use of mouse hovering. This research explores how this strategy can be adapted and expanded to user interaction with interactive surfaces to provide user assistance as well as to help address common surface interaction issues, such as precisions. Design dimensions and considerations are discussed, and potential hover interaction techniques are proposed. These techniques emphasize the use of animation to facilitate user engagement and improve the overall user experience.

Author Keywords
Hovering; animation; interactive surfaces; proximate interaction.

ACM Classification Keywords
H.5.2. User Interfaces – Interaction styles.

General Terms
Human Factors; Design.

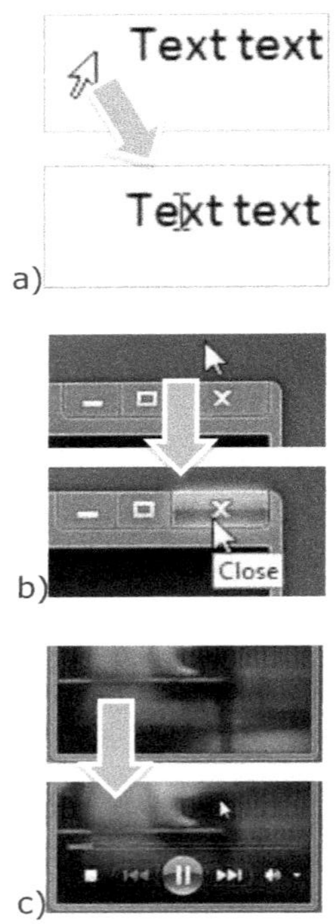

Figure 1. Strategies used with a cursor to provide extra position- and context-dependent information. (a: shape change; b: tooltip; c: revealed controls)

Introduction

Touch-based interactive surfaces respond directly to input from a user's fingers (or hands), without the need for additional input mechanisms, such as a mouse, closely coupling the input and output channels. However, this input model also reduces the state of input to a binary touch or no touch, limiting the expressiveness of a user's input. While various gestures and on-screen menus have been proposed to support user interaction, they require users to learn and memorize steps, often achieved by trial and error.

In the traditional WIMP (Windows, Icons, Menus, Pointer) desktop interaction model, the ability to "point" to an item of interest using a system cursor without activating the item, enables application designers to use position and context information to convey additional information to assist users in their understanding of the interaction process. Such *hovering* (or *mouseover*) capability is commonly used to guide the user through the interaction process by cursor shape change and tooltips (short pieces of text), and timely reveal of controls (see Figure 1).

Hovering allows the system to provide feedback or hints to its user before an action occurs. At the same time, it preserves display space by hiding information or interface components until they are needed. These advantages are widely adopted in various computing applications for both novice and expert users. In contrast, basic touch-based interactive surfaces provide binary input only, and thus, an equivalent hover action is not possible to detect in these systems. However, additional sensors can be added to enable user interaction near the surface, or *proximate interactions*, such as optical sensing [9], or capacitive disruption detection (e.g. Cypress's Real Hover Technology[1]). This proximity sensing can then be used to provide hover-type interaction in surface applications, and provide the potential for designers to leverage the advantages of hover discussed above to improve the overall usability and user experience of touch surface applications.

The aim of this project is to adapt and expand traditional hover interaction design techniques on touch surfaces by taking advantage of proximity sensing capabilities. Moreover, this work focuses on the use of animation as a form of visual feedback to users' proximate interactions. To set the context for this work, we first briefly overview some related work. Next, we discuss our design concepts and future plans for the project.

Related Work

Several techniques have been proposed to bring back hovering to interactive surfaces by offsetting the touch location [3,7], or using an additional input level [4]. Though, they are limited to traditional behaviors of a mouse cursor without adapting to interactive surfaces.

Some recent work has investigated interactions close to a touch surface and generalizes them as *near touch interaction* [6,8]. In contrast to these interactions that rely on gestures or precise positioning of the hands, we focus on interface design that facilitates the fundamental touch input via animation, and the guiding ability it possesses.

[1] http://www.cypress.com/touch/hover.cfm

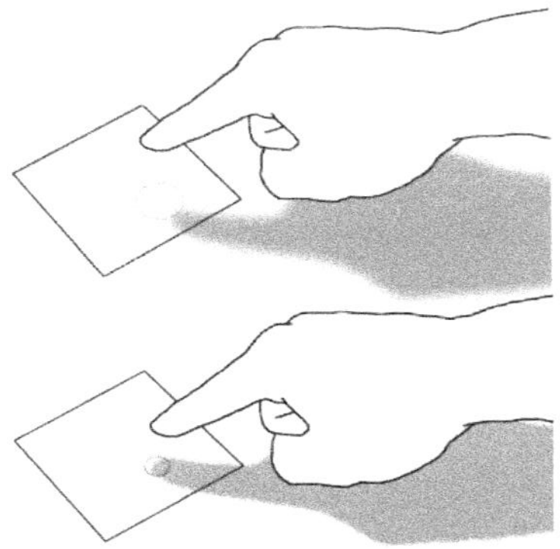

Figure 2. Touch position estimated by the system is shown during hovering as a shrinking halo (multi-state continuous hovering).

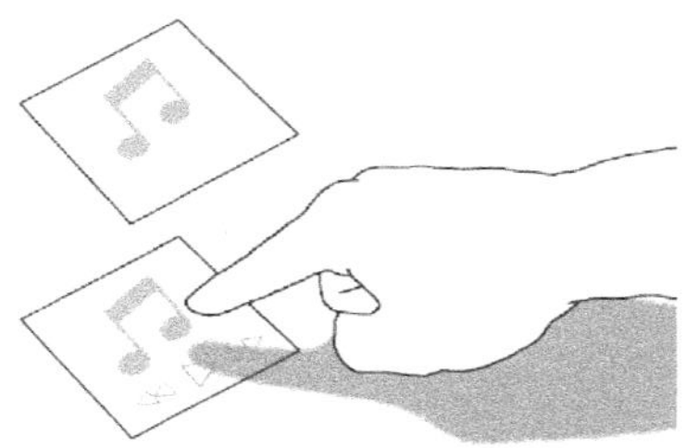

Figure 3. Playback controls appear as the finger approaches (2-state discrete hovering).

Design Dimensions and Considerations

With the additional input modality of proximity in an interactive surface system, an extended set of design dimensions is available with the following parameters: *context* (application status), *position* (planar finger position relative to surface), *proximity* (finger to surface distance), *granularity* (discrete or continuous input), *speed* (rate of approach or depart), and *angle*.

While several modalities of output are possible, this project focuses on the use of animation to provide visual feedback regarding proximate interactions. Previous research has shown that proper use of animation improves decision-making [5] and makes the system more enjoyable and comprehensible [1]. Thus, animation seems an appropriate choice for designing hover interaction on a touch surface that helps to guide user interaction and improve the overall user experience. Various animation parameters are being explored to understand their potential to support hover assistance, including but not limited to *movement* (positional change, rate) and other *appearance* attributes (size, brightness, color, transparency).

When designing animations as feedback to proximate interactions, the following design issues must also be considered:

- *Proximity range.* Proximity sensing provides an additional near and far dimensional range that can be leveraged to provide more sophisticated hover interaction, e.g., multi-state feedback. Also, as hovering is invoked and maintained by the *proximity* of the finger, the invoking height has to be carefully selected: too large creates unnecessary hovering detection and can confuse the user; too small increases the chances of unintentional touches.
- *Feedback complexity*. Duration of each hovering is likely to be short. Thus the visual response from the system has to be immediate and understandable: lengthy words and multiple steps should be avoided.
- *Feedback location*. The animation should take place at the immediate vicinity of the hovering *position*, where the user is currently focusing their attention.
- *Relationship between animation content and proximity*. The relationship between animation content and *proximity* should be consistent with the amount of information needed in the particular context. For instance, increased amounts of animated details could be provided as proximity increases. *Continuity*, *speed* and *angle* could also be considered as determining factors of the user experience context when appropriate.

Interaction Techniques

The project aims to leverage the directness of touch-based systems by adapting traditional hover techniques while providing visual responses for suggestive actions via the use of animation. The animation techniques are grouped based on the *eight uses of animation* proposed by Baecker and Small [1], as described below:

Informative. Informative techniques combine the purpose of *identification* and *choice*. When a hovering event is invoked, the estimated position of touch can be displayed, which is animated in proportion to the finger-surface distance for further cues (see Figure 2). This addresses the occlusion problem by making the estimated point of contact visible before being occluded. Also, some of the hovering techniques in the WIMP paradigm, e.g., appearing controls, can be used, allowing the user to decide ahead if touching at that position leads to the desired outcome (see Figure 3).

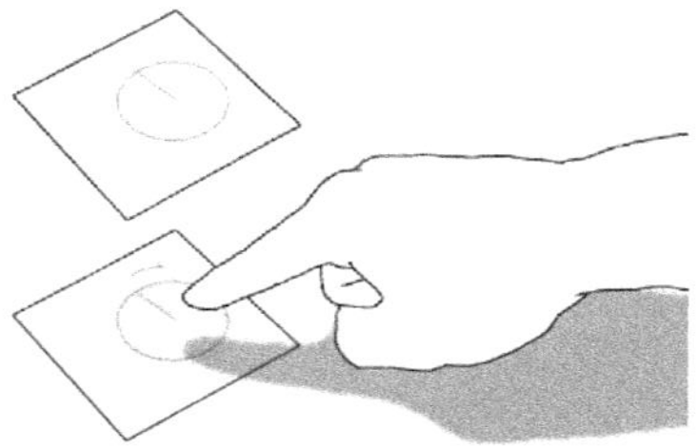

Figure 4. Control guides (glow and arrow) appear upon approach.

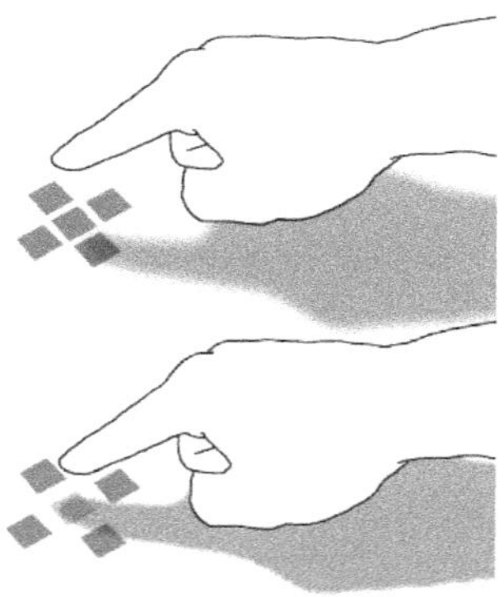

Figure 5. Items move away (and the to-be-selected item lights up) upon approach to prevent selection error.

Guidance. In a more elaborate manner, animation can be used for *demonstration*, providing *feedback*, and showing necessary steps as *guidance* to bring the user through the interaction process. For example, a control that requires adjustment can become increasingly animated (e.g., lights up) upon approach, and displays available options (e.g., arrows, preview of suggested movement) (see Figure 4). In addition, "feedforward" [2] can be used as a preview of an action's outcome.

Preventive. Instead of reporting a user-made error, animation can be used to proactively prevent the error from happening. The key idea is to visually inform the user ahead with the undesirable options, and with smooth transitioning (e.g., slow-in-slow-out) so the user will not be startled. For example, unavailable nearby items can move away slightly during hovering to prevent selection error (see Figure 5). This mitigates the precision problem by both lowering the chances of wrong selection and increasing that of the correct one.

Conclusion & Future Work

Like any other systems, touch-based interactive surfaces require ways to guide their users through the interaction process. We propose the use of hovering and animation to address this issue in a visual and engaging way. In particular, we propose using animation in response to proximate interaction to provide suggestive guides, as well as to deter infeasible interaction to improve the overall interaction process.

In the future we plan to evaluate the design concepts proposed here, with a focus on the subtleties of the implementation parameters, such as threshold of hovering and relationship between animation content and proximity. We will also explore the extension of hovering beyond a single finger. Finally, we intend to investigate how animation could be used during and after the touch event to guide the user further.

ACKNOWLEDGEMENTS

This work was funded by the NSERC SurfNet Network.

References

1. Baecker, R. and Small, I. (1990). Animation at the Interface. In L. Brenda (ed.) *The Art of Human-Computer Interface Design*. Boston, Addison-Wesley Longman Publishing Co., Inc., 251-267.
2. Djajadiningrat, T., Overbeeke, K., and Wensveen, S. (2002). But how, Donald, tell us how?: on the creation of meaning in interaction design through feedforward and inherent feedback. *Proc DIS 2002*, 285-291.
3. Esenther, A. and Ryall, K. (2006). Fluid DTMouse: better mouse support for touch-based interactions. *Proc. AVI 2006*, 112-115.
4. Forlines, C., Shen, C. and Buxton, B. (2005). Glimpse: A Novel Input Model for Mutli-level Devices. *Ext. Abstracts CHI 2005*, 1375-1378.
5. Gonzalez, C. (1996). Does animation in user interfaces improve decision making? *Proc. CHI 1996*, 27-34.
6. Moghaddam, A. B., Svendsen, J., Tory, M., and Albu, A., B. (2011). Integrating touch and near touch interactions for information visualizations. *Ext. Abstracts CHI 2011*, 2347-2352.
7. Potter, R. L., Weldon, L. J., and Shneiderman, B. (1988). Improving the accuracy of touch screens: an experimental evaluation of three strategies. *Proc. CHI 1988*, 27-32.
8. Takeoka, Y., Miyaki, T., and Rekimoto, J. (2010). Z-touch: an infrastructure for 3d gesture interaction in the proximity of tabletop surfaces. *Proc. ITS 2010*, 91-94.
9. Wilson, A. D. (2005). PlayAnywhere: A Compact Interactive Tabletop Projection-vision System. *Proc. UIST 2005*, 83-92.

An Immersive Surface for 3D Interactions

Yusuke Takeuchi
Interaction Technology Lab.
University of Tokyo
7-3-1 Hongo, Bunkyo-ku,
Tokyo, Japan
yusuke@itl.t.u-tokyo.ac.jp

Masanori Sugimoto
Interaction Technology Lab.
University of Tokyo
7-3-1 Hongo, Bunkyo-ku,
Tokyo, Japan
sugi@itl.t.u-tokyo.ac.jp

ITS'12, November 11–14, 2012, Cambridge, Massachusetts, USA.
ACM 978-1-4503-1209-7/12/11.

Abstract
This paper proposes a new tabletop interface that enables a user to visualize projected objects as if they existed on the tabletop surface. It uses head tracking, without the need for any specialized head-mounted hardware, displays, or markers. Nowadays, many interactive tabletop interfaces support interactions above the surface because this is more intuitive. In these 3D interactions, users should be able to gauge the size and height of the projected virtual objects. We evaluate our system quantitatively via a 3D interaction task, by comparing it with a standard tabletop system.

Author Keywords
Kinect; 3D Interaction; 3D Visualization; Immersive Tabletop; Head Tracking

ACM Classification Keywords
H.5.2 [Information interfaces and presentation]: User Interfaces - Interaction styles.

Introduction
Nowadays, interaction methods in tabletop interfaces have evolved from multitouch interactions to interaction above the surface [2, 1] because of enabled higher degrees-of-freedom (DOF) input. However, although users can interact with a projection above the surface, they

Figure 1: System configuration

cannot interact with the 3D models directly because the 3D scene is just projected 2D screen.

In our system, the user can see the 3D models as if they existed on the surface, without the need for any specialized hardware or displays, by means of user head tracking. With this technique, the user can interact with 3D virtual models above the surface.We describe the system's implementation, application scenarios, and future expectations in this paper. Finally, we have evaluated our system empirically, via a pilot study that compares it with other tabletop systems.

Related Works

Many 3D interaction methods are realized by using depth sensors to detect the user's hand and any real objects. [2] and [4] support interaction above the surface by detecting the user's finger tips using depth camera. However, the user cannot know the height of a virtual object because of its 2D surface projection via a fixed program camera. Our research is focused on creating a full 3D experience.

Virtual reality systems provide users with realistic 3D experiences. Many early systems relied on head-mounted video, mobile displays, specialized displays or using markers (cf [3]). We have focused on avoiding any head-mounted equipment or specialized display. Depth-touch [1] is an interface that supports 3D interaction and changing perspective views by movements of the user's head position. However, changing perspective is achieved just by moving the camera position in program. As discussed below, the tabletop interface should take into account the surface inclination.

System Overview

3D Visualization Flow

In this research, the user can see projected objects as if they existed on the surface (referred to as 3D visualization in this paper). 3D visualization is enabled by head tracking, and we use Microsoft's Kinect for this purpose. The proposed tabletop interface has a straightforward configuration(Fig. 1.) We need only a Kinect device and a projection screen of known size. We do not need any specialized displays or head-mounted displays to achieve 3D visualization. Fig. 2 gives an overview of our system.

First, each set of coordinates (Kinect, program, and real world) has to be unified into one coordinate system. We also have to prepare 3D models for our program. We used the XNA Game Studio 4.0 platform for our 3D scene visualization and the JiglibX as physics engine. We generated a plane of the same size as the projection screen and applied the physical engine to it in XNA.

Second, the user's head position is tracked by the Kinect and the XNA camera position is synchronized with the user's head position. Besides, the Kinect distinguishes the user from other people in field of view of kinect. In this way, we can obtain the specific user's-view image (compare Fig. 2 (A) and Fig. 2 (B)). If the camera in XNA image (Fig. 2 B) is projected on the tabletop surface, the user's view is as shown in Fig. 2 (A). The user cannot see the projected object as if it existed on the surface. If (Fig. 2 C) is projected on the surface, the user's view can then be as shown in Fig. 2 (D). We calculate the relation between each pixel in the projector plane and the XNA camera plane, extract color data from the XNA camera's image, and set the color data at the pixel positions in every frame. This produces the correct image (Fig. 2 C) that should be projected on the surface.

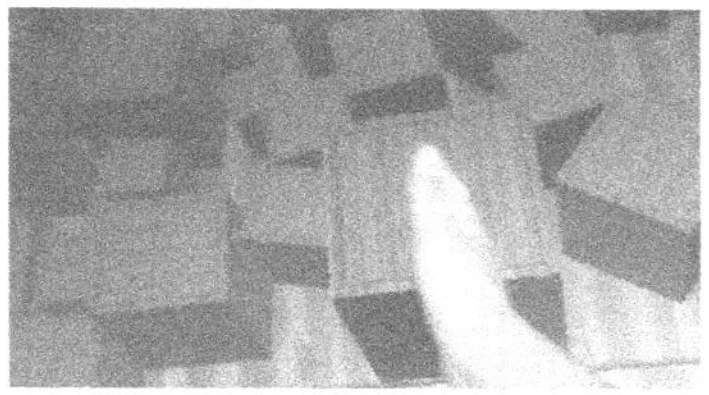

Figure 3: 3D interaction above the tabletop surface

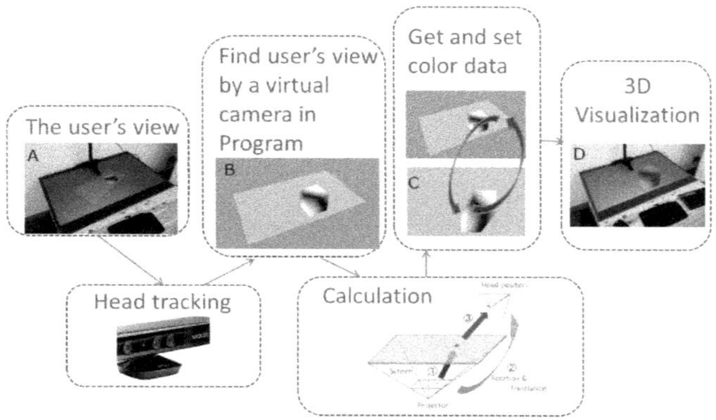

Figure 2: System overview

Morphing Projection
$u = (x, y)$ in projection-plane coordinates is translated to program coordinates $U = (X, Y, Z)$ by a multiplier P: $U = Z \cdot P \cdot [u, 1]$.

P is usually called a projection matrix, where

$$P = \begin{pmatrix} 1/f_x & 0 & -p_x/f_x \\ 0 & 1/f_y & -p_y/f_y \\ 0 & 0 & 1 \end{pmatrix}.$$

Here, f_x, f_y are given by the ratios of the projection width in projection coordinates to the plane width in program coordinates, and p_x, p_y specify the center of projection. Z is the height of the plane in program coordinates. Let F be a representation of a view matrix in the program's camera and let $u' = (x', y')$ be the program's camera plane coordinates. Then, u' is given by a translation from u:

$$u' = F \cdot Z \cdot P \cdot [u, 1].$$

In this way, we can find the relation between the projector and the XNA camera for each pixel. We then obtain and set color data for each pixel in real time. Finally, a correct projection will be specified.

3D Interaction
3D visualization assumes that the tabletop supports 3D interaction above the surface. At this stage, our tabletop interface supports simple 3D interactions involving collisions between the user's hand and virtual physical objects (see Fig. 3). In fact, a physical object is synchronized with the user's hand position, as detected by the Kinect, enabling the user to interact with the virtual objects. As mentioned below, we are planning an additional 3D interaction method.

Pilot Study

We conducted a pilot study to evaluate the performance of the system as an interactive tabletop and to obtain user feedback. In this section, we describe the procedure for this study and its results.

We prepared three types of projection (ProjectionA, Projection B, ProjectionC) using the same surface unit. Projection A is a fixed projection system, as used for many tabletop interfaces able to interact above the surface (e.g., [2].) In this system, the camera in program is fixed in position. Projection B is a projection that camera in program is just synchronized with the user's head position, as used for many interfaces with head tracking (e.g., [1].) Projection C is our 3D visualization system. We compared these three types of tabletop projection and evaluated their performance. We invited eight participants (five male, three female) between the ages of 23 and 30. The participants were required to hit some virtual objects their hands (Fig. 3) and score the performance of each system from 1 to 5 in each of the following respects.

- Direct interaction: How directly did the user feel he/she are touching the object?
- Reality: How well did the user feel immersed in the virtual world?
- Ease of use: How easily could the user manipulate the system?

Results
Fig. 4 shows the mean score for all three systems. A non-parametric statistical test (Friedman test) did not prove significant differences among the systems. However, our proposed system outperformed the other two systems in all the criteria. Many users complained that they could not feel intuitive A and B projection because the user cannot know projected objects's height or interact with them correctly.

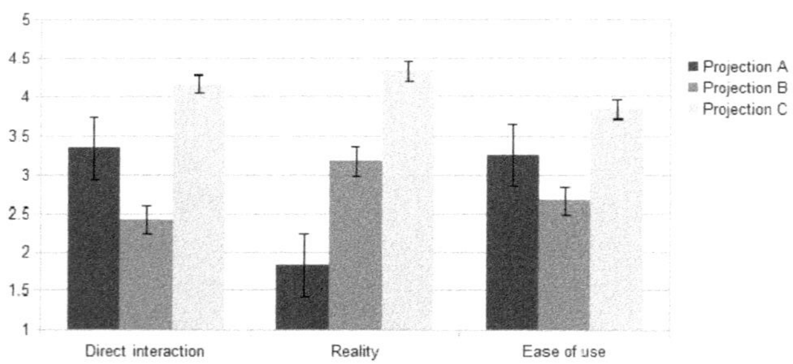

Figure 4: Result of the pilot study.Left: Direct Interaction. Middle: Reality. Right: Ease of use.

Discussion and Future Work
We have designed our first novel tabletop prototype and the system has many interaction possibilities. One of its unique strengths is the ability for users to immerse themselves in a mix of real and virtual worlds. This interplay will lead to interaction gaming possibilities or editing CG. Our system currently is not designed for multiple users because of the 3D visualization. However, we are planning to enable the system to multiplay by connecting two Kinects. Multiple users can share in and interact with a single virtual 3D scene, viewed from different perspectives, at each surface in real time. We are also planning to make the system mobile and implement additional interaction method. We have already tried to detect 3D positions of the user's finger tips by Kinect and going to implement this system.

References
[1] Hrvoje, B., and Andrew, D, W. *DepthTouch: Using Depth-Sensing Camera to Enable Freehand Interactions On and Above the Interactive Surface.* IEEE Work-shop on Tabletops and Interactive Surfaces (11-14), 2008.

[2] Otmar, H., Shahram, I., Andrew, D, W., Steve, H., Armando, G.-M., and Andreas, B. *Interaction in the Air: Adding Further Depth to Interactive Tbletops.* UIST (139-148), 2009.

[3] Papagiannakis, G., and Singh, G. *A survey of mobile and wireless technologies for augmented reality systems.* Comput. Animat. Virtual Worlds 19(3-22), 2008.

[4] Prachyabrued, M., and Borst, C, W. *Dropping the ball: Releasing a virtual grasp.* ACM VRST (59-66), 2011.

Development of a Context-enhancing Surface based on the Entrainment of Embodied Rhythms and Actions Sharing via Interaction

Michiya Yamamoto
Kwansei Gakuin University
2-1 Gakuen Sanda
Hyogo, 669-1337 Japan
michiya.yamamoto@kwansei.ac.jp

Yusuke Shigeno
Kwansei Gakuin University
2-1 Gakuen Sanda
Hyogo, 669-1337 Japan
aof78766@kwansei.ac.jp

Ryuji Kawabe
Kwansei Gakuin University
2-1 Gakuen Sanda
Hyogo, 669-1337 Japan
cmk84511@kwansei.ac.jp

Tomio Watanabe
Okayama Prefectural University
111 Kuboki Soja
Okayama, 719-1197 Japan
watanabe@oka-pu.ac.jp

ITS'12, November 11–14, 2012, Cambridge, Massachusetts, USA.
ACM 978-1-4503-1209-7/12/11.

Abstract
Surfaces with social functions are a recent trend. As the next step in the evolution of these surfaces, we propose a context-enhancing surface, which allows people to entrain and share their embodied rhythms to support their daily lively life. Thus, we developed a prototype system using sensors and screens. We propose a goal-oriented interaction and an entrainment-oriented interaction to support cheering in sports and liveliness in presentation.

Author Keywords
Embodied interaction; entrainment; embodied rhythms; sharing of action; context enhancer

ACM Classification Keywords
H.5.2 User Interfaces - Interaction styles; H.5.3 Group and Organization Interfaces - Collaborative computing

Introduction
Recently, tabletop technologies that allow users to share information intuitively and smoothly face-to-face have evolved into surface technologies with multiple large wall screens or mobile devices. The application of

this technology is also diversifying into education, art, and entertainment, while it also facilitates the sharing and visualization of information. So, what comes next?

We focused on the importance of expanding and deepening interactions between humans. In related studies, Prante et al. introduced zone interaction based on distance-dependent semantics for interaction via the front of a wall [1]. Recently, Ballendat proposed the concept of Proxemic Interaction for interactions using large surfaces and portable devices [2]. The aim of this study was to introduce interpersonal spatial relationships into the surface technology, which is important for human-human social interaction. However, these interaction designs are still focused on the exchange of information. An alternative approach was proposed by Miwa et al. [3] where shadow media were used on large screens to promote the continuous creation of imagery via bodily awareness during stage performances. However, this method had limited applications.

We have focused on the importance of the entrainment of embodied rhythms during human communication [4] and have developed various communication support systems [5, 6]. In this study, we propose the concept of a context-enhancing surface that facilitates the entrainment of embodied rhythms and the sharing of actions via interactions. This system enhances the context of human interactions in daily life directly and indirectly, and it enhances the sense of sharing. We developed a prototype of this system and applied it to sports cheering and presentation.

Concept

In this study, we propose a context-enhancing surface, i.e., a sharing and entraining system for embodied rhythms and actions via interactive surfaces directly and indirectly. Figure 1 shows the concept.

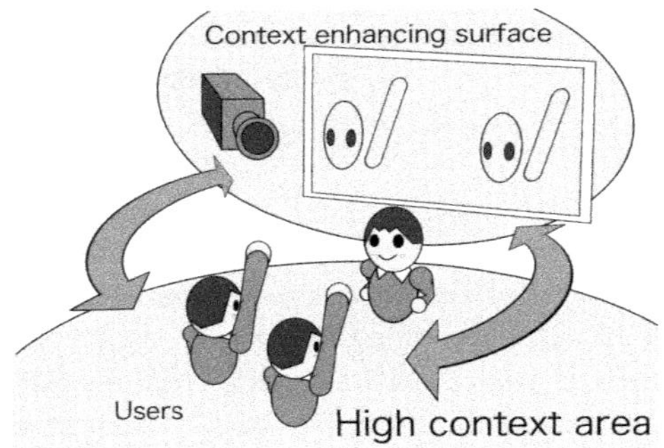

Figure 1. Concept of context-enhancing surface.

During human communication, communicative actions and rhythms are synchronized with each other. As communication becomes livelier, the synchronization becomes much stronger [5]. The rhythmic synchronization experienced during music or dance helps us feel greater enjoyment and a sense of unity [7]. During education, for example, Japanese children learn their multiplication tables in a rhythmic manner and this approach is applicable in many areas. It is also clear that rhythm is useful for walk training with elderly people. These findings suggest that the context of daily life can be enhanced by rhythms even when people are performing the same action. This is why we named this system a context-enhancing surface.

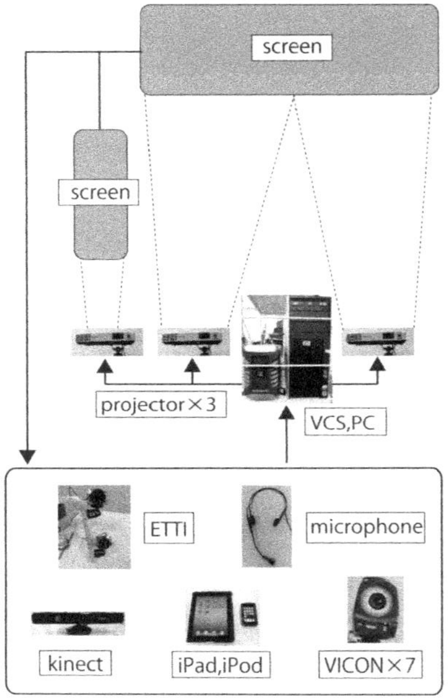

Figure 2. System configuration.

System configuration

The prototype context-enhancing surface consists of sensors, such as a motion capture system (VICON, VICON MX), range sensors (Microsoft Kinect for Windows), and tablet or mobile devices (Apple, iPad, and iPod). These sensors allow the motions of multiple users to be measured simultaneously. We also introduce ETTI (Eye-Tracking Tabletop Interface) [8] for capturing precise gaze information. We used monochromatic cameras (POINT GREY, FFMV-03 MTM) and lenses (ViewPLUS, VP-LE-HC-8S). To provide visual feedback, we used a visual computing system (NVIDIA, Quadroplex 2200), three projectors (EPSON, EB-1735W), and PCs (HP, Z400 Workstation). The screen size was 100 inches across the front and 1.8 m x 5.8 m at the sides. iPads and iPods can also be used as display units. Figure 2 shows the system configuration.

It is important to measure and generate suitable feedbacks using the software. First, we introduce goal-oriented interaction. In our previous study, we analyzed a pointing motion in front of a large surface and we found that the motion does not necessarily express the precise context for humans [9]. Therefore, we produced a livelier context using CG characters and effects, which were presented using sensor data as cues.

Next, we introduce entrainment-oriented interaction. First, the CG characters and effects are presented to the users as encouragement. Based on the sensor data obtained from the users, we determine whether the users should be entrained. The motions and actions of the users are controlled by appropriately driven CGs that enhance context.

Context-enhancing surface for sports cheering

The first prototype was developed for sports cheering based on a goal-oriented interaction. In general, these systems require technologies that duplicate an actual sports stadium. In this study, however, we focused on the importance of sharing and entrainment of cheering actions. Therefore, we arranged many CG cheering characters on the surface. The users placed iPods on their chests and all of the characters jump together if the value of an acceleration sensor exceeded a threshold. This raised the awareness of the importance of embodied actions (as shown in Figure 3) and increased the excitement during sports cheering.

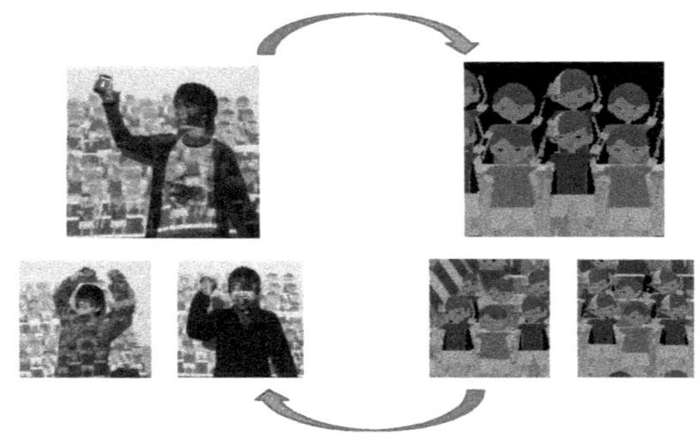

Figure 3. Action of a user is expanded to bigger actions in crowds of cheering characters and other users.

Context-enhancing surface in presentations

In the next step, we developed a presentation room with a context-enhancing surface and implemented two interaction modes. For goal-oriented interactions, we used a real audience of characters who were engaged in a discussion. If a character raised their hand rhythmically, we also raised our hands as shown in Figures 4 and 5.

Figure 4. A character on the surface raises a hand rhythmically.

Figure 5. Users are entrained to the characters.

For the entrainment-oriented interaction, we introduced iRT [4] to the characters. Using iRT, the embodied motions and actions of a speaker and a listener could be generated based only on speech input. This allowed a lively atmosphere and a sense of unity to be generated in the room. By integrating the actual sensor data with the characters, we could control the synchronization level of user actions such as nodding, as shown in Figure 6.

As a further example, we are developing a CG effect that changes the transparency of a slide by calculating the head orientation and gaze direction of users.

Conclusion

In this study, we propose the novel concept of a context-enhancing surface that extends human-human social interactions. We developed prototype systems for sports cheering and presentation, and we confirmed the effectiveness of these systems.

References

[1] Prante, T., Röcker, C., Streitz, N. A., Stenzel, R., Magerkurth, C., van Alphen, D., and Plewe, D. A. Hello.Wall – Beyond Ambient Displays. *Video Track and Adjunct Proceedings of the Fifth International Conference on Ubiquitous Computing (UBICOMP'03)*, (2003), 277-278.

[2] Ballendat, T., Marquardt, N., and Greenberg, S. Proxemic interaction: designing for a proximity and orientation-aware environment. *ACM International Conference on Interactive Tabletops and Surfaces (ITS '10)*, (2010), 121-130.

Figure 6. Lively atmosphere in presentation can be generated with the characters.

[3] Miwa, Y., Itai, S., Watanabe, T., and Nishi H. Shadow awareness: enhancing theater space through the mutual projection of images on a connective slit screen. *ACM SIGGRAPH 2011 Art Gallery (SIGGRAPH '11)*, (2011), 325-333.

[4] Condon, W. S., and Sander L. W. Neonate movement is synchronized with adult speech: Interactional participation and language acquisition. Science, 183, (1974), 99–101.

[5] Watanabe, T., Okubo, M., Nakashige M., and Danbara, R. InterActor: Speech-Driven Embodied Interactive Actor. *International Journal of Human-Computer Interaction 17*, 1 (2004), 43-60.

[6] Osaki, K., Watanabe, T., and Yamamoto, M. Speech-driven embodied entrainment character system with hand motion input in mobile environment. *Proceedings of the 9th international conference on Multimodal interfaces (ICMI '07)*, (2007), 285-290.

[7] Varni, G., Camurri, A., Coletta, P., and Volpe, G., Emotional entrainment in music performance. In Proceedings of 8th International Conference on Automatic Face and Gesture Recognition, IEEE FG2008, (2008), 1-5.

[8] Yamamoto, M., Komeda, M., Nagamatsu, T., and Watanabe, T. Development of Eye-Tracking Tabletop Interface for Media Art Works. ACM International Conference on Interactive Tabletops and Surfaces 2010, (2010), 295-296.

[9] Shigeno, Y., Yamamoto, M., and Watanabe, T. Analysis of Pointing Motions by Introducing a Joint Model for Supporting Embodied Large-Surface Presentation. *ACM International Conference on Interactive Tabletops and Surfaces 2011*, (2011), 250-251.

Development of Wall Amusement with Infrared Radars

Yosuke Kimura
Osaka Electro-Communication University
1170-30 Kiyotaki, Shijonawate, Osaka, Japan
yousukek@hcn.zaq.ne.jp

Haruki Ohta
Osaka Electro-Communication University
1170-30 Kiyotaki, Shijonawate, Osaka, Japan
mw12a006@oecu.jp

Atsushi Karino
Osaka Electro-Communication University
1170-30 Kiyotaki, Shijonawate, Osaka, Japan
m10509@oecu.jp

Tomoyuki Takami
Osaka Electro-Communication University
1170-30 Kiyotaki, Shijonawate, Osaka, Japan
takami@isc.osakac.ac.jp

ITS'12, November 11–14, 2012, Cambridge, Massachusetts, USA.
ACM 978-1-4503-1209-7/12/11.

Abstract
This paper describes a wall amusement system with wall surface and infrared radars. A screen is projected on a wall by an ultra-short throw projector. Interaction between wall surface and players is created by infrared radar measurement. This system can be set up anywhere if there is a certain sized wall. We present here the system using mirrors with infrared radars. This makes both the time and space resolution of infrared radar measurement improved very much. We use this new system to develop exergames with wall surface.

Author Keywords
Exergame; Infrared radar; Multi-touch;

ACM Classification Keywords
H5.2 [Information interfaces and presentation]:User Interfaces. - Input devices and strategies.

Introduction
The multi-touch display system with infrared radars has been developed regarding function enhancement, for example, multi-layerization of touch surface or production of multi-touch library for the system [1, 2]. We present here the system using mirrors with infrared radars. This makes both the time and space resolution of infrared radar measurement improved very much.

We use this new type of the system, interactive wall, to develop exergames with wall surface [3].

System

A screen display is projected on a wall surface by an ultra-short throw projector. This system can be set up anywhere if there is a certain sized wall. Further, as it is assumed that an operator stands in front of a screen, there is a possibility that a body silhouette appears on the screen when normal projectors are used, however, if an ultra-short throw projector is used, the silhouette does not appear on the screen because the main body of the projector can be placed adhered to a wall.

Infrared Radar

The infrared radar we used in this study is SOKUIKI sensor (UBG-04LX-F01, HOKUYO Co., Ltd.), which rotates radar beams with the frequency of 36Hz with a 0.36-degree pitch in fan-shaped flat space with radius 4 m and central angle 240-degree, and can acquire the data of directions and the distances to objects by detecting the reflected near-infrared light from the surface of the objects. The positions of the objects are calculated from these data. In exergame applications described in this paper we use the SOKUIKI sensor to detect the position of a ball or a stick, which are used as a game controller. The space resolution is about 10 mm at the distance of 1 m from the SOKUIKI sensor.

Usage of Mirror

We put two mirrors in the left and right sides of the application screen displayed on the wall surface, in order to reflect the radar beams of SOKUIKI sensor inside. Figure 1 shows this setup. As shown in Figure 1, a radar target is measured by three radar beams. The biggest problem in SOKUIKI sensor system is to come out of the blind spot. Putting mirrors can get rid of this problem as a beam can see the target even if a beam path is cut by obstacles. This mirror system particularly takes advantage of the time resolution of measurement. The chance of measuring a target becomes about three times compared with the system without mirrors.

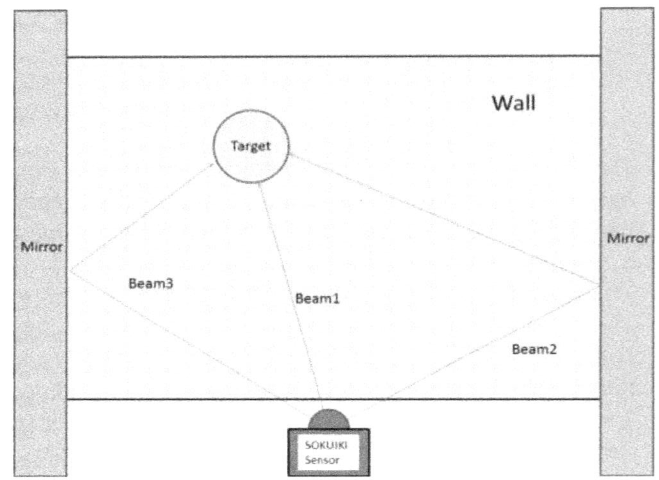

Figure 1. Interactive wall with an infrared radar and mirrors.

Estimation of the Position

As shown in Figure 1, Beam1 directly measures radar targets while Beam2/Beam3 measures virtual images of radar targets formed by mirrors. When the azimuth angle of Beam2/Beam3 is t, the distance between mirror and radar is A and the distance between radar and virtual target is R, the position (X, Y) of real target is as follows: $X=2*A - R*\cos(t)$; $Y=R*\sin(t)$; Here the values of t and R can be estimated by Beam2/Beam3 measurement. The system with mirrors has the following advantages.

- Even if there is an obstacle on the way of the path of Beam1 and Beam2, Beam3 can detect the target. The applications can use more targets.
- As Beam1 measures the front of a target and Beam2/Beam3 measures the side of it, not only the position but also the shape of the target can be estimated.
- Time resolution of radar measurement increses approximately three times as three beams are used.

Multi-touch Library

In this study an ActionScript 3.0 library for the multi-touch interactions and gesture-based interactions is used for programs of exergame applications. This library is very flexible and extensible, giving programmers easy control of multi-touch and gesture-based interaction. They may just write a program for the mouse event instead of the touch event by SOKUIKI sensor measurements. By using this library in the ActionScript 3.0 program, the mouse event can be automatically replaced to the touch event by a ball thrown against wall. Though the mouse event is not dispatched simultaneously, the ball touch event is dispatched simultaneously due to the library.

Production Examples

Production examples of exergames with wall surface are shown in Figure 2 and 3. Both applications use the SOKUIKI sensor to take touch events. Figure 2 is an example using the ball touch and Figure 3 is an example using the stick touch. Several balls and stick can be used simultaneously.

Free Butterflies

Figure 2 shows a screen shot of an exergame, Free Butterflies. Players throw a ball against the wall surface on which an application screen is displayed. In this game players drop colored rectangles by hitting a ball to them. The radar beam of SOKUIKI sensor is scanned along the wall surface. It detects the position where a ball hits with the wall. As SOKUIKI sensor can simultaneously measure several positions of balls, it is no problem that several balls simultaneously hit against the wall. As an ultra-short throw projector is used, there are no silhouettes of players.

Figure 2. A screen shot of Free Butterflies.

Video Puzzle

Figure 3 shows a screen shot of an amusement application, Video Puzzle. This is a puzzle game using the moving image. The radar beam detects the position of a stick that players have as a game controller. Players move a stick along the wall to catch and move a piece of Video Puzzle. Players can see a movie when all pieces are set on the right place. In the screen shot of Figure 3, a player is drugging a piece of video with a stick. The radar is put below the application screen.

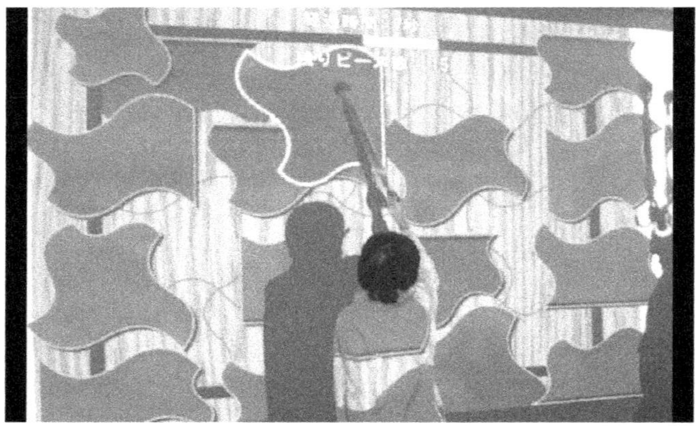

Figure 3. A screen shot of Video Puzzle.

Acknowledgements

We thank the reviewers for their helpful comments.

Summary

We have produced a prototype of the exergame system with wall surface and infrared radars. We introduced content of two exergames in which players throw balls against wall surface or move a stick to control application screen. We can improve the time resolution of SOKUIKI sensor measurement by using mirrors.

References

[1] A. Karino, T. Iwamoto, S. Nakata, M. Hida and T. Takami, "Development of multi-touch table games with real objects," NICOGRAPH International 2010(CD-ROM), 2010.

[2] T. Iwamoto, A. Karino, M. Hida, A. Nishizaki, and T. Takami, "Development of Wall Amusements Utilizing Gesture Input," proceedings of ICEC 2010, pp. 499-501, 2010.

[3] T. Takami, M. Matsumura, T. Yabu, N. Yamawaki, H. Nagai, A. Nishizaki, M. Okamoto, M. Hida, "Design of the Multi-touch Table with Near-Infrared Radars and its Applications to Floor/Wall Display", The Japanese Journal of Game Amusement Society, Vol.4, No.1, pp26-31, 2009.

Tool Support for Developing Scalable Multiuser Applications on Multi-Touch Screens

Ioannis Leftheriotis
Ionian University
Tsirigoti Sq. 7,
Corfu, Greece
and
Norwegian University of
Science and Technology
Sem Sælands vei 7-9,
Trondheim, Norway
iolef@acm.org

Konstantinos Chorianopoylos
Ionian University
Tsirigoti Sq. 7,
Corfu, Greece
choko@acm.org

Letizia Jaccheri
Norwegian University of Science
and Technology
Sem Sælands vei 7-9,
Trondheim, Norway
letizia@idi.ntnu.no

Abstract

MT (Multi-touch) screens are platforms that enhance multiuser collaboration. In this work, we underline the need for novel interaction techniques and toolkits that allow multi-user collaboration on larger MT surfaces. We present ChordiAction toolkit that makes use of a novel chorded interaction technique allowing simultaneous multi-user interaction on scalable MT applications. We describe the design, the architecture and some efficient customizations practices of the toolkit and show how it can be effectively embedded in an application for multiuser interaction. As a proof of concept, we present some example applications using ChordiAction toolkit showing its potentials and discuss our future plans for further evaluation of this technique.

ITS'12, November 11–14, 2012, Cambridge, Massachusetts, USA.
ACM 978-1-4503-1209-7/12/11.

Author Keywords

Toolkit; chords; multi-touch; large multi-touch screens

ACM Classification Keywords

H.5.2. [Information Interfaces]: User Interfaces-Input devices and strategies; graphical user interfaces; prototyping.

Introduction

MT surfaces have become popular platforms during the last years. In addition, a variety of toolkits that support development for MT devices have been presented [2]. There is no doubt that the MT community is vivid and new toolkits are being developed constantly either by practitioners and hobbyists (e.g., Kivy), or researchers. These multi-touch toolkits usually support multiple operating systems and multiple hardware installations. However, the motivation for this work was the fact that despite the considerable quantity of research directed towards MT technologies, a set of standardized UI components have not been developed yet [4], and more importantly there is a lack of tools dedicated to multiuser interaction on larger screens.

Figure 1: Multiple users can articulate different chords. In this screenshot, two users articulate three fingers chord and five fingers inside the colored reserved areas. Chords are not a novel type of interaction [Grossman], but using chords for multi-user interaction is a novel technique.

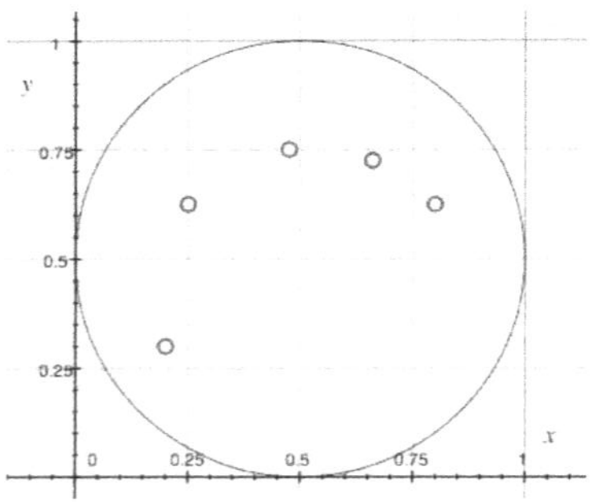

Figure 2: In this graph, the diameter of the circular area is equal to 1. All possible finger-touches and their appropriate positions in relation to the circular chorded area are shown. The positions are based on our own experience. However, positions can be easily changed inside the code.

Although there are Toolkits being focused on MT interaction, only some of them deal with the issue of multi-user synchronous collaboration. In DiamondSpin API, DSFrame DSPanel and DSWindow equivalents of JFrame, JPanel and JWindow of Java are presented. According to Shen et al [5], in order to have multi-user support, multiple menu-bars or concurrent multi-user interaction techniques are needed. In this work, we focus on a novel interaction technique called chords (simultaneous touch of more than one finger on a surface) and we present ChordiAction Toolkit for multi-user interaction on MT surfaces. Hence, the main contribution of our work is: 1) the development of a toolkit that enhances multi-user interaction in larger MT screens, and 2) the proposal and discussion of some characteristics of a multiuser MT toolkit that raised during the development process of our work.

ChordiAction Toolkit

ChordiAction toolkit has been implemented with the PyMT programming framework [1], and it can be easily transferred to any MT Software Development Kit (SDK), because it is based on common MT user interface events, such as touch-down, and touch-up, which are available in any MT toolkit (e.g., Microsoft Surface). Using that event model is a traditional strategy for developing MT applications [1] for a variety of MT toolkits, which make use of this type of events including 2D information such as the coordinates of a touch (e.g. WM_TOUCH).

Design

With ChordiAction toolkit we are dealing two important issues that arise in multi-user MT applications. First, identifying which user has done what on a MT screen and second allowing each user work separately without his actions concerning or even annoying others.

The main idea is the use of a mechanism in order to choose a specific item from a menu without touching the buttons of the menu directly, as well as being able to perform individual interactions within a limited area. A novel multiuser chorded selection technique, where user makes use of a circular chording area that is temporarily (for a number of seconds, e.g. 5 seconds) reserved whenever a user touches the MT screen has been used [3]. In that small area, user has to perform a chord for the selection of the appropriate menu item. With the use of a not-functioning menu bar playing the role of a status indicator (Figure 6), users are able to understand which menu item must be chosen and how many fingers they have to touch on the surface in order to select it.

Multiple users are able to touch different parts of the screen and then different small areas will be temporarily reserved for chorded modifiers accordingly (Figure 1). The reserved area is about the user's hand size, being easy for the user to touch the appropriate number of fingers inside it and thus applying the chord responsible for the selection of the menu item he/she desires. Each time a user makes a selection the appropriate action/function can be activated.

The steps that the system follows for every single user that interacts on the MT screen are the following: a) Initially the systems waits for the first finger touch. b) When this occurs a new chorded area is reserved. c) User has to touch the appropriate number of fingers in the specific chorded area in order to articulate the corresponding chord. d) When user has lifted all his

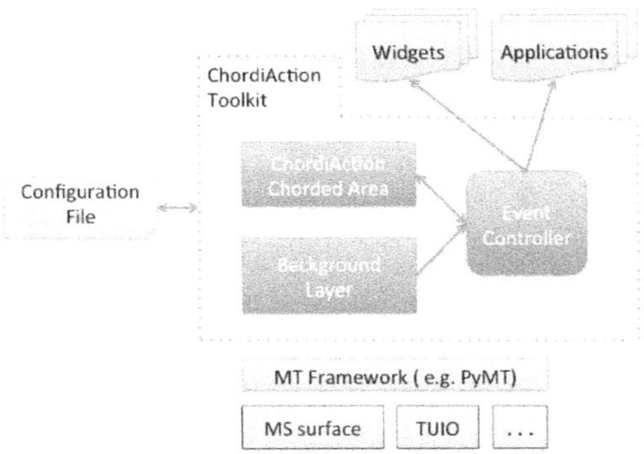

Figure 3: ChordiAction toolkit architecture. The toolkis is developed in PyMT, however, it can be easily migrated to other MT Frameworks.

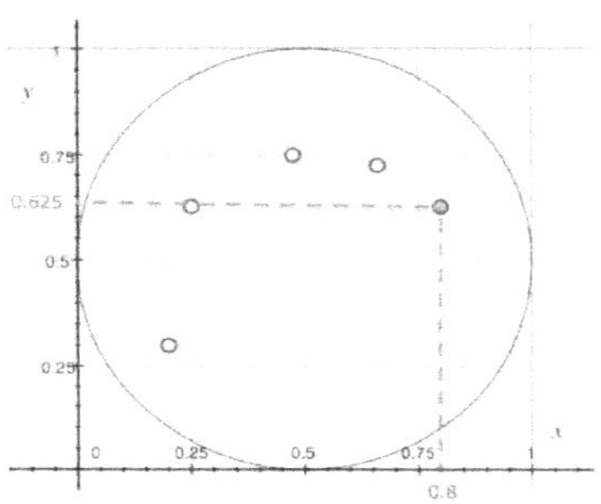

Figure 4: In this example, the circular area pops-up in relation to the fifth finger (pinky). If the pinky enables the chording area, the first touch will be at the (0.8 * circle-diameter, 0.625 * circle-diameter) and the circle will be placed accordingly.

fingers from the screen, the chord interaction area is released. The system then processes the chord and finally, e) The appropriate action or function is enabled.

This five steps strategy of our system stems from the two necessities discussed previously. The system locate the place where the interaction needs to be done, supports us with a method to differentiate what the user needs or which user interact (in our case this method includes chords) and finally, gives the opportunity for undistracted interaction of all users.

Architecture

The architecture of the toolkit is based on PyMT event model [1]. Specifically, there are three separate layers and in order to pass from one level to the next, a touch event is needed. In the background layer, user touches the surface in order to appear the chorded interaction area. When this happens an appropriate event is generated, the chorded area pops up and the user is able to articulate the appropriate chord. Finally, a new layer with a new application or widget or action appears (Figure 3).

In larger MT surfaces where there is enough space for multi-user interaction, the system should allow multiple instances of different applications to run concurrently. That is why we propose that even the toolkits themselves should have multiple instances in a multi-user MT environment where multiple applications may run in parallel. In addition, these tools might be able to be applied in different levels of the widget tree of a MT application. However, each ChodriAction toolkit instance must have its own customization file. Additionally, the toolkit can be used for either selecting among different applications or different widgets/functions.

Toolkit Customization

Along with the toolkit, there is a configuration file that can be modified to express developers' preferences and help them integrate the toolkit inside their own applications. For instance, for every chord that has been articulated, developers can have returned either the position of the first finger of each chord or the (0,0) point of the circular area (Figure 5). Additionally, developers are free to choose which finger will be the first to enable a circular chorded interaction area. Whenever user touches the screen, the circular area pops-up and it is placed accordingly to his/her hand. In Figure 4, an example in which the circle is positioned in relation to the pinky finger is depicted.

Moreover the toolkit allows different sizes of chord interaction circular areas. Additionally, the number of available selection that can be done using chords can be altered. In the case of four different menu objects for instance, there are four different items and thus four different chords: a) two fingers b) three fingers, c) four fingers and d) five fingers. Note that along with the number of selections, a number of different feedback colors (with which the circular area is painted) must be shown to the user. That is why the toolkit allows developers to chose the appropriate color of the circle for each chord. The colors are in RGB format and can be easily altered. For instance, each time the user makes the third selection (by touching four fingers inside the circular chorded interaction area) the circle turns to red color and thus he/she understands that when all his fingers will be released from the MT surface, the action in red is going to be executed.

```
[General]
standard: 0
return_first_touch: 0

[Configurations]
first_finger: 5
circle_diameter: 400
number_of_items: 3
selection1color=(0.3, 0.6, 0.8)
selection2color=(0.9, 0.8, 0.1)
selection3color=(0.9, 0.2, 0.4)
```

Figure 5: The customization file: the circular area pops up according to the fifth finger, there are 3 possible selections/chords and the circle diameter is 400px.

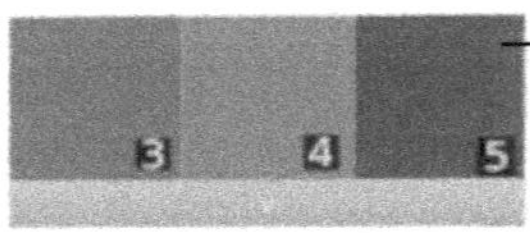

A not functioning status indicator bar that informs users about the available chords.

Figure 7: Drawing application that makes use of ChordiAction in combination to personal windows so as to differentiate users' interactions.

Example applications

We are working on the development of collaborative applications in order to evaluate empirically our chorded technique. We have already developed a collaborative dot-to-dot drawing application where multiple users can draw colored lines in order to connect colored dots and thus draw a sketch. In this application, chords are used for selecting different colors. Chords in combination to personal windows found to be a good technique so as to understand individual actions on the screen. Moreover, we have developed a multiuser word construction application in which ChordiAction is used in order to differentiate user actions (change background letters, create a word etc.)

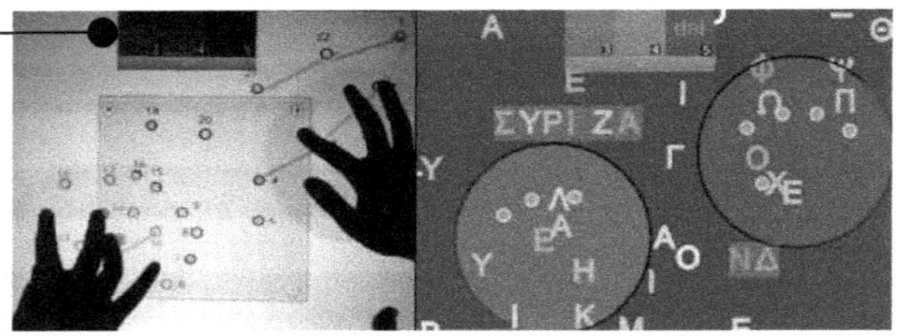

Figure 6: Snapshots of applications using ChordiAction.

Conclusion and Future Work

Considering the possibilities that larger MT surfaces present for collocated multi-user interaction, we presented ChordiAction, which is a toolkit developed as an open-source and ready to use platform that can be easily embedded in MT applications. The need for doing different actions depending on users' needs in the same multi-user application is also apparent. For example, in a scalable multi-user photo editing application one user is changing the brightness of a photo while another is changing the contrast of another. ChordiAction was designed to provide both services.

However, the development of software user interfaces that are rendered on devices with different input and output than those of the development workstation remains an open research issue. Additionally, the need for tools that are going to deal these issues emerges and toolkit developers should be aware of them, so as to design new development tools or improve existing ones for multi-touch devices. Our system was developed for larger vertical surfaces (Figure 7) and we plan to conduct some experiments to evaluate its efficiency with multiple users and compare our technique to other contextual menus or pie menus on large scalable MT surfaces.

References

[1] Hansen T. E., Hourcade J. P., Virble M., Patali S., and Serra T. 2009. PyMT: A Post-WIMP Multi-Touch User Interface Toolkit. Interactive Tabletops and Surfaces. ITS'09. ACM Press, New York, NY, USA.

[2] Kammer D., Keck M., Freitag G., and Wacker M., 2010. Taxonomy and overview of multi-touch frameworks: Architecture, scope and features. Symposium on Engineering Interactive Computre Systems. EICS '10 Workshop on Engineering Patterns for Multi-Touch Interfaces.

[3] Leftheriotis, I., and Chorianopoulos, K., 2011. Multi-user Chorded Toolkit for Multi-touch Screens, Proceedings of EICS ' 11. ACM SIGCHI Symposium on Engineering Interactive Computing Systems, ACM Press. New York, NY, USA.

[4] Lepinski, G. J., Grossman, T., and Fitzmaurice, G., 2010. The Design and Evaluation of Multitouch Marking Menus, Conference of Human Factors in Computing Systems. CHI '10, ACM Press, New York, USA.

[5] Shen C., Vernier, F. D., Forlines C., and Ringel M., 2004. DiamondSpin:An Extensible Toolkit for Around-the-Table Interaction. Conference of Human Factors in Computing Systems. CHI'04. ACM Press, NY, USA.

ITS in the Classroom: Perspectives on Using a Multi-touch Classroom

Emma Mercier
Durham University
School of Education
Leazes Road
Durham, DH1 1TA, UK
emma.mercier@durham.ac.uk

Elizabeth Burd
Durham University
School of Education
Leazes Road
Durham, DH1 1TA, UK
liz.burd@durham.ac.uk

Steven E. Higgins
Durham University
School of Education
Leazes Road
Durham, DH1 1TA, UK
s.e.higgins@durham.ac.uk

James McNaughton
Durham University
School of Education
Leazes Road
Durham, DH1 1TA, UK
j.a.mcnaughton@durham.ac.uk

ITS'12, November 11–14, 2012, Cambridge, Massachusetts, USA.
ACM 978-1-4503-1209-7/12/11.

Abstract
Using interactive surfaces in a classroom requires an understanding of multiple users and stakeholders. While research on how students using tables provides some insight, exploring the roles and needs of the teacher, and the interaction between groups in a classroom, adds an additional dimension to this design challenge. We summarize three years of design and research in a multi-touch classroom, to illuminate some of the issues involved in placing interactive surfaces in the classroom environment. Results indicate that the tables can be used to support joint cognition, that the arrangement of tables in the classroom may influence collaborative interactions, and that allowing the teacher to project content from student tables to a shared interactive whiteboard (IWB) for whole group discussion can facilitate progress within the groups.

Author Keywords
Multi-touch classroom; CSCL; Device Ecology.

ACM Classification Keywords
H.5.m. Information interfaces and presentation (e.g., HCI): Miscellaneous.

Introduction

Research in education has found that collaborative learning can be an effective pedagogic strategy [2,12], and there is increasing recognition of the need to provide students with the skills to collaborate when they enter the work-place [3,13]. However, despite its potential, and the development of many CSCL tools, this strategy is not commonly used in classrooms, and research indicates that even when students are seated in groups, they rarely work in groups [1]. The development of multi-touch tables provides the possibility of redesigning classrooms so that collaborative learning, and teaching collaboration skills, can be more easily supported in classroom [4,8]. However, integrating technology into classrooms requires that the user needs of both students and teachers be considered. In this poster, we review findings from a multi-year study to design a multi-touch classroom (see Fig 1), taking different perspectives on the studies to explore the complexity of designing CSCL for classroom environments.

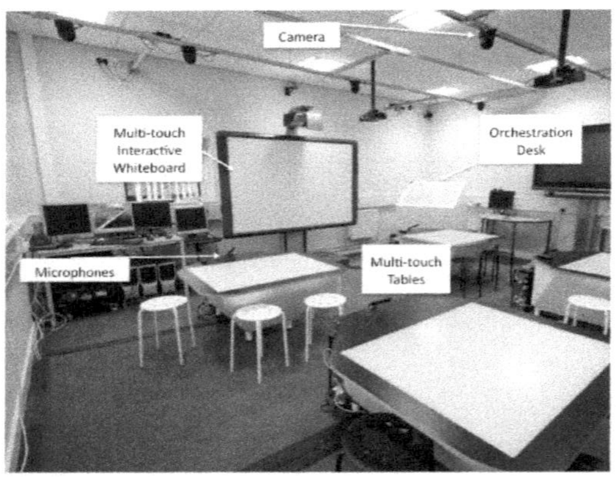

Figure 1: The SynergyNet Classroom

There is a range of research that explores the use of multi-touch tables for collaborative learning activities. This work is generally restricted to the exploration of single groups working around a table, with the focus on understanding how the design of an activity can support collaborative interaction and learning. This work indicates that groups who use multi-touch engaged in more task-focused conversation than groups using single-touch [5] and that the use of a multi-touch table supported the development of a joint problem space and more interactive discussion when compared to paper [7]. Initial work that examines multiple tables in a classroom context indicates that there is potential for increased collaborative learning, but also a need to consider the role of between-group interactions, whole class participation, the learning activities, the role of the teacher and use of tools to support orchestration of the learning experience [6,10].

The design of any CSCL environment requires the integration of multiple perspectives in order to fully understand the range of issues and influences on the learning (and teaching) experiences. In designing and studying a multi-touch enabled classroom, we elaborate on these four aspects, using them to guide the design of different studies in an effort to form a more complete understanding of the use of interactive surfaces for classroom learning. As part of this project, a classroom of multi-touch tables was developed. Over a three year period, a series of experiments were carried out, initially exploring single groups using a multi-touch table with a teacher present, and then bringing up to 16 children from the same class into the lab classroom.

Methods

The interfaces in the classroom each display instances of the SynergyNet framework which was built to support applications designed to be used by students on large horizontal multi-touch interfaces. The multi-touch interfaces in the classroom use diffused illumination [11], a technique where cameras observe the touches users made on the interface. A third party, low-level software framework is used to identify when and where touches are made using information from the cameras. This touch information is transmitted to the SynergyNet framework via the TUIO protocol [9]. The framework is capable of accepting a range of different multi-touch protocols as an input. In addition to this, instances of the SynergyNet framework are able to communicate via a network. This allows for the

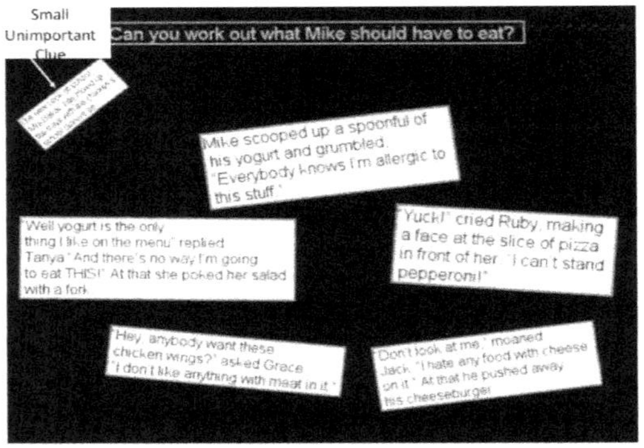

Figure 2: Solved Logic Problem (Start with top clue and move anti-clockwise to solve)

Figure 3: Centered Classroom

sharing of materials and for content on the multi-touch interfaces to be orchestrated remotely by a teacher.

The classroom is equipped with video, audio and screen capture technology to collect data on the groups and classroom interactions. The video, screens and audio were synced, and transcribed for analysis. In the section below, summaries of finding are presented to illustrate how the data will be used to build an understanding about embedding interactive tables in classrooms. The data that the results described are drawn from a study in which six schools (96 students) came to the lab for up to five hours at a time, working on a series of history and mathematical tasks.

Interactive Surfaces and Collaboration

One key question when using interactive surfaces in classrooms is how does the technology influence the way students engage in collaboration. During the study, students worked in groups of four on a logic-reasoning task, using text-based clues to determine the correct answer. This particular task could be solved by making a circular chain of the clues, so that content from the first clue, answered the question in the second, while content from the second answered aspects of the third etc (Fig 2). Results indicated that 13 of the 24 groups solved or were close to solving the task. Video analysis of these groups showed that 12 of those groups, compared to 2 of the 11 groups who did not solve the task, used the tables to externalize their thinking, laying out the solution as they worked towards it. Thus suggesting the interactive surface can support joint cognition in collaborative learning groups.

Interactive Surfaces in the Classroom

By changing the layout of the multi-touch classroom, we explored what effect the room layout might have on the learning opportunities. Three of the schools in the study worked in the classroom when the tables were facing the IWB (Fig 1 & 4), in a traditional classroom manner, while the other three schools worked in the classroom when the tables faced the center of the room (Fig 3). When looking across results from three math mysteries, results indicated that more groups in the front-facing room solved the problems. Analysis of the groups indicated significantly more talk in the center-facing room, however, not more off-topic talk. These results indicate that groups in the center-facing room were engaging in more on-topic conversation. Thus the orientation of the tables influenced the way the students engaged in the activity – with more students collaborating on the task, and thus taking longer to solve the problem (and not finishing before the teacher stopped the task), than students in the forward-facing room.

The Teacher and Orchestration Tools

One benefit of multi-touch tables for classroom use is that they allow for more fluid orchestration of learning activities, giving the teacher more control of distribution of content, and allowing for the projection of content from the tables to a shared display for whole-class discussion. In our study, the teacher controlled the classroom from the orchestration desk. During the history task, the teacher sent content to the tables, and then stopped the groups at two points during the activity to project content from one table and share it with the whole class (Fig 4). Analysis of the groups indicated that there was little change in the levels of reasoning reached during the small group

Figure 4: Whole Class Discussion

interactions after the first whole-class discussion, but that many groups increased in their level of reasoning after the second whole class discussion. While there is some evidence for groups picking up ideas from the whole class discussion, it also appears that presenting their ideas to the whole class, and hearing the teacher's instructions to wrap up their ideas, may have influenced their reasoning in the final stages of the activity. Thus, indicating an important role of the classroom norms and presenting to peers, in collaborative learning activities. The teachers also noted frustration with the orchestration desk, asking for mobile tools to support their orchestration of the classroom. Adaptations in later studies include tablet and gesture based systems to provide more flexibility in how teachers interact with the technology and students.

Conclusions

The three frames used to look at a six-school classroom study illuminate the range of issues that exist when attempts are made to integrate interactive surfaces into classrooms. We will elaborate on these findings and explore principles for designing for classroom environments in light of these and additional findings.

References

1. Baines, E., Rubie - Davies, C., and Blatchford, P. Improving pupil group work interaction and dialogue in primary classrooms: results from a year - long intervention study. *Cambridge Journal of Education 39*, 1 (2009), 95–117.
2. Barron, B. and Darling-Hammond, L. How can we teach for meaningful learning? In L. Darling-Hammond, ed., *Powerful Learning: What we know about teaching for understanding*. Jossey-Bass, 2008, 11–70.
3. Cressey, D. PhDs leave the ivory tower. *Nature 484*, 7392 (2012), 20.
4. Dillenbourg, P. and Evans, M. Interactive tabletops in education. *International Journal of Computer-Supported Collaborative Learning*, July (2011).
5. Harris, A., Rick, J., Bonnett, V., et al. Around the table: are multiple-touch surfaces better than single-touch for children's collaborative interactions? *CSCL* (2009), 335–344.
6. Hatch, A., Higgins, S., Joyce-Gibbons, A., and Mercier, E. NumberNet: Using multi-touch technology to support within and between-group mathematics learning. *CSCL (2011)*
7. Higgins, S., Mercier, E., Burd, L., and Joyce-Gibbons, A. Multi-touch tables and collaborative learning. *BJET* (2011).
8. Higgins, S.E., Mercier, E., Burd, E., and Hatch, A. Multi-touch tables and the relationship with collaborative classroom pedagogies: A synthetic review. *ijCSCL* (2011).
9. Kaltenbrunner, M. reacTIVision and TUIO : A Tangible Tabletop Toolkit. *ITS* (2009), 9–16.
10. Maldonado, R.M., Kay, J., Yacef, K., and Schwendimann, B. Unpacking traces of collaboration from multimodal data of collaborative concept mapping at a tabletop. *ICLS (2012)* 241–245.
11. Matsushita, N. and Rekimoto, J. HoloWall. *UIST '97*, ACM Press (1997), 209–210.
12. O'Donnell, A. The role of peers and group learning. In P. Alexander and P. Winne, eds., *Handbook of educational psychology*. Lawrence Earlbaum, 2006.
13. Whitfield, J. Group theory. *Nature 455*, October (2008), 720–723.

Mobile Assistant: Enhancing Desktop Interaction Using Mobile Phone

Haijun Xia
Dept. of Computer Science
Tsinghua University
Beijing, China
xiahaijun25@gmail.com

Chun Yu
Dept. of Computer Science
Tsinghua University
Beijing, China
yc2pcg@gmail.com

Jingning Zhang
Dept. of Computer Science
Tsinghua University
Beijing, China
mrgaogao9177@gmail.com

Yuanchun Shi
Dept. of Computer Science
Tsinghua University
Beijing, China
shiyc@tsinghua.edu.cn

Yeshuang Zhu
Dept. of Computer Science
Tsinghua University
Beijing, China
yeshuangzhu@gmail.com

ITS'12, November 11–14, 2012, Cambridge, Massachusetts, USA.
ACM 978-1-4503-1209-7/12/11.

Abstract
Touchscreen of mobile phone is an important input channel, whereas most desktop computers have no such a modality. Furthermore, we observe a common situation where ubiquitous mobile phones are placed aside while users operate computers. In this poster, we present Mobile Assistant (MA), which allows a touch mobile phone manipulated by the non-dominant hand to assist desktop interaction without introducing extra devices. To demonstrate this interaction concept, two tasks are investigated: Symbol Input and Button Access. The user study shows that MA can significantly improve the input efficiency for users to complete GUI tasks.

Author Keywords
Mobile Phone; Touchscreen; Non-dominant Hand; Desktop Interaction

ACM Classification Keywords
H.5.2 [Information Interfaces and Presentation]: User Interfaces.

Introduction
Mobile phone has become a necessary personal device for its increasing computing power and network connectivity. It can serve as a ubiquitous human-machine interface for many information systems. However, should we just leave the mobile phone sitting

beside the keyboard quietly when we are working on our computers?

Although there are works on extending desktop interaction with connected handheld devices [4, 5], little research has been done on using touch phones to augment interaction on desktops. Besides, a touch phone is already at hand for everyone, so the re-usage of it could achieve the same goal without introducing extra specially designed devices. On the other hand, researchers have investigated the possibility of having the non-dominant hand controlled devices to enhance human-computer interaction. Buxton [2] and Myers [4] demonstrated that human can perform both concurrent and sequential bimanual operations effectively. Myers [4] also used a Personal Digital Assistant as an auxiliary input device for the non-dominant hand.

Based on these findings, we present MA, which enables a mobile phone operated by the non-dominant hand, typically the left hand, to facilitate desktop operations. The basic idea of this technique is to move those difficult-to-access but frequently used GUI widgets to a phone's touch screen. Users can access these widgets with their non-dominant hand while interacting with other widgets on the computer screen with their dominant hand. Generally speaking, these difficult-to-access widgets can be divided into two categories: too deep in the interface hierarchy (e.g. multi-level menus), and too small or too far to reach. To address both cases, MA currently supports two representative tasks: Symbol Input and Button Access. Preliminary study shows that MA can significantly reduce the task completion time.

Discussion

Introducing a secondary display may lead to two drawbacks.

First, operating another device with the non-dominant hand may be inconvenient when accessing hot-keys, which will decrease interaction efficiency [1]. To address this issue, our design does not require users to move or hold onto the device when tapping or performing a gesture. Therefore, the phone can be placed in close proximity to the keyboard, making both the device and hot-keys within reach of the left hand, as shown in Figure 1. Second, the auxiliary display may cause view separation problems [3], as numerous eye movements are required between the computer screen and mobile phone. However, Tan [6] has shown that the effect of visual separation is relatively small, as our experiment results show how the effect of visual separation can be compensated through the advantages of both direct manipulation and usage of the non-dominant hand.

Figure 1. In our interaction design, both the phone and hot-keys are in the control range of the left hand.

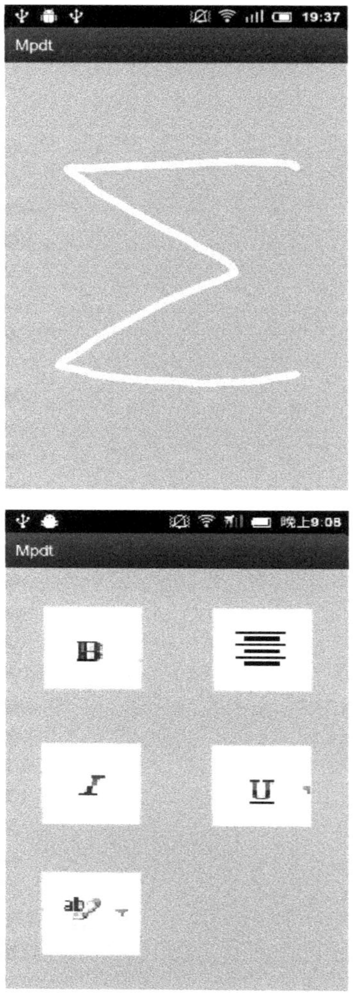

Figure 3. UI of MA for Symbol Input (left) and Button Access (right).

Interaction Design

The current version of MA supports two tasks: 1) Symbol Input, designed to input special symbols by performing gestures on touch phone; 2) Button Access, providing shortcuts on touchscreen for difficult-to-access buttons, making them easy to select with the non-dominant hand.

Technically, MA consists of two parts: a server running on PC and a client application running on a mobile phone. Users can touch the phone's screen with the non-dominant hand to generate corresponding commands. The server receives the command and executes it.

Symbol Input

To input a special symbol, a user can draw it directly on the touchscreen, as shown in Figure 3 (left). The client application can recognize the gesture and inform the server which symbol has been drawn. The server then inserts the symbol at the current location of the cursor. The users can configure the set of supporting gestures and respective symbols. Figure 2 illustrates the gestures and their corresponding symbols in our current implementation.

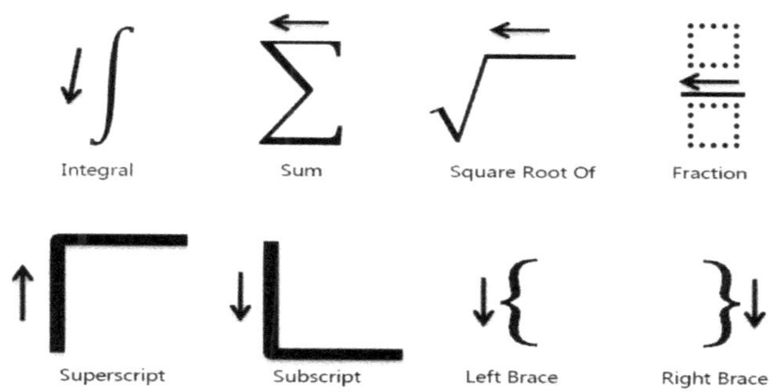

Figure 2. MA gestures for mathematical symbols.

Button Access

The interface of the client application for this task is mainly a table, with adjustable rows and columns. Each table cell contains a particular widget, as shown in Figure 3 (right). When a widget is tapped, the client application sends a TCP message to the server and a corresponding click action is simulated on the desktop.

The interface of server application contains a control panel. Once the user finds a button difficult to click, or without proper hot-keys, he can "move" this button to the phone. This is done by transmitting a screenshot of the target widget to the client. Further, users can personalize the arrangement of button icons. Given that the screen resolution of HTC Desire is 800 × 480 pixels, we recommend dividing the screen into 3 × 2 regions. This layout achieves a reasonable balance between the number of widgets and their accessibility.

User Study

We conducted an experiment investigating its performance when completing tasks in MS Word. Two tasks are designed: inputting a list of mathematical formulas and completing a series of formatting adjustment operations (e.g. adjusting the font and style of words, adjusting paragraph alignment). Users are required to complete these two tasks with and without MA support, which results in 2 x 2 combinations.

Fifteen students were recruited from the campus, all of them right-handed, familiar with MS Word, and using left hand to interact with MA. The completion time and error ratio of each task were recorded. Besides, an interview-based survey was conducted after the experiment.

Results (Table 1) showed that, the completion time of both tasks were significantly reduced (approximately 20%) when using MA; the error rate of MA is acceptable (about 3.6%). The post-experiment interview showed that subjects perceived no difficulty in becoming familiar with MA with the non-dominant hand.

Completion Time (ms) / Error Rate (%)	Without MA Assisted	With MA Assisted
Formula Input	202285 / -	156705 / 3.6
Format Adjustment	121388 / -	97644 / 0.0

Table 1. Results of two experiment tasks.

Conclusion

MA can significantly increase the interaction efficiency, as proved in our user study, by providing shortcuts for those difficultly accessible but frequently used GUI widgets. The proposed method combines advantages of both direct manipulation and the non-dominant hand usage.

Our future work includes improving the gesture recognition ability of MA and applying MA techniques to other desktop tasks. Furthermore, as mobile phones are highly personalized and can be carried around, user information and preferences would also be useful in refining this interaction technique.

References

[1] Balakrishnan, R. and Patel, P. The PadMouse: facilitating selection and spatial positioning for the non-dominant hand. In *Proc. CHI 1998*, ACM Press (1998), 9-16.

[2] Buxton, W. and Myers, B.A. A study in two-handed input. In *Proc. CHI 1986*, ACM Press (1986), 321-326.

[3] Cauchard, J.R., Löchtefeld, M., Irani, P., Schoening, J., Krüger, A., Fraser, M. and Subramanian, S. Visual separation in mobile multi-display environments. In *Proc. UIST 2011*, ACM Press (2011), 451-460.

[4] Myers, B.A., Lie, K.P. and Yang, B.C. Two-handed input using a PDA and a mouse. In *Proc. CHI 2000*, ACM Press (2000), 41-48.

[5] Myers, B.A., Robert, C., Miller, Benjamin, B. and Carl, E. Extending the windows desktop interface with connected handheld computers. In *Proc. WSS 2000*, USENIX Association (2000), 8-8.

[6] Tan, D.S. and Czerwinski, M. Effects of visual separation and physical discontinuities when distributing information across multiple displays. In *Proc. INTERACT 2003*, 252-260.

Amazing Forearm as an Innovative Interaction Device and Data Storage on Tabletop Display

Seiya Koura
Ritsumeikan University
1-1-1 Noji-Higashi, Kusatsu,
Shiga, Japan
koura@rm.is.ritsumei.ac.jp

Shunsuke Suo
Ritsumeikan University
1-1-1 Noji-Higashi, Kusatsu,
Shiga, Japan

Asako Kimura
Ritsumeikan University
1-1-1 Noji-Higashi, Kusatsu,
Shiga, Japan

Fumihisa Shibata
Ritsumeikan University
1-1-1 Noji-Higashi, Kusatsu,
Shiga, Japan

Hideyuki Tamura
Ritsumeikan University
1-1-1 Noji-Higashi, Kusatsu,
Shiga, Japan

ITS'12, November 11–14, 2012, Cambridge, Massachusetts, USA.
ACM 978-1-4503-1209-7/12/11.

Abstract
In this study, we propose interaction techniques that use the forearm on tabletop displays positively. We define the forearm as the part of the arm between the elbow and the hand. On direct input surfaces, users' forearms often create problems such as incorrect recognition and occlusions. Therefore, the forearm is often considered problematic. Conversely, we think it could be possible to use it to create new interaction techniques. We propose new interaction on tabletop displays that use the forearm. In this paper, we describe how users can manipulate menu and data storages by these techniques. Our study offers new possibilities for using the problematic forearm in tabletop displays.

Author Keywords
Forearm; Interaction Techniques; Tabletop Display.

ACM Classification Keywords
H.1.2 [Models and principles]: User/Machine Systems-Human factors; D.4.7 [Operating systems]: Organization and Design - Interactive systems; H.5.2 [Information interfaces and presentation]: User Interfaces - Interaction styles.

Introduction

Many studies have examined direct input surfaces such as tabletop displays. In particular, many researchers have focused on interaction techniques. Wu and Balakrishnan [1] proposed multi-finger and whole-hand gestural interaction techniques for tabletop displays. Weiss et al. developed SLAP Widgets, which support input and adjustment of various values on the computer by buttons, knobs, sliders, and a keyboard placed on a tabletop display [2]. Hinckley et al. observed the motion of the non-dominant hand and proposed a new interaction technique that combines a pen device with gestures [3].

Interaction techniques on tabletop displays can be categorized as those in which the tabletop display is touched directly by the hand and/or finger, and those in which real objects such as pens, knobs, or buttons are used as input devices. However, this classification focuses mainly on objects that are being used actively to interact with the system. If we look at the big picture, it is not only the hand or the input device that frequently comes into contact with the tabletop display, but also the user's forearm.

Users often consciously or unconsciously place their forearms on the tabletop display. However, this creates problems such as occlusion and incorrect recognition. In this paper, we propose interaction techniques that make positive use of the forearm. We propose innovative uses of forearm as menu device and data storage. In the menu device, users can display a menu that is arranged around the hand by placing their forearms on the tabletop display. In the data storage the user's forearm is used as data storage where users can store and retrieve digital objects.

In studies [3, 4], operation was improved by using everyday actions. Therefore, we firstly observed everyday motions of users at a desk and designed interactions that use the forearm on the basis of these motions.

Observation and Interaction Design

observation

We observed the motions of participants working with tools frequently used in desk work, such as a pen and paper. We focused on the following points: How often do people place their forearms on a desk? In what situations and for what purposes did people place their forearms on the desk?

To consider a variety of situations, we observed the following two tasks: Reading several documents and classifying them according to a specified condition (four participants). Create a photo album from several photographs by using tools often used in desk work such as a pen and paper (seven participants).

(1) We observed a strong tendency in the participants to place their forearms on the desk when they were working with tools. In this situation, we think that people placed their forearms on the desk to select and pick up their tools or to facilitate their work to complete the required tasks under steadier conditions. (2) We also observed that the participants often placed their forearms on the table while they are thinking about their tasks. They placed their forearms even when they hear our explanation about the required tasks before beginning our observations. In these situations, we think that the participants acted unconsciously. (3) Some interesting usages of the forearm are observed

that the participants moved or swept objects with their forearms.

Interaction Design
On the basis of our observations, we conclude that when people are working, they frequently place their forearms on the desk. Judging from the frequency with which this action occurred, we believe that placing the forearm on the work surface is natural.
From the observation (1), we propose interaction techniques using forearm as menu device, where users can select functions as if they select and pick up tools in the real world. From the observation (2) and (3), we propose interaction techniques using forearm as data storage. Placed forearm could become a store space with high accessibility. Additionally, if the forearm became a storage box, many desktop data could be gathered with their swipe action.

Implementation

(A) Menu
Our first interaction using the forearm is a menu. Bailly et al. [5] proposed the menu displayed by placing a hand on tabletop display. However, placing only the palm and the fingers without the forearm could be tired. We enable users to easily display a menu by placing the forearm on the tabletop display.

Figure 1 shows the interaction with the menu appearing from the forearm. As with Bailly et al. [5], we used a pie menu so that the menu items are located inside users' range of hand motion and users can easily access each menu item. The users can select an item by the touch gesture. To hide the menu, users can simply lift their forearms up from the tabletop display on their elbows or select the "hide" menu located in the top menu. The menu will then be stored in the forearm

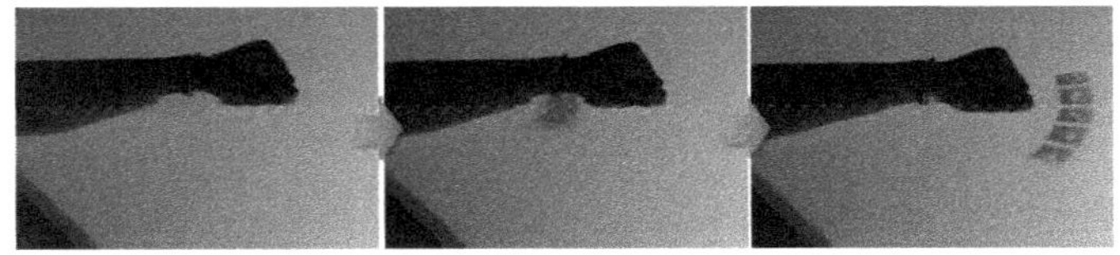

a) Display the menu by placing the forearm

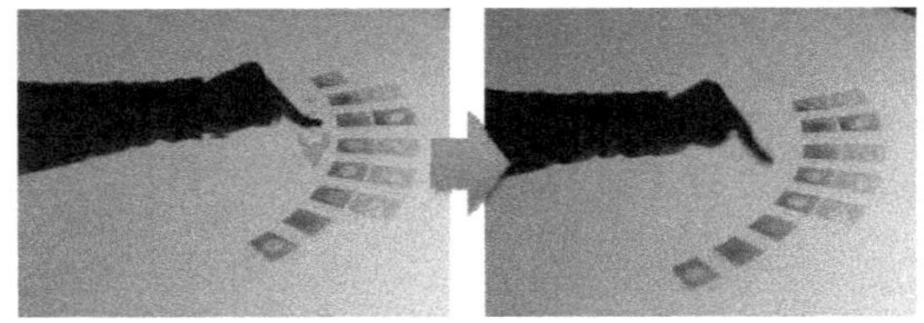

b) Rotate the menu

Figure 1. Interaction with a menu appearing from the forearm.

(disappeared under the forearm). The space between the forearm and the menu items is defined as the gesture area. By sliding a finger in this area, users can rotate the menu in the direction of the finger's motion.

(B) Data Storage
Our second interaction using the forearm is data storage. It can store data such as photos, documents and folders. Figure 2 illustrates how the storage functionality is used.

When users place their forearms on the tabletop display, storage icons are displayed along their forearms. One icon represents one data storage. By tapping the icon, users can open and display the data storage window from the forearm. To hide the window, users tap the icon again.

To store data, users drag the desired data into the storage window or into the forearms directly. If several storage icons are aligned along their forearms, users could drag the data close to the desired icon. Another

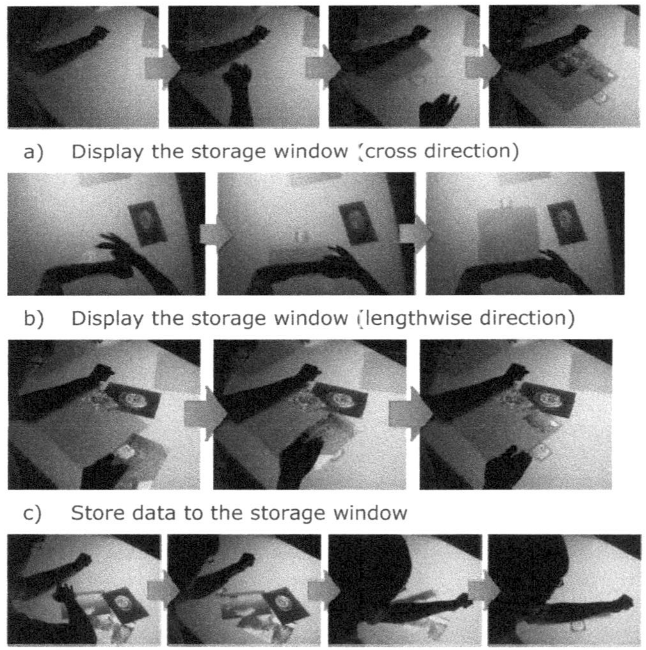

a) Display the storage window (cross direction)

b) Display the storage window (lengthwise direction)

c) Store data to the storage window

d) Interact with collected data by sliding the forearm

Figure 2. Interaction with a data storage in the forearm.

way to store data is to hold the icon a bit longer. This will switch the folder to collection mode. Users can then slide their forearms through on the desired data, and the data is stored automatically.

Users can retrieve the data storage window from the forearm by dragging the storage icon away from the forearm. They can store any data storage window to their forearms by dragging its icon into their forearms.

Conclusion and Future Studies

In this paper, we introduced interaction techniques that make positive use of the forearm on tabletop displays. The data storage can store and retrieve data to the area covered by the forearm by using touch gestures and sliding the forearm. The menu function can display a menu from the area covered by the forearm or store the menu to this area. To change viewpoint, we think that the forearm is not problematic but rather can be used in new interaction techniques.

For our future studies, we plan to create more interaction techniques that users can intuitively use their forearms. For example, when we read books and documents or do some works at desks, we often place our forearms on either side of them. In the same way, if users place their forearms on our tabletop system, a document or an application window on the display could be automatically arranged between their forearms. We also plan to distinguish users' dominant and non-dominant hands to design particularly effective interaction for each hand, and to distinguish forearm user to make the interaction customizable.

References

[1] M. Wu *et al.*: "Multi-finger and whole hand gestural interaction techniques for multi-user tabletop displays," Proc. UIST 2003, pp. 193 - 202, 2003.

[2] M.Weiss *et al.*: "SLAP Widgets: Bridging the gap Between Virtual and Physical Controls on Tabletops," Proc. CHI 2009, pp. 481 - 490, 2009.

[3] K. Hinckley *et al.*: "Pen + Touch = New Tools," Proc. UIST 2010, pp. 27 - 36, 2010.

[4] X. Cao *et al.*: "ShapeTouch: Leveraging Contact Shape on Interactive Surfaces," Proc. TABLETOP 2008, pp. 129 - 136, 2008.

[5] G. Bailly *et al.*: "MultiTouch Menu (MTM)," Proc. IHM 2008, pp. 165 - 168, 2008.

WALDEN: Multi-Surface Multi-Touch Simulation of Climate Change and Species Loss in Thoreau's Woods

Figure 1: Users interacting with WALDEN.

Bertrand Schneider
Harvard University, Cambridge,
Massachusetts, United States
schneibe@seas.harvard.edu

Matthew Tobiasz
University of Calgary,
Calgary, Alberta, Canada
tobiasz@gmail.com

Charles Willis
Duke University, Durham, North
Carolina, United States
charlie.willis@duke.edu

Chia Shen
Harvard University, Cambridge,
Massachusetts, United States
chia_shen@harvard.edu

ITS'12, November 11–14, 2012, Cambridge, Massachusetts, USA.
ACM 978-1-4503-1209-7/12/11.

Abstract
We present a case study of an interactive, multiple heterogeneous-display, multi-touch visualization for informal science education. Our visual simulation application, called WALDEN, has been developed using a Microsoft Surface and a large data wall. Multiple displays offer users the opportunity to interact with large visual datasets and observe complex visual simulations. We discuss the design of our system, findings from our case study, the shortcomings it revealed and how we plan to address them.

Author Keywords
Multi-touch; multiple displays

ACM Classification Keywords
H.5.2

General Terms
Design, Human Factors

Introduction
Translating scientific findings into publicly understandable forms is an important step in making science accessible to the general public, thus is crucial

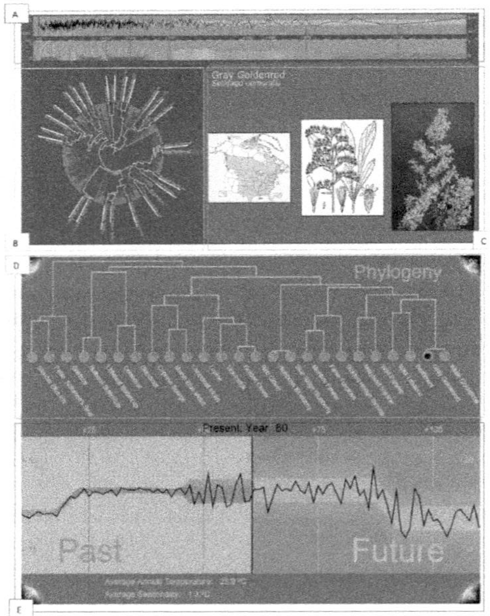

Figure 2: Screen captures of the visual designs of the data wall (above) and the multi-touch tabletop (below) interface.

in the public awareness of our environment, health and well-being. Visualization can be a powerful tool in achieving this translation. The goal of our research is to use interactive visualization coupled with predictive simulation as a fun and engaging informal learning tool for public informal science education. In this paper, we present WALDEN, an interactive visual simulation as a case study to examine whether a large multi-display multi-touch platform is appropriate for this type of visual informal science education. Our research focuses on the design of an interactive visual simulation system for illustrating and predicting the impact of climate change on the *phylogenetic* (evolutionary) patterns of species loss in Thoreau's Woods in Concord, Massachusetts.

WALDEN: a visual simulation for learning

Design Requirements

Visualization designed for informal science education audience needs to be illustrative of the core scientific concepts, and also be self-explanatory for non-biologists. For our particular scientific story, we need to (1) present multiple related concepts and parameters including phylogeny, phenology, warming temperatures, and seasonality, and (2) provide visual illustrations such as imageries of flowering plants, geographic distribution of these plants, and the changing climate. To accommodate this large visual content requirement, we employed a multiple display environment that included a multi-touch tabletop (Microsoft Surface) and a large rear projected display wall of 12x6 ft^2 (3073 by 1536 pixels).

Dynamic Simulation

The WALDEN simulation seeks to model changes in abundance of a select group of plants found in Concord, as a response to climate change and human intervention in the local ecosystem. The stochastic simulation uses empirical plant abundance and climate change data observed in Concord over the last ≈100 years, to make future projections on the floral populations in this area [6].

The abundance change simulation is broken down into three modules: temperature shift (how individual species of plants are able to shift their flowering time (ft) to match fluctuations in annual average temperature; not evolutionary conserved [6]), seasonality (how species are able to respond to fluctuations in temperature from year to year, measured as the standard deviation of average temperatures between years; phylogenetically conserved [6]), and re-growth (the ability of plants to regenerate their populations to their initial equilibrium levels). Each of these modules acts as separate, individual processes that affect the change in abundance of the individual species of plants.

Visualization and Interaction Design

We carried out two rounds of iterative designs to arrive at the visualization and interaction described in this section. The visualization in Figure 2 illustrates how simulated flower populations are affected by changes in annual average temperature and seasonality. People interacting with the simulation can alter the temperature and seasonality values directly on the multi-touch table, and the effect of these changes are presented on the detailed simulation overview on the large wall display.

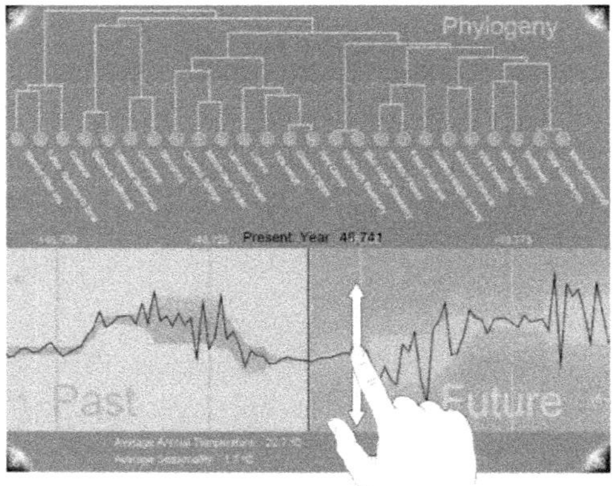

Figure 3: Adjusting the average annual temperature through direct vertical translation.

Visual Design
Figure 2 shows the screen captures of WALDEN's visual design, where the top image is the user interface for the large display data wall, and the bottom image is the multi-touch tabletop. Coordinated multiple views [2] techniques are employed to connect these two displays. The visual encoding of surfaces is subdivided into five distinct areas:

Datawall: (A) Cross the top of the data wall, a dynamic scrolling graph displays the simulated annual average temperature (shown as a black graph line), which is superimposed over the simulated seasonality of that period (yellow band). The abundance values of the currently selected species are shown below. Both graphs use a logarithmic scale on the x-axis in order to visualize a longer time period. (B) On the bottom left is a radial phylogenetic tree of the 429 floral species from the Concord area [6]. The simulation only models a subset of these species, and these nodes are identified within the tree by a label presenting the name of the flower and its current abundance value. The currently selected plant species is highlighted in red. (C) On the bottom right, additional information about the currently selected plant species is presented: a map of the species distribution throughout the USA, a scientific drawing of the species, and an example photo image of the flower.

Tabletop: (D) At the top, a rectilinear phylogenetic tree is presented. This tree only contains the species modeled in the simulation. (E) At the bottom, a graph of the simulated temperature is shown, using the same visual encoding as area A from the data wall: annual average temperature as a black graph line and range of seasonality as a yellow band (Figure 3).

Interaction Design
The user input is through direct touch on the multi-touch tabletop. The touch interaction has been designed to be as simple and intuitive as possible. A user can control three parameters: species selection, annual average temperatures, and seasonality. More specifically, a single finger interaction with the yellow band allows the annual average temperature to be adjusted. By dragging the yellow band vertically up or downward, the temperature value is changed. A two-finger interaction allows the yellow band to be widened or narrowed, adjusting the seasonality (or standard deviation of the simulated temperature value).

EVALUATION
We conducted a qualitative evaluation. The main objective was to assess potential learning gains. In total, 10 users (6 individuals and 2 pairs) participated in the study. We used a think-aloud protocol for prompting comments from individuals. At the beginning of each session, users read a short introduction on phylogeny, and the abstract of Willis' paper [6].

Results
Learning Benefits
Our analysis suggests that every user grasped the main idea that closely related plants tend to react in a similar way to climate changes when using the system. Selected quotes from the participants illustrate this understanding: "I notice that similar species seem to be affected in the same way by similar stimulus", "Species that are close through ancestors have similarities in the abundance behavior", "Closer species were affected quite similarly by changes in temperature".

We also noticed that the setup of tabletop/datawall effectively separated action and reflection: users tended to build hypotheses based on their existing pre-conceptions, make changes on the tabletop and then reflect on the results displayed on the large vertical display. Because users had to wait around 10 seconds to see the effect of climate change on the plants, they took advantage of this time to predict the plants' behavior and elaborate alternative hypotheses.

Related Work

Previous publications have explored user interface design and interaction techniques in combining an interactive tabletop with vertical displays for various experimental application domains [1,2,3] yet none has investigated the cognitive implications for groups verses individuals in for learning. Existing research has also examined the cognitive, social, visual and productivity benefits of large displays [4]. Everitt et al. in [1] investigated interaction techniques for collaborative and flexible document sharing between a multi-touch table and a large interactive whiteboard. Forlines [2] adapted a single-display system to a multi-device multi-display environment. Their system used a multi-touch tabletop as the interaction space while three other vertical displays rendered the same application with different visual perspectives. Wigdor [5] studied a collaborative space for astrophysicists. Their environment enabled the users to bridge private visual data to shared multi-touch displays.

Conclusion

In this paper, we have presented an interactive, multi-touch, multi-display environment for informal science education. Our results suggest that learning environments with multiple large displays can benefit informal learning contexts. Further studies are required to understand the design parameters most suitable for collective use of large multiple display environments.

REFERENCES

1. Everitt, K., Shen, C., Ryall, K., Forlines, C., MultiSpace: Enabling Electronic Document Micro-mobility in Table-Centric, Multi-Device Environments. In *First IEEE Workshop Proceedings of the Horizontal Interactive Human-Computer Systems*, pp. 27-34.
2. Forlines, C., Esenther, A., Shen, C., Wigdor, D., and Ryall, K. Adapting a Single-Display, Single-User Geospatial Application for a Multi-Device, Multi-User Environment. To appear in *Proceedings of the 2006 ACM conference on User Interface Software and Technology,* (Montreux, Switzerland, 2006)
3. Scott, S. D., Grant, K. D., & Mandryk, R. L. (2003). System guidelines for co-located, collaborative work on a tabletop display. In *Proceedings of CSCW 2003*, pp. 159-178.
4. Tan, D. S., Gergle, D., Scupelli, P., & Pausch, R. (2006). Physically large displays improve performance on spatial tasks. *ACM Transactions on Computer-Human Interaction, 13*(1), 71-99.
5. Wigdor, D., Jiang, H., Forlines, C., Borkin, M., & Shen, C. (2009). WeSpace: the design development and deployment of a walk-up and share multi-surface visual collaboration system. *Proceedings of CHI 2009,* Boston, pp. 1237-1246.
6. Willis, C. G., Ruhfel, B., Primack, R. B., Miller-Rushing, A. J., & Davis, C. C. (2008). Phylogenetic patterns of species loss in Thoreau's woods are driven by climate change. *Proceedings of the National Academy of Sciences, 105*(44), 17029-17033.

Comparing the Effect of Interactive Tabletops and Desktops on Students' Cognition

Shima Salehi
Stanford University
School of Education, TLT lab
520 Galvez Mall
Stanford, CA 94305, USA
salehi@stanford.edu

Bertrand Schneider
Stanford University
School of Education, TLT lab
520 Galvez Mall
Stanford, CA 94305, USA
schneibe@stanford.edu

Paulo Blikstein
Stanford University
School of Education, TLT lab
520 Galvez Mall
Stanford, CA 94305, USA
paulob@stanford.edu

ITS'12, November 11–14, 2012, Cambridge, Massachusetts, USA.
ACM 978-1-4503-1209-7/12/11.

Abstract

In this pilot study we investigated the effect of technological platform on the quality of students' cognition when analyzing a computer simulation. As an indicator of performance, we measured the percentage of ideal cycles of cognition; an ideal cycle of cognition is defined as having three distinct steps: planning an action, executing it and evaluating its effects. The results of this study suggest that individuals were not affected by the orientation of display; dyads, however, had twice as many ideal cycles of cognition when interacting with a tabletop than with a desktop. We discuss the implications and limitations of those preliminary results for classroom instruction.

Author Keywords

Education, tabletop, collaborative learning, multi-touch interaction,

ACM Classification Keywords

H.5.m. Information interfaces and presentation: User Interfaces: Miscellaneous-Optional sub-category.

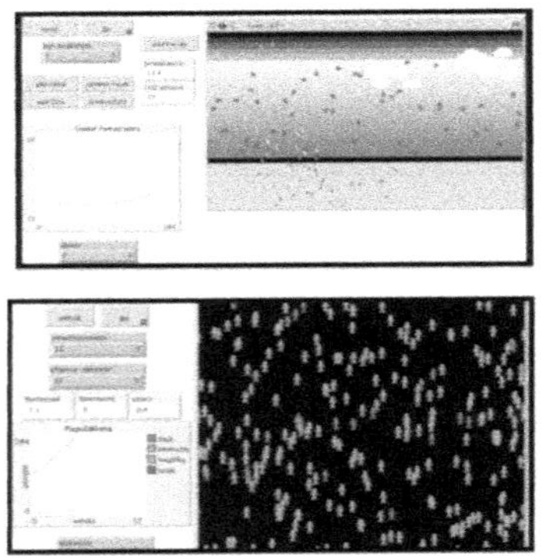

Figure 1. The two agent-based models used in this study. The simulation on top is about climate change, the one on bottom about virus transmission.

Figure 2. Dyads and Individuals working on Tabletop

Introduction

The effects of thinking aloud have been studied in various fields. The results of such studies suggest that verbalizing can have positive effects in learning process. In education, psychologists have highlighted conceptual understanding and memorization of new information [1]. Renkle [7], for instance, has shown that different types of self-explanation could lead to different learning outcomes. However little is known about the effect of technology on people's abilities to think aloud.

For example Rogers and Lindely's study [8] showed that the orientation of a display had a strong influence on group interaction. Our goal is to extend those results by borrowing a concept from cognitive psychology known as "ideal cycles of cognition".

Ideal cycles of cognition

To achieve a goal, human actors should process different information and execute several tasks. Miller et al. [3] suggested test-operate-test-exit model to describe different steps of conducting a task. Other scholars suggested more detailed sequences as goal development–orientation–plan generation–decision–execution– monitoring and feedback for action regulation. Tschan [6] purposed that these different models have major steps in common: plan, execute, and evaluate. She called these three steps ideal cycle of cognition. Sometimes, one of these three steps is missing from the cognition cycle and a cycle is incomplete. Tschan showed that the number of complete ideal cycles of cognition can be used as a mediator to predict performance. According to her study, the greater the number of the complete cycles to overall cycle, the better the performance. Although she has examined the effects of cycle quality on performance for triads, dyads and individuals, she has not investigated variables that can affect cycle quality itself. In this pilot study, we investigated how using a horizontal display instead of a desktop can alter the quality of those cognitive cycles.

Method

Platform

We ran our study on a tabletop called Process Pad. [2] Process Pad is a custom-made multi-touch surface built in our lab, the Transformative Learning Technologies Laboratory (TLTL). We designed it to study how new interactions in this relatively new medium can benefit learning. We are interested in recording multi-modal information about students to facilitate self-reflection. The current study is a first step in this direction; before providing additional tools to learners, we want to know how the form factor of a tabletop influences students' cognition.

Study

This study took place during a month-long workshop on teaching robotics with 13 high school students, nine males and 4 females. From these students, eight high school students (three females and five males) from ninth grade to 12th grade were asked to participate in this study. Four of these students completed the task individually, while the remaining four participants formed two dyads. We used a 2x2 factorial design for our experiment. Each individual or dyad completed two different activities, one on desktop and one on tabletop. We selected two NetLogo [5] models based on their level of complexity and number of variables to explore (Figure 1). In the "climate change" model, participants

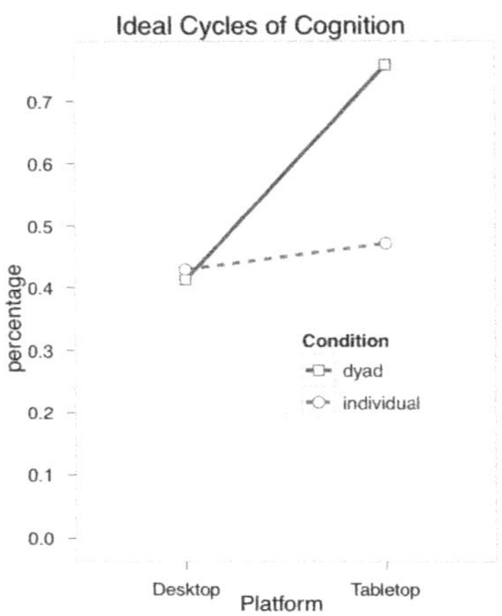

Figure 3. Cycle quality for tabletop and desktop.

could vary the brightness of the sun, the amount of clouds / CO2 in the atmosphere and the albedo (reflection coefficient) of the planet. In the "Virus" model, the users could change the likelihood of being infected, the chance of recovering from an infection and the life expectancy of a virus.

In our experiment, each individual/dyad had to complete two different activities, one on tabletop and one on desktop. For each activity, participants had to interact with a Netlogo simulation. We scaffolded the activity by providing a simple prompt at the beginning of the task. Instructions were kept relatively similar in the two activities to allow for comparison (e.g. "Explore the effect of [variable name] on climate change / the dynamic of a virus spreading in population? Would you evaluate it as a positive or negative effect?"). Participants had 10 minutes to reflect on each model and five minutes after the activity to complete the NASA-TLX (task load questionnaire) and write an answer to the prompt question. Using the NASA-TLX questionnaire, users individually assessed an overall workload of a task based on six different subscales

The experimenter closely observed the participants to count and code cognitive cycles users went through during each task. Before the study, a protocol was defined to distinguish sequences of cycle of cognition. During the study by listening to object and referring to the protocol, for each action, a researcher marked sequences objects conducted in a table At the end of each trial this tables revealed three elements: number of overall actions, number of actions with complete cycle of cognition, and steps missing in an incomplete cycles. A second observer was present during the first three sessions and double-coded the cognitive cycles. Inter-judge reliability was higher than 80%.

Results

We present here the preliminary results of our pilot study. Since we only had a limited sample (N = 8), we did not run any statistical test on our data nor did we include standard deviation to our graph. Rather, we present descriptive results and qualitative observations.

To analyze our data, we used an index called *cycle quality*, which is the percentage of complete cognitive cycles out of the total number of cycles. For both individuals and dyads, the average cycle quality was separately calculated for the tabletop and desktop conditions (Figure 3).

The graph suggests that the cycle quality for individuals is almost equal on both platforms. Interestingly, dyads had a higher percentage of ideal cycles of cognition when working on the tabletop. More precisely, the cycle quality for dyads on tabletop was 0.76%, whereas on desktop, it was 0.41% – quite a remarkable difference. For individuals, the results were respectively 0.47% and 0.43%.

We also analyzed the results from the NASA-TLX questionnaire [4]. We compared the task load for individuals and dyads on both platforms (Figure 4). Interestingly, the average load is relativity similar for individuals on both platforms (10.40 for individuals on desktop, 10.00 on tabletop). Dyads, however, felt that the task was less demanding on the desktop (8.00) than on the tabletop (10.75).

Conclusion

This paper describes preliminary results on the effect of tabletop use on students' cognition. We have examined the quality of cognitive cycles, which has been defined as percentage of complete cycles to overall cycles. Our preliminary results suggest that horizontal surfaces promote a higher quality of cognition among dyads. Interestingly, this result did not apply to individuals: working on a desktop or on a tabletop did not influence their thought process. We also found that dyads judged the task as less demanding when interacting with a desktop; we hypothesize that group coordination was more difficult to achieve on the tabletop, since each user could modify the simulation at any time. On the desktop, only one participant had control of the mouse, which produced a more rigid distribution of roles. This confirms Rogers and Lindley results: horizontal interactive displays are better suited for collaboration.

We also want to stress that these results are preliminary and cannot be considered as strong evidences. Rather, the contribution of this paper is elsewhere: firstly, we tried to define new research questions at the intersection of HCI and education; with the recent advances of tabletop and multi-touch technologies, we want to explore whether new interfaces change the way users approach a problem. Secondly, we introduced a methodology to quantify those differences. Counting the number of ideal cycles of cognition can be an interesting way to measure the quality of participants' thinking process.

In future studies, we plan to: 1) run more participants to test our preliminary results; 2) have a measure of learning after each activity to confirm that ideal cycles of cognition are indeed associated with a positive learning outcomes; 3) conduct an in-depth qualitative analysis to isolate which dimensions of collaboration are mostly affected by horizontal surface.

References

[1] Chi, M. Self-explaining expository texts: the dual processes of generating inferences and repairing inferences and repairing mental models. In R. Glaser (ed.), Advances in Instructional Psychology. Lawrence Erlbaum Associates, Hillsdale, NJ, 2000, 161-238.

[2] Kim, J., Meltzer, C., Salehi, S. and Blikstein, P. Process Pad: A multimedia multi-touch learning platform. In *Proc. ITS 2011*, ACM Press (2011), 272-273.

[3] Miller, G, A.,Galanter, E,.& Pribram, K, H. (1960) Plans and the structure of behavior . New York: Holt.

[4] NASA TLX: Task Load Index. http://humansystems.arc.nasa.gov/groups/TLX/

[5] NetLogo.

http://ccl.northwestern.edu/netlogo/index.shtml

[6] Tschan, F. Ideal cycles of communication (or cognitions) in triads, dyads, and individuals. *Small Group Research 33*, 6 (2002), 615-643.

[7] Renkl, A. Learning from worked-out examples: A study on individual differences. Cognitive Science 21, 1(1997), 1-29.

[8] Rogers, Y. and Lindley, S. Collaborating around vertical and horizontal large interactive display: which way is best? Indiana University Press, Bloomington, IN, USA, 2004.

PiMarking: Co-Located Collaborative Digital Annotating on Large Tabletops

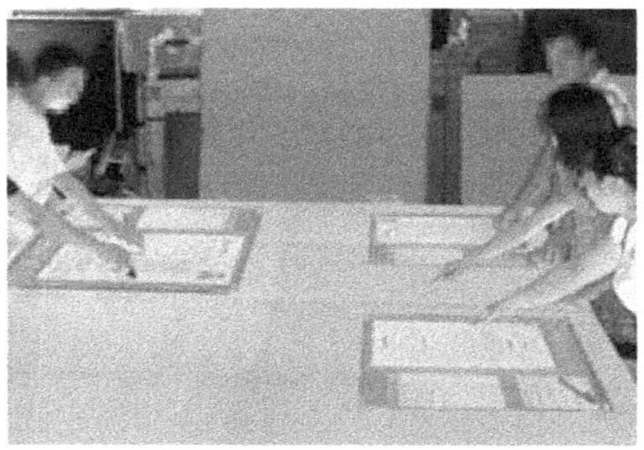

Figure 1: A group of people conducts ɔllaborative marking (annotation) tasks under PiMarking.

Yongqiang Qin
Department of Computer Science,
Tsinghua University
Beijing, 100084 China
qyq08@mails.tsinghua.edu.cn

Chenjun Wu
Department of Computer Science,
Tsinghua University
Beijing, 100084 China
wcj-05@mails.tsinghua.edu.cn

Yuanchun Shi
Department of Computer Science
Tsinghua University
Beijing, 100084 China
shiyc@tsinghua.edu.cn

ITS'12, November 11–14, 2012, Cambridge, Massachusetts, USA.
ACM 978-1-4503-1209-7/12/11.

Abstract
There are situations under which co-located people are required to perform collaborative marking tasks: for example, human resource officers need to review resumes together and teachers need to grade answer sheets after an examination. In this poster, we introduce PiMarking, a collaborative system designed to accommodate user-authenticated marking tasks and face-to-face discussions on large-scale interactive tabletop surfaces. PiMarking makes it easy for user-differentiation, document sharing and synchronized marking among group members. PiMarking puts forward user permission management mechanisms, allowing three modes for document sharing: distributed copy, share display and synchronized marking. We conducted a preliminary study using a realistic resume marking task, which proved the effectiveness of the features provided by PiMarking.

Author Keywords
Co-located, Collaborative Annotation, large tabletop

ACM Classification Keywords
H.5.2 [Information interfaces and presentation]: User Interfaces. - Graphical user interfaces

General Terms
Design, Human Factors

Introduction

There are common and great needs for co-located people to sit together around a table, holding conferences or conducting other collaborative activities such as reviewing resumes or marking papers. In those scenarios, document sharing, collaborative marking, and face-to-face discussions are often needed. For example, resume reviewing is a typical team work: reviewers hold papery resumes and sit around a table, marking them with pens, discussing with each other, and sharing good candidates at the same time. But such un-digital method isn't user-differentiating and always has low efficiency in sharing and synchronized marking aspects. In this paper, we focus on developing a computer supported collaborative annotating system to benefit such kind of co-located collaborative marking works.

Multi-touch tabletop technologies provide a promising plat-form for co-located computer supported tasks. Digital pens can provide more precise input than fingers [1]. In this poster, we present PiMarking, a system designed to support collaborative paper annotating tasks on very large interactive tabletop surfaces. PiMarking enables user-differentiated annotation as well as convenient sharing possibilities. We also conducted laboratory studies using a real co-annotating task.

Design Goals

After interviewing with two teams in need of co-marking and making survey on related literatures, we have concluded with five guidelines that for designing PiMarking system:

- Support authenticated annotating with digital pens, which means the strokes and comments are user-differentiated.
- Support sharing, and synchronized annotating among group users.
- Support awareness among the group members, means one member can easily know what other members are doing.

PiMarking Architecture

PiMarking is implemented on a very large tabletop named uTable [3]. The display area of uTable is 3.8 meters' long by 2 meters' wide, with the resolution of 3840x2048 pixels. uTable leverages DI (Diffused Illumination) to sense multi-touch contacts. It can support up to ten people sitting or standing around and simultaneously interacting.

As of the digital pen, we choose *pPen* [2], a pressure-sensitive digital pen with an active IR emitting tip that works on any vision based tabletop. More importantly, each pPen has a unique ID that can be recognized by RFID technology, which enables possibility of authenticated interaction in PiMarking system: It can recognize each pPen and create connections between users and their pPens, so every marking commands made by pPen is user-differentiated. Based on these technologies, we design PiMarking as Figure 2.

Following are main components of PiMarking:

- *Digital documents*. Each digital document is divided into four parts: input handler, display layer, document container and history recorder.
- *Workspaces*. Workspaces take charge of the digital documents. Each workspace has an ID that

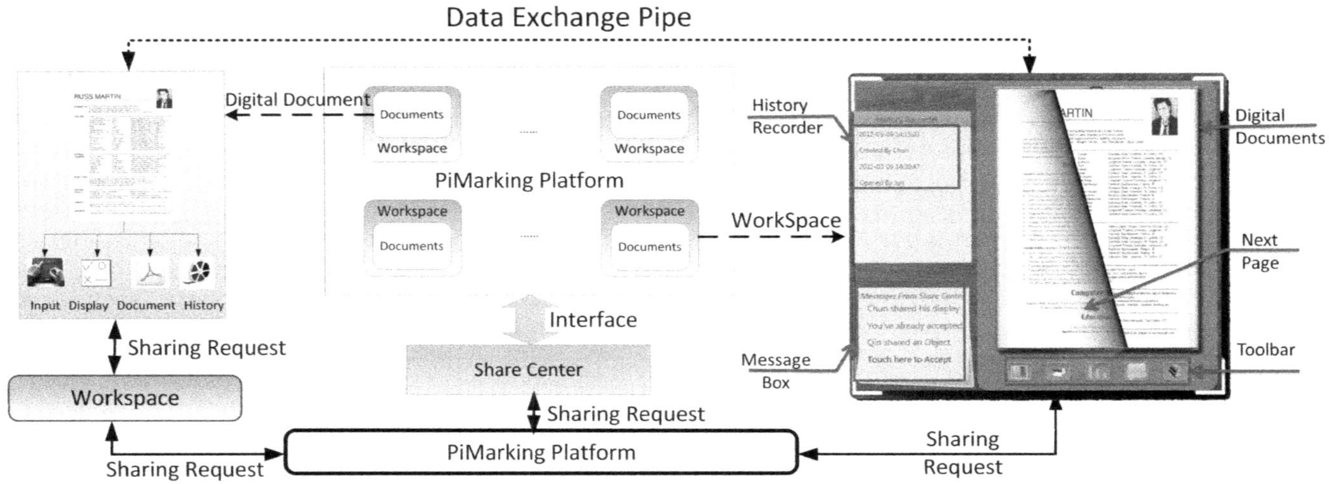

• Figure 2: System architecture of PiMarking. Share center takes charge of all sharing activities, and all requests should passthrough PiMarking Platform, which also takes charge of workspace management.

corresponding to a unique user (via *pPen*). A user without a pPen can only achieve public contents.

- *Share center*. Share center has a database that stores user secret-keys, ID and status of corresponding workspace. It also manages digital objects sharing and co-annotating events.
- *PiMarking platform*. PiMarking platform plays an important role in managing multiple workspaces and communicating with share center. All actions relevant to sharing go through the platform.

User Permission Management

Workspace marks the owner ID (a user ID) and its permission level to each contained object. Among the levels, level 0 is lowest level. As already noted, all *pPen* interaction commands is coming with a user ID (specific user ID, or public user). The workspace will firstly check the user permission level with the object owner and wouldn't allow any user with lower permission level marking on the object. If the two permission levels are equal but without a same user ID, the color of marking strokes will be different. Since finger touch inputs have no user ID attached, all finger touch inputs are interpreted into common interaction gestures other than marking strokes. We defined four basic assembles of interaction gestures: moving, scaling, reorienting, fetching next/pre object, as is shown in Figure 3.

Interaction Design

To create a personal workspace, registered users just need to pick up a *pPen*, draw a circle on PiMarking platform, and write the secret-key he registered to the system on the pop-up hand-writing pad. Users can also create workspaces that with a public ID, which has a lowest permission level 0. A screen shot of workspace is shown in Figure 2 (right part). The history recorder

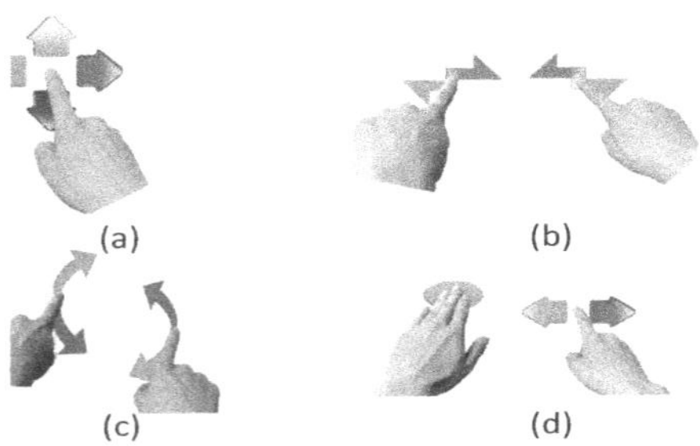

Figure 3: A group of people conducts :ollaborative marking (annotation) tasks under PiMarking.

lies in the upper left of a workspace shows operation history of the object: *when*, *who* opened/created the object, or marked/erased a stroke. If user touches any stroke or comments in the object, the details (i.e. who, when) of the stroke or the comment will appear in the history record area immediately. Another component of the workspace in PiMarking is the message box at the lower left, which displays the news of sharing messages. A hyperlink also exists in the message if user needs to accept the initiator's request.

Sharing

Users can share documents with others by touching the "share" button in the toolbar. There are three modes:

- *Distribute copy.* Initiator sends document copies to recipients so they can save it as their own.
- *Share display.* This mode doesn't create any document copy and recipients can only watch what the initiator is annotating on the document.
- *Synchronized marking.* All users can simultaneously annotating on the same document in their own workspaces and seeing every stroke in real time. In this mode, users have lower permission levels are not able to annotate on the document with a higher level permission.

User Study

We did preliminary study on PiMarking by recruiting 8 participants from the same local university, 20-28 years old. They were randomly divided into two groups. They had 10 minutes training and 15 minutes free playing with PiMarking. They were asked to review 40 resumes and elect a best one. We did post interviews after each trail and found that 1) each participant had a clear idea of the reviewed resumes and 2) they liked to use synchronized marking mode for discussion, as well as touching on a stroke and discuss with the creator face to face.

Conclusion and Furture Work

The PiMarking, a co-located collaborative paper annotating platform running on *uTable*, introduces a set of techniques: personal workspace, authenticated document sharing and synchronized annotating, as well as user permission management. Improvements are also needed to support more customized functions of one's workspace more personal devices (e.g. laptops and mobile phones). A highly integrated co-annotating system will greatly facility people with such requirements.

Acknowledgements

This works is supported by the Natural Science Foundation of China under Grant No.61272230.

References

[1] Amershi, S. and Morris, M.R. CoSearch: A System for Colocated Collaborative Web Search. CHI 2008, 1647-1656.

[2] Brand, P., Forlines, C., Wigdor, D., Haller, M., Shen, C. Combining and Measuring the Benefits of Bimanual Pen and Direct-Touch Interaction on Horizontal Interfaces. In *Proc. AVI'*08, ACM, 153-161.

[3] Morris, M.R., Lombardo, J., and Wigdor, D. WeSearch: Supporting Collaborative Search and Sensemaking on a Tabletop Display. In Proc. CSCW'10. 401-410.

[4] Qin, Y., Yu, C., Jiang, H., Wu, C., Shi, Y. pPen: enabling authenticated pen and touch interaction on tabletop surfaces. In *Proc. ITS* '10. ACM. 283-284.

[5] Qin, Y., Yu, C., Liu, J., Wang, Y., Shi, Y., Su, Z., Shi, Y. uTable: a seamlessly tiled, very large interactive tabletop system. In *Proc*. ITS '11,ACM. 244-245.

uEmergency: A Collaborative System for Emergency Management on Very Large Tabletop

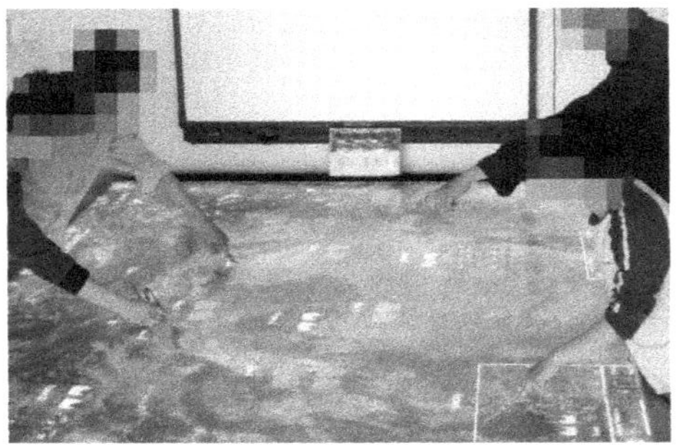

Figure 1. A snapshot of a four people discussing under *uEmergency*.

Yongqiang Qin
Department of Computer Science,
Tsinghua University
Beijing, 100084 China
qyq08@mails.tsinghua.edu.cn

Jie Liu
Department of Computer Science,
Tsinghua University
Beijing, 100084 China
liuj-10@mails.tsinghua.edu.cn

Chenjun Wu
Department of Computer Science,
Tsinghua University
Beijing, 100084 China
wcj-05@mails.tsinghua.edu.cn

Yuanchun Shi
Department of Computer Science,
Tsinghua University
Beijing, 100084 China
shiyc@tsinghua.edu.cn

ITS'12, November 11–14, 2012, Cambridge, Massachusetts, USA.
ACM 978-1-4503-1209-7/12/11.

Abstract
The vertical display, indirect input and distant communication in traditional Emergency Management Information System provide unintuitive human-computer-interaction, and thus reduce the efficiency of decision-making. This paper presents uEmergency, a multi-user collaborative system for emergency management on very large-scale interactive tabletop. It allows people to carry out face-to-face communication based on a horizontal global map. Real-time situation can be browsed and analyzed directly using their fingers and digital pens. In this paper, we also present the results of a study where two groups carried out a task for fighting forest fire based on this system. The results suggest that uEmergency can effectively help people manipulate objects, analyze situation and collaborate for coping with an emergency.

Author Keywords
Emergency, Decision-making, Tabletop, Collaboration.

ACM Classification Keywords
H.5.3. Group and Organization Interfaces.

General Terms
Design, Human Factors

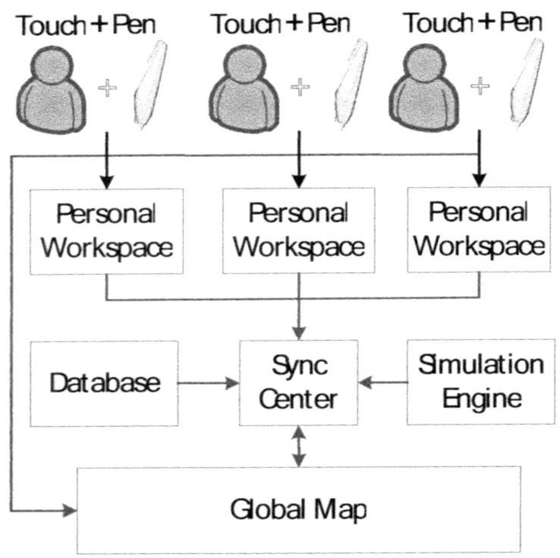

Figure 2. uEmergency Architecture.

Figure 3. Screenshot of uEmergency.

Introduction

The Emergency Management Information System (EMIS) is a computer system designed to support responders during the emergencies by giving them detailed, real-time information [3]. As one of the most important components of EMIS, the decision-making system visualizes emergency situation graphically on vertical display surfaces [1, 2, 6], which usually distorts the real geographical space with 90 degrees rotation. As for the command input, only indirect devices, such as keyboards and mouse, are supported, which make complex commands tough and unnatural to input. Besides, communications are also unintuitive since not all people can directly see each other [4, 5]. These limitations weaken users' understanding of real situation and the efficiency of command inputs for decision-making.

uEmergency, presented in this poster, is the research result to address these issues. It runs on a very Large-scale interactive tabletop, which supports multi-user face-to-face collaborative discussion and multi-touch interaction. In current stage, uEmergency is a simulation game which simulates a forest fire according to existing forest fire records (see **Figure 1**). We conducted a laboratory test and found that the horizontal large-scale interactive display in *uEmergency* can effectively help users make decision by deep understanding of the global situation; the direct input make the manipulation of digital objects more efficient; co-located collaboration facilitates awareness between users by directly seeing other users' actions and words, which is helpful in coordinating work and resolving conflict.

System Design

Figure 2 outlines the uEmergency architecture. uEmergency uses Google Map as its geometry information system; we pre-save map data into database. It is made up of five components: 1) a database storing all map data; 2) a global map for displaying global situation of the emergency; 3) several personal workspaces for different users to browse and annotate a local copy of the global map; 4) a forest fire simulation engine simulating real-time status and 5) a synchronization center to synchronize the fire states of the global map and local maps. Figure 3 is a snapshot of uEmergency: we can clearly see all the status of geographical maps, all fires, houses, fire engines.

Interaction Design

Browsing Map

Users can browse the global map by multi-touch gestures: one-contact moving to translate the map, and two-contacts moving to scale the map. Besides, each user can browser a local map independently in his workspace. This local map provides more flexibility to multi-user collaboration on tabletop since it allows different users to concurrently browse different parts of the map with different scale (figure 4a). In order to coordinate the works of users, each workspace also provides a button that can synchronize the position and scale of the local map with the global map.

Annotating Map

Each workspace contains a markers panel that allows users to make annotation on the map in two ways (figure 4b, 4c): 1) dragging a marker from the panel to the map; 2) select a marker with a digital pen, and directly draw this marker on the map. Although restricted by the input device, the second way makes it

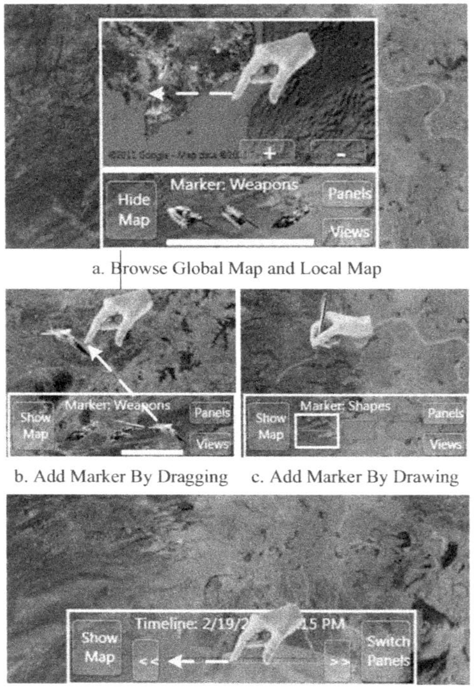

a. Browse Global Map and Local Map

b. Add Marker By Dragging c. Add Marker By Drawing

d. Change the current time point

Figure 4. Interaction design.

easier to repeatedly create the same marker several times. Furthermore, it also allows the user to draw a customized marker, e.g. drawing a curve on the map.

The markers' information keep synchronized among all maps. That is, when a user creates or edits a marker in his local map, it will be immediately seen in the global map and all other local maps. Since marker creation, edit and deletion can be done concurrently by multiple users, conflict can happen. We use a locking policy to resolve this conflict so that when the first user begins to edit a marker, all the copies of this marker in other maps will be locked until the user finishes his operation.

Situation Deduction

Besides position and scale, the map also contains the third dimension: time. At different time point, the map can display different markers to represent different situation. Each workspace has a slider control that can be used to change the time point of its local map (figure 4d). But if the owner of a workspace is the chairman, the time point of the local map can also be configured to keep synchronized or independent with the global map. In this way, every map can be easily looked back or forward for situation deduction.

Multi-user Collaboration

Based on global map and local workspaces, uEmergency provides three kinds of collaboration:

- Work together: all the users focus on the large-scale global map in order to view global situation of the emergency. In this mode, the visible content and controllable area of a user depends on the position he sits. It is very similar to the physical sand table.
- Work independently: each user sits in front of his workspace, and only interact with the system through the interface of that workspace. This mode is similar to traditional EMIS, where each user interacts with his desktop computer and looks up the global situation through a large-scale display wall.
- Mixed focus collaboration: each user can switch between group work and individual work simply by closing or opening his workspace. Traditional tables have been used for this kind of collaboration for a long time, and we believe it can help people complete a task more efficiently [7].

These three kinds of collaboration modes can be switched easily with the change of user position and workspace layout. Therefore, uEmergency also provides a platform for researchers to explore the possibilities of multi-user collaboration in the area of emergency management.

Implementation

uEmergency is implemented under uTableSDK [8], a WPF toolkit for creating multi-user window-based application on interactive tabletop.

User Study

The evaluation was conducted on a large-scale interactive tabletop with 3840*2048 pixel resolution, and a display area of 381*203cm. This tabletop can receive multi-touch inputs, digital pen inputs and multi-mice inputs from 10 persons at the same time, and the response time is less than 30ms.

Eight male participants were recruited to take part in the evaluation, from local universities. They are all familiar with computers and their ages ranged from 24 to 35. Two of them majored in using traditional EMIS for emergency command. Participants were divided into two groups to do the evaluation task respectively. At the beginning of the task, uEmergency displays the

Q1. uEmergency can help users understanding the global situation.
Q2. uEmergency provides good support for collaboration.
Q3. Face-to-face discussion helps users to formulate effective plans.
Q4. Reviewing past procedures can help user to improve their plans in the following fire-fighting tasks.
Q5. Please rate our system from a general view.

Table 1. The questionnaires contains five main questions

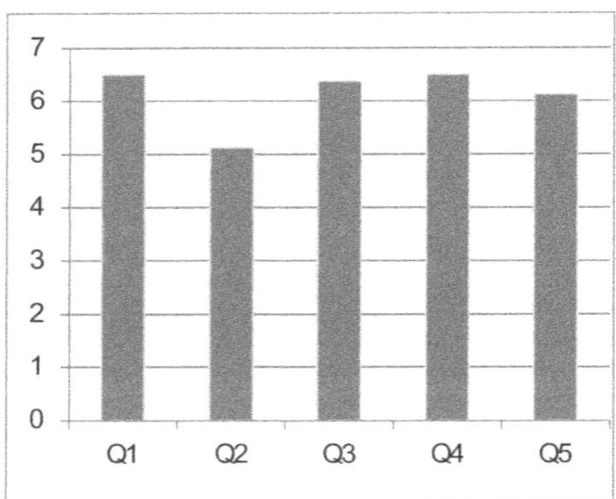

Figure 5. Questionnaire results.

initial situation, including fires, equipment deployment and town position. Participants were asked to send moving and fire-fighting commands to the available equipment so that the fires can be put out as fast as possible, and don't spread to nearby towns. They were instructed to use face-to-face collaboration to finish this task through discussion, division of labor, and use of workspaces. They can freely walk around the table, open or close the workspaces to carry out different types of collaboration.

Every participant was asked to answer 5 questions about uEmergency on a questionnaire (see table 1) to help us with deeper understanding of their feelings on uEmergency. The questionnaire was divided into two parts: the first part is seven-point scales, ranging from "I don't agree" with a value of 1, "hard to say" with a value of 4", and "I totally agree" with a value of 7; the second part consisted with five subjective questions. The results are summarized in figure 5, and the average score is shown for each question. We can find from the figure that participants give high comments on the global situation, face-to-face discussion and situation deduction. They think the support for collaboration can be further improved by stated that "I feel frustrated if the items I want to drag is locked" and "We should have a more detailed discussion to avoid moving the markers back and forth".

Conclusion

In this paper, we introduce *uEmergency* to facilitate decision-making in Emergency Management Information System (EIMS). *uEmergency* takes advantage of very large-scale tabletops, 1)providing an impressive and intuitionistic view of real emergency situation; 2)enabling multiple users' collaboratively direct and indirect input on the interactive surface; 3) providing the possibility of procedure recurrence, which helps users to review the evolution of emergence and make adviser decisions. Controlled evaluation was conducted and the experimental results show that such the system is helpful in EMIS and promising for real use.

Acknowledgements

This works is supported by the Natural Science Foundation of China under Grant No.61272230.

References

[1] Camp P. J, Hudson J. M, Keldorph R. B, Scot L, Mynatt E.D. Supporting communication and collaboration practices in safety-critical situations. In Proc. CHI 2000, ACM. 249-50.

[2] Denef, S., Ramirez, L., Dyrks, T., Stevens, G. Handy Navigation in Ever-Changing Spaces— an Ethnographic Study of Firefighting Practices. In Proc. DIS 2008, ACM, 184-192

[3] Kristensen, M., Kyng, M., Palen, L. Participatory design in emergency medical service: designing for future practice. Proc. CHI 2006, ACM Press, 161—170.

[4] Landgren, J., Nulden, Urban. A Study of Emergency Response Work: Patterns of Mobile Phone Interaction. Proc. CHI 2007, ACM. pp 1323-1332

[5] Li, J., Hara, K. O. Understanding Distributed Collaboration in Emergency Animal Disease Response. Proc. OZCHI 2009, ACM Press, pp 65-72.

[6] Myers B, Malkin R, Bett M, Waibel A, Bostwick B, Miller RC. Flexi-modal and multi-machine user interfaces. In Proc ICMI'02. pp343-348.

[7] Tang, A., Tory, M., Po, B., Neumann, P., Carpendale, S. T. Collaborative coupling over tabletop displays, In Proc. CHI'06, ACM. pp 1181-1190.

[8] uTableSDK. http://utablesdk.codeplex.com

Bridging Private and Shared Interaction Surfaces in Co-located Group Settings

Stacey D. Scott[1,2]
stacey.scott@uwaterloo.ca

Phillip J. McClelland[1]
phil.mcclelland@uwaterloo.ca

Guillaume Besacier[1]
guillaume.becasier@uwaterloo.ca

[1]Games Institute; Systems Design Engineering
[2]English Language and Literature
University of Waterloo
200 University Ave W
Waterloo, ON, N2L 3G1 Canada

ITS'12, November 11–14, 2012, Cambridge, Massachusetts, USA.
ACM 978-1-4503-1209-7/12/11.

Abstract
This work-in-progress paper describes the design of an interaction technique that addresses user interaction challenges with digital object transfer between private and shared surfaces, particularly in co-located group settings. We propose a transfer technique for bridging tablets and digital tables that builds on existing interaction techniques, such as virtual embodiments and multi-display bridging techniques, to improve awareness of the transfer process both for the person performing the transfer and for their collaborators. The technique also minimizes effort involved in the transfer action, enabling people to focus on the activity at hand—or the ongoing conversation—rather than on the technologies being used.

Author Keywords
object transfer; multi-display; private and shared surfaces; co-located collaboration; tablets; digital table

ACM Classification Keywords
H.5.2 [Information Interfaces and Presentation]: User Interfaces: Graphical User Interfaces; H.5.3. [Information Interfaces and Presentation]: Group and Organization Interfaces: Computer Supported Collaborative Work

Introduction

Shared surfaces, such as digital tables, provide many positive benefits to co-located collaborators, including support for communication and coordination [2]. They also place limitations on working with private, secure, or proprietary data, as the whole surface is visible to all group members. To address the issue, personal devices can be combined with shared surfaces to support both individual and shared data access [e.g., 8].

Moving digital objects between private and shared surfaces, however, can be cumbersome. The transfer process can interfere with the activity at hand by capturing the attention of the person performing the transfer. Such technological interruption can be particularly disruptive in a group situation since both the task and the group process can be disturbed.

This project aims to improve the object transfer experience to enable people to remain engaged in the ongoing group activity. In particular, we are exploring a new interaction technique that leverages new low-cost user tracking capabilities (e.g., Microsoft Kinnect) to help integrate and extend existing interaction design concepts to improve the overall transfer process.

The core design concept being investigated is to track someone performing a Pick-and-Drop-style transfer action between their private surface (i.e. tablet) and a shared digital table and to use this tracking information to provide visual feedback on the digital table. This visual feedback depicts the object in transit between devices as an artifact "held" in the hand of the person transferring the object, moving in real-time below the person's hand until the object is released.

The following section overviews existing bridging techniques. We then described the design concept in more detail, along with the specific case study, the Dominion card game, being used to reify the design concept. Finally, we outline future project directions.

Techniques for Bridging Multiple Displays

Common techniques to facilitate digital object transfer typically use one of the following approaches. (For a broader overview of transfer techniques related to multi-touch devices, refer to Bachl et al. [1].)

Contiguous virtual workspace. One approach is for displays to be connected to a common software architecture that maintains awareness of the physical configuration of the displays (which is either static or tracked in real-time). This information is then used to provide a contiguous virtual workspace across devices. Thus, moving an object off the edge of one display moves it to the nearest edge of the adjacent display [e.g., 3, 4, 7, 9]. This technique, however, is not ideal for multi-touch surfaces. For instance, if a digital object is needed on the opposite side of a large digital table from the edge it appears on, the person transferring the object must drag it across the whole display to the desired location. Such interaction would introduce ergonomic issues, especially if the same interaction occurs many times. Given limitations of some multi-touch tables, which can temporarily lose touch input, requiring such long dragging actions can also be a source of frustration for people using it.

Virtual portals. Another technique is to use a virtual portal. The desired digital object is first moved to a specified area (or portal) in the originating display, and then it appears in a corresponding portal in the receiving display [e.g., 1, 4]. Virtual portals have a

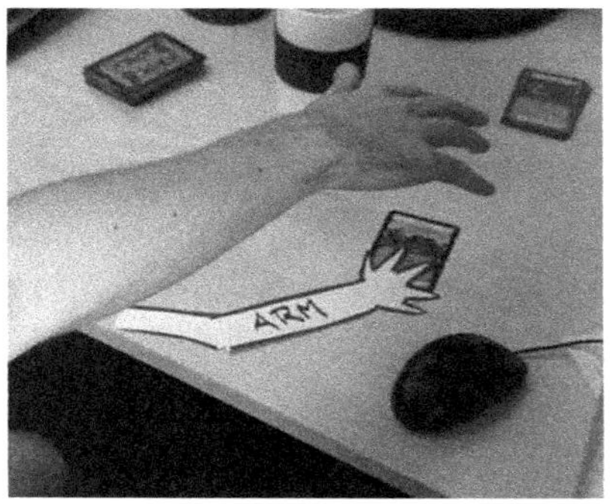

Figure 1. Mocked-up design concept in a card-playing scenario. When the player moves a card from their hand of cards on their tablet (not shown), to the digital table, a visual representation of their card and a visual embodiment of their arm appear on the table. These visualizations will follow the movement of their arm, until the person touches the table to confirm the card transfer.

similar drawback to the previous technique: people are required to drag the object in transit from the virtual portal to the desired location, rather than placing it directly where it is needed on the surface. This creates an additional step in the transfer process.

Bridging using a physical object. Bridging devices can also be accomplished by binding a digital object to a physical object and then moving the physical object to the receiving display. This can be done using an arbitrary physical object [9] or, more commonly, a system-recognized object. For example, Rekimoto's [6] Pick-and-Drop technique allowed someone to "pick up" a digital object using a digital pen and "drop" the object directly onto a different display using the digital pen. Using a digital pen to bind a digital object is not practical on a multi-touch surface as pens are not typically needed (or recognized). The only object that can be assumed across surface systems is the fingers (and by extension, hands) of the people using the system. Our approach leverages this information to enable Pick-and-Drop-style interaction by binding digital objects to a person's hand during the transfer. The next section describes the approach in more detail.

Design Concept

As mentioned, the core design concept is to enable Pick-and-Drop-style bridging by associating a digital object to the hand of the person transferring it. This association will be indicated through visual feedback on the digital table. An example of this concept is shown in Figure 1 in a card-playing scenario, where a player is transferring a playing card from a tablet (not shown) to a digital table. Once the transfer process begins, a virtual representation (or embodiment [5, 10]) of the person performing the transfer action appears on the digital table, along with a virtual representation of the digital object (i.e. the playing card). During the transfer process, the person's hand movement is tracked and the location of their virtual embodiment and associated digital object is updated in real-time. Once the person touches the table, the digital object is transferred to the table at the touch location. The virtual embodiment then disappears. Cancelling the transfer action simply involves touching the originating display (in this case, the tablet) to return the object to the display.

Benefits of the Approach

This approach is designed to improve awareness of the transfer process for the person performing the action, addressing a potential mode error that could result if the person becomes distracted (by the conversation or a collaborator's action) and forgets the ongoing transfer action. It is also designed to provide awareness to others at the table. The virtual embodiment provides a visual cue that a transfer action is occurring, and the virtual representation of the digital object provides information about what is being transferred. Such awareness cues are aimed to help people understand when data are "in the ether" between displays, similar to the *Ubiquitous Cursor* multi-display bridging technique [11].

Active tracking of the transfer action is also intended to minimize the amount of effort involved in the overall transfer process by enabling people to place transferred objects directly where they are needed on the receiving display. Minimizing the transfer effort is intended to enable the person to focus on the activity at hand.

Case Study and Future Work

To investigate this design concept in practice, we selected a popular card-based game, called Dominion[1],

[1] Published by Rio Grande Games, used with permission.

Figure 2. Current prototype of the Dominion game application. A player's hand of cards is displayed on the tablet and the shared card decks and discard piles are displayed on the digital table.

to serve as a case study. Dominion was chosen as it represents a group activity that requires private information (player's hand of cards), shared information (shared card decks), and object transfer between private and shared surfaces (picking up from the shared decks into a player's hand, and playing cards from the player's hand onto the shared surface).

We implemented a Dominion game application that can be played using multiple Samsung Galaxy Tab tablets to hold each player's hand of cards and a custom multi-touch table to serve as the shared gaming surface. Tracking the players' hand movements during object transfer will be done using a Microsoft Kinnect sensor mounted above the digital table. Players' hand movements will be used to provide real-time update of the visual feedback cues on the digital table.

We are currently refining our visual designs for the feedback cues. These visualizations are being modeled on existing *virtual embodiment* techniques for large surfaces, such as Arm Shadows [5, 10].

Once implementation is finalized, we intend to conduct a user study that investigates the effectiveness of this transfer technique in comparison to some of the existing transfer techniques discussed above (e.g., the virtual portals technique). Longer-term, we also intend to investigate the effectiveness of this technique in other application contexts to better understand its advantages and limitations.

Acknowledgements
This research is funded by the NSERC SurfNet Strategic Network. We also thank Dr. Neil Randall.

References
1. Bachl, S., Tomitsch, M., Kappel, K., and Grechenig, T. (2011). The effects of personal displays and transfer techniques on collaboration strategies in multi-touch based multi-display environments. *Proc. of INTERACT'11*, 373-390.
2. Conversy, S., Gaspard-Boulinc, H., Chatty, S., Stephane, V., Dupre, C., and Ollagnon, C. (2011). Supporting air traffic control collaboration with a TableTop system. *Proc. of CSCW'11*, 425-434.
3. Hinckley, K. (2003). Synchronous gestures for multiple persons and computers. *Proc. of UIST'03*, 149-158.
4. Hinckley, K., Ramos, G., Guimbretiere, F., Baudisch, P., and Smith, M. (2004). Stitching: pen gestures that span multiple displays. *Proc. of AVI'04*, 23-31.
5. Pinelle, D., Gutwin, C., and Nacenta, M.A. (2008). The Effects of Co-Present Embodiments on Awareness and Collaboration in Tabletop Groupware. *Proc. of Graphics Interface'08*, 1-8.
6. Rekimoto, J. (1997). Pick-and-drop: a direct manipulation technique for multiple computer environments. *Proc. of UIST'97*, 31–39.
7. Rekimoto, J. and Saitoh, M. (1999). Augmented Surfaces: A spatially continuous workspace for hybird computing environments. *Proc. of CHI'99*, 378-385.
8. Shen, C., Everitt, K.M., and Ryall, K. (2003). UbiTable: Impromptu Face-to-Face Collaboration on Horizontal Interactive Surfaces. *Proc. of UbiComp'03*, 281-288.
9. Streitz, N.A., Tandler, P., and Müller-tomfelde, C. (2001). Roomware: Towards the Next Generation of Human-Computer Interaction Based on an Integrated Design of Real and Virtual Worlds, in J.A. Carroll (ed.). *Human-Computer Interaction in the New Millennium*, Addison-Wesley, 553-578.
10. Tang, A., Boyle, M., and Greenberg, S. (2004). Display and presence disparity in Mixed Presence Groupware. *Proc. of Australasian User Interface Conference*, 73-82.
11. Xiao, R., Nacenta, M.A., Mandryk, R.L., Cockburn, A., and Gutwin, C. (2011). Ubiquitous cursor: a comparison of direct and indirect pointing feedback in multi-display environments. *Proc. of Graphics Interface'11*, 135-142.

BrainExplorer: An Innovative Tool for Teaching Neuroscience

Figure 1. A user interacting with BrainExplorer.

Bertrand Schneider
Stanford University
Stanford, CA 94305, USA
schneibe@stanford.edu

Jenelle Wallace
Stanford University
Stanford, CA 94305, USA
jenellew@stanford.edu

Roy Pea
Stanford University
Stanford, CA 94305, USA
roypea@stanford.edu

Paulo Blikstein
Stanford University
Stanford, CA 94305, USA
paulob@stanford.edu

ITS'12, November 11–14, 2012, Cambridge, Massachusetts, USA.
ACM 978-1-4503-1209-7/12/11.

Abstract
Neuroscience has recently brought many insights into the inner workings of the human brain. The way neuroscience is taught, however, has lagged behind and still relies on direct instruction or textbooks. We argue that the spatial nature of the brain makes it an ideal candidate for hands-on activities coupled with a tangible interface. In this paper we introduce BrainExplorer, a learning environment for teaching neuroscience. BrainExplorer allows users to explore neural pathways on a custom tabletop platform. We conducted an evaluation with 28 participants comparing students who learned neuroscience content through using BrainExplorer with students who learned by reading a textbook chapter. We found that our system promotes learning along 3 dimensions: memorizing scientific terminology, understanding a dynamic system, and transferring knowledge to a new situation.

Author Keywords
Neuroscience; Learning; Tangible Interface; Tabletop

ACM Classification Keywords
H.5.2

General Terms
Design, Human Factors.

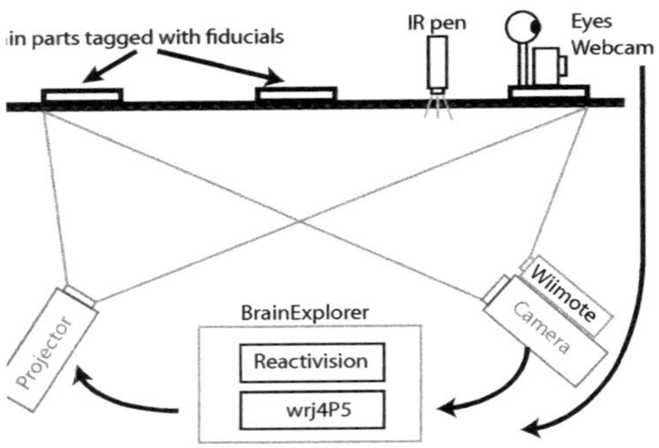

Figure 2. The setup of BrainExplorer.

Introduction
Neuroscience is a rapidly evolving field, and the brain's complexity has traditionally been thought of as the domain of advanced undergraduates and graduate students. However, in recent years, researchers have begun to advocate for the benefits of bringing this topic closer to younger audiences. In this paper, we first describe the construction of BrainExplorer and the way various learning theories informed our design. Following, we present an experimental study comparing the effectiveness of our system as a learning tool compared to textbook instruction.

Related Work: Educational Tabletops and Tangible User Interfaces
The field of education has a long history of using manipulatives for learning: from Pestalozzi, who used to say "things before words, concrete before abstract", Montessori (1870-1952) who constructed a diverse set of manipulatives for poor children in the Italian suburbs, to Bruner who advocated an evolution from enactic to iconic and symbolic reasoning. Researchers have recently regained an interest in this domain now that technology can augment those manipulatives in rich and diversified ways. Projects that embody this idea are called Tangible User Interfaces (TUIs [2]).

Tabletops have been the privileged platform for developing TUIs. We review here a few projects that have tried to take advantage of the specific affordances of physical inputs: in molecular biology, Gillet et al. [1] created a TUI that overlays 3D representations on a molecular model, In geography, Illuminating Clay allows users to explore a landscape augmented with various simulations, such as the influence of water flows or solar radiation [3]. In genomics, Shaer et al. [6] designed and evaluated G-nome Surfer, a tabletop interface for fostering inquiry-based learning of genomics; they found that compared to a multi-mice implementation, their tabletop increased physical participation, encouraged reflection, fostered collaboration and facilitated interaction among participants. Finally, the Tinker Table developed by Zufferey, Jermann & Dillenbourg [7] allows apprentices in logistics to control a simulation of a small-scale warehouse by moving physical shelves (a projector then displays an additional layer of information based on the location of the shelves - e.g. forklifts influencing the fluctuation of the stocks). Based on those studies, We propose that TUIs have an interesting potential to improve education by lowering the degree of abstraction and providing more adequate scaffolds for highly spatial problems. Since the human brain is a complex 3D structure we propose that neuroscience is a particularly well-suited domain for developing neuroscience environments with tangible inputs.

BrainExplorer
Given that the brain is a dynamic 3D system, we propose that it is extremely difficult to teach neuroscience with standard tools. Our system, BrainExplorer, takes advantage of recent technological developments, including infrared camera technology and webcam-based tracking (Fig. 1), to create a tangible user interface to study the human brain.

Design Decision and Process
Our system was targeted to a wide range of educational settings. Its primary purpose is as an inquiry learning tool for middle and high school students to engage in scaffolded investigation about the brain. Our system draws heavily from the constructivist theory of learning

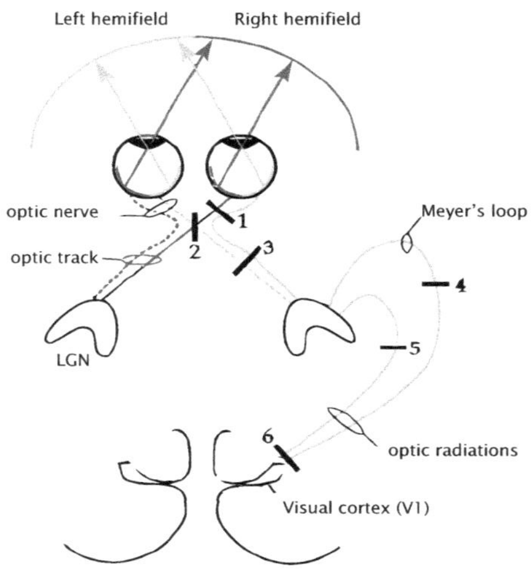

Figure 3. The organization of the visual pathways in the human brain.

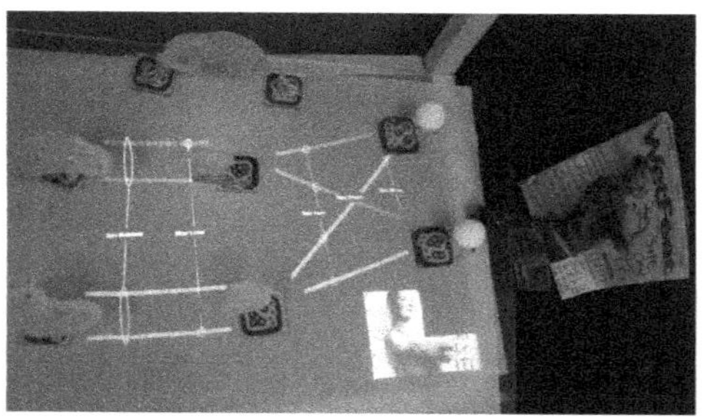

Figure 4. Representation of the visual system in the BrainExplorer environment. In this example, Meyer's loop is severed on the left side of the brain, which occludes the top right quadrant of the vision.

[5], which emphasizes the need for students to construct their own theories about the world based on knowledge and intuitions they already possess. Scientists, including neuroscientists, construct their theories about the world by performing experiments. Therefore, our system is designed to let the user to be the scientist and to allow him or her to replicate experiments that neuroscientists might actually perform in a lab. We also wanted the user to be able to begin with a whole brain and deconstruct it into individual pieces. This design decision was based on users' emotional reactions—taking something apart is a profoundly satisfying way of learning. As a consequence, we built a custom-made table where a physical model of the brain can be taken apart. Departing from a polymer-based replica of the brain sectioned into 6 parts, each part was tagged with a fiducial from the Reactivison toolkit [4].
Figure 1 describes the final setup of our system. A matte surface supports the brain parts tagged with fiducials. Users cut connections by using an infrared pen; the IR signal is detected by a Wiimote underneath the table. A high-resolution, high-frame rate camera (PS3 EyeToy) sees the location of each fiducial and transmits its location to the software. An additional webcam is located between the two eyes of the physical model and "sees" what the brain would perceive based on the lesions made by the user. The program retrieves the input from the Wiimote via Bluetooth and the two cameras images via USB and displays the results through a short throw projector. A custom-made table supports the brain parts, the projector, the Wiimote and the two cameras. Thus, BrainExplorer allow users to cut different visual pathways and observe the impact of their actions on the visual field of the human brain (Fig. 4).

Evaluation

We used a between-subjects design to compare our system with a control condition where users had to read a text on the visual pathways. Our post-test measured learning on 3 dimensions: memorizing scientific terminology, understanding a dynamic system, and transferring knowledge to a new situation.

Participants: 28 undergraduate and graduate students took part in the study (13 males, 15 females; average age = 28.2, SD = 5.7). None of the participants took a class in neuroscience before or had existing knowledge on the topic.

Procedure: The evaluation took place in a private room and both conditions used the same space for the experiment. We kept the lighting conditions identical for each subject in order to assure the stability of the tracking system. Upon their arrivals, users were welcomed and thanked for their participation. An experimenter then explained to them the purpose of the task and tested their existing knowledge on the topic by presenting them a schema similar to Figure 2 (see "Material" for more details). Participants with no prior knowledge were then randomly assigned to one condition ("Text" or "Tabletop") and given specific instructions. In the "Tabletop" condition, subjects were told that they would have 15 minutes to use BrainExplorer in order to explore how the visual system of the human works. Their only task was to find 2 rules that would help them explain to a peer how vision is processed by the brain. Finally, they were also instructed to think aloud during the session. The episode was videotaped for further analyses. Participants in the "text" condition were told to read a text on the same topic for 15 minutes. In both

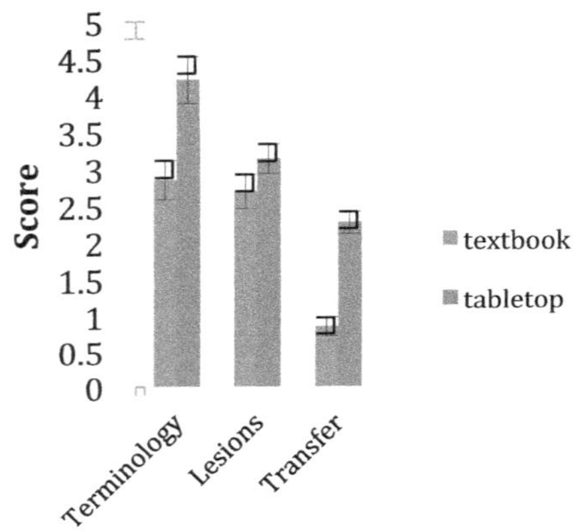

Figure 5. Results of the learning test.

conditions, the experimenter told the users that they would have to complete a test at the end of the activity. After completing the task, subjects filled out a demographic questionnaire and answered a computerized test in which reaction times and answers were recorded (see the "Material" section for more details).

Results: We measured the learning gains with the post-test since none of our participants had prior knowledge in neuroscience. An ANOVA revealed that subjects in the Tabletop condition scored significantly higher than those reading a text: $F(1,26) = 15.77$, $p < .001$ (mean = 9.6, SD = 2.16 for the tabletop condition; mean = 6.38, SD = 2.1 for the text condition); see figure 5 for more details. subjects in the "tabletop" condition significantly outperformed the participants in the "textbook" condition for learning the brain terminology $F(1,26) = 5.18$, $p < .05$, for the transfer questions $F(1,26) = 24.98$, $p < .001$. The difference for the lesions dimension was not significant $F(1,26) = 1.02$, $p = .32$.

Discussion

In our evaluation we found that participants in the tabletop condition learned more about the visual pathways compared to the text condition. Our results have interesting implications for neuroscience education; it shows that tangible systems may have some benefits for teaching the way complex systems work (compared to a traditional instruction). It should be noted that this study has one main limitation; there are confounding variables between our two conditions. In the tabletop condition, users had access to a 3D model of the brain (compared to a 2D schema in the text condition), they were asked to discover concepts by themselves (in the other condition concepts were directly explained to them) and finally they had to think aloud (whereas other users had to read a text). Future work should disentangle those variables to discover how the positive learning effect found in our study takes place.

References

1. Gillet, A., Sanner, M., Stoffler, D., Goodsell, D., et Olson, A. Augmented Reality with Tangible Auto-Fabricated Models for Molecular Biology Applications. *Visualization Conference, IEEE, IEEE Computer Society* (2004), 235-242.
2. Ishii, H. et Ullmer, B. Tangible bits. *Proceedings of the SIGCHI conference on Human factors in computing systems*, (1997), 234-241.
3. Ishii, H., Ratti, C., Piper, B., Wang, Y., Biderman, A., et Ben-Joseph, E. Bringing Clay and Sand into Digital Design — *Continuous Tangible user Interfaces. BT Technology Journal 22,* 4 (2004), 287-299.
4. Kaltenbrunner, M. et Bencina, R. reacTIVision. *Proceedings of the 1st international conference on Tangible and embedded interaction*, (2007), 69.
5. Piaget, J. *The language and thought of the child*. New York: Harcourt, 1928.
6. Shaer, O., Strait, M., Valdes, C., Feng, T., Lintz, M., et Wang, H. Enhancing genomic learning through tabletop interaction. *Proceedings of the 2011 annual conference on Human factors in computing systems*, (2011), 2817.
7. Zufferey, G., Jermann, P., et Dillenbourg, P. A tabletop learning environment for logistics assistants: activating teachers. *Proceedings of the Third IASTED International Conference on Human Computer Interaction*, (2008), 37–42.

Author Index

www.ingramcontent.com/pod-product-compliance
Ingram Content Group UK Ltd.
Pitfield, Milton Keynes, MK11 3LW, UK
UKHW051510290926
15471UKWH00008B/1549

9 781450 319324